Roger Ebert's
Four-Star Reviews
1967–2007

Other Books by Roger Ebert

An Illini Century

A Kiss Is Still a Kiss

Two Weeks in the Midday Sun:
A Cannes Notebook

Behind the Phantom's Mask

Roger Ebert's Little Movie Glossary

Roger Ebert's Movie Home Companion
annually 1986–1993

Roger Ebert's Video Companion
annually 1994–1998

Roger Ebert's Movie Yearbook
annually 1999–2007

Questions for the Movie Answer Man

Roger Ebert's Book of Film: An Anthology

Ebert's Bigger Little Movie Glossary

I Hated, Hated, Hated This Movie

The Great Movies

The Great Movies II

Your Movie Sucks

Awake in the Dark: The Best of Roger Ebert

With Daniel Curley
The Perfect London Walk

With Gene Siskel
The Future of the Movies: Interviews with Martin Scorsese,
Steven Spielberg, and George Lucas

DVD Commentary Tracks
Citizen Kane
Dark City
Casablanca
Floating Weeds
Crumb
Beyond the Valley of the Dolls

Roger Ebert's Four-Star Reviews 1967–2007

Andrews McMeel Publishing, LLC

Kansas City

This book is dedicated
to Chaz

The light at the end of the tunnel

Contents

Introduction

What I Do and How I Do It

Reading over these treasures from four decades, I am reminded of Derek Malcolm's definition of a great movie: a movie you can't stand the thought of never being able to see again. Most of these pass the test. A few don't. The book collects my original reviews of these films, written at the time, and perhaps today I would see some of them differently, filtered through later films and experiences.

In a way, this is the record of a learning experience. When I wrote my first review for the *Chicago Sun-Times,* I had no film education and had hoped to be a professor of English literature. Yes, I went to a lot of movies, and my taste was not bad, but when the paper's previous film critic retired, I think I got the job because I was young, had long hair, and had reviewed the underground films that played at Second City every Monday night.

I bought books by Pauline Kael, Andrew Sarris, Louis Giannetti, and Arthur Knight, and pondered them. In *The Immediate Experience,* a book by Robert Warshaw, I found and underlined this sentence: "A man goes to the movies. The critic must admit that he is this man." I translated that to mean that the critic must place experience above theory, must monitor what he actually thinks and feels during the film, and trust that above all. If the film is by a great director, does that make it a great film? If it comes from a disreputable genre, does that make it unworthy? In the mind of the critic, each film must earn its own living.

I learned about the cinema on the job. It was an education to visit the sets or locations of movies being made by Henry Hathaway, Sam Peckinpah, Billy Wilder, Robert Altman, Ingmar Bergman, Federico Fellini, Luchino Visconti, Gillo Pontecorvo, Bo Widerberg, Otto Preminger, Carol Reed, Norman Jewison, Joseph Mankiewicz, and countless others. In the early days, directors and actors had time for the press; they didn't live in publicity cocoons. I remember nights in restaurants with Jewison, Martin Scorsese, Claude Chabrol, and Brian De Palma, when they engaged in self-analysis, even drawing sketches to diagram shots.

I also learned a lot by teaching. From 1969 until 2005, I taught a weekly film class in the University of Chicago Extension Division, and each class was an opportunity to screen films and prepare comments in areas I wanted to know more about. Silent films, the New Wave, documentaries, the works of Herzog, Hitchcock, Ford, Fassbinder, Truffaut, Kurosawa, Bresson, Powell, Ray. In that class I started using the shot-by-shot approach, where we would go all the way through a film with a stop-action projector, talking about composition, camera movement, lighting, and anything else. I also did that for more than thirty years at the Conference on World Affairs at the University of Colorado, and at many film festivals. It was hands-on; we saw the movie, we talked about what we saw, it was our immediate experience.

When I started on the job, I thought I would do it for perhaps five years. Now it has become a lifetime. I have become convinced in the process that the cinema is the best medium yet devised for observing, sharing, and shaping human experience. We are in the first days. What will *The Godfather, La Dolce Vita, Vertigo, Raging Bull,* or *Rules of the Game* tell those who live five hundred years from now? Will Buster Keaton still be funny? What would we give to have movies from five hundred years ago?

A key element in the love of film is the love of technique: How does the film-maker place or move his camera, and frame his shots? How does he edit? And how is that more important than the story line in revealing his view of the material? A review in a newspaper cannot go into the detail of a David Bordwell, but the newspaper reviewer should be alert to such questions, and not be too shy to introduce them.

As a writer, I have gained a reputation for working fast. It is not that I *write* particularly quickly, I think, as that I spend less time *not* writing. As a sixteen-year-old sports writer at the *Champaign-Urbana News-Gazette,* climbing the stairs at midnight after an out-of-town Friday night game, I would join Bill Lyon in the only lighted corner of the newsroom. He covered Champaign High School, I covered Urbana. He would watch me tear sheet after sheet from my typewriter, crumple it, and throw it away, searching for the perfect lead. "Don't waste time on how it starts until you know how it ends," he advised me. He was two years older than I was, and smoked cigars. He was right. He went on to become a famous columnist in Philadelphia.

I came to believe that the lead paragraphs should not be the beginning of a formal top-down approach, but should read as if we had jumped into the middle of a conversation together. All my reviews began with the invisible words, "So, anyway . . ." I learned not to wait for inspiration, because it would come during the writing process. I found I was taking dictation from that place within my mind that always knew what I should write next.

Another valuable piece of advice was given to me by James Hoge, the *Sun-Times* editor who hired me. "Anyone who has the price of a newspaper should have a fair chance of understanding most of what's written in it," he told me. I tried to write clearly, to use real words and not jargon. Oddly enough, I found that longer sentences could improve clarity, and began flinging in commas, colons, semicolons, and dashes with abandon. As Sam Goldwyn might have observed, "The problem with a period is that it brings a sentence to a complete halt." I think the great tragedy in recent years in the liberal arts is the replacement of coherent writing by pseudo-scientific academic jabberwocky. I believe you can discuss anything about the movies in words that are understandable. Consider the reviews of Stanley Kauffmann, clear as crystal, deep with thought and experience. Or Kael, with her slangy riffs, digging you in the ribs. Or Bordwell, discussing the most subtle intonations in an Ozu film with an undertone of, "Look at this! It's really elegant how he does it."

Should some of these films not be in the book? Undoubtedly. Did I wrongly exclude others? No doubt. Did I just simply miss seeing some that I should have seen? Yes. Have my reviews improved over the years? I hope so. But every review records the experience of a man who went to the movies, and I was that man.

Roger Ebert

Acknowledgments

My editor is Dorothy O'Brien, tireless, cheerful, all-noticing. My friend and longtime editor Donna Martin suggested the yearbook approach to the annual volume; this is a special edition of the yearbook. The design is by Cameron Poulter, the typographical genius of Hyde Park.

My thanks to production editor Christi Clemons Hoffman, who renders Cameron's design into reality. I have been blessed with the expert and discriminating editing of John Barron, Laura Emerick, Miriam DiNunzio, Jeff Wisser, Darel Jevins, Jeff Johnson, Teresa Budasi, and Garry Steckles at the *Chicago Sun-Times*; Sue Roush at Universal Press Syndicate; and Michelle Daniel and David Shaw at Andrews McMeel Publishing. For much advice and counsel, thanks to Jim Emerson, my editor at www.rogerebert.com. Many thanks are also due to the production staff at *Ebert & Roeper,* and to Marsha Jordan at WLS-TV. My gratitude goes to Carol Iwata, my expert personal assistant; to Gregory Isaac, who scanned in hundreds of missing reviews and copy read them with an eagle eye; and to Marlene Gelfond, always helpful at the *Sun-Times*.

And special thanks and love to my wife, Chaz, who was always at my side during a difficult illness, helped see my three previous books through the press, and was a cheerleader for this one. If more film critics had a spouse just like her, the level of cheer in the field would rise.

ROGER EBERT

Key to Symbols

★★★★ A great film

G, PG, PG-13, R, NC-17:
Ratings of the Motion Picture
Association of America

G   Indicates that the movie is
         suitable for general audiences

PG   Suitable for general audiences
         but parental guidance is
         suggested

PG-13   Recommended for viewers
         13 years or above; may contain
         material inappropriate for
         younger children

R   Recommended for viewers
         17 or older

NC-17   Intended for adults only

141 m.   Running time

2007   Year of theatrical release

Four-Star Reviews 1967–2007

A

About Last Night . . .

R, 116 m., 1986

Rob Lowe (Danny), Demi Moore (Debbie), James Belushi (Bernie), Elizabeth Perkins (Joan), George DiCenzo (Mr. Favio), Michael Alldredge (Mother Malone), Robin Thomas (Steve), Joe Greco (Gus). Directed by Edward Zwick and produced by Jason Brett and Stuart Oken. Screenplay by Tim Kazurinsky and Denise DeClue, based on the play *Sexual Perversity in Chicago* by David Mamet.

If one of the pleasures of moviegoing is seeing strange new things on the screen, another pleasure, and probably a deeper one, is experiencing moments of recognition—times when we can say, yes, that's exactly right, that's exactly the way it would have happened. *About Last Night . . .* is a movie filled with moments like that. It has an eye and an ear for the way we live now, and it has a heart, too, and a sense of humor.

It is a love story. A young man and a young woman meet, and fall in love, and over the course of a year they try to work out what that means to them. It sounds like a simple story, and yet *About Last Night . . .* is one of the rarest of recent American movies, because it deals fearlessly with real people, instead of with special effects.

If there's anyone more afraid of a serious relationship than your average customer in a singles bar, it's a Hollywood producer. American movies will cheerfully spend millions of dollars on explosions and chases to avoid those moments when people are talking seriously and honestly to one another. After all, writing good dialogue takes some intelligence.

And intelligence is what sparkles all through *About Last Night . . .* —intelligence and a good, bawdy comic sensibility. The movie stars Rob Lowe as a salesman for a Chicago grocery wholesaler, and Demi Moore as an art director for a Michigan Avenue advertising agency. They meet at a softball game in Grant Park. Their romance blossoms in the singles bars of Rush Street, with a kindly bartender as father figure. At first they are attracted mostly by

biological reasons (they belong to a generation that believes it's kind of embarrassing to sleep with someone for the first time after you know them too well). Then they get to like each other. Then it is maybe even love, although everyone tap-dances around that word. Commitment, in their world, is the moment when Lowe offers Moore the use of a drawer in his apartment. Her response to that offer is one of the movie's high points.

Meanwhile, there is counterpoint, too. Lowe's best friend is his partner at work, played by James Belushi. Moore's best friend is Elizabeth Perkins, her roommate and fellow warrior on the singles scene. While Lowe and Moore start getting really serious about each other, Belushi and Perkins grow possessive— and also develop a spontaneous dislike for one another.

The story is kind of predictable in *About Last Night . . .*, if you have ever been young and kept your eyes open. There are only a limited number of basic romantic scenarios for young people in the city, and this movie sees through all of them. What's important is the way the characters look and sound, the way they talk, the way they reveal themselves, the way they grow by taking chances. Time after time, there are shocks of recognition, as the movie shows how well it understands what's going on.

Lowe and Moore, members of Hollywood's "Brat Pack," are survivors of 1985's awful movie about yuppie singles, *St. Elmo's Fire*. This is the movie *St. Elmo's Fire* should have been. The 1985 movie made them look stupid and shallow. *About Last Night . . .* gives them the best acting opportunities either one has ever had, and they make the most of them. Moore is especially impressive. There isn't a romantic note she isn't required to play in this movie, and she plays them all flawlessly.

Belushi and Perkins are good, too, making us realize how often the movies pretend that lovers live in a vacuum. When a big new relationship comes into your life, it requires an adjustment of all the other relationships, and a certain amount of discomfort and pain.

1

Belushi and Perkins provide those levels for the story, and a lot of its loudest laughs, too.

The movie is based on *Sexual Perversity in Chicago,* a play by David Mamet. The screenplay by Tim Kazurinsky and Denise DeClue smooths out Mamet's more episodic structure, and adds three-dimensional realism. It's a wonderful writing job, and Edward Zwick, directing a feature for the first time, shows a sure touch. His narrative spans an entire year, and the interest never lags.

Why is it that love stories are so rare from Hollywood these days? Have we lost faith in romance? Is love possible only with robots and cute little furry things from the special-effects department? Have people stopped talking? *About Last Night . . .* is a warmhearted and intelligent love story, and one of 1986's best movies.

The Accidental Tourist

PG, 121 m., 1988

William Hurt (Macon Leary), Kathleen Turner (Sarah, His Wife), Geena Davis (Muriel Pritchett), Amy Wright (Rose Leary), David Ogden Stiers (Porter Leary), Ed Begley, Jr. (Charles Leary), Bill Pullman (Julian), Robert Gorman (Alexander), Bradley Mott (Mr. Loomis). Directed by Lawrence Kasdan and produced by Kasdan, Charles Okun, and Michael Grillo. Screenplay by Frank Galati and Kasdan, based on the book by Anne Tyler.

"Yes, that is my son," the man says, identifying the body in the intensive care unit. Grief threatens to break his face into pieces, and then something closes shut inside of him. He has always had a very controlled nature, fearful of emotion and revelation, but now a true ice age begins, and after a year, his wife tells him she wants a divorce. It is because he can not seem to feel anything.

The Accidental Tourist begins on that note of emotional sterility, and the whole movie is a journey toward a smile at the end. The man's name is Macon Leary (William Hurt), and he writes travel books for people who detest traveling. He advises his readers on how to avoid human contact, where to find "American food" abroad, and how to convince themselves they haven't left home. His own life is the same sort of journey, and maybe it began

in childhood; his sister and two brothers still live together in the house where they were born, and any life outside of their routine would be unthinkable.

Macon's wife (Kathleen Turner) moves out, leaving him with the dog, Edward, who does like to travel, and is deeply disturbed by the curious life his masters have provided for him. He barks at ghosts and snaps at strangers. It is time for Macon to make another one of his overseas research trips, so he takes the dog to be boarded at a kennel, and that's where he meets Muriel Pritchett (Geena Davis). Muriel has Macon's number from the moment he walks in through the door. She can see he's a basket case, but she thinks she can help. She also thinks her young son needs a father.

Macon isn't so sure. He doesn't use the number she gives him. But later, when the dog trips him and he breaks his leg, he takes Edward back to the kennel, and this time Macon submits to a little obedience training of his own. He agrees to acknowledge that Muriel exists, and before long they are sort of living together (lust still exists in his body, but it lurks so far from the center of his feelings that sex hardly seems to cheer him up).

The peculiarity about these central passages in the film is that they are quite cheerful and sometimes even very funny, even though Macon himself is mired in a deep depression. Geena Davis, as Muriel, brings an unforced wackiness to her role in scenes like the one where she belts out a song while she's doing the dishes. But she is not as simple as she sometimes seems, and when Macon gets carried away with a little sentimental generalizing about the future, she warns him, "Don't make promises to my son that you are not prepared to keep."

There is also great good humor in the characters in Macon's family: brothers Porter (David Ogden Stiers) and Charles (Ed Begley, Jr.) and sister Rose (Amy Wright), a matriarch who feeds the family, presides over their incomprehensible card games, and supervises such traditional activities as alphabetizing the groceries on the kitchen shelves. One evening Macon takes his publisher, Julian (Bill Pullman), home to dinner, and Julian is struck with a thunderbolt of love for Rose. He eventually marries her, but a few weeks later Julian tells Macon that Rose has moved back home with the boys; she was concerned that they had abandoned regular meals and were eating only gorp.

This emergency triggers the movie's emotional turning point, which is subtle but unmistakable. Nobody knows Rose as well as Macon does, and so he gives Julian some very particular advice: "Call her up and tell her your business is going to pieces. Ask if she could just come in and get things organized. Get things under control. Put it that way. Use those words. 'Get things under control,' tell her."

In context, this speech is hilarious. It is also the first time in the film that Macon has been able to extend himself to help anybody—and it starts him on the road to emotional growth. Clinging to the sterility and loneliness that has been his protection, he doesn't realize at first that he has turned the corner. He still doubts that he needs Muriel, and when she buys herself a ticket and follows him to Paris, he refuses to have anything to do with her. When his wife also turns up in Paris, there is a moment when he thinks they may be able to patch things together again, and then finally Macon arrives at the sort of moment he has been avoiding all of his life: He has to make a choice. But by then the choice is obvious; he has already made it by peeking so briefly out of his shell.

The screenplay for *The Accidental Tourist*, by Lawrence Kasdan and Frank Galati, is able to reproduce a lot of the tone and dialogue of the Anne Tyler novel without ever simply being a movie version of a book. The textures are too specific and the humor is too quirky and well-timed to be borrowed from anywhere; the filmmakers have reinvented the same story in their own terms. The movie is a reunion for Kasdan, Hurt, and Turner, who all three put their careers on the map with *Body Heat* (1981). Kasdan used Hurt again in *The Big Chill* (1983), and understands how to employ Hurt's gift for somehow being likable at the same time he seems to be withdrawn.

What Hurt achieves here seems almost impossible: He is depressed, low-key, and intensely private through most of the movie, and yet somehow he wins our sympathy. What Kasdan achieves is just as tricky; I've never seen a movie so sad in which there was so much genuine laughter. *The Accidental Tourist* was one of the best films of 1988.

Across the Universe

PG-13, 133 m., 2007

Jim Sturgess (Jude), Evan Rachel Wood (Lucy), Joe Anderson (Max), Dana Fuchs (Sadie), Cynthia Loebe (Diner Waitress), Martin Luther (JoJo), T. V. Carpio (Prudence), Heather Janneck (Bowling Alley Dancer), Bono (Dr. Robert), Eddie Izzard (Mr. Kite), James Urbaniak (Bill), Linda Emond (Barbara Carrigan). Directed by Julie Taymor. Produced by Matthew Gross, Jennifer Todd, and Suzanne Todd. Written by Dick Clement, Ian La Frenais, and Taymor.

Here is a bold, beautiful, visually enchanting musical where we walk *into* the theater humming the songs. Julie Taymor's *Across the Universe* is an audacious marriage of cutting-edge visual techniques, heartwarming performances, 1960s history, and the Beatles songbook. Sounds like a concept that might be behind its time, but I believe in yesterday.

This isn't one of those druggy 1960s movies, although it has what the MPAA shyly calls "some" drug content. It's not grungy, although it has Joe Cocker in it. It's not political, which means it's political to its core. Most miraculous of all, it's not dated; the stories could be happening now, and in fact they are.

For a film that is almost wall-to-wall with music, it has a full-bodied plot. The characters, mostly named after Beatles songs, include Lucy (the angelic Evan Rachel Wood), who moves from middle America to New York; Jude (Jim Sturgess), a Liverpool ship welder who works his way to New York on a ship; and Lucy's brother Max (Joe Anderson), a college student who has dropped out (I guess). They now all share a pad in Greenwich Village with their musician friends the Hendrixian JoJo (Martin Luther), the Joplinesque Sadie (Dana Fuchs), and the lovelorn Prudence (T. V. Carpio), who has a thing for Max although the curious cutting of one scene in particular suggests she might have lesbian feelings as well.

Jude and Lucy fall in love, and they all go through a hippie period on Dr. Robert's Magic Bus, where the doctor (Bono) and his bus bear a striking resemblance to Ken Kesey's magical mystery tour. They also get guidance from Mr. Kite (Eddie Izzard), having been some days in preparation. But then things turn serious as

Max goes off to Vietnam and the story gets swept up in the antiwar movement.

Yet when I say "story," don't start thinking about a lot of dialogue and plotting. Almost everything happens as an illustration to a Beatles song. The arrangements are sometimes familiar, sometimes not, and the voices are all new; the actors either sing or synch, and often they find a tone in a song that we never knew was there before. When Prudence sings "I Wanna Hold Your Hand," for example, I realized how wrong I was to ever think that was a happy song. It's not happy if it's a hand you are never, ever, going to hold.

Julie Taymor, famous early as the director of *The Lion King* on Broadway, is a wildly inventive choreographer, such as in a basic training scene where all the drill sergeants look like G. I. Joe; a sequence where inductees in jockey shorts carry the Statue of Liberty through a Vietnam field; and cross-cutting between dancing to the Beatles in an American high school prom and a Liverpool dive bar. There are underwater sequences that approach ballet, a stage performance that turns into musical warfare, strawberries that bleed, rooftop concerts, and a montage combining crashing waves with the Detroit riots.

But all I'm doing here is list making. The experience of the movie is joyous. I don't even want to know about anybody who complains they aren't hearing "the real Beatles." Fred Astaire wasn't Cole Porter, either. These songs are now more than forty years old, some of them, and are timeless, and hearing these fresh young talents singing them (yes, and Bono, Izzard, and Cocker, too) only underlines their astonishing quality.

You weren't alive in the 1960s? Or the '70s, or '80s? You're like the guy on the message board who thought the band was named the "Beetles," and didn't even get it when people made Volkswagen jokes because he hadn't heard of VW Beetles either? All is forgiven. Jay Leno has a Jaywalking spot for you. Just about anybody else is likely to enjoy *Across the Universe*.

I'm sure there were executives who thought it was suicidal to set a "Beatles musical" in the "Vietnam era." But this is a movie that fires its songs like flowers at the way we live now. It's the kind of movie you watch again and again, like listening to a favorite album. It was sched-

uled for the Toronto Film Festival, so was previewed (as several Toronto films were) for critics in major cities. I was drowning in movies and deadlines, and this was the only one I went to see twice. Now do your homework, and rent the DVD of *A Hard Day's Night* if you've never seen it. The thought that there are readers who would get this far in this review and never have seen that film is unbearably sad. Cheer me up. Don't let me down (repeat three times).

Adaptation
R, 114 m., 2002

Nicolas Cage (Charlie/Donald Kaufman), Meryl Streep (Susan Orlean), Chris Cooper (John Laroche), Tilda Swinton (Valerie), Brian Cox (Robert McKee), Cara Seymour (Amelia), Judy Greer (Alice), Maggie Gyllenhaal (Caroline), John Cusack (Himself), Catherine Keener (Herself). Directed by Spike Jonze and produced by Jonathan Demme, Vincent Landay, and Edward Saxon. Screenplay by Charlie Kaufman and Donald Kaufman, based on the book *The Orchid Thief* by Susan Orlean.

What a bewilderingly brilliant and entertaining movie this is—a confounding story about orchid thieves and screenwriters, elegant New Yorkers and scruffy swamp rats, truth and fiction. *Adaptation* is a movie that leaves you breathless with curiosity, as it teases itself with the directions it might take. To watch the film is to be actively involved in the challenge of its creation.

It begins with a book named *The Orchid Thief*, based on a *New Yorker* article by Susan Orlean (Meryl Streep). She writes about a Florida orchid fancier named John Laroche (Chris Cooper), who is the latest in a long history of men so obsessed by orchids that they would steal and kill for them. Laroche is a con man and believes he has found a foolproof way to poach orchids from the protected Florida Everglades: Since they were ancestral Indian lands, he will hire Indians, who can pick the orchids with impunity.

Now that story might make a movie, but it's not the story of *Adaptation*. As the film opens, a screenwriter named Charlie Kaufman (Nicolas Cage) has been hired to adapt the book, and is stuck. There is so *much* about orchids in the book, and no obvious dramatic story line. Having penetrated halfway into the book myself, I understood his problem: It's a great story, but is it a movie?

Charlie is distraught. His producer, Valerie (Tilda Swinton), is on his case. Where is the first draft? He hardly has a first page. He relates his agony in voice-over, and anyone who has ever tried to write will understand his system of rewards and punishments: Should he wait until he has written a page to eat the muffin, or . . .

Charlie has a brother named Donald (also played by Cage). Donald lacks Charlie's ethics, his taste, his intelligence. He cheerfully admits that all he wants to do is write a potboiler and get rich. He attends the screenwriting seminars of Robert McKee (Brian Cox), who breaks down movie classics, sucks the marrow from their bones, and urges students to copy the formula. At a moment when Charlie is suicidal with frustration, Donald triumphantly announces he has sold a screenplay for a million dollars.

What is Charlie to do? To complicate matters, he has developed a fixation, even a crush, on Susan Orlean. He journeys to New York, shadows her, is too shy to meet her. She in turn goes to Florida to interview Laroche, who smells and smokes and has missing front teeth, but whose passion makes him . . . interesting.

And now my plot description will end, as I assure you I have not even hinted at the diabolical developments still to come. *Adaptation* is some kind of a filmmaking miracle, a film that is at one and the same time (a) the story of a movie being made, (b) the story of orchid thievery and criminal conspiracies, and (c) a deceptive combination of fiction and real life. The movie has been directed by Spike Jonze, who with Charlie Kaufman as writer made *Being John Malkovich* the best film of 1999. If you saw that film, you will (a) know what to expect this time, and (b) be wrong in countless ways.

There are real people in this film who are really real, like Malkovich, Jonze, John Cusack, and Catherine Keener, playing themselves. People who are real but are played by actors, like Susan Orlean, Robert McKee, John Laroche, and Charlie Kaufman. People who are apparently not real, like Donald Kaufman, despite the fact that he shares the screenplay credit. There are times when we are watching

more or less exactly what must (or could) have happened, and then a time when the film seems to jump the rails and head straight for the swamps of McKee's theories.

During all of its dazzling twists and turns, the movie remains consistently fascinating not just because of the direction and writing, but because of the lighthearted darkness of the performances. Chris Cooper plays a con man of extraordinary intelligence, who is attractive to a sophisticated New Yorker because he is so intensely *himself* in a world where few people are anybody. Nicolas Cage, as the twins, gets so deeply inside their opposite characters that we can always tell them apart even though he uses no tricks of makeup or hair. His narration creates the desperate agony of a man so smart he understands his problems intimately, yet so neurotic he is captive to them.

Now as for Meryl Streep, well, it helps to know (since she plays in so many serious films) that in her private life she is one of the merriest of women, because here she is able to begin as a studious New Yorker author and end as, more or less, Katharine Hepburn in *The African Queen*.

I sat up during this movie. I leaned forward. I was completely engaged. It toyed with me, tricked me, played straight with me, then tricked me about that. Its characters are colorful because they care so intensely; they are more interested in their obsessions than they are in the movie, if you see what I mean. And all the time, uncoiling beneath the surface of the film, is the audacious surprise of the last twenty minutes, in which—well, to say the movie's ending works on more than one level is not to imply it works on only two.

Affliction

R, 114 m., 1999

Nick Nolte (Wade Whitehouse), Sissy Spacek (Margie Fogg), James Coburn (Glen Whitehouse), Willem Dafoe (Rolfe Whitehouse), Mary Beth Hurt (Lillian), Jim True (Jack Hewitt), Marian Seldes (Alma Pittman), Holmes Osborne (Gordon LaRiviere). Directed by Paul Schrader and produced by Linda Reisman. Screenplay by Schrader, based on the book by Russell Banks.

Nick Nolte is a big, shambling, confident male presence in the movies, and it is startling to see his cocksure presence change into fear in

Paul Schrader's *Affliction*. Nolte plays Wade Whitehouse, the sheriff of a small New Hampshire town, whose uniform, gun, and stature do not make up for a deep feeling of worthlessness. He drinks, he smokes pot on the job, he walks with a sad weariness, he is hated by his ex-wife, and his young daughter looks at him as if he's crazy.

When we meet Glen, his father, we understand the source of his defeat. The older man (James Coburn) is a cauldron of alcoholic venom, a man whose consolation in life has been to dominate and terrorize his family. There are scenes where both men are on the screen together, and you can sense the sheriff shrinking, as if afraid of a sudden blow. The women in their lives have been an audience for cruelty; of the older man's wife, it is said, "Women like this, it's like they lived their lives with the sound turned off. And then they're gone."

Affliction is based on a novel by Russell Banks, whose work also inspired *The Sweet Hereafter*. Both films are set in bleak winter landscapes, and both involve a deep resentment of parental abuse—this one more obviously, since Sheriff Whitehouse's entire unhappy life has been, and still is, controlled by fear of his father. We're reminded of other films Schrader wrote (*Taxi Driver, Raging Bull, The Mosquito Coast*) or directed (*Mishima, Hardcore*), in which men's violence is churned up by feelings of inadequacy. (He also wrote *The Last Temptation of Christ*, in which at least one line applies: "Father, why hast thou forsaken me?")

Wade Whitehouse is a bad husband, a bad father, and a bad sheriff. He retains enough qualities to inspire the loyalty, or maybe the sympathy, of a girlfriend named Margie (Sissy Spacek), but his ex-wife (Mary Beth Hurt) looks at him with deep contempt, and his brother Rolfe (Willem Dafoe), the film's narrator, has been wise to clear out of the town and its poisons.

Early in the film, Wade decides to show a little enterprise on the job. A friend of his has gone out as a hunting guide for a rich man and returned with the man's expensive gun, some bloodstains, and a story of an accident. Wade doesn't believe it was an accident, and like a sleepwalker talking himself back to wakefulness, he begins an investigation that stirs up the stagnant town—and even rouses him into a state where he can be reached, for the first time in years, by fresh thoughts about how his life has gone wrong.

Because there are elements of a crime mystery in *Affliction*, it would be unwise to reveal too much about this side of the plot. It is interrupted, in any event, by another death: Wade and Margie go to the old man's house to find that Wade's mother, Glen's wife, lies dead upstairs and Glen is unable to acknowledge the situation. It is even possible that the sick woman crawled upstairs and was forgotten by a man whose inner eye has long been focused only on his own self-diagnosis: not drunk enough, drunk just right, or too drunk?

Rolfe returns to town for the funeral and to supply missing elements from the story of their childhood, and the film ends in an explosion that seems prepared even in the first frame. Its meaning is very clear: Cruelty to a child is not over in a moment or a day, but is like those medical capsules embedded in the flesh, which release their contents for years.

Nolte and Coburn are magnificent in this film, which is like an expiation for abusive men. It is revealing to watch them in their scenes together—to see how they're able to use physical presence to sketch the history of a relationship. Schrader says he cast Coburn because he needed an actor who was big enough, and had a "great iconic weight," to convincingly dominate Nolte. He found one. Coburn has spent a career largely in shallow entertainments, and here he rises to the occasion with a performance of power.

There is a story about that. "I met with Coburn before the picture began," Schrader told me, "and told him how carefully Nolte prepares for a role. I told Coburn that if he walked through the movie, Nolte might let him get away with it for a day, but on the second day all hell would break loose. Coburn said, 'Oh, you mean you want me to really act? I can do that. I haven't often been asked to, but I can.'" He can.

After Hours

R, 96 m., 1985

Griffin Dunne (Paul Hackett), Rosanna Arquette (Marcy), Linda Fiorentino (Kiki), Verna Bloom (June), Thomas Chong (Pepe), Teri Garr (Julie), John Heard (Bartender), Catherine O'Hara (Gail). Directed by Martin Scorsese and produced by Amy Robinson, Griffin Dunne, and Robert F. Colesberry. Screenplay by Joseph Minion.

Martin Scorsese's *After Hours* is a comedy, according to the strict definition of that word: It ends happily, and there are indications along the way that we're not supposed to take it seriously. It is, however, the tensest comedy I can remember, building its nightmare situation step by insidious step until our laughter is hollow, or defensive. This is the work of a master filmmaker who controls his effects so skillfully that I was drained by this film—so emotionally depleted that there was a moment, two-thirds of the way through, when I wondered if maybe I should pause and gather my thoughts and come back later for the rest of the "comedy."

The movie tells the story of a night in the life of Paul Hackett (Griffin Dunne), a midtown Manhattan word processing specialist who hates his job and his lonely private life. One night in a restaurant he strikes up a conversation with a winsome young woman (Rosanna Arquette). They seem to share some of the same interests. He gets her telephone number. He calls her, she suggests he come downtown to her apartment in Soho, and that is the beginning of his Kafkaesque adventure.

The streets of Soho are dark and deserted. Clouds of steam escape from the pavement, as they did in Scorsese's *Taxi Driver,* suggesting that Hades lurks just below the field of vision. The young woman is staying for a few days in the apartment of a friend (Linda Fiorentino), who makes bizarre sculptures, has kinky sexual tastes, and talks in a strange, veiled way about being burned. In Arquette's bedroom, Dunne makes the usual small talk of a first date, and she gushes that she's sure they'll have a great time, but then everything begins to fall apart.

At first, we think perhaps Dunne is the victim of random bad luck, as he is confronted with nightmares both tragic and trivial: Ominous strangers, escalating subway fares, a shocking suicide, sadomasochistic sexual practices, a punk nightclub where he almost has his head shaved, a street mob that thinks he is a thief. Only later, much later, on this seemingly endless night, do we find how everything is connected—and even then, it doesn't make any logical sense. For Paul Hack-

ett, as for the Job of the Old Testament, the plague of bad luck seems generated by some unexplained divine wrath.

And yet Scorsese does not simply make a horror movie, or some kind of allegory of doom. Each of his characters is drawn sharply, given quirky dialogue, allowed to be offbeat and funny. Teri Garr has a scene as a waitress who has tried to make sense of New York for so long that it has driven her around the bend. Fiorentino has a dry, sardonic angle on things. Arquette speaks wonderingly of a lover who was so obsessed by *The Wizard of Oz* that he always called her Dorothy in bed. John Heard is a bartender who has seen everything walk in through the doors of his all-night saloon and has lost the capacity for astonishment.

After Hours is another chapter in Scorsese's continuing examination of Manhattan as a state of mind; if he hadn't already used the title *New York, New York,* he could have used it this time. The movie earns its place on the list with his great films *Mean Streets, Taxi Driver,* and *Raging Bull.* For New Yorkers, parts of the film will no doubt play as a documentary. In what other city is everyday life such an unremitting challenge?

After Hours is a brilliant film, one of the year's best. It is also a most curious film. It comes after Scorsese's *The King of Comedy,* a film I thought was fascinating but unsuccessful, and continues Scorsese's attempt to combine comedy and satire with unrelenting pressure and a sense of all-pervading paranoia. This time he succeeds. The result is a film that is so original, so particular, that we are uncertain from moment to moment exactly how to respond to it. The style of the film creates, in us, the same feeling that the events in the film create in the hero. Interesting.

After Life

NO MPAA RATING, 118 m., 1999

Arata (Takashi Mochizuki), Taketoshi Naito (Ichiro Watanabe), Erika Oda (Shiori Satonaka), Susumu Terajima (Satoru Kawashima), Takashi Naito (Takuro Sugie), Hisako Hara (Kiyo Nishimura). Directed by Hirokazu Kore-eda and produced by Sato Shiho and Akieda Masayuki. Screenplay by Kore-eda.

The people materialize from out of clear white light as a bell tolls. Where are they? An ordinary building is surrounded by greenery and an indistinct space. They are greeted by staff members who explain, courteously, that they have died and are now at a way station before the next stage of their experience.

They will be here a week. Their assignment is to choose one memory, one only, from their lifetimes: one memory they want to save for eternity. Then a film will be made to reenact that memory, and they will move along, taking only that memory with them, forgetting everything else. They will spend eternity within their happiest memory.

That is the premise of Hirokazu Kore-eda's *After Life,* a film that reaches out gently to the audience and challenges us: What is the single moment in our own lives we treasure the most? One of the new arrivals says that he has only bad memories. The staff members urge him to think more deeply. Surely spending eternity within a bad memory would be—well, literally, hell. And spending forever within our best memory would be, I suppose, as close as we should dare to come to heaven.

The film is completely matter-of-fact. No special effects, no celestial choirs, no angelic flimflam. The staff is hardworking; they have a lot of memories to process in a week, and a lot of production work to do on the individual films. There are pragmatic details to be worked out: Scripts have to be written, sets constructed, special effects improvised. This isn't all metaphysical work; a member of an earlier group, we learn, chose Disney World, singling out the Splash Mountain ride.

Kore-eda, with this film and the 1997 masterpiece *Maborosi,* has earned the right to be considered with Kurosawa, Bergman, and other great humanists of the cinema. His films embrace the mystery of life, and encourage us to think about why we are here and what makes us truly happy. At a time when so many movies feed on irony and cynicism, here is a man who hopes we will feel better and wiser when we leave his film.

The method of the film contributes to the impact. Some of these people, and some of their memories, are real (we are not told which). Kore-eda filmed hundreds of interviews with ordinary people in Japan. The faces on the screen are so alive, the characters seem to be recalling events they really lived through in a world of simplicity and wonder. Although there are a lot of characters in the movie, we have no trouble telling them apart because each is unique and irreplaceable.

The staff members offer a mystery of their own. Who are they, and why were they chosen to work here at the way station instead of moving on to the next stage like everybody else? The solution to that question is contained in revelations I will not discuss, because they emerge so naturally from the film.

One of the most emotional moments in *After Life* is when a young staff member discovers a connection between himself and an elderly new arrival. The new arrival is able to tell him something that changes his entire perception of his life. This revelation, of a young love long ago, has the same kind of deep, bittersweet resonance as the ending of *The Dead,* the James Joyce short story (and John Huston film) about a man who feels a sudden burst of identification with his wife's first lover, a young man now long dead.

After Life considers the kind of delicate material that could be destroyed by schmaltz. It's the kind of film that Hollywood likes to remake with vulgar, paint-by-the-numbers sentimentality. It is like a transcendent version of *Ghost,* evoking the same emotions, but deserving them. Knowing that his premise is supernatural and fantastical, Kore-eda makes everything else in the film quietly pragmatic. The staff labors against deadlines. The arrivals set to work on their memories. There will be a screening of the films on Saturday—and then Saturday, and everything else, will cease to exist. Except for the memories.

Which memory would I choose? I sit looking out the window as images play through my mind. There are so many moments to choose from. Just thinking about them makes me feel fortunate. I remember a line from Ingmar Bergman's film *Cries and Whispers.* After the older sister dies painfully of cancer, her diary is discovered. In it she remembers a day during her illness when she was feeling better. Her two sisters and her nurse join her in the garden, in the sunlight, and for a moment pain is forgotten and they are simply happy to be together. This woman who we have seen die a terrible death has written: "I feel a great gratitude to my life, which gives me so much."

After the Rehearsal

R, 72 m., 1984

Erland Josephson (Henrik Vogler), Ingrid Thulin (Rakel), Lena Olin (Anna Egerman), Nadja Palmstjerna-Weiss (Anna at Twelve). Directed by Ingmar Bergman and produced by Jorn Donner. Screenplay by Bergman.

Ingmar Bergman's *After the Rehearsal* seems to be as simple and direct as a tape recording of actual conversations, and yet look at the thickets of interpretation it has inspired in its critics. After seeing it, I thought I understood the film entirely. Now I am not so sure. Like so many of Bergman's films, and especially the spare "chamber films" it joins *(Winter Light, Persona)*, it consists of unadorned surfaces concealing fathomless depths.

It is safest to begin with the surfaces. All of the action takes place on a stage prepared for a production of Strindberg's *A Dream Play*. An aging director sits among the props, and every chair and table reminds him of an earlier production. The rehearsal has ended some time ago, and now the director simply sits, as if the stage were his room. A young actress returns to the stage for a missing bracelet. But of course the bracelet is an excuse, and she wants to talk to the great man, and perhaps to begin a relationship with him (as, perhaps, she has heard that many other actresses have done over the years). The old director was once the lover of the girl's mother. It is even possible that this girl is his daughter. They talk. Then an older actress enters. She has a few lines in the play, and wants to know—frankly, brutally—if her career as a leading actress is really over because she is known as a drunk. She cries, she rants, she bares her breasts to show the old man that her body is still sound, if sodden. The director is tempted: He was once this woman's lover, and perhaps her daughter is his.

The young girl stays on stage during the extraordinary display of the older actress. When the older woman leaves, the director and ingenue talk again, and this time the old man, who has been through the turmoil of love too many times, talks her through their probable future: We could make love, we could have an affair, we would call it part of our art, you would be the student, I would be the teacher, I would grow tired, you would feel trapped, all

our idealism would turn into ashes. Since the relationship is foredoomed, why bother with it?

Just in terms of these spare passages of dialogue and passion, *After the Rehearsal* is an important and painful confessional, for the old director, of course, bears many points of resemblance to Bergman, whose lovers have included his actresses Harriet Andersson, Bibi Andersson, and Liv Ullmann, among others, and whose daughter by Ullmann appeared in *Face to Face*. But the film is not a scandalous revelation: It is actually more of a sacramental confession, as if Bergman, the son of a Lutheran bishop, now sees the stage as his confessional and is asking the audience to bless and forgive him. (His gravest sin, as I read the film, is not lust or adultery, but the sin of taking advantage of others—of manipulating them with his power and intellect.)

If that were the extent of *After the Rehearsal*, it would be deep enough. But Bergman has surrounded the bare bones of his story with mystifying problems of interpretation. Just as in *Persona* he included scenes in which his characters exchanged personalities and engaged in scenes that might have or might not have been fantasies and dreams, so here, too, he gives us things to puzzle over. Reading the earlier reviews of the film, I discover that one critic realized only belatedly that the younger actress, Anna, was onstage the whole time the older actress, Rakel, poured out her heart. Strange, and yet another critic thought the whole scene with Rakel was the director's own dream. Yet another suggested that Anna represents not only herself but also Rakel's absent daughter. And another theory is that Anna is the daughter of the director and Rakel, and is brought into being by the residual love between them, as a sort of theatrical Holy Spirit. The age of Anna has been variously reported as ranging from twelve to twenty, with one critic reporting that both ages of the character are represented.

Which is the correct interpretation? They are all correct. Each and every one is equally correct; otherwise what is the use of a dream play? The point is not to find the literal meaning, anyway, but to touch the soul of the director, and find out what still hurts him after all these years. After all the sex and all the promises, all the lies and truths and messy affairs, there is still one critical area where he is filled with guilt and passion. It is revealed when Anna tells him she is pregnant. He is enraged. How could she, a young actress given the role of a lifetime, jeopardize her career and his play by getting pregnant? Then she tells him she has had an abortion, for the sake of the play. And then he really is torn in two, for he does not believe, after all, that a play—not even his play—is worth the sacrifice of a life. What we are left with at the end of *After the Rehearsal*, however, is the very strong sense of an artist who has sacrificed many lives for the sake of his art, and now wonders if perhaps one of those lives was his own.

The Age of Innocence

PG, 132 m., 1993

Daniel Day-Lewis (Newland Archer), Michelle Pfeiffer (Ellen Olenska), Winona Ryder (May Welland), Geraldine Chaplin (Mrs. Welland), Mary Beth Hurt (Regina Beaufort), Miriam Margolyes (Mrs. Mingott), Richard E. Grant (Larry Lefferts), Alec McCowen (Sillerton Jackson). Directed by Martin Scorsese and produced by Barbara De Fina. Screenplay by Jay Cocks and Scorsese, based on the book by Edith Wharton.

We live in an age of brutal manners, when people crudely say exactly what they mean, comedy is based on insult, tributes are roasts, and loud public obscenity passes without notice. Martin Scorsese's film *The Age of Innocence*, which takes place in the 1870s, seems so alien it could be pure fantasy. A rigid social code governs how people talk, walk, meet, part, dine, earn their livings, fall in love, and marry. Not a word of the code is written down anywhere. But these people have been studying it since they were born.

The film is based on a novel by Edith Wharton, who died in the 1930s. The age of innocence, as she called it with fierce irony, was over long before she even wrote her book. Yet she understood that the people of her story had the same lusts as we barbaric moderns, and not acting on them made them all the stronger.

The novel and the movie take place in the elegant milieu of the oldest and richest families in New York City. Marriages are like treaties between nations, their purpose not merely to cement romance or produce children, but to provide for the orderly transmission of wealth between the generations. Anything that threat-ens this sedate process is hated. It is not thought proper for men and women to place their own selfish desires above the needs of their class. People do indeed "marry for love," but the practice is frowned upon as vulgar and dangerous.

We meet a young man named Newland Archer (Daniel Day-Lewis), who is engaged to marry the pretty young May Welland (Winona Ryder). He has great affection for her, even though she seems pretty but dim, well-behaved rather than high-spirited. All agree this is a good marriage between good families, and Archer is satisfied—until one night at the opera he sees a cousin who has married and lived in Europe for years. She is Ellen, the Countess Olenska (Michelle Pfeiffer). She has, he is astonished to discover, ideas of her own. She looks on his world with the amusement and detachment of an exile. She is beautiful, yes, but that isn't what attracts Archer. His entire being is excited by the presence of a woman who boldly thinks for herself.

The countess is not quite a respectable woman. First she made the mistake of marrying outside her circle, taking a rich Polish count and living in Europe. Then she made a greater transgression, separating from her husband and returning to New York, where she stands out at social gatherings as an extra woman of undoubted fascination, whom no one knows quite what to do with. It is clear to everyone that her presence is a threat to the orderly progress of Archer's marriage with May.

This kind of story has been filmed, very well, by the Merchant-Ivory team. Their *Howards End, A Room with a View,* and *The Bostonians* know this world. It would seem to be material of no interest to Martin Scorsese, a director of great guilts and energies, whose very titles are a rebuke to the age of innocence: *Mean Streets, Taxi Driver, Raging Bull, GoodFellas.* Yet when his friend and cowriter Jay Cocks handed Scorsese the Wharton novel, he could not put it down, and now he has filmed it, and through some miracle it is all Wharton, and all Scorsese.

The story told here is brutal and bloody, the story of a man's passion crushed, his heart defeated. Yet it is also much more, and the last scene of the film, which pulls everything together, is almost unbearably poignant because it reveals that the man was not the only one with feelings—that others sacrificed for him, that his deepest tragedy was not what he lost, but what he never realized he had.

The Age of Innocence is filmed with elegance. These rich aristocrats move in their gilded circles from opera to dinner to drawing room, with a costume for every role and every time of day. Scorsese observes the smallest of social moments, the incline of a head, the angle of a glance, the subtle inflection of a word or phrase. And gradually we understand what is happening: Archer is considering breaking his engagement to May, in order to run away with the countess, and everyone is concerned to prevent him—while at no time does anyone reveal by the slightest sign that they know what they are doing.

I have seen love scenes in which naked bodies thrash in sweaty passion, but I have rarely seen them more passionate than in this movie, where everyone is wrapped in layers of Victorian repression. The big erotic moments take place in public among fully clothed people speaking in perfectly modulated phrases, and they are so filled with libido and terror that the characters scarcely survive them.

Scorsese, that artist of headlong temperament, here exhibits enormous patience. We are provided with the voice of a narrator (Joanne Woodward), who understands all that is happening, guides us, and supplies the private thoughts of some of the characters.

We learn the rules of the society. We meet an elderly woman named Mrs. Mingott (Miriam Margolyes), who has vast sums of money and functions for her society as sort of an appeals court of what can be permitted and what cannot be.

And we see the infinite care and attention with which May Welland defends her relationship with Newland Archer. May knows or suspects everything that is happening between Newland and the countess, but she chooses to acknowledge only certain information, and works with the greatest cleverness to preserve her marriage while never quite seeming to notice anything wrong.

Each performance is modulated to preserve the delicate balance of the romantic war. Daniel Day-Lewis stands at the center, deluded for a time that he has free will. Michelle Pfeiffer, as the countess, is a woman who sees through society without quite rejecting it, and takes an almost sensuous pleasure in seducing Archer with the power of her mind. At first it seems that little May is an unwitting bystander and victim, but Winona Ryder gradually reveals the depth of her character's intelligence, and in the last scene, as I said, all is revealed and much is finally understood.

Scorsese is known for his restless camera; he rarely allows a static shot. But here you will have the impression of grace and stateliness in his visual style, and only on a second viewing will you realize the subtlety with which his camera does, indeed, incessantly move, insinuating itself into conversations like a curious uninvited guest. At the beginning of *The Age of Innocence*, as I suggested, it seems to represent a world completely alien to us. By the end, we realize these people have all the same emotions, passions, fears, and desires that we do. It is simply that they value them more highly, and are less careless with them, and do not in the cause of self-indulgence choose a moment's pleasure over a lifetime's exquisite and romantic regret.

Akeelah and the Bee

PG-13, 112 m., 2006

Angela Bassett (Tanya Anderson), Keke Palmer (Akeelah Anderson), Laurence Fishburne (Dr. Joshua Larabee), Curtis Armstrong (Mr. Welch), J. R. Villarreal (Javier), Sahara Garey (Georgia), Sean Michael Afable (Dylan), Erica Hubbard (Kiana Anderson). Directed by Doug Atchison and produced by Laurence Fishburne, Sidney Ganis, Nancy Hult Ganis, Daniel Llewelyn, and Michael Romersa. Screenplay by Atchison.

Akeelah Anderson can spell. She can spell better than anyone in her school in south central Los Angeles, and she might have a chance at the nationals. Who can say? She sees the national spelling bee on ESPN and is intrigued. But she is also wary, because in her school there is danger in being labeled a "brainiac," and it's wiser to keep your smarts to yourself. This is a tragedy in some predominantly black schools: Excellence is punished by the other students, possibly as an expression of their own low self-esteem.

The thing with Akeelah (Keke Palmer) is that she *can* spell, whether she wants to or not. Beating time with her hand against her thigh as sort of a metronome, she cranks out the letters and arrives triumphantly at the words. No, she doesn't have a photographic memory, nor is she channeling the occult, as the heroine of *Bee Season* does. She's just a good speller.

The story of Akeelah's ascent to the finals of the National Spelling Bee makes an uncommonly good movie, entertaining and actually inspirational, and with a few tears along the way. Her real chance at national success comes after a reluctant English professor agrees to act as her coach. This is Dr. Joshua Larabee (Laurence Fishburne), on a leave of absence after the death of his daughter. Coaching her is a way out of his own shell. And for Fishburne, it's a reminder of his work in *Searching for Bobby Fischer* (1993), another movie where he coached a prodigy.

Akeelah is not mocked only at school. Her own mother is against her. Tanya Anderson (Angela Bassett) has issues after the death of her husband, and she values Akeelah's homework above all else, including silly after-school activities such as spelling bees. Akeelah practices in secret, and after she wins a few bees, even the tough kids in the neighborhood start cheering for her.

Keke Palmer, a young Chicago actress whose first role was as Queen Latifah's niece in *Barber Shop 2,* becomes an important young star with this movie. It puts her in Dakota Fanning and Flora Cross territory, and there's something about her poise and self-possession that hints she will grow up to be a considerable actress. The movie depends on her, and she deserves its trust.

So far I imagine *Akeelah and the Bee* sounds like a nice but fairly conventional movie. What makes it transcend the material is the way she relates to the professor and to two fellow contestants: a Mexican-American named Javier (J. R. Villarreal) and an Asian-American named Dylan (Sean Michael Afable). Javier, who lives with his family in the upscale Woodland Hills neighborhood, invites Akeelah to his birthday party (unaware of what a long bus trip it involves). Dylan, driven by an obsessive father, treats the spelling bee like life and death, and takes no hostages. Hearing Dylan's father berate him, Akeelah feels an instinctive sympathy. And as for Javier's feelings for Akeelah, at his party he impulsively kisses her.

"Why'd you do that?" she asks him.

"I had an impulse. Are you gonna sue me for sexual harassment?"

The sessions between Akeelah and the professor are crucial to the film, because he is teaching her not only strategy but also how to be willing to win. No, he doesn't use self-help clichés. He is demanding and uncompromising, and he tells her again and again, "Our deepest fear is that we are powerful beyond measure." This quote, often attributed to Nelson Mandela, is actually from Marianne Williamson but is no less true for Akeelah (the movie does not attribute it).

Now I am going to start dancing around the plot. Something happens during the finals of the national bee that you are not going to see coming, and it may move you as deeply as it did me. I've often said it's not sadness that touches me the most in a movie, but goodness. Under enormous pressure, at a crucial moment, Akeelah does something good. Its results I will leave for you to discover. What is ingenious about the plot construction of writer-director Doug Atchison is that he creates this moment so that we understand what's happening, but there's no way to say for sure. Even the judges sense or suspect something. But Akeelah, improvising in the moment and out of her heart, makes it airtight. There is only one person who absolutely must understand what she is doing, and why—and he does.

This ending answers one of my problems with spelling bees and spelling-bee movies. It removes winning as the only objective. Vince Lombardi was dead wrong when he said, "Winning isn't everything. It's the only thing" (a quote, by the way, first said not by Lombardi but in the 1930s by UCLA coach Henry "Red" Sanders—but since everybody thinks Lombardi said it, he won, I guess). The saying is mistaken because to win for the wrong reason or in the wrong way is to lose. Something called sportsmanship is involved.

In our winning-obsessed culture, it is inspiring to see a young woman like Akeelah Anderson instinctively understand, with empathy and generosity, that doing the right thing involves more than winning. That's what makes the film particularly valuable for young audiences. I don't care if they leave the theater wanting to spell better, but if they have learned from Akeelah, they will want to live better.

Alex in Wonderland

R, 109 m., 1971

Donald Sutherland (Alex), Ellen Burstyn (Beth), Meg Mazursky (Amy), Glenna Sergent (Nancy), Viola Spolin (Mother), Paul Mazursky (Hal Stern). Directed by Paul Mazursky and produced by Larry Tucker. Screenplay by Mazursky and Tucker.

"Who are you," said the Caterpillar.

This was not an encouraging opening for a conversation. Alice replied rather shyly. "I— hardly know, Sir, just at present—at least I know who I was when I got up this morning, but I think I must have changed several times since then."

That was exactly the case in Hollywood in the early seventies. Works of genius were showered on us by bright, radical, young, etc., filmmakers who announced their intention to overturn the Hollywood establishment. Occasionally one of their films did make it very big, as *Easy Rider* did. Within weeks, the Hollywood hills were jammed with other would-be geniuses, shooting nihilistic cycle flicks with pseudo-Dylan lyrics. Meanwhile, the original boy wonders . . . have got to make themselves another film. That was the situation for Paul Mazursky and Larry Tucker, who wrote, produced, and directed *Bob & Carol & Ted & Alice*. That movie was an artistic and financial success. It was chosen to open the New York Film Festival. It was argued about in all the best publications. Elliott Gould became a star. Natalie Wood made her comeback. Tucker and Mazursky got rich. The whole enchilada, baby.

Alex in Wonderland was their response to that situation; it's a movie about a director whose first movie is a success and who's at a loss for another project. In this sense, it's autobiographical; not in the details of life, but in the crises. Mazursky himself even appears, as Hal Stern, the doggedly mod movie producer who hopes to interest Donald Sutherland in *Don Quixote* as a Western? Or maybe . . . ?

If the director's dilemma sounds familiar, perhaps you're reminded of Fellini's *8½*. Mazursky and Tucker were. The blocked director's daughter even asks why he doesn't do a movie about not knowing what to do next, and he says, no, Fellini already did that. *Alex in Wonderland* is a deliberately Felliniesque movie, all the same, and all the more

fun for that. Fellini himself appears briefly, to no special purpose, and Fellini trademarks like parades, circuses, and clowns keep turning up in the hero's daydreams.

If *Alex* had been left just on this level, however, it would have been of little interest. What makes it so good is the gift Mazursky, Tucker, and their actors have of fleshing out the small scenes of human contact that give the movie its almost frightening resonance.

Sutherland, as the director, has trouble handling his success. His uncertainty about what to do next spills over into aloofness, even cruelty, toward his wife (Ellen Burstyn) and mother (Viola Spolin). A short scene in a car with his mother, and a long scene in a kitchen with his wife, actually make the rest of the movie work, because they give the character a depth that sticks even through the superficial dream sequences.

And beyond these intimate scenes, there are icily observant portraits of the "new Hollywood." Of aimless "idealistic" arguments on the beach, of luncheon meetings, of idle people trying somehow to be idly committed. These scenes are the 1970 equivalent of Fitzgerald's *The Last Tycoon* or Nathanael West's *The Day of the Locust:* unforgivingly accurate studies of the distance between America and the filmmakers who would be "relevant" about it.

The Fellini elements are laid onto the film and don't quite sink in (although buffs will enjoy them just as parody). But the human story does work, remarkably well, and if the movie doesn't hold together we're not disposed to hold that against it. Half an enchilada is better than none.

Alice Doesn't Live Here Anymore

PG, 113 m., 1974

Ellen Burstyn (Alice Hyatt), Kris Kristofferson (David), Billy Green Bush (Donald), Diane Ladd (Flo), Alfred Lutter (Tommy), Harvey Keitel (Ben). Directed by Martin Scorsese and produced by David Susskind and Audrey Maas. Screenplay by Robert Getchell.

Martin Scorsese's *Alice Doesn't Live Here Anymore* opens with a parody of the Hollywood dream world little girls were expected to carry around in their intellectual baggage a generation ago. The screen is awash with a fake sunset, and a sweet little thing comes strolling along home past sets that seem rescued from *The Wizard of Oz*. But her dreams and dialogue are decidedly not made of sugar, spice, or anything nice: This little girl is going to do things her way.

That was her defiant childhood notion, anyway. But by the time she's thirty-five, Alice Hyatt has more or less fallen into society's rhythms. She's married to an incommunicative truck driver, she has a precocious twelve-year-old son, she kills time chatting with the neighbors. And then her husband is unexpectedly killed in a traffic accident and she's left widowed and—almost worse than that—independent. After all those years of having someone there, can she cope by herself?

She can, she says. When she was a little girl, she idolized Alice Faye and determined to be a singer when she grew up. Well, she's thirty-five, and that's grown-up. She has a garage sale, sells the house, and sets off on an odyssey through the Southwest with her son and her dreams. What happens to her along the way provides one of the most perceptive, funny, occasionally painful portraits of an American woman I've seen.

The movie has been both attacked and defended on feminist grounds, but I think it belongs somewhere outside ideology, maybe in the area of contemporary myth and romance. There are scenes in which we take Alice and her journey perfectly seriously, there are scenes of harrowing reality, and then there are other scenes (including some hilarious passages in a restaurant where she waits on tables) where Scorsese edges into slight, cheerful exaggeration. There are times, indeed, when the movie seems less about Alice than it does about the speculations and daydreams of a lot of women about her age, who identify with the liberation of other women, but are unsure on the subject of themselves.

A movie like this depends as much on performances as on direction, and there's a fine performance by Ellen Burstyn (who won an Oscar for this role) as Alice. She looks more real this time than she did as Cybill Shepherd's available mother in *The Last Picture Show* or as Linda Blair's tormented mother in *The Exorcist*. It's the kind of role she can relax in, be

honest with, allow to develop naturally (although those are often the hardest roles of all). She's determined to find work as a singer, to "resume" a career that was mostly dreams to begin with, and she's pretty enough (although not good enough) to almost pull it off. She meets some generally good people along the way, and they help her when they can. But she also meets some creeps, especially a deceptively nice guy named Ben (played by Harvey Keitel, the autobiographical hero of Scorsese's two films set in Little Italy). The singing jobs don't materialize much, and it's while she's waitressing that she runs into a divorced young farmer (Kris Kristofferson).

They fall warily in love, and there's an interesting relationship between Kristofferson and Alfred Lutter, who does a very good job of playing a certain kind of twelve-year-old kid. Most women in Alice's position probably wouldn't run into a convenient, understanding, and eligible young farmer, but then a lot of the things in the film don't work as pure logic. There's a little myth to them, while Scorsese sneaks up on his main theme.

The movie's filled with brilliantly done individual scenes. Alice, for example, has a run-in with a fellow waitress with an inspired vocabulary (Diane Ladd, an Oscar nominee for this role). They fall into a friendship and have a frank and honest conversation one day while sunbathing. The scene works perfectly. There's also the specific way her first employer backs into offering her a singing job, and the way Alice takes leave from her old neighbors, and the way her son persists in explaining a joke that could only be understood by a twelve-year-old. These are great moments in a film that gives us Alice Hyatt: female, thirty-five, undefeated.

Alice's Restaurant

R, 110 m., 1969

Arlo Guthrie (Arlo), Pat Quinn (Alice), James Broderick (Ray), Michael McClanthan (Shelly), Geoff Outlaw (Roger). Directed by Arthur Penn and produced by Hillard Elkins, Harold Leventhal, and Joe Manduke. Screenplay by Venable Herndon and Arthur Penn, based on the recording by Arlo Guthrie.

Arthur Penn's *Alice's Restaurant* is good work in a minor key. It isn't a great film, but you never get the feeling that it wanted to be. You sense that Penn achieved what he set out to do: to make a relaxed, unstudied portrait of some friends, and some months in their lives, and some births, deaths, and marriages.

To this degree he has been faithful to the spirit of Arlo Guthrie's original recording. A higher-pressure film would have been inappropriate. You almost wish, in fact, that the rudimentary thrusts toward a plot had been left out. *Alice's Restaurant* is at its best when Arlo is on the road, going to college, hitchhiking, playing his guitar, getting drafted, taking his Army physical, going to see his friends Ray and Alice, and things like that.

But it's not as relaxed, and not as confident, in some awkward scenes involving Alice's love life and her relationship with Ray. I guess Alice (Pat Quinn) is an Earth Mother. She folds lost souls to her bosom and tries for a transfusion of life force. Sometimes she succeeds. And to this degree she exudes a healthy sensuality, a generous spirit.

But then Ray keeps turning up, and they fight, and their relationship becomes ambiguous. What are we supposed to think? That she's two-timing him? What does Ray think, for that matter? Penn doesn't make it clear, and as a result the love scenes aren't as positive as they should be.

There's also a difficulty, for me at least, in the decision to bring Arlo's father, Woody, into the film as a character. Woody, played by Joseph Boley, is shown in the last stages of the nerve disorder Arlo may develop someday himself. This is uncomfortably close to life, but we're willing to accept it as part of the film's fundamental honesty.

But the scenes themselves are not handled very well. Woody nods and tries to smile, and Arlo and his mother visit the bedside, and one afternoon Pete Seeger comes to play for his friend. But it's all too staged, somehow. You know they were trying to do the scenes about Woody quietly and tastefully, but still you feel uneasy about it.

These are minor objections, however. For the most part *Alice's Restaurant* is a warm and alive film. You can feel Penn trying to portray a lifestyle rather than a plot with characters in it. He wants to express the spirit of the church Alice and Ray lived in, and the community they presided over. And he does it pretty well;

we are reminded of some of the gentle scenes in *Bonnie and Clyde,* such as the one in the Okie camp, and the time in the gas station when they meet C. W. Moss. This is a new feeling in American movies; it's good to have it.

It is also good to have Arlo Guthrie himself, who is quiet and open and good on camera. His camera presence is so natural, in fact, that it contrasts with the tightness of some of the professional actors (especially James Broderick as Ray). *Alice's Restaurant* finally becomes a synthesis of Arlo's spirit and Arthur Penn's tact.

Ali—Fear Eats the Soul

NO MPAA RATING, 93 m., 1974

Brigitte Mira (Emmi Kurowski), El Hedi ben Salem (Ali), Barbara Valentin (Barbara), Irm Hermann (Krista), Elma Karlowe (Mrs. Kargus). Directed and produced by Rainer Werner Fassbinder. Screenplay by Fassbinder.

Although *Ali—Fear Eats the Soul* was one of the first films by Fassbinder to make an impression outside Germany, his style was already formed and his confidence unshakable. In it, he creates an unlikely social situation and watches it, deadpan, through scenes of excruciating embarrassment and pain. An admirer of the soapy Hollywood melodramas of Douglas Sirk, he liked to add sudden, unexpected dramatic turns, and though in a lesser director they might seem like affectations, in a Fassbinder film they feel more like blows from the fly-swatters of the gods.

Ali is about an unlikely love that grows between a thirty-fiveish Moroccan immigrant laborer and a sixtyish cleaning lady, in a German city that seems to have left them both stranded and lonely. He is handsome and muscular. She is short and pudgy. They meet in a bar, in one of those Fassbinder scenes where silences and mutual embarrassments are stretched out until they pass through comedy and come out as weirdly constrained parody—a cross between TV soap opera and the paintings of Edward Hopper.

Fassbinder borrows from Sirk the technique of framing shots so stringently that the characters seem fenced in, limited in the ways they can move. He'll lock Emmi (Brigitte Mira) in the foreground and Ali (El Hedi Ben Salem) in the background in such a way that neither could move without leaving the frame, and make you aware of that: He's saying visually that they are locked into the same space, without choices. They remain motionless in his carefully composed visual settings while we absorb their dilemma and (gradually) the fact that he's calling attention to it. In the quietest of ways, Fassbinder is breaking his contract with the audience, which expects plausible fiction. He nudges us to get outside the movie and look at it as absurd, as black humor, as comment on these people so hopelessly trapped in their dreary surroundings and by their fates.

Is he sometimes being deliberately funny? I'm sure of it. His style and tone are so adamant that audiences sometimes just sit in silence, uncertain of the right response. With some films, that indicates the director's loss of control over tone. With Fassbinder, it seems to be the response he wants: confusion and curiosity in the face of a new cinematic language that won't use clichés, except to draw them out beyond plausibility.

Consider, for example, a scene where Emmi gathers her family members (one of them played by Fassbinder) to meet in her living room and be introduced to her new husband. They sit stiffly in chairs, lined up, facing the door like panelists on some kind of domestic game show. She summons Ali, who appears in the door. The children and in-laws now realize Emmi is married to a black man half her age. They stare. A silence attenuates until it threatens to snap. Then one of the family stands up and methodically kicks in the screen of her TV set. It is easy to imagine countless ways this scene could have been handled—but only Fassbinder would have approached it this way, with such coldness and cruelty.

There is another scene in which Ali, now more lonely than ever, visits the apartment of the blowzy barmaid at the tavern where he earlier met Emmi. She watched sardonically as their romance developed over Cokes. Now she poses in her doorway like the model for a pulp paperback and asks him what he wants. She does not anticipate his answer: *couscous.*

Ali—Fear Eats the Soul was the third Fassbinder film I saw, after *Merchant of the Four Seasons* (1971) and the magnificent *The Bitter*

Tears of Petra Von Kant, in the early 1970s, when the Chicago Film Festival first introduced him to audiences outside Germany. As I watched those films, a curiosity and excitement grew inside of me. Fassbinder was employing the materials of melodrama, but with a bluntness and love of arbitrary plot development that showed a freedom from the form. What was he saying? That our lives are made of clichés and melodrama? That the movies are made of them—and the more aware of that we are, the better?

Later, after encounters with Fassbinder at the Cannes and Montreal film festivals, I began to understand that his films, apparently so cold, apparently manufactured so cynically out of parts taken off the shelf, were in fact a direct expression of his own personality: his pain, self-loathing, loneliness, compulsiveness, and restless energy. Look here, he seemed to be saying, at these pathetic creatures trapped in a web of someone else's weaving. They do not know they are clichés. And even worse, the clichés themselves are not well-behaved, but break in the middle, leaving them without even the consolation of predictability.

When Fassbinder died in 1982, at thirty-six, of cocaine abuse, I felt a real sense of loss and anger. He was young, prolific, the author of an original vision. He made movies that forced you to deal not just with them, but also with the idea of watching a film. In thirteen years he made more films than most directors make in a lifetime, and threw in the fourteen-part TV series *Berlin Alexanderplatz.* What would he have done next? Or was his work so linked to his self-destructiveness that one would not have been possible without the other?

All or Nothing

R, 128 m., 2002

Timothy Spall (Phil Bassett), Lesley Manville (Penny Bassett), Alison Garland (Rachel Bassett), James Corden (Rory Bassett), Ruth Sheen (Maureen), Marion Bailey (Carol), Helen Coker (Donna). Directed by Mike Leigh and produced by Simon Channing-Williams. Screenplay by Leigh.

Mike Leigh's *All or Nothing* looks behind three doors in a South London public housing estate and finds loneliness, desperation, and a stubborn streak of spunky humor. His characters try to remember a time when they were light-hearted and had hope. But there is little to cheer them now, except for food and sleep, the telly, the pub on Saturday night, and, for the young, thoughtless sex to hurry them along into raising thankless kids of their own.

Phil Bassett, played by the sad-faced and wounded Timothy Spall, is a minicab driver who stares straight ahead as dramas unfold in his backseat. His common-law wife, Penny (Lesley Manville), is a checkout clerk at the Safeway. They have two fat, unattractive children: Rachel (Alison Garland), who is a cleaner at an old-folks' home and buries herself in romance novels, and Rory (James Corden), who lurches from the table to the sofa, his eyes hypnotically fixed on the television, his voice wavering between anger and martyrdom.

Their flat is on an outside corridor of an anonymous housing project, but it has a wooden door with a knocker—a reminder of when they had hopes for it as a home. Now it's a place where they barely meet. Phil sleeps late, his wife goes to work early, Rachel is in a world of her own, and Rory vibrates with hostility. For Penny, there is at least the companionship of neighbors along the corridor; she hangs out with Carol (Marion Bailey) and Maureen (Ruth Sheen), and they go to karaoke night at the pub. Maureen is a single mom whose daughter Donna (Helen Coker) is abused by a boyfriend. Carol, whose husband, Ron, also drives a minicab, is a drunk sliding off into walking hallucinations.

This sounds grim and is grim, but it is not depressing, because Leigh, who in his earlier films might have found a few laughs at the expense of his characters, clearly loves these people and cares for them. They are, we realize, utterly without resources; they lack the skills to enjoy life and are trapped on an economic treadmill. Phil has the makings of a philosopher, and observes sadly that you work all day and sleep all night and then you die. When a fellow driver complains of a car crash, Phil looks on the bright side: "You might have driven around the corner and killed a little girl."

The film pays attention to the neighbors, but its main attention is on the Bassetts, and one day something unforeseen happens—I will not reveal what it is—and it acts as a catalyst to jolt them out of their depression and lethargy. It is the kind of bad thing that good things come from. Watch carefully how it happens, and who reacts to it and how, and you will see that Leigh has made all of the neighbors into characters whose troubles help to define their response.

There are moments in *All or Nothing* of such acute observation that we nod in understanding. Consider the way Maureen learns that Donna is pregnant and how she deals with the news (at first, and then later), and how she treats the boyfriend. Watch joy and beauty flash briefly in the pub when the women are singing. And observe how Timothy Spall goes through an entire life crisis while scarcely saying a word, and tells us all we need to know with his eyes.

There is a scene that establishes the Bassett family as well as any scene possibly could. Phil needs to put together a sum of money, and he visits his wife and children separately. He searches for a coin under Rory's sofa cushion, but Rory finds it and piggishly snatches it. Rachel lends him money as if money is the least of her worries. Penny tries to find out what he is thinking. He keeps repeating that he will pay her back tomorrow. This is his companion of twenty years, and he treats her loan like one he would get in a pub.

Mike Leigh is now the leading British director—ironic, since after his brilliant *Bleak Moments* (1972) he spent long years making TV films because no one would finance his features. He and his actors improvise their scripts during long periods of living as the characters. His subject is usually working- and middle-class life in Britain, although his jolly *Topsy-Turvy* (2000) entered the backstage world of Gilbert and Sullivan. In *All or Nothing* he returns to more familiar material, in one of his very best films.

The closing scenes of the movie are just about perfect. Rory is the center of attention, and notice when, and how, he suddenly speaks in the middle of a conversation about him. When a director gets a laugh of recognition from the audience, showing that it knows his characters and recognizes typical behavior, he has done his job. These people are real as few movie characters ever are. At the end, it looks as if they will be able to admit a little sunshine into their lives, and talk to each other a little more. We are relieved.

All the Real Girls

R., 108 m., 2003

Paul Schneider (Paul), Zooey Deschanel (Noel), Shea Whigham (Tip), Danny McBride (Bust-Ass), Maurice Compte (Bo), Heather McComb (Mary-Margaret), Benjamin Mouton (Leland), Patricia Clarkson (Elvira). Directed by David Gordon Green and produced by Jean Doumanian and Lisa Muskat. Screenplay by Green.

We like to be in love because it allows us to feel idealistic about ourselves. The other person ennobles, inspires, redeems. Our lover deserves the most wonderful person alive, and that person is ourselves. Paul (Paul Schneider), the hero of *All the Real Girls*, has spent his young manhood having sex with any girl who would have sex with him and some who were still making up their minds, but when he meets Noel he doesn't want to rush things. He wants to wait, because this time is special.

Noel (Zooey Deschanel), who has spent the last several years in a girls' boarding school, is crazy in love with him and is a virgin. She is eighteen, an age when all the hormones in our bodies form ranks and hurl themselves against the ramparts of our inhibitions. That they can discuss these matters with romantic idealism does not entirely work as a substitute.

All the Real Girls, David Gordon Green's second film, is too subtle and perceptive, and knows too much about human nature, to treat their lack of sexual synchronicity as if it supplies a plot. Another kind of movie would be entirely about whether they have sex. But Green, who feels tenderly for his vulnerable characters, cares less about sex than about feelings and wild, youthful idealism. He comes from North Carolina, the state where young Thomas Wolfe once prowled the midnight campus, so in love with life that he uttered wild goat cries at the moon.

Most movies about young love trivialize and cheapen it. Their cynical makers have not felt true love in many years, and mock it, perhaps out of jealousy. They find something funny in a twenty-year-old who still doesn't realize he is doomed to grow up to be as jaded as they are. Green is twenty-seven, old enough to be jaded, but he has the soul of a romantic

poet. Wordsworth, after all, was thirty-six when he published

> The rainbow comes and goes,
> And lovely is the rose;

How many guys that age would have that kind of nerve today? Green knows there are nights when lovers want simply to wrap their arms around each other and celebrate their glorious destinies.

He centers these feelings on characters who live in the same kind of rusty, overgrown southern mill town he used for his great first film, *George Washington* (2000). His characters grew up together. They look today on the faces of their first contemporaries. Paul's best friend, Tip (Shea Whigham), has been his best friend almost from birth. That he is Noel's brother is a complication, since Tip knows all about Paul's other girls. And more than a complication, because your best friend's sister embodies a history that includes your entire puberty, and may be the first person you noticed had turned into a girl.

Green likes to listen to his characters talk. They don't have much to do. Some of them work at the few remaining mill jobs, and we learn some details about their lives (an hourly sprinkler system washes the fibers out of the air). They stand around and sit around and idly discuss the mysteries of life, which often come down to whether someone did something, or what they were thinking of when they did it, or if they are ever going to do it. I had relatives who lived in towns like these, and I know that when you go to the salad bar it includes butterscotch pudding.

Paul's single mom, Elvira (Patricia Clarkson), works as a clown at parties and in the children's wards of hospitals. Some critics have mocked this occupation, but let me tell you something: A small-town woman with a family to feed can make better money with a Bozo wig and a putty nose than she can working unpaid overtime at Wal-Mart. People will pay you nothing to clean their houses, but they pay the going rate when their kids have birthdays. The fact that Green knows this and a lot of people don't is an indicator of his comfort with his characters.

Green's dialogue has a kind of unaffected, flat naturalism. ("You feel like waffles or

French toast?" "No, the places I go are usually not that fancy.") That doesn't mean their speech is not poetic. His characters don't use big words, but they express big ideas. Their words show a familiarity with hard times, disappointment, wistfulness; they are familiar with all the concepts on television, but do not lead lives where they apply.

Two emotional upheavals strike at the narrative. One is inevitable; Tip is enraged to learn that Paul and Noel are dating. The other is not inevitable, and I will not even hint about it. There is a scene where it is discussed in a bowling alley, using only body language, in long shot.

The thing about real love is, if you lose it, you can also lose your ability to believe in it, and that hurts even more. Especially in a town where real love may be the only world-class thing that ever happens.

Almost Famous

R, 124 m., 2000

Patrick Fugit (William Miller), Billy Crudup (Russell Hammond), Frances McDormand (Elaine Miller), Kate Hudson (Penny Lane), Jason Lee (Jeff Bebe), Philip Seymour Hoffman (Lester Bangs), Zooey Deschanel (Anita Miller), Michael Angarano (Young William), Noah Taylor (Dick Roswell). Directed by Cameron Crowe and produced by Crowe and Ian Bryce. Screenplay by Crowe.

Oh, what a lovely film. I was almost hugging myself while I watched it. *Almost Famous* is funny and touching in so many different ways. It's the story of a fifteen-year-old kid, smart and terrifyingly earnest, who through luck and pluck gets assigned by *Rolling Stone* magazine to do a profile of a rising rock band. The magazine has no idea he's fifteen. Clutching his pencil and his notebook like talismans, phoning a veteran critic for advice, he plunges into the experience that will make and shape him. It's as if Huckleberry Finn came back to life in the 1970s and, instead of taking a raft down the Mississippi, got on the bus with the band.

The kid is named William Miller in the movie; he's played by Patrick Fugit as a boy shaped by the fierce values of his mother, who drives him to the concert that will change his life, and drops him off with the mantra, "Don't do drugs!" The character and the story are based on the life of Cameron Crowe, the film's writer-director, who indeed was a teenage *Rolling Stone* writer, and who knows how lucky he was. Crowe grew up to write and direct *Say Anything* (1989), one of the best movies ever made about teenagers; in this movie, he surpasses himself.

The movie is not just about William Miller. It's about the band and the early 1970s, when idealism collided with commerce. The band he hooks up with is named Stillwater. He talks his way backstage in San Diego by knowing their names and hurling accurate compliments at them as they hurry into the arena. William wins the sympathy of Russell Hammond (Billy Crudup), the guitarist, who lets him in. Backstage, he meets his guide to this new world, a girl who says her name is Penny Lane (Kate Hudson). She is not a groupie, she explains indignantly, but a Band Aide. She is, of course, a groupie, but she has so much theory about her role it's almost like sex for her is a philosophical exercise.

William's mom, Elaine (Frances McDormand), is a college professor who believes in vegetarianism, progressive politics, and the corrupting influence of rock music. Banning the rock albums of her older daughter Anita (Zooey Deschanel), she holds up an album cover and asks Anita to look at the telltale signs in Simon and Garfunkel's eyes: "Pot!" Anita, who had played the lyrics "I Walked Out to Look for America," leaves to become a stewardess.

William walks out, too, in a way. He intends to be away from school for only a few days. But as Russell and the rest of Stillwater grow accustomed to his presence, he finds himself on the bus and driving far into the Southwest. Along the way, he observes the tension between Russell and Jeff Bebe (Jason Lee), the lead singer, who thinks Russell is getting more attention than his role definition deserves: "I'm the lead singer and you're the guitarist with mystique."

William has two guardian angels to watch over him. One is Penny Lane, who is almost as young as he is, but lies about her age. William loves her, or thinks he does, but she loves Russell, or says she does, and William admires Russell, too, and Russell maintains a reserve that makes it hard to know what he thinks. He has the scowl and the facial hair of a rock star, but is still only in his early twenties, and one of the best moments in the movie comes when William's mom lectures him over the phone about the dangers to her son: "Do I make myself clear?" "Yes, ma'am," he says, reverting to childhood.

William's other angel is the legendary rock critic Lester Bangs (Philip Seymour Hoffman), then the editor of *Creem:* "So you're the kid who's been sending me those articles from your school paper." He ignores the kid's age, trusts his talent, and shares his credo: "Be honest, and unmerciful." During moments of crisis on the road, William calls Lester for advice.

Lester Bangs was a real person, and so are Ben Fong Torres and Jann Wenner of *Rolling Stone,* played by look-alike actors. The movie's sense of time and place is so acute it's possible to believe Stillwater was a real band. As William watches, the band gets a hit record, a hotshot producer tries to take over from the guy who's always managed them, they switch from a bus to an airplane, and there are ego wars, not least when a T-shirt photo places Russell in the foreground and has the other band members out of focus (there's a little *Spinal Tap* here).

Almost Famous is about the world of rock, but it's not a rock film; it's a coming-of-age film about an idealistic kid who sees the real world, witnesses its cruelties and heartbreaks, and yet finds much room for hope. The Penny Lane character is written with particular delicacy, as she tries to justify her existence and explain her values (in a milieu that seems to have none). It breaks William's heart to see how the married Russell mistreats her. But Penny denies being hurt. Kate Hudson has one scene so well acted it takes her character to another level. William tells her, "He sold you to Humble Pie for fifty bucks and a case of beer." Watch the silence, the brave smile, the tear, and the precise spin she puts on the words, "What *kind* of beer?" It's not an easy laugh. It's a whole world of insight.

What thrums beneath *Almost Famous* is Cameron Crowe's gratitude. His William Miller is not an alienated bore, but a kid who had the good fortune to have a wonderful mother and great sister, to meet the right rock star in Russell (there would have been wrong ones), and to have the kind of love for Penny Lane that will arm him for the future and give him a deeper understanding of the mysteries of women. Looking at William—earnestly grasping his tape recorder, trying to get an interview, desperately going to Lester for advice, terrified as Ben Fong Torres rails about deadlines, crushed when it looks like his story will be rejected—we know we're looking at a kid who has the right stuff and will go far. Someday he might even direct a movie like *Almost Famous.*

Note: Why did they give an R rating to a movie perfect for teenagers?

Amadeus

PG, 158 m., 1984

F. Murray Abraham (Salieri), Tom Hulce (Mozart), Elizabeth Berridge (Constanze), Simon Callow (Emanuel Schikaneder), Roy Dotrice (Leopold Mozart), Christine Ebersole (Katerina Cavalieri), Jeffrey Jones (Joseph II). Directed by Milos Forman and produced by Saul Zaentz. Screenplay by Peter Shaffer, based on his play.

Milos Forman's *Amadeus* is one of the riskiest gambles a filmmaker has taken in a long time—a lavish movie about Mozart that dares to be anarchic and saucy, and yet still earns the importance of tragedy. This movie is nothing like the dreary educational portraits we're used to seeing about the Great Composers, who come across as cobwebbed profundities weighed down with the burden of genius. This is Mozart as an eighteenth-century Bruce Springsteen, and yet (here is the genius of the movie) there is nothing cheap or unworthy about the approach. *Amadeus* is not only about as much fun as you're likely to have with a movie, it also is disturbingly true. The truth enters in the character of Salieri, who tells the story. He is not a great composer, but he is a good enough composer to know greatness when he hears it, and that is why the music of Mozart breaks his heart. He knows how good it is, he sees how easily Mozart seems to compose it, and he knows that his own work looks pale and silly beside it.

The movie begins with the suggestion that Salieri might have murdered Mozart. The movie examines the ways in which this possibility might be true, and by the end of the film we feel a certain kinship with the weak and jealous Salieri—for few of us can identify with divine genius, but many of us probably have had dark moments of urgent self-contempt in the face of those whose effortless existence illustrates our own inadequacies. Salieri, played with burning intensity by F. Murray Abraham, sits hunched in a madhouse confessing to a priest. The movie flashes back to his memories of Wolfgang Amadeus Mozart, the child genius who composed melodies of startling originality and who grew up to become a prolific, driven artist.

One of the movie's wisest decisions is to cast Mozart not as a charismatic demigod, not as a tortured superman, but as a goofy, immature, likable kid with a ridiculous laugh. The character is played by Tom Hulce, and if you saw *Animal House,* you may remember him as the fraternity brother who tried to seduce the mayor's daughter, while an angel and a devil whispered in his ears. Hulce would seem all wrong for Mozart, but he is absolutely right, as an unaffected young man filled with delight at his own gifts, unaware of how easily he wounds Salieri and others, tortured only by the guilt of having offended his religious and domineering father.

The film is constructed in wonderfully well-written and -acted scenes—scenes so carefully constructed, unfolding with such delight, that they play as perfect compositions of words. Most of them will be unfamiliar to those who have seen Peter Shaffer's brooding play, on which this film is based; Shaffer and Forman have brought light, life, and laughter to the material, and it plays with grace and ease. It's more human than the play; the characters are people, not throbbing packages of meaning. It centers on the relationships in Mozart's life: with his father, his wife, and Salieri. The father never can be pleased, and that creates an undercurrent affecting all of Mozart's success. The wife, played by delightful, buxom Elizabeth Berridge, contains in one person the qualities of a jolly wench and a loving partner: She likes to loll in bed all day, but also gives Mozart good, sound advice and is a forceful person in her own right. The patrons, especially Joseph II, the Austro-Hungarian emperor, are connoisseurs and dilettantes, slow to take to Mozart's new music but enchanted by the audacity with which he defends it. And then there is Salieri (F. Murray Abraham), the gaunt court composer whose special torture is

to understand better than anybody else how inadequate he is, and how great Mozart is.

The movie was shot on location in Forman's native Czechoslovakia, and it looks exactly right; it fits its period comfortably, perhaps because Prague still contains so many streets and squares and buildings that could be directly from the Vienna of Mozart's day. Perhaps his confidence in his locations gave Forman the freedom to make Mozart slightly *out* of period. Forman directed the film version of *Hair,* and Mozart in this movie seems to share a spirit with some of the characters from *Hair.* Mozart's wigs do not look like everybody else's. They have just the slightest suggestion of punk, just the smallest shading of pink. Mozart seems more a child of the 1960s than of any other age, and this interpretation of his personality—he was an irreverent proto-hippie who trusted, if you will, his own vibes— sounds risky, but works.

I have not mentioned the music. There's probably no need to. The music provides the understructure of the film, strong, confident, above all, *clear* in a way that Salieri's simple muddles only serve to illustrate. There are times when Mozart speaks the words of a child, but then the music says the same things in the language of the gods, and all is clear.

Amadeus is a magnificent film, full and tender and funny and charming—and, at the end, sad and angry, too, because in the character of Salieri it has given us a way to understand not only greatness, but our own lack of it. This movie's fundamental question, I think, is whether we can learn to be grateful for the happiness of others, and that, of course, is a test for sainthood. How many movies ask such questions and succeed in being fun, as well?

Amarcord

R, 127 m., 1974

Magali Noel (Gradisca), Bruno Zamin (Titta), Pupella Maggio (His Mother), Armando Drancia (His Father), Giuseppe Lanigro (His Grandfather), Nando Orfei (Pataca), Chiccio Ingrassia (Uncle Teo), Luigi Rossi (Lawyer). Directed by Federico Fellini and produced by Iranco Cristaldi. Screenplay by Fellini.

Federico Fellini's *Amarcord* takes us back to the small Italian town of his birth and young manhood, and gives us a joyful, bawdy, virtuoso portrait of the people he remembers there. He includes a character undoubtedly meant to be young Federico—earnest, awkward, yearning with all the poignancy of adolescent lust after the town beauties. But the movie's not an autobiography of a character. It's the story of the town itself.

We see it first when the dandelion seeds blow in from the fields, signaling the arrival of spring. The townspeople gather in the piazza to build a ceremonial bonfire and burn the witch of winter, and as they dance around the flames in one of Fellini's beloved processions, we get to know them.

They're of all sizes, sexes, and ages, but they're bound together by their transparent simplicity and a strain of cheerful vulgarity. Fellini likes their weaknesses as much as their virtues, and gives us the pompous lawyer, the egotistical theater owner (who cultivates a resemblance to Ronald Colman), the buxom beautician Gradisca flaunting her delightful derriere, and especially the lustful adolescents and their tormenting fantasies.

Fellini also gives us, in a much more subtle way, some notion of the way fascist Italy of the early 1930s helped to shape these people. In an authoritarian system, the individual has fewer choices to make, and there's a temptation to surrender the responsibilities of freedom. The townspeople are almost children in their behavior, taking delight in the simple joys of eating and making love and parading around the square and gossiping about each other and about the hypnotic Gradisca. Fellini implies that this simple behavior is nourished by a system that encourages a mindless going along—but *Amarcord* isn't a political movie. It is a memory, fond but merciless, of how it was in Italy at a certain time.

It's also absolutely breathtaking filmmaking. Fellini has ranked for a long time among the five or six greatest directors in the world, and of them all, he's the natural. Bergman achieves his greatness through thought and soul-searching, Hitchcock built with meticulous craftsmanship, and Buñuel used his fetishes and fantasies to construct barbed jokes about humanity. But Fellini . . . well, moviemaking for him seems almost effortless, like breathing, and he can orchestrate the most compli-

cated scenes with purity and ease. He's the Willie Mays of movies.

He did hit upon hard critical times, though. After the towering success of *La Dolce Vita* and *8½*, and such 1950s landmarks as *La Strada* and *I Vitelloni*, he began to indulge himself (his critics said). *Juliet of the Spirits* was too fantastical and structureless, and *Satyricon* was an exercise in excess, and *The Clowns* was really only a TV show, and *Fellini Roma* was episodic—a great director spinning out sequences that contained brilliance, yes, but no purpose or direction.

I couldn't agree with those criticisms. I find Fellini's magic spellbinding even when he's only marking time, as he was to some extent in *Roma*. But now, with *Amarcord*, Fellini returns to the very top of his form. And he has the last laugh on the critics of his "structureless" films. Because *Amarcord* seems at first to be a series of self-contained episodes and then reveals a structure so organic and yet so effortless that at its end, we can only marvel at this triumph over ordinary movie forms.

And we can marvel, too, at how universal *Amarcord* is. This is a movie for everybody, even those who hardly ever see foreign or "art" films. Fellini's greatest achievement, in my opinion, was *8½*. But that was a difficult film that revealed its meaning only after a good deal of thought and repeated viewings.

Amarcord, on the other hand, is a totally accessible film. It deals directly, hilariously, and sometimes poignantly with the good people of this small town (actually Fellini's birthplace, Rimini). It's no more complicated than they are, it understands them inside-out, and the audiences I've seen it with (three times) have been moved to horselaughs, stilled by moments of beauty, and then brought back almost to tears. It's not only a great movie, it's a great joy to see.

Someone once remarked that Fellini's movies are filled with symbols, but they're all obvious symbols. At the beginning of *La Dolce Vita*, for example, he wanted to symbolize the gulf between modern, decadent Rome and its history as the center of the Church, so he gave a statue of Christ being helicoptered by pilots who wave and whistle at girls sunning themselves in bikinis. The scene says everything it needs to say, openly and with great economy.

Amarcord is obvious in that way, with a showman's flair for the right effect. There is a night, for example, when all the people of the town get into their boats and sail out to wait for the great new Italian liner to pass by. And when it comes, it towers hundreds of feet above the waves and has thousands of portholes—and is, of course, only a prop built by the special-effects men. It drifts away into invisibility like a candle dying out. The image is of Italy itself in the 1930s: all grandeur and pomp and nationalism, but with an insubstantial soul.

The movie is filled with moments like that, and they're just right. But then there are moments of inexplicable, almost mystical beauty, as when the dandelion seeds drift in on the wind, or when an old lady sweeps up the ashes of the bonfire, or when a peacock spreads its tail feathers in the snow. At moments like that we're almost blinded with delight. Hitchcock once said he wanted to play his audiences like a piano. Fellini requires the entire orchestra.

American Beauty

R, 120 m., 1999

Kevin Spacey (Lester Burnham), Annette Bening (Carolyn Burnham), Thora Birch (Jane Burnham), Wes Bentley (Ricky Fitts), Mena Suvari (Angela Hayes), Chris Cooper (Colonel Fitts), Peter Gallagher (Buddy Kane), Allison Janney (Barbara Fitts). Directed by Sam Mendes and produced by Bruce Cohen and Dan Jinks. Screenplay by Alan Ball.

American Beauty is a comedy because we laugh at the absurdity of the hero's problems. And a tragedy because we can identify with his failure—not the specific details, but the general outline. The movie is about a man who fears growing older, losing the hope of true love, and not being respected by those who know him best. If you never experience those feelings, take out a classified ad. People want to take lessons from you.

Lester Burnham, the hero of *American Beauty*, is played by Kevin Spacey as a man who is unloved by his daughter, ignored by his wife, and unnecessary at work. "I'll be dead in a year," he tells us in almost the first words of the movie. "In a way, I'm dead already." The movie is the story of his rebellion.

We meet his wife, Carolyn (Annette Ben-

ing), so perfect her garden shears are coordinated with her clothing. We meet his daughter, Jane (Thora Birch), who is saving up for breast implants even though augmentation is clearly unnecessary; perhaps her motivation is not to become more desirable to men, but to make them miserable about what they can't have.

"Both my wife and daughter think I'm this chronic loser," Lester complains. He is right. But they are not without their reasons. At an agonizing family dinner, Carolyn plays Mantovanian music that mocks every mouthful; the music is lush and reassuring, and the family is angry and silent. When Lester criticizes his daughter's attitude, she points out correctly that he has hardly spoken to her in months.

Everything changes for Lester the night he is dragged along by his wife to see their daughter perform as a cheerleader. There on the floor, engrossed in a sub-Fosse pom-pom routine, he sees his angel: Angela (Mena Suvari), his daughter's sixteen-year-old classmate. Is it wrong for a man in his forties to lust after a teenage girl? Any honest man understands what a complicated question this is. Wrong morally, certainly, and legally. But as every woman knows, men are born with wiring that goes directly from their eyes to their genitals, bypassing the higher centers of thought. They can disapprove of their thoughts, but they cannot stop themselves from having them.

American Beauty is not about a Lolita relationship, anyway. It's about yearning after youth, respect, power, and, of course, beauty. The moment a man stops dreaming is the moment he petrifies inside, and starts writing snarfy letters disapproving of paragraphs like the one above. Lester's thoughts about Angela are impure, but not perverted; he wants to do what men are programmed to do, with the most beautiful woman he has ever seen.

Angela is not Lester's highway to bliss, but she is at least a catalyst for his freedom. His thoughts, and the discontent they engender, blast him free from years of emotional paralysis, and soon he makes a cheerful announcement at the funereal dinner table: "I quit my job, told my boss to go fuck himself, and blackmailed him for $60,000." Has he lost his mind? Not at all. The first thing he spends money on is perfectly reasonable: a bright red 1970 Pontiac Firebird.

Carolyn and Jane are going through their own romantic troubles. Lester finds out Carolyn is cheating when he sees her with her lover in the drive-thru lane of a fast-food restaurant (where he has a job he likes). Jane is being videotaped by Ricky (Wes Bentley), the boy next door, who has a strange light in his eyes. Ricky's dad (Chris Cooper) is an ex-Marine who tests him for drugs, taking a urine sample every six months; Ricky plays along to keep the peace until he can leave home.

All of these emotional threads come together during one dark and stormy night when there is a series of misunderstandings so bizarre they belong in a screwball comedy. And at the end, somehow, improbably, the film snatches victory from the jaws of defeat for Lester, its hero. Not the kind of victory you'd get in a feel-good movie, but the kind where you prove something important, if only to yourself.

American Beauty is not as dark or twisted as *Happiness,* 1998's attempt to shine a light under the rock of American society. It's more about sadness and loneliness than about cruelty or inhumanity. Nobody is really bad in this movie, just shaped by society in such a way that they can't be themselves, or feel joy. The performances all walk the line between parody and simple realism; Thora Birch and Wes Bentley are the most grounded, talking in the tense, flat voices of kids who can't wait to escape their homes. Bening's character, a Realtor who chants self-help mantras, confuses happiness with success—bad enough if you're successful, depressing if you're not.

And Spacey, an actor who embodies intelligence in his eyes and voice, is the right choice for Lester Burnham. He does reckless and foolish things in this movie, but he doesn't deceive himself; he knows he's running wild—and chooses to, burning up the future years of an empty lifetime for a few flashes of freedom. He may have lost everything by the end of the film, but he's no longer a loser.

American Dream

NO MPAA RATING, 100 m., 1992

A documentary directed by Barbara Kopple and produced by Kopple and Arthur Cohn. Edited by Cathy Caplan, Tom Haneke, and Lawrence Silk.

In 1984, the Hormel meat-packing company offered its Austin, Minnesota, union workers a new contract in which their wage would be cut from $10.69 to $8.25 an hour, and other benefits would be cut by 30 percent. The workers were not overjoyed. The company had just declared an annual profit of $29 million, and the cuts seemed inspired by a management desire to maximize profits at the cost of any other consideration. In the climate of the times—shortly after Reagan had fired all of the striking air controllers—a strike seemed like a dangerous risk, but the meat packers of local P-9 in Austin walked out.

Their decision and its repercussions are the subject of *American Dream,* the documentary by Barbara Kopple that won a 1991 Academy Award. This is the kind of movie you watch with horrified fascination, as families lose their incomes and homes, management plays macho hardball, and rights and wrongs grow hopelessly tangled.

Kopple is the woman who went to Kentucky to document a bitter miner's strike in *Harlan County, U.S.A.,* one of the best documentaries I have ever seen. That strike offered clear-cut choices between good and evil. The Hormel strike, which she follows as it spans long, agonizing months and years, weaves a more tangled web. The local union, which has decided to act independently from its parent international union in Washington, hires a freelance strike consultant named Ray Rogers, who comes in with charts, graphs, and promises of national press attention. He delivers, but at the cost of denying local P-9 the experienced negotiating skills that the international could have supplied.

After P-9's campaign is under way and its position has solidified, the international sends in Lewis Anderson, an experienced negotiator who despairs at the naïveté of the locals. "They made the critical mistake of opening up the whole contract," Anderson says despairingly at one moment. "That allows the company the chance to renegotiate language it took us forty years to win."

Anderson, a chain-smoking everyman with the weary charisma of a Lech Walesa, wants to compromise with Hormel, and arrive at a new contract. The P-9 militants, fired up by Rogers and by their local president, Jim Guyette, want no compromise. They want their $10.69 an hour or else. The company locks out the striking workers and eventually begins to hire replacements, while some dissident local members break away from P-9 and side with Anderson. The international in Washington eventually declares the strike illegal, siezes control of P-9, and negotiates its own deal with Hormel. But the majority of P-9 members remain loyal to the strike, and eventually some 80 percent of them lose their jobs.

The outcome is even more complicated than that. Although Hormel negotiates a compromise wage with the union, it soon closes down half the plant and then rents it to another meat packer who pays $6.50 an hour. As *American Dream* documents these developments, we are torn two ways. We want to see the movie as a battle between right and wrong, good and evil. On the other hand, we also see it as a struggle between two strategies. Would P-9 have been luckier if it had never heard of Ray Rogers and his consulting wizardry, and allowed Lewis Anderson to negotiate a settlement? Or would Hormel have shut down half its plant anyway, in a transparent move to allow the $6.50 operation?

One of the key issues in *American Dream* is the legality of employers who hire permanent replacements for workers who are engaged in a legal strike. Some companies are so cocksure these days that they hire replacements and, if found in violation of labor laws, are happy to pay a fine. They're millions ahead in the long run. In a climate of high unemployment and White House hostility to unions, there are always a lot of workers only too glad to take someone else's job.

The people in this film are so real they make most movie characters look like inhabitants of the funny page. Families are torn apart. One brother goes back to work; another stays on the picket lines. Workers have tears in their eyes as they describe not being able to support their families. It becomes clear that no possible win by the members of P-9 could compensate them for the wages they have already lost—especially as they are striking, not for a raise, but against a pay cut. A nobility creeps onto the scene, as people make enormous financial and personal sacrifices simply for what they believe is morally right. Our hearts are torn, because on the basis of this film we are not sure they have chosen the wisest path.

Stories like the Hormel strike are too long and complicated to be told on a daily basis. Newspapers and TV newscasts are, by their nature, focused on the events of the day—or the week or month at the longest. How can they make sense of a strike that drags on forever, with conflicting loyalties and strategies? Only a documentary like this has a canvas big enough for the whole picture.

Is there a lesson at the end of *American Dream*? I think there is. I think the lesson is that the American tradition of collective bargaining will break down if companies can simply ignore a legal strike, hire replacements, and continue as before. There was a time in American history when such behavior by management would have been seen as not only illegal but immoral. The new management philosophers who won ascendency in the 1980s dismiss such views as sentimentalism. They are concerned only with the bottom line, where they see profits, not people. The White House announced that for a 1992 overseas trip, the video library on *Air Force One* was stocked with *Gone With the Wind*. Next flight, could they take along *American Dream*?

American Graffiti
PG, 112 m., 1973

Ron Howard (Steve), Cindy Williams (Laurie), Richard Dreyfuss (Curt), Paul Le Mat (John), Mackenzie Phillips (Carol), Charles Martin Smith (Terry), Candy Clark (Debbie), Wolfman Jack (Disc Jockey). Directed by George Lucas and produced by Francis Ford Coppola. Screenplay by Lucas, Gloria Katz, and Willard Huyck.

My first car was a '54 Ford and I bought it for $435. It wasn't scooped, channeled, shaved, decked, pinstriped, or chopped, and it didn't have duals, but its hubcaps were a wonder to behold.

On weekends my friends and I drove around downtown Urbana—past the Princess Theater, past the courthouse—sometimes stopping for a dance at the youth center or a hamburger at the Steak 'n' Shake ("In Sight, It Must Be Right"). And always we listened to Dick Biondi on WLS. Only two years earlier, WLS had been the Prairie Farmer Station; now it was the voice of rock all over the Midwest.

When I went to see George Lucas's *American*

Graffiti that whole world—a world that now seems incomparably distant and innocent—was brought back with a rush of feeling that wasn't so much nostalgia as culture shock. Remembering my high school generation, I can only wonder at how unprepared we were for the loss of innocence that took place in America with the series of hammer blows beginning with the assassination of President Kennedy.

The great divide was November 22, 1963, and nothing was ever the same again. The teenagers in *American Graffiti* are, in a sense, like that cartoon character in the magazine ads: the one who gives the name of his insurance company, unaware that an avalanche is about to land on him. The options seemed so simple then: to go to college, or to stay home and look for a job and cruise Main Street and make the scene.

The options were simple, and so was the music that formed so much of the way we saw ourselves. *American Graffiti*'s sound track is papered from one end to the other with Wolfman Jack's nonstop disc jockey show; that's crucial and absolutely right. The radio was on every waking moment. A character in the movie only realizes his car, parked nearby, has been stolen when he hears the music stop: He didn't hear the car being driven away.

The music was as innocent as the time. Songs like "Sixteen Candles" and "Gonna Find Her" and "The Book of Love" sound touchingly naive today; nothing prepared us for the decadence and the aggression of rock only a handful of years later. The Rolling Stones of 1972 would have blown WLS off the air in 1962.

American Graffiti acts almost as a milestone to show us how far (and in many cases how tragically) we have come. Stanley Kauffmann, who liked it, complained in the *New Republic* that Lucas had made a film more fascinating to the generation now between thirty and forty than it could be for other generations, older or younger.

But it isn't the age of the characters that matters; it's the time they inhabited. Whole cultures and societies have passed since 1962. *American Graffiti* is not only a great movie but a brilliant work of historical fiction; no sociological treatise could duplicate the movie's success in remembering exactly how it was to be alive at that cultural instant.

On the surface, Lucas has made a film that seems almost artless; his teenagers cruise Main Street and stop at Mel's Drive-In and listen to Wolfman Jack on the radio and neck and lay rubber and almost convince themselves their moment will last forever. But the film's buried structure shows an innocence in the process of being lost, and as its symbol Lucas provides the elusive blonde in the white Thunderbird—the vision of beauty always glimpsed at the next intersection, the end of the next street.

Who is she? And did she really whisper "I love you" at the last traffic signal? In *8½*, Fellini used Claudia Cardinale as his mysterious angel in white, and the image remains one of his best; but George Lucas knows that for one brief afternoon of American history angels drove Thunderbirds and could possibly be found at Mel's Drive-In tonight . . . or maybe tomorrow night, or the night after.

American Movie

R, 104 m., 2000

Mark Borchardt (Filmmaker), Mike Schank (Friend/Musician), Uncle Bill (Mark's Uncle), Monica Borchardt (Mark's Mom), Cliff Borchardt (Mark's Dad), Chris Borchardt (Mark's Brother), Alex Borchardt (Mark's Brother), Ken Keen (Friend), Joan Petrie (Mark's Girlfriend). A documentary directed by Chris Smith and produced by Sarah Price.

If you've ever wanted to make a movie, see *American Movie*, which is about someone who wants to make a movie more than you do. Mark Borchardt may want to make a movie more than anyone else in the world. He is a thirty-year-old odd-job man from Menomonee Falls, Wisconsin, who has been making movies since he was a teenager, and dreams of an epic about his life, which will be titled *Northwestern*, and be about "rust and decay."

Mark Borchardt is a real person. I have met him. I admire his spirit, and I even admire certain shots in the only Borchardt film I have seen, *Coven*. I saw it at the 1999 Sundance Film Festival—not because it was invited there, but because after the midnight premiere of *American Movie* there wasn't a person in the theater who didn't want to stay and see Mark's thirty-five-minute horror film, which we see him making during the course of the documentary.

American Movie is a very funny, sometimes very sad, documentary directed by Chris Smith and produced by Sarah Price, about Mark's life, his friends, his family, his films, and his dreams. From one point of view, Mark is a loser, a man who has spent his adult life making unreleased and sometimes unfinished movies with titles like *The More the Scarier III*. He plunders the bank account of his elderly Uncle Bill for funds to continue, he uses his friends and hapless local amateur actors as his cast, he enlists his mother as his cinematographer, and his composer and best friend is a guy named Mike Schank who after one drug trip too many seems like the twin of Kevin Smith's Silent Bob.

Borchardt's life is a daily cliff-hanger involving poverty, desperation, discouragement, and die-hard ambition. He's behind on his child support payments, he drinks too much, he can't even convince his ancient Uncle Bill that he has a future as a moviemaker. Bill lives in a trailer surrounded by piles of magazines that he possibly subscribed to under the impression he would win the Publishers' Clearing House sweepstakes. He brightens slightly when Mark shows him the portrait of an actress. "She wants to be in your movie, Bill!" Bill studies the photo: "Oh, my gorsh!" But when Mark tells him about great cinema, what he hears is "cinnamon." And when Bill fumbles countless takes while trying to perform the ominous last line of *Coven* and Mark encourages him to say it like he believes it, Bill answers frankly, "I *don't* believe it."

Smith's camera follows Borchardt as he discusses his theories of cinema (his favorite films: *Night of the Living Dead* and *The Seventh Seal*). We watch as Mark and Bill go to the bank so Bill can grudgingly sign over some of his savings. He is at cast meetings, where one local actor (Robert Jorge) explains in a peeved British accent that *Coven* is correctly pronounced "CO-ven." Not according to Mark, who says *his* film is pronounced "COVE-n." "I don't want it to rhyme with 'oven'!"

Some of the scenes could work in a screwball comedy. One involves an actor being thrown headfirst through a kitchen cabinet. To capture the moment, Mark recruits his long-suffering Swedish-American mother, Monica, to operate the camera, even though she complains she has shopping to do. He gets on the floor behind his actor, who finds out belatedly that Mark's special-effects strategy is simply to ram the actor's head through the door. The first time, the actor's head bounces off. Mark prepares for take two. One reason to see *Coven* is to appreciate that shot knowing what we know now. For another shot, Mark lies flat on the frozen ground to get low-angle shots of his friends, dressed in black cloaks. "Look menacing!" he shouts. That's hard for them to do, since their faces are invisible.

If Mark's mother is supportive, his father stays out of sight, sticking his head around a doorway occasionally to warn against bad language. Mark has two brothers, who are fed up with him; one says he would be "well suited to factory work," and the other observes, "His main asset is his mouth."

And yet Mark Borchardt is the embodiment of a lonely, rejected, dedicated artist. No poet in a Paris garret has ever been more determined to succeed. To find privacy while writing his screenplays, he drives his old beater to the parking lot of the local commuter airport, and composes on a yellow legal pad. To support himself, he delivers the *Wall Street Journal* before dawn and vacuums the carpets in a mausoleum. He has inspired the loyalty of his friends and crew members, and his girlfriend observes that if he accomplishes 25 percent of what he hopes to do, "that'll be more than most people do."

Every year at Sundance young filmmakers emerge from the woodwork, bearing the masterpieces they have somehow made for peanuts, enlisting volunteer cast and crew. Last year's discovery was not *Coven* but *The Blair Witch Project*. It cost $25,000 and so far has grossed $150 million. One day Mark Borchardt hopes for that kind of success. If it never comes, it won't be for lack of trying.

The American President

PG-13, 115 m., 1995

Michael Douglas (Andrew Shepherd), Annette Bening (Sydney Ellen Wade), Martin Sheen (A. J. MacInerney), Michael J. Fox (Lewis Rothschild), Anna Deavere Smith (Robin McCall), Samantha Mathis (Janie Basdin), David Payner (Leon Kodak), Richard Dreyfuss (Senator Rumson), John Mahoney (Leo Solomon), Shawna

Waldron (Lucy Shepherd). Directed and produced by Rob Reiner. Screenplay by Aaron Sorkin.

It is hard to make a good love story. Harder to make a good comedy. Harder still to make an intelligent film about politics. Rob Reiner's *The American President* cheerfully does all three, and is a great entertainment—one of those films like *Forrest Gump* or *Apollo 13* that, however briefly, unites the audience in a reprise of the American dream.

The movie is, above all, a witty and warm romance. The president of the United States, Andrew Shepherd (Michael Douglas), has been a widower for several years. One day he meets an environmental lobbyist, newly arrived in Washington, named Sydney Ellen Wade (Annette Bening). For him there is a powerful attraction at first sight, and he asks one of his aides what the reaction might be if he asked her to be his companion at a state dinner.

The aide asks if he should have a pollster "put together some numbers." But that is precisely the impulse the president is struggling against: the need to measure every action by how it will "play." Andrew gets her number from the FBI, picks up the phone, and calls Sydney—who cannot believe it is really the president because she has just moved in with her sister and has no phone of her own. She hangs up. The president calls back. Convinced she is talking to a prankster, she compliments him on his "great ass."

Because both Douglas and Bening are believable in their roles, and because the power and bureaucracy of the White House have already been credibly established in the opening scenes, this moment works, not as sitcom, but as explosive comedy. Comedy, after all, is a release of tension, and by making the key players both realistic and sympathetic, and then erecting the monumental barrier of the modern presidency between them, the movie creates real stakes: We care, and find ourselves caring throughout the film, whether they will be happy together.

Many of the film's big laughs come from the president's difficulties in doing simple things in ordinary ways. He doesn't want his staff to handle personal matters. But how can he order flowers over the telephone when his credit cards "are in storage with your other stuff in Wisconsin"? How can he bring a date home when the White House is ringed by breathless tabloid reporters? And what about Sydney, a serious career woman who is told by her boss (John Mahoney), "The time it will take you to go from presidential girlfriend to cocktail party joke can be measured on an egg timer."

The screenplay by Aaron Sorkin keeps three elements in tension all during the movie. One is the personal relationship between Shepherd and Wade. Another involves her job, as a lobbyist for an environmental group that needs key votes in order to pass a crucial fuel bill. The third is the situation inside the White House, where Shepherd, a liberal, faces an election-year challenge from a powerful conservative (Richard Dreyfuss) and is trying to get a controversial crime bill passed.

In a standard Hollywood production, the political aspects would be papered over with vague generic terms, and indeed the president would probably not be identified by ideology. What's admirable about *The American President* is that real issues—gun control, the environment—are handled realistically in a series of subplots leading up to a presidential press conference that has a certain resonance even in the current political climate. (The liberal Shepherd learns that he must be decisive and take unpopular stands.)

The movie's center is, of course, the love story, and Douglas and Bening have remarkable chemistry; their scenes are written and played in a way that develops the comedy without sacrificing the notion that two such people might very likely find themselves in such situations. The inevitable strategic questions (like whether the power of "the most powerful man in the free world" extends to his bedroom prowess) are part of the general embarrassment that both feel because the presidency, in a sense, comes between them.

Douglas has recently specialized in more overtly sexual roles, as in *Disclosure,* where he seemed like the hapless instrument of the plot. Here he seems so much more three-dimensional, more vulnerable, smarter, more likable. And Bening is simply luminous; I had hoped to conduct my career as a film critic without ever once writing that a smile "illuminates the screen," but something very like that happens here. Looking around at the audience, I noticed that they were smiling back.

Surrounding Douglas and Bening is a superb supporting cast: Martin Sheen is the president's right-hand man, Michael J. Fox is his ideological conscience, Anna Deavere Smith is his press secretary, David Paymer is a pollster. (His name, Kodak, suggests his snapshots of the national mood, just as Shepherd is an evocative name for a president.) Shawna Waldron plays the president's young adolescent daughter, whose role is as intelligently written and played as everyone else's.

Among the many emotions that *The American President* reawakens, one of the best is simple affection for the presidency. When I was growing up, "Thepresidentoftheunitedstates" was one word, said reverently, and embodying great power and virtue. Now the title is like the butt of a joke; both parties have lessened the office by their potshots at its occupants. Reiner suggests the moral weight of the presidency while at the same time incorporating much of the inside information we now have about the way the White House functions.

Watching *The American President,* I felt respect for the craft that went into it: the flawless re-creation of the physical world of the White House, the smart and accurate dialogue, the manipulation of the love story to tug our heartstrings. It is also a film with a liberal political point of view, and that takes nerve; it would have been easier to create an Identikit president with manufactured issues. This is a great entertainment—one of the year's best films.

American Revolution 2

NO MPAA RATING, 80 m., 1969

A documentary directed by Howard Alk and Mike Gray and produced by the Film Group Inc. as a cooperative venture.

After a preview of *American Revolution 2* this week, a member of the Film Group recalled how it got started: "We finished making a Colonel Sanders commercial and went down to Michigan Avenue and got our heads beat."

The heads got beat in August 1968 during the Democratic National Convention. The events of that week seemed, at the time, to be a watershed. Nothing could ever be the same

afterward. The Daley machine had been mortally wounded. The police themselves, as the Walker Report put it, had been the rioters. And people had seen it all on TV.

Now summer is upon us again, and the question is; has anything really changed? The events of convention week, which will figure so sharply in history, already recede in our minds. Mayor Daley smiles again from the front pages. One battle does not make a revolution. Or does it?

American Revolution 2 isn't really about the convention disturbances. It's about what happened afterward, surprisingly, in the Uptown neighborhood of poor southern whites. While Lincoln Park liberals wrung their hands and signed petitions, an unusual alliance formed a few miles north. It was between the Black Panthers and the Young Patriots. A most unusual alliance: On the side of *their* berets, the Young Patriots wear the Confederate flag.

The film isn't much concerned with the alliance itself, however; it's taken for granted that poor blacks and poor whites should work together. The film is about how a neighborhood had its idea of Chicago permanently altered by the events of convention week. My guess is that the Film Group stumbled onto this theme and had the perception to keep after it.

The film itself began as a collection of footage from those two memorable nights, Wednesday and Thursday, of convention week. It then was expanded to cover several months. The Film Group (a smoothly professional Chicago company that usually makes commercials and sponsored films) made it as a collective effort, and there aren't any credits. Several camera crews worked on and off, first during the convention, then in the ghetto, and then, following their noses, to where the story continued in Uptown.

The result is a film every Chicagoan should see. But that's a cliché. What I want to say is: If you were disturbed by what happened last August and if you wondered, however vaguely, how such a cataclysmic week apparently should have no aftermath, then you should see this film and see what has happened.

The film is an "unnarrated documentary," something both the Film Group and Chicago filmmakers Gerald Temaner and Gordon Quinn have been experimenting with. There's no deep, authoritative voice telling us what is happening. Instead, we see and hear only the people the film is about; they speak for themselves.

One of the film's subtitles is *A Few Honkies Get Their Heads Beat,* and that describes as well as anything the first third of the film. We see again the scenes we remember so well: the demonstrators, the police, the guardsmen, the tear gas, and the march to Dick Gregory's home.

After convention week, a reprise. We get clips of an ABC-TV newscast about the redwood fences Mayor Daley threw up to spare the delegates the sight of empty lots. We hear the boosterism of a Chicago convention official. We get a tour of the Amphitheater neighborhood by a taxi driver ("Here was where they put up the barbed wire; you needed a pass to go any farther").

And then we go into the ghetto: into pool halls, bars, restaurants, to hear black people talking, sometimes angry, sometimes wry, about the honkies who needed to get their heads beat to find out what the ghetto knew all along. In one stunning shot, we begin with a close-up of a black girl who speaks of her experiences and beliefs. Then the camera pulls back to a medium shot revealing her as an armed militant: "I'll have my rifle on one arm and my baby on the other, and I'll fight for what's mine."

By now a smooth editing rhythm has been established, and we're inside the film's logic. (Indeed, this film is as well edited and as high in technical quality as any cinema vérité documentary I've ever seen. The quality of the sound recording outdoors on Michigan Avenue is superior to the sound obtained indoors in, say, *Warrendale.*)

The editing builds up a rhythm of angry and amused black faces, and the rhythm of the film is the rhythm of the words they're saying. This momentum begins to be broken by another kind of face: a white face with a southern accent, saying earnest things. But saying the same things. This is a community leader from Uptown—no, not officially a leader, because the Uptown Council is run by bankers and businessmen and he is "only" a poor white from Appalachia.

We go to a party at which this man and many of his neighbors drink Pepsi and argue passion-ately about their neighborhood, about being poor, about what needs to be done, about the "pigs" who, they say, harass them for the crimes of being poor and living in Uptown. The party includes members of the Young Patriots, a white Uptown street gang—or community organization, depending on your point of view.

Now a revealing scene occurs. A spokesman for the Young Patriots attends a meeting of a group of concerned citizens from Lincoln Park. They're mostly, yes, "white liberals." The spokesman begins to talk about being poor and about the police.

"Oh God," says the chairman, bored, "we've all heard this so many times before." He is resentful: The meeting was called, it appears, by a clique that wished to congratulate itself on its progressive views. How embarrassing to listen to a hillbilly who doesn't even know he's using clichés.

But no. The group decides to let the hillbilly talk. This is the ultimate in liberalism, isn't it? To be bored by someone rather than admit you feel superior to him? And this leads us to the film's most poignant moment of revelation.

For when the liberals from Lincoln Park talk to the Young Patriot and ask him questions, they are condescending! They use simple words. They talk slow-ly, clear-ly, afraid that otherwise he won't understand. And the joke is, the film has already demonstrated that this young man and his friends have a higher degree of verbal facility (talk faster, more colorfully) than these people who condescend to him.

"But what's your program?" a concerned citizen asks him. "If you had a concrete proposal . . ." says another. A third suggests he take his ideas to "his grown-ups." A fourth says that if the Young Patriots could get a program organized, the Lincoln Park group might be able to help . . . might even, indeed, "get it in Royko's column."

The film now shifts permanently to events in Uptown. A Black Panther organizer, Bobby Lee, comes into the neighborhood to offer assistance to the Young Patriots. And Lee, who is quite a remarkable person, dominates the last part of the film.

In an astonishing scene, Lee confronts and wins over a room filled with suspicious, even hostile, Uptown whites. God knows what these people thought of Black Panthers before they met one! Bobby Lee cajoles, reasons, argues, asks questions: "What's bugging you, brother? This black beret? Here, I'll take it off. We been through a lot together. You poor? You ever been in jail?" The man nods, holds up two fingers. "Tell us what you been through," Bobby Lee says.

First one person, then another gets up to speak. Bobby Lee coaches a shy young mother to her feet; she holds her baby. When she finds the courage to talk, the words come in a rush: "The cops had my brother up against the squad car. He was out in front of the house. The cops had a knife, they were pricking him with it. I said, 'What's he done?' They wouldn't answer."

And others: "The cops said, 'What's your height?'" a boy says. "Then they took me over to the wall where there was a measuring stick, and then banged my head up against the wall. If you're poor, they don't care. That's it, man. If you got the bread, the pigs are scared of you." "Right on!" Bobby Lee intones, "Right on!"

The meeting ends in camaraderie and a sense of purpose. These people will constitute a committee to attend the Uptown Council meeting, where a Model Cities program is being decided on—without them.

At this meeting, and at a later meeting with the district police commander, the group finds an identity. The meeting with the policeman is particularly revealing. He begins by congratulating the gang on its name: the Young Patriots. He admits his men may harbor some resentment against people whose appearance doesn't fit their idea of "correct" appearance. "What we're trying to do," he says, "is to teach policemen that everyone isn't like them." But then he says: "The poor neighborhoods have been exploited by a person, or persons, who are less than American. They may be pink or even red."

An outburst of anger from the audience. They've come to share their grievances, to have a dialogue, and now they're being told they're Communist dupes. Obviously, these poor people couldn't have grievances unless a red—a pink, at least—told them they did.

People have been saying for a long time, why don't they make a movie about Chicago? Now one has been made. Not a Hollywood movie, with imported stars and directors, using Chicago merely as a backdrop. But a movie in and of Chicago.

American Revolution 2 shows this much clearly: that in the aftermath of the Democratic convention, a group of formerly voiceless, even opinionless Uptown whites became galvanized into a community that was fed up. That these people were able to understand that their enemy was not the black man (or another stand-in target) but an establishment that dismissed them as poor hillbillies and, therefore, less than equal. That these people formed an alliance with the Black Panthers, borrowing their methods of organization and protest. And that this alliance has created, in the midst of a city largely without a voice (unless you're white, unless you're educated, unless you're affluent, unless you have clout), a community that found its voice and used it.

American Splendor

R, 100 m., 2003

Paul Giamatti (Harvey Pekar), Harvey Pekar (Real Harvey), Hope Davis (Joyce Brabner), Joyce Brabner (Real Joyce), Shari Springer Berman (Interviewer), Earl Billings (Mr. Boats), James Urbaniak (Robert Crumb), Judah Friedlander (Toby Radloff), Robert Pulcini (Bob the Director), Toby Radloff (Real Toby), Madylin Sweeten (Danielle), Danielle Batone (Real Danielle). Directed by Shari Springer Berman and Robert Pulcini and produced by Ted Hope. Screenplay by Berman and Pulcini, based on the comic book series *American Splendor* by Harvey Pekar and *Our Cancer Year* by Joyce Brabner.

One of the closing shots of *American Splendor* shows a retirement party for Harvey Pekar, who is ending his career as a file clerk at a V.A. hospital in Cleveland. This is a real party, and it is a real retirement. Harvey Pekar, the star of comic books, the Letterman show, and now this movie, worked all of his life as a file clerk. When I met Harvey and his wife, Joyce Brabner, at Cannes 2003, she told me: "He's grade G-4. Grade G-2 is minimum wage. Isn't that something, after thirty years as a file clerk?"

Yes, but it got them to Cannes. Pekar is one of the heroes of graphic novels, which are comic books with a yearning toward the light. He had the good fortune to meet the legendary comic artist R. Crumb in the 1970s. He observed with his usual sour pessimism that comics were never written about people like him, and as he talked a lightbulb all but appeared above Crumb's head, and the comic book *American Splendor* was born, with Pekar as writer and Crumb as illustrator.

The books chronicle the life of a man very much indeed like Harvey Pekar. He works at a thankless job. He has friends at work, like the "world-class nerd" Toby Radloff, who share his complaints, although not at the Pekarian level of existential misery. The comic book brings him a visit from a fan named Joyce Brabner, who turns out, improbably, to be able to comprehend his existence while insisting on her own, and eventually they gain a daughter, Danielle Batone, sort of through osmosis (the daughter of a friend, she comes to visit, and decides to stay). The books follow Harvey, Joyce and Danielle as they sail through life, not omitting *Our Cancer Year,* a book retelling his travails after Harvey finds a lump on a testicle.

The comics are true, deep, and funny, precisely because they see that we are all superheroes doing daily battle against twisted and perverted villains. We have secret powers others do not suspect. We have secret identities. Our enemies may not be as colorful as the Joker or Dr. Evil, but certainly they are malevolent— who could be more hateful, for example, than an anal-retentive supervisor, an incompetent medical orderly, a greedy landlord? When Harvey fills with rage, only the graphics set him aside from the Hulk.

The peculiarity and genius of *American Splendor* was always that true life and fiction marched hand in hand. There was a real Harvey Pekar, who looked very much like the one in the comic book, and whose own life was being described. Now comes this magnificently audacious movie, in which fact and fiction sometimes coexist in the same frame. We see and hear the real Harvey Pekar, and then his story is played by the actor Paul Giamatti, sometimes with Harvey commenting on "this guy who is playing me." We see the real Joyce Brabner, and we see Hope Davis playing her. We concede that Giamatti and Davis have mastered not only the looks but the feels and even the souls of these two people. And then there is Judah Friedlander to play Toby Radloff, who we might think could not be played by any-

body, but there the two Tobys are, and we can see it's a match.

The movie deals not merely with real and fictional characters, but even with levels of presentation. There are documentary scenes, fictional scenes, and then scenes illustrated and developed as comic books, with the drawings sometimes segueing into reality or back again. The filmmakers have taken the challenge of filming a comic book based on a life and turned it into an advantage—the movie is mesmerizing in the way it lures us into the daily hopes and fears of this Cleveland family.

The personality of the real Harvey Pekar is central to the success of everything. Pekar's genius is to see his life from the outside, as a life like all lives, in which eventual tragedy is given a daily reprieve. He is brutally honest. The conversations he has with Joyce are conversations like those we really have. We don't fight over trivial things, because nothing worth fighting over is trivial. As Harvey might say, "Hey, it's important to me!"

The Letterman sequences have the fascination of an approaching train wreck. Pekar really was a regular on the program in the 1980s, where he did not change in the slightest degree from the real Harvey. He gave as good as he got, until his resentments, angers, and grudges led him to question the fundamental realities of the show itself, and then he was bounced. We see real Letterman footage, and then a fictional re-creation of Pekar's final show. Letterman is not a bad guy, but he has a show to do, and Pekar is a good guest following his own agenda up to a point, but then he goes far, far beyond that point. When I talked with Pekar at Cannes, he confided that after Letterman essentially fired him and went to a commercial break, Dave leaned over and whispered into Harvey's ear: "You blew a good thing."

Well, he did. But blowing a good thing is Harvey's fate in life, just as stumbling upon a good thing is his victory. What we get in both cases is the unmistakable sense that Pekar does nothing for effect, that all of his decisions and responses proceed from some limitless well of absolute certitude. What we also discover is that Harvey is not entirely a dyspeptic grump, but has sweetness and hope waving desperately from somewhere deep within his despair.

This film is delightful in the way it finds its

own way to tell its own story. There was no model to draw on, but Shari Springer Berman and Robert Pulcini, who wrote and directed it, have made a great film by trusting Pekar's artistic credo, which amounts to: What you see is what you get. The casting of Giamatti and Davis is perfect, but of course it had to be, or the whole enterprise would have collapsed. Giamatti is not a million miles away from other characters he has played, in movies such as *Storytelling, Private Parts,* and *Man on the Moon,* but Davis achieves an uncanny transformation. I saw her in *The Secret Lives of Dentists,* playing a dentist, wife, and mother with no points in common with Joyce Brabner—not in look, not in style, not in identity. Now here she is as Joyce. I've met Joyce Brabner, and she's Joyce Brabner.

Movies like this seem to come out of nowhere, like free-standing miracles. But *American Splendor* does have a source, and its source is Harvey Pekar himself—his life, and what he has made of it. The guy is the real thing. He found Joyce, who is also the real thing, and Danielle found them, and as I talked with her I could see she was the real thing, too. She wants to go into showbiz, she told me, but she doesn't want to be an actress, because then she might be unemployable after forty. She said she wants to work behind the scenes. More longevity that way. Harvey nodded approvingly. Go for the pension.

An Angel at My Table

R, 160 m., 1991

Kerry Fox (Janet), Alexia Keogh (Young Janet), Karen Fergusson (Teenage Janet), Iris Churn (Mum), K.J. Wilson (Dad). Directed by Jane Campion and produced by Bridget Ikin. Screenplay by Laura Jones.

Here is the story of a curly-haired little redhead who grew up to be one of New Zealand's best authors, after enduring ordeals that would have put most people into a madhouse. The irony is that she was already in the madhouse, misdiagnosed as a schizophrenic, and subjected to more than two hundred electroshock treatments even though there was nothing really wrong with her except for shyness and depression.

Janet Frame is today the author of some twenty novels, books of poetry, plays, and autobiography. The first two books were actually written and published while she was in a mental hospital, and it is possible to wonder if the act of writing them saved her life—giving her a place to order her thoughts in the middle of chaos.

Jane Campion's *An Angel at My Table* tells her story in a way that I found strangely engrossing from beginning to end. This is not a hyped-up biopic or a soap opera, but simply the record of a life as lived, beginning in childhood with a talented, dreamy girl whose working-class parents loved her, and continuing to follow her as she was gradually shunted by society into a place that almost killed her. Janet is played in the film by three different actresses (from girlhood through her twenties into her thirties, they are Kerry Fox, Alexia Keogh, and Karen Fergusson), who have uncanny physical and personality similarities, and so we get a real sense of a life as it unfolds, as things go wrong and a strong spirit struggles to prevail.

The movie opens in prewar New Zealand, a green and comfortable land where Janet's father works for the railroad and she fits comfortably into a family including a brother and two sisters that she adores. She is a funny-looking child, with bad teeth and a mop of unruly scarlet hair, but there is something special about her. She has a poet's imagination, and when she writes a poem for grade school, she is absolutely sure what words she wishes to use, and cannot be persuaded by authority to change one word.

She grows up slowly, doesn't date, doesn't have much of a social life. In school, she socializes with the outcasts—the brains, the nonconformists, the arty set—but looks with envy on the popular girls and their boyfriends. It is a world she does not hope to understand. In college, too, she's a loner, shy, keeping to herself, confiding everything to a journal, and then, in her first job as a school teacher, she does not join the other teachers for tea because she cannot think of what to say to them. One day the school inspector comes to visit her class, and she freezes up and cannot say anything.

She is essentially having a panic attack, but one officious and ignorant diagnosis leads to another, and she is committed to a mental home, beginning eight years of unspeakable horror as she is given shock treatments and even threatened with a lobotomy by professionals whose complete ignorance of her condition does not inhibit their cheerful eagerness to deprive her of mind and freedom.

Her books help her keep her mind, and eventually help her win her release—her father, cowed by the professionals, vows he will never let her go back to the asylum again—and at last, in her thirties, her true life begins as she gets a grant to study abroad, and falls in with a group of bohemian writers and painters in Spain. She even finally loses her virginity, and although she will always be a little odd, a loner, wrapped in a cocoon of privacy, we can see her gradually becoming more comfortable with life.

Jane Campion, who directed from a screenplay by Laura Jones, is the author of last year's *Sweetie,* a movie about a family almost destroyed by a disruptive sister. That was a film I had to struggle with. I did not relate to it on the first viewing, but I could sense that something was there, and, eventually, after two more viewings, I came to love it. *An Angel at My Table* does not require a struggle: It is told with a clarity and simplicity that is quietly but completely absorbing. Yes, it is visually beautiful, and, yes, it is well acted, but it doesn't call attention to its qualities. It tells its story calmly and with great attention to human detail, and watching it, I found myself drawn in with a rare intensity.

Another Woman

PG, 81 m., 1988

Gena Rowlands (Marion), Philip Bosco (Sam), Betty Buckley (Cathy), Martha Plimpton (Laura), Blythe Danner (Lydia), Sandy Dennis (Claire), Mia Farrow (Hope), Gene Hackman (Harry), John Houseman (Marion's Father), Ian Holm (Ben). Written and directed by Woody Allen. Produced by Robert Greenhut.

Film is the most voyeuristic medium, but rarely have I experienced this fact more sharply than while watching Woody Allen's *Another Woman*. This is a film almost entirely composed of moments that should be private. At times, privacy is violated by characters in the film. At other times, we invade the privacy of the characters. And the central character is our accomplice, standing beside us, speaking

in our ear, telling us of the painful process she is going through.

This character is named Marion Post (Gena Rowlands), and she is the kind of woman who might feel qualified to advise the rest of us how to organize our lives by "balancing" the demands of home, job, spouse, and friends. She is fearsomely self-contained, well-organized, sane, efficient, and intelligent. *Another Woman* is about the emotional compromises she has had to make in order to earn that description.

She is the head of a university department of philosophy. She is married to a physician, and, childless, has a good relationship with her husband's teenage daughter from an earlier marriage. She dresses in a fashion that is so far above criticism as to almost be above notice. She is writing a book, and to find a place free of distractions, she rents an office in a downtown building. She tells us some of these details on the sound track, describing her life with a dry detachment that seems to hide an edge of concern.

The office is in one of those older buildings with a tricky ventilation system. Sitting at her desk one day, Marion discovers that she can hear every word of a therapy session taking place in the office of the psychiatrist who has his office next door. At first she blocks out the sound by placing pillows against the ventilation outlet. Then, frankly, she begins to listen.

While he is establishing this device of the overheard conversations, Allen does an interesting thing. Not only can Marion Post (and the rest of us) easily eavesdrop on the conversations, but when the pillows are placed against the air shaft, they completely block out every word. The choice—to listen, or not to listen—is presented so clearly that it is unreal. It's too neat, comprehensive, final. Although most of the scenes in *Another Woman* are clearly realistic, I think the treatment of sound in the office is a signal from Allen that the office is intended to be read in another way—as the orderly interior of Marion Post's mind, perhaps. And the cries coming in through the grillwork on the wall are the sounds of real emotions that she has put out of her mind for years. They are her nightmares.

During the course of the next few weeks, Marion Post will find the walls of her mind tumbling down. She will discover that she intimidates people, and that they do not love her as much as she thinks, nor trust her to share their secrets. She will find that she knows little about her husband, little about her own emotions, little about why she married this cold, adulterous doctor instead of another man who truly loved her.

If this journey of discovery sounds familiar, it is because *Another Woman* has a great many elements in common with Ingmar Bergman's *Wild Strawberries,* the story of an elderly doctor whose day begins with a nightmare and continues with a voyage of discovery. The doctor finds that his loved ones have ambiguous feelings about him, that his "efficiency" is seen as sternness, and that he made a mistake when he did not accept passionate love when it was offered to him. Allen's film is not a remake of *Wild Strawberries* in any sense, but a meditation on the same theme—the story of a thoughtful person, thoughtfully discovering why she might have benefited from being a little less thoughtful.

There is a temptation to say that Gena Rowlands has never been better than in this movie, but that would not be true. She is an extraordinary actor who is usually this good, and has been this good before, especially in some of the films of her husband, John Cassavetes. What is new here is the whole emotional tone of her character.

Great actors and great directors sometimes find a common emotional ground, so that the actor becomes an instrument playing the director's song. Cassavetes is a wild, passionate spirit, emotionally disorganized, insecure, and tumultuous, and Rowlands has reflected that personality in her characters for him—white-eyed women on the edge of stampede or breakdown. Allen is introspective, considerate, apologetic, formidably intelligent, and controls people through thought and words rather than through physicality and temper. Rowlands now mirrors that personality, revealing in the process how the Cassavetes performances were indeed *acting* and not some kind of ersatz documentary reality. To see *Another Woman* is to get an insight into how good an actress Rowlands has been all along.

I have not said much about the movie's story. I had better not. More than with many thrillers, *Another Woman* depends upon the audience's gradual discovery of what happens. There are some false alarms along the way. The patient in the psychiatrist's office (Mia Farrow), pregnant and confused, turns up in the "outside" world of the Rowlands character, and we expect more to come of that meeting than ever does. Some critics have asked why the Rowlands and Farrow characters did not interact more deeply—but the whole point is that the philosopher has suppressed everything inside of her that could connect to that weeping, pregnant other woman.

There is also an actual "other woman" in the film, as well as a dry, correct performance by Ian Holm as a man who must have a wife so he can be unfaithful to her. Gene Hackman is precisely cast as the earlier lover whose passion was rejected by Marion, and there is another of Martha Plimpton's bright, somehow sad, teenagers. In the movie's single most effective scene, Betty Buckley plays Holm's first wife, turning up unexpectedly at a social event and behaving "inappropriately," while Holm firmly tries to make her disappear (this scene is so observant of how people handle social embarrassment that it plays like an open wound).

In this last performance before his death, John Houseman finally cut loose from all the appearances of robust immortality and allowed himself to be seen as old, feeble, and spotted—and with immense presence. (In a scene involving the character when he was younger, David Ogden Stiers makes an uncanny Houseman double.)

Another Woman ends a little abruptly. I expected another chapter. And yet I would not have enjoyed a tidy conclusion to this material, because the one thing we learn about Marion Post is that she has got her package so tightly wrapped that she may never live long enough to rummage through its contents. At least by the end of the film she is beginning to remember what it was that she boxed up so carefully, so many years before.

Antonia's Line
NO MPAA RATING, 105 m., 1996

Willeke van Ammelrooy (Antonia), Els Dottermans (Danielle), Jan Decleir (Sebastian), Mil Seghers (Crooked Finger), Marina de Graaf (DeeDee), Jan Steen (Loony Lips), Veerle Van Overloop (Therese), Elsie de

Brauw (Lara). Directed by Marleen Gorris and produced by Hans de Weers. Screenplay by Gorris.

Antonia's Line finds its colors in many cultures, and stirs them in the same jolly pot. They should come out muddy brown, but the rainbow endures. The movie incorporates the magic realism of Latin America, dour European philosophies of death, the everyday realities of rural life, a cheerful feminism, a lot of easygoing sex, and a gallery of unforgettable characters. By the time the film is over, you feel you could walk down its village streets and greet everyone by name.

The movie is about a matriarchy founded by a woman named Antonia (Willeke van Ammelrooy), who after World War II returns to her Dutch village. She and her daughter have come back to bury her old mother. It is not an ordinary funeral; the mother sits up in her coffin to sing *My Blue Heaven*, and a statue of Jesus smiles. Later, in the churchyard, a stone angel uses its wing to smite a priest who refused the last rites to a man who sheltered Jews from the Nazis.

Antonia greets her old friends, among them Russian Olga (who runs the café and is an undertaker and midwife), Crooked Finger (who lives in a room with his books and bitterly insists on the futility of life), and Mad Madonna (who utters wild goat cries at the moon because, as a Catholic, she cannot marry her Protestant lover).

There is also Farmer Bas, who comes courting one day with his five sons, and makes a proposal of marriage centering largely on the boys' need for a mother. Antonia finds this underwhelming, but invites him to come over from time to time to do chores, for which she will pay him with hot breakfasts and cups of tea. "I can get those at home," he observes, but he comes anyway, and eventually Antonia tells him, "You can't have my hand, but you can have the rest." They agree that once a week is enough. Antonia doesn't want "all that confusion" in her house, or his, and so they build a little cottage for their meetings.

And so it goes. In fact, the narrator of *Antonia's Line*, Antonia's great-granddaughter, is very fond of reminding us that so it goes; the movie is punctuated with moments where we are assured that season followed season, and crops were planted and harvested, and life went on, and nothing much changed. e. e. cummings's poem "anyone lived in a pretty how town" comes to mind, and has the same sad, romantic, elegiac, pastoral tone.

Generation follows generation. Antonia's daughter, who wants a child but not a husband, auditions candidates for fatherhood. Local matches are made: Loony Lips and DeeDee, who are both retarded, find happiness together. So does the village priest, who one day flings his cassock in the air, shouts, "I'm free!" settles down, and produces a dozen or so children. There are dark days, two of them involving rape, but the women take direct measures: One miscreant is punctured by a pitchfork, and another receives Antonia's curse.

What we remember most of all is the way Antonia's extended family grows. Children and grandchildren, in-laws and outlaws, neighbors, friends, and drifters all come to sit at her long, long dinner table, and all learn the same simple rule, which is to look for the good in others—and to not criticize those who have found a way to be happy without seriously bothering anybody.

One of the most poignant strands in the story involves Crooked Finger (Mil Seghers), who tutors Antonia's brilliant granddaughter Therese, and who is named, I suppose, after the finger that's always holding a place in a book. His room is a shrine to philosophers, and he believes that life is without meaning, that there is no existence after death, that hope is wasted, that God is dead.

Antonia and the others listen to Crooked Finger but do not subscribe to his gloom. They are not religious in a conventional sense, but they're regular churchgoers, because the church provides a weekly gathering of the community—a spiritual version of their communal dinners.

By the end of the film, we have traveled through fifty years of modern life, through trends and controversies, fads, and fashions (the cars in the village are newer every time we see one). These fancies are not as important as the solid, life-affirming values of Antonia, who is embodied by Willeke van Ammelrooy in a remarkable performance. She ages from her thirties to her eighties, always convincingly, and is a substantial, robust, open-faced woman with a warm smile: In Hollywood, she would be considered fat, but we see she is, quite simply, healthy.

The experience of the film lulls us into a strange and wonderful mood: We are told these stories sometimes as inexplicable as a miracle, sometimes as earthy as a barnyard. Beneath them is a philosophy insisting on itself. The filmmaker, Marleen Gorris, believes women have innate understanding and common sense, and that, left to run things, they will right wrongs and encourage sanity. I hope she is right. Even if she is too optimistic, I am glad her movie made me feel hopeful and cheerful. In one of the opening scenes of the film, as Antonia and her daughter walk through the town, a sign on a wall says WELCOME TO OUR LIBERATORS! It is intended for the American troops. But it could, as it turns out, also apply to them.

Note: The movie won the 1996 Academy Award as best foreign-language film.

Apocalypse Now

R, 139 m., 1979

Marlon Brando (Colonel Kurtz), Robert Duvall (Lieutenant Colonel Kilgore), Martin Sheen (Captain Willard), Frederic Forrest (Chef), Albert Hall (Chief), Sam Bottoms (Lance), Larry Fishburne (Clean), Dennis Hopper (Photographer). Directed and produced by Francis Ford Coppola. Screenplay by John Milius and Coppola.

In his book *The Films of My Life,* the French director François Truffaut makes a curious statement. He used to believe, he says, that a successful film had to simultaneously express "an idea of the world and an idea of cinema." But now, he writes: "I demand that a film express either the joy of making cinema or the agony of making cinema. I am not at all interested in anything in between; I am not interested in all those films that do not pulse."

It may seem strange to begin a review of Francis Coppola's *Apocalypse Now* with those words, but consider them for a moment and they apply perfectly to this sprawling film. The critics who rejected Coppola's film mostly did so on Truffaut's earlier grounds: They had arguments with the ideas about the world and the war in *Apocalypse Now,* or they disagreed

with the very idea of a film that cost $31 million to make and was then carted all over the world by a filmmaker *still* uncertain whether he had the right ending.

That "other" film on the screen—the one we debate because of its ideas, not its images—is the one that caused so much controversy about *Apocalypse Now.* We all read that Coppola took as his inspiration the Joseph Conrad novel *Heart of Darkness,* and that he turned Conrad's journey up the Congo into a metaphor for another journey up a jungle river, into the heart of the Vietnam War. We all read Coppola's grandiose statements (the most memorable: "This isn't a film about Vietnam. This film *is* Vietnam."). We heard that Marlon Brando was paid $1 million for his closing scenes, and that Coppola gambled his personal fortune to finish the film, and, heaven help us, we even read a journal by the director's wife in which she disclosed her husband's ravings and infidelities.

But all such considerations are far from the reasons why *Apocalypse Now* is a good and important film—a masterpiece, I believe. Now, when Coppola's budget and his problems have long been forgotten, *Apocalypse* stands, I think, as a grand and grave and insanely inspired gesture of filmmaking—of moments that are operatic in their style and scope, and of other moments so silent we can almost hear the director thinking to himself.

I should at this moment make a confession: I am not particularly interested in the "ideas" in Coppola's film. Critics of *Apocalypse* have said that Coppola was foolish to translate *Heart of Darkness,* that Conrad's vision had nothing to do with Vietnam, and that Coppola was simply borrowing Conrad's cultural respectability to give a gloss to his own disorganized ideas. The same objection was made to the hiring of Brando: Coppola was hoping, according to this version, that the presence of Brando as an icon would distract us from the emptiness of what he's given to say.

Such criticisms are made by people who indeed are plumbing *Apocalypse Now* for its ideas, and who are as misguided as the veteran Vietnam correspondents who breathlessly reported that *The Deer Hunter* was not "accurate." What idea or philosophy could we expect to find in *Apocalypse Now*—and what good would it really do, at this point after the Vietnam tragedy, if Brando's closing speeches *did* have the "answers"? Like all great works of art about war, *Apocalypse Now* essentially contains only one idea or message, the not-especially-enlightening observation that war is hell. We do not see Coppola's movie for that insight—something Coppola, but not some of his critics, knows well.

Coppola also knows well (and demonstrated in the *Godfather* films) that movies aren't especially good at dealing with abstract ideas—for those you'd be better off turning to the written word—but they *are* superb for presenting moods and feelings, the look of a battle, the expression on a face, the mood of a country. *Apocalypse Now* achieves greatness not by analyzing our "experience in Vietnam," but by re-creating, in characters and images, something of that experience.

An example: The scene in which Robert Duvall, as a crazed lieutenant colonel, leads his troops in a helicopter assault on a village is, quite simply, the best movie battle scene ever filmed. It's simultaneously numbing, depressing, and exhilarating: As the rockets jar from the helicopters and spring through the air, we're elated like kids for a half-second, until the reality of the consequences sinks in. Another wrenching scene—in which the crew of Martin Sheen's Navy patrol boat massacres the Vietnamese peasants in a small boat—happens with such sudden, fierce, senseless violence that it forces us to understand for the first time how such things could happen.

Coppola's *Apocalypse Now* is filled with moments like that, and the narrative device of the journey upriver is as convenient for him as it was for Conrad. That's really why he uses it, and not because of literary cross-references for graduate students to catalog. He takes the journey, strings episodes along it, leads us at last to Brando's awesome, stinking hideaway . . . and then finds, so we've all heard, that he doesn't have an ending. Well, Coppola *doesn't* have an ending, if we or he expected the closing scenes to pull everything together and make sense of it. Nobody should have been surprised. *Apocalypse Now* doesn't tell any kind of a conventional story, doesn't have a thought-out message for us about Vietnam, has no answers, and thus needs no ending.

The way the film ends now, with Brando's fuzzy, brooding monologues and the final violence, feels much more satisfactory than any conventional ending possibly could.

What's great in the film, and what will make it live for many years and speak to many audiences, is what Coppola achieves on the levels Truffaut was discussing: the moments of agony and joy in making cinema. Some of those moments come at the same time; remember again the helicopter assault and its unsettling juxtaposition of horror and exhilaration. Remember the weird beauty of the massed helicopters lifting over the trees in the long shot, and the insane power of Wagner's music, played loudly during the attack, and you feel what Coppola was getting at: Those moments as common in life as art, when the whole huge grand mystery of the world, so terrible, so beautiful, seems to hang in the balance.

Note: See also Hearts of Darkness, *a documentary on the making of* Apocalypse Now.

Apocalypse Now Redux

R, 197 m., 2001

Marlon Brando (Kurtz), Robert Duvall (Kilgore), Martin Sheen (Willard), Frederic Forrest (Chef), Dennis Hopper (Photographer), Aurore Clement (Roxanne), Laurence Fishburne (Clean), Albert Hall (Chief), Harrison Ford (Colonel Lucas). Directed by Francis Ford Coppola and produced by Coppola and Kim Aubry. Screenplay by John Milius and Coppola.

More than ever it is clear that Francis Ford Coppola's *Apocalypse Now* is one of the great films of all time. It shames modern Hollywood's timidity. To watch it is to feel yourself lifted up to the heights where the cinema can take you, but so rarely does. The film is a mirror reflecting our feelings about the war in Vietnam, in all their complexity and sadness. To those who wrote me defending the banality of *Pearl Harbor,* I wrote back: "See *Apocalypse Now* and reflect on the difference."

The movie comes to us now in a new version, forty-nine minutes longer than the original. The most unexpected thing about *Apocalypse Now Redux* may not be the restored footage, however, but the new Technicolor dye-transfer prints. An expert on prints, Jeff Joseph, tells me: "This is essentially a reworking of the old three-strip Technicolor process. Instead of the chemical development of colors, color dyes are transferred to the film directly, resulting in the stunning 'Technicolor' look of the '40s and '50s: lush, gorgeous, bright, sharp, and vivid, with deep, rich, true blacks."

The physical look of the film is therefore voluptuous and saturated. This is what would be at risk with digital projection. Coppola also pushes the envelope with the remastered sound track, and I was reminded of the film's world premiere at Cannes in 1979, when the old Palais was so filled with light and sound that I felt enveloped; the helicopters in the famous village assault could first be heard behind me, and then passed overhead, and yes, there were people who involuntarily ducked. To be able to come home from the hellish production conditions on the Philippines locations with a film of such technical mastery is miraculous.

The story concerns a journey upriver by Captain Willard (Martin Sheen), who commands a patrol boat to penetrate behind enemy lines and discover the secret redoubt of the almost mythical Colonel Kurtz (Marlon Brando)—one of the army's most decorated soldiers, now leading his own band of tribesmen. The story is based on Joseph Conrad's *Heart of Darkness*, but replaces the implacable mystery of the upper reaches of the Congo with the equally unfathomable mystery of the American venture in Vietnam. When you get to the bottom of who Kurtz has become and what he is thinking, you can see how the war transformed the original American idealism.

The movie consists of a series of set pieces. The most famous is the assault on the village, opening with the helicopter loudspeakers blasting Wagner at the terrified students and teachers, and continuing with Lieutenant Kilgore (Robert Duvall) and his swashbuckling bravado on the beach ("I love the smell of napalm in the morning"). Other sequences are also in the permanent memory of moviegoers: the drugged monotony of the river journey, the sudden gunfire that kills everyone on the sampan, the Playboy Playmates entertaining the troops, the dreamlike final approach to Kurtz's compound, the shadowed Kurtz and his bleak aphorisms, and the giggling assent of the stoned photographer (Dennis Hopper), who is the Fool to his Lear.

To the majesty of these scenes in their progression to Kurtz's words "the Horror," Coppola has now added forty-nine minutes, most of them devoted to a visit by the crew to a French plantation, a colonial leftover that somehow survives. At dinner the Americans and French discuss the colonial history of Vietnam, and Willard's eyes meet those of Roxanne (Aurore Clement), a widow who will spend the night in his arms. Other new footage includes dialogue and byplay on the boat, a second encounter with the Playmates, and additional dialogue by Kurtz.

In a note released with the film, Coppola emphasizes that this new material was not simply shoehorned into the original version of the film, but that *Redux* is "a new rendition of the movie from scratch." He and his longtime editor Walter Murch "re-edited the film from the original unedited raw footage—the dailies," he says, and so possibly even some of the shots that look familiar to us are different takes than the ones we saw before. The 1979 version "terrified" him, he says, because it was "too long, too strange and didn't resolve itself in a kind of classic big battle at the end." Facing financial disaster, he shaped it for the "mainstream audience of its day," and twenty years later, seeing it again, he found it "relatively tame."

To consider *Apocalypse Now* mainstream or tame in either form is a bizarre judgment for Coppola to pass on his picture, but then he has a history of incautious and inexplicable remarks about it, going back to the infamous Cannes press conference where he confessed he had "problems with the ending," and many critics thought he was talking about the Kurtz episode, and not (as he was) the closing titles.

My own feeling is that the original cut was neither mainstream nor tame, but epic filmmaking on a scale within the reach of only a few directors—Tarkovsky, Lean, Eisenstein, Kurosawa. The new version therefore triggered my suspicion. I was happy to see the additional footage, and indeed had seen it before, in outtake form. Did the movie require it?

Some of the footage enters seamlessly into the work and disappears, enriching it. That would include the river footage and some moments with the photographer. The new Brando footage, including some more pointed analysis of the war, is a valuable addition. The

Playmate footage simply doesn't work; it was left out of the original because a typhoon prevented him from completing its filming, Coppola says, but "Walter found a way to get in and out of the sequence." Perhaps, but no reason to be there.

It is the French plantation sequence that gives me the most pause. It is long enough, I think, that it distracts from the overall arc of the movie. The river journey sets the rhythm of the film, and too much time on the banks interrupts it (there is the same problem with the feuding families in *Huckleberry Finn*). Yet the sequence is effective and provoking (despite the inappropriate music during the love scene). It helps me to understand it when Coppola explains that he sees the French like ghosts; I questioned how they had survived in their little enclave, and accept his feeling that their spirits survive as a cautionary specter for the Americans.

Longer or shorter, *Redux* or not, *Apocalypse Now* is one of the central events of my life as a filmgoer. To have it in this beautiful print is a luxury. This new version will make its way to DVD and be welcome there, but the place to see it is in a movie theater, sitting not too far back, your eyes and ears filled with its haunting vision. Now this is a movie.

Apollo 13

PG, 135 m., 1995

Tom Hanks (Jim Lovell), Bill Paxton (Fred Haise), Kevin Bacon (Jack Swigert), Gary Sinise (Ken Mattingly), Ed Harris (Gene Kranz), Kathleen Quinlan (Marilyn Lovell), Mary Kate Schellhardt (Barbara Lovell), Emily Ann Lloyd (Susan Lovell). Directed by Ron Howard and produced by Brian Grazer. Screenplay by William Broyles, Jr., and Al Reinert.

There is a moment early in *Apollo 13* when astronaut Jim Lovell is taking some press on a tour of the Kennedy Space Center, and he brags that they have a computer "that fits in one room and can send out millions of instructions." And I'm thinking to myself, hell, I'm writing this review on a better computer than the one that got us to the moon.

Apollo 13 inspires many reflections, and one of them is that America's space program was achieved with equipment that would look like tin cans today. Like Lindbergh, who crossed the Atlantic in the first plane he could string together that might make it, we went to the moon the moment we could, with the tools that were at hand. Today, with new alloys, engines, fuels, computers, and technology, it would be safer and cheaper—but we have lost the will.

Apollo 13 never really states its theme, except perhaps in one sentence of narration at the end, but the whole film is suffused with it: The space program was a really extraordinary thing, something to be proud of, and those who went into space were not just "heroes," which is a cliché, but brave and resourceful.

Those qualities were never demonstrated more dramatically than in the flight of the thirteenth Apollo mission, in April 1970, when an oxygen tank exploded en route to the moon. The three astronauts on board—Jim Lovell, Fred Haise, and Jack Swigert—were faced with the possibility of becoming marooned in space. Their oxygen could run out, they could be poisoned by CO_2 accumulations, or they could freeze to death. If somehow they were able to return to the Earth's atmosphere, they had to enter at precisely the right angle. Too steep an entry, and they would be incinerated; too shallow, and they would skip off the top of the atmosphere like a stone on a pond, and fly off forever into space.

Ron Howard's film of this mission is directed with a single-mindedness and attention to detail that make it riveting. He doesn't make the mistake of adding cornball little subplots to popularize the material; he knows he has a great story, and he tells it in a docudrama that feels like it was filmed on location in outer space.

So convincing are the details, indeed, that I went back to look at *For All Mankind,* the great 1989 documentary directed by Al Reinert, who cowrote *Apollo 13.* It was an uncanny experience, like looking at the origins of the current picture. Countless details were exactly the same: the astronauts boarding the spacecraft, the liftoff, the inside of the cabin, the view from space, the chilling sight of the oxygen venting into space, even the little tape recorder floating in free-fall, playing country music. All these images are from the documentary, all look almost exactly the same in the movie, and that is why Howard has been at pains to emphasize that every shot in *Apollo 13* is new. No documentary footage was used. The special effects—models, animation, shots where the actors were made weightless by floating inside a descending airplane—have re-created the experience exactly.

The astronauts are played by Tom Hanks (Lovell), Bill Paxton (Haise), and Kevin Bacon (Swigert). The pilot originally scheduled for the *Apollo 13* mission was Ken Mattingly (Gary Sinise), who was grounded because he had been exposed to the measles. The key figure at Houston Mission Control is Gene Kranz (Ed Harris). Clean-cut, crew-cut, wearing white collars even in space, the astronauts had been built up in the public mind as supermen, but as Tom Wolfe's book and Phil Kaufman's movie *The Right Stuff* revealed, they were more likely to be hotshot test pilots than straight arrows.

The movie begins with the surprise selection of Lovell's group to crew *Apollo 13*. We meet members of their families, particularly Marilyn Lovell (Kathleen Quinlan); we follow some of the training, and then the movie follows the ill-fated mission, in space and on the ground. Kranz, the Harris character, chain-smoking Camels, masterminds the ground effort to figure out how (and if) *Apollo 13* can ever return.

A scheme is dreamed up to shut down power in the space capsule, and move the astronauts into the Lunar Landing Module, as sort of a temporary lifeboat. The lunar lander will be jettisoned at the last minute, and the main capsule's weakened batteries may have enough power left to allow the crew to return alive.

Meanwhile, the problem is to keep them from dying in space. A scrubber to clean CO_2 from the capsule's air supply is jerry-built out of materials on board (and you can see a guy holding one just like it in *For All Mankind*). And you begin to realize, as the astronauts swing around the moon and head for home, that, given the enormity of the task of returning to Earth, their craft and equipment is only a little more adequate than the rocket sled in which Evil Knievel proposed to hurtle across Snake River Canyon at about the same time.

Ron Howard has become a director who specializes in stories involving large groups of characters: *Cocoon, Parenthood, Backdraft, The Paper*. Those were all films that paid attention to the individual human stories involved; they were a triumph of construction, indeed, in keeping many stories afloat and interesting.

With *Apollo 13*, he correctly decides that the story is in the mission. There is a useful counterpoint in the scenes involving Lovell's wife, waiting fearfully on the ground. (She tells their son, "Something broke on your daddy's spaceship and he's going to have to turn around before he even gets to the moon.") But Howard adds no additional side stories, no little parallel dramas, as a lesser director might have.

This is a powerful story, one of 1995's best films, told with great clarity and remarkable technical detail, and acted without pumped-up histrionics. It's about men trained to do a job, and doing a better one than anyone could have imagined. The buried message is: When we dialed down the space program, we lost something crucial to our vision. When I was a kid, they used to predict that by the year 2000, you'd be able to go to the moon. Nobody ever thought to predict that you'd be able to, but nobody would bother.

The Apostle

PG-13, 133 m., 1998

Robert Duvall (The Apostle E.F.), Farrah Fawcett (Jessie Dewey), Miranda Richardson (Toosie), Todd Allen (Horace), John Beasley (Brother Blackwell), June Carter Cash (Mrs. Dewey Sr.), Walter Goggins (Sam), Billy Joe Shaver (Joe), Billy Bob Thornton (Troublemaker). Directed by Robert Duvall and produced by Rob Carliner. Screenplay by Duvall.

There's a scene early in *The Apostle* where Robert Duvall, as a Pentecostal preacher from Texas, is having a talk with God, who has to do all of the listening. In an upstairs room at his mother's house, he rants and raves at the almighty, asking for a way to see reason in calamity: His cheating wife is stealing his church from him.

So far, the scene could be in a more conventional film. But then the phone rings, and it's a neighbor, complaining to his mother that someone is "carrying on like a wild man." The call establishes that the preacher lives in a real world, with real neighbors, and not on a sound stage where his life is lived in a self-contained drama. His mother tells the neighbor that her son has talked to God ever since he was a boy and she's not going to stop him now.

The Apostle sees its characters in an unusually perceptive light; they have the complexity and spontaneity of people in a documentary. Duvall, who not only plays the preacher but also wrote and directed the film, has seen this preacher—named Eulis "Sonny" Dewey—with great attention and sympathy.

Sonny is different from most movie preachers. He's not a fraud, for one thing; Hollywood tilts toward the Elmer Gantry stereotype. Sonny has a one-on-one relationship with God, takes his work seriously, and in the opening scene of the movie pauses at an auto accident to ask one of the victims to accept Jesus Christ, "who you're going to soon meet." He is flawed, with a quick temper, but he's a good man, and the film is about his struggle back to redemption after his anger explodes.

As the film opens, Sonny is spending a lot of time on the road at revivals (we see him at one of them, made convincing because Duvall cast all the extras from real congregations). His wife (Farrah Fawcett) has taken up with the youth minister, and one night, sitting in a motel room, Sonny figures that out, drives home through the darkness, finds her absent from her bed, and throws a baseball through the minister's bedroom window.

His wife wants out of the marriage. And through legal but shady maneuverings, she also deprives him of his church and his job. Sonny gets drunk, wades into a Little League game being coached by the youth minister, and bangs him on the head with a baseball bat. Then he flees town (there is an overhead shot of his car circling aimlessly around a rural intersection; he has no idea where to go). Eventually he ends up in a hamlet in the Louisiana bayou, where he spends his first night in a pup tent supplied by a man who wants to help him but isn't sure he trusts him.

Sonny changes his name to "The Apostle E.F.," and sets about rebuilding a small rural church given him by a retired black minister. His mostly black congregation is small at first, but grows as the result of broadcasts on the local forty-watt station. We see in countless little ways that Sonny is serious: He wants this church to work, he wants to save souls, he wants redemption. Like the documentary *Say Amen, Somebody*, the film spends enough time at the church services, listening to the music and the preaching, that we get into the spirit; we understand his feelings.

The Apostle became something of a legend in independent film circles, because Duvall was so long in getting it made. The major studios turned him down (of course; it's about something, which scares them). So did old associates who had always promised help, but didn't return his calls on this project. As he waited, Duvall must have rewritten the script many times, because it is astonishingly subtle. There isn't a canned and prefab story arc, with predictable stops along the way. Instead, the movie feels as alive as if it's a documentary of things happening right now.

Consider a sequence where the Apostle E.F., who is a man after all, asks the receptionist at the local radio station out on a date. How will he approach her? How does she see him? He wants to find a way to make his desires clear, without offending her. She knows this. As played by Duvall and Miranda Richardson, the sequence is a brilliant observation of social and sexual strategies.

Many of his scenes develop naturally, instead of along the lines of obligatory clichés. A confrontation with his wife, for example, doesn't end as we think it might. And a face-down with a redneck racist (Billy Bob Thornton) develops along completely unexpected lines. The Apostle E.F. is not easy to read; Duvall's screenplay does what great screenwriting is supposed to do and surprises us with additional observations and revelations in every scene.

Perhaps it's not unexpected that Duvall had to write, direct, and star in this film, and round up the financing himself. There aren't that many people in the film industry gifted enough to make such a film, and fewer still with the courage to deal honestly with a subject both spiritual and complex. (Simpleminded spirituality is no problem; consider the market for angels right now.) *The Apostle* is like a lesson in how movies can escape from convention and penetrate into the hearts of rare characters.

At the Max
R, 89 m., 1992

A documentary featuring the Rolling Stones (Mick Jagger, Keith Richards, Charlie Watts, Ron Wood, and Bill Wyman). Directed by Julien Temple and produced by Michael Cohl and André Picard.

It was probably only a matter of time before the Rolling Stones, billed as the greatest rock 'n' roll band in the world, got together with the IMAX format, which is certainly the greatest movie format in the world. The result is *At the Max*, which in its theatrical impact is the greatest concert film ever made. That doesn't mean it's the best film about a concert; there are some better ones, including *Woodstock*. But no other musical film in my experience has so overwhelmed the eyes and ears, drawing us into the feeling and texture of a rock concert.

If you have been to any of the museums and tourist centers that include an IMAX theater, you are familiar with the format. You are confronted with a screen that is four or five stories high, and surrounded by sound from speakers so powerful that even a whisper sounds like a message from God. The image, projected from special 70mm film, is both enormous in size and dazzling in clarity, and it fills your field of vision so completely that some viewers have actually suffered from vertigo.

This format is usually employed for educational and travelogue material: good films like *Antartica*, which took us inside icebergs, or the NASA documentaries, which took us into space, and bad films like one I saw at the Polynesian Cultural Center, which took a condescending view of Pacific Islanders. Whatever the subject matter, the visual and aural experience at an IMAX film is always startling.

And now here are the Stones, in *At the Max*, recorded and filmed in IMAX during the 1991 Rolling Stones concert tour. All of the concert is here; most IMAX films are limited to forty minutes because the reels of film are so cumbersome the projectors can't handle more, but this one is double-length, with an intermission while the reels are changed.

In its impact on the senses, seeing this film is better than being at a Stones concert. It's like being onstage with the Stones, except that even a member of the band doesn't have an omnipresent point of view, and the cameras do, cutting from one side of the enormous stage to another, and providing close-ups so large and clear that we can count the cigarettes in Bill Wyman's pack.

The film was shot by Julien Temple *(The Great Rock and Roll Swindle)*, using several of the big IMAX cameras, and it has been edited

to preserve the impact of the concert, not to upstage it. Some of the most important shots are taken from far back in the arena, giving an impression of the massive nature of a modern rock concert, with its tens of thousands of spectators. Others are so close we get four-story close-ups of Mick Jagger, although for the most part, aware of the overwhelming nature of the format, Temple keeps his camera back far enough for us to see the full body lengths of the musicians.

The central impression you come away with after any Stones concert, in person or on film, is of Mick Jagger's physical and psychic energy as a performer. Here the camera follows him as he climbs scaffolding to sing a hundred feet above the stage, or when he does a strange duet with huge inflatable dolls. (Those mildly suggestive dolls, and the language, earned the movie an R rating, but most teenagers will hear little to surprise them.) The eerie effect of IMAX is that it takes such passages and makes them both performance and documentary. They work as part of the show, but because the screen is so large and the picture so clear, we also feel like part of the experience; no other movie has communicated so well what it must feel like to be a rock star.

Do I need to write about the music? There are few surprises; this is your basic Stones concert. A lot of the Stones standards are here, and some new songs, and they sound wonderful through the big surround speakers. But the music is not really the point; it's the actual moviegoing experience that makes *At the Max* worth seeing. In the computer world, they talk about "virtual reality," a kind of cyberspace in which computers would take over what we see, hear, and feel, so that we could have the sensation of an experience without actually being there. *At the Max* is a rock concert brought to a point approaching virtual reality.

Note: The movie is available on tape and disc, but see it in an IMAX theater if you can.

Au Revoir les Enfants
PG, 103 m., 1988

Gaspard Manesse (Julien Quentin), Raphael Fejto (Jean Bonnet), Francine Racette (Madame Quentin), Stanislas Carre de Malberg (Francois Quentin), Philippe Morier-Genoud (Father Jean), Francois Berleand

(Father Michel), Francois Negret (Joseph), Peter Fitz (Muller). Directed, written, and produced by Louis Malle.

Which of us cannot remember a moment when we did or said precisely the wrong thing, irretrievably, irreparably? The instant the action was completed or the words were spoken, we burned with shame and regret, but what we had done could never be repaired. Such moments are rare, and they occur most often in childhood, before we have been trained to think before we act. *Au Revoir les Enfants* is a film about such a moment, about a quick, unthinking glance that may have cost four people their lives.

The film was written and directed by Louis Malle, who based it on a childhood memory. Judging by the tears I saw streaming down his face on the night the film was shown at the Telluride Film Festival, the memory has caused him pain for many years. His story takes place in 1944, in a Catholic boarding school in Nazi-occupied France. At the start of a new semester, three new students are enrolled, and we realize immediately that they are Jews, disguised with new names and identities in an attempt to hide them from the Nazis.

To Julien Quentin (Gaspard Manesse), however, this is not at all obvious. Julien, who is intended as Malle's autobiographical double, does not quite understand all of the distinctions involving Jews and gentiles in a country run by Nazis. All he knows is that he likes one of the new boys, Jean Bonnet (Raphael Fejto), and they become friends. Bonnet is not popular with the other students, who follow the age-old schoolboy practice of closing ranks against newcomers, but then Julien is not very popular either; the two boys are a little dreamy and thoughtful—absorbed in themselves and their imaginations, as bright adolescents should be. Malle's film is not filled with a lot of dramatic incidents. Unlike such roughly comparable Hollywood films as *The Lords of Discipline*, it feels no need for strong plotting and lots of dramatic incidents leading up to the big finale. Instead, we enter the daily lives of these boys. We see the classroom routine, the air-raid drills, the way each teacher has his own way of dealing with problems of discipline. More than anything else, we get a feeling for the rhythm of the school. Malle has said that when, years later, he visited the actual site of the boarding school he attended, he found that the building had disappeared and the school was forgotten. But to a student enrolled in such a school, the rules and rituals seem timeless, handed down by innumerable generations and destined to survive forever. A schoolboy cannot be expected to understand how swiftly violence and evil can strike out and change everything.

Julien and Jean play together, study together, look at dirty postcards together. One day, one of those cold early spring days when the shadows seem ominous and there is an unsettling wind in the trees, they go exploring in a nearby forest, and darkness falls. They get lost, or almost lost, and they weather this adventure and become even closer friends. One day, Julien accidentally discovers that "Jean Bonnet" is not his friend's real name. A few days later, when Julien's mother comes to visit, he invites Jean to join them at lunch in a local restaurant, and they witness an anti-Semitic incident as a longtime local customer is singled out because he is Jewish.

That is about all the input that Julien receives, and it is hard to say exactly what he knows, or suspects, about Jean. But when Nazis visit the school, Julien performs in one tragic second an action that will haunt him for the rest of his days. Malle has said that the incident in *Au Revoir les Enfants* does not exactly parallel whatever happened in real life, but the point must be the same: In an unthinking moment, action is taken that can never be retrieved.

Is the film only about guilt? Not at all. It is constructed very subtly to show that Julien only half-realized the nature of the situation, anyway. It isn't as if Julien knew absolutely that Jean was Jewish. It's more as if Julien possessed a lot of information that he had never quite put together, and when the Nazis came looking for hidden Jews, Julien suddenly realized what his information meant. The moment in which he makes his tragic mistake is also, perhaps, the moment when he comprehends for the first time the shocking fact of racism.

Auto Focus

R, 107 m., 2002

Greg Kinnear (Bob Crane), Willem Dafoe (John Carpenter), Maria Bello (Patricia Crane), Rita Wilson

(Anne Crane), Ron Leibman (Lenny). Directed by Paul Schrader and produced by Scott Alexander, Larry Karaszewski, Todd Rosken, Pat Dollard, and Alicia Allain. Screenplay by Michael Gerbosi, based on the book by Robert Graysmith.

Eddie Cantor once told Bob Crane, "Likability is 90 percent of the battle." It seems to be 100 percent of Bob Crane's battle; there is nothing there except likability—no values, no self-awareness, no judgment, no perspective, not even an instinct for survival. Just likability and the need to be liked in a sexual way every single day. Paul Schrader's *Auto Focus*, based on Crane's life, is a deep portrait of a shallow man, lonely and empty, going through the motions of having a good time.

The broad outlines of Crane's rise and fall are well known. How he was a Los Angeles DJ who became a TV star after being cast in the lead of *Hogan's Heroes,* a comedy set in a Nazi prison camp. How his career tanked after the show left the air. How he toured on the dinner theater circuit, destroyed two marriages, and was so addicted to sex that his life was scandalous even by Hollywood standards. How he was found bludgeoned to death in 1978 in a Scottsdale, Arizona, motel room.

Crane is survived by four children, including sons from his first and second marriages who differ in an almost biblical way, the older appearing in this movie, the younger threatening a lawsuit against it, yet running a Web site retailing his father's sex life. So strange was Crane's view of his behavior, so disconnected from reality, that I almost imagine he would have seen nothing wrong with his second son's sales of photos and videotapes of his father having sex. "It's healthy," Crane argues in defense of his promiscuity, although we're not sure if he really thinks that, or really thinks anything.

The movie is a hypnotic portrait of this sad, compulsive life. The director, Paul Schrader, is no stranger to stories about men trapped in sexual miscalculation; he wrote *Taxi Driver* and wrote and directed *American Gigolo*. He sees Crane as an empty vessel, filled first with fame and then with desire. Because he was on TV, he finds that women want to sleep with him, and seems to oblige them almost out of good manners. There is no lust or passion in this film,

only mechanical courtship followed by desultory sex. You can catch the women looking at him and asking themselves if there is anybody at home. Even his wives are puzzled.

Greg Kinnear gives a creepy, brilliant performance as a man lacking in all insight. He has the likability part down pat. There is a scene in a nightclub where Crane asks the bartender to turn the TV to a rerun of *Hogan's Heroes*. When a woman realizes that Hogan himself is in the room, notice how impeccable Kinnear's timing and manner are, as he fakes false modesty and pretends to be flattered by her attention. Crane was not a complex man, but that should not blind us to the subtlety and complexity of Kinnear's performance.

Willem Dafoe is the costar, as John Carpenter, a tech-head in the days when Hollywood was just learning that television could be taped and replayed by devices in the consumer price range. Carpenter hangs around sets, flattering the stars, lending them the newest Sony gadgets, wiring their cars for stereo and their dressing rooms for instant replays. He is the very embodiment of Mephistopheles, offering Crane exactly what he wants to be offered.

The turning point in Crane's life comes on a night when Carpenter invites him to a strip club. Crane is proud of his drumming, and Carpenter suggests that the star could "sit in" with the house band. Soon Crane is sitting in at strip clubs every night of the week, returning late or not at all to his first wife, Anne (Rita Wilson). Sensing something is wrong, he meets a priest one morning for breakfast, but is somehow not interested when the priest suggests he could "sit in" with a parish musical group.

Dafoe plays Carpenter as ingratiating, complimentary, sly, seductive, and enigmatically needy. Despite their denials, is there something homosexual in their relationship? The two men become constant companions, apart from a little tiff when Crane examines a video and notices Carpenter's hand in the wrong place. "It's an orgy!" Carpenter explains, and soon the men are on the prowl again. The video equipment has a curious relevance to their sexual activities; do they have sex for its own sake, or to record it for later editing and viewing? From its earliest days, home video has had an intimate buried relationship with sex. If Tommy Lee and Pamela Anderson ever think to ask themselves why they taped their wedding night, this movie might suggest some answers.

The film is wall-to-wall with sex, but contains no eroticism. The women are never really in focus. They drift in and out of range, as the two men hunt through swinger's magazines, attend swapping parties, haunt strip clubs, and troll themselves like bait through bars. If there is a shadow on their idyll, it is that Crane condescends to Carpenter, and does not understand the other man's desperate need for recognition.

The film is pitch-perfect in its decor, music, clothes, cars, language, and values. It takes place during those heady years between the introduction of the pill and the specter of AIDS, when men shaped as adolescents by *Playboy* in the 1950s now found some of their fantasies within reach. The movie understands how celebrity can make women available—and how, for some men, it is impossible to say no to an available woman. They are hardwired, and judgment has nothing to do with it. We can feel sorry for Bob Crane, but in a strange way, because he is so clueless, it is hard to blame him; we are reminded of the old joke in which God tells Adam he has a brain and a penis, but only enough blood to operate one of them at a time.

The movie's moral counterpoint is provided by Ron Leibman, as Lenny, Crane's manager. He gets him the job on *Hogan's Heroes* and even, improbably, the lead in a Disney film named *Superdad*. But Crane is reckless in the way he allows photographs and tapes of his sexual performances to float out of his control. On the Disney set one day, Lenny visits to warn Crane about his notorious behavior, but Crane can't hear him, can't listen. He drifts toward his doom, unconscious, lost in a sexual fog.

* * *

Postscript: Bob Crane's two sons are on opposite sides in a legal dispute about the biopic *Auto Focus*. Robert David Crane, the son by the first marriage, supports the movie and appears in it as "Bob Crane Jr." Robert Scott Crane, from the second marriage, says it is filled with inaccuracies, and has started a Web site to oppose it. The site somewhat undermines its own position by offering for sale photographs and videos taken by Crane of his sexual indiscretions.

"There is no such person as Bob Crane Jr.," says Lee Blackman, the Los Angeles attorney representing the second wife, Patricia, and her son. "Both sons had Robert as a first name, and different middle names. Bob Crane's own middle name was Edward." In life, he told me, the older son is called Bobby, and the younger, his client, is Scotty.

By taking money for his participation in the movie and billing himself Bob Crane Jr., Blackman said, Bobby has compromised himself. (In the movie, the older son has a small role as a Christian TV interviewer.)

But what about his client Scotty's Web site, with the Crane sex tapes for sale?

"He is trying to set the record straight. The Web site only came into existence because of the film. For example, on Scotty's site you will find the Scottsdale coroner's autopsy on Bob Crane, clearly indicating he never had a penile implant, although the movie claims he did. You will see that his movies were really just homemade comedies: He would edit the sex stuff with cutaways to Jack Benny or Johnny Carson, and a musical sound track."

Other complaints by Blackman and his clients:

> "He was reconciled with Patricia, his second wife, at the time of his death. The movie shows her drinking in the middle of the day, but she has an allergic reaction to hard liquor."

> "DNA tests have proven Scotty is Bob Crane's son, despite implications in the movie that he is not."

> "Bob Crane was not a dark monster. The night he was killed, he was editing *Star Wars* for Scotty, to take out the violence."

> "He didn't meet John Carpenter (the Willem Dafoe character) until 1975. The movie has him meeting him in 1965. It implies Bob needed Carpenter to teach him all that technical stuff, but in fact Bob Crane was very knowledgeable about home electronics, and was making home movies even in the 1950s."

"Legally," said Blackman, "you can defame the dead. This movie has massive quantities of defamation. We're trying to work with the distributor, Sony, to tweak the film in a couple of little places to make it more accurate. When it's released, if it still contains actionable material, we'll determine what to do."

Autumn Sonata

PG, 97 m., 1978

Ingrid Bergman (Charlotte), Liv Ullmann (Eva), Lena Nyman (Helena), Halvor Bjork (Viktor), Georg Lokkeberg (Leonardo), Knut Wigert (The Professor). Directed by Ingmar Bergman. Screenplay by Bergman.

Ingrid Bergman was certainly one of the most beautiful women to ever appear in a film, but that is not the source of her mysterious appeal. There is something there, in that voice and those eyes and in the way her mouth thinks words before she says them, that is, quite simply, unduplicated in the movies. It took Ingmar Bergman thirty-five years to finally cast her in one of his films, and then, in her fortieth year as an actress, Ingrid Bergman called *Autumn Sonata* her last film. Sweden's two most important film artists finally worked together.

The movie is a historic event, taking us back to so many different areas of our memories. We remember Ingrid Bergman from some of the basic cinematic artifacts of all time, movies like *Casablanca* and *Notorious*. But we've never seen her really pushed, really tested, by a director whose commitment to honesty is nothing short of merciless.

Ingmar Bergman didn't cast her for reasons of nostalgia, or sentiment: He cast her because he had an idea for a role she could brilliantly contain and that would contain her, and in *Autumn Sonata* she gives nothing less than the performance of her lifetime. We can only be quietly grateful that she performs opposite Liv Ullmann, who is herself good enough to meet her on the same very high level.

They play mother and daughter. The mother is an internationally famous pianist (and we remember Ingrid Bergman's first great success, as the pianist in *Intermezzo*). She has not seen her daughter for seven years. She's too busy and always traveling and booked up almost every night of the week . . . and, not incidentally, terrified of confronting her daughter.

There are, in fact, two daughters: The one played by Ullmann, who is serious and introspective and filled with guilt and blame and love, and then the other daughter (Lena Nyman), who lives with her, and who suffers from a degenerative nerve disease. The mother's solution to this daughter's illness was to place her in a "home"; Ullmann has taken her out of the institution and brought her home to live with her.

On the morning when the mother arrives for her long-delayed visit, she has no idea that the sick daughter will be there. Her response, on learning that her other daughter is upstairs, is dismay. She's never been able to deal with the illness—but, then, she's never been able to deal at all with the fact of being a mother. She doesn't merely reject the responsibility; she flees from it.

Autumn Sonata then gives us a sort of long day's journey into night in which the pleasantries of the opening hours give way to deeper and deeper terrors and guilts, accusations and renunciations, cries and whispers. And Ingmar Bergman, standing apart from this material and regarding it with clarity and detachment, refuses to find any solutions. There are none, I suppose. A lesser filmmaker would have resolved everything at the end in some sort of neat Freudian bookeeping, but Bergman finds in his story only two people, each demanding love from the other, each doomed by the past to fall just short of the ability to love.

This is excruciatingly difficult material. Ingrid Bergman and Liv Ullmann confront it with a courage and skill that is astonishing. We've always known that Liv Ullmann was a great actress (that is one of the givens of film in the past two decades), and we've known, too, that Ingrid Bergman was a great movie star. But how important that in her sixties, acting in her native language for the first time in four decades, working with one of the supreme film directors, Bergman was able to use not only her star qualities but also every last measure of her artistry and her humanity. It is not just that *Autumn Sonata* was Ingrid Bergman's last film. It's that she knew she had to make it before she died.

Autumn Tale

PG, 112 m., 1999

Marie Riviere (Isabelle), Beatrice Romand (Magali), Alain Libolt (Gerald), Didier Sandre (Etienne), Alexia Portal (Rosine), Stephane Darmon (Leo), Aurelia Alcais (Emilia), Matthieu Davette (Gregoire), Yves Alcais (Jean-Jacques). Directed by Eric Rohmer and

produced by Francoise Etchegaray, Margaret
Menegoz, and Rohmer. Screenplay by Rohmer.

It is hard not to fall a little in love with Magali.
A woman in her late forties, heedless of makeup,
dressed in jeans and a cotton shirt, forever
pushing her unruly hair out of her eyes, she
runs a vineyard in the Rhone district of southern France. She is a widow with a son and
daughter, both grown. She loves her life and
the wines she makes, but, yes, sometimes she
feels lonely. And how will the right man, or
any man, find her while she lives in such splendid isolation?

Her friend Isabelle, happily married, takes
Magali's plight to heart. One day, in an opening scene that effortlessly establishes the characters and their lives, they walk around Magali's
land, talking of the similarities between weeds
and flowers, and the aging of wines and women.
Isabelle (Marie Riviere) asks Magali (Beatrice
Romand) why she doesn't seek a man by placing a personal ad. Magali would rather die. So
Isabelle places the ad herself. She will audition
the candidates and arrange a meeting between
Magali and the chosen man.

There are other characters, in particular
young Rosine (Alexia Portal), who is currently
the girlfriend of Magali's son, Leo, but used
to date an older philosophy professor named
Etienne (Didier Sandre). Rosine doesn't take
Leo seriously ("He's just a filler"), but adores
Magali, and decides to fix her up with Etienne.
Without suspecting it, Magali is headed for
two possible romantic adventures.

Eric Rohmer's *Autumn Tale*, which tells this
story, is the latest in a long, rich series of films
by the perceptive French director, who tells
stories about people we'd like to know, or be.
His movies are about love, chance, life, and
coincidence; he creates plots that unfold in a
series of delights, surprises, and reversals. When
there is a happy ending, it arrives as a relief,
even a deliverance, for characters who spend
much of the movie on the very edge of missing out on their chances for happiness.

Rohmer, now seventy-nine, was the editor
of the famous French film magazine *Cahiers
du Cinema* from 1956 to 1963. He was a founding member of the French New Wave, which
includes Godard, Truffaut, Resnais, Malle, and
Chabrol. He makes his movies in groups. *Six

Moral Tales,* which he said was not so much
about what people did as what they thought
about while they were doing it, included three
that made him famous: *My Night at Maud's*
(1969), *Claire's Knee* (1971), and *Chloe in the Afternoon* (1972). Then came his *Comedies and
Proverbs,* and now his current series, *Tales of
the Four Seasons.*

His films are heavily, craftily plotted, and yet
wear their plots so easily that we feel we're
watching everyday life as it unfolds. Consider
the complexities of *Autumn Tale,* as both Isabelle and Rosine maneuver to arrange meetings
between Magali and the men they've chosen for
her. There are complications and misunderstandings, and Isabelle is almost accused of
being unfaithful to her own husband (whom
she adores, she says, although we never see him
because Rohmer wisely knows he's not needed).

Everything comes together at a virtuoso
scene that Rohmer stages at a wedding party.
Magali is present, reluctantly, and so are the
men, and of course all three misunderstand
almost everything that happens. Since we like
Gerald (Alain Libolt), the guy who answered
the personal ad, and think Etienne is a twerp,
we know who we're cheering for, but Rohmer
creates quiet suspense by elegantly choreo-
graphing the movements at the party—who is
seen, and when, and why, and in what context—
until finally a smile and a nod of approval are
exchanged over a glass of wine, and we feel
like cheering. (The approval is of the wine, not
the characters, but from it all else will follow.)

Even though I enjoy Hollywood romantic
comedies like *Notting Hill,* it's like they wear
galoshes compared to the sly wit of a movie
like *Autumn Tale.* They stomp squishy-footed
through their clockwork plots, while Rohmer
elegantly seduces us with people who have all
of the alarming unpredictability of life. There's
never a doubt that Julia Roberts will live happily ever after. But Magali, now: One wrong
step, and she's alone with her vines forever.

The Aviator

PG-13, 166 m., 2004

Leonardo DiCaprio (Howard Hughes), Cate Blanchett
(Katharine Hepburn), Kate Beckinsale (Ava Gardner),
Alec Baldwin (Juan Trippe), John C. Reilly (Noah
Dietrich), Alan Alda (Senator Brewster), Gwen Stefani

(Jean Harlow), Kelli Garner (Faith Domergue), Adam Scott (Johnny Meyer), Ian Holm (Professor Fitz), Danny Huston (Jack Frye), Jude Law (Errol Flynn), Matt Ross (Glenn Odekirk), Edward Herrmann (Joseph Breen). Directed by Martin Scorsese and produced by Michael Mann, Sandy Climan, Graham King, and Charles Evans Jr. Screenplay by John Logan.

Howard Hughes in his last two decades sealed himself away from the world. At first he haunted a penthouse in Las Vegas, and then he moved to a bungalow behind the Beverly Hills Hotel. He was the world's richest man, and with his billions bought himself a room he never left.

In a sense, his life was a journey to that lonely room. But he took the long way around: As a rich young man from Texas, the heir to his father's fortune, he made movies, bought airlines, was a playboy who dated Hollywood's famous beauties. If he had died in one of the airplane crashes he survived, he would have been remembered as a golden boy. Martin Scorsese's *The Aviator* wisely focuses on the glory years, although we can see the shadows falling, and so can Hughes. Some of the film's most harrowing moments show him fighting his demons; he knows what is normal and sometimes it seems almost within reach.

The Aviator celebrates Scorsese's zest for finding excitement in a period setting, re-creating the kind of glamour he heard about when he was growing up. It is possible to imagine him wanting to be Howard Hughes. Their lives, in fact, are even a little similar: heedless ambition and talent when young, great early success, tempestuous romances, and a dark period, although with Hughes it got darker and darker, while Scorsese has emerged into the full flower of his gifts.

The movie achieves the difficult feat of following two intersecting story arcs, one in which everything goes right for Hughes, and the other in which everything goes wrong. Scorsese chronicled similar life patterns in *GoodFellas, Raging Bull, The King of Comedy, Casino,* actually even *The Last Temptation of Christ.* Leonardo DiCaprio is convincing in his transitions between these emotional weathers; playing madness is a notorious invitation to overact, but he shows Hughes contained, even trapped, within his secrets, able to put on a public act even when his private moments are desperate.

His Howard Hughes arrives in Los Angeles as a good-looking young man with a lot of money, who plunges right in, directing a World War I aviation adventure named *Hell's Angels,* which was the most expensive movie ever made. The industry laughed at him, but he finished the movie and it made money, and so did most of his other films. As his attention drifted from movies to the airplanes in his films, he began designing and building aircraft, and eventually bought his own airline.

Women were his for the asking, but he didn't go for the easy kill. Jean Harlow was no pushover, Ava Gardner wouldn't take gifts of jewelry ("I am not for sale!"), and during his relationship with Katharine Hepburn, they both wore the pants in the family. Hepburn liked his sense of adventure, she was thrilled when he let her pilot his planes, she worried about him, she noted the growing signs of his eccentricity, and then she met Spencer Tracy and that was that. Hughes found Jane Russell and invented a pneumatic bra to make her bosom heave in *The Outlaw,* and by the end he had starlets on retainer in case he ever called them, but he never did.

DiCaprio is nobody's idea of what Hughes looked like (that would be a young Sam Shepard), but he vibrates with the reckless spirit of the man. John C. Reilly plays the hapless Noah Dietrich, his right-hand man and flunky, routinely ordered to mortgage everything for one of Hughes's sudden inspirations; Hughes apparently became the world's richest man by going bankrupt at higher and higher levels.

Scorsese shows a sure sense for the Hollywood of that time, as in a scene where Hughes, new in town, approaches the mogul L. B. Mayer at the Coconut Grove and asks to borrow two cameras for a big *Hell's Angels* scene. He already had twenty-four, but that was not enough. Mayer regards him as a child psychiatrist might have regarded the young Jim Carrey. Scorsese adds subtle continuity: Every time we see Mayer, he seems to be surrounded by the same flunkies.

The women in the film are wonderfully well cast. Cate Blanchett has the task of playing Katharine Hepburn, who was herself so close to caricature that to play her accurately involves some risk. Blanchett succeeds in a performance that is delightful and yet touching;

mannered and tomboyish, delighting in saying exactly what she means, she shrewdly sizes up Hughes and is quick to be concerned about his eccentricities. Kate Beckinsale is Ava Gardner, aware of her power and self-protective; Gwen Stefani is Jean Harlow, whose stardom over-shadows the unknown Texas rich boy; and Kelli Garner is Faith Domergue, "the next Jane Russell" at a time when Hughes became ob-sessed with bosoms. Jane Russell doesn't ap-pear in the movie as a character, but her cleavage does, in a hilarious scene before the Breen office, which ran the Hollywood censor-ship system. Hughes brings his tame meteorol-ogy professor (Ian Holm) to the censorship hearing, introduces him as a systems analyst, and has him prove with calipers and mathe-matics that Russell displays no more cleavage than a control group of five other actresses.

Special effects can distract from a film or enhance it. Scorsese knows how to use them. There is a sensational sequence when Hughes crash-lands in Beverly Hills, his plane's wingtip slicing through living room walls seen from the inside. Much is made of the *Spruce Goose,* the largest airplane ever built, which inspires Senator Owen Brewster (Alan Alda) to charge in congressional hearings that Hughes was a war profiteer. Hughes, already in the spiral to madness, rises to the occasion, defeats Brewster on his own territory, and vows that the plane will fly—as indeed it does, in a CGI sequence that is convincing and kind of awesome.

By the end, darkness is gathering around Hughes. He gets stuck on words, and keeps re-peating them. He walks into a men's room and then is too phobic about germs to touch the doorknob in order to leave; with all his power and wealth, he has to lurk next to the door until someone else walks in and he can sneak through without touching anything. His aides, especially the long-suffering Dietrich, try to protect him, but eventually he disap-pears into seclusion. What a sad man. What brief glory. What an enthralling film—166 minutes, and it races past. There's a match here between Scorsese and his subject, per-haps because the director's own life journey allows him to see Howard Hughes with in-sight, sympathy—and, up to a point, with ad-miration. This is one of the year's best films.

Awakenings

PG-13, 121 m., 1990

Robert De Niro (Leonard Lowe), Robin Williams (Dr. Malcolm Sayer), Julie Kavner (Eleanor Costello), Ruth Nelson (Mrs. Lowe), John Heard (Dr. Kaufman), Anne Meara (Miriam), Lolly Esterman (Lolly), Penelope Ann Miller (Paula). Directed by Penny Marshall and produced by Walter F. Parkes and Lawrence Lasker. Screenplay by Steven Zaillian, based on the book by Oliver Sacks.

We do not know what we see when we look at Leonard. We think we see a human vegetable, a peculiar man who has been frozen in the same position for thirty years, who neither moves nor speaks. What goes on inside his mind? Is he thinking in there? Of course not, a neurologist says, in Penny Marshall's film *Awakenings.* Why not? "Because the implications of that would be unthinkable." Ah, but the expert is wrong, and inside the immobile shell of his body, Leonard is still there. Still waiting.

Leonard is one of the patients in the "gar-den," a ward of a Bronx mental hospital that is so named by the staff because the patients are there simply to be fed and watered. It appears that nothing can be done for them. They were victims of the great "sleeping sickness" epi-demic of the 1920s, and after a period of ap-parent recovery they regressed to their current states. It is 1969. They have many different symptoms, but essentially they all share the same problem: They cannot make their bod-ies do what their minds desire. Sometimes that blockage is manifested through bizarre physical behavior, sometimes through appar-ent paralysis.

One day, a new doctor comes to work in the hospital. He has no experience in working with patients; indeed, his last project involved earth-worms. Like those who have gone before him, he has no particular hope for these ghostly pa-tients, who are there and yet not there. He talks without hope to one of the women, who looks blankly back at him, her head and body frozen. But then he turns away, and when he turns back she has changed her position—appar-ently trying to catch her eyeglasses as they fell. He tries an experiment. He holds her glasses in front of her, and then drops them. Her hand flashes out quickly and catches them.

Yet this woman cannot move through her own will. He tries another experiment, throwing a ball at one of the patients. She catches it. "She is borrowing the will of the ball," the doctor speculates. His colleagues will not listen to this theory, which sounds suspiciously metaphysical, but he thinks he's on to something. What if these patients are not actually "frozen" at all, but victims of a stage of Parkinson's disease so advanced that their motor impulses are canceling each other out—what if they cannot move because all of their muscles are trying to move at the same time, and they are powerless to choose one impulse over the other? Then the falling glasses or the tossed ball might be breaking the deadlock!

This is the great discovery in the opening scenes of *Awakenings*, preparing the way for sequences of enormous joy and heartbreak, as the patients are "awakened" to a personal freedom they had lost all hope of ever again experiencing—only to find that their liberation comes with its own cruel set of conditions. The film, directed with intelligence and heart by Penny Marshall, is based on a famous 1972 book by Oliver Sacks, the British-born New York neurologist whose *The Man Who Mistook His Wife for a Hat* is a classic of medical literature. These were his patients, and the doctor in the film, named Malcolm Sayer and played by Robin Williams, is based on him.

What he discovered in the summer of 1969 was that L-dopa, a new drug for the treatment of Parkinson's disease, might, in massive doses, break the deadlock that had frozen his patients into a space-time lock for endless years. The film follows some fifteen of those patients, particularly Leonard, who is played by Robert De Niro in a virtuoso performance. Because this movie is not a tearjerker but an intelligent examination of a bizarre human condition, it's up to De Niro to make Leonard not an object of sympathy, but a person who helps us wonder about our own tenuous grasp on the world around us.

The patients depicted in this film have suffered a fate more horrible than the one in Poe's famous story about premature burial. If we were locked in a coffin while still alive, at least we would soon suffocate. But to be locked inside a body that cannot move or speak—to look out mutely as even our loved ones talk about us as if we were an uncomprehending piece of furniture! It is this fate that is lifted, that summer of 1969, when the doctor gives the experimental new drug to his patients, and in a miraculous rebirth their bodies thaw and they begin to move and talk once again, some of them after thirty years of self-captivity.

The movie follows Leonard through the stages of his rebirth. He was (as we saw in a prologue) a bright, likable kid, until the disease took its toll. He has been on hold for three decades. Now, in his late forties, he is filled with wonder and gratitude to be able to move around freely and express himself. He cooperates with the doctors studying his case. And he finds himself attracted to the daughter (Penelope Ann Miller) of another patient. Love and lust stir within him for the first time.

Dr. Sayer, played by Williams, is at the center of almost every scene, and his personality becomes one of the touchstones of the movie. He is shut off, too, by shyness and inexperience, and even the way he holds his arms, close to his sides, shows a man wary of contact. He really was happier working with those earthworms. This is one of Robin Williams's best performances, pure and uncluttered, without the ebullient distractions he sometimes adds—the schtick where none is called for. He is a lovable man here, who experiences the extraordinary professional joy of seeing chronic, hopeless patients once again sing and dance and greet their loved ones.

But it is not as simple as that, not after the first weeks. The disease is not an open-and-shut case. And as the movie unfolds, we are invited to meditate on the strangeness and wonder of the human personality. Who are we, anyway? How much of the self we treasure so much is simply a matter of good luck, of being spared in a minefield of neurological chance? If one has no hope, which is better: to remain hopeless, or to be given hope and then lose it again? Oliver Sacks's original book, which has been reissued, is as much a work of philosophy as of medicine. After seeing *Awakenings*, I read it, to know more about what happened in that Bronx hospital. What both the movie and the book convey is the immense courage of the patients and the profound experience of their doctors, as in a small way they re-experienced what it means to be born, to open your eyes, and discover to your astonishment that "you" are alive.

Away from Her

PG-13, 109 m., 2006

Julie Christie (Fiona Anderson), Gordon Pinsent (Grant Anderson), Olympia Dukakis (Marian), Michael Murphy (Aubrey), Kristen Thomson (Kristy), Wendy Crewson (Madeleine), Alberta Watson (Dr. Fischer). Written and directed by Sarah Polley, based on the short story "The Bear Who Came Over the Mountain" by Alice Munro. Produced by Atom Egoyan and Doug Mankoff.

Away from Her is the fifth film I've seen about Alzheimer's in these opening years of the century, and the best, although only one of them has been disappointing. Using sympathy and tenderness for its characters, it tells the story of a marriage that drifts out of the memory of the wife, and of the husband's efforts to deal with that fact. We have two Canadian women to thank for this film: the writer and director, Sarah Polley (born 1979) and the author of the short story that inspired it, Alice Munro (born 1931). Munro in her short fiction has the ability to evoke a lifetime in images and dialogue of almost startling perception. Polley with her camera takes the material, finds an uncanny balance in her casting, and bathes the film in the mercy of simple truth.

Fiona and Grant Anderson (Julie Christie and Gordon Pinsent) have been married more than forty years, mostly happily despite some stumbles. They have the beauty in age they had in youth, although it is weathered now, as a bench on the park looks more inviting when it has spent some seasons in the sun. They have been told she has Alzheimer's disease. The movie spares us the coyness of early scenes where she seems healthy and then starts to slip; she starts right out putting a frying pan into the refrigerator.

They're retired and live in a cottage overlooking fields that are perfect for cross-country skiing. They look robust in their cold-weather gear, and when they come inside from their daily skiing, they look so comfortable with each other that they make us feel cozy. Just as the models in plus-size catalogs always look thin, so the models in retirement ads always look like these two: youthful, athletic, foxy. Fiona has too much respect for herself, and too much pity for Grant, to subject him to what seems her certain decay. She makes a decision on her own to check into a comfortable nearby nursing home, and Grant drives her there, remembering their younger adventures along the same route. An administrator explains that he will not be able to visit for thirty days; it's easier if new patients are cut off from family contact while adjusting to their new lives.

All of this is seen not in darkness and shadows and the early gloom of winter and visions in the night, but in bright focus. Polley told Andrew O'Hehir of Salon: "For me the overriding palette that we were working with was the idea of this very strong, sometimes blinding winter sunlight that should infuse every frame. I didn't want the visual style to draw too much focus to itself. I felt like this needed to be an elegant and simple film, and that it had to have a certain grace."

How can you do that by limiting your palette, instead of making it more complex? I was reminded of Bergman's *Winter Light* (1962), which bathes despair in merciless daylight. The despair here is Grant's. When he returns after thirty days, he finds Fiona almost inseparable from another patient, the mute Aubrey (Michael Murphy). She tends him like her own patient, and seems indifferent, even vague, about Grant. Is she getting even with him for the cheating he did earlier in their marriage? That would almost be a relief, if the alternative is that she is forgetting him. He is deeply wounded.

One reason we get married is that we need a witness to our lives. So says the Susan Sarandon character in Audrey Wells's much-quoted dialogue for *Shall We Dance* (2004). With the death of every person we have known, our mutual memories become only personal, and then when we die the memories die and in a sense those remembered events never happened. Death wipes the slate clean at once, which is a mercy compared to the light of recognition that slowly fades in the eyes of loved ones who have Alzheimer's. Remember the first time we made love? You don't? Who is "we"? What is "love"?

As it turns out, Aubrey has a wife named Marian (Olympia Dukakis), and Grant visits her, at first wondering if she could consider moving her husband to another place. Or whatever. They talk over her kitchen table, Dukakis imparting a sense of implacable truth. She regards reality without blinking. And that is enough about the plot.

The other Alzheimer's movies are Bille August's *A Song for Martin* (2001), Nick Cassavetes's *The Notebook* (2004), and Erik Van Looy's *Memory of a Killer* (2003). All very good, the third perhaps the best. And then there was Richard Eyre's *Iris* (2001), about the decline of the novelist Iris Murdoch, which struck me as cheating because it was too much about young Iris. True, *The Notebook* also moved from present to past, and supplied well-timed moments when the patient's mind opened in perfect clarity and memory. But it proposed to be a romance, not a biography. *A Song for Martin* is about a couple who meet in later life, fall in love passionately, and then have the cloud fall between them. And *Memory of a Killer* stars Jan Decleir as an aging Belgian hit man who wants to retire, and undertakes one last job in which he fights against the fading of his light to bring about an extraordinary outcome. Rent it.

All of these films persist in linking Alzheimer's disease to a story. Sarah Polley, whose film is a heartbreaking masterpiece, has the courage to simply observe the devastation of the disease. Alzheimer's is usually like that. There are few great love stories replayed in the closing days, few books written, few flashbacks as enjoyable for the victims as they are for us. There is only the victim going far, far away, until finally, as if they were falling into a black hole, no signs can ever reach us from them again.

The performances here are carefully controlled, as they must be, so that we see no awareness slipping out from behind the masks; no sense that the Julie Christie character is in touch with a more complete reality than, from day to day, she is. No sense that Gordon Pinsent, as her husband, is finally able to feel revenge, consolation, contrition, or anything else but inescapable loss. No sense that the Olympia Dukakis character deceives herself for a moment. No sense that Michael Murphy's character understands his behavior.

The one aware character is Kristen Thomson as Kristy, the kind nurse who gives Grant practical advice. She has empathy for him, and pity, and she can explain routines and treatments and progressions to him, but she cannot do anything about his grief. She has worked in the home for while. She knows how Alzheimer's is, and must be. I have gotten to know some nurses well over the last year, and seen the sadness in their eyes as they discuss patients (never by name) who they are helpless to help. Thomson finds that precise note.

Sarah Polley, still so young, always until now an actress (*The Sweet Hereafter*, *My Life Without Me*), emerges here as a director who is in calm command of almost impossible material. The movie says as much for her strength of character as for her skills. Anyone who could read Munro's original story and think they could make a film of it, and then make a great film, deserves a certain awe.

B

Baadasssss!

R, 108 m., 2004

Mario Van Peebles (Melvin Van Peebles), Joy Bryant (Priscilla), T. K. Carter (Bill Cosby), Terry Crews (Big T), Khleo Thomas (Mario Van Peebles), Ossie Davis (Grandad), David Alan Grier (Clyde Houston), Nia Long (Sandra), Paul Rodriguez (Jose Garcia), Saul Rubinek (Howie), Len Lesser (Manny/Mort Goldberg). Directed by Mario Van Peebles and produced by Bruce Wayne Gillies, Dennis Haggerty, G. Marq Roswell, and Van Peebles. Screenplay by Van Peebles and Haggerty, based on the book by Van Peebles.

I want to show all the faces that Norman Rockwell never painted.

—Melvin Van Peebles

It would be nice if movies were always made the way they are in Truffaut's *Day for Night*, with idealism and romance, or Minnelli's *The Bad and the Beautiful*, with glamour and intrigue. But sometimes they are made the way they are in Mario Van Peebles's *Baadasssss!*, with desperation, deception, and cunning. Here is one of the best movies I've seen about the making of a movie—a fictionalized eyewitness account by Mario of how and why his father, Melvin Van Peebles, made *Sweet Sweetback's Baadasssss Song*, a landmark in the birth of African-American cinema.

The original 1971 movie was scruffy and raw, the story of a man born in a brothel and initiated to sex at the age of twelve, who grows up as an urban survivor, attacks two racist cops, and eludes capture. That Sweetback got away with it electrified the movie's first audiences, who were intrigued by ad lines like "Rated X by an All-White Jury." Although it was not an exploitation film, it was credited by *Variety* with creating "blaxploitation," a genre that gave us Pam Grier, Shaft, Superfly, and a generation of black filmmakers who moved into the mainstream.

That a big-budget action film is unthinkable today without a black costar is a direct consequence of Melvin Van Peebles's $150,000 fly-by-night movie. *Sweet Sweetback* did astonishing business, proving that a viable market existed for movies made by, for, and about blacks. When the movie opened at the Oriental

Theater in Chicago, the marquee proclaimed: "The Oriental Is Yo-riental Now!"

Mario Van Peebles was thirteen when the movie was being made, and was pressed into service by his father to play Sweetback as a boy. That involved a scene with a hooker in the brothel that still, today, Mario must feel resentment about, since in *Baadasssss!* he makes a point of showing that some of the crew members and his father's girlfriend, Sandra (Nia Long), objected to it. But Melvin was a force of nature, a cigar-chewing Renaissance man who got his own way. Only sheer willpower forced the production ahead despite cash and personnel emergencies, and *Sweet Sweetback* is like a textbook on guerrilla filmmaking.

Aware that he could not possibly afford to pay union wages (there were days when he could pay no wages at all), Melvin disguises the production as a porn film to elude union rules. The day the union reps visit the set is the day he shoots a sex scene—a little more explicit, of course, than the one he would use in the movie. Determined to have a crew that included at least 50 percent minorities (in an industry where most crews were all white), he trained some of them on the job. At the end of *Baadasssss!*, a white sound man has hired his assistant, a tough black street guy who doubles as security, to be his partner; that detail, like most of the film, is based on fact. Surveying the set, he observes, "No crew has ever looked like this."

Mario plays his own father in the movie, and Khleo Thomas plays Mario. It's clear that (the real) Mario admires his father while at the same time harbors some resentment against his old man's strong-willed, single-minded treatment of people. We see Melvin bouncing checks, telling lies, roughing up a crew member who wants to quit, and even getting a free shot courtesy of the Los Angeles Fire Department when their trucks respond to an alarm for a car fire. The car was blown up for a scene in the movie, and Melvin kept the cameras rolling to get the firemen for free.

As a director, Mario keeps the large cast alive, from Melvin's alluring, exasperated assistant, Priscilla (Joy Bryant), to his long-suffering agent, Howie (Saul Rubinek), his hard-pressed producer, Clyde Houston (David Alan Grier), and Bill Cosby (T. K. Carter), whose $50,000 check bailed out Melvin at a crisis point. There is a double role for Len Lesser as Manny and Mort Goldberg, the dubious Detroit exhibitors who premiere *Sweetback* and are ready to close it after one screening, until they see the lines in front of the theater.

Mario could make another movie about the rest of his father's life, which has included being an officer in the U.S. Air Force, making art films in Paris, working as a trader on Wall Street, composing, painting, winning eleven Tony nominations for Broadway plays, and winning the French Legion of Honor. The last shot in the film is a wink and a cloud of cigar smoke from this living legend, now seventy-one.

What's fascinating is the way Mario, working from his father's autobiography and his own memories, has somehow used his firsthand experience without being cornered by it. He keeps a certain objectivity in considering the character of Melvin, seeing him as brave and gifted and determined, but also as a hustler who gets his movie made, in the words of Malcolm X, "by any means necessary." He steps on toes, hurts feelings, expects sacrifices, doesn't hesitate to use his own son in a scene that no professional child actor would have been allowed to touch.

To one degree or another, all low-budget films are like this one, with cast and crew members bludgeoned into hard work at low pay in the service of the director's ego. Mario Van Peebles captures the elusive sense of family that forms on a movie set, the moments of despair, the times when it seems impossible to continue, the sexual intrigue, and (always) the bitching over the food. *Sweet Sweetback's Baadasssss Song* was historically a film of great importance, but in another sense it was just another low-rent, fly-by-night production. *Baadasssss!* manages to get both of those aspects just about right.

Note: This film's original title was How to Get the Man's Foot Outta Your Ass.

Babel

R, 142 m., 2006

Brad Pitt (Richard), Cate Blanchett (Susan), Gael Garcia Bernal (Santiago), Kôji Yakusho (Yasujiro), Adriana Barraza (Amelia), Rinko Kikuchi (Chieko), Said Tarchani (Ahmed), Boubker Ait El Caid (Yussef), Elle Fanning (Debbie), Nathan Gamble (Mike), Mohamed Akhzam (Anwar), Peter Wight (Tom), Abdelkader Bara (Hassan), Mustapha Rachidi (Abdullah), Driss Roukhe (Alarid). Written and directed by Alejandro González Iñárritu. Produced by Iñárritu, Steve Golin, and Jon Kilik.

England and America are two countries separated by a common language.
—George Bernard Shaw

Even more separated are cultures that do not share languages, values, frames of reference, or physical realities. *Babel* weaves stories from Morocco, America, Mexico, and Japan, all connected by the thoughtless act of a child, and demonstrates how each culture works against itself to compound the repercussions. It is the third and most powerful of Alejandro González Iñárritu's trilogy of films in which the action is connected or influenced in invisible ways. Sometimes these are called "hyperlink films." After *Amores Perros* (2000) and *21 Grams* (2003), it shows his mastery of the form, and it surprises us by offering human insight rather than obligatory tragedy.

Without revealing too much, let me chronologically piece together the stories. A Japanese businessman goes on a hunting trip in Morocco, and tips his guide with a rifle. The guide sells the rifle to a friend, who needs it to kill the jackals attacking his sheep. The friend's son shoots toward a tourist bus at a great distance. An American tourist is wounded. The tourist's Mexican nanny, in San Diego, is told to stay with their two children, but doesn't want to miss her son's wedding, and takes the children along with her to Mexico. Police enquiries about the Japanese businessman's rifle lead to consequences for his disturbed daughter.

Yes, but there is so much more to *Babel* than the through-line of the plot. The movie is *not*, as we might expect, about how each culture wreaks hatred and violence on another, but about how each culture tries to behave well and is handicapped by misperceptions. *Babel* could have been a routine recital of man's inhumanity to man, but Iñárritu, the writer-director, has something deeper and kinder to say: When we are strangers in a strange land, we can bring trouble upon ourselves and our hosts. Before our latest Mars probe blasted off, it was scrubbed to avoid carrying Earth microbes to the other planet. All of the characters in this film are carriers of cultural microbes.

Consider the plight of Yussef (Boubker Ait El Caid), the Moroccan boy. He lives happily with his family, tends sheep, plays with his brother Ahmed. Two alien microbes come into his world: a high-powered rifle and a tourist bus. Over a great distance, he childishly shoots at one with the other, and seriously wounds Susan (Cate Blanchett), an American tourist. Her husband, Richard (Brad Pitt), demands doctors, ambulances, helicopters, but has to settle for a friendly local man who takes Susan into his home and summons what the village has in the way of medical care.

American authorities immediately brand the shooting as a terrorist act. The Moroccan government refuses to send a helicopter because it insists it harbors no terrorists. It becomes a worldwide news story, told in clichés. The other tourists on the bus, led by an outraged Brit, insist on leaving the couple behind, in part because the bus driver insists on saving gas by not turning on the air conditioning in this land where the locals have no choice but to live with the heat. As ripples from the original event spread wider, the original reality gets lost.

The American couple lives forty-five minutes north of the Mexican border. Susan has arranged for her sister to watch their children while the nanny (Adriana Barraza) attends her son's wedding. But the sister cannot come, the nanny cannot find a substitute, and in desperation she gets her nephew (Gael Garcia Bernal) to drive them all to the wedding. Returning to America, they are properly questioned by U.S. border authorities, but the nephew (who has been drinking and knows his aunt is an unregistered worker) runs the border, is pursued, and leaves the nanny and children in the desert intending to return. How could the nanny take the children to Mexico? How could she miss her son's wedding? Yes, but how could the nephew leave them in the desert? He drank at the wedding.

Contrary to our expectations, the U.S. border guards are not the villains. Nor, really, is the nanny. Nor did the American couple do anything wrong. Susan was essentially wounded by culture clash. Her husband could not empathize with the nanny because he was too disturbed about his wife. The nanny thought the children, who she loved, would be safe with her and her family. The nephew should not have been drinking, but it was his cousin's wedding and such things have been known to happen. The border guards were correct in questioning two Mexicans, one intoxicated, traveling after midnight with young children not their own.

I could go through each of the stories in this way, showing how carefully Iñárritu portrays the motivations of his characters. Richard, the Pitt character, behaves like an ugly American in one sense, and in another like a man terrified of losing his wife. When Moroccan authorities go looking for the shooter, they behave as we expect, and the sheepherder's family behaves as we would also expect, and children will be children.

In Iñárritu's *21 Grams,* I thought the interlocking stories spun a little out of his control. Everything finally fit together, in a very good film, but there was sometimes the sense that we were more lost than the film really wanted us to be. *Amores Perros,* with its three stories, was easy to follow, and now *Babel* finds Iñárritu in full command of his technique: The writing and editing moves between the stories with full logical and emotional clarity, and the film builds to a stunning impact because it does *not* hammer us with heroes and villains but asks us to empathize with all of its characters. They all have their reasons, they all work with only limited information, they all win our sympathy.

Technically, *Babel* may seem to be an example of the Idiot Plot, in which at many points one word or sentence could clear everything up. But these characters are not idiots and desperately want to utter that word or sentence but are prevented because of (a) the language barrier, (b) their cultural assumptions, (c) the inability of others to comprehend what they are actually saying, and (d) how in that case everyone falls into an established script made of prejudice and misunderstanding. Iñárritu films more in sorrow than anger, and spares most of his characters tragic retribution because he loves and understands them too much to simply grind them in a plot. This is a film about people who do what we might do if we were them. We are not, but then it is useful to reflect that they are not us, either.

Babe: Pig in the City

G, 96 m., 1998

Magda Szubanski (Mrs. Hoggett), James Cromwell (Farmer Hoggett), Mary Stein (The Landlady), Mickey Rooney (Fugly Floom), Roscoe Lee Browne (Narrator). And the voices of: E. G. Daily (Babe), Danny Mann (Ferdinand), Glenne Headly (Zootie), James Cosmo (Thelonious), Stanley Ralph Ross (Bull Terrier). Directed by George Miller and produced by George Miller, Doug Mitchell, and Bill Miller. Screenplay by George Miller, Judy Morris, and Mark Lamprell.

"The first hazard for the returning hero is fame."

So we are assured by the narrator in the opening line of *Babe: Pig in the City*. And what is true of heroes is even more true of sequels. The original *Babe* was an astonishment, an unheralded family movie from Australia that was embraced and loved and nominated for an Oscar as Best Picture. Can the sequel possibly live up to it?

It can and does, and in many ways is more magical than the original. *Babe* was a film in which everything led up to the big sheep-herding contest, in which a pig that worked like a dog turned out to be the best sheep-pig of them all. *Babe: Pig in the City* is not so plot-bound, although it has the required assortment of villains, chases, and close calls. It is more of a wonderment, lolling in its enchanting images—original, delightful, and funny.

It doesn't make any of the mistakes it could have. It doesn't focus more on the human characters—it focuses less, and there are more animals on the screen. It doesn't recycle the first story. It introduces many new characters. It outdoes itself with the sets and special effects that make up "the city." And it is still literate, humane, and wicked. George Miller, who produced, directed, and cowrote the film, has improved and extended the ideas in *Babe* (1995), instead of being content to copy them.

The movie begins with Babe returning in triumph to the farm with his sheepdog trophy. Alas, he soon falls into the well, setting in motion a calamitous chain of events that ends with Farmer Hoggett (James Cromwell) laid

up in bed, and Mrs. Hoggett (Magda Szubanski) forced to exhibit Babe at a state fair in order to save the farm from foreclosure. Alas again, Babe and Mrs. Hoggett miss their connecting flight (she is busted on suspicion of drug possession, that merry, apple-cheeked dumpling of a lady). And they are homeless in the cruel city, where hotels sniff at pigs.

What a city this is! I love imaginary cities in the movies, from *Metropolis* to *Dark City*, and here is one to set beside the great ones. Using elaborate sets that surround the buildings with a canal system, Miller uses f/x to create a skyline that impudently incorporates such landmarks as the Statue of Liberty, the Sydney Opera House, and the Hollywood sign. This is all cities. And in it, Babe finds himself at a boardinghouse whose landlady (Mary Stein) believes animals deserve rooms just like people do.

There is a large cast of animal characters, whose dialogue is lip-synched, and who are colorful and individual—not at all like silly talking animals. One of my favorite scenes involves Ferdinand the duck (voice by Danny Mann), attempting to keep up with the jet plane taking Babe to the city; the rear view of him flapping at breakneck speed is one of the funniest moments in the movie. (He's eventually given a lift by a pelican, who intones, "Go well, noble duck!")

In the boardinghouse, we meet chimpanzees, orangutans, cats, fish, and a dog paralyzed from the waist down, who propels himself on a little cart. Babe is tricked by some of his new housemates into distracting fierce dogs during a desperate raid for food; apparently facing doom, he turns, looks his enemy in the eye, and asks, "Why?" He has a close call with a bull terrier (voice by Stanley Ralph Ross, sounding like a Chicago gangster) who tries to kill him and ends up dangling headfirst in the canal. Babe saves him from drowning, and the dog becomes his fierce protector: "What the pig says, goes!"

The movie is filled with wonders large and small. Little gags at the side of the frame and big laughs in the center. It is in no way just a "children's movie," but one that extends the imagination of everyone who sees it, and there is a wise, grown-up sensibility to its narration, its characters, and a lot of the action. (Other action is cheerfully goofy, as when Mrs. Hoggett gets involved in a weird bungeelike session of chandelier swinging.)

Here is a movie that is all made up. The world and its characters materialize out of the abyss of the imagination, and in their impossibility they seem more real than the characters in many realistic movies. Their hearts are in the right places. And apart from what they do and say, there is the wonderment of the world they live in ("A place just a little to the left of the twentieth century"). I liked *Babe* for all the usual reasons, but I like *Babe: Pig in the City* more, and not for any of the usual reasons, because here is a movie utterly bereft of usual reasons.

Badlands

PG, 94 m., 1974

Martin Sheen (Kit), Sissy Spacek (Holly), Warren Oates (Holly's Father), Ramon Bieri (Cato), Ramon Vint (Deputy). Directed, produced, and written by Terence Malick. Based on the book by James Reinhardt.

They meet for the first time when she is in her front yard practicing baton-twirling. He has just walked off his job on a garbage truck. She thinks he is the handsomest man she's ever seen—he looks just like James Dean. He likes her because he never knew a fifteen-year-old who knew so much: "She could talk like a grown-up woman, without a lot of giggles." Within a few weeks, they will be the targets of a manhunt after he has shot down half a dozen victims.

Terence Malick's *Badlands* calls them Kit and Holly, but his characters are inspired, of course, by Charles Starkweather and Caril Ann Fugate. They went on a wild ride in 1958 that ended with eleven people shot dead. The press named him the Mad Dog Killer, and Sunday supplement psychoanalysts said he killed because the kids at school kidded him about his bowlegs. Starkweather got the electric chair on June 25, 1959. From time to time a story appears about Caril Fugate's appeals to her parole board. She was sentenced to life.

She claimed she was kidnapped and forced to go along with Starkweather. When they first were captured, he asked the deputies to leave her alone: "She didn't do nothing." Later, at his trial, he claimed she was the most trigger-happy person he ever knew, and was responsible for some of the killings. It is a case that is still not closed, although *Badlands* sees her as a child of vast simplicity who went along at first because she was flattered that he liked her: "I wasn't popular at school on account of having no personality and not being pretty."

The film is tied together with her narration, written like an account of a summer vacation crossed with the breathless prose style of a movie magazine. Some of the dialogue is loosely inspired by a book written by James Reinhardt, a criminologist who interviewed Starkweather on death row. Starkweather was offended by his death sentence. He viewed his crimes with total uninvolvement and asked how it was fair for him to die before he'd even been to a big city, or eaten in a fine restaurant, or seen a major-league game. That's what the movie captures, too: The detachment with which Kit views his killings, as Holly eventually draws away from him. He gets no pleasure from killing. He sees it only as necessary. He offers explanations which satisfy her for a while: "I killed them because they was bounty hunters who wanted the reward money. If they was policemen, just being paid for doing their job, that would have been different."

The movie makes no attempt to psychoanalyze Kit Carruthers, and there are no symbols to note or lessons to learn. What comes through more than anything is the enormous loneliness of the lives these two characters lived, together and apart. He is ten years older than she is, but they're both caught up in the same adolescent love fantasy at first, as if Nat King Cole would always be there to sing "A Blossom Fell" on the portable radio while they held their sweaty embrace. He would not. To discourage his daughter from seeing "the kind of a man who collects garbage," her father punishes her by shooting her dog. She is "greatly distressed."

Kit is played by Martin Sheen, in one of the great modern film performances. He looks like James Dean, does not have bowlegs, and plays the killer as a plain and simple soul who has somehow been terribly damaged by life (the real Starkweather, his father explained at the time, was never quite right after being hit between the eyes with a two-by-four). Holly is played by the freckle-faced redhead Sissy

Spacek. She takes her schoolbooks along on the murder spree so as not to get behind. She is in love with Kit at first, but there is a stubborn logic in her makeup and she eventually realizes that Kit means trouble. "I made a resolution never again to take up with any hell-bent types," she confides.

After the first murder and their flight, they never have any extended conversations about anything, nor are they seen to make love, nor is their journey given any symbolic meaning. They hope to reach refuge in the "Far North," where Kit might find employment as a mounted policeman. They follow their case in the newspapers, become aware of themselves as celebrities, and, in a brilliant scene at the end, the captured Kit hands out his comb, his lighter, and his ballpoint pen as souvenirs to the National Guardsmen who had been chasing him.

The movie is very reserved in its attitude toward the characters. It observes them, most of the time, dispassionately. They are strange people, as were their real-life models; they had no rationalizations like Dillinger's regard for the poor or Bonnie and Clyde's ability to idealize themselves romantically. They were just two dumb kids who got into a thing and didn't have the sense to stop. They're something like the kids in Robert Altman's *Thieves Like Us* and the married couple in *The Sugarland Express*. They are in over their heads, incapable of understanding murder as a crime rather than a convenience, inhabitants of lives so empty that even their sins cannot fill them.

Bad Lieutenant

NC-17, 96 m., 1993

Harvey Keitel (Lieutenant), Frankie Thorn (Nun), Brian McElroy (His Son), Frankie Acciarito (His Son No. 2), Peggy Gormley (His Wife), Stella Keitel (His Daughter), Victor Argo (Beat Cop). Directed by Abel Ferrara and produced by Edward R. Pressman and Mary Kane. Screenplay by Zoe Lund and Ferrara.

Bad Lieutenant tells the story of a man who is not comfortable inside his body or soul. He walks around filled with need and dread. He is in the last stages of cocaine addiction, gulping booze to level off the drug high. His life is such a loveless hell that he buys sex just for the sensation of someone touching him, and his at-

tention drifts even then, because there are so many demons pursuing him. Harvey Keitel plays this man with such uncompromised honesty that the performance can only be called courageous; not many actors would want to be seen in this light.

The lieutenant has no illusions about himself. He is bad and knows he is bad, and he abuses the power of his position in every way he can. Interrupting a grocery store stickup, he sends the beat cop away and then steals the money from the thieves. He sells drug dealers their immunity by taking drugs from them. In the film's most harrowing scene, he stops two teenage girls who are driving their parents' car without permission. He threatens them with arrest, and then engages in what can only be described as an act of verbal rape.

Remember the Ray Liotta character in the last sequence of Scorsese's *GoodFellas,* when he is strung out on cocaine and paranoid that the cops are following him? His life speeds up, his thinking is frantic, he can run but he can't hide. The Keitel character in *Bad Lieutenant* is like the same character, many more agonizing months down the road. Life cannot go on like this much longer.

We learn a few things about him. He still lives in a comfortable middle-class home, with a wife and three children who have long since made their adjustment to his madness. There is no longer a semblance of marriage. He comes in at dawn and collapses on the couch, to be wakened by the TV cartoons, which cut through his hangover. He stumbles out into the world again, to do more evil. When he drives the kids to school, his impatience is palpable; he cannot wait to drop them off and get a fix.

The movie does not give the lieutenant a name, because the human aspects of individual personality no longer matter at this stage; he is a bad cop, and those two words, expressing his moral state and his leverage in society, say everything that is still important about him.

A nun is raped. He visits the hospital to see her. She knows who attacked her, but will not name them, because she forgives them. The lieutenant is stunned. He cannot imagine this level of absolution. If a woman can forgive such a crime, is redemption possible even for him?

The film dips at times into madness. In a

church, he hallucinates that Jesus Christ has appeared to him. He no longer knows for sure what the boundaries of reality are. His temporary remedies—drugs and hookers—have stopped working. All that remain are self-loathing, guilt, deep physical disquiet, and the hope of salvation.

Bad Lieutenant was directed by Abel Ferrara, a gritty New Yorker who has come up through the exploitation ranks *(Ms. .45, Fear City)* to low-budget but ambitious films like *China Girl, King of New York,* and *Cat Chaser.* This film lacks the polish of a more sophisticated director, but would have suffered from it. The film and the character live close to the streets. The screenplay is by Ferrara and Zoe Lund, who can be seen onscreen as a hooker, and played the victim in *Ms. .45.* They are not interested in plot in the usual sense. There is no case to solve, no crime to stop, no bad guys except for the hero.

Keitel starred in Martin Scorsese's first film and has spent the last twenty-five years taking more chances with scripts and directors than any other major actor. He has the nerve to tackle roles like this, that other actors, even those with street images, would shy away from. He bares everything here—his body, yes, but also his weaknesses, his hungers. It is a performance given without reservation.

The film has the NC-17 rating, for adults only, and that is appropriate. This is not a film for younger people. But it is not a "dirty movie," and in fact takes spirituality and morality more seriously than most films do. And in the bad lieutenant, Keitel has given us one of the great screen performances in recent years.

Bang the Drum Slowly

PG, 98 m., 1973

Michael Moriarty (Henry Wiggen), Robert De Niro (Bruce Pearson), Vincent Gardenia (Dutch Schnell), Phil Foster (Joe), Ann Wedgeworth (Katie), Patrick McVey (Mr. Pearson). Directed by John Hancock and produced by Maurice and Lois Rosenfield. Screenplay by Mark Harris.

Bang the Drum Slowly is the ultimate baseball movie—and, despite what a plot summary might suggest, I think it's more about baseball than death. It takes place during the last season on this Earth of one Bruce Pearson, an earnest but dumb catcher from Georgia who learns, in the movie's first scene, that he is suffering from an incurable disease. The movie is about that season and about his friendship with Henry Wiggen, a pitcher, who undertakes to see that Bruce at least lives his last months with some dignity, some joy, and a few good games.

On the surface, then, the movie seems a little like *Brian's Song.* But it's not: It's mostly about baseball and the daily life of a major league club on the road. The fact of Bruce's approaching death adds a poignancy to the season, but *Bang the Drum Slowly* doesn't brood about death and it isn't morbid. In its mixture of fatalism, roughness, tenderness, and bleak humor, indeed, it seems to know more about the ways we handle death than a movie like *Love Story* ever guessed. The movie begins at the Mayo Clinic, follows the team through spring training, and then carries it through a season that feels remarkably like a Chicago Cubs year: a strong start, problems during the hot weather, dissension on the team, and then a pennant drive that (in the movie, anyway) is successful. There isn't a lot of play-by-play action, only enough to establish the games and make the character points. So when the team manager and the pitcher conspire to let Bruce finish his last game, despite his illness, the action footage is relevant and moving.

Bang the Drum Slowly was adapted for the screen by Mark Harris, from his observant 1955 novel. He seems to understand baseball players, or at least he can create convincing ones; if real baseball players aren't like the ones in this movie, somehow they should be. The director, John Hancock, is good with his actors and very good at establishing a lot of supporting characters without making a point of it (in this area he reminds me of Robert Altman's shorthand typecasting in *M*A*S*H* and *McCabe and Mrs. Miller*). Some of the best scenes are in the clubhouse, an arena of hope, despair, anger, practical jokes, and impassioned speeches by the manager.

He's played by Vincent Gardenia as a crafty, tough tactician with a heart of gold he tries to conceal. ("When I die," he says during one pre-game pep talk, "in the newspapers they'll write that the sons of bitches of this world have lost their leader.") He knows Bruce and Henry are concealing something, but he doesn't know what, and his efforts to find out are hilariously frustrated. At various times, the midwinter visit to the Mayo Clinic is explained as a fishing trip, a hunting trip, a wenching trip, and a secret mission to rid Bruce of the clap.

Gardenia, as the manager, is the third angle of a triangle that includes very good acting by Michael Moriarty, as Henry, and Robert De Niro, as Bruce. Henry is the All-Star with the $70,000 contract and Bruce is a mediocre catcher who is constantly being ragged by his teammates. Henry's his only friend, until somehow when the team comes together for the pennant stretch, Bruce starts playing the best ball of his life, and the club (somewhat predictably) accepts him.

Hancock and Harris avoid any temptation to structure *Bang the Drum Slowly* as a typical sports movie. Although the team does win the pennant, not much of a point is made of that. There are no telegraphed big moments on the field, when everything depends on a strikeout or a home run or something. Even Bruce's last big hit in his last time at bat is limited, tactfully, to a triple.

Instead of going for a lot of high points, the movie paints characters in their everyday personalities. We get some feeling of life on the road as Henry talks with a hotel telephone operator who's a baseball fanatic, and Bruce moons over the prostitute he's in love with. Phil Foster has a great cameo role as a first-base coach with a genius for luring suckers into card games with remarkably elastic rules. Occupying the background in a lot of shots is the team's Cuban third baseman, who has it written into his contract that he be provided with a translator. And then, as the movie's shape begins to be visible, we realize it's not so much a sports movie as a movie about those elusive subjects, male bonding and work in America. That the males play baseball and that sport is their work is what makes this the ultimate baseball movie; never before has a movie considered the game from the inside out.

The Barbarian Invasions

R, 99 m., 2003

Rémy Girard (Rémy), Stéphane Rousseau (Sébastien), Marie-Josée Croze (Nathalie), Dorothée Berryman (Louise), Louise Portal (Diane), Dominique Michel (Dominique), Yves Jacques (Claude), Pierre Curzi (Pierre), Marina Hands (Gaëlle). Directed by Denys Arcand and produced by Daniel Louis and Denise Robert. Screenplay by Arcand.

Dying is not this cheerful, but we need to think it is. *The Barbarian Invasions* is a movie about a man who dies about as pleasantly as it's possible to imagine; the audience sheds happy tears. The man is a professor named Rémy, who has devoted his life to wine, women, and left-wing causes, and now faces death by cancer, certain and soon. His wife divorced him years ago because of his womanizing, his son is a millionaire who dislikes him and everything he stands for, many of his old friends are estranged, and the morphine is no longer controlling the pain. By the end of the story, miraculously, he will have gotten away with everything, and be forgiven and beloved.

The young embrace the fantasy that they will live forever. The old cling to the equally seductive fantasy that they will die a happy death. This is a fantasy for adults. It is also a movie with brains, indignation, irony, and idealism— a film about people who think seriously and express themselves with passion. It comes from Denys Arcand of Quebec, whose *The Decline of the American Empire* (1986) involved many of the same characters during the fullness of their lives. At that time they either worked in the history department of a Montreal university or slept with somebody who did, and my review noted that "everybody talks about sex, but the real subject is wit . . . their real passion comes in the area of verbal competition."

When people are building their careers, they need to prove they're better than their contemporaries. Those who win must then prove—to themselves—that they're as good as they used to be. Whether Rémy was a good history professor is an interesting point (his son has to bribe three students to visit his bedside, but one of them later refuses to take the money). He certainly excelled in his lifestyle, as the lustiest and most Falstaffian of his circle, but every new conquest meant leaving someone behind— and now, at the end, he seems to have left almost everyone behind.

We've all known someone like Rémy. Frequently their children don't love them as much as their friends do. We have a stake in their passions; they live at full tilt so we don't have to, and sometimes even their castaways come to admire the life force that drives them on to new conquests, more wine, later nights. His former wife, Louise (Dorothée Berryman), calls their son Sébastien (Stéphane Rousseau) in London, where he is a rich trader, to tell him his father is near death, and although he hasn't spoken to the old man in a long time, Sébastien flies home with his fiancée, Gaëlle (Marina Hands).

Their first meeting goes badly; it is a replay of Rémy's socialist rejection of Sébastien's values and his "worthless" job. But Sébastien has learned from the financial world how to get things done, and soon he has bribed a union official to prepare a private room for his father on a floor of the hospital no longer in use. He even wants to fly his father to America for treatment, but Rémy blusters that he fought for socialized medicine and he will stick with it. The movie is an indictment of overcrowded Canadian hospitals and absent-minded caregivers, but it also reveals a certain flexibility, as when the nun caring for Rémy tells his son that morphine no longer kills the pain . . . but heroin would.

How Sébastian responds to that information leads to one of the movie's most delightful sequences, and to the introduction of a drug addict named Nathalie (Marie-Josée Croze), who becomes another of Rémy's caregivers. Nathalie's story and her own problems are so involving that Croze won the best actress award at Cannes in 2003.

Sébastian calls up his father's old friends. Some are Rémy's former lovers. Two are gay. One, Rémy's age, has started a new family. They gather at first rather gingerly around the deathbed of this person they had drifted away from, but eventually their reunion becomes a way to remember their younger days, their idealism, their defiant politics. Rémy is sometimes gray and shaking with pain, but the movie sidesteps the horrendous side effects of chemotherapy and uses heroin as the reason why he can play the graceful and even ebullient host at his own passing. There is a scene at a lakeside cottage that is so perfect and moving that only a churl would wonder how wise it is to leave a terminally ill man outside all night during the Quebec autumn, even with blankets wrapped around him.

The Barbarian Invasions, also written by Arcand, is manipulative without apology, and we want it to be. There's no market for a movie about a man dying a miserable death, wracked by the nausea of chemo. Indeed, Rémy is even allowed his taste for good wines and family feasts. And what a marvel the way his wife and his former (and current!) lovers gather around to celebrate what seems to have been the most remarkable case of priapism any of them have ever encountered. They are not so much forgiving him, I think, as envying his ability to live on his own terms and get away with it. His illusions are all he has, and although they were deceived by them, they don't want Rémy to die without them. As a good friend of mine once observed, nobody on his deathbed ever says, "I'm glad I always flew economy class."

Barfly

R, 110 m., 1987

Mickey Rourke (Henry), Faye Dunaway (Wanda Wilcox), Alice Krige (Tully), Jack Nance (Detective), J. C. Quinn (Jim), Frank Stallone (Eddie), Gloria LeRoy (Grandma Moses). Directed by Barbet Schroeder and produced by Schroeder, Fred Roos, and Tom Luddy. Screenplay by Charles Bukowski.

Louis Armstrong was trying to explain jazz one day, and he finally gave up and said, "There are some folks that, if they don't know, you can't tell 'em." The world of Charles Bukowski could be addressed in the same way. Bukowski is the poet of Skid Row, the Los Angeles drifter who spent his life, until age fifty, in an endless round of saloons and women, all of them cheap, expensive, bad, or good in various degrees. *Barfly*, based on his original screenplay, is a grimy comedy about what it might be like to spend a couple of days in his skin—a couple of the better and funnier days, although they aren't exactly a lark.

The movie takes place in a gutbucket bar down on the bad side of town, where the same regulars take up the same positions on the same bar stools every day. Your private life is nobody's business, but everybody in the joint knows all about it. To this bar, day after day, comes Henry (Mickey Rourke), a drunk who is sometimes also a poet. The day bartender hates him, probably for the same reason all bartenders in gutter saloons hate their customers: It's bad enough that they have to serve these losers, without taking a lot of lip from them, too.

Henry and the bartender head for the back alley to have a fight. Henry is beaten to a pulp. Hawking up spit and blood, he tosses down another drink and heads off for the hovel he calls his room. Another day, another adventure. One day he looks up from his drink and sees, sitting at the other end of the bar, a woman named Wanda (Faye Dunaway). She looks like she belongs in the place, and she doesn't look like she belongs in the place, you know? She looks like a drunk, all right, but she's still kind of classy. Henry and Wanda strike up a conversation, and, seeing that Henry is broke, Wanda invites him home.

The dialogue scenes between Rourke and Dunaway in this movie are never less than a pleasure, but their exchanges on that first night are poetry. She explains that if a guy comes along with a fifth, she is likely to leave with that guy, since when she drinks she always makes bad decisions. He nods. What other kinds of decisions are there when you're drunk? They drink, they talk, they flirt, they coexist. Another day, another adventure.

One day a beautiful rich girl with long hair (Alice Krige) comes to the bar looking for Henry. She publishes a literary magazine and has purchased some of Henry's stuff. He likes this development. They go to her house and drink, talk, flirt, and coexist. The next time she turns up in the bar, Wanda is already there. The rich girl and Wanda do not coexist.

That's basically what the movie is about. *Barfly* is not heavy on plot, which is correct, since in the disordered world of the drinker, one thing rarely leads to another through any visible pattern. Each day is a window that opens briefly after the hangover and before the blackout, and you can never tell what you'll see through that window.

Barfly was directed by Barbet Schroeder, who commissioned the original screenplay by Bukowski and then spent eight years trying to get it made. (At one point, he threatened to cut off his fingers if Cannon Group president Menahem Golan did not finance it; the outcome of the story can be deduced by the fact that this is a Cannon release.) Rourke and Dunaway take their characters as opportuni-ties to stretch as actors, to take chances and do extreme things. Schroeder never tries to impose too much artificial order on the events; indeed, he committed to filming Bukowski's screenplay exactly as written, in all its rambling but romantic detail.

The result is a truly original American movie, a film like no other, a period of time spent in the company of the kinds of characters Saroyan and O'Neill would have understood, the kinds of people we try not to see, and yet might enjoy more than some of our more visible friends. *Barfly* was one of 1987's best films.

Batman Begins
PG-13, 140 m., 2005

Christian Bale (Bruce Wayne/Batman), Michael Caine (Alfred Pennyworth), Liam Neeson (Henri Ducard), Katie Holmes (Rachel Dawes), Morgan Freeman (Lucius Fox), Gary Oldman (Lieutenant James Gordon), Cillian Murphy (Dr. Jonathan Crane), Tom Wilkinson (Carmine Falcone), Rutger Hauer (Richard Earle), Ken Watanabe (Ra's Al Ghul). Directed by Christopher Nolan and produced by Larry J. Franco, Charles Roven, and Emma Thomas. Screenplay by David S. Goyer and Nolan.

Batman Begins at last penetrates to the dark and troubled depths of the Batman legend, creating a superhero who, if not plausible, is at least persuasive as a man driven to dress like a bat and become a vigilante. The movie doesn't simply supply Batman's beginnings in the tradition of a comic book origin story, but explores the tortured path that led Bruce Wayne from a parentless childhood to a friendless adult existence. The movie is not realistic, because how could it be, but it acts as if it is.

Opening in a prison camp in an unnamed nation, *Batman Begins* shows Bruce Wayne (Christian Bale) enduring brutal treatment as a prisoner as part of his research into the nature of evil. He is rescued by the mysterious Henri Ducard (Liam Neeson), who appoints himself Wayne's mentor, teaches him sword-fighting and mind control, and tries to enlist him in his amoral League of Shadows ("We burned London to the ground"). When Wayne refuses to kill someone as a membership requirement, Ducard becomes his enemy; the reclusive millionaire returns to Gotham determined to fight evil, without realizing quite how much trouble he is in.

The story of why he identifies with bats (childhood trauma) and hates evildoers (he saw his parents killed by a mugger) has been referred to many times in the various incarnations of the Batman legend, including four previous films. This time it is given weight and depth.

Wayne discovers in Gotham that the family-owned Wayne Corp. is run by a venal corporate monster (Rutger Hauer), but that in its depths labors the almost-forgotten scientific genius Lucius Fox (Morgan Freeman), who understands that Wayne wants to fight crime and offers him the weaponry. Lucius happens to have on hand a prototype Batmobile, which unlike the streamlined models in the earlier movies is a big, unlovely juggernaut that looks like a Humvee's wet dream. He also devises a Bat Cape with surprising properties.

These preparations, Gotham crime details, and the counsel of the faithful family servant Alfred (Michael Caine) delay the actual appearance of a Batman until the second act of the movie. We don't mind. Unlike the earlier films, which delighted in extravagant special-effects action, *Batman Begins* is shrouded in shadow; instead of high-detail, sharp-edged special effects, we get obscure developments in fog and smoke, their effect reinforced by a superb sound effects design. And Wayne himself is a slow learner, clumsy at times, taking foolish chances, inventing Batman as he goes along ("People need dramatic examples to shake them out of fear and apathy, and I can't do that as a human being").

This, at last, is the Batman movie I've been waiting for. The character resonates more deeply with me than the other comic superheroes, perhaps because when I discovered him as a child he seemed darker and more grown-up than the cheerful Superman. He has secrets. As Alfred muses: "Strange injuries and a nonexistent social life. These things beg the question, what does Bruce Wayne do with his time?"

What he does is create a high profile as a millionaire playboy who gets drunk and causes scenes. This disappoints his friend since childhood, Rachel Dawes (Katie Holmes), who is now an assistant D.A. She and Lieutenant James Gordon (Gary Oldman), apparently

Gotham's only honest cop, are faced with a local crime syndicate led by Carmine Falcone (Tom Wilkinson). But Falcone's gang is child's play compared to the deep scheme being hatched by the corrupt psychiatrist Dr. Jonathan Crane (Cillian Murphy), who in the tradition of Victorian alienists likes to declare his enemies insane and lock them up.

Crane's secret identity as the Scarecrow fits into a scheme to lace the Gotham water supply with a psychedelic drug. Then a superweapon will be used to vaporize the water, citizens will inhale the drug, and it will drive them crazy, for reasons the Scarecrow and his confederates explain with more detail than clarity. Meanwhile, flashbacks establish Wayne's deepest traumas, including his special relationship with bats and his guilt because he thinks he is responsible for his parents' mugging.

I admire, among other things, the way the movie doesn't have the gloss of the earlier films. The Batman costume is an early design. The Bat Cave is an actual cave beneath Wayne Manor. The Batmobile enters and leaves it by leaping across a chasm and through a waterfall. The early Bat Signal is crude and out of focus. The movie was shot on location in Chicago, making good use of the murky depths of Lower Wacker Drive (you may remember it from *Henry: Portrait of a Serial Killer*) and the Board of Trade Building (now the Wayne Corp.). Special effects add a spectacular monorail straight down LaSalle Street, which derails in the best scene along those lines since *The Fugitive*.

Christian Bale is just right for this emerging version of Batman. It's strange to see him muscular and toned, after his cadaverous appearance in *The Machinist*, but he suggests an inward quality that suits the character. His old friend Rachel is at first fooled by his facade of playboy irresponsibility, but Lieutenant Gordon (destined to become in the fullness of time Commissioner Gordon) figures out fairly quickly what Batman is doing, and why. Instead of one villain as the headliner, *Batman Begins* has a whole population, including Falcone, the Scarecrow, the Asian League of Shadows leader Ra's Al Ghul (Ken Watanabe), and a surprise bonus pick.

The movie has been directed by Christopher Nolan, still only thirty-five, whose *Memento* (2000) took Sundance by storm and was followed by *Insomnia* (2002), a police procedural starring Al Pacino. What Warner Bros. saw in those pictures that inspired it to think of Nolan for Batman is hard to say, but the studio guessed correctly, and after an eight-year hiatus the Batman franchise has finally found its way.

I said this is the Batman movie I've been waiting for; more correctly, this is the movie I did not realize I was waiting for, because I didn't realize that more emphasis on story and character and less emphasis on high-tech action was just what was needed. The movie works dramatically in addition to being an entertainment. There's something to it.

A Beautiful Mind

PG-13, 129 m., 2001

Russell Crowe (John Forbes Nash, Jr.), Ed Harris (William Parcher), Jennifer Connelly (Alicia Nash), Paul Bettany (Charles), Adam Goldberg (Sol), Austin Pendleton (Thomas King), Vivien Cardone (Marcee), Judd Hirsch (Helinger), Christopher Plummer (Dr. Rosen). Directed by Ron Howard and produced by Brian Grazer and Howard. Screenplay by Akiva Goldsman, based on the book by Sylvia Nasar.

The Nobel Prize winner John Forbes Nash, Jr. still teaches at Princeton and walks to campus every day. That these commonplace statements nearly brought tears to my eyes suggests the power of *A Beautiful Mind,* the story of a man who is one of the greatest mathematicians, and a victim of schizophrenia. Nash's discoveries in game theory have an impact on our lives every day. He also believed for a time that the Russians were sending him coded messages on the front page of the *New York Times.*

A Beautiful Mind stars Russell Crowe as Nash, and Jennifer Connelly as his wife, Alicia, who is pregnant with their child when the first symptoms of his disease become apparent. It tells the story of a man whose mind was of enormous service to humanity while at the same time betraying him with frightening delusions. Crowe brings the character to life by sidestepping sensationalism and building with small behavioral details. He shows a man who descends into madness and then, unexpectedly, regains the ability to function in the academic world. Nash has been compared to Newton, Mendel, and Darwin, but was also for many years just a man muttering to himself in the corner.

Director Ron Howard is able to suggest a core of goodness in Nash that inspired his wife and others to stand by him, to keep hope, and, in her words in his darkest hour, "to believe that something extraordinary is possible." The movie's Nash begins as a quiet but cocky young man with a West Virginia accent, who gradually turns into a tortured, secretive paranoid who believes he is a spy being trailed by government agents. Crowe, who has an uncanny ability to modify his look to fit a role, always seems convincing as a man who ages forty-seven years during the film.

The early Nash, seen at Princeton in the late 1940s, calmly tells a scholarship winner, "There is not a single seminal idea on either of your papers." When he loses at a game of Go, he explains: "I had the first move. My play was perfect. The game is flawed." He is aware of his impact on others ("I don't much like people, and they don't much like me") and recalls that his first-grade teacher said he was "born with two helpings of brain and a half-helping of heart."

It is Alicia who helps him find the heart. She is a graduate student when they meet, is attracted to his genius, is touched by his loneliness, is able to accept his idea of courtship when he informs her, "Ritual requires we proceed with a number of platonic activities before we have sex." To the degree that he can be touched, she touches him, although often he seems trapped inside himself; Sylvia Nasar, who wrote the 1998 biography that informs Akiva Goldsman's screenplay, begins her book by quoting Wordsworth about "a mind forever voyaging through strange seas of thought alone."

Nash's schizophrenia takes a literal, visual form. He believes he is being pursued by a federal agent (Ed Harris), and finds himself in chase scenes that seem inspired by 1940s crime movies. He begins to find patterns where no patterns exist. One night he and Alicia stand under the sky and he asks her to name any object, and then connects stars to draw it. Romantic, but it's not so romantic when she discovers his office thickly papered with countless bits torn from newspapers and magazines and connected by frantic lines into imaginary patterns.

The movie traces his treatment by an understanding psychiatrist (Christopher Plummer), and his agonizing courses of insulin shock therapy. Medication helps him improve somewhat—but only, of course, when he takes the medication. Eventually newer drugs are more effective, and he begins a tentative re-entry into the academic world at Princeton.

The movie fascinated me about the life of this man, and I sought more information, finding that for many years he was a recluse, wandering the campus, talking to no one, drinking coffee, smoking cigarettes, paging through piles of newspapers and magazines. And then one day he paid a quite ordinary compliment to a colleague about his daughter, and it was noticed that Nash seemed better.

There is a remarkable scene in the movie when a representative for the Nobel committee (Austin Pendleton) comes visiting, and hints that Nash is being "considered" for the prize. Nash observes that people are usually informed they have won, not that they are being considered: "You came here to find out if I am crazy and would screw everything up if I won." He did win, and did not screw everything up.

The movies have a way of pushing mental illness into corners. It is grotesque, sensational, cute, funny, willful, tragic, or perverse. Here it is simply a disease, which renders life almost but not quite impossible for Nash and his wife, before he becomes one of the lucky ones to pull out of the downward spiral.

When he won the Nobel, Nash was asked to write about his life, and he was honest enough to say his recovery is "not entirely a matter of joy." He observes: "Without his 'madness,' Zarathustra would necessarily have been only another of the millions or billions of human individuals who have lived and then been forgotten." Without *his* madness, would Nash have also lived and then been forgotten? Did his ability to penetrate the most difficult reaches of mathematical thought somehow come with a price attached? The movie does not know and cannot say.

Beauty and the Beast

G, 84 m., 1991

With the voices of: Paige O'Hara (Belle), Robby Benson (Beast), Richard White (Gaston), Jerry Orbach (Lumiere), David Ogden Stiers (Cogsworth), Angela Lansbury (Mrs. Potts), Jesse Corti (LeFou). Directed by Gary Trousdale and Kirk Wise and produced by Don Hahn. Screenplay by Linda Woolverton.

Beauty and the Beast slipped around all my roadblocks and penetrated directly into my strongest childhood memories, in which animation looked more *real* than live-action features. Watching the movie, I found myself caught up in a direct and joyous way. I wasn't reviewing an "animated film." I was being told a story, I was hearing terrific music, and I was having fun.

The film is as good as any Disney animated feature ever made—as magical as *Pinocchio, Snow White, The Little Mermaid*. And it's a reminder that animation is the ideal medium for fantasy, because all of its fears and dreams can be made literal. No Gothic castle in the history of horror films, for example, has ever approached the awesome, frightening towers of the castle where the Beast lives. And no real wolves could have fangs as sharp or eyes as glowing as the wolves that prowl in the castle woods.

The movie's story, somewhat altered from the original fable, involves a beauty named Belle, who lives in the worlds of her favorite library books and is repelled by the romantic advances of Gaston, the muscle-bound cretin in her little eighteenth-century French village. Belle's father, a dotty inventor, sets off on a journey through the forest, takes a wrong turn, and is imprisoned in the castle of the Beast. And Belle bravely sets off on a mission to rescue him.

We already know, from the film's opening narration, that the Beast is actually a handsome young prince who was transformed into a hideous monster as a punishment for being cruel. And a beast he will be forever, unless he finds someone who will love him. When Belle arrives at the castle, that lifesaving romance is set into motion—although not, of course, without grave adventures to be overcome.

Like all of the best Disney animated films, *Beauty and the Beast* surrounds its central characters with a large peanut gallery of gossipy, chattering supporting players. The Beast's haunted castle contains his entire serving staff, transformed from humans into household objects, and so we meet Lumiere, a candlestick; Cogsworth, a clock; and Mrs.

Potts, a teapot with a little son named Chip. These characters are all naturally on Belle's side, because if the Beast can end his magic spell, they, too, will become human again.

There are some wonderful musical numbers in the movie, and animation sets their choreography free from the laws of gravity. A hilarious number celebrates the monstrous ego of Gaston, who boasts about his hairy chest and the antlers he uses for interior decoration. "Be Our Guest" is a rollicking invitation to Belle from the castle staff, choreographed like Busby Berkeley running amok. And there is the haunting title song, sung by Mrs. Potts in the voice of Angela Lansbury.

The songs have lyrics by the late Howard Ashman and music by Alan Menken, the same team who collaborated on 1989's *The Little Mermaid,* and they bubble with wit and energy ("Gaston" in particular brings down the house). Lansbury is one of a gifted cast on the sound track, which also includes Paige O'Hara as the plucky Belle; Robby Benson (his voice electronically lowered and mixed with the growls of animals) as the Beast; Jerry Orbach as the candlestick who sounds uncannily like Maurice Chevalier; David Ogden Stiers as the cranky Cogsworth; and Richard White as the insufferable Gaston, who degenerates during the course of the film from a chauvinist pig to a sadistic monster.

Beauty and the Beast, like *The Little Mermaid,* reflects a new energy and creativity from the Disney animation people. They seem to have abandoned all notions that their feature-length cartoons are intended only for younger viewers, and these aren't children's movies but robust family entertainment. Perhaps it is inevitable, in an age when even younger kids see high-voltage special effects films like *Die Hard* or *Terminator II,* that animation could no longer be content with jolly and innocuous fairy tales. What a movie like *Beauty and the Beast* does, however, is to give respect to its audience.

A lot of "children's movies" seem to expect people to buy tickets by default, because of what the movie *doesn't* contain (no sex, vulgarity, etc.). *Beauty and the Beast* reaches back to an older and healthier Hollywood tradition in which the best writers, musicians, and filmmakers are gathered for a project on the assumption that a family audience deserves great entertainment, too.

Bed and Board

PG, 100 m., 1970

Jean-Pierre Leaud (Antoine Doinel), Claude Jade (Christine), Claire Duhamel (Her mother), Daniel Ceccaldi (Her father). Directed by Francois Truffaut and produced by Marcol Berbert and Truffaut. Screenplay by Truffaut, Claude de Givray, and Bernard Revon.

Editor's note: This review contains spoilers.

So here he is for the last time, Antoine Doinel, who has grown up like the rest of us and has finally, apparently, found conjugal peace. He has changed a lot along the way. Francois Truffaut first introduced Antoine in *The 400 Blows* (1959), his first feature. The character was roughly based on Truffaut's own youth and adolescence, when he was the next thing to a juvenile delinquent and prowled the streets of Paris.

The 400 Blows, with Godard's *Breathless* and Chabrol's *Le Beau Serge,* inaugurated the French New Wave and changed the face and style of filmmaking almost overnight. But we don't remember *The 400 Blows* for historical reasons; we remember it because, for many of us, it was our first taste of personal, almost intimate, filmmaking.

The Hollywood movies we saw during the 1950s had grown increasingly sterile and clumsy, with a few exceptions, but now here was a new filmmaker with a relaxed and unstudied manner, who recorded the rhythms of life itself, instead of some arthritic plot. He allowed us to spend some time with the boy Antoine, his parents, his school, and his moody adolescent terrain. There are some movies that are spoken of in hushed tones as "classics" and studied joylessly for their perfection, but *The 400 Blows* will never age like that. It will be one of the movies we can put in a time capsule to convince the next generations that some of us, at least, breathed.

With the exception of an interim short subject, Truffaut didn't return to the autobiographical character of Antoine until *The Stolen Kisses* (1968), which once again starred Jean-Pierre Leaud. It was clear with this movie that Truffaut and Antoine had changed a great deal. *Stolen Kisses* was more on the side of whimsy than pathos and wasn't nearly as serious as the earlier film.

But it was a great film in its own way, showing us young Antoine in a variety of jobs and loves. At the end of *The 400 Blows*, we expected, I think, that Antoine would grow up to be an extraordinary human being of some sort, but we were wrong. Truffaut aged him into a pleasant, rather ordinary young man in his early twenties, and now with *Bed and Board*, Antoine has actually become bourgeois.

He's married Christine, the girl who took him home for that disastrous dinner party in *Stolen Kisses*, and they've settled into a comfortable apartment, decorated with Christine's touch, above the courtyard where Antoine works. (Seemingly unattracted to any vaguely ordinary job, Antoine dyes flowers.) The building is inhabited by the most motley assortment of boarders since the menagerie in *The Fifth Horseman is Fear*, and Truffaut gives us an unstudied notion of the life around the courtyard.

Christine becomes pregnant after a decorous interval, and Antoine gets some sort of inexplicable job operating model boats for an American film. He also falls in love with a beautiful Japanese girl, and the affair picks up such momentum that Christine bars him from their bed. Alas, the other girl is addicted to saying "thank you" much too often, and Antoine finds that he's developing leg cramps trying to eat close to the floor, Japanese style. He longs for Christine again, and she for him, and the movie has a happy ending.

Truffaut himself has changed enormously in the past decade, and Antoine's story has become an autobiography, not of Truffaut's life, but of his art. You get the feeling from his films that he's one of the most gentle and civilized of directors and that he finds the events of ordinary human life just as fascinating as heroic or melodramatic subjects. *Bed and Board* is one of the most decent and loving films I can remember. If it doesn't provide quite the outcome we would have expected for Antoine, it will do.

Bedazzled

PG, 103 m., 1968

Peter Cook (George Spiggott (Satan)), Dudley Moore (Stanley Moon), Eleanor Bron (Margaret Spencer), Raquel Welch (Lilian Lust), Michael Bates (Inspector Clarke), Parnell McGarry (Gluttony). Directed and produced by Stanley Donen. Screenplay by Peter Cook.

There is a certain kind of humor I will always identify with Bob and Ray. Most of their material is based on "normal" situations: a sports interview, a world cruise, a routine police search for a whale lost in Brooklyn.

They approach this material in two ways. Either they play the scene absolutely straight ("We have a few promising leads and we think we can turn up that whale by tomorrow, Mr. Ballou"), or they slowly and logically work themselves out on a limb of pure fantasy ("Good gracious! A woman, apparently thinking the door was in service, has gotten into it and brings this whole World Championship Revolving Door Race to a startling and unexpected conclusion.")

This sort of humor isn't necessarily funny in itself. The audience must supply an attitude toward the material. When Bob and Ray had their radio program years ago, they would supply such lines as "Now Gabriel Heater will do his Sleepeze commercial." Period. Either you found that funny or you didn't. In any case, you couldn't possibly explain its appeal to someone else. *Bedazzled*, Stanley Donen's brilliant new film, is a similar case.

It stars the British comedians Peter Cook and Dudley Moore, whose function in England is similar to Bob and Ray's in this country. After appearing in the *Beyond the Fringe* revue, they starred in the *Not Only . . . But Also* series on British TV and followed it with other programs, commercials, and now *Bedazzled*.

The story is a free remake of the Faust legend, in which a short-order cook (Moore) falls hopelessly in love with a waitress (Eleanor Bron). He sells his soul to the devil (Cook) hoping to win the girl with the seven wishes. Cook and Moore, who wrote or improvised most of the film, break the story up into seven wish elements, plus in-between scenes, much like *Beyond the Fringe* skits.

Their satire, aimed at all the areas of conventional piety, is barbed and contemporary (the devil's magic words are "Julie Andrews" and "LBJ"). It is also often dry and understated, permitting the audience to find the humor without being led to it.

In films of this sort, too often the camera records the fun instead of joining in it. However, that is certainly not the case in this magnificently photographed, intelligent, very funny film.

Bee Season

PG-13, 104 m., 2005

Richard Gere (Saul Naumann), Juliette Binoche (Miriam Naumann), Flora Cross (Eliza Naumann), Max Minghella (Aaron Naumann), Kate Bosworth (Chali), Justin Alioto (Kevin). Directed by Scott McGehee and David Siegel and produced by Albert Berger and Ron Yerxa. Screenplay by Naomi Foner Gyllenhaal, based on the book by Myla Goldberg.

Bee Season involves one of those crazy families that cluster around universities: an intellectual husband who is clueless about human emotions, a wife who married him because she was afraid to be loved and he didn't know how to, a son who rebels by being more like his father than his father is, and a daughter who retreats into secret survival strategies. There are many movies about families sharing problems; in this one the members are isolated by them. They meet mostly at meals, which the father cooks and serves with a frightening intensity.

Like many families without centers, this one finds obsessions to focus on. Saul Naumann (Richard Gere) is a professor at Berkeley, specializing in Jewish theology and the Kabbalah. His wife, Miriam (Juliette Binoche), emotionally wounded by the early loss of her own parents, slips into the homes of strangers to steal small glittering things. Their teenage son, Aaron (Max Minghella), watches his father intimidate students with icy theological superiority and does the one thing best calculated to enrage him; he joins the Hare Krishnas. Their daughter, Eliza (Flora Cross), who is about twelve, seems to be trying to pass as unobserved and ordinary, but her inner life has a fierce complexity.

The father teaches Judaism and follows its forms, but his spiritual life is academic, not mystical. What no one in the family perceives is that Eliza is a genuine mystic, for whom the Kabbalah is not a theory but a reality. One of the things that Kabbalah believes is that words not only reflect reality but in a sense create it. God and the name of God are in this way the same thing.

How could this association enter into the life of a twelve-year-old in a practical way? Eliza finds out when she enters a spelling bee. Because she exists in the same world with words, because words create her world, she doesn't need to "know" how to spell a word. It needs merely to be evoked, and it materializes in a kind of vision: "I see the words." Although this gift gets her into the national finals, *Bee Season* is not a movie about spelling bees. It is a movie about a spiritual choice that calls everyone's bluff; it involves the sort of refusal and rebellion seen in that half-forgotten masterpiece *The Loneliness of the Long-Distance Runner* (1962).

Eliza is at the center of the film, and Cross carries its weight in a performance of quiet, compelling wisdom; the foreground character in the early scenes is Saul, the father. The members of his family swim in and out of focus. He is proud that Miriam is a scientist, in the sense that "my wife is a scientist," but does he know what enormous secrets she keeps from him? He is proud that his son is a gifted musician, and joins him in violin and cello duets. But Eliza is essentially invisible to Saul, because she has no particular accomplishments. Only when she wins a spelling bee does he start to focus on her, "helping" her train, pushing her to the next level, sitting proudly in the audience. He is proud not so much of her as of himself, for fathering such a prodigy.

The performance by Cross is haunting in its seriousness. She doesn't act out; she acts in. She suggests that Eliza has grown up in this family as a wise, often-overlooked observer, who keeps her own counsel and has her own values, the most important being her autonomy. In her father's manic kitchen behavior as he prepares and serves unwanted meals, she sees people-pleasing that exists apart from people who are pleased. In her fellow contestants in the spelling bees, she sees the same thing: Young people who are devoting their lives to mastering useless information for the glory of themselves and their parents. Yes, it is necessary to be able to spell in an ordinary sort of way, but to be able to spell every word is to aim for perfection, and perfection will drive you crazy, because our software isn't designed for it.

The movie, directed by Scott McGehee and David Siegel, is based on a novel by Myla Goldberg, unread by me. They made *Suture* (1993), a film about "identical" brothers played by actors of different races; you can deal with this apparent inconsistency by saying it doesn't matter—but in that case, why doesn't it? And their powerful *Deep End* (2001) starred Tilda Swinton as a mother scarcely less secretive than the Binoche character here.

Neither prepares us for *Bee Season*, which represents Eliza's decision to insist on herself as a being apart from the requirements of theology and authority, a person who insists on exercising her free will. This is a stick in the eye of her father. When people say they are "doing God's will," I am struck by the egotism of such a statement. What Eliza is doing at the end of *Bee Season* is Eliza's will. Does that make her God? No. It makes her Eliza.

Before the Rain

NO MPAA RATING, 114 m., 1995

Rade Serbedzija (Aleksandar), Katrin Cartlidge (Anne), Gregoire Colin (Kiril), Labina Mitevska (Zamira). Directed by Milcho Manchevski and produced by Judy Counihan, Cedomir Kolar, Sam Taylor, and Cat Villiers. Screenplay by Manchevski.

If you are the average consumer of news in North America, you have been hearing about the Bosnians, the Serbians, and the Croats for years now, and you are not sure quite where they all are, or why they are fighting, or which are the people and which are the places. They are basically all a lot of people with mustaches who hate each other, and the UN can't do anything about it.

It's not entirely your fault. The news reports concentrate on today's violent developments; we get stories we can't understand unless we already know so much that we don't need them to begin with. Yet if I were to tell you that *Before the Rain* provides a context for those stories, you would still probably be indifferent, because it's simply not your war.

There is another reason to see *Before the Rain*. This is one of 1995's best films, a brilliant directorial debut for a young man named

Milcho Manchevski, born in Macedonia, educated at Southern Illinois University, now a New Yorker who made award-winning MTV videos before returning home to make this extraordinary film. Work like this is what keeps me going, month after month and film after film: After the junk, this is a reminder of the nobility that film can attain.

The movie is made in three parts, two in Macedonia, one in London. The story circles back on itself, something like *Pulp Fiction*, and there is a paradox, a character who seems to be dead at a time he is still alive. Manchevski was not influenced by Tarantino; they were making their films simultaneously, and in *Before the Rain* the circular structure has a deeper purpose: It shows that the cycle of hate and bloodshed will go on year after year, generation after generation, unless somehow men find the will to break with it.

The London sequence is the most chilling for North American armchair news viewers who think Bosnia is not their concern. I cannot describe it without giving away its shattering surprise. It involves a photographer named Aleksandar (Rade Serbedzija), born in Macedonia but now a citizen of the world, who leaves the war in Bosnia in disgust and returns to London, where a married British woman, Anne (Katrin Cartlidge), has long been his lover. We think this segment will deal with their story, and so it does, but in an unexpected way which shows that no war is really very far away, and no man is an island.

The first and third parts of the film take place in Macedonia, which, like Bosnia and Serbia, was part of Yugoslavia. The fighting has not reached there, but there is great tension between Muslims and Orthodox Christians, and the atmosphere, Manchevski feels, is heavy with anticipation and foreboding, as before a heavy rain. In the first part, an Albanian Muslim girl is suspected of having killed a Christian, and takes refuge in the cell of a beardless youth who, as a monk, has taken a vow of silence. In the third segment, Aleksandar returns to his homeland to see the Muslim woman he once loved, and almost has his throat slit by her grandson.

Manchevski tells his story in a clear, ironic, elliptic style: This is like an art film about war, in which passions replace ideas. The character of Aleksandar is the most compelling one in the film; played by Serbedzija, the best-known movie star in Yugoslavia, he has a world-weary attractiveness, something like Bruno Ganz in *Wings of Desire*. The first and second parts of the film, while working on their own, also function as a setup for the extraordinary payoff, in which he goes home to find that home as he recalls it no longer exists, that childhood playmates are now bitter enemies, rehashing the details of crimes so old they are merely hearsay.

Aleksandar's return is fueled by guilt. "I killed—my camera killed—a man," he explains. While shooting in a war zone, "I complained I wasn't getting anything exciting, so a guard pulled his gun and shot his prisoner for me." He finally decides to remove himself from this circle of hatred, and Manchevski has said in interviews that the seeming "time paradoxes" in his film—the moments when things happen that shouldn't be able to happen—are his way of showing that we are perhaps not trapped by time, that sometimes there is an opening, an escape.

The construction of Manchevski's story is intended, then, to demonstrate the futility of its ancient hatreds. There are two or three moments in the film—I will not reveal them—where hatred of others is greater than love of one's own. Imagine a culture where a man would rather kill his daughter than allow her to love a man from another culture, and you will have an idea of the depth of bitterness in this film, the insane lengths to which men can be driven by belief and prejudice.

Being John Malkovich

R, 112 m., 1999

John Cusack (Craig Schwartz), Cameron Diaz (Lotte Schwartz), Catherine Keener (Maxine), John Malkovich (John Horatio Malkovich), Mary Kay Place (Floris), Orson Bean (Dr. Lester), Byrne Piven (Captain Mertin). Directed by Spike Jonze and produced by Michael Stipe, Sandy Stern, Steve Golin, and Vincent Landay. Screenplay by Charlie Kaufman.

What an endlessly inventive movie this is! Charlie Kaufman, the writer of *Being John Malkovich*, supplies a stream of dazzling inventions, twists, and wicked paradoxes. And the director, Spike Jonze, doesn't pounce on each one like fresh prey, but unveils it slyly, as if there's more where that came from. Rare is the movie where the last half-hour surprises you just as much as the first, and in ways you're not expecting. The movie has ideas enough for half a dozen films, but Jonze and his cast handle them so surely that we never feel hard-pressed; we're enchanted by one development after the next.

John Cusack stars as Craig, a street puppeteer. His puppets are dark and neurotic creatures, and the public doesn't much like them. Craig's wife, Lotte, runs a pet store, and their home is overrun with animal boarders, most of them deeply disturbed. Lotte is played by Cameron Diaz, one of the best-looking women in movies, who here looks so dowdy we hardly recognize her; Diaz has fun with her talent by taking it incognito to strange places and making it work for a living.

The puppeteer can't make ends meet in "today's wintry job climate." He answers a help-wanted ad and finds himself on floor 7½ of a building. This floor, and how it looks, and why it was built, would be inspiration enough for an entire film or a Monty Python sketch. It makes everything that happens on it funny in an additional way, on top of why it's funny in the first place.

The film is so rich, however, that the floor is merely the backdrop for more astonishments. Craig meets a coworker named Maxine (Catherine Keener) and lusts for her. She asks, "Are you married?" He says, "Yeah, but enough about me." They go out for a drink. He says, "I'm a puppeteer." She says, "Waiter? Check, please." Keener has this way of listening with her lips slightly parted, as if eager to interrupt by deconstructing what you just said and exposing you for the fool that you are.

Behind a filing cabinet on the 7½th floor, Craig finds a small doorway. He crawls through it, and is whisked through some kind of temporal-spatial portal, ending up inside the brain of the actor John Malkovich. Here he stays for exactly fifteen minutes, before falling from the sky next to the New Jersey Turnpike.

Whoa! What an experience. Maxine pressures him to turn it into a business, charging people to spend their fifteen minutes inside Malkovich. The movie handles this not as a gimmick but as the opportunity for material that is somehow funny and serious, sad and satirical, weird and touching, all at once. Malkovich himself is part of the magic. He is not playing himself here, but a version of his public image—distant, quiet, droll, as if musing about things that happened long ago and were only mildly interesting at the time. It took some courage for him to take this role, but it would have taken more courage to turn it down. It's a plum.

Why are people so eager to enter his brain? For the novelty, above all. Spend a lifetime being yourself and it would be worth money to spend fifteen minutes being almost anybody else. At one point, there's a bit of a traffic jam. Lotte finds herself inside his mind while Maxine is seducing him. Lotte enjoys this experience, and decides she wants to become a lesbian, or a man. Whatever it takes. This is hard to explain, but trust me.

The movie just keeps getting better. I don't want to steal the surprises and punch lines. Even the Charlie Sheen cameo is inspired. At one point Malkovich enters himself through his own portal, which is kind of like being pulled down into the black hole of your own personality, and that trip results in one of the most peculiar single scenes I've ever seen in the movies. Orchestrating all this, Cusack's character stays cool; to enter another man's mind is, of course, the ultimate puppeteering experience.

Every once in a long, long while a movie comes along that is like no other. A movie that creates a new world for us, and uses it to produce wonderful things. *Forrest Gump* was a movie like that, and so in their different ways were *M*A*S*H*, *This Is Spinal Tap*, *After Hours*, *Babe*, and *There's Something About Mary*. What do such films have in common? Nothing. That's the point. Each one stakes out a completely new place and colonizes it with limitless imagination.

Being There

PG, 130 m., 1980

Peter Sellers (Chance), Shirley MacLaine (Eve Rand), Melvyn Douglas (Ben Rand), Jack Warden (President), Richard Dysart (Dr. Allenby), Richard Basehart (Skrapinov). Directed by Hal Ashby and produced by Andrew Braunsberg. Screenplay by Jerzy Kosinski, based on his book.

There's an exhilaration in seeing artists at the very top of their form: It almost doesn't matter what the form is, if they're pushing their limits and going for broke and it's working. We can sense their joy of achievement—and even more so if the project in question is a risky, off-the-wall idea that could just as easily have ended disastrously.

Hal Ashby's *Being There* is a movie that inspires those feelings. It begins with a cockamamie notion, it's basically one joke told for two hours, and it requires Peter Sellers to maintain an excruciatingly narrow tone of behavior in a role that has him onscreen almost constantly. It's a movie based on an idea, and all the conventional wisdom agrees that emotions, not ideas, are the best to make movies from. But *Being There* pulls off its long shot and is a confoundingly provocative movie.

Sellers plays a mentally retarded gardener who has lived and worked all of his life inside the walls of an elegant Washington town house. The house and its garden are in a decaying inner-city neighborhood, but what goes on outside is of no concern to Sellers: He tends his garden, he watches television, he is fed on schedule by the domestic staff, he is content.

Then one day the master of the house dies. The household is disbanded. Sellers, impeccably dressed in his employer's privately tailored wardrobe, wanders out into the city. He takes along the one possession he'll probably need: His remote-control TV channel switcher. He uses it almost immediately; surrounded by hostile street kids, he imperturbably tries to switch channels to make them go away. He hasn't figured out that, outside his garden, life isn't television.

And that is the movie's basic premise, lifted intact from a Jerzy Kosinski novel. The Sellers character knows almost nothing about real life, but he has watched countless hours of television and he can be pleasant, smile, shake hands, and comport himself; he learned from watching all those guests on talk shows. He knows nothing about *anything*, indeed, except gardening. But when he stumbles into Washington's political and social upper crust, his simple truisms from the garden ("Spring is a time for planting") are taken as audaciously simple metaphors. This guy's a Thoreau! In no time at all, he's the closest confidant of a dying billionaire industrialist (Melvyn Douglas)—and the industrialist is the closest confidant of the president.

This is, you can see, a one-joke premise. It has to be if the Sellers performance is to work. The whole movie has to be tailored to the narrow range within which Sellers's gardener can think, behave, speak, and make choices. The ways in which this movie could have gone out of control, could have been relentlessly boring on the one hand, or manic with its own audacity on the other, are endless. But the tone holds. That's one of the most exhilarating aspects of the joy you can sense, as Ashby pulls this off: Every scene needs the confidence to play the idea completely straight.

There are wonderful comic moments, but they're never pushed so far that they strain the story's premise. Some of them involve: a battle between the CIA and the FBI as to which agency destroyed the gardener's files; Shirley MacLaine unsuccessfully attempts to introduce Sellers to the concept of romance; Sellers as a talk-show guest himself (at last!), and Sellers as the hit of a Washington cocktail party. The movie also has an audacious closing shot that moves the film's whole metaphor into a brand-new philosophical arena.

What is *Being There* about? I've read reviews calling it an indictment of television. But that doesn't fit; Sellers wasn't warped by television, he was retarded to begin with, and has TV to thank for what abilities he *has* to move in society. Is it an indictment of society, for being so dumb as to accept the Sellers character as a great philosophical sage? Maybe, but that's not so fascinating either. I'm not really inclined to plumb this movie for its message, although I'm sure that'll be a favorite audience sport. I just admire it for having the guts to take this weird conceit and push it to its ultimate comic conclusion.

Belle de Jour

R, 100 m., 1967

Catherine Deneuve (Severine Serizy), Jean Sorel (Pierre Serizy), Genevieve Page (Mme. Anais), Michel Piccoli (Henri Husson), Macha Meril (Renee), Francisco Rabal (Hyppolite), Pierre Clementi (Marcel), Georges Marchal (Le Duc). Directed by Luis Buñuel and produced by Robert and Raymond Hakim. Screenplay by Buñuel and Jean Claude Carriere.

Here now is Luis Buñuel's *Belle de Jour,* a movie from 1967, to teach us a lesson about what is erotic in the cinema. We will begin with Catherine Deneuve's face, as she listens to a taxi driver describe a famous Parisian brothel—a place where bored women might work for an afternoon or two every week, to earn some extra money. Her face is completely impassive. The camera holds on it. The taxi driver continues his description. We understand that the Deneuve character is mesmerized by what she hears, and that sooner or later she will be compelled to visit that brothel and have the experience of being a "belle de jour."

We already know something about the character, whose name is Severine. She is married to a rich, bland, young businessman (Jean Sorel). The marriage is comfortable but uneventful. An older friend (the saturnine Michel Piccoli) makes a bold attempt to seduce her, but she does not respond. "What interests me about you is your virtue," he says. Perhaps that is why she is not interested: She desires not a man who thinks she is virtuous, but one who thinks she is not.

Here she is in the street, approaching the luxurious apartment building where Madame Anais presides over the famous brothel. The camera focuses on her feet (Buñuel was famously obsessed with shoes). She pauses, turns away. Eventually she rings the bell and enters. Madame Anais (the elegant, realistic Genevieve Page) greets her, and asks her to wait for a time in her office. Again, Deneuve's face betrays no emotion. None at all. Eventually she learns the rules of the house, and after some thought, agrees to them. She is a belle de jour.

The film will contain no sweaty, steamy, athletic sex scenes. Hardly any nudity, and that discreet. What is sexual in this movie takes place entirely within the mind of Severine. We have to guess at her feelings. All she ever says explicitly is, "I cannot help myself." Much happens off-screen. The most famous scene in *Belle de Jour*—indeed, one of the best-remembered scenes in movie history—is the one where a client presents her with an ornate little box. He shows her what is inside the box. During his hour with Severine, he wants to employ it. She shakes her head, no. What is in the box? We never find out.

Consider that scene. In all the years that have passed since I first saw *Belle de Jour,* I have always wondered what was in the box. Suppose the movie had been dumbed down by modern Hollywood. We would have seen what was in the box. And Severine would have shaken her head the same way, and we would have forgotten the scene in ten minutes.

What is erotic in *Belle de Jour* is suggested, implied, hinted at. We have to complete the link in our own imagination. When we watch the shower scene between Sharon Stone and Sylvester Stallone in *The Specialist,* or the "harassment" scene between Demi Moore and Michael Douglas in *Disclosure,* nothing is left to the imagination. We see every drop of sweat, we see glistening skin, hungry lips, grappling bodies. And we are outside. We are voyeurs, watching them up there on the screen, doing something we are not involved in. It is a technical demonstration.

But in *Belle de Jour,* we are invited into the secret world of Severine. We have to complete her thoughts, and in that process they become our thoughts. The movie understands the hypnotic intensity with which humans consider their own fantasies. When Severine enters a room where a client is waiting, her face doesn't reflect curiosity or fear or anticipation—and least of all lust—because she is not regarding the room, she is regarding herself. What turns her on is not what she finds in the room, but that she is entering it.

Luis Buñuel, one of a small handful of true masters of the cinema, had an insight into human nature that was cynical and detached; he looked with bemusement on his characters as they became the victims of their own lusts and greeds. He also had a sympathy with them, up to a point. He understands why Severine is drawn to the brothel, but he doesn't stop there, with her adventures in the afternoon. He pushes on, to a bizarre conclusion in which she finally gets what she *really* wants.

I will not reveal the ending. But observe, as it is unfolding, a gunfight in the street. Buñuel does not linger over it; in fact, he films it in a perfunctory fashion, as if he was in a hurry to get it out of the way. The gunplay is necessary

in order to explain the next stage of the movie's plot. It has no other function. Today's directors, more fascinated by style than story, would have lingered over the gunfight—would have built it up into a big production number, to supply the film with an action climax that would have been entirely wrong. Not Buñuel.

Best Boy
NO MPAA RATING, 111 m., 1980

A documentary produced, directed, and edited by Ira Wohl.

Sometimes there are movies that absorb you so completely that you forget you're watching them: They're simply happening to you. Ira Wohl's *Best Boy* is a movie like that. To see it is to participate in the lives of other people and to learn just a little more about being human. *Best Boy,* which won the 1980 Academy Award as best documentary, is the story of an only son named Philly, whose parents have always been too protective of him. But as the movie opens, it is time for Philly to go out a little more on his own—to go down to the corner for an ice cream cone, for example, or to look forward to his first day of school. Philly is fifty-two years old. He is mentally retarded, but otherwise, as a psychiatrist explains in the film, "quite normal." He is also warm and lovable, and when Wordsworth wrote that heaven was all about us when we were children, did he guess that would also be true for someone like Philly, who will never really leave childhood?

Best Boy deals intelligently with real people and their problems. It is not simply a documentary; it contains the surprises of true drama, and it is put together so thoughtfully that it takes what could have been a case study and turns it into a cliffhanger. That is largely due to the complete access that the filmmaker, Ira Wohl, had to his subject. Philly is Wohl's cousin, and Philly's parents are Wohl's aunt and uncle. All the time he was growing up, Ira knew Philly—he played with him, presumably, when he was four or five and Philly seemed to be about the same age. Philly stayed four or five. As Wohl grew older, he realized that sooner or later Philly's parents would die, and that Philly's total dependence on them would leave him defenseless.

Philly had been at home almost all his life. The movie begins as his parents make the first reluctant, tentative steps to allow him a little more independence—to set him free. *Best Boy* moves very delicately around this subject, and with good reason: As we watch it, we realize that the parents have come to depend on Philly, too. He provided them with a rationale for their own lives and choices. He is their crutch as well as their burden. And there is yet another drama that unfolds within the film— unfolds so subtly we barely realize it is there, and yet concludes so inevitably that it casts a light back on all the scenes that went before. Philly's father is dying. There is a time in the film when the father clearly knows that and no one else in the film does, but we, strangers, share his secret with him.

You see what I mean when I say *Best Boy* isn't a case study. It's not about what should be done with Philly, and it has little to do with the "problem" of mental retardation. It is so specifically about Philly and his family and their daily choices in life that we almost feel adopted into the family. And we get to like Philly so much! He is sweet and cheerful, patient and good-humored, with a child's logic that cuts right through so much of the confusion adults surround him with. There is a wonderful scene with a psychiatrist, who is trying to administer a series of questions Philly obviously feels are silly. There is a visit to the theater, where Philly is allowed backstage to meet Zero Mostel, and they sing "If I Were a Rich Man" together. Why is it, the movie asks but never answers, that Philly can remember songs better than speech?

Best Boy suffers, I suppose, from being labeled a documentary: Some small-minded people make it a policy never to watch one. But at the Toronto Festival of Festivals, where the patrons are asked to vote for their favorite film, it astonished everyone by defeating all the features in the festival and placing first. It's a wonderfully positive experience.

The Best of Youth

R, 366 m., 2005

Luigi Lo Cascio (Nicola Carati), Alessio Boni (Matteo Carati), Adriana Asti (Adriana Carati), Sonia Bergamasco (Giulia Monfalco), Fabrizio Gifuni (Carlo Tommasi), Maya Sansa (Mirella Utano), Valentina Carnelutti (Francesca Carati), Jasmine Trinca (Giorgia), Andrea Tidona (Angelo Carati), Lidia Vitale (Giovanna Carati). Directed by Marco Tullio Giordana and produced by Angelo Barbagallo. Screenplay by Sandro Petraglia and Stefano Rulli.

Every review of *The Best of Youth* begins with the information that it is six hours long. No good movie is too long, just as no bad movie is short enough. I dropped outside of time and was carried along by the narrative flow; when the film was over, I had no particular desire to leave the theater, and would happily have stayed another three hours. The two-hour limit on most films makes them essentially short stories. *The Best of Youth* is a novel.

The film is ambitious. It wants no less than to follow two brothers and the people in their lives from 1963 to 2000, following them from Rome to Norway to Turin to Florence to Palermo and back to Rome again. The lives intersect with the politics and history of Italy during the period: the hippies, the ruinous flood in Florence, the Red Brigades, kidnappings, hard times and layoffs at Fiat, and finally a certain peace for some of the characters, and for their nation.

The brothers are Nicola and Matteo Carati (Luigi Lo Cascio and Alessio Boni). We meet their parents, Angelo (Andrea Tidona) and Adriana (Adriana Asti), their older sister, Giovanna (Lidia Vitale), and their kid sister, Francesca (Valentina Carnelutti). And we meet their friends, their lovers, and others who drift through, including a mental patient whose life seems to follow in parallel.

As the film opens, Nicola has qualified as a doctor and Matteo is still taking literature classes. Matteo, looking for a job, has been hired as a "logotherapist"—literally, a person who takes mental patients for walks. One of the women he walks with is Giorgia (Jasmine Trinca), who is beautiful, deeply wounded by electroshock therapy, and afraid of the world. On the spur of the moment, Matteo decides to spring her from the institution and take her along when he and Nicola take a summer trip to the "end of the world," the tip of Norway.

Giorgia is found by the police, but has the presence of mind to protect the brothers. Nicola continues on his journey and gets a job as a lumberjack, and Matteo returns to Rome and, impulsively, joins the army. They are to meet again in Florence, where catastrophic floods have drowned the city. Nicola is a volunteer, Matteo is a soldier assigned to the emergency effort, and in the middle of the mud and ruins Nicola hears a young woman playing a piano that has been left in the middle of the street.

This is Giulia (Sonia Bergamasco). Their eyes meet and lock, and so do their destinies. They live together without marrying, and have a daughter, Sara. Giulia is drawn into a secret Red Brigade cell. She draws apart from her family. One night she packs to leave the house. He tries to block her way, then lets her go. She disappears into the terrorist underground.

Matteo meanwhile joins the police, takes an assignment in Sicily because no one else wants to go there, and meets a photographer in a café. This is Mirella (Maya Sansa). She wants to be a librarian, and he advises her to work at a beautiful library in Rome. Years later, he walks into the library and sees her for the second time in his life. They become lovers, but there is a great unexplained rage within Matteo, maybe also self-hatred, and he will not allow anyone very close.

Enough about the plot. These people, all of them, will meet again—even Giorgia, who is found by Nicola in the most extraordinary circumstances, and who will cause a meeting that no one in the movie could have anticipated, because neither person involved knows the other exists. Because of the length of the film, the director, Marco Tullio Giordana, has time and space to work with, and we get a tangible sense of the characters growing older, learning about themselves, dealing with hardship. The journey of Giulia, the radical, is the most difficult and in some ways the most touching. The way Nicola finally finds happiness is particularly satisfying because it takes him so long to realize that it is right there before him for the taking.

The film must have deep resonances for Italians, where it was made for national television; because of its politics, sexuality, and grown-up characters, it would be impossible

on American networks. It is not easy on Italy. As he is graduating from medical school, Nicola is advised by his professor: "Do you have any ambition? Then leave Italy. Go to London, Paris, America if you can. Italy is a beautiful country. But it is a place to die, run by dinosaurs." Nicola asks the professor why he stays. "I'm one of the dinosaurs."

Nicola stays. Another who stays is his brother-in-law, who is marked for kidnapping and assassination but won't leave, "because then they will have won." There is a scene where he stands in front of windows late at night and we feel real dread for him. With the politics and the personal drama there is also the sense of a nation that beneath the turbulent surface is deeply supportive of its citizens. Some of that is sensed through the lives of the parents of the Carati family: The father busies himself with optimistic schemes; the mother meets a grandchild who brings joy into her old age.

The film is being shown in two parts, three hours each, with separate admissions. You don't have to see both parts on the same day, but you may want to. It is a luxury to be enveloped in a good film, and to know there's a lot more of it—that it is not moving inexorably toward an ending you can anticipate, but moving indefinitely into a future that is free to be shaped in surprising ways. When you hear that it is six hours long, reflect that it is therefore also six hours deep.

Betrayal

R, 95 m., 1983

Jeremy Irons (Jerry), Ben Kingsley (Robert), Patricia Hodge (Emma). Directed by David Jones and produced by Sam Spiegel. Screenplay by Harold Pinter.

Love stories have beginnings, but affairs . . . affairs have endings, too. Even sad love stories begin in gladness, when the world is young and the future reaches out cheerfully forever. Then, of course, eventually you get Romeo and Juliet dead in the tomb, but that's the price you have to pay. Life isn't a free ride. Think how much *more* tragic a sad love story would be, however, if you could see into the future, so that even *this* moment, *this* kiss, is in the shadow of eventual despair.

The absolutely brilliant thing about *Betrayal* is that it is a love story told backward. There is a lot in this movie that is wonderful—the performances, the screenplay by Harold Pinter—but what makes it all work is the structure. When Pinter's stage version of *Betrayal* first appeared, back in the late 1970s, there was a tendency to dismiss his reverse chronology as a gimmick. Not so. It is the very heart and soul of this story. It means that we in the audience know more about the unhappy romantic fortunes of Jerry and Robert and Emma at *every moment* than they know about themselves. Even their joy is painful to see.

Jerry is a youngish London literary agent, clever, good-looking, confused about his feelings. Robert, his best friend, is a publisher. Robert is older, stronger, smarter, and more bitter. Emma is Robert's wife and becomes Jerry's lover. But that is telling the story chronologically. And the story begins at the end, with Robert and Emma fighting, and with Robert slapping her, and with Emma and Jerry meeting in a pub for a painful reunion two years after their affair is over. Each additional scene takes place further back in time, and the sections have uncanny titles: Two years earlier. Three years earlier. We aren't used to this. At a public preview of the film, some people in the audience actually *resisted* the backward timeframe, as if the purpose of the playwright was just to get on with the story, damn it all, and stop this confounded fooling around.

The *Betrayal* structure strips away all artifice. It shows, heartlessly, that the very capacity for love itself is sometimes based on betraying not only other loved ones, but even ourselves. The movie is told mostly in encounters between two of the characters; all three are not often on screen together, and we never meet Jerry's wife. These people are smart and they talk a lot—too much, maybe, because there is a peculiarly British reserve about them that sometimes prevents them from quite saying what they mean. They lie and they half-lie. There are universes left unspoken in their unfinished sentences. They are all a little embarrassed that the messy urges of sex are pumping away down there beneath their civilized deceptions.

The performances are perfectly matched.

Ben Kingsley (of *Gandhi*) plays Robert, the publisher, with such painfully controlled fury that there are times when he actually is frightening. Jeremy Irons, as Jerry, creates a man whose desires are stronger than his convictions, even though he spends a lot of time talking about his convictions, and almost none acknowledging his desires. Patricia Hodge, as Emma, loves them both and hates them both and would have led a much happier life if they had not been her two choices. But how could she know that when, in life, you're required by the rules to start at the beginning?

Better Luck Tomorrow

R, 98 m., 2003

Parry Shen (Ben), Jason Tobin (Virgil), Sung Kang (Han), Roger Fan (Daric), John Cho (Steve), Karin Anna Cheung (Stephanie). Directed by Justin Lin and produced by Lin, Ernesto M. Foronda, and Julie Asato. Screenplay by Lin, Foronda and Fabian Marquez.

Justin Lin's *Better Luck Tomorrow* has a hero named Benjamin, but depicts a chilling hidden side of suburban affluence that was unseen in *The Graduate*. Its heroes need no career advice; they're on the fast track to Ivy League schools and well-paying jobs, and their straight-A grades are joined on their résumés by an improbable array of extracurricular credits: Ben lists the basketball team, the academic decathlon team, and the food drive.

What he doesn't mention is the thriving business he and his friends have in selling cheat sheets. Or their drug sideline. Or the box hidden in his bedroom and filled with cash. Ben belongs to a group of overachieving Asian-American students in a wealthy Orange County suburb; they conform to the popular image of smart, well-behaved Asian kids, but although they have ambition they lack values, and step by step they move more deeply into crime. How deep is suggested by the film's opening scene, where Ben (Parry Shen) and his best friend, Virgil (Jason Tobin), are interrupted while sunbathing by the sound of a cell phone ringing on a body they have buried in Virgil's backyard.

Better Luck Tomorrow is a disturbing and skillfully told parable about growing up in today's America. These kids use money as a marker of success, are profoundly amoral, and project a wholesome, civic-minded attitude. They're on the right path to take jobs with the Enrons of tomorrow, in the dominant culture of corporate greed. Lin focuses on an ethnic group that is routinely praised for its industriousness, which deepens the irony, and also perhaps reveals a certain anger at the way white America patronizingly smiles on its successful Asian-American citizens.

Ben, Virgil, and their friends know how to use their ethnic identity to play both sides of the street in high school. "Our straight A's were our passports to freedom," Ben says in his narration. No parents are ever seen in the movie (there are very few adults, mostly played by white actors in roles reserved in most movies for minority groups). The kids get good grades, and their parents assume they are studying while they stay out late and get into very serious trouble.

Better Luck Tomorrow has all the obligatory elements of the conventional high school picture. Ben has a crush on the pretty cheerleader Stephanie Vandergosh (Karin Anna Cheung), but she dates Steve (John Cho), who plays the inevitable older teenager with a motorcycle and an attitude. Virgil is unlucky with girls, but thinks he once spotted Stephanie in a porno film (unlikely, but gee, it kinda looks like her). Han (Sung Kang) comes up with the scheme to sell homework for cash, and Daric (Roger Fan) is the overachiever who has, no doubt, the longest entry under his photo in the school yearbook.

These students never refer to, or are identified by, specific ethnic origin; they're known as the "Chinese Mafia" at school because of their low-key criminal activities, but that's not a name they give themselves. They may be Chinese, Japanese, Korean, Filipino, but their generation no longer obsesses with the nation before the hyphen; they are Orange County Americans, through and through, and although Stephanie's last name and Caucasian little brother indicate she was adopted, she brushes aside Ben's tentative question about her "real parents" by saying, "These are my real parents."

Better Luck Tomorrow is a coming-of-age film for Asian-Americans in American cinema. Like African-American films that take race for granted and get on with the characters and the

story, Lin is making a movie where race is not the point but simply the given. After Ben joins the basketball team, a writer for the high school paper suggests he is the "token Asian" benchwarmer, and when students form a cheering section for him, he quits the team in disgust. He is not a token anything (and privately knows he has beaten the NBA record for free throws).

The story is insidious in the way it moves stealthily into darker waters, while maintaining the surface of a high school comedy. There are jokes and the usual romantic breakthroughs and reversals, and the progress of their criminal careers seems unplanned and offhand, until it turns dangerous. I will not reveal the names of the key characters in the climactic scene, but note carefully what happens in terms of the story; perhaps the film is revealing that a bland exterior can hide seething resentment.

Justin Lin, who directed, cowrote, and coproduced, here reveals himself as a skilled and sure director, a rising star. His film looks as glossy and expensive as a mega-million studio production, and the fact that its budget was limited means that his cinematographer Patrice Lucien Cochet, his art director Yoo Jung Han, and the other members of his crew were very able and resourceful. It's one thing to get an expensive look with money, and another thing to get it with talent.

Lin keeps a sure hand on tricky material; he has obvious confidence about where he wants to go and how he wants to get there. His film is uncompromising, and doesn't chicken out with a U-turn ending. His actors expand and breathe as if they're captives just released from lesser roles (the audition reel of one actor, Lin recalls, showed him delivering pizzas in one movie after another). Parry Shen gives a watchful and wary undertone to his all-American boy, and Karin Anna Cheung finds the right note to deal with a boy she likes but finds a little too goody-goody. *Better Luck Tomorrow* is not just a thriller, not just a social commentary, not just a comedy or a romance, but all of those in a clearly seen, brilliantly made film.

The Big City

NO MPAA RATING, 122 m., 1963

Madhabi Mukherjee (Arati), Anil Chatterjee (Sobrata), Haradhan Banerjee (Mr. Mukherjee), Haren Chatterjee

(Father), Vicky Redwood (Edith Simmons), Java Bhaduri (Sister). Directed by Satyajit Ray and produced by R. D. Bansal. Screenplay by Ray.

The Big City, which has crept quietly into Chicago, is one of the most rewarding screen experiences of our time. I warmly encourage you to see it.

The power of this extraordinary film seems to come in equal parts from the serene narrative style of director Satyajit Ray and the sensitive performances of the cast members. At a time when we are engaged in the annual ritual of choosing our "best actress," it might be useful to see the performance of Madhabi Mukherjee in this film. She is a beautiful, deep, wonderful actress who simply surpasses all ordinary standards of judgment.

She plays Arati, a young housewife. The household consists of her husband (Anil Chatterjee), their children, and his parents. His salary as a bank clerk is not enough to go around, and after a great deal of thought, the couple decide that Arati must find a job. The parents react with shame; no self-respecting man should allow his wife to work. But times have changed.

Arati takes a job demonstrating a knitting machine. The job provides her first real contact with other social levels, and she learns with hesitation to use lipstick, wear dark glasses, and talk without shyness. But there are problems in the home that Ray handles with tact and humor. The old father declares "cold war" on his son and will not speak to him. The husband must reconcile his self-respect with his wife's new status as a breadwinner.

The remarkable thing that Ray accomplishes is to make us really deeply care about the fortunes of this simple family. We can see why it is necessary that the wife work, that the father be reconciled, that the husband and wife understand each other. By contrast, when *Our Man Flint* sets out to save the world from catastrophe it matters not at all, because we don't for a moment believe in Flint or his catastrophe.

That is why I have so much trouble approaching Ray's films as "foreign." They are not foreign. They are about Indians, and I am not Indian, but Ray's characters have more in common with me than I do with the comic-strip characters of Hollywood.

Ray's people have genuine emotions and ambitions, like the people next door and the people in Peoria and the people in Kansas City. There is not a person reading this review who would not identify immediately and deeply with the characters in *The Big City*.

By contrast, Hollywood films with exploding cigarette lighters and gasping starlets and idiot plots are the real "foreign" films. They have nothing at all in common with us, and Satyajit Ray of India understands us better than Jerry Lewis.

The Big Easy
R, 106 m., 1987

Dennis Quaid (Remy McSwain), Ellen Barkin (Anne Osborne), Ned Beatty (Jack Kellom), John Goodman (Andre De Soto), Lisa Jane Persky (McCabe), Ebbe Roe Smith (Ed Dodge), Tom O'Brien (Bobby McSwain), Charles Ludlam (Lamar Parmentel). Directed by Jim McBride and produced by Stephen Friedman. Screenplay by Daniel Petrie, Jr.

The Big Easy happens to be a great thriller. I say "happens," because I believe the plot of this movie is only an excuse for its real strength: the creation of a group of characters so interesting, so complicated, and so original that they make a lot of other movie people look like paint-by-number characters.

The movie takes place in New Orleans, that most mysterious of American cities, a city where you have the feeling you will never really know what goes on down those shadowy passages into those green and humid courtyards so guarded from the street. The heroes of the film are two law enforcement officials: Remy (Dennis Quaid), a homicide detective, and Anne (Ellen Barkin), a special prosecutor for the D.A. They meet after the death of a Mafia functionary, and of course they are immediately attracted to each other.

So far, no surprises. But when they go out to dinner and the restaurant owner won't think of accepting their money, Anne accuses Remy of being on the take and he accuses her of not understanding how the system operates. Later we learn more about the system in New Orleans and come to understand more about Remy. He is an honest cop in the ways that really count and a dishonest cop in small ways he has been able to rationalize. He doesn't have a problem, for example, with the department's illegal "widows and orphans fund," because he's using the money to send his kid brother through college.

There are more killings. There also is, between Anne and Remy, one of the most erotic love scenes I have ever seen in a movie—all the more erotic because the two lovers do not perform like champions in the sexual Olympics, but come to bed with all the insecurity of people who are almost afraid to believe it could, this time, be for real.

The background of their story is populated with characters so well-drawn and with character actors so finely chosen that the movie is fascinating from moment to moment, even when nothing much seems to be happening.

My favorite supporting performance in the movie is by Charles Ludlam, as a defense attorney, impeccable in his Panama hat and summer suit, talking a mile a minute in a shrill Cajun shriek, like a cross between Truman Capote and F. Lee Bailey. Another slick southerner is created by Ned Beatty, in his finest performance in years, as the police captain who sincerely wants to do the right thing and sincerely cannot.

All of these characters inhabit the most convincing portrait of New Orleans I've ever seen. The authentic local Cajun music on the sound track and the instinctive feel for the streets and alleys, the lives and the ways of doing business, the accents and the evasions, make the city itself into a participant in what happens.

In the middle of this riotous gumbo of colorful life, Quaid and Barkin construct a relationship that, by itself, would be enough for a whole movie. They love each other. They are disillusioned. They face each other as enemies in court. They eye each other warily in a wonderful scene at a fish boil and Cajun hootenanny thrown by Quaid's friends.

The movie indeed ends with the obligatory scene of climactic violence that is required in all thrillers, but it's well-handled and the actions at least do seem to be consistent with the characters.

The movie was directed by Jim McBride, whose previous film was *Breathless*, with Richard Gere, a high-style pastiche of 1940s crime movies and 1980s art direction. *The Big Easy* seems to be by a different man, a director not only in full mastery of his materials but in full sympathy with his characters. Forget it's a thriller. See it because you want to meet these people.

Big Night
R, 90 m., 1996

Stanley Tucci (Secondo), Tony Shalhoub (Primo), Isabella Rossellini (Gabriella), Ian Holm (Pascal), Minnie Driver (Phyllis). Directed by Campbell Scott and Stanley Tucci and produced by David Kirkpatrick. Screenplay by Joseph Tropiano and Tucci.

Big Night is one of the great food movies, and yet it is so much more. It is about food not as a subject but as a language—the language by which one can speak to gods, can create, can seduce, can aspire to perfection. There is a moment in the movie when a timpano is sliced open, and the audience sighs with simple delight.

The movie exists in the real world, where you can go broke selling great food. It tells the story of two brothers, recent immigrants to America, who run a restaurant named Paradise. The older brother, named Primo (Tony Shalhoub), is a genius as a chef. The younger brother, named Secondo (Stanley Tucci), knows it. Early in the film, Primo labors all day to create a perfect seafood risotto, but a customer complains she cannot find the seafood. Then she asks for spaghetti and meatballs as a side dish.

Primo is enraged. He will not serve two starches together. Nor will he put meatballs on spaghetti in any event. "She's a philistine!" he cries. "Maybe I put mashed potatoes for the other side!" Secondo, who is keenly aware that customers are rare, tries to placate him but keeps a certain distance: He respects Primo's talent.

Paradise, in any event, is going broke. The bank is foreclosing. Across the street, a man named Pascal (Ian Holm) runs an enormously successful Italian restaurant by giving his customers what they want. When Secondo appeals to him for advice and a loan, Pascal supplies his philosophy: "A guy works all day, he don't want to look at his plate and ask, 'What the - - - - is this?' He wants to look at his plate, see a steak, and say, 'I like steak!'" Pascal will not lend money, but he will do a favor. He is a personal friend of the great Italian-American singer Louis Prima and will arrange for Prima and his band to visit Paradise for a great meal. The visit will be reported in all the papers, business will pick up, and the restaurant will be saved.

Pascal will do this favor, it seems, out of the goodness of his heart. Although he doesn't know it, this is not the first favor he has done Secondo, who has been carrying on a secret affair with Pascal's mistress, Gabriella (Isabella Rossellini). Secondo's life is complicated; while he has steamy meetings with Gabriella, he conducts a more sedate relationship with Phyllis (Minnie Driver), his girlfriend, who has been waiting for a proposal and cannot understand Secondo's reluctance to declare his love.

Big Night sees all of these people with great fascination: It is truly interested in them as individuals. When Primo and Secondo are in the kitchen, for example, notice how absorbed they are in their professional and culinary conversations. They don't seem to be acting, and they don't seem to be in a scene; they seem utterly devoted to the business at hand. There is an unbroken shot in which one prepares a perfect omelet and serves it to the other, and we are left suspecting that anyone who can make a perfect omelet can pass almost any other test life has to offer.

There is a rich feeling to the neighborhood. We meet the baker, the priest, and the woman who sells flowers (Allison Janney). Primo has a crush on her but is very shy. He feeds her a lasagna and tells her, "To eat good food is to be close to God." We even meet the local Cadillac salesman (Campbell Scott), who represents the elusive goal of success, which is not merely to drive a Cadillac, but to drive next year's model this year.

The film ends with the big feast for Louis Prima. The restaurant is filled, and as the diners all wait for Prima to arrive, they begin to eat one magnificent course after another that Primo sends from his kitchen. As these dishes are presented and unveiled, the audience goes into a kind of reverie. I was reminded of other movies where food suggests the possibility of an ideal state: *Like Water for Chocolate, Ba-*

bette's Feast, and *Tampopo,* in which the whole universe is reflected in a perfect bowl of noodle soup.

The movie works smoothly and deeply to achieve its effects, which have to do with more than this night or this feast. The surprises in the plot involve not only secret romance but heartbreak and long-held frustration, for if genius is great, it is nevertheless not easy to be genius's brother. By the end of the movie, we have been through an emotional and a sensual wringer, in a film of great wisdom and delight.

Big Night was written by Joseph Tropiano and Stanley Tucci, and codirected by Tucci and Campbell Scott. Tucci and Scott are familiar from many other roles (Tucci has starred in independent films and in the first season of TV's *Murder One;* Scott was Robert Benchley, Dorothy Parker's lover, in *Mrs. Parker and the Vicious Circle*). To some degree this film must represent a break for them: They have been in good movies before, but not enough of them, and it is said Tucci began working on *Big Night* while making a film he hated.

Now here is their labor of love. Their perfect risotto. They include just what is needed and nothing else. Watching it, I reflected how many Hollywood movies these days seem to come with a side order of spaghetti and meatballs. And mashed potatoes.

The Birds, the Bees, and the Italians
NO MPAA RATING, 115 m., 1967

Virna Lisi (Milena Zulian), Gastore Moschin (Osvaldo Bisigato), Nora Ricci (Gilda Bisigato), Albero Lionello (Toni Gasparini), Olga Villi (Ippolita Gasparini), Franco Fabrizi (Lino Benedetti), Beba Loncar (Noemi Castellan), Gigi Ballista (Giacinto Castellan). Directed by Pietro Germi. Screenplay by Age Scarpelli, Luciano Vincenoni, and Germi.

The Italian marriage has been under steady assault by Pietro Germi for five years now, since his *Divorce—Italian Style* concluded ever so logically that murder was easier and more convenient than divorce. Especially since Italy doesn't permit divorce, but if a man should happen to murder his wife while she was in her lover's arms, well, how could a jury hold that against him?

Germi starts with opinions that every self-respecting Italian shares and then slyly pushes them to their logical outcome. Although *Divorce—Italian Style* is his best-known movie (and inspired almost as many imitations as *Mondo Cane*), his next movie was better. *Seduced and Abandoned* was about a young man who got his girlfriend in the family way and then refused to marry her, because how could any self-respecting Italian marry a woman who, etc., etc.

Now comes Germi's third film on this theme, *The Birds, the Bees, and the Italians*. He branches out. He makes fun of Italian attitudes toward marriage, divorce, chastity, and—incidentally—love. He also demolishes the courts, the police, the church, the family, and the state, leaving no sacred cow unmilked. And he does it at a frantic pace. Nobody ever seems to stand still; every shot opens with somebody already in motion.

There are three stories in the film. The first is about a doctor of whom it is said: "How can I trust a doctor who is always laughing?" The doctor finds it especially hilarious when a patient complains that he is temporarily impotent. But it isn't so funny when the doctor's wife plays Bonnie to his Clyde.

The second, and longest, segment involves a bank clerk (Gastore Moschin) who falls helplessly in love with Virna Lisi, as who wouldn't? But he refuses to observe Italian conventions and make her his mistress. Instead, he abandons his nagging wife and ugly children and goes dancing in the streets proclaiming his love. Society is outraged.

In the third segment, the leading citizens of the town become involved with a lush young peasant girl who, alas, turns out to be under sixteen. The leading citizens join with the other leading citizens in rejoicing that justice will be done and even leading citizens are not immune to it. Meanwhile, they bribe the girl's father to drop the charges.

Germi's films are filled with sheer love of movement and action and could be described as slapstick if they were not written so tightly and aimed so directly at satirical targets. *The Birds, etc.* (which won the grand award at Cannes) is his best and enhances his reputation as an inspired practitioner of film comedy.

Birdy

R, 120 m., 1985

Nicolas Cage (Al), Matthew Modine (Birdy). Directed by Alan Parker and produced by Alan Marshall. Screenplay by Sandy Kroopf and Jack Behr.

The strangest thing about *Birdy*, which is a very strange and beautiful movie indeed, is that it seems to work best at its looniest level, and is least at ease with the things it takes most seriously. You will not discover anything new about war in this movie, but you will find out a whole lot about how it feels to be in love with a canary.

The movie is about two friends from South Philadelphia. One of them, Al, played by Nicolas Cage, is a slick romeo with a lot of self-confidence and a way with the women. The other, nicknamed Birdy (Matthew Modine), is goofy, withdrawn, and absolutely fascinated with birds. As kids, they are inseparable friends. In high school, they begin to grow apart, separated by their individual quests for two different kinds of birds. But they still share adventures, as Birdy hangs upside down from elevated tracks to capture pigeons, or constructs homemade wings that he hopes will let him fly. Then the war comes. Both boys serve in Vietnam and both are wounded. Cage's face is disfigured, and he wears a bandage to cover the scars. Modine's wounds are internal: He withdraws entirely into himself and stops talking. He spends long, uneventful days perched in his room at a mental hospital, head cocked to one side, looking up longingly at a window, like nothing so much as a caged bird.

Because *Birdy* is not told in chronological order, the story takes some time to sort itself out. We begin with an agonizing visit by the Cage character to his friend Birdy. He hopes to draw him out of his shell. But Birdy makes no sign of recognition. Then, in flashbacks, we see the two lives that led up to this moment. We see the adventures they shared, the secrets, the dreams. Most importantly, we go inside Birdy's life and begin to glimpse the depth of his obsession with birds. His room turns into a birdcage. His special pets—including a cocky little yellow canary—take on individual characteristics for us. We can begin to understand that his love for birds is sensual, romantic, passionate. There is a wonderful scene where he brushes his fingers against a feather, showing how marvelously it is constructed, and how beautifully.

Most descriptions of *Birdy* tend to dwell on what seems to be the central plot, the story of the two buddies who go to Vietnam and are wounded, and about how one tries to help the other return to the real world. I felt that the war footage in the movie was fairly routine, and that the challenge of dragging Birdy back to reality was a good deal less interesting than the story of how he arrived at the strange, secret place in his mind. I have seen other, better, movies about war, but I have never before seen a character quite like Birdy.

As you may have already guessed, *Birdy* doesn't sound like a commercial blockbuster. More important are the love and care for detail that have gone into it from all hands, especially from Cage and Modine. They have two immensely difficult roles, and both are handicapped in the later scenes by being denied access to some of an actor's usual tools; for Cage, his face; for Modine, his whole human persona. They overcome those limitations to give us characters even more touching than the ones they started with.

The movie was directed by Alan Parker. Consider this list of his earlier films: *Bugsy Malone, Fame, Midnight Express, Shoot the Moon, Pink Floyd: The Wall*. Each one coming out of an unexpected place, and avoiding conventional movie genres. He was the man to direct *Birdy*, which tells a story so unlikely that perhaps even my description of it has discouraged you—and yet a story so interesting it is impossible to put this movie out of my mind.

Black Hawk Down

R, 143 m., 2002

Josh Hartnett (Eversmann), Ewan McGregor (Grimes), Tom Sizemore (McKnight), Eric Bana (Hoot), William Fichtner (Sanderson), Ewen Bremner (Nelson), Sam Shepard (Garrison), Gabriel Casseus (Kurth), Kim Coates (Wex). Directed by Ridley Scott and produced by Jerry Bruckheimer and Scott. Screenplay by Ken Nolan and Steve Zaillian, based on the book by Mark Bowden.

Ridley Scott's *Black Hawk Down* tells the story of a U.S. military raid that went disastrously wrong when optimistic plans ran into unexpected resistance. In Mogadishu, Somalia, in October 1993, eighteen Americans lost their lives, seventy more were wounded, and within days President Bill Clinton pulled out troops that were on a humanitarian mission. By then some 300,000 Somalians had died of starvation, and the U.S. purpose was to help deliver UN food shipments. Somalian warlords were more interested in protecting their turf than feeding their people—an early warning of the kind of zeal that led to September 11.

The movie is single-minded in its purpose. It wants to record as accurately as possible what it was like to be one of the soldiers under fire on that mission. Hour by hour, step by step, it reconstructs the chain of events. The plan was to stage a surprise raid by helicopter-borne troops, joined by ground forces, on a meeting of a warlord's top lieutenants. This was thought to be such a straightforward task that some soldiers left behind their canteens and night vision gear, expecting to be back at the base in a few hours. It didn't work out that way.

What happened is that enemy rockets brought down two of the helicopters. The warlord's troops gathered quickly and surrounded the U.S. positions. Roadblocks and poor communications prevented a support convoy from approaching. And a grim firefight became a war of attrition. The Americans gave better than they got, but from any point of view the U.S. raid was a catastrophe. The movie's implied message was that America on that day lost its resolve to risk American lives in distant and obscure struggles, and that mind-set weakened our stance against terrorism.

The engagement itself seems to have degenerated into bloody chaos. Ridley Scott's achievement is to render it comprehensible to the audience. We understand, more or less, where the Americans are, and why, and what their situation is. We follow several leading characters, but this is not a star-driven project and doesn't depend on dialogue or personalities. It is about the logistics of that day in October, and how training did help those expert fighters (Army Rangers and Delta Force) to defend themselves as well as possible when all the plans went wrong and they were left hanging out to dry.

His longest day begins with a briefing by Major General William F. Garrison (Sam Shepard), who explains how intelligence has discovered the time and location of a meeting by lieutenants of the warlord Mohamed Farah Aidid. A taxi with a white cross on its roof will park next to the building to guide the airborne troops, who will drop down on ropes, be joined by ground forces, secure the building, and take prisoners. The problem with this plan, as Garrison discovers in steadily more discouraging feedback, is that the opposition is better armed, better positioned, and able to call on quick reinforcements.

We follow several stories. A man falls from a helicopter and is injured when he misses his descent rope. A pilot is taken prisoner. Desperate skirmishes unfold in streets and rubble as darkness falls. The Americans are short on ammo and water, facing enemies not particularly shy about exposing themselves to danger.

Black Hawk Down doesn't have heroic foreground figures like most war movies. The leading characters are played by stars who will be familiar to frequent moviegoers, but may be hard to tell apart for others. They include Josh Hartnett, much more convincing here than in *Pearl Harbor*, as a staff sergeant in command of one of the raiding teams; Ewan McGregor as a Ranger specialist whose specialties are paperwork and coffee making until he is pressed into service; Tom Sizemore as a veteran who provides steady counsel for younger troops; and William Fichtner as a fighter who seems to have internalized every shred of training, and embodies it instinctively.

The cinematography by Slawomir Idziak avoids the bright colors of upbeat combat movies, and its drab, dusty tones gradually drain of light as night falls. The later scenes of the movie feel chilly and forlorn; the surrounded troops are alone and endangered in the night. The screenplay by Ken Nolan and Steve Zaillian, working from a book by Mark Bowden, understands the material and tells it so clearly and efficiently that we are involved not only in the experience of the day but also in its strategies and unfolding realities.

Films like this are more useful than gung ho capers like *Behind Enemy Lines*. They help audiences understand and sympathize with the actual experiences of combat troops, instead of trivializing them into entertainments. Although the American mission in Somalia was humanitarian, the movie avoids speechmaking and sloganeering, and at one point, discussing why soldiers risk their lives in situations like this, a veteran says, "It's about the men next to you. That's all it is."

The Black Stallion

G, 120 m., 1980

Kelly Reno (Alec Ramsey), Mickey Rooney (Henry Dailey), Teri Garr (Alec's Mother), Clarence Muse (Snoe), Hoyt Axton (Alec's Father), Michael Higgins (Neville). The black stallion is portrayed by Cassole, owned by San Antonio Arabians. Directed by Carroll Ballard and produced by Francis Ford Coppola, Fred Roos, and Tom Sternberg. Screenplay by Melissa Mathison, Jeanne Rosenberg and William D. Wittliff.

The first half of *The Black Stallion* is so gloriously breathtaking that the second half, the half with all the conventional excitement, seems merely routine. We've seen the second half before—the story of the kid, the horse, the veteran trainer, and the big race. But the first hour of this movie belongs among the great filmgoing experiences. It is described as an epic, and earns the description.

The film opens at sea, somewhere in the Mediterranean, forty or so years ago, on board a ship inhabited by passengers who seem foreign and fearsome to a small boy. They drink, they gamble, they speak in foreign tongues, they wear caftans and beards and glare ferociously at anyone who comes close to their prize possession, a magnificent black stallion.

The boy and his father are on board this ship for reasons never explained. The father gambles with the foreigners and the boy roams the ship and establishes a shy rapport with the black stallion, and then a great storm sweeps over the ocean and the ship catches fire and is lost. The boy and the stallion are thrown free, into the boiling sea. The horse somehow saves the boy, and in the calm of the next morning they both find themselves thrown onto a deserted island.

THE BLAIR WITCH PROJECT ★ ★ ★ ★ 85

This sequence—the storm, the ship's sinking, the ordeal at sea—is a triumphant use of special effects, miniature models, back projection, editing, and all the tricks of craft that go into the filming of a fantasy. The director, Carroll Ballard, used the big water tank at Cinecitta Studios in Rome for the storm sequences; a model ship, looking totally real, burns and sinks headfirst, its propellers churning slowly in the air, while the horse and boy struggle in the foreground.

The horse in this film (its name is Cassole) is required to perform as few movie horses ever have. But its finest scene is the quietest one, and takes place on the island a few days after the shipwreck. Ballard and his cinematographer, Caleb Deschanel, have already established the mood of the place, with gigantic, quiet, natural panoramas. The boy tries to spear a fish. The horse roams restlessly from the beaches to the cliffs. And then, in a single shot that is held for a long time, Ballard shows us the boy inviting the horse to eat out of his hand.

It is crucial here that this action be seen in a *single* shot; lots of short cuts, edited together, would simply be the filmmakers at work. But the one uninterrupted shot, with the horse at one edge of the screen and the boy at the other, and the boy's slow approach, and the horse's skittish advances and retreats, shows us a rapport between the human and the animal that's strangely moving.

All these scenes of the boy and horse on the island are to be treasured, especially a montage photographed underwater and showing the legs of the two as they splash in the surf. There are also wonderfully scary sequences, such as one in which the boy awakens to find a poisonous snake a few feet away from him on the sand. This scene exploits the hatred and fear horses have for snakes, and is cut together into a terrifically exciting climax.

But then, as all good things must, the idyll on the island comes to an end. The boy and the horse are rescued. And it's here that the film, while still keeping our interest, becomes more routine. The earlier passages of the film were amazing to look at (they were shot, with great difficulty and beauty, on Sardinia). Now we're back to earth again, with scenes shot around an old racetrack in Toronto.

And we've seen the melodramatic materials of the movie's second half many times before. The boy is reunited with his mother, the horse returns home with him, and the boy meets a wise old horse trainer who admits that, yes, that Arabian *can* run like the wind—but the fool thing doesn't have any papers. The presence of Mickey Rooney, who plays the trainer, is welcome but perhaps too familiar. Rooney has played this sort of role so often before (most unforgettably in *National Velvet*) that he almost seems to be visiting from another movie. His Academy Award nomination for the performance is probably a recognition of that.

Still, the melodrama is effective. Everything depends on the outcome of the big race at the film's end. The young boy, of course, is the jockey (the Elizabeth Taylor role, so to speak). Ballard and Deschanel are still gifted at finding a special, epic look for the movie; one especially good scene has the stallion racing against time, in the dark before dawn, in the rain.

The Black Stallion is a wonderful experience at the movies. The possibility remains, though, that in these cynical times it may be avoided by some viewers because it has a G rating—and G movies are sometimes dismissed as being too innocuous. That's sure not the case with this film, which is rated G simply because it has no nudity, profanity, or violence—but it does have terrific energy, beauty, and excitement. It's not a children's movie; it's for adults *and* for kids.

The Blair Witch Project

R, 88 m., 1999

Heather Donahue (Heather), Joshua Leonard (Josh), Michael Williams (Mike). Directed and edited by Eduardo Sanchez and Daniel Myrick. Screenplay by Sanchez and Myrick. Produced by Gregg Hale and Robin Cowie.

We're instinctively afraid of natural things (snakes, barking dogs, the dark), but have to be taught to fear walking into traffic or touching an electrical wire. Horror films that tap into our hard-wired instinctive fears probe a deeper place than movies with more sophisticated threats. A villain is only an actor, but a shark is more than a shark.

The Blair Witch Project, an extraordinarily effective horror film, knows this and uses it. It has no fancy special effects or digital monsters, but its characters get lost in the woods, hear noises in the night, and find disturbing stick figures hanging from trees. One of them discovers slime on his backpack. Because their imaginations have been inflamed by talk of witches, hermits, and child-murderers in the forest, because their food is running out and their smokes are gone, they (and we) are a lot more scared than if they were merely being chased by some guy in a ski mask.

The movie is like a celebration of rock-bottom production values—of how it doesn't take bells and whistles to scare us. It's presented in the form of a documentary. We learn from the opening titles that in 1994 three young filmmakers went into a wooded area in search of a legendary witch: "A year later, their footage was found." The film's style and even its production strategy enhance the illusion that it's a real documentary. The characters have the same names as the actors. All of the footage in the film was shot by two cameras—a color video camcorder operated by the director, Heather (Heather Donahue), and a 16mm black-and-white camera operated by the cameraman, Josh (Joshua Leonard). Mike (Michael Williams) does the sound. All three carry backpacks and are prepared for two or three nights of sleeping in tents in the woods. It doesn't work out that way.

The buried structure of the film, which was written and directed by Eduardo Sanchez and Daniel Myrick, is insidious in the way it introduces information without seeming to. Heather and her crew arrive in the small town of Burkittsville ("formerly Blair") and interview locals. Many have vaguely heard of the Blair witch and other ominous legends; one says, "I think I saw a documentary on the Discovery Channel or something."

We hear that children have been killed in the woods, that bodies have disappeared, that strange things happened at Coffin Rock. But the movie wisely doesn't present this information as if it can be trusted; it's gossip, legend and lore, passed along half-jokingly by local people, and Heather, Josh, and Mike view it as good footage, not a warning.

Once they get into the woods, the situation gradually turns ominous. They walk in circles. Something happens to their map. Nature itself begins to seem oppressive and dead. They find ominous signs. Bundles of twigs. Unsettling stick figures. These crude objects are scarier than more elaborate effects; they look like they were created by a being who haunts the woods, not by someone playing a practical joke. Much has been said about the realistic cinematography—how every shot looks like it was taken by a hand-held camera in the woods (as it was). But the visuals are not just a technique. By shooting in a chill season, by dampening the color palette, the movie makes the woods look unfriendly and desolate; nature is seen as a hiding place for dread secrets.

As fear and desperation grow, the personalities of the characters emerge. "We agreed to a scouted-out project!" one guy complains, and the other says, "Heather, this is *so* not cool!" Heather keeps up an optimistic front; the woods are not large enough to get lost in, she argues, because "this is America. We've destroyed most of our natural resources." Eventually her brave attitude disintegrates into a remarkable shot in which she films her own apology (I was reminded of Scott's notebook entries as he froze to death in Antarctica).

At a time when digital techniques can show us almost anything, *The Blair Witch Project* is a reminder that what really scares us is the stuff we can't see. The noise in the dark is almost always scarier than what makes the noise in the dark. Any kid can tell you that. Not that he believes it at the time.

Blazing Saddles
R, 93 m., 1974

Cleavon Little (Bart), Gene Wilder (Jim, the Waco Kid), Slim Pickens (Taggart), David Huddleston (Olson Johnson), Liam Dunn (Rev. Johnson), Alex Karras (Mongo). Directed by Mel Brooks and produced by Michael Hertzberg. Screenplay by Brooks.

There are some people who literally can get away with anything—say anything, do anything—and people will let them. Other people attempt a mildly dirty joke and bring total silence down on a party. Mel Brooks is not only a member of the first group, he is its lifetime president. At its best, his comedy operates in areas so far removed from taste that (to coin his own expression) it rises below vulgarity.

Blazing Saddles is like that. It's a crazed grab bag of a movie that does everything to keep us laughing except hit us over the head with a rubber chicken. Mostly, it succeeds. It's an audience picture; it doesn't have a lot of classy polish and its structure is a total mess. But of course! What does that matter while Alex Karris is knocking a horse cold with a right cross to the jaw?

The movie is, among other things, a comedy Western. The story line, which is pretty shaky, involves some shady land speculators who need to run a railroad through Ridge Rock and decide to drive the residents out. The last thing they want there is law and order, so the crooks send in a black sheriff (Cleavon Little), figuring the townspeople will revolt.

Well, they almost do, but the sheriff (Black Bart is his name, of course) wins them over and signs up a drunken sharpshooter (Gene Wilder) as his deputy. Meanwhile . . . but what am I saying, meanwhile? Meanwhile, six dozen other things happen. The townspeople decide to stay and make a stand, even though, as the preacher intones, "Our women have been stampeded and our cattle raped." Bart rejects the advances of a man-killing woman who has been sicced on him (Madeline Kahn as Marlene Dietrich—Lili von Shtupp), and the people build a dummy town and lure the bad guys into it.

One of the hallmarks of Brooks's movie humor has been his willingness to embrace excess. In his *The Producers,* one of the funniest movies ever made, we got the immortal "Springtime for Hitler" production number, and Zero Mostel seducing little old ladies in the bushes, and Gene Wilder (again) choreographed with the Lincoln Center water fountain. Brooks's *The Twelve Chairs,* not as funny, still had such great scenes as Brooks himself as an obsequious serf clinging to his master's leg.

And *Blazing Saddles* is like that from beginning to end, except for a couple of slow stretches. The baked bean scene alone qualifies the movie for some sort of Wretched Excess award. Then there's the whole business of Mongo (Alex Karras) who is a kind of dimwitted Paul Bunyan. He rides into town on an ox, sent to eliminate Bart, but is seduced by a black powder bomb in a candygram. It would take too long to explain.

One of the criticisms of *The Producers* was that it took too long to end after "Springtime for Hitler." Determined that *Blazing Saddles* wouldn't end slowly, Brooks has provided for it a totally uninhibited Hollywood fantasy that includes a takeoff on *Top Hat,* a scene at Graumann's Chinese Theater, a pie fight, and, of course, a final fadeout into the sunset.

Bleak Moments
NO MPAA RATING, 111 m., 1971

Anne Raitt (Sylvia), Eric Allan (Peter), Joolia Cappleman (Pat), Ronald Eng (Waiter), Mike Bradwell (Norman), Sarah Stephenson (Hilda). Directed by Mike Leigh and produced by Leslie Blair. Screenplay by Leigh.

There is a new kind of movie emerging in the 1970s that considers, with almost frightening perceptiveness, the ways people really behave toward each other. No other art form is better suited to such subject matter than the movies; plays don't let us get close enough, and novels try to describe things that can only be seen. But these new movies—with their attention to the smallest nuances of human behavior—are scary because they tell us so much about ourselves.

These new movies—I don't have a name for them—are interested in the ways that body language and the territorial imperative operate in human relationships. Most of us don't walk into a saloon like John Wayne or drink a beer like Karen Black, but we do have a set of personal responses and cues that let other people know how to react to us. We have the cues, and we read the cues of others.

Until last week, I had seen only one movie that I felt was completely successful in this new way of telling a story: Eric Rohmer's *My Night at Maud's.* That was a film in which an entire personal drama (between two people who did, or did not, want to make love to each other, at various moments) was told, not in words, but in the ways the characters acted toward each other. Many of their words, in fact, were an evasion of the situation—but Rohmer was able to give us the words to show the evasion.

Now I have seen another film I would place in this category: Mike Leigh's *Bleak Moments*. It is a first film by a young British director who exhibits in every scene a complete mastery of the kind of characterization he is attempting.

This film is a masterpiece, plain and simple, and that is a statement I doubt I will ever have cause to revise. But it is probably not going to appeal to a majority of filmgoers. I still remember the many letters I received—some of them very sincere and thoughtful—asking me why on earth I had praised Rohmer's *My Night at Maud's* and *Claire's Knee.* I had tried to describe the very personal appeal those films had to me, and the ways in which they were different from ordinary cinema; but that is always hard because people still instinctively expect an "advanced" film to be not so very advanced, and they hope to be entertained in the conventional way.

Bleak Moments (the title is awfully apt) is not entertaining in any conventional way. This is not to say for a moment that it is boring or difficult to watch; on the contrary, it is impossible not to watch. After its advance screening, one of my critical colleagues offered an opinion that I suspect may be widespread: "I was riveted to the screen. I could not stop watching the movie. But I could never sit through it again."

I could sit through it again and again, but I understand my colleague's feelings. This movie deals so basically with the pain and utter frustration of life that we may, after all, find it too much to take. Its greatness is not just in direction or subject, but in the complete singularity of the performances. There have never been performances just like this before in the movies; Anne Raitt and Eric Allan have scenes together that are so good, and painful, you find yourself afraid to breathe for fear they will step wrong. They never do.

The movie is about Sylvia (Raitt), a woman who works in an office and comes home at night to care for her sister, who is twenty-nine years old and mentally retarded. Sylvia's best friend at the office is a girl named Pat (Joolia Cappleman), who lives with her invalid mother. Sylvia is a beautiful woman in an austere, gray-eyed, very level and quiet way. She projects intelligence and a cynical amusement about her life and fate; Leigh is good at painting his characters with short, perfectly sculpted scenes, and we feel we know Sylvia after a scene in which she sits in a mussy room, drinks cream sherry, and pages through a book. She isn't an alcoholic; it's just that one might as well drink some sherry in the evening if one is going to feel bloody awful otherwise.

Into Sylvia's life one week come two men. One is a teacher she knows slightly. He asks her out to dinner on a Saturday, and she accepts. The other is a painfully inarticulate hippie, totally awash in his own feelings of self-worthlessness, who comes to run the mimeograph machine after Sylvia's garage is rented by an underground magazine.

Sylvia is the kind of woman, we sense, who has deep wells of humor, of intelligence, of generous and demanding erotic needs. She is not a spinster; she is a captive. The teacher, Peter (Allan), has needs too, and they are as desperate as he is incapable of fulfilling them.

In a situation of authority, he can cope through habit and an acquired manner; at Sylvia's house, he puts down the hippie by treating him as the failed schoolboy he (in fact) happens to be. But Peter cannot cope with women, or anything else that offers a challenge. He clearly feels Sylvia is above him, and he is paralyzed by shyness when he is around her. He can hardly speak. He phrases his words so painfully and doubles back so often in his sentences that what comes out is a kind of apologetic gibberish.

And what is Sylvia to do? As played by Raitt, she is a person who has come to contain her passions within a reserved manner. On their dinner date, they have a painful and (for Peter) humiliating experience with a rude Chinese waiter. This scene, like many in the film, has a great deal of buried humor: We want to cry, and laugh. Then they go back to her apartment, and sit, and sit, and Sylvia drinks sherry and tries to tempt Peter to unwind a little. He never quite does.

This scene in Sylvia's living room, which runs for quite a long time, is the best thing in its line since the celebrated bedroom scene in *My Night at Maud's.* Sylvia clearly wants Peter to do something, but he cannot. God, does he want to! She sits on her couch and subtly uses her body and her face and voice to try to lure him across the room by erotic magnetism, but he will not respond.

The scene is one of the sexiest I can remember; sometimes the repression of passion is more erotic than its immediate fulfillment. What's going on in that room between those two people is as charged with desire—and the anger that frustrated desire can turn into—as anything in the labyrinthine sexual evasion of characters by Henry James.

And then there is a moment: Peter has finally taken a sip from his glass, and Sylvia crosses the room to refill it. But he wants no more. No matter; she fills it to the very brim and looks down at him. "Well, what are you going to do about it?" she says (for now he will have to drink it or spill it). "Hold it as steadily as I can," he says. The buried mutual aggression in this scene is as violent in its way as the farthest reaches of Peckinpah.

Raitt's performance is one of the best I have ever seen. Her role is so tremendously difficult. She has got to let us know everything about her without ever once losing control. Her surface remains unbroken; her manner is most often impassive, or conventionally polite, or kind. But we are somehow inside her mind, understanding how she feels about her sister, her friends, her fate. Sylvia's magnificent personality is trapped inside that desperate life, and Raitt achieves one of the most difficult things an actress can do in convincing us of that fact without ever seeming to try to.

I've never heard of Mike Leigh or his actors before. I don't know where they came from, or what pools of human experience they were able to draw from. And I suspect that the sheer intensity of *Bleak Moments* may prevent it from getting a wide audience. Indeed, this particular story could never have been told in such a way as to appeal to everybody.

It is the task of film festivals to find films like this and give them a showing so they can survive and prevail. The 1972 Chicago festival has been filled with movies worth seeing and remembering. But if it had given us only *Bleak Moments*, it would have sufficiently exercised its mission.

Blood Simple

R, 96 m., 1985

John Getz (Ray), Frances McDormand (Abby), Dan Hedaya (Julian Marty), M. Emmet Walsh (Loren Visser), Samm-Art Williams (Meurice). Directed by Joel Coen and produced by Ethan Coen. Screenplay by Coen and Coen.

A lot has been written about the visual style of *Blood Simple*, but I think the appeal of the movie is more elementary. It keys into three common nightmares: (1) You clean and clean, but there's still blood all over the place; (2) You know you have committed a murder, but you are not sure quite how or why; (3) You know you have forgotten a small detail that will eventually get you into a lot of trouble. *Blood Simple* mixes those fears and guilts into an incredibly complicated plot, with amazingly gory consequences. It tells a story in which every individual detail seems to make sense, and every individual choice seems logical, but the choices and details form a bewildering labyrinth in which there are times when even the murderers themselves don't know who they are.

Because following the plot is one of this movie's most basic pleasures, I will not reveal too much. The movie begins with a sleazy backwoods bar owner's attempt to hire a scummy private detective to murder his wife. The private eye takes the money and then pulls a neat double-cross, hoping to keep the money and eliminate the only witness who could implicate him. Neat. And then it *really* gets complicated.

The movie has been shot with a lot of style, some of it self-conscious, but deliberately so. One of the pleasures in a movie like this is enjoying the low-angle and tilt shots that draw attention to themselves, that declare themselves as being part of a movie. The movie does something interesting with its timing, too. It begins to feel inexorable. Characters think they know what has happened; they turn out to be wrong; they pay the consequences, and it all happens while the movie is marching from scene to scene like an implacable professor of logic, demonstrating one fatal error after another.

Blood Simple was directed by Joel Coen, produced by his brother, Ethan, and written by the two of them. It's their first film, and has the high energy and intensity we associate with young filmmakers who are determined to make an impression. Some of the scenes are virtuoso, including a sequence in which a dead body becomes extraordinarily hard to dispose of, and another one in which two people in adjacent rooms are trapped in the same violent showdown. The central performance in the movie is by the veteran character actor M. Emmet Walsh, who plays the private eye like a man for whom idealism is a dirty word. The other actors in the movie are all effective, but they are obscured, in a way, by what happens to them: This movie weaves such a bloody web that the characters are upstaged by their dilemmas.

Is the movie fun? Well, that depends on you. It is violent, unrelenting, absurd, and fiendishly clever. There is a cliché I never use: "Not for the squeamish." But let me put it this way. *Blood Simple* may make you squeam.

Blow Out

R, 107 m., 1981

John Travolta (Jack), Nancy Allen (Sally), John Lithgow (Burke), Dennis Franz (Manny Karp), Peter Boydon (Sam), Curt May (Donohue). Directed by Brian De Palma and produced by George Litto. Screenplay by De Palma.

There are times when *Blow Out* resembles recent American history trapped in the "Twilight Zone." Episodes are hauntingly familiar, and yet seem slightly askew. What if the "grassy knoll" recordings from the police radio in Dallas had been crossed with Chappaquiddick and linked to Watergate? What if Jack Ruby had been a private eye specializing in divorce cases? What if Abraham Zapruder—the man who took the home movies of President John F. Kennedy's death—had been a sound-effects man? And what if Judith Exner—remember her?—had been working with Ruby? These are some of the inspirations out of which Brian De Palma constructs *Blow Out*, a movie which continues his practice of making cross-references to other movies, other directors, and actual historical events, and which nevertheless is his best and most original work.

The title itself, of course, reminds us of *Blow Up*, the 1966 film by Michelangelo Antonioni in which a photographer saw, or thought he saw, a murder—and went mad while obsessively analyzing his photographs

of the "crime." *Was* there a dead body to be found on that fuzzy negative? Was there even such a thing as reality? In *Blow Out*, John Travolta plays the character who confronts these questions. He's a sound man for a sleazy Philadelphia B-movie factory. He works on cheap, cynical exploitation films. Late one night, while he's standing on a bridge recording owls and other night sounds, he becomes a witness to an accident. A car has a blowout, swerves off a bridge, and plunges into a river. Travolta plunges in after it, rescues a girl inside (Nancy Allen), and later discovers that the car's drowned driver was a potential presidential candidate. Still later, reviewing his sound recording of the event, Travolta becomes convinced that he can hear a gunshot just before the blowout. Was the accident actually murder? He traces down Nancy Allen, discovers that she was part of a blackmail plot against the candidate, and then comes across the trail of a slimy private eye (Dennis Franz) who wanted to cause a blowout, all right, but didn't figure on anybody getting killed.

The plot thickens beautifully. De Palma doesn't have just a handful of ideas to spin out to feature length. He has an abundance. We meet a gallery of violent characters, including Burke (John Lithgow), a dirty-tricks specialist who seems inspired by G. Gordon Liddy. The original crime is complicated by a series of other murders, designed to lay a false trail and throw the police off the scent of political conspiracy.

Meanwhile, the Travolta character digs deeper. For him, it's a matter of competence, of personal pride. Arguing with a cop about his tapes, Travolta denies that he's just imagining things: "I'm a *sound* man!" He stumbles across a series of photos of the fatal accident. In a brilliantly crafted sequence, we follow every step as he assembles the film and his recording into a movie of the event, doggedly extracting what seem to be facts from what looks like chaos.

De Palma's visual images in *Blow Out* invite comparison to many Alfred Hitchcock films, and indeed De Palma invited such comparisons when the posters for *Dressed to Kill* described him as "Master of the Macabre." In *Blow Out* there are such Hitchcock hallmarks as a shower scene (played this time for laughs rather than for the chills of *Dressed to Kill*), several grisly murders in unexpected surroundings, violence in public places, and a chase through Philadelphia on the anniversary of the ringing of the Liberty Bell. This last extended chase sequence reminds us of two Hitchcock strategies: His juxtaposition of patriotic images and espionage, as in *North by Northwest* and *Saboteur,* and his desperate chases through uncaring crowds, reminders of *Foreign Correspondent* and *Strangers on a Train.*

But *Blow Out* stands by itself. It reminds us of the violence of *Dressed to Kill,* the startling images of *The Fury,* the clouded identities of *Sisters,* the uncertainty of historical "facts" from *Obsession,* and it ends with the bleak nihilism of *Carrie.* But it moves beyond those films, because this time De Palma is more successful than ever before at populating his plot with three-dimensional characters. We believe in the reality of the people played by John Travolta, Nancy Allen, John Lithgow, and Dennis Franz. They have all the little tics and eccentricities of life. And although they're caught in the mesh of a labyrinthine conspiracy, they behave as people probably would behave in such circumstances—they're not pawns of the plot.

Best of all, this movie is inhabited by a real cinematic intelligence. The audience isn't condescended to. In sequences like the one in which Travolta reconstructs a film and sound record of the accident, we're challenged and stimulated: We share the excitement of figuring out how things develop and unfold, when so often the movies only need us as passive witnesses.

Blue Collar

R, 114 m., 1978

Richard Pryor (Zeke), Harvey Keitel (Jerry), Yaphet Kotto (Smokey), Ed Begley, Jr. (Bobby Joe), Harry Bellaver (Eddie Johnson), George Memmoli (Jenkins). Directed by Paul Schrader and produced by Don Guest. Screenplay by Paul and Leonard Schrader.

Detroit. Dawn. The next shift arrives for work. On the sound track, music of pounding urgency, suggesting the power of the machines that stamp out car doors from sheets of steel. The camera takes us into the insides of an automobile factory, takes us close enough to almost smell the sweat and shield our eyes against the sparks thrown off by welding torches.

Blue Collar is about life on the Detroit assembly lines, and about how it wears men down and chains them to a lifetime installment plan. It is an angry, radical movie about the vise that traps workers between big industry and big labor. It's also an enormously entertaining movie; it earns its comparison with *On the Waterfront.* And it's an extraordinary directing debut for Paul Schrader, whose credits include *Taxi Driver* and *Rolling Thunder.*

Schrader tells the story of three workers, buddies on and off the job, who are all more or less in the same boat. They work, they drink after work in the bar across the street, they go home to mortgages or bills or kids who need braces on their teeth. One day they get fed up enough to decide to rob the safe in the office of their own union. What they find there is only a few hundred bucks—and a ledger that seems to contain the details of illegal loans of union funds.

The three guys are played by Richard Pryor, Harvey Keitel, and Yaphet Kotto, and they're all three at the top of their forms. Pryor, in particular, is a revelation: He's been good in a lot of movies, but almost always as himself, fast-talking, wise-cracking, running comic variations on the themes suggested by his dialogue. This time, held in rein by Schrader, he provides a tight, convincing performance as a family man.

Yaphet Kotto plays his opposite, an excon who likes to throw all-night parties with lots of sex, booze, and grass. And Harvey Keitel is their white friend, always behind on his loan company payments, who comes home one day to discover that his daughter has tried to bend paper clips over her teeth to convince her friends at school that she's got the braces she should have.

Schrader goes for a nice, raunchy humor in the scenes involving the three guys: The movie is relaxed and comfortable with itself, and we get the precise textures and tones of the society they live in. We understand their friendship, too, because it defies one of the things the movie passionately charges: That unions and management tacitly collaborate on trying to set the rich against the poor, the black against the white, the old against the young, to divide and conquer.

The burglary caper begins innocently enough with Pryor's demand, at a union meeting, that the company repair his locker: He's cut his hand trying to get the damn thing open. But the union representatives seem indifferent to Pryor and just about everyone else, and so Pryor marches into the office of the shaggy, white-maned union leader who was a radical himself, once, back in the 1930s. And while the great statesman is feeding him several varieties of lies, Pryor sees the office safe and gets his idea.

The burglary itself finds the right line between humor and suspense, and then the movie's anger begins to burn. Because when the three men discover that the ledger may be more important than any money in the safe, they're torn between using it for blackmail, or using it to expose the corruption of their own union. Schrader gradually reveals his total vision in the film's second hour: A friendship that was sound and healthy suddenly goes sour. The system drives a wedge between them, as Pryor is offered a union job, Keitel becomes an FBI informer, and Kotto is killed in a scene of great and gruesome power.

It took a measure of courage to make *Blue Collar,* and especially to follow its events through to their inevitable conclusion. The movie could have copped out in its last thirty minutes, and given us a nice, safe Hollywood ending. Instead, it makes criticisms of mass production that social critics like Harvey Swados and Paul Goodman might have agreed with. This isn't a liberal movie but a radical one, and one I suspect a lot of assembly-line workers might see with a shock of recognition.

It took courage to make the movie that honest. But it also took a special filmmaking gift to make it burst with humor, humanity, and suspense as well. Like *On the Waterfront,* it's both an indictment and an entertainment, working just as well on its human levels as with its theoretical concerns. Paul Schrader has been a Hollywood wonder kid ever since negotiating a $450,000 deal for his first screenplay, *The Yakuza.* After *Taxi Driver* and *Obsession,* he was able to demand that he direct his own work, and *Blue Collar* is a

stunning debut, taking chances and winning at them.

The Blue Kite

NO MPAA RATING, 138 m., 1994

Yi Tian (Tietou, infant), Zhang Wenyao (Tietou, child), Chen Xiaoman (Tietou, adolescent), Lu Liping (Mum), Pu Quanxin (Dad), Li Xuejian (Uncle Li [Li Guodong]), Guo Baochang (Stepfather [Lao Wu]). Directed by Tian Zhuangzhuang and produced by Longwick Film Production Ltd. and Beijing Film Studio. Screenplay by Xiao Mao.

I don't know if there really is an ancient Chinese curse that says, "May you live in interesting times," but after seeing *The Blue Kite* I can certainly understand the feeling behind it. During a period which has given us one great Chinese film after another, here is one of the most extraordinary, a sweep of modern Chinese history seen through the eyes of a single family.

Much of the story takes place in the apartments around a small courtyard in Beijing, where the hero, Tietou ("Iron Head"), is born in the early 1950s. His father is a librarian. Times are hard, food is scarce, but spirits are high and we sense the extraordinary camaraderie with which this family and their friends pull together. Events from the outside world, such as the death of Stalin, seem remote compared to the urgency of their daily lives. And as their lives unfold, we become so familiar with the details of life in their small apartment that, if we walked in, we would know where to sit at the table, and how the sleeping arrangements would be made.

But the outside world does intrude into this secure corner, in a scene that is chilling because it shows how lives can be altered by random chance. Political correctness has come to China, and the library staff is called into a meeting. Apparently it has not been self-critical enough, and has not been able to find any reactionaries in its midst. While the discussion continues, Tietou's father leaves the room to visit the toilet. When he returns, he is aware, in a sudden silence, that all eyes are upon him: He has been chosen as the reactionary.

He must leave Beijing and go to work on a

collective farm, for "reeducation." And after he has gone, life will never be as secure or safe for Tietou and his mother. We follow their lives through two more marriages—as she is wed first to an army officer who is an old friend of the family, and later to a good man who is an intellectual.

The Blue Kite follows its characters from the 1950s until the late 1960s, and the Cultural Revolution. And during all of that time, it demonstrates, ordinary life was impossible because a series of political manias swept the land, and zealots sought out those who did not conform, and punished them. At times there is a looking-glass quality to the political movements: Citizens are found guilty because of behavior which only yesterday was proper and correct.

If there had been movies at the time of the American Revolution or the Civil War, they might have had the same excitement as this one, which springs so directly from daily experience and recent memory. No wonder the Chinese government disapproves of the film, and tried to prevent it from being finished and shown. Not enough years have passed for the wounds to heal, and although China is now caught in a capitalist fever, The Blue Kite is a reminder of a time, only a few years ago, when mobs marched through the streets, banging on pans and denouncing fellow citizens for reactionary behavior.

Take, for example, the woman who owns the apartments around the courtyard. She tries to follow first one wind of political orthodoxy and then another, but she can't win, and although she tries to be a good landlady she finds that her class itself makes her guilty. And we see how the pressures of that time caused friends to testify against one another, caused family members to be betrayed, caused the unpredictability of political fashions to make everyone a little crazy.

The Blue Kite was directed by Tian Zhuangzhuang, who is not concerned with big political issues except as they impact on small lives. It is the very everyday, ordinary quality of his story that makes his film important. To some degree The Blue Kite parallels the times and events of another extraordinary Chinese film, Farewell My Concubine, but that film came cloaked in the exoticism of the sexual and personal intrigues at the Peking Opera. The Blue Kite is a movie about people who never go to the opera, who live in one room, but whose lives would nevertheless be warm and rewarding if society would only leave them alone.

Because I have written about the implications of The Blue Kite, I may have given the impression it is an ideological, intellectual movie. Nothing could be more wrong. It is a film made out of daily lives and universal impulses—to form and care for a family, to watch over a child, to be able to depend on parents. The story is narrated by Tietou, who at one point confesses that the more he considers what happened to his family, the less he understands it. It is a shame the Chinese government will not allow this film to be shown in China, because I suspect it would touch a nerve something like Forrest Gump touched here. It gives us a protagonist who is buffeted by the winds of politics and chance—but whose basic human values and needs never change.

Blume in Love

R, 116 m., 1973

George Segal (Blume), Susan Anspach (Nina), Kris Kristofferson (Elmo), Marsha Mason (Arlene), Shelley Winters (Mrs. Cramer), Donald F. Muhich (Analyst), Paul Mazursky (Hellman). Directed, produced, and written by Paul Mazursky.

Paul Mazursky's Blume in Love begins with a busted-up Southern California marriage.

The marriage belonged to Blume, a divorce lawyer, and his wife Nina, a social worker. It busted up all of a sudden one weekday afternoon when Nina came home with a cold and found Blume in bed with his secretary. Why, you may ask (Blume certainly does), could his wife not forgive this indiscretion—especially as Blume is madly in love with Nina and must have her back or die? ("And I don't want to die," he reasons, "so I have to get her back.")

Well, maybe Nina was sort of halfway ready for the marriage to end. She's into her own brand of self-improvement and women's lib, and isn't sure she approves of marriage anymore. She takes up with an out-of-work (for twelve years) musician who lives in a VW truck with his dreams. She gets into yoga and learns to play the guitar and to rely on herself instead of men.

Little good that does Blume, whose love for her becomes a consuming passion. It is complicated by the fact that he gets to like the musician, too: thinks, in fact, that the bearded Elmo is the nicest man he has ever met. Blume even goes so far as to start a beard himself. But nothing will work for him, because of the fact he refuses to accept: Nina simply does not love him anymore. Does not. Period. Blume is driven into a frenzy of love, desire, frustration.

This material, so far, doesn't exactly sound like the stuff of a great film. It sounds more like the brainy, funny dissections of California dreamin' that Mazursky carried out in three previous films, *I Love You, Alice B. Toklas, Bob & Carol & Ted & Alice,* and *Alex in Wonderland.* Those were all fine films—Mazursky is one of the best directors of comedy in Hollywood—but they were all more concerned with the laugh than with reality.

With *Blume in Love,* however, he seems to have pulled off what everybody is always hoping for from Neil Simon: a comedy that transcends its funny moments, that realizes we laugh so we may not cry, and that finally is about real people with real desperations. He's done that in a number of scenes, and yet somehow even during the movie's gloomiest moments he keeps some sort of hope alive. That's probably because Blume is played by the charming George Segal, who seems intrinsically optimistic. No matter what Nina says, he cannot quite give up on her, because he knows she must eventually love him again—because he loves her.

He carries this hope with him on a trip to Venice, which is where the film opens; she's asked him to go away somewhere for a couple of weeks, while she thinks. They had their first and second honeymoons in Venice, but now Blume wanders through Piazza San Marco in the autumn, stranded with a few other lonely tourists looking for love. The story is told in flashbacks from Venice, and it ends there. It ends with a note so unashamedly romantic that Mazursky gets away with "Tristan and Isolde" as his soundtrack music. He's right. The ending would not be believable at all, except as hyperbole.

Nina—thin, earnest, determined to do the right thing and no longer be mastered by mere emotion—is played with a very complex charm by Susan Anspach. We have to like her even though she doesn't like Blume, whom we're cheering for. We do, and we like her boyfriend as much as Blume does. The itinerant musician is played by Kris Kristofferson, who gives evidence once again that he has a real acting talent—particularly in the scene where he hits Segal and then bursts into tears, and in the scene where he tells Segal he's hitting the road again.

Blume in Love has a quality that's hard to analyze but impossible to miss: It sets up an intimate rapport with its audiences.

Bob & Carol & Ted & Alice
R, 105 m., 1969

Robert Culp (Bob), Natalie Wood (Carol), Elliott Gould (Ted), Dyan Cannon (Alice), Donald F. Muhich (Psychiatrist), Greg Mullavey (Group Leader). Directed by Paul Mazursky and produced by Larry Tucker. Screenplay by Tucker and Mazursky.

Bob & Carol & Ted & Alice isn't really about wife swapping at all, but about the epidemic of moral earnestness that's sweeping our society right now. For some curious reason, we suddenly seem compelled to tell the truth in our personal relationships.

Used to be, in the long-ago days of romanticism in the movies, that a girl would peer soulfully into a boy's eyes and say, "Tell me what you really think about me." And then the boy, nobody's fool, would answer quietly: "I think you're wonderful." These days, the boy more likely says, "I think the real reason you want me to answer that question is that you can't answer it for yourself." And then the girl, who looks like a terminal TB case, shivers and says, "You know too much about me. It's scary." And she puffs on her Silva Thin.

Now this sort of honesty is all right for deep conversations over a cup of coffee in the student union, but it's dangerous when practiced by couples over thirty. By then they've got a car and a house and kids, and who knows? If they start telling the truth too much they might have to decide who keeps the kids. That's the dilemma of the in-between generation, the one we overlook in the generation gap, the couples who are too young to be the parents of the revolutionary kids, and too old to be the kids.

The genius of *Bob & Carol & Ted & Alice* is that it understands the peculiar nature of the moral crisis for Americans in this age group, and understands that the way to consider it is in a comedy. What is comedy, after all, but tragedy seen from the outside? So *B&C&T&A* gives us two couples who did their growing up during the Eisenhower years and are sincere enough in wanting to be "contemporary" but, dang it, still have these hang-ups and conventional values.

Their troubles start when Bob (Robert Culp) and Carol (Natalie Wood) spend a weekend at one of those Southern California institutes devoted to telling the truth, working out your hang-ups and letting time and space seep through you. Swept up in the moment, Bob admits he's had an affair. Carol thinks it's wonderful that he's honest enough to admit it to her. His admission sets off a wave of honesty that infects Ted (Elliott Gould) and Alice (Dyan Cannon), their best friends. The two couples gradually become convinced that mutual love and honesty depends upon them trading partners.

The best scene in the movie is the bedroom scene between Gould and Cannon. "You mean you just want to take me, to satisfy yourself, even if I don't feel like it?" she pouts. "That's right," he says. Gould emerges, not so much a star, more of a "personality," like Severn Darden or Estelle Parsons. He's very funny. Culp is the essence of the sagging, dissipated early-middle-age swinger; sort of a young Peter Lawford. Cannon is better than Wood, and Wood is better than I expected.

Some critics have called the ending (when the two couples do not trade partners after all) a cop-out. Not at all. It's consistent with the situation and the development of the characters, and an orgy at the end would have buried the movie's small, but poignant, message. It's a message, incidentally, that I think was missed by the feminist who sent me a postcard saying: "Down with wife swapping, up with husband swapping." They're two sides, wouldn't you say, of the same coin?

Body Snatchers

R, 87 m., 1994

Terry Kinney (Steve Malone), Meg Tilly (Carol Malone), Gabrielle Anwar (Marti Malone), Reilly Murphy (Andy Malone), Billy Wirth (Tim Young), Christine Elise (Jenn Platt), Forest Whitaker (Dr. Collins). Directed by Abel Ferrara and produced by Robert H. Solo. Screenplay by Stuart Gordon, Dennis Paoli, and Nicholas St. John.

Sometimes I'll be looking at someone I know, and a wave of uncertainty will sweep over me. I'll see them in a cold, objective light: "Who is this person—really?" Everything I know about others is based on trust, on the assumption that a "person" is inside them, just as a person clearly seems to be inside me. But what if everybody else only *looks* normal? What if, inside, they're something else altogether, and my world is a laboratory, and I am a specimen?

These spells do not come often, nor do they stay long, nor do I take them seriously. But they reflect a shadowy feeling many people have from time to time. And the classic story of the body snatchers taps into those fears at an elemental level. Since Jack Finney wrote his original novel in the 1940s, his vision of pod people has been filmed three times: in 1956 and 1978 as *Invasion of the Body Snatchers*, by Don Siegel and Philip Kaufman, and now simply as *Body Snatchers*, by Abel Ferrara. The first film fed on the paranoia of McCarthyism. The second film seemed to signal the end of the flower people and the dawn of the Me Generation. And this one? Maybe fear of AIDS is the engine.

Ferrara's version is set on an army base in the South, and told through the eyes of a teenage girl named Marti (Gabrielle Anwar) who has moved there with her family. Her dad (Terry Kinney) is a consultant. She doesn't get along well with her stepmother (Meg Tilly), although she likes her stepbrother (Reilly Murphy). Before the family even arrives on the base, Marti has been grabbed by a runaway soldier in a gas station rest room, who shakes her and says: "They're out there!"

And they are. It gradually becomes clear that visitors from outer space have arrived near the army base, unloading pods, which they store in a nearby swamp. The pods send out tentacles toward sleeping humans, the tendrils snaking up into noses and ears and open mouths and somehow draining out the life force, while the pod swells into a perfect replica of the person being devoured. When the process is complete, the leftover body is a shell, and the new pod person looks and sounds just like someone you know and trust.

There is a catch. They don't look quite right around the eyes. And they don't seem to possess ordinary human emotions, like jealousy. Their goal is to occupy the human race, rent-free. And of course, once Marti understands what is happening, she can't get anyone to believe her.

Ferrara, a talented but uneven director, is capable of making one of the best films of the year (*Bad Lieutenant*, 1993) and one of the worst (*Dangerous Game*, 1993). Here, working in a genre unfamiliar to him, he finds the right note in scene after scene. There is horror here—especially in the gruesome scenes that show us exactly how the pods go about their sneaky business—but there is also ordinary human emotion, as Marti and her boyfriend deal with the fact that people are changing into pods all around them.

Ferrara and his writers are also clever in placing the body-snatching story in the middle of a preexisting family crisis. Marti and her stepmother do not get along, and there is a sense in which the teenage girl already feels that her "real" mother has been usurped by an impostor, and her father subverted. Even her little brother is an enigma: She likes him, but resents having to share love and space with him. So if some of these people turn out to be pods, the psychological basis for her revulsion has already been established.

Ferrara's key scenes mostly take place at night, on the army base, where most of the other people are already podlike in their similar uniforms, language, and behavior. There is a crafty connection made between the army's code of rigid conformity and the behavior of the pod people, who seem like a logical extension of the same code.

Most important, for a horror film, there are scenes of genuine terror. One shot in particular, involving a helicopter, is as scary as anything in *The Exorcist* or *The Silence of the Lambs*. And the fright is generated, not by the tired old slasher trick of having someone jump out of the screen, but by the careful establishing of situations in which we fear, and then our fears are confirmed.

Body Snatchers had its world premiere in May of 1993 in the official competition of the Cannes Film Festival, where the outspoken Ferrara did not endear himself by claiming that Jane Campion's *The Piano* was such a favorite "the jury gave her the award when she got off the plane." Certainly *Body Snatchers* is not the kind of movie that wins festivals: It is a hard-boiled entry in a disreputable genre. But as sheer moviemaking, it is skilled and knowing, and deserves the highest praise you can give a horror film: It works.

Bonnie and Clyde
R, 111 m., 1967

Warren Beatty (Clyde Barrow), Faye Dunaway (Bonnie Parker), Michael J. Pollard (C. W. Moss), Gene Hackman (Buck Barrow), Estelle Parsons (Blanche Barrow), Denver Pyle (Texas Ranger), Dub Taylor (C. W.'s Father), Gene Wilder (Eugene). Directed by Arthur Penn and produced by Warren Beatty. Screenplay by David Newman and Robert Benton.

Bonnie and Clyde is a milestone in the history of American movies, a work of truth and brilliance. It is also pitilessly cruel, filled with sympathy, nauseating, funny, heartbreaking, and astonishingly beautiful. If it does not seem that those words should be strung together, perhaps that is because movies do not very often reflect the full range of human life.

The lives in this case belonged, briefly, to Clyde Barrow and Bonnie Parker. They were two nobodies who got their pictures in the paper by robbing banks and killing people. They weren't very good at the bank robbery part of it, but they were fairly good at killing people and absolutely first-class at getting their pictures in the paper.

Bonnie was a gum-chewing waitress and Clyde was a two-bit hood out on parole. But from the beginning, they both seemed to have a knack for entertaining people. Bonnie wrote ballads and mailed them in with pictures Clyde took with his Kodak. They seemed to consider themselves public servants, bringing a little sparkle to the poverty and despair of the Dust Bowl during the early Depression years.

"Good afternoon," Clyde would say when they walked into a bank. "This is the Barrow Gang." In a way Bonnie and Clyde were pioneers, consolidating the vein of violence in American history and exploiting it, for the first time in the mass media.

Under Arthur Penn's direction, this is a film aimed squarely and unforgivingly at the time we are living in. It is intended, horrifyingly, as entertainment. And so it will be taken. The kids on dates will go to see this one, just like they went to see *Dirty Dozen* and *Born Losers* and *Hells Angels on Wheels.*

But this time, maybe, they'll get more than they counted on. The violence in most American movies is of a curiously bloodless quality. People are shot and they die, but they do not suffer. The murders are something to be gotten over with, so the audience will have its money's worth; the same is true of the sex. Both are like the toy in a Crackerjack box: worthless, but you feel cheated if it's not there.

In *Bonnie and Clyde,* however, real people die. Before they die they suffer, horribly. Before they suffer they laugh, and play checkers, and make love, or try to. These become people we know, and when they die it is not at all pleasant to be in the audience.

When people are shot in *Bonnie and Clyde,* they are literally blown to bits. Perhaps that seems shocking. But perhaps at this time, it is useful to be reminded that bullets really do tear skin and bone and that they don't make nice round little holes like the Swiss cheese effect in Fearless Fosdick.

We are living in a period when newscasts refer casually to "waves" of mass murders, Richard Speck's photograph is sold on posters in Old Town, and snipers in Newark pose for *Life* magazine (perhaps they are busy now getting their ballads to rhyme). Violence takes on an unreal quality. The Barrow Gang reads its press clippings aloud for fun. When C. W. Moss takes the wounded Bonnie and Clyde to his father's home, the old man snorts: "What'd they ever do for you, boy? Didn't even get your name in the paper." Is that a funny line, or a tragic one?

The performances throughout are flawless. Warren Beatty and Faye Dunaway, in the title roles, surpass anything they have done on the screen before and establish themselves (somewhat to my surprise) as major actors.

Michael J. Pollard, as C. W. Moss, the driver and mechanic for the gang, achieves a mixture of moronic good humor and genuine pathos that is unforgettable. When Bonnie tells him, "We rob banks," and asks him to come along,

he says nothing. But the expression on his face and the movements of his body create a perfect, delightful moment.

Gene Hackman and Estelle Parsons play Buck and Blanche Barrow, the other members of the gang, as inarticulate, simple, even good-willed. When Buck is reunited with his kid brother, they howl with glee and punch each other to disguise the truth that they have nothing to say. After the gang has shot its way out of a police trap and Buck is mortally wounded, Blanche's high, mindless scream in the getaway car provides, for me, a very adequate vision of hell.

This is pretty clearly the best American film of the year. It is also a landmark. Years from now it is quite possible that *Bonnie and Clyde* will be seen as the definitive film of the 1960s, showing with sadness, humor, and unforgiving detail what one society had come to. The fact that the story is set thirty-five years ago doesn't mean a thing. It had to be set sometime. But it was made now and it's about us.

Boogie Nights

R, 152 m., 1997

Mark Wahlberg (Eddie Adams/Dirk Diggler), Burt Reynolds (Jack Horner), Julianne Moore (Amber Waves), John C. Reilly (Reed Rothchild), Heather Graham (Rollergirl), Don Cheadle (Buck Swope), Luis Guzman (Maurice T. Rodriguez), Philip Baker Hall (Floyd Gondolli), Philip Seymour Hoffman (Scotty J), Ricky Jay (Kurt Longjohn), William H. Macy (Little Bill), Nina Hartley (Bill's Wife), Robert Ridgely (The Colonel). Directed by Paul Thomas Anderson and produced by Lloyd Levin, John Lyons, Anderson, and Joanne Sellar. Screenplay by Anderson.

Paul Thomas Anderson's *Boogie Nights* is an epic of the low road, a classic Hollywood story set in the shadows instead of the spotlights, but containing the same ingredients: fame, envy, greed, talent, sex, money. The movie follows a large, colorful, and curiously touching cast of characters, as they live through a crucial turning point in the adult film industry.

In 1977, when the story opens, porn movies are shot on film and play in theaters, and a director can dream of making one so good that the audience members would want to stay in the theater even after they had achieved what they came for. By 1983, when the story closes, porn has shifted to video and most of the movies are basically just gynecological loops. There is hope, at the outset, that a porno movie could be "artistic," and less hope at the end.

Boogie Nights tells this story through the life of a kid named Eddie Adams (Mark Wahlberg) from Torrance, who is a dishwasher in a San Fernando Valley nightclub when he's discovered by a Tiparillo-smoking pornographer named Jack Horner (Burt Reynolds). "I got a feeling," Jack says, "that behind those jeans is something wonderful just waiting to get out." He is correct, and within a few months Eddie has been renamed "Dirk Diggler" and is a rising star of porn films.

If this summary makes the film itself sound a little like porn, it is not. Few films have been more matter-of-fact, even disenchanted, about sexuality. Adult films are a business here, not a dalliance or a pastime, and one of the charms of *Boogie Nights* is the way it shows the everyday backstage humdrum life of porno filmmaking. "You got your camera," Jack explains to young Eddie. "You got your film, you got your lights, you got your synching, you got your editing, you got your lab. Before you turn around, you've spent maybe $25,000 or $30,000."

Jack Horner is the father figure for a strange extended family of sex workers; he's a low-rent Hugh Hefner, and Burt Reynolds gives one of his best performances, as a man who seems to stand outside sex and view it with the detached eye of a judge at a livestock show. Horner is never shown as having sex himself, although he lives with Amber Waves (Julianne Moore), a former housewife and mother, now a porn star who makes tearful midnight calls to her ex-husband, asking to speak to her child. When Jack recruits Eddie to make a movie, Amber becomes his surrogate parent, tenderly solicitous of him as they prepare for his first sex scene.

During a break in that scene, Eddie whispers to Jack, "Please call me Dirk Diggler from now on." He falls immediately into star mode, and before long is leading a conducted tour of his new house, where his wardrobe is "arranged according to color and designer." His stardom is based on one remarkable attribute; "everyone is blessed with one special thing," he tells

himself, after his mother has screamed that he'll always be a bum and a loser.

Anderson wisely limits the nudity in the film, and until the final shot we don't see what Jack Horner calls "Mr. Torpedo Area." It's more fun to approach it the way Anderson does. At a pool party at Jack's house, Dirk meets the Colonel (Robert Ridgely), who finances the films. "May I see it?" the silver-haired, business-suited Colonel asks. Dirk obliges, and the camera stays on the Colonel's face as he looks, and a funny, stiff little smile appears on his face; Anderson holds the shot for several seconds, and we get the message.

The large cast of *Boogie Nights* is nicely balanced between human and comic qualities. We meet Rollergirl (Heather Graham), who never takes off her skates, and in an audition scene with Dirk adds a new dimension to the lyrics "I've got a brand-new pair of roller skates, you've got a brand-new key." Little Bill (William H. Macy) is Jack's assistant director, moping about at parties while his wife (porn star Nina Hartley) gets it on with every man she can. (When he discovers his wife having sex in the driveway, surrounded by an appreciative crowd, she tells him, "Shut up, Bill; you're embarrassing me.") Ricky Jay, the magician, plays Jack's cameraman. "I think every picture should have its own look," he states solemnly, although the films are shot in a day or two. When he complains, "I got a couple of tough shadows to deal with," Jack snaps, "There are shadows in life, baby."

Dirk's new best friend is Reed (John C. Reilly). He gets a crush on Dirk and engages him in gym talk ("How much do you press? Let's both say at the same time. One, two . . ."). Buck Swope (Don Cheadle) is a second-tier actor and would-be hi-fi salesman. Rodriguez (Luis Guzman) is a club manager who dreams of being in one of Jack's movies. And the gray eminence behind the industry, the man who is the Colonel's boss, is Floyd Gondolli (Philip Baker Hall), who on New Year's Eve 1980 breaks the news that videotape holds the future of the porno industry.

The sweep and variety of the characters has brought the movie comparisons to Altman's *Nashville* and *The Player*. There is also some of the same appeal as *Pulp Fiction*, in scenes that balance precariously between comedy and violence (a brilliant scene near the end has Dirk and friends selling cocaine to a deranged playboy while the customer's friend throws firecrackers around the room). Through all the characters and all the action, Anderson's screenplay centers on the human qualities of the players. They may live in a disreputable world, but they have the same ambitions and, in a weird way, similar values as mainstream Hollywood.

Boogie Nights has the quality of many great films, in that it always seems alive. A movie can be very good and yet not draw us in, not involve us in the moment-to-moment sensation of seeing lives as they are lived. As a writer and director, Paul Thomas Anderson is a skilled reporter, who fills his screen with understated, authentic details. (In the filming of the first sex scene, for example, the action takes place in an office set that has been built in Jack's garage. Behind the office door we see old license plates nailed to the wall, and behind one wall of the set, bicycle wheels peek out.) Anderson is in love with his camera, and a bit of a showoff in sequences inspired by the famous nightclub entrance in *GoodFellas*, De Niro's rehearsal in the mirror in *Raging Bull*, and a shot in *I Am Cuba* where the camera follows a woman into a pool.

In examining the business of catering to lust, *Boogie Nights* demystifies its sex (that's probably one reason it avoided the NC-17 rating). Mainstream movies use sex like porno films do, to turn us on. *Boogie Nights* abandons the illusion that the characters are enjoying sex; in a sense, it's about manufacturing a consumer product. By the time the final shot arrives and we see what made the Colonel stare, there is no longer any shred of illusion that it is anything more than a commodity. And in Dirk Diggler's most anguished scene, as he shouts at Jack Horner, "I'm ready to shoot my scene *right now!*" we learn that those who live by the sword can also die by it.

Born on the Fourth of July

R, 144 m., 1989

Tom Cruise (Ron Kovic), Willem Dafoe (Charlie), Kyra Sedgwick (Donna), Raymond J. Barry (Mr. Kovic), Jerry Levine (Steve Boyer), Frank Whaley (Timmy), Carolina Kava (Mrs. Kovic), Abbie Hoffman (Strike Organizer), Oliver Stone (News Reporter), Tom Berenger (Recruiting Sergeant), Rob Camilletti (Tommy Finnelli), Sean Stone (Young Jimmy). Directed by Oliver Stone and produced by A. Kitman Ho and Stone. Screenplay by Stone and Ron Kovic, based on the book by Kovic.

For some time we've been reading in the papers about public apologies by governments of the Eastern bloc. The Russians admit they were wrong to invade Afghanistan and Czechoslovakia. The East Germans tear down the wall and denounce the secret luxuries of their leaders. The Poles and Hungarians say Marxism doesn't work very well. There is a temptation for an American reading these articles to feel smug. And yet—hold on a minute here. We had our own disastrous foreign policy mistake: the war in Vietnam. When is anybody going to get up before Congress and read an apology to the Vietnamese?

Never, is the obvious answer. We hail the Soviet bloc for its honesty but see no lessons for ourselves. And yet we have been issuing our own apologies, of a sort. A film like Oliver Stone's *Born on the Fourth of July* is an apology for Vietnam uttered by Stone, who fought there, and Ron Kovic, who was paralyzed from the chest down in Vietnam. Both of them were gung-ho patriots who were eager to answer their country's call to arms. When they came back home, they were still patriots—hurt and offended by the hostility they experienced from the antiwar movement.

Eventually both men turned against the war, Kovic most dramatically. He and his wheelchair were thrown out of the 1972 Republican Convention, but in 1976 he addressed the Democratic Convention, and if you want to you could say his 1976 speech was the equivalent of one of those recent breast-beatings in the Supreme Soviet. We do apologize for our mistakes in this country, but we let our artists do it, instead of our politicians.

Kovic came back from the war with a shattered body, but it took a couple of years for the damage to spread to his mind and spirit. By the time he hit bottom he was a demoralized, spiteful man who sought escape in booze and drugs and Mexican whorehouses. Then he began to look outside of himself for a larger pattern to his life, the pattern that inspired his best-selling autobiography, *Born on the Fourth of July*.

The director, Oliver Stone, who based his earlier film *Platoon* on his own war experiences, has been trying to film the Kovic book for years. Various stars and studios were attached to the project, but it kept being canceled, and perhaps that's just as well, because by waiting this long Stone was able to use Tom Cruise in the leading role. Nothing Cruise has done earlier will prepare you for what he does in *Born on the Fourth of July*. He has been hailed for years now as a great young American actor, but only his first film, *Risky Business*, found a perfect match between actor and role. *Top Gun* overwhelmed him with a special-effects display, *The Color of Money* didn't explain his behavior in crucial final scenes, *Cocktail* was a cynical attempt to exploit his attractive image. Almost always he seemed to be holding something in reserve, standing back from his own presence. In *Born on the Fourth of July*, his performance is so good that the movie lives through it—Stone is able to make his statement with Cruise's face and voice and doesn't need to put everything into the dialogue.

The movie begins in the early 1960s, indeed with footage of John Kennedy on the television exhorting, "Ask not what your country can do for you; ask what you can do for your country." Young Ron Kovic, football star and high school hero, was the kind of kid waiting to hear that message. And when the marine recruiters came to visit his high school, he was ready to sign up. There was no doubt in his mind: There was a war in Vietnam, and his only worry was that he would miss the action. He knew there was a danger of being wounded or killed, but hell, he wanted to make a sacrifice for his country.

His is the kind of spirit all nations must have from time to time. The problem with the Vietnam War is that it did not deserve it. There was no way for a patriotic small-town kid to know that, however, and so we follow young Kovic through boot camp and into the battlefield. In these scenes, Cruise still looks like Cruise—boyish, open-faced—and I found myself wondering if he would be able to make the transition into the horror that I knew was coming. He was.

Oliver Stone was in combat for a year. In *Platoon*, he showed us firefights so confused we (and the characters) often had little idea where the enemy was. In *Born on the Fourth of July*, Stone directs a crucial battle scene with great clarity so that we can see how a mistake was made by Kovic. That mistake, which tortures him for years afterward, probably produced the loss of focus that led to his crippling injury.

The scenes which follow, in a military hospital, are merciless in their honesty. If you have even once, for a few hours perhaps, been helpless in a sickbed and unable to summon aid, all of your impotent rage will come flooding back as the movie shows a military care system that is hopelessly overburdened. At one point, Kovic screams out for a suction pump that will drain a wound that might cost him his leg. He will never have feeling in the leg—but, God damn it, he wants to keep it all the same. It's his. And a hospital orderly absentmindedly explains about equipment shortages and "budget cutbacks" in care for the wounded vets.

Back in civilian life, Kovic is the hero of a Fourth of July parade, but there are peaceniks on the sidewalks, some of them giving him the finger. He feels more rage. But then his emotional tide turns one night in the backyard of his parents' home. He gets drunk with a fellow veteran and finds they can talk about things nobody else really understands. It is from this scene that the full power of the Cruise performance develops. Kovic's life becomes a series of confusions—bar brawls, self-pity, angry confrontations with women he will never be able to make love with in the ordinary way. His parents love him but are frightened of his rage. Eventually it is suggested that he leave home.

In a scene of Dantean evil, Stone shows Kovic in Mexico with other crippled veterans, paying for women and drugs to take away the pain, and finally, shockingly, abandoned in the desert with another veteran with no way to get back to their wheelchairs or to town. It's the sort of thing that happens to people who make themselves unbearable to other people who don't give a damn about them. (In a nod toward *Platoon*, the other crippled veteran in the desert is played by Willem Dafoe, costar of that film; the other costar, Tom Berenger, is the marine who gives the recruitment speech in the opening scenes.)

Born on the Fourth of July is one of those films that steps correctly in the opening moments and then never steps wrongly. It is easy to think of a thousand traps that Oliver Stone, Ron Kovic, and Tom Cruise could have fallen into with this film, but they fall into none of them.

Although this film has vast amounts of pain and bloodshed and suffering in it, and is at home on battlefields and in hospital wards, it proceeds from a philosophical core—it is not a movie about battle or wounds or recovery, but a movie about an American who changes his mind about the war. The filmmakers realize that is the heart of their story and are faithful to it, even though they could have spun off in countless other directions. This is a film about ideology, played out in the personal experiences of a young man who paid dearly for what he learned. Maybe instead of anybody getting up in Congress and apologizing for the Vietnam War, they could simply hold a screening of this movie on Capitol Hill and call it a day.

Bound

R, 109 m., 1996

Jennifer Tilly (Violet), Gina Gershon (Corky), Joe Pantoliano (Caesar), John P. Ryan (Mickey Malnato), Christopher Meloni (Johnnie Marconi), Richard Sarafian (Gino Marzzone), Barry Kivel (Shelly). Directed by Larry Wachowski and Andy Wachowski and produced by Andrew Lazar and Stuart Boros. Screenplay by Larry Wachowski and Andy Wachowski.

Bound is one of those movies that works you up, wrings you out, and leaves you gasping. It's pure cinema, spread over several genres. It's a caper movie, a gangster movie, a sex movie, and a slapstick comedy. It's not often you think of *The Last Seduction* and the Marx Brothers during the same film, but I did during this one—and I also thought about *Blood Simple* and Woody Allen. It's amazing to discover all this virtuosity and confidence in two first-time filmmakers, Larry and Andy Wachowski, self-described college dropouts still in their twenties, from Chicago.

As the film opens, a tough but sexy woman is moving into a new apartment. She rides the elevator to her floor with what looks like a mobster and his ditzy girlfriend. He's a mobster, all right, but she's not as ditzy as she looks. It's more of an act that gives her immunity in a dangerous environment.

The sexy newcomer is Corky (Gina Gershon), a lesbian who has just finished serving a prison sentence. The mobster is Caesar (Joe Pantoliano), a mid-level functionary in the Chicago crime syndicate. His girlfriend is Violet (Jennifer Tilly), whose lust for their new neighbor is so obvious she might as well just turn herself in to Jerry Springer and get it over with ("Violet—afraid to tell Mafioso boyfriend she's a lesbian").

Violet creates an excuse to meet Corky; she uses the routine about how her ring fell down the sink. In old movies this was a ploy to trap men, but for about ten years I've noticed that the only movie characters who seem to do household tasks anymore are lesbians. There's always a scene early in the movie showing them caulking something.

Passion between the two women is instantaneous, steamy, and kind of funny. Gershon and Tilly are electric together, maybe because they understand the humor of their situation and play the sex for delight instead of for solemn, earthshaking, gynecological drudgery. The movie seems to be shaping up as an erotic popcorn masher, but then the plot thickens and keeps on thickening, twisting the characters and the audience ever tighter into a sticky web of murder, blood, sex, and money.

Violet and Corky have secret tête-à-têtes and become lovers. Violet whispers that she wants to escape Caesar so the two women can start a new life together. So far she hasn't been able to get Caesar to listen. ("Caesar, I'm leaving!" she announces. "Why?" he whines. "Did I use a good towel?")

Violet tells Corky that a bag man named Shelly (Barry Kivel) is arriving at Caesar's with $2 million in cash. She thinks they should steal the cash, and she needs Corky's help—since as an ex-con, Corky is presumably an expert criminal.

Now the movie turns into a macabre caper comedy of clockwork virtuosity. The plot depends on split-second timing; if anything goes wrong, they could be dead. Of course everything goes wrong. Shelly arrives with the briefcase, and it appears that he's going to get his fingers cut off one at a time. When this scene played at the Toronto Film Festival, people fled from the theater, so be warned. But also know that the movie never goes as far or shows as much as it seems about to; like *Blood Simple*, it takes us to the edge of the unacceptable, peers over wistfully, and tiptoes away.

To describe what happens in the film's brilliant and long-sustained caper sequence would be unfair. Familiar movie devices are made to feel new. Bodies stack up. The cops arrive and there is evidence of murder right in front of them if they only know where to look. The two lovers are in constant danger of exposure and death.

All of this is somehow constructed like a perfect Marx Brothers routine; the briefcase full of money moves around like the pea in a shell game, powerful Mafia bosses arrive from the East Coast and represent certain death for the increasingly desperate Caesar, and there are little tricks involving things like the redial button on a telephone that have the audience gasping with fear and delight.

The movie is a jubilant comeback for Gina Gershon, whose career now takes a U-turn after the unsuccessful *Showgirls*. She brings an edge and intelligence to her character that reminded me a little of Linda Fiorentino in *The Last Seduction*. Jennifer Tilly takes the giggly showgirl act she introduced in Woody Allen's *Bullets Over Broadway* and uses it to hide a steel will. And Joe Pantoliano has some of the trickiest scenes in the movie, bouncing from paranoia to greed to lust to abject fear like a pinball in the wrong machine.

Bound is shocking and violent, and will offend some audiences. It's that kind of movie. But it's skillful filmmaking, setting a puzzle that involves time, space, money, and danger, and seeing how many different ways it can be solved.

The Bounty

PG, 130 m., 1984

Anthony Hopkins (Captain William Bligh), Mel Gibson (Fletcher Christian), Tevaite Vernette (Mauatua), Laurence Olivier (Admiral Hood), Edward Fox (Captain Greetham), Daniel Day-Lewis (Fryer). Directed by Roger Donaldson and produced by Bernard Williams. Screenplay by Robert Bolt.

The relationship between Fletcher Christian and Captain William Bligh is one of the most familiar in the movies: We've seen it acted between Clark Gable and Charles Laughton, and between Marlon Brando and Trevor Howard, but it's never before been quite as intriguing as in *The Bounty*, the third movie based on the most famous mutiny in the history of the sea. The movie suggests that Bligh and Christian were friends, of all things, and that Bligh—far from being the histrionic martinet of earlier movies—was an intelligent, contemplative man of great complications. The story is well-known, and simple: HMS *Bounty* sets sail for the South Seas, has a difficult voyage that frays everyone's tempers, and then anchors at a Polynesian island. During the trip, the original first mate has been replaced by the young Fletcher Christian, whom Bligh decides to trust. But Christian tires of the voyage and of the dangers and probable death that lie ahead. He falls in love with a native girl and leads a mutiny of sailors who choose to stay on their island paradise.

Bligh is played by Anthony Hopkins in one of the most interesting performances of 1984: He is unyielding, but not mindlessly rigid; certain he is right, but not egotistical; able to be realistic about his fate and his chances, and yet completely loyal to his ideas of a British naval officer's proper duties. When Fletcher Christian leads a mutiny against his command, it is not seen simply as a revolt against cruel authority (as in the earlier movies) but as a choice between a freer lifestyle, and Bligh's placing of duty above ordinary human nature.

Every *Bounty* movie seems to shape its Fletcher Christian somewhat to reflect the actor who plays him. Gable's Christian was a man of action, filled with physical strength and high spirits. Brando's was introverted and tortured. Mel Gibson's is maybe the hardest to figure of the three. He is a man of very few words (the screenplay gives him little to say, and almost no philosophizing), quiet, observant, an enigma. Only in the arms of the woman he comes to love, the Tahitian girl Mauatua, does he find the utter simplicity that perhaps he was looking for when he went to sea. It is a decision of some daring to give Gibson so noticeably little dialogue in this movie, but it works.

This *Bounty* is not only a wonderful movie, high-spirited and intelligent, but something of a production triumph as well. Although this third *Bounty* film was originally conceived as a big-budget, two-part epic to be directed by David *(Doctor Zhivago)* Lean, the current version was prepared and directed after only a few months' notice by a talented young New Zealander named Roger Donaldson, whose previous credits included the brilliant *Smash Palace,* a critical hit and commercial failure. What's interesting is that Donaldson's film doesn't feel like a secondhand treatment; he directs with flair and wit, and the spectacular scenes (like a stormy crossing of the Cape) never allow the special effects to steal the film away from the actors.

The sea voyage is done with the sort of macho confidence that a good sea movie needs, and the land portions do an interesting job of contrasting the proper, civilized British (represented by Laurence Olivier, as an admiral) with the cheerful absolute freedom of Polynesia. The romance between Gibson and the beautiful Tevaite Vernette, as his island lover, is given time to develop instead of just being thrown in as a plot point. And the Polynesians, for once, are all allowed to go topless all the time (the movie nevertheless gets the PG rating, qualifying under the *National Geographic* loophole in which nudity doesn't count south of the equator). *The Bounty* is a great adventure, a lush romance, and a good movie.

Boys Don't Cry

R, 114 m., 1999

Hilary Swank (Brandon Teena), Chloë Sevigny (Lana), Alicia Goranson (Candace), Alison Folland (Kate), Peter Sarsgaard (John), Brendan Sexton III (Tom). Directed by Kimberly Peirce and produced by Eva Kolodner, Jeff Sharp, and John Hart. Screenplay by Peirce and Andy Bienen.

Sex was more interesting when we knew less about it, when we proceeded from murky impulses rather than easy familiarity. Consider the Victorians, slipping off to secret vices, and how much more fun they had than today's Jerry Springer guests ("My girlfriend is a dominatrix"). The intriguing border between the genders must have been more inviting to cross when that was seen as an opportunity rather than a pathology. One of the many virtues of

Boys Don't Cry, one of the best films of 1999, is that never once does it supply the tiresome phrase, "I am a man trapped in a woman's body." Its motto instead could be, "Girls just wanna have fun."

Teena Brandon doesn't think of herself as a sexual case study; nothing in her background has given her that vocabulary. She is a lonely girl who would rather be a boy, and one day she gets a short haircut, sticks a sock down the front of her jeans, and goes into a bar to try her luck. She is not a transsexual, a lesbian, a cross-dresser, or a member of any other category on the laundry list of sexual identities; she is a girl who thinks of herself as a boy, and when she leaves Lincoln, Nebraska, and moves to the small town of Falls City in 1993, that is how she presents herself. By then she has become Brandon Teena, and we must use the male pronoun in describing him.

All of this is true. There is a documentary, *The Brandon Teena Story,* that came out earlier in 1999 and shows us photographs of Brandon, looking eerily like Hilary Swank, who plays the role in *Boys Don't Cry.* In that film we meet some of the women he dated ("Brandon knew how to treat a woman") and we see the two men later charged with Brandon's rape and, after the local law authorities didn't act seriously on that charge, murder a few days later. Like Matthew Shepard in Wyoming, Brandon died because some violent men are threatened by any challenge to their shaky self-confidence.

Boys Don't Cry is not sociology, however, but a romantic tragedy—a *Romeo and Juliet* set in a Nebraska trailer park. Brandon is not the smartest person on Earth, especially at judging which kinds of risks to take, but he is one of the nicest, and soon he has fallen in love with a Falls City girl named Lana (Chloë Sevigny). For Lana, Brandon is arguably the first nice boy she has ever dated. We meet two of the other local studs, John (Peter Sarsgaard) and Tom (Brendan Sexton III), neither gifted with intelligence, both violent products of brutal backgrounds. They have the same attitude toward women that the gun nut has about prying his dying fingers off the revolver.

The film is about hanging out in gas stations and roller rinks, and lying sprawled on a couch looking with dulled eyes at television, and working at soul-crushing jobs, and about six-packs and country bars and Marlboros. There is a reason country music is sad. Into this wasteland, which is all Lana knows, comes Brandon, who brings her a flower.

The Lana character is crucial to the movie, and although Hilary Swank deserves all praise for her performance as Brandon, it is Chloë Sevigny who provides our entrance into the story. Representing the several women the real Brandon dated, she sees him as a warm, gentle, romantic lover. Does Lana know Brandon is a girl? At some point, certainly. But at what point exactly? There is a stretch when she knows, and yet she doesn't know, because she doesn't want to know; romance is built on illusion, and when we love someone, we love the illusion they have created for us.

Kimberly Peirce, who directed this movie and cowrote it with Andy Bienen, was faced with a project that could have gone wrong in countless ways. She finds the right note. She never cranks the story up above the level it's comfortable with; she doesn't underline the stupidity of the local law-enforcement officials because that's not necessary; she sees Tom and John not as simple killers but as the instruments of deep ignorance and inherited anti-social pathology. (Tom knows he's trouble; he holds his hand in a flame and then cuts himself, explaining, "This helps control the thing inside of me so I don't snap out at people.")

The whole story can be explained this way: Most everybody in it behaves exactly according to their natures. The first time I saw the movie, I was completely absorbed in the characters—the deception, the romance, the betrayal. Only later did I fully realize what a great film it is, a worthy companion to those other masterpieces of death on the prairie, *Badlands* and *In Cold Blood*. This could have been a clinical Movie of the Week, but instead it's a sad song about a free spirit who tried to fly a little too close to the flame.

The Boys in Company C

R, 125 m., 1978

Stan Shaw (Tyrone Washington), Andrew Stevens (Billy Ray Pike), James Canning (Alvin Foster), Michael Lembeck (Vinnie Fazio), Craig Wasson (Dave Bisbee), Scott Hylands (Capt. Collins), James Whitmore Jr. (Lt. Archer), Noble Willingham (Sgt. Curry), Lee Ermey (Sgt. Loyce). Directed by Sidney J. Furie and produced by Raymond Chow and Andre Morgan. Screenplay by Furie and Rick Natkin.

Hollywood hasn't been eager to make movies about Vietnam, maybe because the studios fear that the divisions opened up in our society by the war still haven't healed. Only one feature was actually released during the war—John Wayne's hawkish *The Green Berets* (and how long ago it seems when "hawks" and "doves" were emotionally charged words). Three movies about returned Vietnam vets have been released, or will be soon: *Heroes, Rolling Thunder,* and *Coming Home.*

But Sidney J. Furie's *The Boys in Company C* is the first movie since 1968 about actual combat in Vietnam (Francis Coppola's *Apocalypse Now* will be the second, if it ever completes its interminable postproduction). Furie's movie is, in other words, a "war movie," a member of a genre that seemed more brave and thrilling in the days of World War II and Korea, when John Wayne was storming up hills.

And it's being attacked on just those grounds: The newsweeklies charge that it takes the old Hollywood clichés and simply transplants them to Southeast Asia. I don't agree. I think the movie is, first and best, a thrilling entertainment that starts by being funny and ends by being very deeply moving. But I also think it reflects an attitude about Vietnam that wouldn't have been possible in a war movie of the early 1940s.

Vietnam just wasn't like other wars, and you can sense that in the movie's first scenes, as a company of Marine recruits awkwardly tries to find its way through boot camp. If there's an esprit de corps here, it's one the Marines have to find by themselves and on their own. The hard-as-nails, tough-talking drill instructors (cast, by the way, from real life) don't mention duty or patriotism much, but there's a lot of talk about how these guys had better learn to save their asses or they'll come back in body bags. The Marines are seen as a pragmatic instrument to send trained infantry to where they're needed; you don't hear anyone singing "From the Halls of Montezuma."

It's this subtle but definite change in attitude that makes *The Boys in Company C* more than just exciting or entertaining. There aren't many abstract speeches in the movie and nobody gets up and delivers his opinion about Vietnam (except in terms of the most direct cynicism). And yet, in the craziness of the company's first overseas patrol (they get caught in an enemy ambush while transporting luxury goods for a general's birthday party), all of the reality is there. And when, driven by insane demands for larger enemy body counts, they call in firepower on a nonexistent enemy position, their action seems, strangely, almost logical.

The movie bears comparison to *The Dirty Dozen* and *M*A*S*H*, especially in the way it constructs an easy camaraderie among its actors. The mostly young, mostly unknown cast of *Company C* lived together on location in the Philippines while making the movie, and their mutual friendship seems to show through. That's especially true in the case of Chicago native Stan Shaw, who plays the Los Angeles ghetto kid who goes over to 'Nam planning to ship back drugs in body bags—and winds up as the group's natural leader and unifying force. His performance is remarkably strong, and not least when he shows tenderness.

There are also good performances by James Canning, as the kid who keeps a notebook in which he writes, "I'd put down everything that happened today, except that nobody would believe it." And by Andrew Stevens, whose soccer game is good enough that maybe the company's team can get them all transferred out of combat. And, especially, by a former Marine D.I. named Lee Ermey, who originally signed on as a technical advisor and was so convincing he was cast in the film. One of his confrontations with Shaw provides a high point of the movie.

Sidney Furie, the director, hasn't had a substantial hit since *Lady Sings the Blues* (I was not one of the admirers of his *Gable and Lombard*). But he retains the ability to make a picture move, grow on us, and involve us. That's what happens during *The Boys in Company C.*

Boyz N the Hood

R, 107 m., 1991

Cuba Gooding, Jr. (Tre Styles), Ice Cube (Doughboy), Morris Chestnut (Ricky Baker), Larry Fishburne (Furious Styles), Tyra Ferrell (Mrs. Baker). Directed by John Singleton and produced by Steve Nicolaides. Screenplay by Singleton.

There must be few experiences more wounding to the heart than for a parent to look at a child and fear for its future. In inner-city America, where one in every twenty-one young men will die of gunshot wounds, and most of them will be shot by other young men, it is not simply a question of whether the child will do well in school, or find a useful career: It is sometimes whether the child will live or die.

Watching her bright young son on the brink of his teenage years, seeing him begin to listen to his troublesome friends instead of to her, the mother in *Boyz N the Hood* decides that it is best for the boy to go live with his father. The father works as a mortgage broker, out of a storefront office. He is smart and angry, a disciplinarian, and he lays down rules for his son. And then, out in the streets of south-central Los Angeles, the son learns other rules.

As he grows into his teens, his best friends are half brothers, one an athlete, the other drifting into drugs and alcohol. They've known each other for years—and have steered clear, more or less, of the gangs that operate in the neighborhood. They go their own way. But there is always the possibility that words will lead to insults, that insults will lead to a need to "prove their manhood," that with guns everywhere, somebody will be shot dead.

These are the stark choices in John Singleton's *Boyz N the Hood,* one of the best American films of recent years. The movie is a thoughtful, realistic look at a young man's coming of age, and is also a human drama of rare power—Academy Award material. Singleton is a director who brings together two attributes not always found in the same film: He has a subject, and he has a style. The film is not only important, but also a joy to watch, because his camera is so confident and he wins such natural performances from his actors.

The movie's hero, who will probably excel in college and in a profession, if he lives to get that far, is an intelligent seventeen-year-old named Tre Styles (Cuba Gooding, Jr.). His father, Furious Styles (Larry Fishburne), grew up in the neighborhood, survived it, and understands it in two different ways: as a place where young men define their territory and support themselves by violence, and as a real estate market in transition—where, when prices and lives there find their bottom, investors will be able to buy cheap and then make money with gentrification.

Furious Styles also knows the dangers for his son—of gangs, of drugs, of the wrong friends. He lays down strict rules, but he cannot be everywhere and see everything. Meanwhile, Singleton paints the individual characters of the neighborhood with the same attention to detail that Spike Lee used in *Do the Right Thing*. He's particularly perceptive about the Baker family—about the mother (Tyra Ferrell) and her two sons by different fathers, Doughboy (rap artist Ice Cube) and Ricky (Morris Chestnut). Both live at home, where it is no secret in the family that the mother prefers Ricky. He's a gifted athlete who seems headed for a college football scholarship.

Doughboy is not a bad person, but he is into booze and drugs and will sooner or later find bad trouble. He spends most of his days on the front steps, drinking, plotting, feeding his resentments. They live in a neighborhood where violence is a fact of life, where the searchlights from police helicopters are like the guard lights in a prison camp, where guns are everywhere, where a kid can go down to the corner store and not come home alive. In painting the cops as an occupying force, Singleton is especially hard on one self-hating black cop, who uses his authority to mishandle young black men.

In the course of one summer week or two, all of the strands of Tre's life come together to be tested: his girlfriend, his relationship with his father, his friendships, and the dangers from the street gangs of the area. Singleton's screenplay has built well; we feel we know the characters and their motivations, and so we can understand what happens, and why.

A lesser movie might have handled this material in a perfunctory way, painting the characters with broad strokes of good and evil, setting up a confrontation at the end, using a lot of violence and gunfire to reward the good and punish the rest. Singleton cares too much about his story to kiss it off like that. Look, for example, at the scene late in the film—the morning-after scene—where Doughboy walks

across the street and speaks quietly to Tre; he knows what is likely to happen, and yet wants his friend to escape the trap, to realize his future.

Boyz N the Hood has maturity and emotional depth: There are no cheap shots, nothing is thrown in for effect, realism is placed ahead of easy dramatic payoffs, and the audience grows deeply involved. By the end of *Boyz N the Hood*, I realized I had seen not simply a brilliant directorial debut, but an American film of enormous importance.

Breaking Away
PG, 100 m., 1979

Dennis Christopher (Dave), Dennis Quaid (Mike), Daniel Stern (Cyril), Jackie Earle Haley (Moocher), Paul Dooley (Dad), Barbara Barrie (Mom), Robyn Douglass (Katherine). Directed and produced by Peter Yates. Screenplay by Steve Tesich.

Here's a sunny, goofy, intelligent little film about coming of age in Bloomington, Indiana. It's about four local kids, just out of high school, who mess around for one final summer before facing the inexorable choices of jobs or college or the army. One of the kids, Dave (Dennis Christopher), has it in his head that he wants to be a champion Italian bicycle racer, and he drives his father crazy with opera records and ersatz Italian.

His friends have more reasonable ambitions: One (Dennis Quaid) was a high school football star who pretends he doesn't want to play college ball, but he does; another (Jackie Earle Haley) is a short kid who pretends he doesn't want to be taller, but he does; and another (Daniel Stern) is one of those kids like we all knew, who learned how to talk by crossing Eric Sevareid with Woody Allen.

There's the usual town-and-gown tension in Bloomington, between the jocks and the townies (who are known, in Bloomington, as "cutters"—so called after the workers in the area's limestone quarries). There's also a poignant kind of tension between local guys and college girls: Will a sorority girl be seen with a cutter? Dave finds out by falling hopelessly in love with a college girl named Kathy (Robyn Douglass), and somehow, insanely, convincing her he's actually an Italian exchange student.

The whole business of Dave's Italomania provides the movie's funniest running joke: Dave's father (Paul Dooley) rants and raves that he didn't raise his boy to be an Eyetalian, and that he's sick and tired of all the eenees in the house: linguini, fettucini . . . even Jake, the dog, which Dave has renamed Fellini. The performances by Dooley and Barbara Barrie as Dave's parents are so loving and funny at the same time that we remember almost with a shock, that *every* movie doesn't have to have parents and kids who don't get along.

The movie was directed as a work of love by Peter Yates, whose big commercial hits have included *Bullitt* and *The Deep*. The Oscar-winning original screenplay was written by Steve Tesich, who was born in Yugoslavia, was moved to Bloomington at the age of thirteen, won the Little 500 bicycle race there in 1962, and uses it for the film's climax. Yates has gone for the human elements in *Breaking Away*, but he hasn't forgotten how to direct action, and there's a bravura sequence in which Dave, on a racing bicycle, engages in a high-speed highway duel with a semitrailer truck.

In this scene, and in scenes involving swimming in an abandoned quarry, Yates does a tricky and intriguing thing: He suggests the constant possibility of sudden tragedy. We wait for a terrible accident to happen, and none does, but the hints of one make the characters seem curiously vulnerable, and their lives more precious.

The whole movie, indeed, is a delicate balancing act of its various tones: This movie could have been impossible to direct, but Yates has us on his side almost immediately. Some scenes edge into fantasy, others are straightforward character development, some (like the high school quarterback's monologue about his probable future) are heartbreakingly true. But the movie always returns to light comedy, to romance, to a wonderfully evocative instant nostalgia.

Breaking Away is a movie to embrace. It's about people who are complicated but decent, who are optimists but see things realistically, who are fundamentally comic characters but have three full dimensions. It's about a Middle America we rarely see in the movies, yes, but it's not corny and it doesn't condescend. Movies like this are hardly ever made at all;

when they're made this well, they're precious cinematic miracles.

Breaking the Waves

R, 158 m., 1996

Emily Watson (Bess), Stellan Skarsgard (Jan), Katrin Cartlidge (Dodo), Jean-Marc Barr (Terry), Udo Kier (Man on the Trawler), Adrian Rawlins (Dr. Richardson), Jonathan Hackett (The Minister), Sandra Voe (Bess's Mother). Directed by Lars von Trier and produced by Vibeke Windelov and Peter Aalbaek Jensen. Screenplay by von Trier.

Breaking the Waves is emotionally and spiritually challenging, hammering at conventional morality with the belief that God not only sees all, but understands a great deal more than we give Him credit for. It tells the story of Bess, a simple woman of childlike naïveté, who sacrifices herself to sexual brutality to save the life of the man she loves. Is she a sinner? The grim bearded elders of her church think so. But Bess is the kind of person Jesus was thinking of, I believe, when he suffered the little children to come unto him.

The movie takes place in the 1970s, in a remote northern Scottish village. Bess (Emily Watson), a sweet-faced and trusting girl, is "not quite right in the head," and her close-knit community is not pleased by her decision to marry Jan (Stellan Skarsgard), who works on one of the big oil rigs in the North Sea. But she loves Jan so much that when the helicopter bringing him to the wedding is delayed, she hits him in a fury. He is a tall, gentle man with a warm smile, and lets her flail away before embracing her in his big arms.

She is a virgin, but so eager to learn the secrets of marriage that she accosts her new husband in the powder room at the reception after the ceremony, telling him eagerly, "You can love me now!" And then, "What do I do?" The miracle of sexual expression transforms her, and she is grateful to God for having given her Jan and his love and his body. Meanwhile, downstairs at the ceremony, Jan's shipmate and Bess's grandfather scowl at one another; the shipmate crushes a beer can, and the grandfather picks up a lemonade glass and breaks it in his bloody hand.

We learn a little about Bess, who had a

breakdown when her brother died. Her closest friend is her sister-in-law, Dodo (Katrin Cartlidge), a nurse who stays in the remote district mostly because of her. Bess belongs to a strict sect where women do not speak in church, and the sermon over the body at a funeral might be, "You are a sinner and will find your place in hell." Bess's grandfather observes sourly, "We have no bells in our church."

Jan is critically injured in an accident on the rig. He is paralyzed from the neck down, and the local doctor tells Bess he may never walk again. "You don't know Jan!" she says fiercely. One day Jan asks her to find a man and make love to him "for my sake. And then tell me about it." Bess does not like this idea, but she does what Jan asks. Dodo is enraged: "Are you sleeping with other men to feed his sick fantasies? His head's full of scars—he's up to his eyeballs in drugs."

It is indeed never made quite clear why Jan, a good man, has made this request of the woman he loves. That is not the point. The point is that Bess, with her fierce faith, believes that somehow her sacrifice can redeem her husband and even cure him. As his condition grows worse, her behavior grows more desperate; she has herself taken out to a big ship where even the port prostitutes refuse to go because of the way they have been treated there.

The film contains many surprising revelations, including a cosmic one at the end, which I will leave you to discover for yourself. It has the kind of raw power, the kind of unshielded regard for the force of good and evil in the world, that we want to shy away from. It is easier sometimes to wrap ourselves in sentiment and pious platitudes, and forget that God created nature "red in tooth and nail." Bess does not have our ability to rationalize and evade, and fearlessly offers herself to God as she understands him.

This performance by Emily Watson reminds me of what Truffaut said about James Dean, that as an actor he was more like an animal than a man, proceeding according to instinct instead of thought and calculation. It is not a grim performance and is often touched by humor and delight, which makes it all the more touching, as when Bess talks out loud in two-way conversations with God, speaking both voices—making God a stern adult and

herself a trusting child. Her church banishes her and little boys in the village throw stones at her, but she tells a doctor, "God gives everyone something to be good at. I've always been stupid, but I'm good at this."

Breaking the Waves was written and directed by Lars von Trier, from Denmark, who makes us wonder what kinds of operas Nietzsche might have written. He finds the straight pure line through the heart of a story, and is not concerned with what cannot be known: This movie does not explain Jan's cruel request of his wife because Bess does not question it. It shows people who care about her, such as the sister-in-law and the local doctor, and others who do not: religious beancounters like the bearded church elders. They understand nothing about their Christianity except for unyielding rules they have memorized, which means they do not understand Christianity at all. They talk to God as if they expect him to listen and learn. At the end of the film they get their response in a great, savage, ironic peal.

Not many movies like this get made because not many filmmakers are so bold, angry, and defiant. Like many truly spiritual films, it will offend the Pharisees. Here we have a story that forces us to take sides, to ask what really is right and wrong in a universe that seems harsh and indifferent. Is religious belief only a consolation for our inescapable destination in the grave? Or can faith give the power to triumph over death and evil? Bess knows.

A Brief Vacation
PG, 112 m., 1973

Florinda Bolkan (Clara), Renato Salvatori (Husband), Daniel Quenaud (Luigi), Jose Maria Prada (Ciranni), Teresa Gimpera (Gina). Directed by Vittorio de Sica and produced by Marina Cicogna and Arhtur Cohn. Screenplay by Cesare Zavattini.

She leads a grim existence as a factory worker. Her husband has been hit by a motorcycle and is laid off with a broken leg. Her brother-in-law spies on her, and her mother-in-law spits on her. She's been diagnosed as a tuberculosis victim and sent to a sanitorium in the mountains, courtesy of the National Health Service. And now she has met a young man who is desperately in love with her, and she finds she loves him too. "We must try to keep our heads," she tells him, clinging to him. And then after a pause: "But *why* must we try to keep our heads?"

That's the question asked and never answered in Vittorio de Sica's last film, *A Brief Vacation*. De Sica, who died earlier this year, was one of the great directors of the postwar Italian neorealist movement, which represented a large, loud break with Hollywood tradition and dealt with life as it might exist outside sound stages.

In movies such as *Shoeshine* and *Bicycle Thief*, he told the stories of poor people trying to survive in a system geared up to manhandle them. His films grew slicker and more commercial by the 1960s, but he never lost his gift or his heart, and there were masterpieces such as *The Garden of the Finzi-Continis* (1971) and now this final return to a working-class subject.

It's not a movie, though, that offers solutions to the problems it sees; de Sica's communism was outworn long ago. It's a love story, a very brief and poignant one, surrounded by a lot of anger. And it's a "woman's picture" of the new sort, the kind in which women make up their own minds and make their own mistakes. His heroine, Clara (a luminous performance by Florinda Bolkan), is harassed and bone-tired and driven to shouting such things as "I'd do better as a whore" while she faces the bathroom mirror at dawn. But she has resources she never dreamed she owned.

De Sica quotes Appollinaiare: "Sickness is the vacation of the poor." That's the case here, and as the doctor tells Clara of the spot on her lung and prescribes a month or two in the mountains, the faces of her family shrink into meanness and envy. There is the thought, never quite spoken aloud, that her duty as a wife and mother is to stay in Milan and die. But she packs and goes. "Not for myself," she tells her husband in the middle of the night, "but to protect the children."

We realize within the first half hour that Clara is an intelligent woman living a life that makes few demands on intelligence. On the train she meets others going to the sanatorium, and they're all better off than she—a rich man's mistress, a "performer"—but almost from the moment they meet her they identify with her strength. She has coped with conditions of life the rest of them can hardly imagine, and they have left her shy in this new company, but her friends respond to her resiliency and her character.

The sanatorium is like a holiday. People like her and the food is good. When she meets the young man, it is for the second time; on the day she collapsed at work she met him at the clinic. They went next door for a coffee and discussed their jobs. His was a good one at Olivetti, but he had to bend over all the time. She was seen in the cafe and her husband was informed. When she returned home, tired and sick, he slapped her. "Our love began with my husband's slap," she tells the young man.

Their affair lasts only a moment. On Wednesdays the patients are allowed to go into town. They have talked once or twice, and now they come into each other's arms and make love urgently and immediately. Then they talk and dance and he asks her to run away with him to Germany. To get a divorce. "The poor cannot afford a divorce," she says. "And what of my children? Shall I throw them out?"

The love affair, her brief vacation, causes big changes in her ideas about herself. The other women tell her she's really pretty, that she should do something about her nails and learn to walk differently. She was always beautiful and now she allows herself to seem so. And her mind wakes up. A few paperbacks were left behind by a former patient and she reads them. "Who's reading this?" her husband asks during a visit. He is the kind of man who puts on his jacket as if he were lifting weights. "I am," she says. "You learned to read?" "I remembered. It was slow at first but now it goes all right."

This is a woman who tells her husband it will take the police to get her back to Milan, but at the movie's end we're not told what she will finally do. We have a notion, though, and we've met a tough, beautiful person. For the screenplay of *A Brief Vacation*, de Sica returned to his old collaborator Cesare Zavattini, the man who wrote *Bicycle Thief* and *Shoeshine*. It's as if, at seventy-three, he wanted to touch base again in case this was going to be his last film.

Bringing Out the Dead

R, 118 m., 1999

Nicolas Cage (Frank), Patricia Arquette (Mary), John Goodman (Larry), Ving Rhames (Marcus), Tom Sizemore (Walls), Marc Anthony (Noel), Cliff Curtis (Cy Coates), Mary Beth Hurt (Nurse Constance). Directed by Martin Scorsese and produced by Scott Rudin and Barbara De Fina. Screenplay by Paul Schrader, based on the book by Joe Connelly.

"I came to realize that my work was less about saving lives than about bearing witness. I was a grief mop."

The speaker is Frank, a paramedic whose journeys into the abyss of human misery provide the canvas for Martin Scorsese's *Bringing Out the Dead*. There may be happiness somewhere in the city, but the barking voice on Frank's radio doesn't dispatch him there. His job is to arrive at a scene of violence or collapse, and try to bring not only help but encouragement.

"Do you have any music?" he asks the family of a man who seems dead of a heart attack. "I think it helps if you play something he liked." As the old man's Sinatra album plays in the background, he applies the defibrillator to his chest and shouts, "Clear!" The corpse jumps into life like a movie monster. The psychology is sound: Sinatra may not bring the dead to life, but he will give the family something to do, and the song will remind them of their dad's happier times.

Frank is played by Nicolas Cage, seen in the movie's close-up with his eyes narrowed in pain. He cruises the streets of Hell's Kitchen with a series of three copilots, in a three-day stretch during which he drifts in and out of sanity; he has hallucinations of an eighteen-year-old homeless girl named Rose, whose life he failed to save, whose death he wants to redeem. Like Travis Bickle, the hero of Scorsese's *Taxi Driver* (1976), Frank travels the night streets like a boatman on the River Styx, while steam rises from manholes as if from the fires below. Travis wanted to save those who did not want saving. Frank finds those who desperately want help, but usually he is powerless.

The movie is based on a novel by Joe Connelly, himself once a New York paramedic. The screenplay by Paul Schrader is another chapter in the most fruitful writer-director collaboration of the quarter-century *(Taxi Driver, Raging Bull, The Last Temptation of Christ)*. The film wisely has no real plot, because the ambulance driver's days have no beginning or goal, but are a limbo of extended horror. At one point he hallucinates that he is helping pull people's bodies up out of the pavement, freeing them.

To look at *Bringing Out the Dead*—to look, indeed, at almost any Scorsese film—is to be reminded that film can touch us urgently and deeply. Scorsese is never on autopilot, never panders, never sells out, always goes for broke; to watch his films is to see a man risking his talent, not simply exercising it. He makes movies as well as they can be made, and I agree with an observation on the Harry Knowles Web site: You can enjoy a Scorsese film with the sound off, or with the sound on and the picture off.

Now look at *Bringing Out the Dead*. Three days in Frank's life. The first day his copilot is Larry (John Goodman), who deals with the grief by focusing on where his next meal is coming from. To Larry, it's a job, and you can't let it get to you. Day two, Larry works with Marcus (Ving Rhames), who is a gospel Christian and uses emergencies as an opportunity to demonstrate the power of Jesus; bringing one man back to life, he presents it as a miracle. On the third day, the day Christ rose from the dead, Frank's partner is Walls (Tom Sizemore), who is coming apart at the seams and wreaks havoc on hapless patients.

Haunting Frank's thoughts as he cruises with these guys are two women. One is Rose, whose face peers up at him from every street corner. The other is Mary (Patricia Arquette), the daughter of the man who liked Sinatra. After her dad is transferred to an intensive care unit, his life, such as it is, consists of dying and being shocked back to life, fourteen times one day, until Frank asks, "If he gets out, are you gonna follow him around with a defibrillator?" Mary is a former druggie, now clean and straight, and Frank—well, I was going to say he loves her, but this isn't one of those autopilot movies where the action hero has a romance in between the bloodshed. No, it's not love; it's need. He thinks they can save each other.

Scorsese assembles the film as levels in an

inferno. It contains some of his most brilliant sequences, particularly two visits to a high-rise drug house named the Oasis, where a dealer named Cy (Cliff Curtis) offers relief and sur-cease. Mary goes there one night when she cannot stand any more pain, and Frank follows to save her; that sets up a later sequence in which Frank treats Cy while he is dangling near death.

All suffering ends at the same place, the emergency room of the hospital nicknamed Our Lady of Perpetual Misery, where the receiving nurse (Mary Beth Hurt) knows most of the regulars by name. She dispenses the same advice in many forms: Stop what you're doing. But they don't listen, and will be back again. Noel (Marc Anthony) stands for many street people, tied to a gurney, screaming for a glass of water, hour after hour, while the ER team labors to plug the leaks, gaps, and wounds of a night in the city. They make long stories short: "This guy's plant food."

Nicolas Cage is an actor of great style and heedless emotional availability: He will go any-where for a role, and this film is his best since *Leaving Las Vegas*. I like the subtle way he and Scorsese embody what Frank has learned on the job, the little verbal formulas and quiet asides that help the bystanders at suffering. He embodies the tragedy of a man who has necessary work and is good at it, but in a job that is never, ever over.

Bringing Out the Dead is an antidote to the immature intoxication with violence in a film like *Fight Club*. It is not fun to get hit, it is not re-deeming to cause pain, it does not make you a man when you fight, because fights are an admission that you are not smart enough to survive by your wits. *Fight Club* makes a cartoon of the mean streets that Scorsese sees unblinkingly.

Bring Me the Head of Alfredo Garcia

R, 112 m., 1974

Warren Oates (Bennie), Isela Vega (Elita), Kris Kristofferson (Paco), Gig Young (Killer). Directed by Sam Peckinpah and produced by Martin Baum. Screenplay by Gordon T. Dawson and Peckinpah.

Sam Peckinpah's *Bring Me the Head of Alfredo Garcia* is a weird, horrifying film that somehow transcends its unlikely material. It's the story of a drunken and violent odyssey across Mexico by a dropout bartender who, if he returns Alfredo Garcia's head, stands to be paid a million dollars. The head accompanies him in a burlap bag, tossed into the front seat of a beat-up old Ford convertible, and it gathers flies and symbolic meaning at about the same pace.

The movie is some kind of bizarre master-piece. It's probably not a movie that most people would like, but violence, with Peckinpah, sometimes becomes a psychic ballet. His characters don't look for it, they don't like it, and they negotiate it with weariness and resignation. They're too beat up by life to get any kind of exhilaration from a fight. They've been in far too many fights already, and lost most of them, and the violence they encounter is just another cross to bear.

That's the case with Bennie, the antihero of *Bring Me the Head of Alfredo Garcia*. He's played by Warren Oates, one of that breed of movie actors who attract us, somehow, through their negative qualities. He's like some of the characters played by Jack Nicholson or Bruce Dern; we like him because he's suffered so much more than we ever will (we hope) that no matter what horrors he goes through, or inflicts, we still care about him.

Bennie is a bartender and plays a little piano, and he hears about the head of Alfredo Garcia from a couple of bounty hunters who pass through his saloon. They're played, by the way, by the unlikely team of Gig Young and Robert Webber, who between them define dissipation. Garcia's head is worth a million bucks because Garcia, it turns out, has impregnated the daughter of a rich Mexican industrialist. The millionaire is almost a caricature of macho compulsiveness; he simultaneously puts a price on the head of the culprit, and looks forward with pride to the birth of a grandson.

Bennie sees the million dollars as his ticket out of hell, and on the way to finding it he runs across Alfredo Garcia's former lover, Elita (Isela Vega, looking as moistly erotic as anyone since young Anna Magnani). They fall in love, or something; their relationship is complicated by Bennie's crude shyness and her own custom of being abused by men. The most perversely interesting relationship in the movie, however, is the friendship that grows between Bennie and Alfredo's head, once Bennie has gotten possession of it. That's made somewhat easier by the fact that Alfredo, it turns out, is already dead. But there is a gruesome struggle over his grave, and once Bennie finally gets the head he has to kill to protect his prize. His drive across Mexico is fueled by blood and tequila, and about halfway through it we realize why Peckinpah set his movie in the present, instead of in the past; this same material wouldn't have worked as a historical Western. The conventions of the genre would have insulted us from the impact of what happens. There would have been horses and watering holes and clichés. Instead, we get unforgettable scenes of Warren Oates with that grisly burlap bag and the bottle next to him in the front seat, and the nakedness of his greed is inescapable.

Somewhere along the way Oates, as Bennie, makes a compact with the prize he begins to call "Al." They both loved the same woman, they are both being destroyed by the same member of an upper class, they're both poor bastards who never asked for their grief in life. And slowly, out of the haze of the booze and the depths of his suffering, Bennie allies himself with Al and against the slob with the money. *Bring Me the Head of Alfredo Garcia* is Sam Peckinpah making movies flat out, giving us a desperate character he clearly loves, and asking us to somehow see past the horror and the blood to the sad poem he's trying to write about the human condition.

Broadcast News

R, 125 m., 1987

William Hurt (Tom Grunick), Albert Brooks (Aaron Altman), Holly Hunter (Jane Craig), Lois Chiles (Jennifer Mack), Joan Cusack (Blair Litton), Robert Prosky (Bureau Chief). Directed, produced, and written by James L. Brooks.

Broadcast News is as knowledgeable about the TV news-gathering process as any movie ever made, but it also has insights into the more personal matter of how people use high-pressure jobs as a way of avoiding time alone with themselves. The movie was described as being about a romantic triangle, but that's only partly true. It is about three people who toy with the idea of love, but are obsessed by the idea of making television.

Deadline pressure attracts people like that. The newspapers are filled with them, and also ad agencies, brokerages, emergency rooms, show business, sales departments, and police and fire stations. There's a certain adrenaline charge in delivering on a commitment at the last moment, in rushing out to be an instant hero or an instant failure. There's a kind of person who calls you up to shout into the phone, "I can't talk to you now—I'm busy!" This kind of person is always busy, because the lifestyle involves arranging things so you're always behind. Given plenty of time to complete a job, you wait until the last moment to start—guaranteeing a deadline rush.

I know all about that kind of obsession (you don't think I finished this review early, do you?). *Broadcast News* understands it from the inside out, and perhaps the most interesting sequence in the whole movie is a scene where a network news producer sweats it out with a videotape editor to finish a report that is scheduled to appear on the evening news in fifty-two seconds. In an atmosphere like that, theoretical questions get lost. The operational reality, day after day, is to get the job done and beat the deadline and make things look as good as possible. Positive feedback goes to people who deliver. Yesterday's job is forgotten. What have you got for me today?

Right at the center of *Broadcast News* is a character named Jane Craig (Holly Hunter), who is a newswriter-producer for the Washington bureau of one of the networks. She is smart and fast and cherishes certain beliefs about TV news—one of them being that a story should be covered by the person best qualified to cover it. One of her best friends is Aaron Altman (Albert Brooks), a bright, aggressive reporter. He's one of the best in the business, but he's not especially good on camera. During a trip south she meets Tom Grunick (William Hurt), a sportscaster who cheerfully admits he has little education, is not a good reader, and doesn't know much about current events. But he has been hired for the Washington bureau because he looks good and has a natural relationship with the camera.

The Hunter character is only human. She is repelled by this guy's credentials, but she likes his body. After he comes to Washington, he quickly gains the attention of the network brass, while the Brooks character goes into eclipse. Hunter is torn between the two men: Brooks, who says he loves her and is the better reporter, and Hurt, who says he wants to learn, and who is sexier.

The tricky thing about *Broadcast News*—the quality in James L. Brooks's screenplay that makes it so special—is that all three characters have a tendency to grow emotionally absent-minded when it's a choice between romance and work. Frankly, they'd rather work. After Hunter whispers into Hurt's earpiece to talk him through a crucial live report on a Middle East crisis, he kneels at her feet and says it was like sex, having her voice inside his head. He never gets that excited about sex. Neither does she.

Much of the plot of *Broadcast News* centers around a piece that Hurt reports about "date rape." Listening to one woman's story, he is so moved that a tear trickles down his cheek. It means a great deal to Hunter whether that tear is real or faked. Experienced TV people will question why Hunter, a veteran producer, didn't immediately notice the detail that bothers her so much later on. But in a way, *Broadcast News* is not about details, but about the larger question of whether TV news is becoming show business.

Jack Nicholson has an unbilled supporting role in the movie as the network's senior anchorman, an irascible man who has high standards himself, but is not above seeing his ratings assisted by coverage that may be questionable. The implication is that the next anchor will be a William Hurt-type, great on camera, but incapable of discerning authenticity from fakery. Meanwhile, the Albert Brooks types will end up doing superior journalism in smaller "markets" (the TV word for "cities"), and the Holly Hunter types will keep on fighting all the old deadlines, plus a new one, the biological clock.

Broadcast News has a lot of interesting things to say about television. But the thing it does best is look into a certain kind of personality and a certain kind of relationship. Like *Terms of Endearment*, the previous film by James Brooks, it does not see relationships as a matter

of meeting someone you like and falling in love. Brooks, almost alone among major Hollywood filmmakers, knows that some people have higher priorities than love, and deeper fears.

Brokeback Mountain

R, 134 m., 2005

Heath Ledger (Ennis Del Mar), Jake Gyllenhaal (Jack Twist), Michelle Williams (Alma Del Mar), Anne Hathaway (Lureen Twist), Randy Quaid (Joe Aguirre), Linda Cardellini (Cassie Cartwright), Anna Faris (LaShawn Malone). Directed by Ang Lee and produced by Diana Ossana and James Schamus. Screenplay by Larry McMurtry and Ossana, based on the short story by E. Annie Proulx.

Ennis tells Jack about something he saw as a boy. "There were two old guys shacked up together. They were the joke of the town, even though they were pretty tough old birds." One day they were found beaten to death. Ennis says: "My dad, he made sure me and my brother saw it. For all I know, he did it."

This childhood memory is always there, the ghost in the room, in Ang Lee's *Brokeback Mountain*. When he was taught by his father to hate homosexuals, Ennis was taught to hate his own feelings. Years after he first makes love with Jack on a Wyoming mountainside, after his marriage has failed, after his world has compressed to a mobile home, the Laundromat, the TV, he still feels the same pain: "Why don't you let me be? It's because of you, Jack, that I'm like this—nothing, and nobody."

But it's not because of Jack. It's because Ennis and Jack love each other and can find no way to deal with that. *Brokeback Mountain* has been described as "a gay cowboy movie," which is a cruel simplification. It is the story of a time and place where two men are forced to deny the only great passion either one will ever feel. Their tragedy is universal. It could be about two women, or lovers from different religious or ethnic groups—any "forbidden" love.

The movie wisely never steps back to look at the larger picture, or deliver the "message." It is specifically the story of these men, this love. It stays in close-up. That's how Jack and Ennis see it. "You know I ain't queer," Ennis tells Jack after their first night together. "Me neither," says Jack.

Their story begins in Wyoming in 1963, when Ennis (Heath Ledger) and Jack (Jake Gyllenhaal) are about nineteen years old and get jobs tending sheep on a mountainside. Ennis is a boy of so few words he can barely open his mouth to release them; he learned to be guarded and fearful long before he knew what he feared. Jack, who has done some rodeo riding, is a little more outgoing. After some days have passed on the mountain and some whiskey has been drunk, they suddenly and almost violently have sex.

"This is a one-shot thing we got going on here," Ennis says the next day. Jack agrees. But it's not. When the summer is over, they part laconically: "I guess I'll see ya around, huh?" Their boss (Randy Quaid) tells Jack he doesn't want him back next summer: "You guys sure found a way to make the time pass up there. You weren't getting paid to let the dogs guard the sheep while you stemmed the rose."

Some years pass. Both men get married. Then Jack goes to visit Ennis and the undiminished urgency of their passion stuns them. Their lives settle down into a routine, punctuated less often than Jack would like by "fishing trips." Ennis's wife, who has seen them kissing, says nothing about it for a long time. But she notices there are never any fish.

The movie is based on a short story by E. Annie Proulx. The screenplay is by Larry McMurtry and Diana Ossana. Last summer I read McMurtry's *Lonesome Dove* books, and as I saw the movie I was reminded of Gus and Woodrow, the two cowboys who spend a lifetime together. They aren't gay; one of them is a womanizer, and the other spends his whole life regretting the loss of the one woman he loved. They're straight but just as crippled by a society that tells them how a man must behave and what he must feel.

Brokeback Mountain could tell its story and not necessarily be a great movie. It could be a melodrama. It *could* be a "gay cowboy movie." But the filmmakers have focused so intently and with such feeling on Jack and Ennis that the movie is as observant as work by Bergman. Strange but true: The more specific a film is, the more universal, because the more it understands individual characters, the more it applies to everyone. I can imagine someone weeping at this film, identifying with it because he always wanted to stay in the marines, or be an artist or a cabinetmaker.

Jack is able to accept a little more willingly that he is inescapably gay. In frustration and need he goes to Mexico one night and finds a male prostitute. Prostitution is a calling with hazards, sadness, and tragedy, but it accepts human nature. It knows what some people need, and perhaps that is why every society has found a way to accommodate it.

Jack thinks he and Ennis might someday buy themselves a ranch and settle down. Ennis, who remembers what he saw as a boy: "This thing gets hold of us at the wrong time and wrong place and we're dead." Well, wasn't Matthew Shepard murdered in Wyoming in 1998? And Brandon Teena in Nebraska in 1993? Haven't brothers killed their sisters in the Muslim world to defend "family honor"?

There are gentle and nuanced portraits of Ennis's wife, Alma (Michelle Williams), and Jack's wife, Lureen (Anne Hathaway), who are important characters, seen as victims, too. Williams has a powerful scene where she finally calls Ennis on his "fishing trips," but she takes a long time to do that, because nothing in her background prepares her for what she has found out about her husband. In their own way, programs like *Jerry Springer* provide a service by focusing on people, however pathetic, who are prepared to defend what they feel. In 1963 there was nothing like that on TV. And in 2005, the situation has not entirely changed. One of the ads for *Brokeback Mountain*'s Oscar campaign shows Ledger and Williams together, although the movie's posters are certainly honest.

Ang Lee is a director whose films are set in many nations and many times. What they have in common is an instinctive sympathy for the characters. Born Chinese, he makes movies about Americans, British, Chinese, straights, gays; his sci-fi movie *Hulk* was about a misunderstood outsider. Here he respects the entire arc of his story, right down to the lonely conclusion.

A closing scene involving a visit by Ennis to Jack's parents is heartbreaking in what is said, and not said, about their world. A look around Jack's childhood bedroom suggests what he overcame to make room for his feelings. What we cannot be sure of is this: In the flashback, are we witnessing what really happened to Jack, or how Ennis sees it in his imagination? Ennis, whose father "made sure me and my brother saw it."

Broken Flowers

R, 105 m., 2005

Bill Murray (Don Johnston), Jeffrey Wright (Winston), Sharon Stone (Laura), Frances Conroy (Dora), Jessica Lange (Carmen), Tilda Swinton (Penny), Julie Delpy (Sherry), Alexis Dziena (Lolita), Chloë Sevigny (Carmen's Assistant), Chris Bauer (Dan). Directed by Jim Jarmusch and produced by Jon Kilik and Stacey Smith. Screenplay by Jarmusch.

Broken Flowers stars Bill Murray as Don Johnston, a man who made his money in computers and now doesn't even own one. To sit at the keyboard would mean moving from his sofa, where he seems to be stuck. As the film opens, his latest girlfriend (Julie Delpy) is moving out. She doesn't want to spend any more time with "an over-the-hill Don Juan." After she leaves, he remains on the sofa, listening to music. He reaches out for a glass of wine, changes his mind, lets the hand drop.

This is a man whose life is set on idle. His neighbor Winston (Jeffrey Wright), on the other hand, is a go-getter from Ethiopia who supports a wife and five kids with three jobs and still has time to surf the Net as an amateur detective. One day, Don receives a letter suggesting that twenty years ago he fathered a son and that a nineteen-year-old boy may be searching for him at this very moment. Don is unmoved by this intelligence, but Winston is energized; he extracts from Don the names of all the women who could possibly be the mother, and he supplies Don with plane tickets and an itinerary so that he can visit the candidates and figure out which one might have sent the letter.

"The letter is on pink stationery," Winston says. "Give them pink flowers and watch their reaction." Don nods, barely, and embarks on his journey—not to discover if he has a child so much as to discover if he wants a child. At one point, he phones Winston from the road, complaining that he has been supplied with conventional rental cars. Why couldn't he have a Porsche? "I'm a stalker in a Taurus."

No actor is better than Murray at doing nothing at all and being fascinating while not doing it. Buster Keaton had the same gift for contemplating astonishing developments with absolute calm. Keaton surrounded himself with slapstick, and in *Broken Flowers,* Jim Jarmusch surrounds Murray with a parade of formidable women.

First stop, Laura (Sharon Stone). Her husband was a NASCAR champion but "died in a wall of flame." Her daughter (Alexis Dziena), who is named Lolita, offers Don her Popsicle and, unmistakably, herself. Neither daughter nor mother seems to know that the name Lolita has literary associations. Don does in fact spend the night with the mother, but we do not see precisely what goes on, and it's just as well: The sight of this passive and withdrawn man making love might be sad beyond calculation.

Second woman: Dora (Frances Conroy), who with her husband, Dan (Chris Bauer), is a Realtor, specializing in selling "quality prefabs" and currently living in a "wonderful example." Don's dinner with Dora and Dan grows unspeakably depressing after he asks the wrong question.

Third woman: Carmen (Jessica Lange), protected by her ambiguous assistant (Chloë Sevigny). Carmen is an "animal communicator," who talks to people's pets on their behalf. The movie doesn't take cheap shots at this occupation but suggests Carmen may be the real thing. "Is he saying something?" Don asks, as Carmen converses with her cat. Carmen: "He says you have a hidden agenda."

The fourth woman, Penny (Tilda Swinton), has a front yard full of motorcycles and lives in an atmosphere that makes Don feel threatened, not without reason. There was a fifth possible candidate, who has been eliminated from Don's list because, well, she's dead.

Were any of these women the mother of his child? I will leave that for you, and Don, to discover. After the film's premiere at Cannes, I observed: "Some actors give the kinds of performances where we want to get out of the room, stand on the lawn, and watch them through a window. Murray has the uncanny ability to invite us into his performance, into his stillness and sadness. I don't know how he does it. A Bill Murray imitation would be a pitiful sight: Passive immobility, small gestures of the eyes, enigmatic comments, yes, those would be easy, but how does he suggest the low tones of crashing chaotic uncertainty?"

Jarmusch first came into focus in 1984 with *Stranger than Paradise*, about a slick New Yorker who gets an unexpected visit from his Hungarian cousin, who is sexy and naive and soon leaves to visit her aunt in Cleveland. Then followed a series of films of various degrees of wonderfulness; I have admired them all except for *Dead Man* (1995); the critic Jonathan Rosenbaum regards me sadly every time this title is mentioned. Jarmusch makes films about outsiders, but they're not loners; they're soloists. Murray's character here is the ultimate Jarmusch soloist, in that he lacks even an instrument. His act is to walk onto the stage and not play.

How did Don fascinate these women in the first place? Why are most of them (relatively) happy to see him again? Perhaps they were simply curious. Perhaps they embodied nature, and he embodied a vacuum. At the end, there is an enigmatic scene that explains little or nothing. Still, it opens up the possibility that if Don ever did discover he had a son, he would try to do the right thing. That would mean he was doing something, and that would be a start.

A Bronx Tale

R, 121 m., 1993

Robert De Niro (Lorenzo), Chazz Palminteri (Sonny), Lillo Brancato (Calogero, age 17), Francis Capra (Calogero, age 9), Taral Hicks (Jane), Kathrine Narducci (Rosina), Clem Caserta (Jimmy Whispers), Joe Pesci (Carmine). Directed by De Niro and produced by Jane Rosenthal, Jon Kilik, and De Niro. Screenplay by Palminteri.

A boy comes of age in an Italian-American neighborhood in the Bronx. His father gives him a piece of advice: "Nothing is more tragic than a wasted talent." A street-corner gangster gives him another piece of advice: "Nobody really cares." These pieces of advice seem contradictory, but the boy finds that they make a nice fit.

The movie starts when he is nine. Sitting on his front stoop, he sees Sonny, the gangster,

shoot a man in what looks like a fight over a parking space. Then Sonny looks him in the eyes, hard, and the kid gets the message: "Don't squeal!" Sonny (Chazz Palminteri) wants to do something for the kid, and offers a cushy $150-a-week paycheck to his father, Lorenzo (Robert De Niro). Lorenzo turns him down. He is a working man, proud that he supports his family by driving a bus. He doesn't like the Mafia and doesn't want the money.

The kid, whose name is Calogero but who is called C, idolizes Sonny. He likes the way Sonny exercises a quiet authority, and talks with his hands, and dresses well. When C is seventeen, he goes to work for Sonny, against his father's wishes. And in the year when most of the film is set, he learns lessons that he will use all of his life.

A Bronx Tale was written for the stage by Palminteri, who plays Sonny with a calm grace in the film, but was Calogero in real life. There have been a lot of movies about neighborhood mafiosi (Martin Scorsese's *Good-Fellas* was the best), but this movie isn't like the others. It doesn't tell some dumb story about how the bus driver and the mobster have to shoot each other, or about how C is the hostage in a tug-of-war. It's about two men with some experience of life, who love this kid and want to help him out.

Lorenzo, the bus driver, gives sound advice: "You want to see a real hero? Look at a guy who gets up in the morning and goes off to work and supports his family. That's heroism." But Sonny gives sound advice, too. One of the things he tells C is that you cannot live your life on the basis of what other people think you should do, because when the chips are down, nobody really cares. You're giving them a power they don't really have. That sounds like deep thinking for a guy who hangs on the corner and runs a numbers racket, but Sonny, as played by Palminteri, is a complex, lonely character, who might have been a priest or a philosopher had not life called him to the vocation of neighborhood boss.

It is 1968. Blacks are moving into the next neighborhood. C's friends entertain themselves by beating up on black kids who ride past on their bikes. C has other things on his mind. On his father's bus, he has seen a lovely black girl named Jane (Taral Hicks), and been struck with the thunderbolt of love. From the way she smiles back, she likes him, too. When he discovers that they go to the same school, he knows his fate is to ask her out.

But he is troubled, because in 1968 this is not the thing for a kid from his neighborhood (or hers) to do. He questions both his father and Sonny, posing a hypothetical case, and although neither bursts into liberalspeak about the brotherhood of man, both tell him about the same thing, which is that you have to do what you think is right, or live with the consequences.

C's romance is a sweet subplot of the movie, which is filled with life and memories. There are, for example, the characters in Sonny's crowd, including a guy who is such bad luck he has to go stand in the bathroom when Sonny is rolling the dice. And another guy with a complexion so bad he looks like raisin bread. And strange visitors from outside the neighborhood—bikers and hippies and black people—who remind us that C lives in a closed and insular community.

The climax of the film finds C inside a car he does not want to occupy, going with his friends to do something he doesn't want to do. This part is very true. Peer pressure is a terrible thing among teenage boys. It causes them to do things they desperately wish they could avoid. They're afraid to look chicken, or different. C is no exception. His whole life hinges on the outcome of that ride.

A Bronx Tale is a very funny movie sometimes, and very touching at other times. It is filled with life and colorful characters and great lines of dialogue, and De Niro, in his debut as a director, finds the right notes as he moves from laughter to anger to tears. What's important about the film is that it's about values. About how some boys grow up into men who can look at themselves in the mirror in the morning, and others just go along with the crowd, forgetting after a while that they ever had a choice.

Brother's Keeper

NO MPAA RATING, 104 m., 1992

Directed, produced, and edited by Joe Berlinger and Bruce Sinofsky.

For as long as anyone in the central New York hamlet of Munnsville (population 500) could remember, the Ward boys had run a dairy farm outside of town. Everybody knew them—by sight, anyway—and figured them for harmless old coots. They didn't bathe or shave overmuch, and rode into town arrayed on their tractor. They lived in a two-room shack that few of their neighbors had much desire to visit, or get downwind from.

Then, on a June morning in 1990, William Ward, at sixty-four the second-oldest brother, was discovered dead in bed. He had been feeling poorly for quite some time, and given his general condition, it was reasonable to assume he died of natural causes. But a hotshot local lawman smelled foul play, and within a day the youngest brother, Delbert, fifty-nine, was charged with murder. *Brother's Keeper* is an extraordinary documentary about what happened next, as a town banded together to stop what it saw as a miscarriage of justice.

"Hell," one of the townspeople observes, "when they asked Delbert if he was ready to waive his rights, he didn't know the difference between that and waving to someone on the road."

The Ward boys are none of them any too bright, although it's a good question whether they are retarded or simply completely out of touch with modern life. Their cows and pigs live in greater comfort on their farm than they do, not to mention the poultry they raise in an old school bus. They farmed for many decades, keeping to themselves, working long hours, sitting in front of a TV at night, turning in early.

The controversy over the Wards quickly hit the national media. It had everything: quaint rural hayseeds, dark hints of fratricide, doubts over the due process of law. Connie Chung and other media stars turned up to interview the Ward boys, and so did documentary filmmakers Joe Berlinger and Bruce Sinofsky and their cinematographer, Douglas Cooper.

They kept coming back, for more than a year; the passage of the seasons provides an undercurrent for the film. They filmed hearings and trials, community meetings, and even the benefits held to raise money for Delbert's defense. The irony was that after trouble found the Wards, they became more popular and accepted in Munnsville than ever before, and it's quite a sight, seeing them square dancing at a fund-raiser and loading up their plates at the buffet table.

Berlinger and Sinofsky were patient with Delbert and his two surviving brothers, Roscoe, seventy, and Lyman, sixty-two. They won their trust, and soon it was a common sight in Munnsville to see the brothers followed by the small camera team. We gradually begin to get a sense of the three men, whose values and daily rhythms reflect lives of hard manual labor as they might have been lived centuries ago.

The film wisely never takes a position on the actual guilt of Delbert (and I would not dream of revealing the outcome of his legal process, which unfolds as a courtroom drama). Instead, it tries to see into their lives, to understand that for unlearned men who had lived so close to the harsh realities of farming, life and death itself had a more fundamental meaning. Did Delbert smother William with a pillow, as the prosecution charged, in order to put him out of his misery—as he might have put down a sick animal? Or did William die in his sleep? Or are there darker possibilities?

Brother's Keeper, 1992's best documentary, has an impact and immediacy that most fiction films can only envy. It tells a strong story, and some passages are truly inspirational, as the neighbors of Munnsville become determined that Delbert will not be railroaded by some ambitious prosecutor more concerned with bringing charges than with understanding the reality of the situation. Seeing this film, I got a new appreciation for how deeply the notion of civil liberties is embedded in our national consciousness. None of the people on the Delbert Ward defense committee ever went to law school. But they know a lot more about fair play and due process than the people in this film who did.

Bubble

R, 73 m., 2006

Debbie Doebereiner (Martha), Dustin James Ashley (Kyle), Misty Dawn Wilkins (Rose), Omar Cowan (Martha's Dad), Laurie Lee (Kyle's Mother), David Hubbard (Pastor), Kyle Smith (Jake), Decker Moody (Detective Don). Directed by Steven Soderbergh and produced by Gregory Jacobs. Screenplay by Coleman Hough.

Steven Soderbergh's *Bubble* approaches with awe and caution the rhythms of ordinary life itself. He tells the stories of three Ohio factory workers who have been cornered by life. They work two low-paying jobs, they dream of getting a few bucks ahead, they eat fast food without noticing it, two of them live with their parents, one of them has a car. Their speech is such a monotone of commonplaces that we have to guess about how they really feel, and sometimes, we suspect, so do they.

I haven't made the movie sound enthralling. But it is. The characters are so closely observed and played with such exacting accuracy and conviction that *Bubble* becomes quietly, inexorably hypnotic. Soderbergh never underlines, never points, never uses music to suggest emotion, never shows the characters thinking ahead, watches appalled as small shifts in orderly lives lead to a murder.

Everything about the film—its casting, its filming, its release—is daring and innovative. Soderbergh, the poster boy of the Sundance generation (for *sex, lies . . . and videotape* sixteen years ago), has moved confidently ever since between commercial projects *(Ocean's Eleven)* and cutting-edge experiments like *Bubble.* The movie was cast with local people who were not actors. They participated in the creation of their dialogue. Their own homes were used as sets. The film was shot quickly in high-definition video.

And when it opens in theaters, it will simultaneously play on HDNet cable and four days later be released on DVD. Here is an experiment to see if there is a way to bring a small art film to a larger audience; most films like this would play in a handful of big-city art houses, and you'd read this review and maybe reflect that it sounded interesting and then lose track of it. In a time when audiences are pounded into theaters with multimillion-dollar ad campaigns, here's a small film with a big idea behind it.

As the film opens, Martha (Debbie Doebereiner) awakens, brings breakfast to her elderly father, picks up Kyle (Dustin James Ashley) at his mobile home, stops at a bakery, and arrives at the doll factory where they both work. He operates machinery to create plastic body parts. She paints the faces and adds the eyelashes and hair. During their lunch hour in a room of Formica and fluorescence, they talk about nothing much. He doesn't have time to date. He'd like to get the money together to buy a car. He'd like a ride after work to his other job. Martha, who is fat and ten or fifteen years older than Kyle, watches him carefully, looking for clues in his shy and inward speech.

Rose (Misty Dawn Wilkins) begins work at the factory. She is introduced to the workforce and provides Kyle with a smile so small he may not even see it, but Martha does. How should we read this? In a conventional movie, Kyle would be attracted to Rose, and Martha would be jealous. But *Bubble* is more cautiously modulated. Martha, I believe, has never allowed herself to think Kyle would be attracted to her. What she wants from him is what she already has: a form of possession in the way he depends on her for rides and chats with her at lunch. Nor does Kyle seem prepared to go after Rose. He is shy, quiet, and withdrawn, smokes pot at home, keeps a low profile at work.

Rose at least represents change. She takes Martha along to a suburban house that she cleans, and Martha is shocked to find her taking a bubble bath. Rose explains that her apartment, which she shares with her two-year-old daughter, has only a shower. "I'm not too sure about her," Martha tells Kyle. "She scares me a little."

Rose asks Kyle out. In a bar, they share their reasons for dropping out of high school. Their date goes nowhere—not even when Rose gets herself asked into his bedroom—because Kyle is too passive to make a move, or maybe even to respond to one. He's too beaten down by life. "I'm very ready to get out of this area," says Rose, who observes that everybody is poor and there are no opportunities.

I am describing the events but not the fascination they create. The uncanny effect comes in large part from the actors. I learn that Debbie Doebereiner is the manager of a KFC. That Misty Dawn Wilkins is a hairdresser, and her own daughter plays her daughter in the movie.

They are not playing themselves, but they are playing people they know from the inside out, and although Soderbergh must have worked closely with them, his most important work was in the casting: Not everybody could carry a feature film made of everyday life and make it work, but these three do. The movie feels so real a hush falls upon the audience, and we are made aware of how much artifice there is in conventional acting. You wouldn't want to spend the rest of your life watching movies like this, because artifice has its uses, but in this film, with these actors, something mysterious happens.

I said there was a murder. That's all I'll say about it. The local police inspector (Decker Moody) handles the case. He is played by an actual local police inspector. We have seen a hundred or a thousand movies where a cop visits the crime scene and later cross-examines people. There has never been one like this. In the flat, experienced, businesslike way he does his job, and in the way his instincts guide him past misleading evidence, the inspector depends not on crime-movie suspense but on implacable logic. *Bubble* ends not with the solution to a crime but with the revelation of the depths of a lonely heart.

Some theater owners are boycotting *Bubble* because they hate the idea of a simultaneous release on cable and DVD. I think it's the only hope for a movie like this. Let's face it. Even though I call the film a masterpiece (and I do), my plot description has not set you afire with desire to see the film. Unless you admire Soderbergh or can guess what I'm saying about the performances, you'll be there in line for *Annapolis* or *Nanny McPhee*. But maybe you're curious enough to check it out on cable, or rent it on DVD, or put it in your Netflix queue. That's how movies like this can have a chance. And how you can have a chance to see them.

Bugsy
R, 135 m., 1991

Warren Beatty (Bugsy Siegel), Annette Bening (Virginia Hill), Harvey Keitel (Mickey Cohen), Ben Kingsley (Meyer Lansky), Elliott Gould (Harry Greenberg), Joe Mantegna (George). Directed by Barry Levinson and produced by Mark Johnson, Levinson, and Beatty. Screenplay by James Toback.

He's a real smoothie, Warren Beatty, and when he plays one in a movie he is almost always effective. But his title role in *Bugsy* is more than effective; it's perfect for him—showing a man who not only creates a seductive vision, but falls in love with it himself. Beatty plays Benjamin "Bugsy" Siegel, who if he were not a gangster might have been honored on a postage stamp by now as the father of Las Vegas.

Siegel ventured west with some of the eastern mob's investment funds in the early 1940s, and fell in love almost immediately with a leggy starlet named Virginia Hill (Annette Bening). He also fell in love with the movies, and with his slick good looks even got a screen test, although his best scenes were all to be played in mob boardrooms.

His great role in history came to him as he stood in a sleazy, low-rent casino in Vegas, which was then an obscure crossroads in a state that permitted legalized gambling. Ben Siegel had a vision of a Las Vegas that was not an obscure backwater, but a town with big, classy casinos that had name acts in their show rooms. Nobody shared his vision. But he knew that if he built it, they would come. And he did build one casino, the Flamingo, its name inspired by Virginia Hill's legs. He spent so much of the mob's money on it, in fact, that he was rubbed out before he could see the modern city spring from his dream.

This story is told in *Bugsy*, not as history, but as a romance. The screenplay by James Toback, developed with Beatty and then directed by Barry Levinson, shows Siegel as a smooth, charming, even lovable guy, even though he was also a coldhearted killer. The two sides of his character hardly seem to acknowledge one another; on the one hand, he is a family man with a wife and children, who goes to work every day. On the other hand, he is an adulterer whose business involves killing people, and who defies the Mafia itself by spending more of its money than he has quite gotten around to accounting for.

Watching Beatty and Annette Bening in this movie, it is impossible not to be reminded of the famous ad line for *Bonnie and Clyde* (1967), the greatest moment in Beatty's career: "They're young, they're in love . . . and they kill people." Hill does not kill, but she is as hard and calculating, and seductive, as the Bonnie Parker character, and there are times here when Bugsy and Virginia and Bonnie and Clyde all seem to be playing the same tunes on their libidos.

Levinson is back in the same period he used for key scenes of his last picture, *Avalon*, and the 1940s look roomy and plush here; it was a decade that had many of the same inventions we now take for granted, like automobiles and telephones, but back then they were full size and made out of materials that would not break. Bugsy moves into a big Beverly Hills house (he makes the owner an offer he cannot refuse), he hangs out in the right restaurants and clubs, he makes the right contacts, he gets a lot of publicity, and his image is summed up in a headline: Gangster or Star?

It's a question the mob is asking, too. Levinson's movie strikes a different tone than the *Godfather* pictures, but like them, it shows the Mafia as essentially a business, depending on discipline. Levinson and Toback are interested in a different strata of organized crime than Francis Coppola and Mario Puzo, however; the *Godfather* pictures were mostly about Italian-Americans, and most of the key characters in *Bugsy* are Jewish. There's Ben Kingsley, as Meyer Lansky, the only Mafia leader who perhaps fully understood what made Bugsy tick; Harvey Keitel, as Mickey Cohen, an unforgiving killer; and Elliott Gould, as Harry Greenberg, the hapless friend for whom Bugsy will walk a mile, but no further.

For Toback, the screenplay touches on obsessions that are deep in his previous work. His first notable screenplay was *The Gambler* (1974), starring James Caan as a compulsive bettor, and in Toback's own movies as a director (*Fingers, Exposed, The Pick-Up Artist*) are the twin themes of men obsessively attracted to women, and men driven to extend themselves financially to the point of actual physical danger, usually from criminals.

Here, Bugsy Siegel scarcely seems to comprehend the danger he is hurtling toward. Distracted by his passionate love affair, besotted by his vision of a gambling temple in the desert, he listens to the warnings of Lansky and others, but does not seem to understand them. Meanwhile, the movie develops a sly, fascinating subplot involving Virginia Hill's own tangled motives. Does she really love Bugsy or money? Does she really know?

Bugsy moves with a lightness that belies its strength. It is a movie that vibrates with optimism and passion, with the exuberance of the con man on his game. Bugsy Siegel is not a good man and no doubt does not deserve a good end, but somehow we are carried along with him because he seems so innocent (even of his own bloody sins). At the end of the movie there's one of those "crawls," as Hollywood calls them, where we're told what eventually happened—how Las Vegas became a $200 billion industry, how Virginia Hill finally died. It's the kind of crawl you'd get at the end of a movie about a great man. This time, with Bugsy, you don't get a lump in your throat, but you do think, jeez, it's too bad the guy didn't at least live to see Glitter Gulch.

Bullitt
PG, 113 m., 1968

Steve McQueen (Bullitt), Robert Vaughn (Chalmers), Jacqueline Bisset (Cathy), Don Gordon (Delgetti), Robert Duvall (Weissberg), Simon Oakland (Capt. Bennett), Norman Fell (Baker). Directed by Peter Yates and produced by Philip D'Antoni. Screenplay by Alan R. Trustman and Harry Kleiner.

Steve McQueen is sometimes criticized for only playing "himself" in the movies. This misses the boat, I think. Stars such as McQueen, Bogart, Wayne, or Newman aren't primarily actors, but presences. They have a myth, a personal legend they've built up in our minds during many movies, and when they try to play against that image it usually looks phony.

McQueen was a bomb as Thomas Crown, for example, because the character clashed with McQueen's own personality. But McQueen is great in *Bullitt*, and the movie is great, because director Peter Yates understands the McQueen image and works within it. He winds up with about the best action movie of recent years.

McQueen plays a San Francisco cop assigned as bodyguard to a syndicate witness. The witness gets shotgunned—in the most brutally direct ten seconds of film I can remember—and McQueen becomes a political

football. Robert Vaughn (better than usual) is the politician who puts on the heat, and it's up to McQueen to hide the victim's body until he can untangle the case.

It's a very tangled case, too. The beautiful thing is that Yates and his writers keep everything straight. There's nothing worse than a complicated plot that loses track of itself (as in *The Lady in Cement*, which I defy anyone to explain).

Bullitt is Yates's second film; his first was *Robbery*, a superior movie about England's great train robbery, that played Chicago earlier this year. *Robbery* had a great chase sequence in it, involving a running machine-gun battle, all sorts of near-misses in heavy traffic, lots of blood, and remarkable photography.

Bullitt, as everybody has heard by now, also includes a brilliant chase scene. McQueen (doing his own driving) is chased by, and chases, a couple of gangsters up and down San Francisco's hills. They slam into intersections, bounce halfway down the next hill, scrape by half a dozen near-misses, sideswipe each other, and leave your stomach somewhere in the basement for about eleven minutes.

One trouble: They couldn't be satisfied with a cop movie, I guess; they had to have sex appeal, and so they brought in Jacqueline Bisset (a lovely sight, true) to be McQueen's girl. And every line she recites is disastrously inappropriate. She has one speech so awful it takes the movie five minutes to recover.

Yates pulled the same trick in *Robbery*, giving Stanley Baker a wife he didn't need so the movie could have three unnecessary scenes with her. And Lee Remick cluttered up *The Detective*. And Inga Stevens was extra baggage in *Madigan*. They ought to leave the girls out or make them policewomen, like *Coogan's Bluff* did, come to think of it.

Bully
NO MPAA RATING, 112 m., 2001

Brad Renfro (Marty Puccio), Rachel Miner (Lisa Connelly), Nick Stahl (Bobby Kent), Bijou Phillips (Ali Willis), Michael Pitt (Donny Semenec), Kelli Garner (Heather Swaller), Daniel Franzese (Derek Dzvirko), Leo Fitzpatrick (Hit Man). Directed by Larry Clark and produced by Chris Hanley, Don Murphy, and Fernando Sulichin. Screenplay by Zachary Long and Roger Pullis, based on the book *Bully: A True Story of High School Revenge* by Jim Schutze.

Larry Clark's *Bully* calls the bluff of movies that pretend to be about murder but are really about entertainment. His film has all the sadness and shabbiness, all the mess and cruelty and thoughtless stupidity of the real thing. Based on a real incident from 1993, it tells the story of a twisted high school bully and a circle of friends who decide to kill him. But this is not about the evil sadist and the release of revenge; it's about how a group of kids will do something no single member is capable of. And about the moral void these kids inhabit.

Clark moved to the Hollywood, Florida, suburb where the actual murder took place, and sees it as a sterile expanse of identikit homes, strip malls, and boredom, where the kids drift from video arcades to fast-food hangouts, and a car means freedom. There is no doubt a parallel universe in this same suburb, filled with happy, creative, intelligent people and endless opportunities—there always is—but these kids are off that map. They are stupid by choice, not necessity; they have fallen into a slacker subculture that involves leading their lives in a void that can be filled only by booze, drugs, sex, and the endless, aimless analysis of their pathetic emptiness.

The movie is brilliantly and courageously well acted by its young cast; it's one of those movies so perceptive and wounding that there's no place for the actors to hide, no cop-out they can exercise. Their characters bleed with banality and stupid, doped reasoning. Their parents are not bad and, for the most part, not blamed; their children live in a world they do not understand or, in some cases, even see.

We meet Marty Puccio (Brad Renfro) and Bobby Kent (Nick Stahl). For as long as Marty can remember, Bobby has picked on him, and we see it as a daily ordeal: the ear twisting, the hard punches, the peremptory orders ("Get back in the car now!"), the demands that he go where he doesn't want to go and do what he doesn't want to do. In a key scene, Bobby takes him to a gay strip club and makes him dance on the stage while patrons stuff bills into his shorts. Marty is not gay. Bobby may be; certainly his relationship with Marty is sublimated S&M.

Marty and Bobby meet Lisa and Ali (Rachel Miner and Bijou Phillips). Bobby eventually rapes both girls. He also likes to watch Marty and Lisa in the backseat. He is, we sense, evil to the core; something has gone very wrong in his life, and maybe it was engendered by the authoritarian style of his father, who likes to dominate people under the guise of only doing what's right for them.

The movie establishes these kids in a larger circle of friends, including the tall, strong, and essentially nice Donny (Michael Pitt), the anything-goes Heather (Kelli Garner), and Derek (Daniel Franzese), along for the ride. It watches as they drift from coffee shops to malls to each other's cars and bedrooms, engaged in an endless loop of speculation about the only subject available to them, their lives. The leadership in this circle shifts according to who has a strongly held opinion; the others drift into line. A consensus begins to form that Bobby deserves to be killed. At one point, Lisa simply says, "I want him dead."

It's chilling, the way the murder is planned so heedlessly. The kids decide they don't know enough to do it themselves and need to hire a "hit man." This turns out to be Leo Fitzpatrick (from Clark's powerful first film, *Kids*), who is essentially a kid himself. The conspirators vaguely think his family is "Mafia," although his qualifications come into question when he worries that car horns will bother the neighbors; eventually we get the priceless line, "The hit man needs a ride."

The details of the murder are observed unblinkingly in a scene of harrowing, gruesome sadness. It is hard, messy work to kill someone. Once the body is disposed of, the arguments begin almost immediately: Everybody had a hand in the assault, but nobody actually can be said to have delivered the fatal blow, and we watch incredulously as these kids cave in to guilt, remorse, grief, blaming each other, and the irresistible impulse to tell an outsider what happened.

Clark's purpose in the film is twofold. He wants to depict a youth culture without resources, and to show how a crowd is capable of actions its members would never commit on their own. In *Kids* (1995) and in this film, the adult society has abandoned these characters—done little to educate or challenge them, or to create a world in which they have purpose. One of Bobby's sins, which I neglected to mention, is that he is still in high school and plans to go to college; the others live with fast-food jobs and handouts from parents, and Ali has a revealing line: "I was married once, for about three weeks. I have a little boy, but it's no big deal—my parents take care of him." *Kids* takes place in Manhattan and *Bully* in south Florida, but these kids occupy essentially the same lives, have the same parents, share the same futures.

It may be that *Bully* helps to explain the high school shootings. We sense the chilling disconnect between an action and its consequences, the availability of firearms, the buildup of teenage resentments and hatreds, the moral vacuum, the way they can talk themselves into doing unthinkable things, and above all, the need to talk about it. (So many high school shooters leave diaries and Web pages, and tell their friends what they plan to do.) Yes, Bobby Kent is a bully (and one of the most loathsome characters I've seen in a movie). But he dies not for his sins, but because his killers are so bored and adrift, and have such uncertain ideas of themselves.

Larry Clark is obviously obsessed by the culture of floating, unplugged teenagers. Sometimes his camera seems too willing to watch during the scenes of nudity and sex, and there is one particular shot that seems shameless in its voyeurism (you'll know the one). But it's this very drive that fuels his films. If the director doesn't have a strong personal feeling about material like this, he shouldn't be making movies about it. Clark is not some objectified outside adult observer, making an after-school special, but an artist who has made a leap into this teenage mindscape. Some critics have attacked him as a dirty old man with a suspect relationship to his material; if this film had been directed by a twenty-five-year-old, some of these same critics might be hailing it. I believe *Bully* is a masterpiece on its own terms, a frightening indictment of a society that offers absolutely nothing to some of its children—and an indictment of the children, who lack the imagination and courage to try to escape. Bobby and his killers deserve one another.

Burden of Dreams

NO MPAA RATING, 94 m., 1982

Featuring Werner Herzog, Klaus Kinski, Claudia Cardinale, Jason Robards, and Mick Jagger. Directed and produced by Les Blank, with Maureen Gosling.

Les Blank's *Burden of Dreams* is one of the most remarkable documentaries ever made about the making of a movie. There are at least two reasons for that. One is that the movie being made, Werner Herzog's *Fitzcarraldo,* involved some of the most torturous and dangerous on-location shooting experiences in film history. The other is that the documentary is by Les Blank, himself a brilliant filmmaker, who is unafraid to ask difficult questions and portray Herzog, warts and all.

The story of Herzog's *Fitzcarraldo* is already the stuff of movie legend. The movie was shot on location deep within the rain forests of South America, one thousand miles from civilization. When the first version of the film was half-finished, its star, Jason Robards, was rushed back to New York with amoebic dysentery and forbidden by his doctors to return to the location. Herzog replaced Robards with Klaus Kinski (star of his *Aguirre, the Wrath of God*), but meanwhile, costar Mick Jagger left the production because of a commitment to a concert tour. Then the Kinski version of *Fitzcarraldo* was caught in the middle of a border war between tribes of Indians. The whole production was moved twelve hundred miles, to a new location where the mishaps included plane crashes, disease, and attacks by unfriendly Indians. And all of those hardships were on top of the incredible task Herzog set himself to film: He wanted to show his obsessed hero using teams of Indians to pull an entire steamship up a hillside using only block and tackle!

Blank and his associate, Maureen Gosling, visited both locations of Herzog's film. Their documentary includes the only available record of some of the earlier scenes with Robards and Jagger. It also includes scenes in which Herzog seems to be going slowly mad, blaming the evil of the jungle and the depth of his own compulsions. In *Fitzcarraldo,* you can see the incredible strain as men try to pull a steamship up a sharp incline, using only muscle power and a few elementary principles of mechanics. In *Burden of Dreams*, Blank's camera moves back one more step, to show the actual mechanisms by which Herzog hoped to move his ship. A giant bulldozer is used to augment the block-and-pulley, but it proves barely equal to the task, and at one point the Brazilian engineer in charge of the project walks off, warning that lives will be lost.

What drives Herzog to make films that test his sanity and risk his life and those of his associates? Stanley Kauffmann, in the *New Republic*, argued that, for Herzog, the purpose of film is to risk death, and each of his films is in some way a challenge hurled at the odds. Herzog has made films on the slopes of active volcanoes, has filmed in the jungle and in the middle of the Sahara, and has made films about characters who live at the edges of human achievement. *Burden of Dreams* gives us an extraordinary portrait of Herzog trapped in the middle of one of his wildest dreams.

Butley

R, 94 m., 1974

Alan Bates (Ben Butley), Jessica Tandy (Edna Shaft), Richard O'Callaghan (Joey Keyston), Susan Engel (Anne Butley). Directed by Harold Pinter and produced by Henry T. Weirstein. Screenplay by Simon Gray.

Once, in the dim recesses of his alcoholic past, Ben Butley was an authority on T. S. Eliot. But now his photograph of Eliot is peeling from the wall, and Butley is peeling, too. During the course of Simon Gray's *Butley*, which was brilliantly directed for the American Film Theater by Harold Pinter, Butley peels off one layer, and then another, and finally comes down to his self-hating, desperately lonely core.

Butley is one of the most affecting characters of modern theater. He tries to bind people to himself with sarcasm, insult, and a merciless eye for their vulnerabilities. Eventually, it seems, he always fails. But the way Alan Bates plays him (and Bates, who created the role on the London stage, knows him as well as anybody), his mind is still resilient and panther-quick, with a streak of saving humor. So we don't pity him, even though we should. He somehow doggedly weathers each crisis, and we even feel a sneaky affection for him. Maybe

that's the way the role is written, or maybe it's because of the double-reverse charm Bates brings to it; I couldn't quite tell.

The film takes place during a day in an office shared by two English instructors at Queen Mary's College, London. One is Butley, who, as he approaches middle age, has abandoned the difficulties of Eliot and taken up nursery rhymes. The other is Joey, who began as Butley's protégé, then became his roommate, and then (after Butley's marriage and separation) became his roommate again. Joey is as meticulous as Butley is a shambles. Butley spends his day in psychological warfare against the truths that would batter him down. His wife tells him she intends to marry another man. Bad enough. But then Joey acknowledges that he's leaving, too—also for another man. Butley faces being left totally alone, and he fights back with wit, with obscenity, with insult, with booze.

Butley was born lonely, I'd say. He needs to have somebody there. After his marriage fails, he needs Joey again, because Joey had at least admired him at one time. It doesn't really seem to be relevant that Joey is a homosexual; Butley's needs are not sexual but psychological. Butley doesn't have much affection for women: He has some feeling left for his wife but conceals it well, and he has contempt for the other women in his day—the spinster Byron scholar (Jessica Tandy) and the would-be tutorial student (Georgina Hale). True, but he doesn't succeed in acting much better with the men. His loneliness seems to be asexual, if anything. And his tragedy is that he can't admit his hungers and needs—not until the play's end, anyway, when he makes an oblique but honest assessment of his current situation. Butley attempts to keep Joey by attacking his weaknesses, and he taunts Reg, Joey's new friend, in a futile attempt to drive him away. He's a dazzler with words, and even during the most pathetic scenes, he still somehow doesn't lose the poetry.

The Bates performance reminded me of how good he was in a movie that never got a proper American playoff, *A Day in the Death of Joe Egg*. He gives the character so much spirit that the material never feels as depressing as it sounds. We get the feeling that here's one old campaigner who will stay on his feet no matter what and give the bastards as good as he gets. The supporting cast (especially Richard O'Callaghan as Joey) is also good, and Pinter's direction moves with such awareness of what the play is about that we're hardly conscious of any sense of filmed theater. The play hasn't been opened up so much as opened in: The camera gets closer to the characters and sees more. What it sees in Butley is a man with a desperate problem. He needs other people, and his only strategy for attracting them is to drive them away.

Bye Bye Brazil

NO MPAA RATING, 100 m., 1979

Jose Wilker (Lord Gypsy), Betty Faria (Salome), Fabio Junior (Cico), Zaira Zambelli (Desdo), Principe Nabor (Swallow). Directed by Carlos Diegues and produced by L. C. Barreto. Screenplay by Diegues.

It's rare to come across truly great movie images, and we share them like treasured souvenirs—images like Jack Nicholson in the football helmet in *Easy Rider,* the bone turning into a spaceship in *2001,* the peacock spreading its feathers in the snow in *Amarcord,* and the helicopter assault in *Apocalypse Now.*

To the short list of great images, a film named *Bye Bye Brazil* adds one more. A small, raggedy troupe of traveling entertainers is putting on a show in a provincial Brazilian town. The townspeople sit packed together in a sweaty, smoky room, while the magician creates for brief moments the illusion that both he and his audience are more sophisticated than they are. It is time for the climax of his act, and he springs a completely unexpected image on his audience, and on us: Bing Crosby sings "White Christmas" while it snows on his amazed patrons.

That moment provides more than an image. It provides a neatly summarized little statement about *Bye Bye Brazil,* a film which exists exactly on the fault line between Brazil's modern civilization and the simple backwaters of its provinces. The film sees Brazil as a nation where half-assimilated Western culture (in the form of Bing Crosby, public address systems, and politicians) coexists with poverty, superstition, simple good nature, and the permanent fact of the rain forest.

The movie is about the small troupe of entertainers, who travel the backroads in a truck that contains living quarters, a generator, and the props for their nightly shows. The troupe is led by Lord Gypsy, a young man who is half-hippie, half-nineteenth-century medicine show huckster. At his side is Salome, a damply sultry beauty who is his assistant but also has a tendency to do business on her own. Swallow, a strongman, doubles as crew and supporting act.

These three pick up two hitchhikers, a young accordion player and his pregnant wife. And then *Bye Bye Brazil* tells the story of the changing relationships among the five people, and their checkered success with roadshow vaudeville.

Having said that, I've conveyed almost no notion of this movie's special charms. It shows us a society that most American audiences never have seen in the movies, the world of very old, very small Brazilian towns perched precariously along the roads that link them to far-away, half-understood cities.

Television has not come to most of these towns. Electricity is uncertain. The traveling entertainers provide more than music and magic; they provide a link with style that is more fascinating to the audiences than the magician's tricks. People do not pay to see the show, so much as to wonder at these strange performers who speak the same language but could be from another planet.

C

Cabaret Balkan
NO MPAA RATING, 100 m., 1999

Nikola Ristanovski (Boris), Nebojsa Glogovac (Taxi Driver), Miki Manojlovic (Michael), Marko Urosevic (Alex), Bogdan Diklic (John), Dragan Nikolic (John's Boxer Friend), Mira Banjac (Bosnian Serb Mother), Danil Bata Stojkovic (Viktor). Directed by Goran Paskaljevic and produced by Antoine de Clermont-Tonnerre and Paskaljevic. Screenplay by Dejan Dukovski and Paskaljevic, based on Dukovski's play *Bure Baruta*.

Cabaret Balkan is a scream of agony over the madness in Kosovo and the neighboring lands where blood feuds run deep and the macho virus is a killer epidemic. It's a film about violence, sadism, brutality, and the hatred of women, which seems to go hand in hand with those pastimes. The director, Goran Paskaljevic, opens his film with a taxi driver telling a returning citizen: "This is a goddamned lousy country; why would anyone want to come back?" The film shows us nothing to contradict his statement.

Yes, I know, the "former Yugoslavia," as we now wistfully refer to it, contains beauty and greatness. But what is going on there now, the film argues, is ugliness. The dark side has taken over and decent citizens on both sides flee for their lives, or choose the lesser of evils. It's hard at times to tell which side the characters are on, a New York critic complains. Yes, this film might reply, but what difference does it make? They're all doomed.

The movie's device is a series of interlocking, self-contained stories. Some of the same characters turn up from time to time, like haunting reminders. After a while many of the dominant males seem to blur together into one composite: an alcoholic middle-aged man with an absurd mustache, lurching through the world killing, vomiting, urinating, bleeding, belching, swearing, and entertaining himself by terrorizing women.

Some of the episodes end with surprises—not because we don't see them coming, but because we can't believe that the characters are complete monsters. We are inevitably disappointed: None of the men in this movie are nice, except for a few bewildered older men (one of whom crushes a lout's skull and then cradles him, sobbing, "My boy, my boy"). Small events escalate into exercises in terror, and the men in the film seem to be consumed by violence. None of the killings in the film are overtly political; *Cabaret Balkan* seems to argue that monstrous behavior is so ingrained in a sick culture that ethnic cleansing is just an organized form of everyday behavior.

Example: Bus passengers are terrorized by a cretin who hijacks the bus. The elderly driver eventually kills him. A woman passenger, the target of the hijacker's sexual rage, stumbles out of the bus and into the car of her boyfriend, who instantly flies into a jealous rage and accuses her of encouraging the other man. As the two argue, two other men approach, hold them both at gunpoint, and start the next act. Or consider an ordinary traffic accident that escalates: The wronged driver finds the apartment of the other driver's parents and breaks everything in sight. (The other driver got into the crash in the first place because he was cruising the streets harassing single women.)

The most harrowing episode, which starts quietly and escalates, involves a war widow traveling on a train. A large menacing man comes in, sits down, wants her to smoke and drink with him, forces his conversation on her, orders another passenger out of the compartment, and begins the preliminaries to rape. She breaks free and desperately grabs a grenade from her bag. He wrenches the grenade away from her and contemptuously pulls the pin, holding the grenade with one hand as he holds her with the other.

The buried argument of *Cabaret Balkan* seems to be that violence and macho sexual insecurity are closely linked. I was reminded of *Savior* (1998), the film where Dennis Quaid plays a mercenary fighting for the Serbs; he finds himself protecting a woman who has been raped, and whose father and brother want to kill her—because, you see, she has therefore brought dishonor on her family. It is not a crime to rape, but to be raped. Such diseased values, *Cabaret Balkan* seems to suggest, almost inevitably lead to savagery, and indeed the intimidation of women is the primary way the men in this movie express their manhood.

Amazingly, *Cabaret Balkan* is an enormous hit in its homeland, no doubt among the many good citizens who are fed up. Societies can rip themselves to pieces only so long before they are forced to wonder how their values could possibly survive the cost of fighting for them. When war leaves no ideals worth defending, there is only the consolation of depriving the other side of any shreds of remaining standards. Of all the movies about all the tragic places where old hatreds fester over ethnic, racial, and religious animosity, this is the angriest, and therefore possibly the bravest.

Note: The film was released "unrated." Of course, no film that considers violence this unblinkingly and bravely can qualify for an R; that rating is more hospitable toward films that make it look like fun.

Caché

R, 121 m., 2006

Daniel Auteuil (Georges Laurent), Juliette Binoche (Anne Laurent), Maurice Benichou (Majid), Annie Girardot (Georges' Mom), Bernard Le Coq (Georges' Editor), Daniel Duval (Pierre), Lester Makedonsky (Pierrot Laurent), Walid Afkir (Majid's Son). Directed by Michael Haneke and produced by Veit Heiduschka. Screenplay by Haneke.

The opening shot of Michael Haneke's *Caché* shows the facade of a townhouse on a side street in Paris. As the credits roll, ordinary events take place on the street. Then we discover that this footage is a video and that it is being watched by Anne and Georges Laurent (Juliette Binoche and Daniel Auteuil). It is their house. They have absolutely no idea who took the video, or why it was sent to them.

So opens a perplexing and disturbing film of great effect, showing how comfortable lives are disrupted by the simple fact that someone is watching. Georges is the host of a TV program about books; yes, in France they have shows where intellectuals argue about books and an audience that actually watches them. Georges and Anne live in their book-lined house with their son, Pierrot Laurent (Lester Makedonsky), a teenager who is sulky and distracted in the way that teenagers can be when

they have little to complain about except their discontent.

Another video arrives, showing the farmhouse where Georges and his family lived when he was a child. All the videos they receive will have the same style: a camera at some distance, simply looking. Many of the shots in the film itself are set up and filmed in the same way, so that *Caché* could be watching itself just as the videos watch the Laurents. No comment is made in the videos through camera position, movement, editing—or perhaps there is the same comment all the time: Someone wants them to know that they are being watched.

Another video arrives, showing a journey down a suburban street and into a building. Georges is able to freeze a frame and make out a street name; going off alone, he follows the path of the video and finds himself in front of a door in an apartment building. The person inside is someone he knows, but this person (whom I will not describe) is unlikely to be the author of the alarming videos.

Georges conceals the results of his trip from his wife. Then another video arrives, showing him speaking with the occupant of the apartment. Now there is a fierce argument between Georges and Anne: She cannot trust him, she feels. He must tell her who the person is. He will not. In a way, he cannot. She feels threatened by the videos, and now threatened because her husband may be withholding information she needs to know. Binoche trembles with fury as the wife who feels betrayed by her husband; Auteuil, a master of detachment, folds into himself as a man who simply cannot talk about his deepest feelings.

Meanwhile, their lives continue. Georges does the TV show. Their son goes to school. There is a dinner party, at which a story about a dog will give you something to recycle with great effect at your own next dinner party. Georges goes to visit his mother. He asks about events that happened in 1961, when he was a boy. His mother asks him if something is wrong. He denies it. She simply regards him. She knows her son, and she knows something is wrong.

I have deliberately left out a great deal of information, because the experience of *Caché* builds as we experience the film. There are parallels, for example, between the TV news that is often on in the background, and some of the events in Georges' past. We expect that the mystery of the videos will be solved, explained, and make sense. But perhaps not. Here is a curious thing: In some of the videos, the camera seems to be in a position where anyone could see it, but no one ever does.

When *Caché* played at Cannes 2005 (where it won the prize for best direction), it had an English title, *Hidden*. That may be a better title than *Caché*, which can also be an English word, but more obscure. In the film, the camera is hidden. So are events in Georges' life. Some of what he knows is hidden from his wife. The son keeps secrets from his parents, and so on. The film seems to argue that life would have gone on well enough for the Laurents had it not been for the unsettling knowledge that they had become visible, that someone knew something about them, that someone was watching.

The last shot of the film, like many others, is taken from a camera that does not move. It regards events on the outside staircase of a building. There are a lot of people moving around. Closer to us than most of them is a figure with her back turned, placed just to the right of center; given basic rules of composition, this is where our eye will fall if all else in the shot is equal. Many viewers will not notice another element in the shot. Stop reading now if you plan to see the film, and save the review . . .

. . . and now observe that two people meet and talk on the upper left-hand side of the screen. They are two characters we recognize, and who should not know each other or have any way of meeting. Why do they know each other? What does it explain, that they do? Does it explain anything? Are there not still questions without answers? *Caché* is a film of bottomless intrigue. "The unexamined life is not worth living," said Socrates. An examined life may bring its own form of disquiet.

When *Caché* played at Cannes, some critics deplored its lack of a resolution. I think it works precisely because it leaves us hanging. It proposes not to solve the mystery of the videos but to portray the paranoia and distrust that they create. If the film merely revealed in its closing scenes who was sending the videos and why, it would belittle itself. We are left feeling as the characters feel, uneasy, violated, spied upon, surrounded by faceless observers. The nonexplanation supplied by the enigmatic last scene opens a new area of specula- tion that also lacks any solution or closure. And the secrets of Georges' past reach out their guilty tendrils to the next generation.

California Split
R, 109 m., 1974

George Segal (Bill Denny), Elliott Gould (Charlie Waters), Ann Prentiss (Barbara Miller), Gwen Welles (Susan Peters), Edward Walsh (Lew), Joseph Walsh (Sparkle), Bert Remsen ("Helen Brown"). Directed by Robert Altman and produced by Altman and Joseph Walsh, based on a screenplay by Walsh.

They meet in a California poker parlor. One wins, despite a heated discussion with a loser over whether or not a dealt card hit the floor. They drink. They become friends after they are jointly mugged in the parking lot by the sore loser.

They did not know each other before, and they don't know much about each other now, but they know all they need to know: They're both compulsive gamblers, and the dimensions of the world of gambling equal the dimensions of the world they care anything about. It is a small world and a flat one, like one of those maps of the world before Columbus, and they are constantly threatened with falling over the edge.

They're the heroes (or at least the subjects) of *California Split*, the magnificently funny, cynical film by Robert Altman. Their names are Bill and Charlie, and they're played by George Segal and Elliott Gould with a combination of unaffected naturalism and sheer raw nervous exhaustion. We don't need to know anything about gambling to understand the odyssey they undertake to the tracks, to the private poker parties, to the bars, to Vegas, to the edge of defeat, and to the scene of victory. Their compulsion is so strong that it carries us along. The movie will be compared with *M*A*S*H*, the first big hit by Altman (who is possibly our best and certainly our most diverting American director). It deserves that comparison, because it resembles *M*A*S*H* in several big ways: It's funny, it's hard-boiled, it gives us a bond between two frazzled heroes trying to win by the rules in a game where the rules require defeat. But it's a better movie than *M*A*S*H* because here Altman gets it all together. Ever since *M*A*S*H,* he's been trying to make a kind of movie that would function like a comedy but allow its laughs to dig us deeper and deeper into the despair underneath.

Bill and Charlie are driven. We laugh at their hangovers, their bruises (treated with hot shaving cream), the kooky part-time prostitutes who serve them breakfasts of Froot Loops and beer. We move easily through the underworld of their friends, casually introduced through Altman's gift of overlapping dialogue and understated visual introductions, so that we're not so much shown a new character as encouraged to assume we knew him all along. And because Joseph Walsh's screenplay is funny and Segal and Gould are naturally engaging, we have a good time.

But then there are moments that take on bleaker meanings. At one point, for example, at the ragged edge of sleep, boozed out, defeated, Bill and Charlie cling desperately to a bar and very seriously bet with each other on the names of the Seven Dwarfs (There was Droopy. . . Sleepy. . . Dumbo?). And at another time, cornered with their winnings in still another parking lot by still another mugger, this one armed, they hand over half their winnings and bet him that's all they have.

He takes it and runs; they win; they could have been killed but their gambler's instinct forced them to make the try. At the end of *California Split* we realize that Altman has made a lot more than a comedy about gambling; he's taken us into an American nightmare, and all the people we met along the way felt genuine and looked real. This movie has a taste in its mouth like stale air-conditioning, and no matter what time it seems to be, it's always five in the morning in a second-rate casino.

As always, Altman fills his movie with quirky supporting roles—people who have somehow become caricatures of themselves. At the private poker game, Segal stands at the bar, surveys the table, and quietly describes every player. He's right about them, although he (and we) have never seen them before. We know he's right because these people wear their styles and destinies on their faces.

So do the hookers (played with a kind of tart-next-door wholesomeness by Ann Prentiss and Gwen Welles). So does "Helen Brown," one of their customers who's a middle-aged man who likes drag as much as he's terrified of the cops (inspiring a scene of true tragicomedy). Altman's movies always seem full, somehow; we don't have the feeling of an empty screen into which carefully drawn characters are introduced, but of a camera plunging into a boiling sea of frenzied human activity.

What Altman comes up with is sometimes almost a documentary feel; at the end of *California Split* we know something about organized gambling in this country we didn't know before. His movies always seem perfectly at home wherever they are, but this time there's an almost palpable sense of place. And Altman has never been more firmly in control of his style. He has one of the few really individual visual styles among contemporary American directors; we can always see it's an Altman film. He bases his visual strategies on an incredibly attentive sound track, using background noises with particular care so that our ears tell us we're moving through these people—instead of that they're lined up talking to us. *California Split* is a great movie and it's a great experience, too; we've been there with Bill and Charlie.

Capote

R, 114 m., 2005

Philip Seymour Hoffman (Truman Capote), Catherine Keener (Nelle Harper Lee), Clifton Collins, Jr. (Perry Smith), Chris Cooper (Alvin Dewey), Bruce Greenwood (Jack Dunphy), Bob Balaban (William Shawn), Amy Ryan (Marie Dewey), Mark Pellegrino (Dick Hickock). Directed by Bennett Miller and produced by Caroline Baron, William Vince, and Michael Ohoven. Screenplay by Dan Futterman, based on the book *Capote* by Gerald Clarke.

On November 15, 1959, Truman Capote noticed a news item about four members of a Kansas farm family who were shotgunned to death. He telephoned William Shawn, editor of the *New Yorker,* wondering if Shawn would be interested in an article about the murders. Later in his life Capote said that if he had known what would happen as a result of this impulse, he would not have stopped in Holcomb, Kansas, but would have kept right on going "like a bat out of hell."

At first Capote thought the story would be

about how a rural community was dealing with the tragedy. "I don't care one way or the other if you catch who did this," he tells an agent from the Kansas Bureau of Investigation. Then two drifters, Perry Smith and Richard Hickock, are arrested and charged with the crime. As Capote gets to know them, he's consumed by a story that would make him rich and famous, and destroy him. His "nonfiction novel," *In Cold Blood*, became a best seller and inspired a movie, but Capote was emotionally devastated by the experience and it hastened his death.

Bennett Miller's *Capote* is about that crucial period of fewer than six years in Capote's life. As he talks to the killers, to law officers, and to the neighbors of the murdered Clutter family, Capote's project takes on depth and shape as the story of conflicting fates. But at the heart of his reporting is an irredeemable conflict: He wins the trust of the two convicted killers and essentially falls in love with Perry Smith, while needing them to die to supply an ending for his book. "If they win this appeal," he tells his friend Harper Lee, "I may have a complete nervous breakdown." After they are hanged on April 14, 1965, he tells Harper, "There wasn't anything I could have done to save them." She says: "Maybe, but the fact is you didn't want to."

Capote is a film of uncommon strength and insight, about a man whose great achievement requires the surrender of his self-respect. Philip Seymour Hoffman's precise, uncanny performance as Capote doesn't imitate the author so much as channel him, as a man whose peculiarities mask great intelligence and deep wounds.

As the story opens, Capote is a well-known writer (of *Breakfast at Tiffany's*, among others), a popular guest on talk shows, a man whose small stature, large ego, and affectations of speech and appearance make him an outsider wherever he goes. Trying to win the confidence of a young girl in Kansas, he tells her: "Ever since I was a child, folks have thought they had me pegged because of the way I am, the way I talk." But he was able to enter a world far removed from Manhattan and write a great book about ordinary Midwesterners and two pathetic, heartless killers. Could anyone be less like Truman Capote than Perry Smith? Yet they were both mistreated and passed around as children, had issues with distant and remote

mothers, had secret fantasies. "It's like Perry and I grew up in the same house, and one day he went out the back door and I went out the front," he tells Harper Lee.

The film, written by Dan Futterman and based on the book *Capote* by Gerald Clarke, focuses on the way a writer works on a story and the story works on him. Capote wins the wary acceptance of Alvin Dewey (Chris Cooper), the agent assigned to the case. Over dinner in Alvin and Marie Dewey's kitchen, he entertains them with stories of John Huston and Humphrey Bogart. As he talks, he studies their house like an anthropologist. He convinces the local funeral director to let him view the mutilated bodies of the Clutters. Later, Perry Smith will tell him he liked the father, Herb Clutter: "I thought he was a very nice, gentle man. I thought so right up until I slit his throat."

On his trips to Kansas, Capote takes along a southern friend from childhood, Harper Lee (Catherine Keener). So long does it take him to finish his book that Lee in the meantime has time to publish her famous novel, *To Kill a Mockingbird*, sell it to the movies, and attend the world premiere with Gregory Peck. Harper Lee is a practical, grounded woman who clearly sees that Truman cares for Smith and yet will exploit him for his book. "Do you hold him in esteem, Truman?" she asks, and he is defensive: "Well, he's a gold mine."

Perry Smith and Dick Hickock are played by Clifton Collins, Jr. and Mark Pellegrino. Hickock is not developed as deeply as in Richard Brooks's film *In Cold Blood* (1967), where he was played by Scott Wilson; the emphasis this time is on Smith, played in 1967 by Robert Blake and here by Collins as a haunted, repressed man in constant pain who chews aspirin by the handful and yet shelters a certain poetry; his drawings and journal move Capote, who sees him as a man who was born a victim and deserves not forgiveness but pity.

The other key characters are Capote's lover, Jack Dunphy (Bruce Greenwood), and his editor at the *New Yorker*, William Shawn (Bob Balaban). "Jack thinks I'm using Perry," Truman tells Harper. "He also thinks I fell in love with him in Kansas." Shawn thinks *In Cold Blood*, when it is finally written, is "going to change how people write." He prints the entire book in his magazine.

The movie *In Cold Blood* had no speaking role for Capote, who in a sense stood behind the camera with the director. If *Capote* had simply flipped the coin and told the story of the Clutter murders from Capote's point of view, it might have been a good movie, but what makes it so powerful is that it looks with merciless perception at Capote's moral disintegration.

"If I leave here without understanding you," Capote tells Perry Smith during one of many visits to his cell, "the world will see you as a monster. I don't want that." He is able to convince Smith and Hickock to tell him what happened on the night of the murders. He learns heartbreaking details, such as that they "put a different pillow under the boy's head just to shoot him." Capote tells them he will support their appeals and help them find another lawyer. He betrays them. Smith eventually understands that and accepts his fate. "Two weeks, and finito," he tells Capote as his execution draws near. Another good line for the book.

Carmen

R, 95 m., 1983

Antonio Gades (Antonio), Laura Del Sol (Carmen), Paco De Lucia (Paco), Cristina Hoyos (Cristina). Sung by Regina Resnik and Maria Del Monaco. Directed by Carlos Saura and produced by Emiliano Piedra. Screenplay by Saura and Antonio Gades.

Carlos Saura's *Carmen* is an erotic roller coaster of a movie, incorporating dance into its story more effectively than any other movie I can remember. It isn't a "ballet movie," and it's not like one of those musicals where everybody is occasionally taken with the need to dance. It's a story of passion and jealousy— the story of Bizet's *Carmen*—with dance as part and parcel of its flesh and blood. The movie is based on the opera by Bizet, keeping the music and the broad outlines of the story of a poor girl whose fierce romantic independence maddens the men who become obsessed with her. Everything else is new. Saura, the greatest living Spanish film director, has collaborated with Antonio Gades, the Spanish dancer and choreographer, to make this *Carmen* into a muscular, contemporary story. Their strategy is to make a story within a story. The film begins with Gades as a dance

teacher who is looking for the "perfect" Carmen. He finds one in a flamenco dancing school, and as he attempts to mold her into Carmen, their relationship begins to resemble the story of the opera.

Given this approach, *Carmen* could easily have turned into an academic exercise, one of those clever movies in which all the pieces fit but none of them matter. That doesn't happen, and one of the reasons it doesn't is the casting of a young woman named Laura Del Sol as Carmen. She is a twenty-one-year-old dancer who combines convincing technique with a healthy, athletic sexiness, and her dance duets (and duels) with Gades are bold, erotic, and uninhibited. What's fascinating is the way Saura is able to blend the dance, the opera, and the "modern" story. For example, Del Sol and Gades use dance to create a scene that begins as an argument, develops into fierce declarations of independence, and then climaxes in passionate romance. In another scene, a routine day in a dance studio becomes charged by the unexpected appearance of Carmen's other lover, an ex-convict.

I have an ambivalence about dance on film. I begin with the assumption that the ideal way to see dance is live, on a stage. Everything in dance begins with the fact that the dancers are physically present and are using their bodies to turn movement into art. Movies, with their complete freedom over time and space, break that contract between real time and the dancer. Dances can be constructed out of many different shots and even out of the work of more than one dancer (see *Flashdance*). If I can't see dancing on a stage, then my preference is for classical movie dancing, by which I mean frankly artificial constructions of the Astaire and Rogers variety. Serious dance on film usually feels like a documentary. The great achievement of *Carmen* is that it takes serious dance and music, combines them with a plausible story, suspends our disbelief, and gives us a mesmerizing, electric experience.

Carmen

PG, 152 m., 1984

Julia Migenes-Johnson (Carmen), Placido Domingo (Don Jose), Ruggero Raimondi (Escamillo), Faith Esham

(Micaela), JeanPhilippe Lafont (Dancairo). Directed by Francesco Rosi and produced by Patrice Ledoux.

Bizet's *Carmen* is what movies are all about. It's one of the few modern movies that requires one of those legendary Hollywood advertising men who'd cook up copy like, for example . . .

Cheer! As Bizet's towering masterpiece blazes across the screen! Cry bravo! To passion, romance, adventure! From the bullrings of Spain to the innermost recesses of her gypsy heart, Carmen drives men mad and immortalizes herself as a romantic legend! Thrill! To the golden voice of Placido Domingo, and the tempestuous screen debut of the smouldering Julia Migenes-Johnson!

The temptation, of course, is to approach a film like this with hushed voice and bended knee, uttering reverent phrases about art and music. But to hell with it: This movie is the *Indiana Jones* of opera films, and we might as well not beat around the bush. *Carmen* is a Latin soap opera if ever there was one, and the sheer passionate joy of Bizet's music is as vulgar as it is sublime, as popular as it is classical. *Carmen* is one of those operas ideally suited to the movies, and this version by Francesco Rosi is exciting, involving, and entertaining.

You are doubtless already familiar with the music. The sound track was recorded in Paris with Lorin Maazel conducting the National Orchestra of France. Placido Domingo is in great voice, and a relatively unknown American soprano named Julia Migenes-Johnson not only can sing the title role but, perhaps just as importantly, can look it and act it. There is chemistry here, and without the chemistry—without the audience's belief that the scornful gypsy Carmen could enslave the soldier Don Jose—there would only be an illustrated sound track. After the recording was completed, the movie was shot on locations in Spain by Francesco Rosi, the Italian director of *Three Brothers* and *Christ Stopped at Eboli*. He has discovered lush, sun-drenched villages on hillsides, and a bullring of such stark Spanish simplicity that the ballet within the ring for once seems as elegant as the emotions it is reflecting. He also has found moonlight, rich firelight, deep reds and yellows—colors so glowing that the characters seem to warm themselves at his palette.

Opera films are traditionally not successful. They play in festivals, they find a small audience of music lovers, maybe they make some money in Italy. Domingo broke that pattern with his *La Traviata* (1983), directed by Franco Zeffirelli. It had good long runs around the United States, and even broke through to audiences beyond the core of opera lovers. But we Americans are so wary of "culture." Opera for many of us still consists of the fat lady on "The Ed Sullivan Show." And for many of the rest, it is something that inhabits a cultural shrine and must be approached with reverence. Maybe it takes the movies, that most popular of art forms, to break that pattern. Rosi, Domingo, and Migenes-Johnson have filmed a labor of love.

Carnal Knowledge

R, 98 m., 1971

Jack Nicholson (Jonathan), Candice Bergen (Susan), Art Garfunkel (Sandy), Ann-Margret (Bobbie), Rita Moreno (Louise), Cynthia O'Neal (Cindy), Carol Kane (Jennifer). Directed and produced by Mike Nichols. Screenplay by Jules Feiffer.

Mike Nichols's *Carnal Knowledge* opens on a darkened screen, and we hear the traditional Glenn Miller arrangement of *Moonlight Serenade*. And then we hear two young men earnestly talking of young women, and sex, and their ambitions in those two directions.

We learn that the first young man hopes to meet a high-class girl, one with morals, who will tell him things he never knew about himself. We learn that the second young man wants exactly that kind of girl too, only with big boobs. And then . . .

We find ourselves at a college mixer sometime in the late 1940s. Candice Bergen drifts past the two intense young men, who are leaning in a doorway and checking out the talent, and she finds herself a perch on a windowsill. "She's yours. I'm giving her to you," Jack Nicholson (who doesn't have her to give) tells Art Garfunkel (who doesn't know how to take her).

After a pep talk from Nicholson, Garfunkel finally musters the courage to wander over toward Bergen, but he's too shy to speak. He stops in front of her, pretends to look out the window at something tremendously interesting (if invisible) on the other side, and then returns to Nicholson, defeated.

With the perception and economy that mark their entire film, Nichols and his writer, Jules Feiffer, have established the theme of *Carnal Knowledge* in this handful of shots: The film will be about men who are incapable of reaching, touching, or deeply knowing women.

We meet the two men during their college years and follow them for maybe twenty years afterward as they drift through a marriage apiece and several frustrating liaisons with the kinds of women they think they desire. Both men rely a great deal on their supposed sexual prowess, but both are insecure sexually, and the Nicholson character finally becomes impotent.

Their problem, to the degree they share one, is that they try to find their fantasy woman in the flesh, and discover when the fantasy becomes real that the real woman is all too real for them to live with and understand. The thing is, they both want to be dominated by women—only not really.

Carnal Knowledge never finds its male characters at "fault," exactly, and the movie isn't concerned with fixing blame. It chooses the tragedy form, not the essay. At the end, we're left with people who have experienced as much suffering as they've caused through their inability to accept women as fellow human beings. The Nicholson character is reduced to highly complicated charades with a prostitute (Rita Moreno), and the Garfunkel character is still kidding himself. In his early forties, he's grown a mustache, affected a hip lifestyle, and shacked up with a seventeen-year-old. "She may only be seventeen," he tells his old classmate, "but in many ways, I'm telling you, she's older than me."

Carnal Knowledge is clearly Mike Nichols's best film. It sets out to tell us certain things about these few characters and their sexual crucifixions, and it succeeds. It doesn't go for cheap or facile laughs, or inappropriate symbolism, or a phony kind of contemporary feeling.

The Ann-Margret role is the best example, I think, of Nichols's determination to stay within the diameters of his characters. Ann-Margret has been in a lot of bad movies, and done some bad acting in them, and this role

could have degenerated into a parody with no trouble at all. Instead, it's an artistic triumph.

Nicholson, who is possibly the most interesting new movie actor since James Dean, carries the film, and his scenes with Ann-Margret are masterfully played. Garfunkel tends to be a shade transparent, although not to the degree that the film suffers, and Bergen is very good, but in the kind of role she plays too often, the sweet-bitchy-classy college girl.

As I've suggested, *Carnal Knowledge* stays within the universe of its characters and inhabits it totally. And within that universe, men and women fail to find sexual and personal happiness because they can't break through their patterns of treating each other as objects.

Carrington

R, 122 m., 1995

Emma Thompson (Carrington), Jonathan Pryce (Lytton Strachey), Steven Waddington (Ralph Partridge), Samuel West (Gerald Brenan), Rufus Sewell (Mark Gertler), Penelope Wilton (Lady Ottoline Morrell), Janet McTeer (Vanessa Bell), Peter Blythe (Phillip Morrell). Directed by Christopher Hampton and produced by Ronald Shedlo and John McGrath. Screenplay by Hampton.

The first time Lytton Strachey saw Dora Carrington, he asked, "Who is that ravishing boy?" When he discovered she was a girl with a tomboy haircut, he was struck dumb; at their first meeting, conversation came to a complete stall, and in embarrassment he picked up a book and pretended to read. He was a homosexual in his mid-thirties, dry, bearded, reserved. She was a painter, fifteen years younger. Nothing could have been more out of character than for him to suddenly lean over and kiss her, while they were on a walk through the countryside. But he did.

The opening scenes of *Carrington* try to explain the beginnings of one of the oddest romances of the Bloomsbury Group, that gathering of British geniuses, eccentrics, and self-publicists that produced no romances that were not odd. In Christopher Hampton's film version, Carrington (she hated the "Dora" and dropped it) visits Strachey's bedside with scissors to chop off his beard in retaliation for the kiss. But then, regarding his sleeping face, she undergoes a sudden conversion into love. Strachey awakens and sees her looming over him: "Have you brought me my breakfast?"

Carrington (Emma Thompson) and Strachey (Jonathan Pryce) were in love, after their manner, for seventeen years, until his death, followed shortly by her own. During much of that time they occupied Ham Spray House in Berkshire with a series of other lovers, some of them shared. Carrington eventually married Rex Partridge, who Strachey said should change his name to Ralph, which he did. In one scene, the three of them share the same bed, somewhat uneasily ("There are times when I feel like a character in a play by Molière," Strachey said).

Although physical passion no doubt figured at some time, in some way, in all of their lives, they were so reserved about it that the movie leaves us wondering if they wouldn't really engage in repartee rather than sex. "Ah, semen!" says Strachey. "What is it about that ridiculous white secretion that pulls down the corners of an Englishman's mouth?" The movie's single sex scene is so discreet that we can only presume what is happening; during it, Strachey has the facial expression of a person being inoculated.

What they did share was a platonic love, which was real, and endured. Strachey was famous above all for *Eminent Victorians* (1918), the myth-shattering book that treated such icons as Florence Nightingale to portraits written with skepticism and irony. Like all the Bloomsbury circle, he was famous for his verbal wit, and Pryce is meticulous in the way he speaks in epigrams while somehow sounding spontaneous. Startled by the pop of a champagne cork, he exclaims, "Good lord, imagine what the war will be like!" Even on his deathbed he was still in production: "If this is dying, then I don't think much of it."

The screenplay for *Carrington* was written some twenty years ago by Hampton, a playwright *(Tales From Hollywood)* who won an Oscar for his script for *Dangerous Liaisons*. He decided to direct the film only after Mike Newell *(Four Weddings and a Funeral)* dropped out. Pryce, famous on the London stage for *Miss Saigon* and on American television for the Infiniti commercials, was already on board, as was Thompson, who had developed a specialty in unrequited love *(Remains of the Day, Howards End)*.

What they are up against is a "romance" that fits no conventional mold and is not expressed in ordinary ways. Even at the film's end, when we get the line, "No one will ever know the happiness of our lives together," we're tempted to think, "And no wonder." Since Pryce's Strachey is so deeply reserved, it is up to Thompson to project the warmth they both presumably felt, and she does that with her eyes and her silences; she looks at him like a woman in love.

All of the Bloomsbury crowd (Virginia and Leonard Woolf, Roger Fry, John Maynard Keynes, E. M. Forster, Clive and Vanessa Bell, Duncan Grant) were known for their freedom, even recklessness, in their choices of romantic partners. A diagram of their love affairs would look like an underground system where every train stopped at every station. And yet they were all so reined in by the British upper-class trait of repressed emotion that when anger and jealousy do emerge (as they do twice in *Carrington*), the breach of manners is almost more shocking than the sexual infidelity under complaint. We are left to guess what emotions seethed beneath the surface of wit and acceptance.

There is one scene in *Carrington* that suggests the depths of Carrington's heart better than any dialogue ever could. One evening after dinner, she wanders on the lawn at Ham Spray House, and through the open, brightly lit windows, she is able to observe her lovers, past and present, paired off with their present lovers. As her gaze goes from one window to another, we see her as an outsider. But that is not the whole story, because you could take any of the partners from *Carrington* and put them on the lawn, and pair off the others inside, and the effect would be the same. Somehow, for all of them, standing outside on the lawn must have been part of the fun.

Casino

R, 175 m., 1995

Robert De Niro (Sam "Ace" Rothstein), Sharon Stone (Ginger McKenna), Joe Pesci (Nicky Santoro), James Woods (Lester Diamond), Don Rickles (Billy Sherbert), Alan King (Andy Stone), Kevin Pollak (Phillip Green),

L. Q. Jones (Pat Webb). Directed by Martin Scorsese and produced by Barbara De Fina. Screenplay by Nicholas Pileggi and Scorsese, based on the book by Pileggi.

If the Mafia didn't exist, it would be necessary to invent it. The same is true of Las Vegas. There is a universal need to believe in an outfit that exists outside the rules and can get things done. There's a related need for a place where the rules are suspended, where there's no day or night, where everything has a price, where if you're lucky you go home a millionaire. Of course, people who go to Vegas lose money, and people who deal with the mob regret it. But hope is what we're talking about. Neither the mob nor Vegas could exist if most people weren't optimists.

Martin Scorsese's fascinating new film *Casino* knows a lot about the Mafia's relationship with Las Vegas. It's based on a book by Nicholas Pileggi, who had full access to a man who once ran four casinos for the mob, and whose true story inspires the plot of the movie. Like *The Godfather*, it makes us feel like eavesdroppers in a secret place.

The movie opens with a car bombing, and the figure of Sam (Ace) Rothstein floating through the air. The movie explains how such a thing came to happen to him. The first hour plays like a documentary; there's a narration, by Rothstein (Robert De Niro) and others, explaining how the mob skimmed millions out of the casinos.

It's an interesting process. Assuming you could steal 25 percent of the slot-machine take—what would you do with tons of coins? How would you convert them into bills that could be stuffed into the weekly suitcase for delivery to the mob in Kansas City? *Casino* knows. It also knows how to skim from the other games, and from food service and the gift shops. And it knows about how casinos don't like to be stolen from.

There's an incident where a man is cheating at blackjack, and a couple of security guys sidle up to him, and jab him with a stun gun. He collapses, the security guys call for medical attention, and hurry him away to a little room where they pound on his fingers with a mallet and he agrees that he made a very bad mistake.

Rothstein, based on the real-life figure of Frank (Lefty) Rosenthal, starts life as a sports oddsmaker in Chicago, attracts the attention of the mob because of his genius with numbers, and is assigned to run casinos because he looks like an efficient businessman who will encourage the Vegas goose to continue laying its golden eggs. He is a man who detests unnecessary trouble. One day, however, trouble finds him, in the person of Ginger McKenna (Sharon Stone), a high-priced call girl.

Scorsese shows him seeing Ginger on a TV security monitor, and falling so instantly in love that the image becomes a freeze-frame. Ace showers her with gifts, which she is happy to have, but when he wants to marry her she objects; she's been with a pimp named Lester Diamond (James Woods) since she was a kid, and she doesn't want to give up her profession. Rothstein will make her an offer she can't refuse: cars, diamonds, furs, a home with a pool, and the key to his safe-deposit box. She marries him. It is Ace's first mistake.

Another mistake was to ever meet Nicky Santoro (Joe Pesci) when they were both kids in Chicago. Nicky is a thief and a killer, who comes to Vegas, forms a crew, and throws his weight around. After he squeezes one guy's head in a vise, the word goes out that he's the mob's enforcer. Not true, but people believe it, and soon Nicky's name is being linked with his old pal Ace in all the newspapers.

Scorsese tells his story with the energy and pacing he's famous for, and with a wealth of little details that feel just right. Not only the details of tacky 1970s period decor, but little moments like when Ace orders the casino cooks to put "exactly the same amount of blueberries in every muffin." Or when airborne feds are circling a golf course while spying on the hoods, and their plane runs out of gas, and they have to make an emergency landing right on the green. And when crucial evidence is obtained because a low-level hood kept a record of his expenses. And when Ace hosts a weekly show on local TV—and reveals a talent for juggling.

Meanwhile, Ginger starts drinking, and Ace is worried about their kid, and they start having public fights, and she turns to Nicky for advice that soon becomes consolation, and when Ace finds out she may be fooling around he utters a line that, in its way, is perfect: "I just hope it's not somebody who I think it might be."

"It was," the narration tells us, "the last time street guys would ever be given such an opportunity." All the mob had to do was take care of business. But when Ace met Ginger and when Nicky came to town, the pieces were in place for the mob to become the biggest loser in Vegas history. "We screwed up good," Nicky says, not using exactly those words. Scorsese gets the feel, the mood, almost the smell of the city just right; De Niro and Pesci inhabit their roles with unconscious assurance, Sharon Stone's call girl is her best performance, and the supporting cast includes people like Don Rickles, whose very presence evokes an era (his job is to stand impassively beside the boss and look very sad about what might happen to whomever the boss is talking to).

Unlike his other Mafia movies (*Mean Streets* and *GoodFellas*), Scorsese's *Casino* is as concerned with history as with plot and character. The city of Las Vegas is his subject, and he shows how it permitted people like Ace, Ginger, and Nicky to flourish, and then spit them out, because the Vegas machine is too profitable and powerful to allow anyone to slow its operation. When the Mafia, using funds from the Teamsters Union, was ejected in the late 1970s, the 1980s ushered in a new source of financing: junk bonds. The guys who floated *those* might be the inspiration for *Casino II.* "The big corporations took over," the narration observes, almost sadly. "Today, it works like Disneyland."

Which brings us back to our opening insight. In a sense, people *need* to believe a town like Vegas is run by guys like Ace and Nicky. In a place that breaks the rules, maybe you can break some, too. For the gambler mentality, it is actually less reassuring to know that giant corporations, financed by bonds and run by accountants, operate the Vegas machine. They know all the odds and the house always wins. With Ace in charge, who knows what might happen?

Casino Royale
PG-13, 144 m., 2006

Daniel Craig (James Bond), Eva Green (Vesper Lynd), Mads Mikkelsen (Le Chiffre), Judi Dench (M), Jeffrey Wright (Felix Leiter), Giancarlo Giannini (Mathis). Directed by Martin Campbell and produced by Barbara Broccoli and Michael G. Wilson. Written by Neal Purvis, Robert Wade, and Paul Haggis. Based on the book by Ian Fleming.

Casino Royale has the answers to all my complaints about the forty-five-year-old James Bond series, and some I hadn't even thought of. It's not that I didn't love some of the earlier films, like some, dislike others, and so on, as that I was becoming less convinced that I ever had to see another one.

This movie is *new* from the get-go. It could be your first Bond. In fact, it was the first Bond; it was Ian Fleming's first 007 novel, and he was still discovering who the character was. The longtime Saltzman-Broccoli producing team could never get their hands on the rights until now, despite earlier misadventures by others using the same title, and maybe it's just as well, because it provides a fresh starting place. And it returns to the family fold; with her father's passing, Barbara Broccoli is producer.

Yes, Daniel Craig makes a superb Bond: leaner, more taciturn, less sex-obsessed, able to be hurt in body and soul, not giving a damn if his martini is shaken or stirred. That doesn't make him the "best" Bond, because I've long since given up playing that pointless ranking game; Sean Connery was first to plant the flag, and that's that. But Daniel Craig is bloody damned great as Bond, in a movie that creates a new reality for the character.

Year after year, attending the new Bond was like observing a ritual. There was the opening stunt sequence that served little purpose except to lead into the titles; the title song; Miss Moneypenny; M with an assignment of great urgency to the Crown; Q with some new gadgets; an arch-villain; a series of babes, some treacherous, some doomed, all frequently in stages of undress; the villain's master plan; Bond's certain death and a lot of chases. It could be terrific, it could be routine, but you always knew about where you were in the formula.

With *Casino Royale*, we get to the obligatory concluding lovey-dovey on the tropical sands, and then the movie pulls a screeching U-turn and starts up *again* with the most sensational scene I have ever seen set in Venice, or most other places. It's a movie that keeps on giving.

This time, no Moneypenny, no Q, and Judi Dench is unleashed as M, given a larger role, and allowed to seem hard-eyed and disapproving to the reckless Bond. This time, no dream of world domination but just a bleeding-eyed rat who channels money to terrorists. This time a poker game that is interrupted by the weirdest trip to the parking lot I've ever seen. This time, no laser beam inching up on Bond's netherlands, but a nasty knotted rope actually whacking his hopes of heirs.

And this time, no Monte Carlo, but Montenegro, a fictional casino resort, where Bond checks into the Hotel Splendid, which is in fact, yes, the very same Grand Hotel Pupp in Karlovy Vary where Queen Latifah had her culinary vacation in *Last Holiday*. That gives me another opportunity to display my expertise on the Czech Republic by informing you that "Pupp" is pronounced "poop," so no wonder it's the Splendid.

I never thought I would see a Bond movie where I cared, actually cared, about the people. But I care about Bond, and about Vesper Lynd (Eva Green), even though I know that (here it comes) a Martini Vesper is shaken, not stirred. Vesper Lynd, on the other hand, is definitely stirring, as she was in Bernardo Bertolucci's wonderful *The Dreamers*. Sometimes shaken, too. Vesper and James have a shower scene that answers, at last, why nobody in a Bond movie ever seems to have any real emotions.

A review should not be a list. So I should not enumerate all the scenes I liked. But I learn from IMDb that the special credit for the "free running" scenes of Sebastien Foucan refers to the sensational opening Madagascar foot chase in which Foucan practices "parkour," or the ability to run at walls and angles and bounce off them to climb or change direction; Jackie Chan could do similar feats.

Which brings up another thing. Most of the chases and stunts in *Casino Royale* take place in something vaguely approximating real space and time. Of course I know they use doubles and deceptive camera angles and edits to cover impossibilities, but the point is: They try to make it look real.

Recently, with the advent of portable cameras and computerized editing, action movies have substituted visual chaos for visual elegance. I think the public is getting tired of action sequences that are created in postproduction. I've been swamped with letters complaining about *The Bourne Ultimatum*. One guy said, "Why don't critics admit they're tired of it?" Actually, we're tired of writing about how tired of it we are.

The plot centers on a marathon high-stakes poker game, in which Bond will try to deprive Le Chiffre (Mads Mikkelsen) of ten million or more pounds that would go to finance terrorism. Le Chiffre (The Cypher) has problems on his own because he owes money big-time to the people who supply it to him. The director, Martin Campbell, builds suspense in the extended poker game by not being afraid to focus for long seconds on the eyes of the two main opponents, which is all the more effective because Le Chiffre's left eye has tears of blood, inspiring a classic Bond line. Bond's absences from the table are of more than ordinary interest.

This is Campbell's second Bond picture, after *GoldenEye* (1995), but he breaks with his own and everyone else's tradition. He's helped by Craig, who gives the sense of a hard man, wounded by life and his job, who nevertheless cares about people and right and wrong. To a certain degree, the earlier Bonds were lustful technicians. With this one, since he has a big scene involving a merchant's house in Venice, we can excuse ourselves for observing that if you prick him, he bleeds.

The Cell
R, 108 m., 2000

Jennifer Lopez (Catherine Deane), Vince Vaughn (Agent Novak), Vincent D'Onofrio (Carl Stargher), Marianne Jean-Baptiste (Dr. Miriam Kent), Jake Weber (Agent Ramsey), Dylan Baker (Henry West), Patrick Bauchau (Lucien Baines), Gerry Becker (Dr. Cooperman), James Gammon (Teddy Lee), Catherine Sutherland (Anne Marie Vicksey), Jake Thomas (Young Stargher), Pruitt Taylor Vince (Dr. Reid). Directed by Tarsem and produced by Julio Caro and Eric McLeod. Screenplay by Mark Protosevich.

The Cell is a bizarre mixture of science fiction and serial murders, mind games and pop psychology, wild images and haunting special effects. It's a thriller and a fantasy, a police movie and a venture into the mind of a killer so perverse he could see Hannibal Lecter and raise him. For all of its visual pyrotechnics, it's also a story where we care about the characters; there's a lot at stake at the end, and we're involved. I know people who hate it, finding it pretentious or unrestrained; I think it's one of the best films of the year.

Jennifer Lopez stars, as Catherine Deane, a social worker who has a knack for establishing rapport with troubled clients. She is recruited for a project in which experimental technology is used to establish a link between her mind and that of a little boy locked inside a coma. Can she coax him out? The opening images, of black stallions and desert vistas, show her riding across the sands in a flowing white dress, and then finding the little boy in a landscape filled with stark Dali trees, and almost making contact, before . . .

The director, named Tarsem, uses this story to establish the mind-sharing methodology. The mind-trips take place in a sci-fi laboratory, with earnest scientists peering through plate-glass windows at their eerie subjects, who are suspended in midair wearing virtual reality gear. We meet the millionaire parents of the little boy, learn about his problems, and get to know Catherine, who is played by Lopez as quiet, grave, and confident.

In a parallel story, the FBI finds the body of the latest victim of a serial killer who drowns his captives and then makes them up to look like dolls. Vince Vaughn plays an agent named Novak, who believes the killer has a ritual he goes through—a ritual that means his latest victim has only hours to live before a clockwork mechanism brings about her death. Using slim clues and brilliant lab work, the FBI is able to capture the killer, a vile man named Carl Stargher (Vincent D'Onofrio). But how to get him to reveal where his latest captive is hidden? The FBI turns to Catherine Deane and the scientists in charge (Marianne Jean-Baptiste, Dylan Baker, and Pruitt Taylor Vince), who warn that she risks psychic harm by venturing into Stargher's unwholesome subconscious.

The screenplay, by Mark Protosevich, is ingenious in the way it intercuts three kinds of stories. On one level The Cell is science fiction about virtual reality, complete with the ominous observation that if your mind thinks it's real, then it is real, and it could kill you. On

another level the movie is a wildly visionary fantasy in which the mind-spaces of Stargher and Deane are landscapes by Jung out of Dali, with a touch of the Tarot deck, plus light-and-sound trips reminiscent of 2001. On the third level, the movie is a race against time, in which a victim struggles for her life while the FBI desperately pieces together clues; these scenes reminded me of The Silence of the Lambs. The intercutting is so well done that at the end there is tension from all three directions, and what's at stake is not simply the life of the next victim, but also the soul of Carl Stargher, who lets Catherine get glimpses of his unhappy childhood.

Stargher's sexual practices are also suggested, somewhat obliquely. Like the predators in Seven, The Silence of the Lambs, and Hannibal, Stargher is a creature of neo-S&M, a seriously twisted man whose libido needs such complicated tending it hardly seems worth the trouble. We are left with a few technical questions (how did he embed the hooks in his own back?), but a movie like this is more concerned with suggesting weirdness than explaining it.

The Cell is one of those movies where you have a lot of doubts at the beginning, and then one by one they're answered, and you find yourself seduced by the style and story. It plays fair all the way through—it develops its themes and delivers on them, instead of copping out like Hollow Man by making a U-turn into a slasher film. It's not often the imagination and the emotions are equally touched by a film, but here I was exhilarated by the boldness of the conception while still involved at a thriller level.

I don't seek out advance information about movies because I like to go in with an open mind. Walking into the screening of The Cell, I knew absolutely nothing about the plot or premise, but a TV producer in New York made a point of telling me how much she hated it, and various on-line correspondents helpfully told me how bad they thought it was. Did we see the same movie?

We live in a time when Hollywood shyly ejects weekly remakes of dependable plots, terrified to include anything that might confuse the dullest audience member. The new studio guidelines prefer PG-13 cuts from directors, so we get movies like Coyote Ugly that start out with no brains and now don't have any sex, either. Into this wilderness comes a movie like *The Cell*, which is challenging, wildly ambitious, and technically superb, and I dunno: I guess it just overloads the circuits for some people.

Tarsem (he dropped his surname, Duamdwar) is a first-time director who comes to movies via music videos and commercials (indeed his title sequence in the desert looks like it could lead into a beer ad as easily as a psychological fantasy). He must have seized this project with eager ambition. Like other emerging directors (Spike Jonze, David O. Russell, Paul Thomas Anderson) he likes to take big chances; he reminds me of how Spike Lee and Oliver Stone came lunging out of the starting gate.

Tarsem is an Indian, like M. Night Shyamalan of *The Sixth Sense*, and comes from a culture where ancient imagery and modern technology live side by side. In the 1970s, Pauline Kael wrote, the most interesting directors were Altman, Scorsese, and Coppola, because they were Catholics whose imaginations were enriched by the church of pre-Vatican II, while most other Americans were growing up on Eisenhower's bland platitudes. Now our whole culture has been tamed by marketing and branding, and mass entertainment has been dumbed down. It is possible the next infusion of creativity will come from cultures like India, still rich in imagination, not yet locked into malls.

Changing Lanes

R, 100 m., 2002

Ben Affleck (Gavin Banek), Samuel L. Jackson (Doyle Gipson), Toni Collette (Michelle), Sydney Pollack (Delano), William Hurt (Doyle's Sponsor), Amanda Peet (Cynthia), Kim Staunton (Valerie Gipson), Dylan Baker (Fixer). Directed by Roger Michell and produced by Scott Rudin. Screenplay by Chap Taylor and Michael Tolkin.

"One wrong turn deserves another," say the ads for *Changing Lanes*. Yes, both of the movie's dueling hotheads are in the wrong—but they are also both in the right. The story involves two flawed men, both prey to anger, who get involved in a fender bender that brings out all of their worst qualities. And their best. This is not a dumb formula film about revenge. It doesn't use rubber-stamp lines like, "It's payback time." It is about adults who have minds as well as emotions, and can express themselves with uncommon clarity. And it's not just about the quarrel between these two men, but about the ways they have been living their lives.

The story begins with two men who need to be in court on time. Gavin Banek (Ben Affleck) needs to file a signed form proving that an elderly millionaire turned over control of his foundation to Banek's law firm. Doyle Gipson (Samuel L. Jackson) needs to show that he has loan approval to buy a house for his family; he hopes that will persuade his fed-up wife to stay in New York and not move with the kids to Oregon. Banek and Gipson get into a fender bender. It's not really anybody's fault.

Of course they are polite when it happens: "You hurt?" Nobody is. Banek, who is rich and has been taught that money is a solution to human needs, doesn't want to take time to exchange insurance cards and file a report. He hands Gipson a signed blank check. Gipson, who wants to handle this the right way, doesn't want a check. Banek gets in his car and drives away, shouting, "Better luck next time!" over his shoulder, and leaving Gipson stranded in the middle of the expressway with a flat tire.

Gipson gets to court twenty minutes late. The case has already been settled. In his absence, he has lost. The judge isn't interested in his story. Banek gets to court in time, but discovers that he is missing the crucial file folder with the old man's signature. Who has it? Gipson.

At this point, in a film less intelligent and ambitious, the vile Banek would pull strings to make life miserable for the blameless Gipson. But *Changing Lanes* doesn't settle for the formula. Gipson responds to Banek's rudeness by faxing a page from the crucial file to Banek with "Better luck next time!" scrawled on it. Banek turns to his sometime mistress (Toni Collette), who knows a guy who "fixes" things. The guy (Dylan Baker) screws with Gipson's credit rating so his home mortgage falls through. Gipson finds an ingenious way to counterattack. And so begins a daylong struggle between two angry men.

Ah, but that's far from all. *Changing Lanes* is a thoughtful film that by its very existence shames studio movies that have been dumbed down into cat-and-mouse cartoons. The screenplay is by Chap Taylor, who has previously worked as a production assistant for Woody Allen, and by Michael Tolkin, who wrote the novel and screenplay *The Player* and wrote and directed two extraordinary films, *The Rapture* and *The New Age*. The writers, rookie and veteran, want to know who these men are, how they got to this day in their lives, what their values are, what kinds of worlds they live in. A dumb film would be about settling scores after the fender bender. This film, which breathes, which challenges, which is excitingly alive, wants to see these men hit their emotional bottoms. Will they learn anything?

Doyle Gipson is a recovering alcoholic. His AA meetings and his AA sponsor (William Hurt) are depicted in realistic, not stereotyped terms. He's sober, but still at the mercy of his emotions. As he stands in the wreckage of his plans to save his marriage, his wife (Kim Staunton) tells him, "This is the sort of thing that always happens to you—and never happens to me unless I am in your field of gravity." And his sponsor tells him, "Booze isn't really your drug of choice. You're addicted to chaos." At one point, seething with rage, Gipson walks into a bar and orders a shot of bourbon. Then he stares at it. Then he gets into a fight that he deliberately provokes, and we realize that at some level he walked into the bar not for the drink but for the fight.

Gavin Banek leads a rich and privileged life. His boss (Sydney Pollack) has just made him a partner in their Wall Street law firm. It doesn't hurt that Banek married the boss's daughter. It also doesn't hurt that he was willing to obtain the signature of a confused old man who might not have known what he was signing, and that the firm will make millions as a result. His wife (Amanda Peet) sees her husband with blinding clarity. After Banek has second thoughts about the tainted document, Pollack asks his daughter to get him into line, and at lunch she has an extraordinary speech.

"Did you know my father has been cheating on my mother for twenty years?" she asks him. He says no, and then sheepishly adds, "Well, I didn't know it was for twenty years." Her mother

knew all along, his wife says, "but she thought it would be unethical to leave a man for cheating on his marriage, after she has enjoyed an expensive lifestyle that depends on a man who makes his money by cheating at work." She looks across the table at her husband. "I could have married an honest man," she tells him. She did not, choosing instead a man who would go right to the edge to make money. You don't work on Wall Street if you're not prepared to do that, she says.

And what, for that matter, about the poor old millionaire whose foundation is being plundered? "How do you think he got his money?" Pollack asks Affleck. "You think those factories in Malaysia have day-care centers?" He helpfully points out that the foundation was set up in the first place as a tax dodge.

Such speeches are thunderbolts in *Changing Lanes*. They show the movie digging right down into the depths of the souls, of the values of these two men. The director, Roger Michell, has made good movies, including *Persuasion* and *Notting Hill*, but this one seems more like Neil LaBute's *In the Company of Men*, or Tolkin's work. It lays these guys out and X-rays them, and by the end of the day, each man's own anger scares him more than the other guy's. This is one of the best movies of the year.

Chariots of Fire

PG, 123 m., 1981

Ben Cross (Harold Abrahams), Ian Charleson (Eric Liddell), Nigel Havers (Lord Andrew Lindsay), Ian Holm (Coach Mussabini), Sir John Gielgud (Master of Trinity), Lindsay Anderson (Master of Caius), David Yelland (Prince of Wales), Nicholas Farrell (Aubrey Montague). Directed by Hugh Hudson and produced by David Puttnam. Screenplay by Colin Welland.

This is strange. I have no interest in running and am not a partisan in the British class system. Then why should I have been so deeply moved by *Chariots of Fire*, a British film that has running and class as its subjects? I've toyed with that question since I first saw this remarkable film in May 1981 at the Cannes Film Festival, and I believe the answer is rather simple: Like many great films, *Chariots of Fire* takes its nominal subjects as occasions for much larger statements about human nature.

This is a movie that has a great many running scenes. It is also a movie about British class distinctions in the years after World War I, years in which the establishment was trying to piece itself back together after the carnage in France. It is about two outsiders—a Scot who is the son of missionaries in China, and a Jew whose father is an immigrant from Lithuania. And it is about how both of them use running as a means of asserting their dignity. But it is about more than them, and a lot of this film's greatness is hard to put into words. *Chariots of Fire* creates deep feelings among many members of its audiences, and it does that not so much with its story or even its characters as with particular moments that are very sharply seen and heard.

Seen, in photography that pays grave attention to the precise look of a human face during stress, pain, defeat, victory, and joy. Heard, in one of the most remarkable sound tracks of any film in a long time, with music by the Greek composer Vangelis Papathanassiou. His compositions for *Chariots of Fire* are as evocative, and as suited to the material, as the different but also perfectly matched scores of such films as *The Third Man* and *Zorba the Greek*. The music establishes the tone for the movie, which is one of nostalgia for a time when two young and naturally gifted British athletes ran fast enough to bring home medals from the 1924 Paris Olympics.

The nostalgia is an important aspect of the film, which opens with a 1979 memorial service for one of the men, Harold Abrahams, and then flashes back sixty years to his first day at Cambridge University. We are soon introduced to the film's other central character, the Scotsman Eric Liddell. The film's underlying point of view is a poignant one: These men were once young and fast and strong, and they won glory on the sports field, but now they are dead and we see them as figures from long ago.

The film is unabashedly and patriotically British in its regard for these two characters, but it also contains sharp jabs at the British class system, which made the Jewish Abrahams feel like an outsider who could sometimes feel the lack of sincerity in a handshake, and placed the Protestant Liddell in the position of having to explain to the peeved Prince of Wales why he could not, in conscience, run on the Sabbath. Both men are essentially proving themselves, their worth, their beliefs, on the track. But *Chariots of Fire* takes an unexpected approach to many of its running scenes. It does not, until near the film's end, stage them as contests to wring cheers from the audience. Instead, it sees them as *efforts,* as endeavors by individual runners—it tries to capture the exhilaration of running as a celebration of the spirit.

Two of the best moments in the movie: A moment in which Liddell defeats Abrahams, who agonizingly replays the defeat over and over in his memory. And a moment in which Abrahams' old Italian-Arabic track coach, banned from the Olympic stadium, learns who won his man's race. First he bangs his fist through his straw boater, then he sits on his bed and whispers, "My son!"

All of the contributions to the film are distinguished. Neither Ben Cross, as Abrahams, nor Ian Charleson, as Liddell, are accomplished runners but they are accomplished actors, and they *act* the running scenes convincingly. Ian Holm, as Abrahams' coach, quietly dominates every scene he is in. There are perfectly observed cameos by John Gielgud and Lindsay Anderson, as masters of Cambridge colleges, and by David Yelland, as a foppish, foolish young Prince of Wales. These parts and others make up a greater whole.

Chariots of Fire is one of the best films of recent years, a memory of a time when men still believed you could win a race if only you wanted to badly enough.

Children of Heaven

PG, 87 m., 1999

Amir Naji (Ali's Father), Amir Farrokh Hashemian (Ali), Bahare Seddiqi (Zahra), Nafise Jafar-Mohammadi (Roya), Fereshte Sarabandi (Ali's Mother), Kamal Mir Karimi (Assistant), Behzad Rafiee (Trainer), Dariush Mokhtari (Ali's Teacher). Directed by Majid Majidi and produced by the Institute for the Intellectual Development of Children and Young Adults. Screenplay by Majidi.

Children of Heaven is very nearly a perfect movie for children, and of course that means adults will like it too. It lacks the cynicism and smart-mouth attitudes of so much American entertainment for kids, and glows with a kind of good-hearted purity. To see this movie is to be reminded of a time when the children in movies were children, and not miniature stand-up comics.

The movie is from Iran. Immediately you think kids would not be interested in such a movie. It has subtitles. Good lord!—kids will have to read them! But its subtitles are easy for eight- or nine-year-olds, who can whisper them to their siblings, and maybe this is their perfect introduction to subtitles. As for Iran: The theme of this movie is so universal there is not a child who will not be wide-eyed with interest and suspense.

The film is about a boy who loses his sister's shoes. He takes them to the cobbler for repairs, and on the way home, when he stops to pick up vegetables for his mother, a blind trash-collector accidentally carries them away. Of course the boy, named Ali, is afraid to tell his parents. Of course his sister, named Zahra, wants to know how she is supposed to go to school without shoes. The children feverishly write notes to each other, right under their parents' noses.

The answer is simple: Zahra will wear Ali's sneakers to school every morning, and then run home so that Ali can put them on for his school in the afternoon. But Zahra cannot always run fast enough, and Ali, who is a good student, gets in trouble for being late to class. And there is a heartbreaking scene where Zahra solemnly regards her own precious lost shoes, now on the feet of the ragpicker's daughter.

I submit that this situation is scarier and more absorbing for children than a movie about Godzilla or other manufactured entertainments. When you're a kid, you know you're not likely to be squished by a giant lizard, but losing something that has been entrusted to you? And getting in trouble at school? That's big time.

Majid Majidi's film has a wonderful scene where Ali and his father bicycle from the almost medieval streets and alleys of the old town to the high-rises and luxury homes where the rich people live. The father hopes for work as a gardener, but he is intimidated by the challenge of speaking into the intercoms on the gates of the wealthy. His son jumps in with offers of pruning, weeding, spraying, and trimming. It is a great triumph.

And then there is a footrace for the poor children of the quarter. The winner gets two weeks in a summer camp and other prizes. Ali doesn't care. He wants to place third, because the prize is a new pair of sneakers, which he can give to his sister. My guess is that the race and its outcome will be as exciting for many kids as anything they've seen at the movies.

Children of Heaven is about a home without unhappiness. About a brother and sister who love one another, instead of fighting. About situations any child can identify with. In this film from Iran, I found a sweetness and innocence that shames the land of Mutant Turtles, Power Rangers, and violent video games. Why do we teach our kids to see through things before they even learn to see them?

Children of Men

R, 108 m., 2006

Clive Owen (Theo Faron), Julianne Moore (Julian Taylor), Michael Caine (Jasper), Chiwetel Ejiofor (Luke), Charlie Hunnam (Patric), Clare-Hope Ashitey (Kee), Pam Ferris (Miriam), Danny Huston (Nigel), Peter Mullan (Syd). Directed by Alfonso Cuarón. Produced by Armyan Bernstein and Thomas A. Bliss. Written by Cuarón and Timothy J. Sexton, based on P. D. James's book.

It is above all the look of *Children of Men* that stirs apprehension in the heart. Is this what we are all headed for? The film is set in 2027, when assorted natural disasters, wars, and terrorist acts have rendered most of the world ungovernable, uninhabitable, or anarchic. Britain stands as an island of relative order, held in line by a fearsome police state. It has been eighteen years since earth has seen the birth of a human child.

We see today on the news the devastation of Baghdad, the latest city that has fallen through the safety net of civilization. We remember the war zones of Beirut, Algiers, Belfast, Vietnam. Surely it could not happen here? For a time after 9/11 it seemed anarchy might be unloosed upon our world, but now we have domestic calm, however transient.

Watching *Children of Men*, which creates a London in ruins, I realized after a point that the sets and art design were so well done that I took it as a real place. Often I fear it will all come to this, that the rule of law and the rights of men will be destroyed by sectarian mischief and nationalistic recklessness. Are we living in the last good times?

There is much to be said about the story of *Children of Men,* directed by Alfonso Cuarón and based on a lesser-known novel by P. D. James, who usually writes about a detective. But the story, like the stories of *Metropolis, Nosferatu,* or *Escape from New York* is secondary to the visual world we are given to regard. Guerilla fighters occupy abandoned warehouse. The homeless live in hovels. Immigrants are rounded up and penned in cages. The utilities cannot be depended upon. There are, most disturbing of all, no children. Only dogs and cats remain to be cared for and cherished.

As the film opens, the TV news reports that the world's youngest person has been stabbed to death in Buenos Aires, because he declined to give an autograph. Theo Faron (Clive Owen), the film's hero, watches the news in a café and then leaves with his paper cup in his hand. Seconds later, a bomb destroys the café. This is essential: Faron is terrified. He crouches and fear freezes his face. This will not be like action pictures, where the hero never seems to fear death.

Owen's character, indeed, seems to be central to the film's mood. He is tired, depressed, fearful, pessimistic. So is everyone else. They will all grow old and die, and then there won't be anybody else. We could imagine an aging society in which everyone lived in condos and the world was a vast retirement haven, but who would till the fields? Can you imagine a retirement home in which the decrepit fight over cans of peaches?

Britain, as the last functioning nation, has closed its borders, is deporting anyone who is not a citizen, is engaged in a war between the establishment and a band of rebels who support immigrant rights. Faron is kidnapped by this group, headed by Julian Taylor (Julianne Moore), who was once his lover; they lost a child. Her associate, Luke (Chiwetel Ejiofor, in another unexpected character) backs her up with muscle and wisdom. Interestingly, there seems to be no racial prejudice in this

Britain; they don't care what color you are, as long as you were on board before they pulled up the rope. Julian's group wants Faron's influence to get travel papers for Kee (Clare-Hope Ashitey), so the young woman can be smuggled out of the country and to refuge in a rumored safe haven. Kee is a key to the future; the movie's advertising tells you why, but I will not.

The center of the film involves the journey toward the coast that Faron and Kee undertake with Julian, Luke, and Miriam (Pam Ferris), who is both watchdog and nurse. Along the way they are pursued by Homeland Security troops, and there is a chase scene with one of the most sudden and violent moments I have ever seen in a film. Not all of the chases in all of the Bournes equal this one, shot in a single take by one camera, for impact.

Their journey involves a rest stop at the country hideaway of an aging hippie (Michael Caine), who has known Faron for years; we are reminded again of how sweet Caine can seem in a character, how solicitous and concerned. It is a small but perfect performance. The journey continues toward the coast, and then there is a running gun battle (in the middle of an existing battle) down ruined streets of rubble and death. Many of the shots are, or seem, uninterrupted; there is the sense that this city is not a set but extends indefinitely in every direction, poisoned and lethal.

Here again, the action scenes seem rooted in sweat and desperation. Too many action scenes look like slick choreography, but Cuaron and Owen get the scent of fear and death, and nobody does anything that is particularly impossible. Small details: Even in the midst of a firefight, dogs scamper in the streets. Faron's hand reaches out to touch and reassure the nearest animal, and I was reminded of Jack London's belief that dogs (not cats so much) see us as their gods. Apparently sterility affects only humans on earth; when we are gone, will the dogs still tirelessly search for us?

I have been using Hitchcock's term MacGuffin too much lately, but there are times when only it will do. The lack of children and the possibility of children are the MacGuffins in *Children of Men* inspiring all the action, but the movie significantly never tells us why children stopped being born, or how they might become possible again. The children-as-MacGuffin is simply a dramatic device to avoid actual politics while showing how the world is slipping away from civility and coexistence. The film is not really about children; it is about men and women, and civilization, and the way that fear can be used to justify a police state.

I admire that plot decision. I would have felt let down if the movie had a more decisive outcome; it is about the struggle, not the victor, and the climax in my opinion is openended. The performances are crucial, because all of these characters have so completely internalized their world that they make it palpable, and themselves utterly convincing.

Alfonso Cuarón (born in 1961 in Mexico City) is not new to enormous sets and vast scopes. He was the director of *Harry Potter and the Prisoner of Azkaban* (2004), and I have long admired his overlooked *Great Expectations* (1998) and *A Little Princess* (1995), both of which created self-contained worlds of their own. They were in English; he returned to Spanish to make the worldwide hit *Y tu Mamá También* (2001).

Here he fulfills the promise of futuristic fiction; the characters do not wear strange costumes or visit the Moon, and the cities are not plastic hallucinations but look just like today, except tired and shabby. Here is certainly a world ending not with a bang but a whimper, and the film serves as a cautionary warning. The only thing we will have to fear in the future, we learn, is the past itself. Our past. Ourselves.

The China Syndrome

PG, 122 m., 1979

Jane Fonda (Kimberly Wells), Jack Lemmon (Jack Godell), Michael Douglas (Richard Adams), Scott Brady (Herman DeYoung), James Hampton (Bill Gibson), Peter Donat (Don Jacovich), Wilford Brimley (Ted Spindler). Directed by James Bridges and produced by Douglas. Screenplay by Mike Gray, T. S. Cook, and Bridges.

The China Syndrome is a terrific thriller that incidentally raises the most unsettling questions about how safe nuclear power plants really are. It was received in some quarters as a political film, and the people connected with it make no secret of their doubts about nuclear power. But the movie is, above all, entertainment: well-acted, well-crafted, scary as hell.

The events leading up to the "accident" in *The China Syndrome* are indeed based on actual occurrences at nuclear plants. Even the most unlikely mishap (a stuck needle on a graph causing engineers to misread a crucial water level) really happened at the Dresden plant outside Chicago. And yet the movie works so well not because of its factual basis, but because of its human content. The performances are so good, so consistent, that *The China Syndrome* becomes a thriller dealing in personal values. The suspense is generated not only by our fears about what might happen, but by our curiosity about how, in the final showdown, the characters will react.

The key character is Godell (Jack Lemmon), a shift supervisor at a big nuclear power plant in Southern California. He lives alone, quietly, and can say without any selfconsciousness that the plant is his life. He believes in nuclear power. But when an earthquake shakes his plant, he becomes convinced that he felt an aftershock—caused not by an earthquake but by rumblings deep within the plant.

The quake itself leads to the first "accident." Because a two-bit needle gets stuck on a roll of graph paper, the engineers think they need to lower the level of the water shield over the nuclear pile. Actually, the level is already dangerously low. And if the pile were ever uncovered, the result could be the "China syndrome," so named because the superheated nuclear materials would melt directly through the floor of the plant and, theoretically, keep on going until they hit China. In practice, there'd be an explosion and a release of radioactive materials sufficient to poison an enormous area.

The accident takes place while a TV news team is filming a routine feature about the plant. The cameraman (Michael Douglas) secretly films events in the panicked control room. And the reporter (Jane Fonda) tries to get the story on the air. Her superiors refuse, influenced by the power industry's smoothly efficient public relations people. But the more Fonda and Douglas dig into the accident, the less they like it.

Meanwhile, obsessed by that second

tremor, Lemmon has been conducting his own investigation. He discovers that the X-rays used to check key welds at the plant have been falsified. And then the movie takes off in classic thriller style: The director, James Bridges, uses an exquisite sense of timing and character development to bring us to the cliffhanger conclusion.

The performances are crucial to the movie's success, and they're all the more interesting because the characters aren't painted as antinuclear crusaders, but as people who get trapped in a situation while just trying to do their jobs. Fonda is simply superb as the TV reporter; the range and excellence of her performance are a wonder. Douglas is exactly right as the bearded, casually antiestablishment cameraman. And Jack Lemmon, reluctant to rock the boat, compelled to follow his conscience, creates a character as complex as his Oscar-winning businessman in *Save the Tiger*.

Chinatown

R, 131 m., 1974

Jack Nicholson (J. J. Gittes), Faye Dunaway (Evelyn Mulwray), John Huston (Noah Cross), Perry Lopez (Escobar), John Hillerman (Yelburton), Darrell Zwerling (Hollis Mulwray), Diane Ladd (Ida Sessions), Roman Polanski (Man with Knife). Directed by Polanski and produced by Robert Evans. Screenplay by Robert Towne.

Roman Polanski's *Chinatown* is not only a great entertainment, but something more, something I would have thought almost impossible: It's a 1940s private-eye movie that doesn't depend on nostalgia or camp for its effect, but works because of the enduring strength of the genre itself. In some respects, this movie actually could have been made in the 1940s. It accepts its conventions and categories at face value and doesn't make them the object of satire or filter them through a modern sensibility, as Robert Altman did with *The Long Goodbye*. Here's a private-eye movie in which all the traditions, romantic as they may seem, are left intact.

At its center, of course, is the eye himself: J. J. Gittes, moderately prosperous as a result of adultery investigations. He isn't the perennially broke loner like Philip Marlowe, inhab-

iting a shabby office and buying himself a drink out of the office bottle. He's a successful investigator with a two-man staff, and he dresses well and is civilized and intelligent. He does, however, possess the two indispensable qualities necessary for any traditional private eye. He is deeply cynical about human nature, and he has a personal code and sticks to it.

There is also, of course, the woman, who comes to the private eye for help but does not quite reveal to him the full dimensions of her trouble. And there are the other inevitable ingredients of the well-crafted private-eye plot, as perfected by Raymond Chandler and Dashiell Hammett and practiced by Ross Macdonald. There's the woman's father, and the skeletons in their family closet, and the way that a crime taking place now has a way of leading back to a crime in the past.

These plots work best when they start out seeming impossibly complicated and then end up with watertight logic, and Robert Towne's screenplay for *Chinatown* does that with consummate skill. But the whole movie is a tour de force; it's a period movie, with all the right cars and clothes and props, but we forget that after the first ten minutes. We've become involved in the movie's web of mystery, as we always were with the best private-eye stories, whether written or filmed. We care about these people and want to see what happens to them.

And yet, at the same time, Polanski is so sensitive to the ways in which 1940s' movies in this genre were made that we're almost watching a critical essay. Godard once said that the only way to review a movie is to make another movie, and maybe that's what Polanski has done here. He's made a perceptive, loving comment on a kind of movie and a time in the nation's history that are both long past. *Chinatown* is almost a lesson on how to experience this kind of movie.

It's also a triumph of acting, particularly by Jack Nicholson, who is one of the most interesting actors now working and who contributes one of his best performances. He inhabits the character of J. J. Gittes like a second skin; the possession is so total that there are scenes in the movie where we almost have telepathy; we *know* what he's thinking, so he doesn't have to tell us. His loyalty is to the woman, but on several occasions, evidence turns up that seems to incriminate her. And then he must pull back, because his code will not admit clients who lie to him. Why he's this way (indeed, even the fact that he is this way) is communicated by Nicholson almost solely in the way he plays the character; dialogue isn't necessary to make the point.

The woman is Faye Dunaway, looking pale and neurotic and beautiful, and justifying for us (if not always for him) J. J.'s trust in her. And then there are all the other characters, who revolve around a complicated scheme to float a bond issue and build a dam to steal water for Los Angeles, in a time of drought. Because the film depends so much on the exquisite unraveling of its plot, it would be unfair to describe much more; one of its delights is in the way that dropped remarks and chance clues gradually build up the portrait of a crime.

And always at the center, there's the Nicholson performance, given an eerie edge by the bandage he wears on his nose after it's slit by a particularly slimy character played by Polanski himself. The bandage looks incongruous, we don't often see a bandaged nose on a movie private eye, but it's the kind of incongruity that's creepy and not funny. The film works similar ground: Drifting within sight of parody every so often, it saves itself by the seriousness of its character.

Chloe in the Afternoon
R, 97 m., 1972

Zouzou (Chloe), Bernard Verley (Frederick), Francoise Verley (Helene). Directed by Eric Rohmer and produced by Pierre Cottrell. Screenplay by Rohmer.

Chloe in the Afternoon, the last of Eric Rohmer's "Six Moral Tales," is the best of those I've seen. It is also the most fully rounded, lacking the one-dimensional tone of some of his earlier tales. It's as if he were striking notes in the previous works and is now bringing them all together into a chord; the final scene in *Chloe* is his last comment on the series, and Rohmer is telling us to, for God's sake, stop playing games and embrace each other with honesty.

Game-playing is always his subject. He doesn't approve of it, but he's become ob-sessed with studying it. He isn't interested in making movies about people with shallow motives and obvious personalities (which is to say, about 90 percent of the characters in movies). Rohmer's work contains surprises. People develop in unexpected ways. We don't know how to relate to them until well into the movie; they don't telegraph their intentions.

Perhaps the most interesting thing about Rohmer's characters is that they seem to retain free will. They aren't doomed, for example, to climb into the sack with each other at the end of the movie just because that's what usually happens. *Chloe in the Afternoon,* like *My Night at Maud's,* is in fact about an extended flirtation that doesn't get anywhere, and about the reaffirmation of an original love.

Rohmer's hero this time is Frederick (Bernard Verley), a pleasant if somewhat cool business executive who inhabits a marriage of the greatest simplicity and mutual respect. He and his wife, Helene (Francoise Verley), live like students—not because they can't afford better, but because they enjoy the lack of bourgeois physical and mental clutter. It's one of those marriages that outsiders call "perfect."

But then Chloe (Zouzou) materializes, right there in the middle of Frederick's afternoon. Frederick is a man who loves Paris and who has arranged his work schedule so that he has his afternoons free for a sandwich, a little wandering, and his fantasies about the women of the city. It isn't that he desires them (although he daydreams of a magic amulet that could seduce them all) but that their beauty affirms his choice of a wife.

Chloe is one of these people blessed with the ability to insinuate themselves into your life while seeming to leave it. She forms an attachment with Frederick during a period when (he thinks) she is merely passing through. They meet in the afternoons. They flirt, but not too much. They talk.

It eventually develops that Chloe has selected Frederick to be the father of her baby. That's what Chloe says, anyway, and Frederick believes her; she's one of these modern women who would never get married but would rather fancy having a perfect baby. (Cut to Bernard Shaw's famous retort to another such woman: "But, madam, what if the child had *your* brains and *my* body?")

You'll have to decide for yourself if Chloe really wants a baby. My personal notion is that she sees Frederick as merely a difficult exercise in seduction. She's a plain-beautiful woman who has just enough insecurity about herself to want to use her looks to confirm her attractiveness. For Frederick, however, it's a moral problem: How can he make love to Chloe when (as he believes) he is totally and deeply in love with his wife? Oh, you kid!

This description of the movie may make it sound inconsequential and meandering, but then Rohmer's movies always sound like that. Who else would make a whole movie, as he did, about Jerome's desire to caress the knee of Claire? Particularly as Jerome was not even a knee fetishist? What makes Rohmer's films so sparkling and intelligent is the way in which he watches his characters. Nothing escapes him, and he uses the angle of a glance, the tilt of a head, the precise set of a mouth, to create wonderfully complex characters.

The ending of *Chloe in the Afternoon* releases an emotional time bomb that places the movie in a new, and deeper, context. When we see Rohmer's great last scene, the "moral tales" fall into place. He has not been so very sophisticated after all, we realize; he has just been very good at seeing sophistication for what it is—the highly developed art of avoiding simple, direct human relationships.

Chocolat

PG-13, 105 m., 1989

Isaach De Bankole (Protee), Giulia Boschi (Aimee Dalens), Francois Cluzet (Marc Dalens), Cecile Ducasse (France Dalens [Child]), Jean-Claude Adelin (Luc Segalen), Kenneth Cranham (Jonathan Boothby). Directed by Claire Denis and produced by Alain Belmondo and Gerard Crosnier. Screenplay by Denis and Jean-Pol Fargeau.

Of all the places I have visited, Africa is the place where the land exudes the greatest sadness and joy. Outside the great cities, the savannah seems ageless, and in the places where man has built his outposts, he seems to huddle in the center of a limitless space.

The land seems smaller at night than during the day. The horizon draws closer, containing strange rustlings and restlessness and the coughs of wild beasts, and voices carry a great distance—much farther than the lights from the verandah.

Chocolat evokes this Africa better than any other film I have ever seen. It knows how quiet the land can be, so that thoughts can almost be heard—and how patient, so that every mistake is paid for sooner or later. The film is set in a French colony in West Africa in the days when colonialism was already doomed but did not yet realize it. At an isolated outpost of the provincial government, a young girl lives with her father and mother and many Africans, including Protee, the houseboy, who embodies such dignity and intelligence that he confers status upon himself in a society that will allow him none.

The story is told partly through the eyes of the young girl, and the film opens in the present, showing her as an adult in 1988, going back to visit her childhood home. But what is most important about the story are the things the young girl could not have known, or could have understood only imperfectly. And the central fact is that Protee is the best man, the most capable man, in the district—and that her mother and Protee feel a strong sexual attraction to one another.

Protee moves through the compound almost silently, always prompt, always courteous, always tactful. He sees everything. His employer is a French woman in her thirties, attractive, slender, with a few good dresses and the ability to provide a dinner party in West Africa with some of the chic of Paris. She has a workable marriage with her husband, whom she loves after the fashion of a dutiful bourgeois wife. But when the husband goes away on government business, the silence in the compound seems charged with tension; the man and woman who are left in charge become almost painfully aware of each other.

Daily life for the young girl is a little lonely for a child, but she shares secrets with Protee, too, and as she moves around the compound she has glimpses of a vast, unknown reality reaching out in all directions from the little patch of alien French society which has been planted there.

One day there is great excitement. An airplane makes an emergency landing in the district, bearing various visitors who seem exotic in this quiet place. One of them, young and bold, makes an implied proposition to the Frenchwoman. She is not interested, and yet there is a complicated dynamic at work here: She is drawn to Protee, yet cannot have him because of the racist basis of her society. And as is often the case, the master resents the servant, as if prejudice and segregation were the fault of the class that is discriminated against. In a way so subtle that some viewers of the film may miss it, the French woman behaves with the visiting male in such a way as to take revenge on Protee, whom she taunts because she cannot embrace.

Chocolat is a film of infinite delicacy. It is not one of those steamy, melodramatic interracial romances where love conquers all. It is a movie about the rules and conventions of a racist society, and how two intelligent adults, one black, one white, use their mutual sexual attraction as a battleground on which, very subtly, to hurt each other. The woman of course has the power; all of French colonial society stands behind her. But the man has the moral authority, as he demonstrates in the movie's most important scene, which is wordless, brief, and final.

Chocolat is one of those rare films with an entirely mature, adult sensibility; it is made with the complexity and subtlety of a great short story, and it assumes an audience that can understand what a strong flow of sex can exist between two people who barely even touch each other. It is a deliberately beautiful film—many of the frames create breathtaking compositions—but it is not a travelogue and it is not a love story. It is about how racism can prevent two people from looking each other straight in the eyes, and how they punish each other for the pain that causes them.

Chuck Berry Hail! Hail! Rock 'n' Roll

PG, 120 m., 1987

Featuring Chuck Berry, Keith Richards, Eric Clapton, Robert Cray, Etta James, Johnnie Johnson, Julian Lennon, and Linda Ronstadt. Directed by Taylor Hackford and produced by Stephanie Bennett. Music produced by Richards.

I expected *Chuck Berry Hail! Hail! Rock 'n' Roll!* to be a great concert film, and it is.

What I did not expect was that it would also be a tantalizing mystery, a study of Chuck Berry that makes him seem as shrouded and enigmatic as Charles Foster Kane. Here is a sixty-year-old man singing *Sweet Little Sixteen*, and he sings it with total conviction, and we have no idea what he means, or ever meant, by it.

The argument of this film is that Chuck Berry was a crucial figure in the development of rock 'n' roll, that fusion of black gospel and rhythm and blues with mainstream pop and teenage trauma. A good case is made, especially when Eric Clapton and Keith Richards explain precisely which chords and guitar strategies Berry used, and how you can still hear them today. There is a moment in the film when Berry and Richards are rehearsing, and Berry makes Richards do the same passage over and over again until he duplicates an effect that was first heard on records thirty years ago. It still sounds exactly right.

The film is a documentary about the sixtieth birthday concert that Berry performed in his hometown of St. Louis in 1987. The concert was the inspiration of Richards, lead guitarist for The Rolling Stones, who says he wanted to repay Berry for all the things the Stones and other rock groups have stolen from him. The way he wanted to do that was by producing a concert in which Berry would be backed by Richards and—for once—a first-rate, well-rehearsed band.

We quickly learn that this is not the way Berry has been operating in recent years. In testimony from Bruce Springsteen (who once opened for Berry) and in documentary footage of Berry himself, we learn that Berry has reduced his public appearances to an absolute routine. He travels alone, arrives backstage minutes before showtime, requires a local back-up band that knows his hit songs, walks onstage, does his thing, collects his money, and gets out of town.

Money seems to be very important to Berry. He discusses his original decision to become a full-time musician entirely in terms of money; he describes his guitar as "tax deductible," and he shows off some vintage Cadillacs that he refuses to sell until he gets his price. He never discusses his music with a tenth of the interest he has for his bank account.

And yet the man is a terrific musician, and his songs retain an elemental, driving power that defines rock 'n' roll. There is a lot of concert footage in the film, and the audience I saw it with was rocking in their seats. Although Berry is a tough customer during the rehearsals (at one point, he shouts at Richards, "I been doin' it my way for sixty years"), the concert is a magnificent celebration of Berry's work as a composer and performer.

Berry is all over the stage, doing his famous duck walk, assaulting the microphone, nailing the beat, exuding the kind of forbidden anarchic sexuality that startled the bland teenagers of the 1950s. He sings, he says, about the things that mattered to kids: school, romance, and cars.

Berry is backed up onstage by a band including Johnnie Johnson, the piano player who led the original trio where Berry got his start. There is some speculation that Johnson may have helped originate Berry's style, but he seems happier in the background, pounding out the beat. Richards oversees the band and plays lead guitar to Berry's rough rhythm, and there are several guest artists including Clapton, Julian Lennon, Robert Cray, Linda Ronstadt, and, stealing the show, Etta James.

It's one hell of a concert, a joyous celebration of the music, yet always lurking just offstage is the sense of Berry's obsessive privacy about his personal life. One of the movie's quietest moments is unforgettable. We see Berry's wife on camera. She introduces herself. She is asked a question. We hear Berry's voice from off camera: "OK, that's enough." The screen goes black, and we never see her again. Behind the man who helped create a music that let it all hang out, there is another man who plays it all very close to the vest.

City of God

R, 135 m., 2003

Matheus Nachtergaele (Sandro Cenoura), Seu Jorge (Knockout Ned), Alexandre Rodrigues (Rocket), Leandro Firmino da Hora (L'il Zé), Phellipe Haagensen (Bené [Benny]), Jonathan Haagensen (Cabeleira [Shaggy]), Douglas Silva (Dadinho), Roberta Rodriguez Silvia (Berenice), Graziela Moretto (Marina), Renato de Souza (Goose). Directed by Fernando Meirelles and produced by Andrea Barata Ribeiro and Mauricio Andrade Ramos. Screenplay by Bráulio Mantovani, based on the book by Paulo Lins. In Portuguese with English subtitles.

City of God churns with furious energy as it plunges into the story of the slum gangs of Rio de Janeiro. Breathtaking and terrifying, urgently involved with its characters, it announces a new director of great gifts and passions. Fernando Meirelles. Remember the name. The film has been compared with Martin Scorsese's *Good-Fellas,* and it deserves the comparison. Scorsese's film began with a narrator who said that for as long as he could remember he wanted to be a gangster. The narrator of this film seems to have had no other choice.

The movie takes place in slums constructed by Rio to isolate the poor people from the city center. They have grown into places teeming with life, color, music, and excitement—and also with danger, for the law is absent and violent gangs rule the streets. In the virtuoso sequence opening the picture, a gang is holding a picnic for its members when a chicken escapes. Among those chasing it is Rocket (Alexandre Rodrigues), the narrator. He suddenly finds himself between two armed lines: the gang on one side, the cops on the other.

As the camera whirls around him, the background changes and Rocket shrinks from a teenager into a small boy, playing soccer in a housing development outside Rio. To understand his story, he says, we have to go back to the beginning, when he and his friends formed the Tender Trio and began their lives of what some would call crime and others would call survival.

The technique of that shot—the whirling camera, the flashback, the change in colors from the dark brightness of the slum to the dusty, sunny browns of the soccer field—alert us to a movie that is visually alive and inventive as few films are. Meirelles began as a director of TV commercials, which gave him a command of technique—and, he says, trained him to work quickly, to size up a shot, and get it and move on. Working with the cinematographer César Charlone, he uses quick-cutting and a mobile, handheld camera to tell his story with the haste and detail it deserves. Sometimes those devices can create a film that is merely busy, but *City of God* feels like sight itself, as we look here and then there, with danger or opportunity everywhere.

The gangs have money and guns because they sell drugs and commit robberies. But they are not very rich because their activities are limited to the City of God, where no one has much money. In an early crime, we see the stickup of a truck carrying cans of propane gas, which the crooks sell to homeowners. Later there is a raid on a bordello, where the customers are deprived of their wallets. (In a flashback, we see that raid a second time, and understand in a chilling moment why there were dead bodies at a site where there was not supposed to be any killing.)

As Rocket narrates the lore of the district he knows so well, we understand that poverty has undermined all social structures in the City of God, including the family. The gangs provide structure and status. Because the gang death rate is so high, even the leaders tend to be surprisingly young, and life has no value except when you are taking it. There is an astonishing sequence when a victorious gang leader is killed in a way he least expects, by the last person he would have expected, and we see that essentially he has been killed not by a person but by the culture of crime.

Yet the film is not all grim and violent. Rocket also captures some of the Dickensian flavor of the City of God, where a riot of life provides ready-made characters with nicknames, personas, and trademarks. Some, like Benny (Phellipe Haagensen), are so charismatic they almost seem to transcend the usual rules. Others, like Knockout Ned and L'il Zé, grow from kids into fearsome leaders, their words enforced by death.

The movie is based on a novel by Paulo Lins, who grew up in the City of God, somehow escaped it, and spent eight years writing his book. A note at the end says it is partly based on the life of Wilson Rodriguez, a Brazilian photographer. We watch as Rocket obtains a (stolen) camera that he treasures, and takes pictures from his privileged position as a kid on the streets. He gets a job as an assistant on a newspaper delivery truck, asks a photographer to develop his film, and is startled to see his portrait of an armed gang leader on the front page of the paper.

"This is my death sentence," he thinks, but no: The gangs are delighted by the publicity, and pose for him with their guns and girls. And during a vicious gang war, he is able to photograph the cops killing a gangster—a murder they plan to pass off as gang-related. That these events throb with immediate truth is indicated by the fact that Luiz Inacio Lula da Silva, the president of Brazil, actually reviewed and praised *City of God* as a needful call for change.

In its actual level of violence, *City of God* is less extreme than Scorsese's *Gangs of New York,* but the two films have certain parallels. In both films, there are really two cities: the city of the employed and secure, who are served by law and municipal services, and the city of the castaways, whose alliances are born of opportunity and desperation. Those who live beneath rarely have their stories told. *City of God* does not exploit or condescend, does not pump up its stories for contrived effect, does not contain silly and reassuring romantic sidebars, but simply looks, with a passionately knowing eye, at what it knows.

City of Hope

R, 129 m., 1991

Vincent Spano (Nick), Joe Morton (Wynn), Tony Lo Bianco (Joe), Barbara Williams (Angela), Angela Bassett (Reesha), David Strathairn (Asteroid), John Sayles (Carl). Directed by Sayles and produced by Sarah Green and Maggie Renzi. Screenplay by Sayles.

John Sayles's *City of Hope* is like a wheel of torture to which the characters are chained. It goes around and around, sometimes through fire, sometimes through ice, and there is no way for them to free themselves. The film takes place in a fictional big city in New Jersey, where everyone is connected and where all the connections seem tainted by greed, graft, dishonesty, and corruption. Some of the players are on one side of the law and some on the other, but there is little to choose between them.

Sayles's method of telling the story of this city and the people trapped there is audacious. He fills his canvas with many characters—I didn't count, but I'm told there are thirty-six—and follows them through their days and nights as they run into one another, make deals, tell lies, seek happiness, and find mostly compromise and disappointment.

There are idealists in this city, but we watch as their idealism is shattered, as they learn the ways of clout and bribery, arson and perjury. The central character is a young man named Nick (Vincent Spano), whose father (Tony Lo Bianco) is a local contractor. That means Nick has a cushy union job that requires him to sit around all day on a construction site, doing nothing, and eventually even this task is too much for him, and he walks off the job.

He leaves not because he is lazy, but because his ego can no longer deal with the pain of being paid to do nothing. "You don't *have* to just sit around all day!" his father shouts at him. "I could arrange for you to have some more responsibility." Yes, but that's not what Nick wants, either. He wants . . . well, if he could put it in words, his wish would be to live in a world with different rules. But in this world he drifts and falls into a romance with a woman named Angela (Barbara Williams), who has a kid and used to be married to a cop who beat her.

We meet the cop. We meet a couple of cops, one worried by his partner's dangerous temper. We meet the mayor, and the local fat cats, and a small-time crook (Sayles) who runs an auto repair shop, and a black alderman (Joe Morton) who wants to protect a housing development against developers who want to use urban renewal to make a fortune.

We meet a lot of people, and the surprise is that Sayles is able to make it so clear who they are, how they relate to one another, and why they matter. This movie is like a mapped-out version of *Slacker*, the independent film that wandered through Austin, Texas, allowing the camera to follow first one character, then another, drifting in and out of lives and conversations. Sayles is not working at random, and he advances his plot toward a conclusion of some urgency, but his camera seems to have the same random drift. He's telling us that it doesn't matter where he looks in this New Jersey town, he'd find more of the same sickness and greed. He's suggesting he doesn't need a plot to organize his indictment; it's there to be seen.

John Sayles is a director of many different genres and moods, and a festival of his work would show astonishing diversity, from *The Return of the Secaucus Seven* to *Eight Men Out*,

from *Lianna* to *Matewan,* from *Baby, It's You* to *The Brother From Another Planet.* I felt that with both *Matewan*, about a bitter southern labor dispute, and *Eight Men Out*, about the Black Sox scandal, he allowed his large casts to grow too diffuse; we weren't always sure who was who or how they related. With *City of Hope,* he uses the large canvas and his most complex story with complete assurance, and this time we get wrapped up; we care.

The movie is not simply story-driven, or only concerned with the politics and plotting of its characters. There is great attention to nuances of dialogue in scenes like the one where the Sayles character spars with a policeman who knows he has information. There is emotional subtlety in the scenes involving Spano and Williams, who are faced with creating the idealism necessary for love in a city where idealism is mocked. There is enormous power in the scenes between Spano and Lo Bianco—a man who wants to do the right thing and finds he is not strong enough.

One strong thread of the plot involves the dilemma of the black alderman, played by Morton as a reformer who finds he cannot really get anything accomplished unless he goes along. He's trapped between the white establishment and black militants, and turns for advice to a retired black mayor of a nearby town (Ray Aranha), who talks about the hard lessons that destroyed his own idealism.

City of Hope is a powerful film, and an angry one. It is impossible not to find echoes of its despair on the front pages every day. It asks a hard question: Is it possible for a good person to prevail in a corrupt system, just simply because right is on his side? The answer, in the short run, is that power is stronger than right. The notion of the long run, of course, is all that keeps hope alive.

Claire's Knee

PG, 103 m., 1971

Jean-Claude Brialy (Jerome), Aurora Cornu (Aurora), Beatrice Romand (Laura), Laurence de Monaghan (Claire). Directed by Eric Rohmer and produced by Pierre Cottrell. Screenplay by Rohmer.

Now if I were to say, for example, that *Claire's Knee* is about Jerome's desire to caress the knee of Claire, you would be about a million miles from the heart of this extraordinary film. And yet, in a way, *Claire's Knee* is indeed about Jerome's feelings for Claire's knee, which is a splendid knee.

Jerome encounters Claire and the other characters in the film during a month's holiday he takes on a lake between France and Switzerland. He has gone there to rest and reflect before he marries Lucinda, a woman he has loved for five years. And who should he run into but Aurora, a novelist who he's also been a little in love with for a long time.

Aurora is staying with a summer family that has two daughters: Laura, who is sixteen and very wise and falls in love with Jerome, and Claire, who is beautiful and blonde and full of figure and spirit. Jerome and Aurora enter into a teasing intellectual game, which requires Jerome to describe to Aurora whatever happens to him during his holiday. When they all become aware that Laura has fallen in love with the older man, Jerome encourages her in a friendly, platonic way. They have talks about love and the nature of life, and they grow very fond of each other, although of course the man does not take advantage of the young girl.

But then Claire joins the group, and one day while they are picking cherries, Jerome turns his head and finds that Claire has climbed a ladder and he is looking directly at her knee. Claire herself, observed playing volleyball or running, hand-in-hand, with her boyfriend, is a sleek animal, and Jerome finds himself stirring with desire.

He doesn't want to run away with Claire, or seduce her, or anything like that; he plans to marry Lucinda. But he tells his friend Aurora that he has become fascinated by Claire's knee; that it might be the point through which she could be approached, just as another girl might respond to a caress on the neck, or the cheek, or the arm. He becomes obsessed with desire to test this theory, and one day has an opportunity to touch the knee at last.

As with all the films of Eric Rohmer, *Claire's Knee* exists at levels far removed from plot (as you might have guessed while I was describing the plot). What is really happening in this movie happens on the level of character, of thought, of the way people approach each other and then shy away. In some movies,

people murder each other and the contact is casual; in a work by Eric Rohmer, small attitudes and gestures can summon up a universe of humanity.

Rohmer has an uncanny ability to make his actors seem as if they were going through the experiences they portray. The acting of Beatrice Romand, as sixteen-year-old Laura, is especially good in this respect; she isn't as pretty as her sister, but we feel somehow she'll find more enjoyment in life because she is a . . . well, a better person underneath. Jean-Claude Brialy (Jerome) is excellent in a difficult role. He has to relate with three women in the movie, and yet remain implicitly faithful to the unseen Lucinda. He does, and since the sexuality in his performance is suppressed, it is, of course, all the more sensuous. *Claire's Knee* is a movie for people who still read good novels, care about good films, and think occasionally.

The Clockmaker

NO MPAA RATING, 105 m., 1976

Philippe Noiret (Descombes), Jean Rochefort (Inspector Guiboud), Sylvain Rougeria (Bernard), Andree Tainsy (Madeline). Directed by Bertrand Tavernier and produced by Ralph Baum. Screenplay by Jean Ayrenche, based on the book by Georges Simenon.

The Clockmaker, which is based on a novel by Georges Simenon, begins with the report of a murder and ends as the portrait of a personality. It has that in common with a lot of books by Simenon and other crime writers who understand that people, not crimes, are their real subject (I'm thinking also of Nicholas Freeling and P. D. James). What's unusual about *The Clockmaker*, though, is its angle of attention: It's not about the killer, but about the killer's father. And it presents him so eloquently that it becomes one of the year's best films. The father is played by Philippe Noiret. You may not recognize the name, but you will recognize the face from a dozen movies: sad-eyed, thoughtful, resigned to middle age. Noiret plays a clockmaker who lives and works in a quiet quarter of Lyons. He is not quite a widower. ("My wife and I separated, and then she died—what does that make me?") He lives with a son who comes and goes according to his own schedule. One day a police inspector visits the clockmaker's shop to inform him that his son has committed a murder.

There's not the slightest doubt, unfortunately: It was the son, and it was murder. Noiret nods gravely. He and the inspector talk about what it is in young people that makes them do these things. Noiret thinks that perhaps he did not pay close enough attention to his son—didn't display the affection that he felt for him. The inspector listens with sympathy, asks Noiret to report any news of the son and leaves. The clockmaker sits in his son's room and runs through his thoughts again and again.

We think now that perhaps the movie will be about an investigation; that it will involve elements of a thriller. But *The Clockmaker* is much too good to do that; it transcends the crime genre and becomes a totally original work. And it does that very simply, by revealing characters to us. There will be few surprises and little violence, but the film's people will absorb our attention and occupy our memories. And by its end, very gracefully, it will turn out to have been about two relationships: one between Noiret and the inspector, the other between Noiret and his son. The clockmaker and the policeman find themselves becoming friendly during the several days of the investigation. In a Simenon novel, there is always a lot of sending out for beer and sandwiches, and *The Clockmaker* is in the tradition. The two men meet for meals, they talk about human nature, they respect each other's privacy, and eventually they become so friendly that they can even be quiet together. Through the father, the inspector begins to understand some of the son's motives.

The murder, it appears, was politically motivated, not motivated out of overwrought adolescent radicalism, but inspired purely and directly by the behavior of the victim, an overbearing shop steward in the factory where the son's girlfriend works. The son applied a process of reasoning to the situation and arrived at a decision to murder the foreman. Very simple. No regrets.

The son is eventually captured and brought to trial. By now, Noiret has had a long time to think about the case. He discovers, somewhat to his surprise, that in a complex way he is

proud of what his son did—that he can disapprove of murder and yet understand this murder. Noiret says as much during the trial. And, curiously enough, the inspector in his own way also understands.

The film ends with a quiet, understated reconciliation between father and son. Here, as everywhere else in the film, director Bertrand Tavernier has total faith in his characters. He tells us neither too much nor too little; he looks at them, as Simenon himself so often does, with straightforward acceptance and compassion. *The Clockmaker* is an extraordinary film—the more so because it attempts to show us the very complicated workings of the human personality, and to do it with grace, some humor, and a great deal of style.

Close Encounters of the Third Kind: The Special Edition

PG, 152 m., 1978

Richard Dreyfuss (Roy Neary), Francois Truffaut (Claude Lacombe), Teri Garr (Ronnie Neary), Melinda Dillon (Jillian Guiler). Directed and written by Steven Spielberg and produced by Julia Phillips and Michael Phillips.

Close Encounters of the Third Kind: The Special Edition is the movie Steven Spielberg wanted to make in the first place. The changes Spielberg has made in his original 1978 film are basic and extensive, adding up to essentially a new moviegoing experience. Spielberg's changes fall into four categories:

• He's provided an entirely new conclusion, taking us inside the alien spaceship that visits at the end of the film.

• He's provided more motivation for the strange behavior of the Richard Dreyfuss character—who is compelled by "psychic implanting" to visit the Wyoming mountain where the spaceship plans to land.

• He's added additional manifestations of UFO intervention in earthly affairs—including an ocean-going freighter deposited in the middle of the Gobi Desert.

• In addition to the sensational ending, he's added more special effects throughout the film. One shot seems like a lighthearted quote from Spielberg's own *Jaws*. In that film, a high-angle shot showed the shadow of the giant shark passing under a boat. In this one, a high-angle shot shows the shadow of a giant UFO passing over a pickup truck.

Spielberg's decision to revise the original version of *Close Encounters* is all but unprecedented. Some directors have remade their earlier films (Hitchcock did British and American versions of *The Man Who Knew Too Much*), and others have thought out loud about changes they'd like to make (Robert Altman wanted to edit a nine-hour version of *Nashville* for TV). And countless directors, of course, have given us sequels—"part two" of their original hits.

Spielberg's *Special Edition* is sort of a *Close Encounters: Part 1½*. It is also a very good film. I thought the original film was an astonishing achievement, capturing the feeling of awe and wonder we have when considering the likelihood of life beyond the Earth. I gave that first version a four-star rating. This new version gets another four stars: It is, quite simply, a better film—so much better that it might inspire the uncharitable question, "Why didn't Spielberg make it this good the *first* time?"

His changes fall into three categories. He has (1) thrown away scenes that didn't work, like the silly sequence in which Dreyfuss dug up half of his yard in an attempt to build a model of the mountain in his vision; (2) put in scenes he shot three years ago but did not use, such as the Gobi sequence and Dreyfuss flipping out over the strange compulsion that has overtaken him, and (3) shot some entirely new scenes.

The most spectacular of these is the new ending, which shows us what Dreyfuss sees when he enters the spacecraft. He sees a sort of extraterrestrial cathedral, a limitless interior space filled with columns of light, countless sources of brilliance, and the machinery of an unimaginable alien technology. (The new special effects were designed by the underground artist R. Cobb, I understand; no credit is given.) This new conclusion gives the movie the kind of overwhelming final emotional impact it needed; it adds another dimension to the already impressive ending of the first version.

The movie gains impact in another way. Spielberg has tightened up the whole film. Dead ends and pointless scenes have been dropped. New scenes do a better job of establishing the characters—not only of Dreyfuss, but also of Francois Truffaut, as the French scientist. The new editing moves the film along at a faster, more absorbing pace to the mind-stretching conclusion. *Close Encounters*, which was already a wonderful film, now transcends itself; it's one of the great moviegoing experiences. If you've seen it before, I'm afraid that now you'll have to see it again.

Closer
R, 101 m., 2004

Julia Roberts (Anna), Jude Law (Dan), Natalie Portman (Alice), Clive Owen (Larry). Directed by Mike Nichols and produced by Cary Brokaw, John Calley, and Nichols. Screenplay by Patrick Marber, based on his play.

Mike Nichols's *Closer* is a movie about four people who richly deserve one another. Fascinated by the game of love, seduced by seduction itself, they play at sincere, truthful relationships that are lies in almost every respect except their desire to sleep with each other. All four are smart and ferociously articulate, adept at seeming forthright and sincere even in their most shameless deceptions.

"The truth," one says. "Without it, we're animals." Actually, truth causes them more trouble than it saves, because they seem compelled to be most truthful about the ways in which they have been untruthful. There is a difference between confessing you've cheated because you feel guilt and seek forgiveness, and confessing merely to cause pain.

The movie stars, in order of appearance, Jude Law, Natalie Portman, Julia Roberts, and Clive Owen. Law plays Dan, who writes obituaries for his London newspaper; Portman is Alice, an American who says she was a stripper and fled New York to end a relationship; Roberts is Anna, an American photographer; and Owen is Larry, a dermatologist. The characters connect in a series of Meet Cutes that are perhaps no more contrived than in real life.

In the opening sequence, the eyes of Alice and Dan (Portman and Law) meet as they approach each other on a London street. Eye contact leads to an amused flirtation, and then Alice, distracted, steps into the path of a taxicab. Knocked on her back, she opens her eyes, sees

Dan, and says "Hello, stranger." Time passes. Dan writes a novel based on his relationship with Alice, and has his book jacket photo taken by Anna, whom he immediately desires. More time passes. Dan, who has been with Anna, impersonates a woman named "Anna" on a chat line, and sets up a date with Larry, a stranger. When Larry turns up as planned at the aquarium, Anna is there, but when he describes "their" chat, she disillusions him: "I think you were talking with Daniel Wolf."

Eventually both men will have sex with both women, occasionally as a round trip back to the woman they started with. There is no constancy in this crowd: When they're not with the one they love, they love the one they're with. It is a good question, actually, whether any of them are ever in love at all, although they do a good job of saying they are.

They are all so very articulate, which is refreshing in a time when literate and evocative speech has been devalued in the movies. Their words are by Patrick Marber, based on his award-winning play. Consider Dan as he explains to Alice his job writing obituaries. There is a kind of shorthand, he tells her: "If you say someone was 'convivial,' that means he was an alcoholic. 'He was a private person' means he was gay. 'Enjoyed his privacy' means he was a raging queen."

Forced to rank the four characters in order of their nastiness, I would place Dr. Larry at the top of the list. He seems to derive genuine enjoyment from the verbal lacerations he administers, pointing out the hypocrisies and evasions of the others. Dan is an innocent by comparison; he wants to be bad, but isn't good at it. Anna, the photographer, is accurately sniffed out by Alice as a possible lover of Dan. "I'm not a thief, Alice," she says, but she is. Alice seems the most innocent and blameless of the four until the very end of the movie, when we are forced to ask if everything she did was a form of stripping, in which much is revealed, but little is surrendered. "Lying is the most fun a girl can have without taking her clothes off," she tells Dr. Larry, "but it's more fun if you do."

There's a creepy fascination in the way these four characters stage their affairs while occupying impeccable lifestyles. They dress and present themselves handsomely. They fit right in at the opening of Anna's photography exhi-

bition. (One of the photos shows Alice with tears on her face as she discerns that Dan was unfaithful with Anna; that's the stuff that art is made of, isn't it?) They move in that London tourists never quite see, the London of trendy restaurants on dodgy streets, and flats that are a compromise between affluence and the exorbitant price of housing. There is the sense that their trusts and betrayals are not fundamentally important to them; "You've ruined my life," one says, and is told, "You'll get over it."

Yes, unless, fatally, true love does strike at just that point when all the lies have made it impossible. Is there anything more pathetic than a lover who realizes he (or she) really is in love, after all the trust has been lost, all the bridges burnt, and all the reconciliations used up?

Mike Nichols has been through the gender wars before, in films like *Carnal Knowledge* and *Who's Afraid of Virginia Woolf?* Those films, especially *Woolf*, were about people who knew and understood each other with a fearsome intimacy, and knew all the right buttons to push. What is unique about *Closer*, making it seem right for these insincere times, is that the characters do not understand each other, or themselves. They know how to go through the motions of pushing the right buttons, and how to pretend their buttons have been pushed, but do they truly experience anything at all except their own pleasure?

Cold Turkey
PG, 99 m., 1971

Dick Van Dyke (The Reverend Clayton Brooks), Pippa Scott (Natalie Brooks), Tom Poston (Mrs. Stopworth), Edward Everett Horton (Hiram C. Grayson), Bob and Ray (TV Personalities), Bob Newhart (Merwin Wren). Directed and produced by Norman Lear. Screenplay by Lear and William Price Fox, Jr.

I was musing the other day that there aren't enough fat men in movies, and especially not enough mean fat men filled with malice and avarice. Too many movie fat men are jolly these days, and we don't have the Sidney Greenstreets with ice in their eyes.

Which set me to thinking that, fat men aside, we don't have enough malice and avarice in the movies these days, either. Movies are getting to be too damn nice. Especially comedies. If there's anything I can't stand, it's a heartwarming comedy, filled with warmth and sunshine and happy endings, in which the essential goodness of human nature, etc., is demonstrated in the end.

No. What we need are mean comedies, filled with mean and petty people who hate and envy each other, and exhibit the basest of human motives. Comedies like that canonized W. C. Fields, and it was Groucho Marx's fundamental hatefulness that made his stuff so much more than slapstick. Lately, though, the movie comedy has fallen on hard times in America. Until the past couple of weeks.

Now there are two new comedies that I can recommend to cynics and malcontents with little fear they'll be disappointed: *A New Leaf,* reviewed last week, and Norman Lear's *Cold Turkey.* Both of them assume as a matter of course that the human being is powered with unworthy motives, especially greed. *A New Leaf* gets a little sentimental at the end, but not too much, and *Cold Turkey* ends with the scoundrels being shot by their own cigarette lighter.

The movie, as everybody knows by now, concerns an attempt by a small town in Iowa to qualify for a $25 million award by signing all its citizens to a thirty-day no-smoking pledge. That somehow doesn't sound like the world's greatest idea for a comedy, but Lear makes it work by a brilliant masterstroke: He gets the comedy not out of people trying to stop smoking, but out of the people themselves. So instead of lots of scenes of characters sneaking puffs, you have them preening their vanity as national television crews descend upon the town. For, of course, Eagle Rock, Iowa, has become famous overnight.

The television personalities are all played by Bob and Ray, who do a ruthless job as Walter Chronic, David Chetley, and others, confirming (as I've always suspected) that the *CBS Evening News* is itself a send-up of Bob and Ray's pioneering Wally Ballou. President Nixon tries to force his way into Eagle Rock to share the limelight, and various folks such as Spiro Agnew turn up, too.

The townsfolk love it, especially Dick Van Dyke as an ambitious minister who sleeps with hair-curlers and dreams of being transferred to a rich congregation in Dearborn, Michigan. We meet the minister, the mayor, the town drunk, and a little old lady in tennis shoes whose favorite word contains eight letters, the least of which are "bull," during a series of vignettes handled by Lear with an unfailing eye for human frailty. Even if you don't smoke, you'll find *Cold Turkey* funny. You're greedy, aren't you?

The Color Purple

PG-13, 155 m., 1985

Danny Glover (Mister), Whoopi Goldberg (Celie), Margaret Avery (Shug Avery), Oprah Winfrey (Sofia), Willard Pugh (Harpo), Akosua Busia (Nettie), Adolph Caesar (Old Mister), Rae Dawn Chong (Squeak), Dana Ivey (Miss Millie). Directed by Steven Spielberg and produced by Kathleen Kennedy, Frank Marshall, Quincy Jones, and Spielberg. Screenplay by Menno Meyjes, based on the book by Alice Walker.

There is a moment in Steven Spielberg's *The Color Purple* when a woman named Celie smiles and smiles and smiles. That was the moment when I knew this movie was going to be as good as it seemed, was going to keep the promise it made by daring to tell Celie's story. It is not a story that would seem easily suited to the movies.

Celie is a black woman who grows up in the rural South in the early decades of this century, in a world that surrounds her with cruelty. When we first see her, she is a child, running through fields of purple flowers with her sister. But then she comes into clear view, and we see that she is pregnant, and we learn that her father has made her pregnant, and will give away the child as he has done with a previous baby.

By the time Celie is married—to a cruel, distant charmer she calls only "Mister"—she will have lost both her children and the ability to bear children, will have been separated from the sister who is the only person on earth who loves her, and will be living in servitude to a man who flaunts his love for another woman.

And yet this woman will endure, and in the end she will prevail. *The Color Purple* is not the story of her suffering but of her victory, and by the end of her story this film had moved me and lifted me up as few films have. It is a great, warm, hard, unforgiving, triumphant movie, and there is not a scene that does not shine with the love of the people who made it.

The film is based on the novel by Alice Walker, who told Celie's story through a series of letters, some never sent, many never received, most addressed to God. The letters are her way of maintaining sanity in a world where few others ever cared to listen to her. The turning point in the book, and in the movie, comes after Celie's husband brings home the fancy woman he has been crazy about for years—a pathetic, alcoholic juke-joint singer named Shug Avery, who has been ravaged by life yet still has an indestructible beauty.

Shug's first words to Celie are: "You as ugly as sin." But as Shug moves into the house, and Celie obediently caters to her husband's lover, Shug begins to see the beauty in Celie, and there is a scene where they kiss, and Celie learns for the first time that sex can include tenderness, that she can dare to love herself. A little later, Celie looks in Shug's eyes and allows herself to smile, and we know that Celie didn't think she had a pretty smile until Shug told her so. That is the central moment in the movie.

The relationship between Shug and Celie is a good deal toned down from the book, which deals in greater detail with sexual matters. Steven Spielberg, who made the movie, is more concerned with the whole world of Celie's life than he is with her erotic education. We meet many members of the rural black community that surrounds Celie. We meet a few of the local whites, too, but they are bit players in this drama.

Much more important are people like Sofia (Oprah Winfrey), an indomitable force of nature who is determined to marry Harpo, Mister's son by a first marriage. When we first see Sofia, hurrying down the road with everyone trying to keep up, she looks like someone who could never be stopped. But she is stopped, after she tells the local white mayor to go to hell, and the saddest story in the movie is the way her spirit is forever dampened by the beating and jailing she receives. Sofia is counterpoint to Celie: She is wounded by life, Celie is healed.

Shug Avery is another fascinating character, played by Margaret Avery as a sweetfaced, weary woman who sings a little bit like Billie Holiday and has long since lost all of her illusions about men and everything else. Her contact with Celie redeems her; by giving her somebody to be nice to, it allows her to get in touch with what is still nice inside herself.

Mister, whose real name is Albert, is played by Danny Glover, who was the field hand in *Places in the Heart*. He is an evil man, his evil tempered to some extent by his ignorance; perhaps he does not fully understand how cruel he is to Celie. Certainly he seems outwardly pleasant. He smiles and jokes and sings, and then hurts Celie to the quick—not so much with his physical blows as when he refuses to let her see the letters she hopes are coming from her long-lost sister.

And then, at the center of the movie, Celie is played by Whoopi Goldberg in one of the most amazing debut performances in movie history. Goldberg has a fearsomely difficult job to do, enlisting our sympathy for a woman who is rarely allowed to speak, to dream, to interact with the lives around her. Spielberg breaks down the wall of silence around her, however, by giving her narrative monologues in which she talks about her life and reads the words in the letters she composes.

The wonderful performances in this movie are contained in a screenplay that may take some of the smoking edges off Walker's novel, but keeps all the depth and dimension. The world of Celie and the others is created so forcibly in this movie that their corner of the South becomes one of those movie places—like Oz, like Tara, like Casablanca—that lay claim to their own geography in our imaginations. The affirmation at the end of the film is so joyous that this is one of the few movies in a long time that inspires tears of happiness, and earns them.

Coming Home
R, 127 m., 1978

Jane Fonda (Sally Hyde), Jon Voight (Luke Martin), Bruce Dern (Bob Hyde), Robert Carradine (Bill Munson), Penelope Milford (Vi Munson), Robert Ginty (Sergeant Mobley). Directed by Hal Ashby and produced by Jerome Hellman. Screenplay by Waldo Salt and Robert C. Jones.

Sally Hyde makes an ideal wife for a marine: She is faithful, friendly, sexy in a quiet way, and totally in agreement with her husband's loyalties. Since his basic loyalty is to the Marine Corps, that presents difficulties at times. ("You know what they tell them," a girlfriend says. "'If the Marine Corps had wanted you to have a wife, they would have issued you one.'") Still, she's reasonably happy in the spring of 1968, as her husband prepares to ship out for a tour of duty in Vietnam. There's every chance he'll get a promotion over there. And the war, of course, is for a just cause, isn't it? It has to be, or we wouldn't be fighting it.

That is the Sally Hyde at the beginning of Hal Ashby's *Coming Home,* an extraordinarily moving film. The Sally Hyde at the end of the film—about a year later—is a different person, confused in her loyalties, not sure of her beliefs, awakened to new feelings within her. She hasn't turned into a political activist or a hippie or any of those other radical creatures of the late 1960s. But she is no longer going to be able to accept anything simply because her husband, or anybody else, says it's true.

Coming Home considers a great many subjects, but its heart lies with that fundamental change within Sally Hyde. She is played by Jane Fonda as the kind of character you somehow wouldn't expect the outspoken, intelligent Fonda to play. She's reserved, maybe a little shy, of average intelligence and tastes. She was, almost inevitably, a cheerleader in high school. She doesn't seem to have a lot of ideas or opinions. Perhaps she even doubts that it's necessary for her to have opinions—her husband can have them for her.

When her husband (Bruce Dern) goes off to fight the war, though, she finds herself on her own for the first time in her life. There's no home, no high school, no marriage, no Officers' Club to monitor her behavior. And she finds herself stepping outside the role of a wife and doing . . . well, not strange things, but things that are a little unusual for her. Like buying a used sports car. Like renting a house at the beach. Like volunteering to work in the local Veterans' Administration hospital. That's where she meets Luke (Jon Voight), so filled with his pain, anger, and frustration. She knew him vaguely before; he was the captain of the football team at her high school. He

went off to fight the war, came home paralyzed from the waist down, and now, strapped on his stomach to a table with wheels, uses canes to propel himself furiously down hospital corridors. In time, he will graduate to a wheelchair. He has ideas about Vietnam that are a little different from her husband's.

Coming Home is uncompromising in its treatment of Luke and his fellow paraplegics, and if that weren't so the opening sequences of the film wouldn't affect us so deeply. Luke literally runs into Sally on their first meeting, and his urine bag spills on the floor between them. That's the sort of embarrassment he has to learn to live with—and she too, if she is serious about being a volunteer.

She is, she finds. Luke in the early days is a raging troublemaker, and the hospital staff often finds it simpler just to tranquilize him with medication. Zombies are hardly any bother at all. Sally tries to talk to Luke, gets to know him, invites him for dinner. He begins to focus his anger away from himself and toward the war; he grows calmer, regains maturity. One day, he tells her, softly: "You know there's not an hour goes by that I don't think of making love with you."

They do eventually make love, confronting his handicap in a scene of great tenderness, beauty, and tact. It is the first time Sally has been unfaithful. But it isn't really an affair; she remains loyal to her husband, and both she and Luke know their relationship will have to end when her husband returns home. He does, too soon, having accidentally wounded himself, and discovers from Army Intelligence what his wife has been up to. The closing scenes show the film at its most uncertain, as if Ashby and his writers weren't sure in their minds how the Dern character should react. And so Dern is forced into scenes of unfocused, confused anger before the film's not very satisfying ending. It's too bad the last twenty minutes don't really work, though, because for most of its length *Coming Home* is great filmmaking and great acting.

And it is also greatly daring, since it confronts the relationship between Fonda and Voight with unusual frankness—and with emotional tenderness and subtlety that is, if anything, even harder to portray.

Consider. The film has three difficulties to confront in this relationship, and it handles all three honestly. The first is Voight's paralysis: "You aren't one of these women that gets turned on by gimps?" he asks. She is not. The second is the sexual and emotional nature of their affair, an area of enormous dramatic danger, which the movie handles in such a straightforward way, and with such an obvious display of affection between the characters, that we accept and understand.

The third is the nature of the *friendship* between Voight and Fonda, and here *Coming Home* works on a level that doesn't depend on such plot elements as the war, the husband, the paralysis, the time and place, or anything else. Thinking about the movie, we realize that men and women have been so polarized in so many films, have been made into so many varieties of sexual antagonists or lovers or rivals or other couples, that the mutual human friendship of these two characters comes as something of a revelation.

The Confession

PG, 139 m., 1970

Yves Montand (Gerard), Simone Signoret (Lise), Gabriele Farzetti (Kehoutek), Michel Vitold (Smole), Jean Bouise (Boss). Directed by Costa-Gavras and produced by Robert Dortmann and Bertrand Javal. Screenplay by Jorge Semprun, based on a story by Lise and Artur London.

"Confession is the highest form of self-criticism."
—Party official in *The Confession*

Costa-Gavras's first film since *Z* is, once again, a study of the way lies can be made to seem good as truth. All it takes to work this miracle is sufficient power. If you control not only a man's life but also his mind, you can get him to believe anything. In *Z*, the power was fascist and of the right. In *The Confession*, we're shown fascism of the left in the form of the 1952 Communist Party show trials in Czechoslovakia.

The film is inspired almost entirely by fact, by the memoirs of Artur London, one of the thirteen Czech communist leaders who were indicted as traitors, Trotskyists, Titoists, Zionists, or what have you, and one of the three who were not executed. It is not a thriller like *Z*, and it couldn't be, because there is no justice to emerge at the end and no scoundrels to unmask. As nearly as seems possible, the totalitarian system itself kept the show trials running, and they persisted so well that the party officials who began them turned up as defendants, too. No, it's not a thriller but a penetration into the mind, and Yves Montand is able to express the state of his character's mind perfectly by showing him, after nearly twenty months of torture and cross-examination, watching his captor eat a sausage as if it were not lunch but the Holy Grail. The movie itself is a wearing experience, as it was meant to be. We begin to wonder toward the end how even the inquisitors could stand up to the inhuman grind of cross-examination.

Costa-Gavras seems to be trying in his latest two films to take the facts themselves and mold them into a sort of fiction beyond truth. There is nothing he can tell us about the execution of ten innocent Czech leaders that he hasn't shown us already with a shot of their ashes being dumped onto a snow-covered road to help a car get traction. Images like this are beyond explaining. In the current *New York Review of Books*, Alfred Kazin considers Capote's *In Cold Blood* and Mailer's *Of a Fire on the Moon* in much the same way, as the reactions of storytellers to stories that are too real to be reduced to fiction.

The style of *The Confession* reminds us of *Z*, particularly in the quick cutting and the sure-footed use of flashbacks. The structure becomes complex but never confusing, and Costa-Gavras always seems to be urgently on the move, wanting to tell us more than can be told. His characters are always moving when a shot opens on them. His editor hurries ahead to the next image while the voice from the last finishes a sentence. The camera itself seems afraid that by staying too long on one image, it is missing others. And we feel ourselves buried in this mass of information, our rational minds somehow trying to make sense of a system where nothing is "true" but everything must be "correct."

There is a controversy in European Communist circles over *The Confession*, I'm told. It's been banned in a lot of countries, including Russia and Czechoslovakia, and it has been embraced by anti-communist movements as an indictment of communism. But

Costa-Gavras has made a point of insisting that the movie is anti-Stalinist, not anti-Communist. For that matter, we had some show trials trying to get themselves under way in this country in 1952.

I suppose the conclusion you come to after seeing *The Confession* is that mankind has a terrifying ability to persecute and execute its members on the strength of an idea that may turn out, a few years later, to have been forgotten. Daniel Berrigan, S. J., sent an open letter to the Weathermen recently in which he said that no cause was worth the sacrifice of a single human life. That inspired a lot of head scratching in newspaper editorials, philosophy classrooms, and elsewhere. But see *The Confession* and think about it.

The Constant Gardener

R, 129 m., 2005

Ralph Fiennes (Justin Quayle), Rachel Weisz (Tessa Quayle), Danny Huston (Sandy Woodrow), Hubert Kounde (Arnold Bluhm), Bill Nighy (Sir Bernard Pellegrin), Pete Postlethwaite (Marcus Lorbeer). Directed by Fernando Meirelles and produced by Simon Channing-Williams. Screenplay by Jeffrey Caine, based on the book by John le Carre.

They meet as strangers who plunge at once into sudden sex. They catch their breath, marry, and begin to learn about each other. Justin is an official in the British government. Tessa is an activist. She goes to Africa with Justin, her motives unclear in his mind, and witnesses what she thinks is murder in an African hospital. Then she is murdered at a crossroads, along with her African driver. And a doctor named Arnold, whom she works with, is found dead, too. But why, Justin needs to know, did Tessa receive an e-mail asking her, "What were you and Arnold doing in the Nairobi Hilton Friday night? Does Justin know?"

The murder of Tessa takes place right at the start of *The Constant Gardener*, so it is not revealing too much to mention it. The movie is a progress back into her life, and a journey of discovery for Justin, who learns about a woman he never really knew. The flashback structure, told in remembered moments, passages of dialogue, scenes that are interrupted and completed later, is typical of John le Carre, whose

novels resemble chess problems in which one solution is elegant and all of the others take too many moves. It is a style suited to the gifts of the Brazilian director Fernando Meirelles, whose great *City of God* (2003) told a story that was composed of countless tributaries that all flowed together into a mighty narrative stream.

The fragmented style is the best way to tell this story, for both the novel and the movie. *The Constant Gardener* is not a logical exercise beginning with mystery and ending at truth, but a circling around of an elusive conspiracy. Understand who the players are and how they are willing to compromise themselves, and you can glimpse cruel outlines beneath the public relations facade. As the drug companies pour AIDS drugs into Africa, are they using their programs to mask the test of other drugs? "No drug company does something for nothing," le Carre has a character observe.

The Constant Gardener may be the angriest story le Carre has ever told. Certainly his elegant prose and the oblique shorthand of the dialogue show the writer forcing himself to turn fury into style. His novel involves drug companies that test their products on the poor of the Third World, and are willing to accept the deaths that may occur because, after all, those people don't count. Why not? Because no one is there to count them.

Do drug companies really do this? Facts are the bones beneath the skin of a le Carre novel. Either he knows what he's talking about, or he is uncommonly persuasive in seeming to. *The Constant Gardener* at times plays like a movie that will result in indictments. What makes it extraordinary is that it also plays as a love story, and as an examination of the mysteries of the heart.

The performances need to be very good to carry us through sequences in which nobody, good or evil, seems very sure of the total picture. Ralph Fiennes plays Justin as a bureaucrat who seems detached from issues; he's the opposite of Tessa. As he tries to get to the bottom of her death, he sifts through his discoveries like an accountant unwilling to go home for the day until the books are balanced.

One way of looking at Tessa's death is that she was a hothead who had an affair with a handsome African man, went where she shouldn't have been, and got caught in one of those African border killings where toll-collecting soldiers with AK-47s enforce whatever they think is the law. Another way to look at it is to give her the benefit of the doubt. To wonder what was behind the embarrassing questions she asked at a press conference. To ask why statistics seem to be missing, if a drug study is designed to generate them.

As he probes through the wreckage of his wife's life, Justin encounters an array of characters who could have been airlifted in from Graham Greene—or from other le Carre novels, of course. Hubert Kounde plays Arnold Bluhm, the African who is not, in fact, Tessa's driver, but a doctor who is her colleague. Danny Huston, tall and courtly like his father, John, and like John often smiling at a private joke, plays Sandy Woodrow, the British high commissioner on the scene. Bill Nighy, that actor who often seems to be frowning through a migraine, is Sir Bernard Pellegrin, head of the Foreign Office and thus Justin and Sandy's boss. And Pete Postlethwaite, looking as if he has been left out too long in the weather, is Lorbeer, a drug company man who works in the field—at what, it is dangerous to say.

The Constant Gardener begins with a strong, angry story and peoples it with actors who let it happen to them, instead of rushing ahead to check off the surprises. It seems solidly grounded in its Kenyan locations; like *City of God*, it feels organically rooted. Like many le Carre stories, it begins with grief and proceeds with sadness toward horror. Its closing scenes are as cynical about international politics and commerce as I can imagine. I would like to believe they are an exaggeration, but I fear they are not. This is one of the year's best films.

The Contender

R, 126 m., 2000

Joan Allen (Laine Hanson), Gary Oldman (Shelly Runyon), Jeff Bridges (President Jackson Evans), Christian Slater (Reginald Webster), Sam Elliott (Kermit Newman), William Petersen (Jack Hathaway), Saul Rubinek (Jerry Toliver), Philip Baker Hall (Oscar Billings), Mike Binder (Lewis Hollis). Directed by Rod Lurie and produced by Marc Frydman, Douglas Urbanski, Willi Baer, and James Spies. Screenplay by Lurie.

The Contender, a thriller about the first woman nominated to be vice president, hinges on a question from her past: Did she more or less willingly participate in group sex while she was in college? "That's Hanson getting gangbanged," an investigator says, smacking his lips over an old photo from a sorority party. If it really is, she's going to have trouble getting congressional confirmation.

The movie is frankly partisan. Its sentiments are liberal and Democratic, its villains conservative and Republican. When I asked its star, Jeff Bridges, if the plot was a veiled reference to Monicagate, he smiled. "Veiled?" he said. "I don't think it's so veiled." The difference between Senator Laine Hanson (Joan Allen) and President Bill Clinton is that when zealots start sniffing her laundry, she simply refuses to answer their questions. "It's none of your business," she tells GOP Representative Shelly Runyon (Gary Oldman), whose inquiring mind wants to know.

As the movie opens, an incumbent vice president has died in office. It is universally assumed that a man will be named to replace him, and a leading candidate is Senator Jack Hathaway (William Petersen), who has recently made headlines as a hero. While he was on a fishing trip, a car plunged off a bridge near his boat and he dove into icy waters in an unsuccessful attempt to save the woman trapped inside. It is an adventure like this, not a lifetime of service, that the image-mongers like, but the senator's misfortune is that his rescue attempt failed. "A girl died and you let it happen," he's told sorrowfully by presidential advisers, and President Jackson Evans (Jeff Bridges) consoles him cryptically: "You're the future of the Democratic Party, and you always will be."

The president wants to make history by appointing a woman, and Senator Hanson looks like the best choice. She is happily married, has a young child, and when we first see her is having robust sex (on a desktop) with her husband. Runyon, the Oldman character, doubts any woman should be trusted with the nuclear trigger: What if she has her period or something? He is delighted with evidence she may have been the life of the party on campus.

The movie's story of confirmation hearings, backstage politics, and rival investigations unfolds as a political thriller based on suspense and issues. Senator Hanson flatly refuses to answer any questions about her sexual past, and for a time it looks as if the president may have to dump her as a nominee. Is she really taking an ethical stand, or covering up something? There is a remarkable scene between Hanson and Runyon, who have lunch together in a private club, the Republican shoveling down his meal and talking with his mouth full as if he would like to chew on her too.

The movie was written and directed by Rod Lurie, a former Los Angeles film critic who is the son of the political cartoonist Ranan Lurie. He grew up with politics discussed at every meal, he says; his first movie, *Deterrence*, starred Kevin Pollack as a president faced with a nuclear crisis. I liked the way that film dealt with issues and ideas, but *The Contender* is a leap forward, more assured, more exciting, more biting.

Most American movies pretend there are no parties; even in political movies, characters rarely reveal their affiliations. *The Contender* does take sides, most obviously in the character of the GOP congressman Runyon, who is played by Oldman as an unprincipled power broker with an unwholesome curiosity about other people's sex lives. Whether you are in sympathy with the movie may depend on which you found more disturbing: the questions of the Starr Commission or Clinton's attempts to avoid answering them. Full disclosure: I could imagine myself reacting as Clinton did, but to ask Starr's questions would have filled me with self-disgust.

Joan Allen is at the center of the movie, in one of the strongest performances of the year. Some actresses would have played the role as too sensual, others as too cold; she is able to suggest a woman with a healthy physical life who nevertheless has ethical standards that will not bend. She would rather lose the vice presidency than satisfy Runyon's smutty curiosity, and through her the movie argues that we have gone too far in our curiosity about private behavior.

Jeff Bridges plays the president as a man who got elected by seeming a great deal more affable and down-home than he really is. He's forever ordering food and pressing it upon his guests, in gestures that are not so much hospitality as decoys. His top aides, played by Sam Elliott and Saul Rubinek, have a terse shorthand that shows they understand the folksy act but aren't deceived by it. And Christian Slater has a slippery role as a freshman Democratic congressman who is prepared to barter his vote for a seat on Runyon's committee.

And what about Runyon, in Gary Oldman's performance? Oldman is one of the great actors, able to play high, low, crass, noble. Here he disappears into the character, with owly glasses, a feral mouth, and curly locks teased over baldness. He plays the kind of man who, in high school, would rather know who was sleeping with the cheerleaders than sleep with one himself. There are two revealing scenes involving his wife, who knows him better than anyone should have to.

Of course, if he is right about Hanson, then he is not a bad man—merely an unpleasant one. But even if he is right he is wrong, because he opposed the nominee because she is a woman; her shady past is only a means of attacking her. This is one of those rare movies where you leave the theater having been surprised and entertained, and then start arguing. *The Contender* takes sides and is bold about it. Most movies are like puppies that want everyone to pet them.

The Conversation
PG, 113 m., 1974

Gene Hackman (Harry Caul), John Cazale (Stan), Allen Garfield (Bernie Moran), Frederic Forrest (Mark), Cindy Williams (Ann), Michael Higgins (Paul). Directed by Francis Ford Coppola and produced by Fred Roos. Screenplay by Coppola.

As he is played by Gene Hackman in *The Conversation*, an expert wiretapper named Harry Caul is one of the most affecting and tragic characters in the movies; he ranks with someone like Willy Loman in *Death of a Salesman* or the pathetic captives of the middle class in John Cassavetes's *Faces*. Hackman is such a fine actor in so many different roles, from his action roles like *The French Connection* to this introverted, frightened, paranoid who is "the best bugger on the West Coast." He is, indeed, maybe the best wiretapper in the country, but he hasn't gone back to the East Coast since a bugging assignment there led to the deaths of three people. He tries to force himself not to care. He goes to confession and begs forgiveness for not paying for some newspapers, but not for bringing about a murder—because the murder, you see, was none of his business. He is only a professional. He does his job and asks no questions: doesn't *want* to know the answers.

His latest job has been a tactical masterpiece. The assignment: Bug a noon-hour conversation between two young people as they walk in a crowded plaza. He does it by tailing them with a guy who's wired for sound, and also by aiming parabolic microphones at them from buildings overlooking the plaza. This gives him three imperfect recordings of their conversation, which he can electronically marry into one fairly good tape. He is a good craftsman, and, although the film doesn't belabor his techniques, it does show us enough of how bugging is done to give us a cynical education.

It's a movie not so much about bugging as about the man who does it, and Gene Hackman's performance is a great one. He does not want to get involved (whenever he says anything like that, it sounds in italics)—but he does. After he has recorded the conversation, he plays it again and again and becomes convinced that a death may result from it, if he turns the tape in. The ways in which he interprets the tape, and the different nuances of meaning it seems to contain at different moments, remind us of Antonioni's *Blow Up.* Both movies are about the unreality of what seems real: We have here in our hands a document that is maddeningly concrete and yet refuses to reveal its meaning. And the meaning seems to be a matter of life and death.

The movie is a thriller with a shocking twist at the end, but it is also a character study. Hackman plays a craftsman who has perfected his skill at the expense of all other human qualities; he lives in paranoia in a triple-locked apartment, and is terrified when it turns out his landlady has a key. She explains she might have to get in in case of some emergency—his furniture might burn up or something. He explains that none of his possessions is important to him—except his keys.

He has no friends, but he does have acquaintances in the bugging industry, and they're in town for a convention. One of them (played by Allen Garfield) is a truly frightening character. He's the one who talks about the three murders, and he's the one whose hateful envy reveals to us how good Harry Caul really is. A boozy scene in Harry's workshop, with some colleagues and their random dates, provides a perfect illustration of the ways in which even Harry's pathetically constrained social life is expressed through his work.

The Conversation is about paranoia, invasion of privacy, bugging—and also about the bothersome problem of conscience. The Watergate crew seems, for the most part, to have had no notion that what they were doing was objectively wrong. Harry wants to have no notion. But he does, and it destroys him.

The Cook, the Thief, His Wife and Her Lover
NO MPAA RATING, 120 m., 1990

Richard Bohringer (Richard), Michael Gambon (Albert), Helen Mirren (Georgina), Alan Howard (Michael), Tim Roth (Mitchel), Ciaran Hinds (Cory), Gary Olsen (Spangler), Ewan Stewart (Harris). Directed by Peter Greenaway and produced by Kees Kasander. Screenplay by Greenaway.

Rarely has a movie title been more—or less—descriptive than Peter Greenaway's *The Cook, the Thief, His Wife and Her Lover.* On one level you can describe the movie simply in terms of the characters and the lustful and unspeakable things they do to one another. On another level, there is no end to the ideas stirred up by this movie, which was threatened with an X rating in America while creating a furor in Great Britain because of its political content. So, which is it? Pornographic, a savage attack on Margaret Thatcher, or both? Or is it simply about a cook, a thief, his wife, and her lover?

The thief's thuggish personality stands astride the movie and browbeats the others into submission. He is a loud, large, reprehensible criminal, played by Michael Gambon as the kind of bully you can only look at in wonder that God does not strike him dead. He presides every night over an obscene banquet in a London restaurant, where the other customers exhibit remarkable patience at his hoglike behavior. He surrounds himself with his cronies, hit men, and hangers-on, and with his long-suffering wife (Helen Mirren), for whom martyrdom has become a lifestyle. No behavior is too crude for the thief, who delights in making animal noises, who humiliates his underlings, who beats and degrades his wife, and whose treatment of the chef in the opening scene may send some patrons racing for the exits before the real horror show has even begun.

At another table in the restaurant sits the lover (Alan Howard), a book propped up so that he can read while he eats. He ignores the crude displays of the thief; his book distracts him. Then one night his eyes meet the eyes of the thief's wife. Lightning strikes, and within seconds they are making passionate love in the ladies' room. The sex scenes in this movie are as hungry and passionate as any I have seen, and yet they are upstaged by the rest of the film, which is so uncompromising in its savagery that the sex seems tranquil by comparison.

Night after night the charade goes on—the thief acting monstrously, the cook being humiliated, the wife and her lover meeting to make love in the toilet, the kitchen, the meat room, the refrigerator, anywhere that is sufficiently inappropriate and uncomfortable. (Greenaway gives a nightmare tinge to these scenes by using a different color scheme for every locale—red for the dining room, white for the toilets—and having the color of the character's costumes change as they walk from one to another.) Then the thief discovers that he is a cuckold, and in a rage orders his men to shove a book on the French Revolution down the lover's throat, one page at a time. That is the prelude to the movie's conclusion, which I will merely describe as cannibalism, to spare your feelings.

So. What is all this about? Greenaway is not ordinarily such a visceral director, and indeed his earlier films (*The Draughtsman's Contract, A Zed and Two Noughts, In the Belly of the Architect*) have specialized in cerebral detachment. What is his motivation here? I submit it is anger—the same anger that inspired large and sometimes violent British crowds to demonstrate against Margaret Thatcher's poll tax that whipped the poor and coddled the rich. Some British critics read the movie this way:

Cook = Civil servants, dutiful citizens.

Thief = Thatcher's arrogance and support of the greedy.

Wife = Britannia.

Lover = Ineffectual opposition by leftists and intellectuals.

This provides a neat formula and allows us to read the movie as a political parable. (It is easily as savage as Swift's "modest proposal" that if the Irish were starving and overcrowded, they could solve both problems by eating their babies.) But I am not sure Greenaway is simply making an Identikit protest movie, leaving us to put the labels on the proper donkeys. I think *The Cook, the Thief, His Wife and Her Lover* is more of a meditation on modern times in general. It is about the greed of an entrepreneurial class that takes over perfectly efficient companies and steals their assets, that marches roughshod over timid laws in pursuit of its own aggrandizement, that rapes the environment, that enforces its tyranny on the timid majority—which distracts itself with romance and escapism to avoid facing up to the bullyboys.

The actors in this movie exhibit a rare degree of courage. They are asked to do things that few human beings would have the nerve or the stomach for, and they do them because they believe in the power of the statement being made. Mirren, Gambon, and Howard are three of the most distinguished actors in Britain—among them, they've played many of the principal roles in Shakespeare—and here they find the resources to not only strip themselves of all their defenses, but to do so convincingly.

This isn't a freak show; it's a deliberate and thoughtful film in which the characters are believable and we care about them. Gambon makes the thief a study in hatefulness. At the end of the film, I regretted it was over because it let him too easily off the hook. Mirren's character transformation is almost frightening—she changes from submissive wife to daring lover to vicious seeker of vengeance. And watch the way she and Howard handle their sex scenes together, using sex not as joy, not as an avenue to love, but as sheer escapism; lust is their avenue to oblivion.

The Cook, the Thief, His Wife and Her Lover is not an easy film to sit through. It doesn't simply make a show of being uncompromising—it is uncompromised in every single shot from beginning to end. Why is it so extreme? Because it is a film made in rage, and rage cannot be modulated. Those who think it is only about gluttony, lust, barbarism, and bad table manners will have to think again. It is a film that uses the most basic strengths and weaknesses of the human body as a way of giving physical form to the corruption of the human soul.

Cookie's Fortune

PG-13, 118 m., 1999

Glenn Close (Camille Dixon), Julianne Moore (Cora Duvall), Liv Tyler (Emma Duvall), Chris O'Donnell (Jason Brown), Charles S. Dutton (Willis Richland), Patricia Neal (Cookie Orcutt), Ned Beatty (Lester Boyle), Niecy Nash (Deputy Wanda), Lyle Lovett (Manny Hood), Donald Moffat (Jack Palmer), Courtney B. Vance (Otis Tucker), Ruby Wilson (Josie Martin). Directed by Robert Altman and produced by Altman and Etchie Stroh. Screenplay by Anne Rapp.

Cookie's Fortune is Robert Altman's sunniest film, a warmhearted comedy that somehow manages to deal with death and murder charges without even containing a real villain. True, the Glenn Close character comes close to villainy by falsifying a death scene, but since she's in the middle of directing the Easter play at her church, maybe it's partly a case of runaway theatrical zeal.

The movie takes place in the small town of Holly Springs, Mississippi, where Altman assembles a large cast of lovable characters. He's a master of stories that interconnect a lot of people (*M*A*S*H, Nashville, The Player, Short Cuts*), and here one of the pleasures is discovering the hidden connections.

The film begins with a false alarm. A black man named Willis (Charles S. Dutton) wanders out of a bar, seems to break into a home, and studies the guns displayed in a cabinet. An elderly white woman (Patricia Neal) comes downstairs and finds him, and then we discover they're best friends. Neal plays Cookie, a rich widow who misses her husband fiercely. Glenn Close is Camille Dixon, her niece, who before long discovers Cookie's dead body and

rearranges the death scene to make it look like a break-in and a murder.

Meanwhile, Altman's camera strolls comfortably around town, introducing us to Cora (Julianne Moore), Camille's dim sister; Emma (Liv Tyler), Cora's daughter, who takes a pass on genteel society and works at the catfish house; and the forces down at the police station, including the veteran officer Lester (Ned Beatty), Jason the doofus rookie (Chris O'Donnell), and Wanda the deputy (Niecy Nash). Some of these people have roles in the Easter play, which is *Salome* (the letterboard in front of the church says it's "by Oscar Wilde and Camille Dixon").

The key dramatic event in the film is the arrest of Willis on suspicion of murder, even though everyone in the town is convinced he could not have committed such a crime. His fingerprints are indeed on the guns in Cookie's house, but no wonder, since he just finished cleaning them.

> "He's innocent. You can trust me on that," declares Lester the cop.
> "What makes you so sure of that?"
> "Because—I fish with him."

Emma also believes he's innocent, and demonstrates her confidence by moving into his jail cell. The cell door is kept open, which is convenient for Emma and Jason the doofus deputy, since they are desperately in love and sneak off behind the Coke machine for rumpy-pumpy whenever possible.

"They read you your rights?" the lawyer (Donald Moffat) asks Willis. "Yeah, and gave me a cup of coffee and an issue of *Field and Stream*." Also a Scrabble board. Meanwhile, Camille and Cora (who has been sworn to secrecy about the falsified death scene) are beside themselves: They like Willis and are horrified he's under arrest, but to free him would involve incriminating themselves.

Altman and his writer, Anne Rapp, use the crime story as a way to reveal connections of one sort or another between almost everyone in the movie. They also show a small southern town that is not seething with racism, classism, and ignorance, but is in fact a sort of heavenly place where most people know and like one another, and are long accustomed to each other's peculiarities. (There's a lovely scene where the bar owner tries to explain to the cops, without really saying so, that it is Willis's custom to steal a half-pint of Southern Comfort when he's broke, and return it when he's in funds.)

Altman has always been good with sly humor at the edges of his frame. He doesn't only focus on the foreground action, but allows supporting characters to lead their own lives on the edges. Notice in particular the delightful character of Wanda (Niecy Nash), the African-American deputy, who wields a tape recorder with great drama. There's a scene where a state investigator arrives from Jackson to look into the case, and is a handsome black man (Courtney B. Vance). He interviews the blues singer at the bar (Ruby Wilson), while Wanda mans the tape recorder, and both women subtly but shamelessly flirt with him.

Cookie's Fortune is the kind of comedy with a lot of laughs, and even more smiles. The cast blends so smoothly you can believe they all live in the same town. There is a great warmth at the center of the story, in the performance by Charles S. Dutton, who is one of the most likable characters in any Altman film (his scenes with Liv Tyler include some very tricky revelations, which they both handle with perfect simplicity). Glenn Close has the richest comedy in the film, as the meddling, stage-struck director ("The two of you keep forgetting this is ancient Galilee!"). Patricia Neal's role is brief, but crucial and touching. Ned Beatty's sheriff uses fishing as his metaphor for life.

Altman's films are sometimes criticized for being needlessly enigmatic and elliptical, for ending at quixotic moments, for getting too cute with the asides. He does sometimes commit those sins, if sins they are, but in the service of creating movies that are fresh and original. *Cookie's Fortune* has no ragged edges or bothersome detours, and flows from surprise to delight. At the end, when just desserts are handed out, it arrives at a kind of perfection.

Cool Hand Luke

PG, 126 m., 1967

Paul Newman (Lucas "Luke" Jackson), George Kennedy (Dragline), J. D. Cannon (Society Red), Lou Antonio (Koko), Strother Martin (Captain). Directed by Stuart Rosenberg and produced by Gordon Carroll. Screenplay by Donn Pearce, based on his book.

Editor's Note: This review contains spoilers.

A key moment in the development of the movie antihero came right at the end of *The Wild One*, when Marlon Brando gave out with that slow, sickeningly sweet smile. For the first time, here was a leading character who didn't give a damn what you thought of him.

There had been antiheroes in the movies before, but they were really heroes in disguise. The audience identified with them even though they were on the wrong side of the law, were unwashed, had rotten luck, were physically repugnant, or were just plain bad guys.

But in the early 1950s, a new breed of antihero started to develop. He didn't want your sympathy or understanding. In fact, he despised social workers, and audiences who thought like social workers. Brando's belly-scratching, undershirted Stanley Kowalski in *A Streetcar Named Desire* was a leading character like that. And then, two years later in 1954, Brando made *The Wild One* and Hollywood had invented a new kind of film.

In a few movies every year, the central character seemed to be rejecting the values of the audience and stomping on its sympathy. Not all the roles went as far as Brando's motorcycle hoodlum. But Rod Steiger's *Pawnbroker* was a pretty tough case, and James Dean's entire career descended directly from Brando's early style. Lee Marvin and Steve McQueen have made several apiece. Anthony Quinn is practically a professional unwashed antihero, although *Zorba* was an old-style lovable rebel. And then you have the case of Paul Newman.

Newman used to be just another good-looking movie star. But he went through a gradual shift in image, starting with *Exodus*, and finally he was convincing enough that you didn't snicker when he shouted, "Follow me, men," and went over the top. The ability to pull off a line like that is important, and the actors who can do it last forever, such as John Wayne and Richard Widmark.

But then Newman did something else. He could have gone the Charlton Heston route, getting more noble in every picture until finally he was heroic enough to paint the ceiling of the Sistine Chapel, drive chariots, part the Red Sea, and take dictation from God.

But he hasn't been making that kind of movie. Instead, he's been in movies where he is a fairly ordinary guy in a fairly ordinary situation. He's more or less like the people he hangs around with, except he won't be pushed. He knows his own mind.

The bad guys in his movies don't like that, so they try to break him. And he fights back, no matter how much it hurts. If the characters he has played stopped there, they would be more or less conventional heroes. But they don't. Although they exhibit heroic stubbornness and integrity, they're not very likable.

For one thing, they're loners. For another, they don't seem to have basic human feelings. They do rotten things and don't feel bad. They're cold and aloof, and their enemies are usually fairly average people, with a sense of humor. People just like us. We'd break a guy like Paul Newman if we had the chance, because he's a troublemaker, a malcontent, a loner. Won't have a drink with the boys. Doesn't give to the United Fund. That's the kind of guy he played in all those movies, beginning with H (*The Hustler, Hud, Harper, Hombre*). He smiled at the idiots who were crossing him. He didn't care what people thought. And a subtle change took place: The hero stopped wanting to be a hero.

In *The Hustler*, Newman played Eddie Felson, a pool expert in love with his own image as a champion. Jackie Gleason, as Minnesota Fats, was the guy the audience identified with because they didn't like Newman's attitude. In the end, Fast Eddie got his thumbs broken, and audiences weren't all that sorry. Yet Newman was the central character of the movie, the "hero."

In *Hud,* once again, Newman was the outsider. He didn't share his father's sentiment for the ranch and the cattle, and although his little brother idolized him, Newman did all he could to disillusion the kid and discourage his admiration. *Harper* was a more-or-less similar character, a private detective in the Bogart mold but even less open to ordinary human contact than Sam Spade.

Then, in the recent *Hombre* the Newman character gained a degree of self-understanding. Newman played a white man who had been raised by Indians and adopted their way of life. He becomes joined to a party of travelers who are all incapable of protecting themselves and coping with the Western badlands.

So Newman is the hero, the guy who can handle things and defend the weak. Only he doesn't want to. He despises the travelers and sees no need to endanger his own life to save theirs. They talk about courage and duty, and he says he doesn't know what the words mean. In the end, he does sacrifice himself to save a member of the party, but he doesn't feel good about it. His death just proves the uselessness of being a hero. Where will it get you?

Now in his latest film, *Cool Hand Luke,* Newman brings this character to the end of its logical development, playing a hero who becomes an antihero because he despises the slobs who worship him. Luke is on a southern chain gang. He's the only prisoner with guts enough to talk back to the bosses and the only one with nerve enough to escape.

He begins the movie as a likable enough guy, always smiling, always ready for a little fun. He eats fifty hard-boiled eggs on a bet and collects all the money in the camp. That Luke, he's a cool hand.

His biggest admirer is a slack-jawed hillbilly named Dragline (admirably played by George Kennedy, the cop who never got the swinging gate fixed in *In the Heat of the Night*). Dragline figures that as long as Luke keeps escaping, it's almost as good as escaping yourself. Once when Luke escapes he mails the boys a photo of himself with a couple of beautiful girls, and when he's returned to the camp, he can't convince them the photo was faked.

At about this point, the fun of being a hero begins to pale. When Luke is returned to the camp after each escape, he is driven to the brink of madness and death by whippings, solitary confinement, work details, and more refined tortures.

After one punishment session, Luke pleads for mercy from the boss. The boys on the chain gang are stunned; how could good old Luke ever break down and surrender? Their vicarious hero has failed them and now they are left with nothing but their own cowardice.

When Luke finally does escape for the last time, he isn't smiling so much. The whole hero business has become fatal, and this time he is escaping for himself, not his buddies. Dragline gets sucked into coming along, to his own surprise and Luke's weary resignation, and there is a scene at the end in which the hero turns in his mantle and allows Dragline to see him as he is: a desperate, discouraged man who despises his admirers and will no longer pay the price necessary to entertain them.

The movie hero used to be an inspiration, but recently he has become a substitute. We no longer want to be heroes ourselves, but we want to know that heroes are on the job in case we ever need one. This has resulted in an interesting flip-flop of stereotypes.

Used to be the antihero was a bad guy we secretly liked. Then, with Brando, we got a bad guy we didn't like. And now, in *Cool Hand Luke*, we get a good guy who becomes a bad guy because he doesn't like us.

Luke is the first Newman character to understand himself well enough to tell us to shove off. He's through risking his neck to make us happy. With this film, Newman completes a cycle of five films over six years, and together they have something to say about the current status of heroism. Whether this was anyone's original intention is doubtful. But *Cool Hand Luke* does draw together threads from the earlier movies, especially *Hombre*, and it is a tough, honest film with backbone.

The Cotton Club

R, 121 m., 1984

Richard Gere (Dixie Dwyer), Gregory Hines (Sandman Williams), Diane Lane (Vera Cicero), Lonette McKee (Lila Rose Oliver), Bob Hoskins (Owney Madden), James Remar (Dutch Schultz), Fred Gwynne (Frenchy). Directed by Francis Ford Coppola and produced by Robert Evans. Screenplay by William Kennedy and Coppola.

After all the rumors, all the negative publicity, all the stories of fights on the set and backstage intrigue and imminent bankruptcy, Francis Ford Coppola's *The Cotton Club* is, quite simply, a wonderful movie. It has the confidence and momentum of a movie where every shot was premeditated—and even if we know that wasn't the case, and this was one of the most troubled productions in recent movie history, what difference does that make when the result is so entertaining?

The movie takes place in New York in the 1920s and 1930s, where Irish and Jewish gangsters battled the Italians for the rackets. Most of their intrigues were played out in public, in flashy settings like the Cotton Club, a Harlem nightclub that featured the nation's most talented black entertainers on stage—playing before an all-white audience. By telling us two love stories, Coppola shows us both sides of that racial divide. He begins by introducing Dixie Dwyer (Richard Gere), a good-looking young musician who saves the life of a gangster and is immediately recruited into the hood's inner circle. There he meets the gangster's teenage girlfriend (Diane Lane), and they immediately fall in love—but secretly, because they'll live longer that way. Then we meet Sandman Williams (Gregory Hines), a black tap dancer who dreams of appearing at the Cotton Club, and falls in love with a member of the chorus line (Lonette McKee), a mulatto who talks about her secret life among people who think she is white.

The two love stories are developed against a background of a lot of very good jazz, some great dancing, sharply etched character studies of the gang bosses, and a couple of unexpected bursts of violence that remind us, in their sudden explosion, of moments in Coppola's *Godfather* films. Indeed, there's a lot of *The Godfather* in *The Cotton Club*, especially in the movie's almost elegiac sadness: We get the feeling of time passing, and personal histories being written, and some people breaking free and other people dying or surrendering to hopelessness.

There's another reminder of *The Godfather* movies, and that's in the brilliant, indepth casting. There's not an uninteresting face or a boring performance in this movie, but two supporting characters really stand out: Bob Hoskins, as a crooked club owner named Madden, and Fred Gwynne, as a towering hulk named Frenchy. They are friends. They also are criminal associates. Hoskins is a bantamweight filled with hostility; Gwynne is a giant with a deep voice and glowering eyes. After Gwynne is kidnapped and Hoskins pays the ransom, the scene between the two of them begins as a routine confrontation and unfolds into something surprisingly funny and touching.

Coppola has a way, in this film, of telling all the different stories without giving us the impression he's jumping around a lot. Maybe the music helps. It gives the movie a continuity and an underlying rhythm that makes all of the characters' lives into steps in a sad ballet. We like some of the characters, but we don't have much respect for them, and the movie doesn't bother with clear distinctions between good and evil. *The Cotton Club* is a somewhat cynical movie about a very cynical time, and along with the music and the romance there is racism, cruelty, betrayal, and stunning violence. Romance with a cutting edge.

The performances are well-suited to the material. Richard Gere is especially good as Dixie Dwyer, maybe because the camera has a way of seeing him off-balance, so that he doesn't dominate the center of each shot like a handsome icon; Coppola stirs him into the action. Diane Lane, herself still a teenager, is astonishing as the party girl who wants to own her own club. Gregory Hines and his brother, Maurice, create a wonderful moment of reconciliation when they begin to tap dance and end by forgiving each other for a lifetime's hurts. And Hoskins, the British actor who played the unforgettable mob chief in *The Long Good Friday*, is so woundup and fierce and funny as the mobster that he takes a cliché and turns it into an original.

The Cotton Club took months to shoot, and they claim they have another 200,000 feet of footage as good as this movie. I doubt it. Whatever it took to do it, Coppola has extracted a very special film out of the checkered history of this project.

Crash

R, 100 m., 2005

Sandra Bullock (Jean), Don Cheadle (Graham), Matt Dillon (Officer Ryan), Jennifer Esposito (Ria), William Fichtner (Flanagan), Brendan Fraser (Rick), Terrence Dashon Howard (Cameron), Ludacris (Anthony), Thandie Newton (Christine), Ryan Phillippe (Officer Hansen), Larenz Tate (Peter), Shaun Toub (Farhad), Michael Pena (Daniel). Directed by Paul Haggis and produced by Haggis, Mark R. Harris, Robert Moresco, Cathy Schulman, and Tom Nunan. Screenplay by Haggis and Moresco.

Crash tells interlocking stories of whites, blacks, Latinos, Koreans, Iranians, cops and criminals, the rich and the poor, the powerful and powerless, all defined in one way or another by racism. All are victims of it, and all are guilty of it. Sometimes, yes, they rise above it, although it is never that simple. Their negative impulses may be instinctive, their positive impulses may be dangerous, and who knows what the other person is thinking?

The result is a movie of intense fascination; we understand quickly enough who the characters are and what their lives are like, but we have no idea how they will behave because so much depends on accident. Most movies enact rituals; we know the form and watch for variations. *Crash* is a movie with free will, and anything can happen. Because we care about the characters, the movie is uncanny in its ability to rope us in and get us involved.

Crash was directed by Paul Haggis, whose screenplay for *Million Dollar Baby* led to Academy Awards. It connects stories based on coincidence, serendipity, and luck, as the lives of the characters crash against each other like pinballs. The movie presumes that most people feel prejudice and resentment against members of other groups, and observes the consequences of those feelings.

One thing that happens, again and again, is that peoples' assumptions prevent them from seeing the actual person standing before them. An Iranian (Shaun Toub) is thought to be an Arab, although Iranians are Persian. Both the Iranian and the white wife of the district attorney (Sandra Bullock) believe a Mexican-American locksmith (Michael Pena) is a gang member and a crook, but he is a family man.

A black cop (Don Cheadle) is having an affair with his Latino partner (Jennifer Esposito), but never gets it straight which country she's from. A cop (Matt Dillon) thinks a light-skinned black woman (Thandie Newton) is white. When a white producer tells a black TV director (Terrence Dashon Howard) that a black character "doesn't sound black enough," it never occurs to him that the director doesn't "sound black," either. For that matter, neither do two young black men (Larenz Tate and Ludacris), who dress and act like college students, but have a surprise for us.

You see how it goes. Along the way, these people say exactly what they are thinking, without the filters of political correctness. The district attorney's wife is so frightened by a street encounter that she has the locks changed, then assumes the locksmith will be back with his "homies" to attack them. The white cop can't get medical care for his dying father, and accuses a black woman at his HMO of taking advantage of preferential racial treatment. The Iranian can't understand what the locksmith is trying to tell him, freaks out, and buys a gun to protect himself. The gun dealer and the Iranian get into a shouting match.

I make this sound almost like episodic TV, but Haggis writes with such directness and such a good ear for everyday speech that the characters seem real and plausible after only a few words. His cast is uniformly strong; the actors sidestep clichés and make their characters particular.

For me, the strongest performance is by Matt Dillon, as the racist cop in anguish over his father. He makes an unnecessary traffic stop when he thinks he sees the black TV director and his light-skinned wife doing something they really shouldn't be doing at the same time they're driving. True enough, but he wouldn't have stopped a black couple or a white couple. He humiliates the woman with an invasive body search, while her husband is forced to stand by powerless, because the cops have the guns—Dillon, and also a unseasoned rookie (Ryan Phillippe), who hates what he's seeing but has to back up his partner.

That traffic stop shows Dillon's cop as vile and hateful. But later we see him trying to care for his sick father, and we understand why he explodes at the HMO worker (whose race is only an excuse for his anger). He victimizes others by exercising his power, and is impotent when it comes to helping his father.

Then the plot turns ironically on itself, and both of the cops find themselves, in very different ways, saving the lives of the very same TV director and his wife. Is this just manipulative storytelling? It didn't feel that way to me because it serves a deeper purpose than mere irony: Haggis is telling parables, in which the characters learn the lessons they have earned by their behavior.

Other cross-cutting Los Angeles stories come to mind, especially Lawrence Kasdan's more optimistic *Grand Canyon* and Robert Altman's more humanistic *Short Cuts*. But *Crash* finds a way of its own. It shows the way we all leap to conclusions based on race—yes, all of us, of all races, and however fair-minded we may try to be—and we pay a price for that.

If there is hope in the story, it comes because as the characters crash into one another, they learn things, mostly about themselves. Almost all of them are still alive at the end, and are better people because of what has happened to them. Not happier, not calmer, not even wiser, but better. Then there are those few who kill or get killed; racism has tragedy built in.

Not many films have the possibility of making their audiences better people. I don't expect *Crash* to work any miracles, but I believe anyone seeing it is likely to be moved to have a little more sympathy for people not like themselves. The movie contains hurt, coldness, and cruelty, but is it without hope? Not at all.

Stand back and consider. All of these people, superficially so different, share the city and learn that they share similar fears and hopes. Until several hundred years ago, most people everywhere on Earth never saw anybody who didn't look like them. They were not racist because, as far as they knew, there was only one race. You may have to look hard to see it, but *Crash* is a film about progress.

Cries and Whispers
R, 106 m., 1973

Harriet Andersson (Agnes), Kari Sylwan (Anna), Ingrid Thulin (Karin), Liv Ullmann (Maria), Erland Josephson (Lakaren), Henning Moritzen (Joakim). Directed, produced, and written by Ingmar Bergman.

Cries and Whispers is like few movies we'll ever see. It is hypnotic, disturbing, frightening. It envelops us in a red membrane of passion and fear, and in some way that I do not fully understand, it employs taboos and ancient superstitions to make its effect. We slip lower in our seats, feeling claustrophobia and sexual disquiet, realizing that we have been surrounded by the vision of a filmmaker who has absolute mastery of his art. *Cries and Whispers* is about dying, love, sexual passion, hatred, and death—in that order.

The film inhabits a manor house set on a vast country estate. The rooms of the house open out from each other like passages in the human body; with the exception of one moment when Agnes, the dying woman, opens her window and looks at the dawn, the house offers no views. It looks in upon itself.

Three women stay in the house with Agnes (Harriet Andersson), waiting for her to die. She is in the final stages of cancer and in great pain. The women are Karin and Maria, her sisters, and Anna, the stout, round-cheeked servant. In elliptical flashbacks (intended to give us emotional information, not to tell a story), we learn that the three sisters have made little of their lives. Karin (Ingrid Thulin) is married to a diplomat she despises. Maria (Liv Ullmann) is married to a cuckold, and so she cuckolds him (what is one to do?). Agnes, who never married, gave birth to a few third-rate watercolors. Now, in dying, she discovers at last some of the sweetness of life.

The sisters remember that they were close in childhood, but somehow in growing up they lost the ability to love, to touch. Only Anna, the servant, remembers how. When Agnes cries out in the night, in fear and agony, it is Anna who cradles her to her bosom, whispering soft endearments. The others cannot stand to be touched. In a moment of conjured nostalgia, Maria and Karin remember their closeness as children. Now, faced with the fact of their sister's death, they deliberately try to synthesize feeling and love. Quickly, almost frantically, they touch and caress each other's faces, but their touching is a parody and by the next day they have closed themselves off again.

These two scenes—of Anna embracing Agnes, and of Karin and Maria touching like frightened kittens—are two of the greatest Bergman has ever created. The feeling in these scenes—I should say, the way they force us to feel—constitutes the meaning of this film. It has no abstract message; it communicates with us on a level of human feeling so deep that we are afraid to invent words for the things found there.

The camera is as uneasy as we are. It stays at rest mostly, but when it moves it doesn't always follow smooth, symmetrical progressions. It darts, it falls back, is stunned. It lingers on close-ups of faces with the impassivity of God. It continues to look when we want to turn away; it is not moved. Agnes lies thrown on her deathbed, her body shuddered by horrible, deep gasping breaths, as she fights for air, for life. The sisters turn away, and we want to, too. We know things are this bad— but we don't want to know. Bergman's camera stays and watches.

The movie is drenched in red. Bergman has written in his screenplay that he thinks of the inside of the human soul as a membranous red. Color can be so important; in *Two English Girls*, a movie about the absence of passion, Francois Truffaut kept red out of his compositions until the movie's one moment of unfeigned feeling, and then he filled his screen with red.

All of *Cries and Whispers* is occupied with passion—but the passion is inside, the characters can't get it out of themselves. None of them can, except Anna (Kari Sylwan). The film descends into a netherworld of the supernatural; the dead woman speaks (or is it only that they think they hear her?). She reaches out and grasps for Karin (or does Karin move the dead arms?—Bergman's camera doesn't let us see).

The movie, like all supernatural myths, like all legends and fables (and like all jokes— which are talismans to take the pain from truth) ends in a series of threes. The dead woman asks the living women to stay with her, to comfort her while she pauses within her dead body before moving into the great terrifying void. Karin will not. Maria will not. But Anna will, and makes pillows of her breasts for Agnes. Anna is the only one of them who remembers how to touch and love. And she is the only one who believes in God.

We saw her in the morning, praying. We learned that she had lost her little daughter, but is resigned to God's will. Is there a God in Bergman's film, or is there only Anna's faith? The film ends with a scene of astonishing, jarring affirmation: We see the four women some months earlier, drenched with the golden sun, and we hear Anna reading from Agnes's diary: "I feel a great gratitude to my life, which gives me so much." And takes it away.

Crimes and Misdemeanors
PG-13, 107 m., 1989

Caroline Aaron (Barbara), Alan Alda (Lester), Woody Allen (Cliff Stern), Claire Bloom (Miriam Rosenthal), Mia

Farrow (Halley Reed), Joanna Gleason (Wendy Stern), Anjelica Huston (Dolores Paley), Martin Landau (Judah Rosenthal), Jenny Nichols (Jenny), Jerry Orbach (Jack Rosenthal), Sam Waterston (Ben). Directed by Allen and produced by Robert Greenhut. Screenplay by Allen.

Woody Allen's *Crimes and Misdemeanors* is a thriller about the dark nights of the soul. It shockingly answers the question most of us have asked ourselves from time to time: Could I live with the knowledge that I had murdered someone? Could I still get through the day and be close to my family and warm to my friends knowing that because of my own cruel selfishness, someone who had loved me was lying dead in the grave?

This is one of the central questions of human existence, and society is based on the fact that most of us are not willing to see ourselves as murderers. But in the world of this Woody Allen film, conventional piety is overturned, and we see into the soul of a human monster. Actually, he seems like a pretty nice guy.

He's an eye doctor with a thriving practice, he lives in a modern home on three acres in Connecticut, he has a loving wife and nice kids and lots of friends, and then he has a mistress who is going crazy and threatening to start making phone calls and destroy everything. This will not do. He has built up a comfortable and well-regulated life over the years and is respected in the community. He can't let some crazy woman bring a scandal crashing around his head.

Crimes and Misdemeanors tells his story with what Allen calls realism, and what others might call bleak irony. He also tells it with a great deal of humor. Who else but Woody Allen could make a movie in which virtue is punished, evildoing is rewarded, and there is a lot of laughter—even subversive laughter at the most shocking times?

Martin Landau stars in the film as the opthalmologist who has been faithful to his wife (Claire Bloom) for years—all except for a passionate recent affair with a flight attendant (Anjelica Huston). For a few blessed months he felt free and young again, and they walked on the beach, and he said things that sounded to her like plans for marriage. But he is incapable of leaving his wife, and when she finally realizes that she becomes enraged.

What can the doctor do? It's a *Fatal Attraction* situation, and she's sending letters to his wife (which he barely intercepts) and calling up from the gas station down the road threatening to come to his door and reveal everything. In desperation, the doctor turns to his brother (Jerry Orbach), who has Mafia connections. And the brother says that there's really no problem, because he can make one telephone call and the problem will go away.

Are we talking . . . murder? The doctor can barely bring himself to say the word. But his brother is more realistic and certainly more honest, and soon the doctor is forced to ask, and answer, basic questions about his own values. Allen uses flashbacks to establish the childhood of both brothers, who grew up in a religious Jewish family with a father who solemnly promised them that God saw everything, and that, even if He didn't, a good man could not live happily with an evil deed on his conscience.

The story of the doctor's dilemma takes place at the center of a large cast of characters—the movie resembles Allen's *Hannah and Her Sisters* in the way all of the lives become tangled. Among the other important characters are Allen himself, as a serious documentary filmmaker whose wife's brother (Alan Alda) is a shallow TV sitcom producer of great wealth and appalling vanity. Through his wife's intervention, Allen gets a job making a documentary about the Alda character—and then both men make a pass at the bright, attractive production assistant (Mia Farrow). Which will she choose? The dedicated documentarian or the powerful millionaire?

Another important character is a rabbi (Sam Waterston), who is going blind. The eye doctor treats him and then turns to him for moral guidance, and the rabbi, who is a good man, tells him what we would expect to hear. But the rabbi's blindness is a symbol for the dark undercurrent of *Crimes and Misdemeanors*, which seems to argue that God has abandoned men, and that we live here below on a darkling plain, lost in violence, selfishness, and moral confusion.

Crimes and Misdemeanors is not, properly speaking, a thriller, and yet it plays like one. In fact, it plays a little like those *film noir* classics of the 1940s, like *Double Indemnity*, in which a man thinks of himself as moral, but finds out otherwise. The movie generates the best kind of suspense, because it's not about what will happen to people, it's about what decisions they will reach. We have the same information they have. What would we do? How far would we go to protect our happiness and reputation? How selfish would we be? Is our comfort worth more than another person's life? Woody Allen does not evade this question, and his answer seems to be, yes, for some people. Anyone who reads the crime reports in the daily papers would be hard put to disagree with him.

Crouching Tiger, Hidden Dragon
PG-13, 119 m., 2000

Chow Yun Fat (Li Mu Bai), Michelle Yeoh (Yu Shu Lien), Zhang Ziyi (Jen Yu), Chang Chen (Lo), Lung Sihung (Sir Te), Cheng Pei Pei (Jade Fox), Li Fa Zeng (Governor Yu), Gao Xian (Bo). Directed by Ang Lee and produced by Bill Kong, Hsu Li Kong, and Lee. Screenplay by James Schamus, Wang Hui Ling, and Tsai Kuo Jung, based on the book by Wang Du Lu.

The best martial arts movies have nothing to do with fighting and everything to do with personal excellence. Their heroes transcend space, gravity, the limitations of the body, and the fears of the mind. In a fight scene in a Western movie, it is assumed the fighters hate each other. In a martial arts movie, it's more as if the fighters are joining in a celebration of their powers.

To be sure, people get killed, but they are either characters who have misused their powers, or anonymous lackeys of the villain. When the hero stands in the center of a ring of interchangeable opponents and destroys them one after another, it's like a victory for the individual over collectivism—a message not lost in the Asian nations where these movies are most loved. The popularity of strong heroines is also interesting in those patriarchal societies.

Ang Lee's Crouching Tiger, Hidden Dragon is the most exhilarating martial arts movie I have seen. It stirred even the hardened audience at the 8:30 A.M. press screening at Cannes. There is a sequence near the beginning of the film involving a chase over rooftops, and as the characters run up the sides of walls and leap impossibly from one house to another,

the critics applauded, something they rarely do during a film, and I think they were relating to the sheer physical grace of the scene. It is done so lightly, quickly, easily.

Fight scenes in a martial arts movie are like song-and-dance numbers in a musical: After a certain amount of dialogue, you're ready for one. The choreography of the action scenes in Crouching Tiger was designed by Yuen Wo-Ping, whose credits include The Matrix, and who understands that form is more important than function. It's not who wins that matters (except to the plot, of course); it's who looks most masterful.

There's also a competition to find unlikely settings for martial arts scenes. In Legend of Drunken Master, the recently rereleased Jackie Chan movie, a bed of glowing coals is suspended in the air next to an elevated factory railway. Why? So Chan can fall into them. In Crouching Tiger, Hidden Dragon, Ang Lee and Yuen Wo-Ping give us a scene of startling daring and beauty when two protagonists cling to the tops of tall, swaying trees and swing back and forth during a swordfight.

Watching this scene, I assumed it was being done with some kind of computer trickery. I "knew" this because I "knew" the actors were not really forty feet in the air holding onto those trees. I was wrong. Everything we see is real, Lee told me. Computers were used only to remove the safety wires that held the actors. "So those were stunt people up there?" I asked, trying to hold onto some reserve of skepticism. "Not for the most part," he said. "Maybe a little stunt work, but most of the time you can see their faces. That's really them in the trees." And on the rooftops too, he told me.

The film stars Chow Yun Fat and Michelle Yeoh—she a veteran martial arts star who has extraordinary athletic abilities (as Jackie Chan and many of the other stars of the genre also do). Two other key characters are played by Zhang Ziyi (as Jen Yu) and Cheng Pei Pei (as Jade Fox). Long rehearsal and training went into their scenes, but what's unusual about Crouching Tiger, Hidden Dragon is the depth and poetry of the connecting story, which is not just a clothesline for action scenes, but has a moody, romantic, and even spiritual nature.

The story involves Li Mu Bai (Chow Yun Fat), a warrior who has vowed to avenge the death of his master. He has for many years been in love with Yu Shu Lien (Michelle Yeoh), and she with him, but their personal feelings wait upon vengeance and upon their attempts to recapture Green Destiny, a sword that once belonged to Li Mu Bai's master. That brings Yu Shu Lien into contact with the governor's daughter, Jen Yu (Zhang Ziyi), who has a secret I will leave you to discover. The other major character, Jade Fox (Cheng Pei Pei), stands between the heroes and their dreams.

This story, like all martial arts stories, is at some level just plain silly, but Ang Lee (*The Ice Storm, Sense and Sensibility*) and his longtime collaborator James Shamus (who wrote the screenplay with Wang Hui Ling and Tsai Kuo Jung) are unusually successful in bringing out the human elements, especially the unrealized love between the Chou Yun Fat and Michelle Yeoh characters. There are times when they're together that you forget about the swords and are just watching a man and a woman, tenderly cherishing the unspoken bond between them. Zhang Ziyi's character, the governor's daughter, is also intriguing because she chafes at the rules that limit her and realizes a secret fantasy life.

There are those, I know, who will never go to a martial arts movie, just as some people hate Westerns and Jack Warner once told his producers, "Don't make me any more movies where the people write with feathers." But like all ambitious movies, *Crouching Tiger, Hidden Dragon* transcends its origins and becomes one of a kind. It's glorious, unashamed escapism, and surprisingly touching at the same time. And they're really up there in those trees.

Crumb

R, 119 m., 1995

Directed by Terry Zwigoff and produced by Lynn O'Donnell and Zwigoff.

People who have been damaged by life can make the most amazing adjustments in order to survive and find peace. Sometimes it is a toss-up whether to call them mad, or courageous. Consider the case of R. Crumb. He was the most famous comics artist of the 1960s, whose images like "Keep on Truckin'" and "Fritz the Cat" and his cover for the Janis Joplin "Cheap Thrills" album helped to fix the visual look of the decade. He was also a person hanging onto sanity by his fingernails, and it is apparently true that his art saved his life.

Crumb, which is one of the most remarkable and haunting documentaries ever made, tells the story of Robert Crumb, his brothers Max and Charles, and an American childhood which looks normal in the old family photographs but concealed deep wounds and secrets. It is the kind of film that you watch in disbelief, as layer after layer is peeled away and you begin to understand the strategies that have kept Crumb alive and made him successful, when one of his brothers became a recluse in an upstairs bedroom and the other passes his time quite literally sitting on a bed of nails.

Movies like this do not usually get made because the people who have lives like this usually are not willing to reveal them. *Crumb* was directed by Terry Zwigoff, who had two advantages: He had known Crumb well for many years, and he was himself so unhappy and suicidal during the making of the film that in a sense Crumb let him do it as a favor.

Of Crumb's importance and reputation there is not much doubt. His original illustrations and the first editions of his 1960s and 1970s underground comic books command high prices. His new work is shown in galleries, and is in important collections. No less an authority than Robert Hughes, the art critic of *Time* magazine, appears in *Crumb* to declare him "the Brueghel of the last half of the twentieth century."

But *Crumb* is not really about the art, although it will cause you to look at his familiar images with a new eye. It is about the artist, who grew up in a dysfunctional family led by a father who was an overbearing tyrant—a depressive, sadistic bully who, according to this film, beat his sons and lost few opportunities to demean them. (There were also two sisters, who declined to participate in the film.)

All three brothers retreated into fantasies in an attempt to cope with their home life. It was Charles, the oldest, who first started to draw comic strips, and then Robert began to copy him. The brothers seem to have had strong fantasy relationships with comic characters; Charles began to pretend he was Long John Silver. And while it is one thing to learn that

Robert masturbated while looking at comics, especially his own, it is another to learn that his prime erotic fixation was with Bugs Bunny.

Many of the people in Crumb's life talk with great frankness about him, including his brothers, his mother, his first wife, Dana (who says he began to develop a "new vision" in 1966 after experimenting with drugs), and his present wife, Aline Kominsky, who recounts bizarre details of his lifestyle with acceptance and understanding. We learn most from Robert himself, however.

He was intensely unhappy in high school, nursed deep grudges against his contemporaries, and uses high school enemies as the models for many of the unattractive caricatures in his work. It is surprising to learn how closely autobiographical some of his drawings are; in his comics men are fixated by callipygian women, and dream of riding them piggyback, and then we see Robert doing the same thing at a gallery opening. He pages through the faces in a high school yearbook, and then we see their look-alikes in his cartoons.

If Robert was unhappy in high school, Charles found it an ordeal from which he never really recovered. In a trip to the family home, occupied by Charles and his mother, we visit the upstairs room that he rarely left, and with Robert essentially acting as the interviewer, he remembers, "I was good-looking, but there was something wrong with my personality; I was the most unpopular kid in school." On a visit to Max, we find him living as a monk, drawing a long linen tape through his body to clean his intestines, and showing recent oil paintings of considerable skill (he still has his mail-order test from the Famous Artists School).

Mrs. Crumb, interviewed while sprawled on a sofa and worrying darkly about the window shades, seems complacent about the fact that Charles never leaves the house: "At least he's not out taking illegal drugs or making some woman miserable."

Zwigoff shows us details of many Crumb comic strips which are intensely violent, sadistic, and hateful toward women. And he interviews such voices of sanity as Dierdre English, former editor of *Mother Jones,* who finds his work pornographic—"an arrested juvenile vision." So it is, and her voice ex-

presses not Puritanism but concern and simple observation. Yet as I left the film I felt that if anyone had earned the right to express Crumb's vision, it was Crumb, since his art is so clearly a coping mechanism that has allowed him to survive, and deal with his pain. *Crumb* is a film that gives new meaning to the notion of art as therapy.

The Crying Game

R, 108 m., 1992

Stephen Rea (Fergus), Jaye Davidson (Dil), Forest Whitaker (Jody), Miranda Richardson (Jude), Adrian Dunbar (Maguire), Breffini McKenna (Tinker), Joe Savino (Eddie). Directed by Neil Jordan and produced by Stephen Woolley. Screenplay by Jordan.

Some movies keep you guessing. Some movies make you care. Once in a long while a movie comes along that does both things at the same time. It's not easy. Neil Jordan's *The Crying Game* keeps us involved and committed through one plot twist after another. It was one of the best films of 1992.

Jordan's wonderful film does what Hitchcock's *Psycho,* a very different film, also did: It involves us deeply in its story, and then it reveals that the story is really about something else altogether. We may have been fooled, but so was the hero, and as the plot reveals itself we find ourselves identifying more and more with him. The movie doesn't make it easy; we have to follow him through a crisis of the heart, but the journey is worth it.

The movie opens in Northern Ireland, where a British soldier (Forest Whitaker) is kidnapped by the IRA. In a secluded forest hideout, he is guarded by a team including Fergus (Stephen Rea), who has become a committed terrorist and yet is still a person with kindness in his soul. The soldier may be executed if the British government doesn't release IRA prisoners. Meanwhile, he must be guarded, and as Fergus spends a long night with him, they get to know and even like one another. The soldier shows Fergus a snapshot of his girlfriend, back in London, and asks him to look her up someday—if, as the soldier suspects, he is going to die soon.

This is a version of the classic Irish short story *A Guest of the Nation,* by Frank O'Connor, in which IRA men in the 1920s make the mistake of becoming friendly with the man they will have to kill. But the movie resolves this dilemma with an unexpected development. And then, the next time we see Fergus, he is in London, under a new name, working as a laborer on a construction site.

He still has the snapshot. He goes looking for the soldier's girlfriend, and finds her working in a beauty salon. On an impulse he goes in to get his hair cut. After work she goes to a nearby pub. They begin a conversation, using the bartender as a middle man in one of the many unexpected narrative touches in an entirely original film. The girlfriend, named Dil (Jaye Davidson), is an original, too, with a delightful dry way of understating herself, of keeping her cool while seeming amused at the same time. She reminds us there is such a thing as verbal style; too much modern movie dialogue is flat and plot-driven.

Fergus and Dil are attracted to one another. But there are fundamental unacknowledged deceptions between them—not least, the fact that Fergus is the man who shares responsibility for the boyfriend's death. The most fascinating passages in the film follow the development of their relationship, which becomes an emotional fencing match as it survives one revelation after another. Then the IRA tracks Fergus to his hiding place, and has another job for him to do.

The peculiar thing about *The Crying Game* is that this story outline, while true, hardly suggests the actual content of this film. It is much more complex and labyrinthine—both in terms of simple plotting, and in terms of the matters of the heart that follow. Most movie love stories begin as a given; we know from the first frame who will be together in the last. Here, there are times when we know nothing, and times when we know less than that. Yet because we care about the characters—we can't help liking them—it's surprising, how the love story transcends all of the plot turns to take on an importance of its own.

One of the keys to the movie is the casting. The ironic, vulnerable Dil is a real original, a person who arrives on the screen not as a writer's notion but with a convincing, engaging personality. Stephen Rea, as Fergus, is an essentially good person who has gotten involved in a life that requires him to be violent and ruthless. He doesn't have much heart for it; maybe Dil has deeper resources. And Miranda Richardson has a key role as an IRA terrorist who toys with Fergus, early and late, confusing sexual power with political principles.

Neil Jordan first came to view as the writer-director of *Mona Lisa* (1987), with Bob Hoskins as the chauffeur who has a love-hate relationship with a prostitute (Cathy Tyson). His films since then have been widely varied, from the odd supernatural comedy *High Spirits* to last year's winsome fable *The Miracle,* which many liked more than I did. Now comes *The Crying Game,* one of a very few films that want to do something unexpected and challenging, and succeed even beyond their ambitions.

D

Daguerreotypes

NO MPAA RATING, 80 m., 1976

A documentary produced, directed, written, and edited by Agnes Varda.

The notion for Agnes Varda's *Daguerreotypes* must first have suggested itself to her as a pun. She lives, as she tells us, on the rue Daguerre in Paris. And here is her simple and sometimes charming documentary about the people, the types, who are her neighbors.

I remember her cheerful 1968 documentary *Uncle Janco*, about a relative who lived, painted, and loved in utter contentment on a houseboat in San Francisco Bay. *Daguerreotypes*, so different in its locale and subject matter, has the same directness of tone. Here are my friends, she seems to be telling us. Some of them, I can see right through. Others remain mysterious to me. I love them all.

The people in the shops along her street come mostly, it seems, from the provinces. They were apprenticed at early ages and grew up in their trades; they're good at what they do. We meet the baker and his wife. The butcher, expertly slicing steaks "not too thick" for one customer, "not too thin" for another. We meet an accordion player and a laundress and, most memorably of all, a very old couple that run a shop selling perfumes and buttons.

Buttons? Well, the shop is a perfumery, and the old man explains that he makes some of his scents himself and buys the others, and has been making perfume for years and years. Customers come into the store for a little of this scent or that, and get to select the bottle of their choice from his shelf of odd-shaped empties. But then someone comes in who needs a button, and, yes, he has just the right button.

The old man's wife is described as a "mysterious captive." She hardly ever speaks, is consumed by shyness, and "sometimes she starts to go out in the street," the man says, "but she never does." He speaks of their courtship years ago. The others on the street also talk about how they met, how they got started in business, how they take life. Before Varda's cameras they are reserved, amused, themselves.

Varda finds an inspired device to hold her material together; a magician gives a performance for the people of the street, and his tricks reflect and comment on aspects of their daily lives. I don't know whether Varda staged the magic show or simply used it, but it works perfectly: As the magician pretends to cut someone's arm, the butcher winces and then we see him trimming a cut of meat. The others on the street also find themselves commented on, sometimes gravely, sometimes with wit, by the magician's tricks. And they all react, except for the wife of the perfumer. She looks with wide eyes—whether amazed or amused or passive, we cannot guess.

Damage

R, 111 m., 1993

Jeremy Irons (Dr. Stephen Fleming), Juliette Binoche (Anna Barton), Miranda Richardson (Ingrid), Rupert Graves (Martyn), Ian Bannen (Edward Lloyd), Leslie Caron (Elizabeth Prideaux). Directed and produced by Louis Malle. Screenplay by David Hare, based on the book by Josephine Hart.

One of the most sublime and hazardous moments in human experience comes when two people lock eyes and realize that they are sexually attracted to one another. They may not act on the knowledge. They may file it away for future reference. They may deny it. They may never see each other again. But the moment has happened, and for an instant all other considerations are insignificant.

Early in Louis Malle's *Damage*, such a moment takes place between Dr. Stephen Fleming, a British government official, and Anna Barton, a young woman he has met at a reception. But it is wrong to describe it as a moment. They speak briefly, their eyes meet, and then each holds the other's gaze for one interminable second after another, until so much time has passed that we, in the audience, realize we are holding our breath.

There might have been a moment when they could have broken the spell, but both chose not to, continuing the moment far beyond the bounds of propriety or reason—particularly since Anna (Juliette Binoche) has just told Stephen (Jeremy Irons) that she is his son's fiancée.

This moment is followed by another that is remarkable for being so abrupt. Stephen sits at his desk. The telephone rings. A voice: "It's Anna." He replies: "Tell me where you are and I'll be there within an hour." And so begins their love affair, passionate and obsessive, reckless and heedless of harm to others. It is not that they want to hurt anyone, and it is not even that they want a sexual dalliance. This is something different. Indeed, they both love Martyn (Rupert Graves), Stephen's son, and plans for the marriage of Martyn and Anna continue uninterrupted.

Damage is not about romance but about obsession, about erotomania on the part of the older man, and about complex and hidden feelings on the part of the young woman. She is attracted to Stephen, yes, but there is more than that. When she was young she suffered a traumatic loss, and she describes herself as "damaged." She would not hurt him, not by an overt act, but her presence will eventually lead to harm. Watching this movie is like watching an emotional traffic accident as it unfolds.

The film is based on the best seller by Josephine Hart, which had a certain undeniable power, but the right place for this material is the screen, I think, because it can show exactly how the two look at one another. This is a movie about sight; from the first moment the two meet, it is filled with what is seen and what is not seen, as Stephen suffers through a dinner party with his wife, his son, Anna, and her mother—and some observe, and some do not, what has happened.

Casting is everything here. Stephen could easily come to seem like a fool, and some actors could have played him no other way. Jeremy Irons, gaunt and consumed, brings no fleshy pleasure to the role. Love makes him look like a condemned man, and he feels guilty about sleeping with his son's fiancée, but he must, he cannot help himself, and so he does. The heart knows what it must have.

Juliette Binoche also embodies qualities that are essential to the film. She is attractive, but not in a conventional movie way; her face is solemn and serious, and she is capable of showing nothing and yet suggesting multitudes. Godard chose her for the title role of his *Hail Mary*, Andre Techine cast her as a sexual tigress in *Rendezvous*, and in Phil Kaufman's *The Unbearable Lightness of Being*, she was the young woman who the doctor saw for a moment in a train station, and who came to stay with him, and who he could not deny. It is clear that all three directors saw her as somehow outside the norm, as an actress who could portray sexuality without descending to its usual displays.

Louis Malle is a director who has specialized in varieties of forbidden sex. His credits include *Pretty Baby*, about a photographer's child model, and *Murmur of the Heart*, about incest. His screenplay is by the playwright David Hare, who does an excellent job of surrounding these people with convincing characters whose very ordinariness underlines the madness of their actions. Miranda Richardson plays Jeremy Irons's wife, and is magnificently angry in the film's powerful closing scenes. Leslie Caron is Anna's mother, who knows her daughter well, and sees what is happening. And Rupert Graves is warm and likable as the son, who must seem worthy of Anna's love, but irrelevant.

Damage, like *Last Tango in Paris* and *The Unbearable Lightness of Being*, is one of those rare movies that is about sexuality, not sex; about the tension between people, not "relationships"; about how physical love is meaningless without a psychic engine behind it. Stephen and Anna are wrong to do what they do in *Damage*, but they cannot help themelves. We know they are careening toward disaster. We cannot look away.

Dances with Wolves
PG-13, 181 m., 1990

Kevin Costner (Lieutenant Dunbar), Mary McDonnell (Stands with a Fist), Graham Greene (Kicking Bird), Rodney A. Grant (Wind in His Hair), Floyd Red Crow Westerman (Ten Bears), Tantoo Cardinal (Black Shawl), Annie Costner (Christine). Directed by Costner and produced by Jim Wilson and Costner. Screenplay by Michael Blake.

They meet at first in the middle of the prairie, holding themselves formally and a little awkwardly, the infantry officer and Sioux Indians. There should be instant mistrust between them, but they take each other's measure and keep an open mind. A civilized man is a person whose curiosity outweighs his prejudices, and these are curious men.

They know no words of each other's languages. Dunbar, the white man, tries to pantomime a buffalo. Wind in His Hair, the chief, looks at the charade and says, "His mind is gone." But Kicking Bird, the holy man, thinks he understands what the stranger is trying to say, and at last they exchange the word for "buffalo" in each other's languages. These first halting words are the crucial moments in Kevin Costner's *Dances with Wolves,* a film about a white man who goes to live with Indians and learns their civilization firsthand.

In real life, such contacts hardly ever took place. The dominant American culture was nearsighted, incurious, and racist, and saw the Indians as a race of ignorant, thieving savages, fit to be shot on sight. Such attitudes survived until so recently in our society—just look at the B Westerns of the 1940s—that we can only imagine how much worse they were one hundred years ago. In a sense, *Dances with Wolves* is a sentimental fantasy, a "what if" movie that imagines a world in which whites were genuinely interested in learning about a Native American culture that lived more closely in harmony with the natural world than any other before or since. But our knowledge of how things turned out—of how the Indians were driven from their lands by genocide and theft—casts a sad shadow over everything.

The movie, which won the Academy Award as the best picture of 1990, is a simple story, magnificently told. It has the epic sweep and clarity of a Western by John Ford, and it abandons the contrivances of ordinary plotting to look, in detail, at the way strangers get to know one another. The film is seen from the point of view of Dunbar (Costner), a lieutenant in the Union army, who runs away from a field hospital as his foot is about to be amputated and invites death by riding his horse in a suicidal charge at the Confederate lines. When he miraculously survives, he is decorated and given his choice of any posting, and he chooses the frontier, because "I want to see it before it's gone."

He draws an isolated outpost in the Dakotas, where he is the only white man for miles around. He is alone, but at first not lonely; he keeps a journal and writes of his daily routine, and after the first contact with the Sioux, he documents the way they slowly get to know one another. Dunbar possesses the one quality he needs to cut through the entrenched racism of his time: He is able to look another man in the eye, and see the man, rather than his attitudes about the man.

As Dunbar discovers the culture of the Sioux, so do we. The Indians know the white man is coming, and they want to learn more about his plans. They have seen other invaders in these parts: the Spanish, but they always left. Now the Indians fear the white man is here to stay. They want Dunbar to share his knowledge, but at first he holds back. He does not wish to discourage them. And when he finally tells how many whites will be coming ("As many as the stars in the sky"), the words fall like a death knell.

At first, Dunbar and the Indians meet on the open prairie. One day they bring along Stands With a Fist (Mary McDonnell), a white woman who as a girl came to live with the tribe after her family was killed. She remembers a little English. With a translator, progress is quicker, until one day Dunbar comes to live with the tribe, and is eventually given the name Dances with Wolves.

There are some of the plot points we would expect in a story like this. The buffalo hunt (thrillingly photographed). A bloody fight with a hostile tribe. The inevitable love story between Dunbar and Stands with a Fist. But all is done with an eye to detail, with a respect for tradition, and with a certain sweetness of disposition. The love story is especially delicate; this isn't one of those exercises in romantic cliché, but a courtship conducted mostly through the eyes, through these two people looking at one another. There is a delicate, humorous sequence showing how the tribe observes and approves of the romance when the chief's wife, Black Shawl (Tantoo Cardinal), tells her husband it is time for Stands with a Fist to stop mourning her dead husband and accept this new man into her arms.

Meanwhile, we get to know many members of the Sioux tribe, most especially Kicking Bird (Graham Greene), Wind in His Hair (Rodney A. Grant), and the old wise man Ten Bears (Floyd Red Crow Westerman). Each has a strong personality; these are men who know exactly who they are, and at one point, after Dunbar has killed in battle beside them, he realizes he never knew who "John Dunbar" was, but he knows who Dances with Wolves is. Much of the movie is narrated by Dunbar, and his speech at this point is a center for the film: He observes that the battle with the enemy tribe was not fought for political purposes, but for food and land, and it was fought to defend the women and children who were right there in the midst of battle. The futility he felt on his suicidal day as a Union officer has been replaced by utter clarity: He knows why he was fighting, and he knows why he was willing to risk losing his life.

Dances with Wolves has the kind of vision and ambition that is rare in movies today. It is not a formula movie, but a thoughtful, carefully observed story. It is a Western at a time when the Western is said to be dead. It asks for our imagination and sympathy. It takes its time, three hours, to unfold. It is a personal triumph for Kevin Costner, the intelligent young actor of *Field of Dreams,* who directed the film and shows a command of story and of visual structure that is startling; this movie moves so confidently and looks so good it seems incredible that it's a directorial debut. Costner and his cinematographer, Dean Semler, are especially gifted at explaining things visually. Many of their most important points are made with a glance, a close-up, a detail shot.

In 1985, before he was a star, Costner played a small role in a good Western called *Silverado* simply because he wanted to be in a Western. Now he has realized his dream by making one of the best Westerns I've seen. The movie makes amends, of a sort, for hundreds of racist and small-minded Westerns that went before it. By allowing the Sioux to speak in their own tongue, by entering their villages and observing their ways, it sees them as people, not as whooping savages in the sights of an infantry rifle.

Dance with a Stranger

R, 102 m., 1985

Miranda Richardson (Ruth Ellis), Rupert Everett (David Blakely), Ian Holm (Desmond Cussen), Matthew Carroll (Andy), Tom Chadbon (Anthony Findlater), Jane Bertish (Carole Findlater). Directed by Mike Newell and produced by Roger Randall Cutler. Screenplay by Shelagh Delaney.

Ruth Ellis and David Blakely were a tragedy waiting to happen. She was a B-girl, pouring drinks and massaging men's egos in a sleazy little 1950s London nightclub. He was a rich young brat, whose life centered around his career as a race driver. They met one boozy night in the club, and there was an instant spark of lust between them—Ruth, whose profession was to keep her distance from men, and David, who had never felt love in his life.

Dance with a Stranger is the story of their affair, which led to one of the most famous British murder trials of the decade. After Ellis shot Blakely dead in the street outside a pub, she was brought to trial, convicted, and executed with heartless speed; her trial began on June 20, 1955, and she was hanged on July 19—the last woman to receive the death penalty in England.

In the thirty years since Blakely and Ellis died, the case has fascinated the British, perhaps because it combines sexuality and the class system, two of their greatest interests. Blakely was upper-class, polished, affected, superior. Ellis was a working-class girl who made herself up to look like Marilyn Monroe and used the business of bar hostess as a way to support her young son and maintain her independence from men. Ironically, she was finally undone by her emotional dependence on Blakely, who gave and then withdrew his affection in a way that pushed her over the edge.

Their story is told by Mike Newell in a film of astonishing performances and moody, atmospheric visuals. Ruth Ellis is the emotional center of the film, and she is played by a newcomer, Miranda Richardson, as a woman who prides herself on not allowing men to hurt her, and who almost to the end cannot believe that the one man she loves would hurt her the most.

We see her first in the nightclub, where her blond Monroe looks supply the only style in the whole shabby room. We meet her regular "friends," including Desmond Cussen (Ian Holm), a quiet, loyal bachelor who adores her in an unpossessive way. Then Blakely (played by Rupert Everett) walks into her life, and in an instant there is erotically charged tension between them; the way they both flaunt their indifference is a clue. Their relationship falls into a pattern: lust, sex, tears, quarrels, absences, and then lust and sex again. Newell tells the story only in terms of the events and characters themselves. There are no detours into shallow psychology; just the patterns of attraction and repulsion.

For Ruth Ellis, a woman living at a time when women's options were cruelly limited, the obsession with Blakely becomes totally destructive. She loses her job. She grows more dependent as he grows more cold and unpredictable, and everything is complicated by their mutual alcoholism. Cussen, the inoffensive, long-suffering admirer, takes her in, and she makes an effort to shape up, but Blakely sounds chords in her that she cannot ignore.

By the end of the movie, Blakely has done things to her that she cannot forgive. And they are not the big, melodramatic things like the violence that breaks out between them. They are little unforgivable things, as when he raises her hopes and then disappoints her. By the end, he is hardly even hurting her intentionally. He drinks in the company of fawning friends, he ignores responsibilities, he disappears into his own drunken absent-mindedness, and forgets her. And then one night outside a pub, she reminds him, once and for all.

Danton

PG, 136 m., 1983

Gerard Depardieu (Danton), Wojciech Pszoniak (Robespierre), Anne Alvaro (Camille). Directed by Andrzej Wajda and produced by Emmanuel Schlumberger. Screenplay by Jean-Claude Carriere.

The two poles of the French Revolution were the passionate idealism of the republic and the utter finality of the guillotine. *Danton* finds itself comfortable at those two extremes and leaves the parts in the middle—the facts, the issues, the minor personalities—to the historians.

This movie may not be an accurate record of the events of 1793 and 1794, and indeed in Paris the critics are up in arms over its inaccuracies. But as a record of the fiery passions and glorious personalities of the Revolution, it is absolutely superb. I remember a moment in *Napoleon,* the silent 1927 classic by Abel Gance, when Gance tied his camera to a rope and made it into a pendulum that swung back and forth above the inflamed debate in the French Senate. That is the spirit in which this film was made.

The name of the director may help to ex-

plain the wounded sensibilities of the French. He is Andrzej Wajda, one of the two greatest Polish directors, and winner of the 1982 Cannes Film Festival for his *Man of Iron,* about the Solidarity movement. Wajda is temporarily living in Paris, where it is possible that the subject of the Revolution reminded him of the same populist passions in Solidarity.

In any event, he has made a great historical picture, and one with sweat and grime all over it. Whenever I go to see any movie set in the past, I'm reminded of Jack L. Warner's immortal instructions to his producers at Warner Bros., after a series of historical movies had bombed: "Don't make me any more movies where the people write with feathers." The people in *Danton* write with feathers, and they wear wigs and strike poses, but they do it in scenes of such fierce belief that we forget everything except the moment.

The movie is basically about the conflict between two of the most striking personalities of the period, the two revolutionary leaders Danton and Robespierre, who were on the same side at the beginning but came to have fundamental philosophical differences that only the guillotine could settle.

Danton is played by Gerard Depardieu, that large, proletarian French actor who is so useful in roles where high-flown emotions need some sort of grounding. He makes his hoarse-voiced, idealistic speeches to the Senate sound like a football coach at halftime.

Robespierre is played by a Polish actor, Wojciech Pszoniak, as a self-obsessed hypochondriac whose political strategy seems largely determined by his need to make his headaches go away.

Wajda's camera moves through eighteenth century Paris with complete familiarity. He fills the city with the poor, with street people, with crooks and prostitutes and inflamed rabble, and there is always the sense of those crowds pressing outside as the Senate meets. And then he shows Danton and Robespierre, each perfectly aware of the other's motives and of the possibility of the guillotine, conducting an intellectual duel. The scene of the great confrontation between the two of them is so well acted and directed that, for the first time in any movie about the French Revolution, I felt I was listening to people and not speeches.

Dark Circle

NO MPAA RATING, 82 m., 1983

A documentary directed by Chris Beaver and Judy Irving and produced by Irving and Ruth Landry.

In a new documentary named *Dark Circle* we learn:

• That the blueprints for the "earthquake-proofing" of California's Diablo Canyon nuclear reactor were accidentally reversed, resulting in a design that would not have withstood earthquakes.

• That the levels of plutonium downwind from the Rocky Flats nuclear bomb factory outside Denver are far higher than government safety standards, and that neat little split-level subdivisions are what lie downwind.

• That U.S. soldiers were flown through a radioactive mushroom cloud, without their consent, during a series of tests in which thousands of soldiers were carelessly exposed to dangerous levels of radiation.

• That nuclear waste can affect your property values.

• That if the present rate of plutonium poisoning continues, it is likely that America's nuclear bombs will kill more Americans than anybody else—striking us through our lungs, our drinking water, and mothers' milk.

• And that the U.S. government once ran an experiment to see if pigs could be protected from a nuclear blast by being outfitted in little aluminum foil overcoats. They could not.

Dark Circle, which is one of the most horrifying films I've seen, also sometimes is one of the funniest (if you can laugh at the same things in real life that you found amusing in *Dr. Strangelove*). Using powers granted by the Freedom of Information Act, and sleuthing that turned up government film the government didn't even know it had, the producers of this film have created a mosaic of the Atomic Age.

It is a record of reckless mishandling of nuclear waste, criminal disregard for the rights of American citizens being poisoned in their own homes, and bizarre nuclear experiments that resemble nothing so much as a bunch of mad scientists playing with their toys.

Dark Circle is a big, ambitious, rambling documentary. It could use more focus. It tries to cover everything—from the victims of Hiroshima and Nagasaki, to the first postwar bomb tests, to the fallout scares of the 1950s, right up to the present plutonium nightmare outside Denver. It is a tribute to the power of the material, and to the relentless digging of the filmmakers, that the movie is completely riveting.

Of all this film's material, the best, I think, deals with the people living downwind from Rocky Flats. *Dark Circle* documents the situation there, where plutonium is turning up all over the place, cattle are dying, chickens are not reproducing, and children are getting cancer at a statistically alarming rate. The movie doesn't just recite these figures. It brings them home, by interviewing families who live beneath the poisonous winds of Rocky Flats.

One young mother vows to sell her house and move; she won't let her children continue to live there. Later, in the film's most heartbreaking scene, we revisit that mother. She has sold her house. She and her children are moving. She averts her face. She does not want to talk about the fact that the buyers she found . . . are another family with small children.

Dark City

R, 103 m., 1998

Rufus Sewell (John Murdoch), William Hurt (Inspector Bumstead), Kiefer Sutherland (Dr. Daniel Schreber), Jennifer Connelly (Emma Murdoch), Richard O'Brien (Mr. Hand), Ian Richardson (Mr. Book), Bruce Spence (Mr. Wall), Colin Friels (Walenski). Directed by Alex Proyas and produced by Andrew Mason and Proyas. Screenplay by Proyas, Lem Dobbs, and David S. Goyer.

Dark City by Alex Proyas is a great visionary achievement, a film so original and exciting it stirred my imagination like Lang's *Metropolis* or Kubrick's *2001*. If it is true, as the German director Werner Herzog believes, that we live in an age starved of new images, then *Dark City* is a film to nourish us. Not a story so much as an experience, it is a triumph of art direction, set design, cinematography, special effects—and imagination.

Like *Blade Runner*, it imagines a city of the future. But while *Blade Runner* extended existing trends, *Dark City* leaps into the unknown. Its vast *noir* metropolis seems to exist in an alternative time line, with elements of our present and past combined with visions from a futuristic comic book. Like the first *Batman*, it presents a city of night and shadows, but it goes far beyond *Batman* in a richness of ominous, stylized sets, streets, skylines, and cityscapes. For once a movie city is the equal of any city we could picture in our minds; this is the city *The Fifth Element* teased us with, without coming through.

The story combines science fiction with *film noir*—in more ways than we realize and more surprising ways than I will reveal. Its villains, in their homburgs and flapping overcoats, look like a nightmare inspired by the thugs in *M*, but their pale faces would look more at home in *The Cabinet of Dr. Caligari*—and, frighteningly, one of them is a child. They are the Strangers, shape-changers from another solar system, and we are told they came to Earth when their own world was dying. (They create, in the process, the first space vessel since *Star Wars* that is newly conceived—not a clone of that looming mechanical vision.)

They inhabit a city of rumbling, elevated, streamlined trains, dank flophouses, scurrying crowds, and store windows that owe something to Edward Hopper's *Night Owls*. In this city lives John Murdoch (Rufus Sewell), who awakens in a strange bathtub beneath a swinging ceiling lamp, to blood, fear, and guilt. The telephone rings; it is Dr. Schreber (Kiefer Sutherland), gasping out two or three words at a time, as if the need to speak is all that gives him breath. He warns Murdoch to flee, and indeed three Strangers are at the end of the corridor and coming for him.

The film will be the story of Murdoch's flight into the mean streets, and his gradual discovery of the nature of the city and the Strangers. Like many science-fiction heroes, he has a memory shattered into pieces that do not fit. But he remembers the woman he loves, or loved—his wife, Emma (Jennifer Connelly), who is a torch singer with sad eyes and wounded lips. And he remembers . . . Shell Beach? Where was that? He sees it on a billboard and old longings stir.

There is a detective after him, Inspector Bumstead (William Hurt). Murdoch is wanted in connection with the murders of six prostitutes. Did he kill them? Like the hero of Kafka's *The Trial*, he feels so paranoid he hardly knows. Rufus Sewell plays Murdoch like a man caught in a pinball machine, flipped back into danger every time it looks like the game is over.

The story has familiar elements made new. Even the hard-boiled detective, his eyes shaded by the brim of his fedora, seems less like a figure from *film noir* than like a projection of an alien idea of *noir*. Proyas and his co-screenwriters, Lem Dobbs and David S. Goyer, use dream logic to pursue their hero through the mystery of his own life. Along the way, Murdoch discovers that he alone, among humans, has the power of the Strangers—an ability to use his mind in order to shape the physical universe. (This power is expressed in the film as a sort of transparent shimmering projection aimed from Murdoch's forehead into the world, and as klutzy as that sounds, I found myself enjoying its very audacity: What else would mind power look like?)

Murdoch's problem is that he has no way of knowing if his memories are real, if his past actually happened, if the woman he loves ever existed. Those who offer to help him cannot be trusted. Even his enemies may not be real. The movie teasingly explores the question that babies first ask in peek-a-boo: When I can't see you, are you there? It's through that game that we learn the difference between ourselves and others. But what if *we're* not there, either?

The movie is a glorious marriage of existential dread and slam-bang action. Toward the end, there is a thrilling apocalyptic battle that nearly destroys the city, and I scribbled in my notes: "For once, a sequence where the fire and explosions really work, and don't play just as effects." Proyas and his cinematographer, Dariusz Wolski, capture the kinetic energy of great comic books; their framing and foreshortening and tilt shots and distorting lenses shake the images and splash them on the screen, and it's not "action" but more like action painting.

Proyas was the director of *The Crow* (1994), the visually inspired film that was almost doomed when its star, Brandon Lee, was killed in an accident. I called that film "the best version of a comic book universe I've seen," but *Dark City* is miles beyond it. Proyas's background was in music videos, usually an ominous sign, but not here: His film shows the obsessive concentration on visual detail that's the hallmark of directors who make films that are short and expensive. There's such a wealth on the screen, such an overflowing of imagination and energy, of sets and effects. Often in f/x movies the camera doesn't feel free because it must remain within the confines of what has been created for it to see. Here we feel there's no limit.

Is the film for teenage boys and comic book fans? Not at all, although that's the marketing pitch. It's for anyone who still has a sense of wonder and a feeling for great visual style. This is a film containing ideas and true poignancy, a story that has been all thought out and has surprises right up to the end. It's romantic and exhilarating. Watching it, I thought of the last dozen films I'd seen and realized they were all essentially about people standing around and talking to one another. *Dark City* has been created and imagined as a new visual *place* for us to inhabit. It adds treasure to our notions of what can be imagined.

Das Boot

R, 210 m., 1981 (rereleased 1997)

Jurgen Prochnow (Captain), Klaus Wenneman (Chief Engineer), Erwin Leder (Johan), Herbert Groenemeyer (Correspondent), Hubertus Bengsch (1st Lieutenant). Directed by Wolfgang Petersen and produced by Mark Damon, John W. Hyde, and Edward R. Pressman. Screenplay by Petersen and Lothar-Gunther Buchheim, based on the book by Buchheim.

The interior dimensions of the German U-boat in *Das Boot* are 10 feet by 150 feet. The officers' mess is so cramped that when a crew member wants to move from the front to the back, he asks "permission to pass," and an officer stands up to let him squeeze by. War is hell. Being trapped in a disabled submarine is worse.

Das Boot is not about claustrophobia, however, because the crew members have come to terms with that. It is about the desperate, dangerous, and exacting job of manning a submarine. In a way we can focus on that better

because it is a German submarine. If it were an American sub, we would assume the film ends in victory, identify with the crew, and cheer them on. By making it a German boat, the filmmakers neatly remove the patriotic element and increase the suspense. We identify not with the mission but with the job.

When *Das Boot* was first released in the United States, it ran 145 minutes and won huge audiences and no less than six Oscar nominations—unheard of for a foreign film. This 1997 release of Wolfgang Petersen's director's cut is not a minor readjustment but a substantially longer film, running 210 minutes.

The film is like a documentary in its impact. Although we become familiar with several of the characters, it is not their story, really, but the story of a single U-boat mission, from beginning to end. There is a brief opening sequence in which the boat sets out to sea from a French base, and a refueling sequence near the end, but all the other scenes are shot inside the cramped sub, or on the bridge.

And it's not shot in tidy setups, either; the cinematographer, Jost Vacano, hurtles his camera through the boat from one end to the other, plunging through cramped openings, hurdling obstacles on the deck, ducking under hammocks and swinging light fixtures. There are long sequences here—especially when the boat is sinking out of control—when we feel trapped in the same time and space as the desperate crew.

The boat's captain (Jurgen Prochnow) is the rock the others depend on. Experienced, steady, he's capable of shouting "I demand proper reports!" even as the boat seems to be breaking up. He is not a Nazi, and the movie makes that clear in an early scene where he ridicules Goering and other leaders for their "brilliant strategy." For this mission (an assignment to torpedo Allied ships in the North Atlantic), a journalist has been assigned to join the crew. Played by Herbert Groenemeyer, he probably represents Lothar-Gunther Buchheim, whose novel was based on these wartime events. The addition of this character is useful, because it gives the captain a reason to explain things that might otherwise go unsaid.

The centerpiece of the film is an attack on

an Allied convoy; the U-boat torpedoes three ships. We share the experience of the hunt; they drift below the surface, waiting for the explosions that signal hits. And then they endure a long and thorough counterattack, during which destroyers criss-cross the area, dropping depth charges. The chase is conducted by sound, the crew whispering beneath the deadly hunters above.

Then comes the episode that was endlessly discussed when the film came out in 1981. Having finally outlasted the destroyers, the sub surfaces to administer a coup de grace—a final torpedo to a burning tanker. As the ship explodes, the captain is startled to see men leaping from its deck: "What are they doing still on board?" he shouts. "Why haven't they been rescued?" Drowning sailors clearly can be seen in the flames from the tanker. They swim toward the U-boat, their pitiful cries for help carrying clearly across the water. The captain orders his boat to reverse at half speed, to keep it away from them. What does he think of having let the victims drown? He does not say. Only one sentence in the ship's log ("assumed no men were on board") gives a hint. It is against the instinct of every sailor to let another sailor drown in the sea. But in war, it is certainly not practical for a submarine to take prisoners. Somehow it is easier when the targets are seen through periscope sights, and the cries of victims cannot be heard.

That scene supplies another example of why it is effective that Das Boot is a German sub. One cannot easily imagine a Hollywood film in which American submariners are shown allowing drowning men to die. The German filmmakers regard their subject dispassionately; it is a record of the way things were.

Wolfgang Petersen's direction is an exercise in pure craftsmanship. The film is constructed mostly out of closeups and cramped two- and three-shots. All of the light sources are made to seem visible (when the lights fail, flashlight beams dance in the darkness). Long, involved shots are constructed with meticulous detail; when a sailor races toward the torpedo room, the reactions from the other men seem exactly right.

The sound adds another dimension. During the destroyer attacks, the boat rocks with explosions and reverberates with desperate cries and commands. During the cat-and-mouse chases, we can hear the sonar pings bouncing off the U-boat's hull. When the boat dives below its rated depth, rivets come loose like rifle bullets. When it appears the boat may be trapped at the bottom of the Straits of Gibraltar, the sailors lie on their hammocks, gasping oxygen like dying men.

Francois Truffaut said it is impossible to make an antiwar film, because films tend to make war look exciting. In general, Truffaut was right. But his theory doesn't extend to *Das Boot.*

Dawn of the Dead

R, 126 m., 1979

With David Emge, Ken Foree, Scott H. Reiniger, and Gaylen Ross. Directed by George A. Romero and produced by Richard P. Rubenstein. Screenplay by Romero.

Dawn of the Dead is one of the best horror films ever made—and, as an inescapable result, one of the most horrifying. It is gruesome, sickening, disgusting, violent, brutal, and appalling. It is also (excuse me for a second while I find my other list) brilliantly crafted, funny, droll, and savagely merciless in its satiric view of the American consumer society. Nobody ever said art had to be in good taste.

It's about a mysterious plague that sweeps the nation, causing the recently dead to rise from their graves and roam the land, driven by an insatiable hunger for living flesh. No explanation is offered for this behavior—indeed, what explanation would suffice?—but there is a moment at which a survivor solemnly intones: "When there is no more room in hell, the dead will walk the Earth."

Who's that a quotation from? From George A. Romero, who wrote and directed *Dawn of the Dead* as a sequel to his *Night of the Living Dead,* which came out in 1968 and now qualifies as a cult classic. If you have seen *Night,* you will recall it as a terrifying horror film punctuated by such shocking images as zombies tearing human flesh from limbs. *Dawn* includes many more scenes like that, more graphic, more shocking, and in color. I am being rather blunt about this because there are many people who will *not* want to see this film. You know who you are. Why are you still reading?

Well . . . maybe because there's a little of the ghoulish voyeur in all of us. We like to be frightened. We like a good creepy thrill. It's just, we say, that we don't want a movie to go *too* far. What's too far? *The Exorcist*? *The Omen*? George Romero deliberately intends to go too far in *Dawn of the Dead*. He's dealing very consciously with the ways in which images can affect us, and if we sit through the film (many people cannot) we make some curious discoveries.

One is that the fates of the zombies, who are destroyed wholesale in all sorts of terrible ways, don't affect us so much after a while. They aren't being killed, after all: They're already dead. They're even a little comic, lurching about a shopping center and trying to plod up the down escalator. Romero teases us with these passages of humor. We relax, we laugh, we see the satire in it all, and then— *pow!* Another disembowelment, just when we were off guard.

His story opens in a chaotic television studio, where idiotic broadcasters are desperately transmitting inaccurate information (one hopes the Emergency Broadcast System will do a whole lot better). National Guard troops storm public housing, where zombies have been reported. There are ten minutes of unrelieved violence, and then the story settles down into the saga of four survivors who hijack a helicopter, land on the roof of a suburban shopping center, and barricade themselves inside against the zombies.

Their eventual fates are not as interesting as their behavior in the meantime; there is nothing quite like a plague of zombies to wonderfully focus your attention on what really matters to you. Romero has his own ideas, too, and the shopping center becomes a brilliant setting for a series of comic and satiric situations: Some low humor, some exquisitely sly.

But, even so, you may be asking, how can I defend this depraved trash? I do not defend it. I praise it. And it is not depraved, although some reviewers have seen it that way. It is *about* depravity. If you can see beyond the immediate impact of Romero's imagery, if you can experience the film as being more than

just its violent extremes, a most unsettling thought may occur to you: The zombies in *Dawn of the Dead* are not the ones who are depraved. They are only acting according to their natures, and, gore dripping from their jaws, are blameless.

The depravity is in the behavior of the healthy survivors, and the true immorality comes as two bands of human survivors fight each other for the shopping center: *Now* look who's fighting over the bones! But *Dawn* is even more complicated than that, because the survivors have courage, too, and a certain nobility at times, and a sense of humor, and loneliness and dread, and are not altogether unlike ourselves. A-ha.

The Day After Trinity

NO MPAA RATING, 88 m., 1980

A documentary produced and directed by Jon Else. Written by David Peoples, Janet Peoples, and Else.

There is a scene in *The Day After Trinity* showing the world's first atomic device being hoisted atop a steel frame tower that looks barely adequate to hold a windmill. The scene is not shot gracefully. The bomb looks like a giant steel basketball with some tubes and wires stuck onto it. In the background, the sky is a washed-out blue. In the next shot, the bomb is back on the ground again and a man is posing next to it, somewhat self-consciously. In 1945, the Russians would have killed for this footage.

On the sound track, the narrator reads sections of a personal diary kept by one of the scientists at Los Alamos, New Mexico, where the government ran its top-secret project to develop the atom bomb: *Gadget is in place . . . should we have the chaplain here?* It is all somewhat banal until, on reflection, it becomes emotionally shattering. The greatest achievement of *The Day After Trinity* is that it counts down those final days before nuclear weapons became a fact of our lives.

This is a documentary that develops more suspense than most of the thrillers I have seen. It includes photographs and film footage from the Los Alamos laboratory, and it begins and ends with the story of J. Robert Oppenheimer, the brilliant scientist who was the "father of the atomic bomb" and then, a few years later, was branded as a security risk by Senator Joseph McCarthy. It includes newsreel footage of World War II, including the devastation of Hiroshima and Nagasaki, and more footage of Oppenheimer after the war and testifying before the McCarthy committee. And there are present-day interviews with some of the scientists who worked at Los Alamos.

All of this is gripping, especially the second thoughts of Oppenheimer and others about the wisdom of dropping the bomb. Of the wisdom of *developing* the bomb there seems to have been no doubt: The bomb was theoretically possible, it was technologically feasible, if we did not build it, the Russians would, and so we built it first, hurrah! Oppenheimer's brother, Frank, remembers that Robert's initial reaction to the first nuclear explosion (the "Trinity" blast) was, "it worked!" It wasn't until after Hiroshima, he says, that it occurred to him that it killed people.

The most riveting sections of the film deal with the establishment of Los Alamos and the weeks and days leading up to the Trinity test. The New Mexico base was a jerry-built collection of temporary housing, muddy streets, 6,000 people, and paranoid secrecy. But it seems to have been a glorious time for the people who were there: It was like a summer camp for Ph.D.s, with Glenn Miller records playing on the jukebox and bright young nuclear whiz kids given the full resources of the government.

Those who were there on the day of Trinity remember that nobody really knew what would happen. One scientist took side bets that New Mexico would be incinerated. In the event, it was just a very big bang. A woman who was driving through the desert with her sister remembers that her sister saw the blast from hundreds of miles away; her sister was blind. Today, physicist Robert Wilson asks himself why he—why *they*—didn't just all walk away from the bomb after they saw what it could do. But of course they did not.

Day for Night

PG, 116 m., 1974

Francois Truffaut (Ferrand), Jean-Pierre Aumont (Alexandre), Jacqueline Bisset (Julie), Jean-Pierre Leaud (Alphonse), Valentina Cortese (Séverine). Directed by Truffaut and produced by Marcel Bébert. Screenplay by Truffaut, Jean-Louis Richard, and Suzanne Shiffman.

Movies about movies usually don't quite get things right. The film business comes out looking more romantic and glamorous (or more corrupt and decadent) than it really is, and none of the human feeling of a movie set is communicated. That is not the case with Francois Truffaut's funny and touching film, *Day for Night*, which is not only the best movie ever made about the movies but is also a great entertainment.

A movie company, especially if it's away from home on a location somewhere, is a family that's been thrown into close and sometimes desperate contact; strangers become friends and even intimates in a few weeks, and in a few more weeks they're scattered to the winds. The family is complicated by the insecurities and egos of the actors, and by the moviemaking process itself: We see the result, but we don't see the hours and days spent on special effects, on stunts, on making it snow or making it rain or making an allegedly trained cat walk from A to B. *Day for Night* is about all of these aspects of moviemaking; about the technical problems, the boredom between takes (a movie set is one of the most boring places on earth most of the time), and about the romances and intrigues. It's real; this is how a movie set really looks, feels, and smells. Truffaut's story involves a movie company on location in Nice. They're making a melodrama called *Meet Pamela*, of which we see enough to know it's doomed at the box office. But good or bad, the movie must be made; Truffaut, who plays the director in his own film, says at one point: "When I begin a film, I want to make a great film. Halfway through, I just hope to finish the film."

His cast includes a beautiful American actress (Jacqueline Bisset); an aging matinee idol (Jean-Pierre Aumont), and his former mistress, also past her prime (Valentina Cortese); the young, lovestruck male lead (Jean-Pierre Leaud), and the entire crew of script girls, camera operators, stunt men, and a henpecked production manager. (And if you have ever wondered what the key grip does in a movie, here's your chance to find out.) Truffaut sets half a dozen stories in motion, and follows them all so effortlessly it's almost as if we're gossiping with him about his colleagues. The movie set is a microcosm: there is a pregnancy and a death; a love affair ended, another begun, and a third almost but not quite destroyed; and new careers to be nourished and old careers to be preserved.

Truffaut was always a master of quiet comedy, and there are fine touches like the aging actress fortifying herself with booze and blaming her lack of memory on her makeup girl. Then there's the young male lead's ill-fated love for Jacqueline Bisset; she is happily married to a doctor, but unwisely extends her sympathy to the youth, who repays her by very nearly destroying her marriage as well as himself. And all the time there is the movie to be made: Truffaut gives us a hilarious session with the "trained" cat, and shows us without making a point of it how snow is produced on a set, how stunt drivers survive car crashes, and how third-floor balconies can exist without buildings below them.

What we see on the screen is nothing at all like what happens on the set—a truth the movie's title reflects. ("Day for night" is the technical term for "night" scenes shot in daylight with a special filter. The movie's original French title, *La Nuit Americaine*, is the French term for the same process—acknowledging their debt to Hollywood.)

The movie is just plain fun. Movie buffs will enjoy it like *Singin' in the Rain* (that perfect musical about the birth of talkies), but you don't have to be a movie buff to like it. Truffaut knows and loves the movies so much it's infectious; one of *Day for Night*'s best scenes is a dream in which the adult director remembers himself, as a little boy, slinking down a darkened street to steal a still from *Citizen Kane* from in front of a theater. We know who the little boy grew up to be, and that explains everything to us about how he feels now.

The Day of the Jackal
PG, 150 m., 1973

Edward Fox (The Jackal), Terence Alexander (Lloyd), Michel Auclair (Colonel Rolland), Alan Badel (The Minister), Tony Britton (Inspector Thomas), Denis Carey (Casson), Olga Georges-Picot (Denise), Cyril Cusack (The Gunsmith). Directed by Fred Zinnemann and produced by John Woolf. Screenplay by Kenneth Ross, based on the book by Frederick Forsyth.

Fred Zinnemann's *The Day of the Jackal* is one hell of an exciting movie. I wasn't prepared for how good it really is: it's not just a suspense classic, but a beautifully executed example of filmmaking. It's put together like a fine watch. The screenplay meticulously assembles an incredible array of material, and then Zinnemann choreographs it so that the story—complicated as it is—unfolds in almost documentary starkness.

The "jackal" of the title is the code name for a man who may (or may not) be a British citizen specializing in professional assassinations. He allegedly killed Trujillo of the Dominican Republic in 1961 and, now, two years later, he has been hired by a group of Frenchmen who want de Gaulle assassinated. His price is $500,000; he says, "and considering that I'm handing you France, I wouldn't call that expensive."

Zinnemann, working from Frederick Forsyth's bestseller, tells both sides of the story that unfolds during the summer of 1963. The jackal prepares two disguises and three identities, gets a legal passport by applying in the name of a child who died in 1931, and calls on European experts for his materials. An old gunsmith handmakes a weird-looking lightweight rifle with silencer, sniper scope, and explosive bullets. A forger provides French identity papers and a driver's license (and comes to an unexpected end). And then the jackal enters France.

Meanwhile, the government has received information that an attempt will be made on de Gaulle's life. The general absolutely insists that he will make no changes in his public schedule, and that any attempt to prevent an assassination must be made in secret. The French police cooperate "unofficially" with the top police forces of other nations in attempting an apprehension. But they don't even know who the jackal is.

How can they stop him? The movie provides a fascinating record of police investigative work, which combines exhaustive checking with intuition. But the jackal is clever, too, particularly when he's cornered. Some of the movie's finest moments come after the jackal's false identity is discovered and his license plates and description are distributed. He keeps running—and always convincingly; this isn't a movie about a killer with luck, but about one of uncommon intelligence and nerve.

Playing the jackal, Edward Fox is excellent. The movie doesn't provide much chance for a deep characterization, but he projects a most convincing persona. He's boyishly charming, impeccably groomed, possessed of an easy laugh, and casually ruthless. He will kill if there's the slightest need to. Fox's performance is crucial to the film, of course, and the way he carries it off is impressive.

The others on the case are uniformly excellent, especially Tony Britton as a harried police inspector and Cyril Cusack, in a nicely crafted little vignette, as the gunsmith. The movie's technical values (as is always the case with a Zinnemann film) are impeccable. The movie was filmed at great cost all over Europe, mostly on location, and it looks it. A production of this scope needs to appear absolutely convincing, and Zinnemann has mastered every detail—including the casting of a perfect de Gaulle look-alike.

The Day of the Jackal is two and a half hours long and seems over in about fifteen minutes. There are some words you hesitate to use in a review, because they sound so much like advertising copy, but in this case I can truthfully say that the movie is spellbinding.

Days of Heaven

PG, 95 m., 1978

Richard Gere (Bill), Brooke Adams (Abby), Sam Shepard (The Farmer), Linda Manz (Linda), Robert Wilke (Foreman), Jackie Shultis (Linda's Friend), Stuart Margolin (Mill Foreman). Directed by Terence Malick and produced by Bert and Harold Schneider. Screenplay by Malick.

Can any description of Terence Malick's *Days of Heaven* quite evoke the sense of wonder this film inspires? It's about a handful of people who find themselves shipwrecked in the middle of the Texas Panhandle—grain country—sometime before World War I. They involve themselves in a tragic love triangle, but their secrets seem insignificant, almost pathetic, seen against the awesome size of their world. Our wonder is that they endure at all in the face of the implacable land.

The land is farmed by a sick young man (Sam Shepard) who is widely believed to be on the edge of death. In the autumn, he and his foreman hire crews of itinerant laborers who ride out from the big cities on the tops of boxcars: swaggering, anonymous men who will follow the harvest north from Texas to Canada. Others pass through to entertain them and live off their brief periods of wage earning: aerial barnstormers, circus troupes, all specks on the great landscape.

We meet three people who set out together from the grime of Chicago, looking for harvest work: A strong young man (Richard Gere), his kid sister (Linda Manz), and the woman he lives with and also claims, for convenience, as his sister (Brooke Adams). They arrive at the farm of the sick young man, who falls in love with the older "sister."

Because they are so poor, because the farmer has a house, land, and money, the three keep quiet about his mistake and eventually the farmer and the "sister" marry. Her "brother"—her man—works on the farm and observes the marriage from a resentful, festering distance. The younger girl also observes, and the film's narration comes from her comments, deeply cynical, pathetically understated.

So goes the story of *Days of Heaven*, except that Malick's film doesn't really tell a story at all. It is an evocation of emptiness, loneliness, desolation, the slow accumulation of despair in a land too large for its inhabitants and blind to their dreams. Willa Cather wrote novels about such feelings—*The Lost Lady, Death Comes for the Archbishop,* the middle section of *The Professor's House*—and now Malick joins her company. This is a huge land we occupy. The first people to settle it must have wondered if they could ever really possess it.

Malick's vision of the land, indeed, is so sweeping that an ordinary, human-scale "story" in the foreground would be a distraction. We get a series of scenes, like tableaux, as the characters involve themselves in their mutual tragedy. The visual compositions often place them against vast backdrops (this is one of the most beautifully photographed films ever made), but Malick finds terror, too, in extreme close-ups of grasshoppers, of a germinating seed, of the little secrets with which nature ultimately builds her infinite secret.

When it develops that the girl has really fallen in love with her new husband, that she is not a con artist but just another victim, we might expect, in another movie, all sorts of blame and analysis. A director not sure of this material could have talked it away. But Malick brings a solemnity to his revelations, as the farmer gradually discovers the deception, as the laborer discovers his loss, as the little sister loses what little childhood she had.

Days of Heaven is a unique achievement—I can't think of another film anything like it. It's serious, yes, very solemn, but not depressing. More than anything else, it wants to re-create its time and place, as if Malick believes the decisions of his characters (and maybe his very characters themselves) come out of the time and place, and are caused by them.

So many movies are jammed with people talking to each other all the time, people obsessed with the conviction they're saying something. The people of *Days of Heaven* are so overwhelmed by the sheer force of nature, by the weight of the land, the bounty of the harvest, the casual distraction of fire and plague, the sharp, involuntary impulses of their passions, that they hardly know what to say. When you look at it that way, who does?

Dead Again

R, 107 m., 1991

Kenneth Branagh (Church/Strauss), Emma Thompson (Grace/Margaret), Andy Garcia (Gray Baker), Derek Jacobi (Madson), Hanna Schygulla (Inga). Directed by Branagh and produced by Charles H. Maguire. Screenplay by Scott Frank.

Dead Again is like *Ghost* for people who grew up on movies that were not afraid of grand gestures. This is a romance with all the stops out, a story about intrigue, deception, and bloody murder—and about how the secrets of the present are unraveled through a hypnotic trance that reveals the secrets of the past. I am

a particular pushover for movies like this, movies that could go on the same list with *Rebecca, Wuthering Heights,* or *Vertigo.*

Murder! screams the first word on the screen. Headlines tell of a Hollywood scandal in the 1940s involving the death of the beautiful young wife of a European composer. We cut to the present day. The musical score by Patrick Doyle is ominous and insinuating. We see a threatening old Gothic mansion, we meet a cynical private eye, there is a beautiful woman who has lost her memory, a devious hypnotist who wants to regress her in a search for clues. And of course the murder in the 1940s holds the clue to the woman's amnesia.

Dead Again is Kenneth Branagh once again demonstrating that he has a natural flair for bold theatrical gesture. If *Henry V,* the first film he directed and starred in, caused people to compare him with Olivier, *Dead Again* will inspire comparisons with Welles and Hitchcock—and the Olivier of Hitchcock's *Rebecca.* I do not suggest Branagh is already as great a director as Welles and Hitchcock, although he has a good start in that direction. What I mean is that his spirit, his daring, is in the same league. He is not interested in making timid movies.

This film is made of Grand Guignol setting and mood, music and bold stylized camera angles, coincidence and shock, melodrama and romance. And it is also suffused with a strange, infectious humor; Branagh plays it dead seriously, but sees that it is funny. Consider, for example, the character of Madson (Derek Jacobi), the old antiques dealer who dabbles in hypnotism on the side. As he regresses his clients in a search for the details of their earlier lives, he has a little sideline, autosuggesting that they keep a lookout for any interesting antiques they see along the way, so that he can track them down and snap them up cheap.

The movie stars Branagh and his wife, Emma Thompson, in dual roles. In the present day, they are Church, a detective specializing in tracking down missing heirs, and Grace, a young woman who has lost her memory. In black-and-white flashbacks to the lush Hollywood of the postwar 1940s, they are Strauss, a composer who fled from Hitler and is now the toast of Los Angeles, and Margaret,

Strauss's beautiful new wife. Lurking in the background of the Hollywood marriage is Inga, the sinister German maid (Hanna Schygulla), and her little boy. Inga is forever lurking on a stair landing, eavesdropping on conversations while painful emotions churn in her memories.

Margaret, the new bride, is not happy with the ominous Inga lurking in the shadows, but Strauss cannot dismiss her because she did, after all, save him from Hitler and deliver him safely to America. But if Margaret is jealous of Inga, Strauss is jealous, too—of Gray Baker (Andy Garcia), the sleek, darkly handsome newspaper reporter who falls for Margaret on the day of her wedding to the older man. Are they having an affair? Can Strauss trust her?

The plot shuttles back and forth between past and present, as the sins of one generation are visited on the next. The dual roles are a way of suggesting that the uneasy spirits of the 1940s characters might have found new hosts in the present to resolve their profound psychic unease. And the old hypnotist, established in the baroque shadows of his cluttered antique shop, may hold the key to everything (the photography here is right out of *The Third Man*).

The screenplay, by Scott Frank, is oldfashioned (if you will allow that to be a high compliment). It takes grand themes—murder, passion, reincarnation—and plays them at full volume. Yet there is room for wit, for turns of phrase, for subtle little sardonic touches, for the style that transforms plot into feeling. Kenneth Branagh's direction, here as in *Henry V* (1989), shows a flair for the memorable gesture, for theatricality, for slamming the screen with a stark emotional image and then circling it with suspicions of corruption. When his characters kiss, we do not feel they do so merely to give or receive sexual pleasure; no, they are swept into each other's arms by a great passionate tidal force greater than either one of them, a compulsion from outside of time. You get the idea.

Dead Man Walking
R, 122 m., 1996

Susan Sarandon (Sister Helen Prejean), Sean Penn (Matthew Poncelet), Robert Prosky (Hilton Barber), Raymond J. Barry (Earl Delacroix), R. Lee Ermey (Clyde Percy), Celia Weston (Mary Beth Percy), Scott Wilson (Prison Chaplain). Directed by Tim Robbins and produced by Jon Kilik, Robbins, and Rudd Simmons. Screenplay by Robbins, based on the book by Prejean.

After seeing *Dead Man Walking*, I paused outside the screening to jot a final line on my notes: "This film ennobles filmmaking." That is exactly what it does. It demonstrates how a film can confront a grave and controversial issue in our society, see it fairly from all sides and not take any shortcuts, and move the audience to a great emotional experience without unfair manipulation. What is remarkable is that the film is also all the other things a movie should be: absorbing, surprising, technically superb, and worth talking about for a long time afterward.

The movie begins with a Louisiana nun, Helen Prejean (Susan Sarandon), who works in an inner-city neighborhood. One day she receives a letter from an inmate on death row, asking her to visit him. So she visits him. The prison chaplain (Scott Wilson) doesn't think much of her visit, and briefs her on the ways that prisoners can manipulate outsiders. He obviously thinks of her as a bleeding heart. Her answer is unadorned: "He wrote to me and asked me to come."

The inmate, named Matthew Poncelet (Sean Penn), has been convicted along with another man of participating in the rape and murder of two young people on a lover's lane. We see him first through the grating of a visitor's pen, so that his face breaks into jigsaw pieces. In looks and appearance he is the kind of person you would instinctively dread: He has the mousy little goatee and elaborate pompadour of a man with deep misgivings about his face. His voice is halting and his speech is ignorant. He smokes a cigarette as if sneaking puffs in a grade school washroom. He tells her, "They got me on a greased rail to the Death House here."

He wants her to help with his appeal. At one point, he mentions that they don't have anything in common. Sister Helen thinks about that and says, "You and I have something in common. We both live with the poor." His face looks quietly stunned, as if for the first time in a long time he has been confronted with an insight about his life that is not solely ego-driven. She says she will come to see him again, and that she will help him file a last-minute appeal against his approaching execution.

Sister Helen, as played here by Sarandon and written and directed by Tim Robbins (from the memoir by the real Helen Prejean), is one of the few truly spiritual characters I have seen in the movies. Movies about "religion" are often only that—movies about secular organizations that deal in spirituality. It is so rare to find a movie character who truly does try to live according to the teachings of Jesus (or anyone else, for that matter) that it's a little disorienting: This character will behave according to what she thinks is right, not according to the needs of a plot, the requirements of a formula, or the pieties of those for whom religion, good grooming, polite manners, and prosperity are all more or less the same thing.

But wait. The film is not finished with its bravery. At this point in any conventional story, we would expect developments along familiar lines. Take your choice: (1) The prisoner is really innocent, and Sister Helen leads his eleventh-hour defense as justice is done; (2) they fall in love with one another, she helps him escape, and they go on a doomed flight from the law; or, less likely (3) she converts him to her religion, and he goes to his death praising Jesus.

None of these things happen. Instead, Sister Helen experiences all of the complexities, contradictions, and hard truths of the situation, and we share them. In movies like this you rarely see the loved ones of the victims, unless they are presented in hate-filled caricatures of blood lust. Here it is not like that. Sister Helen meets the parents of the dead girl and the father of the dead boy. (The father is seen among packing cases—moving, after a separation from his wife, who felt it was time for them to "get on with their lives," which he can never do.) She begins to understand that Matthew may indeed have been guilty. She has to face the anger of the parents, who cannot see why anyone would want to befriend a murderer ("Are you a Communist?"). There is a scene of agonizing embarrassment, as the girl's parents make a basic mistake about her motives for visiting them.

And there is more. Matthew, we come to realize, is the product of an impoverished cultural background. He has been supplied with only a few clichés to serve him as a philosophy: He believes in "taking things like a man," and "showing people," and there on death row he even makes a play for Sister Helen, almost as a reflex. "Death is breathing down your neck," she tells him, "and you're playing your little man-on-the-make games." He parrots a racist statement from his prison buddies in the Aryan Nation, which does his case no good, and later, when he bitterly resents his stupidity in saying those things, we realize he didn't even think about them; nature abhors a vacuum, and racism abhors an empty mind and pours in to fill it.

The movie comes down to a drama of an entirely unexpected kind: a spiritual drama, involving Matthew's soul. Christianity teaches that all sin can be forgiven, and that no sinner is too low for God's love. Sister Helen believes that. Truly believes it, with every atom of her being. And yet she does not press Matthew for a "religious" solution to his situation. What she hopes for is that he can go to his death in reconciliation with himself and his crime. The last half-hour of this movie is overwhelmingly powerful—not least in Matthew's strained eleventh-hour visit with his family, where we see them all trapped in the threadbare clichés of a language learned from television shows and saloon jukeboxes.

The performances in this film are beyond comparison, which is to say that Sarandon and Penn find their characters and make them into exactly what they are without reference to other movies or conventions. Penn proves again that he is the most powerful actor of his generation, and as for Sarandon—in film after film, she finds not the right technique for a character so much as the right humanity. It's as if she creates a role out of a deep understanding of the person she is playing.

Tim Robbins, Sarandon's longtime companion, has directed once before (*Bob Roberts*, an intelligent political drama). With this film, he leaps far beyond his earlier work and makes that very rare thing, a film that is an exercise of philosophy. This is the kind of movie that spoils us for other films because it reveals so starkly how most movies fall into conventional routine and lull us with the reassurance that they will not look too hard, or probe too deeply, or make us think beyond the boundaries of what is comfortable. For years, critics of the movies have asked for more films that deal, say, with the spiritual side of life. I doubt if *Dead Man Walking* was what they were thinking of, but this is exactly how such a movie looks and feels.

Dear America: Letters Home from Vietnam

PG-13, 86 m., 1988

Directed by Bill Couturie and produced by the Couturie Co. and Vietnam Veterans Ensemble Theater Company. Screenplay by Richard Dewhurst and Couturie.

Surf's up, and the Beach Boys are singing. American kids dive into the waves and come up wet and grinning, and there's a cooler of beer waiting under the palm trees. It looks like Vietnam is going to be a fun place. The opening scenes of *Dear America: Letters Home from Vietnam* are so carefree, so lighthearted, that it doesn't even seem strange that most of the soldiers look exactly like the kids they are—high school graduates drafted straight into war.

On the sound track, we hear the voices of these soldiers, in the words they wrote home. They speak of patriotism, of confidence, of new friendships. In their letters there is a sense of wonder at this new world they have found, a world so different from the American cities and towns they left behind. And then gradually the tone of their letters begins to change.

There have been several great movies about Vietnam. This is the one that completes the story, that has no plot except that thousands of young men went to a faraway country and had unspeakable experiences there, and many of them died or were wounded for life in body or soul. This movie is so powerful precisely because it is so simple—the words are the words of the soldiers themselves, and the images are taken from their own home movies, and from TV news footage of the war.

There are moments here that cannot be forgotten, and most of them are due to the hard work of the filmmaker, director Bill Couturie, who has not taken just any words and any old footage, but precisely the right words to go with the images. Couturie began with an anthology of letters written home by U.S. soldiers in Vietnam. Then he screened the *entire* archive of TV news footage shot by NBC-TV from 1967 to 1969—two million feet of film totaling 926 hours. He also gained access to footage from the Department of Defense, including previously classified film of action under fire. Much of the footage in this film has never been seen publicly before, and watching it, you know why.

What Couturie and his researchers have done is amazing. In many cases, they have matched up individual soldiers with their letters—we see them as we hear their words, and then we discover their fates. "I tell you truthfully I doubt if I'll come out of this alive," a private named Raymond Griffiths writes home to his girlfriend. "In my original squad, I'm the only one left unharmed." He died in action on the Fourth of July, 1966.

There are amateur 8-mm home movies here, of GIs clowning in front of the camera, and cracking beers, and cleaning their weapons. There are frightening firefights, and unflinching shots of men in the process of dying. And there are chilling scenes such as the one when General William Westmoreland greets the survivors from a bloodbath, and his words are the words of an automaton, with utterly no emotion in his voice as he "chats" with his troops. He is so false, it seems like a bad performance. If this footage had been shown on TV at the time, he might have been forced to resign.

The movie follows a chronology that roughly corresponds to a soldier's year in Vietnam. From the first days of swimming in the surf to the last exhausted days of fear and despair, it never looks away. And the words of the soldiers have the eloquence of simple truth. One soldier writes of the bravery of men who rescued their comrades under enemy fire. Another writes of a momentary hush in a tank battle on Christmas Eve, and of hearing someone begin to sing "Silent Night" and others joining in.

The words in the letters are read by some forty different actors and actresses, whose voices you can sometimes identify, until you stop thinking in those terms. The voices include Robert De Niro, Martin and Charlie Sheen, Kathleen Turner, Tom Berenger, Brian Dennehy, Howard Rollins, Jr., Sean Penn, Matt Dillon, Michael J. Fox. The music on the sound track is all from the period, and then, at the end of the movie, there is a heartbreaking flash-forward to the Vietnam War Memorial in Washington fifteen years later, and we hear Bruce Springsteen's "Born in the USA" as Ellen Burstyn reads from a letter that the mother of a dead veteran left at the foot of the wall of names:

"Dear Bill, Today is February 13, 1984. I came to this black wall again to see and touch your name, William R. Stocks, and as I do I wonder if anyone ever stops to realize that next to your name, on this black wall, is your mother's heart. A heart-broken fifteen years ago today, when you lost your life in Vietnam.

"They tell me the letters I write to you and leave here at this memorial are waking others up to the fact that there is still much pain left, after all these years, from the Vietnam War.

"This I know. I would rather have had you for twenty-one years, and all the pain that goes with losing you, than never to have had you at all. Mom."

Choose any film as the best movie ever made about Vietnam, and this is the other half of the same double feature. Francois Truffaut once wrote that it was impossible to make an "antiwar film," because any war film, no matter what its message, was sure to be exhilarating. He did not live to see this film.

The Death of Mr. Lazarescu

R, 154 m., 2006

Ion Fiscuteanu (Mr. Lazarescu), Luminita Gheorghiu (Mioara Avram), Gabriel Spahiu (Leo), Doru Ana (Sandu Sterian), Dana Dogaru (Miki Sterian), Florin Zamfirescu (Dr. Ardelean), Mimi Branescu (Dr. Mirica). Directed by Cristi Puiu and produced by Alexandru Munteanu. Screenplay by Puiu and Razvan Radulescu.

It must be like this with many people, and not just in Romania. A smelly old drunk calls for an ambulance after having a headache for four days. The ambulance service asks him so many questions, he doubts they believe him, and he asks his neighbors for help. They stretch him out on a sofa, ask him how he feels, and complain about the stink of his cats. They call the ambulance again.

The Death of Mr. Lazarescu will follow this dying man for most of the night, as he gradually slips away from the world and the world

little notices. The movie is not heartless, but it is matter-of-fact and makes no attempt to heighten the drama. In its relentless gaze at exactly what happens, it reminds me of the Dardenne brothers *(The Son, The Child)*, whose films see everything but do not intervene.

Mr. Lazarescu (Ion Fiscuteanu) has long lived in his cluttered Bucharest apartment. He has a sister in a nearby town and a child in Canada, neither much concerned with him. He gives such information to his neighbors, while slowly drifting out of contact with reality. Then the ambulance arrives, with the attendant Mioara (Luminita Gheorghiu) and the driver Leo (Gabriel Spahiu). In the course of this night, they will take him to four hospitals. It is a long night and a long film, but not a slow one because we are drawn so deeply into it.

At hospitals, the obviously incompetent Mr. Lazarescu is asked to fill out forms, sign consents, and answer questions he does not understand. Each hospital suggests sending him to another one. He is nevertheless given a scan that reveals a blood clot on his brain, and a problem with his liver that "nobody," a doctor observes, "is going to be able to do anything about." One of the CT scan technicians almost rejoices: "These neoplasms are Discovery Channel stuff!"

The film's focus is never on Mr. Lazarescu, who becomes disoriented and finally almost speechless, and who was probably not good company on his best days. It does not help that he wets himself during a CT scan, then soils his pants. We focus on the ambulance attendant, who is given one opportunity after another to dump her patient but stubbornly wants to be sure someone actually pays him attention. Her job is to take sick people to hospitals. If they are not admitted, her life is meaningless.

She is not portrayed as a heroine and indeed is passive in the face of sarcasm by a smart-ass resident who mocks her description of Mr. Lazarescu's problems. She knows that what he needs immediately is brain surgery to relieve the clot. One doctor who agrees with this diagnosis nevertheless insists on a signature of consent: "If I operate without his signature, I could go to jail." The doctor's solution is a perfect catch-22: "Drive him for a while until he's comatose and then bring him back."

At the fourth hospital, Mioara finds a doctor who is just ending her shift but wearily agrees to take the patient. And only then can Mioara leave—and disappear from the film because we follow the dying body of Mr. Lazarescu through the hands of all these strangers who have only an immediate role in his final day. Even in the first three hospitals, he has continued to wear his ratty stocking cap and threadbare knit sweater. Now at last he is undressed and bathed, the nurses sponging him and shaving his head with quiet professionalism.

The film, directed and cowritten by Cristi Puiu, has been described as a criticism of the health services in Romania. At least in Romania he is not asked for his insurance company, and he has a theoretical right to free medical care. On Cinematical.com, a doctor posted this message: "As a Romanian physician, I would say it's worse than shown. The misery of Romanian hospitals is not shown at all. By the way, this is based on a true story of a man turned down at five Bucharest hospitals in 1997 and eventually left in the street by the paramedics and found dead next morning (the paramedic got fired)."

There is no need to fire Mioara and her driver, although in the film's final shot we wonder whether Mr. Lazarescu is still alive. I have undergone various medical adventures in recent years and have been moved by the unfailing competence and care of the doctors and nurses I have come into contact with; I admire them even more because I sense this movie is accurate about many hospitals everywhere, in which everyone is overworked, there are more problems than solutions, and the smelly, incoherent Mr. Lazarescu seems doomed no matter what is done. He is not a candidate for triage.

I keep thinking about Mioara. She is insulted by young residents whose experience is far less than hers. She carries Mr. Lazarescu's X-rays around with her from one set of uncaring eyes to another. She could get angry, but she has been on the job too long for that. They all have. Here are no E.R.-style interns calling for transfusions or racing down corridors with gurneys. In *The Death of Mr. Lazarescu,* the patient is another detail in an endless series of impossible situations and exhausting overnight shifts. If you start thinking of Lazarescu, of all the Lazarescus, as people who deserve your full concern and attention, you could go mad. Yes, the doctors and nurses chat about getting an espresso or using each other's cell phones. Life goes on.

There is a rule about the movies: Never take an expert to a movie about his or her specialty. *The Death of Mr. Lazarescu* is an exception. I suspect medical professionals would see much they recognize in this movie. The credits include a long list of technical advisers, but it doesn't take an adviser to convince you the movie is authentic. Like *United 93* and the work of the Dardenne brothers, it lives entirely in the moment, seeing what happens as it happens, drawing no conclusions, making no speeches, creating no artificial dramatic conflicts, just showing people living one moment after another, as they must.

Note: The man's full name is Dante Remus Lazarescu. Dante wrote of the circles of hell. Remus was a cofounder of ancient Rome, killed by his twin. "Lazarescu" reminds us of Lazarus, who was lucky enough to find someone who could raise him from the dead.

The Deer Hunter
R, 183 m., 1978

Robert De Niro (Michael), John Cazale (Stan), John Savage (Steven), Christopher Walken (Nick), Meryl Streep (Linda), George Dzundza (John), Chuck Aspegren (Axel). Directed by Michael Cimino and produced by Barry Spikings, Michael Deeley, Cimino, and John Peverall. Screenplay by Deric Washburn.

Michael Cimino's *The Deer Hunter* is a three-hour movie in three major movements. It is a progression from a wedding to a funeral. It is the story of a group of friends. It is the record of how the war in Vietnam entered several lives and altered them terribly forever. It is not an antiwar film. It is not a pro-war film. It is one of the most emotionally shattering films ever made.

It begins with men at work, at the furnaces of the steel mills in a town somewhere in Ohio or Pennsylvania. The klaxon sounds, the shift is over, the men go down the road to a saloon for a beer. They sing "I Love You *Bay*-bee" along with the jukebox. It is still morning on the last day of their lives that will belong to them before Vietnam.

The movie takes its time with these opening scenes, with the steel mill and the saloon and especially with the wedding and the party in the American Legion Hall. It's important not simply that we come to know the characters, but that we feel absorbed into their lives, that the wedding rituals and rhythms feel like more than just ethnic details. They do.

The opening moment is lingered over; it's like the wedding celebration in *The Godfather,* but celebrated by hard-working people who have come to eat, dance, and drink a lot and wish luck to the newlyweds and to say good-bye to the three young men who have enlisted in the army. The party goes on long enough for everyone to get drunk who is ever going to, and then the newlyweds drive off and the rest of the friends go up into the mountains to shoot some deer. There is some Hemingwayesque talk about what it means to shoot deer: We are still at a point where shooting something is supposed to mean something.

Then Vietnam occupies the screen, suddenly, with a wall of noise, and the second movement of the film is about the experiences that three of the friends (Robert De Niro, John Savage, and Christopher Walken) have there. At the film's center comes one of the most horrifying sequences ever created in fiction, as the three are taken prisoner and forced to play Russian roulette while their captors gamble on who will, or will not, blow out his brains.

The game of Russian roulette becomes the organizing symbol of the film: Anything you can believe about the game, about its deliberately random violence, about how it touches the sanity of men forced to play it, will apply to the war as a whole. It is a brilliant symbol because, in the context of this story, it makes any ideological statement about the war superfluous.

The De Niro character is the one who somehow finds the strength to keep going and to keep Savage and Walken going. He survives the prison camp and helps the others. Then, finally home from Vietnam, he is surrounded by a silence we can never quite penetrate. He is touched vaguely by desire for the girl that more than one of them left behind, but does not act decisively. He is a "hero," greeted shyly, awkwardly, by the hometown people.

He delays for a long time going to the VA hospital to visit Savage, who has lost his legs. While he is there he learns that Walken is still in Vietnam. He had promised Walken—on a drunken moonlit night under a basketball hoop on a playlot, the night of the wedding—that he would never leave him in Vietnam. They were both thinking, romantically and naively, of the deaths of heroes, but now De Niro goes back in an altogether different context to retrieve the living Walken. The promise was adolescent stuff, but there is no adolescence left when De Niro finds Walken still in Saigon, playing Russian roulette professionally.

At about this point in a review it is customary to praise or criticize those parts of a film that seem deserving: the actors, the photography, the director's handling of the material. It should be said, I suppose, that *The Deer Hunter* is far from flawless, that there are moments when its characters do not behave convincingly, such as implausible details involving Walken's stay and fate in Vietnam, and unnecessary ambiguities in the De Niro character. It can also be said that the film contains greatly moving performances, and that it is the most impressing blending of "box office" and "art" in American movies since *Bonnie and Clyde, The Godfather,* and *Nashville.* All of those kinds of observations will become irrelevant as you experience the film: It gathers you up, it takes you along, it doesn't let up.

The Deer Hunter is said to be about many subjects: About male bonding, about mindless patriotism, about the dehumanizing effects of war, about Nixon's "silent majority." It is about any of those things that you choose, if you choose, but more than anything else it is a heartbreakingly effective fictional machine that evokes the agony of the Vietnam time.

If it is not overtly "anti-war," why should it be? What *The Deer Hunter* insists is that we not *forget* the war. It ends on a curious note: The singing of "God Bless America." I won't tell you how it arrives at that particular moment (the unfolding of the final passages should occur to you as events in life) but I do want to observe that the lyrics of "God Bless America" have never before seemed to me to contain such an infinity of possible meanings, some tragic, some unspeakably sad, some few still defiantly hopeful.

A Delicate Balance

PG, 132 m., 1973

Katharine Hepburn (Agnes), Paul Scofield (Tobias), Lee Remick (Julia), Kate Reid (Claire), Joseph Cotten (Harry), Betsy Blair (Edna). Directed by Tony Richardson and produced by Ely A. Landau. Screenplay by Edward Albee based on his play.

A Delicate Balance is a play about a family in which that balance has been clung to precariously for too many years. It's a family of four: Tobias, the patriarch, who has constructed a respectable middle-class shell around his empty interior; Agnes, his wife, who skippers the family ship on its aimless voyage; Julia, their daughter, who has climbed back on board after the failure of her fourth marriage; and Claire, Agnes's sister, who mocks the whole arrangement between her frequent trips to the bar. It's a family like many others, held together by habit and shared memories and made bearable by the anesthesia of a great many very-dry martinis.

Enter Harry and Edna, the very best friends of Tobias and Agnes. They haven't come to visit; they've come to live. They were sitting at home, Harry explains, and he was reading a book and Edna was doing her needlepoint, when suddenly they were filled with a vast, nameless terror. Afraid to death, they have come for shelter and protection. Agnes, the dutiful host, gives them Julia's room and they go upstairs. And then a terrible night and morning of self-examination begins. What Edward Albee achieved with his 1967 Pulitzer Prize play almost defies description because (unlike the generation of playwrights that preceded him) he isn't interested in explanations or messages. We leave his play filled with emotions but without words for it; he's shown us how his family feels and suggested why, but he's left them in more trouble than they began with. Before, they were only sterile and unhappy. Now they know that they are.

The American Film Theater engaged Tony Richardson to make the play into a movie, and he has delivered with a fine, tough, lacerating production. It's suitable that *A Delicate Balance* follows Harold Pinter's *The Homecoming* in the AFT series, because both involve similar situations, settings, and lengths of time. The difference is in the light-years of style that separate the visions of Pinter and Albee. Both probe unspeakable psychic depths, but Pinter stylizes more visibly; Albee sometimes seems to be simply recording a family history. The only problem with his families is that they always seem to have something moaning and snuffling at the bottom of the garden.

Richardson's cast could hardly be better. I suppose Katharine Hepburn and Paul Scofield will get the most notice for their Agnes and Tobias, and that's as it should be: The tightrope-balancing act is theirs, and when we leave them they're working without a net. But the supporting performances are what really make the play work. Joseph Cotten, whose acting ability hasn't been adequately used in the movies lately, is stunning as Harry; he describes the sudden terror that visited him, and we taste it. Kate Reid, who plays the alcoholic Claire, also contributes a finely realized performance; even when she's not on we sense her hovering off screen and waiting for everyone to stop talking so she can suggest another little drinkie-poo. Some percentage of the AFT subscriber list no doubt must be not unlike Agnes and Tobias, and it's a tribute to this production that they may possibly wish they hadn't seen it.

Note: American Film Theater was the brainchild of producer Ely Landau in the early 1970s—a subscription-based program of great plays turned into films by prominent directors and casts. Among the AFT productions (released on DVD) are Albee's A Delicate Balance, *Eugene O'Neill's* The Iceman Cometh *(directed by John Frankenheimer and starring Lee Marvin, Fredrich March, Robert Ryan, and Jeff Bridges), Harold Pinter's* The Homecoming *(directed by Peter Hall and starring Cyril Cusack and Ian Holm), Eugene Ionesco's* Rhinoceros *(directed by Tom O'Horgan and starring Gene Wilder, Zero Mostel, and Karen Black), and Chekhov's* Three Sisters *(directed by Laurence Olivier and starring Joan Plowright and Alan Bates).*

The Departed

R, 151 m., 2006

Leonardo DiCaprio (Billy Costigan), Matt Damon (Colin Sullivan), Jack Nicholson (Frank Costello), Mark Wahlberg (Sean Dignam), Martin Sheen (Oliver Queenan), Ray Winstone (Mr. French), Vera Farmiga (Madolyn Madden), Anthony Anderson (Brown), Alec Baldwin (George Ellerby). Directed by Martin Scorsese and produced by Brad Pitt, Brad Grey, and Graham King. Screenplay by William Monahan.

Most of Martin Scorsese's films have been about men trying to realize their inner image of themselves. That's as true of Travis Bickle as of Jake LaMotta, Rupert Pupkin, Howard Hughes, the Dalai Lama, Bob Dylan, or, for that matter, Jesus Christ. *The Departed* is about two men trying to live public lives that are the radical opposites of their inner realities. Their attempts threaten to destroy them, either by implosion or fatal betrayal. The telling of their stories involves a moral labyrinth, in which good and evil wear each other's masks.

The story is inspired by *Infernal Affairs* (2002) by Alan Mak and Andrew Lau, the most successful Hong Kong film of recent years. Indeed, having just reread my 2004 review of that film, I find I could change the names, cut and paste it, and be discussing this film. But that would only involve the surface, the plot, and a few philosophical quasi-profundities. What makes this a Scorsese film, and not merely a retread, is the director's use of actors, locations, and energy—and its buried theme. I am fond of saying that a movie is not about what it's about; it's about how it's about it. That's always true of a Scorsese film.

This one, a cops-and-gangster picture set in Boston rather than, say, New York or Vegas, begins with a soda fountain scene that would be at home in *GoodFellas*. What is deliberately missing, however, is the initial joy of that film. Instead of a kid who dreamed of growing up to be a mobster, we have two kids who grow up as imposters: One becomes a cop who goes undercover as a gangster, and the other becomes a gangster who goes undercover as a cop.

Leonardo DiCaprio and Matt Damon star. Damon is Colin Sullivan, the kid spotted in that soda fountain by mob boss Frank Costello (Jack Nicholson). He enlists in the state police after Costello hand-picks him so many years before as a promising spy. DiCaprio is Billy Costigan, an ace police cadet who is sent undercover by Captain Queenan (Martin Sheen) to infiltrate Costello's gang. Both men succeed with their fraudulent identities; Colin rises in the force, and Billy rises in the mob.

The story's tension, which is considerable, depends on human nature. After several years, both men come to identify with, and desire the approval of, the men they are deceiving. This may be a variant of the Stockholm Syndrome; for that matter, we see it all the time in politicians who consider themselves public servants even though they are thieves. If you are going to be a convincing gangster, you have to be prepared to commit crimes. If a convincing cop, you have to be prepared to bust bad guys, even some you know. Protect your real employers and you look fishy. *The Departed* turns the screw one more time because each man is known to only one or a few of the men on the side he's working for. If Billy's employer, Capt. Queenan, gets killed, who can testify that Billy is really a cop?

Ingenious additional layers of this double-blind are added by the modern devices of cell phones and computers. When the paths of the two undercover men cross, as they must, will they eventually end up on either end of the same phone call? And when the cops suspect they have an informer in their midst, what if they assign the informer to find himself? The traps and betrayals of the undercover life are dramatized in one of my favorite moments, when one of the characters is told, "I gave you the wrong address. But you went to the right one."

Although many of the plot devices are similar in Scorsese's film and the Hong Kong "original," this is Scorsese's film all the way, because of his understanding of the central subject of so much of his work: guilt. It is reasonable to assume that Boston working-class men named Costigan, Sullivan, Costello, Dignam, and Queenan were raised as Irish-American Catholics, and that if they have moved outside the church's laws they have nevertheless not freed themselves of a sense of guilt. The much-married Scorsese once told me that he thought he would go to hell for violating the church's rules on marriage and divorce, and I believed him. Now think of the guilt when you are simultaneously (1) committing crimes, and (2) deceiving the men who depend on you. Both Billy and Colin are doing that, although perhaps only a theologian could name their specific sin. A theologian, or Shakespeare, whose advice from Polonius they do not heed: "To thine own self be true, and it must follow, as the night the day, thou canst not then be false to any man."

Another amateur theologian, Hemingway, said it's good if you feel good afterward, and bad if you feel bad afterward. Colin and Billy feel bad all the time, and so their lives involve a performance that is a lie. And that is the key to the performances of DiCaprio and Damon: It is in the nature of the movies that we believe most characters are acting or speaking for themselves. But in virtually every moment in this movie, except for a few key scenes, they are not. Both actors convey this agonizing inner conflict so that we can sense and feel it, but not see it; they're not waving flags to call attention to their deceptions. In that sense, the most honest and sincere characters in the movie are Queenan (Sheen), Costello (Nicholson), and Costello's right-hand man, French (Ray Winstone, that superb British actor who invests every line with the authority of God dictating to Moses).

It's strange that Jack Nicholson and Scorsese have never worked together, since they seem like a natural fit; he makes Frank Costello not a godfather, not a rat, not a blowhard, but a smart man who finally encounters a situation no one could fight free of, because he simply lacks all the necessary information. He has a moment and a line in this movie that stands beside Joe Pesci's work at a similar moment in *GoodFellas*.

There is another character who is caught in a moral vise and may sense it although she cannot for a long time know it. That is Madolyn (Vera Farmiga), a psychologist who works for the police and who coincidentally comes to know both Colin and Billy. Her loyalty is not to her employer but to her client—but, oh, what a tangled web that becomes.

It is intriguing to wonder what Scorsese saw in the Hong Kong movie that inspired him to make the second remake of his career (after *Cape Fear*, 1991). I think he instantly recognized that this story, at a buried level, brought two sides of his art and psyche into equal focus. We know that he, too, was fascinated by gangsters. In making so many films about them, about what he saw and knew growing up in Little Italy, about his insights into their natures, he became, in a way, an informant. I have often thought that many of Scorsese's critics and admirers do not realize how deeply the Catholic Church of pre-Vatican II could

burrow into the subconscious, or in how many ways Scorsese is a Catholic director. This movie is like an examination of conscience, when you stay up all night trying to figure out a way to tell the priest: I know I done wrong, but, oh, Father, what else was I gonna do?

Derby

R, 92 m., 1971

With Ann Calvello, Lydia Clay, Janet Earp, Eddie Krebs, Charlie O'Connell, Butch Snell, Christina Snell, and Mike Snell. A documentary directed by Robert Kaylor and produced by L. S. Fields and William Richert.

The kid's name is Mike Snell and he builds tires for a living in Dayton, Ohio. He is twenty-three years old and pays eighty-five dollars a month rent on a house he occupies with his wife, Christina, two children, and his younger brother, Butch. Butch lives in a basement room which he has decorated himself: There are posters on the walls and the floor is wall-to-wall mattress. Here Butch hangs out reading *Playboy* sideways, scratching his pot-belly, and waiting to be drafted. The army does not appeal to Butch: "I'm a lover, not a killer."

Mike has an ambition in life, and that is to be a professional Roller Derby star. The starting pay is $12,000 a year, which is what he makes building tires, but the glamour and the glory of the Roller Derby is worth an uncountable amount. Mike thinks he would be good: "In a couple years I could be making the big money. Charlie O'Connell makes fifty grand a year."

Charlie O'Connell is in his thirties and is the star of the San Francisco Bay Bombers. He is to the Derby what DiMaggio was to baseball. The Derby has been kind to him, and he tells us something about his life. He started out in a park in New York, forming his first Roller Derby team with nine or ten kids from the neighborhood. They skated around and around a cast-iron railing in the park. "The kids today," he says, "don't do nothing. Look at them, just walking around and throwing dirt."

Because Charlie had skill and determination, however, he lives today in a beautiful two-level ranch-style home with a kidney-shaped swimming pool where, one night not long ago, he threw a great pool party. It is a hard life on the road, however, driving from city to city, staring bleakly at motel walls, putting on your uniform in the john. "After a while," one of Charlie's teammates says, "I don't even have to put the damn thing on. It just leaps at me."

Derby, which is one of the most engaging movies I have seen in a long time, is about Mike Snell and Charlie O'Connell and about why the Roller Derby is, in some respects, a mirror held up to the American lower middle class. The movie never quite made it commercially; it played for a week as the bottom half of a double bill at the McVickers, and now it has surfaced for a very short time at the 400 Theater in Rogers Park. In this muggy summer season of brainless mass entertainments, of snakes and rats and vampires, it is the best thing in town.

Robert Kaylor, who directed *Derby*, seems to have started out to make a conventional cinema verité documentary of the game and its players. But then Mike Snell wandered into the dressing room in Dayton one night and asked Charlie O'Connell how a guy could get started in skating. Mike is a true American original: a hustler, looking for angles, a ladies' man who is said by his best friend to have had, at one time, five girlfriends in addition to his wife. He is also engaging and smart.

Kaylor took his camera into the home life of the Snells and came out with some footage that can hardly be believed. There is the scene, for example, where Mike's wife and her best girlfriend confront a local go-go dancer who is, they allege, having affairs with their husbands. The camera is right there, we know, but these young women are so engrossed they forget about it, and we look through a window into their lives, lives that seem learned from a book by Nelson Algren.

There is also a lot of action; Kaylor cuts back and forth between the Snells, Charlie, and actual Roller Derby games. I watch the Derby sometimes on Channel 32—it's just about the only thing on commercial TV worth watching—and I have never been able to understand why several players are not killed in every game. It is all here, the gouging and the hair-pulling and the running jumps

that land your skates on an opponent's stomach. And then there's a little five-year-old fan there with her grandma who says, the little darling, that she likes the Derby because she digs the action. Welcome to the United States of America.

P.S. After *Derby* was filmed, Mike Snell bought a used motorcycle, drove out to San Francisco, and graduated from Roller Derby school. He is now a jammer with the Midwest Pioneers.

Dick Tracy
PG, 105 m., 1990

Warren Beatty (Dick Tracy), Al Pacino (Big Boy Caprice), Madonna (Breathless Mahoney), Glenne Headly (Tess Trueheart), Charlie Korsmo (Kid), Seymour Cassel (Sam Catchem), James Keane (Pat Patton), Charles Durning (Chief Brandon), Mandy Patinkin (88 Keys), Paul Sorvino (Lips Manlis), Dustin Hoffman (Mumbles), Dick Van Dyke (D.A. Fletcher). Directed and produced by Beatty. Screenplay by Jim Cash and Jack Epps, Jr.

There was always something inbred about the *Dick Tracy* comic strip, some suggestion that all of its characters had been mutated by the same cosmic rays, and then locked together in a bizarre loony bin of crime. *Tracy* was the first comic strip I encountered after I outgrew funny animals, and what struck me was that the physical appearance of the characters always mirrored their souls, or occupations. They looked like what they were, and what you saw was what you got, from the square-jawed Tracy barking into his wrist radio, to Pruneface, Flattop, and the others.

Warren Beatty's production of *Dick Tracy* approaches the material with the same fetishistic glee I felt when I was reading the strip. The Tracy stories didn't depend really on plot—they were too spun-out for that—and of course they didn't depend on suspense—Tracy always won. What they were about was the interaction of these grotesque people, doomed by nature to wear their souls on their faces. We see this process at work in one of the film's first scenes, where a poker game is in progress, and everyone around the table looks like a sideshow attraction, from Little Face, whose features are at the middle of a sea of dissipation, to The Brow, always deep in shallow thought.

Another of the movie's opening shots establishes, with glorious excess, the Tracy universe. The camera begins on a window, and pulls back, and moves up until we see the skyline of the city, and then it seems to fly through the air, turning as it moves so that we sweep above an endless urban vista. Skyscrapers and bridges and tenements and elevated railways crowd each other all the way to the distant horizon, until we realize this is the grandest and most squalid city that ever was. It's more than a place. It's the distillation of the idea of City—of the vast, brooding, mysterious metropolis spreading in all directions forever, concealing millions of lives and secrets.

And then the camera moves in on one of those buildings, and as we see people again we realize that everything we have seen before— every skyscraper, every bridge—was created in a movie studio. *Dick Tracy* is a masterpiece of studio artificiality, of matte drawings and miniatures and optical effects. It creates a world that never could be. There is a scene where a giant locomotive roars down upon the fleeing figure of a small boy, and he jumps in front of it and we actually flinch. The whole fearsome train is actually a model and the running figure has been combined with it in an optical process, but don't tell that to anyone watching the movie because they won't believe you.

Into this theater of the night comes striding the peculiar figure of a man in a yellow hat and a yellow raincoat—Dick Tracy. When Chester Gould first conceived him all those years ago, did it seem unlikely that a police detective would wear yellow? Maybe not, since Tracy didn't live in a city but in a comic strip, and the primary colors had to jump off the page. Beatty's decision to shoot *Dick Tracy* only in the seven basic colors of comic strips is a good one, because this is a movie about creatures of the imagination, about people who live in rooms where every table lamp looks like a Table Lamp and every picture on the wall represents only a Picture on the Wall. It was necessary for Tracy to wear the essence of hats and coat, and so of course they were yellow; anything less would have been too ordinary.

Tracy in the comics was always an enigma, a figure without emotion or complexity. Warren Beatty plays his Tracy as a slightly more human figure, a cop who does have a personality, however slight. To the degree that the human side of Tracy peeks through, I believe, the character is diminished; the critics who have described Tracy as too shallow have missed the entire point, which is that we are not talking about real people here, but about archetypes. Tracy should be as square as his jaw.

Surrounding him are the characters who provide the real meat of the movie, and the scene-stealer is Big Boy Caprice, played by Al Pacino with such grotesque energy that we seem to have stumbled on a criminal from Dickens. Consider the scene where Big Boy rehearses the chorus line in his nightclub. He dashes and darts behind the girls, pushing them, slapping them, acting more like a dog trainer than a choreographer. There is an edge of cruelty to his behavior, and later we see that some of his cruelty is directed toward himself. Unlike most of the villains of modern movies, he does not flaunt his evil, but is ashamed of it, and this Victorian trait makes him more interesting.

In the shadows around Big Boy are a gallery of other human grotesqueries—characters who have been named for their physical abnormalities, like Lips Manlis and Shoulders, or for other handicaps, like Mumbles (Dustin Hoffman), who talks so fast he cannot be heard. Because these characters are glimpsed rather quickly, their makeup can be more bizarre; the characters who are onscreen all the time look more normal, and among them are the two women in Tracy's life, the faithful Tess Trueheart (Glenne Headly) and the seductive Breathless Mahoney (Madonna).

Pop sociologists have made a specialty out of Madonnaology, claiming she changes images so quickly that she is always ahead of her audience, always on the cutting edge. Her very appearance in each new tour is a clue to her latest message about pop imagery, we're told. Her mistake in *Dick Tracy,* I think, is that she frankly reaches back to Marilyn Monroe and tries to make Breathless into a Monroe clone, right down to the lighting and costuming in some numbers, which seems inspired by Monroe in *Some Like It Hot.* It doesn't work.

She's not Monroe and she's not Madonna, either. Breathless should have come out of a new place in her mind.

That's not a crucial flaw in the movie because Tracy himself is so bloodless that we barely believe he can be seduced. The deepest emotional attachment in the detective's life, indeed, is not even Tess Trueheart, but Kid (Charlie Korsmo), an orphan Tracy takes under his wing, and the movie's emotional high point is probably when Kid decides to call himself Dick Tracy, Jr.

Last summer's *Batman,* a movie I found disappointing, was at least a triumph of special effects—of set design and art direction. *Dick Tracy,* which is a sweeter, more optimistic movie, outdoes even *Batman* in the visual departments. This is a movie in which every frame contains some kind of artificial effect. An entire world has been built here, away from the daylight and the realism of ordinary city streets. And *Dick Tracy* also reflects the innocence of the comic strip that inspired it. Unlike the movie version of *Batman,* which hyped up the level of its violence to a degree that could have been truly disturbing to younger viewers, the PG-rated *Dick Tracy* contains no obscenity, no blood, and no "realistic" violence. It is one of the most original and visionary fantasies I've seen on a screen.

The Discreet Charm of the Bourgeoisie

PG, 100 m., 1972

Fernando Rey (Ambassador), Stephane Audran (Mrs. Scnechal), Delphine Seyrig (Mrs. Thevenot), Bulle Ogier (Florence), JeanPierre Cassel (Senechal), Michel Piccoli (Secretary of State). Directed by Luis Buñuel and produced by Serge Silberman. Screenplay by Buñuel and Jean-Claude Carriere.

"The best explanation of this film is that, from the standpoint of pure reason, there is no explanation."

—Buñuel's preface to
The Exterminating Angel

There is never quite an explanation in the universe of Luis Buñuel. His characters slip in and out of each other's fantasies, driven by compulsions that are perhaps not even their own. Buñuel doesn't like characters who have free will; if they inhabit his films, they will do what he tells them. And his fancies are as unpredictable as they are likely to be embarrassing.

His theme is almost always entrapment. His characters cannot get loose. He places them in either literal or psychological bondage, and forces them to watch with horror as he demonstrates the underlying evil of the universe. Buñuel is the most pessimistic of filmmakers, the most negative, certainly the most cynical. He is also the most obsessive, returning again and again to the same situations and predicaments; it's as if filmmaking, for him, is a grand tour of his favorite fetishes.

The Discreet Charm of the Bourgeoisie (which won the Oscar as 1972's best foreign film) has nothing new in it; but Buñuel admirers don't want anything new. They want the same old stuff in a different way, and Buñuel doesn't—perhaps cannot—disappoint them. The most interesting thing about *Discreet Charm* is the way he neatly reverses the situation in his *Exterminating Angel* (1967).

In that film, one of my favorites, a group of dinner guests finds itself in an embarrassing predicament: After dinner, no one can leave the drawing room. There is nothing to prevent them; the door stands wide open. But, somehow, they simply . . . can't leave. They camp out on the floor for several days of gradually increasing barbarism, black magic, death, suicide, and visits from a bear and two sheep (which they capture and barbecue).

The film, as Buñuel noted in his opening title, makes no sense. Not that it needs to; it gives us an eerie feeling, and we look at his trapped characters with a mixture of pity and the notion that they got what was coming to them. In *The Discreet Charm of the Bourgeoisie,* Buñuel reverses the mirror; this time, his characters are forever sitting down to dinner—but they never eat.

The consummation of their feast is prevented by a series of disasters—some real, some dreams, some obviously contrived to feed some secret itch of Buñuel's. At first there is a simple misunderstanding; the guests have arrived on the wrong night. Later, at an inn, their appetites are spoiled when it develops that the owner has died and is laid out in the next room. Still later, there are interruptions from the army, the police . . . and the guests' own dreams. All of the fantasies of public embarrassment are here, including a scene in which the guests sit down to eat and suddenly find themselves on a stage in front of an audience.

The movie isn't about anything in particular, I suppose, although devoted symbolmongers will be able to make something of the ambassador who is a cocaine smuggler and the bishop who gets off by hiring himself out as a gardener. Buñuel seems to have finally done away with plot and dedicated himself to filmmaking on the level of pure personal fantasy.

Since the form of a movie is so much more important than the content anyway, this decision gives Buñuel's immediately preceding films (*Tristana, Belle de Jour*) a feeling almost of relief. We are all so accustomed to following the narrative threads in a movie that we want to *make* a movie make "sense," even if it doesn't. But the greatest directors can carry us along breathlessly on the wings of their own imaginations, so that we don't ask questions; we simply have an experience. Ingmar Bergman's *Cries and Whispers* did that; now here comes old Buñuel to show that he can, too.

Diva

R, 123 m., 1981

Wilhelmenia Wiggins Fernandez (Cynthia,) Frédéric Andrei (Jules), Richard Bohringer (Gordorish), Thay An Luu (Alba), Jacques Fabbri (Saporta), Chantal Deruaz (Nadia). Directed by Jean-Jacques Beineix and produced by Irene Silberman. Screenplay by Beineix and Jean Van Hamme.

The opening shots inform us with authority that *Diva* is the work of a director with an enormous gift for creating visual images. We meet a young Parisian mailman. His job is to deliver special-delivery letters on his motor scooter. His passion is opera, and, as *Diva* opens, he is secretly tape-recording a live performance by an American soprano. The camera sees this action in two ways. First, with camera movements that seem as lyrical as the operatic performance. Second, with almost surreptitious observations of the electronic eavesdropper at work. His face shows the intensity of a fanatic: He does not simply admire this woman, he adores her. There is a tear in his eye. The operatic performance takes on a greatness, in this scene, that is absolutely necessary if we're to share his passion. We do. And, doing so, we start to like this kid.

He is played by Frédéric Andrei, an actor I do not remember having seen before. But he could be Antoine Doinel, the subject of *The 400 Blows* and several other autobiographical films by Francois Truffaut. He has the same loony idealism, coexisting with a certain hard-headed realism about Paris. He lives and works there, he knows the streets, and yet he never quite believes he could get into trouble. *Diva* is the story of the trouble he gets into. It is one of the best thrillers of recent years but, more than that, it is a brilliant film, a visual extravaganza that announces the considerable gifts of its young director, Jean-Jacques Beineix. He has made a film that is about many things, but I think the real subject of *Diva* is the director's joy in making it. The movie is filled with so many small character touches, so many perfectly observed intimacies, so many visual inventions—from the sly to the grand—that the thriller plot is just a bonus. In a way, it doesn't really matter what this movie is about; Pauline Kael has compared Beineix to Orson Welles and, as Welles so often did, he has made a movie that is a feast to look at, regardless of its subject.

But to give the plot its due: *Diva* really gets under way when the young postman slips his tape into the saddlebag of his motor scooter. Two tape pirates from Hong Kong know that the tape is in his possession, and, since the American soprano has refused to ever allow any of her performances to be recorded, they want to steal the tape and use it to make a bootleg record. Meanwhile, in a totally unrelated development, a young prostitute tape-records accusations that the Paris chief of police is involved in an international white-slavery ring. The two cassette tapes get exchanged, and *Diva* is off to the races.

One of the movie's delights is the cast of characters it introduces. Andrei, who plays the hero, is a serious, plucky kid who's made his own accommodation with Paris. The diva herself, played by Wilhelmenia Wiggins Fernandez, comes into the postman's life after a most unexpected event (which I deliberately will not reveal, because the way in which it happens, and *what* happens, are enormously surprising). We meet others: A young Vietnamese girl who seems so blasé in the face of Paris that we wonder if anything truly excites her; a wealthy man-about-town who specializes in manipulating people for his own amusement; and a grab bag of criminals.

Most thrillers have a chase scene, and mostly they're predictable and boring. *Diva's* chase scene deserves ranking with the alltime classics, *Raiders of the Lost Ark, The French Connection,* and *Bullitt.* The kid rides his motorcycle down into the Paris Metro system, and the chase leads on and off trains and up and down escalators. It's pure exhilaration, and Beineix almost seems to be doing it just to show he knows how. A lot of the movie strikes that note: Here is a director taking audacious chances, doing wild and unpredictable things with his camera and actors, just to celebrate moviemaking.

There is a story behind his ecstasy. Jean-Jacques Beineix has been an assistant director for ten years. He has worked for directors ranging from Claude Berri to Jerry Lewis. But the job of an assistant director is not always romantic and challenging. Many days, he's a glorified traffic cop, shouting through a bullhorn for quiet on the set, and knocking on dressing room doors to tell the actors they're wanted. Day after day, year after year, the assistant director helps set up situations before the director takes control of them. The director gives the instructions, the assistant passes them on. Perhaps some assistants are always thinking of how *they* would do the shot. Here's one who finally got his chance.

Do the Right Thing
R, 120 m., 1989

Danny Aiello (Sal), Ossie Davis (Da Mayor), Ruby Dee (Mother Sister), Richard Edson (Vito), Giancarlo Esposito (Buggin Out), Spike Lee (Mookie), Bill Nunn (Radio Raheem), John Turturro (Pino), Paul Benjamin (ML), Frankie Faison (Coconut Sid). Directed, produced, and written by Lee.

Spike Lee's *Do the Right Thing* is the kind of film people find they have to talk about afterward. Some of them are bothered by it—they think it will cause trouble. Others feel the message is confused. Some find it too militant, others find it the work of a middle-class director who is trying to play street-smart. All of those reactions, I think, are simply different ways of avoiding the central fact of this film, which is that it comes closer to reflecting the current state of race relations in America than any other movie of our time.

Of course it is confused. Of course it wavers between middle-class values and street values. Of course it is not sure whether it believes in liberal pieties, or militancy. Of course some of the characters are sympathetic and others are hateful—and of course some of the likable characters do bad things. Isn't that the way it is in America today? Anyone who walks into this film expecting answers is a dreamer or a fool. But anyone who leaves the movie with more intolerance than they walked in with wasn't paying attention.

The movie takes place during one long, hot day in the Bedford-Stuyvesant neighborhood of Brooklyn. But this is not the typical urban cityscape we've seen in countless action movies about violence and guns and drugs. People live here. It's a neighborhood like those city neighborhoods in the urban movies of the Depression—people know each other, and accept each other, and although there are problems there is also a sense of community.

The neighborhood is black, but two of the businesses aren't. Sal's Famous Pizzeria has been on the same corner since before the neighborhood changed, and Sal (Danny Aiello) boasts that "these people have grown up on my pizza." And in a nearby storefront that had been boarded up for years, a Korean family has opened a fruit and vegetable stand. Nobody seems to quite know the Koreans, but Sal and his sons are neighborhood fixtures—they know everybody, and everybody knows them.

Sal is a tough, no-nonsense guy who basically wants to get along and tend to business. One of his sons is a vocal racist—in private, of course. The other is more open toward blacks. Sal's ambassador to the community is a likable local youth named Mookie (Spike Lee), who delivers pizzas and also acts as a messenger of news and gossip. Mookie is good at his job, but his heart isn't in it; he knows there's no future in delivering pizzas.

We meet other people in the neighborhood. There's Da Mayor (Ossie Davis), a kind of everyman who knows everybody. Buggin Out (Giancarlo Esposito), a vocal militant. Radio Raheem (Bill Nunn), whose boom box defines his life, and provides a musical cocoon to insulate him from the world. Mother Sister (Ruby Dee), who is sort of the neighborhood saint. And there's the local disk jockey, whose program provides a running commentary, and a retarded street person who wanders around selling photos of Martin Luther King and Malcolm X, and then there are three old guys on the corner who comment on developments, slowly and at length.

This looks like a good enough neighborhood—like the kind of urban stage the proletarian dramas of the 1930s liked to start with. And for a long time during *Do the Right Thing*, Spike Lee treats it like a backdrop for a Saroyanesque slice of life. But things are happening under the surface. Tensions are building. Old hurts are being remembered. And finally the movie explodes in racial violence.

The exact nature of that violence has been described in many of the articles about the film—including two I wrote after the movie's tumultuous premiere at the Cannes Film Festival—but in this review I think I will not outline the actual events. At Cannes, I walked into the movie cold, and its ending had a shattering effect precisely because I was not expecting it. I would like you to have the experience for yourself, and think about it for yourself. Since Spike Lee does not tell you what to think about it, and deliberately provides surprising twists for some of the characters, this movie is more open-ended than most. It requires you to decide what you think about it.

Do the Right Thing is not filled with brotherly love, but it is not filled with hate, either. It comes out of a weary urban cynicism that has settled down around us in recent years. The good feelings and many of the hopes of the 1960s have evaporated, and today it would no longer be accurate to make a movie about how the races in America are all going to love one another. I wish we could see such love, but instead we have deepening class divisions in which the middle classes of all races flee from what's happening in the inner city, while a series of national administrations provides no

hope for the poor. *Do the Right Thing* tells an honest, unsentimental story about those who are left behind.

It is a very well-made film, beautifully photographed by Ernest Dickerson, and well-acted by an ensemble cast. Danny Aiello has the pivotal role, as Sal, and he suggests all of the difficult nuances of his situation. In the movie's final scene, Sal's conversation with Mookie holds out little hope, but it holds out at least the possibility that something has been learned from the tragedy, and the way Aiello plays this scene is quietly brilliant. Lee's writing and direction are masterful throughout the movie; he knows exactly where he is taking us, and how to get there, but he holds his cards close to his heart, and so the movie is hard to predict, hard to anticipate. After we get to the end, however, we understand how, and why, everything has happened.

I believe that any good-hearted person, white or black, will come out of this movie with sympathy for all of the characters. Lee does not ask us to forgive them, or even to understand everything they do, but he wants us to identify with their fears and frustrations. *Do the Right Thing* doesn't ask its audiences to choose sides; it is scrupulously fair to both sides, in a story where it is our society itself which is not fair.

Down and Out in Beverly Hills

R, 103 m., 1986

Nick Nolte (Jerry Baskin), Richard Dreyfuss (Dave Whiteman), Bette Midler (Barbara Whiteman), Little Richard (Orvis Goodnight), Tracy Nelson (Jenny Whiteman), Elizabeth Pena (Carmen). Directed and produced by Paul Mazursky. Screenplay by Mazursky and Leon Capetanos.

Buddy Hackett once said that the problem with Beverly Hills is, you go to sleep beside your pool one day and when you wake up you're seventy-five years old. *Down and Out in Beverly Hills* understands that statement inside-out.

It tells the story of a rich family that lives in the timeless comfort of a Beverly Hills mansion—in the kind of house where they use *Architectural Digest* for pornography. One day a bum wanders down the alley and into their backyard and tries to drown himself in their swimming pool. After he is saved, he changes their lives forever.

In its broad outlines, this story is borrowed from Jean Renoir's classic film *Boudo Saved from Drowning*. But this isn't just a remake. The director, Paul Mazursky, makes his whole film depend on the very close observation of his characters. Mazursky knows Beverly Hills (he lives there, on the quiet cloistered flatlands below Sunset Boulevard), and he knows the deceptions and compromises of upper-middle-class life (his credits include *An Unmarried Woman* and *Bob & Carol & Ted & Alice*). With great attention and affection, he shows us the lives that are disrupted by the arrival of the derelict—this seedy failure whose whole life is an affront to the consumer society.

The film's heroes are the Whitemans, Dave and Barbara (Richard Dreyfuss and Bette Midler), and the bum, Jerry Baskin. He is played by Nick Nolte as the kind of guy who didn't set out in life to be a failure, but just sort of drifted from one plateau down to the next one, until finally he was spending most of his time talking to his dog.

It is, indeed, the dog's disappearance that inspires Nolte's suicide attempt, and it will be the Whitemans' own amazing dog, named Matisse, that gets some of the loudest laughs in the movie. Maybe Mazursky is trying to tell us something about the quality of human relationships in Beverly Hills.

The Dreyfuss character is a coat-hanger manufacturer. He didn't set out in life to be rich (one of his favorite conversational gambits involves his own good luck and assurances that it could have happened to you as easily as to him—nice if you are him, but not if you are you). Here he is, living in a manicured mansion, exploiting wetback labor, sleeping with the Mexican maid, driving a Rolls convertible, selling 900 million coat hangers to the Chinese, and yet, somehow, something is missing. And almost from the first moment he sets eyes on the Nolte character, he realizes what it is: the authenticity of poverty.

The movie has a quiet, offhand way of introducing us to the rich man's milieu. We meet his wife, whose life involves long sessions with masseurs, yogis, and shrinks (even her dog has a doggie psychiatrist). We meet his daughter (Tracy Nelson), a sunnyfaced, milk-fed child of prosperity. We meet the Whitemans' neighbor, played by Little Richard with an incongruous mixture of anger and affluence (he complains that he doesn't get full service from the police; when he reports prowlers, they don't send helicopters and attack dogs).

We meet Carmen (Elizabeth Pena), the maid, who greets her employer lustily in her servant's quarters, but who grows, during the movie, from a soap opera addict into a political radical. We also meet the extended family and friends of the Whitemans, each one a perfectly written vignette, right down to the dog's analyst.

Down and Out in Beverly Hills revolves around the fascination that Dreyfuss feels for Nolte's life of dissipation and idleness. He is drawn to the shiftless sloth like a moth to a flame. A bum's life seems to have more authenticity than his own pampered existence. And, indeed, perhaps the last unreachable frontier of the very rich, the one thing they cannot buy, is poverty. Dreyfuss spends a night down on the beach with Nolte and his bum friends, and there is a breathtaking moment at sundown when Nolte (who claims to be a failed actor) recites Shakespeare's lines beginning "What a piece of work is a man!"

Certain predictable things happen. Nolte not only becomes Dreyfuss's good buddy, but is enlisted by all of the women in the household—the wife, the daughter, and the maid—as a sex therapist. Dreyfuss will put up with almost anything, because he really likes this guy, and Nolte's best hold on them is the threat to leave. Mazursky makes the most of that paradox, and gradually we see the buried theme of the movie emerging, and it is the power of friendship. What these people all really lacked, rich and poor, sane and crazy alike, was the power to really like other people.

The movie should get some kind of award for its casting. Dreyfuss, who has been so good in the past as a hyperactive overachiever, succeeds here in slightly deflecting that energy. He has the success, but is bedazzled by it, as if not quite trusting why great wealth should come to him for doing so little. He channels his energy, not into work, but into enthusiasms—and Nolte becomes his greatest enthusiasm.

For Bette Midler, Barbara Whiteman is the perfect character, all filled with the distractions of living up to her level of consumption. Nolte in some ways has the subtlest role to play, although when we first see it, it seems the broadest. His shiftless drifter has to metamorphose into a man who understands his hosts so deeply that he can play them like a piano.

The supporting roles are so well filled, one after another, that we almost feel we recognize the characters before they're introduced. And Mike, the dog, should get an honorary walk-on at the Oscars.

Perhaps I have made the movie sound too serious. Mazursky has a way of making comedies that are more intelligent and relevant than most of the serious films around; his last credit, for example, was the challenging *Moscow on the Hudson.* So let me just say that *Down and Out in Beverly Hills* made me laugh longer and louder than any film I've seen in a long time.

Downfall

R, 155 m., 2005

Bruno Ganz (Adolf Hitler), Alexandra Maria Lara (Traudl Junge), Juliane Kohler (Eva Braun), Corinna Harfouch (Magda Goebbels), Thomas Kretschmann (Hermann Fegelein), Ulrich Matthes (Joseph Goebbels), Heino Ferch (Albert Speer), Christian Berkel (Dr. Schenck), Ulrich Noethen (Heinrich Himmler). Directed by Oliver Hirschbiegel and produced by Bernd Eichinger. Screenplay by Eichinger, based on the book *Inside Hitler's Bunker* by Joachim Fest and the book *Bis zur letzten Stunde* by Junge and Melissa Muller.

Downfall takes place almost entirely inside the bunker beneath Berlin where Adolf Hitler and his inner circle spent their final days, and died. It ventures outside only to show the collapse of the Nazi defense of Berlin, the misery of the civilian population, and the burning of the bodies of Hitler, Eva Braun, and Joseph and Magda Goebbels. For the rest, it occupies a labyrinth of concrete corridors, harshly lighted, with a constant passage back and forth of aides, servants, guards, family members, and Hitler's dog, Blondi. I was reminded, oddly, of the claustrophobic sets built for *Das Boot,* which took place mostly inside a Nazi submarine.

Our entry to this sealed world is Traudl Junge (Alexandra Maria Lara), hired by Hitler as a secretary in 1942 and eyewitness to Hitler's decay in body and mind. She wrote a memoir about her experiences, which is one of the sources of this film, and *Blind Spot* (2002) was a documentary about her memories. In a clip at the end of *Downfall,* filmed shortly before her death, she says she now feels she should have known more than she did about the crimes of the Nazis. But like many secretaries the world over, she was awed by the power of her employer and not included in the information loop. Yet she could see, as anyone could see, that Hitler was a lunatic. Sometimes kind, sometimes considerate, sometimes screaming in fits of rage, but certainly cut loose from reality.

Against the overarching facts of his personal magnetism and the blind loyalty of his lieutenants, the movie observes the workings of the world within the bunker. All power flowed from Hitler. He was evil, mad, ill, but long after Hitler's war was lost he continued to wage it in fantasy. Pounding on maps, screaming ultimatums, he moved troops that no longer existed, issued orders to commanders who were dead, counted on rescue from imaginary armies.

That he was unhinged did not much affect the decisions of acolytes like Joseph and Magda Goebbels, who decided to stay with him and commit suicide as he would. "I do not want to live in a world without National Socialism," says Frau Goebbels, and she doesn't want her six children to live in one, either. In a sad, sickening scene, she gives them all a sleeping potion and then, one by one, inserts a cyanide capsule in their mouths and forces their jaws closed with a soft but audible crunch. Her oldest daughter, Helga, senses there is something wrong; senses, possibly, she is being murdered. Then Magda sits down to a game of solitaire before she and Joseph kill themselves. (By contrast, Heinrich Himmler wonders aloud, "When I meet Eisenhower, should I give the Nazi salute, or shake his hand?")

Hitler is played by Bruno Ganz, the gentle soul of *Wings of Desire,* the sad-eyed romantic or weary idealist of many roles over thirty years. Here we do not recognize him at first, hunched over, shrunken, his injured left hand fluttering behind his back like a trapped bird. If it were not for the 1942 scenes in which he hires Frau Junge as a secretary, we would not be able to picture him standing upright. He uses his hands as claws that crawl over battlefield maps, as he assures his generals that this or that impossible event will save them. And if not, well: "If the war is lost, it is immaterial if the German people survive. I will shed not one tear for them." It was his war, and they had let him down, he screams: betrayed him, lied to him, turned traitor.

Frau Junge and two other secretaries bunk in a small concrete room, and sneak away to smoke cigarettes, which Hitler cannot abide. Acting as a hostess to the death watch, his mistress, Eva Braun (Juliane Kohler), presides over meals set with fine china and crystal. She hardly seems to engage Hitler except as a social companion. Although we have heard his rants and ravings about the Jews, the Russians, his own treacherous generals, and his paranoid delusions, Braun is actually able to confide to Junge, toward the end: "He only talks about dogs and vegetarian meals. He doesn't want anyone to see deep inside of him." Seeing inside of him is no trick at all: He is flayed bare by his own rage.

Downfall was one of 2005's Oscar nominees for Best Foreign Film. It has inspired much debate about the nature of the Hitler it presents. Is it a mistake to see him, after all, not as a monster standing outside the human race, but as just another human being?

David Denby, *The New Yorker*: "Considered as biography, the achievement (if that's the right word) of *Downfall* is to insist that the monster was not invariably monstrous—that he was kind to his cook and his young female secretaries, loved his German shepherd, Blondi, and was surrounded by loyal subordinates. We get the point: Hitler was not a supernatural being; he was common clay raised to power by the desire of his followers. But is this observation a sufficient response to what Hitler actually did?"

Stanley Kauffman, *The New Republic*: "Ever since World War II, it has been clear that a fiction film could deal with the finish of Hitler and his group in one of two ways: either as ravening beasts finally getting the fate they deserved or as consecrated idealists who believed in what they had done and were willing to pay with their lives for their actions. The historical evidence of the behavior in the bunker supports the latter view .... *Downfall,* apparently faithful to the facts, evokes—torments us with—a discomfiting species of sympathy or admiration."

Admiration I did not feel. Sympathy I felt in the sense that I would feel it for a rabid dog, while accepting that it must be destroyed. I do not feel the film provides "a sufficient response to what Hitler actually did," because I feel no film can, and no response would be sufficient. All we can learn from a film like this is that millions of people can be led, and millions more killed, by madness leashed to racism and the barbaric instincts of tribalism.

What I also felt, however, was the reality of the Nazi sickness, which has been distanced and diluted by so many movies with so many Nazi villains that it has become more like a plot device than a reality. As we regard this broken and pathetic Hitler, we realize that he did not alone create the Third Reich, but was the focus for a spontaneous uprising by many of the German people, fueled by racism, xenophobia, grandiosity, and fear. He was skilled in the ways he exploited that feeling, and surrounded himself with gifted strategists and propagandists, but he was not a great man, simply one armed by fate to unleash unimaginable evil. It is useful to reflect that racism, xenophobia, grandiosity, and fear are still with us, and the defeat of one of their manifestations does not inoculate us against others.

Downhill Racer

NO MPAA RATING, 101 m., 1969

Robert Redford (Chappellet), Gene Hackman (Coach Claire), Camilla Sparv (Carole), Joe Jay Jalbert (Tommy Erb), Timothy Kirk (D. K. Bryan), Dabney Coleman (Mayo). Directed by Michael Ritchie and produced by Richard Gregson. Screenplay by James Salter, based on *The Downhill Racers* by Oakley Hall.

Some of the best moments in *Downhill Racer* are moments during which nothing special seems to be happening. They're moments devoted to capturing the angle of a glance, the curve of a smile, an embarrassed silence. Together they form a portrait of a man that is so complete, and so tragic, that *Downhill Racer* becomes the best movie ever made about sports—without really being about sports at all.

The champions in any field have got to be, to some degree, fanatics. To be the world's best skier, or swimmer, or chess player, you've got to overdevelop that area of your ability while ignoring almost everything else. This is the point we miss when we persist in describing champions as regular, all-around Joes. If they were, they wouldn't be champions.

This is the kind of man *Downhill Racer* is about: David Chappellet, a member of the U.S. skiing team, who fully experiences his humanity only in the exhilaration of winning. The rest of the time, he's a strangely cut-off person, incapable of feeling anything very deeply, incapable of communicating with anyone, incapable of love, incapable (even) of being very interesting.

Robert Redford plays this person very well, even though it must have been difficult for Redford to contain his own personality within such a limited character. He plays a man who does nothing well except ski downhill—and does that better than anyone.

But this isn't one of those rags-to-riches collections of sports clichés, about the kid who fights his way up to champion. It's closer in tone to the stories of the real champions of our time: Sandy Koufax, Muhammad Ali, Joe Namath, who were the best and knew they were the best and made no effort to mask their arrogance. There is no humility at all in the racer's character: not that there should be. At one point, he's accused by a fellow American of not being a good "team man." Another skier replies: "Well, this isn't exactly a team sport."

It isn't; downhill racing is an intensely individual sport, and we feel that through some remarkable color photography. More often than not, races are shot from the racer's point of view, and there are long takes that nearly produce vertigo as we hurtle down a mountain. Without bothering to explain much of the technical aspect of skiing, *Downhill Racer* tells us more about the sport than we imagined a movie could.

The joy of these action sequences is counterpointed by the daily life of the ski amateur. There are the anonymous hotel rooms, one after another, and the deadening continual contact with the team members, and the efforts of the coach (Gene Hackman in a superb performance) to hold the team together and placate its financial backers in New York.

And there is Chappellet's casual affair with a girl (Camilla Sparv) who seems to be a sort of ski groupie. She wants to make love to him, and does, but he is so limited, so incapable of understanding her or anything beyond his own image, that she drops him. He never does quite understand why.

The movie balances nicely between this level and the exuberance of its outdoor location photography. And it does a skillful job of involving us in the competition without really being a movie about competition. In the end, *Downhill Racer* succeeds so well that instead of wondering whether the hero will win the Olympic race, we want to see what will happen to him if he does.

The Draughtsman's Contract

R, 103 m., 1983

Anthony Higgins (Mr. Neville), Janet Suzman (Mrs. Herbert), Anne Louise Lambert (Mrs. Talmann). Directed by Peter Greenaway and produced by David Payne. Screenplay by Greenaway.

What we have here is a tantalizing puzzle, wrapped in eroticism and presented with the utmost elegance. I have never seen a film quite like it. *The Draughtsman's Contract* seems to be telling us a very simple story in a very straightforward way, but after it's over you may need hours of discussion with your friends before you can be sure (if even then) exactly what happened.

The film takes place in 1694, in the English countryside. A rich lady (Janet Suzman) hires an itinerant artist to make twelve detailed drawings of her house. The artist (Anthony Higgins) strikes a hard bargain. In addition to his modest payment, he demands "the unrestricted freedom of her most intimate hospitality." Since the gentleman of the house is away on business, the lady agrees, and thus begins a pleasant regime divided between the easel and the boudoir.

All of this is told in the most precise way. All of the characters speak in complete, elegant, literary sentences. All of the camera strategies are formal and mannered. The movie advances with the grace and precision of a well-behaved novel. There is even a moment, perhaps, when we grow restless at the film's deliberate pace. But then, if we are sharp, we begin to realize that strange things are happening under our very noses.

The draughtsman demands perfection. There must be no change, from day to day, in the view he paints. He aims for complete realism. But little changes do creep in. A window is left open. A ladder is found standing against a wall. There are things on the lawn that should not be on the lawn. The lady's daughter calls on the artist and suggests that a plot may be under way and that her father, the lord of the manor, may have been murdered. Furthermore, the artist may be about to be framed for the crime. As a payment for her friendship, the daughter demands the same payment in "intimate hospitality" as her mother. Now the artist is not only draughtsman but lover to mother and daughter *and* the possible object of a plot to frame him with murder.

There is more. There is a lot more, all allowed to unfold at the same deliberate pace. There is a mysterious statue in the garden. An eavesdropper. Misbehaving sheep. The raw materials of this story could have been fashioned into a bawdy romp like *Tom Jones*. But the director, Peter Greenaway, has made a canny choice. Instead of showing us everything, and explaining everything, he gives us the clues and allows us to draw our own conclusions. His movie is like a crossword puzzle for the senses.

The Dreamers

NC-17, 115 m., 2004

Michael Pitt (Matthew), Eva Green (Isabelle), Louis Garrel (Theo), Robin Renucci (Father), Anna Chancellor (Mother). Directed by Bernardo Bertolucci. and produced by Jeremy Thomas. Screenplay by Gilbert Adair, based on his book.

In the spring of 1968, three planets—Sex, Politics, and the Cinema—came into alignment and exerted a gravitational pull on the status quo. In Paris, what began as a protest over the ouster of Henri Langlois, the legendary founder of the Cinématheque Français, grew into a popular revolt that threatened to topple the government. There were barricades in the streets, firebombs, clashes with the police, a crisis of confidence. In a way that seems inexplicable today, the director Jean-Luc Godard and his films were at the center of the maelstrom. Other New Wave directors and the cinema in general seemed to act as the agitprop arm of the revolution.

Here are two memories from that time. In the spring of 1968, I was on vacation in Paris. Demonstrators had barricaded one end of the street where my cheap Left Bank hotel was located. Police were massed at the other end. I was in the middle, standing outside my hotel, taking it all in. The police charged, I was pushed out in front of them, and rubber truncheons pounded on my legs. "Tourist!" I shouted, trying to make myself into a neutral. Later I realized they might have thought I was saying "tourista!" which is slang for diarrhea. Unwise.

The second memory is more pleasant. In April 1969, driving past the Three Penny Cinema on Lincoln Avenue in Chicago, I saw a crowd lined up under umbrellas on the sidewalk, waiting in the rain to get into the next screening of Godard's *Weekend.* Today you couldn't pay most Chicago moviegoers to see a film by Godard, but at that moment, the year after the Battle of Grant Park, at the height of opposition to the Vietnam War, it was all part of the same alignment.

Oh, and sex. By the summer of 1969, I was in Hollywood, writing the screenplay for Russ Meyer's *Beyond the Valley of the Dolls.* It would be an X-rated movie from 20th Century-Fox, and although it seems tame today (R-rated, probably), it was part of a moment when sex had entered the mainstream and was part of a whole sense of society in flux.

I indulge in this autobiography because I have just seen Bernardo Bertolucci's *The Dreamers* and am filled with poignant and powerful nostalgia. To be sixteen in 1968 is to be fifty-two today, and so most younger moviegoers will find this film as historical as *Cold Mountain.* For me, it is yesterday; above all, it evokes a time when the movies—good movies, both classic and newborn—were at the center of youth culture. "The Movie Generation," *Time* magazine called us in a cover story. I got my job at the *Sun-Times* because of it; they looked around the feature department and appointed the longhaired new kid who had written a story about the underground films on Monday nights at Second City.

Bertolucci is two years older than I am, an Italian who made his first important film, *Before the Revolution,* when he was only twenty-four. He would, in 1972, make *Last Tango in Paris,* a film starring Marlon Brando and the unknown Maria Schneider in a tragedy about loss, grief, and sudden sex between two strangers who find it a form of urgent communication. Pauline Kael said, "Bertolucci and Brando have altered the face of an art form." Well, in those days we talked about movies that way.

It is important to have this background in mind when you go to see *The Dreamers* because Bertolucci certainly does. This film, like *Last Tango,* takes place largely in a vast Parisian apartment. It is about transgressive sex. Outside the windows, there are riots in the streets, and indeed, in a moment of obvious symbolism, a stone thrown through a window saves the lives of the characters, the revolution interrupting their introverted triangle.

The three characters are Matthew (Michael Pitt), a young American from San Diego who is in Paris to study for a year, but actually spends all of his time at the Cinématheque, and the twins Isabelle (Eva Green) and Theo (Louis Garrel), children of a famous French poet and his British wife. They also spend all of their time at the movies. Almost the first thing Isabelle tells Matthew is, "You're awfully clean for someone who goes to the cinema so much." He's clean in more ways than one; he's a naive, idealistic American, and the movie treats him to these strange Europeans in the same way Henry James sacrifices his Yankee innocents on the altar of continental decadence.

These are the children of the cinema. Isabelle tells Matthew, "I entered this world on the Champs Élysées in 1959, and my very first words were *New York Herald Tribune!*" Bertolucci cuts to the opening scene in Godard's *Breathless* (1959), one of the founding moments of the New Wave, as Jean Seberg shouts out those words on the boulevard. In other words, the New Wave, not her parents, gave birth to Is-

abelle. There are many moments when the characters quiz each other about the movies, or reenact scenes they remember; a particularly lovely scene has Isabelle moving around a room, touching surfaces, in a perfect imitation of Garbo in *Queen Christina.* And there's a bitter argument between Matthew and Theo about who is greater—Keaton or Chaplin? Matthew, the American, of course, knows that the answer is Keaton. Only a Frenchman could think it was Chaplin.

But *The Dreamers* is not Bertolucci's version of Trivial Pursuit. Within the apartment, sex becomes the proving ground and then the battleground for the revolutionary ideas in the air. Matthew meets the twins at the Cinématheque during a demonstration in favor of Langlois (Bertolucci intercuts newsreel footage of Jean-Pierre Leaud in 1968 with new footage of Leaud today, and we also get glimpses of Truffaut, Godard, and Nicholas Ray). They invite him back to their parents' apartment. The parents are going to the seaside for a month, and the twins invite him to stay.

At first it is delightful. "I have at last met some real Parisians!" Matthew writes his parents. Enclosed in the claustrophobic world of the apartment, he finds himself absorbed in the sexual obsessions of the twins. He glimpses one night that they sleep together, naked. Isabelle defeats Theo in a movie quiz and orders him to masturbate (on his knees, in front of a photo of Garbo). Theo wins a quiz and orders Matthew to make love to his sister. Matthew is sometimes a little drunk, sometimes high, sometimes driven by lust, but at the bottom he knows this is wrong, and his more conventional values set up the ending of the film, in which sex and the cinema are engines, but politics is the train.

The film is extraordinarily beautiful. Bertolucci is one of the great painters of the screen. He has a voluptuous way here of bathing his characters in scenes from great movies, and referring to others. Sometimes his movie references are subtle, and you should look for a lovely one. Matthew looks out a window as rain falls on the glass, and the light through the window makes it seem that the drops are running down his face. This is a quote from a famous shot by Conrad L. Hall in Richard Brooks's *In Cold Blood*

(1967). And although Michael Pitt usually looks a little like Leonardo DiCaprio, in this shot, at that angle, with that lighting, he embodies for a moment the young Marlon Brando. Another quotation: As the three young people run down an outdoor staircase, they are pursued by their own giant shadows, in a nod to *The Third Man.*

The movie is rated NC-17, for adults only, because of the themes and because of some frontal nudity. So discredited is the NC-17 rating that Fox Searchlight at first thought to edit the film for an R, but why bother to distribute a Bertolucci film except in the form he made it? The sexual content evokes that time and place. The movie is like a classic argument for an A rating, between the R and NC-17, which would identify movies intended for adults but not actually pornographic. What has happened in our society to make us embrace violence and shy away from sexuality?

Bertolucci titled his film *The Dreamers,* I think, because his characters are dreaming, until the brick through the window shatters their cocoon and the real world of tear gas and Molotov cocktails enters their lives. It is clear now that Godard and sexual liberation were never going to change the world. It only seemed that way for a time. The people who really run things do not go much to the movies, or perhaps think much about sex. They are driven by money and power. Matthew finds he cannot follow the twins into whatever fantasy the times have inspired in them. He turns away and disappears into the crowd of rioters, walking in the opposite direction. Walking into a future in which, perhaps, he will become the director of this movie.

The Dresser

PG, 118 m., 1984

Albert Finney (Sir), Tom Courtenay (Norman), Edward Fox (Oxenby), Zena Walker (Her Ladyship). Directed and produced by Peter Yates. Screenplay by Ronald Harwood.

Much of mankind is divided into two categories, the enablers and the enabled. Both groups accept the same mythology, in which the enablers are self-sacrificing martyrs and the enabled are egomaniacs. But the roles are sometimes reversed; the stars are shaken by insecurities that are subtly encouraged by enablers who, in their heart of hearts, see themselves as the real stars. It's human nature. Ever hear the one about the guy who played the gravedigger in *Hamlet?* He was asked what the play was about, and he answered, "It's about this gravedigger . . ."

The Dresser is about a guy like that, named Norman. He has devoted the best years of his life to the service of an egomaniacal actor, who is called Sir even though there is some doubt he has ever been knighted. Sir is an actor-manager who runs his own traveling theatrical troupe, touring the provinces to offer a season of Shakespeare. One night he plays King Lear. The next night, Othello. The next, Richard III. Most nights he has to ask his dresser what role he is playing. Dressers in the British theater do a great deal more than dress their employers. In *The Dresser,* Norman is also Sir's confidant, morale booster, masseur, alter ego, and physician, nursing him through hangovers with medicinal amounts of brandy. Norman has been doing this job for years, and Sir is at the center of his life. Sir, however, takes Norman very much for granted, and it is this difference between them that provides the emotional tension.

The Dresser is a backstage movie, based on a backstage play, but the movie leaves the theater for a few wonderful additions to the play, as when Sir commands a train to stop, and the train does. Mostly, though, the action is in a little provincial theater, where tonight's play is *King Lear,* and Sir looks as if he had spent the last week rehearsing the storm scene. It is Norman's job to whip him into shape. Sir is seriously disoriented. He is so hung over, shaky, and confused that he can't even remember how the play begins—indeed, he starts putting on the makeup for *Othello.* There are other problems for Norman to handle, such as Sir's relationships with his wife, his adoring stage manageress, and a young actress he is considering for Cordelia (she is slim, and would be easier to carry onstage). There are also an angry supporting player and a quaking old trouper who is being pressed into service as the Fool.

The minor characters are all well-drawn, but *The Dresser* is essentially the story of two people, and the movie has been well-cast to make the most of both of them; no wonder both actors won Oscar nominations. Norman is played by Tom Courtenay, who had the role on stage in London and New York and will also be remembered from all those British Angry Young Men films like *Billy Liar* and *Loneliness of the Long Distance Runner.* He is perfect for playing proud, resentful, self-doubting outsiders. Sir is played by Albert Finney, who manages to look far older than his forty-seven years and yet to create a physical bravura that's ideal for the role. When he shouts "Stop . . . that . . . train!" we are not too surprised when the train stops.

On the surface, the movie is a wonderful collection of theatrical lore, detail, and superstition (such as the belief that it is bad luck to say the name "Macbeth" aloud—safer to refer always to "the Scottish tragedy"). The physical details of makeup and costuming are dwelled on, and there is a great backstage moment when the primitive thunder machine is rattled to make a storm. Beneath those details, though, a human relationship arrives at a crisis point and is resolved, in a way. Sir and Norman come to the end of their long road together, and, as is the way with enablers and enabled, Norman finally understands the real nature of their relationship, while Sir, of course, can hardly be bothered. This is the best sort of drama, fascinating us on the surface with color and humor and esoteric detail, and then revealing the truth underneath.

Driving Miss Daisy

PG, 99 m., 1989

Morgan Freeman (Hoke Colburn), Jessica Tandy (Daisy Werthan), Dan Aykroyd (Boolie Werthan), Patti Lupone (Florine Werthan), Esther Rolle (Idella), Joann Havrilla (Miss McClatchey), William Hall, Jr. (Oscar), Alvin M. Sugarman (Dr. Weil), Clarice F. Geigerman (Nonie). Directed by Bruce Beresford and produced by Richard D. Zanuck and Lili Fini Zanuck. Screenplay by Alfred Uhry, based on his play.

Driving Miss Daisy is a film of great love and patience, telling a story that takes twenty-five years to unfold, exploring its characters as few films take the time to do. By the end of the film, we have traveled a long way with the two most important people in it—Miss Daisy Werthan, a proud old southern lady, and Hoke Colburn, her chauffeur—and we have developed a real stake in their feelings.

The movie spans a quarter-century in the lives of its two characters, from 1948, when Miss Daisy's son decides it is time she stop driving herself and employ a chauffeur, to 1973, when two old people acknowledge the bond that has grown up between them. It is an immensely subtle film, in which hardly any of the most important information is carried in the dialogue, and in which body language, tone of voice, or the look in an eye can be the most important thing in a scene. After so many movies in which shallow and violent people deny their humanity and ours, what a lesson to see a film that looks into the heart.

The movie contains a performance nominated for an Academy Award by Morgan Freeman, as Hoke, and an Academy Award–winning role by Jessica Tandy, who at the age of eighty creates the best performance of her career as Miss Daisy. As the movie opens, Miss Daisy still lives in proud self-sufficiency, with only her cook to help out, and she drives herself around in a big new 1948 Packard. One day she drives the Packard over the wall and into the neighbor's yard, and her son (Dan Aykroyd) lays down the law: It is time that she have a chauffeur.

She refuses. She needs no such thing. It is a nuisance to have servants in the house, anyway—they're like children, always underfoot. But her son hires a chauffeur anyway, and in their first interview he tells Hoke that it is up to him to convince Miss Daisy to let herself be driven. Thus commences a war of wills that continues, in one way or another, for twenty-five years, as two stubborn and proud old people learn to exist with one another.

Hoke's method is the employment of infinite patience, and Morgan Freeman's performance is a revelation, based on close observation and quiet nuance. Hoke is not obsequious. He is not ingratiating. He is very wise. His strategy is to express verbal agreement in such a way that actual agreement is withheld. If Miss Daisy does not want to be driven to the Piggly Wiggly, very well then, Hoke will not drive her. He will simply follow her in the car. The car by this time is a shiny new 1949 Hudson, and Hoke somehow defuses the situation by making the car itself the subject, rather than himself. It is a shame, he observes, that a fine new car like that is left sitting in the driveway, not being used. It's good for a car to be driven. . . .

Eventually Miss Daisy agrees to be driven, and eventually, over the years, she and Hoke begin to learn about one another. Neither one is quick to reveal emotion. And although Miss Daisy prides herself on being a southern Jewish liberal, she is not always very quick to see the connections between such things as an attack on her local synagogue and the Klan's attacks on black churches. Indeed, much of Hoke's relationship with her consists of helping her to see certain connections. When she goes to listen to a speech by Martin Luther King, for example, she has Hoke drive her—but although she has an extra ticket it never occurs to her to invite him to come inside. "Things have changed," she observes complacently in another scene, referring to race relations in the South, and he replies that they have not changed all *that* much.

"Is Morgan Freeman the greatest American actor?" Pauline Kael once asked, reviewing his performance as a steel-eyed pimp in *Street Smart* (1987). It is when you compare that performance with this one in *Driving Miss Daisy* and another film, *Glory*, that you begin to understand why the question can be asked. The three performances have almost nothing in common; all three are works of the imagination in which Freeman creates three-dimensional characters that are completely convincing. In *Street Smart*, he created an aura of frightening violence. In *Lean on Me*, early in 1989, he was school principal Joe Clark, a man of unassailable self-confidence and bullheaded determination. In *Glory*, he was an ignorant grave digger who becomes a soldier in the Civil War. In *Miss Daisy*, he is so gentle, so perceptive, so patient, it is impossible to get a glimpse of those other characters.

It is a great performance, and matched by Miss Tandy's equally astonishing range, as she ages from a sprightly and alert widow in her sixties to an infirm old woman drifting in and out of senility in her nineties. Hers is one of the most complete portraits of the stages of old age I have ever seen in a film.

Driving Miss Daisy was directed by Bruce Beresford, an Australian whose sensibilities seem curiously in tune with the American South. His credits include the superb *Tender Mercies* and *Crimes of the Heart*, as well as the underrated and overlooked 1986 film about an aborigine teenager, *The Fringe Dwellers*. Working from a screenplay by Alfred Uhry, based on Uhry's play (and on Uhry's memories of a grandmother and a chauffeur in his own family), Beresford is able to move us, one small step at a time, into the hearts of his characters. He never steps wrong on his way to a luminous final scene in which we are invited to regard one of the most privileged mysteries of life: the moment when two people allow each other to see inside.

Drugstore Cowboy

R, 100 m., 1989

Matt Dillon (Bob), Kelly Lynch (Diane), James Le Gros (Rick), Heather Graham (Nadine), Max Perlich (David), James Remar (Gentry), Grace Zabriskie (Bob's Mother), Beah Richards (Drug Counselor), William S. Burroughs (Tom the Priest). Directed by Gus Van Sant, Jr., and produced by Cary Brokaw. Screenplay by Van Sant and Daniel Yost.

Drugstore Cowboy is one of the best films in a long tradition of American outlaw road movies—a tradition that includes *Bonnie and Clyde, Easy Rider, Midnight Cowboy,* and *Badlands*. It is about criminals who do not intend to be particularly bad people, but whose lives run away with them. The heroes of these films always have a weakness, and in *Drugstore Cowboy* the weakness is drug abuse.

The movie stars Matt Dillon in one of the great recent American movie performances, as the leader of a pack of two young couples who are on the prowl in Washington and Oregon. It is 1971 and they are the rear guard of the love generation. They drift from one rented apartment or motel room to another, in an aimless migration in search of drugs. They will use almost anything, but their favorites are prescription drugs, and they have developed a smooth method of stealing them from drugstores.

We see them at work. The four enter a store separately. One of them creates a commotion—pretending to have a fit, let's say. Under cover of the confusion, Dillon sneaks behind the prescription counter and scoops up as many drugs as he can identify. What drugs they can't use, they sell. And when they aren't stealing or on the road, their lives fall into a listless routine of getting high, watching TV, smoking, talking, waiting.

Sex is not high on Dillon's list of enthusiasms. Like a lot of drug abusers, he is more turned on by drugs than sex—by the excitement of setting up a job, the fear during the actual stealing, and the payoff afterward when he gets high. He has apparently been with the same girlfriend (Kelly Lynch) since they were in high school, and at some point along the road they got married, but their eyes are turned toward drugs, not each other. They travel with a goofy sidekick (James Le Gros) and his girlfriend, a pathetic teenage drifter (Heather Graham). Together, they're a family.

Strangely enough, it is the family feeling that makes *Drugstore Cowboy* so poignant and effective. This is not a movie about bad people, but about sick people. They stick together and try to help one another in the face of the increasing desperation of their lives. The movie is narrated by Dillon, whose flat voice doesn't try to dramatize the material; he could be telling his story at an AA meeting. He knows that it is sad, but he also knows that it is true, and he is not trying to glamorize it, simply trying to understand it.

There is humor in their lives—craziness almost always breeds humor—and there is also deeply buried hurt, as in the scene where the Dillon character goes to visit his mother (Grace Zabriskie). Up until this point in the movie we have seen him primarily through his own eyes and have grown to like him, a little, for the resourceful way he is trying to lead his team of losers. Then his mother refuses to let him into the house—not because she doesn't love him, but because she knows him too well and knows he will steal anything to get money for drugs. The way he has to stand there and accept this, and try to shrug it off, provides one of the most painful scenes in the movie.

Life falls into a rhythm of excitement and ennui. And their lives drift imperceptibly from bad to worse. There is a way in which desperate people can accept the conditions of their lives up to a point, and then there is the unmistakable day when that point has been passed. For this family, that day comes when the teenage girl overdoses and they are stuck with a corpse in their room at a motel where a deputy sheriffs' convention is being held. It is a tribute to the sure hand of the director, Gus Van Sant, Jr., that this scene works through irony and desperation, instead of through the cheap laughs another director might have settled for.

Drugstore Cowboy is a story told with a threat of insane logic that makes it one of the most absorbing movies in a long time. It is a logic that many drug abusers would understand. It goes like this: I feel bad and drugs make me feel good, although they are also why I feel bad. But since they make me feel good now and bad later, I will worry about later when the time comes. Eventually, for the Dillon character, the time does come, and he tells his wife that he is heading back to Seattle to get into some kind of a program and try to kick drugs. He has the intelligence to see that things are out of control, that he can no longer make them hold together, that he has lost the fight and had better surrender before his corpse is somebody else's problem.

The movie then inserts a small supporting performance by William Burroughs that is like a guest appearance by Death. Sitting in a fleabag hotel room, playing a defrocked priest addicted to heroin, Burroughs talks to Dillon in a gallows voice about drugs. We sense two things about the character: that he should have died long ago, and that death would not have been unwelcome compared to his earthly purgatory. This cameo appearance has been criticized by some writers as the movie's single flaw. It's distracting to see Burroughs in a fiction film, they say. But with his skull shining through his eyes and his dry voice and his laugh like a smoker's cough, Burroughs creates a perfect moment. The Dillon character looks at him and sees one of the fates he is free to choose.

Like all truly great movies, *Drugstore Cowboy* is a joyous piece of work. I believe that the subject of a film does not determine whether it makes us feel happy or sad. I am unutterably depressed after seeing stupid comedies that insult my ingelligence, but I felt exhilarated after seeing *Drugstore Cowboy* because every person connected with this project is working at top form. It's a highwire act of daring, in which this unlikely subject matter becomes the occasion for a film about sad people we come to care very deeply about.

At the end of the film, the Dillon character seems to have broken out of drugs. His wife is still on the road. "Are you crazy?" she asks him when he says he wants to kick his habit. She cannot imagine life without drugs. He can. That is the difference between them, and in painting that difference, this movie shows the distance between hope and despair.

A Dry White Season

R, 106 m., 1989

Donald Sutherland (Ben du Toit), Janet Suzman (Susan), Zakes Mokae (Stanley), Jurgen Prochnow (Captain Stolz), Susan Sarandon (Melanie), Marlon Brando (McKenzie), Winston Ntshona (Gordon), Thoko Ntshinga (Emily). Directed by Euzhan Palcy and produced by Paula Weinstein. Screenplay by Colin Welland and Palcy, based on the book by Andre Brink.

When you are safe and well-off, and life has fallen into a soothing routine, there is a tendency to look the other way when trouble happens—especially if it hasn't happened to you. Say, for example, that you are a white schoolmaster in South Africa, and live in a comfortable suburban home with your wife and two children. Suppose your African gardener's son disappears one day. How do you feel? You feel sorry, of course, because you have humanitarian instincts. But what if it appears that the boy was the victim of police brutality and may be imprisoned illegally? What do you do then? In a country where the gardener has little hope of lodging an effective appeal, do you stick your neck out and help him?

That is the question posed to Ben du Toit (Donald Sutherland) in the opening passages of *A Dry White Season*. His answer is almost instinctive: "Best to let it go," he tells the gardener. "No doubt they'll see they made a mistake and release him. There's nothing to be done." This is a sensible answer, if the boy is not your son. But Gordon Ngubene (Winston Ntshona), the gardener, cannot accept it. With the help of an African lawyer, he tries to get some answers, to find out why and how his son disappeared. And it is not very long until Gordon has disappeared, too.

A Dry White Season is set in the 1970s, at the time when the schoolchildren of Soweto, an African township outside Johannesburg, held a series of protests. They wanted to be educated in English, not Afrikaans (a language spoken only in South Africa). The protests resulted in the deaths of many marchers, but the government weathered the storm and clapped a lid on the possibility of a civil uprising, as it always has.

In 1989, we have arrived at another season of protest in South Africa, where, to the general amazement of almost everyone involved, peaceful antigovernment marches were permitted by the government in Cape Town and Johannesburg. As someone who has visited South Africa and studied for a year at the University of Cape Town, I wonder what the average American reader makes of the headlines. How does he picture South Africa? What does he think life is like there? Does he see these marches in the same context as American freedom marches? Does he ask how six million whites can get away with ruling twenty-four million Africans?

This film, based on a novel by Andre Brink, provides a series of bold images to go with the words and the concepts in the stories out of South Africa. Like *A World Apart* (1988), it is set mostly in the pleasant world of white suburbia, an easy commute from the skyscrapers of downtown (some Americans, I believe, still see South Africa in images from old Tarzan movies, and do not know the country is as modern and developed as any place in Europe or North America). We meet the schoolteacher, a decent and quiet man, a onetime Springbok sports hero, who finds it easy not to reflect overlong on the injustices of his society. He disapproves of injustice in principle, of course, but finds it prudent not to rock the boat.

Then disaster strikes into the life of the gardener, who also loves his family, and who also lives a settled family life, in a township outside the city. Jonathan, the gardener's son, is a clever lad, and the schoolteacher is helping him with a scholarship. Jonathan is arrested almost at random and jailed with many other demonstrators, and then a chain of events is set into motion that leads Ben du Toit into a fundamental difference with the entire structure of his society.

The movie follows him step by step as he sees things he can hardly believe, and begins to suspect the unthinkable—that the boy and his father have been ground up inside the justice system and spit out as "suicides." He meets with the African lawyer (Zakes Mokae) and with the gardener's wife (Thoko Ntshinga). He finds one catch-22 being piled on another. (After her husband is reported dead, the widow no longer has a legal right to stay in her house and must be deported to a "homeland" she has never seen, from where it will be impossible to lodge a legal protest.)

As a respected white man, the schoolteacher is allowed access to the system—until it becomes obvious that he is asking the wrong questions and adopting the wrong attitude. Then he is ostracized. He loses his job. Shots are fired through his windows. His wife (Janet Suzman, brittle and unforgiving) is furious that he has betrayed his family by appearing to be a "kaffir lover." His daughter finds him a disgrace. Only his young son seems to understand that he is wearily, doggedly, trying to do what is right.

A Dry White Season is a powerfully serious movie, but the director, Euzhan Palcy, provides a break in the middle, almost as Shakespeare used to bring on pantomime before returning to the deaths of kings. A famous South African lawyer, played by Marlon Brando, is brought in to lodge an appeal against the finding that one of the dead committed suicide. The Brando character knows the appeal is useless, that his courtroom appearance will be a charade, and yet he goes ahead with it anyway—using irony and sarcasm to make his points, even though the outcome is hopeless.

Brando, in his first movie appearance since 1980, has fun with the role in the way that Charles Laughton or Orson Welles would have approached it. He allows himself theatrical gestures, droll asides, astonished double takes. His scenes are not a star turn, but an effective performance in which we see a lawyer with a brilliant mind, who uses it cynically and comically because that is his form of protest.

At the center of the film, Donald Sutherland is perfectly cast and quietly effective as a man who will not be turned aside, who does not wish misfortune upon himself or his family, but cannot ignore what has happened to the family of his friend. Like *A World Apart* and *Cry Freedom*, the movie concentrates on a central character who is white (because the movie could not have been financed with a black hero), but *A Dry White Season* has much more of the South African black experience in it than the other two films.

It shows daily life in the townships, which are not slums but simply very poor places where determined people struggle to live decently. It hears the subtleties of voice when an intelligent African demeans himself before a white policeman, appearing humble to gain a hearing. It shows some of the details of police torture that were described in Joseph Lelyveld's *Move Your Shadow,* the most comprehensive recent book about South Africa. It provides mental images to go with the columns of text in the newspapers. American network TV coverage of South Africa all but ended when the government banned the cameras (proving that the South African government was absolutely right that the networks were interested only in sensational footage, and not in the story itself). Here are some pictures to go with the words.

Here is also an effective, emotional, angry, subtle movie. Euzhan Palcy, a gifted filmmaker, is a thirty-two-year-old from Martinique, whose first feature was the masterpiece about poor black Caribbean farm workers, *Sugar Cane Alley.* Here, with a larger budget and stars in the cast, she still has the same eye for character detail. This movie isn't just a plot trotted out to manipulate us, but the painful examination of one man's change of conscience. For years he has been blind, perhaps willingly. But once he sees, he cannot deny what he feels is right.

E

Eastern Promises
R, 96 m., 2007

Viggo Mortensen (Nickolai Luzhin), Naomi Watts (Anna Khitrova), Vincent Cassel (Kirill), Armin Mueller-Stahl (Semyon), Sinéad Cusack (Helen), Jerzy Skolimowski (Stepan Khitrov), Donald Sumpter (Yuri). Directed by David Cronenberg and produced by Robert Lantos and Paul Webster. Screenplay by Steven Knight.

David Cronenberg's *Eastern Promises* opens with a throat slashing and a young woman collapsing in blood in a drugstore, and connects these events with a descent into an underground of Russians who have emigrated to London and brought their crime family with them. Like the Corleone family, but with a less wise and more fearsome patriarch, the Vory V Zakone family of the Russian Mafia operates in the shadows of legitimate business—in this case, a popular restaurant.

The slashing need not immediately concern us. The teenage girl who hemorrhages is raced to a hospital and dies in childbirth in the arms of a midwife named Anne Khitrova (Naomi Watts). Fiercely determined to protect the helpless surviving infant, she uses her Russian-born parents (Sinéad Cusack and Jerzy Skolimowski) to translate the dead girl's diary, and it leads her to a restaurant run by Semyon (Armin Mueller-Stahl), the head of the Mafia family. Her father begs her to go nowhere near that world.

Semyon has a vile son named Kirill (Vincent Cassel) and a violent but loyal driver and bodyguard, Nickolai (Viggo Mortensen). And the gears of the story shift into place when the diary, the midwife, and the crime family become interlocked.

Eastern Promises is no ordinary crime thriller, just as Cronenberg is no ordinary director. Beginning with low-rent horror films in the 1970s, because he could get them financed, Cronenberg has moved film by film into the top rank of directors, and here he wisely reunites with Mortensen, star of their *A History of Violence* (2005). No, Mortensen is not Russian, but don't even think about the problem of an accent; he digs so deeply into the role you may not recognize him at first.

Naomi Watts, playing an Anglicized second-generation immigrant, has no idea at first what she has gotten herself into and why the diary is of vital importance to these people. All she cares about is the baby, but she learns fast that the baby's life and her own are both at great risk. In fact, her entry into that world has driven a wedge into it that sets everybody at odds and challenges long assumptions.

The screenplay is by Steven Knight, author of the powerful film *Dirty Pretty Things* (2002), about a black market in body parts. It was set in London and had scarcely a native-born Londoner in it. He's fascinated by the worlds within the London world. Here, too. And his lines of morality are more murkily drawn here, as allegiances and loyalties shift and old emotions turn out to be forgotten, but not dead.

Mortensen's Nikolai is the key player, trusted by Semyon. We are reminded of Don Corleone's trust in an outsider, Tom Hagen, over his own sons, Sonny and Fredo. Here Semyon depends on Nikolai more than Kirill, who has an ugly streak that sometimes interferes with the orderly conduct of business. Anna (Watts) senses she can trust Nikolai, too, even though it is established early on that this tattooed warrior is capable of astonishing violence. At a time when movie "fight scenes" are as routine as the dances in musicals, Nikolai engages in a fight in this film that sets the same kind of standard that *The French Connection* set for chases. Years from now, it will be referred to as a benchmark.

Cronenberg has said he's not interested in crime stories as themselves. "I was watching *Miami Vice* the other night," he told Adam Nayman of *Toronto's Eye Weekly,* "and I realized I'm not interested in the mechanics of the mob . . . but criminality and people who live in a state of perpetual transgression—that is interesting to me." And to me as well. What the director and writer do here is not unfold a plot, but flay the skin from a hidden world. Their story puts their characters to a test: They can be true to their job descriptions within a hermetically sealed world where everyone shares the same values and expectations, and where outsiders are by definition the prey. But what happens when their cocoon is broached? Do they still possess fugitive feelings instilled by a long-forgotten babushka? And what if they do?

"Just don't give the plot away," Cronenberg begged in that interview. He is correct that it would be fatal, because this is not a movie of what or how, but of *why*. And for a long time you don't see the *why* coming. It's that way with stories about plausible human beings, which is why I prefer them to stories about characters who are simply elements in fiction. There was a big surprise in *A History of Violence* that pretty much everybody entering the theater already knew. But *Eastern Promises* had its world premiere at the Toronto Film Festival on September 8, 2007, and opened in major North American markets six days later; I have studied its trailer, and it doesn't give away a hint of its central business.

So let's leave it that way and simply regard the performances. I write little about casting directors, because I can't know what really goes on, and of course directors make the final choice for key roles. But whatever Deirdre Bowen and Nina Gold had to do with the choices in this movie, including what might seem the unlikely choice of Mortensen, was pitch-perfect. The actors and the characters merge and form a reality above and apart from the story, and the result is a film that takes us beyond crime and London and the Russian Mafia and into the mystifying realms of human nature.

Easy Rider

R, 95 m., 1969

Peter Fonda (Wyatt), Dennis Hopper (Billy), Antonio Mendoza (Jesus), Phil Spector (Connection), Jack Nicholson (George Hanson). Directed by Hopper and produced by Fonda. Screenplay by Fonda, Hopper, and Terry Southern.

Henry Fonda is said to have come out of *Easy Rider* a confused and puzzled man. He had worked in movies for thirty-five years and made some great ones, and now his son Peter was going to be a millionaire because of a movie Henry couldn't even understand.

Where did those two guys come from? he wanted to know. What was their background? How did they set up that drug-smuggling deal? Where were they going? And what, oh what, did the movie mean?

I suspect many members of Hollywood's older generation believe, sincerely and deeply, that *Easy Rider* doesn't have a story, and doesn't mean anything, and that the kids are all crazy these days.

But in fact, director Dennis Hopper has done an old and respectable thing. He has told his story in cinematic shorthand, instead of spelling it out in dreary detail. Fifty years ago, Hollywood figured out that if you put the good guys in white hats you could eliminate ten minutes of explanation from every Western. Hopper has applied this technique to the motorcycle movie. (He also has made a great film, but more of that later.)

Everybody "knows" that *Easy Rider* is tremendously popular with high school and college-age kids. But these kids apparently sprang into existence full-blown, and did not grow up or go to any other movie before they found this one. That's the way Hollywood sees it. Hollywood believes in magic.

In fact, the same kids who did *Easy Rider* were on dates in the drive-ins a few years ago when *The Wild Angels* and *Hells Angels on Wheels* and all the other motorcycle pictures came along. When the Hollywood establishment was dismissing motorcycle movies as an unpleasant low-budget fad, the kids already knew that something was happening here. Because the Hells Angel, like the gangster, was a bad guy produced by the society he victimized and tied to it by a love-hate relationship that created some really neat sex and violence scenes.

And it was inevitable that a great film would come along someday, utilizing the motorcycle genre the same way the great Westerns suddenly made everyone realize they were a legitimate American art form. *Easy Rider* is the picture.

In all the exploitation-type motorcycle movies, the central characters were outlaws from conventional society. They rejected the establishment values (but took them seriously enough to attach importance to putting them down). They used drugs and beat up each other, and cops hated them on sight. There was usually an ounce of worth in the hero, however.

Actors such as Peter Fonda and Adam Roarke played gang leaders in the tradition of Brando.

But, unlike Brando (in *The Wild One*) they usually repented when they saw the suffering they'd caused. They didn't repent all over the place, but they did repent, and if you looked close you could catch them at it in the last scene.

Easy Rider takes the gang leader (Fonda) and condenses his gang into one uptight archetype (played by director Hopper). It takes the aimless rebellion of the bike gangs and channels it into specific rejection of the establishment (by which is meant everything from rednecks to the Pentagon to hippies on communes).

Fonda and Hopper specifically break with the establishment by smuggling cocaine across the Mexican border; that's a no-no. But during most of the picture they have cash money hidden in their gas tanks, not dope. They sold their dope to the establishment (represented ironically by rock tycoon Phil Spector in a Rolls-Royce). They sold out, that is. And now they want to go to Florida and retire.

So Fonda and Hopper the dope-smugglers are symbols of every earnest, hardworking, law-abiding, middle-class wage-slave selling his integrity to the establishment every day (whether you believe this is immaterial to the symbolism, which works anyway).

But it's hard to identify with the Fonda and Hopper characters. So Hopper and his co-writers, Fonda and Terry Southern, write in a brilliant character, Old George (played magnificently by Jack Nicholson). And when this alcoholic, tragic ACLU lawyer from a small southern town enters the picture, suddenly that's us there on the bike with Fonda. And the movie starts to work.

If you follow the story closely in *Easy Rider*, you find out it isn't there. The rough cut of the movie reportedly ran over three hours, and Hopper edited it to a reasonable length by throwing out the story details and keeping the rest. So the heroes are suspended in an invisible story, like falcons on an invisible current of air. You can't see it, but it holds them up.

All of this divests a motorcycle movie of its weak point (the story) and develops its strong point (the role of the self-proclaimed rebel in a conformist society). It's not just bike freaks who get in trouble when they challenge the establishment—it's everybody, even Old George.

And yet, *Easy Rider* suggests, it's not as simple as that. We almost forget that the Fonda and Hopper characters have also sold out. Victims can sell out just as well as their persecutors. They sold out because what they were trying to be was the mirror image of the rednecks in the truck, and neither lifestyle is healthy. And so there they were, their gas tanks stuffed full of bribes from the establishment, and you remember hearing somewhere that, in the South, "easy rider" is slang for a prostitute's lover.

Elephant
R, 81 m., 2003

Alex Frost (Alex), Eric Deulen (Eric), John Robinson (John), Elias McConnell (Elias), Jordan Taylor (Jordan), Carrie Finklea (Carrie), Nicole George (Nicole), Brittany Mountain (Brittany). Directed by Gus Van Sant and produced by Dany Wolf. Screenplay by Van Sant.

Gus Van Sant's *Elephant* is a record of a day at a high school like Columbine, on the day of a massacre much like the one that left thirteen dead. It offers no explanation for the tragedy, no insights into the psyches of the killers, no theories about teenagers or society or guns or psychopathic behavior. It simply looks at the day as it unfolds, and that is a brave and radical act; it refuses to supply reasons and assign cures so that we can close the case and move on.

Van Sant seems to believe there are no reasons for Columbine and no remedies to prevent senseless violence from happening again. Many viewers will leave this film as unsatisfied and angry as *Variety*'s Todd McCarthy, who wrote after it won the Golden Palm at Cannes 2003 that it was "pointless at best and irresponsible at worst." I think its responsibility comes precisely in its refusal to provide a point.

Let me tell you a story. The day after Columbine, I was interviewed for the Tom Brokaw news program. The reporter had been assigned a theory and was seeking sound bites to support it.

"Wouldn't you say," she asked, "that killings like this are influenced by violent movies?"

No, I said, I wouldn't say that.

"But what about *The Basketball Diaries*?" she asked. "Doesn't that have a scene of a boy walking into a school with a machine gun?"

The obscure 1995 Leonardo DiCaprio movie did indeed have a brief fantasy scene of that nature, I said, but the movie failed at the box office (it grossed only $2.5 million), and it's unlikely the Columbine killers saw it.

The reporter looked disappointed, so I offered her my theory.

"Events like this," I said, "if they are influenced by anything, are influenced by news programs like your own. When an unbalanced kid walks into a school and starts shooting, it becomes a major media event. Cable news drops ordinary programming and goes around the clock with it. The story is assigned a logo and a theme song; these two kids were packaged as the Trench Coat Mafia.

"The message is clear to other disturbed kids around the country: 'If I shoot up my school, I can be famous. The TV will talk about nothing else but me. Experts will try to figure out what I was thinking. The kids and teachers at school will see they shouldn't have messed with me. I'll go out in a blaze of glory.'"

In short, I said, events like Columbine are influenced far less by violent movies than by CNN, the *NBC Nightly News,* and all the other news media who glorify the killers in the guise of "explaining" them. I commended the policy at the *Sun-Times,* where our editor said the paper would no longer feature school killings on page one.

The reporter thanked me and turned off the camera. Of course, the interview was never used. They found plenty of talking heads to condemn violent movies, and everybody was happy.

Van Sant's *Elephant* is a violent movie in the sense that many innocent people are shot dead. But it isn't violent in the way it presents those deaths. There is no pumped-up style, no lingering, no release, no climax. Just implacable, poker-faced, flat, uninflected death. Van Sant has made an antiviolence film by draining violence of energy, purpose, glamour, reward, and social context. It just happens.

I doubt that *Elephant* will ever inspire anyone to copy what they see on the screen. Much more than the insipid message movies shown in social studies classes, it might inspire useful discussion and soul-searching among high school students.

Van Sant simply follows a number of students and teachers as they arrive at the school and go about their daily routines. Some of them intersect with the killers, and many of those die. Others escape for no particular reason.

The movie is told mostly in long tracking shots; by avoiding cuts between close-ups and medium shots, Van Sant also avoids the film grammar that goes along with such cuts, and so his visual strategy doesn't load the dice or try to tell us anything. It simply watches.

At one point he follows a tall, confident African-American student in a very long tracking shot as he walks into the school and down the corridors, and all of our experience as filmgoers leads us to believe this action will have definitive consequences; the kid embodies all those movie heroes who walk into hostage situations and talk the bad guy out of his gun. But it doesn't happen like that, and Van Sant sidesteps all the conventional modes of movie behavior and simply shows us sad, sudden death without purpose.

"I want the audience to make its own observations and draw its own conclusions," Van Sant told me at Cannes. "Who knows why those boys acted as they did?"

He is honest enough to admit that he does not. Of course a movie about a tragedy that does not explain the tragedy—that provides no personal or social "reasons" and offers no "solutions"—is almost against the law in the American entertainment industry. When it comes to tragedy, Hollywood is in the catharsis business.

Van Sant would have found it difficult to find financing for any version of this story (Columbine isn't "commercial"), but to tell it on a small budget, without stars or a formula screenplay, is unthinkable. He found the freedom to make the film, he said, because of the success of his *Good Will Hunting,* which gave him financial independence: "I came to realize since I had no need to make a lot of money, I should make films I find interesting, regardless of their outcome and audience."

El Norte

R, 141 m., 1983

Zaide Silvia Gutierrez (Rosa), David Villalpando (Enrique), Ernesto Gomez Cruz (Father), Alicia del Lago (Mother), Trinidad Silva (Monty). Directed by Gregory Nava and produced by Anna Thomas. Screenplay by Nava and Thomas.

From the very first moments of *El Norte,* we know that we are in the hands of a great movie. It tells a simple story in such a romantic and poetic way that we are touched, deeply and honestly, and we know we will remember the film for a long time. The movie tells the story of two young Guatemalans, a brother and sister named Rosa and Enrique, and of their long trek up through Mexico to *el Norte*—the United States. Their journey begins in a small village and ends in Los Angeles, and their dream is the American Dream.

But *El Norte* takes place in the present, when we who are already Americans are not so eager for others to share our dream. Enrique and Rosa are not brave immigrants who could have been our forefathers, but two young people alive now, who look through the tattered pages of an old *Good Housekeeping* for their images of America. One of the most interesting things about the film is the way it acknowledges all of the political realities of Latin America and yet resists being a "political" film. It tells its story through the eyes of its heroes, and it is one of the rare films that grants Latin Americans full humanity. They are not condescended to, they are not made to symbolize something, they are not glorified, they are simply themselves.

The movie begins in the fields where Arturo, their father, is a *bracero*—a pair of arms. He goes to a meeting to protest working conditions and is killed. Their mother disappears. Enrique and Rosa, who are in their late teens, decide to leave their village and go to America. The first part of the film shows their life in Guatemala with some of the same beauty and magical imagery of Gabriel Garcia Marquez's *One Hundred Years of Solitude*. The middle section shows them going by bus and foot up through Mexico, which is as harsh on immigrants from the south as America is. At the border they try to hire a "coyote" to guide them across, and they finally end up crawling to the promised land through a rat-infested drainage tunnel.

The final section of the film takes place in Los Angeles, which they first see as a glittering carpet of lights, but which quickly becomes a cheap motel for day laborers, and a series of jobs in the illegal, shadow job market. Enrique becomes a waiter. Rosa becomes a maid. Because they are attractive, intelligent, and have a certain naive nerve, they succeed for a time, before the film's sad, poetic ending.

El Norte is a great film, one of 1983's best, for two different kinds of reasons. One is its stunning visual and musical power; the approach of the film is not quasi-documentary, but poetic, with fantastical images that show us the joyous hearts of these two people.

The second reason is that this is the first film to approach the subject of "undocumented workers" solely through *their* eyes. This is not one of those docu-dramas where we half-expect a test at the end, but a film like *The Grapes of Wrath* that gets inside the hearts of its characters and lives with them.

The movie was directed by Gregory Nava and produced by Anna Thomas, who wrote it together. It's been described by *Variety* as the "first American independent epic," and it is indeed an epic film made entirely outside the studio system by two gifted filmmakers (their credits include *The Confessions of Amans*, which won a Gold Hugo at the Chicago Film Festival, and *The Haunting of M*, one of my favorite films from 1979). This time, with a larger budget and a first-rate cast, they have made their breakthrough into the first ranks of filmmaking.

El Topo

NO MPAA RATING, 125 m., 1970

Alejandro Jodorowsky (El Topo), Brontis Jadorowsky (Son of El Topo, as a boy), Jose Legarreta (Dying Man). Directed by Alejandro Jodorowsky and produced by Roberto Viskin. Screenplay by Jodorowsky.

Shot on a fairly large budget in Mexico, it began its American existence as an underground cult object, playing midnight shows in New York for six months. It surfaced to a normal run last November amid loud controversy. Its director, author, and star, Alejandro Jodorowsky, was attacked in some quarters for using the symbols to make the violence digestible, and in other quarters for using the blood to sell the symbols. I don't think you can take the movie apart that way; *El Topo* is all of a piece, and you've got to take the concrete with the fantasy, the spirit with the flesh.

Jodorowsky lifts his symbols and mythologies from everywhere: Christianity, Zen, discount-store black magic, you name it. He makes not the slightest attempt to use them so they sort out into a single logical significance. Instead, they're employed in a shifting, prismatic way, casting their light on each other instead of on the film's conclusion. The effect resembles Eliot's *The Waste Land*, and especially Eliot's notion of shoring up fragments of mythology against the ruins of the post-Christian era.

Jodorowsky's hero, El Topo (the mole), devotes his life to a spaced-out quest that's first cousin to the journeys in the Lord of the Ring book trilogy, *Stranger in a Strange Land*, maybe *Easy Rider*, certainly *2001*, and most obviously to the goalless, introspective missions of Eastwood's Man with No Name.

The movie begins with an observation about the mole (he spends his life digging tunnels to the sky, and when he finally sees the sun, he goes blind), then sets its hero to actual and symbolic tunnel-digging. What he digs his way into and out of, mostly, is the Italian Western genre. The movie has echoes here of Godard's *Pierrot le Fou*, in which the characters make their way out of a gangster movie and into a musical, and wind up against their will in a Western.

In the version according to Jodorowsky, the West is peopled largely with corpses of men and animals, and the survivors are gross, obscene caricatures who follow phony gospelmongers and practice slavery. When El Topo moves out of this world, he goes first to do battle with the Four Masters of the Desert (who have black-magic connotations probably inspired by the work of Aleister Crawley), and later to help free a colony of deformed and incestuously mutated cripples.

These quests supply most of the film's generous supply of killings, tortures, disembowelments, hangings, boilings, genocides, and so on. *El Topo's* violence is extreme and unremitting, and more callous even than Ken Russell's in *The Devils*. And yet, somehow, *The Devils* came over as a violent exploitation film, and *El Topo* doesn't. Maybe that's because Jodorowsky dazzles us with such delicate mythological footwork that the violence becomes distanced, somehow, and we accept it like the slaughters in the Old Testament.

I'm not sure. *El Topo* is a movie it's very hard to be sure about after a single viewing. It weaves a web about you, and you're left with two impulses. One is to accept it on its own terms, as a complex fantasy that uses violence as the most convenient cinematic shorthand for human power relationships. The other is to reject it as the work of a cynic, who is simply supplying more jolts and shocks per minute than most filmmakers. The first impulse seems sounder to me, because if Jodorowsky were simply in the blood-and-gut sweepstakes he could have made a much simpler, less ambitious movie that would have had the violence of *El Topo* but not its uncanny resonance.

Elvira Madigan

PG, 91 m., 1967

Pia Degermark (Elvira Madigan), Thommy Berggren (Sixten Sparre). Directed and produced by Bo Widerberg. Screenplay by Widerberg.

Somewhere in these pages today there is doubtless an advertisement describing *Elvira Madigan* as the most beautiful film ever made. That has been the New York critical line, expressed in turn by the *New York Times*, *Newsweek*, and the *New Yorker*. I think it does an injustice to Bo Widerberg's great film.

Elvira Madigan is indeed remarkably beautiful. Almost every frame would make a painting, and yet the film is alive and cinematic, not simply photographs of pretty pictures. Widerberg composes his shots of muted colors—usually white, yellow, and green—and of the remarkably attractive faces of his stars, Pia Degermark and Thommy Berggren.

But then he uses a style of moving his camera away from the direction of the movement on the screen. The camera moves left, for example, as Berggren, on the left, passes a glass of wine to Degermark, on the right. Conventional camera work, I suppose, would require the camera to follow the action. What Widerberg establishes is both the static beauty of the scene and the subtle sense that the "art" is moving against the "reality."

This sense, I believe, is what *Elvira Madigan* really conveys. And that is why it is so similar to *Bonnie and Clyde*, although on any objective level the two films are unlike. Widerberg started with a legend well known in Sweden, and he has directed and photographed it with a very smooth, beautiful surface. But what is underneath is altogether different.

The story is a simple one. Elvira Madigan, a beautiful sixteen-year-old tightrope walker, ran away from her family's circus in the summer of 1889. Count Sixten Sparre, a young lieutenant with two children, abandoned his family and deserted from the army. After a summer together, they committed suicide in the autumn.

Widerberg begins his story with a scene in a sunny clearing. Sixten removes the brass military buttons from his uniform. He shaves off his beard to avoid recognition. They make love. Mozart's Piano Concerto No. 21 provides the sound track. The scene, and most of the following ones, are pure romanticism and are intended to be.

But small events take place. During a picnic, Elvira spills a bottle of red wine and it gurgles into the ground like blood. When the couple are forced to flee detection, the woman who warned them hurries to return Elvira's knitting: "You'll need it when the autumn comes." The couple runs out of money, and a charming early scene in which they dip raspberries into cream is contrasted now with a scene in which Elvira, driven by hunger, crawls on the ground eating nuts and mushrooms until she vomits.

What we have here is the story of two beautiful, stupid, selfish, romantic people, intoxicated by the legendary aspect of their own love affair. Although they seem at the beginning to be simply a young couple in love, the degree of their fanaticism becomes clear in their decision to commit suicide. This is a tribute not to love, but to the human ego.

The Emigrants

PG, 151 m., 1971

Max von Sydow (Karl Oskar), Liv Ullmann (Kristina). Directed by Jan Troell and produced by Bengt Forslund. Screenplay by Forslund and Troell, based on the novels by Vilhelm Moberg.

The Emigrants isn't the kind of movie we used to be shown in grade school, a movie all about the tired and huddled masses and Samuel Gompers and melting pots.

No, it tells a simple story (and one closer to the truth, most likely) about European peasants caught in an impossible situation. Their land is poor and their crops scarce, their greatest efforts only force them more deeply into debt, and the social system will not allow them to better themselves. Eventually they arrive at a reasonable course of action: They will go to America and see if things are not better there. Their dream is naive, desperate, and brave—all at the same time. Nobody has told them the streets are paved with gold (and they are too filled with Swedish common sense to believe that, anyway.) But they have heard stories about the prosperity to be found in America, and it seems as if every mother has a son in Minnesota who owns a hundred acres of land. That must have sounded impressive to anyone who had not seen the Minnesota of 150 years ago.

Two boys, bound under contract for a year to a stern and sadistic farmer, read a booklet about the Promised Land: "Even the slaves have a higher standard of living than most European peasants. They are allowed to own their own chickens and market the produce themselves." "I'm going to sign on as a slave," one of the young boys exclaims, his eyes alight with the wonder of his opportunity.

And later, on board a paddle-wheel steamer that is taking them through the Great Lakes to Minnesota, the emigrants in steerage look up in admiration to the rich first-class passengers on the upper deck. "I thought you said there were no commoners and gentry in America," one says.

"I said there isn't a *class* system," the other explains. "The way it works is, those people who have been here long enough are already rich. We're still poor because we just got here. It takes a little time." The reasoning seems sound as a bell, and Jan Troell's film masterpiece is made up of dozens of moments like this, moments when hope and reality clash, and the new Americans take measure of the actual situation they find themselves in. There's not a one of us—not even the Indians, who came first—whose ancestors didn't come to this continent from another, and yet we so easily forget this most historic of all movements of people. We think we were here always.

Troell's epic film, more than two and a half hours long and infinitely absorbing and moving, is based on *Upon a Good Land,* the bestselling series of Swedish novels by Vilhelm Moberg. At nearly $2 million, this is the most expensive and ambitious Swedish film ever made and one of the handful of foreign films ever to be shot partly on location in America. (Troell used the Great Lakes, Minnesota, northern Wisconsin—and Galena, Illinois.) It tells the story of Swedish immigrants but it might as well be about any group of people. The voyage would have been just as long, the illnesses and deaths just as heartbreaking, the spirit as indomitable. Troell is considered perhaps the best of the post-Bergman generation of Swedish filmmakers; like his contemporary Bo Widerberg (*Elvira Madigan, Adalen 31*) he has a feeling for the historical past, and for the meaning and beauty of ordinary lives. Troell's first film, *Here's Your Life,* won our 1967 Chicago Film Festival, and his *Ole Dole Duff* won again in 1969 (he shares with Peru's Armando Robles Godoy the distinction of having won twice).

Both films dealt with common life in Sweden, and *Here's Your Life* was an extraordinarily beautiful story of a young man's coming of age in the years before World War I. It is said that Moberg—who had refused to have his novels filmed—saw this work by Troell and decided he had found, at last, the right director.

Troell, in turn, has found the perfect casting for his emigrant couple in those two splendid Swedish actors, Max von Sydow and Liv Ullmann. With the rest of the excellent cast, they bring a purity, a grit, and a depth of purpose to their roles that, we feel, the original settlers must have had.

The Emigrants is a special film in that it's Swedish and yet somehow American—in the sense that it tells the story of what America meant for so many millions. When it was over the other evening, the audience applauded; that's a rare thing for a Chicago audience to do, but then *The Emigrants* is a very rare film.

Note: There is a sequel, The New Land.

The Empire Strikes Back

PG, 127 m., 1980 (rereleased 1997)

Mark Hamill (Luke Skywalker), Harrison Ford (Han Solo), Carrie Fisher (Princess Leia), Billy Dee Williams (Lando Calrissian), Anthony Daniels (C-3PO), Frank Oz (Yoda), David Prowse (Darth Vader), James Earl Jones (Vader's Voice), Alec Guinness (Ben [Obi-Wan] Kenobi). Directed by Irvin Kershner and produced by Gary Kurtz. Screenplay by Leigh Brackett and Lawrence Kasdan, based on a story by George Lucas.

The Empire Strikes Back is the best of the three *Star Wars* films, and the most thought-provoking. After the space opera cheerfulness of the original film, this one plunges into darkness and even despair, and surrenders more completely to the underlying mystery of the story. It is because of the emotions stirred in *Empire*

that the entire series takes on a mythic quality that resonates back to the first and ahead to the third. This is the heart.

The film was made in 1980 with full knowledge that *Star Wars* had become the most successful film of all time. If corners were cut in the original budget, no cost was spared in this one, and it is a visual extravaganza from beginning to end, one of the most visionary and inventive of all films.

Entirely apart from the story and the plot, the film is worth seeing simply for its sights. Not for the scenes of space battle, which are more or less standard (there's nothing here to match the hurtling chase through the high walls of the Death Star). But for such sights as the lumbering, elephantlike Imperial Walkers (was ever a weapon more impractical?). Or for the Cloud City, on its spire high in the sky. Or for the face of a creature named Yoda, whose expressions are as convincing as a human's, and as subtle. Or for the dizzying, vertiginous heights that Luke Skywalker dangles over, after nearly plunging to his death.

There is a generosity in the production design of *The Empire Strikes Back.* There are not only the amazing sights before us, but plenty more in the corners of the screen, or everywhere the camera turns. The whole world of this story has been devised and constructed in such a way that we're not particularly aware of sets or effects—there's so *much* of this world that it all seems seamless. Consider, for example, an early scene where an Empire "probe droid" is fired upon on the ice planet Hoth. It explodes. We've seen that lots of times. But then hot pieces of it shower down on the snow in the foreground, in soft, wet plops. That's the kind of detail that George Lucas and his team live for.

There is another moment. Yoda has just sent Luke Skywalker into a dark part of the forest to confront his destiny. Luke says a brave farewell. There is a cut to R2-D2, whirling and beeping. And then a cut back to Yoda, whose face reflects a series of emotions: concern, sadness, a hint of pride. You know intellectually that Yoda is a creature made by Frank Oz in a Muppet shop. But Oz and Lucas were not content to make Yoda realistic. They wanted to make him a good actor too. And they did; in his range of wisdom and emotion, Yoda may actually give the best performance in the movie.

The worst, I'm afraid, is Chewbacca's. This character was thrown into the first film as window dressing, was never thought through, and as a result has been saddled with one facial expression and one mournful yelp. Much more could have been done. How can you be a space pilot and not be able to communicate in any meaningful way? Does Han Solo really understand Chewy's monotonous noises? Do they have long chats sometimes?

Never mind. The second movie's story continues the saga set up in the first film. The Death Star has been destroyed, but Vader, of course, escaped, and now commands the Empire forces in their ascendancy against the rebels. Our heroes have a secret base on Hoth, but flee it after the Empire attack, and then the key characters split up for parallel stories. Luke and R2-D2 crash-land on the planet Dagobah and Luke is tutored there by Yoda in the ways of the Jedi and the power of the Force. Princess Leia, Han Solo, Chewbacca, and C-3PO evade Empire capture by hiding their ship in plain sight, and then flee to the Cloud City ruled by Lando (Billy Dee Williams), an old pal of Han's and (we learn) the original owner of the Millennium Falcon, before an unlucky card game.

There are a couple of amusing subplots, one involving Han's easily wounded male ego, another about Vader's knack of issuing sudden and fatal demotions. Then comes the defining moment of the series. Can there be a person alive who does not know (read no further if you are that person) that Luke discovers Darth Vader is his father? But that is not the moment. It comes after their protracted (and somewhat disorganized) laser-sword fight, when Luke chooses to fall to his death rather than live to be the son of Vader.

He doesn't die, of course (there is a third movie to be made); he's saved by some sort of chute I still don't understand, only to dangle beneath the Cloud City until his rescue, and a conclusion that only by sheer effort of will doesn't have the words "To be continued" superimposed over it.

Perhaps because so much more time and money was spent on *The Empire Strikes Back* in the first place, not much has been changed in this restored and spruced-up 1997 rerelease. I do not recall the first film in exact detail, but learn from the *Star Wars* Web pages that the look of the Cloud City has been extended and enhanced, and there is more of the Wampa ice creature than before. I have no doubt there are many improvements on the sound track, but I would have to be a dog to hear them.

In the glory days of science fiction, critics wrote about the "sense of wonder." That's what *The Empire Strikes Back* creates in us. Like a lot of traditional science fiction, it isn't psychologically complex or even very interested in personalities (aside from some obvious character traits). That's because the characters are not themselves—they are us. We are looking out through their eyes, instead of into them, as we would in more serious drama. We are on a quest, on a journey, on a mythological expedition. The story elements in the *Star Wars* trilogy are as deep and universal as storytelling itself. Watching these movies, we're in a receptive state like that of a child—our eyes and ears are open, we're paying attention, and we are amazed.

The English Patient

R, 160 m., 1996

Ralph Fiennes (Almasy), Juliette Binoche (Hana), Willem Dafoe (Caravaggio), Kristin Scott Thomas (Katharine Clifton), Naveen Andrews (Kip), Colin Firth (Geoffrey Clifton), Julian Wadham (Madox), Kevin Whately (Hardy). Directed by Anthony Minghella and produced by Saul Zaentz. Screenplay by Minghella, based on the book by Michael Ondaatje.

Backward into memory, forward into loss and desire, *The English Patient* searches for answers that will answer nothing. This poetic, evocative film version of the novel by Michael Ondaatje circles down through layers of mystery until all of the puzzles in the story have been solved, and only the great wound of a doomed love remains. It is the kind of movie you can see twice—first for the questions, the second time for the answers.

The film opens with a prewar biplane flying above the desert, carrying two passengers in its open cockpits. The film will tell us who these passengers are, why they are in the plane, and what happens next. All of the rest of the story is prologue and epilogue to the reasons for this flight. It is told with the sweep and visual richness of a film by David Lean, with an attention to fragments of memory that evoke feelings even before we understand what they mean.

The "present" action takes place in Italy, during the last days of World War II. A horribly burned man, the "English patient" of the title, is part of a hospital convoy. When he grows too ill to be moved, a nurse named Hana (Juliette Binoche) offers to stay behind to care for him in the ruins of an old monastery. Here she sets up a makeshift hospital, and soon she is joined by two bomb disposal experts and a mysterious visitor named Caravaggio (Willem Dafoe).

The patient's skin is so badly burned it looks like tortured leather. His face is a mask. He can remember nothing. Hana cares for him tenderly, perhaps because he reminds her of other men she has loved and lost during the war. ("I must be a curse. Anybody who loves me— who gets close to me—is killed.") Caravaggio, who has an interest in the morphine Hana dispenses to her patient, is more cynical: "Ask your saint who he's killed. I don't think he's forgotten anything."

The nurse is attracted to one of the bomb disposal men, a handsome, cheerful Sikh officer named Kip (Naveen Andrews). But as she watches him risk his life to disarm land mines, she fears her curse will doom him; if they fall in love, he will die. Meanwhile, the patient's memories start to return in flashes of detail, spurred by the book that was found with his charred body—an old leather-bound volume of the histories of Herodotus, with drawings, notes, and poems pasted or folded inside.

I will not disclose the crucial details of what he remembers. I will simply supply the outlines that become clear early on. He is not English, for one thing. He is a Hungarian count named Laszlo de Almasy (Ralph Fiennes) who, in Egypt before the war, was attached to the Royal Geographic Society as a pilot who flew over the desert, making maps that could be used for their research—which was the cover story— but also used by English troops in case of war.

In the frantic social life of Cairo, where everyone is aware that war is coming, Almasy meets a newly-married woman at a dance. She is Katharine Clifton (Kristin Scott Thomas). Her husband, Geoffrey (Colin Firth), is a disappointment to her. Almasy follows her home one night, and she confronts him and says,

"Why follow me? Escort me, by all means, but to follow me . . ." It is clear to both of them that they are in love. Eventually they find themselves in the desert, part of an expedition, and when Geoffrey is called away (for reasons that later are revealed as good ones), they draw closer together. In a stunning sequence, their camp is all but buried in a sandstorm, and their relief at surviving leads to a great romantic sequence.

These are the two people—the count and the British woman—who were in the plane in the first shot. But under what conditions that flight was taken remains a mystery until the closing scenes of the movie, as do a lot of other things, including actions by the count that Caravaggio, the strange visitor, may suspect. Actions that may have led to Caravaggio having his thumbs cut off by the Nazis.

All of this back story (there is much more) is pieced together gradually by the dying man in the bed, while the nurse tends to him, sometimes kisses him, bathes his rotting skin, and tries to heal her own wounds from the long war. There are moments of great effect: one in which she plays hopscotch by herself. A scene involving the nurse, the Sikh, and a piano. Talks at dusk with the patient, and with Caravaggio. All at last become clear.

The performances are of great clarity, which is a help to us in finding our way through the story. Binoche is a woman whose heart has been so pounded by war that she seems drawn to its wounded as a distraction from her own hurts. Fiennes, in what is essentially a dual role, plays a man who conceals as much as he can—at first because that is his nature, later because his injuries force him to. Thomas is one of those bright, energetic British women who seem perfectly groomed even in a sandstorm, and whose core is steel and courage. Dafoe's character must remain murkier, along with his motives, but it is clear he shelters a great anger. And Andrews, as the bomb disposal man, lives the closest to daily death and seems the most grateful for life.

Ondaatje's novel has become one of the most widely read and loved of recent years. Some of its readers may be disappointed that more is not made of the Andrews character; the love between the Sikh and the nurse could provide a balance to the doomed loves elsewhere. But the novel is so labyrinthine that it's a miracle it was filmed at all, and the writer-director, Anthony Minghella, has done a creative job of finding visual ways to show how the rich language slowly unveils layers of the past.

Producers are not always creative contributors to films, but the producer of *The English Patient*, Saul Zaentz, is in a class by himself. Working independently, he buys important literary properties *(One Flew Over the Cuckoo's Nest, Amadeus, The Unbearable Lightness of Being, At Play in the Fields of the Lord)* and savors their difficulties. Here he has created with Minghella a film that does what a great novel can do: Hold your attention the first time through with its story, and then force you to think back through everything you thought you'd learned, after it is revealed what the story is *really* about.

The Enigma of Kaspar Hauser

NO MPAA RATING, 110 m., 1974

Bruno S. (Kaspar Hauser) Walter Ladengast (Professor Daumer), Brigitte Mira (Kathe, Servant), Willy Semmerogge (Circus Director). Directed and produced by Werner Herzog. Screenplay by Herzog.

Werner Herzog's films do not depend on "acting" in the conventional sense. He is most content when he finds an actor who embodies the essence of a character, and then he studies that essence with a fascinated intensity. Consider the case of Bruno S., a street performer and forklift operator whose last name was long concealed. He is the center of two Herzog films *The Enigma of Kaspar Hauser* (1974) and *Stroszek* (1977). The son of a prostitute, he was locked for twenty-three years in mental institutions, even though Herzog believes he was not insane.

Bruno is however very strange, bullheaded, with the simplicity and stubbornness of a child. In *Kaspar Hauser,* he looks anywhere he wants to, sometimes even craftily sideways at the camera, and then it feels not like he's looking at the audience but through us. He can't possibly play any role other than himself, but that is what Herzog needs him for. On the commentary track Herzog says he was vilified in Germany for taking advantage of an unfortunate, but if you study Bruno sympathetically you may see that, by his lights, he is taking advantage of Herzog.

On his commentary track, Herzog describes him as "the unknown soldier of the cinema."

Kaspar Hauser was a real historical figure who in 1828 appeared in a town square early one morning clutching the Bible and an anonymous letter. In the movie, as apparently in reality, an unknown captor kept him tied up in a cellar for about the first twenty years of his life. Adopted by the town and a friendly couple, he learns to read and write and even play the piano (in life Bruno also plays accordion and glockenspiel). Kaspar speaks as a man to whom every day is a mystery: "What are women good for?" "My coming to this world was a terribly hard fall." And think of the concept being expressed when he says, "It dreamed to me. . . ."

In Herzog the line between fact and fiction is a shifting one. He cares not for accuracy but for effect, for a transcendent ecstasy. *Kaspar Hauser* tells its story not as a narrative about its hero, but as a mosaic of striking behavior and images: A line of penitents struggling up a hillside, a desert caravan led by a blind man, a stork capturing a worm. These images are unrelated to Kaspar except in the way they reflect and illuminate his struggle. The last thing Herzog is interested in is "solving" this lonely man's mystery. It is the mystery that attracts him.

All through the work of this great director, born in 1942, maker of fifty-four films, you can find extraordinary individuals who embody the qualities Herzog wants to evoke. In *Heart of Glass* (1976), challenged to depict a village deprived of its livelihood, he hypnotized the entire cast. In *Land of Silence and Darkness* (1971) and *Even Dwarfs Started Small* (1970), he tied to imagine the inner lives of the blind and deaf, and dwarfs. These people are not the captives of their limitations but freed by them to enter realms that are barred from us.

Herzog made two films about a German named Dieter Dengler, the documentary *Little Dieter Needs to Fly* (1977) and the fiction film *Rescue Dawn* (2006). In the first, Dengler, who enlisted in the navy, plays himself, retracing a torturous escape through the jungle from a Viet Cong prison camp. In the second, he is played by Christian Bale. But Herzog has explained that he made up some of the incidents in the documentary, and the feature is in a way a document about the ordeal of making the film; Bale looks like a scarecrow; the real

Dengler was down to eighty-five pounds. His performance in a way resembles the dedication of Timothy Treadwell, the man who thought he could walk unprotected among bears in *Grizzly Man*, a 2005 documentary based on video footage he took before finding himself mistaken. And there is Jouko Ahola, a Finnish weight lifter, twice named the world's strongest man, who Herzog uses as the hero of *Invincible* (2001), about a Polish strong man, Jewish, who poses as an Aryan ideal in Hitler's Berlin. Not an actor, but the right person for the role.

Bale is a professional actor, yes, but hired for what he can embody, as much as for what he can do. Consider also the case of Klaus Kinski, the star of Herzog's films *Aguirre, the Wrath of God* (1972), *Fitzcarraldo* (1982), *Nosferatu* (1979), *Cobra Verde* (1987), and *Woyzeck* (1979). An actor in one hundred thirty-five films, yes, but he told me he had seen only two or three of them. A man of towering rages and terrifying rampages, which at one point had him at gunpoint with Herzog. The subject of *My Best Fiend* (1999), Herzog's savage documentary about the man he loved and reviled. To see Kinski in a Herzog film is to see a man used not as an actor, but as an instrument through which to force the film.

In some ways the most emblematic film of Herzog's career is *The Ecstasy of the Woodcarver Steiner* (1974), a documentary about a ski jumper who must start halfway down the slope, because otherwise he is too good and would fly over the landing zone and into the parking lot. His limitation is his gift, and he dreams of flying forever. So many of Herzog's protagonists, real and fictional, have such dreams of escape, and are so intensely *themselves* that they carry his purpose unthinkingly.

The Enigma of Kaspar Hauser is a lyrical film about the least lyrical of men. Bruno S. has the solidity of the horses and cows he is often among, and as he confronts the world I was reminded of W. G. Sebold's remark that men and animals regard each other across a gulf of mutual incomprehension. The film's landscapes, its details from nature, its music all embody the dream world Kaspar entered when he escaped the unchanging reality of his cellar. He never dreamed in the cellar, he explains. I think it was because he knew of nothing else than the cellar to dream about.

The film is often linked with Truffaut's *The Wild Child* (1970), set in the same century, about a boy who emerged from the forest possibly having been raised by animals. A psychologist tries to "civilize" him, but cannot change his essential nature. Kaspar is also the subject of study, and there is a professor in the film who tests Kaspar with the riddle about the two villages, one populated by those who could not tell the truth, and the other by those who could not lie. When you meet a man on a path to the two villages, Kaspar is asked, what is the one question you must ask him to determine which village he comes from? "I would ask him if he is a tree frog," Kaspar answers with some pride.

Then there is the foppish English dandy Lord Stanhope, who introduces Kaspar as his "protégé," only to find that his protégé does not like being on exhibit at fancy dress balls. Kaspar seems happy enough to allow the village to pay off its debts by displaying him as an exhibit in a sideshow, however, along with a Brazilian flautist who believes that if he ever stops playing, the village will die. To prove he is Brazilian, he speaks in his own tongue, forgetting his prophecy.

The film's German title translates as *Every Man for Himself and God Against All*. That seems to summarize Kaspar's thinking. The mystery of the captive's origins has occupied investigators ever since he first appeared. Was he the secret heir to a throne? A rich man's love child? We have glimpses of the man who held him prisoner and then set him free, standing behind him and kicking his boots to force him to walk. Who is this man? He is never explained. He may be the embodiment of Kaspar's fate. We may all have somebody behind us, kicking our boots. We are poor mortals, but it dreams to us that we can fly.

E.T.—The Extra-Terrestrial

PG, 115 m., 1982

Henry Thomas (Elliott), Dee Wallace (Mary), Peter Coyote (Keys), Robert MacNaughton (Michael), Drew Barrymore (Gertie). Directed by Steven Spielberg and produced by Spielberg and Kathleen Kennedy. Screenplay by Melissa Mathison.

This movie made my heart glad. It is filled with innocence, hope, and good cheer. It is also wickedly funny and exciting as hell. *E.T.—The Extra-Terrestrial* is a movie like *The*

Wizard of Oz, that you can grow up with and grow old with, and it won't let you down. It tells a story about friendship and love. Some people are a little baffled when they hear it described: It's about a relationship between a little boy and a creature from outer space that becomes his best friend. That makes it sound like a cross between *The Thing* and *National Velvet.* It works as science fiction, it's sometimes as scary as a monster movie, and at the end, when the lights go up, there's not a dry eye in the house.

E.T. is a movie of surprises, and I will not spoil any of them for you. But I can suggest some of the film's wonders. The movie takes place in and around a big American suburban development. The split-level houses march up and down the curved drives, carved out of hills that turn into forest a few blocks beyond the backyard. In this forest one night, a spaceship lands, and queer-looking little creatures hobble out of it and go snuffling through the night, looking for plant specimens, I guess. Humans arrive—authorities with flashlights and big stomping boots. They close in on the spaceship, and it is forced to take off and abandon one of its crew members. This forlorn little creature, the *E.T.* of the title, is left behind on Earth—abandoned to a horrendous world of dogs, raccoons, automobile exhausts, and curious little boys.

The movie's hero is one particular little boy named Elliott. He is played by Henry Thomas in what has to be the best little boy performance I've ever seen in an American film. He doesn't come across as an overcoached professional kid; he's natural, defiant, easily touched, conniving, brave, and childlike. He just *knows* there's something living out there in the backyard, and he sits up all night with his flashlight, trying to coax the creature out of hiding with a nearly irresistible bait: Reese's Pieces. The creature, which looks a little like Snoopy but is very, very wise, approaches the boy. They become friends. The E.T. moves into the house, and the center section of the film is an endless invention on the theme of an extra-terrestrial's introduction to bedrooms, televisions, telephones, refrigerators, and six-packs of beer. The creature has the powers of telepathy and telekinesis, and one of the ways it communicates is to share its emotions with Elliott. That's how Elliott knows that the E.T. wants to go home.

And from here on out, I'd better not describe what happens. Let me just say that the movie has moments of sheer ingenuity, moments of high comedy, some scary moments, and a very sad sequence that has everybody blowing their noses.

What is especially wonderful about all of those moments is that Steven Spielberg, who made this film, creates them out of legitimate and fascinating plot developments. At every moment from its beginning to its end, *E.T.* is really *about* something. The story is quite a narrative accomplishment. It reveals facts about the E.T.'s nature; it develops the personalities of Elliott, his mother, brother, and sister; it involves the federal space agencies; it touches on extra-terrestrial medicine, biology, and communication, and *still* it inspires genuine laughter and tears.

A lot of those achievements rest on the very peculiar shoulders of the E.T. itself. With its odd little walk, its high-pitched squeals of surprise, its tentative imitations of human speech, and its catlike but definitely alien purring, E.T. becomes one of the most intriguing fictional creatures I've ever seen on a screen. The E.T. is a triumph of special effects, certainly; the craftsmen who made this little being have extended the boundaries of their art. But it's also a triumph of imagination, because the filmmakers had to imagine E.T., had to see through its eyes, hear with its ears, and experience this world of ours through its utterly alien experience in order to make a creature so absolutely convincing. The word for what they exercised is empathy. *E.T.—The Extra-Terrestrial* is a reminder of what movies are for. Most movies are not for any one thing, of course. Some are to make us think, some to make us feel, some to take us away from our problems, some to help us examine them. What is enchanting about *E.T.* is that, in some measure, it does all of those things.

Everyone Says I Love You
R, 101 m., 1997

Alan Alda (Bob), Woody Allen (Joe), Drew Barrymore (Skylar), Goldie Hawn (Steffi), Julia Roberts (Von), Tim Roth (Charles Ferry), Lukas Haas (Scott), Gaby Hoffmann (Lane), Natasha Lyonne (D.J.), Edward Norton (Holden), Natalie Portman (Laura), David Ogden Stiers (Holden's Father). Directed by Allen and produced by Jean Doumanian and Robert Greenhut. Screenplay by Allen.

Sometimes, when I am very happy, I sing to myself. Sometimes, when they are very happy, so do the characters in *Everyone Says I Love You,* Woody Allen's magical new musical comedy. I can't sing. Neither can some of Allen's characters. Why should that stop them? Who wants to go through life not ever singing?

Here is a movie that had me with a goofy grin plastered on my face for most of its length. A movie that remembers the innocence of the old Hollywood musicals and combines it with one of Allen's funniest and most labyrinthine plots, in which complicated New Yorkers try to recapture the simplicity of first love. It would take a heart of stone to resist this movie.

Allen's most inspired decision was to allow all of his actors to sing for themselves, in their own voices (all of them except for Drew Barrymore, who just plain can't sing). Some of them are accomplished (Alan Alda, Goldie Hawn, Edward Norton). The rest could hold their own at a piano bar. Allen knows that the musical numbers are not about performance or technical quality or vocal range; they're about feeling.

"Cuddle Up a Little Closer." "My Baby Don't Care for Pearls." "Looking at You." "I'm Through With Love." "I'm a Dreamer." "Makin' Whoopee." "Enjoy Yourself, It's Later Than You Think." These are songs that perhaps suffer a little when they're sung too well (just as trained opera singers always overdo it in musical comedy). They're for ordinary, happy voices, and from the first moment of the film, when Edward Norton turns to Drew Barrymore and sings "Just You, Just Me," the movie finds a freshness and charm that never ends.

The story involves a lot of Allen's familiar elements. His character, named Joe, is unlucky in love; he's a writer who lives in Paris, where his French girlfriend Giselle has just dumped him. He contemplates suicide, and debates the wisdom of taking the Concorde to New York before killing himself (with the time gain, he could get an extra three hours of stuff done and still be dead on schedule).

He returns to New York to be comforted by his best friends, who are his first wife, Steffi (Goldie Hawn), and her current husband, Bob

(Alan Alda). The extended family is a yours, mine, and ours situation. D.J. (Natasha Lyonne) is Joe's daughter with Steffi. She serves as the narrator. Then there are Skylar (Drew Barrymore), who has just gotten engaged; Scott (Lukas Haas), who has the family concerned with his newfound conservatism; and his sisters Lane (Gaby Hoffmann) and Laura (Natalie Portman), who are just discovering boys and have unfortunately discovered the same one.

The plot is simultaneously featherweight and profound, like a lot of Allen's movies: Big questions are raised and then dispatched with a one-liner, only to keep eating away at the hero until an eventually happy ending. Most of the questions have to do, of course, with unwise or inappropriate romances.

Joe decides to get away from it all by taking his daughter D.J. to Venice. Here we get one of the movie's loveliest moments, Allen singing "I'm Through With Love" on a balcony overlooking the Grand Canal. Of course he is not; soon after, he sees the enticing Von (Julia Roberts) in Venice, and falls in love at first sight. Amazingly, D.J. is able to supply him with useful insights into this mystery woman. D.J.'s best friend's mother is Von's psychiatrist, and the kids have eavesdropped on therapy sessions, so D.J. knows Von's likes (Tintoretto) and dislikes (her current husband), and coaches her father. This is, of course, dishonest and unethical, and delicious.

Joe's inside knowledge makes him irresistible to Roberts, although their romance is doomed from the start. Meanwhile, D.J. falls in love with a gondolier and announces an impending marriage. Back in New York, Holden (Edward Norton) has bought an engagement ring for Skylar (while the salesmen at Harry Winston's celebrate in a song and dance). Also meanwhile, Steffi, a liberal who wears her heart on her sleeve, arranges the release of a prisoner (Tim Roth) she thinks has been unfairly treated, and he steals Skylar's heart, for a time, anyway—and also contributes to an unusual dinner party.

Oh, there's more. Including the scene where Skylar accidentally swallows her $8,000 engagement ring and is told by the doctor examining the X rays, "I could have got it for you for $6,000." And a miraculous cure for Scott's conservatism. And a fanciful song-and-dance scene involving some ghosts in a funeral home. And the absolutely wonderful long closing sequence, which begins at a New Year's Eve party in Paris where everyone is dressed like Groucho Marx.

Steffi's family is visiting Paris, and at dawn she and Joe walk off alone to the café where their romance started many years ago. Was their divorce a mistake? Should Steffi dump Bob and come back to Joe? At dawn in a romantic café in Paris all sorts of seductive ideas can occur, but the movie segues away from hard decisions and into a dance number involving Allen and Hawn on the banks of the Seine, Goldie floating effortlessly in a scene that combines real magic with the magic of the heart.

Watching that scene, I thought that perhaps *Everyone Says I Love You* is the best film Woody Allen has ever made. Not the most profound, or the most daring, or the most successful in every one of its details—but simply the best, because he finds the right note for every scene, and dances on a tightrope between comedy and romance, between truth and denial, between what we hope and what we know.

Not many musicals are made these days. They're hard to do, and the fashion for them has passed. This one remembers the musicals of the 1930s, the innocent ones starring Astaire and Rogers, or Powell and Keeler, and to that freshness it adds a sharper, contemporary wit. Allen knows that what modern musicals are missing is not the overkill of multimillion-dollar production numbers, or the weight of hit songs from the charts, but the feeling that some things simply cannot be said in words and require songs to say them. He is right. Attempt this experiment: Try to say "Cuddle up a little closer, baby mine" without singing. Can't be done. Should rarely be attempted.

Eve's Bayou

R, 109 m., 1997

Jurnee Smollett (Eve Batiste), Meagan Good (Cisely Batiste), Samuel L. Jackson (Louis Batiste), Lynn Whitfield (Roz Batiste), Debbi Morgan (Mozelle Batiste Delacroix), Jake Smollett (Poe Batiste), Ethel Ayler (Gran Mere), Diahann Carroll (Elzora), Vondie Curtis Hall (Julian Grayraven). Directed by Kasi Lemmons and produced by Caldecot Chubb and Jackson. Screenplay by Lemmons.

"Memory is a selection of images, some elusive, others printed indelibly on the brain. The summer I killed my father, I was ten years old."

With those opening words, *Eve's Bayou* coils back into the past, into the memories of a child who grew up in a family both gifted and flawed, and tried to find her own way to the truth. The words explain the method of the film. This will not be a simpleminded story that breathlessly races from A to B. It is a selection of memories, filtered through the eyes of a young girl who doesn't understand everything she sees—and filtered, too, through the eyes of her older sister, and through the eyes of an aunt who can foretell everyone's future except for her own.

As these images unfold, we are drawn into the same process Eve has gone through: We, too, are trying to understand what happened in that summer of 1962, when Eve's handsome, dashing father—a doctor and womanizer—took one chance too many. And we want to understand what happened late one night between the father and Eve's older sister, in a moment that was over before it began. We want to know because the film makes it perfectly possible that there is more than one explanation; *Eve's Bayou* studies the way that dangerous emotions can build up until something happens that no one is responsible for and that can never be taken back.

All of these moments unfold in a film of astonishing maturity and confidence; *Eve's Bayou,* one of the very best films of the year, is the debut of its writer and director, Kasi Lemmons. She sets her story in Southern Gothic country, in the bayous and old Louisiana traditions that Tennessee Williams might have been familiar with, but in tone and style she earns comparison with the family dramas of Ingmar Bergman. That Lemmons can make a film this good on the first try is like a rebuke to established filmmakers.

The story is told through the eyes of Eve Batiste, played with fierce truthfulness by Jurnee Smollett. Her family is descended from a slave, also named Eve, who saved her master's life and was rewarded with her freedom and with sixteen children. In 1962, the Batistes are the premiere family in their district, living in a big old mansion surrounded by rivers and swampland. Eve's father, Louis (Samuel L. Jackson), is the local doctor. Her mother, Roz (Lynn

Whitfield), is "the most beautiful woman I ever have seen." Her sister, Cisely (Meagan Good), is on the brink of adolescence, and the apple of her father's eye; Eve watches unhappily at a party and afterwards asks her father, "Daddy, why don't you ever dance with me?" Living with them is an aunt, Mozelle (Debbi Morgan), who has lost three husbands, "is not unfamiliar with the inside of a mental hospital," and has the gift of telling fortunes.

Dr. Batiste is often away from home on house calls—some of them legitimate, some excuses for his philandering. He is a weak but not a bad man, and not lacking in insight: "To a certain type of woman, I am a hero," he says. "I need to be a hero." On the night that her father did not dance with her, Eve steals away to a barn and falls asleep, only to awaken and see her father apparently making love with another man's wife. Eve tells Cisely, who says she was mistaken, and the doubt over this incident will echo later, on another night when much depends on whether Cisely was mistaken.

Lemmons surrounds her characters with a rich setting. There is a marketplace, dominated by the stalls of farmers and fishermen, and by the presence of a voodoo woman (Diahann Carroll) whose magic may or may not be real. Certainly Aunt Mozelle's gift is real; her prophecies have a terrifying accuracy, as when she tells a woman her missing son will be found in a Detroit hospital on Tuesday. But Mozelle cannot foresee her own life: "I looked at each of my husbands," she says, "and never saw a thing." All three died. So when a handsome painter (Vondie Curtis Hall) comes into the neighborhood and Mozelle knows she has found true love at last, she is afraid to marry him, because it has been prophesied that any man who marries her will die.

The film has been photographed by Amy Vincent in shadows and rich textures, where even a sunny day contains dark undertones; surely she looked at the Bergman films photographed by Sven Nykvist in preparing her approach. There is a scene of pure magic as Mozelle tells Eve the story of the death of one of her husbands, who was shot by her lover; the woman and the girl stand before a mirror, regarding the scene from the past, and then Mozelle slips out of the shot and reappears in the past.

There is also great visual precision in the scenes involving the confused night when the doctor comes home drunk, and Cisely goes downstairs to comfort him. What happened? We get two accounts and we see two versions, and the film is far too complex and thoughtful to try to reduce the episode to a simple formula like sexual abuse; what happens lasts only a second, and is charged with many possibilities for misinterpretation, all of them prepared for by what has gone before.

Eve's Bayou resonates in the memory. It called me back for a second and third viewing. It is a reminder that sometimes films can venture into the realms of poetry and dreams.

The Exorcist

R, 121 m., 1973

Ellen Burstyn (Chris), Linda Blair (Regan), Jason Miller (Father Karras), Max von Sydow (Father Merrin), Kitty Winn (Sharon), Lee J. Cobb (Kinderman). Directed by William Friedkin and produced by William Peter Blatty. Screenplay by Blatty, based on his book.

Nineteen seventy-three began and ended with cries of pain. It began with Ingmar Bergman's *Cries and Whispers*, and it closed with William Friedkin's *The Exorcist*. Both films are about the weather of the human soul, and no two films could be more different. Yet each in its own way forces us to look inside, to experience horror, to confront the reality of human suffering. The Bergman film is a humanist classic. The Friedkin film is an exploitation of the most fearsome resources of the cinema. That does not make it evil, but it does not make it noble, either.

The difference, maybe, is between great art and great craftsmanship. Bergman's exploration of the lines of love and conflict within the family of a woman dying of cancer was a film that asked important questions about faith and death, and was not afraid to admit there might not be any answers. Friedkin's film is about a twelve-year-old girl who either is suffering from a severe neurological disorder or—perhaps—has been possessed by an evil spirit. Friedkin has the answers; the problem is that we doubt he believes them.

We don't necessarily believe them ourselves, but that hardly matters during the film's two hours. If movies are, among other things, opportunities for escapism, then *The Exorcist* is one of the most powerful ever made. Our objections, our questions, occur in an intellectual context after the movie has ended. During the movie there are no reservations, but only experiences. We feel shock, horror, nausea, fear, and some small measure of dogged hope.

Rarely do movies affect us so deeply. The first time I saw *Cries and Whispers,* I found myself shrinking down in my seat, somehow trying to escape from the implications of Bergman's story. *The Exorcist* also has that effect—but we're not escaping from Friedkin's implications, we're shrinking back from the direct emotional experience he's attacking us with. This movie doesn't rest on the screen; it's a frontal assault.

The story is well-known; it's adapted, more or less faithfully, by William Peter Blatty from his own best seller. Many of the technical and theological details in his book are accurate. Most accurate of all is the reluctance of his Jesuit hero, Father Karras, to encourage the ritual of exorcism: "To do that," he says, "I'd have to send the girl back to the sixteenth century." Modern medicine has replaced devils with paranoia and schizophrenia, he explains. Medicine may have, but the movie hasn't. The last chapter of the novel never totally explained in detail the final events in the tortured girl's bedroom, but the movie's special effects in the closing scenes leave little doubt that an actual evil spirit was in that room, and that it transferred bodies. Is this fair? I guess so; in fiction the artist has poetic license.

It may be that the times we live in have prepared us for this movie. And Friedkin has admittedly given us a good one. I've always preferred a generic approach to film criticism; I ask myself how good a movie is of its type. *The Exorcist* is one of the best movies of its type ever made; it not only transcends the genre of terror, horror, and the supernatural, but it transcends such serious, ambitious efforts in the same direction as Roman Polanski's *Rosemary's Baby.* Carl Dreyer's *The Passion of Joan of Arc* is a greater film—but, of course, not nearly so willing to exploit the ways film can manipulate feeling.

The Exorcist does that with a vengeance. The film is a triumph of special effects. Never for a moment—not when the little girl is possessed by the most disgusting of spirits, not when the bed is banging and the furniture flying and the vomit is welling out—are we less than convinced. The film contains brutal shocks, almost indescribable obscenities. That it received an R rating and not the X is stupefying.

The performances are in every way appropriate to this movie made this way. Ellen Burstyn, as the possessed girl's mother, rings especially true; we feel her frustration when doctors and psychiatrists talk about lesions on the brain and she *knows* there's something deeper, more terrible, going on. Linda Blair, as the little girl, has obviously been put through an ordeal in this role, and puts us through one. Jason Miller, as the young Jesuit, is tortured, doubting, intelligent.

And the casting of Max von Sydow as the older Jesuit exorcist was inevitable; he has been through so many religious and metaphysical crises in Bergman's films that he almost seems to belong on a theological battlefield the way John Wayne belonged on a horse. There's a striking image early in the film that has the craggy von Sydow facing an ancient, evil statue; the image doesn't so much borrow from Bergman's famous chess game between von Sydow and Death (in *The Seventh Seal*) as extend the conflict and raise the odds.

I am not sure exactly what reasons people will have for seeing this movie; surely enjoyment won't be one, because what we get here aren't the delicious chills of a Vincent Price thriller, but raw and painful experience. Are people so numb they need movies of this intensity in order to feel anything at all? It's hard to say.

Even in the extremes of Friedkin's vision there is still a feeling that this is, after all, cinematic escapism and not a confrontation with real life. There is a fine line to be drawn there, and *The Exorcist* finds it and stays a millimeter on this side.

Exotica

R, 103 m., 1995

Bruce Greenwood (Francis), Mia Kirshner (Christina), Don McKellar (Thomas), Arsinee Khanjian (Zoe), Elias Koteas (Eric), Sarah Polley (Tracey), Victor Garber (Harold), Calvin Green (Customs Officer). Directed by Atom Egoyan and produced by Egoyan and Camelia Frieberg. Screenplay by Egoyan.

Exotica is a movie labyrinth, winding seductively into the darkest secrets of a group of people who should have no connection with one another, but do. At the beginning, the film seems to be about randomly selected strangers. By the end, it is revealed that these people are so tightly wound up together that if you took one away, their world would collapse.

Christina (Mia Kirshner) works in a "gentleman's club," so called because few gentlemen go there. She has a regular client named Francis (Bruce Greenwood). He pays her an hourly rate to come and "dance" seductively at his table. No touching is allowed in this club, but Francis has no desire to touch. What he needs from Christina is not physical. And Christina . . . what does she need? We sense an odd private bond between them.

Eric is the deejay in the club, spinning suggestive fantasies about the dancers, drumming up business for the tables. He was once Christina's lover. Now he watches jealously, possessively, as she lingers for hours with Francis. Zoe owns the club. It was started by her late mother, whose "sense of freedom" she admired so much that she even dresses in her mother's clothes. Zoe is pregnant, sweet, honest; she sees the club as a place where lonely people can be less lonely for a few hours. No one there is lonelier than her.

Who are these other characters? Who is the customs officer, and what is his real connection with the man who picks him up at the ballet—the man who owns a pet shop? Why does he steal precious eggs from the man's incubator? And why does Francis hire a babysitter to stay at his house when he goes to the gentleman's club, since he has no children?

It's easy for a director to play these games all night, setting up mysteries and then revealing deeper mysteries inside of them. That is not Atom Egoyan's game. His plot for *Exotica* coils back upon itself, revealing one layer of mystery after another, but this is not an exercise in style. It is a movie about people whose lives,

once we understand them, reveal a need and urgency that only these mysteries can satisfy.

Egoyan, a Canadian director whose imagination and originality have not always been under such masterful control, has been moving toward *Exotica* in his other recent films, like *The Adjuster* (1992). Of that film, he wrote, "I wanted to make a movie about believable people doing believable things in an unbelievable way." It was a good film, but you could see the gears turning. *Exotica* is his best yet, a film in which the characters seem completely real even while they seem to be acting without any apparent explanation—and then seem even more real when we understand them.

Many of the actors come from his stock company. Elias Koteas, who was the adjuster, now plays the deejay; in the earlier film he served others, but this time he serves only himself. Arsinee Khanjian (Egoyan's wife) is Zoe, the club owner, suffusing the sleazy surroundings with a gentle innocence. Mia Kirshner, an actress new to me, combines sexual allure with a kindness that makes her all the more appealing. Indeed, the intriguing thing about Egoyan's work here is how he sets the story in a hothouse of sex, and then works around the sex, getting to the feelings, revealing how most of the characters are much nicer than at first they seem.

In the months after *Pulp Fiction* opened, I talked to a lot of people who were stimulated by its plot structure, the way it played with apparent paradoxes. Those people are likely to admire the plot of *Exotica* even more: We begin with desperation and need, and move to satisfaction and fulfillment, and at the same time Egoyan astonishingly finds a way to add melodrama, blackmail, and an ingenious deception. The movie is a series of interlocking surprises and delights, and, at the end, it is heartbreaking as well. It's quite a performance, announcing Egoyan's arrival in the first rank of filmmakers.

F

Faces
PG-13, 130 m., 1968

John Marley (Richard Forst), Gena Rowlands (Jeannie Rapp), Lynn Carlin (Maria Forst), Seymour Cassel (Chet), Fred Draper (Freddie). Directed by John Cassavetes and produced by Maurice McEndree. Screenplay by Cassavetes.

John Cassavetes's *Faces* is the sort of film that makes you want to grab people by the neck and drag them into the theater and shout: "Here!" It would be a triumphant shout. Year after year, we get a tide of bilge that passes for "the American way of life" in the movies.

We know it isn't like that. We don't live that way and neither does anyone we know. What Cassavetes has done is astonishing. He has made a film that tenderly, honestly, and uncompromisingly examines the way we really live.

The central characters are middle-aged, middle-class, and rather ordinary: a man and his wife. They have everything in the world they desire, except love and a sense of personal accomplishment. They've become consumers in the most cruel sense of that word: Their only identity is as economic beings who earn and spend money to sustain a meaningless existence. They don't do anything, or make anything, or create anything. They use.

This is not only a crisis but a trap, because society has left them stranded without any means of breaking out. During a long night when their marriage reaches the breaking point, they discover only two ways to kick loose: alcohol and adultery. One of the problems with this class of society is that it provides so few ways to boil over.

The film begins with the man (John Marley), a fairly prosperous executive, stopping off at a prostitute's apartment on his way home. The hooker (Gena Rowlands) and her roommate are already entertaining two men, and there is some alcoholic give-and-take punctuated with stale dirty jokes. (Has anybody noticed that dirty jokes have simply passed out of the repertory of most people under thirty?)

Marley eventually goes on home, and there is a scene with his wife (Lynn Carlin) that is one of the best single scenes I've ever seen.

They sit at the dining room table and talk about sex, and just in the way they form their sentences you can see they're terribly "sophisticated" and verbal, but really very frightened and repressed.

In a burst of alcoholic ethics, Marley announces he wants a divorce and telephones the call girl while his wife watches. We then follow two stories, Marley's evening with the prostitute and his wife's outing with three female friends.

Handled incorrectly, these scenes could all be mawkish stereotypes. But Cassavetes has pressed beneath the stereotypes and down to the level where these things really do happen.

Among the five awards *Faces* won at the Venice Film Festival was one to John Marley, as best actor. It was deserved, but Seymour Cassel also deserves mention, and perhaps an Academy Award supporting actor nomination, for his performance as the hippie.

Lynn Carlin reportedly was a secretary at Screen Gems when Cassavetes cast her as Marley's wife. This is her first professional role; she brings depth and truth to it.

Rowlands (in real life, Cassavetes's wife) avoids the heart-of-gold clichés and plays a prostitute who has her own problems and a deep reservoir of human sympathy as well.

The Falcon and the Snowman
R, 131 m., 1985

Timothy Hutton (Christopher Boyce), Sean Penn (Daulton Lee), Pat Hingle (Mr. Boyce), Joyce Van Patten (Mrs. Boyce), David Suchet (Alex), Boris Leskin (Mikhail). Directed by John Schlesinger and produced by Gabriel Katska and Schlesinger. Screenplay by Steven Saillian.

A few years ago there were stories in the papers about a couple of California kids who were caught selling government secrets to the Russians. The stories had an air of unreality about them. Here were a couple of middle-class young men from suburban backgrounds, who were prosecuted as spies and traitors and who hardly seemed to have it quite clear in their own minds how they had gotten into the spy business. One of the many strengths of *The Falcon and the Snowman* is that it succeeds, in an admirably matter-of-fact way, in showing us exactly how these two young men got in way over their heads. This is a movie about spies, but it is not a thriller in any routine sense of the word; it's just the meticulously observant record of how naiveté, inexperience, misplaced idealism, and greed led to one of the most peculiar cases of treason in American history.

The movie stars Timothy Hutton as Christopher Boyce, a seminarian who has a crisis of conscience, drops out of school, and ends up working almost by accident for a message-routing center of the CIA. Sean Penn is his best friend, Daulton Lee. Years ago, they were altar boys together, but in recent times their paths have diverged; while Boyce was studying for the priesthood, Lee was setting himself up as a drug dealer. By the time we meet them, Boyce is earnest and clean-cut, just the kind of young man the CIA might be looking for (it doesn't hurt that his father is a former FBI man). And Lee, with a mustache that makes him look like a failed creep, is a jumpy, paranoid drug dealer who is one step ahead of the law.

The whole caper begins so simply. Boyce, reading the messages he is paid to receive and forward, learns that the CIA is engaged in dirty tricks designed to influence elections in Australia. He is deeply offended to learn that his government would be interfering in the affairs of another state, and the more he thinks about it, the more he wants to do something. For example, supply the messages to the Russians. He doesn't want to be a Russian *spy*, you understand, just to bring this injustice to light. Lee has some contacts in Mexico, where he buys drugs. One day, in a deceptively casual conversation by the side of a backyard swimming pool, the two friends decide to go into partnership to sell the information to the Soviet Embassy in Mexico City. Lee takes the documents south and launches them both on an adventure that is a lark at first, and then a challenge, and finally just a very, very bad dream.

These two young men have one basic problem. They are amateurs. The Russians don't necessarily like that any better than the Americans would; indeed, even though the Russians are happy to have the secrets that are for sale, there is a definite sense in some scenes that the key Russian contact agent, played by David Suchet, is almost offended by the sloppy way Penn deals in espionage. The only thing Penn seems really serious about is the money.

The Falcon and the Snowman never steps wrong, but it is best when it deals with the relationship between the two young American spies. The movie was directed by John Schlesinger, an Englishman whose understanding of American characters was most unforgettably demonstrated in *Midnight Cowboy*, and I was reminded of Joe Buck and Ratso Rizzo from that movie as I watched this one. There is even a quiet, understated quote to link Ratso with the Penn character: a moment in a parking garage when Penn defies a car to pull in front of him, and we're reminded of Ratso crossing a Manhattan street and hurling the line "I'm *walking* here!" at a taxi that dares to cut him off. Instead of relying on traditional methods for creating the suspense in spy movies, this one uses the energy generated between the two very different characters, as the all-American Boyce gradually begins to understand that his partner is out of control. *The Falcon and the Snowman*, like most good movies, is not really about its plot but about its characters. These two young men could just as easily be selling stolen IBM programs to Apple, instead of CIA messages to the Russians; the point is that they begin with one set of motives and then the implacable real world supplies them with another, harder, more unforgiving set of realities.

Just as with *Midnight Cowboy*, it's hard to say who gives the better performance this time: Sean Penn, with his twitching intensity as he angles for respect from the Russians, or Timothy Hutton, the straight man, earnestly telling his girlfriend that she should remember he really loves her—"no matter what you may hear about me in a few days from now."

Falling from Grace
PG-13, 101 m., 1992

John Mellencamp (Bud Parks), Mariel Hemingway (Alice Parks), Claude Akins (Specs Parks), Dub Taylor (Grandpa Parks), Kay Lenz (P. J. Parks). Directed by

Mellencamp and produced by Harry Sandler.
Screenplay by Larry McMurtry.

Thomas Wolfe told us, "You can't go home again," and people who have never read a word of his novels remember that warning, perhaps because it is so obviously true. And still people try to go back home. In *Falling from Grace,* John Mellencamp's powerful and perceptive movie, a country-rock star returns to his small town in Indiana, hoping to throw back a few brews and hang out with his old buddies at the pool hall. It doesn't work out that way.

The Mellencamp character left more than memories behind in Indiana. He also left an alcoholic father (Claude Akins), whose idea of an ideal male role falls somewhere between patriarch and rapist. And he left behind an old girlfriend (Kay Lenz), who has now married the hero's brother but who has spent a lot of years thinking the singer should have taken her along when he left for the big time.

John Mellencamp, of course, is a rock star who comes from Indiana himself, and often goes back there—so often it is unlikely *Falling from Grace* is autobiographical except in its broadest and least personal outlines. What he has done, I imagine, is to combine Larry McMurtry's uncommonly good original screenplay with his own small-town insights, and the experiences of all sorts of other people he's met or worked with on the road. They all come together in this story where old wounds never heal.

One of the strangest truths about high school reunions is that all of the old jealousies and resentments of years before are still remembered so clearly; the people who sat together in the school lunchroom now sit together at the reunion banquet, as if the years in between haven't made a difference. We get that same sense of wounded memory in the opening scenes of *Falling from Grace,* as Mellencamp's private plane arrives at the local airport, disgorging the singer, his wife (Mariel Hemingway), and his entourage.

Word quickly gets around town that Mellencamp is back, and it is especially quick to reach Kay Lenz, the sister-in-law. The situation resembles, I suppose, a script from *Dallas* or *Dynasty* (returning rock star still feels chemistry with sexy old flame, now married

to his brother), but McMurtry doesn't write it that way. His screenplay is too intelligent, and too observant.

Kay Lenz has many of the best scenes in the movie. She plays a woman who has achieved some degree of material comfort (she lives in one of the best houses in town), but no psychic or emotional satisfaction. She fools around all the time, and everyone in town knows it, and she doesn't care that they know.

The Mellencamp character comes back to town with the idea that everyone will be more or less happy to see him. He is wrong. His friends and relatives have spent a long time thinking about his life in the fast lane, and there are a lot of jealousies and resentments. Lenz is particularly angry. She knows she was smart enough and pretty enough for him to take along when he made his break, and if he's going to come back she isn't going to simply smile and bite the bullet.

While Hemingway, as the singer's wife, sits around bored and ignored, and pawed by the singer's randy father—who treats her like a toy that his son brought home for Dad—Mellencamp and Lenz engage in a hostile and risky flirtation. This could have been soap opera material, but McMurtry's screenplay is based on a lot of psychological insight, and we see how old issues and old wounds are still able to affect the present and change lives.

A lot of rock stars and other showbiz heroes have the notion that because they're successful in other areas, they can direct a movie, too. Usually they're wrong. But Mellencamp turns out to have a real filmmaking gift. His film is perceptive and subtle, and doesn't make the mistake of thinking that because something is real, it makes good fiction. The characters created here with McMurtry are three-dimensional and fully realized—and the Lenz character is probably even better-seen than Mellencamp's. At the end of the movie we are left with the possibility that although you may be able to go home again, it might be a good idea not to.

Falstaff/Chimes at Midnight

NO MPAA RATING, 115 m., 1967

Orson Welles (Falstaff), Jeanne Moreau (Doll Tearsheet), Margaret Rutherford (Mistress Quickly),

John Gielgud (Henry IV), Marina Vlady (Kate Percy), Keith Baxter (Prince Hal), Norman Rodway (Henry Percy). Directed by Orson Welles and produced by Allesandro Tasca. Screenplay by Raphael Holinshed, based on a play by William Shakespeare.

Orson Welles's *Falstaff* has some sound track difficulties, but they hardly affect the greatness of his film. Working on location in Spain and dubbing the voices of the extras he used in many roles, Welles saved money but sometimes lost clarity.

Nevertheless, his film is a brilliant tribute to Falstaff; perhaps Welles felt a comradeship with his subject this time. One imagines that Falstaff would have made this film much as Welles has, with lots of lusty wenches, flagons of ale, a tavern big enough for a battalion, a castle romantically vast, and a really gung-ho battle scene—all done, of course, as a fitting backdrop to kind, sweet, fat Jack Falstaff.

Welles himself plays Falstaff, of course, and selects from Shakespeare's *Henry IV* plays to bring the political and historic events around to Falstaff's point of view. He has done this, however, without using a single word of dialogue not written by Shakespeare.

The film should not be avoided, then, by purists who usually dislike screen "treatments" of Shakespeare. The great events in the kingdom march forward despite Falstaff's celebrations, and there is sufficient background for us to understand the full impact when, at his coronation, Hal refuses to recognize his dear old friend.

The story is suited to Welles's personal camera style. Low-angle shots exaggerate the enormous bulk of Falstaff's armor-clad frame. Deep-focus photography makes the king (John Gielgud) seem terribly lonely at the foot of the towering pillars in the castle, and the sun's rays cut across his path like prison bars. Welles has made Falstaff's tavern not a crowded Elizabethan pub but a cavernous place with a loft above for Doll Tearsheet to ply her trade.

To this basic accomplishment, Welles brings several passages of genius. The battle scene is the best I have seen. It is edited quickly, to give a sense of confusion and violence—providing an ironic backdrop for the frightened Falstaff himself, running from tree to tree to hide from the combatants. Welles looks something like a Sherman tank on legs as he hustles his three-hundred pounds out of the way.

Gielgud supplies a traditional reading of Shakespeare, as if he were in the "real" play and not in this version about Falstaff. Jeanne Moreau is a fond and moving Doll Tearsheet. As Mistress Quickly, Margaret Rutherford gives a touching description of Falstaff's death ("He babbled 'a green fields . . ."). The closing shot, of pallbearers struggling to carry away Jack Falstaff's improbably, pathetically oversize coffin, is a touch only Welles would have supplied: dramatic, emotional, just a touch of schmaltz. Here is a film to treasure.

Fanny and Alexander

R, 197 m., 1983

Pernilla Allwin (Fanny Ekdahl), Bertil Guve (Alexander Ekdahl), Jan Malmsjo (Bishop Vergerus), Erland Josephson (Isak Jacobi), Kabi Laretei (Aunt Emma), Gunn Wallgren (Helena Ekdahl), Ewa Froling (Emilie Ekdahl), Gunnar Bjornstrand (Filip Landahl). Directed by Ingmar Bergman and produced by Jorn Donner. Screenplay by Bergman.

There was a time when Ingmar Bergman wanted to make films reflecting the whole of human experience. He asked the big questions about death, sex, and God, and he wasn't afraid of the big, dramatic image, either. Who else (except Woody Allen) has had the temerity to show a man playing chess with Death? Bergman was swinging for the fences in those deliberately big, important films. But he has discovered that a better way to encompass all human experience is to be specific about a small part of it and let the audience draw its own conclusions. In *The Seventh Seal* (1956), he portrayed Death as a symbolic grim reaper. But in *Cries and Whispers* (1973), by showing one particular woman dying painfully while her sisters and her maid stood by helplessly, he said infinitely more about death.

His film *Fanny and Alexander* is one of the most detailed and specific he's ever made, and therefore one of the most universal. It comes directly out of his experiences as a Swede in his mid-sixties who was born into a world of rigid religious belief, grew up in a world of war and turmoil, and is now old enough, wise enough, and resigned enough to develop a sort of philosophical mysticism about life. In its chronology, the film covers only a handful of years. But in its buried implications about life, I believe, it traces the development of Bergman's thought from his school days until the day before yesterday.

Fanny and Alexander is a long film that contains many characters and many events. Very simply: In a Swedish provincial town in the early years of this century, two children are growing up within the bosom of a large, jolly extended family. Their father dies and their mother remarries. Their new stepfather is a stern, authoritarian clergyman who means well but is absolutely incapable of understanding the feelings of others. Escape from his household leads them, by an indirect path, into the life of an old Jewish antique dealer whose life still has room for the mysticism and magic of an earlier time. Not everything is explained by the end of the film, but everything is reconciled.

Bergman has confessed that a great deal of the movie is autobiographical—if not literally, then in terms of its feelings. He had, for example, a father who was a strict clergyman. But it's too easy to assume the bishop in the movie represents only Bergman's father: Can he not also represent Bergman himself, who is seen within the circle of his collaborators as an authoritarian figure with a tendency to know what is right for everyone else? Bergman has hinted that there's a little of himself, indeed, in *all* the male characters in his movies. Looking for Bergman's autobiography in his characters is one thing. I think we also can see *Fanny and Alexander* as the autobiography of his career. The warm humanism of the early scenes reflects his own beginnings in naturalism. The stern aestheticism of the middle scenes reflects his own middle period, with its obsession with both philosophical and stylistic black-and-white. The last third of the film, like the last third of his career, admits that there are more things in heaven and on Earth than dreamed of in his philosophy.

Fanny and Alexander is a big, exciting, ambitious film—more of a beginning than, as Bergman claims, the summary of his career. If you've followed him on his long trek of discovery, this will feel like a film of resolution. If you're coming fresh to Bergman, it may, para-doxically, seem to burst with the sort of invention we associate with young first-time directors. It's a film for all seasons.

Farewell My Concubine

R, 156 m., 1993

Leslie Cheung (Cheng Dieyi), Zhang Fengyi (Duan Xiaolou), Gong Li (Juxian), Lu Qi (Guan Jifa), Ying Da (Na Kun), Ge You (Master Yuan), Li Chun (Xiao Si, Teenage), Lei Han (Xiao Si, Adult), Tong Di (Old Man Zhang). Directed by Chen Kaige and produced by Hsu Feng. Screenplay by Lilian Lee and Lu Wei.

Farewell My Concubine is two films at once: an epic spanning a half century of modern Chinese history, and a melodrama about life backstage at the famed Peking Opera. The idea of viewing modern China through the eyes of two of the opera's stars would not, at first, seem logical: How could the birth pangs of a developing nation have much in common with the death pangs of an ancient and ritualistic art form? And yet the film flows with such urgency that all its connections seem logical. And it is filmed with such visual splendor that possible objections are swept aside.

The film opens on a setting worthy of Dickens, as two young orphan boys are inducted into the Peking Opera's harsh, perfectionist training academy. The physical and mental hardships are barely endurable, but they produce, after years, classical performers who are exquisitely trained for their roles.

We meet the delicate young Douzi (Leslie Cheung), who is assigned to the transvestite role of the concubine in a famous traditional opera, and the more masculine Shitou (Zhang Fengyi), who will play the king. Throughout their lives they will be locked into these roles onstage, while their personal relationship somehow survives the upheavals of World War II, the communist takeover of China, and the Cultural Revolution.

Under the stage names of Cheng Dieyi (Leslie Cheung) and Duan Xiaolou (Zhang Fengyi), the two actors become wildly popular with Peking audiences. But they are politically unsophisticated, and Cheng in particular makes unwise decisions during the Japanese occupation, leading to later charges of collaborating with the enemy.

Their personal relationship is equally unsettled. Dieyi, a homosexual, feels great love for Xiaolou, but the "king" doesn't share his feelings, and eventually marries the beautiful prostitute Juxian, played by China's leading actress, Gong Li. Dieyi is resentful and jealous, but during long years of hard times Juxian stands heroically by both men.

That the Peking Opera survives at all during five decades of upheaval is rather astonishing; apparently its royalist and bourgeois origins are balanced against its long history as a Chinese cultural tradition, so that even the Red Chinese accept it in all of its anachronistic glory. What almost does it in, however, is the Cultural Revolution, as shrill young ideologues impose their instant brand of political correctness on the older generations, and characters are forced to denounce one another. Xiaolou even denounces Dieyi as a homosexual, and Dieyi counterattacks by denouncing his friend's wife as a prostitute.

The movie's director is Chen Kaige, who knows about the Cultural Revolution at first hand. Born in 1952, he was sent in 1969 to a rural area to do manual labor; the scenes involving the Peking Opera's youth training programs may owe something to this experience. The son of a filmmaker, he was a Red Guard and a soldier before enrolling in film school, and at one point actually denounced his own father, an act for which he still feels great shame. (The father, sentenced to hard labor for several years, worked with his son as artistic director of this film.)

Farewell My Concubine won the Grand Prix at Cannes in 1993, but Chen Kaige returned home to find his film first shown, then banned, then shown again and banned again in China. His particular offense was to show a suicide taking place in 1977, a year in which, government orthodoxy holds, life in China did not justify such measures. The Chinese authorities were also uneasy about the homosexual aspects in the story.

What is amazing, given the conditions under which the film was made, is the freedom and energy with which it plays. The story is almost unbelievably ambitious, using no less than the entire modern history of China as its backdrop, as the private lives of the characters reflect their changing fortunes: The toast of the nation at one point, they are homeless outcasts at another, and nearly destroyed by their political naïveté more than once. (It is perhaps an unfair quibble that although they must be sixtyish by the end of the story, they look only somewhat older than when they were young men.)

The Peking Opera itself is filmed in lavish detail; the costumes benefit from the rich colors of the world's last surviving threestrip Technicolor lab, in Shanghai, and the backstage intrigues and romances are worthy of a soap opera. Leslie Cheung's concubine is never less than convincing, and his private life—he is essentially raised by the opera as a homosexual whether or not he consents—contains labyrinthine emotional currents. Gong Li, as the prostitute, is sometimes glamorous, sometimes haggard, and always at the mercy of two men whose work together has defined their individual personalities.

The epic is a threatened art form at the movies. Audiences seem to prefer less ambitious, more simpleminded stories, in which the heroes control events, instead of being buffeted by them. *Farewell My Concubine* is a demonstration of how a great epic can function. I was generally familiar with the important moments in modern Chinese history, but this film helped me to feel and imagine what it was like to live in the country during those times. Like such dissimilar films as *Dr. Zhivago* and *A Passage to India*, it took me to another place and time, and made it emotionally comprehensible.

Farewell, My Lovely

R, 95 m., 1975

Robert Mitchum (Philip Marlowe), Charlotte Rampling (Velma), John Ireland (Lieutenant Nulty), Sylvia Miles (Mrs. Nulty), Jack O'Halloran (Moose Malloy), Anthony Zerbe (Brunette), Harry Dean Stanton (Billy Rolfe), Walter McGinn (Tommy Ray). Directed by Dick Richards and produced by George Pappas and Jerry Bruckheimer. Screenplay by David Zelag Goodman, based on the book by Raymond Chandler.

Los Angeles, 1941. A run-down street of seedy shop fronts and blinking neon signs. Music from a lonely horn. The camera pans up to a second-story window of a flophouse. In the window, his hat pushed back, his tie undone,

Philip Marlowe lights another cigarette and waits for the cops to arrive. He is ready to tell his story.

These opening shots are so evocative of Raymond Chandler's immortal Marlowe, archetypical private eye, haunting the underbelly of Los Angeles, that if we're Chandler fans we hold our breath. Is the ambience going to be maintained, or will this be another campy rip-off? Half an hour into the movie, we relax. *Farewell, My Lovely* never steps wrong. It is, indeed, the most evocative of all the private-detective movies we have had in the last few years. It is not as great as Roman Polanski's *Chinatown*, which was concerned with larger subjects, but in the genre itself there hasn't been anything this good since Hollywood was doing Philip Marlowe the first time around. One reason is that Dick Richards, the director, takes his material and character absolutely seriously. He is not uneasy with it, as Robert Altman was when he had Elliott Gould flirt with seriousness in *The Long Goodbye*. Richards doesn't hedge his bet.

And neither does Robert Mitchum, in what becomes his definitive performance. Mitchum is one of the great screen presences. He was born to play the weary, cynical, doggedly romantic Marlowe. His voice and his face and the way he lights his cigarette are all exactly right, and seem totally effortless. That's his trademark. In a good Mitchum performance, we are never aware he is acting. And it is only when we measure the distances between his characters that we can see what he is doing. Mitchum is at home on the kinds of streets Philip Marlowe worked: streets of one-room furnished flats and pink stucco hotels, out-of-town newsstands and seedy bars, and always the drowsy commonness of the flatlands leading up to the baroque mansions in the hills and canyons.

Farewell, My Lovely gets all of this just right—Angelo Graham's art direction is a triumph—and then places Mitchum's Marlowe in the center of it and leads him through one of Chandler's tortuous plots. Although everything does finally tie together in this one (as it never did in Chandler's labyrinthine *The Big Sleep*), it doesn't matter that much. What's important is the gallery of characters Marlowe encounters, each grotesque and beautiful in his own way.

The most touching is Moose Malloy, played by an ex-prizefighter named Jack O'Halloran. Moose towers over everyone in the film, both in stature and in the immensity of his need. Seven years ago he fell in love with a hooker named Velma and they were going to be married, but something went wrong during a bank job, and Moose took the rap. When he gets out of prison, he hires Marlowe to find his Velma.

Marlowe's quest for Velma, a faded memory from a hopeless love affair, leads him, as we might have known, into a case a lot larger and more important than he could have suspected. There is an odyssey through a lurid whorehouse and a killing in a ghetto bar, and a midnight rendezvous that ends in another death, and always there is Lieutenant Nulty, of the Los Angeles Police Department, trying to figure out why Marlowe winds up attached to so many dead bodies. Richards's approach, with screenplay by David Zelag Goodman, is to start the story at the end with Marlowe trying to explain things to Nulty and then flash back to the beginning and let Marlowe elaborate on the story voice-over. It is a strategy that is often distracting in movies. But not this time, because it borrows from Chandler's own first-person narrative. And it provides great one-liners, as when the elusive Velma (Charlotte Rampling) sizes Marlowe up and down and he says, "She threw me a look I caught in my hip pocket."

Farewell, My Lovely is a great entertainment and a celebration of Robert Mitchum's absolute originality. The day after you view it, you might find yourself quoting lines to friends, which is always the test in these cases, because most of the time private-eye stories have no meaning at all unless it is in the way their heroes behave in the face of the most unsettling revelations about human nature. This time Philip Marlowe behaves very well.

Far from Heaven

PG-13, 107 m., 2002

Julianne Moore (Cathy Whitaker), Dennis Quaid (Frank Whitaker), Dennis Haysbert (Raymond Deagan), Patricia Clarkson (Eleonor Fine), Viola Davis (Sybil), James Rebhorn (Dr. Bowman), Celia Weston (Mona Lauder). Directed by Todd Haynes and produced by Jody Patton and Christine Vachon. Screenplay by Haynes.

Todd Haynes's *Far from Heaven* is like the best and bravest movie of 1957. Its themes, values, and style faithfully reflect the social melodramas of the 1950s, but it's bolder and says out loud what those films only hinted at. It begins with an ideal suburban Connecticut family, a husband and wife "team" so thoroughly absorbed into corporate culture they're known as "Mr. and Mrs. Magnatech." Then it develops that Mr. Magnatech is gay, and Mrs. Magnatech believes that the black gardener is the most beautiful man she has ever seen.

They are the Whitakers, Cathy and Frank (Julianne Moore and Dennis Quaid). They live in a perfect split-level house on a perfect street, where the autumn leaves are turning to gold. Their little son is reprimanded for rude language like "Aw, shucks." Of course she drives a station wagon. Mona Lauder (Celia Weston), the local society editor, is writing a profile about their perfection.

One slight shadow clouds the sun. While being interviewed by Celia, Cathy sees a strange black man in the yard and walks outside to ask, ever so politely, if she can "help" him. He introduces himself: Raymond Deagan (Dennis Haysbert), son of their usual gardener, who has died. Cathy, who has a good heart, instinctively reaches out to touch Raymond on the shoulder in sympathy, and inside the house the gesture is noted by Celia, who adds to her profile that Cathy is a "friend to Negroes."

Frank Whitaker is one of those big, good-looking guys who look like a college athlete gone slightly to seed, or drink. One night Cathy has to pick him up at the police station after an incident involving "one lousy cocktail." In another scene we see him enter a gay bar, where in these days long before Stonewall, the men exchange furtive, embarrassed glances as if surprised to find themselves there. One night Cathy makes the mistake of taking Frank his dinner when he works late, and opens his office door to find him kissing a man.

The movie accurately reflects the values of the 1950s, and you can see that in a scene where Frank says his homosexuality makes him feel "despicable," but he's "going to lick this problem." The key to the power of *Far from Heaven* is that it's never ironic; there is never a wink or a hint that the filmmakers have more enlightened ideas than their characters. This is not a movie that knows more than was known in 1957, but a movie that knows exactly what mainstream values were in 1957—and traps us in them, along with its characters.

Frank and Cathy have no sex life. Cathy is not attracted to Raymond so much sexually, however, as she's in awe of his kindness and beauty, which is so adamantly outside her segregated world. She hardly knows how to talk with him. At one point she says that "Mr. Whitaker and I support equal rights for the Negro." Raymond looks at her level-eyed and says, "I'm happy to hear that." He has a business degree, but has inherited the same gardening business that supported his father; a widower, he dotes on his eleven-year-old daughter.

The plot advances on a public and a private front. Publicly, word starts to get around that Cathy has been "seen" with the black gardener. Only that—"seen." Once when they take a ride in his truck, they enter a black diner, where their reception is as frosty as it would have been in a white place. Neither race approves of mixed couples. Soon people start to "talk," and Frank, the hypocrite, screams at her about all he's done to build up the reputation of the family, only to hear these stories.

Frank's homosexuality, of course, remains deeply buried. A psychiatrist (James Rebhorn) muses about "aversion therapy" but warns that the "majority of cases cannot be cured." Frank drinks heavily and turns ugly, and Cathy's feelings for Raymond grow, but she has no idea how to act on them. Mr. and Mrs. Magnatech need a repairman.

Far from Heaven uses superb craftsmanship to make this film look and feel like a film from the 1950s. Todd Haynes says he had three specific inspirations: Douglas Sirk's *All That Heaven Allows* (1955), which starred Jane Wyman and Rock Hudson in the story of a middle-aged widow and her handsome young gardener; Sirk's *Imitation of Life* (1959), with Lana Turner as a rich woman whose maid's daughter (Susan Kohner) passes for white; and Max Ophuls's *The Reckless Moment* (1949), about blackmail. In Sirk's films you often have the feeling that part of the plot is in code, that one kind of forbidden love stands for another.

The movie benefits enormously from its cinematography by Ed Lachman, who faithfully reproduces the lush 1950s studio style; the opening downward crane shot of autumn leaves is matched by the closing upward crane shot of spring blossoms, and every shot has the studied artifice of 1950s "set decoration," which was not so different, after all, from 1950s "interior decoration." The musical score, by Elmer Bernstein, is true to the time, with its underlining of points and its punching-up of emotions. Haynes said in an interview that "every element" of his film has been "drawn from and filtered through film grammar."

One detail is particularly true to the time: Interracial love and homosexual love are treated as being on different moral planes. The civil rights revolution predated gay liberation by about ten years, and you can see that here: The movie doesn't believe Raymond and Cathy have a plausible future together, but there is bittersweet regret that they do not. When Frank meets a young man and falls in love, however, the affair is not ennobled but treated as a matter of motel rooms and furtive meetings. Haynes is pitch-perfect here in noting that homosexuality, in the 1950s, still dared not speak its name.

Because the film deliberately lacks irony, it has a genuine dramatic impact; it plays like a powerful 1957 drama we've somehow never seen before. The effect is oddly jolting: Contemporary movies take so many subjects for granted that they never really look at them. Haynes, by moving back in time, is able to bring his issues into focus. We care about the characters in the way its period expected us to. (There is one time rupture; Frank uses the f-word to his wife and the fabric of the film breaks, only to be repaired when he apologizes.)

Julianne Moore, Dennis Quaid, and Dennis Haysbert are called on to play characters whose instincts are wholly different from their own. By succeeding, they make their characters real, instead of stereotypes. The tenderness of Cathy and Raymond's unrealized love is filled with regret that is all the more touching because they acknowledge that their society will not accept them as a couple. When Raymond and his daughter leave town, Cathy suggests maybe she could visit them sometime in Baltimore, but Raymond gently replies, "I'm not sure that would be a good idea."

Fargo

R, 98 m., 1996

Frances McDormand (Marge Gunderson), William H. Macy (Jerry Lundegaard), Steve Buscemi (Carl Showalter), Peter Stormare (Gaear Grimsrud), Harve Presnell (Wade Gustafson), Kristin Rudrud (Jean Lundegaard), John Carroll Lynch (Norm Gunderson). Directed by Joel Coen and produced by Ethan Coen. Screenplay by the Coens.

Fargo begins with an absolutely dead-on familiarity with small-town life in the frigid winter landscape of Minnesota and North Dakota. Then it rotates its story through satire, comedy, suspense, and violence, until it emerges as one of the best films I've seen. To watch it is to experience steadily mounting delight, as you realize the filmmakers have taken enormous risks, gotten away with them, and made a movie that is completely original, and as familiar as an old shoe—or a rubber-soled hunting boot from L.L. Bean, more likely.

The film is "based on a true story" that took place in Minnesota in 1987.* It has been filmed on location, there and in North Dakota, by the Coen brothers, Ethan and Joel, who grew up in St. Louis Park, a suburb of Minneapolis, and went on to make good movies like *Blood Simple, Miller's Crossing,* and *Barton Fink,* but never before a film as wonderful as this one, shot in their own backyard.

To describe the plot is to risk spoiling its surprises. I will tread carefully. A car salesman named Jerry Lundegaard (William H. Macy) desperately needs money for a business deal— a parking lot scheme that can save him from bankruptcy. He is under the thumb of his rich father-in-law (Harve Presnell), who owns the car agency and treats him like a loser. Jerry hires a couple of scrawny lowlifes named Showalter and Grimsrud (Steve Buscemi and Peter Stormare) to kidnap his wife (Kristin Rudrud), and promises to split an $80,000 ransom with them. Simple enough, except that everything goes wrong in completely unanticipated ways, as the plot twists and turns and makes a mockery of all of Jerry's best thinking.

Showalter is nervous, sweaty, talkative, mousy. Grimsrud is a sullen slug of few words. During the course of the kidnapping, he unexpectedly kills some people ("Oh, Daddy!" says

Showalter, terrified). The bodies are found the next morning, frozen beside the highway in the barren lands between Minneapolis and Brainerd, Minnesota, which is, as we are reminded every time we see the hulking statue outside town, the home of Paul Bunyan.

Brainerd's police chief is a pregnant woman named Marge Gunderson (Frances McDormand). She talks like one of the MacKenzie Brothers, in a Canadian-American-Scandinavian accent that's strong on cheerful folksiness. Everybody in the movie talks like that, with lines like "You're dern tootin'." When she gets to the big city, she starts looking for a place with a good buffet.

Marge Gunderson needs a jump to get her patrol car started in the morning. But she is a gifted cop, and soon after visiting the murder site, she reconstructs the crime—correctly. Eyewitnesses place two suspects in a tan Ciera. She traces it back to Jerry Lundegaard's lot. "I'm a police officer from up Brainerd," she tells him, "investigating some malfeasance."

Jerry, brilliantly played by Macy, is a man weighed down by the insoluble complexities of the situation he has fumbled himself into. He is so incompetent at crime that, when the kidnapping becomes unnecessary, he can't call off the kidnappers, because he doesn't know their phone number. He's being pestered with persistent calls from GMAC, inquiring about the illegible serial number on the paperwork for the same missing tan Ciera. He tries sending faxes in which the number is smudged. GMAC isn't fooled. Macy creates the unbearable agony of a man who needs to think fast, and whose brain is scrambled with fear, guilt, and the crazy illusion that he can somehow still pull this thing off.

Fargo is filled with dozens of small moments that make us nod with recognition. When the two low-rent hoods stop for the night at a truck stop, for example, they hire hookers. Cut to a shot of bored mercenary sex. Cut to the next shot: They're all sitting up in bed, watching The Tonight Show on TV. William H. Macy, who has played salesmen and con men before (he's a veteran of David Mamet's plays), finds just the right note in his scenes in the auto showroom. It's fascinating to watch him in action, trying to worm out of a lie involving an extra charge for rustproofing.

Small roles seem bigger because they're so well written and observed. Kristin Rudrud has few scenes as Jerry's wife, but creates a character out of them, always chopping or stirring something furiously in the kitchen. Their teenage son, who excuses himself from the table to go to McDonald's, helps establish the milieu of the film with a bedroom that has a poster on its wall for the Accordion King. Marge, discussing a hypothetical killer who has littered the highway with bodies, observes matter-of-factly, "I doubt he's from Brainerd." Harve Presnell is a typical self-made millionaire in his insistence on delivering the ransom money himself: He earned it, and by God if anyone is going to hand it over, it'll be him. He wants his money's worth. And on the way to the violent and unexpected climax, Marge has a drink in her hotel buffet with an old high school chum who obviously still lusts after her, even though she's married and pregnant. He explains, in a statement filled with the wistfulness of the downsizable, "I'm working for Honeywell. If you're an engineer, you could do a lot worse."

Frances McDormand has a lock on an Academy Award nomination with this performance, which is true in every individual moment, and yet slyly, quietly over the top in its cumulative effect. The screenplay is by Ethan and Joel Coen (Joel directed, Ethan produced), and although I have no doubt that events something like this really did take place in Minnesota in 1987, they have elevated reality into a human comedy—into the kind of movie that makes us hug ourselves with the way it pulls off one improbable scene after another. Films like Fargo are why I love the movies.

The Coen brothers later admitted that they made up the "true story" attribution.

Fast, Cheap & Out of Control
PG, 82 m., 1997

Dave Hoover (Animal Trainer), George Mendonca (Topiary Gardener), Ray Mendez (Mole-Rat Specialist), Rodney Brooks (Robot Scientist). Directed by Errol Morris and produced by Morris, Julia Sheehan, Mark Lipson, and Kathy Trustman.

Life is a little like lion taming, wouldn't you say? Here we are in the cage of life, armed only with a chair and a whip, trying to outsmart the teeth and the claws. If we are smart enough or know the right lore, sometimes we survive, and are applauded.

Errol Morris's magical film *Fast, Cheap & Out of Control* is about four people who are playing the game more strangely than the rest of us. They have the same goal: to control the world in a way that makes them happy. There is a lion tamer, a man who designs robots, a gardener who trims shrubs so they look like animals, and a man who is an expert on the private life of the naked mole rat.

Morris weaves their dreams together with music and images, into a meditation. To watch the movie is to reflect that no matter how hard we work, our lives are but a passing show. Maybe Rodney Brooks, the robot scientist from MIT, has the right idea: We should develop intelligent robots that can repair themselves, and send them out into the universe as our proxies. Instead of a few incredibly expensive manned space missions, why not send up thousands of robots that are fast, cheap, and out of control—and trust that some of them will work?

Consider the lifework of George Mendonca, who is a topiary gardener, and must sometimes reflect that he has spent fifty years or more practicing an art that most people cannot even name. What is a topiary? A shrub that has been trained, clipped, and trimmed in such a way that it looks like a giraffe, or a bear, or a geometric shape. That is not in the nature of shrubs, and Mendonca, who is in his seventies, reflects that a good storm could blow his garden away, and that the moment he stops clipping, nature will go to work undoing his art. There is a beautiful slow-motion shot of him in the rain, at night, walking past his creations as if he, too, were a topiary waiting to be overcome by nature.

And consider Ray Mendez. Here is a happy man. When he first learned of the discovery of the naked mole rat, he felt the joy of a lottery winner. There are not supposed to be mammals like this. They have no hair and no sweat glands because they live always in a controlled environment—their tunnels beneath the African savanna, where they organize themselves like insects. Mendez lives with mole rats in his office, and creates museum environ-ments for them. That means he has to ask himself a question no scientist before him has ever asked: What makes a mole rat happy? So that they can tell the members of one colony from another, they roll cheerfully in their communal feces—but where do they like to do that? In a room at the end of a tunnel system or in the middle? Like the architect of a luxury hotel, Mendez wants his guests to feel comfortable.

Dave Hoover is a lion tamer. He goes into a cage with animals whose nature it is to eat him. He outsmarts them. He explains why animal trainers use chairs: Not to hold off a savage beast, but to confuse it. "Lions are very single-minded. When you point the four legs of a chair at them, they get confused. They don't know where to look, and they lose their train of thought."

Hoover has lived his life in the shadow of a man he readily acknowledges as his superior: Clyde Beatty, the famous animal trainer who also starred in movie serials and radio programs. "There will never be another Clyde Beatty," he says, as we watch images from *Darkest Africa,* a serial in which Beatty and a little fat kid in a loincloth do battle in a hidden city with soldiers who wear large cardboard wings. It is clear that Beatty captured Hoover's imagination at an early age—that Hoover is a lion tamer because Beatty was, so that, in a way, Hoover is carrying out Beatty's programming just as Rodney Brooks's robots are following instructions, and the mole rats are crapping where Ray Mendez wants them to.

Morris's film assembles these images not so much as a documentary might, but according to musical principles: Caleb Sampson's score creates a haunting, otherworldly, elegiac mood that makes all of the characters seem noble and a little sad. The photography uses a lot of styles and textures, from 35mm to Super 8, from film to the handheld feel of home video. The cinematographer is Robert Richardson, who achieved a similar effect for Oliver Stone in *JFK* and *Natural Born Killers.* (Morris adds the year's most memorable end credit: "Mole Photography Sewercam by Roto Rooter.")

Errol Morris has long since moved out of the field of traditional documentary. Like his subjects, he is arranging the materials of life according to his own notions. They control shrubs, lions, robots, and rats, and he controls them. *Fast, Cheap & Out of Control* doesn't fade from the mind the way so many assembly-line thrillers do. Its images lodge in the memory. To paraphrase the old British beer ad, Errol Morris refreshes the parts the others do not reach.

The Fast Runner

NO MPAA RATING, 172 m., 2002

Natar Ungalaaq (Atanarjuat), Sylvia Ivalu (Atuat), Peter-Henry Arnatsiaq (Oki), Lucy Tulugarjuk (Puja), Madeline Ivalu (Panikpak), Paul Qulitalik (Qulitalik), Eugene Ipkarnak (Sauri, the Chief), Pakkak Innushuk (Amaqjuaq). Directed by Zacharias Kunuk and produced by Paul Apak Angilirq, Norman Cohn, and Kunuk. Screenplay by Angilirq.

We could begin with the facts about *The Fast Runner*. It is the first film shot in Inuktitut, the language of the Inuit peoples who live within the Arctic Circle. It was made with an Inuit cast, and a 90 percent Inuit crew. It is based on a story that is at least one thousand years old. It records a way of life that still existed within living memory.

Or we could begin with the feelings. The film is about romantic tensions that lead to tragedy within a small, closely knit community of people who depend on one another for survival, surrounded by a landscape of ice and snow. It shows how people either learn to get along under those circumstances, or pay a terrible price.

Or we could begin with the lore. Here you will see humans making a living in a world that looks, to us, like a barren wasteland. We see them fishing, hunting, preparing their kill, scraping skins to make them into clothing, tending the lamps of oil that illuminate their igloos, harvesting the wild crops that grow in the brief summertime, living with the dogs that pull their sleds.

Or we could begin with the story of the film's production. It was shot with a high-definition digital video camera, sidestepping the problems that cinematographers have long experienced while using film in temperatures well below zero. Its script was compiled from versions of an Inuit legend told by eight elders. The film won the Camera d'Or, for best first film, at Cannes, and was introduced at Telluride by the British stage director Peter Sellars; telling the story of its origin, he observed, "In most cultures, a human being is a library."

We could begin in all of those ways, or we could plunge into the film itself, an experience so engrossing it is like being buried in a new environment. Some find the opening scene claustrophobic. It takes place entirely inside an igloo, the low lighting provided only by oil lamps, most of the shots in close-up, and we do not yet know who all the characters are. I thought it was an interesting way to begin: to plunge us into this community and share its warmth as it shelters against the cold, and then to open up and tell its story.

We meet two brothers, Amaqjuaq (Pakkak Innushuk), known as the Strong One, and Atanarjuat (Natar Ungalaaq), known as the Fast Runner. They are part of a small group of Inuit including the unpleasant Oki (Peter-Henry Arnatsiaq), whose father is the leader of the group. There is a romantic problem. Oki has been promised Atuat (Sylvia Ivalu), but she and Atanarjuat are in love. Just like in Shakespeare. In the most astonishing fight scene I can recall, Atanarjuat challenges Oki, and they fight in the way of their people: They stand face to face while one solemnly hits the other, there is a pause, and the hit is returned, one blow after another, until one or the other falls.

Atanarjuat wins, but it is not so simple. He is happy with Atuat, but eventually takes another wife, Puja (Lucy Tulugarjuk), who is pouty and spoiled and put on Earth to cause trouble. During one long night of the midnight sun, she is caught secretly making love to Amaqjuaq, and banished from the family. It is, we gather, difficult to get away with adultery when everybody lives in the same tent.

Later there is a shocking murder. Fleeing for his life, Atanarjuat breaks free, and runs across the tundra—runs and runs, naked. It is one of those movie sequences you know you will never forget.

At the end of the film, over the closing titles, there are credit cookies showing the production of the film, and we realize with a little shock that the film was made now, by living people, with new technology. There is a way in which the intimacy of the production and the 172-minute running time lull us into accepting the film as a documentary of real life. The actors, many of them professional Inuit performers, are without affect or guile: They seem sincere, honest, revealing, as real people might, and although the story involves elements of melodrama and even soap opera, the production seems as real as a frozen fish.

I am not surprised that *The Fast Runner* has been a box-office hit in its opening engagements. It is unlike anything most audiences will ever have seen, and yet it tells a universal story. What's unique is the patience it has with its characters: The willingness to watch and listen as they reveal themselves, instead of pushing them to the front like little puppets and having them dance through the story. *The Fast Runner* is passion, filtered through ritual and memory.

Fat City

PG, 100 m., 1972

Stacy Keach (Tully), Jeff Bridges (Ernie), Susan Tyrrell (Oma), Candy Clark (Faye). Directed by John Huston and produced by Huston and Ray Stark. Screenplay by Leonard Gardner, based on his book.

Two men, barely ten years apart in age, one with a lifetime of emptiness ahead of him, one with an empty lifetime already behind. This is what John Huston has to work with in *Fat City* and he treats it with a level, unsentimental honesty and makes it into one of his best films.

The young man is one of those cool, muscular youths who seem to be bursting with energy in their last year of high school. Then you run into them two years later and they're pumping gas and daydreaming about refinements they can make on their cars. The older man was a boxer once, and he came close enough to greatness to be haunted by it, but now he is a drifter and the next thing to a bum. Leonard Gardner's novel *Fat City* placed these men in Stockton, California, and contrasted the hopelessness of their lives with the dogged persistence of their optimism.

Huston's film owes a great deal to the Gardner novel, but it also has something that is all Huston's own: his fascination with underdogs and losers. The characters in Huston movies hardly ever achieve what they're aiming for. Sam Spade, in *The Maltese Falcon*, Huston's first film, ends up minus one partner and one woman he thought he could trust. Everyone is a loser in *The Treasure of the Sierra Madre*, and the gold blows back into the dust and is lost in it. Ahab, in *Moby Dick*. Marlon Brando's career army officer in *Reflections in a Golden Eye*, even Bogart and Hepburn in *The African Queen*—they all fall short of their plans. *The African Queen* does have a happy ending, but it feels tacked-on and ridiculous, and the *Queen* destroys itself in destroying the German steamer.

So this is a theme we find in Huston's work, but rarely does he fit it to characters and a time and place so well as in *Fat City*. Maybe that's because Huston knows the territory: He was a professional boxer himself for a while, and not a very good one.

The Stockton in his film exists in an America we tend to forget about these days. It is the other side of the image preferred by chambers of commerce. The characters live their lives in fly-stained walk-ups with screen doors that bang in the wind. They hang out in the kind of bar that advertises in its window the price of a shot and a beer. They know in their bones it will take a miracle to get them out of their lives, because they know (accurately) that they don't have what it takes. So they dream, and bank on long shots. Even after all the hours of training and roadwork and pep talks, the boxers in *Fat City* feel little confidence in themselves. They substitute brag for optimism.

Huston's boxers are Stacy Keach, the electrifying New York stage actor who was mostly overlooked in such films as *Doc* and *End of the Road*, and Jeff Bridges, who was the young man who went away to Korea in *The Last Picture Show*. Keach plays Tully, whose boxing career is all over, although he miraculously pulls himself together for one final victory. Bridges plays Ernie, who never even has what Tully lost; he does have a strong body and a few good moves, but basically he's a pushover.

Huston tells his story in a slow, atmospheric way, and characters drift into it and stay because they have no place else to go. There's Oma (Susan Tyrrell), a youngish but bloated alcoholic who picks up with Tully while her black lover is serving a little time. She is dumb, vulgar, sluttish, and all the other things we think about people who never had an education and drink cream sherry all day. But she has a heart, by God, and she believes in all the naive clichés that do for her philosophy.

Belief is important to these people because there is nothing else—not even the realization of belief. Take Ruben (Nicholas Colusanto), who runs the local gym, manages fighters, and promotes bouts when he can. He is old and poor and in a dying industry, but when a new kid comes in to the gym, he blinks once and sees Marciano. He drives his boxers over to the next town for a fight and drives them back when they have lost, all the time talking about Madison Square Garden.

The movie's edges are filled with small, perfect character performances. Candy Clark is vulnerable and vacuously hopeful as Ernie's young, pregnant bride. She has exercised a little instinctive cunning to lure him into marriage, hardly anticipating what a cheerless future she's won for herself. Curtis Cokes, as Earl, Oma's black lover, has a self-respect that will not give way to jealousy; when he gets out of jail and moves back in with Oma, he treats Tully with man-to-man dignity.

The one performance in the movie I'm sure I will never forget comes from Sixto Rodriguez, an actor who doesn't have a single line of dialogue. He plays a Mexican fighter who once, briefly, had a reputation, and is brought in by bus to fight Tully. He comes to the stadium surrounded by a vast silence and loneliness. He urinates, and there is blood, and we know his secret. He is in such pain he can barely stand. But he goes out and fights and loses, and gives Tully a moment of glory that (we know) is so small as to hardly be measurable.

A few critics of *Fat City* found it too flat, too monochromatic. But this material won't stand jazzing up. If Huston and Gardner had forced the story into a conventional narrative of suspense, climax, and resolution, it would have seemed obscene. There just isn't going to be any suspense, climax, or resolution in the lives of these people: just a few moments of secondhand hope that don't even seem worth getting very worked up about at the time.

Fellini Satyricon

R, 129 m., 1970 (rereleased 2001)

Martin Potter (Encolpio), Hiram Keller (Ascilto), Max Born (Gitone), Salvo Randone (Eumolpo), Mario Romagnoli (Trimalcione), Magali Noel (Fortunata), Capucine (Trifena), Alain Cuny (Lica), Fanfulla (Vernacchio). Directed by Federico Fellini and produced by Alberto Grimaldi. Screenplay by Fellini and Bernardino Zapponi, based on the book by Petronius.

I am examining ancient Rome as if this were a documentary about the customs and habits of the Martians.

—Fellini in an interview, 1969

Fellini Satyricon was released in 1970, and I was ready for it: "Some will say it is a bloody, depraved, disgusting film," I wrote in a fever. "Indeed, people by the dozens were escaping from the sneak preview I attended. But *Fellini Satyricon* is a masterpiece all the same, and films that dare everything cannot please everybody." Today I'm not so sure it's a masterpiece, except as an expression of the let-it-all-hang-out spirit of the 1970 world that we both then occupied. But it is so much more ambitious and audacious than most of what we see today that simply as a reckless gesture, it shames these timid times. Films like this are a reminder of how machine-made and limited recent product has become.

The movie is based on a book that retold degenerate versions of Roman and Greek myth. Petronius's *Satyricon*, written at the time of Nero, was lost for centuries and found in a fragmented form, which Fellini uses to explain his own fragmented movie; both book and film end in midsentence. Petronius was a sensualist who celebrated and mocked sexual decadence at the same time. So does Fellini, who observes that although the wages of sin may be death, it's nice work if you can get it.

The movie was made two years after the Summer of Love—it came out at about the same time as the documentary *Woodstock*—and it preserves the postpill, pre-AIDS sexual frenzy of that time, when penalty-free sex briefly seemed to be a possibility (key word: seemed). The characters in the Fellini film may be burned alive, vivisected, skewered, or crushed, but they have no concerns about viruses, guilt, or psychological collapse. Like most of the characters in ancient myth, indeed, they have no psychology; they act according to their natures, without introspection or the possibility of change. They are hard-wired by the myths that contain them.

The film loosely follows the travels and adventures of several characters, notably the students Encolpio (Martin Potter) and Ascilto (Hiram Keller), as they fight over the favors of the comely slave boy Gitone (Max Born). Gitone is won by Ascilto, who sells him to the repulsive actor Vernacchio (Fanfulla), whose performances include mutilation of prisoners. True to the nature of the film, Gitone doesn't mind such treatment and indeed rather enjoys the attention, but the story moves on, presenting a series of masters and slaves in moments of grotesque drama and lurid fantasy. It is all phantasmagoria, said Pauline Kael, who hated the film, and wrote, "Though from time to time one may register a face or a set or an episode, for most of the time one has the feeling of a camera following people walking along walls."

Well, yes and no. There are scenes that are complete playlets, as when a patrician couple free their slaves and then commit suicide, or when a dead rich man's followers gather on the seashore to consider his final request that his body be eaten. These moments pop out from the fresco as they must have popped out of Petronius, but Fellini is unconcerned with beginnings, middles, and ends, and wants us to walk through the film as through a gallery in which an artist tries variations on a theme. This would increasingly be his approach in the films that followed; set against this ancient Rome is the fragmented modern city in *Fellini's Roma*, which is a series of episodes in search of a destination, and lacks the structure of his great Roman film, *La Dolce Vita* (1959).

Does *Satyricon* work? Depends. Certainly the visuals are rich (Kael's wall-image doesn't do justice to their grungy, spermy, tactile fertility). Is there anyone we care about as we watch the film? We share the joy during a couple of sexual romps, and are touched by the suicides of the patricians, but—no, we don't care about them, because they seem defined not by their personalities but by their mythical programming. Like the figures in Keats's "Ode on

a Grecian Urn," they are forever caught in the act of demonstrating their natures, without prologue or outcome.

In no other Fellini film do we see a more abundant demonstration of his affection for human grotesques (although *Fellini Casanova* comes close). I visited the set of this film one day, on the coast near Rome, when he was shooting the funeral of the man who wanted to be cannibalized. We were surrounded by dwarfs and giants, fat people and beanpoles, hermaphrodites and transvestites, some grotesquely painted or costumed, some deformed by nature or choice. "People ask, where did you find these faces?" Fellini said. "None of them are professional actors; these faces come from my private dreams. I opened a little office in Rome and asked funny-looking people to come in. Did you know Nero had a hang-up on freaks? He surrounded himself with them." And so does Fellini, perhaps because ordinary-looking extras would bring too much normality into his canvas.

What is the sum of all this effort? A film that deals in visual excess like no other, showing a world of amorality, cruelty, self-loathing, and passion. Did Fellini see his *Satyricon* as a warning to modern viewers, an object lesson? Not at all, in my opinion. He found an instinctive connection between Petronius and himself—two artists fascinated by deviance and excess—and in the heady days of the late 1960s saw no reason to compromise. *Fellini Satyricon* is always described as a film about ancient Rome, but it may be one of the best films about the Summer of Love—not celebrating it, but displaying the process of its collapse. What is fun for a summer can be hard work for a lifetime.

Fellini's Roma
R, 128 m., 1973

Featuring Peter Gonzales, Stefano Majore, Britta Barnes, Pia de Doses, Fiona Florence, Marno Maitland, Giovannoli Renato, Anna Magnani, Gore Vidal, and Federico Fellini. Directed by Fellini. Screenplay by Bernardino Zapponi and Fellini.

Federico Fellini first included his name in the title of one of his movies with *Fellini Satyricon* (1970), and then for legal reasons: A quickie

Italian version of the *Satyricon* was being palmed off in international film markets as the real thing. Once having savored the notion, however, Fellini found it a good one, and so we have *Fellini's Roma*, which was followed by *Fellini Casanova.*

The name in the title doesn't seem conceited or affected, as it might from another director (*Peckinpah's Albuquerque?*). This *is* Fellini's Rome and nobody else's, just as all of his films since *La Dolce Vita* have been autobiographical musings and confessions from the most personal—and the best—director of his time. Any connection with a real city on the map of Italy is libelous. Fellini's Rome gets its suburbs trimmed when he goes for a haircut.

The movie isn't a documentary, although sometimes he lets it look like one. It's a rambling essay, meant to feel like free association. There's a very slight narrative thread, about a young man named Fellini who leaves the little town of Rimini and comes to the great city and is overwhelmed by its pleasures of body and spirit. He moves into a mad boarding house that would make a movie all by itself; he dines with his neighbors in great outdoor feasts when the summer heat drives everyone into the piazzas; he attends a raucous vaudeville show and he visits his first whorehouse . . . and then his second.

This material, filmed with loving attention to period detail, exists by itself in the movie; there's no effort to link the naive young Fellini with the confident genius who appears elsewhere in the movie. It's as if Fellini, the consummate inventor of fantasies, didn't grow out of his young manhood—he created it from scratch.

The autobiographical material is worked in between pseudodocumentary scenes that contain some of the most brilliant images Fellini has ever devised. The movie opens with a monumental Roman traffic jam that, typically, becomes important because Fellini has deigned to photograph it. He swoops above it on a crane, directing his camera, his movie, and the traffic. A blinding rainstorm turns everything into a hellish apparition, and then there's a final shot, held just long enough to make its point, of the autos jammed around the Colosseum.

The image is both perfect and natural; as someone commented about *Fellini's 8½*, his movies are filled with images, and they're all obvious. If Bergman is the great introvert of the movies, forever probing more and more deeply, Fellini is the joyous exponent of surfaces and excess, of letting more hang out than there is.

The obviousness of his images gives his movies a curious kind of clarity; he isn't reaching for things to say, but finding ways to say the same things more memorably. The decadence of Rome has been one of his favorite subjects throughout his career, and who could forget Anita Ekberg in the fountain, or the Mass procession at dawn, in *La Dolce Vita*?

But in *Roma*, he is even more direct, more stark: An expedition to inspect progress on the Rome subway system suddenly becomes transcendent when workmen break through to an underground crypt from pre-Christian times. The frescoes on the walls are so clear they might have been painted yesterday—until the air of the modern city touches them.

Rome, the eternal city, has historically been as carnal as it has been sacred. Fellini won't settle for one or the other; he uses scenes of carnality to symbolize a blessed state, and vice versa. Nothing could be more eternal, more patient, and more resigned than Fellini's use of a weary prostitute standing beside a highway outside Rome. She is tall, huge-bosomed, garishly made up, and her feet are tired. She stands among the broken stones of the Roman Empire, expecting nothing, hoping for nothing.

The prostitute, so often used as a symbol of fleeting moments and insubstantial experiences, becomes eternal; and the Church, always the symbol of the unchanging, the rock, becomes temporal. In his most audacious sequence, Fellini gives us an "ecclesiastical fashion show," with roller-skating priests, and nuns whose habits are made of blinking neon lights. What is unreal, and where is the real? Fellini doesn't know, and he seems to believe that Rome has never known. Rome has simply endured, waiting in the hope of someday finding out.

Fellini's Roma was attacked in some circles as an example of Fellini coasting on his genius. I find this point of view completely incomprehensible. Critics who would force

Fellini back into traditional narrative films are missing the point; Fellini isn't just giving us a lot of flashy scenes, he's building a narrative that has a city for its protagonist instead of a single character.

The only sly thing is that the city isn't Rome—it's Fellini, disguised in bricks, mortar, and ruins. Fellini, who cannot find his way between the flesh and the spirit, who cannot find the connection between his youth and his greatness, and whose gift is to make movies where everything is obvious and nothing is simple. That was the dilemma that the Fellini character faced in 8½, when he couldn't make sense of his life, and it's the dilemma we all face every day, isn't it?

Femme Fatale

R, 110 m., 2002

Rebecca Romijn-Stamos (Laure Ash), Antonio Banderas (Nicolas Bardo), Peter Coyote (Bruce Hewitt Watts), Eriq Ebouaney (Black Tie), Edouard Montoute (Racine), Rie Rasmussen (Veronica), Thierry Frémont (Serra). Directed by Brian De Palma and produced by Tarak Ben Ammar and Marina Gefter. Screenplay by De Palma.

Sly as a snake, Brian De Palma's *Femme Fatale* is a sexy thriller that coils back on itself in seductive deception. This is pure filmmaking, elegant and slippery. I haven't had as much fun second-guessing a movie since *Mulholland Dr.* Consider such clues as the overflowing aquarium, the shirt still stained with blood after many days, the subtitles for dialogue that is not spoken, the story that begins in 2001 and then boldly announces: "Seven years later."

The movie opens with a $10 million diamond theft, with a difference: The diamonds adorn the body of a supermodel attending a premiere at the Cannes Film Festival, and they are stolen with erotic audacity as the model is seduced in a rest room of the Palais du Cinema by the tall, brazen Laure Ash (Rebecca Romijn-Stamos). Her team includes the usual crew of heist-movie types, and we get the usual details, like the guy in the wet suit, the laser cutter, and the TV spycam that attracts the attention of an inquisitive cat. But the movie announces its originality when none of these characters perform as they expect to, and Laure Ash steals the

diamonds not only from the model but also from her fellow criminals.

No, I have not given away too much. The fact is, I have given away less than nothing, as you will fully appreciate after seeing the film. The long opening sequence, about forty minutes by my clock, is done almost entirely without dialogue, and as De Palma's camera regards these characters in their devious movements, we begin to get the idea: This is a movie about watching and being watched, about seeing and not knowing what you see.

Romijn-Stamos plays Laure Ash as a supremely self-confident woman with a well-developed sense of life's ironies. Chance plays a huge role in her fate. Consider that not long after the theft, while trying to avoid being spotted in Paris, she is mistaken for a grieving widow, taken home from a funeral, and finds herself in possession of an airplane ticket to New York and a passport with a photo that looks exactly like her. And then . . .

But no. I cannot tell any more. I will, however, describe her relationship with Nicolas Bardo (Antonio Banderas), a paparazzo who photographs her in 2001 on that day she is mistaken for the widow, and photographs her again seven years later (!) when she returns to Paris as the wife of the American ambassador (Peter Coyote). She wants that film: "I have a past here." And then . . .

Well, the movie's story, written by De Palma, is a series of incidents that would not be out of place in an ordinary thriller, but here achieve a kind of transcendence since they are what they seem, and more than they seem, and less than they seem. The movie tricks us, but not unfairly, and for the attentive viewer there are markers along the way to suggest what De Palma is up to.

Above all he is up to an exercise in superb style and craftsmanship. The movie is very light on dialogue, and many of the words that are spoken come across as if the characters are imitating movie actors (the film opens with Laure watching *Double Indemnity*—for pointers in how to be a vixen, no doubt). I've seen *Femme Fatale* twice; it's one of those films like *Memento* that plays differently the second time. Only on the second viewing did I spot the sly moment when the subtitles supply standard thriller dialogue—but the lips of the actors are not moving. This is a movie joke worthy of Buñuel.

Rebecca Romijn-Stamos may or may not be a great actress, but in *Femme Fatale* she is a great Hitchcock heroine—blond, icy, desirable, duplicitous—with a knack for contemptuously manipulating the hero. She is also very sexy, and let it be said that De Palma, at least, has not followed other directors into a sheepish retreat from nudity, seduction, desire, and erotic wordplay. The man who made *Body Double* is still prepared to make a movie about a desirable woman, even in these days of buddy movies for teenage boys. When it comes to sex, the characters in *Femme Fatale* have all been around the block a few times, but it takes this scenario to make them wonder what side of the street they're on.

De Palma deserves more honor as a director. Consider also these titles: *Sisters, Blow Out, The Fury, Dressed to Kill, Carrie, Scarface, Wise Guys, Casualties of War, Carlito's Way, Mission: Impossible.* Yes, there are a few failures along the way *(Snake Eyes, Mission to Mars, The Bonfire of the Vanities),* but look at the range here, and reflect that these movies contain treasure for those who admire the craft as well as the story, who sense the glee with which De Palma manipulates images and characters for the simple joy of being good at it. It's not just that he sometimes works in the style of Hitchcock, but that he has the nerve to.

Field of Dreams

PG, 107 m., 1989

Kevin Costner (Ray Kinsella), Amy Madigan (Annie Kinsella), Gaby Hoffman (Karin Kinsella), Ray Liotta (Shoeless Joe Jackson), Timothy Busfield (Mark), James Earl Jones (Terence Mann), Burt Lancaster (Dr. "Moonlight" Graham), Frank Whaley (Archie Graham), Dwier Brown (John Kinsella). Directed by Phil Alden Robinson and produced by Lawrence Gordon and Charles Gordon. Screenplay by Robinson, based on the book by W. P. Kinsella.

The farmer is standing in the middle of a cornfield when he hears the voice for the first time: "If you build it, he will come." He looks around and doesn't see anybody. The voice speaks again, soft and confidential: "If you build it, he will come." Sometimes you can get too much sun, out there in a hot Iowa cornfield in the middle of the season. But this isn't a case of sunstroke.

Up until the farmer (Kevin Costner) starts hearing voices, *Field of Dreams* is a completely sensible film about a young couple who want to run a family farm in Iowa. Ray and Annie Kinsella (Costner and Amy Madigan) have tested the fast track and had enough of it, and they enjoy sitting on the porch and listening to the grass grow. When the voice speaks for the first time, the farmer is baffled, and so was I: Could this be one of those religious pictures where a voice tells the humble farmer where to build the cathedral?

It's a religious picture, all right, but the religion is baseball. And when he doesn't understand the spoken message, Ray Kinsella is granted a vision of a baseball diamond, right there in his cornfield. If he builds it, the voice seems to promise, Joe Jackson will come and play on it—Shoeless Joe, who was a member of the infamous 1919 Black Sox team but protested until the day he died that he played the best he could.

As *Field of Dreams* developed this fantasy, I found myself being willingly drawn into it. Movies are often so timid these days, so afraid to take flights of the imagination, that there is something grand and brave about a movie where a voice tells a farmer to build a baseball diamond so that Shoeless Joe Jackson can materialize out of the cornfield and hit a few fly balls. This is the kind of movie Frank Capra might have directed and James Stewart might have starred in—a movie about dreams.

It is important not to tell too much about the plot. (I was grateful I knew nothing about the movie when I went to see it, but the ads gave away the Shoeless Joe angle.) Let it be said that Annie Kinsella supports her husband's vision, and that he finds it necessary to travel east to Boston so he can enlist the support of a famous writer (James Earl Jones) who has disappeared from sight, and north to Minnesota to talk to what remains of a doctor (Burt Lancaster) who never got the chance to play with the pros.

The movie sensibly never tries to make the slightest explanation for the strange events that happen after the diamond is constructed. There is, of course, the usual business about how the bank thinks the farmer has gone haywire and wants to foreclose on his mortgage (the Capra and Stewart movies always had evil bankers in them). But there is not a corny, stupid payoff at the end. Instead, the movie depends on a poetic vision to make its point.

The director, Phil Alden Robinson, and the writer, W. P. Kinsella, are dealing with stuff that's close to the heart (it can't be a coincidence that the author and the hero have the same last name). They love baseball, and they think it stands for an earlier, simpler time when professional sports were still games and not industries. There is a speech in this movie about baseball that is so simple and true that it is heartbreaking. And the whole attitude toward the players reflects that attitude. Why do they come back from the great beyond and materialize here in this cornfield? Not to make any kind of vast, earth-shattering statement, but simply to hit a few and field a few, and remind us of a good and innocent time.

It is very tricky to act in a movie like this; there is always the danger of seeming ridiculous. Kevin Costner and Amy Madigan create such a grounded, believable married couple that one of the themes of the movie is the way love means sharing your loved one's dreams. Jones and Lancaster create small, sharp character portraits—two older men who have taken the paths life offered them, but never forgotten what baseball represented to them in their youth.

Field of Dreams will not appeal to grinches and grouches and realists. It is a delicate movie, a fragile construction of one goofy fantasy after another. But it has the courage to be about exactly what it promises. "If you build it, he will come." And he does.

The Fifth Horseman Is Fear

NO MPAA RATING, 100 m., 1968

Miroslav Machacek (Dr. Braun), Olga Scheinpflugova (Music teacher), Jiri Adamira (Mr. Vesely), Illia Prachar (Butcher), Josef Vinklar (Mr. Fanta), Zdenka Prochazkova (Mrs. Vesely), Slavka Budinova (Mrs. Wlenerova), Jiri Virtala (Inspector). Directed by Zbynek Brynych and produced by the Barrandov Studio. Screenplay by Brynych.

The Fifth Horseman Is Fear is such a nearly perfect film that it comes as a shock, in the last

ten minutes, to discover how deeply involved you have become.

In this sense, it resembles Fellini's 8½. The technique itself is such a pleasure to observe that the emotion steals unnoticed into the back of your mind. Then, at the end, the director pulls the strings and you realize the tragic meaning of the things you have seen.

The Fifth Horseman is the first film shown in this country by Zbynek Brynych, a forty-one-year-old director from Czechoslovakia. Yet it is unmistakably the work of a master, and I can only wonder whether Brynych has made other films or if his ability is natural, as Fellini's seems to be.

I mention Fellini because this film seems to have what Fellini and very few other directors are able to achieve: a sense of rhythm. It is not a series of scenes cut together, not a series of statements made one after another, but a total film, conceived as one complete idea.

The story is about an old Jewish doctor who has been forbidden by the Nazis to practice medicine. He works in a large warehouse as a clerk, cataloging confiscated Jewish property.

At first we do not realize exactly where we are, and as the old man moves through rooms filled with clocks and violins and teacups, his existence seems almost dreamlike. But soon enough we discover that this is Prague, the city of Kafka, and that the man's life is indeed quite real.

A wounded partisan is brought to the doctor for medical attention. He treats him, hides him, and goes on a search through Prague for morphine to deaden the man's pain.

His trip is like a journey through the underworld. It takes him to a house of prostitution, to a madhouse and to a nightclub known as the Desperation Bar, where Jews have gathered to drink and listen to the piano and try to ignore the significance of the Nazis in the streets outside.

This scene in the nightclub is one of singular brilliance. Brynych uses his camera as Fellini does, moving almost in rhythm with the music, catching faces and attitudes for all time against plain white backgrounds. The use of music in this scene, and throughout the picture, is perhaps the best since *La Dolce Vita*. There, too, the sound of a cocktail orchestra seemed inexplicably tragic.

After the old man has gotten the morphine, he goes back to his rooming house. We have already met the other tenants: a minor Nazi functionary, a wealthy lawyer, a music teacher, an eccentric.

It is difficult to describe what happens then without destroying the impact of the last minutes. But I will say that Brynych finds a subtle way to demonstrate that the roomers of that building, each in his own way, are as guilty as the Nazis for the event that takes place.

The Fifth Horseman Is Fear is a beautiful, distinguished work. I imagine it will win this year's Academy Award for the best foreign film.

Editor's Note: The Fifth Horseman Is Fear *was not nominated for an Academy Award. The entry from Czechoslovakia for best foreign film of 1967 was Jiri Menzel's* Closely Watched Trains *(it won); the entry for 1968 was Milos Forman's* The Firemen's Ball *(it lost to the Russian* War and Peace.*)*

Finding Nemo

G, 101 m., 2003

With the voices of: Albert Brooks (Marlin), Ellen DeGeneres (Dory), Alexander Gould (Nemo), Willem Dafoe (Gill), Geoffrey Rush (Nigel), Brad Garrett (Bloat), Barry Humphries (Bruce), Allison Janney (Peach). Directed by Andrew Stanton and produced by Graham Walters. Screenplay by Stanton.

Finding Nemo has all of the usual pleasures of the Pixar animation style—the comedy and wackiness of *Toy Story* or *Monsters Inc.* or *A Bug's Life.* And it adds an unexpected beauty, a use of color and form that makes it one of those rare movies where I wanted to sit in the front row and let the images wash out to the edges of my field of vision. The movie takes place almost entirely under the sea, in the world of colorful tropical fish—the flora and fauna of a shallow warm-water shelf not far from Australia. The use of color, form, and movement make the film a delight even apart from its story.

There is a story, though, one of those Pixar inventions that involves kids on the action level while adults are amused because of the satire and human (or fishy) comedy. The movie involves the adventures of little Nemo, a clownfish born with an undersized fin and an oversized curiosity. His father, Marlin, worries

obsessively over him because Nemo is all he has left: Nemo's mother and all of her other eggs were lost to barracudas. When Nemo goes off on his first day of school, Marlin warns him to stay with the class and avoid the dangers of the drop-off to deep water, but Nemo forgets and ends up as a captive in the saltwater aquarium of a dentist in Sydney. Marlin swims off bravely to find his missing boy, aided by Dory, a bright blue Regal Tang fish with enormous eyes whom he meets along the way.

These characters are voiced by actors whose own personal mannerisms are well known to us; I recognized most of the voices, but even the unidentified ones carried buried associations from movie roles, and so somehow the fish take on qualities of human personalities. Marlin, for example, is played by Albert Brooks as an overprotective, neurotic worrywart, and Dory is played by Ellen DeGeneres as helpful, cheerful, and scatterbrained (she has a problem with short-term memory).

The Pixar computer animators, led by writer-director Andrew Stanton, create an undersea world that is just a shade murky, as it should be; we can't see as far or as sharply in sea water, and so threats materialize more quickly, and everything has a softness of focus. There is something dreamlike about *Finding Nemo*'s visuals, something that evokes the reverie of scuba diving.

The picture's great inspiration is to leave the sea by transporting Nemo to that big tank in the dentist's office. In it we meet other captives, including the Moorish Idol fish Gill (voice by Willem Dafoe), who are planning an escape. Now it might seem to us that there is no possible way a fish can escape from an aquarium in an office and get out of the window and across the highway and into the sea, but there is no accounting for the ingenuity of these creatures, especially since they have help from a conspirator on the outside—a pelican with the voice of Geoffrey Rush.

It may occur to you that many pelicans make a living by eating fish, not rescuing them, but some of the characters in this movie have evolved admirably into vegetarians. As Marlin and Dory conduct their odyssey, for example, they encounter three carnivores who have formed a chapter of Fish-Eaters Anonymous and chant slogans to remind themselves that they abstain from fin-based meals.

The first scenes in *Finding Nemo* are a little unsettling, as we realize the movie is going to be about fish, not people (or people-based characters like toys and monsters). But of course animation has long since learned to enlist all other species in the human race, and to care about fish quickly becomes as easy as caring about mice or ducks or Bambi.

When I review a movie like *Finding Nemo*, I am aware that most members of its primary audience do not read reviews. Their parents do, and to them and adults who do not have children as an excuse, I can say that *Finding Nemo* is a pleasure for grown-ups. There are jokes we get that the kids don't, and the complexity of Albert Brooks's neuroses, and that enormous canvas filled with creatures that have some of the same hypnotic beauty as—well, fish in an aquarium. They may appreciate another novelty: This time the dad is the hero of the story, although in most animation it is almost always the mother.

Finian's Rainbow

G, 145 m., 1968

Fred Astaire (Finian McLonergan), Petula Clark (Sharon McLonergan), Don Francks (Woody Mahoney), Keenan Wynn (Judge Rawkins), Al Freeman, Jr. (Howard), Tommy Steele (Leprechaun). Directed by Francis Ford Coppola and produced by Joseph Landon. Screenplay by E. Y. Harburg and Fred Saidy.

Finian's Rainbow is the best of the recent roadshow musicals, perhaps because it's the first to cope successfully with the longer roadshow form. The best musicals of the past (Astaire and Rogers in the 1930s, Gene Kelly's and Stanley Donen's productions in the 1950s) were rather modest in length and cost. They depended on charm and the great talents of their performers.

Since *The Sound of Music*, unhappily, musicals have been locked into the reserved-seat format. That, in turn, apparently means they have to be long, expensive, weighed down with unnecessary production values and filled with pretension. It was a gloomy sight to see the great songs and performances of *Camelot* trying to get out from beneath the dead weight of its expensive, unnecessary, distracting sets and costumes.

Movies are a faster medium than the stage.

They don't have entrances, exits, curtains, scene changes. Yet recent film "versions" actually tend to be longer than Broadway productions, and the second half is often an ordeal. Movie musicals shouldn't be much more than two hours long, I think.

Finian's Rainbow is an exception. It gives you that same wonderful sense you got from *Swing Time* or *Singin' in the Rain* or any of the great musicals: that it knows exactly where it's going and is getting there as quickly and with as much fun as possible. Remarkably, because it is only Francis Ford Coppola's second film, it is the best-directed musical since *West Side Story*. It is also enchanting, and that's a word I don't get to use much.

A lot of the fine things in the film come from Fred Astaire, who possibly danced better thirty years ago but has never achieved a better characterization. In most of the Astaire musicals we remember, he was really playing himself, and the plot didn't make much of an effort to conceal that. This time he plays arthritic, wizened, wise Finian McLonergan (with some songs and dances the original stage Finian didn't have). And it is a remarkable performance.

It is so good, I suspect, because Astaire was willing to play it as the screenplay demands. He could have rested on his laurels and his millions easily enough, turning out a TV special now and then, but instead he created this warm old man, Finian, and played him wrinkles and all. Astaire is pushing seventy, after all, and no effort was made to make him look younger with common tricks of lighting, makeup, and photography. That would have been unnecessary: He has a natural youthfulness. I particularly want to make this point because of the cruel remarks on Astaire's appearance in the *New York Times* review by Renata Adler. She is mistaken.

All the same, this isn't Astaire's movie. One of its strengths is that a lot of characters are involved, and their roles are well balanced. The story is familiar: Finian and his daughter (Petula Clark) journey to America with a pot of gold stolen from a leprechaun (Tommy Steele). They pitch up in Rainbow Valley, a rural co-operative near Fort Knox. It is inhabited by black and white farmers who raise tobacco, by a redneck sheriff and by a southern senator (Keenan Wynn) who is even more stereotyped than Strom Thurmond. There is an intrigue involving the back taxes on the co-op, a couple of romances, race relations, and the pot of gold.

Petula Clark is a surprise. I knew she could sing, but I didn't expect much more. She is a fresh addition to the movies: a handsome profile, a bright personality, and a singing voice as unique in its own way as Streisand's. Tommy Steele, as always, is a shade overdone, but perhaps a leprechaun should be a shade overdone.

Al Freeman, Jr., who plays an earnest young Negro botanist, has a hilarious moment as he brings the senator a bromo with the official darky shuffle. Barbara Hancock, an accomplished dancer, is fetching as Susan the Silent. Don Francks, as Petula's boyfriend, is clean-cut and pleasant, alas. And after the racist senator (Wynn) is magically turned black, there's a bravura scene. He joins up with one of the most improbable gospel quartets ever assembled.

The movie's message is a sort of subliminal plea for racial understanding but not much is made of it. Perhaps that's just as well. *Camelot* got mired in its involved philosophy, and *My Fair Lady* succeeded because it dumped a lot of Shaw's preaching.

For the rest, *Finian's Rainbow* is a marvelous evening right up to its last shot of Astaire walking away down a country road. Unfortunately, the management of the Bismarck turned on the house lights before Astaire was finished walking; for that, I would gladly turn them into little green toads.

The Firemen's Ball

NO MPAA RATING, 73 m., 1969

Jan Vostroll (Jan), Josef Sebanek (Josef). Directed and produced by Milos Forman. Screenplay by Forman, Ivan Passer and Jaroslav Papousek.

The firemen decide to have a ball. There'll be a drawing for prizes, a lot to eat and drink, a beauty contest, and a ceremony to honor the old retired chief. Everyone in town will come. The old chief really should have been honored last year, but the firemen didn't get around to it. They meant to, but something came up and they didn't. Now the old chief is dying, as everybody knows, and so it's obvious he will have to be honored this year or not at all.

Most likely he will suspect something. He may feel he's being honored only because everyone knows he's dying. Perhaps under the circumstances, the old chief would rather not be honored this year. But the old chief is not the only person to think about. It would be a terrible thing not to honor him at all. Not that he would care—but could the firemen look each other in the eye? So the old chief will be honored, even though it would be kinder to forget about it.

It's like that so often. We start out with the best of intentions, but we foul things up. And then we don't know whether to laugh or cry. And that is exactly the case with Milos Forman's *The Firemen's Ball*, a small, warm jewel of a movie from Czechoslovakia.

Just about everything goes wrong at the fireman's ball, of course. People walk off with the raffle prizes, the young men drink too much, and the beauty contest is a shambles. A committee is appointed to choose the finalists from among the girls at the dance. A lot of pretty girls are there, but the committee botches the job. Proud mothers force their daughters on the judges, while the pretty girls all have mothers who won't hear of a beauty contest. One fat girl gets selected by accident. An ugly girl is selected by misunderstanding.

When the judges look at the pathetic lineup of finalists, they hold their heads in their hands. What's worse, they have no idea how to run the contest. They'd like to see the girls in bathing suits, of course—but it's the middle of the winter. Any way you look at it, the local beauty contest is no match for the glamorous Miss Universe photographs the judges study for inspiration.

Forman (who also made the memorable *Loves of a Blonde*) develops his material with loving care. He never laughs at his characters; instead, he sees them as victims of human nature. It's too bad that all the raffle prizes— even the glazed ham—are stolen. But if some of the prizes are already missing, isn't it only fair to steal one yourself since you bought a ticket? When the fire chief orders the lights be turned out so the prizes can be returned, isn't it only natural his wife will be caught with a prize in her hands when the lights go back on? Who is to throw the first stone?

This is a very warm, funny movie, and perhaps the best way you could spend an evening in a theater just now. It is a relief to find a director who doesn't force his material, who trusts us to understand what's funny without being told.

Some say *The Firemen's Ball* is an allegory of Czechoslovakia in the years before the Dubcek reforms—and the years after, as things turned out. Perhaps it is. But Forman is never obvious about it.

And even if it's allegory, there's also something immediate and human about the advice the firemen give an old man whose house burns down. They arrive too late to save the house—they were at the dance—and now the old man is out in the snow and he's cold. Thoughtfully, they suggest he move his chair closer to the fire.

A Fish Called Wanda

R, 108 m., 1988

John Cleese (Archie), Jamie Lee Curtis (Wanda), Kevin Kline (Otto), Michael Palin (Ken), Maria Aitken (Wendy), Tom Georgeson (George), Patricia Hayes (Mrs. Coady). Directed by Charles Crichton and produced by Michael Shamberg. Screenplay by Cleese and Crichton.

This may be a purely personal prejudice, but I do not often find big-scale physical humor very funny. When squad cars crash into each other and career out of control, as they do in nine out of ten modern Hollywood comedies, I stare at the screen in stupefied silence. What is the audience laughing at? The creative bankruptcy of filmmakers who have to turn to stunt experts when their own ideas run out?

I do, on the other hand, laugh loudly at comedies where eccentric people behave in obsessive and eccentric ways, and other, equally eccentric, people do everything they can to offend and upset the first batch. In *A Fish Called Wanda*, for example, a character played by Kevin Kline is very particular about one thing: "Don't you *ever* call me stupid!" He is then inevitably called stupid on a number of occasions, leading to the payoff when his girlfriend explains to him in great detail why and how he is stupid, and lists some of the stupid

things he believes. ("The London Underground is not a political movement.")

I also like it when people have great and overwhelming passions—passions that rule their lives and are so outsized they seem like comic exaggerations—and then their passions are deliberately tweaked. In *A Fish Called Wanda*, for example, Michael Palin is desperately in love with a tank of tropical fish, and so Kevin Kline, who is equally desperate about discovering the whereabouts of some stolen jewels, eats the fish, one at a time, in an attempt to force Palin to talk. (The fact that Kline also stuffs French fries up Palin's nose gives the scene a nice sort of fish-and-chips symmetry.)

Another thing I like is when people are appealed to on the basis of their most gross and shameful instincts, and surrender immediately. When Jamie Lee Curtis wants to seduce an uptight British barrister, for example, she simply wears a low-cut dress and blinks her big eyes at him and tells him he is irresistible, and this illustrates a universal law of human nature, which is that every man, no matter how resistible, believes that when a woman in a low-cut dress tells him such things she must certainly be saying the truth.

Many of these things that I like come together in *A Fish Called Wanda*, which is the funniest movie I have seen in a long time; it goes on the list with *The Producers, This Is Spinal Tap,* and the early Inspector Clouseau movies.

One of its strengths is its mean-spiritedness. Hollywood may be able to make comedies about mean people (usually portrayed as the heroes), but only in England are the sins of vanity, greed, and lust treated with the comic richness they deserve. *A Fish Called Wanda* is sort of a mid-Atlantic production, with flawless teamwork between its two American stars (Curtis and Kline) and its British Monty Python veterans (Cleese and Palin). But it is not a compromise; this is essentially a late-1950s-style British comedy in which the Americans are employed to do and say all of the things that would be appalling to the British characters.

The movie was directed by Charles Crichton, who co-wrote it with Cleese, and Crichton is a veteran of the legendary Ealing Studio, where he directed perhaps its best comedy, *The Lavender Hill Mob.* He understands why it is usually funnier to *not* say something, and let the audience know what is not being said, than to simply blurt it out and hope for a quick laugh. He is a specialist at providing his characters with venal, selfish, shameful traits, and then embarrassing them in public. And he is a master at the humiliating moment of public unmasking, as when Cleese the barrister, in court, accidentally calls Jamie Lee Curtis "darling."

The movie involves an odd, ill-matched team of jewel thieves led by Tom Georgeson, a weaselly thief who is locked up in prison along with the secret of the jewels. On the outside, Palin, Kline, and Curtis plot with and against each other, and a great deal depends on Curtis's attempts to seduce several key defense secrets out of Cleese.

The film has one hilarious sequence after another. For classic farce, nothing tops the scene in Cleese's study, where Cleese's wife almost interrupts Curtis in mid-seduction. Curtis and Kline are both behind the draperies while the mortified Cleese tries to explain a bottle of champagne and a silver locket. The timing in this scene is as good as anything since the Marx Brothers.

And then there is the matter of the three murdered dogs. One friend of mine said she wouldn't see *A Fish Called Wanda* because she heard that dogs die in it (she is never, of course, reluctant to attend movies where people die). I tried to explain to her that the death of a pet is, of course, a tragic thing. But when the object is to inspire a heart attack in a little old lady who is a key prosecution witness, and when her little darling is crushed by a falling safe, well, you've just got to make a few sacrifices in the name of comedy.

Fitzcarraldo

PG, 157 m., 1982

Klaus Kinski (Fitzcarraldo), Claudia Cardinale (Molly), Jose Lewgoy (Don Aquilino), Miguel Angel Fuentes (Cholo). Directed by Werner Herzog. Screenplay by Herzog.

Werner Herzog's *Fitzcarraldo* is a movie in the great tradition of grandiose cinematic visions. Like Coppola's *Apocalypse Now* or Kubrick's *2001*, it is a quest film in which the hero's quest is scarcely more mad than the filmmaker's. Movies like this exist on a plane apart from ordinary films. There is a sense in which *Fitzcarraldo* is not altogether successful—it is too long, we could say, or too meandering—but it is still a film that I would not have missed for the world. The movie is the story of a dreamer named Brian Sweeney Fitzgerald, whose name has been simplified to "Fitzcarraldo" by the Indians and Spanish who inhabit his godforsaken corner of South America. He loves opera. He spends his days making a little money from an ice factory and his nights dreaming up new schemes. One of them, a plan to build a railroad across the continent, has already failed. Now he is ready with another: He seriously intends to build an opera house in the rain jungle, twelve hundred miles upstream from the civilized coast, and to bring Enrico Caruso there to sing an opera.

If his plan is mad, his method for carrying it out is madness of another dimension. Looking at the map, he becomes obsessed with the fact that a nearby river system offers access to hundreds of thousands of square miles of potential trading customers—if only a modern steamship could be introduced into that system. There is a point, he notices, where the other river is separated only by a thin finger of land from a river that already is navigated by boats. His inspiration: Drag a steamship across land to the other river, float it, set up a thriving trade, and use the profits to build the opera house—and then bring in Caruso! This scheme is so unlikely that perhaps we should not be surprised that Herzog's story is based on the case of a real Irish entrepreneur who tried to do exactly that.

The historical Irishman was at least wise enough to disassemble his boat before carting it across land. In Herzog's movie, however, Fitzcarraldo determines to drag the boat up one hill and down the other side in one piece. He enlists engineers to devise a system of blocks-and-pulleys that will do the trick, and he hires the local Indians to work the levers with their own muscle power. And it is here that we arrive at the thing about *Fitzcarraldo* that transcends all understanding: Werner

Herzog determined to literally drag a real steamship up a real hill, using real tackle and hiring the local Indians! To produce the movie, he decided to do personally what even the original Fitzgerald never attempted.

Herzog finally settled on the right actor to play Fitzcarraldo, author of this plan: Klaus Kinski, the shock-haired German who starred in Herzog's *Aguirre, the Wrath of God* and *Nosferatu*, is back again to mastermind the effort. Kinski is perfectly cast. Herzog's original choice for the role was Jason Robards, who is also gifted at conveying a consuming passion, but Kinski, wild-eyed and ferocious, consumes the screen. There are other characters important to the story, especially Claudia Cardinale as the madam who loves Fitzcarraldo and helps finance his attempt, but without Kinski at the core it's doubtful this story would work.

The story of Herzog's own production is itself well-known, and has been told in Les Blank's *Burden of Dreams*, a brilliant documentary about the filming. It's possible that every moment of *Fitzcarraldo* is colored by our knowledge that Herzog was "really" doing the things we see Fitzcarraldo do. (The movie uses no special effects, no models, no opticals, no miniatures.) Perhaps we're even tempted to give the movie extra points because of Herzog's ordeal in the jungle. But *Fitzcarraldo* is not all sweat and madness. It contains great poetic images of the sort Herzog is famous for: An old phonograph playing a Caruso record on the deck of a boat spinning out of control into a rapids; Fitzcarraldo frantically oaring a little rowboat down a jungle river to be in time to hear an opera; and of course the immensely impressive sight of that actual steamship, resting halfway up a hillside.

Fitzcarraldo is not a perfect movie, and it never comes together into a unified statement. It *is* meandering, and it is slow and formless at times. Perhaps the conception was just too large for Herzog to shape. The movie does not approach perfection as *Aguirre* did. But as a document of a quest and a dream, and as the record of man's audacity and foolish, visionary heroism, there has never been another movie like it.

See also Burden of Dreams, *a documentary on the making of* Fitzcarraldo.

Five Easy Pieces

R, 98 m., 1970

Jack Nicholson (Robert Dupea), Karen Black (Rayette), Susan Anspach (Catherine), Billy Green Bush (Elton), Helena Kallianiotes (Hitchhiker), Ralph Waite (Carl Dupea), William Challee (Nicholas Dupea), John Ryan (Spicer). Directed by Bob Rafelson and produced by Richard Wechsler and Rafelson. Screenplay by Adrien Joyce.

The title of *Five Easy Pieces* refers not to the women its hero meets along the road, for there are only three, but to a book of piano exercises he owned as a child. The film, one of the best American films, is about the distance between that boy, practicing to become a concert pianist, and the need he feels twenty years later to disguise himself as an oil-field rigger. When we sense the boy, tormented and insecure, trapped inside the adult man, *Five Easy Pieces* becomes a masterpiece of heartbreaking intensity.

At the outset, we meet only the man—played by Jack Nicholson with the same miraculous offhandedness that brought *Easy Rider* to life. He's an irresponsible roustabout, making his way through the oil fields, sleeping with a waitress (Karen Black) whose every daydreaming moment is filled with admiration for Miss Tammy Wynette. The man's name is Robert Eroica Dupea. He was named after Beethoven's Third Symphony and he spends his evenings bowling and his nights wearily agreeing that, yes, his girl sings "Stand By Your Man" just like Tammy.

In these first marvelous scenes, director Bob Rafelson calls our attention to the grimy life textures and the shabby hopes of these decent middle Americans. They live in a landscape of motels, highways, TV dinners, dust, and jealousy, and so do we all, but they seem to have nothing else. Dupea's friends are arrested at the mental and emotional level of about age seventeen; he isn't, but thinks or hopes he is.

Dupea discovers his girl is pregnant (his friend Elton breaks the news out in the field, suggesting maybe it would be good to marry her and settle down). He walks out on her in a rage, has a meaningless little affair with a slut from the bowling alley, and then discovers more or less by accident that his father is dying. His father, we discover, is a musical genius who moved his family to an island and tried to raise them as Socrates might have. Dupea feels himself to be the only failure.

The movie bares its heart in the scenes on the island, where Dupea makes an awkward effort to communicate with his dying father. The island is peopled with eccentrics, mostly Dupea's own family, but including a few strays. Among their number is a beautiful young girl who's come to the island to study piano with Dupea's supercilious brother. Dupea seduces this girl, who apparently suggests the early life he has abandoned. He does it by playing the piano; but when she says she's moved, he says he isn't—that he played better as a child and that the piece was easy anyway.

This is possibly the moment when his nerve fails and he condemns himself, consciously, to a life of self-defined failure. The movie ends, after several more scenes, on a note of ambiguity; he is either freeing himself from the waitress or, on the other hand, he is setting off on a journey even deeper into anonymity. It's impossible to say, and it doesn't matter much. What matters is the character during the time covered by the film: a time when Dupea tentatively reapproaches his past and then rejects it, not out of pride, but out of fear.

The movie is joyously alive to the road life of its hero. We follow him through bars and bowling alleys, motels and mobile homes, and we find him rebelling against lower middle-class values even as he embraces them. In one magical scene, he leaps from his car in a traffic jam and starts playing the piano on the truck in front of him; the scene sounds forced, described this way, but Rafelson and Nicholson never force anything, and never have to. Robert Eroica Dupea is one of the most unforgettable characters in American movies.

Flirting

NO MPAA RATING, 102 m., 1992

Noah Taylor (Danny Embling), Thandie Newton (Thandie Adjewa), Nicole Kidman (Nicola Radcliffe), Bartholomew Rose ("Gilby Fryer"), Felix Nobis (Jock Blair), Josh Picker ("Baka" Bourke), Kiri Paramore ("Slag" Green). Directed by John Duigan and produced by George Miller, Doug Mitchell, and Terry Hayes. Screenplay by Duigan.

Flirting is one of those rare movies with characters I cared about intensely. I didn't simply observe them on the screen; I got involved in their decisions and hoped they made the right ones. The movie is about two teenagers at private schools in Australia in the 1960s, a white boy and an African girl, who fall in love and do a little growing up, both at the same time.

The boy is Danny (Noah Taylor), awkward, a stutterer, the target of jokes from some of his classmates. He has a fine offbeat mind, which questions authority and doubts conventional wisdom. He is gawky in that way teenage boys can be before the parts grow into harmony with the whole. The girl is Thandie (Thandie Newton), very pretty, very smart, attracted to Danny because alone of the boys in her world he possesses a sense of humor and rebellion. She first sees him during a get-together between their twin schools, which are on either side of a lake, and looks at him boldly until he meets her gaze. Not long after, they are on opposing debate teams, and carry on a subtle little flirtation by disagreeing with the arguments of their own sides.

The girl's mother was British; her stepmother is African, like her father, who is a diplomat. Uganda is newly independent and is approaching the agony of the Idi Amin years. Events far away in Africa will decide whether the boy and girl will be able to carry on a normal teenage flirtation, or whether she will be swept away by the tide of history. Meanwhile, their eyes wide open, with joy and solemnity, they try to honor their love.

The movie is not about "movie teenagers," those unhappy creatures whose interests are limited and whose values are piggish. Most movies have no idea how thoughtful and responsible many teenagers are— how seriously they take their lives, how carefully they agonize over personal decisions. Only a few recent films, like *Say Anything* and *Man in the Moon*, have given their characters the freedom that *Flirting* grants—for kids to grow up by trying to make the right choices.

In *Flirting*, every scene serves a purpose. We go to classrooms and dormitories, to Parents' Day and sporting events, and we see the wit and daring with which Thandie and Danny arrange to meet under the eyes of their teachers. We also get a sense of the schools; the boys' school, where one of the teachers is too fond of caning, and another too fond of building model airplanes, and the girls' academy, where one of the older girls (Nicole Kidman) is responsible for Thandie, but secretly admires her willingness to break the rules.

Scene after scene is written with delicacy and wit. For example, a scene in which the young lovers' parents meet. Neither set of parents knows their child is dating at all; the way they all behave in this social setting, in a time and place where interracial dating raises eyebrows, is written with subtlety and tact. The adult actors bring a kind of awkward grace to the scene that is somehow very moving. The little nonconversation between Danny's parents, after they are alone again, is priceless.

Race itself is not the issue in *Flirting,* however; the movie is a coming-of-age drama (and comedy) about the ways in which these two young people balance lust with mutual respect, and how the girl, who is wiser and more mature, is also enormously tactful in guiding and protecting the boy that she loves. There is a scene in which they explore one another sexually, but it is not a "sex scene" in any conventional sense of the term, and the way it is handled is a rebuke to the way so many movies cheapen physical love.

Flirting came to me out of the blue, without advance notice, and I was deeply affected by it. Then I discovered it is a sequel to an earlier Australian film, *The Day My Voice Broke,* unseen by me, and that Danny will be seen again in a third film still to be made by the writer-director, John Duigan. I have gone searching for the first film, which I remember having heard good things about, but I know from experience that it is possible to see *Flirting* all by itself.

So often we settle for noise and movement from the movie screen, for stupid people indulging unworthy fantasies. Only rare movies like *Flirting* remind us that the movies are capable of providing us with the touch of other lives, that when all the conditions are right we can grow a little and learn a little, just like the people on the screen. This movie is joyous, wise, and life-affirming, and certainly one of 1992's best films.

The Fog of War
PG-13, 106 m., 2004

A documentary directed by Errol Morris and produced by Morris, Michael Williams, and Julie Ahlberg. Screenplay by Morris.

How strange the fate that brought together Robert McNamara and Errol Morris to make *The Fog of War.* McNamara, considered the architect of the Vietnam War, an Establishment figure who came to Washington after heading the Ford Motor Company and left to become the president of the World Bank. And Morris, the brilliant and eccentric documentarian who has chronicled pet cemeteries, death row, lion tamers, robots, naked mole rats, a designer of electric chairs, people who cut off their legs for the insurance money, and Stephen Hawking's *A Brief History of Time.*

McNamara agreed to talk with Morris for an hour or so, supposedly for a TV special. He eventually spent twenty hours peering into Morris's "Interrotron," a video device that allows Morris and his subjects to look into each other's eyes while also looking directly into the camera lens. Whether this invention results in better interviews is impossible to say, but it does have the uncanny result that the person on the screen never breaks eye contact with the audience.

McNamara was eighty-five when the interviews were conducted—a fit and alert eighty-five, still skiing the slopes at Aspen. Guided sometimes by Morris, sometimes taking the lead, he talks introspectively about his life, his thoughts about Vietnam, and, taking Morris where he would never have thought to go, his role in planning the firebombing of Japan, including a raid on Tokyo that claimed one hundred thousand lives. He speaks concisely and forcibly, rarely searching for a word, and he is not reciting boilerplate and old sound bites; there is the uncanny sensation that he is thinking as he speaks.

His thoughts are organized as *Eleven Lessons from the Life of Robert S. McNamara,* as extrapolated by Morris, and one wonders how the planners of the war in Iraq would respond to lesson Nos. 1 and 2 ("Empathize with your enemy" and "Rationality will not save us"), or for that matter, No. 6 ("Get the data"), No. 7

("Belief and seeing are both often wrong"), and No. 8 ("Be prepared to reexamine your reasoning"). I cannot imagine the circumstances under which Donald Rumsfeld, the current secretary of defense, would not want to see this film about his predecessor, having recycled and even improved upon McNamara's mistakes.

McNamara recalls the days of the Cuban missile crisis, when the world came to the brink of nuclear war (he holds up two fingers, almost touching, to show how close—"this close"). He recalls a meeting, years later, with Fidel Castro, who told him he was prepared to accept the destruction of Cuba if that's what the war would mean. He recalls two telegrams to Kennedy from Khrushchev, one more conciliatory, one perhaps dictated by Kremlin hard-liners, and says that JFK decided to answer the first and ignore the second. (Not quite true, as Fred Kaplan documents in an article at Slate.com.) The movie makes it clear that no one was thinking very clearly, and that the world avoided war as much by luck as by wisdom.

And then he remembers the years of the Vietnam War, inherited from JFK and greatly expanded by Lyndon Johnson. He began to realize the war could never be won, he says, and wrote a memo to the president to that effect. The result was that he resigned as secretary. (He had dinner with Kay Graham, publisher of the *Washington Post,* and told her, "Kay, I don't know if I resigned or was fired." "Oh, Bob," she told him, "of course you were fired.") He didn't resign as a matter of principle, as a British cabinet minister might; it is worth remembering that a few months later Johnson, saying he would not stand for reelection, did effectively resign.

McNamara begins by remembering how, at the age of two, he witnessed a victory parade after World War I, and engages in painful soul-searching about his role in World War II. He was a key aide to General Curtis LeMay, the hard-nosed warrior whose strategy for war was simplicity itself: kill them until they give up. Together, they planned the bombing raids before the atomic bomb ended the war, and Morris supplies a chart showing the American cities equivalent in size to the ones they targeted. After the war, McNamara says, in one of the film's most astonishing moments, LeMay observed to him that if America had lost, they would have been tried as war criminals. Thinking of the one hundred thousand burned alive in Tokyo, McNamara finds lesson No. 5: "Proportionality should be a guideline in war." In other words, I suppose, kill enough of the enemy but don't go overboard. Lesson No. 9: "In order to do good, you may have to engage in evil."

McNamara is both forthright and elusive. He talks about a Quaker who burned himself to death below the windows of his office in the Pentagon, and finds his sacrifice somehow in the same spirit as his own thinking—but it is true he could have done more to try to end the war and did not, and will not say why he did not, although now he clearly wishes he had. He will also not say he is sorry, even though Morris prompts him; maybe he's too proud, but I get the feeling it's more a case of not wanting to make a useless gesture that could seem hypocritical. His final words in the film make it clear there are some places he is simply not prepared to go.

Although McNamara is photographed through the Interrotron, the movie is far from offering only a talking head. Morris is uncanny in his ability to bring life to the abstract, and here he uses graphics, charts, moving titles, and visual effects in counterpoint to what McNamara is saying. There's also a lot of historical footage, including some shots of Curtis LeMay with his cigar clenched between his teeth—images that describe whatever McNamara neglected to say about him. There are tape recordings of Oval Office discussions involving McNamara, Kennedy, and Johnson. And archival footage of McNamara's years at Ford (he is proud of introducing seat belts). Underneath all of them, uneasily urging the movie along, is the Philip Glass score, which sounds—what? Mournful, urgent, melancholy, driven?

The effect of *The Fog of War* is to impress upon us the frailty and uncertainty of our leaders. They are sometimes so certain of actions that do not deserve such certitude. The farce of the missing weapons of mass destruction is no less complete than the confusion in the Kennedy White House over whether there were really nuclear warheads in Cuba. Some commentators on the film, notably Kaplan in his informative Slate essay, question McNamara's facts. What cannot be questioned is his ability to question them himself. At eighty-five, he knows what he knows, and what he does not know, and what cannot be known. Lesson No. 11: "You can't change human nature."

Forrest Gump
PG-13, 135 m., 1994

Tom Hanks (Forrest Gump), Robin Wright (Jenny Curran), Gary Sinise (Lieutenant Dan), Mykelti Williamson (Bubba), Sally Field (Mama Gump), Michael Humphreys (Young Forrest), Hanna Hall (Young Jenny). Directed by Robert Zemeckis and produced by Wendy Finerman, Steve Tisch, and Steve Starkey. Screenplay by Eric Roth.

I've never met anyone like Forrest Gump in a movie before, and for that matter I've never seen a movie quite like *Forrest Gump*. Any attempt to describe him will risk making the movie seem more conventional than it is, but let me try. It's a comedy, I guess. Or maybe a drama. Or a dream.

The screenplay by Eric Roth has the complexity of modern fiction, not the formulas of modern movies. Its hero, played by Tom Hanks, is a thoroughly decent man with an IQ of seventy-five, who manages between the 1950s and the 1980s to become involved in every major event in American history. And he survives them all with only honesty and niceness as his shields.

And yet this is *not* a heartwarming story about a mentally retarded man. That cubbyhole is much too small and limiting for *Forrest Gump*. The movie is more of a meditation on our times, as seen through the eyes of a man who lacks cynicism and takes things for exactly what they are. Watch him carefully and you will understand why some people are criticized for being "too clever by half." Forrest is clever by just exactly enough.

Tom Hanks may be the only actor who could have played the role. I can't think of anyone else as Gump, after seeing how Hanks makes him into a person so dignified, so straight-ahead. The performance is a breathtaking balancing act between comedy and sadness, in a story rich in big laughs and quiet truths.

Forrest is born to an Alabama boardinghouse owner (Sally Field), who tries to correct his posture by making him wear braces, but who never criticizes his mind. When Forrest is called "stupid," his mother tells him, "Stupid is as stupid does," and Forrest turns out to be incapable of doing anything less than profound. Also, when the braces finally fall from his legs, it turns out he can run like the wind.

That's how he gets a college football scholarship, in a life story that eventually becomes a running gag about his good luck. Gump the football hero becomes Gump the Medal of Honor winner in Vietnam, and then Gump the Ping-Pong champion, Gump the shrimp boat captain, Gump the millionaire stockholder (he gets shares in a new "fruit company" named Apple Computer), and Gump the man who runs across America and then retraces his steps.

It could be argued that with his IQ of seventy-five Forrest does not quite understand everything that happens to him. Not so. He understands everything he needs to know, and the rest, the movie suggests, is just surplus. He even understands everything that's important about love, although Jenny, the girl he falls in love with in grade school and never falls out of love with, tells him, "Forrest, you don't know what love is." She is a stripper by that time.

The movie is ingenious in taking Forrest on his tour of recent American history. The director, Robert Zemeckis, is experienced with the magic that special effects can do (his credits include the *Back to the Future* movies and *Who Framed Roger Rabbit*), and here he uses computerized visual legerdemain to place Gump in historic situations with actual people.

Forrest stands next to the schoolhouse door with George Wallace, he teaches Elvis how to swivel his hips, he visits the White House three times, he's on the Dick Cavett show with John Lennon, and in a sequence that will have you rubbing your eyes with its realism, he addresses a Vietnam-era peace rally on the Mall in Washington. Special effects are also used in creating the character of Forrest's Vietnam friend Lieutenant Dan (Gary Sinise), a Ron Kovic type who quite convincingly loses his legs.

Using carefully selected TV clips and dubbed voices, Zemeckis is able to create some hilarious moments, as when LBJ examines the wound in what Forrest describes as "my butt-ox." And the biggest laugh in the movie comes after Nixon inquires where Forrest is staying in Washington, and then recommends the Watergate. (That's not the laugh, just the setup.)

As Forrest's life becomes a guided tour of straight-arrow America, Jenny (played by Robin Wright) goes on a parallel tour of the counterculture. She goes to California, of course, and drops out, tunes in, and turns on. She's into psychedelics and flower power, antiwar rallies and love-ins, drugs and needles. Eventually it becomes clear that between them Forrest and Jenny have covered all of the landmarks of our recent cultural history, and the accommodation they arrive at in the end is like a dream of reconciliation for our society. What a magical movie.

Four Friends

R, 114 m., 1981

Craig Wasson (Danilo Prozor), Jodi Thelen (Georgia Miles), Jim Metzler (Tom Donaldson), Michael Huddleston (David Levine), Reed Birney (Louie Carnahan), Julie Murray (Adrienne Carnahan), Miklos Simon (Mr. Prozor). Directed by Arthur Penn and produced by Penn and Gene Lasko. Screenplay by Steven Tesich.

Somewhere in the middle of *My Dinner with André*, Andre Gregory wonders aloud if it's not possible that the 1960s were the last decade when we were all truly alive—that since then we've sunk into a bemused state of self-hypnosis, placated by consumer goods and given the illusion of excitement by television. Walking out of *Four Friends*, I had some of the same thoughts. This movie brings the almost unbelievable contradictions of that decade into sharp relief, not as nostalgia or as a re-creation of times past, but as a reliving of all of the agony and freedom of the weirdest ten years any of us is likely to witness.

The movie is told in the form of a looseknit autobiography, somewhat inspired by the experiences of Steve Tesich, the son of Yugoslavian parents who moved to this country as a boy and lived in the neighborhoods of East Chicago, Indiana, that provide the film's locations. If the film is his emotional autobi-

ography, it is also perhaps the intellectual autobiography of Arthur Penn, the film's director, whose *Bonnie and Clyde* was the best American film of the 1960s and whose *Alice's Restaurant* (1969) was an earlier examination of that wonderful and haunted time.

Their movie tells the stories of four friends. When we meet them, they're entering their senior year of high school. It is 1961. That is so long ago that nobody has yet heard of the Beatles. One of the friends is a young woman (Jodi Thelen), who imagines she is the reincarnation of Isadora Duncan, and who strikes attitudes and poses in an attempt to appear altogether too much of an artistic genius for East Chicago to contain. The other three friends are male classmates. They all love the girl in one way or another, or perhaps it's just that they've never seen anyone like her before. In the ten years to follow, these four people will have lives that were not imaginable in 1961. They will have the opportunity to break out of the sedate conservatism of the Eisenhower era and into the decade of "alternative lifestyles."

The movie is ambitious. It wants to take us on a tour of some of the things that happened in the 1960s, and some of the ways four midwestern kids might have responded to them. It also wants to be a meditation on love, and on how love changes during the course of a decade. When Thelen turns up at the bedroom window of her "real" true love (Craig Wasson) early in the movie and cheerfully offers to sleep with him, Wasson refuses, not only because he's a high school kid who's a little afraid of her—but also because he's too much in love with his idea of her to want to make it real. By the time they finally do come back together, years later, they've both been through bad scenes, through madness, drug abuse, and the trauma of the war in Vietnam. They have also grown up, some. The wonder is not that *Four Friends* covers so much ground, but that it makes many of its scenes so memorable that we learn more, even about the supporting characters, than we expect to.

There are individual scenes in this movie that are just right. One of them involves a crowd of kids walking home in the dusk after school. Another happens between Wasson and Miklos Simon, who plays his gruff, defensive Yugoslavian father, and who finally, painfully, breaks down and smiles after a poker-faced lifetime. A relationship between Wasson and a dying college classmate (Reed Birney) is well drawn, to remind us of undergraduate friendships based on idealism and mutual discovery. And the scene where Wasson and Thelen see each other after many years is handled tenderly and with just the right notes of irony.

Four Friends is a very good movie. Like *Breaking Away*, the story of growing up in Bloomington, Indiana (for which Tesich also wrote the original screenplay), this is a movie that remembers times past with such clarity that there are times it seems to be making it all up. Did we really say those things? Make those assumptions? Live on the edge of what seemed to be a society gone both free and mad at once? Some critics have said the people and events in this movie are not plausible. I don't know if they're denying the movie's truth, or arguing that from a 1980s point of view the '60s were just a bad dream. Or a good one.

4 Little Girls

NO MPAA RATING, 102 m., 1997

A documentary directed by Spike Lee and produced by Lee and Sam Pollard.

Spike Lee's *4 Little Girls* tells the story of the infamous Birmingham church bombing of September 15, 1963, when the lives of an eleven-year-old and three fourteen-year-olds, members of the choir, were ended by the explosion. More than any other event, that was the catalyst for the civil rights movement, the moment when all of America could look away no longer from the face of racism. "It was the awakening," says Walter Cronkite in the film.

The little girls had gone to church early for choir practice, and we can imagine them, dressed in their Sunday best, meeting their friends in the room destroyed by the bomb. We can fashion the picture in our minds because Lee has, in a way, brought them back to life through photographs, through old home movies, and especially through the memories of their families and friends.

By coincidence, I was listening to the radio not long after seeing *4 Little Girls,* and I heard a report from Charlayne Hunter-Gault. In 1961, when she was nineteen, she was the first black woman to desegregate the University of Georgia. Today she is an NPR correspondent. That is what happened to her. In 1963, Carole Robertson was fourteen, and her Girl Scout sash was filled with merit badges. Because she was killed that day, we will never know what would have happened in her life.

That thought keeps returning: The four little girls never got to grow up. Not only were their lives stolen, but their contributions to ours. I have a hunch that Denise McNair, who was eleven when she died, would have made her mark. In home videos, she comes across as poised and observant, filled with charisma. Among the many participants in the film, two of the most striking are her parents, Chris and Maxine McNair, who remember a special child.

Chris McNair talks of a day when he took Denise to downtown Birmingham, and the smell of onions frying at a store's lunch counter made her hungry. "That night I knew I had to tell her she couldn't have that sandwich because she was black," he recalls. "That couldn't have been any less painful than seeing her with a rock smashed into her head."

Lee's film re-creates the day of the bombing through newsreel footage, photographs, and eyewitness reports. He places it within a larger context of the southern civil rights movement, the sit-ins and the arrests, the marches, the songs, and the killings.

Birmingham was a tough case. Police commissioner Bull Connor is seen directing the resistance to marchers and traveling in an armored vehicle—painted white, of course. Governor George Wallace makes his famous vow to stand in the schoolhouse door and personally bar any black students from entering. Though they could not know it, their resistance was futile after September 15, 1963, because the hatred exposed by the bomb pulled all of their rhetoric and all of their rationalizations out from under them.

Spike Lee says he has wanted to make this film since 1983, when he read a *New York Times Magazine* article by Howell Raines about the bombing. "He wrote me asking permission back then," Chris McNair told me in an interview. "That was before he had made any of his films." It is perhaps good that Lee waited, because he is more of a filmmaker now, and events have supplied him a denouement in the conviction of a man named Robert Chambliss ("Dynamite Bob") as the bomber. He was, said Raines, who met quite a few, "the most pathological racist I've ever encountered."

The other two victims were Addie Mae Collins and Cynthia Wesley, both fourteen. In shots that are almost unbearable, we see the bodies of the victims in the morgue. Why does Lee show them? To look full into the face of what was done, I think. To show racism's handiwork. There is a memory in the film of a big, burly, white Birmingham policeman who in the aftermath of the bombing tells a black minister, "I really didn't believe they would go this far."

The man was a Klansman, the movie says, but in using the word "they" he unconsciously separates himself from his fellows. He wants to dissociate himself from the crime. So did others. Before long even George Wallace was apologizing for his behavior and trying to define himself in a different light. There is a scene in the film where the former governor, now old and infirm, describes his black personal assistant, Eddie Holcey, as his best friend. "I couldn't live without him," Wallace says, dragging Holcey in front of the camera, insensitive to the feelings of the man he is tugging over for display. Why is that scene there? It's sort of associated with the morgue photos, I think. There is mostly sadness and regret at the surface in *4 Little Girls*, but there is anger in the depths, as there should be.

The Fox

NO MPAA RATING, 111 m., 1968

Sandy Dennis (Jill), Keir Dullea (Paul), Anne Heywood (March). Directed by Mark Rydell and produced by Raymond Stross. Screenplay by Lewis John Carlino and Howard Koch, based on the story by D. H. Lawrence.

Do not see *The Fox* because of its subject matter, and do not stay away for that reason. The scenes that disturbed Chicago's reactionary censors are filmed with quiet taste and an intuitive knowledge of human nature. And they are only a small part of a wholly natural film.

Indeed, it is the natural ease of the film that is so appealing. Departing from the original setting in D. H. Lawrence's story, director Mark Rydell decided to shoot on location during a Canadian winter. The delicately constructed atmosphere of cold and snow, of early sunsets and chill lingering in the corners, establishes the tone. This will be a film about love, but not about passion. The characters will come together tentatively, unsure that any warm season will follow this cold.

The events take place on a small farm that two young women (Sandy Dennis and Anne Heywood) are attempting to manage. It was their idea to become independent, to get away from the pettiness of the city. Although the film's publicity would indicate otherwise, the two women are not necessarily presented as homosexual.

They are free spirits, fresh out of college, trying to make a success of the farm; the brief lesbian scene that follows the crisis in their lives can be seen, I believe, more as a pouring over of strong emotion than as a "perversion."

The crisis arrives in the form of Paul (Keir Dullea), whose grandfather once lived on the farm. He offers to stay for a few weeks and help with the work. Dennis, who plays an unsure, spontaneous character, agrees enthusiastically. Heywood, who is reserved and lonely, allows herself to be persuaded.

Rydell sets these events securely into the context of the farm life in winter. His photography establishes the farm not only as isolated but also, paradoxically, as serene. The only threat to the small community comes from a fox that preys on the chickens. Heywood cannot quite bring herself to kill the fox, although she sees it several times. Dullea finally shoots it; but, of course, Dullea is also a fox, preying on the two women.

Dennis has a difficult role; after Dullea and Heywood announce that they plan to be married, she must behave badly, annoying them in a childish way. The role could have become ridiculous, but Dennis manages it well.

Dullea is also stronger than he has been in other recent performances. Since *David and Lisa*, he has been trapped into playing a series of insecure, weak characters; this time, as the dominant personality, he is altogether successful. And he meets his match in Heywood, who must love him without being over-whelmed by his personality.

Rydell has been faithful to Lawrence in the way he develops the love relationship. Lawrence rarely used conventional plot development to bring his lovers together. Instead, they were drawn together by something compelling in each other's personalities. Done awkwardly, this is unconvincing. Lawrence, and Rydell after him, make it believable. What results is a quiet, powerful masterpiece.

Frailty

R, 100 m., 2002

Bill Paxton (Dad), Matthew McConaughey (Fenton Meiks), Powers Boothe (Agent Wesley Doyle), Matthew O'Leary (Young Fenton Meiks), Jeremy Sumpter (Young Adam Meiks), Luke Askew (Sheriff Smalls), Derk Cheetwood (Agent Griffin Hull), Blake King (Eric). Directed by Paxton and produced by David Blocker, David Kirschner, and Corey Sienega. Screenplay by Brent Hanley.

Heaven protect us from people who believe they can impose their will on us in this world, because of what they think they know about the next. *Frailty* is about such a man, a kind and gentle father who is visited by an angel who assigns him to murder demons in human form. We are reminded that Andrea Yates believed she was possessed by Satan and could save her children by drowning them. *Frailty* is as chilling: The father enlists his two sons, who are about seven and ten, to join him in the murders of victims he brings home.

This is not, you understand, an abusive father. He loves his children. He is only following God's instructions: "This is our job now, son. We've got to do this." When the older son, terrified and convinced his father has gone mad, says he'll report him to the police, his father explains, "If you do that, son, someone will die. The angel was clear on this." The pressure that the children are under is unbearable and tragic, and warps their entire lives.

Frailty is an extraordinary work, concealing in its depths not only unexpected story turns but also implications, hidden at first, that make it even deeper and more sad. It is the first film directed by the actor Bill Paxton, who also plays the father, and succeeds in making "Dad" not a villain but a sincere man lost within his delusions. Matthew Mc-Conaughey plays one of his sons as a grown man, and Powers Boothe is the FBI agent who is investigating the "God's Hand" serial murders in Texas when the son comes to him one night, with the body of his brother parked outside in a stolen ambulance.

The movie works in so many different ways that it continues to surprise us right until the end. It begins as a police procedural, seems for a time to be a puzzle like *Usual Suspects*, reveals itself as a domestic terror film, evokes pity as well as horror, and reminded me of *The Rapture*, another film about a parent who is willing to sacrifice a child in order to follow the literal instructions of her faith.

As the film opens, Matthew McConaughey appears in the office of FBI agent Wesley Doyle (Powers Boothe), introduces himself as Fenton Meiks, and says he knows who committed the serial killings that have haunted the area for years. His story becomes the narration of two long flashbacks in which we see Paxton as the elder Meiks, and Matthew O'Leary and Jeremy Sumpter as young Fenton and Adam. Their mother is dead; they live in a frame house near the community rose garden, happy and serene, until the night their father wakes them with the news that he has been visited by an angel.

The film neither shies away from its horrifying events nor dwells on them. There is a series of ax murders, but they occur offscreen; this is not a movie about blood, but about obsession. The truly disturbing material involves the two boys, who are played by O'Leary and Sumpter as ordinary, happy kids whose lives turn into nightmares. Young Adam simply believes everything his father tells him. Fenton is old enough to know it's wrong: "Dad's brainwashed you," he tells Adam. "It's all a big lie. He murders people and you help him."

The construction of the story circles around the angel's "instructions" in several ways. The sons and father are trapped in a household seemingly ruled by fanaticism. There is, however, the intriguing fact that when Dad touches his victims, he has graphic visions of their sins—he can see vividly why they need to be killed. Are these visions accurate? We see them, too, but it's unclear whether through Dad's eyes or the movie's narrator—if that makes a difference. Whether they are objectively true is something I, at least, believe no man can know for sure about another. Not just by touching him, anyway. But the movie contains one shot, sure to be debated, that suggests God's hand really is directing Dad's murders.

Perhaps only a first-time director, an actor who does not depend on directing for his next job, would have had the nerve to make this movie. It is uncompromised. It follows its logic right down into hell. We love movies that play and toy with the supernatural, but are we prepared for one that is an unblinking look at where the logic of the true believer can lead? There was just a glimpse of this mentality on the day after 9/11, when certain TV preachers described it as God's punishment for our sins, before backpedaling when they found such frankness eroded their popularity base.

On the basis of this film, Bill Paxton is a gifted director; he and his collaborators, writer Brent Hanley, cinematographer Bill Butler, and editor Arnold Glassman, have made a complex film that grips us with the intensity of a simple one. We're with it every step of the way, and discover we hardly suspect where it is going.

Note: Watching the film, I was reminded again of the West Memphis Three (www.wm3.org), those three Arkansas teenagers convicted of the brutal murder of three children. One faces death and the other two long sentences. The documentaries Paradise Lost *(1992) and* Paradise Lost 2: Revelations *(2000) make it clear they are probably innocent (a prime suspect all but confesses on-screen), but the three are still in jail because they wore black, listened to heavy metal music, and were railroaded by courts and a community convinced they were Satanists—which must have been evidence enough, since there wasn't much else, and the boys could prove they were elsewhere.*

The French Connection

R, 104 m., 1971

Gene Hackman (Detective Jimmy "Popeye" Doyle), Fernando Rey (Alain Charnier), Roy Scheider (Detective Buddy "Cloudy" Russo), Tony Lo Bianco (Salvatore "Sal" Boca). Directed by William Friedkin and produced by G. David Schine and Philip D'Antoni. Screenplay by Ernest Tidyman, based on the book by Robin Moore.

The French Connection is routinely included, along with *Bullitt, Diva,* and *Raiders of the Lost Ark,* on the short list of movies with the greatest chase scenes of all time. What is not always remembered is what a good movie it is apart from the chase scene. It featured a great early Gene Hackman performance that won an Academy Award, and it also won Oscars for best picture, direction, screenplay, and editing.

The movie is all surface, movement, violence, and suspense. Only one of the characters really emerges into three dimensions: Popeye Doyle (Gene Hackman), a New York narc who is vicious, obsessed, and a little mad. The other characters don't emerge because there's no time for them to emerge. Things are happening too fast.

The story line hardly matters. It involves a $32 million shipment of high-grade heroin smuggled from Marseilles to New York hidden in a Lincoln Continental. A complicated deal is set up between the French people, an American money man and the Mafia. Doyle, a tough cop with a shaky reputation who busts a lot of street junkies, needs a big win to keep his career together. He stumbles on the heroin deal and pursues it with a single-minded ferocity that is frankly amoral. He isn't after the smugglers because they're breaking the law; he's after them because his job consumes him.

Director William Friedkin constructs *The French Connection* so surely that it leaves audiences stunned. And I don't mean that as a reviewer's cliché: It is literally true. In a sense, the whole movie is a chase. It opens with a shot of a French detective keeping the Continental under surveillance, and from then on the smugglers and the law officers are endlessly circling and sniffing each other. It's just that the chase speeds up sometimes, as in the celebrated car-train sequence.

In *Bullitt,* two cars and two drivers were matched against each other at fairly equal odds. In Friedkin's chase, the cop has to weave through city traffic at 70 mph to keep up with a train that has a clear track: The odds are off-balance. And when the train's motorman dies and the train is without a driver, the chase gets even spookier: A man is matched against a machine that cannot understand risk or fear. This makes the chase psychologically more scary, in addition to everything it has going for it visually.

The movie was shot during a cold and gray New York winter, and it has a doomed, gritty look. The landscape is a wasteland, and the characters are hardly alive. They move out of habit and compulsion, long after ordinary human feelings have lost the power to move them. Doyle himself is a bad cop, by ordinary standards; he harasses and brutalizes people, he is a racist, he endangers innocent people during the chase scene (which is a high-speed ego trip). But he survives. He wins, too, but that hardly matters. *The French Connection* is as amoral as its hero, as violent, as obsessed, and as frightening.

The key to the chase is that it occurs in an ordinary time and place. No rules are suspended; Popeye's car is racing down streets where ordinary traffic and pedestrians can be found, and his desperation is such that we believe, at times, he is capable of running down bystanders just to win the contest. I had an opportunity at the Hawaii Film Festival in 1992 to analyze the sequence a shot at a time, using a stop-action laserdisc approach, at a seminar honoring the work of the cinematographer, Owen Roizman. He recalled the way the whole chase was painstakingly storyboarded and then broken down into shots that were possible and safe, even though actual locations were being employed. Lenses were chosen to play with distance, so that the car sometimes seemed closer to hazards than it was. But essentially, the chase looked real because its many different parts were real: A car threads through city streets, chasing an elevated train.

The other key element in the film, of course, is Hackman. He was already well known in 1971, after performances in such films as *Bonnie and Clyde, Downhill Racer,* and *I Never Sang for My Father.* But it's probably *The French Connection* that launched his long career as a leading character star—a man with the unique ability to make almost any dialogue plausible. As Popeye Doyle, he generated an almost frightening single-mindedness, a cold determination to win at all costs, which elevated the stakes in the story from a simple police cat-and-mouse chase into the acting-out of Popeye's pathology. The chase

scene has, in a way, been a mixed blessing, distracting from the film's other qualities.

Frenzy

R, 116 m., 1972

Jon Finch (Richard Blaney), Barry Foster (Rusk), Barbara Leigh-Hunt (Brenda Blaney), Anna Massey (Babs Mulligan), Alec McCowen (Chief Inspector Oxford), Vivien Merchant (Mrs. Oxford). Directed by Alfred Hitchcock. Associate producer William Hill. Screenplay by Anthony Shaffer.

Alfred Hitchcock's *Frenzy* is a return to old forms by the master of suspense, whose newer forms have pleased movie critics but not his public. This is the kind of thriller Hitchcock was making in the 1940s, filled with macabre details, incongruous humor, and the desperation of a man convicted of a crime he didn't commit.

The only 1970s details are the violence and the nudity (both approached with a certain grisly abandon that has us imagining *Psycho* without the shower curtain). It's almost as if Hitchcock, at seventy-three, was consciously attempting to do once again what he did better than anyone else. His films since *Psycho* struck out into unfamiliar territory and even got him involved in the Cold War *(Torn Curtain)* and the fringes of fantasy *(The Birds).* Here he's back at his old stand.

Frenzy, which allegedly has a loose connection with a real criminal case, involves us in the exploits of a murderer known as The Necktie Killer (Barry Foster). And involvement is the sensation we feel, I think, since we know his identity from the beginning and sometimes cannot help identifying with him. There is a scene, for example, in which he inadvertently gets himself trapped in the back of a potato truck with a sack containing the body of his latest victim. We know he is a slimy bastard, but somehow we're sweating along with him as he crawls through the potatoes trying to regain a bit of incriminating evidence. He is the killer but, as is frequently the case with Hitchcock, another man seems much more guilty. This is Richard Blaney (Jon Finch), an ex-RAF hero who is down on his luck and has just lost his job. Through a series of unhappy coincidences which I'd better not give away, he's caught red-handed with the evidence while the killer walks away.

Hitchcock sets his action in the crowded back alleys of Covent Garden, where fruit and vegetable vendors rub shoulders with prostitutes, third-rate gangsters, bookies, and barmaids. A lot of the action takes place in a pub, and somehow Hitchcock gets more feeling for the location into his films than he usually does. With a lot of Hitchcock, you have the impression every frame has been meticulously prepared. This time, the smell and tide of humanity slops over. (There is even one tide in the movie which does a little slopping over humanity itself—but never mind.)

It's delicious to watch Hitchcock using the camera. Not a shot is wasted, and there is one elaborate sequence in which the killer goes upstairs with his victim. The camera precedes them up the stairs, watches them go in a door, and then backs down the stairs, alone, and across the street to look at the outside of the house. This shot is not for a moment a gimmick; the melancholy of the withdrawing camera movement is one of the most touching effects in the film, despite the fact that no people inhabit it.

There's a lot of humor, too, including two hilarious gourmet meals served to the Chief Inspector (Alec McCowen) by his wife (Vivien Merchant). There is suspense, and local color ("It's been too long since the Christie murders; a good colorful crime spree is good for tourism") and, always, Hitchcock smacking his lips and rubbing his hands and delighting in his naughtiness.

Fresh

R, 109 m., 1994

Sean Nelson (Fresh), Giancarlo Esposito (Esteban), Samuel L. Jackson (Sam), N'Bushe Wright (Nichole), Ron Brice (Corky), Jean LaMare (Jake), Jose Zuniga (Lieutenant Perez), Luis Lantigua (Chuckie). Directed by Boaz Yakin and produced by Lawrence Bender and Randy Ostrow. Screenplay by Yakin.

Characters are never at a loss for words in the movies. They talk quickly, never hesitating or repeating themselves. Kids are especially articulate, like well-trained little word machines. Movies are getting to be more and more like television, where there's never a moment to spare. *Fresh* isn't like that. Here's a movie filled with drama and excitement, unfolding a plot of brilliant complexity, in which the central character is solemn and silent, saying only what he has to say, revealing himself only strategically.

Fresh is a twelve-year-old boy who lives in Brooklyn. He is a runner for drug dealers. Because he is smart and honest, they respect him. Fresh lives with eleven other children in the spotless, orderly apartment of his aunt, who is a saint, he agrees, but who is helpless against the dangers that children face in the streets. Sometimes he sees his dad, an alcoholic who lives in a camper and supports himself by hustling chess games for cash. Sometimes he sees his sister, who has moved out of their aunt's apartment to live with a dealer. Her days pass in a sad haze of drugs.

Fresh knows a lot about drugs, and has a good relationship with a local dealer named Esteban, who is not a bad man as drug dealers go, and who is proud of Fresh—thinking of him almost like a son. Fresh's life, and the city that formed it, are drawn carefully in the early scenes of *Fresh*, which was written and directed by Boaz Yakin, a sometime writer of Hollywood thrillers *(The Rookie)*, who dropped out, moved to Paris, and told himself he would return to the movies only when he had something to say, and control over how it was said. *Fresh* meets those qualifications.

You may think, having seen an urban thriller or two, that you can guess how *Fresh* feels and sounds. You would be wrong. The sound track is not filled with loud, angry music. The plot is not manic but focused and perceptive. Fresh, the central character, is played in an extraordinary performance by Sean Nelson, as a boy who sees and understands much, and keeps his own counsel.

It is important that the film establish its world. We will need to understand it in order to appreciate the remarkable last act of this movie, in which Fresh pulls off a plan that is part scam and part revenge—an unforgiving retribution against the system that is destroying the lives of those he loves.

The early scenes are fascinating. Fresh is doted on by the dealers (Giancarlo Esposito is engaging as Esteban). A great future is predicted for him. He doesn't use drugs himself, and his opinion of those who do is indifference laced with contempt—except in the case of his older sister (N'Bushe Wright), who makes his heart weep. Fresh saves his money, and has a lot of it. He has some friends his own age, especially Chuckie (Luis Lantigua), who talks too much—a mistake Fresh never makes.

To fill the great vacuum in his life, the need for love and discipline, he returns to his father (Samuel L. Jackson), a man who might have been a great chess champion, and is still almost unbeatable in the rough school of New York street chess. His father, who is never far from a bottle purchased with his winnings, does the best he can for Fresh, using chess as a metaphor for life. It is during one of his chess lectures that Fresh conceives the audacious scheme he pulls off. Seeing the movie at the 1994 Cannes Film Festival, I thought I was hearing some chess advice. Seeing it the second time, I realized that the actual outcome of the movie was being predicted.

Fresh is barely old enough to be noticing girls, but there is one he does notice, and as she smiles sweetly at him, he feels his heart sing for perhaps the first time in his life. It is the outcome of this first schoolyard crush that influences all the rest of the movie. The movie is well constructed; no event is unmotivated, and Yakin's screenplay establishes all of the emotional reasons, too, so that nothing is unexplained, even what seems at first like the gratuitous death of a dog.

Sudden, violent death is a fact of life in America today. Guns have made our cities unsafe for children. What *Fresh* does is bring a new perspective to those facts, in the form of both drama and thriller. This is not an action film, not a clever, superficial thriller, but a story of depth and power, in which the dangerous streets are seen through the eyes of a twelve-year-old who reacts with the objectivity he has learned from chess, and the anger taught to him by his life.

The Friends of Eddie Coyle

R, 102 m., 1973

Robert Mitchum (Eddie Coyle), Peter Boyle (Dillon), Richard Jordan (Dave Foley), Steven Keats (Jackie), Alex Rocco (Scalise), Joe Santos (Artie Van).

Directed by Peter Yates and produced and written by Paul Monash, based on the book by George Higgins.

Someone remarks of Eddie, about halfway through *The Friends of Eddie Coyle*, that for a two-bit hood, he has fingers in a lot of pies. Too many, as it turns out. Without ever rising to the top, Eddie has been employed in organized crime for most of his life. He's kind of a utility infielder, ready to trade in some hot guns, drive a hijacked truck, or generally make himself useful.

Eddie got the nickname "Fingers" some years ago after a gun deal. The buyers he supplied got caught. Their friends slammed Eddie's fingers in a drawer. He understood. There is a certain code without which it would be simply impossible to go on doing business.

But as the movie opens, Eddie is in trouble, and it looks like he'll have to break the code. He's facing a two-year stretch in New Hampshire, and he wants out of it. He doesn't want to leave his wife and kids and see them go on welfare. He is, at heart, just a small businessman; he deals in crime but is profoundly middle class. He thinks maybe he can make a deal with the state's attorney and have a few good words put in for him up in New Hampshire.

The movie is as simple as that. It's not a high-strung gangster film, it doesn't have a lot of overt excitement in it, and it doesn't go in for much violence. It gives us a man, invites our sympathy for him, and then watches almost sadly as his time runs out. And *The Friends of Eddie Coyle* works so well because Eddie is played by Robert Mitchum, and Mitchum has perhaps never been better.

He has always been one of our best screen actors: sardonic, masculine, quick-witted, but slow to reveal himself. More than half his films have been conventional action melodramas, and it is a rare summer without at least one movie in which Mitchum wears a sombrero and lights bombs with his cigar. But give him a character and the room to develop it, and what he does is wonderful. Eddie Coyle is made for him: a weary middle-aged man, but tough and proud; a man who has been hurt too often in life not to respect pain; a man who will take chances to protect his own territory.

The movie is drawn from a knowledgeable novel by George V. Higgins, himself a state's attorney, and has been directed by one of the masters of this sort of thing, Peter Yates *(Robbery, Bullitt)*. Paul Monash's screenplay stays close to the real-life Massachusetts texture of the novel, and the dialogue sounds right. The story isn't developed in the usual movie way, with lots of importance being given to intricacies of plot; instead, Eddie's dilemma occurs to him as it occurs to us, and we watch him struggle with it.

If the movie has a flaw, it's that we don't really care that much about the bank robberies that are counterpointed with Eddie's situation. We're interested in him. We can get the bank robberies in any summer's caper picture. It's strange that a movie's interest should fall off during its action scenes. But this is Eddie Coyle's picture, and Mitchum's.

The Fugitive

PG-13, 133 m., 1993

Harrison Ford (Dr. Richard Kimble), Tommy Lee Jones (Deputy U.S. Marshal Gerard), Jeroen Krabbe (Dr. Charles Nichols), Joe Pantoliano (Renfro), Andreas Katsulas (Sykes), Sela Ward (Helen Kimble), Daniel Roebuck (Biggs), L. Scott Caldwell (Poole), Tom Wood (Newman). Directed by Andrew Davis and produced by Arnold Kopelson. Screenplay by Jeb Stuart and David Twohy.

Andrew Davis's *The Fugitive* is a tense, taut, and expert thriller that becomes something more than that: an allegory about an innocent man in a world prepared to crush him. Like the cult television series that inspired it, the film has a Kafkaesque view of the world. But it is larger and more encompassing than the series: Davis paints with bold visual strokes so that the movie rises above its action-film origins and becomes operatic.

The story involves a cat-and-mouse game between a man unjustly accused of having murdered his wife, and a law officer who tracks him with cunning ferocity. This was, of course, Hitchcock's favorite theme, touching on the universal dread of the innocent man wrongly accused. The man is Dr. Richard Kimble (Harrison Ford), a respected Chicago surgeon, who returns home one night to find his wife fatally beaten by a one-armed man who flees after a struggle. All of the evidence points to Kimble's guilt, and his story of the intruder is brushed away in a courtroom scene of such haste and finality that, like a lot of the film, it only looks realistic while actually functioning on the level of a nightmare.

Kimble is sentenced to death, but escapes during a collision between his prison bus and a train. The crash sequence is as ambitious and electric as any I have seen, with Kimble fleeing for his life while a locomotive bears down on him (the echo here is of Harrison Ford's famous sequence in *Raiders of the Lost Ark* in which he is nearly crushed by a giant stone ball).

Free for the time being, but isolated in a cold winter landscape of hostile stones, icy water, and barren trees, Kimble is pursued in a manhunt directed by a deputy U.S. marshal (Tommy Lee Jones). It seems incredible that he could remain free, and even pursue attempts to prove his innocence, but he does, in a film that never relaxes its tension even for an instant. This is pure filmmaking on a master scale.

Tommy Lee Jones has become one of the great craggy presences of the screen, often cast as a villain, but with a half-masked amusement that borders on contempt for lesser beings: He has the charm of a hangman promising to make things as comfortable as possible. In *The Fugitive*, his role is more complex than at first it seems. As the chase continues, he gradually becomes convinced of the innocence of his prey, but this conviction is wisely never spelled out in dialogue, and remains ambivalent, expressed in the look in his eyes, or his pauses between words.

Ford is once again the great modern movie everyman, dogged, determined, brave, and not demonstrative. As an actor, nothing he does seems merely for show, and in the face of this melodramatic material he deliberately plays down, lays low, gets on with business instead of trying to exploit the drama in meaningless acting flourishes.

The director, Andrew Davis, has come up through a series of superior action films. His gift was apparent in one of his earlier features, the Chuck Norris thriller *Code of Silence*, which remains Norris's best film and one of the best, most atmospheric uses of Chicago locations ever achieved. Davis's good films continued with the Steven Seagal thriller *Above the Law*, *The Package* with Gene Hackman, and 1992's superb *Under Siege*. Here he transcends genre and shows an ability to marry action and artistry that deserves comparison with Hitchcock, yes, and also with David Lean and Carol Reed.

The device of the film is to keep Kimble only a few steps ahead of his pursuers. It is a dangerous strategy, and could lead to laughable close calls and near-misses, but Davis tells the story of the pursuit so clearly on the tactical level that we can always understand why Kimble is only so far ahead, and no farther. As always, Davis uses locations not simply as the place where action occurs, but as part of the reason for the action. Consider his virtuoso opening chase sequence, which after the train crash leads to a series of drainage tunnels (echoes here of *The Third Man*) and finally to a spectacular dam, where Kimble risks death for a chance of freedom, and dives into the cascading waters in a moment that can only be called Wagnerian.

Jones's "Deputy," as he likes to be called, has much more dialogue than Kimble, and in the screenplay by Jeb Stuart and David Twohy it always serves an intelligent purpose. You never have the feeling the characters are saying things simply to give us information; instead, a little at a time, they reveal the way they are thinking. Jones is surrounded by good character actors, who for once sound like Chicago cops in their words and inflections, instead of like transplants from a TV police drama. Strangely, although the film is relentlessly manipulative, it plays like real events. Nothing can really be believed in retrospect, but Davis and his actors ground all the action and dialogue in reality, so we don't consider the artifice while it's happening.

Thrillers are a much-debased genre these days, depending on special effects and formula for much of their content. *The Fugitive* has the standards of an earlier, more classic time, when acting, character, and dialogue were meant to stand on their own, and where characters continued to change and develop right up until the last frame.

Funny Girl
G, 151 m., 1968

Barbra Streisand (Fanny Brice), Omar Sharif (Nick Arnstein), Kay Medford (Rose Brice), Anne Francis (Georgia James), Walter Pidgeon (Flo Ziegfeld). Directed by William Wyler and and produced by Wyler and Ray Stark. Screenplay by Isobel Lennart, based on the musical by Jule Styne and Bob Merrill.

The trouble with *Funny Girl* is almost everything except Barbra Streisand. She is magnificent.

But the film itself is perhaps the ultimate example of the roadshow musical gone overboard. It is over-produced, over-photographed, and over-long. The second half drags badly. The supporting characters are generally wooden. And in this movie, believe me, everyone who ain't Barbra Streisand is a supporting character.

That makes the movie itself kind of schizo. It is impossible to praise Miss Streisand too highly; hard to find much to praise about the rest of the film.

She turns out, curiously enough, to be a born movie star. It was her voice that made her famous, and that's fair enough. But it will be her face and her really splendid comic ability that make her a star. She has the best shtick since Mae West, and is more fun to watch than anyone since the young Katharine Hepburn.

She doesn't actually sing a song at all; she acts it. She does things with her hands and face that are simply individual; that's the only way to describe them. They haven't been done before. She sings, and you're really happy you're there.

Unfortunately, one gathers Miss Streisand is a rather set-minded lady as well as a star. She wants her way on the set, they say; and Miss Streisand has been heard to claim William Wyler didn't direct her, she directed herself. I doubt that. But someone, Wyler or someone, should have directed the rest of the movie. The sets (Hollywood sound stages mostly) and the supporting roles seem designed merely to backdrop the magnificent Barbra. And in the end, that hurts the movie.

Take Omar Sharif, for example. Until now, he has always been a human being on the screen. He has walked, talked, breathed, moved around. In *Funny Girl,* he becomes a cigar-store Indian. There has rarely been a more wooden male performance in a musical. I guess we're supposed to look at Miss Streisand, who is nearly always on the screen, instead.

Well, this is her first film and that is a pleasant task. But it would certainly have been a better musical if more attention had been given to the total effect, and less to Barbra's admittedly great talent. As it is, the more modest *Finian's Rainbow* is better this season as a well-balanced musical.

Funny Girl is lopsided; good when Barbra's there, transcendent during her best numbers ("Don't Rain On My Parade," "My Man," and a roller-skating sequence), and curiously flat the rest of the time, as if everyone were waiting until she got back.

G

The Gambler

R, 111 m., 1974

James Caan (Axel), Paul Sorvino (Hips), Lauren Hutton (Billie), Morris Carnovsky (A. R. Lowenthal), Jacqueline Brooks (Naomi), Burt Young (Carmine). Directed by Karel Reisz and produced by Irwin Winkler and Robert Chartoff. Screenplay by James Toback.

"Jeez, Axel, I never seen such bad cards," Axel Freed's friend tells him consolingly. They're standing in the kitchen of a New York apartment, and gray dawn is seeping through the smoke. Axel has never seen such bad cards either. His disbelief that anyone could draw so many lousy poker hands in a row has led him finally $44,000 into debt. He doesn't have the money, but it's been a bigtime game, and he has to find it somewhere or be in heavy trouble.

And that's how Karel Reisz's *The Gambler* begins: with a problem. The way Axel solves his problem is only fairly difficult. He borrows the money from his mother, who is a doctor. But then we discover that his problem is greater than his debt, because there is some final compulsion within him that won't let him pay back the money. He needs to lose, to feel risk, to place himself in danger. He needs to gamble away the forty-four grand on even more hopeless bets because in a way it isn't gambling that's his obsession—it's danger itself.

"I play in order to lose," he tells his bookie at one point. "That's what gets my juice going. If I only bet on the games I know, I could at least break even." But he doesn't want that. At one point, he's driven to bet money he doesn't really have on college basketball games picked almost at random out of the sports pages.

And yet Axel Freed is not simply a gambler, but a very complicated man in his midthirties who earns his living as a university literature teacher. He teaches Dostoyevski, William Carlos Williams, Thoreau. But he doesn't seem to teach their works so much as what he finds in them to justify his own obsessions. One of the students in his class has Axel figured out so completely that she always has the right answer, when he asks what Thoreau is saying, or

what Dostoyevski is saying. They're saying, as Axel reads them, to take risks, to put the self on the line.

"Buffalo Bill's defunct," he says, quoting the e. e. cummings poem, and the death of the nineteenth-century age of heroes obsesses him. In that earlier age, he could have tested himself more directly. His grandfather came to America flat broke, fought and killed to establish himself, and still is a man of enormous vitality at the age of eighty. The old man is respectable now (he owns a chain of furniture stores), but the legend of his youth fascinates Axel, who recites it poetically at the eightieth birthday party.

Axel finds nothing in 1974 to test himself against, however. He has to find his own dangers, to court and seduce them. And the ultimate risk in his life as a gambler is that behind his friendly bookies and betting cronies is the implacable presence of the Mafia, the guys who take his bets like him, but if he doesn't pay, there's nothing they can do. "It's out of my hands," his pal Hips explains. "A bad gambling debt has got to be taken care of." And that adds an additional dimension to *The Gambler*, which begins as a portrait of Axel Freed's personality, develops into the story of his world, and then pays off as a thriller. We become so absolutely contained by Axel's problems and dangers that they seem like our own. There's a scene where he soaks in the bathtub and listens to the last minutes of a basketball game, and another scene where he sits in the stands and watches a basketball game he has tried to fix (while a couple of hit men watch him), and these scenes have a quality of tension almost impossible to sustain.

But Reisz sustains them, and makes them all the more real because he doesn't populate the rest of his movie with stock characters.

Axel Freed, as played by James Caan, is himself a totally convincing personality, and original. He doesn't derive from other gambling movies or even from other roles he's played.

And the people around him also are specific, original creations. His mother Naomi (Jacqueline Brooks) is a competent, independent person who gives him the money because she fears for his life, and yet understands that his problem is deeper than gambling. His grandfather, marvelously played by Morris Carnovsky, is able to imply by his behavior why he fascinates Axel so. The various bookies and collectors he comes across aren't Mafia stereotypes. They enforce more in sorrow than in anger. Only his girlfriend (Lauren Hutton) fails to seem very real. Here's still another demonstration of the inability of contemporary movies to give us three-dimensional women under thirty.

There's a scene in *The Gambler* that has James Caan on screen all by himself for two minutes, locked in a basement room, waiting to meet a Mafia boss who will arguably instruct that his legs be broken. In another movie, the scene could have seemed too long, too eventless.

But Reisz, Caan, and screenwriter James Toback have constructed the character and the movie so convincingly that the scene not only works, but works two ways: first as suspense, and then as character revelation. Because as we look into Axel Freed's caged eyes we see a person who is scared to death and yet stubbornly ready for this moment he has brought down upon himself.

Gandhi

PG, 188 m., 1982

Ben Kingsley (Mahatma Gandhi), Candice Bergen (Margaret Bourke-White), Edward Fox (General Dyer), John Gielgud (Lord Irwin), Trevor Howard (Judge Broomfield), John Mills (The Viceroy), Martin Sheen (Walker), Rohini Hattangady (Kasturba Gandhi), Ian Charleson (Charlie Andrews), Athol Fugard (General Smuts). Directed and produced by Richard Attenborough. Screenplay by John Briley.

In the middle of this epic film there is a quiet, small scene that helps explain why *Gandhi* is such a remarkable experience. Mahatma Gandhi, at the height of his power and his fame, stands by the side of a lake with his wife of many years. Together, for the benefit of a visitor from the West, they reenact their marriage vows. They do it with solemnity, quiet warmth, and perhaps just a touch of shyness; they are simultaneously demonstrating an aspect of Indian culture and touching on something very personal to them both. At the end of the ceremony, Gandhi says, "We were thirteen at the time." He shrugs. The marriage had been arranged. Gandhi and his wife had not been in love, had not been old enough for love, and yet love had grown between them. But that is not really the point of the scene. The point, I think, comes in the quiet smile with which Gandhi says the words. At that moment we believe that he is fully and truly human, and at that moment, a turning point in the film, *Gandhi* declares that it is not only a historical record but a breathing, living document.

This is the sort of rare epic film that spans the decades, that uses the proverbial cast of thousands, and yet follows a human thread from beginning to end: *Gandhi* is no more overwhelmed by the scope of its production than was Gandhi overwhelmed by all the glory of the British Empire. The movie earns comparison with two classic works by David Lean, *Lawrence of Arabia* and *Dr. Zhivago*, in its ability to paint a strong human story on a very large canvas.

The movie is a labor of love by Sir Richard Attenborough, who struggled for years to get financing for his huge but "noncommercial" project. Various actors were considered over the years for the all-important title role, but the actor who was finally chosen, Ben Kingsley, makes the role so completely his own that there is a genuine feeling that the spirit of Gandhi is on the screen. Kingsley's performance is powerful without being loud or histrionic; he is almost always quiet, observant, and soft-spoken on the screen, and yet his performance comes across with such might that we realize, afterward, that the sheer moral force of Gandhi must have been behind the words. Apart from all its other qualities, what makes this movie special is that it was obviously made by people who believed in it.

The movie begins in the early years of the century, in South Africa. Gandhi moved there from India in 1893, when he was twenty-three. He already had a law degree, but, degree or not, he was a target of South Africa's system of racial segregation, in which Indians (even though they are Caucasian, and thus should "qualify") are denied full citizenship and manhood. Gandhi's reaction to the system is, at first, almost naive; an early scene on a train doesn't quite work only because we can't believe the adult Gandhi would still be so ill-informed about the racial code of South Africa. But Gandhi's response sets the tone of the film. He is nonviolent but firm. He is sure where the right lies in every situation, and he will uphold it in total disregard for the possible consequences to himself.

Before long Gandhi is in India, a nation of hundreds of millions, ruled by a relative handful of British. They rule almost by divine right, shouldering the "white man's burden" even though they have not quite been requested to do so by the Indians. Gandhi realizes that Indians have been made into second-class citizens in their own country, and he begins a program of civil disobedience that is at first ignored by the British, then scorned, and finally, reluctantly, dealt with, sometimes by subterfuge, sometimes by brutality. Scenes in this central passage of the movie make it clear that nonviolent protests could contain a great deal of violence. There is a shattering scene in which wave after wave of Gandhi's followers march forward to be beaten to the ground by British clubs. Through it all, Gandhi maintains a certain detachment; he is convinced he is right, convinced that violence is not an answer, convinced that sheer moral example can free his nation—as it did. "You have been guests in our home long enough," he tells the British, "Now we would like for you to leave."

The movie is populated with many familiar faces, surrounding the newcomer Kingsley. Where would the British cinema be without its dependable, sturdy, absolutely authoritative generation of great character actors like Trevor Howard (as a British judge), John Mills (the British viceroy), John Gielgud, and Michael Hordern? There are also such younger actors as Ian Bannen, Edward Fox, Ian Charleson, and, from America, Martin Sheen as a reporter and Candice Bergen as the photographer Margaret Bourke-White.

Gandhi stands at the quiet center. And Ben Kingsley's performance finds the right note and stays with it. There are complexities here; *Gandhi* is not simply a moral story with a happy ending, and the tragedy of the bloodshed between the Hindu and Muslim popula-

tions of liberated India is addressed, as is the partition of India and Pakistan, which we can almost literally feel breaking Gandhi's heart.

I imagine that for many Americans, Mahatma Gandhi remains a dimly understood historical figure. I suspect a lot of us know he was a great Indian leader without quite knowing why and—such is our ignorance of Eastern history and culture—we may not fully realize that his movement did indeed liberate India, in one of the greatest political and economic victories of all time, achieved through nonviolent principles. What is important about this film is not that it serves as a history lesson (although it does) but that, at a time when the threat of nuclear holocaust hangs ominously in the air, it reminds us that we are, after all, human, and thus capable of the most extraordinary and wonderful achievements, simply through the use of our imagination, our will, and our sense of right.

The Garden of the Finzi-Continis
R, 90 m., 1971

Dominique Sanda (Micol), Lino Capolicchio (Giorgio), Helmut Berger (Alberto), Fabrio Tesel (Malnate), Romolo Valli (Giorgio's Father). Directed by Vittorio de Sica and produced by Gianni Hecht Lucari. Screenplay by Ugo Pirro and Vittorio Bonicelli.

The Garden of the Finzi-Continis, as nearly as I can tell, is not an enclosed space but an enclosed state of mind. Eager for an afternoon of tennis, the young people ride into it on their bicycles one sunny Sunday afternoon. The Fascist government of Mussolini has declared the ordinary tennis clubs off limits for Italian Jews—but what does that matter, here behind these tall stone walls that have faithfully guarded the Finzi-Contini family for generations?

Micol, the daughter, welcomes her guests and gives some of them a little tour: That tree over there is said to be five hundred years old and might even have been planted by the Borgias. If it has stood for all those years in this garden, she seems to believe, what is there to worry about in the world outside?

She is a tall blond girl with a musical laugh and a way of turning away from a man just as he reveals himself to her. Giorgio, who has been helplessly in love with her since they were both children, deceives himself that she loves him. But she cannot quite love anyone, although she carries on an affair with a tall, athletic young man who is about to be drafted into the army. Giorgio's father says of the Finzi-Continis: "They're different. They don't even seem to be Jewish."

They're different because wealth and privilege and generations of intellectual and social position have bred them into a family as proud as it is vulnerable. The other Jews in the town react to Mussolini's edicts in various ways: Giorgio is enraged; his father is philosophical. But the Finzi-Continis hardly seem to know, or care, what is happening. They are above mere edicts; they chose to live behind their walls long before the Fascists said they must.

This is the situation as Vittorio de Sica sketches it for us at the outset of *The Garden of the Finzi-Continis,* which was a true surprise from a director who had seemed to lose his early genius. De Sica's previous two or three films (especially the disastrous *A Place for Lovers*) were embarrassments from the director of *Bicycle Thief* and *Shoeshine.*

But here he returned with a film that seems to owe little to his previous work. It is not neorealism; it is not a comic mixture of bawdiness and sophistication; it is most of all not the dreamy banality of his previous few films. In telling of the disintegration of the Jewish community in one smallish Italian town, de Sica merges his symbols with his story so that they evoke the meaning of the time.

It was a time in which many people had no idea what was really going on. Giorgio's younger brother, sent to France to study, finds out to his horror about the German concentration camps. There has been no word of them in Italy, of course. Italy in those final prewar years is painted by de Sica as a perpetual wait for something no one admitted would come: war and the persecution of the Jews.

The walled garden of the Finzi-Continis is his symbol for this waiting period. It seems to promise that nothing will change, and even the Jews who live in the village seem to cling to the apparent strength of the Finzi-Continis as assurance of their own power to survive.

In presenting the garden to us, de Sica uses an interesting visual strategy; he never completely orients us visually, and so we don't know its overall size and shape. Therefore, visually, we can't count on it: We don't know when it will give out. It's an uneasy feeling to be inside an undefined space, especially if you may need to hide or run, and that's exactly the feeling de Sica gets.

The ambiguity of the garden's space is matched by an understated sexual ambiguity. Nothing happens overtly, but de Sica uses looks and body language to suggest the complex varieties of sexual attractions among his characters. When Micol is discovered by Giorgio with her sleeping lover, she does a most interesting thing. She covers him, not herself, and stares at Giorgio until he goes away.

The thing is, you can't count on anything. And nothing permanent can be permitted to take place during this period of waiting. De Sica's film creates a feeling of nostalgia for a lost time and place, but it isn't the nostalgia of looking back. It's the nostalgia of the time itself, when people still inhabiting their world could sense it slipping away, and already missed what they had not yet lost.

Gates of Heaven

NO MPAA RATING, 85 m, 1978

A documentary produced, directed, and written by Errol Morris.

There are many invitations to laughter during this remarkable documentary, but what *Gates of Heaven* finally made me feel was an aching poignancy about its subjects. They say you can make a great documentary about almost anything, if only you see it well enough and truly, and this film proves it. *Gates of Heaven,* which has no connection with the unfortunate *Heaven's Gate,* is a documentary about pet cemeteries and their owners. It was filmed in Southern California, so of course we immediately anticipate a sardonic look at peculiarities of the Moonbeam State. But then *Gates of Heaven* grows ever so much more complicated and frightening, until at the end it is about such large issues as love, immortality, failure, and the dogged elusiveness of the American Dream.

The film was made by a California filmmaker named Errol Morris, and it has been the subject of notoriety because Werner Herzog, the West German director, promised to eat his shoe if Morris ever finished it. Morris did finish it, and at the film's premiere in Berkeley, Herzog indeed boiled and ate his shoe.

Gates of Heaven is so rich and thought provoking, it achieves so much while seeming to strain so little, that it stays in your mind for tantalizing days. It opens with a monologue by a kind-looking, somewhat heavyset paraplegic, with a slight lisp that makes him sound like a kid. His name is Floyd McClure. Ever since his pet dog was run over years ago by a Model A Ford, he has dreamed of establishing a pet cemetery. The movie develops and follows his dream, showing the forlorn, bare patch of land where he founded his cemetery at the intersection of two superhighways. Then, with cunning drama, it gradually reveals that the cemetery went bankrupt and the remains of 450 animals had to be dug up. Various people contribute to the story: One of McClure's investors, a partner, two of the women whose pets were buried in his cemetery, and an unforgettable old woman named Florence Rasmussen, who starts on the subject of pets, and switches, with considerable fire, to her no-account son. Then the action shifts north to the Napa Valley, where a go-getter named Cal Harberts has absorbed what remained of McClure's dream (and the 450 dead pets) into his own pet cemetery, the Bubbling Well Pet Memorial Park. It is here that the movie grows heartbreaking, painting a portrait of a lifestyle that looks chillingly forlorn, and of the people who live it with relentless faith in positive thinking.

Harberts, a patriarch, runs his pet cemetery with two sons, Phil and Dan. Phil, the older one, has returned home after a period spent selling insurance in Salt Lake City. He speaks of having been overworked. Morris lets the camera stay on Phil as he solemnly explains his motivational techniques, and his method of impressing a new client by filling his office with salesmanship trophies. He has read all of Clement Stone's books on "Positive Mental Attitude," and has a framed picture of Stone on his wall. Phil looks neat, presentable, capable. He talks reassuringly of his positive approach to things, "mentally wise." Then we

meet the younger brother, Dan, who composes songs and plays them on his guitar. In the late afternoon, when no one is at the pet cemetery, he hooks up his 100watt speakers and blasts his songs all over the valley. He has a wispy mustache and looks like a hippie. The family hierarchy is clear. Cal, in the words of Phil, is "El Presidento." Then Dan comes next, because he has worked at the cemetery longer. Phil, the golden boy, the positive thinker, is maintaining his P.M.A. in the face of having had to leave an insurance business in Salt Lake City to return home as third in command at a pet cemetery.

The cemetery itself is bleak and barren, its markers informing us, "God is love; dog is god backwards." An American flag flies over the little graves. Floyd McClure tells us at the beginning of the film that pets are put on Earth for two reasons: to love and to be loved. At the end of this mysterious and great movie, we observe the people who guard and maintain their graves, and who themselves seem unloved and very lonely. One of the last images is of old Cal, the patriarch, wheeling past on his forklift, a collie-sized coffin in its grasp.

George Washington

NO MPAA RATING, 89 m., 2001

Candace Evanofski (Nasia), Donald Holden (George), Curtis Cotton III (Buddy), Eddie Rouse (Damascus), Paul Schneider (Rico Rice), Damian Jewan Lee (Vernon), Rachael Handy (Sonya), Jonathan Davidson (Euless), Janet Taylor (Ruth). Directed by David Gordon Green and produced by Green, Sacha W. Mueller, and Lisa Muskat. Screenplay by Green.

There is a summer in your life that is the last time boys and girls can be friends until they grow up. The summer when adolescence has arrived, but has not insisted on itself. When the stir of arriving sexuality still makes you feel hopeful instead of restless and troubled. When you feel powerful instead of unsure. That is the summer *George Washington* is about, and all it is about. Everything else in the film is just what happened to happen that summer.

This is such a lovely film. You give yourself to its voluptuous languor. You hang around with these kids from the poor side of town, while they kill time and share their pipe dreams. A tragedy happens, but the movie is not about the tragedy. It is about the discovery that tragedies can happen. In the corresponding summer of my life, a kid tried to be a daredevil by riding his bicycle up a ramp, and fell off and broke his leg, and everybody blamed that when he got polio. I tell you my memory instead of what happens in this film, because the tragedy in the film comes so swiftly, in the midst of a casual afternoon, that it should be as surprising to you as to the kids.

The movie takes place in a rusting industrial landscape, which the weeds are already returning to nature. It is in North Carolina. We meet some black kids, between ten and thirteen, and a few white kids. They're friends. They are transparent to one another. They are facts of life. You wake up every morning and here they are, the other kids in your life. They are waiting to grow up. There are some adults around, but they're not insisted upon. Some of them are so stranded by life they kill time with the kids. Nothing better to do.

Buddy (Curtis Cotton III) has a crush on Nasia (Candace Evanofski). She leaves him for George (Donald Holden). This is all momentous because it is the first crush and the first leaving of their lives. Buddy asks for one last kiss. "Do you love me?" asks Nasia. Buddy won't say. He wants the kiss voluntarily. No luck. George has his own problems: The plates in his skull didn't meet right, and he wears a football helmet to protect his skull. "When I look at my friends," Nasia muses, "I know there's goodness. I can look at their feet, or when I hold their hands, I pretend I can see the bones inside."

George fears for his dog because his uncle Damascus (Eddie Rouse) doesn't like animals. "He just don't like to get bothered," says Aunt Ruth (Janet Taylor). "Do you remember the first time we made love to this song?" Damascus asks Ruth. "We were out in that field. You buried me in that grass." "Why is it," Ruth asks him, "every time you start talkin', you sound like you gonna cry?"

The heat is still, the days are slow, there is not much to do. A kid with freckles gets in trouble in the swimming pool and George jumps in to save him, even though he's not supposed to get his head wet. Then George starts wearing a cape, like a superhero. Buddy wears a Halloween dinosaur mask while he stands in a rest room, which is one of their hangouts, and delivers a soliloquy that would be worthy of Hamlet, if instead of being the prince of Denmark, Hamlet had been Buddy. Buddy disappears. Nasia thinks he ran away "because he still has his crush on me." Others know why Buddy disappeared but simply do not know what to do with their knowledge. Vernon (Damian Jewan Lee) has a soliloquy beginning with the words "I wish," that would be worthy of Buddy, or Hamlet.

The film has been written, produced, and directed by David Gordon Green. The cinematography, by Tim Orr, is the best of the year. The mood and feel of the film has been compared to the work of Terence Malick, and Green is said to have watched *The Thin Red Line* over and over while preparing to shoot. But this is not a copy of Malick; it is simply in the same key. Like Malick's *Days of Heaven*, it is not about plot, but about memory and regret. It remembers a summer that was not a happy summer, but there will never again be a summer so intensely felt, so alive, so valuable.

Get on the Bus

R, 122 m., 1996

Ossie Davis (Jeremiah), Charles S. Dutton (George), Andre Braugher (Flip), Richard Belzer (Rick), Thomas Jefferson Byrd (Evan Thomas, Sr.), Harry Lennix (Randall), Isaiah Washington (Kyle), Roger Guenveur Smith (Gary), De'Aundre Bonds (Junior), Hill Harper (Xavier), Gabriel Casseus (Jamal), Wendell Pierce (Wendell). Directed by Spike Lee and produced by Reuben Cannon, Barry Rosenbush, and Bill Borden. Screenplay by Reggie Rock Bythewood.

Spike Lee's *Get on the Bus* is a movie made in haste and passion, and that may account for its uncanny effect: We feel close to the real, often unspoken, issues involving race in America without the distance that more time and money might have provided. The film follows a group of about twenty black men on a cross-country bus trip to the Million Man March on October 16, 1995, and it opens exactly one year later.

Lee made the movie quickly, after fifteen black men invested in the enterprise. He shot in 16mm and video, always in and around the bus, using the cross section of its passengers to show hard truths, and falsehoods too. If the movie's central sadness is that we identify with our own group and suspect outsiders, the movie's message is that we have been given brains in order to learn to empathize.

There are all kinds of men on the bus. The tour leader (Charles S. Dutton) will be an inspiration and a referee. Another steadying hand is supplied by the oldest man on board, Jeremiah (Ossie Davis), a student of black history who delights in informing white cowboys that a black cowboy invented steer wrestling.

Also on board are a father (Thomas Jefferson Byrd) and his young son (De'Aundre Bonds), who have been shackled together by a court order; the irony of going to the march in chains is not lost on the others. An ex marine (Isaiah Washington), who is gay, boards the bus with his lover (Harry Lennix) and they're singled out for persecution by a homophobic would-be actor (Andre Braugher). And a light-skinned man (Roger Guenveur Smith) is revealed as a cop assigned to South Central. Then there's a UCLA film student (Hill Harper), who is shooting a video documentary. And a member of the Nation of Islam (Gabriel Casseus), in black suit, bow tie, and dark glasses, who says not one word during the journey.

During the course of the trip, conversations will be philosophical, humorous, sad, nostalgic, angry, and sometimes very personal. The homosexual couple provokes the hostility of the gay-hater; prejudice knows no color line. That's true, too, in the attitudes toward the cop, whose skin is so light that he could pass, and who, it is revealed, became a cop in part because his black father, also a cop, was killed ("yes," he says, "by a brother").

"The man says he's black, he's black," pronounces Ossie Davis. But then the cop himself is revealed to have blinkers on. Another man reveals he's a former gang member, "cripping since I smoked a guy on my thirteenth birthday," but that now he does social work with "kids at risk." No matter; the cop warns him: "When we get back to L.A., I'm going to have to arrest you."

For many white people, a distressing element of the Million Man March was the racial slant of its convener, Louis Farrakhan, who has made many anti-Semitic and antiwhite slurs. Lee could have ducked this area, but doesn't. When the bus breaks down, the replacement driver (Richard Belzer) is a Jewish man who keeps quiet as long as he can, and then speaks out about Farrakhan's libels against Jews. "At least my parents did their part," he says; they were civil rights activists. He cites Farrakhan's statements that Judaism is a "gutter religion" and "Hitler was a great man." After some of the tour members recycle old clichés about Jewish landlords, the Belzer character says, "I wouldn't expect you to drive a bus to a Klan meeting," and walks away from the bus at a rest stop. Dutton takes over driving.

This is, I think, a forthright way to deal with Farrakhan's attitudes; the bus driver expresses widely felt beliefs in the white community and acts on his moral convictions. For the men on the bus, quite simply, "this march is not about Farrakhan." We expect that the Nation of Islam member will speak up to defend his leader, but he never does, and his silence, behind his dark glasses, acts as a powerful symbol of a religion that none of the other men on the bus seem to relate to, or even care much about.

As the journey continues, Lee brings in other characters who illustrate the complexity of race in America. There is a satiric cameo by Wendell Pierce as a prosperous Lexus dealer, who boards the bus in mid-journey and puffs on a cigar while airily expressing self-hating clichés about blacks. Then, in Tennessee, the reason for the march comes into sharp focus when the bus is pulled over by white cops. They bring a drug-sniffing dog on board, and treat the men in a subtle but unmistakably racist way. When the cops leave, Lee gives us a series of close-ups of silent, thoughtful faces: Every black man in America has at one time or another felt charged by the police with the fact of being black.

What makes *Get on the Bus* extraordinary is the truth and feeling that go into its episodes. Spike Lee and his actors face one hard truth after another, in scenes of great power. I have always felt Lee exhibits a particular quality of fairness in his films. *Do the Right Thing* was so even-handed that it was possible for a black viewer to empathize with Sal, the pizzeria owner, and a white viewer to empathize with Mookie, the black kid who starts the riot that burns down Sal's Pizzeria.

Lee doesn't have heroes and villains. He shows something bad—racism—that in countless ways clouds all of our thinking. *Get on the Bus* is fair in the same sense. It is more concerned with showing how things are than with scoring cheap rhetorical points. This is a film with a full message for the heart, and the mind.

Getting It Right

R, 102 m., 1989

Jesse Birdsall (Gavin Lamb), Helena Bonham Carter (Minerva Munday), Peter Cook (Mr. Adrian), John Gielgud (Sir Gordon Munday), Jane Horrocks (Jenny), Lynn Redgrave (Joan), Shirley Anne Field (Anne), Pat Heywood (Mrs. Lamb), Bryan Pringle (Mr. Lamb). Directed by Randal Kleiser and produced by Jonathan D. Krane and Kleiser. Screenplay by Elizabeth Jane Howard, based on her book.

Getting It Right is a late-1980s version of all those driven, off-center London films like *Darling, Georgy Girl,* and *Morgan*—movies in which a wide-eyed innocent journeys through the jungle of the eccentric, the depraved, and the blasé, protected only by a good heart and limitless naïveté.

The movie tells the story of Gavin Lamb, a hairdresser who shampoos the coiffures and the miseries of his ancient clients, and returns every night to the home of his parents—where his mother serves awesomely inedible dinners promptly at the stroke of six. Gavin is thirty-one and still a virgin, and his bedroom is a sanctuary where he keeps his precious collection of recorded music, meticulously arranged.

At first we can't get a reading on Gavin Lamb. He is pleasant, friendly, a little standoffish. Life doesn't seem to have happened to him yet. The character is played close to the vest by Jesse Birdsall, a young actor who manages to look thoroughly ordinary most of the time, and sublimely crafty the rest of the time. It's a performance a little like Dustin Hoffman's in *The Graduate,* where society is criticized by the character's very indifference to it.

One day Gavin is taken to a party that seems to be a last-gasp attempt to resurrect Swinging London. It's held in the spectacular penthouse of a garish divorcée (Lynn Redgrave), whose red wig and outlandish costumes look like a conscious attempt to keep people at arm's length. But she likes Gavin, and takes pity on him, and invites him to a secret inner sanctum in the vast apartment—the only room, apparently, where she feels free to take off her wig and be herself. Her secret identity turns out to be sweet and tender, and Gavin is started down the road toward losing his virginity and gaining his independence.

There is another woman at the party—a girl, really—who is dark and intense and small and determined. Her name is Minerva Munday (Helena Bonham Carter) and her father is fearsomely old and rich and eccentric (Sir John Gielgud has great relish with the role). Suddenly Gavin is catapulted out of his safe orbit of the hairdressing salon and life with Mum and Dad, and finds his romantic life more eventful than he could have dreamed.

Getting It Right is a character film, not a plot film, and so the point is not what happens, but who it happens to. The screenplay is by Elizabeth Jane Howard, based on her own novel, and it shows a novelist's instinct for character and dialogue. This is not one of those mechanically plotted forced marches through film school script formulas, but a story that lives and breathes and gives the characters the freedom to surprise us.

Smaller roles, like Peter Cook's cameo as the owner of the hairdressing salon, are enriched with asides that suggest the entire character. And some of the characters sneak up on us— like Jenny (Jane Horrocks), who is Gavin's assistant at the salon. He has barely looked at her in two years, but now, emboldened by his late flowering, he looks at everyone in a new light, and Jenny begins to blossom.

Getting It Right was directed by Randal Kleiser, whose big hit film *Grease,* in 1978, has been followed by a career with no discernible pattern (can the same director have made *The Blue Lagoon, Flight of the Navigator,* and *Big Top Pee-wee?*).

With this film, however, Kleiser has gotten everything right; he is often dealing with the most delicate nuances, in which the whole point of some scenes depends on subtle reactions or small shifts of tone, and he doesn't step wrong. Look, for example, at his control of a scene where Gavin takes a date to a birthday party for a gay friend who breaks up with his lover right there on the spot; the scene is poignant, and yet still works as a comedy of embarrassment. There is a delicious delight seeing the film find its way into the lives of so many bright, lonely, mixed-up people. And *Getting It Right* does not box them into a plot, but allows them to be themselves.

Ghost World

R, 111 m., 2001

Thora Birch (Enid), Scarlett Johansson (Rebecca), Steve Buscemi (Seymour), Brad Renfro (Josh), Illeana Douglas (Roberta), Bob Balaban (Enid's Dad), Teri Garr (Maxine). Directed by Terry Zwigoff and produced by Lianne Halfon, John Malkovich, and Russell Smith. Screenplay by Daniel Clowes and Zwigoff, based on the comic book by Clowes.

There's a small tomb in Southwark Cathedral that I like to visit when I am in London. It contains the bones of a teenage girl who died three centuries ago. I know the inscription by heart:

> *This world to her*
> *Was but a tragic play.*
> *She came, saw, dislik'd,*
> *And passed away.*

I thought of those words while I was watching *Ghost World,* the story of an eighteen-year-old girl from Los Angeles who drifts forlorn through her loneliness, cheering herself up with an ironic running commentary. The girl is named Enid, she has just graduated from high school, and she has no plans for college, marriage, a career, or even next week. She's stuck in a world of stupid, shallow phonies, and she makes her personal style into a rebuke.

Unfortunately, Enid is so smart, so advanced, and so ironically doubled back upon herself that most of the people she meets don't get the message. She is second-level satire in a one-level world, and so instead of realizing, for example, that she is mocking the 1970s punk look, stupid video store clerks merely think she's twenty-five years out of style.

Enid is played by Thora Birch, from *Ameri-*

can Beauty, and in a sense this character is a continuation of that one—she certainly looks at her father the same way, with disbelief and muted horror. Her running mate is Rebecca (Scarlett Johansson). There's a couple like this in every high school: the smart outsider girls who are best friends for the purpose of standing back-to-back and fighting off the world. At high school graduation, they listen to a speech from a classmate in a wheelchair, and Enid whispers: "I liked her so much better when she was an alcoholic and drug addict. She gets in one stupid car crash and suddenly she's Little Miss Perfect."

But now Rebecca is showing alarming signs of wanting to get on with her life, and Enid is abandoned to her world of thrift shops, strip malls, video stores, and 1950s retro diners. One day, in idle mischief, she answers a personal ad in a local paper, and draws into her net a pathetic loner named Seymour (Steve Buscemi). At first she strings him along. Then, unexpectedly, she starts to like him—this collector who lives hermetically sealed in a world of precious 78 rpm records and old advertising art.

By day, Seymour is an insignificant fried chicken executive. By night, he catalogs his records and wonders how to meet a woman. Why does Enid like him? "He's the exact opposite of all the things I hate." Why does he like her? Don't get ahead of the story. *Ghost World* isn't a formula romance where opposites attract and march toward the happy ending. Seymour and Enid are too similar to fall in love; they both specialize in complex personal lifestyles that send messages no one is receiving. Enid even offers to try to fix up Seymour, but he sees himself as a bad candidate for a woman: "I don't want to meet someone who shares my interests. I hate my interests."

Seymour resembles someone I know, and that person is Terry Zwigoff, who directed this movie. It's his first fiction film. Zwigoff earlier made two docs, the masterpiece *Crumb* (1995), about the comic artist R. Crumb, and *Louie Bluie,* about the old-timey Chicago string band Martin, Bogan, and the Armstrongs. He looks a little like Buscemi, and acts like a Buscemi character: worn down, dubious, ironic, resigned. Zwigoff was plagued by agonizing back pain all during the period when he was making *Crumb,* and slept with a gun under his pillow, he told me, in case he had to end his misery in the middle of the night. When Crumb didn't want to cooperate with the documentary, Zwigoff threatened to shoot himself. Crumb does not often meet his match, but did with Zwigoff.

Both Zwigoff and his character Seymour collect old records that are far from the mainstream. Both are morose and yet have a bracing black humor that sees them through. Seymour and Enid connect because they are kindred spirits, and it's hard to find someone like that when you've cut yourself off from mankind.

The movie is based on a graphic novel by Daniel Clowes, who cowrote the screenplay with Zwigoff. It listens carefully to how people talk. Illeana Douglas, for example, has a perfectly observed role as the art teacher in Enid's summer makeup class, who has fallen for political correctness hook, line, and sinker, and praises art not for what it looks like but for what it "represents." There are also some nice moments from Teri Garr, who plays the take-charge girlfriend of Enid's father (Bob Balaban).

One scene I especially like involves a party of Seymour's fellow record collectors. They meet to exchange arcane information, and their conversations are like encryptions of the way most people talk. This event must seem strange to Enid, but see how she handles it. It's Seymour's oddness, his tactless honesty, his unapologetic aloneness, that Enid responds to. He works like the homeopathic remedy for angst: His loneliness drives out her own.

I wanted to hug this movie. It took such a risky journey, and never stepped wrong. It created specific, original, believable, lovable characters, and meandered with them through their inconsolable days, never losing its sense of humor. The Buscemi role is one he's been pointing toward during his entire career; it's like the flip side of his alcoholic barfly in *Trees Lounge*, who also becomes entangled with a younger girl, not so fortunately.

The movie sidesteps the happy ending Hollywood executives think lobotomized audiences need as an all-clear to leave the theater. Clowes and Zwigoff find an ending that is more poetic, more true to the tradition of the classic short story, in which a minor character finds closure that symbolizes the next step for everyone.

Ghost World is smart enough to know that Enid and Seymour can't solve their lives in a week or two. But their meeting has blasted them out of lethargy, and now movement is possible. Who says that isn't a happy ending?

Girl with a Pearl Earring
PG-13, 95 m., 2003

Scarlett Johansson (Griet), Colin Firth (Johannes Vermeer), Tom Wilkinson (Van Ruijven), Judy Parfitt (Maria Thins), Essie Davis (Catharina), Cillian Murphy (Pieter), Joanna Scanlan (Tanneke), Alakina Mann (Cornelia). Directed by Peter Webber and produced by Andy Paterson and Anand Tucker. Screenplay by Olivia Hetreed, based on the book by Tracy Chevalier.

Girl with a Pearl Earring is a quiet movie, shaken from time to time by ripples of emotional turbulence far beneath the surface. It is about things not said, opportunities not taken, potentials not realized, lips unkissed. All of these elements are guessed at by the filmmakers as they regard a painting made in about 1665 by Johannes Vermeer. The painting shows a young woman regarding us over her left shoulder. She wears a simple blue headband and a modest smock. Her red lips are slightly parted. Is she smiling? She seems to be glancing back at the moment she was leaving the room. She wears a pearl earring.

Not much is known about Vermeer, who left about thirty-five paintings. Nothing is known about his model. You can hear that it was his daughter, a neighbor, a tradeswoman. You will not hear that she was his lover, because Vermeer's household was under the iron rule of his mother-in-law, who was vigilant as a hawk. The painting has become as intriguing in its modest way as the *Mona Lisa*. The girl's face turned toward us from centuries ago demands that we ask, who was she? What was she thinking? What was the artist thinking about her?

Tracy Chevalier's novel speculating about the painting has now been filmed by Peter Webber, who casts Scarlett Johansson as the girl and Colin Firth as Vermeer. I can think of many ways the film could have gone wrong, but it goes right because it doesn't cook up melodrama and romantic intrigue but tells a story that's content with its simplicity. The painting is contemplative, reflective, subdued, and the film must be too: We don't want lurid revelations breaking into its mood.

Sometimes two people will regard each other over a gulf too wide to ever be bridged and know immediately what could have happened, and that it never will. That is essentially the message of *Girl with a Pearl Earring*. The girl's name is Griet, according to this story. She lives nearby. She is sent by her blind father to work in Vermeer's house, where several small children are about to be joined by a new arrival. The household is run like a factory with the mother-in-law, Maria Thins (Judy Parfitt), as foreman. She has set her daughter to work producing babies while her son-in-law produces paintings. Both have an output of about one a year, which is good if you are a mother, but not if you are a painter.

Nobody ever says what they think in this house except for Maria, whose thoughts are all too obvious anyway. Catharina (Essie Davis), Vermeer's wife, sometimes seems to be standing where she hopes nobody will see her. It becomes clear that Griet is intelligent in a natural way, but has no idea what to do with her ideas. Of course she attracts Vermeer's attention; she's a hard worker and responds instinctively to the manual labor of painting—to the craft, the technique, the strategy, even the chemistry (did you know that the color named Indian Yellow is distilled from the urine of cows fed on mango leaves?).

In one flawless sequence, Griet is alone in Vermeer's studio and looks at the canvas he is working on, looks at what he is painting, looks back, looks forth, and then moves a chair away from a window. When he returns and sees what she has done, he studies the composition carefully and removes the chair from his painting. Eventually he has her move up to the attic, closer to his studio, where she can mix his paints, which she does very well.

And then of course they start sleeping together? Not in this movie. Vermeer has a rich patron named Van Ruijven (Tom Wilkinson). If Vermeer is too shy to reveal feelings for his maid, Van Ruijven is not. He wants a painting of the girl. This, of course, would be unacceptable to Catharina Vermeer, whose best-developed quality is her insecurity—but it is not unacceptable to her mother, who must keep a rich patron happy. Thus Griet becomes a model.

There is a young man in the town, Pieter (Cillian Murphy), a butcher's apprentice, who is attracted to Griet. He would make her a good husband, in this world where status and opportunity are assigned by caste. Griet likes him. It's not that she likes Vermeer more; indeed, she's so intimidated she barely speaks to the artist. It's that—well, Griet could never be a butcher, but she could be a painter.

Mankind has Shakespeares who were illiterate, Mozarts who never heard a note, Picassos who never touched a brush. Griet *could* be a painter. Whether a good or bad one, she will never know. Vermeer senses it. The moments of greatest intimacy between the simple peasant girl and the famous artist come when they sit side by side in wordless communication, mixing paints, both doing the same job, both understanding it.

Do not believe those who think this movie is about the "mystery" of the model, or Vermeer's sources of inspiration, or medieval gender roles, or whether the mother-in-law was the man in the family. A movie about those things would have been a bad movie. *Girl with a Pearl Earring* is about how they share a professional understanding that neither one has in any way with anyone else alive. I look at the painting and I realize that Griet is telling Vermeer, without using any words, "Well, if it were *my* painting, I'd have her stand like this."

The Gleaners and I

NO MPAA RATING, 82 m., 2001

A documentary by Agnes Varda.

In our alley we see men searching through the garbage for treasure. *The Gleaners and I* places them in an ancient tradition. Since 1554, when King Henry II affirmed the right of gleaning, it has been a practice protected by the French Constitution, and today the men and women who sift through the Dumpsters and markets of Paris are the descendants of gleaners who were painted by Millet and van Gogh.

Gleaners traditionally follow the harvest, scavenging what was missed the first time around. In Agnes Varda's meditative new film we see them in potato fields and apple orchards, where the farmers actually welcome them (tons of apples are missed by the first pickers, because the professionals work fast and are not patient in seeking the hidden fruit). Then we meet urban gleaners, including an artist who finds objects he can make into sculpture, and a man who has not paid for his food for more than ten years.

Everybody seems to know this practice is protected by law, but no one seems to know quite what the law says. Varda films jurists standing in the fields with their robes and law books, who say gleaning must take place between sunup and sundown, and she shows oyster-pickers in rubber hip boots, who say they must come no closer than ten, or twenty, or twelve, or fifteen yards from the oyster beds, and cannot take more than eight, or twenty, or ten pounds of oysters—not that anybody is weighing them.

In a provincial city, Varda considers the case of young unemployed people who overturned the Dumpsters of a supermarket after the owner drenched the contents with bleach to discourage them. Perhaps both parties were violating the law; the young people had the right to glean, but not to vandalize. But as she talks to the young layabouts in the town square, we realize they don't have the spirit of the other gleaners, and in their own minds see themselves as getting away with something instead of exercising a right. They have made themselves into criminals, although the French law considers gleaning a useful profession.

The true gleaner, in Varda's eyes, is a little noble, a little idealistic, a little stubborn, and deeply thrifty. We meet a man who gleans for his meals and to find objects he can sell, and follow him back to a suburban homeless shelter where for years he has taught literature classes every night. We look over the shoulders of him and his comrades as they find perfectly fresh tomatoes left after a farmer's market. Varda and her cinematographer find a clock without hands—worthless, until she places it between two stone angels in her house, and it reveals a startling simplicity of form.

Agnes Varda, of course, is a gleaner herself. She is gleaning the gleaners. And in what appears to be a documentary, she conceals a tender meditation about her own life, and life itself. Who is this woman? I have met her, with her bangs cut low over her sparkling eyes in a round and merry face, and once had lunch in the house she shared with her late husband,

the director Jacques Demy (The Umbrellas of Cherbourg). The house itself was in the spirit of gleaning: not a luxury flat for two famous filmmakers, but a former garage, with the bays and rooms around a central courtyard parceled out, one as a kitchen, one as Jacques's office, one a room for their son, Mathieu, one Agnes's workroom, etc.

Varda is seventy-two and made her first film when she was twenty-six. She was the only woman director involved in the French New Wave, and has remained truer to its spirit than many of the others. Her features include such masterpieces as One Sings, the Other Doesn't, Vagabond, and Kung Fu Master (which is not about kung fu but about love). Along the way she has made many documentaries, including Uncle Yanco (1968), about her uncle who lived on a houseboat in California and was a gleaner of sorts, and Daguerreotypes (1975), about the other people who live on her street. Her A Hundred and One Nights (1995) gleaned her favorite moments from a century of cinema.

In The Gleaners and I, she has a new tool—a modern digital camera. We sense her delight. She can hold it in her hand and take it anywhere. She is liberated from cumbersome equipment. "To film with one hand my other hand," she says, as she does so with delight. She shows how the new cameras make a personal essay possible for a filmmaker—how she can walk out into the world and, without the risk of a huge budget, simply start picking up images as a gleaner finds apples and potatoes.

"My hair and my hands keep telling me that the end is near," she confides at one point, speaking confidentially to us as the narrator. She told her friend Howie Movshovitz, the critic from Boulder, Colorado, how she had to film and narrate some scenes while she was entirely alone, because they were so personal. In 1993, she directed Jacquot de Nantes, the story of her late husband, and now this is her story of herself, a woman whose life has consisted of moving through the world with the tools of her trade, finding what is worth treasuring.

The Godfather
R, 171 m., 1972

Marlon Brando (Don Vito Corleone), Al Pacino (Michael Corleone), James Caan (Sonny Corleone), Robert Duvall

(Tom Hagen), Richard Castellano (Clemenza). Directed by Francis Ford Coppola and produced by Albert S. Ruddy. Screenplay by Coppola and Mario Puzo, based on Puzo's book.

We know from Gay Talese's book *Honor Thy Father* that being a professional mobster isn't all sunshine and roses. More often, it's the boredom of stuffy rooms and a bad diet of carry-out food, punctuated by brief, terrible bursts of violence. This is exactly the feel of *The Godfather,* which brushes aside the flashy glamour of the traditional gangster picture and gives us what's left: fierce tribal loyalties, deadly little neighborhood quarrels in Brooklyn, and a form of vengeance to match every affront.

The remarkable thing about Mario Puzo's novel was the way it seemed to be told from the inside out; he didn't give us a world of international intrigue, but a private club as constricted as the seventh grade. Everybody knew everybody else and had a pretty shrewd hunch what they were up to.

The movie (based on a script labored over for some time by Puzo and then finally given form, I suspect, by director Francis Ford Coppola) gets the same feel. We tend to identify with Don Corleone's family not because we dig gang wars, but because we have been with them from the beginning, watching them wait for battle while sitting at the kitchen table and eating chow mein out of paper cartons.

The Godfather himself is not even the central character in the drama. That position goes to the youngest, brightest son, Michael, who understands the nature of his father's position while revising his old-fashioned ways. The Godfather's role in the family enterprise is described by his name; he stands outside the next generation which will carry on and, hopefully, angle the family into legitimate enterprises.

Those who have read the novel may be surprised to find Michael at the center of the movie, instead of Don Corleone. In fact, this is simply an economical way for Coppola to get at the heart of the Puzo story, which dealt with the transfer of power within the family. Marlon Brando, who plays the Godfather as a shrewd, unbreakable old man, actually has the character lead in the movie; Al Pacino, with a brilliantly developed performance as Michael, is the lead.

But Brando's performance is a skillful throwaway, even though it earned him an Academy Award for best actor. His voice is wheezy and whispery, and his physical movements deliberately lack precision; the effect is of a man so accustomed to power that he no longer needs to remind others. Brando does look the part of old Don Corleone, mostly because of acting and partly because of the makeup, although he seems to have stuffed a little too much cotton into his jowls, making his lower face immobile.

The rest of the actors supply one example after another of inspired casting. Although *The Godfather* is a long, minutely detailed movie of some three hours, there naturally isn't time to go into the backgrounds and identities of such characters as Clemenza, the family lieutenant; Jack Woltz, the movie czar; Luca Brasi, the loyal professional killer; McCluskey, the crooked cop; and the rest. Coppola and producer Al Ruddy skirt this problem with understated typecasting. As the Irish cop, for example, they simply slide in Sterling Hayden and let the character go about his business. Richard Castellano is an unshakable Clemenza. John Marley makes a perfectly hateful Hollywood mogul (and, yes, he still wakes up to find he'll have to cancel his day at the races).

The success of *The Godfather* as a novel was largely due to a series of unforgettable scenes. Puzo is a good storyteller, but no great shakes as a writer. The movie gives almost everything in the novel except the gynecological repair job. It doesn't miss a single killing; it opens with the wedding of Don Corleone's daughter (and attendant upstairs activity); and there are the right number of auto bombs, double crosses, and garrotings.

Coppola has found a style and a visual look for all this material so *The Godfather* becomes something of a rarity: a really good movie squeezed from a bestseller. The decision to shoot everything in period decor (the middle and late 1940s) was crucial; if they'd tried to save money as they originally planned, by bringing everything up-to-date, the movie simply wouldn't have worked. But it's uncannily successful as a period piece, filled with sleek, bulging limousines and post-war fedoras. Coppola and his cinematographer,

Gordon Willis, also do some interesting things with the color photography. The earlier scenes have a reddish-brown tint, slightly overexposed and feeling like nothing so much as a 1946 newspaper rotogravure supplement.

Although the movie is three hours long, it absorbs us so effectively it never has to hurry. There is something in the measured passage of time as Don Corleone hands over his reins of power that would have made a shorter, faster moving film unseemly. Even at this length, there are characters in relationships you can't quite understand unless you've read the novel. Or perhaps you can, just by the way the characters look at each other.

Godspell

G, 102 m., 1973

Victor Garber (Jesus), David Haskell (John, Judas), Jerry Sroka (Jerry), Lynne Thigpen (Lynne), Katie Hanley (Katie), Robin Lamont (Robin), Gilmer McCormick (Gilmer), Joanne Jonas (Joanne), Merrell Jackson (Merrell), Jeffrey Mylett (Jeffrey). Directed by David Greene and produced by Edgar Lansbury. Screenplay by Green and John-Michael Tebelak, based on Tebelak's book.

The thing about *Godspell* that caught my heart was its simplicity, its refusal to pretend to be anything more than it is. It's not a message for our times, or a movie to cash in on the Jesus movement, or even quite a youth movie. It's a series of stories and songs, like the Bible is, and it's told with the directness that simple stories need: with no tricks, no intellectual gadgets, and a lot of openness.

This was the quality that attracted me to the stage version. I had to be almost dragged to the play, because its subject matter sounded so depressingly contemporary. But after I finally got into the theater and sat down and let *Godspell* relax me, I found myself simply letting it happen. For a musical based on the Gospel according to St. Matthew, *Godspell* is strangly irreverent, wacky, and endearing.

The stage version has been opened up into a movie by taking the whole of New York as a set. Except for the scenes at the beginning and end—which show the city as a temple of mammon and a rat nest—the movie is populated only by its cast; we don't see anybody else,

and the ten kids dance, sing, and act out parables in such unlikely places as the World Trade Center and a tugboat. This is a new use for New York, which looks unusually clean; even its tacky skyscrapers edge toward grandeur when the vast long shots engulf them.

Against this wilderness of steel and concrete, the characters come on like kids at a junior high reunion, clothed in comic book colors and bright tattered rags. Only two have names: Jesus, and a character who plays both John (who ushered Jesus into the Bible) and Judas (who hastened him out). The other eight characters, who seem to represent an on-the-spot gathering of disciples, are just themselves.

What's nice about the casting—which gives us all new faces—is that the characters don't look like professional stage youths. Remember *West Side Story*, where all the allegedly teenage dancers looked like hardened theatrical professionals in greaser wigs? *Godspell*'s cast is not only young but is allowed to look like a collection of individuals. These could conceivably be real people, and their freshness helps put the material over even when it seems pretty obvious. For some blessed reason the director, David Greene, has resisted any temptation to make the movie visually fancy. With material of this sort, there must have been an impulse to go for TV-commercial trendiness, but Greene's style is unforced, and goes well with the movie's freshness and basic colors.

The movie characters, like the stage characters, are given little watercolor designs on their faces by Jesus. A girl gets a little yellow flower, a boy gets a tiny red star, and so on. It was necessary in the stage version to exaggerate this makeup to make it visible, but the movie underplays it and it was gentle and nice. It occurred to me, about an hour into the film, that maybe young people will pick up on this. Tattoos were big in the '70s-little butterflies and stars-so why not facepaint zigzags and pinwheels and flowers? Anything to brighten up this miserable world: Which is what *Godspell* is saying, anyway.

Goin' Down the Road

NO MPAA RATING, 90 m., 1971

Doug McGrath (Peter), Paul Bradley (Joey), Jayne Eastwood (Betty), Cayle Chernin (Celina), Nicole Morin

(Nicole), Pierre La Roche (Plant Foreman). Directed and produced by Donald Shebib. Screenplay by William Fruet.

Don Shebib's *Goin' Down the Road* feels at times like a film realization of Studs Terkel's *Hard Times*, until you remind yourself that the movie is fiction and the time is now. It tells the story of two young men from Canada's Maritime Provinces who come to the big city, Toronto, lured by the possibility of good jobs and good times. They find none of the former and precious few of the latter—a few beery, brawling evenings and a few easy girls aside—but they're game and they keep pushing until the urban monster grinds them down.

The film's special accomplishment is its treatment of the characters and the city itself with an absolutely unsentimental levelheadedness. It tells a story that contains joy, silliness, love, and despair. But these things are kept organic to the story; the film itself doesn't pretend to be other than a record. Shebib achieves a documentary objectivity that touches us more deeply than tear jerking could.

I don't know if I've put that clearly enough. What I mean is that *Goin' Down the Road* doesn't pander. Too many films about young people today betray a desperate need on the part of their makers to be accepted by the young audience. *Fools* is the most extreme example: a film so obsessed with being "contemporary" that it mires in self-parody. Shebib, who is twenty-eight and made *Goin' Down the Road* with about $80,000, most of it borrowed, doesn't wave any credentials to prove he's plugged in. He just gets on with his story.

He's aided immeasurably by his two leading actors, Paul Bradley and Doug McGrath (who shared Canada's 1970 best-actor award, while the film was named Canada's best of the year). They play straight young men from the Maritimes who drive to Toronto in a beat-up old Chevy with flames painted on the sides. They aren't hip or radical or even, as you think at first, greasers. They're in Toronto for the action.

They get a job in a bottling plant and hit the streets on Saturday night with paychecks in their pockets. And they come flat up against the loneliness of any big city. Of pretty girls who seem unapproachable. Of lots of other guys with dates, but they have none. Of time on their hands. Of boozing and messing around. Of fascination with the office girl in the factory, the one with the big knockers who's supposed to be stuck up and won't date any of the guys. And even of actually getting a date with her and feeling all the more dumped because, up close, she's ten times as unapproachable.

Shebib, directing Bradley and McGrath, makes these scenes so poignant and so accurate that they could represent, if necessary, the human condition. The easy male camaraderie of the two friends is so unforced that it betrays similar scenes in *Husbands* for what they are: three professional actors narcissistically killing time. In *Goin' Down the Road,* Shebib does what the Cassavetes of *Shadows* knew how to do, and he does it better.

There are other scenes, of jobs in car washes and bowling alleys, of meeting a couple of waitresses, of Bradley getting married and moving into an apartment and buying three rooms of furniture on time payments. Then winter comes. They're laid off at the bottling plant, and that would seem too obvious in a more contrived film, but in this film it's just simply what happens. *Goin' Down the Road* is about hard times here and now, and it's the best movie to hit town in a long time.

Goodbye, Mr. Chips

G, 148 m., 1969

Peter O'Toole (Arthur Chipping), Sian Phillips (Ursula Mossbank), Petula Clark (Katherine), Michael Bryant (Max Staefel), Sir Michael Redgrave (Headmaster). Directed by Herbert Ross and produced by Arthur Jacob. Screenplay by Terence Rattigan, based on the book by James Hilton.

Note: This review contains spoilers.

Sure, big-budget road-show musicals are on their way out. But that's no reason to dislike them on principle, and some of the silliest reviews of *Goodbye, Mr. Chips* have criticized it for costing too much. That would make sense if the millions had been spent to buy vulgarity (as they were in *Star!*) or offensive overproduction (*Camelot*).

But *Goodbye, Mr. Chips* uses its budget quietly, with good taste, and succeeds in being a big movie without being a gross one. I think I enjoyed it about as much as any road show since *Funny Girl*. And that surprised me, since so much of the critical reaction has been negative. Even at its worst, *Chips* is inoffensive in its sentimentality. At its best, it's the first film since *The Two of Us* that I genuinely feel deserves to be called heartwarming.

James Hilton's novel of a gentle English schoolmaster was first made into a movie in 1939, and Robert Donat won an Academy Award as Chips. In the current version, writer Terence Rattigan has moved the action from the late nineteenth century to a period between about 1922 and the end of World War II.

I don't object to this; the Hilton story was a best seller but hardly a work of art. By modernizing the action, Rattigan has made it possible for the movie to mirror changes in the English class structure during the two decades when it was most obviously becoming obsolete. And social class was the pillar supporting the exclusive boarding schools like the one where Chips teaches.

Strange to say, Rattigan's screenplay not only makes this possible, but also does it. In an unobtrusive way, never lecturing, *Goodbye, Mr. Chips* does capture the flavor of a time when (as Chips reflects) schoolboys were taught Latin and Greek, which they couldn't use, but were also taught decency and assorted other civilized virtues, which perhaps they could.

English boarding schools at their best did attempt this (although, as George Orwell points out in several essays, at their worst they usually did the opposite). Luckily, Chips teaches in the very best of schools, a beautiful old institution made up mostly of stones, moss, and wooden beams.

But he is not getting along with his students very well as the movie opens. He is dedicated to the ethics of the teaching profession, but finds it difficult to get through to his students on a human level. This changes after he (improbably, I suppose) meets a beautiful musical-comedy star during a summer vacation in Italy. They marry, weather the storms of scandal, and create a warm, delicate marriage during the fifteen years when Chips really reaches greatness as a teacher.

As the schoolmaster and his wife, Peter O'Toole and Petula Clark are exactly right.

O'Toole succeeds in creating a character that is aloof, chillingly correct, terribly reserved—and charming all the same. He resists the temptation to play Chips as a dear old Robert Morley type. Wisely, I think, director Herbert Ross has assisted this effort by giving O'Toole only about two and a half songs. The performance is otherwise so consistent that we'd be distracted if he kept breaking into song.

Clark carries most of the musical duties in the film, and carries them well. She's especially effective in a scene during a school assembly, when her behavior onstage turns a dreary school song into a rouser. In other musical scenes, Ross frequently cuts away from the singers to provide a visual interpretation of the song. This is not a new technique, but it's not a bad one; it saves us the distraction of seeing two dramatic characters suddenly become musical performers.

Indeed, one of the best things about *Chips* is that Ross has concentrated on telling his story and hasn't let the songs intrude. That's particularly lucky since Leslie Bricusse's music and lyrics are sublimely forgettable; there's not a really first-rate song in the movie.

There are a couple of other objections. The movie, of course, should end on that magnificent scene when Chips retires as headmaster. Instead, it provides two superfluous scenes in the aging teacher's rooms—scenes that are dramatically pointless and dissipate the emotion of the ending. And the death of Chips's wife is badly handled (*must* we see it from the point of view of an aerial bomb?). But these are lapses in an otherwise admirable film, in which an engaging human being is shown to live a useful and civilized life. *Goodbye, Mr. Chips* is a lot better than you might have expected.

GoodFellas
R, 148 m., 1990

Robert De Niro (James Conway), Ray Liotta (Henry Hill), Joe Pesci (Tommy DeVito), Lorraine Bracco (Karen Hill), Paul Sorvino (Paul Cicero), Frank Sivero (Frankie Carbone), Catherine Scorsese (Tommy's Mother). Directed by Martin Scorsese and produced by Irwin Winkler. Screenplay by Nicholas Pileggi and Scorsese, based on the book *Wiseguy* by Pileggi.

There really are guys like this. I've seen them in restaurants and I've met them on movie sets, where they carefully explain that they are retired and are acting as technical consultants. They make their living as criminals, and often the service they provide is that they will not hurt you if you pay them. These days there is a certain guarded nostalgia for their brand of organized crime, because at least the mob would make a deal with you for your life, and not just kill you casually, out of impatience or a need for drugs.

Martin Scorsese's *GoodFellas* is a movie based on the true story of a mid-level professional criminal named Henry Hill, whose only ambition, from childhood on, was to be a member of the outfit. We see him with his face at the window, looking across the street at the neighborhood Mafiosi, who drove the big cars and got the good-looking women and never had to worry about the cops when they decided to hold a party late at night. One day the kid goes across the street and volunteers to help out, and before long he's selling stolen cigarettes at a factory gate and not long after that the doorman at the Copacabana knows his name.

For many years, it was not a bad life. The rewards were great. The only thing you could complain about was the work. There is a strange, confused evening in Hill's life when some kidding around in a bar leads to a murder, and the guy who gets killed is a "made man"—a man you do not touch lightly, because he has the mob behind him—and the body needs to be hidden quickly, and then later it needs to be moved, messily. This kind of work is bothersome. It fills the soul with guilt and the heart with dread, and before long Henry Hill is walking around as if there's a lead weight in his stomach.

But the movie takes its time to get to that point, and I have never seen a crime movie that seems so sure of its subject matter. There must have been a lot of retired technical consultants hanging around. Henry Hill, who is now an anonymous refugee within the federal government's witness protection program, told his life story to the journalist Nicholas Pileggi, who put it into the best seller *WiseGuy*, and now Pileggi and Scorsese have written the screenplay, which also benefits from Scorsese's firsthand observations of the Mafia while he

was a kid with his face in the window, watching the guys across the street.

Scorsese is in love with the details of his story, including the Mafia don who never, ever talked on the telephone and held all of his business meetings in the open air. Or the way some guys with a body in the car trunk will stop by to borrow a carving knife from one of their mothers, who will feed them pasta and believe them when they explain that they got blood on their suits when their car hit a deer. Everything in this movie reverberates with familiarity; the actors even inhabit the scenes as if nobody had to explain anything to them.

GoodFellas is an epic on the scale of *The Godfather,* and it uses its expansive running time to develop a real feeling for the way a lifetime develops almost by chance at first, and then sets its fateful course. Because we see mostly through the eyes of Henry Hill (Ray Liotta), characters swim in and out of focus; the character of Jimmy Conway (Robert De Niro), for example, is shadowy in the earlier passages of the film and then takes on a central importance. And then there's Tommy De-Vito (Joe Pesci), always on the outside looking in, glorying in his fleeting moments of power, laughing too loudly, slapping backs with too much familiarity, pursued by the demon of a raging anger that can flash out of control in a second. His final scene in this movie is one of the greatest moments of sudden realization I have ever seen; the development, the buildup, and the payoff are handled by Scorsese with the skill of a great tragedian.

GoodFellas isn't a myth-making movie, like *The Godfather.* It's about ordinary people who get trapped inside the hermetic world of the mob, whose values get worn away because they never meet anyone who disagrees with them. One of the most interesting characters in the movie is Henry Hill's wife, Karen (Lorraine Bracco), who is Jewish and comes from outside his world. He's an outsider himself—he's half-Irish, half-Italian, and so will never truly be allowed on the inside—but she's so far outside that at first she doesn't even realize what she's in for. She doesn't even seem to know what Henry does for a living, and when she finds out, she doesn't want to deal with it. She is the conarrator of the film, as if it were a documentary, and she talks about how she never goes anywhere or does anything except in the company of other mob wives. Finally she gets to the point where she's proud of her husband for being willing to go out and steal to support his family, instead of just sitting around like a lot of guys.

The parabola of *GoodFellas* is from the era of "good crimes," like stealing cigarettes and booze and running prostitution and making book, to bad crimes involving dope. The godfather in the movie (Paul Sorvino) warns Henry Hill about getting involved with dope, but it's not because he disapproves of narcotics (like Brando's Don Corleone); it's because he seems to sense that dope will spell trouble for the mob, will unleash street anarchy and bring in an undisciplined element. What eventually happens is that Hill makes a lot of money with cocaine but gets hooked on it as well, and eventually spirals down into the exhausted paranoia that proves to be his undoing.

Throbbing beneath the surface of *GoodFellas,* providing the magnet that pulls the plot along, are the great emotions in Hill's makeup: a lust for recognition, a fear of powerlessness, and guilt. He loves it when the headwaiters know his name, but he doesn't really have the stuff to be a great villain—he isn't brave or heartless enough—and so when he does bad things, he feels bad afterward. He begins to hate himself. And yet, he cannot hate the things he covets. He wants the prizes, but he doesn't want to pay for the tickets.

And it is there, on the crux of that paradox, that the movie becomes Scorsese's metaphor for so many modern lives. He doesn't parallel the mob with corporations or turn it into some kind of grotesque underworld version of yuppie culture. Nothing is that simple. He simply uses organized crime as an arena for a story about a man who likes material things so much that he sells his own soul to buy them—compromises his principles, betrays his friends, abandons his family, and finally even loses contact with himself. And the horror of the film is that, at the end, the man's principal regret is that he doesn't have any more soul to sell.

Good Morning, Vietnam

R, 119 m., 1988

Robin Williams (Adrian Cronauer), Forest Whitaker (Edward Garlick), Tung Thanh Tran (Tuan), Chintara Sukapatana (Trinh), Bruno Kirby (Lieutenant Hauk), Robert Wuhl (Marty Lee Dreiwitz), J. T. Walsh (Sergeant Dickerson), Noble Willingham (General Taylor). Directed by Barry Levinson and produced by Mark Johnson and Larry Brezner. Screenplay by Mitch Markowitz.

Like most of the great stand-up comedians, Robin Williams has always kept a certain wall between himself and his audience. If you watch his concert videos, you see him trying on a bewildering series of accents and characters; he's a gifted chameleon who turns into whatever makes the audience laugh. But who is inside?

With George Carlin, Richard Pryor, Steve Martin, Billy Crystal, Eddie Murphy, we have an idea—or think we do. A lot of their humor depends on confessional autobiography. With Robin Williams, the wall remains impenetrable. Like Groucho Marx, he uses comedy as a strategy for personal concealment.

Williams's best movies *(Popeye, The World According to Garp, Moscow on the Hudson)* are the ones where he is given a well-written character to play, and held to the character by a strong director. In his other movies, you can see him trying to do his stand-up act on the screen, trying to use comedy to conceal not only himself from the audience—but even his character. The one-liners and adlibs distance him from the material and from his fellow actors. Hey, he's only a visitor here.

What is inspired about *Good Morning, Vietnam,* which contains far and away the best work Williams has ever done in a movie, is that his own tactics are turned against him. The director, Barry Levinson, has created a character who *is* a stand-up comic—he's a fast-talking disc jockey on Armed Forces Radio during the Vietnam War, directing a nonstop monologue at the microphone. There is absolutely no biographical information about this character. We don't know where he comes from, what he did before the war, whether he's ever been married, what his dreams are, what he's afraid of. Everything in his world is reduced to material for his program.

Levinson used Mitch Markowitz's script as a starting point for a lot of Williams's monologues, and then let the comedian improvise.

Then he put together the best parts of many different takes to create sequences that are undeniably dazzling and funny. Williams is a virtuoso.

But while he's assaulting the microphone, Levinson is doing something fairly subtle in the movie around him. He has populated *Good Morning, Vietnam* with a lot of character actors who are fairly complicated types, recognizably human, and with the aid of the script, they set a trap for Williams. His character is edged into a corner where he *must* have human emotions, or die.

The character (his name is Adrian Cronauer) resists. At one point his Jeep breaks down in the middle of the jungle in Viet Cong territory, and he starts using one-liners on the trees. He meets a Vietnamese girl he likes, and uses one-liners on her, too, in a genuine exercise in cynicism since she doesn't understand any of his humor. He runs afoul of top army brass that doesn't approve of his anti-establishment tone on the radio, and he wisecracks at them, too, trying to insist that he's always on stage, that nothing is real, that the whole war is basically just material.

And then things happen. To impress the girl and her brother, he starts teaching an English-language class for the Vietnamese. He finds that he likes them. He witnesses (and barely survives) a particularly gruesome terrorist attack. He gets thrown off the radio. He meets some kids who are going into battle, and who admire him, and in their eyes he sees something that makes him start to take himself a little more seriously. By the end of the movie, Cronauer has turned into a better, deeper, wiser man than he was at the beginning; the movie is the story of his education.

I know there are other ways to read this material. *Good Morning, Vietnam* works as straight comedy, and it works as a Vietnam era *M*A*S*H*, and even the movie's love story has its own bittersweet integrity. But they used to tell us in writing class that if we wanted to know what a story was really about, we should look for what changed between the beginning and the end. In this movie, Cronauer changes. War wipes the grin off of his face. His humor becomes a humanitarian tool, not simply a way to keep him talking and us listening.

In a strange, subtle way, *Good Morning,*

Vietnam is not so much about war as it is about stand-up comedy, about the need that compels people to get up in front of the room and try to make us laugh—to control us.

Why do comics do that? Because they need to have their power proven and vindicated. Why do they need that? Because they are the most insecure of earth's people (just listen to their language—they're gonna kill us, unless they die out there). How do you treat low self-esteem? By doing estimable things and then saying, hey, I did that! What happens to Cronauer in this movie? Exactly that. By the end of the film he doesn't wisecrack all the time because he doesn't need to. He no longer thinks he's the worthless (although bright, fast, and funny) sack of crap that got off the plane. In the early scenes of the movie, the character's eyes are opaque. By the end, you can see what he's thinking.

Good Night, and Good Luck

PG, 93 m., 2005

David Strathairn (Edward R. Murrow), Patricia Clarkson (Shirley Wershba), George Clooney (Fred Friendly), Jeff Daniels (Sig Mickelson), Robert Downey, Jr. (Joe Wershba), Frank Langella (William Paley), Ray Wise (Don Hollenbeck), Dianne Reeves (Jazz Singer). Directed by George Clooney and produced by Grant Heslov. Screenplay by Clooney and Heslov.

Good Night, and Good Luck is a movie about a group of professional newsmen who with surgical precision remove a cancer from the body politic. They believe in the fundamental American freedoms, and in Senator Joseph McCarthy they see a man who would destroy those freedoms in the name of defending them. Because McCarthy is a liar and a bully, surrounded by yes-men, recklessly calling his opponents traitors, he commands great power for a time. He destroys others with lies and then himself is destroyed by the truth.

The instrument of his destruction is Edward R. Murrow, a television journalist above reproach, whose radio broadcasts from London led to a peacetime career as the most famous newsman in the new medium of television. Murrow is offended by McCarthy. He makes bold to say so, and why. He is backed by his producers and reporters and is supported by the leadership of his network, CBS, even though it loses sponsors, and even though McCarthy claims Murrow himself is a member of a subversive organization.

There are times when it is argued within CBS that Murrow has lost his objectivity, that he is not telling "both sides." He argues that he is reporting the facts, and if the facts are contrary to McCarthy's fantasies, they are nevertheless objective. In recent years, few reporters have dared take such a stand, but at the height of Hurricane Katrina, we saw many reporters in the field who knew by their own witness that the official line on hurricane relief was a fiction, and said so.

Murrow is played in *Good Night, and Good Luck* by David Strathairn, that actor of precise inward silence. He has mastered the Murrow mannerisms, the sidelong glance from beneath lowered eyebrows, the way of sitting perfectly still and listening and watching others, the ironic underplayed wit, the unbending will. He doesn't look much like Murrow, any more than Philip Seymour Hoffman looks much like Truman Capote, but both actors create their characters from the inside, concealing behind famous mannerisms the deliberate actions that impose their will. In that they are actually a little alike.

George Clooney costars as Fred Friendly, Murrow's producer, who remained active into the 1990s. Clooney also directed and cowrote the movie. Because his father was a newscaster, he knows what the early TV studios looked like, and it is startling to see how small was Murrow's performance space: He sits close to the camera, his famous cigarette usually in the shot, and Friendly sits beside the camera, so close that he can tap Murrow's leg to cue him. They are also close as professionals who share the same beliefs about McCarthy and are aware that they risk character assassination from the Wisconsin senator.

The other key character is McCarthy himself, and Clooney uses a masterstroke: He employs actual news footage of McCarthy, who therefore plays himself. It is frightening to see him in full rant, and pathetic to see him near meltdown during the Army-McCarthy hearings, when the Army counsel Joseph Welch famously asked him, "Have you no decency?" His wild attack on Murrow has an element of humor; he claims the broadcaster is a member of the Industrial Workers of the World, the anarchist "Wobblies," who by then were more a subject of nostalgic folk songs than a functioning organization.

The movie is entirely, almost claustrophobically, about politics and the news business. Even its single subplot underlines the atmosphere of the times. We meet Shirley and Joe Wershba (Patricia Clarkson and Robert Downey, Jr.), who work for CBS News and keep their marriage a secret because company policy forbids the employment of married couples. Their clandestine meetings and subtle communications raise our own suspicions and demonstrate in a way how McCarthyism works.

Apart from the Wershbas, the movie is entirely about the inner life of CBS News. Every substantial scene is played in the CBS building, except for a banquet, a bar, a bedroom, and the newsreel footage. Murrow and Friendly circulate in three arenas: their production offices, the television studio, and the offices of their boss, William Paley (Frank Langella), who ran the network as a fiefdom but granted Murrow independence and freedom from advertiser pressure.

The movie is not really about the abuses of McCarthy but about the process by which Murrow and his team eventually brought about his downfall (some would say his self-destruction). It is like a morality play, from which we learn how journalists should behave. It shows Murrow as fearless but not flawless. Paley observes that when McCarthy said that Alger Hiss was convicted of "treason," Murrow knew Hiss was convicted not of treason but of perjury and yet did not correct McCarthy. Was he afraid of seeming to support a communist, Paley asks, perhaps guessing the answer. He has a point. Murrow's response indicates he might have been a great poker player.

There are small moments of humor. After one broadcast fraught with potential hazards, Murrow waits until he's off the air and then there is the smallest possible movement of his mouth: Could that have been almost a smile? David Strathairn is a stealth actor, revealing Murrow's feelings almost in code. Clooney by contrast makes Friendly an open, forthright kinduva guy, a reliable partner for Murrow's enigmatic reserve.

As a director, Clooney does interesting things. One of them is to shoot in black and white, which is the right choice for this material, lending it period authenticity and a matter-of-factness. In a way, black and white is inevitable, since both Murrow's broadcasts and the McCarthy footage would have been in black and white. Clooney shoots close, showing men (and a few women) in business dress, talking in anonymous rooms. Everybody smokes all of the time. When they screen footage, there is an echo of *Citizen Kane*. Episodes are separated by a jazz singer (Dianne Reeves), who is seen performing in a nearby studio; her songs don't parallel the action but evoke a time of piano lounges, martinis, and all those cigarettes.

Clooney's message is clear: Character assassination is wrong, McCarthy was a bully and a liar, and we must be vigilant when the emperor has no clothes and wraps himself in the flag. It was Dr. Johnson who said, "Patriotism is the last refuge of the scoundrel." That was more than two-hundred years ago. The movie quotes a more recent authority, Dwight Eisenhower, who is seen on TV defending the basic American right of habeas corpus. How many Americans know what "habeas corpus" means, or why people are still talking about it on TV?

Gosford Park

R, 137 m., 2002

Eileen Atkins (Mrs. Croft), Bob Balaban (Morris Weissman), Alan Bates (Jennings), Charles Dance (Lord Stockbridge), Stephen Fry (Inspector Thompson), Michael Gambon (Sir William McCordle), Richard E. Grant (George), Derek Jacobi (Probert), Kelly Macdonald (Mary Maceachran), Helen Mirren (Mrs. Wilson), Jeremy Northam (Ivor Novello), Clive Owen (Robert Parks), Ryan Phillippe (Henry Denton), Maggie Smith (Constance, Countess of Trentham), Kristin Scott Thomas (Lady Sylvia McCordle), Emily Watson (Elsie). Directed by Robert Altman and produced by Altman, Balaban, and David Levy. Screenplay by Julian Fellowes, based on an idea by Altman and Balaban.

Robert Altman's *Gosford Park* is above all a celebration of styles—the distinct behavior produced by the British class system, the personal styles of a rich gallery of actors, and his own style of introducing a lot of characters and letting them weave their way through a labyrinthine plot. At a time when too many movies focus every scene on a $20 million star, an Altman film is like a party with no boring guests. *Gosford Park* is such a joyous and audacious achievement it deserves comparison with his very best movies, such as *M*A*S*H*, *McCabe and Mrs. Miller, Nashville, The Player, Short Cuts,* and *Cookie's Fortune*.

It employs the genre of the classic British murder mystery, as defined by Agatha Christie: Guests and servants crowd a great country house, and one of them is murdered. But *Gosford Park* is a Dame Agatha story in the same sense that *M*A*S*H* is a war movie, *McCabe* is a Western, and *Nashville* is a musical: Altman uses the setting, but surpasses the limitations and redefines the goal. This is no less than a comedy about selfishness, greed, snobbery, eccentricity, and class exploitation, and Altman is right when he hopes people will see it more than once; after you know the destination, the journey is transformed.

The time is November 1932. Sir William McCordle (Michael Gambon) and Lady Sylvia McCordle (Kristin Scott Thomas) have invited a houseful of guests for a shooting party. They include Sir William's sister Constance, the countess of Trentham (Maggie Smith), who depends on an allowance he is constantly threatening to withdraw. And Lady Sylvia's sister Louisa (Geraldine Somerville), who like Sylvia had to marry for money (they cut cards to decide who would bag Sir William). And Louisa's husband, Commander Anthony Meredith (Tom Hollander). And their sister Lavinia (Natasha Wightman), married to Raymond, Lord Stockbridge (Charles Dance). And the Hollywood star Ivor Novello (Jeremy Northam). And Morris Weissman (Bob Balaban), a gay Hollywood producer who has brought along his "valet," Henry Denton (Ryan Phillippe).

Below stairs we meet the butler Jennings (Alan Bates), the housekeeper Mrs. Wilson (Helen Mirren), the cook Mrs. Croft (Eileen Atkins), the footman George (Richard E. Grant), and assorted other valets, maids, grooms, and servers. When the American Henry comes to take his place at the servants' table and says his name is Denton, Jennings sternly informs him that servants are addressed below stairs by the names of their masters, and he will be "Mr. Weissman" at their table—where, by the way, servants are seated according to the ranks of their employers.

It has been said that the most enjoyable lifestyle in history was British country house life in the years between the wars. That is true for some of the people upstairs in this movie, less true of most of those downstairs. Altman observes exceptions: Some of the aristocrats, like Lady Constance, are threatened with financial ruin, and others, like Novello, have to sing for their supper; while below stairs, a man like Jennings is obviously supremely happy to head the staff of a great house.

The classic country house murder story begins with perfect order, in which everyone up and down the class ladder fits securely into his or her place—until murder disrupts that order and discloses unexpected connections between the classes. That's what happens here, when one of the characters is poisoned and then stabbed, suggesting there are two murderers to be apprehended by Inspector Thompson (Stephen Fry).

Half of those in the house have a motive for the murder, but the investigation isn't the point, and Altman has fun by letting Thompson and his assistant Constable Dexter (Ron Webster) mirror the relative competence of the upper and lower classes in the house. Thompson, like the aristocrats, sets great store by his title and dress (he puffs a pipe that will be recognized by anyone who knows the name Monsieur Hulot). Dexter, like the servants, just gets on with it, doggedly pointing out clues (footprints, fingerprints on a tea cup, a secret door) that Thompson ignores.

The cast of *Gosford Park* is like a reunion of fine and familiar actors (I have not yet even mentioned Derek Jacobi, Kelly Macdonald, Clive Owen, Emily Watson, and James Wilby). This is like an invitation for scene-stealing, and Maggie Smith effortlessly places first, with brittle comments that cut straight to the quick. When Novello entertains after dinner with one song, and then another, and then another, and shows no sign of stopping, Smith crisply asks, "Do you think he'll be as long as he usually is?" and then stage-whispers, "Don't encourage him."

Altman has a keen eye and ear for snobbery. Note the way that when Mr. Weissman introduces himself, Lady Sylvia asks him to repeat his name, and then she repeats it herself. Just that, but she is subtly underlining his ethnicity. And the way Constance puts Novello in his place by mentioning his most recent film and observing, ostensibly with sympathy, "It must be rather disappointing when something flops like that."

The screenplay by Julian Fellowes, based on an idea by Altman and Balaban, is masterful in introducing all of the characters and gradually making it clear who they are, what they've done, and what it means. Like guests at a big party, we are confused when we first arrive: Who are all these people? By the end, we know. No director has ever been better than Altman at providing the audience with bearings to find its way through a large cast. The sense of place is also palpable in this film; the downstairs and attics were entirely constructed on sound stages by production designer Steven Altman, Altman's son, who also supervised the real country house used for the main floors. Andrew Dunn's photography is sumptuous upstairs, while making the downstairs look creamy and institutional. The editor, Tim Squyres, must have been crucial in keeping the characters in play.

Gosford Park is the kind of generous, sardonic, deeply layered movie that Altman has made his own. As a director he has never been willing to settle for plot; he is much more interested in character and situation, and likes to assemble unusual people in peculiar situations and stir the pot. Here he is, like Prospero, serenely the master of his art.

The Graduate
PG, 105 m., 1967

Anne Bancroft (Mrs. Robinson), Dustin Hoffman (Benjamin Braddock), Katharine Ross (Elaine Robinson), William Daniels (Mr. Braddock), Murray Hamilton (Mrs. Braddock), Brian Avery (Carl Smith), Buck Henry (Room Clerk). Directed by Mike Nichols and produced by Nichols and Lawrence Turman. Screenplay by Calder Willingham and Henry, based on the book by Charles Webb.

The Graduate, the funniest American comedy of the year, is inspired by the free spirit the young British directors have brought into their movies. It is funny, not because of sight gags and punch lines and other tired rubbish, but because it has a point of view. That is to say, it is against something. Comedy is naturally subversive, no matter what Doris Day thinks.

Most Hollywood comedies have non-movie assumptions built into them. One of the most persistent is that movie characters have to react to funny events in the same way that stage actors do. So we get Jerry Lewis mugging. But in the direct style of new British directors, the audience is the target of the joke, and the funny events do not happen in the movie—they are the movie.

This theory is based upon a belief that audiences, having seen hundreds of movies, come into the theater with an instinctive knowledge of film shorthand. So the new-style British comedies (*The Knack, Morgan, Alfie, Tom Jones, A Hard Day's Night*) go against standard practice, and their use of film itself is part of the comedy. When something funny happens, the actors don't react; the movie itself reacts by what it shows next.

This is the case with *The Graduate*, in which Mike Nichols announces himself as a major new director.

He introduces us to a young college graduate (Dustin Hoffman) who returns to a ferociously stupid upper-middle-class California suburb. He would like the chance to sit around and think about his future for several months. You know—think?

His family and their social circle demand that he perform in the role of Successful Young Upward-Venturing Clean-Cut All-American College Grad. At the end of two weeks Benjamin is driven to such a pitch of desperation that he demonstrates a new scuba outfit (birthday present from proud dad) by standing on the bottom of the family pool: Alone at last.

One of his parents' contemporaries (Anne Bancroft) seduces Benjamin, who succumbs mostly out of weariness and disbelief. Then he falls in love with her daughter (Katharine Ross) and sets in motion a fantastic chain of events that ends with Miss Ross (just married to a handsome blond Nordic pipe-smoking fraternity boy) being kidnapped from the altar by Benjamin. He jams a cross into the church door to prevent pursuit, and they escape on a bus.

This is outrageous material, but it works in *The Graduate* because it is handled in a straightforward manner. Hoffman is so painfully awkward and ethical that we are forced to admit we would act pretty much as he does, even in his most extreme moments. Bancroft, in a tricky role, is magnificently sexy, shrewish, and self-possessed enough to make the seduction convincing.

Nichols stays on top of his material. He never pauses to make sure we're getting the point. He never explains for the slow-witted. He never apologizes. His only flaw, I believe, is the introduction of limp, wordy Simon and Garfunkel songs and arty camera work to suggest the passage of time between major scenes. Otherwise, *The Graduate* is a success and Benjamin's acute honesty and embarrassment are so accurately drawn that we hardly know whether to laugh or to look inside ourselves.

Grand Canyon
R, 134 m., 1992

Danny Glover (Simon), Kevin Kline (Mack), Steve Martin (Davis), Mary McDonnell (Claire), Mary-Louise Parker (Dee), Alfre Woodard (Jane). Directed by Lawrence Kasdan and produced by Lawrence Kasdan, Charles Okun, and Michael Grillo. Screenplay by Lawrence Kasdan and Meg Kasdan.

Lawrence Kasdan's *Grand Canyon* begins in much the same way as *The Bonfire of the Vanities*, as a white man driving a luxury car strays off his usual route and finds himself threatened by black youths in a deserted urban landscape. But at that point the two stories take different paths, because this is a film about possibilities, not fears. At first, to be sure, the white man (Kevin Kline) believes he is going to be killed by the ominous black muggers, one of whom displays a gun. But then a tow truck arrives, driven by another black man (Danny Glover), who talks to the leader of the would-be thieves and defuses the situation.

The dialogue in this scene, and throughout the movie, does not simply exist to push along the plot. It is the way we really think and talk in various situations. "Do you respect me, or do you respect my gun?" the gang leader asks Glover, who looks him in the eye and says,

"You don't have that gun, there's no way we're having this conversation." And that honesty somehow satisfies the man with the gun.

Honesty is all through *Grand Canyon*, which is about several characters who would never, in the ordinary course of events, meet one another. Kline plays a wealthy immigration attorney attached to the entertainment industry; Glover is a divorced, hardworking tow truck driver. A few days after the street incident, Kline seeks out Glover for a cup of coffee because, he says, he wants to thank the man who saved his life. He doesn't want it to be just a chance meeting in the night.

This impulse—to break down the barriers society erects between people—is what *Grand Canyon* is about. It takes place in a Los Angeles that is painted as ominous and threatening, an alienating landscape where rich people pile up bulwarks of money and distance to protect them from the dangers of poverty and despair. But the Kline character believes that he has been granted a new life, and he wants to lead it a little differently this time. Like the characters in two other Kasdan movies, *The Big Chill* and *The Accidental Tourist*, he finds that the nearness of death can be an inspiration to live more thoughtfully.

His wife (Mary McDonnell) feels the same way. Their son is about to leave for college, and as the empty nest looms, a miracle falls into her life: She hears crying in the bushes along her daily jogging route, and finds an abandoned baby. She brings it home and wants to keep it. Kline is opposed at first to the notion of raising another child, but eventually comes around to the logic of the situation: Just as Glover appeared from nowhere to save Kline, so Kline's wife appeared to save the baby.

Grand Canyon is not all about coincidences. Much of it is about daily life in a big American city. Glover tells Kline he's worried about his sister's son, who seems to be getting involved with gangs. Kline says he knows a man who owns an apartment building in a better neighborhood. But that neighborhood turns out to have its own sorts of dangers, including policemen who believe that the sight of a jogging young black man is automatically suspicious.

It is uncanny, the way the movie tunes in to the kinds of fears that are all around us in the cities—even those we're not always aware of. In a film that vibrates with an impending sense of danger, the single most terrifying scene is a driving lesson. Kline takes his son out for a drive, during which they are going to practice left turns, and as this scene develops, there is something about Owen Roizman's camera work and James Newton Howard's music that creates a frightening undercurrent. It's only a *driving lesson*, for chrissakes, but by the end of it Kline is explaining to his son that you only have a split second to act, or you'll get creamed. How many of those split-second choices do we make every day without even thinking about them?

Various kinds of romance act as counterpoint to the dangers in this film. Kline arranges a blind date between Glover and Alfre Woodard, a single woman who works in his office, and later that evening, the two of them, realizing he hardly really knows either one, surmise they may be the only two black people he knows. McDonnell falls in love with the baby she has found. A regard develops between Kline and Glover. And so on.

There is another character in *Grand Canyon*, a producer of violent action pictures, played by Steve Martin. Early in the movie, he's complaining because an editor has left out the "money shot" (a bus driver getting his brains sprayed on a windshield). Then a mugger shoots Martin in the leg, and he feels real pain, and has a great awakening and vows not to make any more violent movies. We doubt that he will keep his promise. But the symbolism is there: In a time when our cities are wounded, movies like *Grand Canyon* can help to heal.

The Great Santini

PG, 118 m., 1980

Robert Duvall (Bull Meechum), Blythe Danner (Lillian Meechum), Michael O'Keefe (Ben Meechum), Lisa Jane Persky (Mary Anne Meechum), Stan Shaw (Toomer Smalls), Theresa Merritt (Arrabelle Smalls). Directed by Lewis John Carlino and produced by Charles A. Pratt. Screenplay by Carlino.

Like almost all of my favorite films, *The Great Santini* is about people more than it's about a

300 ★ ★ ★ ★   THE GREEN WALL

story. It's a study of several characters, most unforgettably the Great Santini himself—played by Robert Duvall. Despite his name, he is not a magician or an acrobat but a lieutenant colonel in the marines with the real name of Bull Meechum. He sees himself as the Great Santini, an ace pilot, great marine, heroic husband and father and, in general, a sterling man among men. His family is expected to go along with this—and to go along with him, as he's transferred to a duty camp in South Carolina in the early 1960s.

There are five other members of the Meechum family. His wife (Blythe Danner) is a sweet southern girl who calls her kids "sugar" and understands her maverick husband with a love that is deep but unforgiving. His oldest son (Michael O'Keefe) is just turning eighteen and learning to stand up to a father who issues "direct orders," calls everyone "sports fan," and expects to be called "sir." There are two daughters and one more son, but the movie's main relationship is between the father and the oldest boy.

Santini, you understand, is one hell of a guy. All he understands is competition. He's a royal pain in the ass to his marine superiors, because he's always pulling damn fool stunts and making a spectacle out of himself. But he's a great pilot and he's said to be a good leader (even though his first briefing session for the men under him in South Carolina leaves them totally bewildered). Santini wants to win at everything, even backyard basketball with his son.

But the son is learning to be his own man. And there's a subplot involving a friendship between O'Keefe and the intense actor Stan Shaw, who plays the son of the family's black maid. Marine kids grow up nowhere and everywhere, we learn, and in South Carolina these two kids go shrimping together, trade lore together, become friends. It's a nice relationship, although a little tangential to the main thrust of the movie.

It's Robert Duvall who really makes the movie live—Duvall and Blythe Danner in a stunning performance that nothing she's done before (in *1776*, *Hearts of the West*, etc.) prepares us for. Although *The Great Santini* is set about ten years before *Apocalypse Now*, Duvall is playing essentially the same charac-ter in both films—we remember his great scene in *Apocalypse*, shouting that napalm smells to him like victory, as he gives his gung-ho speeches in this movie.

Duvall and O'Keefe go hard at each other, in the father-son confrontation, and there's an especially painful scene where the father bounces a basketball off his son's head, egging him on. But this movie is essentially a comedy—a serious, tender one, like *Breaking Away*, which is also about a son getting to know his father.

There are wonderful little moments in the dialogue (as when the Great Santini's daughter wonders aloud if females are allowed full Meechum family status, or are only sort of one-celled Meechums). There are moments straight out of left field, as when Duvall and the family's new maid (the formidable Theresa Merritt) get into an impromptu shoulder-punching contest. There are moments so unpredictable and yet so natural they feel just like the spontaneity of life itself. And the movie's conclusion is the same way: sentimental without being corny, a tearjerker with dignity.

The Great Santini is a movie to seek out and to treasure.

The Green Wall

R, 110 m., 1970

Julio Aleman (Mario), Sandra Rive (Delba), Raul Martin (Romulo), Jorie Montoro (Chief of Jungle Region). Directed by Armondo Robles Godoy and produced by Manuel Yori. Screenplay by Juan Cuadros, based on the book by Omar Aramayo.

It is so rare to find a movie that people reach out to and embrace, a movie that makes you feel cleaner and more alive. *The Green Wall* is a movie like that. It came to the 1970 Chicago Film Festival with little advance publicity (all we knew was that it was the fourth feature ever made in Peru). But the Chicago critics fell in love with it at a preview, and their advance reviews helped inspire a sold-out house for its festival screening.

When it was over, the audience rose in a joyous standing ovation. Its director, a big bear of a man named Armando Robles Godoy, stood there grinning through his shaggy moustache, and there were tears in his eyes. There was a feeling in the theater that we had been present when a great movie came into the world.

The Green Wall is inspired, to some degree, by Robles Godoy's own life experience. It is about an office worker who sickens of the big-city chaos of Lima and enlists himself and his family in a government program to colonize the forest. He is given a large tract of land in the wilderness, clears the rich soil, and grows coffee. He builds a simple, comfortable bamboo home for his wife and his small boy, and it has a cool veranda that overlooks a little stream.

The boy loves the trickle of water and builds his own tiny city there out of blocks and pieces of tin and glass and string. There is a waterwheel that goes around and around and tinkles against a glass jar. Its music is part of the soft murmur of the forest: the bird cries, the leaves brushing against each other, the calls and coughs of the animals.

In these days of a movement away from the urban clutter and back to a more natural life, *The Green Wall* is a poem about the life a lot of us would like to lead. It isn't in any sense an adventure saga about survival in the jungle; these are intelligent, self-sufficient pioneers who understand the land and love it. What frustrates them is not the challenge of colonization, but the stupid government bureaucracy that runs the settlement program.

The movie opens with one of the most beautiful evocations of love I can remember in a film. The man and his wife make love tenderly and with deep affection, and their little son, who is supposed to be napping, watches them with clear-eyed contentment; because they love each other, he feels good. He is a quiet child because he has no friends to play with, but the world of his imagination is a busy place and we are allowed into it.

Then an accident happens; the boy is bitten by a snake. The father goes by boat and Jeep into the nearest town to get serum—but the serum is locked up, and the bureaucrat with the key is at a political rally in the next town. As the father races desperately to save his own son's life, Godoy gives us a bitter commentary on the ways bureaucracy frustrates humanity. And then the film closes with a procession of boats on the river, simple and stately and filled with an enormous dignity—and a weary embrace between the man and his wife that says whatever a movie can say about the deepness of love.

The Green Wall is beautiful in so many different ways—in its story, its photography, in the construction of its images—that it becomes not simply a movie but an affirmation of life. There is not a false note in it, nothing that lies or is trickery, and we're reminded of *The Bicycle Thief* and *The Wild Child*.

And then we wonder . . . how could this movie come from Peru, with its "undeveloped" movie industry? The answer, of course, is that great films have nothing to do with the industry. They come from great filmmakers, who might be found in Peru as well as anywhere. The Chicago Film Festival honored *The Green Wall* with its Golden Hugo and its special Critics' Prize, and that helped Godoy with his entry into the cutthroat American movie market. Now *The Green Wall* is back with us, and that is a very good thing.

The Grey Automobile

NO MPAA RATING, 90 m., 1919 (rereleased 2003)

In the film: Juan Manuel Cabrera (Himself), Gang Members (Themselves). On the stage: Irene Akiko Iida (Japanese Benshi), Enrique Arreola (Spanish Dialogue), Thomasi McDonald (English Dialogue), Ernesto Gomez Santana (Pianist). A live performance with a 1919 Mexican silent film. Film originally directed by Enrique Rosas; interpreted, augmented, and staged by Claudio Valdes-Kuri.

A little-known 1919 Mexican silent film . . . and already your attention is drifting, right? You've been meaning to catch up on the Mexican silent cinema, but somehow the time is never right. Now the time has come. *The Grey Automobile* provides the inspiration for an astonishing theatrical experience.

By the Marx Brothers out of Gilbert and Sullivan and incorporating an early Japanese film tradition, the event devised by director Claudio Valdes-Kuri is slapstick, surrealist, charming, and lighthearted, especially considering that an actual automobile gang is literally executed during the course of the film. A Japanese benshi, a Mexican actor, and an

English "interpreter" join the film on the stage, as a pianist supplies the score.

To begin with benshis. During the silent film era, Japanese exhibitors supplied a benshi, or interpreting actor, to stand next to the screen and explain films. The benshis might or might not understand the Western stories and characters any more than the audience did, but that didn't matter, because benshis evolved a performance tradition of their own—not only explaining, but praising, criticizing, sympathizing, and applauding, in parallel with the film. Benshis became so popular that their names were billed above the stars, they had theaters of their own, and silent films survived in Japan for almost a decade after the introduction of sound—because audiences could not do without their beloved benshis.

Claudio Valdes-Kuri, an avant-garde theatrical director from Mexico City, discovered the benshi tradition during a visit to Japan, where benshis still flourish, many of them trained in a line going back to the original artists. Back home in Mexico, he decided to adapt the tradition to *The Grey Automobile,* said to be Mexico's finest silent film, which is about the real-life Grey Automobile Gang.

This film, originally a serial, has existed in many forms over the years, but it is safe to say that no one associated with it could have imagined the ninety-minute version now presented by Valdes-Kuri and his Certain Inhabitants Theater. The film stars Juan Manuel Cabrera, the actual detective who apprehended the gang, playing himself. The real gang members also appear, briefly to be sure, in a startling scene where they are (really) executed. Other scenes are fiction.

It is impossible to say, on the basis of this presentation, whether *The Grey Automobile* is a good film or not—my four-star rating refers to the entire theatrical experience. As the performance opens, Irene Akiko Iida, a Japanese-Mexican actress dressed in a traditional kimono, joins the pianist, Ernesto Gomez Santana, by the side of the screen and provides a traditional benshi commentary in Japanese. Then she is joined by Enrique Arreola, who begins a Spanish commentary. Then they are joined by Thomasi McDonald, who supplies commentary and translation in English.

But that sounds straightforward, and the performance quickly jumps the rails into sublime zaniness. Other languages—German, French, and Russian—creep into the commentary. The film seems to have no subtitles, but suddenly generates them, and then the titles leave the bottom of the screen and begin to emerge from the mouths of the movie actors in a variety of typefaces; the words coil around the screen and take on lives of their own. Then the actors begin to interpret the on-screen dialogue so freely that at times they have the characters barking at one another. At one point the action stops for a little song-and-dance number, and at another Ms. Iida performs a tap dance.

But this description fails to do justice to the technical virtuosity of the verbal performers. For long stretches, they create perfect lip-synch with the actors on-screen while talking at breakneck speed, never missing a cue or a beat; what they do is so difficult, and done so effortlessly, that it suggests a Zenlike identification with the material. I avoid clichés such as "You've never seen anything like this before," but the fact is, you haven't.

Grey Gardens
PG, 100 m., 1975

Featuring Edith Bouvier Beale and Edie Beale. A documentary directed by David and Albert Maysles, Ellen Hovde, Muffie Meyer, and Susan Froemke and produced by the Maysles.

Edith Bouvier Beale sits on her bed, wrapped in a housecoat, surrounded by cats, singing in a reverie: "Tea for two, and two for tea . . ." And we wonder if it occurs to her that the song is the story of the last, long chapter of her life. For more than twenty years, she and her daughter, Edie, have lived together in a crumbling old mansion by the sea. They are surrounded on both sides by the summer homes of the wealthy—of people from their class—but Grey Gardens stands in Gothic decay.

The house was beautiful once, and so were the Beales. They look through old scrapbooks, this woman of eighty-two and her fifty-six-year-old daughter, and we see them when they were the cream of society. Edith on her wedding day. Edie modeling at a charity fashion show. Now a slow disintegration has set in; rooms of their mansion and areas of their lives have been closed off, one at a time, left to the forages of raccoons and memories.

Still, they've preserved a few things, while abandoning so much. They still have wit, style, and what I would define as sanity. *Grey Gardens,* one of the most haunting documentaries in a long time, preserves their strange existence, and we're pleased that it does. It expands our notions of the possibilities. It's about two classic eccentrics, two people who refuse to live the way they're supposed to, but by the film's end we see that they live fully, in ways of their own choosing.

The film was made almost by accident. Albert and David Maysles, the directors of such documentaries as *Salesman* and *Gimme Shelter,* were approached by the two Bouvier sisters, Jacqueline Onassis and Lee Radziwell. Would the Maysles like to make a movie about the Bouviers? They might. Jackie and Lee supplied them with information about the family, including their two reclusive cousins in East Hampton, New York. The Maysles shot, on and off, for several months. Then they reviewed their footage and decided there wasn't a movie in Jackie and Lee—but there seemed to be one in Edith and Edie.

They went back to Grey Gardens and all but moved in for two months, using portable cameras to follow the Beales in their daily routines. Many of the routines seem intended for the stage. Mrs. Beale, once a highly regarded concert singer, sings several songs for them. Edie, who'd always dreamed of a career as a dancer, improvises a soft shoe to the Virginia Military Institute fight song. And the two women, in ways that have been exquisitely refined over the years, fight a little among themselves.

It is here that the film has its fascinating, mysterious center. We gradually realize that these two women are absolutely dependent on each other, that they form a composite personality (or, as the Maysles put it, a "closed system"). Edie never married. She brought a few boys home, but her mother didn't like them. So that's one thing to fight about. "That was just after the fall of France," Edie says at one time, dating a memory. "France fell," her mother says, "but Edie didn't." The house is surrounded, as Edie observes, by a "sea of green." The grounds have grown wild. "I lost a lovely blue scarf in there one day and never found it again," she muses. Inside, plaster is crumbling from the walls, and raccoons coexist amicably with the Beales and a large family of cats. Old phonograph records are played once again, and on Sunday night the girls tune in Norman Vincent Peale from New York. "First, think," he advises. "Then, try . . ."

Edie dresses up in bizarre costumes. She likes to wear skirts upside down. She is never seen without a turban. She dresses in lace curtains, in bedspreads, in bathing suits that were last seen on the cover of *Life,* circa 1948. She and her mother talk all the time, sometimes at the same time—they both know all the words. And out of this existence comes a movie that, curiously enough, is comic and bright, as well as sobering. It's hard not to find these two odd women likable.

Moments: Edie feeding the raccoons a loaf of Wonder Bread. Edith placidly observing that a cat is defecating behind her portrait. Edie, nearsighted, standing on a scale and reading her weight with binoculars. Edith confessing that she can't turn around just at the moment because her bathing suit has no back. The two women at night, alone in their room, the crumbling mansion extending around them, listening to old songs and replaying old memories. Me for you, and you for me, can't you see, how happy we will be . . .

The Grey Zone
R, 108 m., 2002

David Arquette (Hoffman), Daniel Benzali (Schlermer), Steve Buscemi (Abramowics), David Chandler (Rosenthal), Allan Corduner (Dr. Nyiszli), Harvey Keitel (Muhsfeldt), Natasha Lyonne (Rosa), Mira Sorvino (Dina), Kamelia Grigorova (Girl). Directed by Tim Blake Nelson and produced by Pamela Koffler, Nelson, and Christine Vachon. Screenplay by Nelson, based on the play by Nelson and the book *Auschwitz: A Doctor's Eyewitness Account* by Miklos Nyiszli.

"How can you know what you'd really do to stay alive, until you're asked? I know now that the answer for most of us is—anything."

So says a member of the Sonderkommandos, a group of Jews at the Auschwitz II–Birkenau death camp, who sent their fellow Jews to die in the gas chambers and then disposed of the ashes afterward. For this duty they were given clean sheets, extra food, cigarettes, and an extra four months of life. With the end of the war obviously drawing closer, four months might mean survival. Would you refuse this opportunity? Would I?

Tim Blake Nelson's *The Grey Zone* considers moral choices within a closed system that is wholly evil. If everyone in the death camp is destined to die, is it the good man's duty to die on schedule, or is it his duty to himself to grasp any straw? Since both choices seem certain to end in death, is it more noble to refuse or cooperate? Is hope itself a form of resistance?

These are questions no truthful person can answer without having been there. The film is inspired by the uprising of October 7, 1944, when members of the 12th Sonderkommando succeeded in blowing up two of the four crematoria at the death camp; because the ovens were never replaced, lives were saved. But other lives were lost as the Nazis used physical and mental torture to try to find out how the prisoners got their hands on gunpowder and weapons.

I have seen a lot of films about the Holocaust, but I have never seen one so immediate, unblinking, and painful in its materials. *The Grey Zone* deals with the daily details of the work gangs—who lied to prisoners, led them into gas chambers, killed them, incinerated their bodies, and disposed of the remains. All of the steps in this process are made perfectly clear in a sequence that begins with one victim accusing his Jewish guard of lying to them all, and ends with the desperate sound of hands banging against the inside of the steel doors. "Cargo," the workers called the bodies they dealt with. "We have a lot of cargo today."

The film has been adapted by Nelson from his play, and is based in part on the book *Auschwitz: A Doctor's Eyewitness Account,* by Miklos Nyiszli, a Jewish doctor who cooperated on experiments with the notorious Dr. Josef Mengele, and is portrayed in the film by Allan Corduner.

Is it a fact of human nature that we are hardwired to act for our own survival? That those able to sacrifice themselves for an ethical ideal are extraordinary exceptions to the rule? Consider a scene late in the film when Rosa and Dina (Natasha Lyonne and Mira Sorvino), two women prisoners who worked in a nearby mu-

nitions factory, are tortured to reveal the secret of the gunpowder. When ordinary methods fail, they are lined up in front of their fellow prisoners. The interrogator repeats his questions, and every time they do not answer, his arm comes down and another prisoner is shot through the head. What is the right thing to do? Betray the secrets and those who collaborated? Or allow still more prisoners to be murdered? And if all will die eventually anyway, how does that affect the choice? Is it better to die now, with a bullet to the brain, than after more weeks of dread? Or is any life at all worth having?

The film stars David Arquette, Daniel Benzali, Steve Buscemi, and David Chandler as the leaders of the Sonderkommandos, and Harvey Keitel as Muhsfeldt, an alcoholic Nazi officer in command of their unit. Although these faces are familiar, the actors disappear into their roles. The Jewish workforce continues its grim task of exterminating fellow Jews, while working on its secret plans for a revolt.

Then an extraordinary thing happens. In a gas chamber, a young girl (Kamelia Grigorova) is found still alive. Arquette rescues her from a truck before she can be taken to be burned, and now the Jews are faced with a subset of their larger dilemma: Is this one life worth saving if the girl jeopardizes the entire revolt? Perhaps not, but in a world where there seem to be no choices, she presents one, and even Dr. Nyiszli, so beloved by Mengele, helps to save the girl's life. It is as if this single life symbolizes all the others.

In a sense, the murders committed by the Nazis were not as evil as the twisted thought that went into them and the mental anguish they caused for the victims. Death occurs thoughtlessly in nature every day. But death with sadistic forethought, death with a scenario forcing the victims into impossible choices, and into the knowledge that those choices are inescapable, is mercilessly evil. The Arquette character talks of one victim: "I knew him. We were neighbors. In twenty minutes his whole family and all of its future was gone from this Earth." That victim's knowledge of his loss was worse than death.

The Grey Zone is pitiless, bleak, and despairing. There cannot be a happy ending, except that the war eventually ended. That is no consolation for its victims. It is a film about making choices that seem to make no difference, about attempting to act with honor in a closed system where honor lies dead. One can think: If nobody else knows, at least I will know. Yes, but then you will be dead, and then who will know? And what did it get you? On the other hand, to live with the knowledge that you behaved shamefully is another kind of death—the death of the human need to regard ourselves with favor. *The Grey Zone* refers to a world where everyone is covered with the grey ash of the dead, and it has been like that for so long they do not even notice anymore.

The Grifters

R, 119 m., 1991

Anjelica Huston (Lily Dillon), John Cusack (Roy Dillon), Annette Bening (Myra Langtry), Pat Hingle (Bobo Justus), Henry Jones (Simms), J. T. Walsh (Cole), Charles Napier (Hebbing). Directed by Stephen Frears and produced by Martin Scorsese, Robert Harris, and James Painten. Screenplay by Donald E. Westlake, based on the book by Jim Thompson.

Con men are more appealing than run-of-the-mill villains, who want to take your money because they are stronger or more dangerous than you are. Con men want to take it because they're smarter than you are. And there is hardly ever a con man who isn't likable, because, after all, if he can't win your confidence, how can he take your money? Movies about con men are seductive because the audience is on both sides of the moral issues: We want to see justice done, of course, but at the same time we're intrigued by the audacity of this character who is trying to outthink his opposition.

You can see some of that seductiveness at work in David Mamet's *House of Games* (1987), where a woman psychologist grows fascinated by a con man and asks him to teach her some of the tricks of his trade. Does he ever. The con man is sweet and almost gentle as he devastates his victim. In a sense, he really does like her. In Stephen Frears's *The Grifters*, there aren't any outsiders to be seduced, because the three central characters are all confidence tricksters. So they seduce each other.

The movie is based on a 1950s novel, but it's set in the present day. There are a few details that don't translate very well—today's con man probably wouldn't stay in a colorful fleabag hotel, but in a downtown executive suite—but the underlying story is universal. It involves the archetypal triangle of the lover, the loved one, and the authority figure who would separate them. The lover is Roy Dillon (John Cusack), a con man in his twenties, who isn't very good and pulls mostly small-time cons. The loved one is Myra Langtry (Annette Bening), who looks young and sexy, but is probably older than she looks and certainly more dangerous than Roy realizes. And the authority figure is Roy's mother, Lily (Anjelica Huston), who has been pulling cons since a very early age and considers everyone a potential victim. That list would certainly include her son.

Myra has knocked around the country a good deal, working as a sexy decoy for bigtime con operators. Lily has an arrangement with a major sports gambling operation and travels from one racetrack to another, placing large bets at the last minute to improve the odds. Roy isn't in their league. He's still pulling nickel-and-dime stuff like walking into a bar and getting change for a twenty dollar bill and then switching to a smaller bill. One day, a bartender catches him at it and beats him up so badly that he almost dies.

It's in his hospital room that the two women meet and unsheathe their claws. Roy doesn't realize it, but he's doomed right from the moment of their meeting, because, for each of these women, it is more important to win than to love, and poor, dumb, sentimental Roy doesn't play in that league. He loves too easily, perhaps, and the movie suggests Oedipal possibilities long before the shocking final confrontation.

The Grifters is the first American production by Stephen Frears, one of the best new British directors. His credit list is short but distinguished: *My Beautiful Laundrette, Prick Up Your Ears, Sammy and Rosie Get Laid,* and *Dangerous Liaisons.* All four films deal with labyrinths of passion, with characters deceiving others about the true nature of their loves. The story of *The Grifters* comes from a pulp novel by the recently rediscovered Jim

Thompson, a poet of *film noir,* whose books exist in a world of cynicism and despair, where characters put up a big front but are being gnawed inside by fear, guilt, and low self-esteem. The screenplay is by another distinguished crime novelist, Donald Westlake, and, for once, here is a new movie that exudes the *film noir* spirit from its very pores, instead of just adding a few cosmetic touches to a modern chase-and-crash story.

The performances are all insidiously powerful. Cusack provides a sympathetic center for the film, as a kid with a burning ambition to be good at the con game, but with no particular talent and without the ruthlessness he will need. Anjelica Huston was an Academy Award nominee as his mother, who had this child when she was a teenager, and who has never fully accepted the fact that he is her son. And Annette Bening has some of that same combination of sexiness, danger, and vulnerability you could see in Gloria Grahame in movies like *The Big Heat* and *In a Lonely Place.*

One of the strengths of *The Grifters* is how everything adds up, and it all points toward the conclusion of the film, when all secrets will be revealed and all debts collected. This is a movie of plot, not episode. It's not just a series of things that happen to the characters, but a web, a maze of consequences; by the end, when Roy and his mother are facing each other in their last desperate confrontation, the full horror of their lives is laid bare.

Why do confidence operators do what they do? Why do they need to win our love and trust, and then betray us? In *The Grifters,* it's pretty clear that they're locked into an old pattern of trust and betrayal that goes back to childhood, and that they're trying to get even. Poor Roy. He thinks he wants to be a great con man, and all he really wants is to find just one person he can safely love, one person who isn't trying to con him.

Grizzly Man

R, 103 m., 2005

As themselves: Timothy Treadwell, Amie Huguenard, Medical Examiner Franc G. Fallico, Jewel Palovak, Willy Fulton, Sam Egli. Directed by Werner Herzog and produced by Erik Nelson. Screenplay by Herzog.

"If I show weakness, I'm dead. They will take me out, they will decapitate me, they will chop me up into bits and pieces—I'm dead. So far, I persevere. I persevere."

So speaks Timothy Treadwell, balanced somewhere between the grandiose and the manic in Werner Herzog's *Grizzly Man.* He is talking about the wild bears he came to know and love during thirteen summers spent living among them in Alaska's Katmai National Park and Preserve. In the early autumn of 2003, one of the bears took him out, decapitated him, chopped him up into bits and pieces, and he was dead. The bear also killed his girlfriend.

In happier times, we see Treadwell as a guest on the David Letterman show. "Is it going to happen," Letterman asks him, "that we read a news item one day that you have been eaten by one of these bears?" Audience laughter. Later in the film, we listen to the helicopter pilot who retrieved Treadwell's bones a few days after he died: "He was treating them like people in bear costumes. He got what he deserved. The tragedy of it is, he took the girl with him."

Grizzly Man is unlike any nature documentary I've seen; it doesn't approve of Treadwell, and it isn't sentimental about animals. It was assembled by Herzog, the great German director, from some ninety hours of video that Treadwell shot in the wild, and from interviews with those who worked with him, including Jewel Palovak of Grizzly People, the organization Treadwell founded. She knew him as well as anybody.

Treadwell was a tanned, good-looking man in his thirties with a Prince Valiant haircut who could charm people and, for thirteen years, could charm bears. He was more complex than he seemed. In rambling, confessional speeches recorded while he was alone in the wilderness, he talks of being a recovering alcoholic, of his love for the bears and his fierce determination to "protect" them—although others point out that they were safe enough in a national park, and he was doing them no favor by making them familiar with humans. He had other peculiarities, including a fake Australian accent to go with his story that he was from down under and not from New York.

"I have seen this madness on a movie set before," says Herzog, who narrates his film. "I have seen human ecstasies and darkest human turmoil." Indeed, madness has been the subject of many of his films, fact and fiction, and watching Treadwell I was reminded of the ski-jumper Steiner in another Herzog doc, the man who could fly so far that he threatened to overshoot the landing area and crash in the parking lot. Or the hero of *Fitzcarraldo,* obsessed with hauling a ship across land from one river to another.

"My life is on the precipice of death," Treadwell tells the camera. Yet he sentimentalizes the bears and is moved to ecstasy by a large steaming pile of "Wendy's poop," which is still warm, he exults, and was "inside of her" just minutes earlier. He names all the bears and provides a play-by-play commentary as two of the big males fight for the right to court "Satin."

During his last two or three years in the wilderness, Treadwell was joined by his new girlfriend, Amie Huguenard. Herzog is able to find only one photograph of her, and when she appears in Treadwell's footage (rarely), her face is hard to see. Treadwell liked to give the impression that he was alone with his bears, but Herzog shows one shot that is obviously handheld—by Huguenard, presumably.

Ironically, Treadwell and Huguenard had left for home in the September when they died. Treadwell got into an argument with an Air Alaska employee, canceled his plans to fly home, returned to the "Grizzly Maze" area where most of the bears he knew were already hibernating, and was killed and eaten by an unfamiliar bear that, it appears, he photographed a few hours before his death.

The cap was on his video camera during the attack, but audio was recorded. Herzog listens to the tape in the presence of Palovak and then tells her: "You must never listen to this. You should not keep it. You should destroy it because it will be like the elephant in your room all your life." His decision not to play the audio in his film is a wise one, not only out of respect to the survivors of the victims, but because to watch him listening to it is, oddly, more effective than actually hearing it. We would hear, he tells us, Treadwell screaming for Huguenard to run for her life, and we would hear the sounds of her trying to fight off the bear by banging it with a frying pan.

The documentary is an uncommon meeting between Treadwell's loony idealism and Herzog's bleak worldview. Treadwell's footage is sometimes miraculous, as when we see his close bond with a fox that has been like his pet dog for ten years. Or when he grows angry with God because a drought has dried up the salmon run and his bears are starving. He *demands* that God make it rain and, what do you know, it does.

Against this is Herzog, on the sound track: "I believe the common character of the universe is not harmony, but hostility, chaos, and murder." And over footage of one of Treadwell's beloved bears: "This blank stare" shows not the wisdom Treadwell read into it but "only the half-bored interest in food."

"I will protect these bears with my last breath," Treadwell says. After he and Huguenard become the first and only people to be killed by bears in the park, the bear that is guilty is shot dead. His watch, still ticking, is found on his severed arm. I have a certain admiration for his courage, recklessness, idealism, whatever you want to call it, but here is a man who managed to get himself and his girlfriend eaten, and you know what? He deserves Werner Herzog.

Guelwaar
NO MPAA RATING, 115 m., 1994

Omar Seck (Gora), Mame Ndoumbe Diop (Nogoy Marie Thioune), Thierno Ndiaye (Pierre Henri Thioune [Guelwaar]), Ndiawar Diop (Barthelemy), Moustapha Diop (Aloys), Marie-Augustine Diatta (Sophie), Samba Wane (Gor Mag). Directed by Ousmane Sembene and produced by Sembene and Jacques Perrin. Screenplay by Sembene.

Most moviegoers hardly ever get the opportunity to see a film like *Guelwaar,* and even fewer take advantage of it. Does anyone care that Ousmane Sembene, the foremost African filmmaker, has made a film that tells a simple story and yet touches on some of the most difficult questions of our time? Moviegoers have little curiosity. Most of them have never seen a film about Africans, by Africans, in modern Africa, shot on location. They see no need to start now (and this indifference extends, of course, to African-Americans). Movies can show us worlds and societies we will never otherwise glimpse, but most of the time we prefer to watch slick fictions with lots of laughs and action.

Enough of the sermon. What about the movie. *Guelwaar* is the name of a man who is dead at the beginning of Sembene's film. He was, we gather, quite a guy—a district leader in Senegal who made a fiery speech against foreign aid. He felt it turned those who accepted it into slaves. Soon after, he was found dead, and by the end of the film we more or less know why he died, although this is not a whodunit.

It is, in fact, the story of his funeral. His family gathers: The older son flies home from France; a daughter who works as a prostitute returns from Dakar, the capital; and the youngest son is still in the village. Then there is a problem. Guelwaar's body disappears from the morgue.

Sembene uses this disappearance, and the search for the body, to tell us a story about modern Senegal, which is a former French colony on the west coast of Africa, with a population of about eight million. In the district where the story takes place, the majority of people are Islamic, but there is a sizable Roman Catholic minority, including Guelwaar's family. At first it is suspected that the body has been snatched by members of a fetishistic cult who might use it in their ceremonies, but there is a much more mundane explanation: Through a mixup at the morgue, Guelwaar has been confused with a dead Muslim, and has already been buried in the Islamic cemetery.

Sembene tells this story in a series of conversations which reveal, subtly and casually, how things work in modern Senegal. The Catholics and Muslims live side by side in relative harmony, but when a controversy arises there are always troublemakers who attempt to fan it up into sectarian hatred. As the Catholics march out to the cemetery to try to retrieve the body, they are met by a band of angry Muslims who intend to defend the graves of their ancestors from sacrilege.

One of the few cool heads belongs to a district policeman, himself a Muslim, but fairminded. He thinks it sensible that the misplaced body should be reburied in its rightful grave. He sets up a meeting between the priest and the Imam of the district, both reasonable men, although sometimes hotheaded. There are moments of hair-trigger tension, when the wrong word could set off a bloody fight which might spread far beyond this small local case. And when the situation is almost resolved, an officious government official arrives ("Park the Mercedes in the shade"), and tries to play to the crowd.

The struggle over the body and its burial provides Sembene's main plot line. But curling around and beneath it are many other matters. One of the most interesting encounters in the film is between the priest and a prostitute (a friend of the sister from Dakar), who tells him she is proud to be helping a brother through medical school, and to not be a beggar. She has arrived in the village wearing a revealing costume. The priest listens silently, and then simply says, "Try to put on something more decent." He does not condemn her for her prostitution, and indeed the passionate message of Sembene's film is that anything is better than begging—or accepting aid.

We learn that for long years the country fed and provided for itself. Now a drought has caused starvation. But even more fatally, Sembene suggests, the country's political bureaucracy has grown fat and distant, fed on corruption, enriched by stealing and reselling the aid shipments from the West. In a shocking scene late in the film, sacks of grain and rice (marked "Gift of the USA") are thrown in the road, and the people walk over them, in a homage to Guelwaar, who spoke against aid.

Guelwaar's words are: "Make a man dependent on your charity and you make him your slave." He argues that aid has destroyed the Senegalese economy and created a ruling class of thieves. And he shows how these facts have been obscured because political demagogues have fanned Muslim-Catholic rivalries, so that the proletariat fights among itself instead of against its exploiters.

The film is astonishingly beautiful. The serene African landscape is a backdrop for the struggle over the cemetery, and the sere colors of the landscape frame the bright colors of the African costumes. We see something of the way the people live, and what their values are, and how their traditional ways interact with the new forms of government. And it is a joy to listen to the dialogue, in which intelligent people seriously discuss important matters; not one Hollywood film in a dozen allows its characters to seem so in control of what they think and say.

Sembene's message is thought-provoking. He does not blame the hunger and poverty of Senegal on buzz-words like colonialism or racism. He says they have come because self-respect has been worn away by thirty years of living off foreign aid. Like many stories that are set in a very specific time and place, this one has universal implications.

Ousmane Sembene is seventy-one years old. This is his seventh feature. Along the way he has also made many short subjects, founded a newspaper, written a novel. I am happy to have seen two of his other films (*Black Girl* and *Xala*), and with *Guelwaar* he reminds me that movies can be an instrument of understanding, and need not always pander to what is cheapest and most superficial.

Guess Who's Coming to Dinner

NO MPAA RATING, 108 m., 1967

Spencer Tracy (Matt Drayton), Katharine Hepburn (Christina Drayton), Sidney Poitier (John Prentice), Katharine Houghton (Joey Drayton), Cecil Kellaway (Messenger Ryan), Beah Richards (Mrs. Prentice), Roy E. Glenn, Sr. (Mr. Prentice), Isabell Sanford (Tillie). Directed and produced by Stanley Kramer. Screenplay by William Rose.

Yes, there are serious faults in Stanley Kramer's *Guess Who's Coming to Dinner*, but they are overcome by the virtues of this delightfully old-fashioned film. It would be easy to tear the plot to shreds and catch Kramer in the act of copping out. But why? On its own terms, this film is a joy to see, an evening of superb entertainment.

Entertainment, I think, is the key word here. Kramer has taken a controversial subject (interracial marriage) and insulated it with every trick in the Hollywood bag. There are glamorous star performances by Katharine Hepburn and Spencer Tracy made more poignant by his death. There is shameless schmaltz (the title song, so help me, advises

folks to give a little, take a little, let your poor heart break a little, etc.). The minor roles are filled with crashing stereotypes, like a Negro maid who must be Rochester's sister and an Irish monsignor with a brogue so fey and eyes so twinkling he makes Bing Crosby look like a Protestant.

And there is the plot, borrowed from countless other drawing room comedies about "ineligible" suitors. Only this time the controversial suitor is not a socialist (*Man and Superman*), a newspaper reporter (*The Philadelphia Story*) or even a spinster (*Cactus Flower*)—but a Negro.

Of course, the Negro is Sidney Poitier. He is a noble, rich, intelligent, handsome, ethical medical expert who serves on United Nations committees when he's not hurrying off to Africa, Asia, Switzerland, and all those other places where his genius is required. During a vacation in Hawaii, he meets Katharine Houghton, and they fall in love and come home to break the news to her parents.

Hepburn takes the news rather well ("Just let me sit down a moment and I'll be all right"), but Tracy has his doubts. Although he is a liberal newspaper publisher and a crusader against prejudice, he doesn't want to be hurried into making up his mind. And that's the trouble. Poitier has to catch the 10 P.M. flight to Geneva, you see, so Tracy has to decide before then.

It is easy to ridicule this deadline as contrived and artificial, and it is easy to argue that Poitier's character is too perfect to be convincing. But neither of these aspects bothered me. The artificial deadline is a convention of drawing room comedies. It provides automatic suspense and keeps the action within a short span of time. And Poitier's "perfect Negro" is no more perfect than Houghton's perfect liberal daughter, Hepburn's perfect Rock of Gibraltar mother, and Tracy's perfect Spencer Tracy.

The things that did bother me were more subtle. Despite Poitier's reluctance, Miss Houghton insists that *his* parents also be invited to dinner. They are a pleasant middle-aged couple (Roy E. Glenn, Sr. and Beah Richards), who turn out to be the most believable characters in the story. But their presence leads to two troublesome scenes.

The first occurs when Poitier (who has been unfailingly polite and deferential to Tracy) backs his own father into a corner and lectures him. The Negro father, like the white one, opposes interracial marriage. And Poitier, who has already agreed to abide by Tracy's decision, cruelly attacks his own father's position.

The words ring false. Poitier accuses his father of being an Uncle Tom: "Your generation will always think of itself as Negro first and a man second. I think of myself as a man." In a cruel switch, he threatens to disown his father if he opposes the marriage. This speech doesn't seem consistent with Poitier's character elsewhere in the film. Contrasted with Poitier's awe of Tracy, it seems to establish the older Negro as a second-class father.

The second bothersome scene is similar to the first. Poitier's mother lectures Tracy, informing him that he really opposes the marriage because he has forgotten what it means to be in love. Tracy has successfully weathered all other arguments, but this one shakes him. After a long period of thought, he agrees to the marriage.

What it boils down to, then, is that the two fathers are overcome by implied attacks on their masculinity. The race question becomes secondary; what Tracy really has to decide is if he feels inadequate as a man. Kramer accomplishes this transition so subtly you hardly notice it. But it is the serious flaw in his plot, I think.

Still, perhaps Kramer was being more clever than we imagine. He has pointed out in interviews that his film does accomplish its purpose, after all. And it does. Here is a film about interracial marriage that has the audience throwing rice. The women in the audience can usually be counted on to identify with the love story. I suppose. But what about those men? Will love conquer prejudice? I wonder if Kramer isn't sneaking up on one of the underlying causes of racial prejudice when he implies that the fathers feel their masculinity threatened.

All of these deep profundities aside, however, let me say that *Guess Who's Coming to Dinner* is a magnificent piece of entertainment. It will make you laugh and may even make you cry. When old, gray-haired, weather-beaten Spencer Tracy turns to Katharine Hepburn and declares, by God, that he *does* remember what it is like to be in love, there is nothing to do but believe him.

H

Hagbard and Signe/
The Red Mantle

R, 92 m., 1967

Gitte Haenning (Signe), Oleg Vidov (Hagbard), Gunnar Bjornstrand (King Sigvor), Eva Dahlbeck (His Wife), Lisben Movin (Bengrerd), Johannes Meyer (Bilvis), Henning Palmer (Hake). Directed by Gabriel Axel and produced by Bent Christensen and Johan Bonnier. Screenplay by Axel and Frank Jaeger.

Hagbard and Signe is a beautiful, lean, spare film, that reaches back into the legends of the past to find its strength. I think it must be reckoned the sleeper of the year; I had not heard of it previously, either under the present title or as *The Red Mantle* (its title as the Danish entry at Cannes).

Director Gabriel Axel set his story in the year 1100 and shot entirely on location in Iceland to find the virgin landscapes of the Middle Ages. His experiment was a splendid success: From scenes of conflict, the camera often looks up to unbroken panoramas of mountains, ice, mist, and tough green vegetation.

The plot has the simplicity of legend, as if it had been retold for many years until only the most important contours remained. The film involves three brothers who come to avenge their father's death.

They fight the king's three sons with sword and spear, but the match is a standoff, and at day's end the king declares a truce. The brothers spend the night at his castle. One of them, Hagbard, falls in love with the king's daughter, Signe, and she with him.

What follows has its roots in a dozen folk tales from as many lands; I would rather praise the marvelous craft of this film. There is a battle scene halfway through that is among the most perfect and brutal I have ever seen; it ranks with the battle in Orson Welles's *Falstaff*.

In most battle scenes, we become aware that we are shown first one swordsman, then the other, but never both actually chopping at each other. Here, however, we are drawn right into the heart of battle. Then there are the horses; enormous, muscular, slow, strong warhorses. Not since the short *Dreams of the Wild Horses* have horses been shown with such effect on film.

The actors are more than accomplished. The king and queen are played by Gunnar Bjornstrand and Eva Dahlbeck, two veteran members of Ingmar Bergman's repertory company. The young lovers are physically and spiritually lovely: Gitte Haenning (Signe) is a greater beauty, in my eyes, than Pia Degermark of *Elvira Madigan.*

Two more things need to be said. The dialogue is rare and sparse; for long passages, we hear nothing but natural sounds, and when the characters do speak they say only what is necessary. This helps to establish the film as legend; talking too much would only get us bogged down. The other thing that must be mentioned is the photography by Henning Bendtsen. He places us so firmly in the breathtaking, lonely vastness of Iceland that we can believe only heroes could inhabit this land.

Hair

R, 118 m., 1979

John Savage (Claude), Beverly D'Angelo (Sheila), Dorsey Wright (Hud), Cheryl Barnes (Hud's Fiancée), Treat Williams (Berger), Annie Golden (Jeannie), Don Dacus (Woof). Directed by Milos Forman and produced by Lester Persky and Michael Butler. Screenplay by Michael Weller.

I walked into *Hair* with the gravest doubts that this artifact of 1960s social shock would transfer to our current, sleepier times. In the 1960s we went to angry musicals; now we line up for *La Cage aux Folles.* My doubts disappeared with the surge and bold authority of the first musical statement: *This is the dawning of the Age of Aquarius!*

So maybe it isn't, really, and maybe the sun set on that particular age back around the time they pinched the Watergate burglars. But Milos Forman's *Hair* opens with such confidence and joy, moves so swiftly and sustains itself so well that I wonder why I had any doubts. *Hair* is, amazingly, not a period piece but a freshly conceived and staged memory of the tribulations of the mid-sixties.

It is also a terrific musical. The songs, of

311

course, were good to begin with: The glory of "Hair" and "Let the Sun Shine In" and "Age of Aquarius" and the sly, silly warmth of "Black Boys/White Boys." But to the original music, the film version adds a story that works well with it, airy and open photography, and glorious choreography by Twyla Tharp.

I said I lost my doubts about *Hair* during "Age of Aquarius." To be more precise, they disappeared during Tharp's opening scene in Central Park, when the dancers were joined by the horses of mounted policemen. Anyone who can sit through that opening dance sequence and not be thrilled should give up musicals.

The original play, you may recall, didn't exactly have what you could call much of a plot. The screenplay, by Michael Weller, remedies that, but not too much. Weller provides a framework structured around the experiences of a young Midwestern farmboy (John Savage) who takes the bus to Manhattan to be inducted into the army and makes instant friends with a family of hippies living in Central Park.

Savage is just right as the shy, introspective kid who feels suspicious of the hippies—and, indeed, of any alternative lifestyle. But he knows nobody else in New York, so he hangs around with these kids and suddenly a vision enters his life: a beautiful girl on horseback (Beverly D'Angelo), a debutante passing through Central Park and probably out of his life.

She comes from an incredibly wealthy family, he learns. They have nothing in common. But she's drawn, sort of, to the easy freedom of the hippies. And the leader of the hippies (Treat Williams, of *Jesus Christ Superstar*) leads them all in a high-spirited invasion of the girl's debutante party. It's one of the movie's best scenes, somehow finding a fresh way to handle the old cliché of the uninvited street people at a millionaire's party.

The movie also evokes the stylistic artifacts of the flower-power time. The love beads and vests and headbands and fringed jackets and all the other styles that were only yesterday, already look more dated than costumes from the 1940s. And it remembers the conflicts in lifestyles, mostly strikingly in scenes between the young black man (Dorsey Wright) who has joined the hippies, and the mother of his child (Cheryl Barnes), whom he left behind.

The movie's final sequences center on Savage's induction, leading to the hilarious "Black Boys/White Boys" number, an omnisexual showstopper. Twyla Tharp's choreography here is wonderfully happy and grin inducing, as enlisted men rub legs under the table.

This number, like a lot of the movie, is loosely structured around the political attitudes of the Vietnam era, but the politics isn't heavy-handed. The movie's ideas are handled with grace and style. And it's interesting how it recalls *Hair*'s myths of the 1960s—especially the image of the youth culture as a repository, simultaneously, of ancient American values and the new values aborning in the Age of Aquarius.

That this time and spirit could be evoked so well and so naturally is a tribute to the director, Forman. His accomplishment is all the more remarkable when you reflect that when *Hair* first occupied a stage, the Russians were in the process of occupying Forman's native Czechoslovakia, and he was in the process of becoming a filmmaker without a country.

He has since, however, shown an uncanny feeling for the textures of American life, in his *Taking Off*, with its runaway children, in his *One Flew Over the Cuckoo's Nest*, and now in *Hair*. Maybe it's just as well that this version had to wait a decade to be filmed so Forman could be hired to do it. He brings life to the musical form in the same way that *West Side Story* did, the last time everyone was saying the movie musical was dead.

Halloween
R, 93 m., 1978

Donald Pleasence (Dr. Sam Loomis), Jamie Lee Curtis (Laurie Strode), P. J. Soles (Lynda van der Klok), and Nancy Loomis (Annie Brackett). Directed by John Carpenter and produced by Irving Yablans. Screenplay by Carpenter and Debra Hill.

I enjoy playing the audience like a piano.
       —Alfred Hitchcock

So does John Carpenter. *Halloween* is an absolutely merciless thriller, a movie so violent and scary that, yes, I *would* compare it to *Psycho*. It's a terrifying and creepy film about what one of the characters calls Evil Personified. Right. And that leads us to the one small piece of plot I'm going to describe. There's this six-year-old kid who commits a murder right at the beginning of the movie, and is sent away, and is described by his psychiatrist as someone he spent eight years trying to help, and then the next seven years trying to keep locked up. But the guy escapes. And he returns on Halloween to the same town and the same street where he committed his first murder. And while the local babysitters telephone their boyfriends and watch *The Thing* on television, he goes back into action.

Period: That's all I'm going to describe, because *Halloween* is a visceral experience—we aren't seeing the movie, we're having it happen to us. It's frightening. Maybe you don't like movies that are *really* scary: Then don't see this one. Seeing it, I was reminded of the favorable review I gave a few years ago to *The Last House on the Left,* another really terrifying thriller. Readers wrote to ask how I could possibly support such a movie. But it wasn't that I was supporting it so much as that I was describing it: You don't want to be scared? Don't see it. Credit must be paid to filmmakers who make the effort to really frighten us, to make a good thriller when quite possibly a bad one might have made as much money. Hitchcock is acknowledged as a master of suspense; it's hypocrisy to disapprove of other directors in the same genre who want to scare us too.

It's easy to create violence on the screen, but it's hard to do it well. Carpenter is uncannily skilled, for example, at the use of foregrounds in his compositions, and everyone who likes thrillers knows that foregrounds are crucial: The camera establishes the situation, and then it pans to one side, and something unexpectedly looms up in the foreground. Usually it's a tree or a door or a bush. Not always. And it's interesting how he paints his victims. They're all ordinary, everyday people—nobody's supposed to be the star and have a big scene and win an Academy Award. The performances are all the more absorbing because of that; the movie's a slice of life that is carefully painted (in drab daylights and impenetrable nighttimes) before its human monster enters the scene.

We see movies for a lot of reasons. Sometimes we want to be amused. Sometimes we want to escape. Sometimes we want to laugh,

or cry, or see sunsets. And sometimes we want to be scared. I'd like to be clear about this. If you don't want to have a really terrifying experience, don't see *Halloween.*

Hamlet
PG-13, 238 m., 1997

Kenneth Branagh (Hamlet), Derek Jacobi (Claudius), Julie Christie (Gertrude), Kate Winslet (Ophelia), Richard Briers (Polonius), Charlton Heston (Player King), Nicholas Farrell (Horatio), Michael Maloney (Laertes), Timothy Spall (Rosencrantz), Reece Dinsdale (Guildenstern), Billy Crystal (First Gravedigger), Gérard Depardieu (Reynaldo), Richard Attenborough (English Ambassador), John Gielgud (Priam), Robin Williams (Osric), Rosemary Harris (Player Queen), Judi Dench (Hecuba), Jack Lemmon (Marcellus), Brian Blessed (Ghost), John Mills (Old Norway). Directed by Branagh and produced by David Barron. Screenplay adapted by Branagh from the play by William Shakespeare.

There is early in Kenneth Branagh's *Hamlet* a wedding celebration, the Danish court rejoicing at the union of Claudius and Gertrude. The camera watches, and then pans to the right to reveal the solitary figure of Hamlet, clad in black. It always creates a little shock in the movies when the foreground is unexpectedly occupied. We realize the subject of the scene is not the wedding, but Hamlet's experience of it. And we enjoy Branagh's visual showmanship: In all of his films, he reveals his joy in theatrical gestures.

His *Hamlet* is long but not slow, deep but not difficult, and it vibrates with the relief of actors who have great things to say and the right ways to say them. And in the 70mm version, it has a visual clarity that is breathtaking. It is the first uncut film version of Shakespeare's most challenging tragedy, the first 70mm film since *Far and Away* in 1992, and at 238 minutes the second-longest major Hollywood production (one minute shorter than *Cleopatra*). Branagh's Hamlet lacks the narcissistic intensity of Laurence Olivier's (in the 1948 Academy Award winner), but the film as a whole is better, placing Hamlet in the larger context of royal politics and making him less a subject for pity.

The story provides a melodramatic stage for inner agonies. Hamlet (Branagh), the prince of Denmark, mourns the untimely death of his father. His mother, Gertrude, rushes with unseemly speed into marriage with Claudius, her husband's brother. Something is rotten in the state of Denmark. And then the ghost of Hamlet's father appears and says he was poisoned by Claudius.

What must Hamlet do? He desires the death of Claudius but lacks the impulse to action. He despises himself for his passivity. In tormenting himself he drives his mother to despair, kills Polonius by accident, speeds the kingdom to chaos, and his love, Ophelia, to madness.

What is intriguing about *Hamlet* is the ambiguity of everyone's motives. Tom Stoppard's *Rosenkrantz and Guildenstern Are Dead* famously filtered all the action through the eyes of Hamlet's treacherous school friends. But how does it all look to Gertrude? To Claudius? To the heartbroken Ophelia? The great benefit of this full-length version is that these other characters become more understandable.

The role of Claudius (Derek Jacobi) is especially enriched: In shorter versions, he is the scowling usurper who functions only as villain. Here, with lines and scenes restored, he seems more balanced and powerful. He might have made a plausible king of Denmark, had things turned out differently. Yes, he killed his brother, but regicide was not unknown in the twelfth century, and perhaps the old king was ripe for replacement; this production shows Gertrude (Julie Christie) as lustfully in love with Claudius. By restoring the original scope of Claudius's role, Branagh emphasizes court and political intrigue instead of enclosing the material in a Freudian hothouse.

The movie's very sets emphasize the role of the throne as the center of the kingdom. Branagh uses costumes to suggest the nineteenth century, and shoots his exteriors at Blenheim Castle, seat of the duke of Marlborough and Winston Churchill's childhood home. The interior sets, designed by Tim Harvey and Desmond Crowe, feature a throne room surrounded by mirrored walls, overlooked by a gallery, and divided by an elevated walkway. The set puts much of the action onstage (members of the court are constantly observing) and allows for intrigue (some of the mirrors are two-way, and lead to concealed chambers and corridors).

In this very public arena Hamlet agonizes, and is observed. Branagh uses rapid cuts to show others reacting to his words and meanings. And he finds new ways to stage familiar scenes, renewing the material. Hamlet's most famous soliloquy ("To be, or not to be . . .") is delivered into a mirror, so that his own indecision is thrust back at him. When he torments Ophelia, a most private moment, we spy on them from the other side of a two-way mirror; he crushes her cheek against the glass and her frightened breath clouds it. When he comes upon Claudius at his prayers and can kill him, many productions imagine Hamlet lurking behind a pillar in a chapel. Branagh is more intimate, showing a dagger blade insinuating itself through the mesh of a confessional.

One of the surprises of this uncut *Hamlet* is the crucial role of the play within the play. Many productions reduce the visiting troupe of actors to walk-ons; they provide a hook for Hamlet's advice to the players, and merely suggest the performance that Hamlet hopes will startle Claudius into betraying himself. Here, with Charlton Heston magnificently assured as the Player King, we listen to the actual lines of his play (which shorter versions often relegate to dumb-show at the back of the stage). We see how ingeniously and cleverly they tweak the conscience of the king, and we see Claudius's pained reactions. The episode becomes a turning point; Claudius realizes that Hamlet is on to him.

As for Hamlet, Branagh (like Mel Gibson in the 1990 film) has no interest in playing him as an apologetic mope. Branagh is an actor of exuberant physical gifts and energy (when the time comes, his King Lear will bound about the heath). Consider the scene beginning, "Oh, what a rogue and peasant slave am I . . . ," in which Hamlet bitterly regrets his inaction. The lines are delivered not in bewilderment but in mounting anger, and it is to Branagh's credit that he pulls out all the stops; a quieter Hamlet would make a tamer *Hamlet*.

Kate Winslet is touchingly vulnerable as Ophelia, red-nosed and snuffling, her world crumbling about her. Richard Briers makes Polonius not so much a foolish old man as an adviser out of his depth. Of the familiar faces, the surprise is Heston: How many great performances have we lost while he visited the

Planet of the Apes? Billy Crystal is a surprise, but effective, as the gravedigger. But Robin Williams, Jack Lemmon, and Gérard Depardieu are distractions, their performances not overcoming our shocks of recognition.

At the end of this *Hamlet*, I felt at last as if I was getting a handle on the play (I never expect to fully understand it). It has been a long journey. I read it in high school, underlining the famous lines. I saw the Richard Burton film version, and later Olivier's. I studied it in graduate school. I have seen it on stage in England and America (most memorably in Aidan Quinn's punk version, when he sprayed graffiti on the wall: "2B=?"). Zeffirelli's version with Gibson came in 1990. I learned from them all.

One of the tasks of a lifetime is to become familiar with the great plays of Shakespeare. *Hamlet* is the most opaque. Branagh's version moved me, entertained me, and made me feel for the first time at home in that doomed royal court. I may not be able to explain *Hamlet*, but at last I have a better idea than Rosencrantz and Guildenstern.

Hannah and Her Sisters

PG-13, 107 m., 1985

Woody Allen (Mickey), Michael Caine (Elliot), Mia Farrow (Hannah), Carrie Fisher (April), Barbara Hershey (Lee), Lloyd Nolan (Hannah's Father), Maureen O'Sullivan (Hannah's Mother), Daniel Stern (Dusty), Max von Sydow (Frederick), Dianne Wiest (Holly). Directed by Allen and produced by Robert Greenhut. Screenplay by Allen.

Woody Allen's *Hannah and Her Sisters*, the best movie he has ever made, is organized like an episodic novel, with acute self-contained vignettes adding up to the big picture.

Each section begins with a title or quotation on the screen, white against black, making the movie feel like a stately progression through the lives of its characters. Then the structure is exploded, time and again, by the energy and the passion of those characters: an accountant in love with his wife's sister, a TV executive who fears he is going to die, a woman whose cocaine habit has made her life a tightrope of fear, an artist who pretends to be strong but depends pitifully on his girlfriend.

By the end of the movie, the section titles and quotations have made an ironic point: We try to organize our lives according to what we have read and learned and believed in, but our plans are lost in a tumult of emotion.

The movie spans two years in the lives of its large cast of characters—New Yorkers who labor in Manhattan's two sexiest industries, art and money. It begins and ends at family Thanksgiving dinners, with the dinner in the middle of the film acting as a turning point for several lives.

It is hard to say who the most important characters are, but my memory keeps returning to Elliot, the accountant played by Michael Caine, and Lee, the artist's girlfriend, played by Barbara Hershey. Elliot is married to Hannah (Mia Farrow), but has been blind-sided with a sudden passion for Lee. She lives in a loft with the tortured artist Frederick (Max von Sydow), who treats her like his child or his student. He is so isolated from ordinary human contact that she is actually his last remaining link with reality.

Lee and Hannah have a third sister, Holly (Dianne Wiest). They form parts of a whole. Hannah is the competent, nurturing one. Lee is the emotional, sensuous earth mother. Holly is a bundle of tics and insecurities. When they meet for lunch and the camera circles them curiously, we sense that in some ways the movie knows them better than they will ever know themselves. And to talk about the movie that way is to suggest the presence of the most important two characters in the movie, whom I will describe as Woody Allen and Mickey.

Mickey is the character played by Allen; he is a neurotic TV executive who lives in constant fear of death or disease. He was married to Hannah at one time. Even after Hannah's marriage to Elliot, Mickey remains a member of the family, circling its security with a winsome yearning to belong.

The family itself centers on the three women's parents, played by Maureen O'Sullivan and Lloyd Nolan as an aging showbusiness couple who have spent decades in loving warfare over his cheating and her drinking and their mutual career decisions.

If Mickey is the character played by Woody Allen in the movie, Allen also provides another, second character in a more subtle way. The entire movie is told through his eyes and his sensibility; not Mickey's, but Allen's. From his earlier movies, especially *Annie Hall* and *Manhattan,* we have learned to recognize the tone of voice, the style of approach.

Allen approaches his material as a very bright, ironic, fussy, fearful outsider; his constant complaint is that it's all very well for these people to engage in their lives and plans and adulteries because they do not share his problem, which is that he sees through everything, and what he sees on the other side of everything is certain death and disappointment.

Allen's writing and directing style is so strong and assured in this film that the actual filmmaking itself becomes a narrative voice, just as we sense Henry James behind all of his novels, or William Faulkner and Iris Murdoch, behind theirs.

The movie is not a comedy, but it contains big laughs, and it is not a tragedy, although it could be if we thought about it long enough. It suggests that modern big-city lives are so busy, so distracted, so filled with ambition and complication that there isn't time to stop and absorb the meaning of things. Neither tragedy nor comedy can find a place to stand; there are too many other guests at the party.

And yet, on reflection, there is a tragedy buried in *Hannah and Her Sisters,* and that is the fact of Mickey's status as the perennial outsider. The others get on with their lives, but Mickey is stuck with his complaints. Not only is he certain there is no afterlife, he is very afraid that this life might also be a sham. How he ever married Hannah in the first place is a mystery; it must have been an intermediate step on his journey to his true role in life, as the ex-husband and hanger-on.

There is a scene in the movie where Michael Caine confronts Barbara Hershey and tells her that he loves her. She is stunned, does not know what to say, but does not categorically deny that she has feelings for him. After she leaves him, he stands alone on the street, ecstatic, his face glowing, saying "I've got my answer! I've got my answer!"

Underlying all of *Hannah and Her Sisters* is the envy of Mickey (and Woody) that anyone could actually be happy enough and lucky enough to make such a statement. And yet, by the end of the movie, in his own way, Mickey has his answer, too.

Happiness

NO MPAA RATING, 140 m., 1998

Jane Adams (Joy Jordan), Lara Flynn Boyle (Helen Jordan), Cynthia Stevenson (Trish Maplewood), Dylan Baker (Bill Maplewood), Philip Seymour Hoffman (Allen), Camryn Manheim (Kristina), Louise Lasser (Mona Jordan), Ben Gazzara (Lenny Jordan), Rufus Read (Billy Maplewood), Jared Harris (Vlad), Jon Lovitz (Andy Kornbluth), Elizabeth Ashley (Diane Freed), Marla Maples (Ann Chambeau). Directed by Todd Solondz and produced by Ted Hope and Christine Vachon. Screenplay by Solondz.

Todd Solondz's *Happiness* is a film that perplexes its viewers, even those who admire it, because it challenges the ways we attempt to respond to it. Is it a portrait of desperate human sadness? Then why are we laughing? Is it an ironic comedy? Then why its tenderness with these lonely people? Is it about depravity? Yes, but why does it make us suspect, uneasily, that the depraved are only seeking what we all seek, but with a lack of ordinary moral vision?

In a film that looks into the abyss of human despair, there is the horrifying suggestion that these characters may *not* be grotesque exceptions, but may in fact be part of the stream of humanity. Whenever a serial killer or a sex predator is arrested, we turn to the paper to find his neighbors saying that the monster "seemed just like anyone else."

Happiness is a movie about closed doors—apartment doors, bedroom doors, and the doors of the unconscious. It moves back and forth between several stories, which often link up. It shows us people who want to be loved, and who never will be—because of their emotional incompetence and arrested development. There are lots of people who do find love and fulfillment, but they are not in this movie.

We meet Joy (Jane Adams), who has just broken up with the loser she's been dating (Jon Lovitz). He gives her a present, an engraved reproduction ashtray he got through mail order, but after she thanks him ("It almost makes me want to learn to smoke"), he viciously grabs it back: "This is for the girl who loves me for who I am."

We meet Allen (Philip Seymour Hoffman), who describes pornographic sexual fantasies to his psychiatrist (Dylan Baker) and then concludes that he will never realize them because he is too boring. The psychiatrist, named Bill, is indeed bored. Later he buys a teen-idol magazine and masturbates while looking at the photos.

We meet Joy's two sisters, Trish (Cynthia Stevenson) and Helen (Lara Flynn Boyle). Trish is a chirpy housewife, who is married to Bill the psychiatrist but knows nothing of his pedophilia. Helen is a poet who drops names ("Salman is on the line") and describes the countless men who lust for her. The parents of the three sisters, Mona and Lenny (Louise Lasser and Ben Gazzara), have been married for years, but now Lenny wants to leave. Not to fool around. Just to be alone.

We meet Kristina (Camryn Manheim), a fat girl who lives down the hall from the solitary Allen, and knocks on his door to announce that Pedro, the doorman, has been murdered. (His body has been dismembered and put in plastic bags: "Everyone uses Baggies. That's why we can relate to this crime.") Allen doesn't want to know. He leafs through porno magazines, gets drunk, and makes obscene phone calls. One of his calls goes to the woman he fantasizes about. It is Helen, the "popular" sister, who enjoys his heavy breathing and calls him back.

We get the sense of warehouses of strangers—of people stacked into the sky in lonely apartments, each one hiding secrets. We watch in sadness and unease as Bill the shrink attends his son Billy's Little League game and becomes enraptured by one of his teammates. When the other boy has a "sleepover" with Billy, Bill drugs his family and molests the young boy (not on-screen).

Later, there is a heartbreaking conversation between Billy and his father. (Billy is isolated in close-up and we assume the young actor is reading the lines without knowing what the older actor is saying.) Their talk lingers in uneasy memory. The boy has been told at school that his father is a molester. He asks his dad if it is true. His father says it is. In a scene of pain and sadness, the boy asks more questions and the father answers simply, briefly, and com-pletely honestly. A friend who saw the movie told me, "Instead of lying, he kept telling him the truth, regardless of how hard that was for both of them. The honesty may be the one thing that saves the son from the immense damage done by the father." Well, I hope so.

Happiness belongs to the emerging genre of the New Geek Cinema, films that occupy the shadowland between tragedy and irony. Todd Solondz also made *Welcome to the Dollhouse* (1996), about an unpopular eleven-year-old girl who defiantly improvises survival tactics. *Happiness* is harder to take, and yet equally attentive to the suffering of characters who see themselves outside the mainstream—geeks, if you will, whose self-images are formed by the conviction that the more people know about them, the less people will like them.

Why see the film? *Happiness* is *about* its unhappy characters in a way that helps us see them a little more clearly, to feel sorry for them, and at the same time to see how closely tragedy and farce come together in the messiness of sexuality. Does *Happiness* exploit its controversial subjects? Finally, no: It sees them as symptoms of desperation and sadness. It is more exploitative to create a child molester as a convenient villain, as many movies do; by disregarding his humanity and seeing him as an object, such movies do the same thing that a molester does.

These are the kinds of thoughts *Happiness* inspires. It is not a film for most people. It is certainly for adults only. But it shows Todd Solondz as a filmmaker who deserves attention, who hears the unhappiness in the air and seeks its sources.

Hardcore

R, 106 m., 1979

George C. Scott (Jake VanDorn), Peter Boyle (Andy Mast), Season Hubley (Niki), Dick Sargent (Wes DeJong), Leonard Gaines (Ramada), David Nichols (Kurt), Gary Rand Graham (Tod), Larry Block (Burrows). Directed by Paul Schrader and produced by Buzz Feitshans. Screenplay by Schrader.

Hardcore is said to be the story of a father's search for a daughter who has disappeared into the underworld of pornography and prostitution. That does indeed describe its beginning and ending. But there are moments in between when it becomes something much more interesting: The story of a tentative, trusting human relationship between the father and the young prostitute he enlists in his search.

The man is played by George C. Scott, the girl by Season Hubley. They have moments in the movie when they talk, really talk, about what's important to them—and we're reminded of how much movie dialogue just repeats itself, movie after movie, year after year. There's a scene in *Hardcore* where the man (who is a strict Calvinist) and the prostitute (who began selling herself in her early teens) talk about sex, religion, and morality, and we're almost startled by the belief and simple poetry in their words.

This relationship, between two people with nothing in common, who meet at an intersection in a society where many have nothing in common, is at the heart of the movie, and makes it important. It is preceded and followed by another of those story ideas that Paul Schrader seems to generate so easily. His movies are about people with values, in conflict with society. He wrote *Taxi Driver* and *Rolling Thunder* and wrote and directed *Blue Collar*. All three are about people prepared to defend (with violence, if necessary) their steadfast beliefs.

The Scott character is a fundamentalist from Grand Rapids, Michigan—Schrader's own hometown. The opening scenes establish the family setting, at Christmas, with a fairly thick theological debate going on around the dinner table. (The small boy listening so solemnly, Schrader has said, can be taken for himself.) A few days later, Scott's daughter leaves home for a church rally in California. She never returns. Scott hires a private detective (Peter Boyle) to try to find her, and Boyle does find her—in an 8-millimeter porno movie. Can it be traced? Boyle says not: "Nobody made it. Nobody sold it. Nobody *sees* it. It doesn't exist."

But Scott vows to follow his daughter into the sexual underworld and bring her back. His efforts to trace her, through San Francisco and Los Angeles and San Diego, make *Hardcore* into a sneakily fascinating guided tour through massage parlors, whorehouses, and the world of porno movies. Schrader some-

times seems to be having it both ways, here: Scott is repelled by the sex scenes he explores, but is the movie?

That doesn't matter so much after he meets Niki (Season Hubley), who might know some people who might know where his daughter is. She is in many ways like all the other lost young girls who drift to California and disappear. But she has intelligence and a certain insight into why she does what she does, and so their talks together become occasions for mutual analysis.

She has a deep psychological need for a father figure, a need she thinks Scott can meet. She also has insights into Scott's own character, insights his life hasn't previously made clear to him. There's a scene near the waterfront in San Diego that perfectly illuminates both of their personalities, and we realize how rare it is for the movies to show us people who are speaking in real words about real things.

The movie's ending is a mess, a combination of cheap thrills, a chase, and a shootout, as if Schrader wasn't quite sure how to escape from the depths he found. The film's last ten minutes, in fact, are mostly action, the automatic resolution of the plot; the relationship between Scott and Hubley ends without being resolved, and in bringing his story to a "satisfactory" conclusion, Schrader doesn't speak to the deeper and more human themes he's introduced. Too bad. But *Hardcore*, flawed and uneven, contains moments of pure revelation.

Harlan County, U.S.A.
PG, 103 m., 1976

A documentary directed and produced by Barbara Kopple.

One moment among many in *Harlan County, U.S.A.*: The striking miners are holding an all-day rally and picnic. A big tent has been pitched, and it's filled with people—some of them familiar to us by now, others new. There are speeches and songs and union battle cries, and then an old woman takes the microphone. The words she sings are familiar: *They say in Harlan County, there are no neutrals there. You'll either be a union man or a thug for Sheriff Blair.* And then the whole tent-full joins in the chorus: *Which side are you on?*

The woman who is leading the singing wrote the song fifty years ago, during an earlier strike in the county the miners call "Bloody Harlan." And here it is 1973, in a county where the right of workers to organize has presumably long since been won, and the song is not being sung out of nostalgia. It is being sung by striking coal miners in Harlan County, where it still applies.

That's the most uncomfortable lesson we learn in Barbara Kopple's magnificent documentary: That there are still jobs for scabs and strike breakers, that union organizers still get shot at and sometimes get killed, and that in Harlan County, Kentucky, it still matters very much which side you're on. And so a song we know best from old Pete Seeger records suddenly proves itself still frighteningly relevant.

The movie, which won the 1976 Academy Award for best feature-length documentary, was shot over a period of eighteen months in eastern Kentucky, after the miners at the Brookside mine voted to join the United Mine Workers. The Duke Power Company refused to sign the UMW contract, fought the strike, and was fought in turn by the miners and—most particularly—their wives.

Barbara Kopple and her crew stayed in Harlan County during that entire time, living in the miners' homes and recording the day-by-day progress of the strike. It was a tumultuous period, especially since the mine workers' union itself was deep in the midst of the Tony Boyle-Jock Yablonsky affair. But what emerges from the film is not just the documentation of a strike, but an affecting, unforgettable portrait of a community.

The cameras go down into the mines to show us the work, which is backbreaking, dirty, and brutal. We get to meet many of the miners, and to notice a curious thing about the older ones: They tend to talk little, as if their attentions are turned inward to the source of the determination that takes them back down the mine every day. Their wives, on the other hand, seem born to lead strikes. The film shows them setting up committees, organizing picket lines, facing (and sometimes reciprocating) violence, and becoming eloquent orators.

Ms. Kopple is a feminist, and her work includes *Year of the Women*. In *Harlan County*, though, she doesn't seem to have gone looking for examples of capable, competent, strong women: They were simply inescapable. There are talents, energies, and intelligences revealed in this film that could, if we would tap them, transform legislatures and bring wholesale quantities of common sense to public life. There are tacticians, strategists, and philosophers in *Harlan County, U.S.A.* who make the UMW theoreticians look tame—and the company spokesmen look callow and inane.

The movie is a great American document, but it's also entertaining; Kopple structures her material to provide tension, brief but vivid characterizations, and dramatic confrontations (including one incredibly charged moment when the sheriff attempts to lead a caravan of scabs past the picket line). There are gunshots in the film, and a death, and also many moments of simple warmth and laughter. The many union songs on the sound track provide a historical context, and also help Kopple achieve a fluid editing rhythm. And most of all there are the people in the film, those amazing people, so proud and self-reliant and brave.

Harry and Tonto

PG, 115 m., 1974

Art Carney (Harry), Ellen Burstyn (Shirley), Chief Dan George (Indian), Geraldine Fitzgerald (Jessie). Directed and produced by Paul Mazursky. Screenplay by Mazursky and Josh Greenfield.

Paul Mazursky's *Harry and Tonto* tells the story of a feisty seventy-two-year-old who is carried forcibly from his New York apartment one step ahead of the wrecker's ball. He was happy with his life in the city (apart from the four muggings so far this year) and content to talk to his old cronies and to his cat, Tonto. But life without a home isn't easy. He goes for a while to live with his son on Long Island, where he's welcomed, sort of, into a household on the edge of insanity. One of his grandsons thinks the other one is crazy. The other won't respond because, you see, he has taken a vow of silence. Harry sizes up the situation, packs Tonto in a carrying case, and hits the road. The road becomes a strange and wonderful place for Harry, mostly because of his own resilient personality. He's played by

Art Carney as a man of calm philosophy, gentle humor, and an acceptance of the ways people can be. He is also not a man in a hurry. When he can't carry Tonto onto an airplane, he takes the bus. When the bus can't wait for Tonto to relieve himself, he buys a used car and picks up hitchhikers.

One of them is a young girl who becomes his friend. She talks of her life, and he talks of his, including his long-ago romance with a member of the Isadora Duncan troupe. The last he'd heard of her, she was living in Peru, Indiana, as the wife of a pharmacist. The girl talks him into stopping in Indiana and looking the old woman up. And he does so, in a scene of rare warmth and tenderness. The woman, Jessie (played by Geraldine Fitzgerald), has a very shaky memory, but she does recall being a dancer, and in the calm of the recreation room at her nursing home, the old couple dances together one last time.

And then Harry's back on the road to Chicago, where he has a daughter who runs a bookstore. He spends a few days with her, walking on the beach and talking things over. His silent grandson has broken his vow and flown to Chicago to try to talk the old man into coming back to New York. But, no, Harry doesn't think he will. ("You're talking now?" he asks his grandson. "Garbo speaks," the kid shrugs.)

He heads vaguely westward. His young hitchhiker has fallen in love with his grandson, and they think they'll aim for a commune in Colorado. Harry gives them a lift because that's more or less where he's going, but he declines, just now, to join the commune. He gives them his car, hitches a ride with a Las Vegas hooker, is (to his vast surprise) seduced by her, has a good time in Vegas, and, alas, is arrested for having a few too many.

This leads to the film's most hilarious scene. Harry is tossed into a cell already occupied by an ancient Indian (Chief Dan George) who has been arrested for practicing medicine without a license. The two old men gravely discuss recent television shows and the problem of bursitis, and the chief cures Harry's aching shoulder in return for an electric blender. Chief Dan George is so solemn, so understated, with Mazursky's dialogue that the result is a great comic scene.

Harry and Tonto drift on west toward the Pacific, and we begin to get the sense that this hasn't been your ordinary road picture, but a sort of farewell voyage by a warm and good old man who is still, at seventy-two, capable of being thankful for the small astonishments offered by life. The achievement is partly Mazursky's, partly Carney's.

Mazursky has established himself as the master of a kind of cinema he calls "serious comedy"—movies that make us laugh and yet have a special attitude toward their material and American society. His earlier films have included *Bob & Carol & Ted & Alice* and the remarkable *Blume in Love*.

Art Carney has, of course, fashioned a distinguished career for himself on the stage after all those years as Norton on *The Honeymooners*. Here, he flowers as a movie star. The performance is totally original, all his own, and worthy of the Academy Award it received. It's not easy to make comedies that work as drama, too. But Carney's acting is so perceptive that it helps this material succeed.

Harry Potter and the Chamber of Secrets

PG, 161 m., 2002

Daniel Radcliffe (Harry Potter), Rupert Grint (Ron Weasley), Emma Watson (Hermione Granger), Jason Isaacs (Lucius Malfoy), Alan Rickman (Professor Snape), Maggie Smith (Professor McGonagall), Robbie Coltrane (Hagrid the Giant), David Bradley (Mr. Argus Filch), Kenneth Branagh (Gilderoy Lockhart), Miriam Margolyes (Professor Sprout), John Cleese (Nearly Headless Nick), Richard Harris (Professor Dumbledore), Tom Felton (Draco Malfoy), Bonnie Wright (Ginny Weasley), Harry Melling (Dudley Dursley). Directed by Chris Columbus and produced by David Heyman. Screenplay by Steve Kloves, based on the book by J. K. Rowling.

The first movie was the setup, and this one is the payoff. *Harry Potter and the Chamber of Secrets* leaves all of the explanations of wizardry behind and plunges quickly into an adventure that's darker and scarier than anything in the first Harry Potter movie. It's also richer: The second in a planned series of seven Potter films is brimming with invention and new ideas, and its Hogwarts School seems to expand and deepen before our very eyes into a world large enough to conceal unguessable secrets.

What's developing here, it's clear, is one of the most important franchises in movie history, a series of films that consolidate all of the advances in computer-aided animation, linked to the extraordinary creative work of J. K. Rowling, who has created a mythological world as grand as *Star Wars*, but filled with more wit and humanity. Although the young wizard Harry Potter is nominally the hero, the film remembers the golden age of moviemaking, when vivid supporting characters crowded the canvas. The story is about personalities, personal histories, and eccentricity, not about a superstar superman crushing the narrative with his egotistical weight.

In the new movie, Harry (Daniel Radcliffe, a little taller and deeper-voiced) returns with his friends Ron Weasley (Rupert Grint) and Hermione Granger (Emma Watson, in the early stages of babehood). They sometimes seem to stand alone amid the alarming mysteries of Hogwarts, where even the teachers, even the august headmaster Albus Dumbledore (Richard Harris), even the learned professors Snape (Alan Rickman) and McGonagall (Maggie Smith), even the stalwart Hagrid the Giant (Robbie Coltrane) seem mystified and a little frightened by the school's dread secrets.

Is there indeed a Chamber of Secrets hidden somewhere in the vast pile of Hogwarts? Can it only be opened by a descendent of Salazar Slytherin, the more sinister of the school's cofounders? Does it contain a monster? Has the monster already escaped, and is it responsible for paralyzing some of the students, whose petrified bodies are found in the corridors, and whose bodies are carried to the infirmary still frozen in a moment of time? Do the answers to these questions originate in events many years ago, when even the ancient Dumbledore was (marginally) younger? And does a diary by a former student named Tom Marvolo Riddle—a book with nothing written in it, but whose pages answer questions in a ghostly handwriting—provide the clues that Harry and his friends need? (Answer to all of the above: probably.)

This puzzle could be solved in a drab and routine movie with characters wandering down old stone corridors, but one of the pleasures of Chris Columbus's direction of *Harry Potter and the Chamber of Secrets* is how visually alive it is. This is a movie that answers any objection to computer animation with glorious or creepy sights that blend convincingly with the action. Hogwarts itself seems to have grown since the first movie, from a largish sort of country house into a thing of spires and turrets, vast rooms and endlessly convoluted passageways, lecture halls and science labs, with as much hidden below the ground as is visible above it. Even the Quidditch game is held in a larger stadium (maybe rich alumni were generous?). There are times, indeed, when the scope of Hogwarts seems to approach that of Gormenghast, the limitless edifice in the trilogy by Mervyn Peake that was perhaps one of Rowling's inspirations.

The production designer is Stuart Craig, returning from *Harry Potter and the Sorcerer's Stone*. He has created (there is no other way to put it) a world here, a fully realized world with all the details crowded in, so that even the corners of the screen are intriguing. This is one of the rare recent movies you could happily watch with the sound turned off, just for the joy of his sets, the costumes by Judianna Makovsky and Lindy Hemming, and the visual effects (the Quidditch match seems even more three-dimensional, the characters swooping across the vast field, as Harry finds himself seriously threatened by the odious Malfoy).

There are three new characters this time, one delightful, one conceited, one malevolent. Professor Sprout (Miriam Margolyes) is on the biology faculty and teaches a class on the peculiar properties of the mandrake plant, made all the more amusing by students of John Donne who are familiar with the additional symbolism of the mandrake only hinted at in class. The more you know about mandrakes, the funnier Sprout's class is.

She is the delightful addition. The conceited new faculty member, deliciously cast, is Gilderoy Lockhart (Kenneth Branagh), author of the autobiography *Magical Me*, who thinks of himself as a consummate magician but whose spell to heal Harry's broken arm has unfortunate results. And then there is Lucius Malfoy (Jason Isaacs), father of the supercilious Draco, who skulks about as if he should be hated just on general principles.

These characters and plot elements draw together in late action sequences of genuine power, which may be too intense for younger viewers. There is a most alarming confrontation with spiders and a scary late duel with a dragon, and these are handled not as jolly family movie episodes, but with the excitement of a mainstream thriller. While I am usually in despair when a movie abandons its plot for a third act given over entirely to action, I have no problem with the way *Harry Potter and the Chamber of Secrets* ends, because it has been pointing toward this ending, hinting about it, preparing us for it, all the way through. What a glorious movie.

Harry Potter and the Sorcerer's Stone

PG, 152 m., 2001

Daniel Radcliffe (Harry Potter), Rupert Grint (Ronald Weasley), Emma Watson (Hermione Granger), Tom Felton (Draco Malfoy), Richard Harris (Albus Dumbledore), Maggie Smith (Professor Minerva McGonagall), Alan Rickman (Professor Severus Snape), Ian Hart (Professor Quirrell), Robbie Coltrane (Gamekeeper Rubeus Hagrid), Julie Walters (Mrs. Weasley), Harry Melling (Dudley Dursley), Warwick Davis (Professor Flitwick), Zoe Wanamaker (Madame Hooch). Directed by Chris Columbus and produced by David Heyman. Screenplay by J. K. Rowling and Steven Kloves, based on the book by Rowling.

Harry Potter and the Sorcerer's Stone is a red-blooded adventure movie, dripping with atmosphere, filled with the gruesome and the sublime, and surprisingly faithful to the novel. A lot of things could have gone wrong, and none of them have: Chris Columbus's movie is an enchanting classic that does full justice to a story that was a daunting challenge.

The novel by J. K. Rowling was muscular and vivid, and the danger was that the movie would make things too cute and cuddly. It doesn't. Like an *Indiana Jones* for younger viewers, it tells a rip-roaring tale of supernatural adventure, where colorful and eccentric characters alternate with scary stuff like a three-headed dog, a pit of tendrils known as the Devil's Snare, and a two-faced immortal who drinks unicorn blood. Scary, yes, but not too scary—just scary enough.

Three high-spirited, clear-eyed kids populate the center of the movie. Daniel Radcliffe plays Harry Potter, he with the round glasses, and like all of the young characters, he looks much as I imagined him, but a little older. He once played David Copperfield on the BBC, and whether Harry will be the hero of his own life in this story is much in doubt at the beginning. Deposited as a foundling on a suburban doorstep, he is raised by his aunt and uncle as a poor relation, then summoned by a blizzard of letters to become a student at Hogwarts School, an Oxbridge for magicians.

Our first glimpse of Hogwarts sets the tone for the movie's special effects. Although computers can make anything look realistic, too much realism would be the wrong choice for *Harry Potter*, which is a story in which everything, including the sets and locations, should look a little made-up. The school, rising on ominous Gothic battlements from a moonlit lake, looks about as real as Xanadu in *Citizen Kane*, and its corridors, cellars, and Great Hall, although in some cases making use of real buildings, continue the feeling of an atmospheric book illustration.

At Hogwarts, Harry makes two friends and an enemy. The friends are Hermione Granger (Emma Watson), whose merry face and tangled curls give Harry nudges in the direction of lightening up a little, and Ronald Weasley (Rupert Grint), all pluck, luck, and untamed talents. The enemy is Draco Malfoy (Tom Felton), who will do anything, and plenty besides, to be sure his house places first at the end of the year.

The story you either already know or do not want to know. What is good to know is that the adult cast, a who's who of British actors, play their roles more or less as if they believed them. There is a broad style of British acting, developed in Christmas pantomimes, that would have been fatal to this material; these actors know that, and dial down to just this side of too much. Watch Alan Rickman drawing out his words until they seem ready to snap, yet somehow staying in character.

Maggie Smith, still in the prime of Miss Jean Brodie, is Professor Minerva McGonagall, who assigns newcomers like Harry to one of the school's four houses. Richard Harris is Headmaster Dumbledore, his beard so long that in an Edward Lear poem birds would nest in it. Robbie Coltrane is the gamekeeper, Hagrid, who has a record of misbehavior and a way of saying very important things and then not believing that he said them.

Computers *are* used, exuberantly, to create a plausible look in the gravity-defying action scenes. Readers of the book will wonder how the movie visualizes the crucial game of Quidditch. The game, like so much else in the movie, is more or less as I visualized it, and I was reminded of Stephen King's theory that writers practice a form of telepathy, placing ideas and images in the heads of their readers. (The reason some movies don't look like their books may be that some producers don't read them.)

If Quidditch is a virtuoso sequence, there are other set pieces of almost equal wizardry. A chess game with life-size, deadly pieces. A room filled with flying keys. The pit of tendrils, already mentioned, and a dark forest where a loathsome creature threatens Harry but is scared away by a centaur. And the dark shadows of Hogwarts's library, cellars, hidden passages, and dungeons, where an invisibility cloak can keep you out of sight but not out of trouble.

During *Harry Potter and the Sorcerer's Stone,* I was pretty sure I was watching a classic, one that will be around for a long time, and make many generations of fans. It takes the time to be good. It doesn't hammer the audience with easy thrills, but cares to tell a story and to create its characters carefully. Like *The Wizard of Oz, Willy Wonka and the Chocolate Factory, Star Wars,* and *E.T.,* it isn't just a movie but a world with its own magical rules. And some excellent Quidditch players.

The Haunting of M

NO MPAA RATING, 98 m., 1981

Sheelagh Gilbey (Marianna), Nini Pitt (Halina), Evie Garratt (Daria), Alan Hay (Karol), Jo Scott Matthews (Aunt Teresa), William Bryan (Marion), Isolde Cazalet (Yola). Written, directed, and produced by Anna Thomas.

Anna Thomas's *The Haunting of M* is an absolutely spellbinding ghost story in the late-Victorian tradition of Henry James, M. R. James, and that forgotten master, Oliver Onions. It is not, that is to say, concerned with blood and gore and shock effects. It works more insidiously upon our imaginations. And like all great ghost stories, it finds the correct balance between eroticism and fear.

The classic ghosts of literature are usually not there simply to frighten us. They come attached to strong sexual connotations. They threaten to seduce us because (in an ironic twist) they can see through us. They belong to the next life and know all our weaknesses and secrets. If we surrender to them, perhaps we can obtain forbidden pleasures and dangerous knowledge.

This cerebral approach to ghosts is deliciously attractive to me, and perhaps that is why I admire *The Haunting of M* so much. It is a languorous, visually beautiful film set in a small, perfectly tended Scottish castle at the beginning of this century. The castle's rooms are filled with flowers and solemn young ladies who whisper secrets to one another. On the sound track, the romantic eroticism of Mahler gives everything a tone of impending discovery.

By the time a character solemnly observes, "Someone is walking in this house at night," we suspect this is the simple truth. We think we have already seen him. He is a young man with a yearning, lonely look on his face, and he has inexplicably appeared in a photograph of the family. His clothes are forty years out of date.

Who is he? His name is Marian. He was the lover of the family's spiteful old grandmother, who was forbidden to marry him, and who is even now hanging onto the last shreds of life. He threatens to become (if she will have him) the ghostly lover of the woman's granddaughter. There are glances across a room at nightfall, and a rendezvous on a foggy lake . . . and the scene where the ghost and the girl reach out their hands to each other is as emotionally charged as anything of the sort I can remember.

Apart from its appeal as a thinking person's ghost story, *The Haunting of M* is also an extraordinary film to watch. It achieves a certain deliberate tone in its camera placements and editing rhythms, so that the solemnity of its supernatural content is not interrupted by flashy distractions.

Anna Thomas, who wrote and directed it, seems to have been completely sure of what she wanted before she began filming; there's no moment when the film seems to falter or lose its direction. Indeed, its singleness of intention from beginning to end is one of the reasons it works.

The film was photographed by Gregory Nava, Thomas's husband. Both are known to Chicago Film Festival audiences; his own first film, *The Confessions of Amans,* won the best first-feature prize here four years ago.

They make their films on very little money, but there's no moment in *The Haunting of M* when you're aware of that. Every location is authentic, the costumes and decor are all from the period, and Thomas has filled the frame with an astonishing variety of visual delights: with fire eaters, circus elephants, a ballroom scene, a formal dinner, portentous arrivals of horse-drawn carriages, and, of course, the mystical presence of the ghost.

When this film played here in the 1979 Chicago Film Festival, I wrote that it was "the most audacious, ambitious, and generally successful debut film since *Citizen Kane.*" I meant that. I do not mean to say it's as great a film as *Citizen Kane,* but that it was as joyous a debut, because Thomas seems to be celebrating the gift of filmmaking at the limit of her powers.

The Haunting of M is obviously the work of someone who loves what you can do with film. It wants to astonish us with pomp and pride, seduce us with music, let us eavesdrop on old family secrets, and engage in a fantasy of ghosts. Its actors are almost all unknowns, and some of their accents are shaky, but they are so fresh-faced, so earnestly naive in their solemn confidences, that we believe them. Something may be walking in the house at night.

Heartbreakers

R, 98 m., 1984

Peter Coyote (Arthur Blue), Nick Mancuso (Eli Kahn), Carole Laure (Liliane), Max Gail (King), Carol Wayne (Candy), James Laurenson (Terry Ray), Jamie Rose (Libby), Kathryn Harrold (Cyd). Directed by Bobby Roth and produced by Bob Weis and Roth. Screenplay by Roth.

You can play the field only so long. Then you get stuck in it. You become a person so adept at avoiding commitment that it eventually becomes impossible for you to change your own rules, and so there you are, trapped in your precious freedom. Bobby Roth's *Heartbreakers* is about a group of people like that, a mixed bag of loners that includes a couple of artists, a businessman, a gallery owner, an aerobics instructor, and a model who specializes in telephone sex. During the course of a few weeks, their lives cross in ways that make it particularly hard for each one of them to deny his own unhappiness.

The movie stars Peter Coyote as an angry young artist and Nick Mancuso as his best friend, a businessman who is confused about women and a great many other things. They've been pals for a long time, through good times and bad, but the one thing they've never been able to do is break down and talk about what they're really feeling. During the course of the film, they both fall in love with a beautiful young woman (Carole Laure) who works in an art gallery, and whose body is available but whose mind always seems to be somewhere else.

These three characters are in a movie populated with a lot of other interesting characters, the sort of mixed bag of people who find themselves thrown together in a big city like Los Angeles. Kathryn Harrold plays Coyote's longtime lover, who finally can't take his irresponsibility any longer and moves in with another artist (Charles King), who is big and powerful but surprisingly gentle—his character is developed against type, in interesting ways. Jamie Rose plays an aerobics instructor who is attracted to Mancuso, but he is attracted to Laure, although not in a way that is likely to get him anywhere.

All of the threads of these lives seem to come together during one long night that Mancuso and Coyote spend with the busty, mid-thirties blond who models for Coyote's kinky paintings. She is played by Carol Wayne, who had regular walk-ons on the Johnny Carson program until she drowned in Mexico not long after completing her work on this movie. Her performance is so good, so heartbreaking, if you will, that it pulls the whole movie together; her character's willingness to talk about what she really feels places the other characters in strong contrast.

When we first see her, she's an enigma at the

edge of the screen—a seemingly dumb blonde with big boobs who dresses up in leather to model for Coyote's strange, angry paintings. Later, the two men, adrift and unhappy about their respective love lives, end up in her apartment, and what begins as a ménage à trois ends up as her own startlingly direct confessional. She makes a frank assessment of her body, her appearance, her prospects. She talks about what she had hoped for from life, and what she has received. There is an uncanny feeling that, to some degree, we are listening here to the real Carol Wayne, the real person beneath the image on the Carson show. It is one of the best movie scenes in a long time.

The rest of the movie is also very good, in the way it examines the complex relationships in its Los Angeles world of art, sex, and business, and in the way it shows how arid the Mancuso-Coyote buddy relationship is. The people in this movie might seem glamorous if you glimpsed just a small corner of their lives. But *Heartbreakers* sees them whole, and mercilessly.

Heartland

PG, 95 m., 1981

Conchata Ferrell (Elinore Randall), Rip Torn (Clyde Stewart), Barry Primus (Jack), Lilia Skala (Grandma), Megan Folsom (Jerrine). Directed by Richard Pearce and produced by Annick Smith, Michael Hausman, and Beth Ferris. Screenplay by Ferris.

Richard Pearce's *Heartland* is a big, robust, joyous movie about people who make other movie heroes look tentative. It takes place in 1910, out in the unsettled frontier lands of Wyoming, and it's about a determined young widow who packs up her daughter and moves out west to take a job as the housekeeper on a ranch. At first she is completely baffled by the rancher who has hired her ("I can't talk about anything with that man"), but in the end she marries him and digs in to fight an endless battle with the seasons, the land, and the banks.

A movie newcomer named Conchata Ferrell plays the widow, Elinore Randall. She's a big-boned, clear-eyed, wide-hipped woman of about thirty who makes us realize that most of the women in Westerns look as if they're about to collapse under the strain. She is extremely clear about her motivations. She gives a full day's work for a full day's pay, but she is tired of working for others, and would like to own her own land someday. She does not, however, speak endlessly about her beliefs and ambitions, because *Heartland* is a movie of few words. That is partly because of the character of Clyde Stewart (Rip Torn), the rancher she goes to work for. He hardly ever says anything. He is a hard man, a realist who knows that the undisciplined Western land can break his back. But he is not unkind, and in the scene where he finally proposes to marry her, his choice of words contains understated wit that makes us smile.

Everything in this movie affirms life. Perhaps that is why *Heartland* can also be so unblinking in its consideration of death. The American West was not settled by people who spent all their time baking peach cobbler and knitting samplers, and this movie contains several scenes that will shock some audiences because of their forthright realism. We see a pig slaughtered, a calf birthed, cattle skinned, and a half-dead horse left out in the blizzard because there is simply nothing to feed it.

All of *Heartland* is stunningly photographed on and around a Montana ranch. (The movie is based on the real life of a settler named Elinore Randall Stewart.) It contains countless small details of farming life, put in not for "atmosphere" but because they work better than dialogue to flesh out the characters. The desolation of the frontier is suggested in small vignettes, such as one involving a family that could get this far and no farther, and lives huddled inside a small wagon. Among the many scenes that delight us with their freshness is one moment right after the wedding, when Ferrell realizes she got married wearing her apron and work boots, and another when she is about to give birth and her husband rides off into the storm to fetch the midwife from the next farm. We settle back here in anticipation of the obligatory scene in which the midwife arrives and immediately orders everyone to boil hot water, lots of it—but this time we're surprised. The husband returns alone; the midwife was not at her farm. Quiet little developments like that help expose the weight of cliché that holds down most Westerns.

In a movie filled with wonderful things, the

very best thing in *Heartland* is Conchata Ferrell's voice. It is strong, confident, clear as a bell, and naturally musical. It is a fine instrument, bringing authenticity to every word it says. It puts this movie to a test, because we could not quite accept that voice saying words that sounded phony and contrived. In *Heartland*, we never have to.

Heidi Fleiss, Hollywood Madam

NO MPAA RATING, 106 m., 1996

A documentary featuring Heidi Fleiss, Ivan Nagy, Madam Alex, Victoria Sellers, Cookie, Daryl Gates, L'Hua Reid, and others. Directed and produced by Nick Broomfield.

Eventually we'll never know each other. Probably very soon.
　　　　　　　—Heidi Fleiss on Ivan Nagy

Oh, the face of evil can be charming. Remember Hannibal Lecter. Or consider, in the real world, the case of Ivan Nagy. He is a sometime Hollywood movie director who was also—if you can believe his detractors—a pimp, a drug dealer, and a police informer who betrayed his lover while still sleeping with her. He has an impish little smile that he allows to play around his face, and it implicates you in his sleaze. "Come on," the smile suggests, "who are we kidding? We're all men of the world here; we know this stuff goes on."

Ivan Nagy was a key player in the life of Heidi Fleiss, the Hollywood Madam, who was sentenced to three years for procuring prostitutes for an A-list of top Hollywood players and free-spending Arabs. Heidi was not an innocent when she met Nagy. At sixteen, she was already the lover of the millionaire financial swindler Bernie Cornfield. But it was Nagy who (according to the legendary Madam Alex) "sold" Heidi to Alex for $500, then used her as a mole to take over Alex's thriving call girl operation. And it was Nagy who eventually turned Heidi over to the police—again, if Madam Alex can be believed.

What is intriguing about *Heidi Fleiss, Hollywood Madam* is that no one can necessarily be believed. This is an endlessly suggestive, tantalizing documentary in which the young life of Heidi Fleiss is reflected back at us from

funhouse mirrors: now she is a clever businesswoman, now a dupe, now a cynical hooker, now an innocent wrapped around the little finger of a manipulative hustler. Watching the film, we hear several versions of the same stories. Someone is lying, yes—but is anyone telling the truth?

Nick Broomfield is an enterprising documentary filmmaker for the BBC who tracks his prey with a lightweight camera and sound equipment that can hear around corners. This film is the record of his six months on the case of Heidi Fleiss. She might seem like an insignificant, even pathetic figure, but by the time Broomfield is finished, she has become a victim, and almost sympathetic, if only in contrast with the creatures she dealt with. She wanted to be bad, but had absolutely no idea what she was getting into. "As much bravado as she displays, to me she's still a little kid," her mother tells Broomfield.

Her *mother* participated in this documentary? Most certainly. And so did Heidi and Nagy and Victoria Sellers (Peter's daughter and Heidi's best friend) and Madam Alex and former Los Angeles police chief Daryl Gates. They participated because Broomfield paid them to talk. Madam Alex counts out her cash carefully, and we see Gates pocketing $2,500 before submitting to Broomfield's questions.

What we learn is that Alex was for many years the most successful madam in Los Angeles. Arrested for tax evasion, she got off with probation after an LAPD detective testified she was a valuable police informant. She allegedly used Nagy, a filmmaker with a respectable front, to obtain airline tickets for her since she couldn't get a credit card. Perhaps he also located cocaine for her clients. She says Nagy "sold" her Heidi, at around the age of twenty, and that Heidi helped Nagy steal away her empire. Heidi was the front, but Nagy was always the power and the brains.

Nagy says Madam Alex was "one of the most evil women I've met in my life." He smiles. He asks Broomfield, "Do I look like I need $500?" Then he sells him a home video of himself and Heidi. In the video, he tries to get her to take off her clothes, and she observes with concern but not alarm that "some green stuff" is coming out of that part of a man's anatomy he least desires to produce green stuff. A man who would sell that video needs $500.

Broomfield finds Mike Brambles, an LAPD detective (now in jail for robbery), who says Heidi's problem was that she was a bad police informant. She didn't cooperate, and so Nagy set her up to take the fall. Heidi doesn't seem to know if this is true. She describes her business (her clients wanted "typical untouched Southern California eighteen-year-old girls-next-door. No high heels. Blondes, blondes, blondes"). She is realistic ("A lot of times they'd hire us just to watch them do drugs"). She confesses to always having been attracted to older men ("Over forty, they're all the right age to me").

There is talk of a shadowy Israeli named Cookie, who everyone in the film seems frightened of. If Nagy is the power behind Heidi, is Cookie behind everything? No one will say. Broomfield is tireless in poking his nose, and camera, into these lives. During one visit to Alex he finds her maid using incense to purify the apartment against evil spirits. Nagy conducts a tour of his art collection. Heidi is interviewed in front of her bookshelf, which contains a set of the Great Books of the Western World: Did she buy them or did a client trade them in?

At the end of the film, after Heidi has been found guilty and is going to prison, and she has every reason to hate Nagy, there is a remarkable scene. Nagy calls her on the phone and lets us eavesdrop as he sweet-talks her. You can tell she still falls for him. Nagy smiles to the camera, helplessly: "There you go," he says. Charming.

A Hero Ain't Nothin' but a Sandwich

PG, 107 m., 1978

Cicely Tyson (Sweets), Paul Winfield (Butler), Larry B. Scott (Benjie), Helen Martin (Mrs. Bell), Glynn Turman (Nigeria), David Groh (Cohen), Kevin Hooks (Tiger). Directed by Ralph Nelson and produced by Robert B. Radnitz. Written by Alice Childress, based on her book.

A Hero Ain't Nothin' but a Sandwich opens with Benjie, a bright thirteen-year-old black kid, poised exactly on the brink of his future. He's good in school. He has an original, creative mind. He has a lot of stubbornness, and

a lot of anger, too. And some of the anger is directed at Butler, the man who lives with his mother. Benjie needs a father figure, or maybe a hero figure, but he's too smart to believe very easily in heroes.

Being smart, though, is one thing. Surviving in one piece as a teenager growing up in Watts is another. One of Benjie's friends, already hooked on heroin, recruits him for just a taste, y'know—supplied free by a neighborhood pusher. Benjie likes it. He tries it again. He isn't addicted, he tells himself. He can stop when he wants to, do without it, stay in control. The pusher agrees: How many times has he heard those same boasts?

Things aren't easy at home. Benjie's father walked out on the family three years ago, and now Benjie lives with his grandmother, his mother (Cicely Tyson), and her lover (Paul Winfield). He coexists with the boyfriend in an uneasy truce, resentful that he's taking the place of his real father, suspicious that he'll hurt his mother, too. There are doubts on both sides; Winfield is uncertain about how much of a father's role he should play. And Benjie's natural thirteen-year-old rebelliousness complicates things.

When he steals money from his grandmother to buy junk, his family discovers his addiction. And it almost tears them apart, threatening to destroy the relationship between Winfield and Tyson. And now the film's underlying purpose begins to become clear: This is a movie about the teenage heroin epidemic in the ghetto, yes, but it's also a film about family structure, about values, about trusting people.

Benjie undergoes a painful withdrawal process in a drug detoxification center (and there's a tremendously touching scene involving an encounter group). And when he comes back home, the four people in the family group begin to learn from each other about the possibilities of becoming a family.

A Hero Ain't Nothin' but a Sandwich is enormously rich in human values, touching the same kinds of truths as *Sounder,* the great 1972 film also starring Cicely Tyson and Paul Winfield (and made by the same producer, Robert Radnitz). It dares to be honest with its subject matter: It doesn't water it down to make it more commercial, or turn its eyes away from its harshest realities. But it still might have been no more than a praiseworthy effort if it weren't for the strength of its performances.

Tyson and Winfield are, of course, superb actors. But *Hero* had to succeed or fail on the basis of the actor playing Benjie. And Larry B. Scott succeeds brilliantly; it would be an insult to use that old term "child actor" in his case, because he completely holds the screen in one difficult scene after another in an Academy Award–caliber performance. We're reminded, from time to time, of another young black actor, Kevin Hooks, who was the proud son in *Sounder* (and who turns up here as the pusher).

A Hero Ain't Nothin' but a Sandwich is an important human document, a serious film about the breakup of the traditional family and the cynical ways in which drugs destroy lives and potential. That it's also a movie with tremendous warmth and heart pushes it over the border between being important and being a masterpiece.

High Fidelity

R, 120 m., 2000

John Cusack (Rob), Iben Hjejle (Laura), Todd Louiso (Dick), Jack Black (Barry), Lisa Bonet (Marie), Catherine Zeta-Jones (Charlie), Joan Cusack (Liz), Tim Robbins (Ian). Directed by Stephen Frears and produced by Tim Bevan and Rudd Simmons. Screenplay by D. V. Devincentis, Steve Pink, John Cusack, and Scott Rosenberg, based on the book by Nick Hornby.

In its unforced, whimsical, quirky, obsessive way, *High Fidelity* is a comedy about real people in real lives. The movie looks like it was easy to make—but it must not have been, because movies this wry and likable hardly ever get made. Usually a clunky plot gets in the way, or the filmmakers are afraid to let their characters seem too smart. Watching *High Fidelity*, I had the feeling I could walk out of the theater and meet the same people on the street—and want to, which is an even higher compliment.

John Cusack stars as Rob, who owns a used-record store in Chicago and has just broken up with Laura, his latest girlfriend. He breaks up a lot. Still hurting, he makes a list of the top five girls he's broken up with, and cackles that

Laura didn't make it. Later he stands forlornly on a bridge overlooking the Chicago River and makes lists of the top five reasons he misses her.

The key design elements in Rob's apartment are the lumber bookshelves for his alphabet-ized vinyl albums. He has two guys working for him in his store. Each was hired for three days a week, but both come in six days a week, maybe because they have no place else to go. These guys are the shy, sideways Dick (Todd Louiso) and the ultraconfident Barry (Jack Black). They are both experts on everything, brains stocked with nuggets of information about popular culture.

Rob is the movie's narrator, guiding us through his world, talking directly to the camera, soliloquizing on his plight—which is that he seems unable to connect permanently with a girl, maybe because his attention is elsewhere. But on what? He isn't obsessed with his business, he isn't as crazy about music as Dick and Barry, and he isn't thinking about his next girl—he's usually moping about the last one. He seems stuck in the role of rejected lover, and never likes a girl quite as much when she's with him as after she's left.

Laura (Iben Hjejle) was kind of special. Now she has taken up with an unbearably supercil-ious, ponytailed brainiac named Ian (Tim Rob-bins), who comes into the store to "talk things over" and inspires fantasies in which Rob, Dick, and Barry dream of kicking him senseless. "Conflict resolution is my job," he offers help-fully. Whether Ian is nice or not is of no consequence to Rob; he simply wants Laura back.

The story unspools in an unforced way. Barry and Dick involve Rob in elaborate de-bates about music minutiae. They take him to a nightclub to hear a new singer (Lisa Bonet). Rob gets advice from Laura's best friend (Joan Cusack), who likes him but is fed up with his emotional dithering. Rob seeks out former girlfriends like Charlie (Catherine Zeta-Jones), who tells him why she left him in more detail than he really wants to hear. Rob decides that his ideal girl would be a singer who would "write songs at home and ask me what I thought of them—and maybe even include one of our private little jokes in the liner notes."

High Fidelity is based on a 1995 novel by Nick Hornby, a London writer, and has been directed by Stephen Frears, also British. Frears and his screenwriters (D. V. Devincentis, Steve Pink, Cusack, and Scott Rosenberg) have transplanted the story to Chicago so successfully that it feels like it grew organically out of the funky soil of Lincoln Avenue and Halsted, Old Town and New Town, Rogers Park and Hyde Park, and Wicker Park, where it was shot—those neighborhoods where the workers in the alternative lifestyle industry live, love, and labor.

This is a film about, and also for, not only obsessed clerks in record stores, but the video store clerks who have seen all the movies, and the bookstore employees who have read all the books. Also for bartenders, waitresses, greengrocers in health food stores, kitchen slaves at vegetarian restaurants, the people at GNC who know all the herbs, writers for alternative weeklies, disc jockeys on college stations, salespeople in retro-clothing shops, tattoo artists and those they tattoo, poets, artists, musicians, novelists, and the hip, the pierced, and the lonely. They may not see themselves, but they will recognize people they know.

The Cusack character is someone I have known all my life. He is assembled out of my college friends, the guys at work, people I used to drink with. I also recognize Barry, the character played by Jack Black; he's a type so universal it's a wonder he hasn't been pinned down in a movie before: a blowhard, a self-appointed expert on all matters of musical taste, a monologuist, a guy who would rather tell you his opinion than take your money. Jack Black is himself from this world; he's the lead singer of the group Tenacious D, and it is a measure of his acting ability that when he does finally sing in this movie, we are surprised that he can.

The women I recognize too. They're more casual about romance than most movie characters, maybe because most movies are simpleminded and pretend it is earthshakingly important whether this boy and this girl mate forever, when a lot of young romance is just window-shopping and role-playing, and everyone knows it. You break up, you sigh, you move on. The process is so universal that with some people, you sigh as you meet them, in anticipation.

I am meandering. All I want to say is that *High Fidelity* has no deep significance, does not grow exercised over stupid plot points, savors the rhythms of these lives, sees how pop music is a sound track for everyone's autobiography, introduces us to Rob and makes us hope that he finds happiness, and causes us to leave the theater quite unreasonably happy.

High Hopes

no mpaa rating, 110 m., 1989

Philip Davis (Cyril), Ruth Sheen (Shirley), Edna Dore (Mrs. Bender), Philip Jackson (Martin), Heather Tobias (Valerie), Lesley Manville (Laetitia), David Bamber (Rupert). Written and directed by Mike Leigh and produced by Simon Channing-Williams and Victor Glynn. Screenplay by Leigh.

The characters in *High Hopes* exist on either side of the great divide in Margaret Thatcher's England, between the new yuppies and the die-hard socialists.

Cyril and Shirley, quasi-hippie survivors of the 1970s, live in comfortable poverty in a small flat, supported by Cyril's earnings as a motorcycle messenger. Cyril's sister, Valerie, lives in an upscale home surrounded by modern conveniences with her husband, Martin, who sells used cars. In their language, their values, and the way they furnish their lives, each couple serves as a stereotype for their class: Cyril and Shirley are what Tories think leftists are like, and Valerie and Martin stand for all the left hates most about Thatcherism.

Sometimes these two extremes literally live next door to each other. Cyril and Valerie's mother, a bitter, withdrawn old woman named Mrs. Bender, lives in solitude in the last council flat on a street that has otherwise been gentrified. Her next-door neighbors are two particularly frightening examples of the emerging social class the British call Hooray Henrys (and Henriettas). Paralyzed by their affected speech and gestures, they play out a grotesque parody of upper-class life in their own converted row house, which they like to forget was recently public housing for the poor.

All of these lives, and a few others, collide during the course of a few days in *High Hopes*, which was written and directed by Mike Leigh with the participation of the actors, who developed their scenes and dialogue in improvisational sessions. Leigh is a legendary figure in modern British theater, for his plays and television films that mercilessly dissect the British class system, using as their weapon the one emotion the British fear most, embarrassment.

Leigh has made only one other film, the brilliant *Bleak Moments*, some eighteen years ago. He cannot easily find financing for his films because, at the financing stage, they do not yet have scripts; he believes in developing the material as he goes along.

The backing for *High Hopes* came partly from Channel Four, the innovative alternative British TV channel, and with its money he has produced one of those rare films in which anger and amusement exist side by side—in which the funniest scenes are also the most painful ones.

Consider, for example, the dilemma of the old mother, Mrs. Bender, when she locks herself out of her council house. She naturally turns for help to her neighbors. But Rupert and Laetitia, who live next door, are upwardly mobile yuppies who treat the poor as a disease they hope not to catch. As the old woman stands helplessly at the foot of the steps, grasping her shopping cart, her chic neighbor supposes she must, after all, give her shelter, and says, "Hurry up, now. Chop, chop!"

Mrs. Bender calls her daughter, Valerie, who can hardly be bothered to come and help her, until she learns that her mother is actually inside the yuppie house next door. Then she's there in a flash, hoping to nose about and see what they've "done" with the place. Some of her dialogue almost draws blood, as when she looks into Rupert's leather-and-brass den and shouts, "Mum, look what they've done with your coal-hole!"

This sort of materialism and pride in possessions is far from the thoughts of Cyril and Shirley, the left-wing couple, who still sleep on a mattress on the floor and decorate their flat with posters and cacti. Lacking in ambition, they make enough from Cyril's messenger job to live on, and they smooth over the rough places with hashish. They are kind, and the movie opens with them taking a bewildered mental patient into their home; he has been wandering the streets of London, a victim of Thatcher's dismantled welfare state. (America and Britain are indeed cousins across the waters; we are reminded that the Reagan administration benevolently turned thousands of our own mentally ill out onto the streets.)

Most of the action in *High Hopes* centers around two set pieces, both involving the mother: the crisis of the lost keys, and then the mother's birthday party, which the hysterical Valerie stages as a parody of happy times. As the confused Mrs. Bender sits in bewilderment at the head of the table, her daughter shouts encouragement at her with a shrill desperation. The evening ends with a bitter quarrel between the daughter and her husband, while Cyril and Shirley pack the miserable old lady away home.

High Hopes is not a movie with a simple message; it's not left-wing propaganda in which all kindness resides with the Labourites and all selfishness with the Conservatives. Leigh shows us a London that exists beyond such easy distinctions, and it is possible he is almost as angry at Cyril and Shirley—laidback, gentle, ineffectual potheads—as at the movie's cruel upward-strivers.

Much of the movie's concern seems to center around Shirley's desire to have a child, and Cyril's desire that they should not. Their conflict is not the familiar old one of whether or not to "bring" a child into "this world." It seems to center more around the core of Cyril's laziness. He cannot be bothered. Of course, he stands for all good things and opposes all bad ones, in principle—but in practice, it's simpler to light up a joint.

High Hopes is an alive and challenging film, one that throws our own assumptions and evasions back at us. Leigh sees his characters and their lifestyles so vividly, so mercilessly, and with such a sharp satirical edge, that the movie achieves a neat trick: We start by laughing at the others, and end by feeling uncomfortable about ourselves.

The Homecoming

PG, 111 m., 1973

Cyril Cusack (Sam), Ian Holm (Lenny), Michael Jayston (Teddy), Vivien Merchant (Ruth), Terence Rigby (Joey), Paul Rogers (Max). Directed by Peter Hall and produced by Mort Abrahams, Otto Plaschkes, and Henry T. Weinstein. Screenplay by Harold Pinter, based on his stage play.

Harold Pinter's *The Homecoming* almost cried out to be filmed, unlike so many plays that seem stagy or claustrophobic as films. It works even better—because it *is* stagy and claustrophobic. And because it depends for its effect on sometimes minute adjustments among a family at war, the camera helps by getting us so close we sometimes want to duck.

It's a difficult play, one that has never been very popular with audiences—but seeing it as a movie helped me understand it better than I've ever been able to before. If this is what Ely Landau means when he says his American Film Theater will present movies based on stage plays—and not merely photographed plays—then the AFT has come through on its first try.

The play takes place during one interminable day and night in a drab Cockney flat in London. Drab is the word, all right; the movie is in color, but the sets are deliberately ugly variations on white, gray, and black (and so are the souls of the characters). We're introduced to a family: Max the patriarch; his sons, Lenny the pimp and Joey the would-be boxer; and his brother, Sam the chauffeur. These people hate each other with a violence and depth that must have taken long, bitter years to perfect.

It's literally a household: The house holds them in like a psychic prison. They turn on each other because there are no other targets. Distant reports are received from the outside world; a box of cigars, for example, is presented as a gift from one of Sam's customers. But somehow we can't believe there's anyone outside; these are the last people alive, like Vladimir and Estragon in *Waiting for Godot*. Then, almost shockingly, two more characters appear: Teddy, a third son, who is a teacher of philosophy in America, and Ruth, his wife. The family has never met Ruth before, but they pounce on her with sadistic glee, accusing her of being a prostitute and not a very expensive one at that. Teddy halfheartedly defends his wife, but before the play is over (1) he has decided to return to America alone; (2) she has agreed to stay as the resident sex object for the other males in the family and turn a few tricks on the side, and (3) Sam has collapsed on the floor, making it necessary for the others to step around him while giving the final twists to their psychic thumbscrews. Peter Hall, who did the original production for the Royal Shakespeare Company, has assembled many of the original cast members (Cyril Cusack is new), and they are so fierce with Pinter's words that even the silences hurt. No effort has been made to "open up" the play just because it's a movie now; the two or three exterior shots aren't for the scenery but to show us what we suspected all along: The London outside is an abandoned ruin bathed in a hellish red glow. So we admire the movie's technical excellence but are left with the problem of what it all means.

The movie's meaning is in the experience we have while we're watching it, I think. Pinter has a single purpose: to create uncomfortable emotional states within us, to fabricate for us (against our will, if necessary) a cluster of painful feelings.

"The play is about love," he explained, not very helpfully, back in 1967. When you think about it, he's right. The play is about love the way night is about day. The one has no meaning without the other. The play is an enclosed sphere with love on the outside. Determined realists are still left with such questions as, why doesn't Teddy object when Joey is having at Ruth on the living room couch while everybody watches?

The answer, I guess, is that if you expect Pinter characters to react decently, you're a lot more of an optimist than he is. These people are so far beyond decency, they can't even joke about it, because they've forgotten it.

It's weird. The most improbable things happen in *The Homecoming*, and its characters treat each other with total contempt, and yet somehow we *are* moved.

We don't think we will be; we spend the first half of the movie trying to reject its premises, but then Pinter sucks us in. We realize, consciously or not, that the people in that room have to care about each other very much, in order to hate each other so thoroughly. One aspect of love is, perhaps, to value another, and what would these sadomasochists do without their laboriously maintained relationships? They'd be at a loss. Here's a movie about dependence and need and . . . love?

Homicide

R, 102 m., 1991

Joe Mantegna (Bobby Gold), William H. Macy (Tim Sullivan), Natalija Nogulich (Chava), Ving Rhames

(Randolph), Rebecca Pidgeon (Miss Klein), Vincent Guastaferro (Senna), Lionel Mark Smith (Olcott), Jack Wallace (Frank). Directed by David Mamet and produced by Michael Hausman and Edward R. Pressman. Screenplay by Mamet.

There is a moment in David Mamet's *Homicide* when the hero does not know he is being overheard. He is a police detective, using the telephone in the library of a wealthy Jewish doctor who has complained about shots being fired on a nearby rooftop. The detective does not take the charges very seriously; he resents being pulled off a glamorous drug bust because the doctor, who has clout, has asked for him.

Standing at the phone, the detective unleashes a tightly knit, brilliantly arranged, flawlessly executed stream of four-letter obscenities and anti-Semitic remarks. Only David Mamet could write, and perhaps only one of his favorite actors, Joe Mantegna, could deliver, this dialogue so bluntly and forcibly, and yet with such verbal slickness that it has the freedom of a jazz improvisation. It's so well done, it gets an audience response just on the basis of the delivery.

Then the cop turns around and he sees that he is not alone in the room. The doctor's daughter has heard every foul, bitter word. She knows something we also know: This cop himself is Jewish. And because she heard him, she forces him to listen to himself. To hear what he's really saying.

Homicide is about a man waking up to himself. As the movie opens, Detective Bobby Gold, the Mantegna character, is a cop who places his job first and his personal identity last. He does not think much about being Jewish. He gets in a scrape with a superior officer, who is black, and when the officer calls him a "kike," he is ready to fight—but we sense his anger grows more out of departmental rivalries than a personal sense of insult. Throughout the movie, Mamet's characters use the bluntest street language in their racial and sexual descriptions, as if somehow getting the ugliness out into the open is progress. (The language in this film, like the dialogue in Sidney Lumet's 1990 *Q & A*, is staccato gutter dialect.)

Gold is angry with the doctor because the doctor's mother got murdered, and the murder resulted in Gold being pulled off the big case. The mother, a stubborn old lady, ran a corner store in a black ghetto. She didn't need the money, but she refused to budge from the store, and she is shot dead in a robbery. Bobby, speeding toward the drug bust with his partner (William H. Macy), happens on the scene of the crime accidentally. "This isn't my case," he keeps saying. "I'm not here. You didn't see me." But the old woman's son, who has the clout downtown, wants him assigned to the case. Since Bobby Gold is Jewish, the doctor thinks, maybe he'll really care.

The doctor has the wrong man. What Mamet is trying to do in *Homicide*, I think, is combine the structure of a thriller with the content of a soul-searching conversion process. The two cases get all mixed up throughout the film—the black drug dealer on the run, the murdered old lady—and in a sense Bobby is not going to be able to figure out who did anything until he decides who *he* is.

The movie crackles with energy and life, and with throwaway slang dialogue by Mamet, who takes realistic speech patterns and simplifies them into a kind of hammer-and-nail poetry. This is his third film as a writer-director (after *House of Games* and *Things Change*), and he is a filmmaker with a clear sense of how he wants to proceed. He uses the elements of traditional genres—the con game, the mistaken identity, the personal crisis, the cop picture—as a framework for movies that ask questions like, Who's real? Who can you trust? What do people really want?

Here he has several of his favorite actors, who have grown up in Mamet stage productions: Mantegna, Macy, Jack Wallace, J. J. Johnston—substantial guys with good haircuts who smoke cigarettes like they need to. This isn't a cast of aging teen idols. These are men, middle-aged, harassed, run down. They've seen it all. We sense that Bobby Gold is not in touch with his Jewishness because, like a lot of his partners, he has let the job take over from the person. Gold has become so hard-boiled, he doesn't even know how he sounds, until he hears himself through that woman's ears.

Hoop Dreams

PG-13, 165 m., 1994

Directed by Steve James and produced by Frederick Marx, James, and Peter Gilbert. Screenplay by James, Marx, and Gilbert.

A film like *Hoop Dreams* is what the movies are for. It takes us, shakes us, and makes us think in new ways about the world around us. It gives us the impression of having touched life itself.

Hoop Dreams is, on one level, a documentary about two black kids named William Gates and Arthur Agee, from Chicago's inner city, who are gifted basketball players and dream of someday starring in the NBA. On another level, it is about much larger subjects: about ambition, competition, race, and class in our society. About our value structures. And about the daily lives of people like the Agee and Gates families, who are usually invisible in the mass media, but have a determination and resiliency that is a cause for hope.

The movie spans six years in the lives of William and Arthur, starting when they are in the eighth grade, and continuing through the first year of college. It was intended originally to be a thirty-minute short, but as the filmmakers followed their two subjects, they realized this was a much larger, and longer, story. And so we are allowed to watch the subjects grow up during the movie, and this palpable sense of the passage of time is like walking in their shoes.

They're spotted during playground games by a scout for St. Joseph's High School in suburban Westchester, a basketball powerhouse. Attending classes there will mean a long daily commute to a school with few other black faces, but there's never an instant when William or Arthur, or their families, doubt the wisdom of this opportunity: St. Joseph's, we hear time and again, is the school where another inner-city kid, Isiah Thomas, started his climb to NBA stardom.

One image from the film: Gates, who lives in the Cabrini Green project, and Agee, who lives on Chicago's South Side, get up before dawn on cold winter days to begin their daily ninety-minute commute to Westchester. The street lights reflect off the hard winter ice, and

we realize what a long road—what plain hard work—is involved in trying to get to the top of the professional sports pyramid. Other high school students may go to "career counselors," who steer them into likely professions. Arthur and William are working harder, perhaps, than anyone else in their school—for jobs that, we are told, they have only a 0.00005 percent chance of winning.

We know all about the dream. We watch Michael Jordan and Isiah Thomas and the others on television, and we understand why any kid with talent would hope to be out on the same courts someday. But *Hoop Dreams* is not simply about basketball. It is about the texture and reality of daily existence in a big American city. And as the film follows Agee and Gates through high school and into their first year of college, we understand all of the human dimensions behind the easy media images of life in the "ghetto."

We learn, for example, of how their extended families pull together to help give kids a chance. How if one family member is going through a period of trouble (Arthur's father is fighting a drug problem), others seem to rise to periods of strength. How if some family members are unemployed, or if the lights get turned off, there is also somehow an uncle with a big backyard, just right for a family celebration. We see how the strong black church structure provides support and encouragement—how it is rooted in reality, accepts people as they are, and believes in redemption.

And how some people never give up. Arthur's mother asks the filmmakers, "Do you ever ask yourself how I get by on $268 a month and keep this house and feed these children? Do you ever ask yourself that question?" Yes, frankly, we do. But another question is how she finds such determination and hope that by the end of the film, miraculously, she has completed her education as a nursing assistant. *Hoop Dreams* contains more actual information about life as it is lived in poor black city neighborhoods than any other film I have ever seen.

Because we see where William and Arthur come from, we understand how deeply they hope to transcend—to use their gifts to become pro athletes. We follow their steps along the path that will lead, they hope, from grade school to the NBA.

The people at St. Joseph's High School were not pleased with the way they appear in the film, saying among other things that they were told the film would be a nonprofit project to be aired on PBS, not a commercial venture. The filmmakers responded that they, too, thought it would—that the amazing response that found it a theatrical release was a surprise to them. The movie simply turned out to be a masterpiece, and its intended noncommercial slot was not big enough to hold it. The St. Joseph suit reveals understandable sensitivity, because not all of the St. Joseph people come out looking like heroes.

It is as clear as day that the only reason Arthur Agee and William Gates are offered scholarships to St. Joseph's in the first place is because they are gifted basketball players. They are hired as athletes as surely as if they were free agents in pro ball; suburban high schools do not often send scouts to the inner city to find future scientists or teachers.

Both sets of parents are required to pay a small part of the tuition costs. When Gates's family cannot pay, a member of the booster club pays for him—because he seems destined to be a high school all-American. Arthur at first does not seem as talented. And when he has to drop out of the school because his parents have both lost their jobs, there is no sponsor for him. Instead, there's a telling scene where the school refuses to release his transcripts until the parents have paid their share of his tuition.

The morality here is clear: St. Joseph's wanted Arthur, recruited him, and would have found tuition funds for him if he had played up to expectations. When he did not, the school held the boy's future as hostage for a debt his parents clearly would never have contracted if the school's recruiters had not come scouting grade school playgrounds for the boy. No wonder St. Joseph's feels uncomfortable. Its behavior seems like something out of Dickens. The name Scrooge comes to mind.

Gene Pingatore, the coach at St. Joseph's, felt he was seen in an unattractive light. I thought he came across fairly well. Like all coaches, he believes athletics are a great deal more important than they really are, and there is a moment when he leaves a decision to Gates that Gates is clearly not well prepared to make. But it isn't Pingatore but the whole system that is brought into question: What does it say about the values involved, when the pro sports machine reaches right down to eighth-grade playgrounds?

But the film is not only, or mostly, about such issues. It is about the ebb and flow of life over several years, as the careers of the two boys go through changes so amazing that, if this were fiction, we would say it was not believable. The filmmakers (Steve James, Frederick Marx, and Peter Gilbert) shot miles of film, 250 hours in all, and that means they were there for several of the dramatic turning points in the lives of the two young men. For both, there are reversals of fortune—life seems bleak, and then is redeemed by hope and even sometimes triumph. I was caught up in their destinies as I rarely am in a fiction thriller, because real life can be a cliffhanger, too.

Many filmgoers are reluctant to see documentaries, for reasons I've never understood; the good ones are frequently more absorbing and entertaining than fiction. *Hoop Dreams,* however, is not only a documentary. It is also poetry and prose, muckraking and exposé, journalism and polemic. It is one of the great moviegoing experiences of my lifetime.

Hoosiers

PG, 114 m., 1987

Gene Hackman (Norman Dale), Barbara Hershey (Myra Fleener), Dennis Hopper (Shooter), Sheb Wooley (Cletus), Fern Parsons (Opal Fleener), Chelcie Ross (George), Robert Swan (Rollin), Michael O'Guinne (Rooster). Directed by David Anspaugh and produced by Carter De Haven and Angelo Pizzo. Screenplay by Pizzo.

I was a sportswriter once for a couple of years in downstate Illinois. I covered mostly high school sports, and if I were a sportswriter again, I'd want to cover them again. There is a passion to high school sports that transcends anything that comes afterward; nothing in pro sports equals the intensity of a really important high school basketball game.

Hoosiers knows that. This is a movie about a tiny Indiana high school that sends a team all the way to the state basketball finals in the days when schools of all sizes played in the same tournaments and a David could slay a Goliath. The school in the movie is so small that it can barely field a team, especially after the best player decides to drop out. Can schools this small actually become state champs? Sure. That's what high school sports are all about.

Hoosiers is a comeback movie, but it's not simply about a comeback of this small team, the Hickory Huskers. It's also about the comeback of their coach, a mysterious middle-age guy named Norman Dale (Gene Hackman), who seems to be too old and too experienced to be coaching in an obscure backwater like Hickory.

And it's also the comeback story of Shooter, the town drunk (played by Dennis Hopper, whose supporting performance won an Oscar nomination). Everybody in this movie seems to be trying to start over in life, and, in a way, basketball is simply their excuse.

Hoosiers has the broad overall structure of most sports movies: It begins with the problem of a losing team, introduces the new coach, continues with the obligatory training sequences and personality clashes, arrives at the darkest hour, and then heads toward triumph. This story structure is almost as sacred to Hollywood as basketball is to Indiana.

What makes *Hoosiers* special is not its story, however, but its details and its characters. Angelo Pizzo, who wrote the original screenplay, knows small-town sports. He knows all about high school politics and how the school board and the parents' groups always think they know more about basketball than the coach does. He knows about gossip, scandal, and vengeance. And he knows a lot about human nature.

All of this knowledge, however, would be pointless without Hackman's great performance at the center of this movie. Hackman is gifted at combining likability with complexity—two qualities that usually don't go together in the movies. He projects all of the single-mindedness of any good coach, but then he contains other dimensions, and we learn about the scandal in his past that led him to this one-horse town. David Anspaugh's direction is good at suggesting Hackman's complexity without belaboring it.

Hickory High School is where Hackman

hopes to make his comeback, but he doesn't think only of himself. He meets Shooter (Hopper), the alcoholic father of one of his team members, and enlists him as an assistant coach with one stipulation: no more drinking. That doesn't work. In a way, Hackman knows it won't work, but by involving Shooter once again in the life of the community, he's giving him a reason to seek the kind of treatment that might help.

Hackman finds that he has another project on his hands, too: the rehabilitation of his heart. He falls in love with a teacher at the school (Barbara Hershey), and their relationship is interesting, as far as it goes, although it feels like key scenes have been cut out of the romance. Maybe another movie could have been made about them; this movie is about basketball.

The climax of the movie will come as no great surprise to anyone who has seen other sports movies. *Hoosiers* works magic, however, in getting us to really care about the fate of the team and the people depending on it. In the way it combines sports with human nature, it reminded me of another wonderful Indiana sports movie, *Breaking Away*. It's a movie that is all heart.

Hotel Rwanda

PG-13, 110m., 2004

Don Cheadle (Paul Rusesabagina), Sophie Okonedo (Tatiana), Nick Nolte (Colonel Oliver), Joaquin Phoenix (Jack). Directed by Terry George and produced by George and A. Kitman Ho. Screenplay by Keir Pearson and George.

You do not believe you can kill them all?

Why not? Why not? We are halfway there already.

In 1994 in Rwanda, a million members of the Tutsi tribe were killed by members of the Hutu tribe, in a massacre that took place while the world looked away. *Hotel Rwanda* is not the story of that massacre. It is the story of a hotel manager who saved the lives of twelve hundred people by being, essentially, a very good hotel manager.

The man is named Paul Rusesabagina, and he is played by Don Cheadle as a man of quiet, steady competence in a time of chaos. This is not the kind of man the camera silhouettes against mountaintops, but the kind of man who knows how things work in the real world, and uses his skills of bribery, flattery, apology, and deception to save these lives who have come into his care.

I have known a few hotel managers fairly well, and I think if I were hiring diplomats they would make excellent candidates. They speak several languages. They are discreet. They know how to function appropriately in different cultures. They know when a bottle of Scotch will repay itself six times over. They know how to handle complaints. And they know everything that happens under their roof, from the millionaire in the penthouse to the bellboy who can get you a girl (the wise manager fires such bellboys, except perhaps for one who is prudent and trustworthy and a useful resource on certain occasions).

Paul is such a hotel manager. He is a Hutu, married to a Tutsi named Tatiana (Sophie Okonedo). He has been trained in Belgium and runs the four-star Hotel Des Milles Collines in the capital city of Kigali. He does his job very well. He understands that when a general's briefcase is taken for safekeeping, it contains bottles of good Scotch when it is returned. He understands that to get the imported beer he needs, a bribe must take place. He understands that his guests are accustomed to luxury, which must be supplied even here in a tiny central African nation wedged against Burundi, Tanzania, Uganda, and the Congo (formerly Zaire). Do these understandings make him a bad man? Just the opposite. They make him an expert on situational ethics. The result of all the things he knows is that the hotel runs well and everyone is happy.

Then the genocide begins, suddenly, but after a long history. Rwanda's troubles began, as so many African troubles began, when European colonial powers established nations that ignored traditional tribal boundaries. Enemy tribes were forced into the same land. For years in Rwanda under the Belgians, the Tutsis ruled, and killed not a few Hutu. Now the Hutus are in control, and armed troops prowl the nation, killing Tutsis.

There is a United Nations "presence" in Rwanda, represented by Colonel Oliver (Nick Nolte). He sees what is happening, informs his superiors, asks for help and intervention, and is ignored. Paul Rusesabagina informs corporate headquarters in Brussels of the growing tragedy, but the hotel in Kigali is not the chain's greatest concern. Finally it comes down to these two men acting as freelancers to save more than a thousand lives they have somehow become responsible for.

When *Hotel Rwanda* premiered at Toronto in 2004, two or three reviews criticized the film for focusing on Rusesabagina and the colonel, and making little effort to "depict" the genocide as a whole. But director Terry George and writer Keir Pearson have made exactly the correct decision. A film cannot be about a million murders, but it can be about how a few people respond. Paul Rusesabagina, as it happens, is a real person, and Colonel Oliver is based on one, and *Hotel Rwanda* is about what they really did. The story took shape after Pearson visited Rwanda and heard of a group of people who were saved from massacre.

Don Cheadle's performance is always held resolutely at the human level. His character intuitively understands that only by continuing to act as a hotel manager can he achieve anything. His hotel is hardly functioning, the economy has broken down, the country is ruled by anarchy, but he puts on his suit and tie every morning and fakes business as usual—even on a day he is so frightened he cannot tie his tie.

He deals with a murderous Hutu general, for example, not as an enemy or an outlaw, but as a longtime client who knows that the value of a good cigar cannot be measured in cash. Paul has trained powerful people in Kigali to consider the Hotel Des Milles Collines an oasis of sophistication and decorum, and now he pretends that is still the case. It isn't, but it works as a strategy because it cues a different kind of behavior; a man who has yesterday directed a mass murder might today want to show that he knows how to behave appropriately in the hotel lobby.

Nolte's performance is also in a precise key. He came to Rwanda as a peace-keeper, and now there is no peace to keep. The nations are united in their indifference toward Rwanda. Nolte's bad-boy headlines distract from his acting gifts; here his character is steady, wise, cynical, and a master of the possible. He makes a considered choice in ignoring his orders and doing what he can do, right now, right here, to save lives.

How the twelve hundred people come to be "guests" in the hotel is a chance of war. Some turn left, some right, some live, some die. Paul is concerned above all with his own family. As a Hutu he is safe, but his wife is Tutsi, his children are at threat, and in any event he is far beyond thinking in tribal terms. He has spent years storing up goodwill, and now he calls in favors. He moves the bribery up another level. He hides people in his hotel. He lies. He knows how to use a little blackmail: Sooner or later, he tells a powerful general, the world will take a reckoning of what happened in Kigali, and if Paul is not alive to testify for him, who else will be believed?

This all succeeds as riveting drama. *Hotel Rwanda* is not about hotel management, but about heroism and survival. Rusesabagina rises to the challenge. The film works not because the screen is filled with meaningless special effects, formless action, and vast digital armies, but because Don Cheadle, Nick Nolte, and the filmmakers are interested in how two men choose to function in an impossible situation. Because we sympathize with these men, we are moved by the film. Deep movie emotions for me usually come not when the characters are sad, but when they are good. You will see what I mean.

Note: The character of Colonel Oliver is based on Lieutenant General Romeo Dallaire, a Canadian who was the UN force commander in Rwanda. His autobiography, Shake Hands with the Devil, *was published in October 2004.*

Household Saints

R, 124 m., 1993

Vincent Phillip D'Onofrio (Joseph Santangelo), Tracey Ullman (Catherine), Lili Taylor (Teresa), Victor Argo (Lino Falconetti), Judith Malina (Joseph's Mother), Michael Imperioli (Leonard Villanova). Directed by Nancy Savoca and produced by Richard Guay and Peter Newman. Screenplay by Savoca and Guay.

Saints are a great inconvenience. They interfere with the plans of ordinary people. When a modern family finds itself with a saint in its midst, there is a tendency to send for the psychiatrist. *Household Saints* is about Italian-Americans in New York City who begin with a form of madness they are comfortable with, and end with a madness only a saint could understand.

Like many stories of miracles, this one begins with a pinochle game. The local butcher, Joseph Santangelo, has fallen in love with Catherine, the daughter of his card-playing buddy, Lino Falconetti. The stakes in their game go higher and higher one night, until finally Joseph wants to play for the right to marry Catherine. Lino agrees, and loses, and goes home and orders his daughter to fix a nice dinner because the Santangelos are coming over.

"I want you to make a meal so good a man would get married to eat like that every night," he says. "I got news for you," she says. "Nobody gets married for the food." And particularly not her cooking, which is so haphazard that Joseph's mother insults the cooking right there at the table.

But Joseph (Vincent D'Onofrio) and Catherine (Tracey Ullman) do get married. And gradually they change. As young people they look like the "before" pictures in an ad for a beauty school. Catherine is particularly careless, with her lank hair and her tendency to spend the day locked up with a book. But eventually prosperity touches them. Joseph grows a mustache and goes to a better barber. Catherine tints her hair and uses makeup.

It is a constant trial, living with Joseph's shrill and hateful mother (Judith Malina), who spends Catherine's first pregnancy pumping her full of horrifying old wives' tales—superstitions about all the things that can lead to miscarriages or the birth of monsters. When Mrs. Santangelo finally dies, Catherine paints the dark old apartment in bright pastels and buys Tupperware, and the family enters the twentieth century.

To them a daughter is born. Teresa (Lili Taylor) is a quiet, serious girl who grows up as a devout Catholic. She is attracted to that uncompromising thread of Catholicism that challenges her to become a saint. She prays, meditates, and spends her days in penance and good works. She develops a special devotion to her namesake, St. Teresa, known as the Little Flower of Jesus. She agrees with the saint that it is not necessary to do great things in the world to be holy; one can do God's work anywhere, and there is grace to be won by scrubbing floors.

Teresa is a child who would be completely understood by her superstitious grandmother. Her parents have become modernized, however, and while of course they are Catholics, they don't see any need to get carried away with things. When Teresa shyly announces her hope to enter the convent, her father explodes: "I don't want no daughter of mine lining the Pope's pockets."

By now it is about 1970. Change is in the air. Teresa enrolls in college, where most of the students are on the floor in sit-ins, not prayer. She meets a young man named Leonard Villanova (Michael Imperioli), who explains that he has a Life Plan: "First, I get the St. John's law degree. Then I want a Lincoln Continental. I want a family, and a town house on the upper East Side, and I want membership in all those clubs that always turned up their noses to the Italians." He plans a career in "television law." Teresa is impressed: "You mean like Perry Mason?"

Household Saints is a wonderful movie, without a second that isn't blessed by the grace of its special humor and tenderness. But the closing scenes are transcendent, as Teresa drifts away from the Villanova Plan and into a plan of her own, for loving Jesus. The fact is that modern people *do* worship false gods, and that a life devoted to getting a big car and a town house is seen as eminently more sane than a life devoted to God. You can decide for yourself if Teresa goes mad. In an earlier age, people would have known how to think of her.

This warmhearted jewel of a movie was directed by Nancy Savoca, whose previous films are *True Love* and *Dogfight* (which also starred the priceless Lili Taylor). She treasures eccentricity in people. Another director might have started right off with the story of Teresa. But Savoca's subject is larger: She wants to show how, in only three generations, an Italian family that is comfortable with the mystical turns into an American family that is threatened by it. And she wants to explore the possibilities of sainthood in these secular days. That she sees great humor in her subject is perfect; it is always easier to find the truth through laughter.

There will be people who question Teresa's devotion to the Little Flower. For me, the movie rang one bell of memory after another. I went to Catholic school in the 1950s—that age of Latin, incense, and mystery before Vatican II repainted the Church in politically correct pastels. I know this movie is closer to the literal truth of those days than many non-Catholics will believe. When was it, I wonder, that it became madness to want to be a saint?

Housekeeping
PG, 117 m., 1988

Christine Lahti (Sylvie), Sara Walker (Ruth), Andrea Burchill (Lucille), Anne Pitoniak (Aunt Lily), Barbara Reese (Aunt Nona). Directed by Bill Forsyth and produced by Robert F. Colesberry. Screenplay by Forsyth, based on the book by Marilynne Robinson.

In a land where the people are narrow and suspicious, where do they draw the line between madness and sweetness? Between those who are unable to conform to society's norm, and those who simply choose not to, because their dreamy private world is more alluring? That is one of the many questions asked, and not exactly answered, in Bill Forsyth's *Housekeeping*, which was one of the strangest and best films of 1988.

The movie, set some thirty or forty years ago in the Pacific Northwest, tells the story of two young girls who are taken on a sudden and puzzling motor trip by their mother to visit a relative. Soon after they arrive, their mother commits suicide, and before long her sister, their aunt Sylvie, arrives in town to look after them.

Sylvie, who is played by Christine Lahti as a mixture of bemusement and wry reflection, is not an ordinary type of person. She likes to sit in the dusk so much that she never turns the lights on. She likes to go for long, meandering walks. She collects enormous piles of newspapers and hundreds of tin cans—carefully washing off their labels and then polishing them and arranging them in gleaming pyramids. She is nice to everyone and generally seems cheerful, but there is an enchantment about her that some people find suspicious.

Indeed, even her two young nieces are divided. One finds her "funny," and the other loves her, and eventually the two sisters will take separate paths in life because they differ about Sylvie. At first, when they are younger, she simply represents reality to them. As they grow older and begin to attend high school, however, one of the girls wants to be "popular," and resents having a weird aunt at home, while the other girl draws herself into Sylvie's dream.

The townspeople are not evil, merely conventional and "concerned." Parties of church ladies visit, to see if they can "help." The sheriff eventually gets involved. But *Housekeeping* is not a realistic movie, not one of those disease-of-the-week docudramas with a tidy solution. It is funnier, more offbeat, and too enchanting to ever qualify on those terms.

The writer-director, Bill Forsyth, has made all of his previous films in Scotland (they make a list of whimsical, completely original comedies: *Gregory's Girl, Local Hero, Comfort and Joy, That Sinking Feeling*). For his first North American production, he began with a novel by Marilynne Robinson that embodies some of his own notions, such as that certain people grow so amused by their own conceits that they cannot be bothered to pay lip service to yours.

In Christine Lahti, he has found the right actress to embody this idea. Although she has been excellent in a number of realistic roles (she was Gary Gilmore's sister in *The Executioner's Song,* and Goldie Hawn's best friend in *Swing Shift*), there is something resolutely private about her, a sort of secret smile that is just right for Sylvie. The role requires her to find a delicate line; she must not seem too mad or willful, or the whole charm of the story will be lost. And although there are times in the film when she seems to be indifferent to her nieces, she never seems not to love them.

Forsyth has surrounded that love with some extraordinary images, which help to create the magical feeling of the film. The action takes place in a house near a lake that is crossed by a majestic, forbidding railroad bridge, and it is a local legend that one night decades ago, a passenger train slipped ever so lazily off the line and plunged down, down into the icy waters of the frozen lake. The notion of the passengers in their warm, well-lit carriages, plunging down to their final destination, is one that Forsyth somehow turns from a tragedy into a notion of doomed beauty. And the bridge becomes important at several moments in the film, especially the last one.

The pastoral setting of the film (in British Columbia) and the production design by Adrienne Atkinson are also evocative; it is important that the action takes place in a small, isolated community, in a place cut off from the world where whimsies can flourish and private notions can survive. At the end of the film, I was quietly astonished; I had seen a film that could perhaps be described as being about a madwoman, but I had seen a character who seemed closer to a mystic, or a saint.

House of Flying Daggers
PG-13, 119 m., 2004

Zhang Ziyi (Mei), Takeshi Kaneshiro (Jin), Andy Lau (Leo), Song Dandan (Yee). Directed by Zhang Yimou and produced by William Kong and Yimou. Screenplay by Feng Li, Bin Wang, and Yimou.

Movie imagery, which has grown brutal and ugly in many of the new high-tech action pictures, may yet be redeemed by the elegance of martial arts pictures from the East. Zhang Yimou's *House of Flying Daggers,* like his *Hero* (2004) and Ang Lee's *Crouching Tiger, Hidden Dragon* (2000), combines excitement, romance, and astonishing physical beauty; to Pauline Kael's formula of "kiss kiss bang bang" we can now add "pretty pretty."

Forget about the plot, the characters, the intrigue, which are all splendid in *House of Flying Daggers,* and focus just on the visuals. There are interiors of ornate, elaborate richness, costumes of bizarre beauty, landscapes of mountain ranges and meadows, fields of snow, banks of autumn leaves, and a bamboo grove that functions like a kinetic art installation.

The action scenes set in these places are not broken down into jagged short cuts and incomprehensible foreground action. Zhang stands back and lets his camera regard the whole composition, wisely following Fred Astaire's belief that to appreciate choreography you must be able to see the entire body in motion. Tony Scott of the *New York Times* is on to something when he says the film's two most accomplished action scenes are likely to be "cherished like favorite numbers from *Singin' in the Rain* and *An American in Paris.*" Try making that claim about anything in *The Matrix* or *Blade: Trinity*.

The scenes in question are the Echo Game and a battle in a tall bamboo grove. The Echo Game takes place inside the Peony Pavilion, a luxurious brothel that flourishes in the dying days of the Tang Dynasty, A.D. 859. An undercover policeman named Jin (Takeshi Kaneshiro) goes there on reports that the new dancer may be a member of the House of Flying Daggers, an underground resistance movement. The dancer is Mei (Zhang Ziyi, also in *Hero* and *Crouching Tiger*), and she is blind; martial arts pictures have always had a special fondness for blind warriors, from the old *Zatoichi* series about a blind swordsman to Takeshi Kitano's *Zatoichi* remake (2004).

After Mei dances for Jin, his fellow cop Leo (Andy Lau) challenges her to the Echo Game, in which the floor is surrounded by drums on poles, and he throws a nut at one of the drums. She is to hit the same drum with the weighted end of her long sleeve. First one nut, then three, then countless nuts are thrown, as Mei whirls in midair to follow the sounds with beats of her own; like the house-building sequence in the Kitano picture, this becomes a ballet of movement and percussion.

Jin and Mei form an alliance to escape from the emperor's soldiers, Mei not suspecting (or does she?) that Jin is her undercover enemy. On their journey, supposedly to the secret headquarters of the House of Flying Daggers, they fall in love; but Jin sneaks off to confer with Leo, who is following them with a contingent of warriors, hoping to be led to the hideout. Which side is Jin betraying?

Still other warriors, apparently not aware of the undercover operation, attack the two lovers, and there are scenes of improbable delight, as when four arrows from one bow strike four targets simultaneously. Indeed most of the action in the movie is designed not to produce death, but the pleasure of elegant ingenuity. The impossible is cheerfully welcome here.

The fight in the bamboo grove inspires comparison with the treetop swordfight in *Crouching Tiger,* but is magnificent in its own way. Warriors attack from above, hurling sharpened bamboo shafts that surround the lovers, and then swoop down on tall, supple bamboo trees to attack at close range. The sounds of the whooshing bamboo spears and the click of dueling swords and sticks have a musical effect; if these scenes are not part of the sound track album, they should be.

The plot is almost secondary to the glorious action, until the last act, which reminded me a little of the love triangle in Hitchcock's *Notorious*. In that film, a spy sends the woman he loves into danger, assigning her to seduce an enemy of the state, which she does for patriotism and her love of her controller. Then the spy grows jealous, suspecting the woman really loves the man she was assigned to deceive. In *House of the Flying Daggers* the relationships contain additional levels of discovery and betrayal, so that the closing scenes in the snowfield are operatic in their romantic tragedy.

Zhang Yimou has made some of the most visually stunning films I've seen *(Raise the Red Lantern)* and others of dramatic everyday realism *(To Live).* Here, and with *Hero,* he wins for mainland China a share of the martial arts glory long claimed by Hong Kong and its acolytes like Ang Lee and Quentin Tarantino. The film is so good to look at and listen to that, as with some operas, the story is almost beside the point, serving primarily to get us from one spectacular scene to another.

House of Games
R, 102 m., 1987

Lindsay Crouse (Margaret Ford), Joe Mantegna (Mike), Mike Nussbaum (Joey), Lilia Skala (Dr. Littauer), J. T. Walsh (Businessman), Jack Wallace (Bartender). Directed by David Mamet and produced by Michael Hausman. Screenplay by Mamet.

This movie is awake. I have seen so many films that sleepwalk through the debris of old plots and secondhand ideas that it was a constant pleasure to watch *House of Games,* a movie about con men that succeeds not only in conning its viewers, but also in creating a series of characters who seem imprisoned by the need to con or be conned.

The film stars Lindsay Crouse as a psychiatrist who specializes in addictive behavior, possibly as a way of dealing with her own compulsions. One of her patients is a gambler who fears he will be murdered over a bad debt. Crouse walks through lonely night streets to the neon signs of the House of Games, a bar where she thinks she can find the gambler who has terrorized her client. She wants to talk him out of enforcing the debt.

The gambler (Joe Mantegna) has never heard anything like this before. But he offers her a deal: If she will help him fleece a high-roller Texan in a big-stakes poker game, he will tear up the marker. She does so. She also becomes fascinated by the back-room reality of these gamblers who have reduced life to a knowledge of the odds. She comes back the next day, looking for Mantegna. She tells him she wants to learn more about gamblers and con men, about the kind of man he is. By the end of this movie, does she ever.

House of Games was written and directed by David Mamet, the playwright *(Glengarry Glen Ross)* and screenwriter *(The Untouchables),* and it is his directorial debut. Originally it was intended as a big-budget movie with an established director and major stars, but Mamet took the reins himself, cast his wife in the lead and old acting friends in the other important roles, and shot it on the rainy streets of Seattle. Usually the screenwriter is insane to think he can direct a movie. Not this time. *House of Games* never steps wrong from beginning to end.

The plotting is diabolical and impeccable, and I will not spoil the delight of its unfolding by mentioning the crucial details. What I can mention are the performances, the dialogue, and the setting. When Lindsay Crouse enters the House of Games, she enters a world occupied by characters who have known each other so long and so well, in so many different ways, that everything they say is a kind of shorthand. At first we don't fully realize that, and there is a strange savor to the words they use. They speak, of course, in Mamet's distinctive dialogue style, an almost musical rhythm of stopping, backing up, starting again, repeating, emphasizing, all the time with the hint of deeper meanings below the surfaces of the words. The leading actors, Joe Mantegna and Mike Nussbaum, have appeared in countless performances of Mamet

plays over the years, and they know his dialogue the way other actors grow into Beckett or Shakespeare. They speak it as it is meant to be spoken, with a sort of aggressive, almost insulting, directness. Mantegna has a scene where he "reads" Lindsay Crouse—where he tells her about her "tells," those small giveaway looks and gestures that poker players use to read the minds of their opponents. The way he talks to her is so incisive and unadorned it is sexual.

These characters and others live in a city that looks, as the Seattle of *Trouble in Mind* did, like a place on a parallel time track. It is a modern American city, but like none we have quite seen before; it seems to have been modeled on the paintings of Edward Hopper, where lonely people wait in empty public places for their destinies to intercept them. Crouse is portrayed as an alien in this world, a successful, best-selling author who has never dreamed that men like this exist, and the movie is insidious in the way it shows her willingness to be corrupted.

There is in all of us a fascination for the inside dope, for the methods of the confidence game, for the secrets of a magic trick. But there is an eternal gulf between the shark and the mark, between the con man and his victim. And there is a code to protect the secrets. There are moments in *House of Games* when Mantegna instructs Crouse in the methods and lore of the con game, but inside every con is another one.

I met a woman once who was divorced from a professional magician. She hated this man with a passion. She used to appear with him in a baffling trick where they exchanged places, handcuffed and manacled, in a locked cabinet. I asked her how it was done. The divorce and her feelings meant nothing compared to her loyalty to the magic profession. She looked at me coldly and said, "The trick is told when the trick is sold." The ultimate question in *House of Games* is, who's buying?

House of Sand and Fog

R, 126 m., 2003

Jennifer Connelly (Kathy Nicolo), Ben Kingsley (Massoud Amir Behrani), Ron Eldard (Lester Burdon), Shohreh Aghdashloo (Nadi Behrani), Jonathan Ahdout

(Esmail Behrani), Frances Fisher (Connie Walsh).
Directed by Vadim Perelman and produced by Michael
London and Perelman. Screenplay by Perelman and
Shawn Lawrence Otto, based on the book by Andre
Dubus III.

It's so rare to find a movie that doesn't take sides. Conflict is said to be the basis of popular fiction, and yet here is a film that seizes us with its first scene and never lets go, and we feel sympathy all the way through for everyone in it. To be sure, they sometimes do bad things, but the movie *understands* them and their flaws. Like great fiction, *House of Sand and Fog* sees into the hearts of its characters, and loves and pities them. It is based on a novel by Andre Dubus III, and there must have been pressure to cheapen and simplify it into a formula of good and evil. But no. It stands with integrity, and breaks our hearts.

The story is simply told. Kathy Nicolo (Jennifer Connelly), a recovering alcoholic, has been living alone since her husband walked out eight months ago. She has fallen behind on the taxes for her modest split-level home that has a view, however distant, of the California shore. She neglects warnings from the county, the house is put up for auction, and it is purchased by Massoud Amir Behrani (Ben Kingsley), an Iranian immigrant who was a colonel in the Shah's air force but now works two jobs to support his family, and dreams that this house is the first step in rebuilding the lives of his wife and son.

The director, producer, and cowriter, Vadim Perelman, doesn't lay out the plot like bricks on a wall, but allows it to reveal itself. We see Massoud working on a highway construction gang, washing himself in a rest room, getting into a Mercedes, and driving to his other job, as an all-night clerk in a roadside convenience store. When the wealthy have a fall, the luxury car is often the last treasure to go; better an expensive old car than a cheap new one. And they are a reminder. Yes, Massoud has memories of the good life they led and their shore cottage in Iran.

Kathy has memories, too. The house was left to her and her brother when their father died. The brother lives in the East, sometimes loans her money, is not sure he believes she is clean and sober. She hasn't had a drink in three years, but is depressed by the departure of her hus-

band, has started smoking again, has needed this shock to blast her out of her lethargy. After she is evicted, she drives past her house in disbelief, seeing this foreigner with his family and his furniture, and one night she sleeps in her car, right outside the gate.

Both of these people desperately need this house. Both have a moral claim to it. Neither can afford to let go of it. Yes, Kathy should have opened her mail and paid her taxes. Yes, perhaps, Massoud should agree with Kathy's public defender (Frances Fisher) and sell the house back for what he paid. But we know, from looking into his books (where every Snickers bar is accounted for), that he is almost broke. This is his last chance to keep up appearances for his wife and son, and to look substantial in the eyes of his daughter's new Iranian husband and her in-laws.

Into the lives of these two blameless parties comes a third, Lester Burdon (Ron Eldard), the deputy sheriff who evicts Kathy but is touched by her grief, then stirred by her beauty. If we are keeping a moral accounting, then his is the blame for what eventually happens. It is fair enough to fight for your home and family, but not fair to misuse your uniform—not even if your excuse is love, or what is spoken of as love. Lester says he will leave his wife and family for Kathy, and although maybe he will, he certainly shouldn't. There is a moment when they start sharing an empty cottage in the woods, and as he leaves she asks if he'll come back, and then quickly adds, "I'll understand if you don't." But he holds himself to a bargain he should not have made and cannot fulfill, and because he is not a moral man he brings unimaginable suffering into the lives of Kathy and the Behrani family, who in all of their dealings after all acted only as good people would from strong motives.

There is much more that the movie will unfold to you, but although I will not reveal it, it isn't in the nature of a surprise plot development. At every step, we feel we are seeing what could and would naturally happen next—not because of coincidence or contrivance, but because of the natures of the people involved.

Not much is said about Massoud Amir Behrani's background in Iran; he has nightmares, he lived in a bad time, but now has pulled back to the simplest things: to find a house for his wife and a wife for his son. Kingsley is such an unbending actor when he needs to be, has such reserves of dignity, that when the deputy attempts to intimidate him with the uniform and the badge, Massoud stands his ground and says, "I don't know who you think you're talking to," and we see at once that he is the man and the deputy is the boy.

As for Kathy, misfortune and injury follow her. Even new love is bad luck. There are scenes involving her being taken back into her old house. And a crisis when the Behranis, whose family is threatened by this woman, simplify everything with one simple sentence: "We have a guest in the house." And a subtle subtext in the way Nadi Behrani (Shohreh Aghdashloo), Massoud's wife, treats the sad girl as a mother would, while hardly understanding a word she says.

I have not read the novel by Andre Dubus III, and no doubt changes have been made in the adaptation—they always are. But I sense that the essential integrity has been defended. *House of Sand and Fog* relates not a plot with its contrived ups and downs, but a story. A plot is about things that happen. A story is about people who behave. To admire a story you must be willing to listen to the people and observe them, and at the end of *House of Sand and Fog* we have seen good people with good intentions who have their lives destroyed because they had the bad luck to come across a weak person with shabby desires. And finally there is a kind of love and loyalty, however strange to us, that reveals itself in the marriage of Massoud and Nadi, and must be respected.

Howards End

PG, 140 m., 1992

Anthony Hopkins (Henry Wilcox), Vanessa Redgrave (Ruth Wilcox), Emma Thompson (Margaret Schlegel), Helena Bonham Carter (Helen Schlegel), Joseph Bennett (Paul Wilcox), James Wilby (Charles Wilcox), Sam West (Leonard Bast). Directed by James Ivory and produced by Ismail Merchant. Screenplay by Ruth Prawer Jhabvala, based on the book by E. M. Forster.

Howards End, a film at once civilized and passionate, is named for a house in the English countryside. It has been in the Wilcox family for a long time—or, more properly, in the family of Mrs. Wilcox, who makes it the center of her life

and retreats to its peace when the noise of life in London with Mr. Wilcox grows too deafening.

In America, where we change our address as easily as we change our telephone number, the meaning of such a house is harder to understand. We do not often grow up in the same rooms where our grandparents were born. But in a country such as England, until quite recently, many families had such houses in their histories, and *Howards End* is about the passing of the traditional and humanist values that could flourish in such places.

The story of the house and the people who pass through it is told by E. M. Forster, in the best of his novels and one of the last (after *A Passage to India, A Room With a View, Where Angels Fear to Tread,* and *Maurice*) to be filmed.

The year is 1910. Mrs. Wilcox (Vanessa Redgrave) develops an admiration for Margaret Schlegel (Emma Thompson), who belongs to a musical family with a British mother and a German father (but not "Germans of the dreadful sort," Forster confides). She finds she can talk to Margaret—she recognizes a spark in the girl that reminds her of herself. When she dies, her family is horrified to discover a scrawled, unsigned coda to her will, leaving the house to Margaret. They burn the scrap of paper ("Mother couldn't have meant it"), and agree to say nothing about it.

But life has a way of correcting errors. Margaret, who is young and beautiful by our standards but old enough to be on the edge of spinsterhood by the standards of her day, catches the eye of the bereaved Mr. Wilcox, a very rich, shy, abrupt industrialist played by Anthony Hopkins. He proposes, or more exactly croaks out some tortured syllables that seem to express esteem and desire. She interprets, and accepts. And she comes home to Howards End.

But this is not a melodrama about inheritances. It is a film about values. Other characters are involved, especially Margaret's sister, Helen (Helena Bonham Carter), and the desperately poor and unhappy Mr. Leonard Bast (Sam West), who meets the Schlegels through an incident of a lost umbrella, and becomes the victim of their attempts to help him. Mr. Wilcox, asked for advice on Mr. Bast's job prospects, advises him to leave a thriving company and join one that soon goes bankrupt, and when the girls cry out that poor Mr. Bast is now worse off than he was before, Wilcox replies, not complacently, "The poor are the poor, and one's sorry for them—but there it is."

The fiery Helen will not stand for this, and indeed produces poor Mr. Bast at Wilcox's daughter's wedding fete on the lawns of Howards End, where Bast, the leper at the feast, discovers along with everyone else that his slovenly wife knows Mr. Wilcox far better than she should. This development leads to the story's angry outcry against hypocrisy, as Helen denounces her sister and Margaret denounces her husband—not for immorality, but for failing to apply to himself the same standards he would apply to others.

Howards End is one of the best novels of the twentieth century. Read it. This film adaptation, by the team of director James Ivory, writer Ruth Prawer Jhabvala, and producer Ismail Merchant, is one of the best movies of the year—one of the best collaborations ever by these three, who specialize in literate adaptations of novels of manners *(A Room with a View, The Bostonians, Mr. and Mrs. Bridge)*.

Howards End is such a good story, partly because Forster himself was a master storyteller who was particularly gifted at strong endings, and partly because the splendid cast embodies the characters so fully that the events actually seem to be happening to them, instead of unfolding from a screenplay.

Emma Thompson is superb in the central role: quiet, ironic, observant, with steel inside. Helena Bonham Carter has never been better than she is here, as the hothead who commits her mind and body to the radical new social ideas of the day. Anthony Hopkins gives a heartbreaking performance as a man who wants to change and wants to love, but finally cannot quite bring himself to break through the hidebound, reactionary impulses that protect him from his better nature. And Vanessa Redgrave, as the dying Mrs. Wilcox, casts a spell over the whole movie; if we do not believe in her values, and understand what she sees in Margaret and why she wants her to have the house, we miss the whole point.

What a beautiful film it is: not an overdecorated "period" adaptation, but a film in which the people move easily through town and country homes and landscapes that frame and define them. The house used as Howards End in the film is the very same house, I am informed, that Forster used as a model in writing his novel. It is easy to imagine standing on the lawn and understanding what such a house could mean. Paul Goodman once wrote, "As an architect draws, men live," by which, among other things, he possibly meant that good houses inspire good lives. Here is a house that sets such a test that a whole society is challenged.

The Hunchback of Notre Dame

G, 95 m., 1996

With the voices of: Tom Hulce (Quasimodo), Demi Moore (Esmeralda), Tony Jay (Frollo), Kevin Kline (Phoebus), Paul Kandel (Clopin), Jason Alexander (Hugo [Gargoyle]), Charles Kimbrough (Victor [Gargoyle]), Mary Wickes (Laverne [Gargoyle]), David Ogden Stiers (Archdeacon). Directed by Gary Trousdale and Kirk Wise and produced by Don Hahn. Screenplay by Tab Murphy, Bob Tzudiker, Irene Mecchi, Noni White, and Jonathan Roberts, based on an animation story by Murphy from the Victor Hugo book *Notre Dame de Paris*.

When I first heard about the project, I wondered if *The Hunchback of Notre Dame* could possibly work as a Disney animated feature—if the fearsome features and fate of its sad hero Quasimodo would hold audiences at arm's length. When I saw the preview trailers for the film, with its songs about "Quasi," I feared Disney had gone too far in an attempt to popularize and neutralize the material. I was wrong to doubt, and wrong to fear: *The Hunchback of Notre Dame* is the best Disney animated feature since *Beauty and the Beast*— a whirling, uplifting, thrilling story with a heart-touching message that emerges from the comedy and song.

The story involves the lonely life of the deformed Quasimodo (voice by Tom Hulce), born a "monster" and thrown down a well before being rescued and left to be raised by the priests of Notre Dame Cathedral in Paris. The vast, gloomy, Gothic shadows of the cathedral become his playground, and his only friends are three stone gargoyles. But his life changes on the day of the Festival of Fools, when he ventures out of the cathedral, is elected "King of the Fools," and then hears Clopin, king of the gypsies, gasp: "That's no mask!"

Quasimodo is made a captive by the mob and tied down at the orders of the heartless Judge Frollo, but is rescued by the gypsy girl Esmeralda (voice by Demi Moore). He rescues her in turn, giving her sanctuary inside the cathedral. And then he finds himself in the center of a battle to save the gypsies of Paris from Frollo's troops, led by Phoebus (voice by Kevin Kline), captain of the guard. But Phoebus is not a bad man, and besides, he has fallen in love with the fiery Esmeralda. But ... so has Quasimodo.

This is not such a simple story. There are depths and shadows to it, the ending cannot be simple, and although the heroes may live ever after, it may not be happily. This is the first Disney animated film I can recall with two heroes who both love the girl, which makes heartbreak inevitable.

The movie is forthright in its acceptance of Quasimodo's appearance ("You've got a look that's all your own, kid"), and doesn't look away from his misshapen face. One of Alan Menken's songs even looks on the bright side: "Those other guys that she could dangle / All look the same from every boring point of view—You're a surprise from any angle ..."

But Quasimodo is an enormously sympathetic character; we grow accustomed to his face. And we follow him into a series of locations in which the Disney animators unveil some of their most breathtaking visual inventions. The Festival of Fools is a riotous celebration in the shadow of Notre Dame. Then Quasi finds himself in the gypsies' Court of Miracles, in the catacombs beneath Paris, for a display of animation and music that is breathtaking in its freedom over time and space.

The cathedral itself is a character in the film, with its rows of stone saints and church fathers, and its limitless vaults of shadows and mystery. Quasimodo moves through its upper reaches like a child on a jungle gym, and there are scary sequences in which he and his friends risk dashing their brains out on the stones below. The thing that animation can do better than any other film form is show human movement freed from the laws of gravity, and as Quasi clambers up and down the stone walls of Notre Dame, the camera swoops freely along with him creating dizzying perspectives and exhilarating movement.

The buried story of the film—the lesson some younger viewers may learn for the first time—is that there is room in the world for many different kinds of people, for hunchbacks and gypsies as well as for those who scornfully consider themselves the norm. Judge Frollo wants to rid Paris of its gypsies, and assigns Phoebus to lead the genocide, but the captain instinctively feels this cannot be right. And when he meets Esmeralda, gypsies suddenly gain a human face for him, and he changes sides.

As for Quasimodo, who has lived so long in isolation, there is a kind of release in discovering the gypsies ("Were you once an outcast too?"). He understands that he is not unique in being shunned, that the need to create outsiders is a weakness of human nature.

The Hunchback of Notre Dame, directed by Gary Trousdale and Kirk Wise, is a high point in the renaissance of Disney animation that began in 1989 with *The Little Mermaid*. It blends Menken's songs, glorious animation, boundless energy and the real substance of the story into a movie of heart and joy. More than *Aladdin* or *The Lion King,* certainly more than *Pocahontas,* it is as good for its story and message as for its animation. It reminds us, as all good animation does, that somehow these cartoons of lines and colors and movements can create a kind of life that is more archetypal, more liberating, than images that are weighed down by human bodies and the gravity that traps them.

I

Iceman
PG, 99 m., 1984

Timothy Hutton (Dr. Shephard), John Lone (Iceman), Lindsay Crouse (Dr. Diane Brady). Directed by Fred Schepisi and produced by Norman Jewison and Patrick Palmer. Screenplay by John Drimmer and Chip Proser.

Iceman begins in almost exactly the same way as both versions of *The Thing*, with a team of Arctic scientists chopping a frozen mammal out of the ice. But somehow we're more interested in this discovery because the frozen object isn't simply a gimmick at the beginning of a horror picture; it is presented with real curiosity and awe.

What is it? As a helicopter lifts the discovery aloft, we can glimpse its vague, shadowy outline through the block of forty-thousand-year-old ice. It seems almost to be a man, with its arms outstretched. If we remember Fellini's *La Dolce Vita*, we're reminded of its famous opening scene, as the helicopter flew above Rome with the statue of Christ. In both cases, a contrast is made between the technological gimmicks of man and an age-old mystery. In both cases, also, we're aware that we are in the hands of a master director. *Iceman* is by Fred Schepisi, the Australian who made *The Chant of Jimmy Blacksmith* and Willie Nelson's *Barbarosa*. Both of those movies were about men who lived entirely apart from modern society, according to rules of their own, rules that we eventually realized made perfect sense (to them, at least). Now Schepisi has taken that story idea as far as it will go.

The block of ice is thawed. As each drop of water trickles down a stainless steel table to the floor, we feel a real excitement. We're about to discover something, just as we were when the apes found the monolith in *2001*. Inside the block of ice is a Neanderthal man, perfectly preserved, frozen in an instant with his hands pushing out and his mouth open in a prehistoric cry of protest. Such a discovery is at least theoretically possible; mastodons have been found in Russia, frozen so quickly in a sudden global catastrophe that the buttercups in their stomachs had still not been digested. Why not a man? Of course, the man's cell tissue would have been destroyed by the freezing

process, right? Not according to *Iceman*, which advances an ingenious theory.

The scene in which the Neanderthal is brought back to life is one of those emergency room dramas we're familiar with from the TV medical shows, with medics pounding on the chest and administering electrical shocks. Then the movie leaves the familiar, and begins an intriguing journey into the past of the man. The Neanderthal (his name sounds like "Charlie") is placed in a controlled environment. Two scientists (Timothy Hutton and Lindsay Crouse) establish a relationship with him. Elementary communication is started— although here the movie makes a basic error in showing the scientists teaching Charlie to speak English, when of course they would want to learn his language instead.

The rest of the movie develops a theory about how Charlie was frozen and what he was looking for when that surprising event took place. There is also an argument between two branches of science: Those who are more interested in what they can learn from Charlie's body and those who want to understand his mind. This conflict seems to have been put in to generate suspense (certainly no responsible scientist, presented with a living Neanderthal man, would suggest any experiment that would endanger his life). But never mind; before it turns into conflict between good and evil, *Iceman* departs in an unexpected, mystical direction.

This movie is spellbinding storytelling. It begins with such a simple premise and creates such a genuinely intriguing situation that we're not just entertained, we're drawn into the argument. What we feel about Charlie reflects what we feel about ourselves. And what he knows—that we've forgotten—illuminates the line between man the firebuilder, and man the stargazer. Think how much more interesting *The Thing* would have been if its frozen life form had been investigated rather than destroyed, and you have an idea of *Iceman*'s appeal.

The Iceman Cometh
PG, 241 m., 1973

Lee Marvin (Hickey), Robert Ryan (Larry), Fredric March (Harry Hope), Jeff Bridges (Don Parritt), Evans

Evans (Cora), George Voskovec (The General), John McLiam (Jimmy Tomorrow). Directed by John Frankenheimer and produced by Ely A. Landau. Screenplay by Thomas Quinn Curtis, based on the play by Eugene O'Neill.

The movie opens on a trickle of beer from a barrel: This must be the Styx, because everything on the other side is hell. The camera tracks to the back room of an Irish saloon in Greenwich Village, summer 1912, where the regulars are tossed about like sleeping rag dolls. Snores, snorts, and cries of terror from fearful dreams. In the corner, one man remains awake, his cynicism too deep to allow easy dreams.

The man's name is Larry, and he used to be a Wobbly before he abandoned the movement for his own personal scorn of faith. The bartender wearily joins him at the table and they wait for the day. There are so many men in the room that it seems impossible we will eventually get to know them all, but we will, and the three whores upstairs, and especially the man they are all waiting for, the iceman, Hickey.

The owner of the bar is named, ironically, Harry Hope. He has so long ago abandoned any hope that he has not even stepped outside his establishment in twenty years. This place is the end of the road, the bottom of the sea, Larry says. But every man except Larry has a "pipe dream"— something to keep him going. Tomorrow one of them will sober up and get his job back. Tomorrow the assistant bartender will marry one of the whores and make her respectable. Tomorrow. Eugene O'Neill's *The Iceman Cometh* is the work of a man who has very nearly abandoned all hope. The only characters in it who summon up the courage to act (not to act positively, but to act at all) are Hickey, who kills his wife, and the boy Don, who kills himself. Larry, who is always the most intelligent man in the room, comes to the conclusion at the end of the play that death is not to be avoided but even to be welcomed.

And yet the play sings with a defiant urge to live. The derelicts who inhabit the two rooms of this seedy saloon depend upon each other with a ferociousness born of deep knowledge of each other. The two old soldiers, for example, one British and the other Boer in the South African War, have almost gotten to love each other, so deeply do they depend on their ancient hate.

O'Neill's play was not only so despairing but also so long (four hours and one minute in the film version) that it was not produced on the stage until 1946, seven years after he finished it. It's staged infrequently, despite its stature as the most ambitious play of America's greatest playwright. The American Film Theater production of it, directed by John Frankenheimer, is thus all the more welcome. The play was clearly too difficult to be done as an ordinary commercial movie, but now it has been preserved, with a series of brilliant performances and a virtuoso directing achievement, in what has to be a definitive film version.

There isn't a bad performance in the film, but there are three of such greatness they mesmerize us. The best is by the late Robert Ryan, as Larry, and this is possibly the finest performance of his career. There is such wisdom and sadness in his eyes, and such pain in his rejection of the boy Don (who may be his own son), that he makes the role almost tender despite the language O'Neill gives him. It would be a tribute to a distinguished career if Ryan were nominated posthumously for an Academy Award.

Lee Marvin, as Hickey, has a more virtuoso role: He plays a salesman who has been coming to Harry's saloon for many years to have a "periodical drunk." This time he's on the wagon, he says, because he has found peace. We discover his horrible peace when he confesses to the murder. Marvin has recently been playing in violent action movies that require mostly that he look mean; here he is a tortured madman hidden beneath a true believer.

I also liked old Fredric March, as Harry Hope. He's a pathetic pixie who tolerates his customers for the security they give him. To be the proprietor of a place like this is, at least, better than being a customer. But not much better. And so for four hours we live in these two rooms and discover the secrets of these people, and at the end we have gone deeper, seen more and will remember more than with most of the other movies of our life.

The Ice Storm

R, 112 m., 1997

Kevin Kline (Ben Hood), Joan Allen (Elena Hood), Henry Czerny (George Clair), Sigourney Weaver (Janey

Carver), Jamey Sheridan (Jim Carver), Christina Ricci (Wendy Hood), Tobey Maguire (Paul Hood), Elijah Wood (Mikey Carver), Adam Hann-Byrd (Sandy Carver), David Krumholtz (Francis Davenport), Michael Cumpsty (Reverend Philip Edwards). Directed by Ang Lee and produced by Ted Hope, James Schamus, and Lee. Screenplay by Schamus, based on the book by Rick Moody.

The Ice Storm takes place as an early winter storm descends on Connecticut, casting over Thanksgiving a shroud of impending doom. In a wooded suburb, affluent adults stir restlessly in their split-level homes, depressed not only by their lives but by their entertainments and even by their sins. Their teenage children have started experimenting with the same forms of escape: booze, pot, and sex.

The Hood family is held together by quiet desperation. Ben (Kevin Kline) is having an affair with a neighbor (Sigourney Weaver). His wife, Elena (Joan Allen), is a shoplifter who is being hit on by a longhaired minister. The children sip wine in the kitchen. Young Wendy Hood's grace before Thanksgiving dinner is to the point: "Thanks for letting us white people kill all the Indians and steal all their stuff." Ben and Elena observe later, "The only big fight we've had in years is about whether to go back into couples therapy."

The film, based on a novel by Rick Moody, has been directed by Ang Lee, whose previous credit was an adaptation of Jane Austen's *Sense and Sensibility.* Both films are about families observing protocol and exchanging visits. Only the rules have changed. When Ben Hood visits Janey Carver (Weaver) for an adulterous liaison, he wanders into Janey's rec room to find his own daughter, Wendy (Christina Ricci), experimenting with Janey's son Mikey (Elijah Wood). Wendy, who is fourteen, has also conducted an exploratory session with Mikey's kid brother, Sandy. The father asks his daughter what she's doing there. She could as easily have asked him.

The early 1970s were a time when the social revolution of the 1960s had seeped down, or up, into the yuppie classes, who wanted to be "with it" and supplemented their martinis with reefers. The sexual revolution is in full swing for the characters in this movie, leading to Ben Hood's lecture to his son on the facts of life: "Masturbating in the shower wastes water and electricity." When Janey Carver finds her son and the Hood girl playing "I'll show you mine if you'll show me yours," her response is a bizarre speech on Margaret Mead's book about coming of age in Samoa.

The literate, subtle screenplay by James Schamus cuts between the children and their parents, finding parallels. Paul takes the train into the city to visit the apartment of the girl he likes; he sneaks sleeping pills into the drink of his rival to put him out of the picture, but she, of course, wants a pill of her own, and passes out. Meanwhile in New Caanan, the adults are attending a "key party," which turns into a sort of race: Can they swap their wives before they pass out? Elena Hood even finds Philip, the longhaired minister (Michael Cumpsty), there. "Sometimes the shepherd needs the comfort of the sheep," he explains tolerantly. She answers: "I'm going to try hard not to understand the implications of that."

There is a sense of gathering tragedy, symbolized in one scene where a child balances on an icy diving board over an empty pool. When disaster does strike, it releases helpless tears for one of the characters; we reflect on how very many things he has to cry about. Despite its mordant undertones, the film is often satirical and frequently very funny, and quietly observant in its performances, as when the Weaver character takes all she can of Kline's musings about his dislike of golf, and finally tells her lover: "You're boring me. I have a husband. I don't feel the need for another."

They all feel the need for something. What we sense after the film is that the natural sources of pleasure have been replaced with higher-octane substitutes, which have burnt out the ability to feel joy. Going through the motions of what once gave them escape, they feel curiously trapped.

Il Ladro di Bambini

NO MPAA RATING, 116 m., 1993

Enrico Lo Verso (Antonio), Valentina Scalici (Rosetta), Giuseppe Ieracitano (Luciano), Florence Darel (Martine), Marina Golovine (Nathalie), Fabio Alessandrini (Grignani). Directed by Gianni Amelio and produced by Angelo Rizzoli. Screenplay by Amelio, Sandro Petraglia, and Stefano Rulli.

The Italian title *Il Ladro di Bambini* translates as *The Thief of Children*, and the movie's English title is *Stolen Children*, but both titles have to be read with great irony, because here is a film about a man who only steals children away from great unhappiness, and allows them to see for a few days that life can contain joy, as well. Like *Cinema Paradiso*, but in a different way, the movie tells a heartwarming story about an older man who acts as a parent and friend for kids who need one.

The movie opens in Milan, where Rosetta, an eleven-year-old girl, and her brother Luciano, a year younger, live with their mother, who forces the girl to work as a child prostitute. This element of the story, tragic and unsavory, is not dwelled on; the movie properly begins when the two children are taken away from the mother and placed in the care of Antonio (Enrico Lo Verso), a young policeman, whose job is to take them to a children's home.

The cop doesn't much relish the job, especially after his partner cooks up a scam where Antonio will do the work while the partner takes an unscheduled vacation. Antonio believes he doesn't care for children—and the kids return the favor. After years of emotional and physical abuse, they are withdrawn, sullen, and suspicious.

But that will change during the course of the story. The children are turned away from the church-run children's home, apparently out of fear that their past might infect the other students. Naively taking the case into his own hands, without authorization, Antonio next takes them to Sicily. As they travel all the way down the length of Italy, stopping even for a feast at the home of Antonio's parents, a bond grows between the three travelers.

The movie is a road picture, in a sense; the people and experiences along the way are part of the education of Antonio, Rosetta, and Luciano, and what we see through the car windows is a cross-section of modern Italy, good and bad. But what happens in the car is more important, as Antonio learns to love the children, and they learn to trust an adult for the first time in their lives.

There are no big episodes, until the end. Instead, the director and cowriter, Gianni Amelio, takes small events, the daily routine, and shows how the behavior of the travelers gradually changes. There is also a magical day at the beach, where the children from a dark, oppressive slum breathe fresh air and run on the sand in the sunshine, and Antonio realizes how much he has come to care for them.

With child abuse in all the headlines, it is unlikely this story could be told today as an American movie; our thinking on such subjects has been poisoned by too many talk shows and tabloids, and the cop's genuine love might seem suspect. But somehow the fact that the film is Italian creates the right perspective on the material. It seems more innocent, more filled with grace, more plausible.

Unknown to Antonio and the children, however, a scandal is brewing over their "disappearance." The policeman has operated outside the rules, on his own authority, and although we see that he has done nothing wrong, the authorities assume he has stolen the children, and a manhunt gets under way. The resolution is as satisfactory as in any film since, oh, *Cinema Paradiso*.

Maybe Hollywood films have grown so slick and sophisticated that simple stories like this can no longer be told in the big commercial genres. I don't know. I do know that in the early months of 1993, the best films I've seen have mostly been from other countries. *Il Ladro di Bambini*, *Like Water for Chocolate*, *Léolo*, and *The Last Days of Chez Nous* all have a freshness and daring that's in contrast to the assembly-line stories. Here is a movie with the spontaneity of life; watching it is like living it.

I Married a Shadow

NO MPAA RATING, 110 m., 1983

Nathalie Baye (Helene/Patricia), Francis Huster (Pierre), Richard Bohringer (Frank), Madeleine Robinson (Lena), Guy Trejan (Msseur. Meyrand), Victoria Abril (Fifo). Directed by Robin Davis and produced by Alain Sarde. Screenplay by Patrick Laurent and Davis, based on the book *I Married a Dead Man* by William Irish (pseudonym of Cornell Woolrich).

Note: This review contains spoilers.

This movie is a small but valuable discovery, a mystery that turns into an exploration of loneliness and love. If I seem to be telling you too much of the story, don't be alarmed. The mystery element is over in twenty minutes and serves only to set up a much deeper, more startling story.

I Married a Shadow begins as the story of a pregnant woman whose lover is a beast who mistreats her and finally throws her out. She takes a train ride to nowhere in particular. On the train, she meets a married couple. Like her, the other woman is eight months pregnant. She is invited to their compartment to rest, she tries on the other woman's wedding band, and then there is a train crash and the couple are killed. Naturally, she is mistaken for the other woman. And as she meets her new "in-laws," she discovers that she is the widow of a very rich man.

All of that is just plot. The reasons to see this movie begin after the woman decides to assume her new identity. The woman is played by Nathalie Baye, the finest actress now working in French films. She is sweet, quiet, painfully shy. She loves her new little baby and decides to accept the new identity so that her son will have a better chance in life.

The family she has entered owns a large, famous vineyard in the south of France. Her new father-in-law is a loving, sensitive man. Her new mother-in-law is a dying woman with the single regret that she has not loved enough. Her new brother-in-law is a quiet, withdrawn type who quickly falls in love with her. And that is enough of the plot.

I Married a Shadow is based on a novel by Cornell Woolrich, who wrote it under the name William Irish. Woolrich is worth a movie in his own right. He was a rich, reclusive, eccentric alcoholic who lived in a series of hotel rooms and wrote moody, quirky thrillers that movie directors have loved to film. Hitchcock's *Rear Window* and Truffaut's *The Bride Wore Black* are based on his books. He loved opening sentences (I quote from memory) such as, "The night was young, and so was I, but the night was gay, and I was sour."

There was not much happiness in his books. But there is happiness in this story. What happens is a little unexpected: Instead of making the story into a mystery plot, with clues, suspicions, and threats, the movie takes another approach altogether. Everybody learns the woman's secret when they need to, and then they behave out of surprisingly generous motives. There is forgiveness and redemption—and, of course, a proper amount of blackmail, murder, deception, cheating, and scandal. At the end of the movie, you feel good, and this is the kind of movie where that is the last way you expect to feel.

In America
PG-13, 103 m., 2003

Paddy Considine (Johnny), Samantha Morton (Sarah), Sarah Bolger (Christy), Emma Bolger (Ariel), Djimon Hounsou (Mateo). Directed by Jim Sheridan and produced by Arthur Lappin and Jim Sheridan. Screenplay by Jim Sheridan, Naomi Sheridan, and Kirsten Sheridan.

In America has a moment when everything shifts, when two characters face each other in anger and there is an unexpected insight into the nature of their relationship. It is a moment sudden and true; we realize how sluggish many movies are in making their points, and how quickly life can blindside us.

The moment takes place between Johnny (Paddy Considine), the father of an Irish immigrant family recently arrived in New York, and Mateo (Djimon Hounsou), the angry Nigerian painter who lives below them in a shabby tenement. Mateo is known as "the man who screams" because his anguish sometimes echoes up the stairs. But when Johnny's young daughters knock on his door for trick-or-treating, he is unexpectedly gentle with them. Johnny's wife, Sarah (Samantha Morton), invites Mateo to dinner, he becomes friendly with the family during a time when Paddy is feeling hard-pressed and inadequate, and slowly Paddy begins to suspect that romantic feelings are developing between his wife and the man downstairs.

All of that grows slowly in the movie, in the midst of other events, some funny, some sad, all rich with life. It is a suspicion rustling beneath the surface, in Paddy's mind and ours. Finally Paddy confronts Mateo: "Do you want to be in my place?"

"I might," says Mateo.

"Do you love my wife?"

"I love your wife. And I love you. And I love

your children," Mateo says, barking the words ferociously.

There is a silence, during which Paddy's understanding of the situation changes entirely. I will not reveal what he believes he has discovered (it may not be what you are thinking). The rest of the film will be guided by that moment, and what impressed me was the way the dialogue uses the techniques of short fiction to trigger the emotional shift. This is not a "surprise" in the sense of a plot twist, but a different way of seeing—it's the kind of shift you find in the sudden insight of the young husband at the end of Joyce's *The Dead*. It's not about plot at all. It's about how you look at someone and realize you have never really known them.

The screenplay is by Jim Sheridan, the director, and his daughters Naomi and Kirsten. It is dedicated "to Frankie," and in the movie the family has two young daughters, and there was a son named Frankie who died of a brain tumor after a fall down the stairs. *In America* is not literally autobiographical (the real Frankie was Sheridan's brother, who died at ten), but it is intensely personal. It's not the typical story of turn-of-the-century immigrants facing prejudice and struggle, but a modern story, set in the 1980s and involving new sets of problems, such as racism and drug addiction in the building and the neighborhood.

It is also about the way poverty humiliates those who have always prided themselves on being able to cope. It is a very hot summer in New York, the apartment is sweltering, and there is a sequence involving the purchase of a cheap air conditioner that is handled perfectly: We see a father trying to provide for his family and finding shame, in his own eyes, because he does not do as well as he wants to.

The film is also about the stupid things we do because we are human and flawed. Consider the scene at the street carnival, where Johnny gets involved in a "game of skill"—throwing balls at a target, hoping to win a prize for his daughters. The film knows exactly how we try to dig ourselves out, and only dig ourselves deeper.

The mother is played by Samantha Morton, who in film after film (as the mute in *Sweet and Lowdown* and one of the psychics in *Minority Report*) reveals the power of her silences, her quiet, her presence. The two young girls are played by real sisters, Sarah and Emma Bolger,

who are sounding boards and unforgiving judges as the family's troubles grow. "Don't 'little girl' me," Christy says. "I've been carrying this family on my back for over a year."

Paddy Considine is new to me; I saw him in *24 Hour Party People*, I guess, but here he makes an impression: He plays Johnny as determined, insecure, easily wounded, a man who wants to be an actor but fears his spirit has been broken by the death of his son. Djimon Hounsou, given his first big role by Steven Spielberg in *Amistad*, often plays strong and uncomplicated types (as in *Gladiator*). Here, as an artist despairing for his art and his future, he reveals true and deep gifts.

From Ireland and Nigeria, from China, the Philippines, Poland, India, Mexico, and Vietnam, we get the best and the brightest. I am astonished by the will and faith of the recent immigrants I meet. Think what it takes to leave home, family, and even language, to try for a better life in another country. *In America* is not unsentimental about its new arrivals (the movie has a warm heart and frankly wants to move us), but it is perceptive about the countless ways in which it is hard to be poor and a stranger in a new land.

In Cold Blood

R, 134 m., 1967

Robert Blake (Perry Smith), Scott Wilson (Dick Hickock), John Forsythe (Alvin Dewey), Charles McGraw (Smith's Father), John McLiam (Herb Clutter), Brenda C. Currin (Nancy Clutter). Directed and produced by Richard Brooks. Screenplay by Brooks, based on the book by Truman Capote.

In Cold Blood is an eerie case. Not a movie. A case. The film itself, which is fantastically powerful despite its flaws, is the last episode in a chain that began eight years ago when the Herbert Clutter family was murdered near Holcomb, Kansas. Without that murder, Richard Brooks would have been hard-pressed to make this movie, and Truman Capote would have found little employment as the *New Yorker's* rural correspondent.

When I was typing up the cast credits, I came to the line "based on the book by Truman Capote." Some grim humor suggested that I could keep on typing: " . . . and the murders by Perry Smith and Dick Hickock." In an important sense, this movie was created by Smith and Hickock. They spent most of their lives compiling biographies that prepared them for their crime.

Perry came from a violent childhood. His mother drank, his father flew into explosive rages, he was beaten in orphanages. Dick came from marginal poverty, a rootless existence without values. So both were "victims of society," in the way defense attorneys use that term. For their own victims, they chose the Clutter family—a well-off, middle-class, God-fearing family that, in every respect, lived in an opposite world.

If this had been fiction, the themes could not have been more obvious. Two opposed cultures collide. The outsiders kill the insiders in the first round, then lose the second to the hangman. But the film is not based on fiction; the Clutter murders actually happened. If you look at the list of characters you will find such names as Herb Clutter and Perry Smith. Real names. Also featured in the cast are Sadie Truitt and Myrtle Clare playing themselves. They were residents of Holcomb on the night of the murders, and they still are today.

Considerations like that make it difficult to review In Cold Blood as a movie. This is not a work of the imagination, but a masterpiece of copying. Richard Brooks and Truman Capote brought technical skill to their tasks in re-creating the murders, but imagination was not needed. All the events had already happened. And every detail of the film—from the physical appearance of the actors to the use of actual locations, such as the Clutter farmhouse—was chosen to make the film a literal copy of those events.

I do not object to this. Men have always learned about themselves by studying the things their fellows do. If mass murders of this sort are possible in American society (and many have been), then perhaps it is useful to see a thoughtful film about one of them.

And to the degree that In Cold Blood is an accurate, sensitive record of actual events, it succeeds overpoweringly. The actors, Robert Blake (Smith) and Scott Wilson (Hickock), are so good they pass beyond performances and almost into life. Many other performances also have the flat, everyday, absolutely genuine

ring of truth to them. At times one feels this is not a movie but a documentary where the events are taking place now.

What does bother me is the self-conscious "art" that Brooks allows into his film. It does not mix with the actual events. The music on the sound track, for example, is almost conventional Hollywood spook music, as if these murders had to be made convincing. The sounds of the landscape—the wind and weather—would have been music enough. Again some of the photography is staged and distracting. We see Herb Clutter shaving, and fade to one of the killers shaving. We see Perry's bus transform itself into a Santa Fe train passing through Holcomb. Gimmicks like this belong in TV commercials.

Another of Brooks's mistakes, I think, was his decision to write a liberal reporter into the script. This figure obviously represents Capote. He hangs around during the last half of the film, tells about death row, narrates the hangings, and provides instant morals about capital punishment. He is useless and distracting. Brooks should have used either Capote himself or no one.

What we are left with, however, is a film that this Hollywood artiness does not damage very much. The sheer evocative power of the actual events and places sweeps over the music and the trick photography and humbles them. The story itself emerges as bleak and tragic as the day the murders first occurred. The questions raised by Smith and Hickock's senseless crime and the deaths of their undeserving victims are still as impossible to answer.

An Inconvenient Truth

PG, 100 m., 2006

Featuring Al Gore. A documentary directed by Davis Guggenheim and produced by Lawrence Bender, Scott Burns, and Laurie David.

I want to write this review so that every reader will begin it and finish it. I am a liberal, but I do not intend this as a review reflecting any kind of politics. It reflects the truth as I understand it, and it represents, I believe, agreement among the world's experts.

Global warming is real.

It is caused by human activity.

Mankind and governments must begin immediate action to halt and reverse it.

If we do nothing, in about ten years the planet may reach a "tipping point" and begin a slide toward destruction of our civilization and most of the other species on this planet.

After that point is reached, it would be too late for any action.

These facts are stated by Al Gore in the documentary *An Inconvenient Truth.* Forget that he ever ran for office. Consider him a concerned man speaking out on the approaching crisis. "There is no controversy about these facts," he says in the film. "Out of 925 recent articles in peer-review scientific journals about global warming, there was no disagreement. Zero."

He stands on a stage before a vast screen, in front of an audience. The documentary is based on a speech he has been developing for six years and is supported by dramatic visuals. He shows the famous photograph "Earthrise," taken from space by the first American astronauts. Then he shows a series of later space photographs, clearly indicating that glaciers and lakes are shrinking, snows are melting, shorelines are retreating.

He provides statistics: The ten warmest years in history were in the past fourteen years. Last year, South America experienced its first hurricane. Japan and the Pacific are setting new records for typhoons. Hurricane Katrina passed over Florida, doubled back over the Gulf, picked up strength from unusually warm Gulf waters, and went from Category 1 to Category 5. There are changes in the gulf stream and the jet stream. Cores of polar ice show that carbon dioxide is much, much higher than it has been in a quarter of a million years.

It once was thought that such things went in cycles. Gore stands in front of a graph showing the ups and downs of carbon dioxide over the centuries. Yes, there is a cyclical pattern. Then, in recent years, the graph turns up and keeps going up, higher and higher, off the chart.

The primary manmade cause of global warming is the burning of fossil fuels. We are taking energy stored over hundreds of millions of years in the form of coal, gas, and oil and releasing it suddenly. This causes global warming, and there is a pass-along effect. Since glaciers and snow reflect sunlight but seawater absorbs it, the more the ice melts, the more of the sun's energy is retained by the sea.

Gore says that although there is "100 percent agreement" among scientists, a database search of newspaper and magazine articles shows that 57 percent question the fact of global warming, while 43 percent support it. These figures are the result, he says, of a disinformation campaign started in the 1990s by the energy industries to "reposition global warming as a debate." It is the same strategy used for years by the defenders of tobacco. My father was a Luckys smoker who died of lung cancer in 1960, and twenty years later it still was "debatable" that smoking and lung cancer were linked. Now we are talking about the death of the future, starting in the lives of those now living.

"The world won't 'end' overnight in ten years," Gore says. "But a point will have been passed, and there will be an irreversible slide into destruction."

In England, Sir James Lovelock, the scientist who proposed the Gaia hypothesis (that the planet functions like a living organism), has published a new book saying that in one hundred years mankind will be reduced to "a few breeding couples at the poles." Gore thinks "that's too pessimistic. We can turn this around just as we reversed the hole in the ozone layer. But it takes action right now, and politicians in every nation must have the courage to do what is necessary. It is not a political issue. It is a moral issue."

When I said I was going to a press screening of *An Inconvenient Truth,* a friend said, "Al Gore talking about the environment! Bor . . . ing!" This is not a boring film. The director, Davis Guggenheim, uses words, images, and Gore's concise litany of facts to build a film that is fascinating and relentless. In thirty-nine years I have never written these words in a movie review, but here they are: You owe it to yourself to see this film. If you do not, and you have grandchildren, you should explain to them why you decided not to.

Am I acting as an advocate in this review? Yes, I am. I believe that to be "impartial" and "balanced" on global warming means one must take a position like Gore's. There is no other view that can be defended. Senator James Inhofe of Oklahoma, who chairs the Senate Environment Committee, has said, "Global warming is the greatest hoax ever perpetrated on the American people." I hope he takes his job seriously enough to see this film. I think he has a responsibility to do that.

What can we do? Switch to and encourage the development of alternative energy sources: solar, wind, tidal, and, yes, nuclear. Move quickly toward hybrid and electric cars. Pour money into public transit and subsidize the fares. Save energy in our houses. I did a funny thing when I came home after seeing *An Inconvenient Truth.* I went around the house turning off the lights.

Indiana Jones and the Temple of Doom
PG, 118 m., 1984

Harrison Ford (Indiana Jones), Kate Capshaw (Willie Scott), Ke Huy Quan (Short Round), Amrish Puri (Mola Ram), Philip Stone (Captain Blumburtt), Roshan Seth (Chattar Lal). Directed by Steven Spielberg and produced by George Lucas. Screenplay by Willard Huyck and Gloria Katz.

Steven Spielberg's *Indiana Jones and the Temple of Doom* is one of the greatest Bruised Forearm Movies ever made. You know what a Bruised Forearm Movie is. That's the kind of movie where your date is always grabbing your forearm in a viselike grip, as unbearable excitement unfolds on the screen. After the movie is over, you've had a great time but your arm is black-and-blue for a week. This movie is one of the most relentlessly nonstop action pictures ever made, with a virtuoso series of climactic sequences that must last an hour and never stop for a second. It's a roller-coaster ride, a visual extravaganza, a technical triumph, and a whole lot of fun. And it's not simply a retread of *Raiders of the Lost Ark,* the first Indiana Jones movie. It works in a different way, and borrows from different traditions.

Raiders was inspired by Saturday afternoon serials. It was a series of cliff-hanging predicaments, strung out along the way as Indiana Jones traveled from San Francisco to Tibet, Egypt, and other romantic locales. It was an exotic road picture. *Indiana Jones* mostly takes place on one location, and belongs more to the great tradition of the Impregnable Fortress Impregnated. You know the kind of fortress I'm talking about. You see them all the time in James Bond pictures. They involve unbelievably bizarre hideaways, usually buried under the earth, beneath the sea, on the moon, or inside a volcano. They are ruled over by megalomaniac zealots who dream of conquest, and they're fueled by slave labor. Our first glimpse of an Impregnable Fortress is always the same: An ominous long shot, with Wagnerian music, as identically uniformed functionaries hurry about their appointed tasks.

The role of the hero in a movie like this is to enter the fortress, steal the prize, and get away in one piece. This task always involves great difficulty, horrendous surprises, unspeakable dangers, and a virtuoso chase sequence. The very last shots at the end of the sequence are obligatory: The fortress must be destroyed. Hopefully, there will be great walls of flame and water, engulfing the bad guys as the heroes race to freedom, inches ahead of certain death.

But enough of intellectual film criticism. Let's get back to Indiana Jones. As *Temple of Doom* opens, Indiana is in a nightclub somewhere in Shanghai. Killers are after him. He escapes in the nick of time, taking along a beautiful nightclub floozy (Kate Capshaw), and accompanied by his trusty young sidekick, Short Round (Ke Huy Quan). Their getaway leads them into a series of adventures: A flight over the Himalayas, a breathtaking escape from a crashing plane, and a meeting with a village leader who begs Indiana to find and return the village's precious magic jewel—a stone that disappeared along with all of the village's children. Indiana is a plucky chap and agrees. Then there's a dinner in the palace of a sinister local lord. The dinner scene, by the way, also is lifted from James Bond, where it's an obligatory part of every adventure: James is always promised a sure death, but treated first to an elegant dinner with his host, who boasts of his power and takes inordinate pride in being a sophisticated host. After Indiana and Willie retire for the night, there's the movie's only slow sequence, in which such matters as love are discussed. (Make some popcorn.)

Then the movie's second half opens with a breathtaking series of adventures involving the mines beneath the palace—mines that have been turned into a vision of hell.

The set design, art direction, special effects, and sound effects inside this underground Hades are among the most impressive achievements in the whole history of Raiders and Bond-style thrillers. As dozens of little kids work on chain gangs, the evil maharajah keeps them in slavery by using the sinister powers of the missing jewel and its two mates. Indiana and his friends look on in astonishment, and then Indiana attempts to steal back the jewel. Some of the film's great set pieces now take place: Human victims are lowered into a subterranean volcano in a steel cage, weird rituals are celebrated, and there is a chase scene involving the mine's miniature railway. This chase has to be seen to be believed. Spielberg has obviously studied Buster Keaton's *The General,* that silent classic that solved the obvious logistic problem of a chase on railway tracks (i.e., what to do about the fact that one train seemingly always has to be behind the other one). As Indiana and friends hurtle in the little out-of-control mine car, the pursuers are behind, ahead, above, below, and beside them, and the scene will wring you out and leave you breathless. *Indiana Jones and the Temple of Doom* makes no apologies for being exactly what it is: Exhilarating, manic, wildly imaginative escapism.

No apologies are necessary. This is the most cheerfully exciting, bizarre, goofy, romantic adventure movie since *Raiders,* and it is high praise to say that it's not so much a sequel as an equal. It's quite an experience. You stagger out with a silly grin—and a bruised forearm, of course.

I Never Sang for My Father

PG, 92 m., 1971

Melvyn Douglas (Tom), Gene Hackman (Gene), Dorothy Stickney (Margaret), Estelle Parsons (Alice, The Sister), Elizabeth Hubbard (Peggy). Directed and produced by Gilbert Cates. Screenplay by Robert Anderson, based on his play.

At the beginning and again at the end of *I Never Sang for My Father,* we see a grainy snapshot of an old man and a middle-aged man, arms thrown about each other's shoulders, peering uncertainly into the camera as if they're not quite sure what drew them out into the sunshine to pose this day. And we hear Gene Hackman's voice: "Death ends a life. But it does not end a relationship." This film takes that simple fact and uses it to make a poignant and ultimately tragic statement about parents and children, life and death, and all the words that go unspoken. The man is played by Melvyn Douglas, and Hackman plays his son, and the film is about the fierce love they bear for each other, and about their inability to communicate that love, or very much of anything else.

The story takes place at a time when the old man's life is ending, but he won't admit it, and when the younger man's life is about to permit a new beginning. The old man is eighty-one, and a long time ago he was the mayor and the school board president—one of the town's most important citizens. But now he has largely been forgotten, left to live a comfortable life in the rambling old family home. He lives there with his wife and his memories, and a fierce possessiveness for his son.

What he wants from the son is a show of devotion. He doesn't communicate with him; indeed, he spends a lot of time falling asleep in front of the television set. But he wants him there, almost as a hostage, because he has a hunger for affection left over from his own neglected childhood. The son tries to go through the motions. But his own wife died a year ago, and now, at forty-four, he has decided to marry a woman doctor who lives in California. This will mean leaving the hometown, and that would be heresy to his father.

The situation becomes urgent when the old man's wife dies. He seems to accept the death as an inconvenience, transferring his grief to memories of his own mother's death half a century before. But his dependence upon his son becomes almost total. His daughter (Estelle Parsons) comes home for the funeral; in a fit of rage, the old man had banished her for marrying a Jew. Now she explains to Hackman, with an objectivity that sounds cruel but springs from love, that an arrangement is going to have to be made about their father. He can't live in the big house by himself.

The trouble is, his pride makes him refuse to hire the housekeeper he could easily afford. He expects his son to watch over him. And Hackman has not gathered the courage to reveal his marriage plans. He goes to look at a couple of old people's homes, but he finds them depressing and he knows his father would never, ever, go to one. So there you have the son's dilemma. The father should not live alone. A nursing home seems impossible. For a moment, the children consider gaining power of attorney and insisting on a housekeeper. But then, in a scene of remarkable emotional impact, the son watches as his father finally breaks down and reveals his grief, and the son invites him to come and live in California. But that, of course, is also unacceptable to the old man, whose pride will not allow him to admit that others could make his decisions, and whose stubbornness makes him insist on having everything his way, no matter what.

These bare bones of plot hardly give any hint of the power of this film. I've suggested something of what it's about, but almost nothing about the way the writing, the direction, and the performances come together to create one of the most unforgettably human films I can remember.

Robert Anderson's screenplay is from his autobiographical play, and it rings with truth. His dialogue is direct and revealing, without the "literary" touches or sophistication that could have sabotaged the characters. Eugene O'Neill was writing a different kind of dialogue for different purposes in *Long Day's Journey into Night*, a somewhat similar work that comes to mind. But for Anderson's story, which depends on everyday realism and would find symbolism dangerous, the unadorned dialogue is essential.

Gilbert Cates's direction also respects the fact that this is a movie not about visual style or any other fashionably cinematic selfconsciousness. With the exception of an inappropriate song which sneaks onto the sound track near the film's beginning, Cates has directed solely to get those magnificent performances onto the screen as movingly as possible. Much of the film is just between the two of them and the characters seem to work so well because Douglas and Hackman respond to each other in every shot;

the effect is not of acting, but as if the story were happening right now while we see it.

The film tells us that death ends a life, but not a relationship. That's true of all close and deep human relationships; when one person dies, the other continues long afterwards to wonder what could have been said between them, but wasn't.

I Never Sang for My Father has the courage to remain open-ended; the father dies, but the problems between father and son remain unresolved. That is really more tragic than the fact of death, because death is natural, but human nature cries out that parents and children should understand each other.

Innocence

NO MPAA RATING, 94 m., 2001

Julia Blake (Claire), Charles "Bud" Tingwell (Andreas), Terry Norris (John), Kristien Van Pellicom (Young Claire), Kenny Aernouts (Young Andreas). Directed and produced by Paul Cox. Screenplay by Cox.

Here is the most passionate and tender love story in many years, so touching because it is not about a story, not about stars, not about a plot, not about sex, not about nudity, but about *love itself*. True, timeless, undefeated love. *Innocence* tells the story of two people who were lovers in Belgium as teenagers and discover each other, incredibly, both living in Adelaide, Australia, in their late sixties. They meet for tea and there is a little awkward small talk and then suddenly they realize that all the old feelings are still there. They are still in love. And not in some sentimental version of love for the twilight years, but in mad, passionate, demanding, forgiving, accepting love.

Paul Cox's *Innocence* is like a great lifting up of the heart. It is all the more affirming because it is not told in grand, phony gestures, but in the details of the daily lives of these two people. Life accumulates routines, obligations, habits, and inhibitions over the years, and if they are going to face their feelings then they're going to have to break out of long, safe custom and risk everything.

Their names are Claire (Julia Blake) and Andreas (Charles "Bud" Tingwell). Both actors are respected in Australia, both unknown in North America, which is all the better, because the purity of this story would be diffused by the presence of familiar faces (perhaps, for example, *The Bridges of Madison County* would have seemed riskier without the familiarity of Clint Eastwood and Meryl Streep). Andreas is a retired music teacher. His wife died thirty years ago. Claire has long been married to John (Terry Norris), in a marriage she thinks, in that bittersweet phrase, will see her out. Both Claire and Andreas have children, friends, people who count on their predictability. How, for example, does Andreas's housekeeper of many years feel when she discovers (as a housekeeper must) that he is sleeping with someone?

Not that sleeping with someone is that easy. In the movies, characters fall into bed with the casual ease of youth or experience, and no film ever stops to consider that questions of modesty, fear, or shyness might be involved. Paul Cox is a director who never loses sight of the humor even in the most fraught situations, and there is a moment in the film that is just about perfect, when Claire and Andreas find themselves at last unmistakably alone in a bedroom, and she says: "If we're going to do this—let's do it like grown-ups. First, close the curtains. Then, close your eyes."

Innocence has no villains. The treatment of John, Claire's husband, is instructive. He is not made into a monster who deserves to be dumped. He is simply a creature of long habit, a man who is waiting it out, who wears the blinders of routine, who expects his life will continue more or less in the same way until accident or illness brings it to a close. When Claire decides to tell him about Andreas ("I'm too old to lie"), his reaction is a study in complexities, and Paul Cox knows human nature deeply enough to observe that in addition to feeling betrayed, disappointed, and hurt, John also feels—well, although he doesn't acknowledge it, somehow grateful for the excitement. At last something unexpected has happened in the long slow march of his life.

The casting of Blake and Tingwell must have been a delicate matter. It is necessary for them to look their age (unlike aging Hollywood stars who seem stuck at forty-five until they die). But they must not seem dry and brittle, as if left on the shelf too long. Both of them seem touchable, warm, healthy, alive to tenderness and

humor. And there is a sweet macho stubbornness in Tingwell's Andreas, who refuses to accept the world's verdict that he must be over "that sort of thing" at "his age." He is not over it, because, as he writes her in the letter that brings them together, he always imagined them on a journey together, and if she is still alive then the possibility of that journey is alive. If sixty-nine is a little late to continue what was started at nineteen—what is the alternative?

Many things happen in the movie that I have not hinted at. You must share their discoveries as they happen. By the end, if you are like me, you will feel that something transcendent has taken place. This is the kind of film that makes critics want to reach out and shake their readers. Andrew Sarris, for example, who usually maintains a certain practiced objectivity, writes: "The climax of the film is accompanied by a thrilling musical score that lifts the characters to a sublime metaphysical level such as is seldom attained in the cinema." Then he goes on to call *Innocence* a "film for the ages." You see what I mean.

For myself, *Innocence* is a song of joy and hope, and like its characters it is grown up. Here is a movie that believes love leads to sex, made at a time when movies believe that sex leads to love. But sex is only mechanical unless each holds the other like a priceless treasure, to be defended against all of the hazards of the world. This movie is so wise about love it makes us wonder what other love stories think they are about.

Innocence Unprotected

NO MPAA RATING, 75 m., 1967

Dragoljub Aleksic (Acrobat Aleksic), Bratoljub Gligorijevic (Mr. Petrovic), Vera Jovanovic (The Wicked Stepmother), Ana Milosavljevic (Nada the Orphan). Directed by Dusan Makavejev. Screenplay by Makavejev and Branko Vucicevic.

Innocence Unprotected, directed by Dusan Makavejev of Yugoslavia, is one of the most delightful films I've ever seen, and one of the hardest to describe: It's funny, tragic, filled at one moment with black humor and at the next with disarming naïvéte and in form and style totally original.

I saw it a week ago in a preview, and since

then I've engaged in three or four unsuccessful attempts to describe it. Imagine if you will, a film that includes the entire footage of the first Serbian language talkie (produced by an anti-Nazi underground in 1942). Imagine that this film is a melodrama about an orphan girl, a cruel stepmother, her sadistic lover, and a heroic acrobat.

Imagine that twenty-five years later a film was made about the people in this film. Imagine that it was done in a semi-documentary style incorporating color, black-and-white, wide screen, square screen, subtitles, flashbacks, old Hitler newsreels, picnics in graveyards, a man who suffered a fall and became precisely 4.5 centimeters shorter, and the acrobat standing on his head on the seat of a unicycle whose wheel is balanced on the wheel of another unicycle balanced by its seat on a tall pole.

Imagine, in addition, that the 1942 film and the 1967 film both had the same name: *Innocence Unprotected*. That the 1942 stars were not totally aware of the approach the 1967 director was taking. That underlying their optimism there is a hint of tragedy. That the film pretends to be a documentary, but in fact has a dramatic structure that only becomes apparent at the end. And that people quite seriously say things like: "Gentlemen, I assure you the entire Yugoslavian cinema came out of my navel. In fact, I have made certain inquiries, and I am in a position to state positively that the entire Bulgarian cinema came out of my navel as well."

As you can see, the movie indeed resists being written about. More than any director since Jean-Luc Godard, Makavejev is able to leap nimbly back and forth over the line dividing a film from reality. This is a film within a film, but it's also a film about a film that has a film within it. That may sound nonsensical, but I mean it literally. Makavejev works in a world of his own.

Note: The film won the Gold Hugo, first prize, in the 1968 Chicago Film Festival.

Interiors

PG, 93 m., 1978

Kristin Griffith (Flyn), Mary Beth Hurt (Joey), Richard Jordan (Frederick), Diane Keaton (Renata), E. G. Marshall (Arthur), Geraldine Page (Eve), Maureen Stapleton (Pearl), Sam Waterston (Mike). Directed by Woody Allen and produced by Charles H. Joffe. Screenplay by Allen.

Yes, the opening *does* remind us of Bergman: The static shots, held for a moment's contemplation, of the rooms and possessions of a family. But then people enter the rooms, and their lives and voices have a particularly American animation; Woody Allen is right to say that his drama, *Interiors*, belongs more in the tradition of Eugene O'Neill than of Ingmar Bergman. But what's this? Here we have a *Woody Allen* film, and we're talking about O'Neill and Bergman and traditions and influences? Yes, and correctly. Allen, whose comedies have been among the cheerful tonics of recent years, is astonishingly assured in his first drama.

He gives us a time of crisis in a family, and develops it in counterpoint with the countless smaller joys and crises that are a family. He is very spare: Every scene counts, and the dialogue has the precision of a J. D. Salinger short story. There's nothing thrown in for effect unless the effect contributes specifically to the direction of the complete film.

Allen's central character is the family's mother, Eve, played by Geraldine Page as a heartbreaking showdown between total self-confidence in the past and catastrophic breakdown in the present. She is a designer, and her rooms are some, but not all, of the interiors of the title. She aims for a cool perfectionism in her rooms, for grays and greens and pale blues, for a look of irreproachable sterility. Her science and art is to know the correct place for a lamp, within a fraction of an inch.

She is married to a wealthy lawyer (E. G. Marshall). She has three daughters: A poet (Diane Keaton), a movie star (Kristin Griffith), and a searcher for meaningful occupation (Mary Beth Hurt). Keaton lives with an alcoholic would-be novelist (Richard Jordan). Hurt lives with a filmmaker (Sam Waterston). Marshall announces that he wants a trial separation from Page, and later introduces a woman he's met on a cruise and wants to marry (Maureen Stapleton).

There you have them, the eight people of this movie. Allen, who thought nothing in *Annie Hall* of producing Marshall McLuhan from behind a theater lobby display for a comic walk-on, isolates his characters in *Interiors* so thoroughly, we're reminded of O'Neill's family in *Long Day's Journey into Night*, coming and going in an old house with no access to any world outside.

There are hurts in this family that have been buried for years, and guilts that still hold it together. One daughter finally blurts out an accusation against her mother, who had thought herself so perfect and yet was as capable as anyone of pettiness and cruelty. We get the feeling, indeed, that the family has been together much too long, and that family life is not necessarily a blessing.

If there is a common wish shared by all the characters in the film, it's to live a life of their own. The father, defending to his daughters his decision to marry a woman they call a "vulgarian," argues not unreasonably that he's paid the bills and maintained the household for years—that now, in his early sixties, he's *earned* his right to some years of his own choosing.

The others have earned their rights, too, but each at the expense of the others. That is how each sees it, anyway. The same charge passes again and again around the family circle: That if the others had not been so demanding, or selfish, or jealous, or vindictive, then *this* person would have been set free to realize himself or herself.

Allen treats these themes in scenes that have an elegant economy of expression. The scene around the dinner table, for example, as the father announces his decision to leave, is handled in a way that etches the feelings of every member of the family, in just the right tones of anger, disbelief, or defiance. Scenes involving the daughters and their men suggest in different ways that the problems of this family will not end in this generation.

The funniest and saddest scene begins with the father's second marriage; Maureen Stapleton is wonderful as the "vulgarian," sweeping in with her red gown and finding Page's rooms "so gray. . . ." The dinner table conversation this time allows Allen to regard the Stapleton character with a mixture of tenderness and satire so delicately balanced, it's virtuoso.

The wonderment is that it's "serious." Yes, it is, but to be serious is not always to be good, and a movie both serious and bad is a great depression for everyone. *Interiors* becomes serious by intently observing complex adults as they fend and cope, blame and justify. Because it illuminates some of the ways we all act, it is serious but not depressing; when it's over, we may even find ourselves quietly cheered that Allen has seen so clearly how things can be.

In the Bedroom

R, 130 m., 2001

Tom Wilkinson (Matt Fowler), Sissy Spacek (Ruth Fowler), Nick Stahl (Frank Fowler), William Mapother (Richard Strout), Marisa Tomei (Natalie Strout), William Wise (Willis Grinnel), Celia Weston (Katie Grinnel), Karen Allen (Marla Keyes). Directed by Todd Field and produced by Field, Ross Katz, and Graham Leader. Screenplay by Robert Festinger and Field, based on a short story by Andre Dubus.

Todd Field's *In the Bedroom* only slowly reveals its real subject, in a story that has a shocking reversal at the end of the first act, and then looks more deeply than we could have guessed into the lives of its characters. At first it seems to be about a summer romance. At the end, it's about revenge—not just to atone for a wound, but to prove a point. The film involves love and violence, and even some thriller elements, but it is not about those things. It is about two people so trapped in opposition that one of them must break.

The story opens in sunshine and romance. Frank Fowler (Nick Stahl) is in love with Natalie Strout (Marisa Tomei). He'll be a new graduate student in the autumn. She is in her thirties, has two children, is estranged from Richard (William Mapother), who is a rich kid and an abusive husband. Frank's parents are worried.

"This is not some sweetie from Vassar you can visit on holidays," his mother tells him. "You're not in this alone."

"We're not serious, Mom," Frank says. "It's a summer thing."

"I see," says his mother. She sees clearly that Frank really does love Natalie—and she also sees that Frank's father may be vicariously enjoying the relationship, proud that his teenage son has conquered an attractive woman.

Ruth Fowler (Sissy Spacek) is a choral director at the local high school. Her husband, Matt (Tom Wilkinson), is the local doctor in their Maine village. On the local social scale, they are a step above the separated Natalie and her husband, whose money comes from the local fish business. Is she a snob? She wouldn't think so. The Fowlers pride themselves on being intelligent, open-minded, able to talk about things with their son (who does not want to talk about anything with them). We sense that their household accommodates enormous silences; that the parents and their son have each retreated to a personal corner to nurse wounds.

Then something happens. A review should not tell you what it is. It changes our expectations for the story, which turns out to be about matters more deeply embedded in the heart than we could have imagined. The film unfolds its true story, which is about the marriage of Matt and Ruth—about how hurt and sadness turns to anger and blame. There are scenes as true as movies can make them, and even when the story develops thriller elements, they are redeemed, because the movie isn't about what happens, but about why.

In the Bedroom is the first film directed by Todd Field, an actor *(Eyes Wide Shut, The Haunting)*, and one of the best-directed films this year. It's based on a story by the late Andre Dubus, the Massachusetts-based writer who died in 1999, and who worked with Field on the adaptation before his death. It works with indirection; the events on the screen are markers for secret events in the hearts of the characters, and the deepest insight is revealed, in a way, only in the last shot.

Every performance has perfect tone: Nick Stahl as the man who is half in love with a woman and half in love with being in love; Marisa Tomei, who is wiser than her young lover, and protective toward him, because she understands better than he does the problems they face; William Mapother as the abusive husband, never more frightening than when he tries to be conciliatory and apologetic; William Wise and Celia Weston as the Grinnels, the Fowlers' best friends.

And Sissy Spacek and Tom Wilkinson. They know exactly what they're doing, they understand their characters down to the ground, they are masters of the hidden struggle beneath the surface. Spacek plays a reasonable and civil wife and mother who has painful issues of her own; there is a scene where she slaps someone, and it is the most violent and shocking moment in a violent film. Wilkinson lives through his son more than he admits, and there is a scene where he surprises Frank and Natalie alone together, and finds a kind of quiet relish in their embarrassment. When Matt and Ruth lash out at each other, when the harsh accusations are said aloud, we are shocked but not surprised; these hard notes were undertones in their civilized behavior toward each other. Not all marriages can survive hard times.

Most movies are about plot, and chug from one stop to the next. Stephen King, whose book *On Writing* contains a lot of good sense, argues for situation over plot, suggests that if you do a good job of visualizing your characters, it is best to put them into a situation and see what happens, instead of chaining them to a plot structure. Todd Field and Andre Dubus use the elements of plot, but only on the surface, and the movie's title refers not to sex but to the secrets, spoken, unspoken, and dreamed, that are shared at night when two people close the door after themselves.

In the Company of Men

R, 93 m., 1997

Aaron Eckhart (Chad), Stacy Edwards (Christine), Matt Malloy (Howard), Michael Martin (Coworker 1), Mark Rector (John), Chris Hayes (Coworker 2), Jason Dixie (Intern), Emily Cline (Suzanne). Directed by Neil LaBute and produced by Mark Archer and Stephen Pevner. Screenplay by LaBute.

Now here is true evil: cold, unblinking, reptilian. The character Chad in *In the Company of Men* makes the terrorists of the summer thrillers look like boys throwing mud pies. And for every Chad there is a Howard, a weaker man, ready to go along, lacking the courage to disagree and half intoxicated by the stronger will of the other man. People like this are not so uncommon. Look around you.

The movie takes place in the familiar habitats of the modern corporate male: hotel corridors, airport "courtesy lounges," corporate cubicles, and meeting rooms. The men's room is an invaluable refuge for private conversations. We never find out what the corporation makes, but what does it matter? Modern business administration techniques have made the corporate environment so interchangeable that an executive from Pepsi, say, can transfer seamlessly to Apple and apply the same "management philosophy" without missing a beat.

Chad (Aaron Eckhart) and Howard (Matt Malloy) have been assigned for six weeks to a regional office of their company. Waiting for their flight, they talk. Chad is unhappy and angry because he's been dumped by his girlfriend ("The whole fade-out thing"). He proposes a plan: "Say we were to find some girl vulnerable as hell . . ." In their new location, they'll select a young woman who doesn't look like she has much of a social life. They'll both shower her with attention—flowers, dinner dates—until she's dizzy, and then, "out comes the rug, both of us dropping her!"

Chad explains this plan with the blinkered, formal language of a man whose recreational reading consists of best-selling primers on excellence and wealth. "Life is for the taking—is it not?" he asks. And, "Is that not ideal? To restore a little dignity to our lives?" He hammers his plan home in a men's room, while Howard, invisible behind a cubicle door, says he guesses he agrees.

The "girl" they choose for their target turns out to be deaf—a bonus. Her name is Christine (Stacy Edwards). She is pleasant, pretty, articulate; it is easy to understand everything she says, but Chad is cruel as he describes her to Howard: "She's got one of those voices like Flipper. You should hear her going at it, working to put the simplest sounds together." Chad makes a specialty of verbal brutality. Christine is not overwhelmed to be dating two men at once, but she finds it pleasant, and eventually she begins to really like Chad.

In the Company of Men, written and directed by Neil LaBute, is a continuing series of revelations, because it isn't simply about this sick joke. Indeed, if the movie were only about what Chad and Howard do to Christine and how she reacts, it would be too easy, a one-note attack on these men as sadistic predators. The movie deals with much more and it cuts deeper, and by the end we see it's about a whole system of values in which men as well as women are victims, and monstrous selfishness is held up as the greatest good.

Environments like the one in this film are poisonous, and many people have to try to survive in them. Men like Chad and Howard are dying inside. Personal advancement is the only meaningful goal. Women and minorities are seen by white males as unfairly advantaged. White males are seen as unfairly advantaged by everyone else.

There is an incredibly painful scene in *In the Company of Men* where Chad tells a young black trainee, "They asked me to recommend someone for the management training program," and then requires the man to humiliate himself in order to show that he qualifies. At first you see the scene as racist. Then you realize Chad and the trainee are both victims of the corporate culture they occupy, in which the power struggle is the only reality. Something forces both of them to stay in the room during that ugly scene, and it is job insecurity.

On a more human level, the story becomes poignant. Both Howard and Chad date Christine. There is an unexpected emotional development. I will not reveal too much. We arrive at the point where we thought the story was leading us, and it keeps on going. There is another chapter. We find a level beneath the other levels. The game was more Machiavellian than we imagined. We thought we were witnessing evil, but now we look on its true face.

What is remarkable is how realistic the story is. We see a character who is depraved, selfish, and evil, and he is not a bizarre eccentric, but a product of the system. It is not uncommon to know personally of behavior not unlike Chad's. Most of us, of course, are a little more like Howard, but that is small consolation. "Can't you see?" Howard says. "I'm the good guy!" In other words, I am not as bad as the bad guy, although I am certainly weaker.

Christine survives, because she knows who she is. She is deaf, but less disabled than Howard and Chad, because she can hear on frequencies that their minds and imaginations do not experience. *In the Company of Men* is the kind of bold, uncompromising film that insists on being thought about afterward—talked about, argued about, hated if necessary, but not ignored. "How does it feel right now, deep down inside?" one of the characters asks. The movie asks us the same question.

In the Shadow of the Moon

PG, 100 m., 2007

With Buzz Aldrin, Alan Bean, Eugene Cernan, Michael Collins, Jim Lovell, John Young, Charlie Duke, Edgar D. Mitchell, Harrison Schmitt, and Dave Scott. Directed by David Singleton and produced by Duncan Copp.

We think of the Apollo voyages to the moon more in terms of the achievement than the ordeal. On the night of July 20, 1969, we looked up at the sky and realized that men, who had been gazing at the moon since before they were men, had somehow managed to venture there and were walking on its surface.

Yes, but consider the journey. Three men were packed like sardines in a tiny space capsule ("Spam in a can," the Gemini astronauts called themselves) and sent on a 480,000-mile round trip in a vessel whose electrical wiring was so questionable it had already burned three of them alive on a test pad. The capsule sat atop a rocket that had a way of blowing up. They had no way of knowing where, on the moon, they would land, if they got there. Compared to them, Evel Knievel was a Sunday driver.

Yes, but they took their chances, and they made it. Six of the seven Apollo missions landed on he moon, and the saga of *Apollo 13* was a masterpiece of ingenuity in the face of catastrophe. Now here is a spellbinding documentary interviewing many of the surviving astronauts, older men now, about their memories of the adventure. One who is prominently missing is Neil Armstrong, first man on the moon, who says he was first only by chance and gets too much attention. Gene Siskel sat next to him on an airplane once, and thought to himself, "Here is a man who is very weary of being asked what it was like to walk on the moon." So they talked about other things.

Of the others, every one is still sharp and lively and youthful in mind, even often in body. I attended the Conference on World Affairs in Boulder several times with Rusty Schweickart, and noticed that he tended to be on panels that were about everything but space exploration. Yet here, in front of the cameras, they open up in a heartfelt way. The most stunning moment reveals how desper-

ately they wanted to be part of the missions: Gus Grissom, one of the three astronauts killed in the launch-pad fire, earlier told John Young he doubted the safety of the wiring in the 100-percent oxygen atmosphere of the capsule but didn't dare complain because he might be booted out of the program for a negative attitude.

When you were on the moon, they remember, you could blank out the earth by holding up your thumb in front of your face. Yet they were struck by how large the planet was, and how thin and fragile its atmosphere, floating in an infinite void and preserving this extraordinary thing, life. And below, we were poisoning it as fast as we could.

The interviews with the astronauts are intercut with footage that is new, in great part, and looks better than it has any right to do. A researcher for this production spent years screening NASA footage that was still, in many cases, in its original film cans and had never been seen. The film was cleaned up and restored, the color refreshed, and the result is beautiful and moving. The Apollo missions were, after all, the most momentous steps ever taken by mankind; our species, like all living things, was evolved to live and endure on the planet of its origin. Random life spores may have traveled from world to world by chance, but this was the first time any living thing looked up and said, "I'm going there." These astronauts are still alive, but as long as mankind survives, their journeys will be seen as the turning point—to what, it is still to be seen.

In the Valley of Elah

R, 120 m., 2007

Tommy Lee Jones (Hank Deerfield), Charlize Theron (Detective Emily Sanders), Jason Patric (Lieutenant Kirklander), Susan Sarandon (Joan Deerfield), Jonathan Tucker (Mike Deerfield), Brent Briscoe (Detective Hodge), Joseph Bertot (Juan), Victor Wolf (Jose Ortiez), James Franco (Sergeant Dan Camelli). Directed by Paul Haggis and produced by Patrick Wachsberger, Steven Samuels, Darlene Caamano Loquet, Haggis, and Larry Becsey. Screenplay by Haggis.

I don't know Tommy Lee Jones at all. Let's get that clear. I've interviewed him, and at Cannes we had one of those discussions at the American Pavilion. He didn't enjoy doing it, but he felt duty-bound to promote his great film *The Three Burials of Melquiades Estrada*. During my questions he twisted his hands like a kid in the principal's office. He remains a mystery to me, which is why I feel free to share some feelings about him. I'm trying to understand why he is such a superb actor.

Look at the lines around his eyes. He looks concerned, under pressure from himself, a man who has felt pain. Look at his face. It seems to conceal hurtful emotion. He doesn't smile a lot, but when he does, its like clouds are lifting. Listen to his voice, filled with authority and hard experience. Notice when he speaks that he passes out words as if they were money he can't afford. Whether these characteristics are true of the private man, I have no way of knowing.

Paul Haggis's *In the Valley of Elah* is built on Tommy Lee Jones's persona, and that is why it works so well. The same material could have been banal or routine with an actor trying to be "earnest" and "sincere." Jones isn't trying to be anything at all. His character is simply compelled to do what he does, and has a lot of experience doing it. He plays a Vietnam veteran named Hank Deerfield, now hauling gravel in Tennessee. He gets a call from the Army that his son Mike, just returned from a tour in Iraq, is AWOL from his squad at Fort Rudd. That sounds wrong. He tells his wife Joan (Susan Sarandon) that he's going to drive down there and take a look into things. "It's a two-day drive," she says. "Not the way I'll drive it."

He checks into a cheap motel. His investigations in the area of Fort Rudd take him into topless bars, chicken shacks, the local police station, the base military police operation, and a morgue where he's shown something cut into pieces and burned, and he IDs the remains as his son. Looking through his son's effects, he asks as a distraction if he can have his Bible, while he's pocketing his son's cell phone. It's been nearly destroyed by heat, but a friendly technician salvages some video from it, filled with junk artifacts but still retaining glimpses of what it recorded on video: Glimpses of hell.

To describe the many avenues of his investigation would be pointless, and diminish the film's gathering tension. I'd rather talk about what Haggis, also the cowriter and coproducer, does with the performance. Imagine the first violinist playing a note to lead the orchestra into tune. Haggis, as director, draws that note from Jones, and the other actors tune to it. They include Charlize Theron as a city homicide detective, Jason Patric as a military policeman, Sarandon as Deerfield's wife, and various other police and military officers and member's of Mike's unit in Iraq.

None of these characters are heightened. None of them behave in any way as if they're in a thriller. Other directors might have pumped them up, made them colorful or distinctive in some distracting way. Theron could (easily) be sexy. Patric could (easily) be a bureaucratic paper-pusher. Sarandon could (easily) be a hysterical worrier, or an alcoholic, or push it any way you want to. You know how movies make supporting actors more colorful than they need to be, and how happily a lot of actors go along with that process.

Not here. Theron, who is actually the costar, so carefully modulates her performance that she even ignores most of the sexism aimed at her at the police station. Nor is there any hint of sexual attraction between her and anybody else, nor does she sympathize with Hank Deerfield and work on his behalf. Nor, for that matter does she compete with him. She simply does her job and raises her young son.

I don't think there's a scene in the movie that could be criticized as "acting," with quotation marks. When Sarandon, who has already lost one son to the Army, now finds she has lost both, what she says to Jones over the telephone is filled with bitter emotion but not given a hint of emotional spin. She says it the way a woman would, if she had held the same conversation with this man for a lifetime. The movie is about determination, doggedness, duty, and the ways a war changes a man. There is no release or climax at the end, just closure. Even the final dramatic gesture only says exactly what Deerfield explained earlier that it says, and nothing else.

That tone follows through to the movie's consideration of the war itself. Those who call *In the Valley of Elah* anti-Iraq-war will not have been paying attention. It doesn't give a damn where the war is being fought. Hank

Deerfield isn't politically opposed to the war. He just wants to find out how his son came all the way home from Iraq and ended up in charred pieces in a field. Because his experience in Vietnam apparently had a lot to do with crime investigation, he's able to use intelligence as well as instinct. And observe how Theron, as the detective, observes him, takes what she can use, and adds what she draws from her own experience.

Paul Haggis is making good films these days. He directed *Crash* and wrote *Million Dollar Baby*, both Oscar winners, and was nominated as cowriter of *Letters from Iwo Jima*. He and his casting directors assembled an ideal ensemble for this film, which doesn't sensationalize but just digs and digs into our apprehensions. I have been trying to think who else could have carried this picture except Tommy Lee Jones, and I just can't do it. Who else could tell Theron's young son the story of David and Goliath (which took place in the alley of Elah) and make it sound like instruction in the tactics of being brave?

Into the Wild

R, 150 m., 2007

Emile Hirsch (Christopher McCandless), Vince Vaughn (Wayne Westerberg), Marcia Gay Harden (Billie McCandless), William Hurt (Walt McCandless), Hal Holbrook (Ron Franz), Catherine Keener (Jan Burres), Kristen Stewart (Tracy), Jena Malone (Carine McCandless), Zach Galifianakis (Kevin). Written and directed by Sean Penn. Based on the book by Jon Krakauer. Produced by David Blocker, Frank Hildebrand, and John J. Kelly.

For those who have read Thoreau's *Walden*, there comes a time, maybe only lasting a few hours or a day, when the notion of living alone in a tiny cabin beside a pond and planting some beans seems strangely seductive. Certain young men, of which I was one, lecture patient girlfriends about how such a life of purity and denial makes perfect sense. Christopher McCandless did not outgrow this phase.

Jon Krakauer's *Into the Wild*, which I read with a fascinated dread, tells the story of a twenty-year-old college graduate who cashes in his law school fund and, in the words of Mark Twain, lights out for the territory. He

drives west until he can drive no farther, and then north into the Alaskan wilderness. He has a handful of books about survival and edible wild plants, and his model seems to be Jack London, although he should have devoted more attention to that author's *To Build a Fire*.

Sean Penn's spellbinding film adaptation of this book stays close to the source. We meet Christopher (Emily Hirsch) as an idealistic dreamer, in reaction against his proud parents (William Hurt and Marcia Gay Hardin) and his bewildered sister (Jena Malone). He had good grades at Emory; his future in law school was right there in his grasp. Why did he disappear from their lives, why was his car found abandoned, where was he, and why, why, why?

He keeps journals in which he sees himself in the third person as a heroic loner, renouncing civilization, returning to the embrace of nature. In centuries past such men might have been saints, retreating to a cave or hidden hermitage, denying themselves all pleasures except subsistence. He sees himself not as homeless, but as a man freed from homes.

In the book, Krakauer traces his movements through the memories of people he encounters on his journey. It was an impressive reporting achievement to track them down, and Penn's film affectionately embodies them in strong performances. These are people who take in the odd youth, feed him, shelter him, give him clothes, share their lives, mentor him—and worry as he leaves to continue his quest, which seems to them, correctly, as doomed.

By now McCandless has renamed himself Alexander Supertramp. He is validated by his lifestyle choice. He meets such people as Rainey and Jan (Brian Dieker and Catherine Keener), leftover hippies still happily rejecting society, and Wayne (Vince Vaughn), a hard-drinking, friendly farmer. The most touching contact he makes is with Ron (Hal Holbrook), an older man who sees him clearly and with apprehension, and begins to think of him as a wayward grandson. Christopher lectures this man, who has seen it all, on what he is missing, and asks him to follow him up a steep hillside to see the next horizon. Ron tries, before he admits he is no longer in condition.

And then McCandless disappears from the maps of memory, into unforgiving Alaska.

Yes, it looks beautiful. It is all he dreamed of. He finds an abandoned bus where no bus should be, and makes it his home. He tries hunting, not very successfully. He lives off the land, but the land is a zero-tolerance system. From his journals and other evidence, Penn reconstructs his final weeks. Emile Hirsch plays him in a hypnotic performance, turning skeletal, his eyes sinking into his skull while they still burn with zeal. It is great acting, and more than acting.

This is a reflective, regretful, serious film, about a young man swept away by his uncompromising choices. Two of the more truthful statements in recent culture is that we need a little help from our friends, and that sometimes we must depend on the kindness of strangers. If you don't know those two things and accept them, you will end up eventually in a bus of one kind or another. Sean Penn himself, fiercely idealistic, uncompromising, a little less angry now, must have read the book and reflected that there, but for the grace of God, went he. The movie is so good partly because it means so much, I think, to its writer-director. It is a testament like the words that Christopher carved into planks in the wilderness.

I grew up in Urbana three houses down from the Sanderson family—Milton and Virginia and their boys, Steve and Joe. My close friend was Joe. His bedroom was filled with aquariums, terrariums, snakes, hamsters, spiders, and butterfly and beetle collections. I envied him like crazy. After college he hit the road. He never made a break from his parents, but they rarely knew where he was. Sometimes he came home and his mother would have to sew $100 bills into the seams of his blue jeans. He disappeared in Nicaragua. His body was later identified as a dead Sandinista freedom fighter. From a nice little house surrounded by evergreens at the other end of Washington Street, he left to look for something he needed to find. I believe in Sean Penn's Christopher McCandless. I grew up with him.

Invincible

PG-13, 133 m., 2002

Tim Roth (Erik-Jan Hanussen), Jouko Ahola (Zishe Breitbart), Anna Gourari (Marta Farra), Max Raabe (Master of Ceremonies), Jacob Wein (Benjamin), Gustav-Peter Wöhler (Landwehr). Directed by Werner Herzog and produced by Gary Bart and Herzog. Screenplay by E. Max Frye and Herzog.

Werner Herzog's *Invincible* tells the astonishing story of a Jewish strongman in Nazi Germany, a man who in his simple goodness believes he can be the "new Samson" and protect his people. He is a blacksmith in Poland in 1932 when discovered by a talent scout, and soon becomes the headliner in the Palace of the Occult in Berlin, which is run by the sinister Hanussen (Tim Roth), a man who dreams of becoming minister of the occult in a Nazi government.

The strongman, named Zishe Breitbart, is played by a Finnish athlete named Jouko Ahola, twice winner of the title World's Strongest Man. Much of the movie's uncanny appeal comes from the contrast between Ahola's performance, which is entirely without guile, and Roth's performance, which drips with mannered malevolence. Standing between them is the young woman Marta (Anna Gourari), who is under Hanussen's psychological power, and whom the strongman loves.

Invincible is based, Herzog says, on the true story of Breitbart, whose great strength contradicted the Nazi myth of Aryan superiority. I can imagine a dozen ways in which this story could be told badly, but Herzog has fashioned it into a film of uncommon fascination, in which we often have no idea at all what could possibly happen next. There are countless movies about preludes to the Holocaust, but I can't think of one this innocent, direct, and unblinking. In the face of gathering evil, Zishe trusts in human nature, is proud of his heritage, and believes strength and goodness (which he confuses) will triumph.

The movie has the power of a great silent film, unafraid of grand gestures and moral absolutes. Its casting of the major characters is crucial, and instinctively correct. Tim Roth is a sinister charlatan, posing as a man with real psychic powers, using trickery and showmanship as he jockeys for position within the emerging Nazi majority. There is a scene where he hypnotizes Marta, and as he stares boldly into the camera I wondered, for a moment, if it was possible to hypnotize a movie audience that way. Late in the film there is a scene where his secrets are revealed, and he makes a speech of chilling, absolute cynicism. Another actor in another movie might have simply gnashed his teeth, but Roth and Herzog take the revelations as an opportunity to show us the self-hatred beneath the deception.

As for Jouko Ahola, this untrained actor, who seems by nature to be good-hearted and uncomplicated, may never act again, but he has found the one perfect role, as Maria Falconetti did in *The Passion of Joan of Arc*. He embodies the simple strongman. The camera can look as closely as it wants and never find anything false. As a naive man from a backward town, not especially devout, he gets into a fight when Polish customers in a restaurant insult him and his little brother as Jews. A little later, entering a circus contest, he watches as the strongman lifts a boulder—and then puts an end to the contest by lifting the strongman *and* the boulder.

The talent scout takes him to see his first movie. Soon he is in Berlin, where Hanussen sizes him up and says, "We will Aryanize you. A Jew should never be as strong as you." Zishe is outfitted with a blond wig and a Nordic helmet, and presented as "Siegfried." He becomes a great favorite of Nazi brownshirts in the audience, as Hanussen prattles about "the strength of the body against the dark powers of the occult." But Zishe's mind works away at the situation until finally he has his solution, tears off the helmet and wig, and identifies himself as a Jew.

Here as throughout the film Herzog avoids the obvious next scene. Is Hanussen outraged? To a degree. But then he reports: "There's a line three blocks long outside! It's the Jews. They all want to see the new Samson." And then, at a time when Hitler was on the rise but the full measure of Jewish persecution was not yet in view, the Palace of the Occult turns into a dangerous pit where audience members are potentially at one another's throats.

This is the first feature in ten years from Werner Herzog, one of the great visionaries among directors. He strains to break the bonds of film structure in order to surprise us in unexpected ways. His best films unashamedly yearn to lift us into the mythical and the mystical. "Our civilization is starving for new images," he once told me, and in *Invincible* there is

an image of a bleak, rocky seashore where the sharp stones are littered with thousands or millions of bright red crabs, all mindlessly scrabbling away on their crabby missions. I think this scene may represent the emerging Nazi hordes, but of course there can be no literal translation: Perhaps Herzog wants to illustrate the implacable Darwinian struggle from which man can rise with good heart and purpose.

The strongman in *Invincible* is lovable and so deeply moving precisely because he is not a cog in a plot, has no plan, is involved in no machinations, but is simply proud of his parents, proud to be a Jew, in love with the girl, and convinced that God has made him strong for a reason. He may be wrong in his optimism, but his greatest strength is that he will never understand that. The Roth character is equally single-minded, but without hope or purpose—a conniver and manipulator.

Watching *Invincible* was a singular experience for me, because it reminded me of the fundamental power that the cinema had for us when we were children. The film exercises the power that fable has for the believing. Herzog has gotten outside the constraints and conventions of ordinary narrative, and addresses us where our credulity keeps its secrets.

Iphigenia

NO MPAA RATING, 127 m., 1977

Irene Papas (Clytemnestra), Costa Kazakos (Agamemnon), Costa Carras (Menelaus), Tatiana Papamoskou (Iphigenia), Christos Tsangas (Ulysses), Panos Michalopoulos (Achilles). Directed, produced, and written by Michael Cacoyannis, based on the play by Euripides.

Forget for the moment that *Iphigenia* is based on a Greek tragedy by Euripides. Accept it instead as the story of a carefree young girl on the eve of her wedding. See her surrounded by her playmates, see her coddled by her mother, and know that she is, in fact, never going to be married. That her father has promised her instead as a sacrifice to the gods.

It's possible for us to relate to *Iphigenia* on this simple human level because its director, Michael Cacoyannis, has filmed it that way. There's a tendency sometimes to overplay classical Greek drama, as if the production had to be overwrought to do justice to the emotions contained.

Cacoyannis never does that here, and he didn't, either, in *Electra* (1962), the first of the three films he's made about the Trojan Wars. He keeps his focus firmly on the characters and their stories; he isn't reverential in the face of classical material, and so its elemental force comes through—the same kind of force we felt in Zeffirelli's *Romeo and Juliet.* These aren't classroom productions; they're movies.

And *Iphigenia* is heartbreaking in its events. It's the third of Cacoyannis's films about the Trojan Wars (*Electra* was followed in 1971 by *The Trojan Woman*, which I didn't admire as much). But it's the first in chronological order, telling of the days when Helen eloped with Paris, and the Greeks joined together to avenge the honor of her husband, Menelaus.

The film opens with the vast Greek fleet becalmed: The wind will not take them to Troy. Agamemnon, the older brother of Menelaus, shoots game to feed the troops, and one of his arrows strikes a sacred deer. Disaster; the oracle orders him to sacrifice his first-born child to appease the gods and cause the wind to blow.

Up until this point in the film, what we're given is pretty straightforward narrative. But then the film's two key characters enter: Iphigenia, played by the gravely beautiful young actress Tatiana Papamoskou, and her mother, Clytemnestra, played by Irene Papas, who combines beauty with dignity in a way that approaches the elemental.

The young girl is told by a messenger that she must come at once to the seashore; she is to marry the handsome young Achilles. Because we know her fate, we find the scenes of her marriage preparations heartbreaking. The little scenes between Iphigenia and her playmates, the small tendernesses between mother and daughter, the exhaustions of the journey, are all building to a final hour of extraordinary emotion.

There are three key movements. The first involves the moral bind that Agamemnon finds himself in: As his armies chant with terrifying blood lust for a sacrifice, he's torn between love for his daughter, a superstitious regard for the oracle and Greek tradition, and his own weakness. There is a message here

about the nature of men and armies, but Cacoyannis doesn't press it. He doesn't have to.

The other two movements are contained in the film's two great scenes. One is the confrontation between Agamemnon and Clytemnestra, and here Irene Papas surpasses herself. As Cacoyannis's camera cuts on movements to present Agamemnon as surrounded on all sides by the wrath of his wife, she attacks him with withering scorn while begging for the life of their child. And then there is the scene, as moving in its simplicity as the other was in its force, in which the child begs for her own life, and then accepts her fate with dignity.

Cacoyannis is simply incapable of taking such a story and filming it as a sort of Classics Illustrated. He goes straight to the heart of the story, he tells it simply and directly (with no "these" and "thous" and similar anachronisms in the subtitles), and at the end we're wrung out.

A lot has happened since his *Electra* won the grand prix at Cannes in 1962. Cacoyannis had his greatest international success in 1964, with *Zorba the Greek* (which in some respects *The Greek Tycoon* is still ripping off). But then there was the Greek military junta—and exile for Cacoyannis, his composer Mikis Theodorakis, and stars such as Irene Papas and Melina Mercouri. There was *The Trojan Woman*, shot in exile and not necessarily benefiting from the interpretations of such non-Greek actresses as Katharine Hepburn and Vanessa Redgrave. But now, back on his native soil, shooting more simply, Cacoyannis with *Iphigenia* has found his roots again.

Ivans xtc.

NO MPAA RATING, 94 m., 2002

Danny Huston (Ivan Beckman), Peter Weller (Don West), Lisa Enos (Charlotte White), Adam Krentzman (Barry Oaks), Alex Butler (Brad East), Morgan Vukovic (Lucy Lawrence), Tiffani-Amber Thiessen (Marie Stein), James Merendino (Danny McTeague), Caroleen Feeney (Rosemary). Directed by Bernard Rose and produced by Enos. Screenplay by Rose and Enos, based on the story *The Death of Ivan Ilyich* by Leo Tolstoy.

There is much sadness but little mourning at the funeral of Ivan Beckman. All agree he brought about his own death. He had few close friends. It is said he died from cancer. Insiders whisper, "The cancer is a cover story." You know you have lived your life carelessly when cancer is your cover story.

Ivans xtc., a remarkable film by Bernard Rose, stars Danny Huston, the rich-voiced, genial, tall son of John Huston, as a powerful Hollywood agent whose untidy personal life becomes a legend. Cocaine was the solution to his problems, which were caused by cocaine. He is headed for a shipwreck anyway when the diagnosis of lung cancer comes, but instead of looking for medical help he bulldozes ahead with cocaine, denial, and call girls.

The film opens with his funeral. There is a fight between a writer fired from a new movie and the star (Peter Weller) who fired him. Their disagreement cannot wait upon death. In voice-over, we hear the voice of the dead agent, who says that at the end, "the pain was so bad I took every pill in the house." And he tried, he says, "to find one simple image to get me through it."

Then we flash back through his life, as Ivan appears on-screen, one of those charming but unknowable men who have perfect courtesy, who lean forward with the appearance of great attention, and whose minds seem to be otherwise involved. As it happens, that is precisely the impression I had of John Huston on the three or four occasions when I met him: He was a shade too courteous, too agreeable, too accommodating, leaning forward too attentively from his great height, and I felt that he was playing a nice man while thinking about other things.

Danny Huston plays Ivan Beckman as the sort of man who believes he cannot be touched. Who has been given a pass. To whom all things come because they must, and for whom addictions like cocaine do not bring the usual ravages. I am told that if you have enough money for enough cocaine you can hold out like that for quite a while, which is not good, because you are building up a deficit in your mind and body that eventually cannot be repaid.

When Ivan doesn't return phone calls, when he doesn't appear at the office, when clients can't find him, he doesn't get in the same kind of trouble that a less legendary agent might experience, because—well, that's Ivan. When his girlfriend Charlotte (Lisa Enos) can't find him, and then discovers he was partying with hookers—well, who did she think he was when she started going out with him? Surely she heard the stories? Surely this doesn't come as news? When his bosses grow restless at his irresponsibility—hey, he has the big client list. If the clients like him, then the agency must.

The diagnosis of cancer comes like a telegram that should have been delivered next door. It is the final, irrefutable reply to his feeling of immunity. There are two painful scenes where he tries, in one way or another, to deal with this news. One comes in a meeting with his father, whose ideas have made him a stranger. One comes during a party with two call girls, who are happy with the money, happy with the cocaine, happy to be with Ivan Beckman, and then increasingly unhappy and confused as their services are needed, not to pretend, but to be real. You cannot hire someone to really care about you.

The movie is allegedly inspired by *The Death of Ivan Ilyich* by Leo Tolstoy. I say "allegedly," because Bernard Rose has charged that the powerful Creative Artists Agency tried to prevent the film, seeing it as a transparent version of the life of Jay Moloney, an agent who at one time (I learn from a news story) represented Leonardo DiCaprio, Steven Spielberg, Bill Murray, Uma Thurman, Tim Burton—and Rose himself. Fired from CAA in 1996 because of cocaine, the story says, he moved to the Caribbean and killed himself in 1999.

Well, the story could be based on a lot of lives. The parabola of serious addiction often looks the same. If the victim has more money, the settings are prettier. The tragedy of Ivan Beckman is that he doesn't know how to call for help, and has no one to call if he did. It is important to recognize that he is not a bad man. He can be charming, does not wish to cause harm, is grateful for company, and, as such people like to say, "If I'm hurting anybody, I'm only hurting myself." It is not until too late that he discovers how much it hurts.

Note: The story of the making of Ivans xtc. *is the story of how a lot of movies can now be made, according to Bernard Rose, its director.*

Because of its controversial subject matter and because the Hollywood establishment has no wish to fund the thinly veiled story of the death of one of its own, the movie could not find conventional financing.

"So we went ahead and filmed it anyway,"

Rose told me after the film's screening at Cannes 2001. "We got a 24-fps digital video camera, and we shot it in our own homes, and the crew was the cast and the cast was the crew and we took care of catering by calling for carryout."

Rose, forty-two, is the British-born director of a number of commercial hits, notably Candyman (1992) and Immortal Beloved (1995), and he is known for the power of his visual imagery. In Paperhouse (1989), he created a real landscape based on a child's imaginary drawings. In Immortal Beloved, a boy runs through the woods at night and plunges into a lake, floating on his back as the camera pulls back to show him surrounded by the reflections of countless stars.

Ivans xtc., made on a $500,000 budget, did not support or require such images. Produced by Lisa Enos, who also stars in it, it was directed by Rose on high-def video, which looks—appropriate, I think, is the word. Some shots are beautiful, others are functional, and there are no shots that do not work.

"We finished the movie, we took it to Artisan Entertainment, and we made a deal," he said. "A 50-50 split of all the proceeds from dollar one. It was made so cheaply that we'll make out and so will they."

Does he wish he'd had film? "It's no use saying you'd rather have film, because this project on film could not have existed."

J

Jackie Brown

R, 154 m., 1997

Pam Grier (Jackie Brown), Samuel L. Jackson (Ordell Robbie), Robert Forster (Max Cherry), Bridget Fonda (Melanie), Michael Keaton (Ray Nicolette), Robert De Niro (Louis Gara), Michael Bowen (Mark Dargus), Chris Tucker (Beaumont Livingston), Lisa Gay Hamilton (Sheronda), Tommy "Tiny" Lister, Jr. (Winston), Hattie Winston (Simone), Aimee Graham (Billingsley Sales Girl). Directed by Quentin Tarantino and produced by Lawrence Bender, Richard N. Gladstein, Paul Hellerman, Elmore Leonard, Bob Weinstein, and Harvey Weinstein. Screenplay by Tarantino, adapted from the book *Rum Punch* by Leonard.

I like the moment when the veins pop out on Ordell's forehead. It's a quiet moment in the front seat of a van, he's sitting there next to Louis, he's just heard that he's lost his retirement fund of $500,000, and he's thinking hard. Quentin Tarantino lets him think. Just holds the shot, nothing happening. Then Ordell looks up and says, "It's Jackie Brown."

He's absolutely right. She's stolen his money. In the movies, people like him hardly ever need to think. The director has done all their thinking for them. One of the pleasures of *Jackie Brown*, Tarantino's new film based on a novel by Elmore Leonard, is that everybody in the movie is smart. Whoever is smartest will live.

Jackie (Pam Grier) knows she needs to pull off a flawless scam or she'll be dead. Ordell (Samuel L. Jackson) will pop her, just like that guy they found in the trunk of the car. So she thinks hard, and so do her bail bondsman (Robert Forster) and the ATF agent (Michael Keaton). Everyone has a pretty good idea of exactly what's happening: They just can't figure it out fast enough to stay ahead of Jackie. The final scenes unfold in a cloud of delight, as the audience watches all of the threads come together.

This is the movie that proves Tarantino is the real thing, and not just a two-film wonder boy. It's not a retread of *Reservoir Dogs* or *Pulp Fiction* but a new film in a new style, and it evokes the particular magic of Elmore Leonard—who elevates the crime novel to a

form of sociological comedy. There is a scene here that involves the ex-con Louis (Robert De Niro) and Ordell's druggie mistress (Bridget Fonda) discussing a photograph pinned to the wall, and it's so perfectly written, timed, and played that I applauded it.

Tarantino has a lot of scenes that are good in this movie. The scene where one character lures another to his death by tempting him with chicken and waffles. The scene where a nagging woman makes one suggestion too many. The scene where a man comes around in the morning to get back the gun a woman borrowed the night before. The moment when Jackie Brown uses one line of dialogue, perfectly timed, to solve all of her problems.

This movie is about texture, not plot. It has a plot, all right, but not as the whole purpose of the film. Jackie Brown, forty-four years old, is an attendant on the worst airline in North America and supplements her meager salary by smuggling cash from Mexico to Los Angeles for Ordell, who is a gun dealer. Beaumont (Chris Tucker), one of Ordell's hirelings, gets busted by an ATF agent (Keaton) and a local cop (Michael Bowen). So they know Jackie is coming in with $50,000 of Ordell's money, and bust her.

Ordell has Jackie bailed out by Max Cherry (Robert Forster), a bondsman who falls in love the moment he sees her, but keeps that knowledge to himself. Jackie knows Ordell will kill her before she can cut a deal with the law. Maybe she could kill Ordell first, but she's not a killer, and besides, she has a better idea. The unfolding of this idea, which involves a lot of improvisation, occupies the rest of the movie.

At the heart of the story is the affection that grows between Jackie and Max. In a lesser thriller, there would be a sex scene. Tarantino reasonably believes that during a period when everyone's in danger and no one's leveling about their real motives, such an episode would be unlikely.

Max silently guesses part of what Jackie is up to, and provides a little crucial help. Jackie takes the help without quite acknowledging it. And their attraction stays on an unspoken level, which makes it all the more intriguing.

In *Jackie Brown*, as in *Pulp Fiction*, we get the sense that the characters live in spacious worlds and know a lot of people (in most thrillers the characters only know one another). Ordell has women stashed all over Southern California, including a dim runaway from the South who he keeps in Glenwood, which he has told her is Hollywood. Max Cherry has a partner (Tiny Lister) who is referred to long before he goes into action.

The sides of the film's canvas are free to expand when it's necessary. If Tarantino's strengths are dialogue and plotting, his gift is casting. Pam Grier, the goddess of 1970s tough-girl pictures, here finds just the right note for Jackie Brown; she's tired and desperate. Robert Forster has the role of a career as the bail bondsman, matter-of-fact about his job and the law; he's a plausible professional, not a plot stooge.

Jackson, as Ordell, does a harder, colder version of his hit man in *Pulp Fiction,* and once again uses the word "nigger" like an obsession or a mantra (that gets a little old). De Niro, still in a longtime convict's prison trance, plays Louis as ingratiatingly stupid. Bridget Fonda's performance is so good it's almost invisible; her character's lassitude and contempt coexist with the need to be high all the time.

A lot of crime films play like they were written by crossword puzzle fans who fill in the easy words and then call the hotline for the solution. (The solution is always: Abandon the characters and end with a chase and a shoot-out.) Tarantino leaves the hardest questions for last, hides his moves, conceals his strategies in plain view, and gives his characters dialogue that is alive, authentic, and spontaneous. You savor every moment of *Jackie Brown.* Those who say it is too long have developed cinematic attention deficit disorder. I wanted these characters to live, talk, deceive, and scheme for hours and hours.

Jail Bait

NO MPAA RATING, 102 m., 1977

Eva Mattes (Hanni), Harry Baer (Franz), Jorg von Liebenfels (Hanni's Father), Ruth Drexel (Hanni's Mother). Directed by Rainer Werner Fassbinder and produced by Rolf Defrank and Gerhard Freund. Screenplay by Fassbinder, based on a book by Franz Xaver Kroetz.

Some movies evaporate so quickly in the memory that their beginnings are already fading before their ends finally come. Other films, like Rainer Werner Fassbinder's *Jail Bait,* take up permanent residence in that place where we store the curious, the bizarre and the unforgettable.

I saw it months ago, during a festival of new German films. It remains as immediate in my mind as the book I just put down; Fassbinder, that perverse genius, proves here once again that he's the most interesting of the new European directors of the 1970s.

The movie's original English title was *Game Pass.* The retitling is perfect, not only because *Jail Bait* describes the title character, but because it catches the movie's tone. This is a movie about young love and motorcycles and trashy rock songs and the inexhaustible myth of James Dean. It's a movie, if you will, about the teenagers who went to see the teenage movies of the 1950s and early 1960s and saw on the screen a naïveté they could only yearn for in their own lives.

The girl is fourteen, very ripe for her age, self-centered and secretive. The boy is nineteen, into motorcycles, leather jackets, and ducktail haircuts. He begins their relationship by seducing her, hardly suspecting that his moment of triumph in an empty barn represents the end of his autonomy. His will is no match for her own. And whatever has been going on in that strange, repressed family of hers will eventually lead to his destruction.

Fassbinder is a master of painfully banal relationships, mercilessly explored. He submerges us in the girl's family life from his very first shot, a virtuoso use of a long pan that explores both the girl's home and the relationships within it. She's an only child; her father is strict and gruff and has troublesome incestuous feelings, and her mother is good-hearted but completely cowed. The family is outwardly harmonious, but there's something beneath the surface here, something they've all always known and will never acknowledge.

The boy, in getting involved with this girl, enlists without knowing it on her side of the family warfare. And he has a rough campaign. She becomes pregnant, he's sent off to prison for corrupting the morals of a minor, and then she's there waiting when he gets out. This time she wants him to murder her father. He does, in a scene where Fassbinder uses a bicycle, of all things, as his instrument for turning violence into pathos.

Fassbinder tells the story, as usual, at a deliberate pace. He doesn't show us just the outcomes, but things in the process of happening. He allows pauses, silences, embarrassing lulls in behavior. His films are sometimes described as artificial and mannered, but sometimes, as in *Jail Bait*, he's simply recording awkwardly revealing behavior. And doing it with a mesmerizing vividness.

Jaws

PG, 124 m., 1975

Roy Scheider (Brody), Robert Shaw (Quint), Richard Dreyfuss (Hooper), Lorraine Gary (Ellen Brody), Murray Hamilton (Mayor). Directed by Steven Spielberg and produced by Richard Zanuck and David Brown. Screenplay by Peter Benchley and Carl Gottlieb, based on the book by Benchley.

Steven Spielberg's *Jaws* is a sensationally effective action picture—a scary thriller that works all the better because it's populated with characters that have been developed into human beings we get to know and care about. It's a film that's as frightening as *The Exorcist*, and yet it's a nicer kind of fright, somehow more fun because we're being scared by an outdoor-adventure saga instead of by a brimstone-and-vomit devil.

The story, as I guess everyone knows by now, involves a series of attacks on swimmers by a great white shark, the response of the threatened resort island to its loss of tourist business, and, finally, the epic attempt by three men to track the shark and kill it. There are no doubt supposed to be all sorts of levels of meanings in such an archetypal story, but Spielberg wisely decides not to underline any of them. This is an action film content to stay entirely within the perimeters of its story, and none of the characters has to wade through speeches expounding on the significance of it all. Spielberg is very good, though, at presenting those characters in a way that makes them individuals. Before the three men get on that leaky old boat and go forth to do battle with what amounts to an elemental natural force, we know them well enough to be genuinely interested in the ways they'll respond. There's Brody (Roy Scheider), the police chief, who came to the island from New York looking, so he thought, for a change from the fears of the city. There's Quint (Robert Shaw), a caricature of the crusty old seafaring salt, who has a very particular personal reason for hating sharks. And there's Hooper (Richard Dreyfuss), the rich kid turned oceanographer, who knows best of all what a shark can do to a man, and yet is willing to get into the water with one.

All three performances are really fine. Scheider is the character most of us identify with. He's actually scared of the water, doesn't like to swim and, when he sees the giant shark swim past the boat for the first time, we believe him when he informs Quint, very sincerely, "We need a bigger boat." Shaw brings a degree of cheerful exaggeration to his role as Quint, stomping around like a cross between Captain Queeg and Captain Hook, and then delivering a compelling five-minute monologue about the time the *Indianapolis* went down and he was one of more than a thousand men in the water. By the time rescue came, two-thirds of them had been killed by sharks.

Probably the most inspired piece of casting in the movie is the use of Richard Dreyfuss as the oceanographer. He made this film soon after playing the driven, scheming, overwhelmingly ambitious title character in *The Apprenticeship of Duddy Kravitz,* and the nice kid, college-bound, in *American Graffiti.* Here he looks properly young, engaging, and scholarly, and introduces the technical material about sharks in a way that reinforces our elemental fear of them.

Which brings us to the shark itself. Some of the footage in the film is of an actual great white shark. The rest uses a mechanical shark patterned on the real thing. The illusion is complete. We see the shark close up, we look in its relentless eye, and it just plain feels like a shark. *Jaws* is a great adventure movie of the kind we don't get very often any more. It's clean-cut adventure, without the gratuitous violence of so many action pictures. It has the necessary amount of blood and guts to work—but none extra. And it's one hell of a good story, brilliantly told.

JFK

R, 188 m., 1991

Kevin Costner (Jim Garrison), Sissy Spacek (Liz Garrison), Joe Pesci (David Ferrie), Tommy Lee Jones (Clay Shaw), Gary Oldman (Lee Harvey Oswald), Jay O. Sanders (Lou Ivon), Donald Sutherland ("X"), Michael Rooker (Bill Broussard), Laurie Metcalf (Susie Cox), Brian Doyle-Murray (Jack Ruby), Ed Asner (Guy Bannister), Jack Lemmon (Jack Martin), John Candy (Dean Andrews), Kevin Bacon (Willie O'Keefe). Directed by Oliver Stone and produced by A. Kitman Ho and Stone. Screenplay by Stone and Zachary Sklar.

Oliver Stone's *JFK* builds up an overwhelming head of urgency that all comes rushing out at the end of the film in a tumbling, angry, almost piteous monologue—the whole obsessive weight of Jim Garrison's conviction that there was a conspiracy to assassinate John F. Kennedy. With the words come images, faces, names, snatches of dialogue, flashbacks to the evidence, all marshaled to support his conclusion that the murder of JFK was not the work of one man.

Well, do you know anyone who believes Lee Harvey Oswald acted all by himself in killing Kennedy? I don't. I've been reading the books and articles for the last twenty-five years, and I've not found a single convincing defense of the Warren Commission report, which arrived at that reassuring conclusion. It's impossible to believe the Warren report because the physical evidence makes its key conclusion impossible: One man with one rifle could not physically have caused what happened on November 22, 1963, in Dallas. If one man could not have, then there must have been two. Therefore, there was a conspiracy.

Oliver Stone's *JFK* has been attacked by those who believe Stone has backed the wrong horse in the Kennedy assassination sweepstakes—by those who believe the hero of this film, former New Orleans District Attorney Jim Garrison, was a loose cannon who attracted crackpot conspiracy theories the way a dog draws fleas.

The important point to make about *JFK* is that Stone does not subscribe to all of Garrison's theories, and indeed rewrites history to supply his Garrison character with material he could not have possessed at the time of these events. He uses Garrison as the symbolic center of his film because Garrison, in all the United States in all the years since 1963, is the only man who has attempted to bring anyone into court in connection with the fishiest political murder of our time.

Stone's film is truly hypnotically watchable. Leaving aside all of its drama and emotion, it is a masterpiece of film assembly. The writing, the editing, the music, the photography, are all used here in a film of enormous complexity to weave a persuasive tapestry out of an overwhelming mountain of evidence and testimony. Film students will examine this film in wonder in the years to come, astonished at how much information it contains, how many characters, how many interlocking flashbacks, what skillful interweaving of documentary and fictional footage. The film hurtles for 188 minutes through a sea of information and conjecture, and never falters and never confuses us.

That is not to say that we are quite sure, when it is over and we try to reconstruct the experience in our minds, exactly what Stone's final conclusions are. *JFK* does not unmask the secrets of the Kennedy assassination. Instead, it uses the Garrison character as a seeker for truth who finds that the murder could not have happened according to the official version. Could not. Those faded and trembling images we are all so familiar with, the home movie Abraham Zapruder took of the shooting of Kennedy, have made it forever clear that the Oswald theory is impossible—and that at least one of the shots *must* have come from in front of Kennedy, not from the Texas Schoolbook Depository behind him.

Look at me, emphasizing the word "must." The film stirs up that kind of urgency and anger. The CIA and FBI reports on the Kennedy assassination are sealed until after most of us will be long dead, and for what reason? Why can't we read the information our government gathered for us on the death of our president? If Garrison's investigation was so pitiful—and indeed it was flawed, underfunded, and sabotaged—then where are the better investigations by Stone's attackers? A U.S. Senate select committee found in 1979 that Kennedy's assassination was probably a conspiracy. Why, twelve years later, has the case not been reopened?

Stone's film shows, through documentary footage and reconstruction, most of the key elements of those 1963 events. The shooting. The flight of Air Force One to Washington. Jack Ruby's murder of Oswald. And it shows Garrison in New Orleans, watching the same TV reports we watched, and then stumbling, hesitantly at first, into a morass of evidence suggesting that various fringe groups in New Orleans, pro- and anti-Castro, may have somehow been mixed up with the CIA and various self-appointed soldiers of fortune in a conspiracy to kill JFK.

His investigation leads him to Clay Shaw, respected businessman, who is linked by various witnesses with Lee Harvey Oswald and other possible conspirators. Some of those witnesses die suspiciously. Eventually Garrison is able to bring Shaw to trial, and although he loses his case, there is the conviction that he was onto something. He feels Shaw perjured himself, and in 1979, five years after Shaw's death and ten years after the trial, Richard Helms of the CIA admits that Shaw, despite his sworn denials, was indeed an employee of the CIA.

Most people today, I imagine, think of Garrison as an irresponsible, publicity-seeking hothead who destroyed the reputation of an innocent man. Few know Shaw perjured himself. Was Garrison the target of the same kind of paid misinformation floated in defense of Michael Milkin? A good PR campaign can do a better job of destroying a reputation than any Louisiana D.A. Stone certainly gives Garrison a greater measure of credibility than he has had for years, but the point is not whether Garrison's theories are right or wrong—what the film supports is simply his seeking for a greater truth.

As Garrison, Kevin Costner gives a measured yet passionate performance. "You're as stubborn as a mule," one of his investigators shouts at him. Like a man who has hold of an idea he cannot let go, he forges ahead, insisting that there is more to the assassination than meets the eye. Stone has surrounded him with an astonishing cast, able to give us the uncanny impression that we are seeing historical figures. There is Joe Pesci, squirming and hyperkenetic as David Ferrie, the alleged getaway pilot. Tommy Lee Jones as Clay Shaw,

hiding behind an impenetrable wall of bemusement. Gary Oldman as Lee Harvey Oswald. Donald Sutherland as "X" (actually Fletcher Prouty), the high-placed Pentagon official who thinks he knows why JFK was killed. Sissy Spacek, in the somewhat thankless role of Garrison's wife, who fears for her family and marriage. And dozens of others, including Jack Lemmon, Ed Asner, Walter Matthau, and Kevin Bacon in small, key roles, their faces vaguely familiar behind the facades of their characters.

Stone and his editors, Joe Hutshing and Pietro Scalia, have somehow triumphed over the tumult of material here and made it work—made it grip and disturb us. The achievement of the film is not that it answers the mystery of the Kennedy assassination, because it does not, or even that it vindicates Garrison, who is seen here as a man often whistling in the dark. Its achievement is that it tries to marshal the anger that ever since 1963 has been gnawing away on some dark shelf of the national psyche. John F. Kennedy was murdered. Lee Harvey Oswald could not have acted alone. Who acted with him? Who knew?

Johnny Got His Gun
R, 111 m., 1971

Timothy Bottoms (Joe Bonham), Kathy Fields (Kareen), Jason Robards (Joe's Father), Diane Varsi (Fourth Nurse), Donald Sutherland (Jesus Christ), Eduard Franz (General Tillery). Directed by Dalton Trumbo and produced by Bruce Campbell. Screenplay by Trumbo.

I've never much liked anti-war films. They've never much stopped war, for one thing. For another, they attract hushed and reverential praise which speaks of their universality and the urgency of their messages. Most anti-war films come so burdened with universality and urgency that the ads for them read like calls to sunrise services.

Dalton Trumbo's *Johnny Got His Gun* smelled like that kind of anti-war film. It came out of the Cannes Film Festival with three awards and a slightly pious aroma, as if it had been made for joyless Student Peace Union types of thirty-five years ago. But it isn't like that at all. Trumbo has taken the most difficult sort of material—the story of a soldier who lost his arms, his legs, and most of his face in a World War I shell burst—and handled it, strange to say, in a way that's not so much anti-war as pro-life. Perhaps that's why I admire it. Instead of belaboring ironic points about the "war to end war," Trumbo remains stubbornly on the human level. He lets his ideology grow out of his characters, instead of imposing it from above. In this sense, his film resembles Joseph Losey's *King and Country* which also turned its back on the war in order to consider one ordinary, unremarkable soldier.

Trumbo's soldier is Joe Bonham (Timothy Bottoms), who comes from an American background that is clearly modeled on Trumbo's own. The boy works in a bakery, supports his mother and sisters after his father's death, is in love with an open-faced and sweet Irish girl, and enlists in the army because "it's the sort of thing a fellow ought to do, when his country is in trouble." Months later, he's sent on a patrol into no-man's land to bury a corpse that was offending a colonel's nose. A shell lands near him, and he wakes up in a hospital.

The army is convinced he has no conscious mind. They decide to keep him alive simply to learn from him. But he can think, and gradually the enormity of his injuries is revealed to him. He is literally the prisoner of his mind, for years, until he finds a way of communicating with a sympathetic nurse (Diane Varsi).

Trumbo uses flashbacks and fantasies to make Joe alive for us, while he exists in a living death. The most charming flashback is the first, when Joe and his girl kiss in her living room and are interrupted by her father. He's an old Wobbly who sends them both into the bedroom, and there is a love scene of such tenderness and beauty that its echoes resound through the entire film. Other scenes develop Joe's relationship with his father (Jason Robards) and with Jesus Christ (Donald Sutherland), whom he consults in fantasies. Christ really doesn't have much to suggest; he has no answers, in Joe's fantasies, because there are no answers.

The movie ends with no political solutions and without, in fact, even a political position. It simply states a case. Here was a patriotic young man who went off and was grievously wounded for no great reason, and whose conscious mind remains a horrible indictment of the system that sent all the young men away to kill each other. The soldier's own answer to his situation seems like the only possible one. He wants them to put him in a sideshow, where, as a freak, he can cause people a moment's thought about war. If they won't do that, he wants them to kill him. The army won't do either, of course.

The Joy Luck Club
R, 135 m., 1993

The Mothers: Kieu Chinh (Suyuan), Tsai Chin (Lindo), France Nuyen (Ying Ying), Lisa Lu (An Mei). The Daughters: Ming-Na Wen (June), Tamlyn Tomita (Waverly), Lauren Tom (Lena), Rosalind Chao (Rose). Directed by Wayne Wang and produced by Wang, Amy Tan, Ronald Bass, and Patrick Markey. Screenplay by Tan and Bass, based on the book by Tan.

The Joy Luck Club comes rushing off the screen in a torrent of memories, as if its characters have been saving their stories for years, waiting for the right moment to share them. That moment comes after a death and a reunion that bring the past back in all of its power, and show how the present, too, is affected—how children who think they are so very different are deeply affected by the experiences of their parents.

The movie, based on Amy Tan's 1989 best-selling novel, tells the story of four women who were born in China and eventually came to America, and of their daughters. Around these eight women circle innumerable friends and relatives, both there and here, Chinese and not, in widening circles of experience. What is about to be forgotten are the origins of the women, the stories of how they were born and grew up in a time and culture so very different from the one they now inhabit.

The Joy Luck Club of the title is a group of four older Chinese ladies who meet once a week to play mah-jongg, and compare stories of their families and grandchildren. All have made harrowing journeys from prerevolutionary China to the comfortable homes in San Francisco where they meet. But those old days are not often spoken about, and sometimes the whole truth of them is not known.

June (Ming-Na Wen), the narrator, is the

daughter of one of the women, Suyuan (Kieu Chinh). After her mother's death, she decides to take a trip to China, to meet for the first time two half-sisters who still live there. The movie opens at a farewell party, and then, in a series of flashbacks, tells the secrets and stories of all four of the "aunties." In a screenplay remarkable for its complexity and force, *The Joy Luck Club* moves effortlessly between past and present, between what was, and how it became what is. Many different actresses are used to play the daughters and mothers at different ages, and there are many stories, but the movie proceeds with perfect clarity.

We see that the China of the 1930s and 1940s, before the revolution, was an unimaginably different place than it is today. Women were not valued very highly. Those with independent minds and spirits were valued even less than the docile, obedient ones. Life was cheap, especially in wartime. A mother's ability to care for her children was precarious. In many cases, issues from those hard days still affect later generations: The ability of the mothers to relate to their daughters depends on things that have never been said out loud.

How, for example, could June's mother have told of abandoning her firstborn twin girls by the roadside? Suyuan, starving and sick, was sure she would die, and felt her girls would have a better chance of survival if they were not linked to the "bad luck" of a dead mother.

Other stories fall equally hard on Americanized ears. There is the auntie who became the fourth wife of a rich man, and when she bore him the son he desired so much, the boy child was taken from her by the second wife. There are humorous stories, too, including the auntie who prayed before her arranged marriage for a husband "not too old," and got a ten-year-old boy ("Maybe I prayed too hard!").

In America, the mothers find it hard to understand the directions their daughters are taking. Some marry whites, who have bad table manners. They move out of the old neighborhood into houses that seem too modern and cold. One daughter despairs of ever satisfying her mother, who criticizes everything she does.

These stories are about Chinese and Chinese-American characters, but they are universal stories. Anyone with parents or children, which is to say, everyone, will identify with the way that the hopes of one generation can become both the restraints and the inspirations of the next.

The movie is a celebration, too, of the richness of Asian-American acting talent; all of the performers here have appeared in many other films and plays, and I could list their credits, from the old days of *South Pacific* and *The World of Suzie Wong* to recent films like *1,000 Pieces of Gold* and *Come See the Paradise*. But often they were marginalized, or used in "exotic" roles, or placed in stories that were based on what made them different from the dominant culture, instead of what makes them human and universal. *The Joy Luck Club* is like a flowering of talent that has been waiting so long to be celebrated.

Junebug

R, 107 m., 2005

Alessandro Nivola (George), Amy Adams (Ashley), Embeth Davidtz (Madeleine), Scott Wilson (Eugene), Benjamin McKenzie (Johnny), Frank Hoyt Taylor (David Wark), Celia Weston (Peg). Directed by Phil Morrison and produced by Mike Ryan and Mindy Goldberg. Screenplay by Angus MacLachlan.

Junebug is a movie that understands, profoundly and with love and sadness, the world of small towns; it captures ways of talking and living I remember from my childhood with the complexity and precision of great fiction. It observes small details that are important *because* they are small. It has sympathy for every character in the story and avoids two temptations: It doesn't portray the small-town characters as provincial hicks, and it doesn't portray the city slickers as shallow materialists. Phil Morrison, who directed this movie, and Angus MacLachlan, who wrote it, understand how people everywhere have good intentions, and how life can assign them roles where they can't realize them.

Tone is everything in this movie; it's not so much what people say, as how they say it, and why. Consider this dialogue:

Peg: You comin' to bed?

Eugene: Not now. I'm looking for something. My Phillips-head.

That much is exactly right. A certain kind of person (my father was one) finds a Phillips-head screwdriver easier to lose than almost everything else. So now wait until it's later at night, and observe Eugene in the kitchen. He looks in the refrigerator and then he says: "Now where would I be if I was a screwdriver?"

If you get that right, you get everything else right, too. And here is other dialogue that rings with clarity and truth:

> Ashley to Johnny: God loves you just the way you are, but he loves you too much to let you stay that way.

> Peg, under her breath at a baby shower, after her son's new wife from the city has given her other daughter-in-law a silver spoon: That won't go in the dishwasher.

Who are these people? The story begins in Chicago, where an art dealer named Madeleine (Embeth Davidtz) is holding a benefit for Jesse Jackson Jr. At the event, she meets George (Alessandro Nivola), and they fall in love and get married. His family from North Carolina is invited but doesn't attend. Six months later, she learns of a folk artist named David Wark (Frank Hoyt Taylor), who lives near George's family in the Winston-Salem area. They decide to kill two birds with one stone: She'll sign up the artist and meet the family.

Here is the family she meets. Peg (Celia Weston) is the matriarch who criticizes everyone, second-guesses every decision, and is never wrong, according to her. Eugene (Scott Wilson) is her husband, who has withdrawn into a deep silence and a shadowy presence, and spends many hours in his basement wood-carving corner. Johnny (Benjamin McKenzie) is George's younger brother, newly married to his high school sweetheart, Ashley (Amy Adams). She is pregnant.

As George and Madeleine arrive, Ashley is about to give birth. Johnny is responding to this, as he does to everything, by withdrawing, not talking to anybody, working under his car in the garage. Ashley, on the other hand, is always chatty: She's a good soul, cheerful, optimistic, supportive. The four people in this household are so locked into their roles that the arrival of the Chicagoans is like a bomb dropping.

Madeleine, the outsider, smiles all the time. If she feels that this family is strange and disturbing, she doesn't say so. George behaves as he knows he should but remains enigmatic: We don't find out what he really thinks about his family until the movie's last line, if then.

The artist, David Wark, is a profound eccentric with an accent and values that seem to have been imported from the eighteenth century. His folk art incorporates imperfectly controlled images from a half-understood world. "I like all the dog heads and computers," Madeleine tells him, "and the scrotums." This is not intended as a funny line. Wark has just finished an allegorical painting about the freeing of the slaves. He explains that he can't paint a face unless it belongs to somebody he knows, and he doesn't know any black people, which is why all the slaves have white faces.

There is tension between George and Johnny, between Ashley and Johnny, between the world and Johnny. He spends long hours away from everyone, but watch him in the family room when a documentary about meerkats comes on TV. He knows his wife "loves meerkats." He races around desperately to find a blank video so he can tape the show. It would mean so much to him to give her this video. He fails. Ashley explains about the tab that keeps you from recording over something, but he responds with anger and, of course, takes it out on her.

Two events happen at once. Madeleine believes she can win David Wark away from a New York gallery, and Ashley goes into labor. George thinks Madeleine's place is with the family, at the hospital. She doesn't agree: "I'll be over as soon as I do this. You know how important this is to me."

Now here is the question: How important is Ashley and Johnny's baby to George? (Johnny, of course, is nowhere to be found, certainly not at the hospital.) If he were in Chicago, George certainly would not fly down to be at the hospital. But when he moves into his family's house, he follows its rules. This leads to a scene of incredible power between Ashley and her brother-in-law, in which we see that Ashley truly is good, and brave, and sweeter than peaches. Small wonder that Amy Adams won the Sundance acting award.

Junebug is a great film because it is a true film. It humbles other films that claim to be about family secrets and eccentricities. It understands that families are complicated and their problems are not solved during a short visit, just in time for the film to end. Families and their problems go on and on, and they aren't solved; they're dealt with.

Consider a guarded moment between Madeleine and Eugene, her father-in-law. She observes cautiously of his wife, "She's a very strong personality." This is putting it mildly. Eugene replies quietly, "That's just her way. She hides herself. She's not like that inside." And then he adds two more words: "Like most." Thank God for actors like Wilson, who know how those two words must be said. They carry the whole burden of the movie.

K

Kagemusha

PG, 160 m., 1980

Tatsuya Nakadai (Shingen and Kagemusha), Tsutomu Yamazaki (Nobukado), Kenichi Hagiwara (Katsuyori), Jinpachi Nezu (Bodyguard), Shuji Otaki (Fire General). Directed by Akira Kurosawa and produced by Kurosawa and Tomoyuki Tanaka. Screenplay by Kurosawa and Masato Ide.

Kagemusha, we learn, means "shadow warrior" in Japanese, and Akira Kurosawa's great film tells the story of a man who becomes the double, or shadow, of a great warrior. It also teaches the lesson that shadows or appearances are as important as reality, but that men cannot count on either shadows or reality.

Kagemusha is a samurai drama by the director who most successfully introduced the genre to the West (with such classics as *The Seven Samurai* and *Yojimbo*), and who, at the age of seventy, made an epic that dares to wonder what meaning the samurai code—or any human code—really has in the life of an individual man. His film is basically the story of one such man, a common thief who, because of his astonishing resemblance to the warlord Shingen, is chosen as Shingen's double. When Shingen is mortally wounded in battle, the great Takeda clan secretly replaces him with the double—so their enemies will not learn that Shingen is dead. Thus begins a period of three years during which the kagemusha is treated by everyone, even his son and his mistresses, as if he were the real Shingen. Only his closest advisers know the truth.

But he is not Lord Shingen. And so every scene is undercut with irony. It is important that both friends and enemies believe Shingen is alive; his appearance, or shadow, creates both the respect of his clan and the caution of his enemies. If he is unmasked, he is useless; as Shingen's double, he can send hundreds of men to be killed, and his own guards will willingly sacrifice their lives for him. But as himself, he is worthless, and when he *is* unmasked, he's banished into the wilderness.

What is Kurosawa saying here? I suspect the answer can be found in a contrast between two kinds of scenes. His film contains epic battle scenes of astonishing beauty and scope. And then there are the intimate scenes in the throne room, the bedroom, the castles, and battlefield camps. The great battle scenes glorify the samurai system. Armies of thousands of men throw themselves heedlessly at death, for the sake of pride. But the intimate scenes undermine that glorious tradition; as everyone holds their breath, Shingen's double is tested in meetings with his son, his mistresses, and his horse. They know him best of all. If they are not fooled, all of the panoply and battlefield courage is meaningless, because the Takeda clan has lost the leader who is their figurehead; the illusion that he exists creates the clan's reality.

Kurosawa made this film after a decade of personal travail. Although he is often considered the greatest living Japanese director, he was unable to find financial backing in Japan when he first tried to make *Kagemusha*. He made a smaller film, *Dodeskaden*, which was not successful. He tried to commit suicide, but failed. He was backed by the Russians and went to Siberia to make the beautiful *Dersu Uzala* (1976), about a man of the wilderness. But *Kagemusha* remained his obsession, and he was finally able to make it only when Hollywood directors Francis Ford Coppola and George Lucas helped him find U.S. financing.

The film he finally made is simple, bold, and colorful on the surface, but very thoughtful. Kurosawa seems to be saying that great human endeavors (in this case, samurai wars) depend entirely on large numbers of men sharing the same fantasies or beliefs. It is entirely unimportant, he seems to be suggesting, whether or not the beliefs are based on reality—all that matters is that men accept them. But when a belief is shattered, the result is confusion, destruction, and death. At the end of *Kagemusha*, for example, the son of the real Lord Shingen orders his troops into a suicidal charge, and their deaths are not only unnecessary but meaningless, because they are not on behalf of the sacred person of the warlord.

There are great images in this film: Of a breathless courier clattering down countless steps, of men passing in front of a blood-red sunset, of a dying horse on a battlefield. But Kurosawa's last image—of the dying kagemusha floating in the sea, swept by tidal currents past the fallen standard of the Takeda clan—summarizes everything: ideas and men are carried along heedlessly by the currents of time, and historical meaning *seems* to emerge when both happen to be swept in the same way at the same time.

Kalifornia

R, 117 m., 1993

Brad Pitt (Early Grayce), Juliette Lewis (Adele Corners), David Duchovny (Brian Kessler), Michelle Forbes (Carrie Laughlin), Sierra Pecheur (Mrs. Musgrave), Gregory Mars Martin (Walter Livesy). Directed by Dominic Sena and produced by Steve Golin, Aris McGarry, and Joni Sighvatsson. Screenplay by Tim Metcalfe.

Be careful what you ask for. You may get it.
—Old saying

Once in a very long while I see a film that cuts through the surface of movie violence and says something important about the murderous energies at loose in society. *Kalifornia* is such a film—terrifying and horrifying, yes, but also unflinchingly honest, and so well acted that for most of the film I abandoned any detachment and just watched it as if I were observing the lives of real people.

The film brings together four people who are, by themselves, fairly recognizable types. But while an ordinary film would simply plug them into a story, this film forces them to actually deal with one another, so that we see a confrontation between voyeurs who are turned on by violence (as long as it's at arm's length) and those who are actually capable of killing.

The movie introduces us to two couples. Brian and Carrie are smart, ambitious yuppies. Early and Adele are wretched white trash. Brian (David Duchovny) is a writer with an interest in mass murderers. Carrie (Michelle Forbes) is a photographer, a would-be Mapplethorpe with a low, no-nonsense voice and a certain cool detachment. They want to move to California, and Brian suggests a cross-country tour of the sites of famous mass murders. She can take the pictures, he can write the text, and they can get a book out of it.

Early and Adele, played by Brad Pitt and Juliette Lewis in two of the most harrowing and convincing performances I've ever seen, live in a slovenly rented trailer. He's on parole. She's a slack-jawed child-woman who repeats clichés that seem to have been imperfectly learned from television. The landlord is on their case about the rent.

Brian and Carrie need someone to share the gas and driving for their trip out West. They put up a card on the bulletin board at the university. Bad luck: Early, who has been sent over to the campus by his parole officer to take a job as a janitor, sees the card and decides it's time to take off for California with Adele. Of course, that's a parole violation, but what the hell: Before he leaves, he murders and buries his landlord to teach him a lesson about bugging people for the rent.

Most of the film takes place on the road, as the writer and photographer gradually become aware of the nature of the people who are sharing the ride. It is here that the movie reveals its greatness. A lesser film would simply be a thriller in which the protagonists would desperately scheme to escape from the killers in their car. *Kalifornia* is much more subtle than that. It's about the strange fascination that some people feel for those who seem tougher and more "authentic." Usually those who romanticize in that way have never had to deal with anyone who hurts others just for the entertainment value.

There's a deep class difference between the two couples—between Brian, with his yuppie sportswear, and Early, with his greasy hair and careless tattoos and smelly socks. And between the feminist Carrie and Adele, who observes curiously, "I used to smoke, but Early broke me of it." The yuppies, though, with their liberals' reluctance to show bad manners, try to "accept" these two strangers and to make allowances for their behavior.

A certain bond even grows between Brian and Early. Brian, for example, has never fired a gun. Early has. Brian is fascinated by Early's gun (Carrie is terrified). Early lets him shoot out some windows in an abandoned factory, and Brian is like a kid with a toy. It's also exciting—a rush, a high—when the two guys go out drinking one night, and when a guy in the bar takes offense to Brian's appearance, Early steps in and kicks the guy almost to death.

Early is not stupid, and has a better sense of Brian than Brian has of him. As Carrie gradually discovers that Early beats Adele and is probably a sociopath, Brian is being halfway seduced by Early's lawlessness. Not that he wants to get involved, of course. But it's intriguing to be so close to it.

Gradually, by slow, logical steps, the director, Dominic Sena, and the writer, Tim Metcalfe, reveal to Brian and Carrie the full reality of the situation they've gotten themselves into. Here's a middle-class couple who thought it would be a gas to revisit the scenes of mass murders, and whaddaya know? They end up with a real mass murderer, right in the same car, and it isn't fun. Not at all.

Dominic Sena is a director unknown to me, but he shows the kind of mastery of material here that I've seen in other early films such as Martin Scorsese's *Mean Streets*, Terence Malick's *Badlands*, John McNaughton's *Henry: Portrait of a Serial Killer*, and Carl Franklin's *One False Move*. The suspense screws up tighter than a drumhead. The characters remain believable; we have a conflict of personalities, not stereotypes. The action coexists seamlessly with the message.

A woman sitting behind me at the screening objected out loud, from time to time, to the movie's "depravity." If she hates it so much, I wondered, why doesn't she leave? Afterward, she admitted it was "very well made," but that she feared "the wrong people could see it and get bad ideas." I think the point of *Kalifornia* is that it's altogether too comforting to believe that people need inspiration to hurt and kill. Some people, the movie says, are simply evil. They lack all values and sympathy. And they don't need anybody to give them ideas.

The Karate Kid

PG, 126 m., 1984

Ralph Macchio (Daniel), Noriyuki "Pat" Morita (Miyagi), Elisabeth Shue (Ali), Martin Kove (Kreese), William Zabka (Johnny). Directed by John G. Avildsen and produced by Jerry Weintraub. Screenplay by Robert Mark Kamen.

I didn't want to see this movie. I took one look at the title and figured it was either (a) a sequel to *Toenails of Vengeance*, or (b) an adventure pitting Ricky Schroeder against the Megaloth Man. I was completely wrong. *The Karate Kid* was one of the nice surprises of 1984—an exciting, sweet-tempered, heartwarming story with one of the most interesting friendships in a long time. The friends come from different worlds. A kid named Daniel (Ralph Macchio) is a New Jersey teenager who moves with his mother to Los Angeles. An old guy named Miyagi (Pat Morita) is the Japanese janitor in their apartment building. When Daniel starts to date the former girlfriend of the toughest kid in the senior class, the kid starts pounding on Daniel's head on a regular basis. Daniel tries to fight back, but this is a Southern California kid, and so of course he has a black belt in karate. Enter Mr. Miyagi, who seems to be a harmless old eccentric with a curious hobby: He tries to catch flies with chopsticks. It turns out that Miyagi is a karate master, a student not only of karate fighting but of the total philosophy of the martial arts. He agrees to take Daniel as his student.

And then begins the wonderful center section of *The Karate Kid*, as the old man and the kid from Jersey become friends. Miyagi's system of karate instruction is offbeat, to say the least. He puts Daniel to work shining cars, painting fences, scrubbing the bottoms of pools. Daniel complains that he isn't learning karate, he's acting as free labor. But there is a system to Mr. Miyagi's training.

The Karate Kid was directed by John G. Avildsen, who made *Rocky*. It ends with the same sort of climactic fight scene; Daniel faces his enemies in a championship karate tournament. But the heart of this movie isn't in the fight sequences, it's in the relationships. And in addition to Daniel's friendship with Miyagi, there's also a sweet romantic liaison with Ali (Elisabeth Shue), who is your standard girl from the right side of town and has the usual snobbish parents.

Macchio is an unusual, interesting choice for Daniel. He's not the basic handsome Hollywood teenager but a thin, tall, intense kid with a way of seeming to talk to himself. His delivery always sounds natural, even offhand; he never seems to be reading a line. He's a good, sound, interesting lead, but the movie really belongs to Pat Morita, an actor who has been around a long time (he was Arnold on

Happy Days) without ever having a role any- where near this good. Morita makes Miyagi into an example of applied serenity. In a cou- ple of scenes where he has to face down a hos- tile karate coach, Miyagi's words are so carefully chosen they don't give the other guy any excuse to get violent; Miyagi uses the lan- guage as carefully as his hands or arms to ward off blows and gain an advantage. It's refresh- ing to see a completely original character like this old man. *The Karate Kid* is a sleeper with a title that gives you the wrong idea: It's one of 1984's best movies.

Kes

PG, 110 m., 1969

Directed by Ken Loach and produced by Tony Garnett. Screenplay by Barry Hines, based on his book, *A Kestrel for a Knave*.

It isn't often that Academy Award winners completely fail to open in Chicago, but that's what happened with *Kes*. In the event that the movie's name doesn't exactly sound familiar, I should add that *Kes* won the 1970 British Acad- emy Award, as England's best film of the year. It picked up a lot of other honors, too, includ- ing the grand prize at Edinburgh and lots of praise at the 1970 New York Film Festival. But it was never released commercially in America.

For that matter, it never got very good bookings in England, either—the distributors were afraid that audiences wouldn't under- stand the movie's Yorkshire accents. This is the typical sort of blind muddling that seems to go on whenever a good film comes along that's slightly out of the ordinary; nobody was afraid of Michael Caine's accent in *Alfie*, maybe because *Alfie* had enough sex scenes to carry the day. None of this would be impor- tant if *Kes* were not one of the best, the warmest, the most moving films of recent years. After a couple of years in limbo, it was finally picked up for 16-mm distribution in 1972 and had its Chicago premiere in April 1972. The movie is about a teenager and his trained kestrel, and it's perhaps inevitable that it took Loyola's Biological Honor Society to arrange the booking—were they interested in the movie, or the kestrel?

Kes was directed by Ken Loach, a young British filmmaker who now has made three movies of high quality and disappointing commercial performance. His *Poor Cow*, with Carol White, was an ambitious but somewhat confusing movie about a barmaid who be- comes pregnant; it would have fared better, I think, in these latter days of women's lib. After *Kes*, he made *Family Life*, which got good no- tices at the 1972 Cannes festival and opened in New York in fall 1972 as *Wednesday's Child*. This was the story of a misfit adolescent girl and her uptight parents, and it was effective in a grim, slice-of-life way.

But *Kes* is Loach at his best. He shot it on a very low budget, on location, using most local nonprofessionals as his leads. His story is about a boy who's caught in England's class- biased educational system. He reaches school- leaving age and decides to leave but doesn't have anything else he much cares about. He's the butt of jokes and hostility at home (where his older brother rules) and inarticulate with his contemporaries.

One day he finds a small kestrel hawk and trains it to hunt. The bird becomes his avenue to a free and natural state—the state his soul needs, and that his home and school deny him. And then the system, alarmed or offended by his freedom, counterattacks. The film has a heartbreaking humanity.

Kill Bill: Volume 1

R, 93 m., 2003

Uma Thurman (The Bride), Lucy Liu (O-Ren Ishii), Daryl Hannah (Elle Driver), Vivica A. Fox (Vernita Green), Michael Parks (Sheriff), Sonny Chiba (Hattori Hanzo), Chiaki Kuriyama (Go Go Yubari), Julie Dreyfus (Sofie Fatale), David Carradine (Bill), Michael Madsen (Budd). Directed by Quentin Tarantino and produced by Lawrence Bender and Tarantino. Screenplay by Tarantino.

Kill Bill: Volume 1 shows Quentin Tarantino so effortlessly and brilliantly in command of his technique that he reminds me of a virtuoso vi- olinist racing through "Flight of the Bumble Bee"—or maybe an accordion prodigy setting a speed record for "Lady of Spain." I mean that as a sincere compliment. The movie is not about anything at all except the skill and humor of its making. It's kind of brilliant.

His story is a distillation of the universe of martial arts movies, elevated to a trancelike mastery of the material. Tarantino is in the Zone. His story engine is revenge. In the opening scene, Bill kills all of the other members of a bridal party, and leaves The Bride (Uma Thurman) for dead. She survives for years in a coma, and is awakened by a mosquito's buzz. (Is QT thinking of Emily Dickinson, who heard a fly buzz when she died? I am reminded of Manny Farber's definition of the auteur theory: "A bunch of guys standing around trying to catch someone shoving art up into the crevices of dreck.")

The Bride is no Emily Dickinson. She reverses the paralysis in her legs by "focusing." Then she vows vengeance on the Deadly Viper Assassination Squad, and as *Volume 1* concludes she is about half-finished. She has wiped out Vernita Green (Vivica A. Fox) and O-Ren Ishii (Lucy Liu), and in *Volume 2* will presumably kill Elle Driver (Daryl Hannah), Budd (Michael Madsen), and, of course, Bill (David Carradine). If you think I have given away plot details, you think there can be doubt about whether the heroine survives the first half of a two-part action movie, and should seek help.

The movie is all storytelling and no story. The motivations have no psychological depth or resonance, but are simply plot markers. The characters consist of their characteristics. Lurking beneath everything, as it did with *Pulp Fiction,* is the suggestion of a parallel universe in which all of this makes sense in the same way that a superhero's origin story makes sense. There is a sequence here (well, it's more like a third of the movie) where The Bride single-handedly wipes out O-Ren Ishii and her entire team, including the Crazy 88 Fighters, and we are reminded of Neo fighting the clones of Agent Smith in *The Matrix Reloaded,* except the Crazy 88 Fighters are individual human beings, I think. Do they get their name from the Crazy 88 blackjack games on the Web, or from Episode 88 of the action anime *Tokyo Crazy Paradise,* or should I seek help?

The Bride defeats the eighty-eight superb fighters (plus various bodyguards and specialists) despite her weakened state and recently paralyzed legs because she is a better fighter than all of the others put together. Is that because of the level of her skill, the power of her focus, or the depth of her need for vengeance? Skill, focus, and need have nothing to do with it: She wins because she kills everybody without getting killed herself. You can sense Tarantino grinning a little as each fresh victim, filled with foolish bravado, steps forward to be slaughtered. Someone has to win in a fight to the finish, and as far as the martial arts genre is concerned, it might as well be the heroine. (All of the major characters except Bill are women, the men having been emasculated right out of the picture.)

Kill Bill: Volume 1 is not the kind of movie that inspires discussion of the acting, but what Thurman, Fox, and Liu accomplish here is arguably more difficult than playing the nuanced heroine of a Sundance thumb-sucker. There must be presence, physical grace, strength, personality, and the ability to look serious while doing ridiculous things. The tone is set in an opening scene, where The Bride lies near death and a hand rubs at the blood on her cheek, which will not come off because it is clearly congealed makeup. This scene further benefits from being shot in black and white; for QT, all shots in a sense are references to other shots—not particular shots from other movies, but archetypal shots in our collective moviegoing memories.

There's b&w in the movie, and slo-mo, and a name that's bleeped entirely for effect, and even an extended sequence in anime. The animated sequence, which gets us to Tokyo and supplies the backstory of O-Ren Ishii, is sneaky in the way it allows Tarantino to deal with material that might, in live action, seem too real for his stylized universe. It deals with a Mafia kingpin's pedophilia. The scene works in animated long shot; in live action close-up it would get the movie an NC-17.

Before she arrives in Tokyo, The Bride stops off to obtain a sword from Hattori Hanzo ("special guest star" Sonny Chiba). He has been retired for years, and is done with killing. But she persuades him, and he manufactures a sword that does not inspire his modesty: "This my finest sword. If in your journey you should encounter God, God will be cut." Later the sword must face the skill of Go Go Yubari (Chiaki Kuriyama), O-Ren's teenage bodyguard and perhaps a major in medieval studies, since her weapon of choice is the mace and chain. This is in the comic-book tradition by which characters are defined by their weapons. To see The Bride's God-slicer and Go Go's mace clashing in a field of dead and dying men is to understand how women have taken over from men in action movies. Strange, since women are not nearly as good at killing as men are. Maybe they're cast because the liberal media wants to see them succeed. The movie's women warriors remind me of Ruby Rich's defense of Russ Meyer as a feminist filmmaker (his women initiate all the sex and do all the killing).

There is a sequence in which O-Ren Ishii takes command of the Japanese Mafia and beheads a guy for criticizing her as half-Chinese, female, and American. O-Ren talks Japanese through a translator, but when the guy's head rolls on the table everyone seems to understand her. Soon comes the deadly battle with The Bride, on a two-level set representing a Japanese restaurant. Tarantino has the wit to pace this battle with exterior shots of snowfall in an exquisite formal garden. Why must the garden be in the movie? Because gardens with snow are iconic Japanese images, and Tarantino is acting as the instrument of his received influences.

By the same token, Thurman wears a costume identical to one Bruce Lee wore in his last film. Is this intended as coincidence, homage, impersonation? Not at all. It can be explained by quantum physics: The suit can be in two movies at the same time. And when the Daryl Hannah character whistles the theme from *Twisted Nerve* (1968), it's not meant to suggest she is a Hayley Mills fan but that leakage can occur between parallel universes in the movies. Will *Volume 2* reveal that Mr. Bill used to be known as Mr. Blond?

Kill Bill: Volume 2

R, 137 m., 2004

Uma Thurman (The Bride), David Carradine (Bill), Daryl Hannah (Elle Driver), Michael Madsen (Budd), Gordon Liu (Pei Mei). Directed by Quentin Tarantino and produced by Lawrence Bender and Tarantino. Screenplay by Tarantino and Uma Thurman.

Quentin Tarantino's *Kill Bill: Volume 2* is an exuberant celebration of moviemaking, coasting with heedless joy from one audacious chapter to another, working as irony, working as satire, working as drama, working as pure action. I liked it even more than *Kill Bill* (2003). It's not a sequel but a continuation and completion, filmed at the same time; now that we know the whole story, the first part takes on another dimension. *Volume 2* stands on its own, although it has deeper resonance if you've seen *Kill Bill*.

The movie is a distillation of the countless grind house kung-fu movies Tarantino has absorbed, and which he loves beyond all reason. Web sites have already enumerated his inspirations—how a sunset came from this movie, and a sword from that. He isn't copying, but transcending; there's a kind of urgency in the film, as if he's turning up the heat under his memories.

The movie opens with a long close-up of The Bride (Uma Thurman) behind the wheel of a car, explaining her mission, which is to kill Bill. There is a lot of explaining in the film; Tarantino writes dialogue with quirky details that suggest the obsessions of his people. That's one of the ways he gives his movies a mythical quality; the characters don't talk in mundane, everyday dialogue, but in a kind of elevated geekspeak that lovingly burnishes the details of their legends, methods, beliefs, and arcane lore.

Flashbacks remind us that the pregnant Bride and her entire wedding party were targeted by the Deadly Viper Assassination Squad in a massacre at the Two Pines Wedding Chapel. Bill was responsible—Bill, whom she confronts on the porch of the chapel for a conversation that suggests the depth and weirdness of their association. He's played by David Carradine in a performance that somehow, improbably, suggests that Bill and The Bride had a real relationship despite the preposterous details surrounding it. (Bill is deeply offended that she plans to marry a used record store owner and lead a normal life.)

The Bride, of course, improbably survived the massacre, awakened after a long coma, and in the first film set to avenge herself against the Deadly Vipers and Bill. That involved extended action sequences as she battled Vernita Green (Vivica A. Fox) and O-Ren Ishii (Lucy Liu), not to mention O-Ren's teenage bodyguard Go Go Yubari (Chiaki Kuriyama) and the martial arts team known as the Crazy 88.

Much of her success came because she was able to persuade the legendary sword maker

Hattori Hanzo (Sonny Chiba) to come out of retirement and make her a weapon. He presented it without modesty: "This my finest sword. If in your journey you should encounter God, God will be cut."

In *Volume 2*, she meets another Asian legend, the warrior master Pei Mei, played by Gordon Liu. Pei Mei, who lives on the top of a high, lonely hill reached by climbing many stairs, was Bill's master, and in a flashback, Bill delivers his protégé for training. Pei Mei is a harsh and uncompromising teacher, and The Bride sheds blood during their unrelenting sessions.

Pei Mei, whose hair and beard are long and white and flowing, like a character from the pages of a comic book, is another example of Tarantino's method, which is to create lovingly structured episodes that play on their own while contributing to the legend. Like a distillation of all wise, ancient, and deadly martial arts masters in countless earlier movies, Pei Mei waits patiently for eons on his hilltop until he is needed for a movie.

The training with Pei Mei, we learn, prepared The Bride to begin her career with Bill ("jetting around the world making vast sums of money and killing for hire"), and is inserted in this movie at a time and place that makes it function like a classic cliff-hanger. In setting up this scene, Tarantino once again pauses for colorful dialogue; The Bride is informed by Bill that Pei Mei hates women, whites, and Americans, and much of his legend is described. Such speeches function in Tarantino not as long-winded detours, but as a way of setting up characters and situations with dimensions it would be difficult to establish dramatically.

In the action that takes place "now," The Bride has to fight her way past formidable opponents, including Elle Driver (Daryl Hannah), the one-eyed master of martial arts, and Budd (Michael Madsen), Bill's beer-swilling brother, who works as a bouncer in a strip joint and lives in a mobile home surrounded by desolation. Neither one is a pushover for The Bride—Elle because of her skills (also learned from Pei Mei), Budd because of his canny instincts.

The showdown with Budd involves a sequence where it seems The Bride must surely die after being buried alive. (That she does not is a given, considering the movie is not over and Bill is not dead, but she sure looks doomed.)

Tarantino, who began the film in black and white before switching to color, plays with formats here, too; to suggest the claustrophobia of being buried, he shows The Bride inside her wooden casket, and as clods of earth rain down on the lid, he switches from wide-screen to the classic 4x3-screen ratio.

The fight with Elle Driver is a virtuoso celebration of fight choreography; although we are aware that all is not as it seems in movie action sequences, Thurman and Hannah must have trained long and hard to even seem to do what they do. Their battle takes place inside Budd's trailer home, which is pretty much demolished in the process, and provides a contrast to the elegant nightclub setting of the fight with O-Ren Ishii; it ends in a squishy way that would be unsettling in another kind of movie, but here all the action is so ironically heightened that we may cringe and laugh at the same time.

These sequences involve their own Tarantinian dialogue of explanation and scene-setting. Budd has an extended monologue in which he offers The Bride the choice of Mace or a flashlight, and the details of his speech allow us to visualize horrors worse than any we could possibly see. Later, Elle Driver produces a black mamba, and in a sublime touch reads from a Web page that describes the snake's deadly powers.

Of the original *Kill Bill*, I wrote: "The movie is all storytelling and no story. The motivations have no psychological depth or resonance, but are simply plot markers. The characters consist of their characteristics." True, but one of the achievements of *Volume 2* is that the story is filled in, the characters are developed, and they do begin to resonate, especially during the extraordinary final meeting between The Bride and Bill—which consists not of nonstop action but of more hypnotic dialogue, and ends in an event that is like a quiet, deadly punch line.

Put the two parts together, and Tarantino has made a masterful saga that celebrates the martial arts genre while kidding it, loving it, and transcending it. I confess I feared that *Volume 2* would be like those sequels that lack the intensity of the original. But this is all one film, and now that we see it whole, it's greater than its two parts; Tarantino remains the most brilliantly oddball filmmaker of his generation, and this is one of the best films of the year.

Killer of Sheep

NO MPAA RATING, 80 m., 2007

Henry Gayle Sanders (Stan), Kaycee Moore (Stan's Wife). Directed, produced, and written by Charles Bennett.

Ordinary daily life is one of the hardest things for a movie to portray, because so many other movies have trained us to expect patterns and plots. In my 1977 review of Charles Burnett's *Killer of Sheep* I made that mistake of expectation, in a sentence so wrong-headed it cries out to be corrected: "But instead of making a larger statement about his characters, he chooses to show them engaged in a series of daily routines, in the striving and succeeding and failing that make up a life in which, because of poverty, there is little freedom of choice."

Surely I should have seen that what Burnett chooses to show is, in fact, a larger statement. In this poetic film about a family in Watts he observes the quiet nobility of lives lived with values but without opportunities. The lives go nowhere, the movie goes nowhere, and in staying where they are they evoke a sense of sadness and loss.

The film centers on Stan (Henry Gayle Sanders) a slaughterhouse worker, who labors to exhaustion at his work, and then returns to jobs at home: fixing the sink, putting down new linoleum, raising the kids. In this is he joined by his wife (Kaycee Moore), a beautiful but tired women, who freshens her makeup to welcome him home, even though he can hardly notice. Burnett regards their faces, lives, children, friends, neighbors, in a loosely strung-together series of episodes that don't add up to much, while they somehow add up to everything. His black-and-white images and deliberate editing create a sense of serene resignation; this is how it is, and ever shall be.

Killer of Sheep became a legend while hardly being seen. I cannot remember, indeed, why I was able to see it in 1977. Filmed by Burnett for $10,000 as his master's thesis at the UCLA film school, it did not find distribution because Burnett could not afford the rights to the music on his sound track. Now, thirty years later, the film has been beautifully restored by UCLA and blown up from 16 to 35 mm, while retaining its original music (the rights cost

$150,000). The movie's Web site, www.killerof-sheep.com, tells the story and describes the extraordinary music selection: Etta James; Dinah Washington; Gershwin; Rachmaninov; Paul Robeson; Earth, Wind & Fire.

Surely, if he wanted his film seen, Burnett could have used cheaper music? Not at all, because on a deeper level he wanted his film to be a demonstration of the breadth of music by and about African-Americans. One shot at the end, with a backlit Stan and his wife (never named) dancing wearily to Dinah Washington's "This Bitter Earth" demonstrates that it had to be Dinah Washington and no one else, singing that song and no other.

You have to be prepared to see a film like this, or able to relax and allow it to unfold. It doesn't come, as most films do, with built-in instructions about how to view it. One scene follows another with no apparent pattern, reflecting how the lives of its family combine endless routine with the interruptions of random events. The day they all pile into a car to go to the races, for example, a lesser film would have had them winning or losing. In this film, they have a flat tire, and no spare. Thus does poverty become your companion on every journey.

The lives of the adults are intercut with shots of the children at play. One brilliant sequence shows a kid's head darting out from behind a plywood shield once, twice, six times. The camera pulls back to show that two groups of kids are playing at war in a rubbish-strewn wasteland, throwing rocks at one another from behind barriers. A boy gets hit and bleeds and cries. The others forget war and gather around. He's not too badly hurt, and so they idly drift over to railroad tracks and throw rocks at a passing train. All of the scenes of children at play were unrehearsed; Burnett just filmed them.

They have few toys. One child puts on a grotesque rubber Halloween mask and wears it all day, and get roughed up because, somehow, the mask obscures the fact that a child is inside it. At home, Stan works on projects, complains to a friend he cannot sleep, projects deep discouragement. Sitting at the kitchen table, he presses a tea cup against his face and says it reminds him of a feeling just after sex. That kind of tender thought has little place in his world.

We see him at work, herding sheep to their deaths, then stringing them up on a conveyor belt, cutting their throats, watching them bleed. Later, he throws away their inner parts. It is a hard and horrible job. Is there a connection between the sheep, who are content before their ends, and the children at play, happy because they know no better, unaware of the dead end that poverty will bring to some (not all!) of them?

Other scenes. Two men want to involve Stan in a crime. He and his wife send them away. Kids playing in an alley stare as two big boys climb over a back fence with a stolen TV set. We can tell they witness such things all the time. Stan buys a used auto motor, and then the sort of thing happens that is always happening to Stan. He's running, running, just to stay in place.

For an unseen film, *Killer of Sheep* has had a lot of attention. It won the Critics Prize at Berlin; was one of the first fifty titles on the Library of Congress list of American films worthy of permanent preservation; Burnett is "not only the most important African-American director but one of the most distinctive filmmakers this country has ever produced" (Andrew O'Hehir, Salon); and the film deserves "a secure place not only as the greatest achievement in African-American cinema but also as one of the great achievements in cinema, period" (Jeffrey M. Anderson, Cinematical). David Gordon Green names the film as an influence on his own brilliant first feature, *George Washington;* indeed, in homage, he has a kid wearing a Halloween mask.

Charles Burnett was born in 1944 in Mississippi, raised in Watts, and may have learned a lot of things at UCLA but not how to film moneymakers. Among his other titles are *The Glass Shield* (1994) and *To Sleep with Anger* (1990) and a lot of TV and documentary work; he made *The Wedding* (1998) for TV, with Oprah Winfrey producing and Halle Berry starring.

What he captures above all in *Killer of Sheep* is the deadening ennui of hot, empty summer days, the dusty passage of time when windows and screen doors stood open, and the way the breathless day crawls past. And he pays attention to the heroic efforts of this man and wife to make a good home for their children.

Poverty in the ghetto is not the guns and drugs we see on TV. It is more often like life in this movie: Good, honest, hardworking people trying to get by, keep up their hopes, love their children, and get a little sleep.

The Killing Fields

R, 139 m., 1984

Sam Waterston (Sydney Schanberg), Dr. Haing S. Ngor (Dith Pran), John Malkovich (Al Rockoff), Craig T. Nelson (Military Attaché), Athol Fugard (Dr. Sundesval). Directed by Roland Joffe and produced by David Puttnam. Screenplay by Bruce Robinson.

There's a strange thing about stories based on what the movies insist on calling "real life." The haphazard chances of life, the unanticipated twists of fate, have a way of getting smoothed down into Hollywood formulas, so that what might once have happened to a real person begins to look more and more like what might once have happened to John Wayne. One of the risks taken by *The Killing Fields* is to cut loose from that tradition, to tell us a story that does not have a traditional Hollywood structure, and to trust that we'll find the characters so interesting that we won't miss the cliché. It is a risk that works, and that helps make this into a really affecting experience.

The "real-life" story behind the movie is by now well-known. Sydney Schanberg, a correspondent for the *New York Times,* covered the invasion of Cambodia with the help of Dith Pran, a local journalist and translator. When the country fell to the communist Khmer Rouge, the lives of all foreigners were immediately at risk, and Schanberg got out along with most of his fellow Western correspondents. He offered Pran a chance to leave with him, but Pran elected to stay. And when the Khmer Rouge drew a bamboo curtain around Cambodia, Pran disappeared into a long silence. Back home in New York, Schanberg did what he could to discover information about his friend; for example, he wrote about four hundred letters to organizations like the Red Cross. But it was a futile exercise, and Schanberg had given up his friend for dead, when one day four years later word came that Pran was still alive and had made it across the border to a refugee camp. The two friends were reunited, in one of the rare happy endings that come out of a period of great suffering.

As a human story, this is a compelling one. As a Hollywood story, it obviously will not do because the last half of the movie is essentially Dith Pran's story, told from his point of view. Hollywood convention has it that the American should fight his way back into the occupied country (accompanied by renegade Green Berets and Hell's Angels, and Rambo, if possible), blast his way into a prison camp, and save his buddy. That was the formula for *Uncommon Valor* and *Missing in Action*, two box-office hits, and in *The Deer Hunter* one friend went back to Vietnam to rescue another. Sitting in New York writing letters is not quite heroism on the same scale. And yet, what else could Schanberg do? And, more to the point, what else could Dith Pran do, in the four years of his disappearance, but try to disguise his origins and his education, and pass as an illiterate peasant—one of the countless prisoners of Khmer Rouge work camps? By telling his story, and by respecting it, *The Killing Fields* becomes a film of an altogether higher order than the Hollywood revenge thrillers.

The movie begins in the early days of the journalistic coverage of Cambodia. We meet Schanberg (Sam Waterston) and Pran (played by Dr. Haing S. Ngor, whose own story is an uncanny parallel to his character's), and we sense the strong friendship and loyalty that they share. We also absorb the conditions in the country, where warehouses full of Coca-Cola are blown up by terrorists who know a symbolic target when they see one. Life is a routine of hanging out at cafés and restaurants and official briefings, punctuated by an occasional trip to the front, where the American view of things does not seem to be reflected by the suffering that the correspondents witness.

The whole atmosphere of this period is suggested most successfully by the character of an American photographer, played by John Malkovich as a cross between a dopehead and a hard-bitten newsman. He is not stirred to action very easily, and still less easily stirred to caring, but when an occasion arises (for example, the need to forge a passport for Pran), he reveals the depth of his feeling. As the Khmer Rouge victory becomes inevitable, there are

scenes of incredible tension, especially one in which Dith Pran saves the lives of his friends by some desperate fast talking with the cadres of adolescent rebels who would just as soon shoot them. Then there is the confusion of the evacuation of the U.S. Embassy and a last glimpse of Dith Pran before he disappears for four years.

In a more conventional film, he would, of course, have really disappeared, and we would have followed the point of view of the Schanberg character. But this movie takes the chance of switching points of view in midstream, and the last half of the film belongs to Dith Pran, who sees his country turned into an insane parody of a one-party state, ruled by the Khmer Rouge with instant violence and a savage intolerance for any reminders of the French and American presence of the colonial era. Many of the best scenes in the film's second half are essentially played without dialogue, as Pran works in the fields, disguises his origins, and waits for his chance.

The film is a masterful achievement on all the technical levels—it does an especially good job of convincing us with its Asian locations— but the best moments are the human ones, the conversations, the exchanges of trust, the waiting around, the sudden fear, the quick bursts of violence, the desperation. At the center of many of those scenes is Dr. Haing S. Ngor, a nonactor who was recruited for the role from the ranks of Cambodian refugees in California, and who brings to it a simple sincerity that is absolutely convincing. Sam Waterston is effective in the somewhat thankless role of Sydney Schanberg, and among the carefully drawn vignettes are Craig T. Nelson as a military attaché and Athol Fugard as Dr. Sundesval.

The American experience in Southeast Asia has given us a great film epic *(Apocalypse Now)* and a great drama *(The Deer Hunter)*. Here is the story told a little closer to the ground, of people who were not very important and not very powerful, who got caught up in events that were indifferent to them, but never stopped trying to do their best and their most courageous.

King Kong
PG-13, 187 m., 2005

Naomi Watts (Ann Darrow), Jack Black (Carl Denham), Adrien Brody (Jack Driscoll), Andy Serkis (Kong/Lumpy),

Thomas Kretschmann (Captain Englehorn), Colin Hanks (Preston), Kyle Chandler (Bruce Baxter). Directed by Peter Jackson and produced by Jan Blenkin, Carolynne Cunningham, Fran Walsh, and Jackson. Screenplay by Walsh, Philippa Boyens, and Jackson, based on a story by Merian C. Cooper and Edgar Wallace.

It was beauty killed the beast.

There are astonishments to behold in Peter Jackson's new *King Kong,* but one sequence, relatively subdued, holds the key to the movie's success. Kong has captured Ann Darrow and carried her to his perch high on the mountain. He puts her down, not roughly, and then begins to roar, bare his teeth, and pound his chest. Ann, an unemployed vaudeville acrobat, somehow instinctively knows that the gorilla is not threatening her but trying to impress her by behaving as an alpha male—the king of the jungle. She doesn't know how Queen Kong would respond, but she does what she can: She goes into her stage routine, doing backflips, dancing like Chaplin, juggling three stones.

Her instincts and empathy serve her well. Kong's eyes widen in curiosity, wonder, and finally what may pass for delight. From then on, he thinks of himself as the girl's possessor and protector. She is like a tiny, beautiful toy that he has been given for his very own, and before long they are regarding the sunset together, both of them silenced by its majesty.

The scene is crucial because it removes the element of creepiness in the gorilla/girl relationship in the two earlier Kongs (1933 and 1976), creating a wordless bond that allows her to trust him. When Jack Driscoll climbs the mountain to rescue her, he finds her comfortably nestled in Kong's big palm. Ann and Kong in this movie will be threatened by dinosaurs, man-eating worms, giant bats, loathsome insects, spiders, machine guns, and the Army Air Corps, and could fall to their death into chasms on Skull Island or from the Empire State Building. But Ann will be as safe as Kong can make her, and he will protect her even from her own species.

The movie more or less faithfully follows the outlines of the original film, but this fundamental adjustment in the relationship between the beauty and the beast gives it heart, a quality the earlier film was lacking. Yes, Kong in 1933 cares for his captive, but she doesn't care so much for him. Kong was always misunderstood, but in the 2005 film there is someone who knows it. As Kong ascends the skyscraper, Ann screams not because of the gorilla but because of the attacks on the gorilla by a society that assumes he must be destroyed. The movie makes the same kind of shift involving a giant gorilla that Spielberg's *Close Encounters of the Third Kind* did when he replaced 1950s attacks on alien visitors with a very 1970s attempt to communicate with them (by 2005, Spielberg was back to attacking them in *War of the Worlds*).

King Kong is a magnificent entertainment. It is like the flowering of all the possibilities in the original classic film. Computers are used not merely to create special effects but to create style and beauty, to find a look for the film that fits its story. And the characters are not cardboard heroes or villains seen in stark outline but quirky individuals with personalities.

Consider the difference between Robert Armstrong (1933) and Jack Black (2005) as Carl Denham, the movie director who lands an unsuspecting crew on Skull Island. A Hollywood stereotype based on C. B. DeMille has been replaced by one who reminds us more of Orson Welles. And in the starring role of Ann Darrow, Naomi Watts expresses a range of emotion that Fay Wray, bless her heart, was never allowed in 1933. Never have damsels been in more distress, but Fay Wray mostly had to scream, while Watts looks into the gorilla's eyes and sees something beautiful there.

There was a stir when Jackson informed the home office that his movie would run 187 minutes. The executives had something around 140 minutes in mind, so they could turn over the audience more quickly (despite the greedy twenty minutes of paid commercials audiences now have inflicted upon them). After they saw the movie, their objections were stilled. Yes, the movie is a tad too long, and we could do without a few of the monsters and overturned elevated trains. But it is so well done that we are complaining, really, only about too much of a good thing. This is one of the great modern epics.

Jackson, fresh from his *Lord of the Rings* trilogy, wisely doesn't show the gorilla or the other creatures until more than an hour into the movie. In this he follows Spielberg, who fought off producers who wanted the shark in *Jaws* to appear virtually in the opening titles. There is an hour of anticipation, of low, ominous music, of subtle rumblings, of uneasy squints into the fog and mutinous rumblings from the crew, before the tramp steamer arrives at Skull Island—or, more accurately, is thrown against its jagged rocks in the first of many scary action sequences.

During that time we see Depression-era bread lines and soup kitchens, and meet the unemployed heroes of the film: Ann Darrow (Watts), whose vaudeville theater has closed, and who is faced with debasing herself in burlesque; Carl Denham (Black), whose work for a new movie is so unconvincing the backers want to sell it off as background footage; and Jack Driscoll (Adrien Brody), a playwright whose dreams lie off-Broadway and who thrusts fifteen pages of a first-draft screenplay at Denham and tries to disappear.

They all find themselves aboard the tramp steamer of Captain Englehorn (Thomas Kretschmann), who is persuaded to cast off just as Denham's creditors arrive on the docks in police cars. They set course for the South Seas, where Denham believes an uncharted island may hold the secret of a box-office blockbuster. On board, Ann and Jack grow close, but not *too* close, because the movie's real love story is between the girl and the gorilla.

Once they reach Skull Island, the second act of the movie is mostly a series of hair-curling special effects, as overgrown prehistoric creatures endlessly pursue the humans, occasionally killing or eating a supporting character. The bridges and logs over chasms, so important in 1933, are even better used here, especially when an assortment of humans and creatures falls in stages from a great height, resuming their deadly struggle whenever they can grab a convenient vine, rock, or tree. Two story lines are intercut: Ann and the ape, and everybody else and the other creatures.

The third act returns to Manhattan, which looks uncannily evocative and atmospheric. It isn't precisely realistic, but more of a dreamed city in which key elements swim in and out of view. There's a poetic scene where Kong and the girl find a frozen pond in Central Park,

and the gorilla is lost in delight as it slides on the ice. It's in scenes like this that Andy Serkis is most useful as the actor who doesn't so much play Kong as embody him for the f/x team. He adds the body language. Some of the Manhattan effects are not completely convincing (and earlier, on Skull Island, it's strange how the fleeing humans seem to run beneath the pounding feet of the T-rexes without quite occupying the same space). But special effects do not need to be convincing if they are effective, and Jackson trades a little realism for a lot of impact and momentum. The final ascent of the Empire State Building is magnificent, and for once the gorilla seems the same size in every shot.

Although Watts makes a splendid heroine, there have been complaints that Black and Brody are not precisely hero material. Nor should they be, in my opinion. They are a director and a writer. They do not require big muscles and square jaws. What they require are strong personalities that can be transformed under stress. Denham the director clings desperately to his camera no matter what happens to him, and Driscoll the writer beats a strategic retreat before essentially rewriting his personal role in his own mind. Bruce Baxter (Kyle Chandler) is an actor who plays the movie's hero and now has to decide if he can play his role for real. And Preston (Colin Hanks) is a production assistant who, as is often the case, would be a hero if anybody would give him a chance.

The result is a surprisingly involving and rather beautiful movie—one that will appeal strongly to the primary action audience and cross over to people who have no plans to see *King Kong* but will change their minds the more they hear. I think the film even has a message, and it isn't that beauty killed the beast. It's that we feel threatened by beauty, especially when it overwhelms us, and we pay a terrible price when we try to deny its essential nature and turn it into a product, or a target. This is one of the year's best films.

King of the Hill

PG-13, 102 m., 1993

Jesse Bradford (Aaron), Jeroen Krabbe (Mr. Kurlander), Lisa Eichhorn (Mrs. Kurlander), Joseph Chrest (Ben), Spalding Gray (Mr. Mungo), Elizabeth McGovern

(Lydia), Karen Allen (Miss Mathey), Adrien Brody (Lester). Directed by Steven Soderbergh and produced by Albert Berger, Barbara Maltby, and Ron Yerxa. Screenplay by Soderbergh, based on the memoir by A. E. Hotchner.

Steven Soderbergh's *King of the Hill* is the story of a twelve-year-old boy who is left on his own in St. Louis during the Great Depression, and not only survives but thrives, and learns a thing or two. His parents are absent for excellent reasons: His mother is in a TB sanitarium, and his father, a door-to-door salesman, having failed to find much of a market for wickless candles, has left town to travel for a watch company. His younger brother has been shipped away to relatives. That leaves young Aaron (Jesse Bradford) behind in his family's rooms in the Empire Hotel, a transient hotel not quite nice enough to qualify as a brothel.

As a hero, Jesse has some of the qualities of Huckleberry Finn, David Copperfield, or Oliver Twist. He's plucky, smart, and knows his way around people. It is a sad truth that he could not survive in today's unkinder world, but in the 1930s, he finds it possible to support himself and even attend a prestigious local school, all because of his gift of gab and his genius at creative lying.

King of the Hill is based on a 1972 memoir by A. E. Hotchner, who presumably lived through experiences something like these, and who grew up to be the biographer of Ernest Hemingway and Doris Day, as well as others, indicating, among other things, an impressive reach. It's curious that Steven Soderbergh chose this story for his third film, since it has no apparent connection with his first two: *sex, lies and videotape*, which was a sensational debut, and *Kafka*, which was a ponderous and uncompelling followup. Now, with the kind of material you'd never dream of associating with him, he has made his best film.

Some of the credit goes to Bradford, a young actor who looks thoroughly normal and yet has that rare ability to convince us he is thinking when he seems to be doing nothing. His family has fallen on desperate times. His father (Jeroen Krabbe), an immigrant from Germany, is bedeviled by bill collectors and landlords, and tries everything he can think of to make money. Nothing works. His mother (Lisa Eichhorn) is capable and loving, but too ill to help out, and finally has to go to the sanitarium. After the little brother leaves, his father gives him an earnest lecture, tells him he will send money and be back as soon as possible, and leaves him on his own.

The St. Louis where he must survive seems, here, like a glorious city, one of those places that are tough and devious, where you can break your heart or make your fortune. Young Aaron knows his way around the Empire Hotel, with its bribable bellboys and its semi-permanent guests such as the elusive Mr. Mungo (Spalding Gray), who lives across the hallway, occasionally sobering up enough to entertain a prostitute (Elizabeth McGovern) who is slightly less hapless than he is.

The movie follows Aaron's adventures as he talks his way into a private school, creating out of whole cloth a story about his family. He charms a rich girl and is even invited to her house, but he also survives on the streets, and at one point learns to drive, on the spot, when his father's car must be hidden from the collection agency.

This material could make many different kinds of movies. *King of the Hill* could have been a family picture, or a heartwarming TV docudrama, or a comedy. Soderbergh must have seen more deeply into the Hotchner memoir, however, because his movie is not simply about what happens to the kid. It's about how the kid learns and grows through his experiences. It's about growing up, not just about having colorful adventures. And despite the absence of Aaron's family for much of the picture, it's about the support a family can give—even, if it's believed in, when it isn't there.

Kinsey
R, 118 m., 2004

Liam Neeson (Alfred Kinsey), Laura Linney (Clara McMillen), Chris O'Donnell (Wardell Pomeroy), Peter Sarsgaard (Clyde Martin), Timothy Hutton (Paul Gebhard), John Lithgow (Alfred Sequine Kinsey), Tim Curry (Thurman Rice), Oliver Platt (Herman Wells), Dylan Baker (Alan Gregg). Directed by Bill Condon and produced by Gail Mutrux. Screenplay by Condon.

Everybody's sin is nobody's sin. And everybody's crime is no crime at all.

Talk like that made people really mad at Dr. Alfred C. Kinsey. When his first study of human sexual behavior was published in 1947, it was more or less universally agreed that masturbation would make you go blind or insane, that homosexuality was an extremely rare deviation, that most sex was within marriage, and most married couples limited themselves to the missionary position.

Kinsey interviewed thousands of Americans over a period of years, and concluded: Just about everybody masturbates, 37 percent of men have had at least one homosexual experience, there is a lot of premarital and extramarital sex, and the techniques of many couples venture well beyond the traditional male-superior position.

It is ironic that Kinsey's critics insist to this day that he brought about this behavior by his report, when in fact all he did was discover that the behavior was already a reality. There's controversy about his sample, his methods, and his statistics, but ongoing studies have confirmed his basic findings. The decriminalization of homosexuality was a direct result of Kinsey's work, although there are still nine states where oral sex is against the law, even within a heterosexual marriage.

Kinsey, a fascinating biography of the Indiana University professor, centers on a Liam Neeson performance that makes one thing clear: Kinsey was an impossible man. He studied human behavior but knew almost nothing about human nature, and was often not aware that he was hurting feelings, offending people, making enemies, or behaving strangely. He had tunnel vision, and it led him heedlessly toward his research goals without prudent regard for his image, his family and associates, and even the sources of his funding.

Neeson plays Kinsey as a man goaded by inner drives. He began his scientific career by collecting and studying 1 million gall wasps, and when he switched to human sexuality seemed to regard people with much the same objectivity that he brought to insects. Maybe that made him a good interviewer; he was so manifestly lacking in prurient interest that his subjects must have felt they were talking to a confessor imported from another planet. Only occasionally is he personally involved, as when he interviews his strict and difficult father (John

Lithgow) about his sex life, and gains a new understanding of the man and his unhappiness.

The movie shows Kinsey arriving at sex research more or less by accident, after a young couple come to him for advice. Kinsey and his wife, Clara McMillen (Laura Linney), were both virgins on their wedding night (he was twenty-six, she twenty-three) and awkwardly unsure about what to do, but they worked things out, as couples had to do in those days. Current sexual thinking was summarized in a book named *Ideal Marriage: Its Physiology and Technique,* by Theodoor Hendrik van de Velde, a volume whose title I did not need to double-check because I remember so vividly finding it hidden in the basement rafters of my childhood home. Van de Velde was so cautious in his advice that many of those using the book must have succeeded in reproducing only by skipping a few pages.

One of the movie's best scenes shows Kinsey giving the introductory lecture for a new class on human sexuality, and making bold assertions about sexual behavior that were shocking in 1947. His book became a bestseller, Kinsey was for a decade one of the most famous men in the world, and he became the target of congressional witch-hunters who were convinced his theories were somehow linked with the Communist conspiracy. That patriotic middle Americans had contributed to Kinsey's statistics did not seem to impress them, as they pressured the Rockefeller Foundation to withdraw its funding. One of the quiet amusements in the film is the way the foundation's Herman Wells (Oliver Platt) wearily tries to prevent Kinsey from becoming his own worst enemy through tactless and provocative statements.

The movie has been written and directed by Bill Condon, who shows us a Kinsey who is a better scientist than a social animal. Kinsey objectified sex to such an extent that he actually encouraged his staff to have sex with one another and record their findings; this is not, as anyone could have advised him, an ideal way to run a harmonious office. Kinsey didn't believe in secrets, and he brings his wife to tears by fearlessly and tactlessly telling her all of his. Laura Linney's performance as Clara McMillen is a model of warmth and understanding in the face of daily impossibilities;

she loved Kinsey and understood him, acted as a buffer for him, and has an explosively funny line: "I think I might like that."

Kinsey evolved from lecturing to hectoring as he grew older, insisting on his theories in statements of unwavering certainty. His behavior may have been influenced by unwise use of barbiturates, at a time when their danger was not fully understood; he slept little, drove himself too hard, alienated colleagues. And having found that people are rarely exclusively homosexual or heterosexual but exist somewhere between zero and six on the straight-to-gay scale, he found himself settling somewhere around three or four. Condon, who is homosexual, regards Kinsey's bisexuality with the kind of objectivity that Kinsey would have approved; the film, like Kinsey, is more interested in what people do than why.

The strength of *Kinsey* is finally in the clarity it brings to its title character. It is fascinating to meet a complete original, a person of intelligence and extremes. I was reminded of Russell Crowe's work in *A Beautiful Mind* (2001), also the story of a man whose brilliance was contained within narrow channels. *Kinsey* also captures its times, and a political and moral climate of fear and repression; it is instructive to remember that as recently as 1959, the University of Illinois fired a professor for daring to suggest, in a letter to the student paper, that students consider sleeping with each other before deciding to get married. Now universities routinely dispense advice on safe sex and contraception. Of course there is opposition, now as then, but the difference is that Kinsey redefined what has to be considered normal sexual behavior.

Kramer vs. Kramer

PG, 105 m., 1979

Dustin Hoffman (Ted Kramer), Justin Henry (Billy Kramer), Meryl Streep (Joanna Kramer), Howard Duff (Shaunessy), Jane Alexander (Margaret Phelps), George Coe (O'Connor). Directed by Robert Benton and produced by Stanley R Jaffe. Screenplay by Benton, based on the book by Avery Corman.

Kramer vs. Kramer wouldn't be half as good as it is—half as intriguing and absorbing—if the movie had taken sides. The movie's about a situation rich in opportunities for choosing up sides: a divorce and a fight for the custody of a child. But what matters in a story like this (in the movies and in real life, too) isn't who's right or wrong, but if the people involved are able to behave according to their own better nature. Isn't it so often the case that we're selfish and mean-spirited in just those tricky human situations that require our limited stores of saintliness?

Kramer vs. Kramer is about just such a situation. It begins with a marriage filled with a lot of unhappiness, ego, and selfishness, and ends with two single people who have both learned important things about the ways they want to behave. There is a child caught in the middle—their first-grader, Billy—but this isn't a movie about the plight of the kid but about the plight of the parents.

Hollywood traditionally has approached stories like this from the child's point of view, showing him unhappy and neglected by the grown-ups—but what if the grown-ups aren't really grown up? What about a family in which everybody is still basically a kid crying for attention and searching for identity?

That's the case here. The movie stars Dustin Hoffman as a workaholic advertising executive whose thoughts are almost entirely centered on his new account—so much so that when he comes home and his wife announces she's walking out on their marriage, he hardly hears her and doesn't really take her seriously. But his wife (Meryl Streep) is walking out. She needs time to find herself, she says, to discover the unrealized person she left behind when she went into the marriage.

Right away we're close to choosing sides and laying blame: How can she walk out on her home and child? we ask. But we can't quite ask that question in all sincerity, because what we've already seen of Hoffman makes it fairly clear why she might have decided to walk out. She may be leaving the family but he has hardly been a part of it. Harassed, running late, taking his son to school on the first day after his wife has left, he asks him: "What grade are you in?" It's the first. Hoffman didn't know.

The movie leaves Streep off screen during its middle passages, as Hoffman and the kid get to know each other, and as Hoffman's duties as a parent eventually lead to his firing at the ad agency. These scenes are the movie's most heartwarming. The movie's writer and director, Robert Benton, has provided his characters with dialogue that has the ring of absolute everyday accuracy, but in the case of the kid (the young actor is named Justin Henry), he and Hoffman reportedly decided to use improvisation where possible.

Situations are set up and then the young boy is more or less left free to respond in his own words, with Hoffman leading and improvising as well, and many moments have the sense of unrehearsed real life.

What that means is that we can see the father and son learning about each other and growing closer. Another movie might have hedged its bets, but *Kramer vs. Kramer* exists very close to that edge where real people are making real decisions. And that's true, too, when the movie reaches its crisis point: when the Streep character returns and announces that now she feels ready to regain custody of her son.

By now we have no inclination at all to choose sides. Our sympathies do tend to be with the father—we've seen him change and grow—but now we are basically just acting as witnesses to the drama. The movie has encouraged us to realize that these people are deep enough and complex enough, as all people are, that we can't assign moral labels to them.

Kramer vs. Kramer is a movie of good performances, and it had to be, because the performances can't rest on conventional melodrama. Hoffman's acting is about the best in his career, I think, and this movie should win him an Academy Award nomination and perhaps the Oscar. His performance as Ratso in *Midnight Cowboy* (1970) might strike some people as better than this one, but he had the advantage there of playing a colorful and eccentric character. This time he's just a guy in a three-piece suit, trying to figure out the next twenty-four hours. One of his best scenes comes as he applies for a job during an ad agency's office Christmas party and insists on an immediate decision.

Streep certainly has been having quite a year and has appeared in what seems like half the year's best female roles (so far she's been in *The Deer Hunter, The Seduction of Joe Tynan,* and *Manhattan,* and *Holocaust* on TV). In *Kramer vs. Kramer,* Benton asked her to state her character's own case in the big scene where she argues for her child from the witness stand. She is persuasive, but then so is Jane Alexander, who plays her best friend, and whose character is a bystander and witness as Hoffman slowly learns how to be a father.

This is an important movie for Benton, who cowrote *Bonnie and Clyde* and wrote and directed *Bad Company* and *The Late Show.* He spends a great deal of attention on the nuances of dialogue: His characters aren't just talking to each other, they're revealing things about themselves and can sometimes be seen in the act of learning about their own motives. That's what makes *Kramer vs. Kramer* such a touching film: We get the feeling at times that personalities are changing and decisions are being made even as we watch them.

L

La Belle Noiseuse

NO MPAA RATING, 240 m., 1992

Michel Piccoli (Frenhofer), Jane Birkin (Liz), Emmanuelle Béart (Marianne), Marianne Denicourt (Julienne), David Bursztein (Nicolas), Gilles Arbona (Porbus). Directed by Jacques Rivette and produced by Pierre Grise. Screenplay by Pascal Bonitzer, Christine Laurent, and Rivette.

Some movies are worlds that we can sink into, and *La Belle Noiseuse* is one of them. It is a four-hour movie, but not one second too long, in which the process of art and the process of life come into a fascinating conflict. There is something fundamentally sensual about the relationship between an artist and a model, not because of the nudity and other superficial things, which are obvious, but because the artist is trying to capture something intimate and secret from another person and put it on the canvas. It is possible to have sex with someone and not know them, but it is impossible to draw them well and not know them well.

The movie is about an artist in his sixties, who has not painted for many years. In his studio is an unfinished canvas, a portrait of his wife, which leans against the wall like a rebuke for the passion that has died between them. They are still happily married, but their relationship is one of understanding, not hunger. One day a young admirer brings his girlfriend to meet the artist and his wife. Something stirs within the older man, and he asks the girl to pose for him. She agrees, indifferently, and as he begins his portrait a subtle dance of seduction begins.

To understand the dynamic, you will have to picture the actors. The artist is played by Michel Piccoli, veteran of dozens of important French movies, he of the intimidating bald forehead, the vast eyebrows, the face of an aging satyr. The young woman is played by Emmanuelle Béart (*Manon of the Spring*), whose beauty may come from heaven but whose intelligence is all her own. Watching her here, we realize that it would not have been enough simply to cast a beautiful woman in the role, for the artist is entrapped by her mind, not her appearance. The artist's wife is played by Jane Birkin (the daughter in *Daddy Nostalgia*), who knows her husband well enough to warn Béart against him, but not well enough to warn herself.

The sittings begin, and the artistic process takes over. And the film's director, Jacques Rivette, takes a big risk, which works brilliantly. He shows the preliminary sketches, the pencil drawings, charcoals, and watercolor washes, in great detail. The camera looks over the shoulder of the artist and regards his hand as he draws. Sometimes the camera is on the hand for four or five minutes at a time. This may sound boring. It is more thrilling than a car chase. We see a human being taking shape before us. And as the artist tries one approach and then another, we see the process of his mind at work.

It is said that artistic processes take place on the right side of the brain, the side that is liberated from mundane considerations like the passage of time. I know for myself that when I draw, I drop out of time and lose all consciousness of its passing. I even fail to hear people who are talking to me because the verbal side of my mind is not engaged. Most films are a contest between the right and left brains, in which dialogue and plot struggle to make sense, while picture, mood, music, and emotion struggle toward a reverie state. In *La Belle Noiseuse*, the right side, the artistic side, of the viewer's mind is given the freedom to take over, and as the artist draws, something curious happens. We become the artist ourselves, in a way, looking at the model, taking up the tools, plunging into the preliminary drawings.

The artist and his model do not get along very well. He is almost sadistic in his treatment of her, addressing her curtly, asking her to assume uncomfortable poses, keeping an impolite distance between her concerns and his own. She hates him. He does not care. It is a battle of the wills. But Jacques Rivette is an old and wise man, and so this movie doesn't develop along simplistic lines in which love soon rears its inquisitive head. Here is where Béart's intelligence comes in—hers, and her character's. The battle between the two people

395

becomes one of imagination, a chess game of the emotions, in which small moves can have great consequences.

You may think you can guess what will happen. The artist will fall in love with his model. The wife and the boyfriend will be jealous. There will be sex scenes. Perhaps to some degree you are right. To a much larger degree, however, *La Belle Noiseuse* will surprise you, because this is not a movie that limits its curiosity to the question of where everybody's genitals will turn up.

The reason the movie benefits from its length is twofold. First, Rivette takes all of the time he needs to show the actual physical process of drawing. These passages are surprisingly tactile; we hear the whisper of the pencil on the paper, the scratch of the drawing pen, and we see that drawing is a physical process, not, as some people fancy, an exercise in inspiration. Second, having given the artist time to discover his model on his canvas, Rivette then gives himself the time to discover his own models. While the artist and model in the film are investigating one another, Rivette stands at his own canvas and draws both of them.

La Cage aux Folles

R, 91 m., 1979

Ugo Tognazzi (Renato), Michel Serrault (Zaza), Michel Galabru (Charrier), Claire Maurier (Simone), Remy Laurent (Laurent), Benny Luke (Jacob). Directed by Edouard Molinaro and produced by Marcello Danon. Screenplay by Francis Veber and Molinaro.

La Cage aux Folles are "birds of a feather," which are precisely and hilariously what do not flock together in this wonderful comedy from France. It's about the gay owner of a scandalous nightclub in St. Tropez, his transvestite lover, and how the owner reacts after his son returns home one day and announces he's going to marry . . . a girl!

But that's not *really* what it's about: This is basically the first sitcom in drag, and the comic turns in the plot are achieved with such clockwork timing that sometimes we're laughing at what's funny and sometimes we're laughing at the movie's sheer comic invention. This is a great time at the movies.

The nightclub owner is played by Ugo Tognazzi, that grizzled Italian veteran of so many macho roles, and he has lived for twenty years with a drag queen (Michel Serrault) who stars in the club. They're like an old married couple, nostalgic and warm one minute, fighting like cats and dogs the next. Tognazzi sired the son all those years ago and has raised him with the help of "Auntie" Serrault and their live-in "maid," a wickedly funny black transvestite who has perhaps the movie's funniest moment.

Tognazzi and Serrault have trouble at first accepting the notion that their treasured young man is going to get married. They have more trouble, however, accepting the notion that the intended bride is the daughter of the minister of moral standards—and that the in-laws are planning to come to dinner.

This dilemma inspires the film's hilarious middle section, in which Tognazzi's garishly bizarre apartment is severely redecorated in crucifixes and antiques, and Serrault is gently asked by the son if he'd mind being gone for the evening: "I told them my father was a cultural attaché; what'll they think when they find out he lives with a drag queen?"

Tognazzi, meanwhile, goes to visit the woman who bore his son two decades ago, to ask her to portray the mother for one night. She agrees. Too bad, because in the course of the uproariously funny dinner party, at least two reputed mothers are produced, one of them suspiciously hairy around the chest.

Describing a comedy is always a risky business; the bare plot outline is, of course, no hint as to how funny a film is, and to steal the jokes is a misdemeanor. What I can say, though, is that *La Cage aux Folles* gets the audience on its side with immediate ease; it never betrays our confidence; it astonishes us with the inspiration and logic it brings to ringing changes on the basic situation.

And it contains several classic sequences. The best is perhaps the one in which Tognazzi coaches Serrault on how to act "macho," an attribute that apparently consists of knowing how to butter your toast with manly firmness. There's also that extended dinner scene that begins with the minister of moral standards discovering that . . . Greek boys . . . are doing . . . *something* . . . on his soup plate . . . and builds from there.

The Lacemaker

NO MPAA RATING, 107 m., 1978

Isabelle Huppert (Pomme), Yves Beneyton (Francois), Florence Giorgetti (Marylene), Anne Marie Duringer (Pomme's Mother), Renata Schroeter (Francois' Friend), Michel De Re (The Painter). Directed by Claude Goretta and produced by Yves Peyrot. Written by Goretta and Pascal Laine, based on the book by Laine.

Her face, Claude Goretta tells us in the titles at the end of *The Lacemaker*, is one of those remarkable faces that are not quite in fashion. If she had been living during the Renaissance, she might have been included as one of the figures in the background of a painting: a seamstress, perhaps, or a lacemaker. The titles come immediately after she has turned and regarded us gravely for a time.

She's an eighteen-year-old girl named Pomme who works as an assistant in a Paris beauty shop. She's quiet, shy, pretty. She lives with her mother, and they get along well. Her best friend is Marylene, a slightly trampy beautician who works in the same shop, and whose affair with a married man is coming to an unhappy end. So, even though it's late in the season, Pomme and Marylene decide to take a holiday at the seacoast together.

Marylene meets an American tourist and moves into his hotel. Pomme, alone, soberly regards the bathers. She eats a plum in her room. She has solitary ice creams in deserted cafés. One day she meets Francois, a literature student from Paris who is also alone at the resort. They shyly like each other but lose track of each other, and Goretta provides a stunning shot showing Francois walking alone on the beach as the camera then rotates to zoom in on Pomme on a side street a few blocks away.

They do eventually meet again, though, and Goretta quietly celebrates the beginnings of their love. Both are quiet and withdrawn. Both are sexually inexperienced. Both are more in love than perhaps they'll ever be able to articulate. They go back to Paris and take an apartment together after Francois shares an awkward cup of tea with Pomme's mother ("Just so long as she's happy . . ."). But then their relationship grows more complicated, and *The Lacemaker* stops being a love story and starts being a delicate character study.

Because Francois, you see, wants to "improve" Pomme. Thinks she should have a better job than at the beauty parlor. Is proud of her in conversations with his intellectual friends. ("She couldn't go to college, but she has a natural intelligence.") But finds that she has little to contribute when his friends come over for self-conscious discussions about Marxism.

"What do you mean by 'dialectic'?" she asks him, after one such evening. He's very attentive and helpful in his answer although it gradually becomes clear to her, and to us, that he has no idea exactly what he means by "dialectic." She'd never think of pointing that out, though. Instead, she withdraws into herself, becomes very still and silent, and finally acquiesces when he explains why their relationship has to end.

"How did she take it?" one of Francois's intellectual friends asks.

"Better than I expected," he says. "She didn't say anything." What a rat. But a pathetic rat, because he's trapped in his personality, just as she's trapped in hers.

Some of the New York reviews of *The Lacemaker* have found a Marxist line in it: Francois, the bourgeois intellectual, uses and then discards the working-class girl. I don't read it that way. I think Goretta and Pascal Laine, who wrote the screenplay, are looking with compassion on both characters. If Francois drives Pomme to sadness, silence, and disorientation, he does so at great cost to himself because, in ways he doesn't understand and may never understand, he's lost a person who really was precious to him—lost her through convincing himself he wanted a girl different than the one he fell in love with.

The movie's performances are wonderfully subtle. Isabelle Huppert, as Pomme, is good at the very difficult task of projecting the inner feelings of a character whose whole personality is based on the concealment of feeling. (There was a lot of feeling at the 1977 Cannes Film Festival that she should have won as best actress.) And Yves Beneyton, as Francois, looks so skinny and forlorn in the black sweater he usually wears that he almost cries out for sympathy.

The Lacemaker must have been a very difficult film to make because the modulations of emotion have to be so exact. But Goretta, the young Swiss director who also made last year's *The Wonderful Crook*, knows his characters and knows the territory of their souls.

Lacombe, Lucien

R, 141 m., 1974

Pierre Blaise (Lucien Lacombe), Aurore Clement (France Horn), Holger Lowenadler (Albert Horn), Therese Giehse (Bella Horn), Stephane Bouy (Jean-Bernard), Loumi Iacobesco (Betty Beaulieu). Directed by Louis Malle and produced by Malle and Claude Nedjar. Screenplay by Malle and Patrick Modiano.

Louis Malle's *Lacombe, Lucien* opens with a young man cleaning the floors of a hospital ward. Outside, a bird sings. The youth goes to the window, spots the bird, takes a slingshot from his pocket, and kills the bird. He resumes his task of cleaning floors. His face hasn't betrayed any emotion. He seems to have killed the bird purely as a technical exercise, to demonstrate the accuracy of his aim.

The young man is Lucien Lacombe, and he is seventeen in 1944, when the German war machine has started to fall apart. He lives in occupied France, and as we get to know him, we realize he's a moral cipher with no point of view at all toward the momentous events surrounding him. He's not stupid, but his interest in the war is limited mostly to the daily ways it affects him directly.

It affects him at home, where his mother lives with her lover (his father is missing in action). It affects him at work, where he labors in his boring job at the hospital. A lot of the young men in the town are members of the underground resistance movement. They carry guns, are involved in secret schemes, and don't have to mop floors. Lucien approaches the local resistance and asks to join, but he's turned away because he's too young. He wants desperately (if "desperately" isn't too strong a word for such a taciturn character) to break the mold of his life, and since the resistance won't have him, he joins the local Gestapo.

Now he gets to carry a gun (even a machine gun), and he has money in his pocket. It's a good job, as jobs go. He doesn't seem, at first, or even afterward, to have given much thought to the moral issues involved. He doesn't see himself as a traitor to France, or a collaborator with the evil of Nazism, but as a person of some consequence through his power to order and bully. He likes the work.

And that seems to be an underlying theme of Louis Malle's *Lacombe, Lucien*, which is one of a growing number of works examining the role played by ordinary Frenchmen during the German occupation. Marcel Ophuls's landmark documentary, *The Sorrow and the Pity* (1972), first broke this ground two years ago, destroying the myth that most Frenchmen listened faithfully to de Gaulle's broadcasts from London, while only a handful were collaborators. Ophuls's *Hotel Terminus* made the point again in 1987. The truth, Marcel Ophuls and Louis Malle seem to be saying, is that a lot of ordinary people simply went along, passively, because they were so accustomed to obeying authority that they preferred the Germans to the bother of making up their own minds. That was part of what Ophuls had to say, and now, Malle offers a more provocative statement.

His *Lucien* is a case study of a young man of almost total selfishness, who betrays his people and joins the Gestapo primarily to make things easier for himself. His error, of course, is that he becomes a collaborator at a point in the war when the Germans clearly are going to lose. But his horizons aren't wide enough to take account of those faraway possibilities.

His life becomes complicated, however, when he uses the power of the Gestapo to move into a comfortable house that's being occupied by a Jewish tailor from Paris, his mother, and his attractive young daughter. These people are of an intelligence and sophistication beyond a simple thug like Lucien, but in some backward way, he develops a grudging affection for them. He bullies them around, his machine gun having provided a personality where none existed before. But then he falls in love with the girl, and she with him.

This is crazy, we're thinking. Lucien joins the Gestapo almost absentmindedly, and then this bright Jewish girl falls for a guy like that. But Malle's point is a complex one. Neither of these people can quite see beyond their immediate circumstances. They're young, uninformed, and naive, and the fact is that adolescent sex appeal is a great deal more meaningful to them than all the considerations of history.

Lucien (who falls into the bureaucratic mold so effortlessly that he takes to giving his last name first for the convenience of those filling out official forms) is faced now with complications and challenges he simply isn't equal to. He loves the girl, and he has some kind of wary relationship with her father, but his Gestapo membership is eventually going to force him to hurt this family. He doesn't, though. He comes along to their house on a raid with a German officer, but decides at the last minute to kill the officer, and run off to the country with the girl. That wasn't a brave or ideological decision, either. He almost seems to have taken it as a matter of convenience.

Malle, whose previous film was the bittersweet and lovely *Murmur of the Heart* (1971), gave himself a difficult assignment this time. His film isn't really about French collaborators, but about a particular kind of human being, one capable of killing and hurting, one incapable of knowing or caring about his real motives, one who would be a prime catch for basic training and might make a good soldier and not ask questions.

As played by Pierre Blaise, a young forester who had never acted before (and who died in a road crash a few years later), Lucien is a victim trapped in his own provincialism and lack of curiosity. Malle seems almost to be examining the mentality of someone like the war criminals at My Lai—technicians of murder who hardly seemed to be troubled by their actions. That's the achievement of *Lacombe, Lucien*. But what Malle is never quite able to do is to make us care about Lucien, who is so morally illiterate that his choices, even the good ones, seem randomly programmed—perhaps to show that illiteracy is the point of the film.

L.A. Confidential

R, 138 m., 1997

Kevin Spacey (Jack Vincennes), Russell Crowe (Bud White), Guy Pearce (Ed Exley), James Cromwell (Dudley Smith), Kim Basinger (Lynn Bracken), David Strathairn (Pierce Patchett), Ron Rifkin (D. A. Ellis Loew), Danny DeVito (Sid Hudgens). Directed by Curtis Hanson and produced by Arnon Milchan, Hanson, and Michael Nathanson. Screenplay by Brian Helgeland and Hanson, based on the book by James Ellroy.

Confidential was a key magazine of the 1950s, a monthly that sold millions of copies with its seamy exposés of celebrity drugs and sex. I found it in my dad's night table and read it breathlessly, the stories of reefer parties, multiple divorces, wife-swapping, and "leading men" who liked to wear frilly undergarments. The magazine sank in a sea of lawsuits, but it created a genre; the trash tabloids are its direct descendents.

Watching *L.A. Confidential*, I felt some of the same insider thrill that *Confidential* provided: The movie, like the magazine, is based on the belief that there are a million stories in the city, and all of them will raise your eyebrows and curl your hair. The opening is breathlessly narrated by a character named Sid Hudgens (Danny DeVito), who publishes *Hush-Hush* magazine and bribes a cop named Jack Vincennes (Kevin Spacey) to set up celebrity arrests; Jack is photographed with his luckless victims, and is famous as the guy who caught Robert Mitchum smoking marijuana.

It's Christmas Eve 1953, and Bing Crosby is crooning on the radio as cops pick up cartons of free booze to fuel their holiday parties. We meet three officers who, in their way, represent the choices ahead for the LAPD. Vincennes, star-struck, lives for his job as technical adviser to *Badge of Honor*, a *Dragnet*-style show. Bud White (Russell Crowe) is an aggressive young cop who is willing to accommodate the department's relaxed ethics. Ed Exley (Guy Pearce) is a straight arrow, his rimless glasses making him look a little like a tough accountant—one who works for the FBI, maybe.

Ed is an ambitious careerist who wants to do everything by the book. His captain, Dudley Smith (James Cromwell), kindly explains that an officer must be prepared to lie, cheat, and steal—all in the name, of course, of being sure the guilty go to jail. Captain Smith likes to call his men "good lads," and seems so wise we can almost believe him as he administers little quizzes and explains that advancement depends on being prepared to give the "right answers."

L.A. Confidential is immersed in the atmosphere and lore of *film noir*, but it doesn't seem like a period picture—it believes its *noir* values and isn't just using them for decoration. It's based on a novel by James Ellroy, that lanky, sardonic poet of Los Angeles sleaze. Its director, Curtis Hanson *(Bad Influence, The Hand That Rocks the Cradle),* weaves a labyrinthine plot, but the twists are always clear because the characters are so sharply drawn; we don't know who's guilty or innocent, but we know who should be.

The plot involves a series of crimes that take place in the early days of the new year. Associates of Mickey Cohen, the L.A. mob boss, become victims of gangland-style executions. A decomposing body is found in a basement. There's a massacre at an all-night coffee shop; one of the victims is a crooked cop, and three black youths are immediately collared as suspects, although there's evidence that police may have been behind the crime.

We meet a millionaire pornographer named Pierce Patchett (David Strathairn). He runs a high-class call girl operation in which aspiring young actresses are given plastic surgery to make them resemble movie stars; one of them is Lynn Bracken (Kim Basinger), who has been "cut" to look like Veronica Lake. Bud White, the Crowe character, tracks her down, thinking she'll have info about the decomposing corpse, and they fall almost helplessly in love ("You're the first man in months who hasn't told me I look just like Veronica Lake").

At this point, perhaps an hour into the movie, I felt inside a Raymond Chandler novel: not only because of the atmosphere and the dialogue, but also because there seemed to be no way all of these characters and events could be drawn together into a plot that made sense. Not that I would have cared; I enjoy *film noir* for the journey as much as the destination.

But Hanson and his cowriter, Brian Helgeland, do pull the strands together, and along the way there's an unlikely alliance between two cops who begin as enemies. The film's assumption is that although there's small harm in free booze and a little graft, there are some things a police officer simply cannot do and look himself in the mirror in the morning.

The film is steeped in L.A. lore; Ellroy is a student of the city's mean streets. It captures the town just at that postwar moment when it was beginning to become self-conscious about

its myth. Joseph Wambaugh writes in one of his books that he is constantly amazed by the hidden threads that connect the high to the low, the royalty to the vermin, in Los Angeles—where a hooker is only a role from stardom, and vice, as they say, versa.

One of the best scenes takes place in the Formosa Cafe, a restaurant much frequented in the 1940s by unlikely boothfellows. Cops turn up to question Johnny Stompanato, a hood who may know something about the Cohen killings. His date gives them some lip. "A hooker cut to look like Lana Turner is still a hooker," one of them tells her, but Jack Vincennes knows better: "She is Lana Turner," he says with vast amusement.

One of the reasons *L.A. Confidential* is so good, why it deserves to be mentioned with *Chinatown,* is that it's not just plot and atmosphere. There are convincing characters here, not least Kim Basinger's hooker, whose quiet line, "I thought I was helping you," is one of the movie's most revealing moments. Russell Crowe *(Proof)* and Guy Pearce *(The Adventures of Priscilla, Queen of the Desert)* are two Australian actors who here move convincingly into star-making roles, and Kevin Spacey uses perfect timing to suggest his character's ability to move between two worlds while betraying both (he has a wonderful scene where he refuses to cooperate with a department investigation—until they threaten his job on the TV show).

Behind everything, setting the moral tone and pulling a lot of the plot threads, is the angular captain, seemingly so helpful. James Cromwell, who was the kindly farmer in *Babe,* has the same benevolent smile in this role, but the eyes are cold, and in his values can be seen, perhaps, the road ahead to Rodney King. *L.A. Confidential* is seductive and beautiful, cynical and twisted, and one of the best films of the year.

Ladybird, Ladybird

NO MPAA RATING, 102 m., 1995

Crissy Rock (Maggie), Vladimir Vega (Jorge), Sandie LaVelle (Mairead), Mauricic Venegas (Adrian), Ray Winstone (Simon), Clare Perkins (Jill), Jason Stracey (Sean), Luke Brown (Mickey). Directed by Ken Loach and produced by Sally Hibbin. Screenplay by Rona Munro.

Ladybug, ladybug,
Fly away home.
Your house is on fire,
And your children will burn.

—nursery rhyme

This is the story of a troublesome woman. A woman with a big heart and a big temper, who has had four children by four different fathers, and lost custody of all of them because she cannot function responsibly. Or, looking at it differently, it is the story of a woman persecuted by British social workers who slap her down every time she almost has her life together. The strength of the film is that there is truth to both interpretations: Yes, she is treated cruelly by social workers—and, yes, she is her own worst enemy.

The woman's name is Maggie, and she is played by a former barmaid and stand-up comic named Crissy Rock who has never acted before. It is the strongest performance in any film of its year; seeing the movie for the first time at the Telluride Film Festival in September 1994, I walked out of the theater and saw Rock standing there, and wanted to comfort her, she had embodied Maggie's suffering so completely. The Oscar nominations were incomplete because they did not take this performance into account.

If you hang around bars where a lot of steady drinking goes on, you will have met someone like Crissy. She is short, blond, pudgy, in her thirties, with a nice face tending to fat. She's a "character." On karaoke night, she grabs the mike and brings down the house. She's good company, tells jokes, gets bawdy, holds her own. She likes to laugh, but there is sadness inside, and after too many drinks she may start to sob. She's in the bar looking for comfort, reassurance, a sense of belonging, and so she's a pushover for guys who buy her a drink and seem to care.

One night she meets a man who really does care. His name is Jorge (Vladimir Vega), and he is an immigrant from Paraguay with "political problems" at home. He seems almost improbably nice, and for once she dares to hope: Maybe this man will treat her better than the others, who were abusive, irresponsible, drunks, and dopeheads. He watches her singing, and is attracted to her

spirit. Soon they are a couple, and she begins to hope.

We see how hopeless she is as a mother—and as a responsible adult. She was abused as a child, never learned basic survival and social skills, and exists in chaos, moving from one flat to another, treating each meal as a fresh challenge, as if food itself baffles her. We see her exploding; she has a fierce temper, a knack for blowing up when she should lay low. One day she does something that is shockingly irresponsible, and her four children are taken away from her by the social workers. She deserves to lose them. But because *Ladybird, Ladybird* sees her so clearly, we can understand why she acted as she did. Not forgive, but understand.

Now starts her long ordeal. She wants her children back, but sees the photograph of one of them in the newspaper, offered for adoption. Jorge sticks by her, and soon she is pregnant again, but now the social workers watch her like a hawk, and she loses that baby to them—and then another, in a scene where the social workers enter the maternity ward and all but rip the infant from her womb, while a nurse breaks down and sobs.

To witness Crissy Rock in these scenes is to see acting of such elemental power and truth it can hardly be borne. She screams, she cries, she rages against her fate. The rawness of her need and grief is like an open wound. And yet at the same time we acknowledge that she seems unfit to be a mother, although perhaps Jorge could make a new start for her, and his sweetness and good sense could teach her hard lessons of maturity and balance.

The social workers are monstrous precisely because they seem to apply rules without any regard for the human beings in front of them—and yet we can see their reasoning, as Maggie explodes again and again. She is white, her children are of various races, and now her new husband is a foreigner with questionable British immigration papers; the workers never say anything overtly racist, they are too correct for that, but sometimes you can guess what they're thinking.

Ken Loach directed the film. After twenty-five years of specializing in working-class British life (*Kes, Poor Cow*), he has recently made a cluster of particularly fine movies:

Riff-Raff, about the floating population of construction workers; *Raining Stones,* about an unemployed man trying to buy a communion dress for his daughter; and now *Ladybird, Ladybird,* which could have been a predictable tear-jerking docu-drama, but is too honest to stack the deck. What we see here is not a "problem," not a "solution," but simply a painful record from life. The movie is "based on a true story." I never doubted that for a second.

La Guerre Est Finie
NO MPAA RATING, 121 m., 1966

Yves Montand (Diego), Ingrid Thulin (Marianne), Genevieve Bujold (Nadine), Dominique Rozan (Jude), Juan-Francois Remi (Juan). Directed by Alain Resnais and produced by Anatole Dauman, Giselle Rebillon, and Catherine Winter. Screenplay by Jorge Semprun.

Alain Resnais's *La Guerre Est Finie* is exactly about the political dilemma of our time. This seems to be an age when the old and the young cannot agree on what is good or bad. The old (say the young) cling to outworn slogans and are worn down by centralization and bureaucracy. The young (say the old) care nothing for traditional values and seek to destroy society by anarchy.

What Resnais has attempted to do in *La Guerre Est Finie* is to explore the terms of this argument and to see if we can still hope (as we once did) that the ideas of good men can improve society.

For his subject, Resnais has taken the most dramatic political confrontation of the twentieth century: the Spanish civil war. It was a strange war. The communists were the democratically elected, legal government; the fascists were the rebels trying to seize control. Franco was backed by Hitler and Mussolini, and the Nazis perfected their techniques of air warfare by bombing little towns whose names have passed into the human conscience, such as Guernica.

But as Resnais tells us in the title of his film, the war is over. It has been over for nearly thirty years. Franco is an old man but still in command; fascism is still the form of government.

The hero of the film (Yves Montand) is a Spanish citizen who has been engaged ever since the war's end in a variety of underground anti-Franco movements. He is part of a network that moves people and information in and out of Spain, prepares reports, calls general strikes, prints propaganda newspapers, and does everything else that seems to be indicated.

But the members of the underground are weary; they subscribe to political dogmas that no longer seem relevant, except to a few of them; they can show few tangible results.

Resnais conceives his entire film in terms of the one character. He has loyally served the underground, but he begins to believe their decisions are the wrong ones. They sit in Paris and call general strikes, and when he returns from Madrid to protest, they tell him he was "misled by reality."

In the course of exchanging a passport, he meets a young girl (Genevieve Bujold) who is involved in another, much younger movement against Franco. One afternoon after he argues with futility that his superiors are following the wrong policy, he encounters the girl and her young associates.

They plan violence, plastic bombs, anarchy. They believe that the tourist trade can be stopped if terrorists attack popular resorts. Their reasoning is alien to the methodical nature of his own work over three decades, and suddenly he finds himself in the middle, convinced both approaches are wrong, almost convinced at last that nothing can be done.

Resnais's previous films (*Hiroshima, Mon Amour, Last Year at Marienbad*) were explorations of the subconscious. With *La Guerre Est Finie* he unexpectedly gives us not only psychology but an exciting thriller, done with great artistry.

Montand is simultaneously caught in a web of actual danger, and in his own ideological crisis. The women in his life seem to say just the wrong (or right) things, pushing him toward some sort of a moral decision about Spain. The film ends on what some will consider an inconclusive note, but it has made clear that there are no final conclusions to be drawn yet about Spain.

La Lectrice
R, 98 m., 1989

Miou-Miou (Constance/Marie), Christian Ruche (Jean/Philippe), Sylvie Laporte (Françoise), Michel

Raskine (Agency Man), Brigitte Catillon (Eric's Mother/Jocelyn), Regis Royer (Eric), Simon Eine (Hospital Professor), Christian Blanc (Old Teacher). Directed by Michel Deville and produced by Rosalinde Deville. Screenplay by Rosalinde and Michel Deville, based on the book by Raymond Jean.

Constance is in bed with her boyfriend when he asks her to read aloud to him. As she reads, she begins to imagine herself as the heroine of the story. The story Constance reads is about Marie, a young woman who needs employment and takes an ad in the paper, offering to read aloud to people. Marie finds that a surprising number of clients want to take advantage of her services—and, as she reads for them, she begins to enter into their lives.

This is the elegant, Chinese-box structure of Michel Deville's *La Lectrice,* and one of the pleasures of the film is the way Deville moves up and down through the various levels of the story, and then sideways through the sometimes devious motives of the clients who hire the reader. Only someone who loves to read would understand how one person can become another, can enter into the life of a person in a book. That is what happens in this movie.

Marie is played by Miou-Miou as a solemn woman who comes to care about her clients. There are several, each one with a different problem (and probably with a different "real" reason why they want to be read aloud to). There is a young boy who has been gravely injured in an accident and fears for his potency. He wants Marie to read him passionate poetry—and he falls in love with her, identifying her with the poems. An old woman, once filled with fire and conviction, hires Marie to read to her, for one last time, the writers like Tolstoy and Marx who once inspired her. A busy mother hires Marie to read *Alice in Wonderland* to her small daughter. And a rich investor probably wants her to read him pornography, but is reluctant to say so, and so gets respectable erotica instead.

Each client's book reflects the nature of his or her fantasy, and Marie understands that immediately. As she reads to them, a curious process begins to take place. She becomes, in a way, the author of the books. The teenager idealizes her as a romantic. The old lady thinks she is an intellectual. The little girl sees her as a mother figure. And the businessman, of course, wants to sleep with her. What is intriguing is that Marie herself starts to identify with the books, and so is almost able to see herself as lover, confidante, mother, and prostitute.

La Lectrice is a movie in love with words— deliriously intoxicated by the stories and images in the pages that Marie reads. But making a movie about reading is like writing a symphony about looking at paintings: How do you make the leap from one medium to another? In Francois Truffaut's *Fahrenheit 451,* another film about the love of books, the final scene showed human beings who had "become" books in order to preserve their contents in an age of book-burning. One was *David Copperfield,* another was *Pride and Prejudice,* walking back and forth in the snow, reciting the words to themselves. In *La Lectrice,* the words become real in a different way—by having an actual effect. Because the love poems make the teenager amorous, because the eroticism arouses the businessman, the books become like magical talismans.

I hope I have not made *La Lectrice* sound too difficult or dryly intellectual. This is a sensuous film from beginning to end, a film that is all the more seductive because it teases the imagination. As the reader becomes the books she reads, we become the people she reads to. And so, in our imaginations, we see her in all her roles. In some scenes she is sweet, in others thoughtful, in others carnal. The film is a demonstration that we can rarely understand the secret minds of people, so therefore upon their exteriors we project our own fantasies. When the movie was over, I wanted to go out and find the novel by Raymond Jean that the screenplay is based on. I didn't want to read it. I wanted someone to read it to me.

Last Days
R, 97 m., 2005

Michael Pitt (Blake), Lukas Haas (Luke), Asia Argento (Asia), Scott Patrick Green (Scott), Nicole Vicius (Nicole), Ricky Jay (Detective), Thadeus A. Thomas (Salesman). Directed by Gus Van Sant and produced by Van Sant and Dany Wolf. Screenplay by Van Sant.

Gus Van Sant has made three movies in which the camera follows young men as they wander toward their deaths. All three films resolutely refuse to find a message in the deaths. No famous death can take place in our society without being endlessly analyzed by experts, who find trends, insights, motives, and morals with alarming facility. It's brave of Van Sant to allow his characters to simply wander off, in John Webster's words, "to study a long silence."

In *Gerry* (2002), death is accidental, caused by carelessness. Two friends fecklessly wander into a desert, get lost, and don't get found. In *Elephant* (2003), death is preceded by murder and is deliberate but pointless. Two friends carry out a plan to kill students and teachers at their high school, and then they too are shot. Now in *Last Days*, death is a condition that overtakes a character as he mumbles and stumbles into the final stage of drug addiction.

These deaths are not heroic or meaningful, and although they may be tragic, they lack the stature of classical tragedy. They are stupid and careless, and in *Elephant* they are monstrous, because innocent lives are also taken. If Van Sant is saying anything (I am not sure he is), it's that society has created young men who do not live as if they value life.

Last Days is dedicated to the suicide of Kurt Cobain, who led the band Nirvana, influential in the creation of grunge rock. Grunge as a style is a deliberate way of presenting the self as disposable. In a disclaimer that distances itself from Cobain with cruel precision, the movie says its characters are "in part, fictional."

The movie concerns a singer named Blake (Michael Pitt), who wanders about a big stone house in a wet, gloomy forest area. The first scenes show him throwing up, stumbling down a hillside to a stream, bathing himself, drying his clothes at a campfire, and, in the middle of the night, singing "Home on the Range." The movie seems unwilling to look at his face very clearly; it is concealed by lanky hair and a hooded coat, and the camera prefers long shots to close-ups. We notice that he is wearing the sort of wrist tag you get in a hospital. Blake walks aimlessly through the house, prepares meals (Cocoa Puffs, macaroni and cheese), and listens without comment as people talk to him in person and on the phone.

They're worried about him. Kim Gordon of Sonic Youth plays a woman who asks him, "Do you talk to your daughter? Do you say I'm sorry that I'm a rock and roll cliché?" No answer. "I have a car waiting, and I want you to come with me." No answer. A detective (Ricky Jay) turns up, cannot find Blake (who hides in the woods), and relates an anecdote about a magician who could catch a bullet in his teeth (most of the time). A musician turns up and wants Blake's help with a song he is writing about a girl he left behind in Japan. A (real) Yellow Pages salesman (Thadeus A. Thomas) turns up and tries to sell Blake an ad. Harmony Korine turns up (all the characters, except Michael Pitt as Blake, have the same names as the actors) and talks about playing Dungeons & Dragons with Jerry Garcia.

None of this interests Blake. One night he wanders into a nearby town, into a bar, and out of the bar again. No doubt some of the people in the bar know he is a famous rock star, but his detachment is so complete it forms a wall around him; you look at him, and you know nothing is happening there.

There is a moment at the house when some friends are about to leave, and one man pauses and looks for a long time as Blake, seen indistinctly through the windows of a potting shed, moves aimlessly. That is where his body will be found in the morning. In a curious coda to such a minimalist film, Van Sant shows Blake's ghostly image leaving his body and ascending, not by floating up to heaven, but by climbing—using the frames of a window as a ladder.

Last Days is a definitive record of death by gradual drug exhaustion. After the chills and thrills of *Sid & Nancy* and *The Doors*, here is a movie that sees how addicts usually die, not with a bang but with a whimper. If the dead had it to do again, they might wish that, this time, they'd at least be conscious enough to realize what was happening.

The Last Detail

R, 104 m., 1974

Otis Young (Mulhall), Jack Nicholson (Buddusky), Randy Quaid (Meadows), Carol Kane (Prostitute), Michael Moriarty (Marine OD). Directed by Hal Ashby and produced by Gerald Ayres. Screenplay by Robert Towne, based on the book by Darryl Ponicsan.

Meadows is a big hulk of a kid who compulsively shoplifts candy bars and peanut butter sandwiches and eats them for consolation. He has been in the navy only long enough to get busted for stealing a charity box with forty bucks inside, for which he has been sentenced to eight years in the Portsmouth naval brig. Buddusky and Mulhall are the two navy lifers assigned to transport him to Portsmouth, and *The Last Detail* is the story of how they travel there on a series of trains, buses, and drunks. It's a very good movie—and the best thing in it is Jack Nicholson's performance as Buddusky. Nicholson, always one of the most interesting of actors, does in *The Last Detail* what he did in *Easy Rider*. He creates a character so complete and so complex that we stop thinking about the movie and just watch to see what he'll do next.

What he tries to do is show the kid a good time. Now a good time, by Buddusky's standards, is not everybody's idea of a good time. It involves great volumes of time spent drinking great volumes of beer. It involves bitching about the system instead of doing something about it. But it also involves some small measure of human sympathy: Buddusky is personally affronted that the kid is going to be locked up for eight years before his life as a man has even begun.

Mulhall (Otis Young), the other member of this shore patrol, is a serious black man who has spent a lot of years working for his seniority and his retirement rights, and is not going to forfeit everything just by letting one dumb kid escape. But he goes along, within limits, and they take off the kid's handcuffs and try to give him some taste of life. They get him drunk in Washington and take him to a redlight house in New York—and the funny thing is, the kid goes along mostly to please them.

He might be described as a totally unformed youth. He's played superbly by Randy Quaid, who you might remember as the kid with the bottle in his sport-coat pocket in *The Last Picture Show*—the grinning kid in the corner who took Cybill Shepherd skinny-dipping in the next county. His character is the only one that changes in the movie. What happens is that he learns in a very tentative way to assert himself—even to value himself, and make a token protest against his fate.

The direction is by Hal Ashby. How good this movie really is can be gauged by comparing it to *Cinderella Liberty*, another navy movie based on a novel by the same author, Darryl Ponicsan. Both movies have similar world views, and the stories in both move somewhat relentlessly toward inevitable conclusions. But *Cinderella Liberty* just can't be believed, and in *The Last Detail*, we always have the sense that these people are plausible individuals: each limited in his own way, but each somehow coping with life. The movie is ultimately pretty sad, but for most of the way it alternates between being poignant and being very funny. Nicholson plays comedy better than most comedians, because with him the humor seems to well up from the real experiences of his character.

The Last Emperor
PG-13, 160 m., 1987

John Lone (Pu Yi, adult), Joan Chen (Wan Jung), Peter O'Toole (Reginald Johnston), Ying Ruocheng (Governor), Victor Wong (Chen Pao Shen), Dennis Dun (Big Li), Ryuichi Sakamoto (Amakasu), Maggie Han (Eastern Jewel). Directed by Bernardo Bertolucci and produced by Jeremy Thomas. Screenplay by Mark Peploe and Bertolucci.

The boy was three when he first sat on the Dragon Throne as emperor of China, and seven when he abdicated. He had barely reached what in the West is considered the age of reason, and already events beyond his control had shaped his life forever. Bernardo Bertolucci's *The Last Emperor* tells the story of this child, named Pu Yi, in an epic that uses the life of one man as a mirror that reflects China's passage from feudalism through revolution to its current identity crisis.

This is a strange epic because it is about an entirely passive character. We are accustomed to epics about heroes who act on their society—*Lawrence of Arabia*, *Gandhi*—but Pu Yi was born into a world that allowed him no initiative. The ironic joke was that he was emperor of nothing, for there was no power to go with his title, and throughout the movie he is seen as a pawn and victim, acted upon, exploited for the purposes of others, valued for what he wasn't rather than for what he was.

The movie reveals his powerlessness almost at once; scenes of his childhood in the

Forbidden City are intercut with scenes from later in his life, when the Chinese communists had taken power, and he was seized and held in a reeducation camp, where a party official spent a decade talking him through a personal transition from emperor to gardener—which was Pu Yi's last, and perhaps happiest, occupation.

But the process in the communist jail actually starts many years earlier, in one of the most poignant scenes in the film, when young Pu Yi is given a bicycle and excitedly pedals it around the Forbidden City until he reaches its gates to the outer world, and is stopped by his own guards. He is an emperor who cannot do the one thing any other little boy in China could do, which was to go out of his own house.

Bertolucci is able to make Pu Yi's imprisonment seem all the more ironic because this entire film was shot on location inside the People's Republic of China, and he was even given permission to film inside the Forbidden City—a vast medieval complex covering some 250 acres and containing 9,999 rooms (only heaven, the Chinese believed, had 10,000 rooms). It is probably unforgivably bourgeois to admire a film because of its locations, but in the case of *The Last Emperor,* the narrative cannot be separated from the awesome presence of the Forbidden City, and from Bertolucci's astonishing use of locations, authentic costumes, and thousands of extras to create the everyday reality of this strange little boy.

There is a scene early in the film when Pu Yi, seated on the Dragon Throne, attended by his minders and servants, grows restless, as small boys will do. He leaps impatiently from his seat and runs toward the door of the throne room, where at first a vast billowing drapery (a yellow one—the color reserved for only the emperor) obstructs the view. Then the curtain is blown aside, and we see an incredible sight, thousands of the emperor's minions, all of them traditionally costumed eunuchs, lined up in geometric precision as far as the eye can see, all of them kowtowing to the boy.

After he formally abdicates power in 1912, Pu Yi remains on the throne, a figurehead maintained in luxury for the convenience of the real rulers of China. A Scottish tutor named Reginald Johnston (Peter O'Toole) comes out to instruct him in the ways of Europe, and the youth (played in manhood by John Lone) becomes an anglophile, dreaming of "escaping" to Cambridge. Johnston advises him to escape instead into marriage, and he takes an empress (Joan Chen) and a concubine. In 1924, he is thrown out of the Forbidden City, and moves with his retinue back to his native Manchuria, then controlled by the Japanese. In a scene of great elegant irony, Bertolucci shows him in Western clothes, a cigarette in hand, leaning on a piano and crooning "Am I Blue?"

As World War II grows closer, Pu Yi grows increasingly irrelevant, except to the Japanese, who set him up briefly as their puppet in Manchuria. His wife becomes an opium addict and begins a dalliance with a lesbian Japanese spy, his old tutor returns to England, he gives himself over to a life of depravity and drifting, and then everything changes for him when the communists take control of China and he is captured by Russians who turn him over to their new allies.

We might expect the communists to sentence Pu Yi to death (a fate he himself confidently expected), but instead there is the reeducation process, complicated by the fact that this grown man has never done anything for himself and does not know how to tie his own shoes or turn off the tap after filling a glass with drinking water. When we see him at the end of the film, he is working as a gardener in Peking, and seems happy, and we assume that for him, at least, reeducation was a success because it was essentially education in the first place, for a man whose whole life was directed toward making him impotent and irrelevant.

In Orson Welles's *Citizen Kane,* one of the tycoon's friends says, "I was there before the beginning—and now I'm here after the end." *The Last Emperor* ends with an extraordinary sequence, beyond the end, in which an elderly Pu Yi goes to visit the Forbidden City, which is now open to tourists. He sneaks past the velvet rope and climbs onto the Dragon Throne. Once that would have been a fatal offense. And the old man who was once the boy on that throne experiences a complex mixture of emotions. It is an inspired ending for the film, which never makes the mistake of having only one thing to say about the life of a man who embodied all the contradictions and paradoxes of twentieth-century China.

There aren't a lot of action scenes in *The Last Emperor*, and little enough intrigue (even the Japanese spy isn't subtle: "I'm a spy, and I don't care who knows it," she tells the empress on their first meeting). As in *Gandhi*, great historical changes take place during *The Last Emperor*, but, unlike Gandhi, the emperor has no influence on them. His life is a sad irony; his end is a bittersweet elegy. But it is precisely because so little "happens" in this epic that its vast and expensive production schedule is important. When we see those thousands of servants bowing to a little boy, for example, the image is effective precisely because the kowtowing means nothing to the boy, and the lives of the servants have been dedicated to no useful purpose.

Everything involving the life of Pu Yi was a waste. Everything except one thing—the notion that a single human life could have infinite value. In its own way, the Dragon Throne argued that, making an emperor into a god in order to ennoble his subjects. And in its own way, the Chinese revolution argued the same thing by making him into a gardener.

L.A. Story

PG-13, 95 m., 1991

Steve Martin (Harris), Victoria Tennant (Sara), Richard E. Grant (Roland), Marilu Henner (Trudi), Sarah Jessica Parker (SanDeE). Directed by Mick Jackson and produced by Daniel Melnick and Michael Rachmil. Screenplay by Steve Martin.

There are some big laughs in Steve Martin's *L.A. Story*, but also a certain delicacy of tone that is bewitching. Somehow the film evokes an elusive side of Los Angeles that isn't often seen in the movies. We know all about the weirdo Southern California lifestyle, the obsessions with food and physical appearance and lifestyle, and we know all the standard show biz types. We've seen movies about those subjects many times before (and, for that matter, Martin doesn't neglect them).

But there is also a bewitching Los Angeles, a

city I glimpsed on my first visit there many years ago, where, after my team won in the Rose Bowl, I was driven up to Mulholland Drive and the whole city lay glittering beneath, and for a kid from downstate Illinois, there was something enchanting going on down there—there was the promise of not merely success and the fulfillment of lust, but even of happiness and the fulfillment of dreams.

None of that has much to do with the reality of the city, I am aware, and sometimes the dreams seem buried by car washes and minimalls, smog and traffic, and urban wretchedness. But *L.A. Story* is a lighthearted fantasy that asks us to just accept one small possibility, and promises us we may find contentment if we keep an open mind. That possibility is that a giant electrical traffic warning billboard might one day start sending personal messages to a TV weatherman, suggesting how he can make improvements in his life.

The weatherman is named Harris K. Telemacher (Martin), and he specializes in goofy weather reports that have little connection with actual climatic conditions. He makes enough money at his job to move in an affluent circle of beautiful people who seem prepared to sit in the sunshine ordering cappucino for the rest of their lives. Then Telemacher is fired, and discovers that his mistress (Marilu Henner) is having an affair, and with relief and a certain feeling of freedom he walks out of the relationship and takes stock of his life, inspired by the sentient highway sign. (He is not without his own difficulties in believing that the sign is on the level; the first time it talks to him, he looks around in paranoid despair, convinced he's on *Candid Camera*.)

The sign urges him to telephone a number that's been given to him by a friendly Valley Girl in a clothing store, and before long he finds himself in an energetic relationship with SanDeE (Sarah Jessica Parker), who, like many Southern Californians, spells her name as if it were an explosion at the type foundry. SanDeE has a carefree and liberating air, but eventually Telemacher has to admit that the woman he's really attracted to is Sara (Victoria Tennant), a British journalist in town to do a story on L.A. lifestyles.

These stories of love provide the fragile

narrative thread on which Martin (who wrote) and Mick Jackson (who directed) weave their spell. There are scenes that, in other hands, might have seemed obvious (for example, the daily routine of shooting at other drivers while racing down the freeway), but somehow there is a fanciful edge in the way they do it, a way they define all of their material with a certain whimsical tone.

The film is astonishing in the amount of material it contains. Martin has said he worked on the screenplay, on and off, for seven years, and you can sense that as the film unfolds. It isn't thin or superficial; there is an abundance of observation and invention here, and perhaps because the filmmakers know they have so much good material, there's never the feeling that anything is being punched up, or made to carry more than its share. I was reminded of the films of Jacques Tati, in which, calmly, serenely, an endless series of comic invention unfolds.

Steve Martin shows again in this film that he has found the right comic presence for the movies; the lack of subtlety in early films like *The Jerk* has now been replaced by a smoothness and unforced intelligence. The other cast members are basically in support of that character, although Sarah Jessica Parker has figured out a Valley Girl airhead right down to the ground. What you feel here, as you feel in the work of Tati and some of the comedians of the silent era, is that the whole film is the work of comedy—that it isn't about jokes, or a funny individual, but about creating a fictional world which is funny on its own terms.

The Last Picture Show

R, 114 m., 1971

Timothy Bottoms (Sonny), Jeff Bridges (Duane), Cybill Shepherd (Jacy Farrow), Ben Johnson (Sam the Lion), Cloris Leachman (Ruth Popper), Ellen Burstyn (Lois Farrow), Eileen Brennan (Genevieve), Bill Thurman (Coach Popper). Directed by Peter Bogdanovich and produced by Bert Schneider and Stephen J. Friedman. Screenplay by Larry McMurtry and Bogdanovich.

There was something about going to the movies in the 1950s that will never be the same again. It was the decade of the last gasp of the great American movie-going habit, and before my eyes in the middle 1950s the Saturday kiddie matinee died a lingering death at the Princess Theater on Main Street in Urbana. For five or six years of my life (the years between when I was old enough to go alone, and when TV came to town) Saturday afternoon at the Princess was a descent into a dark magical cave that smelled of Jujubes, melted Dreamsicles, and Crisco in the popcorn machine. It was probably on one of those Saturday afternoons that I formed my first critical opinion, deciding vaguely that there was something about John Wayne that set him apart from ordinary cowboys. The Princess was jammed to the walls with kids every Saturday afternoon, as it had been for years, but then TV came to town and within a year the Princess was no longer an institution. It survived into the early 1960s and then closed, to be reborn a few years later as the Cinema. The metallic taste of that word, cinema, explains what happened when you put it alongside the name "Princess."

Peter Bogdanovich's *The Last Picture Show* uses the closing of another theater on another Main Street as a motif to frame a great many things that happened to America in the early 1950s. The theater is the Royal, and along with the pool hall and the all-night cafe it supplies what little excitement and community survives in a little West Texas crossroads named Anarene.

All three are owned by Sam the Lion, who is just about the only self-sufficient and self-satisfied man in town. The others are infected by a general malaise, and engage in sexual infidelities partly to remind themselves they are alive. There isn't much else to do in Anarene, no dreams worth dreaming, no new faces, not even a football team that can tackle worth a damn. The nourishing myth of the Western (*Wagonmaster* and *Red River* are among the last offerings at the Royal) is being replaced by nervously hilarious TV programs out of the East, and defeated housewives are reassured they're part of the *Strike It Rich* audience with a heart of gold.

Against this background, we meet two high school seniors named Sonny and Duane, who are the co-captains of the shameful football squad. We learn next to nothing about their home lives, but we hardly notice the omission because their real lives are lived in a pickup truck and a used Mercury. That was the way it was in high school in the 1950s, and probably always will be: A car was a mobile refuge from adults, frustration, and boredom. When people in their thirties say today that sexual liberation is pale compared to a little prayerful groping in the front seat, they are onto something.

During the year of the film's action, the two boys more or less survive coming-of-age. They both fall in love with the school's only beauty, a calculating charmer named Jacy who twists every boy in town around her little finger before taking this skill away with her to Dallas. Sonny breaks up with his gum-chewing girlfriend and has an unresolved affair with the coach's wife, and Duane goes off to fight the Korean War. There are two deaths during the film's year, but no babies are born, and Bogdanovich's final pan shot along Main Street curiously seems to turn it from a real location (which it is) into a half-remembered backdrop from an old movie. *The Last Picture Show* is a great deal more complex than it might at first seem, and this shot suggests something of its buried structure. Every detail of clothing, behavior, background music, and decor is exactly right for 1951—but that still doesn't explain the movie's mystery.

Mike Nichols's *Carnal Knowledge* began with 1949, and yet felt modern. Bogdanovich has been infinitely more subtle in giving his film not only the decor of 1951, but the visual style of a movie that might have been shot in 1951. The montage of cutaway shots at the Christmas dance; the use of an insert of Sonny's foot on the accelerator; the lighting and black-and-white photography of real locations as if they were sets—everything forms a stylistic whole that works. It isn't just a matter of putting in Jo Stafford and Hank Williams, Sr.

The Last Picture Show has been described as an evocation of the classic Hollywood narrative film. It is more than that; it is a belated entry in that age—the best film of 1951, you might say. Using period songs and decor to create nostalgia is familiar enough, but to tunnel down to the visual level and get that right, too, and in a way that will affect audiences even if they aren't aware how, is one hell of a directing accomplishment. Movies create our dreams as well as reflect them, and when we lose the movies we lose the dreams. I wonder

if Bogdanovich's film doesn't at last explain what it was that Pauline Kael, and a lot of the rest of us, lost at the movies.

The Last Seduction

NO MPAA RATING, 110 m., 1994

Linda Fiorentino (Bridget Gregory), Peter Berg (Mike Swale), J. T. Walsh (Frank Griffith), Bill Nunn (Harlan), Bill Pullman (Clay Gregory), Michael Raysses (Phone Sales Rep), Zack Phifer (Gas Station Attendant). Directed by John Dahl and produced by Jonathan Shestack. Screenplay by Steve Barancik.

There is a kind of deliciousness to the great movie villains. By setting out to do evil, they tempt our own darker natures. By getting away with it, they alarm us: Is there nothing safe or sacred? In crime pictures and thrillers, the villains are almost always more interesting than the heroes, and there is a kind of unconscious sigh in the audience when a really intriguing villain is defeated. Harry Lime doesn't even appear in the first eighty minutes of *The Third Man*, and yet is more fascinating than anyone on the screen.

John Dahl's *The Last Seduction* knows how much we enjoy seeing a character work boldly outside the rules. It gives us a diabolically evil woman, and goes the distance with her. We keep waiting for the movie to lose its nerve, and it never does: This woman is bad from beginning to end, she never reforms, she never compromises, and the movie doesn't tack on one of those contrived conclusions where the morals squad comes in and tidies up.

The woman is named Bridget Gregory, although she goes under other names as the plot develops. She is played by Linda Fiorentino, with a hard voice and cold eyes and a certain fearsome sexiness; she plays Bridget as the kind of woman who has the same effect on a man as a bucket of ice in the bathtub. Her motivation is simple: She wants to get her hands on large amounts of money, and is willing to play any game with any man who will help her. "Are you still a lawyer?" she asks her attorney. "Yeah," he says. "Are you still a self-serving bitch?"

As the movie opens, she and her husband have made a big haul—$700,000 in illegal funds. Then he makes the big mistake of hitting her in the face. He knows it's a mistake: "Hey, you can hit me anywhere, hard." During the course of the movie she will accept his invitation, in her own way.

The plot takes her to a small town, where she meets a guy named Mike (Peter Berg). He tries to pick her up in a bar. This is one of the more unwise moves in his life. She rejects him, then casually decides to toy with him, and eventually ends up recruiting him as an accessory to murder. He never quite catches on to the full depth of her deception.

It would not be fair to *The Last Seduction* to say much more about the plot, which only gradually reveals itself even to Bridget (she has a gift for improvising, moving from one crime to another as a jazzman might sample various melodic lines). Like Billy Wilder's classic *Double Indemnity*, where Barbara Stanwyck mesmerized Fred MacMurray with his own lust, *The Last Seduction* is about the way even a smart guy gets dumb when he starts thinking tumescently.

The Last Seduction is the second amazing film I've seen by John Dahl, whose *Red Rock West* was a sleeper hit in early 1994. Who is this guy? He makes movies so smart and cynical that the American movie industry doesn't know how to handle him.

I loved *Red Rock West* when I saw it in 1993 at the Toronto Film Festival, but distributors wouldn't touch it, and it went to cable and video without a theatrical release. Then a theater in San Francisco started showing it, and set a house record, and soon it had returned from its video grave to play in theaters all over the country. Then came *The Last Seduction*, with the same story: passed over by distributors, played on cable, etc. And then it opened in London and got some of the best reviews of the year, before finally arriving in American theaters.

What is it? Do distributors think American audiences are so dumb they can't appreciate a smart woman who unspools a criminal plan of diabolical complexity, while treating men like disposable diapers? Are they afraid of a female character who is *really* evil—not just pretend—bad, like the saucy heroines of the glossy Hollywood slasher movies? (There's a pop psychology theory that women are weak in American movies because Hollywood executives are terrified of strong women.)

The great quality in *The Last Seduction* is the dry humor with which Linda Fiorentino puts across the role. Look at this movie just a little sideways, and it's a comedy, although you can never quite catch Dahl or Fiorentino smiling. It must have been a lot of fun for her to play the role; there are several scenes where the men in the movie simply cannot believe she's really serious. "You mean this broad is really going to go through with that?" She is.

Fiorentino has played other roles like this. She has a quality about her. In *VisionQuest* (1985), a silly wrestling movie, there was nothing silly about her scenes. In Martin Scorsese's *After Hours,* she was the black widow waiting in the net that the hapless hero stumbled into. What's crucial is that she plays these roles with relish: She seems to enjoy the freedom a script like *The Last Seduction* gives her, and the result is a movie that is not only ingenious and entertaining, but liberating, because we can sense the story isn't going to be twisted into conformity with some stupid formula.

Last Summer

R, 95 m., 1969

Barbara Hershey (Sandy), Richard Thomas (Peter), Bruce Davison (Dan), Cathy Burns (Rhoda), Ernesto Gonzalez (Anibal). Directed by Frank Perry and produced by Alfred W. Crown and Sidney Beckerman. Screenplay by Eleanor Perry, based on the book by Evan Hunter.

From time to time you find yourself wondering if there will ever be a movie that understands life the way you've experienced it. There are good movies about other people's lives, but rarely a movie that recalls, if only for a scene or two, the sense and flavor of life the way you remember it.

Adolescence is a period that most people, I imagine, remember rather well. For the first time in your life important things were happening to you; you were growing up; what mattered to you made a difference. For three or four years, every day had a newness and unfamiliarity to it, and you desperately wanted to act in a way that seemed honorable to yourself. Even if you didn't read Thomas Wolfe you were more idealistic than you ever were likely to be again.

But on top of the desire to be brave and honorable, there was also the compelling desire to be accepted, to be admitted to membership in that adolescent society defined only by those excluded from it. Because you were insecure, like all teenagers still groping for a style and a philosophy, you tended to value other people's opinions above your own. If everybody else disagreed with you, then how could you be right? And so sometimes you repressed your own feelings, rather than risk being shut out. And yet, inside, there was still the strong force of that idealism, and occasionally it occurred to you that the way you handled these years might decide the worth of your life.

Frank Perry's *Last Summer* is about exactly such years and days, about exactly that time in the life of four fifteen- or sixteen-year-old adolescents, and it is one of the finest, truest, most deeply felt movies in my experience.

As *Last Summer* opens we are introduced to three affluent teenagers, two boys and a girl, who are spending the summer on Fire Island with their parents. Sandy, the girl, is more familiar and experienced with sex than the boys, or so she would have them believe. The two boys are, naturally, unsure of themselves. They are not men and yet must be concerned with manhood. In the hot sun, during the long summer, the three friends circle the knowledge of sex like skittish colts.

But the movie is not really about them. It is about Rhoda, a plump and painfully idealistic girl from Ohio who is also staying on the island. She forces herself into the group, her loneliness overcoming her shyness. And although she seems the most insecure of them all, she is the only one who knows her own mind and whose decisions are not determined by insecurity.

What happens then—how the story is brought to a conclusion—is not really important to the greatness of the movie. Indeed, the sensational last scene doesn't strike me as particularly valid. A quieter conclusion would have made the point.

But the movie makes its point anyway, with dialogue, with exquisitely drawn characterizations, with a very accurate examination of the adolescent character. Some months ago I attacked a lousy movie, *The First Time*, because it demonstrated no knowledge of how teenagers really talk and think. Godard tells us that the only valid act of film criticism is to make another movie; *Last Summer* will serve as the definitive criticism of *The First Time*.

One scene: Rhoda has just been taught to swim by her friend Peter. They rest on the beach, and she talks about some of the things she believes in, and then he does, and then with infinite delicacy they realize they "like" each other.

Another scene: Sandy and the two boys sit on the beach, drinking beer, fooling around, skirting the awareness of their own new sexuality. During this scene the friends become unequal; Sandy is now in control.

Another scene: A rainy day. Sandy, Peter, and Dan experiment with pot. On an impulse, they wash each other's hair. They talk. They kill time; Rhoda arrives and feels excluded by the camaraderie. They convince her to tell "the worst thing" in her life. Reluctantly, she does; in a brilliantly acted monologue, she describes the drowning death of her mother. The way Rhoda's ambiguous feelings are presented makes this the best scene in the film.

There are many other things I want to say about *Last Summer,* but I don't want to diminish your experience in seeing the film for the first time. So a longer article will have to wait. But let me add that the performances of the four teenagers are the best that could possibly be hoped for. Cathy Burns, as Rhoda, clearly deserves an Academy Award nomination. Barbara Hershey's character, Sandy, seems easier to play but there is a marvelous subtlety in the way she gradually alters her relationship with the other three. Richard Thomas, as Peter, and Bruce Davison, as Dan, perfectly capture the ambiguity, the self-doubt, of adolescence.

Last Tango in Paris
x, 127 m., 1972

Marlon Brando (Paul), Maria Schneider (Jeanne), Darling Legitimus (Concierge), JeanPierre Leaud (Tom). Directed by Bernardo Bertolucci and produced by Alberto Grimaldi. Screenplay by Bertolucci and Franco Arcalli.

Bernardo Bertolucci's *Last Tango in Paris* is one of the great emotional experiences of our time. It's a movie that exists so resolutely on the level of emotion, indeed, that possibly only Marlon Brando, of all living actors, could have played its lead. Who else can act so brutally and imply such vulnerability and need?

For the movie is about need; about the terrible hunger that its hero, Paul, feels for the touch of another human heart. He is a man whose whole existence has been reduced to a cry for help—and who has been so damaged by life that he can only express that cry in acts of crude sexuality.

Bertolucci begins with a story so simple (which is to say, so stripped of any clutter of plot) that there is little room in it for anything but the emotional crisis of his hero. The events that take place in the everyday world are remote to Paul, whose attention is absorbed by the gradual breaking of his heart. The girl, Jeanne, is not a friend and is hardly even a companion; it's just that because she happens to wander into his life, he uses her as an object of his grief.

The movie begins when Jeanne, who is about to be married, goes apartment-hunting and finds Paul in one of the apartments. It is a big, empty apartment, with a lot of sunlight but curiously little cheer. Paul rapes her, if rape is not too strong a word to describe an act so casually accepted by the girl. He tells her that they will continue to meet there, in the empty apartment, and she agrees.

Why does she agree? From her point of view—which is not a terribly perceptive one—why not? One of the several things this movie is about is how one person, who may be uncommitted and indifferent, nevertheless can at a certain moment become of great importance to another. One of the movie's strengths comes from the tragic imbalance between Paul's need and Jeanne's almost unthinking participation in it. Their difference is so great that it creates tremendous dramatic tension; more, indeed, than if both characters were filled with passion.

They do continue to meet, and at Paul's insistence they do not exchange names. What has come together in the apartment is almost an elemental force, not a connection of two beings with identities in society. Still, inevitably, the man and the girl do begin to learn about each other. What began, on the man's part, as totally depersonalized sex develops into a deeper relationship almost to spite him.

We learn about them. He is an American, living in Paris these last several years with a French wife who owned a hotel that is not quite a whorehouse. On the day the movie begins, the wife has committed suicide. We are never quite sure why, although by the time the movie is over we have a few depressing clues.

The girl is young, conscious of her beauty and the developing powers of her body, and is going to marry a young and fairly inane filmmaker. He is making a movie of their life together; a camera crew follows them around as he talks to her and kisses her—for herself or for the movie, she wonders.

The banality of her "real" life has thus set her up for the urgency of the completely artificial experience that has been commanded for her by Paul. She doesn't know his name, or anything about him, but when he has sex with her it is certainly real; there is a life in that empty room that her fiancé, with all of his *cinema verité*, is probably incapable of imagining.

She finds it difficult, too, because she is a child. A child, because she hasn't lived long enough and lost often enough to know yet what a heartbreaker the world can be. There are moments in the film when she does actually seem to look into Paul's soul and halfunderstand what she sees there, but she pulls back from it; pulls back, finally, all the way— and just when he had come to the point where he was willing to let life have one more chance with him.

A lot has been said about the sex in the film; in fact, *Last Tango in Paris* has become notorious because of its sex. There is a lot of sex in this film—more, probably, than in any other legitimate feature film ever made—but the sex isn't the point, it's only the medium of exchange. Paul has somehow been so brutalized by life that there are only a few ways he can still feel.

Sex is one of them, but only if it is debased and depraved—because he is so filled with guilt and self-hate that he chooses these most intimate of activities to hurt himself beyond all possibilities of mere thoughts and words. It is said in some quarters that the sex in the movie is debasing to the girl, but I don't think it is. She's almost a bystander, a witness at the scene of the accident. She hasn't suffered enough, experienced enough, to more than dimly guess at what Paul is doing to himself with her. But Paul knows, and so does Bertolucci; only an idiot would criticize this movie because the girl is so often naked but Paul never is. That's their relationship.

The movie may not contain Brando's greatest performance, but it certainly contains his most emotionally overwhelming scene. He comes back to the hotel and confronts his wife's dead body, laid out in a casket, and he speaks to her with words of absolute hatred—words which, as he says them, become one of the most moving speeches of love I can imagine.

As he weeps, as he attempts to remove her cosmetic death mask ("Look at you! You're a monument to your mother! You never wore makeup, never wore false eyelashes . . ."), he makes it absolutely clear why he is the best film actor of all time. He may be a bore, he may be a creep, he may act childish about the Academy Awards—but there is no one else who could have played that scene flatout, no holds barred, the way he did, and make it work triumphantly.

The girl, Maria Schneider, doesn't seem to act her role so much as to exude it. On the basis of this movie, indeed, it's impossible to really say whether she can act or not. That's not her fault; Bertolucci directs her that way. He wants a character who ultimately does not quite understand the situation she finds herself in; she has to be that way, among other reasons, because the movie's ending absolutely depends on it. What happens to Paul at the end must seem, in some fundamental way, ridiculous. What the girl does at the end has to seem incomprehensible—not to us; to her.

What is the movie about? What does it all mean? It is about, and means, exactly the same things that Bergman's *Cries and Whispers* was about, and meant. That's to say that no amount of analysis can extract from either film a rational message. The whole point of both films is that there is a land in the human soul that's beyond the rational—beyond, even, words to describe it.

Faced with a passage across that land, men make various kinds of accommodations. Some ignore it; some try to avoid it through temporary distractions; some are lucky enough to have the inner resources for a successful journey. But of those who do not, some turn to the most highly charged resources of the body; lacking the mental strength to face crisis and death, they turn on the sexual mechanism, which can at least be depended upon to function, usually.

That's what the sex is about in this film (and in *Cries and Whispers*). It's not sex at all (and it's a million miles from intercourse). It's just a physical function of the soul's desperation. Paul in *Last Tango in Paris* has no difficulty in achieving an erection, but the gravest difficulty in achieving a life-affirming reason for one.

The Last Temptation of Christ
R, 160 m., 1988

Willem Dafoe (Jesus), Harvey Keitel (Judas), Paul Greco (Zealot), Steven Shill (Centurion), Barbara Hershey (Mary Magdalene), Harry Dean Stanton (Paul), David Bowie (Pontius Pilate), Verna Bloom (Mary the Mother), Andre Gregory (John the Baptist). Directed by Martin Scorsese and produced by Barbara De Fina. Screenplay by Paul Schrader.

Christianity teaches that Jesus was both God and man. That he could be both at once is the central mystery of the Christian faith, and the subject of *The Last Temptation of Christ*. To be fully man, Jesus would have had to possess all of the weakness of man, to be prey to all of the temptations—for as man, he would have possessed God's most troublesome gift, free will. As the son of God, he would of course have inspired the most desperate wiles of Satan, and this is a film about how he experienced temptation and conquered it.

That, in itself, makes *The Last Temptation of Christ* sound like a serious and devout film, which it is. The astonishing controversy that has raged around this film is primarily the work of fundamentalists who have their own view of Christ and are offended by a film that they feel questions his divinity. But in the father's house are many mansions, and there is more than one way to consider the story of Christ—why else are there four Gospels?

Among those who do not already have rigid views on the subject, this film is likely to inspire more serious thought on the nature of Jesus than any other ever made.

That is the irony about the attempts to suppress this film; it is a sincere, thoughtful investigation of the subject, made as a collaboration between the two American filmmakers who have been personally most attracted to serious films about sin, guilt, and redemption. Martin Scorsese, the director, has made more than half of his films about battles in the souls of his characters between grace and sin. Paul Schrader, the screenwriter, has written Scorsese's best films (*Taxi Driver, Raging Bull*) and directed his own films about men torn between their beliefs and their passions (*Hardcore,* with George C. Scott as a fundamentalist whose daughter plunges into the carnal underworld, and *Mishima*, about the Japanese writer who killed himself as a demonstration of his fanatic belief in tradition).

Scorsese and Schrader have not made a film that panders to the audience—as almost all Hollywood religious epics traditionally have. They have paid Christ the compliment of taking him and his message seriously, and have made a film that does not turn him into a garish, emasculated image from a religious postcard. Here he is flesh and blood, struggling, questioning, asking himself and his father which is the right way, and finally, after great suffering, earning the right to say, on the cross, "It is accomplished."

The critics of this film, many of whom did not see it, raised a sensational hue and cry about the final passages, in which Christ on the cross, in great pain, begins to hallucinate and imagines what his life would have been like if he had been free to live as an ordinary man. In his reverie, he marries Mary Magdalene, has children, grows old. But it is clear in the film that this hallucination is sent to him by Satan, at the time of his greatest weakness, to tempt him. And in the hallucination itself, in the film's most absorbing scene, an elderly Jesus is reproached by his aging apostles for having abandoned his mission. Through this imaginary conversation, Jesus finds the strength to shake off his temptation and return to consciousness to accept his suffering, death, and resurrection.

During the hallucination, there is a very brief moment when he is seen making love with Magdalene. This scene is shot with such restraint and tact that it does not qualify in any way as a "sex scene," but instead is simply an illustration of marriage and the creation of children. Those offended by the film object to the very notion that Jesus could have, or even imagine having, sexual intercourse. But, of course, Christianity teaches that the union of man and wife is one of the fundamental reasons God created human beings, and to imagine that the son of God, as a man, could not encompass such thoughts within his intelligence is itself a kind of insult. Was he less than the rest of us? Was he not fully man?

There is biblical precedent for such temptations. We read of the forty days and nights during which Satan tempted Christ in the desert with visions of the joys that could be his if he renounced his father. In the film, which is clearly introduced as a fiction and not as an account based on the Bible, Satan tries yet once again at the moment of Christ's greatest weakness. I do not understand why this is offensive, especially since it is not presented in a sensational way.

I see that this entire review has been preoccupied with replying to the attacks of the film's critics, with discussing the issues, rather than with reviewing *The Last Temptation of Christ* as a motion picture. Perhaps that is an interesting proof of the film's worth. Here is a film that engaged me on the subject of Christ's dual nature, that caused me to think about the mystery of a being who could be both God and man. I cannot think of another film on a religious subject that has challenged me more fully. The film has offended those whose ideas about God and man it does not reflect. But then, so did Jesus.

The Late Show

PG, 94 m., 1977

Art Carney (Ira Wells), Lily Tomlin (Margo), Bill Macy (Charlie Hatter), Eugene Roche (Ron Birdwell), Joanna Cassidy (Laura Birdwell), John Considine (Lamar), Howard Duff (Harry Regan), Ruth Nelson (Mrs. Schmidt). Directed by Robert Benton and produced by Robert Altman. Screenplay by Benton.

It's hard enough for a movie to sustain one tone, let alone half a dozen, but that's just what Robert Benton's *The Late Show* does. It's the story of a strangely touching relationship between two people. It's a violent crime melodrama. It's a comedy. It's a commentary on the private-eye genre, especially its 1940s manifestations. It's a study of the way older people do a balancing act between weariness and experience. It's a celebration of that uncharted continent, Lily Tomlin.

And most of all, it's a movie that dares a lot, pulls off most of it, and entertains us without insulting our intelligence. What's quietly astonishing is that all of it starts with a woman coming to a private eye about a missing cat. The woman is played by Lily Tomlin, who somehow provides scatterbrained eccentricism with a cutting edge. The cat has been missing a couple of days, and she's worried. The private eye is played by Art Carney, who has seen it all twice, when once would have been too much.

He takes the case maybe because he could use the money, maybe because he's intrigued by the client, maybe because he's bored, maybe because he's been taking cases so long it's second nature. He doesn't give a damn about the cat. But then, in a series of plot developments so labyrinthine we should be taking notes, the missing cat leads to a mysterious robbery, a missing stamp collection, a fence with a house full of stolen goods, and a dead body that's in the . . .

But, no, I won't say where the body is, because the way Benton reveals it and then lets Lily Tomlin discover it (when all she was after was a Coke) is one of the movie's many pleasures. A friend of mine objected to the body, and to the movie's violence, as being unnecessary in a comedy. Well, The Late Show is a long way from being only a comedy, and the introductory shot of that body redeems any amount of gratuitous movie violence.

It's the case with most good detective fiction that the puzzle seems impossible to solve until the last chapter, when everything is made transparently clear. That's true here, with Art Carney providing a brilliant analysis of the connections and coincidences just when it's most irrelevant. But the plot's incidental to the movie's center, which has to do with Carney and Lily Tomlin.

You see, they're allowed to be people here. They're allowed to play characters who have no particular connection with clichés or stereotypes or characters who were successful in a box-office hit last year. Yes, Carney's a private eye, but a particular one: Overweight and wheezing, hard of hearing, given to comments that only obliquely refer to the problem at hand.

And Lily Tomlin . . . well, her character employs a form of reasoning that has nothing to do with logic but a lot to do with the good reasons we have for behaving as we do. An example. Art Carney pretends to be mortally ill (never mind why). He is not (never mind why). His ruse has saved their lives (never mind how). Lily Tomlin is not pleased: She could have had a heart attack! Does he think it's funny, playing with his own friend's *emotions* that way? Doesn't he have any *consideration*?

Benton's screenplay is filled with lines that perfectly define their moments (and belong so securely to the characters that they seem to come from them, as some of them probably did). The way in which Tomlin explains why today is the *pits*, for example. The way Carney wonders if it would kill her, for chrissakes, to wear a dress once in a while. The way Carney's sometime partner talks to himself before he dies. The way the fence offers a bribe of a stereo set.

The Late Show is one of three movies from the seventies that had their spiritual origins in the classic private-eye films. The other two were Dick Richards's Farewell, My Lovely (in which Robert Mitchum demonstrated that he was born to play Philip Marlowe), and Robert Altman's The Long Goodbye, (in which Elliott Gould demonstrated that he was not).

Altman produced The Late Show, which is probably another way of saying he made it possible to be filmed, and Benton has brilliantly realized it. Maybe these three films about an all but extinct occupation are telling us something: That the more we become plastic and bland, the more we become fascinated by a strata in our cities we'd like to believe still exists, a society of loners and eccentrics, people brave and crazy and doomed, old private eyes and cat lovers. If they're OK, we're OK.

La Vie en Rose/Fall of the Sparrow
PG-13, 140 m., 2007

Marion Cotillard (Edith Piaf), Clotilde Courau (Anetta Gassion), Jean Paul Rouve (Louis Gassion), Sylvie

Testud (Momone), Pascal Greggory (Louis Barrier), Jean Pierre Martins (Marcel Cerdan), Emmanuelle Seigner (Titine), Gerard Depardieu (Louis Leplee), Catherine Allegret (Louise), Caroline Silhol (Marlene Dietrich), Manon Chevallier (Edith, age five), Pauline Burlet (Edith, age eight). Directed by Olivier Dahan and produced by Alain Goldmar. Screenplay by Dahan and Isabelle Sobelman.

She was the daughter of a street singer and a circus acrobat. She was dumped by her mother with her father, who dumped her with his mother, who ran a brothel. In childhood, diseases rendered her temporarily blind and deaf. She claimed she was cured by St. Therese, whose shrine the prostitutes took her to. One of the prostitutes adopted her, until her father returned, snatched her away, and put her to work in his act. From her mother and the prostitute she heard many songs, and one day when his sidewalk act was doing badly, her father commanded her, "Do something." She sang "La Marseilles." And Edith Piaf was born.

Piaf. The French word for "sparrow." She was named by her first impresario, Louis Leplee. He was found shot dead not long after—possibly by a pimp who considered her his property. She stood four feet, eight inches tall, and so became "the Little Sparrow." She was the most famous and beloved French singer of her time—of the twentieth century, in fact—and her lovers included Yves Montand (whom she discovered) and the middleweight champion Marcel Cerdan. She drank too much, all the time. She became addicted to morphine and required ten injections a day. She grew old and prematurely stooped, and died at forty-seven.

Olivier Dahan's *La Vie en Rose*, one of the best biopics I've seen, tells Piaf's life story through the extraordinary performance of Marion Cotillard, who looks like the singer. The title, which translates loosely as "life through rose-colored glasses," is from one of Piaf's most famous songs, which she wrote herself. She is known for countless other songs, perhaps most poignantly for "Non, Je ne Regrette Rien" ("No, I regret nothing"), which is seen in the film as her final song; if it wasn't, it should have been.

How do you tell a life story so chaotic, jum-bled, and open to chance as Piaf's? Her life did not have an arc but a trajectory. Joy and tragedy seemed simultaneous. Her loves were heartfelt but doomed; after she begged the boxer Cerdan to fly to her in New York, he was killed in the crash of his flight from Paris. Her stage triumphs alternated with her stage collapses. If her life resembled in some ways Judy Garland's, there is this difference: Garland lived for the adulation of the audience, and Piaf lived to do her duty as a singer. From her earliest days, from the prostitutes, her father, and her managers, she learned that when you're paid, you perform.

Oh, but what a performer she was. Her voice was loud and clear, reflecting her early years as a street singer. Such a big voice for such a little woman. At first she sang mechanically but was tutored to improve her diction and express the meaning of her words. She did that so well that if you know what the words "Non, je ne regrette rien" mean, you can essentially feel the meaning of every other word in the song.

Dahan and his cowriter, Isabelle Sobelman, move freely through the pages of Piaf's life. A chronology would have missed the point. She didn't start here and go there; she was always, at every age, even before she had the name, the little sparrow. The action moves back and forth from childhood to final illness, from applause to desperation, from joy to heartbreak (particularly in the handling of Cerdan's last visit to her).

This mosaic storytelling style has been criticized in some quarters as obscuring facts. (Quick: How many times was she married?) But think of it this way: Since there are, in fact, no wedding scenes in the movie, isn't it more accurate to see husbands, lovers, friends, admirers, employees, and everyone else as whirling around her small, still center? Nothing in her early life taught her to count on permanence or loyalty. What she counted on was singing, champagne, infatuation, and morphine.

Many biopics break down in depicting their subjects in old age, and Piaf, at forty-seven, looked old. Gene Siskel once referred to an actor's old-age makeup as making him look like a turtle. In *La Vie en Rose* there is never a moment's doubt. Even the hair is right; her frizzled, dyed, thinning hair in the final scenes matches the real Piaf. The only detail I can question is her resiliency after all-night drinking sessions. I once knew an alcoholic who said, "If I wasn't a drinker and I woke up with one of these hangovers, I'd check myself into the emergency room."

Then there are the songs, a lot of them. I gather from the credits that some are dubbed by other singers, some are sung by Piaf herself, and some, in parts at least, by Cotillard. Piaf choreographed her hands and fingers, and Cotillard has that right, too. If a singer has been dead fifty years and sang in another language, she must have been pretty great to make it onto so many saloon jukeboxes, which is how I first heard her. Now, of course, she's on my iPod, and I'm listening to her right now.

Pour moi toute seule.

Leaving Las Vegas

R, 112 m., 1995

Nicolas Cage (Ben Sanderson), Elisabeth Shue (Sera), Julian Sands (Yuri), Richard Lewis (Peter), Valeria Golino (Terri). Directed by Mike Figgis and produced by Lila Cazes and Annie Stewart. Screenplay by Figgis, based on the book by John O'Brien.

Oh, this movie is so sad! It is sad not because of the tragic lives of its characters, but because of their goodness and their charity. What moves me the most in movies is not when something bad happens, but when characters act unselfishly. In *Leaving Las Vegas*, a man loses his family and begins to drink himself to death. He goes to Vegas, and there on the street he meets a prostitute, who takes him in and cares for him, and he calls her his angel. But he doesn't stop drinking.

The man's name is Ben (Nicolas Cage). The woman's name is Sera (Elisabeth Shue). You could not have seen two better performances in 1995. Midway in the film someone offers Ben the insight that his drinking is a way of killing himself. He smiles lopsidedly and offers a correction: "Killing myself is a way of drinking." At one point, after it is clear that Sera really cares for him, he tells her, "You can never, ever, ask me to stop drinking, do you understand?" She replies in a little voice: "I do, I really do." In a sense, it is a marriage vow.

The movie is not really about alcoholism. It is about great sad passion, of the sort celebrated in operas like *La Bohème*. It takes place in bars and dreary rented rooms and the kind of Vegas poverty that includes a parking space and the use of the pool. The practical details are not quite realistic—it would be hard to drink as much as Ben drinks and remain conscious, and it is unlikely an intelligent prostitute would allow him into her life. We brush those objections aside, because they have nothing to do with the real subject of this movie, which is that we must pity one another and be gentle.

Ben was a movie executive. Something bad happened in his life, and his wife and son are gone. Is he divorced? Are they dead? It is never made clear. "I'm not sure if I lost my family because of my drinking, or if I'm drinking because I lost my family," he muses. The details would not help, because this is not a case history but a sad love song. Cage, a resourceful and daring actor, has never been better.

Consider an opening scene where Ben attempts to make jokey small talk with some former colleagues who have long since written him off as a lost cause. He desperately needs money because he needs a drink—*now! Right now!* He is shaking. He may go into convulsions. Yet he manufactures desperately inane chatter, dropping famous names. Finally one of the former friends takes him aside, gives him some money, and says, "I think it would be best if you didn't contact me again." Minutes later, brought back to life by alcohol, he is trying to pick up a woman at a bar: "You smell good," he says. She catches a whiff of his breath: "You've been drinking all day."

What could possibly attract Sera, the prostitute, to this wounded man? We learn a little about her, in closeups where she talks about her life to an invisible therapist. She is proud of the way she controls her clients and sets the scenarios. She is adamant that none of them is ever really allowed to know her. She has an abusive relationship with a pimp (Julian Sands), and we can guess that she probably also had an abusive father; it usually works out that way. The pimp is soon out of the picture, and *Leaving Las Vegas* becomes simply the story of two people. Perhaps she likes Ben because he is so desperate and honest. She takes him in as she might take in a wet puppy.

It is unclear to what extent he fully understands his circumstances. At times he hallucinates. He calls her his "angel" fancifully, but there are moments when she literally seems to be an angel. He hears voices behind the walls. He shakes uncontrollably. He asks her, "How did our evening go?" There is a curiously effective scene in which he tries to get a check cashed, and his hands shake too much to sign his name. He goes off to drink himself into steadiness, and then it seems he returns and makes obscene suggestions to the teller, but they all take place in his head.

Mike Figgis, who wrote, directed, and composed the music, is a filmmaker attracted to the far shores of behavior. Here he began with a novel by a man named John O'Brien, whose autobiographical sources can be guessed by the information that he killed himself two weeks after selling the book rights. To be sure this project wasn't compromised, Figgis shot it as an independent film, using Super 16 cameras to "grab" Las Vegas locations. The outdoor scenes feel unrehearsed and real.

The movie works as a love story, but really romance is not the point here any more than sex is. The story is about two wounded, desperate, marginal people and how they create for each other a measure of grace. One scene after another finds the right note. If there are two unplayable roles in the stock repertory, they are the drunk and the whore with a heart of gold. Cage and Shue make these two clichés into unforgettable people. Cage's drunkenness is inspired in part by a performance he studied, Albert Finney's alcoholic consul in *Under the Volcano.* You sense an observant intelligence peering out from inside the drunken man, and seeing everything clearly and sadly.

Shue's prostitute is, however, the crucial role, because Sera is the one with a choice. She sees Ben clearly, and decides to stick with him for the rest of the ride. When he lets her down badly toward the end of the movie, she goes out and does something that no hooker should do—gets herself into a motel room with a crowd of drunken college boys—and we see how she needed Ben because she desperately needed to do something good for somebody.

He was her redemption, and when it seems he scorns her gift, she punishes herself.

That such a film gets made is a miracle: One can see how this material could have been softened and compromised, and how that would have been wrong. It is a pure, grand gesture. That he is an alcoholic and she works the streets are simply the turnings they have taken. Beneath their occupations are their souls. And because Ben has essentially given up on his, the film becomes Sera's story, about how even in the face of certain defeat we can, at least, insist on loving and trying.

Hookers often give themselves street names. Sera's makes me think of "Que Sera, Sera"—what will be, will be.

Le Beau Mariage

NO MPAA RATING, 97 m., 1982

Béatrice Romand (Sabine), André Dussollier (Edmond), Féodor Atkine (Simon). Written and directed by Eric Rohmer and produced by Margaret Menegoz.

This is a movie about a young woman who decides it is high time to get married. She chooses the man she will marry—a busy young lawyer. She promises herself and her friends that he will marry her—after all, is she not charming, bright, and all but impossible to resist? More crucially, is it not just the right time in her life, and in his, to leap impulsively into a sensible marriage?

This description of *Le Beau Mariage* makes it sound like something involving Sandra Dee's pursuit of Tab Hunter. And there are plot elements in it that could have been lifted from *I Love Lucy*—particularly the idea of throwing a birthday party as an excuse for inviting the lucky man to the young lady's home. But *Le Beau Mariage* is a lot deeper and a lot wittier than that. It is another film by Eric Rohmer, the French director who has made a career out of examining everyday life with unblinking honesty and cheerful acceptance of human nature.

Rohmer takes a slice of life, a very small slice, and studies it so closely that we recognize ourselves in it. He takes a specific story (about a young French woman who wants to be married, for example) and finds selfishness in it, and timidity, and romance, and courage. He draws no great lessons from his discoveries. He is simply saying, here is the way we live, here are the ways we deceive ourselves and here, too, are the ways we would like to deceive ourselves—if we could get away with it.

The woman's name is Sabine. She is pretty, dark-haired, and alert, very smart. She has just ended an unhappy love affair with a married man and has made an "intellectual" decision to get married herself. (Intellectual decisions, of course, are always made for flagrantly emotional reasons; usually, they're hurt feelings, masquerading as unemotional logic.) She meets a lawyer in his mid-thirties and decides to marry him. He will be unable to resist her charm.

For a time it looks as if she might be right. She is his "type." He likes slender, brainy brunettes. But he is busy. He is so busy that he does not have time for a relationship, and because he knows himself so well, he denies himself the pleasure of her company because, in the long run, it would be unfair to her. His arguments are developed during a long, virtuoso scene in his law office, where she has burst in and demanded an explanation (essentially, she wants to know why he won't marry her) and he provides her with one (basically, it is easier to stay apart in the first place than to break up later).

Rohmer is suspicious of the motives of everyone in this movie. Is the lawyer telling the truth, or only letting the woman down without hurting her feelings? Is the woman more in love with the lawyer, or with the beauty of her own logic? One of the beautiful things about this movie is that you walk out questioning the motives of almost everyone in it. It's not that they're dishonest. It's just that they're so wickedly human.

Le Cercle Rouge

NO MPAA RATING, 140 m., 1970 (rereleased 2003)

Alain Delon (Corey), Gian Maria Volonté (Vogel), Yves Montand (Jansen), André Bourvil (Captain Mattei), François Périer (Santi), Paul Crauchet (The Fence), Pierre Collet (Prison Guard), André Ekyan (Rico). Directed by Jean-Pierre Melville and produced by Robert Dorfmann. Screenplay by Melville.

Gliding almost without speech down the dawn streets of a wet Paris winter, these men in trench coats and fedoras perform a ballet of crime, hoping to win and fearing to die. Some are cops and some are robbers. To smoke for them is as natural as breathing. They use guns, lies, clout, greed, and nerve with the skill of a magician who no longer even thinks about the cards. They share a code of honor that is not about what side of the law they are on, but about how a man must behave to win the respect of those few others who understand the code.

Jean-Pierre Melville watches them with the eye of a concerned god in his 1970 film *Le Cercle Rouge.* His movie involves an escaped prisoner, a diamond heist, a police manhunt, and mob vengeance, but it treats these elements as the magician treats his cards; the cards are insignificant, except as the medium through which he demonstrates his skills.

Melville is a director whose films are little known in America; he began before the French New Wave, died in 1973, worked in genres but had a stylistic elegance that kept his films from being marketed to the traditional genre audiences. His *Bob le Flambeur,* now available on a Criterion DVD, has been remade as *The Good Thief* and inspired elements of the two *Ocean's Eleven* films, but all they borrowed was the plot, and that was the least essential thing about it.

Melville grew up living and breathing movies, and his films show more experience of the screen than of life. No real crooks or cops are this attentive to the details of their style and behavior. Little wonder that his great 1967 film about a professional hit man is named *Le Samourai;* his characters, like the samurai, place greater importance on correct behavior than upon success. (Jim Jarmusch's *Ghost Dog* owes something to this value system.)

Le Cercle Rouge, or *The Red Circle* (restored for 2003 release by his admirer John Woo), refers to a saying of the Buddha that men who are destined to meet will eventually meet, no matter what. Melville made up this saying, but no matter; his characters operate according to theories of behavior, so that a government minister believes all men, without exception, are bad; and a crooked nightclub owner refuses to be a police informer because it is simply not in his nature to inform.

The movie stars two of the top French stars of the time, Alain Delon and Yves Montand, as well as Gian Maria Volonté, looking younger here than in the spaghetti Westerns, and with hair. But it is not a star vehicle—or, wait, it is a star vehicle, but the stars ride in it instead of the movie riding on them. All of the actors seem directed to be cool and dispassionate, to guard their feelings, to keep their words to themselves, to realize that among men of experience almost everything can go without saying.

As the film opens, we meet Corey (Delon) as he is released from prison. He has learned of a way to hold up one of the jewelry stores of Place Vendôme. Then we meet Vogel (Volonté), who is a handcuffed prisoner on a train, but he picks the locks of the cuffs, breaks a window, leaps from the moving train, and escapes from the veteran cop Mattei (André Bourvil).

Fate brings Vogel and Corey together. On the run in the countryside, Vogel hides in the trunk of Corey's car. Corey sees him do this, but we don't know he does. He drives into a muddy field, gets out of his car, stands away from it, and tells the man in the trunk he can get out. The man does, holding a gun that Corey must have known he would find in the trunk. They regard each other, face to face in the muddy field. Vogel wants a smoke. Corey throws him a pack and a lighter.

Notice how little they actually say before Corey says, "Paris is your best chance," and Vogel gets back in the trunk. And then notice the precision and economy of what happens next. Corey's car is being tailed by gunmen for a mob boss he relieved of a lot of money. It was probably due him, but still, that is no way to treat a mob boss. Corey pulls over. The gunsels tell him to walk toward the woods. He does. Then we hear Vogel tell them to drop their guns and raise their hands. Vogel picks up each man's gun with a handkerchief and uses it to shoot the other man—so the fingerprints will indicate they shot each other. Corey risked his life on the expectation that Vogel would know what to do and do it, and Corey was right.

There is one cool, understated scene after another. Note the way the police commissioner talks to the nightclub owner after he knows that the owner's son, picked up in an attempt to pressure the owner, has killed himself. Note what he says and what he doesn't say, and how he looks. And note, too, how Jansen, the Yves Montand character, comes into the plot, and

think for a moment about why he doesn't want his share of the loot.

The heist itself is performed with the exactness we expect of a movie heist. We are a little startled to realize it is not the point of the film. In most heist movies, the screenplay cannot think beyond the heist, and is satisfied merely to deliver it. *Le Cercle Rouge* assumes that the crooks will be skillful at the heist because they are good workmen. The movie is not about their jobs but about their natures.

Melville fought for the French Resistance during the war. Manohla Dargis of the *Los Angeles Times*, in a review of uncanny and poetic perception, writes: "It may sound far-fetched, but I wonder if his obsessive return to the same themes didn't have something to do with a desire to restore France's own lost honor." The heroes of his films may win or lose, may be crooks or cops, but they are not rats.

L'Enfant ★ ★ ★ ★
R, 100 m., 2006

Jeremie Renier (Bruno), Deborah Francois (Sonia), Jeremie Segard (Steve), Fabrizio Rongione (Young Thug), Olivier Gourmet (Plainclothes Officer), Stephane Bissot (Receiver), Mireille Bailly (Bruno's Mother). Directed by Jean-Pierre and Luc Dardenne and produced by Jean-Pierre and Luc Dardenne and Denis Freyd. Screenplay by Jean-Pierre and Luc Dardenne.

We talk about the "point of view" of a film. *L'Enfant* sees with the eye of God. The film has granted free will to its central character, Bruno, and now it watches, intense but detached, to see how he will use it. Bruno is so amoral he doesn't register the meaning of his actions. At first his behavior is evil. He attempts repairs. Whether he is redeemed is a good question. At the end he is weeping, but he cannot weep forever, and he has a limited idea of how to survive and make a living.

But let me just bluntly tell you what happens in the film, while observing that *L'Enfant,* more than almost any film I can think of, is not about plot development but about putting one foot in front of the other. We meet Sonia and Bruno. She has just borne his child. The baby in her arms, she finds Bruno begging from cars at a traffic light, while serving as a lookout for a burglary in progress. She shows him their child. He is as interested as if she had shown him her new phone card.

Sonia (Deborah Francois) looks in her late teens. Bruno (Jeremie Renier) looks older, yet in no way seems an adult, and indeed his criminal pals are all kids of around fourteen. He lives entirely in the moment. While Sonia was in the hospital, he sublet her apartment. When he divides loot from a robbery, he spends his share immediately. He buys a used perambulator because Sonia wants one. He rents an expensive convertible because he wants one. There will always be more money. Working? Working is for losers.

In a café, he meets a woman he does business with. He mentions the baby. She tells him, "People pay to adopt." Promising Sonia to watch the baby for an afternoon, he arranges to sell the child. Bruno lives in a grim world of unfriendly streets; he and Sonia have spent nights huddled on a river bank. But no place in the movie is bleaker than the empty building where the sale of the child takes place. He never sees the buyers. They never see him. The child is left in a room, is taken, the money left behind. He returns to Sonia and proudly shows her the money ("This is ours!"). When she despairingly asks about the baby, he says, "We can have another one." She faints dead away and is taken to the hospital. This is a surprise to him.

L'Enfant, which won the Golden Palm at Cannes 2005, is the new film by the Dardenne brothers, Jean-Pierre and Luc, whose The Son (2003) made such an impact, audiences were moved in a deep, rare way. The Dardennes do not make morality tales. Their character Bruno is not aware that what he does is good or bad. He is unformed. There is a scene where he and Sonia tussle playfully in a car and then romp outside in a park like a couple of kids. Does he love her? Love is outside his emotional range. He takes money, spends it, doesn't even cultivate the persona of a hustler. He is that most terrifying kind of human being, the one who doesn't feel ordinary emotions or even understand that other people do.

The Dardennes achieve their effects through an intense visual focus. They follow their characters as if their camera can look nowhere else. In L'Enfant, their gaze is upon Bruno. They deliberately do not establish the newborn child as a character. Unlike the (equally powerful) Tsotsi, their film doesn't show Bruno caring for the child. The child is simply something he carries, like loot or a video game. The movie also avoids the opportunity to develop Sonia, except as her behavior responds to Bruno's. When she lets out a cry of grief and faints, this is not so much what she does as what Bruno sees her do.

Observe particularly the camera strategy in the last half of the film. Often when a hand-held camera follows a character, it feels subjective; we are invited to identify, as if the camera is a point of view we share with the character. In the passages after Sonia faints in L'Enfant, the camera focuses so intensely on Bruno that everything else seems peripheral vision. But it doesn't "identify" with him, and it doesn't represent his point of view. It watches to see what he will do.

There is a theological belief that God gives us free will and waits to see how we will use it. If he were to interfere, it would not be free will at all. If we choose well, we will spend eternity in the sight of God; if badly, banished from his presence. If God were to issue instructions, what would be the point of his creation? If we are not free to choose evil, where is the virtue in choosing good?

It's with that in mind that the visual strategy of the Dardennes reflects the eye of God. Having made a universe that has set this creature Bruno into motion, God (and we) look to see what he will do. Bruno has little intellectual capital and a limited imagination. He has been so damaged that he lacks ordinary feelings; when he visits his mother to arrange for an alibi, we get some insights into his childhood. After Sonia faints, he sets about trying to get the baby back. Does he do this because he knows that selling the baby was wrong? Or because Sonia is a companion and convenience for him, and he must try to restore her to working order?

The greatness of the Dardennes is that they allow us to realize that these are questions, and leave us free to try to answer them. What happens at the end of the film perhaps suggests grief and a desire to repent. I hope it does. But

L'Enfant is not so simple as to believe that for Bruno there can be a happy ending. Here is a film where God does not intervene, and the directors do not mistake themselves for God. It makes the solutions at the ends of other pictures seem like child's play.

Léolo

NO MPAA RATING, 107 m., 1993

Gilbert Sicotte (Narration), Maxime Collin (Léolo), Ginette Reno (Mother), Julien Guiomar (Grandfather), Pierre Bourgault (The Word Tamer), Giuditta Del Vecchio (Bianca), Andrée Lachapelle (Psychiatrist). Directed by Jean-Claude Lauzon and produced by Lyse Lafontaine and Aimee Danis. Screenplay by Lauzon.

Léolo is an enchanting, disgusting, romantic, depressing, hilarious, tragic movie, and it is quite original—one of 1993's best. I have never seen one like it before. It cannot be assigned a category, or described in terms of other films. I felt alive when I was watching it. If you are one of those lonely film lovers who used to attend foreign films, who used to seek out the offbeat and the challenging, and who has given up on movies because they all seem the same, crawl out of your bunker and look at this one. It will remind you that movies can be wonderful.

Directed by Jean-Claude Lauzon, a young nonconformist from Quebec, it tells the story of the young manhood of Leo, who grows up in an insanely dysfunctional but colorful and not altogether harmful family in Montreal. Leo despises his father, so much so that he has created a fantasy in which his mother was somehow impregnated by a tomato from Sicily, which bore the sperm of the man he imagines was his real father. Leo insists he is therefore Italian, and should be called Léolo.

The film is narrated by him, in a sense. In fact, the narration comes out of a journal he keeps as a child, a journal that falls into other hands some years later—into the hands of an old man who treasures the written word, and plunders garbage cans to save it from destruction. This is the same man who once, visiting Léolo's vast and awesomely maternal mother, stopped the kitchen table from tilting by placing an old book under one of the legs—which is how the only book in Léolo's house got there.

Léolo has a way he can dream, and in his dreams he is visited by his Muse. The rest of his time is fairly grim. It is believed in his household that a bowel movement a day keeps the doctor away, and so he spends long hours locked in the toilet, making convincing sound effects to cover his other activities, which include reading naughty Parisian magazines and plotting the murder of his grandfather.

The grandfather is a vile old codger who is conducting a mercenary relationship with the beautiful young neighbor who Léolo persists in thinking of as virginal, and someday destined to become his own. The scene in which Léolo attempts to actually carry out his death plan, using perfectly understood principles of pulleys and levers but faulty craftsmanship, is one of the more astonishing I have seen.

A streak of madness runs, or more accurately gallops, through Léolo's family. They are all either in the madhouse or headed that way. Léolo is a self-raised boy (his mother's maternalism is as misguided as it is smothering), aware of the family curse, and also clever at keeping his own secrets within the claustrophobic household. He is not a cute Hollywood child, or a *Home Alone* brat, or a little plastic monster. He is a fully formed, difficult, complicated individual, who sees himself clearly, sees through his family, and uses fantasy as an escape and a tonic.

Jean-Claude Lauzon, who wrote as well as directed, made his debut in 1987 with *Night Zoo*, a movie that was sensationally well received in Canada (eleven Genie awards—the equivalent of the Oscar) but left some observers, myself included, less than convinced. Yet I remember it clearly after six years, perhaps because Lauzon's films contain images no other film would dare to show. In *Night Zoo*, for example, the young hero grants his father's dying wish by breaking into the zoo so the old man can hunt big game before he dies.

If I was not sure about *Night Zoo*, I have not the slightest doubt about *Léolo*. It is a work of genius—and the best kind of genius, too, which is deranged genius. Lauzon takes no hostages. He has only scorn for sure-fire box office formulas. He makes his films from scratch. It is amazing how many notes he plays in this 107-minute film. How there is broad burlesque, fanciful dreaming, seamy sex, dire poverty, hope for the future, despair. The structure of the film is another amazement, gradually revealing itself, so that the more we know about how and why the story is being told, the more poignant it becomes.

There is a beer in England that advertises itself as "refreshing the parts the others do not reach." I commend this motto to the distributors of *Léolo,* because here is a film that does exactly the same thing.

Les Carabiniers

NO MPAA RATING, 80 m., 1963

Marino Mase (Michelangelo), Albert Juross (Ulysses), Genevieve Gaela (Venus), Catherine Ribero (Cleopatra). Directed by Jean-Luc Godard and produced by Carlo Ponti and Georges deBeauregard. Screenplay by Roberto Rossellini, Jean Gruault, and Godard, from a play by Benjamin Joppolo.

Note: This review of Jean-Luc Godard's 1963 Les Carabiniers *was written upon the film's American release in 1968.*

If I use a cliché, such as writing that *Les Carabiniers* explodes on the screen with the brilliance of fireworks, let me explain that Jean-Luc Godard's fireworks are black against white.

A false report is spread that the war has been won, and Godard's grubby heroes look up for the fireworks celebration. But Godard shows us the negative instead of the print, and you would be amazed how unceremonious black fireworks look in a white sky. That's the general spirit of this marvelously funny antiwar allegory, Godard's 1963 excursion into black humor.

Godard's movies are originals. With each one he tries to rearrange the relationship between the screen and the audience. He doesn't let you sit there, spongelike and passive, the way you get in front of a pound of Hollywood hamburger. He requires a new way of looking at movies; his style, like his politics, has grown steadily more radical.

For that reason, walking in at the beginning of a new Godard movie is like walking in at the middle of someone else's: You ask yourself what happened before you got there. Many of the people who disliked *La Chinoise* had never seen a Godard film before, I suspect, and you

can't meet the natives until you learn the language.

This wisdom is by the way of encouraging you to see *Les Carabiniers,* an excellent introduction to what Godard has done since and a most effective film in its own right. This was just about the first time Godard revealed political consciousness on the screen. *Breathless* was a spoof on 1930s gangster movies and 1950s love affairs. Then came movies concerned with private lives (*A Woman Is a Woman, My Life to Live*) before this statement about war, inhumanity, and totalitarianism, which was filmed in 1963 but not released in America until this year [1968].

The film involves two cretinous brothers, named Ulysses and Michelangelo for some reason, who live in a shack in a dump with their slatternly wives. One day two carabiniers arrive with a letter from the king: The brothers are cordially invited to attend the war. They are promised everything: They will be allowed to loot, plunder, deface, see the sights, and in general have a smashing time. "Will we be able to slaughter the innocent?" asks Ulysses. "Of course," the carabinier snaps. "This is war." Delighted, the brothers enlist.

What follows is a series of self-contained scenes, separated by postcards the brothers write home. The postcards are presented in longhand on the screen, an early example of Godard's affection for title cards even in talkies. One reads: "Yesterday the war entered its third spring, and therefore no longer offers the prospect of peace." Another: "We captured Santa Cruz and I saw my first movie."

This title begins a hilarious scene, as Michelangelo sits in a movie house (Godard always manages to work the movies into his movies). A woman appears on screen and begins to take a bath. Enraptured, Michelangelo leaps onto the stage to look into the tub. We laugh at his delusion that a movie is real, and in laughing we demonstrate the same delusion.

There are other effective scenes. A young blonde woman calmly recites revolutionary slogans and poetry while standing before a firing squad, and it is a noble gesture but useless. Out of this scene comes the whole conception of *Masculine-Feminine,* in which young people recite, write, distribute, and memorize slogans for a whole movie without accomplishing anything. And out of that came *La Chinoise*, in which they finally talked themselves into action.

The last section of the film is Godard at his best. The soldiers, who were promised the world, come back with postcards. They show them to their wives in a scene nearly ten minutes long that grows steadily more hilarious. One card after another: "The Parthenon . . . the Taj Mahal . . . the Technicolor works in Hollywood . . . the Chicago aquarium . . . Cleopatra (actually Liz Taylor) . . . forms of transportation . . . little green grasshoppers."

This is an antiwar film in the same sense *Breathless* was a gangster movie—that is, Godard has chosen a subject on which to exercise his style. The result is one of his most successful films and, incidentally, one easier to understand and enjoy than his later work.

Less Than Zero

R, 100 m., 1987

Andrew McCarthy (Clay), Jami Gertz (Blair), Robert Downey, Jr. (Julian), James Spader (Rip), Tony Bill (Bradford Easton), Nicholas Pryor (Benjamin Wells), Donna Mitchell (Elaine Easton), Michael Bowen (Hop), Sarah Buxton (Markie). Directed by Marek Kanievska and produced by Jon Avnet and Jordan Kerner. Screenplay by Harley Peyton.

George Carlin was once asked how cocaine made you feel, and he answered: "It makes you feel like having some more cocaine." That inescapable fact is at the bottom of *Less Than Zero*, a movie that knows cocaine inside out and paints a portrait of drug addiction that is all the more harrowing because it takes place in the Beverly Hills fast lane, in a world of wealth, sex, glamour, and helpless self-destruction.

The movie is about three very rich kids who graduate from the same high school. How rich? As a graduation present, the father of one of the kids sets him up in the recording industry. The character's name is Julian, and he is played by Robert Downey, Jr., as a slick, smart, charming young man who takes less than a year to lose everything. His best friend in high school was Clay, played by Andrew McCarthy. Clay, who wears a tie even in

Southern California, goes off to an Ivy League university, leaving behind his girlfriend, Blair (Jami Gertz). By Thanksgiving, Downey and Gertz are sleeping together and doing cocaine together, and by Christmas, a terrified Gertz is calling McCarthy and begging him to come home and rescue Downey, who is in very big trouble.

The problem is, you cannot rescue someone who is addicted to drugs. You can lecture them, to no point, and plead with them, to no avail, but essentially, an outsider is powerless over someone else's addiction. Downey is clearly out of control and headed for bottom. He has lost the recording studio, spent all his money, made a half-hearted stab at a rehab center, gone back to using, and been banished from his home by his father, who practices tough love and tells him, "You can lead your life any way you want, but stay the hell out of mine."

The first hint of this movie's power comes during a Christmas party scene. McCarthy, back from the East, tries to talk to his old friend and his former girlfriend, but they're stoned, and talk too fast and too loud, almost mechanically, and have tiny attention spans. Later, Gertz begs McCarthy to help Downey but what can he do? And then the movie's long middle section functions almost as a documentary of the Beverly Hills fast track, of private clubs that open at midnight, of expensive cars and smooth drug dealers and glamorous hangers-on, and the quiet desperation of a society of once-bright, once-attractive, once-promising young people who talk about a lot of things but essentially think only about cocaine.

The movie's three central performances are flawless: by Jami Gertz, as the frightened girl who witnesses the disintegration of her friend; by Andrew McCarthy, as the quiet, almost cold, witness from outside this group; and especially by Robert Downey, Jr., whose acting here is so real, so subtle, and so observant that it's scary.

His life in the film revolves around the will of a fourth character, his drug dealer (James Spader). He owes the dealer $50,000 and has no money and no prospects, and the most frightening thing about his situation is that the Spader character is actually fairly reasonable, as these characters go. "I'm not the problem," Spader tells McCarthy. "Julian is the problem." He has extended much more credit than he would usually permit, out of "friendship," but now Downey is at the end of the line.

The movie's last thirty minutes are like a kick in the gut, as Downey spirals through the ultimate results of his addiction. He appeals to his father, to his friends, and even to his dealer, and the fact is, he gets more help than perhaps he deserves. He makes firm resolutions to stop using, and vague plans to "get back into rehab," and his friends stand by him as much as they can. The movie's outcome reflects, more or less accurately, what awaits most cocaine addicts who do not get clean.

If this description of *Less Than Zero* makes it sound like a downbeat retread of *The Lost Weekend,* that's because I haven't described the movie's visual style. Director Marek Kanievska and cinematographer Ed Lachman have photographed Beverly Hills, Bel Air, and Palm Springs the way they look in high-priced fashion ads and slick TV commercials. The water in the pools is always an azure blue. The homes look like sets. The people look like models. The discos look like music videos. The whole movie looks brilliantly superficial, and so Downey's predicament is all the more poignant: He is surrounded by all of this, he is in it and of it, and he cannot have it. All he wants to have is a good time, but he is trapped in a paradox: Cocaine is the good time that takes itself away.

Lethal Weapon

R, 110 m., 1987

Mel Gibson (Martin Riggs), Danny Glover (Roger Murtaugh), Gary Busey (Joshua), Mitchell Ryan (The General), Tom Atkins (Michael Hunsaker), Darlene Love (Trish Murtaugh), Traci Wolfe (Rianne Murtaugh). Directed by Richard Donner and produced by Donner and Joel Silver. Screenplay by Shane Black.

Lethal Weapon is another one of those Bruised Forearm Movies, like *Raiders of the Lost Ark,* a movie where you and your date grab each other's arm every four minutes and you end up black and blue and grinning from ear to ear. It's a buddy movie about two homicide cops who chase a gang of drug dealers all over

Southern California, and the plot makes an amazing amount of sense, considering that the action hardly ever stops for it.

The cops are played by Danny Glover, as a homebody who has just celebrated his fiftieth birthday, and Mel Gibson, as a crazed, wild-eyed rebel who has developed a suicidal streak since his wife was killed in a car crash. In the space of less than forty-eight hours, they become partners, share a family dinner, kill several people, survive a shoot-out in the desert, battle with helicopters and machine guns, toss hand grenades, jump off buildings, rescue Glover's kidnapped daughter, drive cars through walls, endure torture by electric shock, have a few beers, and repair the engine on Glover's boat—not in that order.

The movie's so tightly wound up, it's like a rubber band ready to snap. Richard Donner, the director, throws action scenes at us like hardballs, and we don't know when to duck. All of the elements of this movie have been seen many times before—the chases, the explosions, the hostage negotiations—but this movie illustrates a favorite belief of mine, which is that the subject of a movie is much less important than its style. I'm a guy who is bored by shoot-outs and chase scenes. I've seen it all. But this movie thrilled me from beginning to end.

Part of that is because I cared about the characters. Glover has had important roles for several years (in movies as different as *Places in the Heart* and *The Color Purple*), but this movie makes him a star. His job is to supply the movie's center of gravity, while all the nuts and weirdos and victims whirl around him. He's a family man, concerned about those gray hairs he sees in the mirror, not interested in taking unnecessary chances.

Gibson is the perfect counterpoint, with his wild hair, his slob clothing, and his emotional misery. It's a running gag in the movie that Gibson is so suicidal he doesn't care if he lives or dies—and that gives him a definite advantage in showdown situations. That's what happens in a scene where Gibson is up on a rooftop trying to reason with a jumper. I won't spoil the scene; I'll just say the scene ends with one of the few genuinely unexpected surprises in any recent action film.

The supporting cast is strong, and has to be,

to stand out in the midst of the mayhem. Gary Busey, slimmed down and bright of eye, makes an appropriately hateful killer. And Traci Wolfe, as Glover's good-looking daughter, is cute when she gets a teenage crush on Gibson. But most of the attention focuses on Glover and Gibson, and they work easily together, as if they were having fun, their eccentric personal rhythms supplying a counterpoint to the movie's roar of violence.

Now about that matter of style. In a sense, a movie like *Lethal Weapon* isn't about violence at all. It's about movement and timing, the choreography of bodies and weapons in time and space. In lesser movies, the people stand there and shoot at each other and we're bored. In a movie with the energy of this one, we're exhilarated by the sheer freedom of movement; the violence becomes surrealistic and less important than the movie's underlying energy level.

Richard Donner has directed a lot of classy pictures. My favorites are *Inside Moves, Ladyhawke,* and the original *Superman,* which is still the best. This time he tops himself.

Life Is Sweet

NO MPAA RATING, 102 m., 1991

Alison Steadman (Wendy), Jim Broadbent (Andy), Claire Skinner (Natalie), Jane Horrocks (Nicola), Stephen Rea (Patsy), Timothy Spall (Aubrey). Directed by Mike Leigh and produced by Simon Channing-Williams. Screenplay by Leigh.

Most movies begin by knowing everything about their characters. *Life Is Sweet* seems to make discoveries as it goes along; it really feels as if the story is as surprising to the characters as it is to us. The filmmaker, Mike Leigh, works in a unique way: He assembles his actors, and then they spend weeks or months devising the screenplay by improvising together. When it's finished, they start shooting, having invented the characters from the inside out.

With *Life Is Sweet,* that approach combines more humor and more poignancy into the same story than most screenwriters would have dared for. There are scenes here that are funnier than those of any other movie of 1991, and other scenes that weep with the pain of sad family secrets, and when it's over we have

seen some kind of masterpiece. This is one of the best films of 1991.

The story takes place in a small home in a London suburb, where the parents, Wendy and Andy (Alison Steadman and Jim Broadbent), live with twin daughters who are twentyish (Claire Skinner and Jane Horrocks). These daughters are like night and day. Nicola, played by Horrocks, hides behind glasses, tangled hair, and cigarettes, and affects a great contempt for all things conventional, progressive, or healthy. Natalie, played by Skinner, is clean-cut, cheerful, and dutiful. Each sister is a rebuke to the other.

Andy, the father, was athletic when he was younger, but is now going comfortably to seed. He and Wendy were married when they were quite young, and have grown up together, learning some hard lessons along the way, but now they seem to have settled into a comfortable accommodation with one another, inspired partly by Andy's lunatic schemes, and partly by the way Wendy is both horrified and amused by them. There is a moment when Andy leads his wife out into the front of the house with her eyes covered, and then—ta da!—unveils them to reveal his latest scheme for independent living, a mobile hot dog stand.

In his day job, Andy works in the food preparation industry, and hates it. When he trips over a spoon and breaks a leg, there is a wonderful illustration of the way the humor develops in this film. He brings the spoon home with him, hangs it in a place of shame on the wall, and accuses it of treachery in the warmest and most personal terms. It is hard to imagine a screenwriter coming up with this dialogue, but it feels both original and exactly right—the sort of things that would come out of an improvisational investigation.

The funniest passage in the movie actually has little to do with the rest of it; it involves a family friend (the feckless Timothy Spall) who opens a grotty French restaurant on the high road, hires one of the girls as his waitress, and then gets doggedly drunk while waiting for customers and reviewing his implausible menu.

Meanwhile, at home, in such a subtle way we don't at first realize it, the movie reveals its more serious undertones. Nicola really is seriously disturbed—convinced she is ugly and fat—and the sunny cheerfulness of her sister acts only as a daily depressant. The twins know almost everything about each other, but several important secrets have never been openly discussed, and now they are, as the family's underlying problems come out into the open.

I do not want to reveal too much. I especially want to avoid spoiling for you the extraordinary impact of an outburst by Wendy, the mother, who tells her girls some of the sorts of things children do not realize about parents. By the end of *Life Is Sweet* we are treading close to the stuff of life itself—to the way we all struggle and make do, compromise some of our dreams and insist on the others. Watching this movie made me realize how boring and thin many movies are; how they substitute plots for the fascinations of life.

Life Is Sweet has been the greatest success so far in the long, brave career of Mike Leigh, who made a film named *Bleak Moments* that made my "best of the year" list in 1971. He then did not make another film until *High Hopes* in 1989 (that also made my "best ten" list—so he's never made a film that didn't). Film financiers are understandably slow to back a film that doesn't have a screenplay, but Leigh has persisted in his collaborations with actors, working usually on the British stage and TV, where in his own brave and stubborn way he has finally become something of a hero.

What is amazing is that a man can labor against the market forces of the stage and screen for twenty years and still retain his sense of humor. And yet that is what he has done. *Life Is Sweet* is as funny, spontaneous, and free as if it had been made on a lark by a millionaire. This is an almost miraculous coming-together of actors, material, a time and a place, and an attitude. See it, and you will sense the freedom with which movies can be made when they are freed from the lockstep of the assembly line.

Light Sleeper

R, 103 m., 1992

Willem Dafoe (John LeTour), Susan Sarandon (Ann), Dana Delany (Marianne), David Clennon (Robert), Mary Beth Hurt (Teresa). Directed by Paul Schrader and produced by Linda Reisman. Screenplay by Schrader.

People get into situations like this. They start doing drugs when they're young, and then they start dealing drugs in order to pay for them, and then if they survive, the day comes when they get off drugs, because eventually one day you either get off drugs or you die. And then they are left with selling the drugs, because the money is easy and it is the only life they know, and their résumé for a straight job would have a gap representing their adult lifetime.

John LeTour, the hero of *Light Sleeper,* Paul Schrader's brooding, lonely film, delivers drugs to clients in Manhattan. He works for a dealer named Ann, who runs her operation as a business, but dreams of getting into another one—maybe she'll start a cosmetics firm. It's the daydream of anyone who is being paid too much to do something that no longer matters to them; they'll quit one day, and do what they really want to do. But somehow they can never afford that. Maybe a catastrophe would be a blessing in disguise.

Schrader knows this world of insomnia, craving, and addiction. And he knows all about people living in a cocoon of themselves. *Light Sleeper* is the third in his trilogy about alienated night workers, after *Taxi Driver* (he wrote the screenplay, Martin Scorsese directed) and *American Gigolo,* about a man who supplies sex at great cost to himself. Now comes this story about the man who delivers drugs. There are many parallels in the three films; all involve the men in misguided efforts to save or connect with a self-destructive woman, and all end in violence. But, perhaps because he is growing older and wiser, the characters over the years have become better people. The zombie craziness in Travis Bickle, the De Niro character in *Taxi Driver* (1976), has mellowed into a certain gentle resignation in Willem Dafoe's gifted portrait of John LeTour in *Light Sleeper.*

LeTour has been off drugs for a couple of years. He still drinks, and never really got involved in going to meetings. He does his job for money. He has clients who worry him, including one completely strung out guy who has holed up in an apartment with booze and drugs and is going off the deep end. His last trip to this guy's house—where he brutally tells him he's hit bottom, and kicks the guy back down to the floor while making a call to turn him in—is a scene of perfect insight into the world of addiction.

One day LeTour accidentally runs into a woman he loved and lost because of drugs (Dana Delany). She is afraid of him; she keeps edging away, because she's been clean and sober for five years, and she thinks his shaky status might be catching. He pursues her. He tries to tell her he's cleaned up his act. He goes sometimes to a psychic (Mary Beth Hurt), who sees an aura of death around him, and he appeals to her desperately for help and advice. *Light Sleeper* isn't about the help he can get from psychics, however; it's about desperation that makes him project healing qualities upon anyone who is halfway sympathetic.

The movie is familiar with its life of night and need. It finds the real human qualities in a person like Ann, the dealer (Susan Sarandon)—who, in a crisis, reacts with loyalty and quick thinking. It is filled with great weariness and sadness; the party has been over for a long time, and these old druggies, now approaching middle age, have been left behind. Because they were survivors, because they were more intelligent and honest than most, this is the thanks they get: They continue to work in the scene long after they should have been replaced by a new generation of losers.

I've talked to some people who had this or that complaint about the plot of *Light Sleeper,* often that they didn't like the way the ending seemed like an ironic echo of *Taxi Driver.* This movie isn't about plot; it's about a style of life, and the difficulty of preserving selfrespect and playing fair when your income depends on selling people stuff that will make them hate you. In film after film, for year after year, Paul Schrader has been telling this story in one way or another, but never with more humanity than this time.

Like Water for Chocolate

R, 113 m., 1993

Lumi Cavazos (Tita), Marco Leonardi (Pedro), Regina Torne (Mama Elena), Mario Ivan Martinez (John Brown), Ada Carrasco (Nacha), Yareli Arizmendi (Rosaura). Directed and produced by Alfonso Arau. Screenplay by Laura Esquivel, based on the book by Esquivel.

In Mexico, so I have learned, hot chocolate is made with water, not milk. The water is brought to a boil and then the chocolate is spooned into it. A person in a state of sexual excitement is said to be "like water for chocolate." And now here is a movie where everyone seems at the boil, their lives centering around a woman whose sensual life is carried out in the kitchen, and whose food is so magical it can inspire people to laugh, or cry, or run naked from the house to be scooped up and carried away by a passing revolutionary.

Like Water for Chocolate creates its own intense world of passion and romance, and adds a little comedy and a lot of quail, garlic, honey, chilies, mole, cilantro, rose petals, and cornmeal. It takes place in a Mexican border town, circa 1910, where a young couple named Tita and Pedro are deeply in love. But they are never to marry. Mama Elena, Tita's fearsome and unbending mother, forbids it. She sees the duty of her youngest daughter to stay always at home and take care of her. Tita is heartbroken—especially when Pedro marries Rosaura, her oldest sister.

But there is a method to Pedro's treachery. During a dance at the wedding, he whispers into Tita's ear that he has actually married Rosaura in order to be always close to Tita. He still loves only her. Weeping with sadness and joy, Tita prepares the wedding cake, and as her tears mingle with the granulated sugar, sifted cake flour, beaten eggs, and grated peel of lime, they transform the cake into something enchanting that causes all of the guests at the feast to begin weeping at what should be an occasion for joy.

The movie is narrated by Tita's greatniece, who describes how, through the years, Aunt Tita's kitchen produces even more extraordinary miracles. When Pedro gives her a dozen red roses, for example, she prepares them with quail and honey, and the recipe is such an aphrodisiac that everyone at the table is aroused, and smoke actually pours from the ears of the middle sister, Gertrudis. She races to the outhouse, which catches fire, and then, tearing off her burning clothes, is swept into the saddle of a passing bandolero. (She returns many years later, a famous revolutionary leader.)

Like Water for Chocolate is based on a bestselling novel by Laura Esquivel, and has been directed by her husband, Alfonso Arau. Like *Bye Bye Brazil* and parts of *El Norte*, it continues the tradition of magical realism that is central to modern Latin film and literature. It begins with the assumption that magic can change the fabric of the real world, if it is transmitted through the emotions of people in love. And Lumi Cavazos, as Tita, is the perfect instrument for magic, with her single-minded, lifelong devotion to Pedro—a love that transcends even their separation, when the evil Mama Elena dispatches Pedro and Rosaura to another town, where their baby dies for lack of Tita's cooking.

The movie takes the form of an old family legend, and the source is apparently Esquivel. It gains the poignancy of an old story that is already over, so that the romance takes on a kind of grandeur. What has survived, however, is a tattered but beautiful old book containing all of Aunt Tita's recipes, and who has not felt some sort of connection with the past when reading or preparing a favorite recipe from a loved one who has now passed on?

Imagine, for example, melting some butter and browning two cloves of garlic in it. Then adding two drops of attar of roses, the petals of six roses, two tablespoons of honey, and twelve thinly sliced chestnuts to the mixture, and rubbing it all over six tiny quail and browning them in the oven. Serve, of course, with the remaining rose petals. And stand back.

The Lion in Winter

PG, 135 m., 1968

Peter O'Toole (Henry II), Katharine Hepburn (Eleanor), Anthony Hopkins (Richard), Nigel Terry (John), John Castle (Geoffrey), Timothy Dalton (King Philip), Jane Merrow (Alais). Directed by Anthony Harvey and produced by Joseph E. Levine and Martin Poll. Screenplay by James Goldman, based on his play.

One of the joys that movies provide too rarely is the opportunity to see a literate script handled intelligently. *The Lion in Winter* triumphs at that difficult task; not since *A Man for All Seasons* have we had such capable handling of a story about ideas. But *The Lion in Winter* also functions at an emotional level and is the better film, I think.

One of the flaws of *A Man for All Seasons* was that it was so graceful and bloodless. The characters were scrubbed; the sets were ornate; the dialogue was delivered as a sort of free verse, especially when Paul Scofield got rolling. In the last analysis, the film provided a civilized version of a story that you sensed was not nearly so civilized at the time.

That's not the case with *The Lion in Winter*. Henry II rules a world in which kings still kicked aside chickens on their way through the courtyard, and he wears a costume that looks designed to be put on in November and shed layer by layer during April. In this England, 350 years earlier than the time of Thomas More, there are dogs and dirt floors, rough furskins and pots of stew, pigs, mud, dungeons—and human beings. We believe in the complicated intrigue these people get themselves into because we believe in them. They look real and inhabit a world that looks lived in.

The action is mostly contained within one day, a Christmas Eve. Henry II (Peter O'Toole) is fifty years old and wants to choose his heir before he dies. He has three surviving sons: John, his favorite, a sniveling slack-jaw; Richard, the soldier genius; and Geoffrey, reserved and quiet. Henry calls a Christmas court, letting his wife, Eleanor of Aquitaine (Katharine Hepburn) out of prison for the occasion. King Philip II of France is also a visitor. He wants to know when his sister will be married to the heir to the throne. But Henry has not been able to appoint an heir yet, and what's more, the girl has become his mistress.

James Goldman's fine script handles this situation in a series of meetings between the principals. He is as good as Shaw in getting people on and off stage; at one point, he has three people hidden behind tapestries when Henry visits Philip's room, and he gets them all out without faltering in his command of the scene. He gives his characters a most effective language; it seems direct, and yet it has a gracefulness and wit.

Little Big Man

PG, 157 m., 1971

Dustin Hoffman (Jack Crabb), Faye Dunaway (Mrs. Pendrake), Martin Balsam (Merriweather), Richard Mulligan (General Custer), Chief Dan George (Old

Lodge Skins), Jeff Corey (Wild Bill Hickok). Directed by Arthur Penn and produced by Stuart Millar. Screenplay by Calder Willingham.

Arthur Penn's *Little Big Man* is an endlessly entertaining attempt to spin an epic in the form of a yarn. It mostly works. When it doesn't—when there's a failure of tone or an overdrawn caricature—it regroups cheerfully and plunges ahead. We're disposed to go along; all good storytellers tell stretchers once in a while, and circle back to be sure we got the good parts.

It is the very folksiness of Penn's film that makes it, finally, such a perceptive and important statement about Indians, the West, and the American dream. There's no stridency, no preaching, no deep-voiced narrators making sure we got the point of the last massacre. All the events happened long, long ago, and they're related by a 121-year-old man who just wants to pass the story along. The yarn is the most flexible of story forms. Its teller can pause to repeat a point; he can hurry ahead ten years; he can forget an entire epoch in remembering the legend of a single man. He doesn't capture the history of a time, but its flavor. *Little Big Man* gives us the flavor of the Cheyenne nation before white men brought uncivilization to the West. Its hero, played by Dustin Hoffman, is no hero at all but merely a survivor.

Hoffman, or Little Big Man, gets around pretty well. He touches all the bases of the Western myth. He was brought West as a settler, raised as a Cheyenne, tried his hand at gunfighting and medicine shows, scouted for the cavalry, experimented with the hermit life, was married twice, survived Custer's Last Stand, and sat at the foot of an old man named Old Lodge Skins, who instructed him in the Cheyenne view of creation.

Old Lodge Skins, played by Chief Dan George with such serenity and conviction that an Academy Award was mentioned, doesn't preach the Cheyenne philosophy. It is part of him. It's all the more a part of him because Penn has allowed the Indians in the film to speak ordinary, idiomatic English. Most movie Indians have had to express themselves with an "um" at the end of every other word: "Swap-um wamp-um plenty soon," etc. The Indians in *Little Big Man* have dialogue reflecting the idiomatic richness of Indian tongues; when Old Lodge Skins simply refers to Cheyennes as "the Human Beings," the phrase is literal and meaningful and we don't laugh.

Despite Old Lodge Skins, however, Little Big Man doesn't make it as an Indian, or as a white man, either, or as anything else he tries. He looks, listens, remembers, and survives, which is his function. The protagonists in the film are two ideas of civilization: the Indian's and the white man's. Custer stages his bloody massacres and is massacred in turn, and we know that the Indians will eventually be destroyed as an organic community and shunted off to reservations. But the film's movement is circular, and so is its belief about Indians.

Penn has adopted the yarn form for a reason. All the characters who appear in the early stages of the film come back in the later stages, fulfilled. The preacher's wife returns as a prostitute. The medicine-quack, already lacking an arm, loses a leg (physician, heal thyself). Wild Bill Hickok decays from a has-been to a freak show attraction. Custer fades from glory to madness. Only Old Lodge Skins makes it through to the end not merely intact, but improved.

His survival is reflected in the film's structure. Most films, especially ones with violence, have their climax at the end. Penn puts his near the center; it is Custer's massacre of an Indian village, and Little Big Man sees his Indian wife killed and his baby's head blown off. Penn can control violence as well as any American director (remember *Bonnie and Clyde* and *The Left Handed Gun*). He does here. The final massacre of Custer and his men is deliberately muted, so it doesn't distract from Old Lodge Skins's "death" scene.

But Custer stays dead, and Old Lodge Skins doesn't quite die ("I was afraid it would turn out this way"). So he leaves the place of death and invites Little Big Man home to have something to eat. Custer's civilization will eventually win, but Old Lodge Skins's will prevail. William Faulkner observed in his Nobel Prize speech that man will probably endure—but will he prevail? It's probably no accident that we don't smile when Old Lodge Skins explains the difference between Custer and the Human Beings.

Little Dorrit

G, 357 m., 1988

Alec Guinness (William Dorrit), Sarah Pickering (Little Dorrit), Cyril Cusack (Frederick Dorrit), Amelda Brown (Fanny), Derek Jacobi (Arthur Clennam), Joan Greenwood (Mrs. Clennam), Roshan Seth (Mr. Pancks). Directed by Christine Edzard and produced by John Brabourne and Richard Goodwin. Screenplay by Edzard based on the book by Charles Dickens.

I turned on the TV late one night, just in time to catch the closing moments of Truffaut's *Fahrenheit 451*. You remember the scene. In a world where the printed word has been forbidden, a little colony of book-lovers lives by the side of a lake in the woods. Each one has dedicated his life to memorizing the contents of one book. They walk slowly back and forth on paths through the snow, reciting the words over and over, and their voices form a litany of familiar passages.

Little Dorrit is like a film made in the same spirit. It is a six-hour epic, with 242 speaking roles, and yet it was crafted almost by hand. The director, Christine Edzard, and the co-producer, her husband Richard Goodwin, live and work in a converted warehouse in London's dockland. When they are not making films, they manufacture dollhouses. They built the sets for this film inside their warehouse, they sewed all of the costumes on premises, they used their dollhouse skills to build miniature models which are combined with special effects to create a backdrop of Victorian London. And to their studio by the side of the Thames, they lured such actors as Alec Guinness, Derek Jacobi, Cyril Cusack, and Joan Greenwood to appear in a film that was made mostly out of the love of Charles Dickens.

I myself have spent some time in the company of Dickens. I read *Nicholas Nickleby* not long ago, and then *Our Mutual Friend*, and now here is this six-hour film version of *Little Dorrit*, which is so filled with characters, so rich in incident, that it has the expansive, luxurious feel of a Victorian novel. Dickens created worlds large enough that you could move around in them. He did not confine himself to the narrow focus of a few neurotic characters and their shell-shocked egos; he created

worlds, in the closing words of *Little Dorrit*, where "the noisy and the eager, and the arrogant and the froward and the vain, fretted, and chafed, and made their usual uproar."

Little Dorrit opens with the information that the story will be told in two parts, the first through the eyes of Arthur Clennam, the second through the eyes of *Little Dorrit*. The two parts of the film contain many of the same scenes, seen from different points of view and remembered differently, so that half a line of throwaway dialogue in the first version may turn out, in the second version, to have been absolutely crucial. The use of two different points of view is not simply a conceit of the filmmakers, but creates a real romantic tension, because it is clear from the outset that Clennam and *Little Dorrit* are in love with each other—and neither one has any way of admitting that fact.

The film opens in Marshalsea Prison, where the heroine's father, William Dorrit (Alec Guinness) has been confined for twenty years for nonpayment of debt. Although her older sister despises the debtor's prison, Dorrit (Sarah Pickering) has grown to love it, as the only home she has ever known. On its stairs she received her education—learned to read and write, learned her English history in the form of stories told of kings and queens. She is not too proud to be poor.

Near the beginning of the film, Dorrit goes to work in an old, gloomy house occupied by the grasping Mrs. Clennam (Joan Greenwood), who lives there with Flintwinch, her bitter steward (Max Wall). It is there that Dorrit first lays eyes on the old lady's son, Arthur (Derek Jacobi), who has plugged away honorably in life without getting much of anywhere. And it is there that Dorrit discovers the clue to an ancient inheritance that the mother is determined to keep from her son.

Arthur's first glimpse of Dorrit is only momentary. But he wants to know who that young girl was. He wants to know in a tentative, almost frightened voice that lets us know, immediately, that he has fallen irrevocably into love with her. But there are great barriers, of course. One of them is the difference in their ages—although that was not so big a problem in Victorian times, when poor young ladies were often married off for reasons of money rather than love. A greater problem is Dorrit's self-image. Since her father, who she dearly loves, lives in a debtor's prison, her place is at his side. The third problem, of course, is that Arthur and Dorrit can barely endure to be in the same room together, because they love each other so much and cannot admit it.

I saw *Little Dorrit* all in the same day. I think that is a good way to see it, although many people will want to split it into two different evenings. Very long films can create a life of their own. We lose our moorings. We don't know exactly where we stand within the narrative, and so we can't guess what will happen next. People appear and reappear, grow older and die, and we accept the rhythm of the story rather than requiring it to be speeded up.

This kind of timing imparts tremendous weight to the love story. During the course of the film, we ourselves come to love Little Dorrit and Arthur Clennam (who is a good man and a very lonely one). We see all their difficulties. We know all of their fears. We identify with all of their hesitations. When they are finally able to bring themselves to admit that they are in love, it is a joyous moment. And when old Dorrit comes to the time when he must die, Alec Guinness plays the scene with the kind of infinitely muted pathos that has you wiping your eyes even as you're admiring his acting craft.

Many good novels, it is said, begin with a funeral and end with a wedding. *Little Dorrit* more or less travels that route, with another funeral at the end. It is never simply a love story, and it is not structured melodramatically. It is about the accumulation of incident. We are told that old Dorrit, the Guinness character, lives in the prison for twenty years. We begin to feel those years, as he sits in his chair by the window and we inventory the pathetically short list of his possessions. We see the hopelessness and waste of the Victorian debtor system, which Dickens helped to reform with novels such as this. But we also see the hope that could exist in a city where people lived cheek by jowl, rich by poor, everyone in sight of the street.

The Little Mermaid

G, 82 m., 1989

With the voices of: Jodi Benson (Ariel), Kenneth Mars (Triton), Pat Carroll (Ursula), Buddy Hackett (Scuttle), Samuel E. Wright (Sebastian), Rene Auberjonois (Louis), Christopher Daniel Barnes (Eric), Jason Marin (Flounder), Edie McClurg (Carlotta), Ben Wright (Grimsby), Will Ryan (Seahorse). Directed by John Musker and Ron Clements and produced by Howard Ashman and Musker. Screenplay by Musker and Clements, based on a story by Hans Christian Andersen.

Walt Disney's *The Little Mermaid* is a jolly and inventive animated fantasy—a movie that's so creative and so much fun it deserves comparison with the best Disney work of the past. It's based on the Hans Christian Andersen tale about a mermaid who falls in love with a prince, but the Disney animators have added a gallery of new supporting characters, including an octopus named Ursula who is their most satisfying villainess since the witch in *Snow White*.

Watching *The Little Mermaid*, I began to feel that the magic of animation had been restored to us. After the early years of Walt Disney's pathfinding feature-length cartoons, we entered into a long dark age in which frame-by-frame animation was too expensive, and even the great Disney animation team began using shortcuts. Now computers have taken the busywork out of the high-priced hands of humans, who are free to realize even the most elaborate flights of imagination. And that's certainly what they do in this film.

The movie opens far beneath the sea, where the god Triton rules over his underwater kingdom. All obey his commands—except for his daughter, Ariel, a mermaid who dreams of far-off lands. One day Ariel makes a forbidden visit to the surface of the sea, and there she sees a human for the first time—a handsome young prince. She saves him from drowning, but he remembers nothing about the experience except for her voice, which he falls in love with. Triton is angry at Ariel's disobedience, but she can think of nothing but the prince, and eventually she strikes an unwise bargain with the evil Ursula, an octopus who can disguise herself in many different forms. Ursula will take away Ariel's tail and give her human legs so she can follow the prince onto the land—but in exchange Ariel must give up her haunting singing voice, and if the prince doesn't kiss her within three days, she will become Ursula's slave.

Two key elements in the storytelling make *The Little Mermaid* stand apart from lesser recent animated work. One is that Ariel is a fully realized female character who thinks and acts independently, even rebelliously, instead of hanging around passively while the fates decide her destiny. Because she's smart and thinks for herself, we have sympathy for her scheming. The second element involves the plot itself: It's tricky and clever, and involves some suspense as Ariel loses her voice and very nearly loses her prince to the diabolical Ursula (who assumes the form of a *femme fatale* and hijacks Ariel's beautiful voice).

As the plot thickens and the melodrama unwinds, the animators introduce a gallery of new characters who are instantly engaging. Ariel is accompanied most places, for example, by Sebastian, a crab with extraordinary wisdom, by Flounder, a fish who cannot always be counted upon, and by Scuttle, a busybody sea gull who looks and sounds a good deal like Buddy Hackett. They provide comic relief, especially in a sequence that mixes comedy and danger in the best Disney tradition, as Sebastian finds himself captured by a French chef who attempts to cook and serve the little blighter.

What's best about *The Little Mermaid* is the visual invention with which the adventures are drawn. There is a lightness and a freedom about the setting—from Triton's underwater throne room to storms at sea and Ursula's garden of captured souls (they look a little like the tourists buried in Farmer Vincent's backyard in *Motel Hell*). The colors are bright, the water sparkles with reflected light, and there is a sense that not a single frame has been compromised because of the cost of animation.

The songs are good, too. *The Little Mermaid* contains some of the best Disney music since the glory days. My favorite song is a laidback reggae number named *Under the Sea,* sung by Samuel E. Wright in such a splendid blend of animation and music that I recommend it to the cable music channels. The movie was written and directed by John Musker and Ron Clements, who made the entertaining *The Great Mouse Detective* (1986), and the songs are by Alan Menken and the coproducer, Howard Ashman, who did *Little Shop of Horrors.*

Something seems to have broken free inside all of these men, and the animating directors they worked with: Here at last, once again, is the kind of liberating, original, joyful Disney animation that we remember from *Snow White, Pinocchio,* and the other first-generation classics. There has been a notion in recent years that animated films are only for kids. But why? The artistry of animation has a clarity and a force that can appeal to everyone, if only it isn't shackled to a dimwitted story. *The Little Mermaid* has music and laughter and visual delight for everyone.

Little Murders

R, 110 m., 1971

Elliott Gould (Alfred Chamberlain), Marcia Rodd (Patsy Newquist), Vincent Gardenia (Mr. Newquist), Donald Sutherland (Reverend Dupas), Alan Arkin (Lieutenant Practice). Directed by Arkin and produced by Jack Brodsky. Screenplay by Jules Feiffer, based on his play.

Alan Arkin's *Little Murders* is a very New York kind of movie: paranoid, masochistic, and nervous. It left me with a cold knot in my stomach, a vague fear that something was gaining on me. It's a movie about people driven to insanity and desperate acts of violence by the simple experience of living in a large American city.

It falls somewhere within the category of satire, but Arkin has been careful to keep the satire within very tight and self-consistent boundaries. This isn't the kind of satire that lets up occasionally, that opens a window to the merely ridiculous (as *Dr. Strangelove* did), so that we can laugh and relax and brace ourselves for the next stretch of painfulness. No, *Little Murders* is entirely self-contained, and once you get inside it, you've got to stay.

Arkin said, shortly after the film was released, that he'd seen his movie only once in a theater, and he was afraid to go again. When he saw it with an audience, he said, he thought it was a flop because there was no pattern to the laughs. People were laughing as individuals, almost uneasily, as specific things in the movie touched or clobbered them.

That's my feeling about *Little Murders.* One of the reasons it works, and is indeed a definitive reflection of America's darker moods, is that it breaks audiences down into isolated individuals, vulnerable and uncertain. Most movies create a temporary sort of democracy, a community of strangers there in the darkened theater. Not this one. The movie seems to be saying that New York City has a similar effect on its citizens and that it will get you if you don't watch out.

Jules Feiffer's screenplay is about Alfred, "a devout apathist" who gets by in New York, sort of, by deadening himself to the terrible cries, smells, sights, and pains the city keeps lobbing at him like flies and grounders. You can't feel pain if you can't feel anything. If the absence of sensation means a living death, then perhaps zombies are merely creatures thrown up by evolution to live in the urban environment.

Alfred, a zombie, meets Patsy, an optimist, who keeps smiling through a wilderness of muggings, sniping, bombings, and obscene telephone calls because if she lets such things get at her, what'd be the use of living? Indeed. Patsy makes her life in New York a happy one, according to her, by consuming fashionable possessions, places, and opinions. She introduces Alfred to this glorious existence and, sure enough, the good life breaks through his shell. He falls in love.

This stretch of the movie—Patsy's courtship of Alfred—contains some awfully interesting ideas about the materialistic society. It seems to be saying that city life has cut its characters off from simple human emotion, and they've forgotten how to love or be sorry. Sharp, intense experiences can still penetrate the shell: sex, pain, getting fired. But the gentler emotions have atrophied.

Consumer buying power, however, may be a form of salvation. City dwellers can set out on self-improvement programs designed to restore their emotional muscles. By vacationing at expensive resorts, eating in intimate restaurants, possessing fashionable artifacts, people may actually be able to learn (from objects!) how to be people. It's significant here that Patsy is an interior decorator; she sees her own life largely in terms of the possessions and attitudes she has arranged around it.

The city finally defeats her, however, but not before Alfred finds a harbor in her family. Patsy's father, mother, and brother perform a hysterical parody of "family life," and Alfred fits right in. He even helps break down their

apathy. They'd been content to do merely passive things such as install steel shutters on their windows and triple locks on their doors. He buys a rifle and encourages them to start shooting back.

Elliott Gould's performance as Alfred sets the movie's acting tone, which is uptight, barely controlled (but somehow low-key) hysteria. An illustration would be Donald Sutherland's brilliant cameo as a progressive minister who uses the concept of love as a bludgeon. Arkin makes *Little Murders* so much of a piece, so consistent on its own terms, that while you're watching it, it doesn't even feel like satire—just real life, a little farther down the road.

The Lives of Others

R, 137 m., 2006

Ulrich Mühe (Captain Gerd Wiesler), Sebastian Koch (Georg Dreyman), Martina Gedeck (Christa-Maria Sieland), Ulrich Tukur (Lieutenant Colonel Anton Grubitz), Thomas Thieme (Minister Bruno Hempf), Hans-Uwe Bauer (Paul Hauser), Herbert Knaup (Gregor Hessenstein), Volkmar Kleinert (Albert Jerska), Matthias Brenner (Karl Wallner), Charly Hübner (Udo). Written and directed by Florian Henckel von Donnersmarck. Produced by Quirin Berg and Max Widermann.

He sits like a man taking a hearing test, big headphones clamped over his ears, his body and face frozen, listening for a far-away sound. His name is Gerd Wiesler, and he is a captain in the Stasi, the notorious secret police of East Germany. The year is, appropriately, 1984, and he is Big Brother, watching. He sits in an attic day after day, night after night, spying on the people in the flat below.

The flat is occupied by a playwright named Dreyman (Sebastian Koch) and his mistress, the actress Christa-Maria Sieland (Martina Gedeck). Wiesler (Ulrich Mühe) first saw Dreyman at the opening of one of his plays, where he was informed by a colleague that Dreyman was a valuable man: "One of our only writers who is read in the West and is loyal to our government." How can that be? Wiesler wonders. Dreyman is good-looking, successful, with a beautiful lover; he must be getting away with something. Driven by suspicion, or perhaps by envy or simple curiosity, Wiesler has Dreyman's flat wired and begins an official eavesdropping.

He doesn't fine a shred of evidence that Dreyman is disloyal. Not even in whispers. Not even in guarded allusions. Not even during pillow talk. The man obviously believes in the East German version of socialism, and the implication is that not even the Stasi can believe that. They are looking for dissent and subversion because, in a way, they think a man like Dreyman *should* be guilty of them. Perhaps they do not believe in East Germany themselves, but have simply chosen to play for the winning team.

Wiesler is a fascinating character. His face is a mask, trained by his life to reflect no emotion. Sometimes not even his eyes move. As played in Mühe's performance of infinite subtlety, he watches Dreyman as a cat awaits a mouse. And he begins to internalize their lives—easy, because he has no life of his own, no lover, no hobby, no distraction from his single-minded job.

Although the movie won the Academy Award for the best foreign-language film of 2006, you may not have seen it, so I will repress certain developments. I will say that Wiesler arrives at a choice, when his piggish superior officer, the government minister Bruno Hempf (Thomas Thieme), develops a lust for Christa Maria, and orders Wiesler to pin something, anything, on Dreyman so that his rival will be eliminated. But there is nothing to pin on him. A loyal spy must be true to his trade, and now Wiesler is asked to be false to prove his loyalty.

The thing is, Wiesler has no one he can really talk to. He lives in a world of such paranoia that the slightest slip can be disastrous. Consider a scene in the Stasi cafeteria when a young officer unwisely cracks an anti-government joke; Wiesler goes through the motions of laughter, and then coldly asks for the man's name. The same could happen to Wiesler. So as he proceeds through his crisis, he has no one to confide in, and there is no interior monologue to inform us of his thoughts. There is only that blank face, and the smallest indications of what he might be thinking. And then instinctive decisions that choose his course for him.

The Berlin Wall falls in 1989 (the event is seen here), and the story continues for a few more years to an ironic and surprisingly satisfactory conclusion. But the movie is relevant today, as our government ignores habeas corpus, practices secret torture, and asks for the right to wiretap and eavesdrop on its citizens. Such tactics did not save East Germany; they destroyed it, by making it a country its most loyal citizens could no longer believe in. Driven by the specter of aggression from without, it countered it with aggression from within, as sort of an anti-toxin. Fearing that its citizens were disloyal, it inspired them to be. True, its enemies were real. But the West never dropped the bomb, and East Germany and the other USSR republics imploded after essentially bombing themselves.

The Lives of Others is a powerful but quiet film, constructed of hidden thoughts and secret desires. It begins with Wiesler teaching a class in the theory and practice of interrogation; one chilling detail is that suspects are forced to sit on their hands, so that the chair cushion can be saved for possible use by bloodhounds. It shows how the Wall finally fell, not with a bang, but because of whispers.

Note: In the movie, one lover is a government informer. In real life, the actor Mühe discovered that his own wife was a Stasi informant.

Local Hero

PG, 112 m., 1983

Burt Lancaster (Happer), Peter Riegert (Mac), Peter Capaldi (Danny), Fulton McKay (Ben), Denis Lawson (Urquhart). Directed by Bill Forsyth and produced by David Puttnam. Screenplay by Forsyth.

Here is a small film to treasure; a loving, funny, understated portrait of a small Scottish town and its encounter with a giant oil company. The town is tucked away in a sparkling little bay, and is so small that everybody is well aware of everybody else's foibles. The oil company is run by an eccentric billionaire (Burt Lancaster) who would really rather have a comet named after him than own all the oil in the world. And what could have been a standard plot about conglomerates and ecology, etc., turns instead into a wicked study of human nature.

The movie opens in Houston, but quickly moves to the fishing village of Ferness. The oil company assigns an earnest young American (Peter Riegert) and a whimsical Scot (Peter Capaldi) to go to Ferness, and buy it up, lock, stock, and beachline, for a North Sea oil-refining complex. This is a simpler job than it appears, since a lot of the locals are all too willing to soak the oil company for its millions of dollars, sell the beach, and go in search of the bright lights of Edinburgh. But there are complications. One of them is old Ben, the cheerful philosopher who lives in a shack on the beach. It turns out that the beach has been the legal property of Ben's family for four centuries, ever since an ancestor did a favor for the king. And Ben doesn't want to sell: "Who'd look after the beach then? It would go to pieces in a short matter of time."

The local negotiations are handled by the innkeeper, Urquhart (Denis Lawson). He also is the accountant, and sort of the mayor, I guess, and is so much in love with his pretty wife that they're forever dashing upstairs for a quickie. Meanwhile, Riegert and Capaldi fall under the spell of the town, settle into its rhythms, become wrapped up in its intrigues, and, in general, are co-opted by a place whose charms are seductive.

What makes this material really work is the low-key approach of the writer-director, Bill Forsyth, who also made the charming *Gregory's Girl* and has the patience to let his characters gradually reveal themselves to the camera. He never hurries, and as a result, *Local Hero* never drags: Nothing is more absorbing than human personalities, developed with love and humor. Some of the payoffs in this film are sly and subtle, and others generate big laughs. Forsyth's big scenes are his little ones, including a heartfelt, whiskey-soaked talk between the American and the innkeeper, and a scene where the visitors walk on the beach and talk about the meaning of life. By the time Burt Lancaster reappears at the end of the film, to personally handle the negotiations with old Ben, *Local Hero* could hardly have anything but a happy ending. But it's a fairly close call.

Lone Star

R, 136 m., 1996

Chris Cooper (Sam Deeds), Elizabeth Pena (Pilar), Kris Kristofferson (Charlie Wade), Joe Morton (Delmore Payne), Ron Canada (Otis Payne), Clifton James (Hollis Pogue), Matthew McConaughey (Buddy Deeds), Miriam Colon (Mercedes Cruz), Frances McDormand (Bunny), Stephen Mendillo (Cliff), Stephen J. Lang (Mikey). Directed by John Sayles and produced by R. Paul Miller and Maggie Renzi. Screenplay by Sayles.

John Sayles's *Lone Star* contains so many riches it humbles ordinary movies. And yet they aren't thrown before us to dazzle and impress: It is only later, thinking about the film, that we appreciate the full reach of its material. I've seen it twice, and after the second viewing I began to realize how deeply, how subtly, the film has been constructed.

On the surface, it's pure entertainment. It involves the discovery of a skeleton in the desert of a Texas town near the Mexican border. The bones belong to a sheriff from the 1950s, much hated. The current sheriff suspects the murder may have been committed by his own father. As he explores the secrets of the past, he begins to fall in love all over again with the woman he loved when they were teenagers.

Those stories—the murder and the romance—provide the spine of the film and draw us through to the end. But Sayles is up to a lot more than murders and love stories. We begin to get a feel for the people of Rio County, where whites, blacks, Chicanos, and Seminole Indians all remember the past in different ways. We understand that the dead man, Sheriff Charlie Wade, was a sadistic monster who strutted through life, his gun on his hip, making up the law as he went along. That many people had reason to kill him—not least his deputy, Buddy Deeds (Matthew McConaughey). They exchanged death threats in a restaurant shortly before Charlie disappeared. Buddy became the next sheriff.

Now Charlie's skull, badge, and Masonic ring have been discovered on an old army firing range, and Buddy's son, Sam Deeds (Chris Cooper), is the sheriff on the case. He wanders through town, talking to his father's old deputy (Clifton James), and to Big Otis (Ron Canada), who ran the only bar in the county where blacks were welcome, and to Mercedes Cruz (Miriam Colon), who runs the popular Mexican restaurant where the death threat took place.

THE LONG GOOD FRIDAY ★ ★ ★ ★ **437**

Along the way, Sam does a favor. A kid has been arrested for maybe stealing car radios. He releases him to the custody of his mother, Pilar (Elizabeth Pena). He is pleased to see her again. Pilar and Sam were in love as teenagers, but their parents forced them to break up, maybe because both families opposed a Mexican-Anglo marriage. Now, tentatively, they begin to see each other again. One night in an empty restaurant, they play "Since I Met You Baby" on the jukebox and dance, having first circled each other warily in a moment of great eroticism.

All of these events unfold so naturally and absorbingly that all we can do is simply follow along. Sayles has made other films following many threads (his *City of Hope* in 1991 traced a tangled human web through the politics of a New Jersey city). But never before has he done it in such a spellbinding way; like Faulkner, he creates a sure sense of the way the past haunts the present, and how old wounds and secrets are visited upon the survivors.

Lone Star is not simply about the solution to the murder and the outcome of the romance. It is about how people try to live together at this moment in America. There are scenes that at first seem to have little to do with the main lines of the story. A school board meeting, for example, at which parents argue about textbooks (and are really arguing about whose view of Texas history will prevail). Scenes involving the African-American colonel (Joe Morton) in charge of the local army base, whose father was Big Otis, owner of the bar. Another scene involving a young black woman, an army private, whose interview with her commanding officer reveals a startling insight into why people enlist in the army. And conversations between Sheriff Deeds and old widows with long memories.

The performances are all perfectly eased together; you feel these characters have lived together for a long time and known things they have not spoken about for years. Chris Cooper, as Sam Deeds, is a tall, laconic presence who moves through the film, learning something here and something there and eventually learning something about himself. Cooper looks a little like Sayles; they project the same watchful intelligence.

As Pilar, Elizabeth Pena is a warm, rich female presence; her love for Sam is not based on anything simple like eroticism or need, but on a deep, fierce conviction that this should be her man. Kris Kristofferson is hard-edged and mean-eyed as Charlie Wade, and there is a scene where he shoots a man and then dares his deputy to say anything about it. Wade's evil spirit in the past is what haunts the whole film and must be exorcised.

And then there is so much more. I will not even hint at the surprises waiting for you in this film. They're not Hollywood-style surprises—or yes, in a way, they are—but they're also truths that grow out of the characters; what we learn seems not only natural, but instructive, and by the end of the film we know something about how people have lived together in this town, and what it has cost them.

Lone Star is a great American movie, one of the few to seriously try to regard with open eyes the way we live now. Set in a town that until very recently was rigidly segregated, it shows how Chicanos, blacks, whites, and Indians shared a common history, and how they knew each other and dealt with each other in ways that were off the official map. This film is a wonder—the best work yet by one of our most original and independent filmmakers—and after it is over and you think about it, its meanings begin to flower.

The Long Good Friday

R, 118 m., 1982

Bob Hoskins (Harold Shand), Helen Mirren (Victoria), Eddie Constantine (Charlie), Derek Thompson (Jeff), Bryan Marshall (Harris), Paul Freeman (Collin). Directed by John Mackenzie and produced by Barry Hanson. Screenplay by Barrie Keeffe.

Harold is as hard as a rock and he will crush you. He runs the London docks and he wants to put together the biggest real estate deal in Europe. He has Mafia money from America and the tacit cooperation of the London criminal organization. He's short, barrel-chested, with his thinning hair combed forward above a round face and teeth that always seem to be grinding. He cannot believe that in one weekend his whole world can come apart. Harold Shand is a hood, but he lives in a penthouse, anchors a world-class yacht in the Thames, has the love of an intelligent and tactful mistress, and talks obsessively about the ten years of peace he has helped negotiate in the London underground. Then a bomb blows up his Rolls Royce, killing his chauffeur. Another bomb demolishes the lovingly restored landmark pub he owns. A third bomb is found inside Harold's Mayfair casino, but fails to detonate. Who is after him? Who is his enemy? And why has the enemy chosen this worst of all possible times to come after him—the Easter weekend when an American Mafioso is in town to consider investing millions in his real estate project?

The Long Good Friday, which is a masterful and very tough piece of filmmaking, eventually does answer these questions. But the point of the film isn't to analyze Harold Shand's problems. It's to present a portrait of this man. And I have rarely seen a movie character so completely alive. Shand is an evil, cruel, sadistic man. But he's a mass of contradictions, and there are times when we understand him so completely we almost feel affection. He's such a character, such an overcompensating Cockney, sensitive to the slightest affront, able to strike fear in the hearts of killers, but a pushover when his mistress raises her voice to him. Shand is played by a compact, muscular actor named Bob Hoskins, in the most-praised film performance of the year from England. Hoskins has the energy and the freshness of a younger Michael Caine, if not the good looks, of course. There are scenes where he hangs his enemies upside down from meat hooks and questions them about the bombings, and other scenes, moments later, where he solemnly kids with the neighborhood juvenile delinquents and tries to soft-talk the American out of his millions.

He's an operator. He's a con man who has muscled his way to the top by knowing exactly how things work and what buttons to push, and now here he is, impotent before this faceless enemy. *The Long Good Friday* tells his story in a rather indirect way, opening with a montage of seemingly unrelated events, held together by a hypnotic music theme. Everything is eventually explained. It's all a big misunderstanding, based on stupid decisions taken by Shand's underlings and misinterpreted by the IRA. But although we know the real story, and Harold Shand does, the IRA

never does—and the movie's final shots are, quite simply, extraordinary close-ups, held for a long time, of Shand's ratlike face in close-up, as his eyes shift from side to side, and his mouth breaks into a terrified grin, and he realizes how it feels to get a dose of his own medicine. This movie is one amazing piece of work, not only for the Hoskins performance but also for the energy of the filmmaking, the power of the music, and, oddly enough, for the engaging quality of its sometimes very violent sense of humor.

Lorenzo's Oil

PG-13, 135 m., 1993

Nick Nolte (Augusto Odone), Susan Sarandon (Michaela Odone), Peter Ustinov (Professor Nikolais), Zack O'Malley Greenburg (Lorenzo), Kathleen Wilhoite (Deirdre Murphy), Gerry Bamman (Doctor Judalon), Margo Martindale (Wendy Gimble). Directed by George Miller and produced by Doug Mitchell and Miller. Screenplay by Miller and Nick Enright.

You may have heard that *Lorenzo's Oil* is a harrowing movie experience. It is, but in the best way. It takes a heartbreaking story and pushes it to the limit, showing us the lengths of courage and imagination that people can summon when they must. The performances, by Susan Sarandon and Nick Nolte, are daring, too: They play a married couple sometimes too exhausted and obsessed to even be nice to one another. But they share a common goal. They want to save their son's life.

When doctors urge a dying patient to have patience while research continues into the cure for their disease, what they are saying is, please be patient enough to wait until after your death while we work on this. That is not much consolation for the parents when the patient is their little boy, stricken in the dawn of life. Some assume that the doctors know best—as, indeed, usually they do. Some strike out with anger or denial.

Augusto and Michaela Odone, the real-life models for the parents in *Lorenzo's Oil,* went through all of those stages when their son was diagnosed with adrenoleukodystrophy (ALD), a rare nerve disease that strikes only little boys and was always fatal. They decided to take matters into their own hands. Knocking on doors, haunting research libraries, reading everything, talking to the parents of other sick children, using intuition, they actually discovered a treatment for the disease, employing humble olive oil.

The last frames of *Lorenzo's Oil* provide a montage of young boys who are healthy and active today because of the work of the Odones. One doesn't know whether to laugh or weep; their good fortune comes after hundreds of other children were gradually imprisoned inside their own bodies, blind, deaf, unable to touch or taste, because of the disease that was strangling their nervous systems.

The movie has been directed, coproduced, and cowritten by George Miller *(Road Warrior, The Witches of Eastwick)*, a filmmaker who is also a medical doctor. He does not insult the intelligence of the audience by turning this story into a disease-of-the-week docudrama. We follow the thought process of Augusto Odone as he asks questions, makes connections, and uses common sense: If his son's body is breaking down the fatty sheath that protects the nerves, is there a way to replace the fat, or frustrate the process?

While Augusto spends months in research libraries (where the librarians eventually share his quest), his wife maintains a stubborn, even mad, conviction that her boy will get well. The child is moved home to the living room, which is converted into a hospital ward. Nurses are hired around the clock. Convinced that her boy is alive and alert inside the shell of his body, Michaela reads to him by the hour, and hires other readers—firing one employee after another for not sharing her unbending vision.

There is probably as much dialogue in this movie as in two other films. Augusto and Michaela talk to each other in rapid-fire, impatient bursts; there is no time to lose if their child is to be saved. The screenplay incorporates a great deal of technical information, somehow making it comprehensible, so that we can understand the reasoning when scientists like the distinguished Professor Nikolais (Peter Ustinov) debate the Odones.

Nikolais represents the larger medical establishment, which Miller does not portray as a bunch of conservative, unfeeling clods. He shows the doctors and researchers doing their jobs conscientiously, and doubting the claims of the Odones because, after all, they are not the first parents of a dying child to grasp at any straw.

I was distracted at first by the Italian accent Nolte uses in the film, not because it is badly done (he sounds much like the real Odone, who has appeared on talk shows), but because it seems odd to hear Nolte with an accent. But eventually the accent issue fell by the side; this is an immensely moving and challenging movie, and it is impossible not to get swept up in it.

Lost in America
R, 90 m., 1985

Albert Brooks (David Howard), Julie Hagerty (Linda Howard), Garry K. Marshall (Casino Boss), Art Frankel (Job Counselor). Directed by Albert Brooks and produced by Marty Katz. Screenplay by Brooks and Monica Johnson.

Every time I see a Winnebago motor home, I have the same fantasy as the hero of *Lost in America*. In my dream, I quit my job, sell everything I own, buy the Winnebago, and hit the open road. Where do I go? Look for me in the weather reports. I'll be parked by the side of a mountain stream, listening to Mozart on compact discs. All I'll need is a wok and a paperback.

In *Lost in America*, Albert Brooks plays an advertising executive in his thirties who realizes that dream. He leaves his job, talks his wife into quitting hers, and they point their Winnebago down that long, lonesome highway. This is not, however, a remake of *The Long, Long Trailer*. Brooks puts a different spin on things. For example, when movie characters leave their jobs, it's usually because they've been fired, they've decided to take an ethical stand, or the company has gone broke. Only in a movie by Brooks would the hero quit to protest a "lateral transfer" to New York. There's something intrinsically comic about that: He's taking a stand, all right, but it's a narcissistic one. He's quitting because he wants to stay in Los Angeles, he thinks he deserves to be named vice president, and he doesn't like the traffic in New York.

Lost in America is being called a yuppie comedy, but it's really about the much more universal subjects of greed, hedonism, and panic. What makes it so funny is how much we can identify with it. Brooks plays a character who is making a lot of money, but not enough; who lives in a big house, but is outgrowing it; who drives an expensive car, but not a Mercedes-Benz; who is a top executive, but not a vice president. In short, he is a desperate man, trapped by his own expectations.

On the morning of his last day at work, he puts everything on hold while he has a long, luxurious telephone conversation with a Mercedes dealer. Brooks has great telephone scenes in all of his movies, but this one perfectly captures the nuances of consumerism. He asks how much the car will cost—including *everything*. Dealer prep, license, sticker, add-ons, extras, *everything*. The dealer names a price.

"That's *everything?*" Brooks asks.

"Except leather," the dealer says.

"For what I'm paying, I don't get leather?" Brooks asks, aghast.

"You get Mercedes leather."

"*Mercedes* leather? What's that?"

"Thick vinyl."

This is the kind of world Brooks is up against. A few minutes later, he's called into the boss's office and told that he will not get the promotion he thinks he deserves. Instead, he's going to New York to handle the Ford account. Brooks quits, and a few scenes later, he and his wife (Julie Hagerty) are tooling the big Winnebago into Las Vegas. They have enough money, he conservatively estimates, to stay on the road for the rest of their lives. That's before she loses their nest egg at the roulette tables.

Lost in America doesn't tell a story so much as assemble a series of self-contained comic scenes, and the movie's next scene is probably the best one in the movie. Brooks the adman tries to talk a casino owner (Garry K. Marshall) into giving back the money. It doesn't work, but Brooks keeps pushing, trying to sell the casino on improving its image. ("I'm a high-paid advertising consultant. These are professional opinions you're getting.") There are other great scenes, as the desperate couple tries to find work to support themselves: An interview with an unemployment counselor,

who listens, baffled, to Brooks explaining why he left a $100,000-a-year job because he couldn't "find himself." And Brooks's wife introducing her new boss, a teenage boy.

Lost in America has one strange flaw. It doesn't seem to come to a conclusion. It just sort of ends in midstream, as if the final scenes were never shot. I don't know if that's the actual case, but I do wish the movie had been longer and had arrived at some sort of final destination. What we do get, however, is observant and very funny. Brooks is especially good at hearing exactly how people talk, and how that reveals things about themselves. Take that line about "Mercedes leather." A lot of people would be very happy to sit on "Mercedes leather." But not a Mercedes owner, of course. How did Joni Mitchell put it? "Don't it always seem to go, that you don't know what you've got, till it's gone."

Lost in Translation
R, 105 m., 2003

Bill Murray (Bob Harris), Scarlett Johansson (Charlotte), Giovanni Ribisi (John), Anna Faris (Kelly). Directed by Sofia Coppola and produced by Coppola and Ross Katz. Screenplay by Coppola.

The Japanese phrase *mono no aware* is a bittersweet reference to the transience of life. It came to mind as I was watching *Lost in Translation,* which is sweet and sad at the same time it is sardonic and funny. Bill Murray and Scarlett Johansson play two lost souls rattling around a Tokyo hotel in the middle of the night, who fall into conversation about their marriages, their happiness, and the meaning of it all.

Such conversations can really be held only with strangers. We all need to talk about metaphysics, but those who know us well want details and specifics; strangers allow us to operate more vaguely on a cosmic scale. When the talk occurs between two people who could plausibly have sex together, it gathers a special charge: You can only say, "I feel like I've known you for years" to someone you have not known for years. Funny, how your spouse doesn't understand the bittersweet transience of life as well as a stranger encountered in a hotel bar. Especially if drinking is involved.

Murray plays Bob Harris, an American movie star in Japan to make commercials for whiskey. "Do I need to worry about you, Bob?" his wife asks over the phone. "Only if you want to," he says. She sends him urgent faxes about fabric samples. Johansson plays Charlotte, whose husband, John, is a photographer on assignment in Tokyo. She visits a shrine and then calls a friend in America to say, "I didn't feel anything." Then she blurts out: "I don't know who I married."

She's in her early twenties; Bob's in his fifties. This is the classic setup for a May-November romance, since in the mathematics of celebrity intergenerational dating you can take five years off the man's age for every million dollars of income. But *Lost in Translation* is too smart and thoughtful to be the kind of movie where they go to bed and we're supposed to accept that as the answer. Sofia Coppola, who wrote, coproduced, and directed, doesn't let them off the hook that easily. They share something as personal as their feelings rather than something as generic as their genitals.

These are two wonderful performances. Bill Murray has never been better. He doesn't play "Bill Murray" or any other conventional idea of a movie star, but invents Bob Harris from the inside out, as a man both happy and sad with his life—stuck, but resigned to being stuck. Marriage is not easy for him, and his wife's voice over the phone is on autopilot. But he loves his children. They are miracles, he confesses to Charlotte. Not his children specifically, but—children.

He is very tired, he is doing the commercials for money and hates himself for it, he has a sense of humor and can be funny, but it's a bother. She has been married only a couple of years, but it's clear her husband thinks she's in the way. Filled with his own importance, flattered that a starlet knows his name, he leaves her behind in the hotel room because—how does it go?—he'll be working, and she won't have a good time if she comes along with him.

Ingmar Bergman's *Scenes from a Marriage* was about a couple who met years after their divorce and found themselves "in the middle of the night in a dark house somewhere in the world." That's how Bob and Charlotte seem to me. Most of time nobody knows where they are, or cares, and their togetherness is all

that keeps them both from being lost and alone. They go to karaoke bars and drug parties, pachinko parlors and, again and again, the hotel bar. They wander Tokyo, an alien metropolis to which they lack the key. They don't talk in the long, literate sentences of the characters in *Before Sunrise*, but in the weary understatements of those who don't have the answers.

Now from all I've said you wouldn't guess the movie is also a comedy, but it is. Basically, it's a comedy of manners—Japan's, and ours. Bob Harris goes everywhere surrounded by a cloud of white-gloved women who bow and thank him for—allowing himself to be thanked, I guess. Then there's the director of the whiskey commercial, whose movements for some reason reminded me of Cab Calloway performing *Minnie the Moocher*. And the hooker sent up to Bob's room, whose approach is melodramatic and archaic; she has obviously not studied the admirable Japanese achievements in porno. And the B-movie starlet (Anna Faris), intoxicated with her own wonderfulness.

In these scenes there are opportunities for Murray to turn up the heat under his comic persona. He doesn't. He always stays in character. He is always Bob Harris, who *could* be funny, who *could* be the life of the party, who *could* do impressions in the karaoke bar and play games with the director of the TV commercial, but doesn't—because being funny is what he does for a living, and right now he is too tired and sad to do it for free. Except . . . a little. That's where you see the fine-tuning of Murray's performance. In a subdued, fond way, he gives us wry, faint comic gestures, as if to show what he could do, if he wanted to.

Well, I loved this movie. I loved the way Coppola and her actors negotiated the hazards of romance and comedy, taking what little they needed and depending for the rest on the truth of the characters. I loved the way Bob and Charlotte didn't solve their problems, but felt a little better anyway. I loved the moment near the end when Bob runs after Charlotte and says something in her ear, and we're not allowed to hear it. We shouldn't be allowed to hear it. It's between them, and by this point in the movie they've become real enough to deserve their privacy. Maybe he gave her his phone number.

Or said he loved her. Or said she was a good person. Or thanked her. Or whispered, "Had we but world enough, and time . . ." and left her to look up the rest of it.

Lovely and Amazing
R, 89 m., 2002

Catherine Keener (Michelle Marks), Brenda Blethyn (Jane Marks), Emily Mortimer (Elizabeth Marks), Raven Goodwin (Annie Marks), Aunjanue Ellis (Lorraine), Clark Gregg (Bill), Jake Gyllenhaal (Jordan), James LeGros (Paul), Dermot Mulroney (Kevin McCabe), Michael Nouri (Dr. Crane). Directed by Nicole Holofcener and produced by Anthony Bregman, Eric d'Arbeloff, and Ted Hope. Screenplay by Holofcener.

The four women in *Lovely and Amazing* have been described as a dysfunctional family, but they function better than some, and at least they're out there looking. Here is a movie that knows its women, listens to them, doesn't give them a pass, allows them to be real: It's a rebuke to the shallow *Ya-Ya Sisterhood.*

Jane Marks (Brenda Blethyn), the mother, fiftyish, had two daughters at the usual season of her life, and now has adopted a third, eight-year-old Annie (Raven Goodwin), who is African-American. Her grown daughters are Michelle (Catherine Keener), who tries to escape from a pointless marriage through her pointless art, and Elizabeth (Emily Mortimer), who is an actress who cares more about dogs than acting.

All of these women are smart, which is important in a story like this. The mistakes they make come through trying too hard and feeling too insecure. They're not based on dumb plot points. They're the kinds of things real people do. And thank God they have a sense of humor about their lives, and a certain zest: They aren't victims but participants. They're even mean sometimes.

Men are a problem. Michelle's husband, Bill (Clark Gregg), is tired of paying all the bills while she sits at home making twee little chairs out of twigs. She accuses him of stepping on one of the chairs deliberately. He informs her that her "art" is worthless. Indeed her chairs are the sorts of collectibles made by the clueless for the clueless. But there is a deeper impulse at work: Her art allows her a zone free of her husband, a zone that insists she is creative and important.

Elizabeth, the actress, is like most actresses, filled with paralyzing doubt about her looks, her body, her talent. Annie, the adopted child, understandably wonders why she is black when everyone else in the family is white, and asks blunt questions about skin and hair. She also eats too much, and is already learning denial: "I'm not gonna eat *all* this," she tells Michelle, who finds her at McDonald's after she has disappeared from home. "I just couldn't make up my mind."

Where did she learn that reasoning? Perhaps from her mother. As the film opens, Jane has gone into the hospital to have liposuction, and there is a complicated dynamic going on because in some sense she dreams that her handsome surgeon (Michael Nouri) will first improve her, then seduce her.

All of these women are obsessed by body image. There is a scene of uncomfortable truth when Elizabeth sleeps with Kevin, a fellow actor (an indifferent, narcissistic hunk played by Dermot Mulroney), and then stands before him naked, demanding that he subject her body to a minute commentary and critique. When he misses her flabby underarms, she points them out.

When I saw the movie for the first time at Telluride, I noticed a curious thing about the audience. During most nude scenes involving women, men are silent and intent. During this scene, which was not focused on sexuality but on an actual female body, attractive but imperfect, it was the women who leaned forward in rapt attention. Nicole Holofcener, who wrote and directed *Lovely and Amazing,* is onto something: Her movie knows how these women relate to men, to each other, to their bodies, and to their prospects of happiness.

Consider Elizabeth again. She picks up stray dogs—even dogs not much hoping to be adopted. One of them bites her. We have already seen how obsessed she is with her body, and yet she never even mentions the scarring that will result; it's as if the dog bite releases her from a duty to be perfect. Little Annie is certainly obsessed by being plump—she got that from Jane, probably along with the overeating—but she finds another unexpected image problem. An adult black woman, who volunteers to be her big sister, is disappointed: "When I signed up, I thought I was going to get somebody who was poor."

Michelle's husband is manifestly no longer interested in her. When he insists she get a job, she goes to work at a one-hour photo stand, where a fellow employee, a teenage boy (Jake Gyllenhaal), gets a crazy crush on her. She is not impervious to being adored. She likes this kid. She even winds up in his bedroom. And here Holofcener does something almost no other movie ever does: holds an adult woman to the same standard as an adult man. Michelle knows the age difference makes them wrong as a couple. The kid's mother calls the cops and accuses Michelle of statutory rape. There is some doubt about what exactly has taken place, but at least *Lovely and Amazing* doesn't repeat the hypocrisy that it's all right for adult women to seduce boys, but wrong for adult men to seduce girls.

Scene after scene in this movie has the fascination of lives lived by those willing to break loose, to try something new. *Lovely and Amazing* is not about the plight of its women but about their opportunities, and how in their disorganized, slightly goofy way they persist in seeking the good and the true. I hope I haven't made the film sound like a docudrama or a message picture: It has no message, other than to celebrate the lives of these imperfect women, and the joy of their imperfections.

Love Story

PG, 100 m., 1970

Ali MacGraw (Jenny Cavilleri), Ryan O'Neal (Oliver Barrett IV), Ray Milland (Oliver Barrett III), John Marley (Phil Cavilleri). Directed by Arthur Hiller and produced by Howard G. Minsky. Screenplay by Erich Segal, based on his book.

I read *Love Story* one morning in about fourteen minutes flat, out of simple curiosity. I wanted to discover why five and a half million people had actually bought it. I wasn't successful. I was so put off by Erich Segal's writing style, in fact, that I hardly wanted to see the movie at all. Segal's prose style is so revoltingly coy—sort of a cross between a parody of Hemingway and the instructions on a soup can—that his story is fatally infected.

The fact is, however, that the film of *Love Story* is infinitely better than the book. I think it has something to do with the quiet taste of Arthur Hiller, its director, who has put in all the things that Segal thought he was being clever to leave out. Things like color, character, personality, detail, and background. The interesting thing is that Hiller has saved the movie without substantially changing anything in the book. Both the screenplay and the novel were written at the same time, I understand, and if you've read the book, you've essentially read the screenplay. Nothing much is changed except the last meeting between Oliver and his father; Hiller felt the movie should end with the boy alone, and he was right. Otherwise, he's used Segal's situations and dialogue throughout. But the Segal characters, on paper, were so devoid of any personality that they might actually have been transparent. Ali MacGraw and Ryan O'Neal, who play the lovers on film, bring them to life in a way the novel didn't even attempt. They do it simply by being there, and having personalities.

The story by now is so well-known that there's no point in summarizing it for you. I would like to consider, however, the implications of *Love Story* as a three-, four- or five-handkerchief movie, a movie that wants viewers to cry at the end. Is this an unworthy purpose? Does the movie become unworthy, as *Newsweek* thought it did, simply because it has been mechanically contrived to tell us a beautiful, tragic tale? I don't think so. There's nothing contemptible about being moved to joy by a musical, to terror by a thriller, to excitement by a Western. Why shouldn't we get a little misty during a story about young lovers separated by death?

Hiller earns our emotional response because of the way he's directed the movie. The Segal book was so patently contrived to force those tears, and moved toward that object with such humorless determination, that it must have actually disgusted a lot of readers. The movie is mostly about life, however, and not death. And because Hiller makes the lovers into individuals, of course we're moved by the film's conclusion. Why not?

Love Streams

PG-13, 141 m., 1984

Gena Rowlands (Sarah Lawson), John Cassavetes (Robert Harmon), Diahnne Abbott (Susan), Seymour Cassel (Jack Lawson), Margaret Abbott (Margarita). Directed by Cassavetes and produced by Menahem Golan and Yoram Globus. Screenplay by Ted Allan and Cassavetes.

John Cassavetes's *Love Streams* is the kind of movie where a woman brings home two horses, a goat, a duck, some chickens, a dog, and a parrot, and you don't have the feeling that the screenplay is going for cheap laughs. In fact, there's a tightening in your throat as you realize how desperate an act you're witnessing, and how unhappy a person is getting out of the taxi with all those animals. The menagerie scene occurs rather late in the film, after we've already locked into Cassavetes's method. This is a movie about mad people, and they are going to be acting in crazy ways, but the movie isn't going to let us off the hook by making them funny or picaresque or even symbolic (as in *King of Hearts*). They are, quite simply, desperate.

The brother, Robert (played by Cassavetes), is a writer who lives up in the Hollywood Hills in one of those houses that looks like *Architectural Digest* Visits a Motel. He writes trashy novels about bad women. A parade of hookers marches through his life; he gathers them by the taxi load, almost as a hobby, and dismisses them with lots of meaningless words about how he loves them, and how they're sweethearts and babies and dolls. The circular drive in front of his house is constantly filled with the cars of the lonely and the desperate. He is an alcoholic who stays up for two or three days at a stretch, as if terrified of missing one single unhappy moment. The sister, Sarah (Gena Rowlands), is as possessive as her brother is evasive. She is in the process of a messy divorce from her husband (Seymour Cassel), and her daughter is in flight from her. Rowlands thinks that maybe she can buy love: First she buys the animals, later she talks about buying her brother a baby, because that's what he "needs."

At least Cassavetes and Rowlands can communicate. They share perfect trust, although

it is the trust of two people in the same trap. There are other characters in the movie that Cassavetes talks at and around, but not with. They include a bemused young singer (Diahnne Abbott) who goes out with Cassavetes but looks at him as if he were capable of imploding, and a former wife (Michele Conway) who turns up one day on the doorstep with a small boy and tells him: "This is your son." The way Cassavetes handles this news is typical of the movie. The woman wonders if maybe he could baby-sit for a weekend. He says he will. He brings the kid into the house, scares him away, chases him halfway down Laurel Canyon, brings him back, pours him a beer, has a heart-to-heart about "Women, Life and Marriage," and then asks the kid if he'd like to go to Vegas. Cut to Vegas. Cassavetes dumps the kid in a hotel room and goes out partying all night. He is incapable of any appropriate response to a situation requiring him to care about another human being. He fills his life with noise, hookers, emergencies, and booze to drown out the insistent whisper of duty.

The movie is exasperating, because we never know where we stand or what will happen next. I think that's one of its strengths: There's an exhilaration in this roller-coaster ride through scenes that come out of nowhere. This is not a docudrama or a little psychological playlet with a lesson to be learned. It is a raw, spontaneous life, and when we laugh (as in the scene where Cassavetes summons a doctor to the side of the unconscious Rowlands), we wince.

Viewers raised on trained and tame movies may be uncomfortable in the world of Cassavetes; his films are built around lots of talk and the waving of arms and the invoking of the gods. Cassavetes has been making these passionate personal movies for twenty-five years, ever since his *Shadows* helped create American underground movies. His titles include *Minnie and Moskowitz* (in which Rowlands and Cassel got married), *Faces, A Woman Under the Influence, The Killing of a Chinese Bookie, Gloria, Opening Night*, and *Husbands*. Sometimes (as in *Husbands*) the wild truth-telling approach evaporates into a lot of empty talk and play-acting. In *Love Streams*, it works.

Lucas

PG-13, 99 m., 1985

Corey Haim (Lucas), Kerri Green (Maggie), Charlie Sheen (Cappie), Courtney Thorne-Smith (Alise), Guy Bond (Coach). Directed by David Seltzer and produced by Lawrence Gordon and David Nicksay. Screenplay by Seltzer.

The first loves of early adolescence are so powerful because they are not based on romance, but on ideals. When they are thirteen and fourteen, boys and girls do not fall in love with one another because of all the usual reasons that are celebrated in love songs; they fall in love because the other person is perfect. Not smart or popular or goodlooking, but *perfect*, the embodiment of all good.

The very name of the loved one becomes a holy name, as you can see in *Lucas*, when the hero says, "Maggie. Is that short for Margaret?" And then hugs himself to find that it is, because he suddenly realizes that Margaret is the most wonderful name in all the world.

Everybody grows up, and sooner or later love becomes an experience that has limits and reasons. *Lucas* is a movie that takes place before that happens. It is about a very smart kid who looks a little too short and a little too young to be in high school, and when you tell him that, he nods and solemnly explains that he is "accelerated."

One summer day, while riding his bike through the leafy green of a suburb north of Chicago, he sees a red-haired girl practicing her tennis swing. He stops to speak to her, and before long they are fast friends who sit cross-legged in the grass, knees touching knees, and talk about things that begin with capital letters, like Life and Society and Art.

Lucas loves Maggie, but she is just a little older and more mature than he, and has her eye on a member of the football team. Lucas believes, of course, that the whole value system of football and cheerleaders and pep rallies is corrupt. Maggie says she agrees. But how can she argue when the football hero notices her, breaks up with his girlfriend, and asks her if he can have a kiss?

To describe this situation is to make *Lucas* sound like just one more film about teenage romance. But it would be tragic if this film got lost in the shuffle of "teenage movies." This is a movie that is as pure and true to the adolescent experience as Truffaut's *The 400 Blows*. It is true because it assumes all of its characters are intelligent, and do not want to hurt one another, and will refuse to go along with the stupid, painful conformity of high school.

The film centers around the character of Lucas, a skinny kid with glasses and a shock of unruly hair and a gift for trying to talk himself into situations where he doesn't belong. Lucas is played by Corey Haim, who was Sally Field's son in *Murphy's Romance*, and he does not give one of those cute little boy performances that get on your nerves. He creates one of the most three-dimensional, complicated, interesting characters of any age in any recent movie, and if he can continue to act this well he will never become a half-forgotten child star but will continue to grow into an important actor. He is that good.

But the film's other two major actors are just as effective. Kerri Green, who was in *The Goonies*, is so subtle and sensitive as Maggie that you realize she isn't just acting, she understands this character in her heart. As the football hero, Charlie Sheen in some ways has the most difficult role, because we're primed to see him in terms of clichés—the jock who comes along and wins the heart of the girl. Sheen doesn't play the character even remotely that way. It is a surprise to find that he loves Lucas, that he protects him from the goons at school, that although he has won Maggie away from Lucas, he cares very deeply about sparing the kid's feelings.

The last third of the movie revolves around a football game. So many films have ended with the "big match" or the "big game," that my heart started to sink when I saw the game being set up. Surely *Lucas* wasn't going to throw away all its great dialogue and inspired acting on another formula ending? Amazingly, the movie negotiates the football game without falling into predictability. Lucas finds himself in uniform and on the field under the most extraordinary circumstances, but they are plausible circumstances, and what happens then can hardly be predicted.

There are half a dozen scenes in the movie so well-done that they could make little short films of their own. They include: The time Lucas and Maggie listen to classical music and discuss her name; the scene between Maggie and the football hero in the high school's laundry room; the scene in which Lucas is humiliated at a school assembly, and turns the situation to his advantage; the way in which he takes the news that he will not be going to the dance with Maggie; and the very last scene in the whole movie, which is one of those moments of perfect vindication that makes you want to cry.

Lucas was written and directed by David Seltzer, who has obviously put his heart into the film. He has also used an enormous amount of sensibility. In a world where Hollywood has cheapened the teenage years into predictable vulgarity, he has remembered how urgent, how innocent, and how idealistic those years can be. He has put values into this movie. It is about teenagers who are learning how to be good to each other, to care, and not simply to be filled with egotism, lust, and selfishness—which is all most Hollywood movies think teenagers can experience. *Lucas* is one of the year's best films.

M

Maborosi

NO MPAA RATING, 110 m., 1997

Makiko Esumi (Yumiko), Takashi Naitoh (Tamio, Second Husband), Tadanobu Asano (Ikuo, First Husband), Gohki Kashiyama (Yuichi, Yumiko's Son), Naomi Watanabe (Tomoko, Tamio's Daughter), Midori Kiuchi (Michiko, Yumiko's Mother), Akira Emoto (Yoshihiro, Tamio's Father), Mutsuko Sakura (Tomeno). Directed by Hirokazu Kore-Eda and produced by Naoe Gozu. Screenplay by Yoshihisa Ogita, based on a story by Teru Miyamoto.

Maborosi is a Japanese film of astonishing beauty and sadness, the story of a woman whose happiness is destroyed in an instant by an event that seems to have no reason. Time passes, she picks up some of the pieces, and she is even distracted sometimes by happiness. But at her center is a void, a great unanswered question.

The woman, named Yumiko, is played by the fashion model Makiko Esumi. Models are not always good actresses, but Esumi is the right choice for this role. Tall, slender, and grave, she brings a great stillness to the screen. Her character speaks little; many shots show her seated in thought, absorbed in herself. She is dressed always in long, dark dresses—no pants or jeans—and she becomes after a while like a figure in an opera that has no song.

She is twenty when we meet her. She is happily, playfully married to Ikuo (Tadanobu Asano). They have a little boy, and there is a sunny scene where she bathes him. Then an inexplicable event takes place, and she is left a widow. Five years pass, and then a matchmaker finds a husband for her: Tamio (Takashi Naitoh), who lives with his young son in an isolated fishing village. At twenty-five, she starts her life again.

This is the first film by Hirokazu Kore-Eda, a young Japanese director whose love for the work of the great Yasujiro Ozu (1903–1963) is evident. Ozu is one of the four or five greatest directors of all time, and some of his visual touches are visible here. The camera, for example, is often placed at the eye level of someone kneeling on a tatami mat. Shots begin or end on empty rooms. Characters speak while seated side by side, not looking at one another. There are many long shots and few close-ups; the camera does not move, but regards.

In more obvious homage, Kore-Eda uses a technique which Ozu himself borrowed from Japanese poetry: the "pillow shot," inspired by "pillow words," which are words that do not lead out of or into the rest of the poem but provide a resting place, a pause or punctuation. Kore-Eda frequently cuts away from the action to simply look for a moment at something: a street, a doorway, a shop front, a view. And there are two small touches in which the young director subtly acknowledges the master: a characteristic tea kettle in the foreground of a shot, and a scene where the engine of a canal boat makes a sound so uncannily similar to the boat at the beginning of Ozu's *Floating Weeds* (1959) that it might have been lifted from the sound track.

But what, you are asking, do these details have to do with the movie at hand? I mention them because they indicate the care with which this beautiful film has been made, and they suggest its tradition. *Maborosi* is not going to insult us with a simpleminded plot. It is not a soap opera. Sometimes life presents us with large, painful, unanswerable questions, and we cannot simply "get over them."

There isn't a shot in the movie that's not graceful and pleasing. We get an almost physical sensation for the streets and rooms. Here are shots to look for:

The first husband walking off cheerfully down the street, swinging an umbrella. Her joy in bathing the baby. A child playing with a ball on a sloping concrete courtyard. Yumiko and her second husband sitting in front of an electric fan in the hot summertime, too exhausted to make love any longer. Yumiko, wearing a deep blue dress, almost lost in shadow at a bus stop. A funeral procession, framed in a long shot between the earth, the sea, and the sky. And a reconciliation seen at a great distance.

Maborosi is one of those valuable films where you have to actively place yourself in the character's mind. There are times when we do not know what she is thinking, but we are inspired with an active sympathy. We want to understand. Well, so does she. There's real dramatic suspense in the first scenes after she arrives at the little village. Will she like her new husband? Will their children get along? Can she live in such a backwater?

It's lovely how the film reveals the answers to these questions in such small details as a shot where she walks out her back door into the sunshine. Underneath these immediate questions, of course, lurk the bigger ones. "I just don't understand!" she says. "It just goes around and around in my head!" Her second husband offers an answer of sorts to her question. It is based on an experience fishermen sometimes have at sea, when they see a light or mirage that tempts them farther from shore. But what is the reason for the light?

Macbeth

R, 139 m., 1972

Jon Finch (Macbeth), Francesca Annis (Lady Macbeth), Martin Shaw (Banquo), Nicholas Selby (Duncan), John Stride (Ross), Stephen Chase (Malcolm), Paul Shelley (Donalbain), Terence Bayler (Macduff). Directed by Roman Polanski and produced by Andrew Braunsberg. Screenplay by Polanski and Kenneth Tynan.

We have all heard it a hundred times, Macbeth's despairing complaint about life: ". . . it is a tale told by an idiot, full of sound and fury, signifying nothing." But who has taken it more seriously than Roman Polanski, who tells his bloody masterpiece at precisely the level of the idiot's tale?

Macbeth always before seemed reasonable, dealing with a world in which wrongdoing was punished and logic demonstrated. Macbeth's character was not strong enough to stand up under the weight of the crime he committed, so he disintegrated into the fantasies of ignorant superstition, while his flimsy wife went mad.

It all seemed so clear. And at the proper moment, the forces of justice stepped forward, mocked the witches' prophecies which deluded poor Macbeth and set things right for the final curtain. There were, no doubt, those who thought the play was about how Malcolm became king of Scotland.

But in this film Polanski and his collaborator, Kenneth Tynan, place themselves at Macbeth's side and choose to share his point of view, and in their film there's no room at all for detachment. All those noble, tragic Macbeths—Orson Welles and Maurice Evans and the others—look like imposters now, and the king is revealed as a scared kid.

No effort has been made to make Macbeth a tragic figure, and his death moves us infinitely less than the murder of Macduff's young son. Polanski places us in a visual universe of rain and mist, of gray dawns and clammy dusks, and there is menace in the sound of hoofbeats but no cheer in the cry of trumpets. Even the heroic figure of Macduff has been tempered; now he is no longer the instrument of God's justice, but simply a man bent on workaday revenge. The movie ends with the simple fact that a job has been done: Macbeth got what was coming to him.

Polanski has imposed this vision on the film so effectively that even the banquet looks like a gang of highwaymen ready to wolf down stolen sheep. Everyone in the film seems to be pushed by circumstances; there is small feeling that the characters are motivated by ideas. They seem so ignorant at times that you wonder if they understand the wonderful dialogue Shakespeare has written for them. It's as if the play has been inhabited by Hell's Angels who are quick studies.

All of this, of course, makes Polanski's *Macbeth* more interesting than if he had done your ordinary, respectable, awe-stricken tiptoe around Shakespeare. This is an original film by an original film artist, and not an "interpretation." It should have been titled *Polanski's Macbeth*, just as we got *Fellini Satyricon*.

I might as well be honest and say it is impossible to watch certain scenes without thinking of the Charles Manson case. It is impossible to watch a film directed by Roman Polanski and not react on more than one level to such images as a baby being "untimely ripped from his mother's womb." Indeed, Polanski adds his own grim conclusion after Shakespeare's, with a final scene in which Malcolm, now crowned king, goes to consult the same witches who deceived Macbeth. Polanski's characters resemble Manson: They are anti-intellectual, witless, and driven by deep, shameful wells of lust and violence.

Why did Polanski choose to make *Macbeth*, and why this *Macbeth*? I have no way of guessing. This is certainly one of the most pessimistic films ever made, and there seems little doubt that Polanski intended his film to be full of sound and fury—which it is, to the brim—and to signify nothing.

It's at that level that Polanski is at his most adamant: The events that occur in the film must not be allowed to have significance. Polanski and Tynan take only small liberties with Shakespeare, and yet so successfully does Polanski orchestrate *Macbeth*'s visual content that we come out of the film with a horrified realization. We didn't identify with either Macbeth or Macduff in their final duel. We were just watching a sword-fight.

Madame Sousatzka

PG-13, 120 m., 1988

Shirley MacLaine (Madame Sousatzka), Navin Chowdhry (Manek Sen), Peggy Ashcroft (Lady Emily), Shabana Azmi (Sushila), Twiggy (Jenny), Leigh Lawson (Ronnie Blum), Geoffrey Bayldon (Cordle), Lee Montague (Vincent Pick). Directed by John Schlesinger and produced by Robin Dalton. Screenplay by Ruth Prawer Jhabvala and Schlesinger, from the book by Bernice Rubens.

The Indian boy comes every afternoon for piano lessons from Madame Sousatzka, who cannot disguise the love in her voice as she teaches him not only about music, but also about how to sit, how to breathe, how to hold his elbows, and how to think about his talent. Behind her, in the shadows of her musty London apartment, are the photographs of earlier students who were taught the same lessons before they went out into the world—where some of them became great pianists and others became just players of the piano.

Madame Sousatzka believes that this boy, Manek, can be a great pianist, a virtuoso—but we have no objective way to know if she is a great teacher of great musicians, or just a piano teacher who is deluding herself and the boy. That doesn't matter. *Madame Sousatzka* is not a one-level movie in which everything leads up to the cliché of the crucial first concert. This is not a movie about success or failure; it is a movie about soldiering on, about continuing to do your best, day after day, simply because you believe in yourself—no matter what anyone else thinks. Madame believes this sixteen-year-old boy can be a great pianist, and that she—no one else—is the person to guide him on the right path to his destiny.

Madame Sousatzka is a film about her efforts to protect the boy from all the pressures and temptations around him, while simultaneously shoring up the ruins of her own world. As played by Shirley MacLaine, in one of the best performances of her career, she is a faded, aging woman who possesses great stubbornness and conviction. Once, long ago, she failed in her own concert debut. Her own mother pushed her too fast, too soon, and she broke down in the middle of her debut concert and fled from the stage.

That humiliation is still in her nightmares, and still shapes her attitude toward her students. They must not be allowed to perform in public until they are ready. Unfortunately, Madame is hardly ever prepared to admit they are ready, and so sooner or later all of her pupils are forced to make a break with her. Their departures have made her career a series of heartbreaks, and populated the shelves of photographs in her apartment.

Manek, her latest student, is played by Navin Chowdhry as a teenager who apart from his talent is a fairly normal young man. He travels by skateboard despite Madame's explicit orders that he is not to endanger his hands, he enjoys playing the piano and yet is not obsessed by it, and he has a lively interest in the model (Twiggy) who lives upstairs in Madame's eccentric rooming house. His mother (Shabana Azmi) is divorced, and supports them by making gourmet Indian pastries for the food department of Harrod's. She has an admirer, but Manek is jealous of her boyfriend, and wants to make his concert debut so that he—not some strange man—can support his mother. He is encouraged in his ambition by a predatory booking agent who overhears his playing and wants to use him immediately—creating a war of wills between Madame and her pupil.

Madame Sousatzka was directed by John Schlesinger, who plays it in a very particular kind of London household. The shabby rooming house is on a once-distinguished street that has now been targeted by realtors for gentrification. The house is owned by Lady Emily (Dame Peggy

Ashcroft), a sweet-tempered old lady who lives in the basement and peacefully coexists with her tenants, who include Madame, the model, and Cordle (Geoffrey Bayldon), a decayed civil servant type with occasional, furtive homosexual adventures. Although the movie creates affection for the little community within the house, this is not a film about how the developers must be defeated—and you will be relieved to learn that the young pianist does not star in a benefit for Lady Emily.

The film is not about preserving the present, but about being prepared to change, and by the end of the film Lady Emily and Cordle have found that they can live quite comfortably in a little riverside flat, while Madame resolutely soldiers on in the house, undeterred by the noise and dirt of construction. But she has changed in a more important way, by being able to understand for the first time, a little anyway, why a student must eventually be allowed to go out into the world and take his chances.

MacLaine's approach to the role is interesting. She deliberately ages herself, and has put on weight for the role, so that there is relatively little of the familiar Shirley MacLaine to be seen on the screen. Even those traces soon disappear into the role of a woman who loves music, loves to teach, loves her students, and is crippled only by her traumatic failure on the stage. It might have embittered her, but it has not; she holds onto her students not out of resentment but out of pride, and fear.

The screenplay, by Ruth Prawer Jhabvala and Schlesinger, takes the time to be precise about teaching; we may feel by the end that we've had a few lessons ourselves. It is about discipline, about patience, about love of music. Manek tells Sousatzka at one point that when he goes on a stage, he will feel a small core of strength inside himself that she has given him. It is all, besides technique, that any teacher has to offer. *Madame Sousatzka* is an extraordinary movie that loves music and loves the people it is about, and has the patience to do justice to both.

Mad Max Beyond Thunderdome

R, 115 m., 1985

Mel Gibson (Mad Max), Tina Turner (Aunty Entity), Frank Thring (Collector), Angelo Rossitto (Master), Paul Larsson (Blaster), Angry Anderson (Ironbar). Directed by George Miller and George Ogilvie and produced by Miller. Screenplay by Miller and Terry Hayes.

It's not supposed to happen this way. Sequels are not supposed to be better than the movies that inspired them. The third movie in a series isn't supposed to create a world more complex, more visionary, and more entertaining than the first two. Sequels are supposed to be creative voids. But now here is *Mad Max Beyond Thunderdome*, not only the best of the three Mad Max movies, but one of the best films of 1985.

From its opening shot of a bizarre vehicle being pulled by camels through the desert, *Mad Max Three* places us more firmly within its apocalyptic postnuclear world than ever before. We are some years in the future; how many, it is hard to say, but so few years that the frames and sheet metal of 1985 automobiles are still being salvaged for makeshift new vehicles of bizarre design. And yet enough years that a new society is taking shape. The bombs have fallen, the world's petroleum supplies have been destroyed, and in the deserts of Australia, mankind has found a new set of rules and started on a new game.

The driver of the camels is Mad Max (Mel Gibson), former cop, now sort of a freelance nomad. After his vehicle is stolen and he is left in the desert to die, he makes his way somehow to Bartertown, a quasi-Casablanca hammered together out of spare parts. Bartertown is where you go to buy, trade, or sell anything—or anybody. It is supervised by a Sydney Greenstreet-style fat man named the Collector (Frank Thring), and ruled by an imperious queen named Aunty Entity (Tina Turner).

And it is powered by an energy source that is, in its own way, a compelling argument against nuclear war: In chambers beneath Bartertown, countless pigs live and eat and defecate, and from their waste products, Turner's soldiers generate methane gas. This leads to some of the movie's most memorable moments, as Mad Max and others wade knee-deep in piggy-do.

Tina Turner herself lives far above the masses, in a birds'-nest throne room perched high overhead. And as Mad Max first visits

Turner's sky palace, I began to realize how completely the codirector, George Miller, had imagined this future world. It has the crowding and the variety of a movie crossroads, but it also has a riot of hairstyles and costume design, as if these desperate creatures could pause from the daily struggle for survival only long enough to invent new punk fashions. After the clothes, the hair, the crowding, the incessant activity, the spendthrift way in which Miller fills his screen with throwaway details, Bartertown becomes much more than a movie set—it's an astounding address of the imagination, a place as real as Bogart's Casablanca or Orson Welles's Xanadu or the Vienna of *The Third Man*. That was even before the movie introduced me to Thunderdome, the arena for Bartertown's hand-to-hand battles to the death.

Thunderdome is the first really original movie idea about how to stage a fight since we got the first karate movies. The "dome" is a giant upside-down framework bowl. The spectators scurry up the sides of the bowl, and look down on the fighters. But the combatants are not limited to fighting on the floor of the arena. They are placed on harnesses with long elastic straps, so that they can leap from top to bottom and from side to side with great lethal bounds. Thunderdome is to fighting as three-dimensional chess is to a flat board. And the weapons available to the fighters are hung from the inside of the dome: Cleavers, broadaxes, sledgehammers, the inevitable chainsaw.

It is into Thunderdome that Mad Max goes for his showdown with Aunty Entity's greatest warrior, and George Miller's most original creation, a character named MasterBlaster, who is actually two people. Blaster is a giant hulk of a man in an iron mask. Master is a dwarf who rides him like a chariot, standing in an iron harness above his shoulders. The fight between Mad Max and MasterBlaster is one of the great creative action scenes in the movies.

There is a lot more in *Mad Max Beyond Thunderdome*. The descent into the pig world, for example, and the visit to a sort of postwar hippie commune, and of course the inevitable final chase scene, involving car, train, truck, cycle, and incredible stunts. This is a movie that strains at the leash of the possible, a movie of great visionary wonders.

The Madness of King George
NO MPAA RATING, 110 m., 1995

Nigel Hawthorne (George III), Helen Mirren (Queen Charlotte), Ian Holm (Willis), Amanda Donohoe (Lady Pembroke), Rupert Graves (Greville), Rupert Everett (Prince of Wales), Alan Bennett (Second M. P.). Directed by Nicholas Hytner and produced by Stephen Evans and David Parfitt. Screenplay by Bennett, based on his play.

WILLIS: *My patients acquire a better conceit of themselves.*
GEORGE: *I'm the king of England! A man can have no better conceit of himself than that!*
—dialogue between the king and his doctor

The Madness of King George tells the story of the disintegration of a fond and foolish old man, who rules England, yet cannot find his way through the tangle of his own mind. The parallel with *King Lear* is clear, and there is even a moment when George III reads from the play: "I fear I am not in my perfect mind." But the story of George is not tragedy, because tragedy requires a fall from greatness, and George III is not great, merely lovable and confused.

The film opens in 1788, some years after the American colonies have thrown off George's rule. He presides over an establishment that wishes him gone—his own son, the Prince of Wales, waits impatiently in the wings—and over a court scandalized by his erratic behavior. He awakes before dawn, runs in his nightshirt through the fields, pounces on a lady-in-waiting—and, worse still, cannot remember the names of his enemies. His queen, Charlotte, keeps up a brave front ("Smile and wave! It's what you're paid for!" she hisses at the Prince of Wales). When George forces his court to sit through an interminable session of "Greensleeves" being rung on bells and then asks to hear it again, troubled looks are exchanged: The king is losing it.

Alan Bennett's play, now filmed with its original stage star, Nigel Hawthorne, still in the title role, is a fond portrait of this befuddled old man. The action takes place in 1788, when the king was fifty. He lived on until 1820, blind and hopelessly insane the last ten years of his life, but the film wisely focuses on his middle age, when there were periods of clarity, and he struggled bravely to keep his wits and his throne.

The film shows both court and Parliament acutely attuned to the weathers of the king's mind. The Prince of Wales (Rupert Everett) schemes with the opposition leader, Charles James Fox (Jim Carter), to displace his father ("If a few ramshackle colonists in America can send him packing, why not me?"). Fox's archenemy, William Pitt the Younger (Julian Wadham), the king's loyal prime minister, schemes to keep George and his policies in power. And the loving, loyal Queen Charlotte (Helen Mirren), is denied access to her husband by the Prince of Wales—a cruel, foppish man, who complains, with a prescient bow to the present holder of his title, "To be Prince of Wales is not a position; it is a predicament."

All of this could be the material for a solemn historical biopic, but Bennett's play, and the direction by Nicholas Hytner, are more lighthearted than analytical, and the performance by Nigel Hawthorne as the ailing king is barbed and yet lovable: Madness burns in his eyes, but also sweetness and vulnerability, and when he lashes out at his court and accosts its ladies, we sense his suffering.

Medical science at the time could not offer much help: Great attention is lavished on the condition of the king's stools, and particularly their color. The king performs royally upon the pot, but, as a doctor observes sadly, "One may produce a copious, regular evacuation every day of the week and still be a stranger to reason." (Future historians were able to deduce from the medical records that George's mental state was caused by porphyria, a metabolic imbalance.)

What saves the king, at least for a time, is the materialization of a man named Willis (Ian Holm), who has revolutionary ideas about mental health. During a period of George's greatest confusion, the serious face of Willis swims into view, along with his portentious words: "I have a farm. . . ." On that farm he hopes to shock the king into sanity, and the king is shocked, all right:

GEORGE: *I am the king!*
WILLIS: *No, sir! You are the patient!*

The battle of wills between these two strong men is the centerpiece of the movie, and hugely entertaining. Willis, whose approach seems to embody some of the theories of modern psychology, tries to break the king down so he can build him up again. The king resists, aghast that a commoner would so treat the royal personage: "I am the verb, sir! I am not the object!" Holm is perfect for the role, stern, unyielding, and dotty.

It is only when strings are pulled to reunite the king with Queen Charlotte that the pieces fall into place. Reduced from grandeur to a sad little old man, he finds that his mind has cleared, and "I have remembered how to seem myself." The sequence during which he pulls himself together and astounds Parliament is triumphant, and funny.

I am not sure anyone but Nigel Hawthorne could have brought such qualities to this role. Having seen him onstage in London at about the same time the movie was released, in *The Clandestine Marriage*, a play written during George's reign, I was struck again by the way he projects a ferocious façade, and then peeks out from behind it, winking. Through the movie, he punctuates George's dialogue with little verbal tics like "What-what!" and "Yes-yes!" When George emerges briefly from his madness, one of the signs, for those who love him, is the reappearance of "What-what!" The way Hawthorne delivers the line makes it seem, for a moment, as if George has defeated insanity with eccentricity—which, of course, is the madness of the sane.

The Magic Flute
G, 135 m., 1975

Ulrik Cold (Sarastro), Josef Kostlinger (Tamino), Erik Saeden (The Speaker), Birgit Nordin (Queen of the Night), Irma Urrila (Pamina). Directed by Ingmar Bergman and produced by Måns Reuterswärd. Screenplay by Bergman, based on the opera by Wolfgang Mozart.

Ingmar Bergman has never before made a movie so warm, happy, and innocent as this version of Mozart's *The Magic Flute*. It's as if all this joy has been building up inside him during the great decade of metaphysical films beginning with *Persona*. It has been ten years since he made a comedy (the dreadful *All*

These Women) and twenty years since he made a good one (*Smiles of a Summer Night*), and now here's something to make you think he specialized in comic opera.

His *Magic Flute* is directed with a cheerful relish for its fairy-tale adventures, its young lovers and sinister sorcerers and improbable special effects. To film it, he decided to stay in the period, to approach the work head-on and in its own spirit as a sort of spooky, funny bedtime story.

He constructed on a sound stage a replica of Stockholm's tiny old Drottingholm Court Theater—a creaking eighteenth century treasure with machinery, still in working order to create thunder, lightning, and waves. He pretends he's filming an actual performance there, with proscenium arch, footlights, and an audience (the attentive little girl he cuts away to during scene changes is his own daughter). But then as each scene develops, he goes into it, opens it up (but not too much—we still feel we're on a stage), and films it with the most fluid camera work Sven Nykvist ever has provided for him.

It's an agile camera, too; instead of composing the characters into the sometimes static, sterile confrontations of his later films, he surprises them in reaction shots, cuts quickly to create moments of uncertainty, and has fun combining his actors with such props as stuffed animals and an amazing cherub-powered balloon.

And along the way, while remaining faithful to the spirit (if not always the precise story line) of *The Magic Flute,* he succeeds in making it into a movie. I can't recall another opera film I've seen in which that happened; usually we're all too conscious of the stage-bound nature of the performance, and of the difficulty of combining successfully what Pauline Kael calls the two bastard arts. Film and opera are both wonderful at borrowing and plundering other art forms but usually are incompatible with each other. Bergman's attempt succeeds brilliantly.

That's in great part due to his cast. Bergman has put together a group of singers who are filled with life, work naturally together, and look their parts even in close-up (something most opera singers most definitely do not).

My favorite is Hakan Hagegard as the irrepressible Papageno, awed by the supernatural,

delighted by his breakneck escapades, forever romantic.

Josef Kostlinger, as Tamino, is suitably heroic; when he and the magic flute safely guide Princess Pamina through the fearsome tests of fire and water, he looks every bit as capable as the flute. And Ulrik Cold (the name is perfectly suited) plays Sarastro, the sorcerer, with a malevolence that transcends even the ridiculous pointed cap he enters wearing.

Bergman lets us see how the special effects work, he gives us backstage glimpses of the players hurrying to meet cues and relaxing during the intermission, and we're reminded of the many other backstage scenes in his films.

We're supposed to be conscious of watching a performance, and yet at some level Bergman also wants Mozart's fantasy to work as a story, a preposterous tale, and it does. This must be the most delightful film ever made from an opera.

Magnolia
R, 179 m., 2000

Jason Robards (Earl Partridge), Julianne Moore (Linda Partridge), Tom Cruise (Frank Mackey), Philip Seymour Hoffman (Phil Parma), John C. Reilly (Officer Kurring), Melora Walters (Claudia Gator), Jeremy Blackman (Stanley Spector), Michael Bowen (Rick Spector), William H. Macy (Donnie Smith), Philip Baker Hall (Jimmy Gator), Melinda Dillon (Rose Gator), April Grace (Reporter). Directed by Paul Thomas Anderson and produced by Joanne Sellar. Screenplay by Anderson.

Magnolia is operatic in its ambition, a great joyous leap into melodrama and coincidence, with ragged emotions, crimes and punishments, deathbed scenes, romantic dreams, generational turmoil, and celestial intervention, all scored to insistent music. It is not a timid film. Paul Thomas Anderson here joins Spike Jonze (*Being John Malkovich*), David O. Russell (*Three Kings*), and their master, Martin Scorsese (*Bringing Out the Dead*), in beginning the new decade with an extroverted self-confidence that rejects the timid postmodernism of the 1990s. These are not movies that apologize for their exuberance or shield themselves with irony against suspicions of sincerity.

The movie is an interlocking series of episodes that take place during one day in Los Angeles, sometimes even at the same moment. Its characters are linked by blood, coincidence, and by the way their lives seem parallel. Themes emerge: the deaths of fathers, the resentments of children, the failure of early promise, the way all plans and ambitions can be undermined by sudden and astonishing events. Robert Altman's *Short Cuts* was also a group of interlinked Los Angeles stories, and both films illustrate former district attorney Vincent Bugliosi's observation in *Till Death Do Us Part* that personal connections in L.A. have a way of snaking around barriers of class, wealth, and geography.

The actors here are all swinging for the fences, heedless of image or self-protective restraint. Here are Tom Cruise as a loathsome stud, Jason Robards looking barely alive, William H. Macy as a pathetic loser, Melora Walters as a despairing daughter, Julianne Moore as an unloving wife, Michael Bowen as a browbeating father. Some of these people are melting down because of drugs or other reasons; a few, like a cop played by John C. Reilly and a nurse played by Philip Seymour Hoffman, are caregivers.

The film's opening sequence, narrated by an uncredited Ricky Jay, tells stories of incredible coincidences. One has become a legend of forensic lore; it's about the man who leaps off a roof and is struck by a fatal shotgun blast as he falls past a window before landing in a net that would have saved his life. The gun was fired by his mother, aiming at his father and missing. She didn't know the shotgun was loaded; the son had loaded it some weeks earlier, hoping that eventually one of his parents would shoot the other. All (allegedly) true.

This sequence suggests a Ricky Jay TV special, illustrating weird coincidences. But it is more than simply amusing. It sets up the theme of the film, which shows people earnestly and single-mindedly immersed in their lives, hopes, and values, as if their best-laid plans were not vulnerable to the chaotic interruptions of the universe. It's humbling to learn that existence doesn't revolve around us; worse to learn it revolves around nothing.

Many of the characters are involved in television, and their lives reflect on one another.

Robards plays a dying tycoon who produces many shows. Philip Baker Hall, also dying, is a game show host. Cruise is Robards's son, the star of infomercials about how to seduce women; his macho hotel ballroom seminars could have been scripted by Andrew Dice Clay. Walters is Hall's daughter, who doesn't believe anything he says. Melinda Dillon is Hall's wife, who might have been happier without his compulsion for confession. Macy plays "former quiz kid Donnie Smith," now a drunk with a bad job in sales, who dreams that orthodontics could make him attractive to a burly bartender. Jeremy Blackman plays a bright young quiz kid on Hall's program. Bowen plays his father, a tyrant who drives him to excel.

The connections are like a game of psychological pickup sticks. Robards alienated Cruise, Hall alienated Dillon, Bowen is alienating Blackman. The power of TV has not spared Robards or Hall from death. Childhood success left Macy unprepared for life, and may be doing the same thing for Blackman. Both Hall and Robards have employees (a producer, a nurse) who love them more than their families do. Both Robards and Hall cheated on their wives. And around and around.

And there are other stories with their own connections. The cop, played by Reilly, is like a fireman rushing to scenes of emotional turmoil. His need to help is so great that he falls instantly in love with the pathetic drug user played by Walters; her need is more visible to him than her crime. Later, he encounters Macy in the middle of a ridiculous criminal situation brought about to finance braces for his teeth.

There are big scenes here for the actors. One comes as Cruise's cocky TV stud disintegrates in the face of cross-examination from a TV reporter (April Grace). He has another big scene at Robards's deathbed. Philip Baker Hall (a favorite actor of Anderson's since *Hard Eight*) also disintegrates on TV; he's unable to ask, instead of answer, questions. Julianne Moore's breakdown in a pharmacy is parallel to Walters's nervousness with the cop: Both women are trying to appear functional while their systems scream because of drugs.

All of these threads converge, in one way or another, upon an event there is no way for the audience to anticipate. This event is not "cheating," as some critics have argued, because the prologue fully prepares the way for it, as do some subtle references to Exodus. It works like the hand of God, reminding us of the absurdity of daring to plan. And yet plan we must, because we are human, and because sometimes our plans work out.

Magnolia is the kind of film I instinctively respond to. Leave logic at the door. Do not expect subdued taste and restraint but instead a kind of operatic ecstasy. At three hours it is even operatic in length, as its themes unfold, its characters strive against the dying of the light, and the great wheel of chance rolls on toward them.

Malcolm X

PG-13, 201 m., 1992

Denzel Washington (Malcolm X), Angela Bassett (Betty Shabazz), Albert Hall (Baines), Al Freeman, Jr. (Elijah Muhammad), Delroy Lindo (West Indian Archie), Spike Lee (Shorty). Directed by Lee and produced by Marvin Worth and Lee. Screenplay by Arnold Perl and Lee.

Spike Lee's *Malcolm X* is one of the great screen biographies, celebrating the whole sweep of an American life that began in sorrow and bottomed out on the streets and in prison, before its hero reinvented himself. Watching the film, I understood more clearly how we do have the power to change our own lives, how fate doesn't deal all of the cards. The film is inspirational and educational—and it is also entertaining, as movies must be before they can be anything else.

Its hero was born Malcolm Little. His father was a minister who preached the beliefs of Marcus Garvey, the African-American leader who taught that white America would never accept black people, and that their best hope lay in returning to Africa. Years later, Malcolm would also become a minister and teach a variation on this theme, but first he had to go through a series of identities and conversions and hard lessons of life.

His father was murdered, probably by the Klan, which had earlier burned down the family house. His mother was unable to support her children, and Malcolm was parceled out to a foster home. He was the brightest student in his classes, but was steered away from ambitious career choices by white teachers who told him that, as a Negro, he should look for something where he could "work with his hands." One of his early jobs was as a Pullman porter, and then, in Harlem, he became a numbers runner and small-time gangster.

During that stage of his life, in the late 1940s, he was known as "Detroit Red," and ran with a fast crowd including white women who joined him for sex and burglaries. Arrested and convicted, he was sentenced to prison; the movie quotes him that he got one year for the burglaries and seven years for associating with white women while committing them. Prison was the best thing that happened to Detroit Red, who fell into the orbit of the Black Muslim movement of Elijah Muhammad, and learned self-respect.

The movie then follows Malcolm as he sheds his last name—the legacy, the Muslims preached, of slave-owners—and becomes a fiery street-corner preacher who quickly rises until he is the most charismatic figure in the Black Muslims, teaching that whites are the devil and that blacks had to become independent and self-sufficient. But there was still another conversion ahead: During a pilgrimage to Mecca, he was embraced by Muslims of many colors, and returned to America convinced that there were good people of peace in all races. Not long after, in 1965, he was assassinated—probably by members of the Muslim sect he had broken with.

This is an extraordinary life, and Spike Lee has told it in an extraordinary film. Like *Gandhi*, the movie gains force as it moves along; the early scenes could come from the lives of many men, but the later scenes show a great original personality coming into focus. To understand the stages of Malcolm's life is to walk for a time in the steps of many African-Americans, and to glimpse where the journey might lead.

Denzel Washington stands at the center of the film, in a performance of enormous breadth. He never seems to be trying for an effect, and yet he is always convincing; he seems as natural in an early scene, clowning through a railroad club car with ham sandwiches, as in a later one, holding audiences spellbound on street corners, in churches, on television, and at Harvard. He is as persuasive early in the film, wearing a zoot suit and prowling the nightclubs of Harlem, as later, disappearing into a throng of pilgrims to Mecca. Washington is a congenial, attractive actor, and so it is especially effective to see how he shows the anger in Malcolm, the unbending dogmatic side, especially in the early Muslim years.

Lee tells his story against an epic background of settings and supporting characters (the movie is a gallery of the memorable people in Malcolm's life). Working with cinematographer Ernest Dickerson, Lee paints the early Harlem scenes in warm, sensuous colors, and then uses cold, institutional lighting for the scenes in prison. In many of the key moments in Malcolm's life as a public figure, the color photography is intercut with a black-and-white, quasi-documentary style that suggests how Malcolm's public image was being shaped and fixed.

That image, at the time of his death, was of a man widely considered racist and dogmatic—a hate-monger, some said. It is revealing that even Martin Luther King, seen in documentary footage making a statement about Malcolm's death, hardly seems overcome with grief. The liberal orthodoxy of the mid-1960s taught that racism in America could be cured by legislation, that somehow the hopeful words in the folk songs would all come true. Malcolm doubted it would be that simple.

Yet he was not the monolithic ideologue of his public image, and one of the important achievements of Lee's film is the way he brings us along with Malcolm, so that anyone, black or white, will be able to understand the progression of his thinking. Lee's films always have an underlying fairness, an objectivity that is sometimes overlooked.

A revealing scene in *Malcolm X* shows Malcolm on the campus of Columbia University, where a young white girl tells him her heart is in the right place, and she supports his struggle. "What can I do to help?" she asks. "Nothing," Malcolm says coldly, and walks on. His single word could have been the punch line for the scene, but Lee sees more deeply, and ends the scene with the hurt on the young woman's face. There will be a time, later in Malcolm's life, when he will have a different answer to her question.

Romantic relationships are not Lee's strongest suit, but he has a warm, important one in *Malcolm X,* between Malcolm and his wife, Betty (Angela Bassett), who reminds her future husband that even revolutionary leaders must occasionally pause to eat and sleep. Her sweetness and support help him to find the gentleness that got lost in Harlem and prison.

Al Freeman, Jr., is quietly amazing as Elijah Muhammad, looking and sounding like the man himself, and walking the screenplay's tightrope between his character's importance and his flaws. Albert Hall is also effective, as the tough Muslim leader who lectures Malcolm on his self-image, who leads him by the hand into self-awareness, and then later grows jealous of Malcolm's power within the movement. And there is a powerful two-part performance by Delroy Lindo, as West Indian Archie, the numbers czar who first impresses Malcolm with his power, and later moves him with his weakness.

Walking into *Malcolm X,* I expected an angrier film than Spike Lee has made. This film is not an assault but an explanation, and it is not exclusionary; it deliberately addresses all races in its audience. White people, going into the film, may expect to meet a Malcolm X who will attack them, but they will find a Malcolm X whose experiences and motives make him understandable and finally heroic. A reasonable viewer is likely to conclude that, having gone through similar experiences, he might also have arrived at the same place. Black viewers will not be surprised by Malcolm's experiences and the racism he lived through, but they may be surprised to find that he was less one-dimensional than his image, that he was capable of self-criticism and was developing his ideas right up until the day he died.

Spike Lee is not only one of the best filmmakers in America, but one of the most crucially important, because his films address the central subject of race. He doesn't use sentimentality or political clichés, but shows how his characters live, and why.

Empathy has been in short supply in our nation recently. Our leaders are quick to congratulate us on our own feelings, slow to ask us to wonder how others feel. But maybe times are changing. Every Lee film is an exercise in empathy. He is not interested in congratulating the black people in his audience, or condemning the white ones. He puts human beings on the screen, and asks his audience to walk a little while in their shoes.

The Man from Elysian Fields

R, 106 m., 2002

Andy Garcia (Byron Tiller), Mick Jagger (Luther Fox), Julianna Margulies (Dena Tiller), Olivia Williams (Andrea Allcott), James Coburn (Tobias Allcott), Anjelica Huston (Jennifer Adler), Michael Des Barres (Greg). Directed by George Hickenlooper and produced by Garcia, David Kronemeyer, Andrew Pfeffer, and Donald Zuckerman. Screenplay by Phillip Jayson Lasker.

"Elysian Fields is an escort service. We tend to the wounds of lonely women in need of emotional as well as spiritual solace."
"Only women?"
"Call me old-fashioned."

It's not just the reply, it's the way Mick Jagger delivers it. The way only Mick Jagger could deliver it. There is a brave insouciance to it, and George Hickenlooper's *The Man from Elysian Fields* finds that tone and holds it. This is a rare comedy of manners, witty, wicked, and worldly, and one of the best movies of the year. It has seven principal characters, and every one of them is seen sharply as an individual with faults, quirks, and feelings.

With the craftsmanship of a sophisticated film from Hollywood's golden age, with the care for dialogue and the attention to supporting characters that have been misplaced by the star system, the movie is about what people want and need, which are not always the same thing. It contains moments of tender romance, but is not deceived that love can solve anything.

Byron Tiller (Andy Garcia), the hero, is the author of a good first novel and now has written a bad second one. He is afraid to tell his wife, Dena (Julianna Margulies), that his new novel has been rejected, and that they desperately need money. In a bar, he meets a man with the obscurely satanic name Luther Fox (Mick Jagger). Fox runs Elysian Fields, an escort service for wealthy women. Byron agrees to take an assignment, and finds himself with the

lovely Andrea Allcott (Olivia Williams). Why would she need to pay for companionship? It is a form of loyalty to her husband, who is old and diabetic, and whom she loves. It would be cheating to go out with an available man.

Her husband is Tobias Allcott (James Coburn), who has won Pulitzer prizes for his novels. He knows about his wife's arrangement, treats Byron in a dry, civilized manner, and enlists the younger writer's help with his current novel. Soon Byron is providing solace, of different kinds to be sure, to both of the Allcotts. He's a little dazzled by their qualities. And then there are two other characters, who add depth to the peculiar emotional complexity of the escort business: Jennifer Adler (Anjelica Huston), who pays for Luther Fox's services but doesn't want them for free; and Greg (rock star Michael Des Barres), a successful escort who gives Byron helpful tips on the clients.

The literate, sophisticated screenplay by Phillip Jayson Lasker understands that what happens to one character affects how another one feels; there's an emotional domino effect. By working for Elysian Fields, Byron supports his family, but it loses his attention. By risking everything in telling Jennifer that he loves her, Luther discovers his own self-deception. By accepting Byron's help with his novel, Tobias loses stature in his own eyes. Andrea fiercely tells Byron of the old man: "The only thing he has left is his reputation, and when he dies I want him holding onto it." Yes, but she saves it in public by destroying it in private. She isn't very sensitive that way.

This is a grown-up movie, in its humor and in its wisdom about life. You need to have lived a little to understand the complexities of Tobias Allcott, who is played by James Coburn with a pitch-perfect balance between sadness and sardonic wit. Listen to his timing and his word choices in the scene where he opens his wife's bedroom door and finds Byron, not without his permission, in his wife's bed. You can believe he is a great novelist. The scene is an example of the dialogue's grace and irony. Another example: "This business you're in," Byron asks Luther. "Does it ever make you ashamed?" Luther replies: "No. Poverty does that."

Julianna Margulies, as Byron's wife, has what could have been the standard role of the wronged woman, but the screenplay doesn't dismiss her with pathos and sympathy. Dena stands up and fights, holds her ground, is correctly unforgiving. Olivia Williams, as Andrea, has a hint of selfishness: Her concern for Tobias's reputation is connected to the way it reflects on her. There is a scene between Luther and Byron on the beach, where the older man shares a lesson he has just learned; it makes exactly the point it needs to make, and stops. The movie is confident enough it doesn't need to underline everything. It makes its point about the Michael Des Barres character even more economically; for him, the song "Just a Gigolo" is sad or jolly, depending on his mood.

Andy Garcia's performance took some courage because his Byron is not a very strong man. Not strong enough to tell his wife the novel didn't sell. Not strong enough to resist the temptations of Elysian Fields, or the flattery of Tobias's attention. By the time the ending comes around, we observe that it is happy, but we also observe that the movie has earned it: Most movies are too eager to wrap things up by providing forgiveness before it has been deserved. Not this one.

The Manhattan Project

PG-13, 118 m., 1986

John Lithgow (John Mathewson), Christopher Collet (Paul Stephens), Cynthia Nixon (Jenny Anderman), Jill Eikenberry (Elizabeth Stephens). Directed by Marshall Brickman and produced by Brickman and Jennifer Ogden. Screenplay by Brickman and Thomas Baum.

The kid is really smart, but like a lot of smart kids he has learned to hide it, to lay back and observe and keep his thoughts to himself. When the new scientist arrives in town and starts to date the kid's mother, and then tries to make pals by taking the kid on a tour of the research lab where he works, the kid keeps his eyes open and his mouth shut. But he knows the lab is devoted to nuclear weapons research, and he's kind of insulted that the scientist would try to deceive him.

That's the setup for *The Manhattan Project,* a clever, funny, and very skillful thriller about how the kid builds his own atomic bomb. This is not, however, another one of those teenage movies about bright kids and science projects. There have been some good movies in that genre—I liked *WarGames* and *Real Genius*—but this isn't really a teenage movie at all, it's a thriller. And it's one of those thrillers that stays as close as possible to the everyday lives of convincing people, so that the movie's frightening aspects are convincing.

The kid is played by Christopher Collet. He is very, very smart. We know that not just because we are told so, but because the movie has lots of subtle, sometimes funny little ways of demonstrating it—as when the kid solves a puzzle in three seconds flat, just as we were trying to understand it.

The kid lives with his mother (Jill Eikenberry) in an upstate New York college town. John Lithgow plays the scientist who moves into the town and starts to date Eikenberry and makes friends with the kid. The movie is very sophisticated about the relationship between Collet and Lithgow. This isn't a case of the two men competing for the affections of the mother; indeed, there are times when these two bright, lonely males seem to have more in common with each other.

In particular, the Lithgow character isn't allowed to fall into clichés. He isn't a mad scientist, and he isn't a heartless intellectual: He's just a smart man trying to do his job well and still have some measure of simple human pleasure.

After Collet is given his tour of the "research center," he tells his girlfriend (Cynthia Nixon) that he's a little insulted that they thought they could fool him. He knows a bomb factory when he sees one. And so, to prove various things to various people, the kid figures out a way to sneak into the plant, steal some plutonium, and build his own nuclear bomb. He wants to enter it in a New York City science fair.

I love it when movies get very detailed about clever schemes for outsmarting people. *The Manhattan Project* invites us to figure out things along with Collet, as he uses his girlfriend as a decoy and outsmarts the security guards at the plant. Inside, he has it all figured out: how to baffle the automatic alarms, how to anticipate what the guards are going to do, how to get in and out without being detected.

The long closing sequence is probably too predictable, as Lithgow and the federal authorities try to convince the kid to take his bomb out of the science fair and allow them to disarm it before he vaporizes the city. Even here, the movie doesn't depend on ordinary thriller strategies; a lot depends not only on the relationship between the kid and the scientist, but on how they think alike and share some of the same goals.

The Manhattan Project was cowritten, co-produced, and directed by Marshall Brickman, the sometime Woody Allen collaborator *(Annie Hall, Manhattan)* whose own films include *Lovesick* and *Simon*. This movie announces his arrival into the first ranks of skilled American directors. It's a *tour de force,* the way he combines everyday personality conflicts with a funny, oddball style of seeing things, and wraps up the whole package into a tense and effective thriller. It's not often that one movie contains so many different kinds of pleasures.

The Man in the Moon

PG-13, 99 m., 1991

Sam Waterston (Matthew Trant), Tess Harper (Abigail Trant), Gail Strickland (Marie Foster), Reese Witherspoon (Dani Trant), Jason London (Court Foster), Emily Warfield (Maureen Trant). Directed by Robert Mulligan and produced by Mark Rydell. Screenplay by Jenny Wingfield.

When this movie was over, I sat quietly for a moment so that I could feel the arc of its story being completed in my mind. They had done it: They had found a path all the way from the beginning to the end of this material, which is so fraught with peril, and never stepped wrong, not even at the end, when everything could have come tumbling down. *The Man in the Moon* is a wonderful movie, but it is more than that; it is a victory of tone and mood. It is like a poem.

The film takes place on a farm outside a small country town in the 1950s. Two teenage girls are being raised by parents who are strict, but who are also loving and good. One of the girls, Dani, is fourteen years old and has just passed uncertainly into young womanhood. Her sister, Maureen, is about seventeen. On hot summer nights they sleep on the screened-in porch and have girl talks, and

Dani laments that she will never be as beautiful and popular as her sister. Of course, all kid sisters feel that way.

A widow moves onto the farm next door with her son, Court, who is about seventeen. One day he happens upon Dani down at the swimming hole. They fight at first, but then they make up and become friends. Dani, of course, develops an enormous crush on this boy, and for a day or two he seems to feel the same emotions she does. Dani asks Maureen how to kiss, and Maureen gives her lessons. She "practices" on her hand. Then Court kisses her, and she confesses it was the first time she has ever been kissed by a boy. "How was it?" he asks. "Perfect," she says.

The moment is perfect, too, but there is an even better one when she tells him, "I want to know what your hopes are." This isn't just a movie about teenage romance; it's a movie about idealism—about how we idealize what and who we love—and a movie about the meaning of life. Yes, the Meaning of Life, which is a topic teenagers discuss a good deal as their insides churn with hope and doubt, and which adults discuss less and less, the more they could benefit from it.

The way the scenes between Dani and Court are handled is typical of the entire movie, which takes material we may have seen many times before and makes it true and fresh. Maybe it is because of the acting— Reese Witherspoon as Dani and Jason London as Court do justice to the slightest nuance of the scene. Maybe it is the direction, by Robert Mulligan, whose long career includes another fine movie about a young girl, *To Kill a Mockingbird*. Or maybe it is because everyone involved with the film knew that the script, by Jenny Wingfield, was not going to sell out at the end, was not going to contrive an artificial ending, or go for false sentiment, or do anything other than exactly what the material cries out for.

There are some complications surrounding that "perfect" kiss. One of them is that the girls' mother (Tess Harper) is in the last weeks of pregnancy. Another is that the older sister has just had a particularly nasty date with a crude local boy. Another is that their father (Sam Waterston) is fairly strict—not because he is mean, but because he loves them. Another, inevitably and painfully, is that when Court sees the older girl, he forgets about the kid sister with whom he shared the perfect kiss. Life is so direct sometimes in the way it hurts us—and the younger we are, the more universal the hurt.

Now something happens in the story that I cannot tell. It must catch you unprepared. And then the magnificent concluding passages of this film are about how deeply one can be hurt, how hard it is to forgive, how impossible it is to share the deepest feelings.

The Man in the Moon is like a great short story, one of those masterpieces of language and mood where not one word is wrong or unnecessary. It flows so smoothly from start to finish that it hardly even seems like an ordinary film. Usually I am aware of the screenwriter putting in obligatory scenes. I can hear the machinery grinding. Not this time. Although, in retrospect, I can see how carefully the plot was put together, how meticulously each event was prepared for, as I watched the film I was only aware of life passing by.

Of the performances, it is enough to say that each one creates a character that could not be improved on. Tess Harper and Sam Waterston are convincing parents here; they aren't simply stick figures in a plot, used only to move events along, but people we believe could really have raised these girls. There is a moment when Waterston hugs his youngest girl, and the way it arrives and the way it plays are heartbreakingly touching. There is a moment when Harper intuits something about her older girl, and the way she acts on her intuition is so tactful we feel she is giving the girl a lesson on how to be a mother. And Gail Strickland, as the boy's mother, creates moments that are as difficult as they are true.

Then there are the two sisters, Reese Witherspoon and Emily Warfield. Like all sisters of about the same age, they share almost all of their secrets, but the ones they cannot share are the ones that hurt deeply. Their intimate moments together—talking about boys, about growing up—have a special intimacy. But the silences and the hurt body language of some of their later scenes speak of an intimacy betrayed, and are even more special. There is a scene where Court comes over and is asked to stay for dinner, and the way he has eyes only for Maureen—he all but ignores Dani—reflects, we remember, exactly the cruel and thoughtless ways that teenagers deal with affairs of the heart.

Robert Mulligan is a director whose titles range from *Inside Daisy Clover* to *Blood Brothers* to *The Other.* He made *Summer of '42,* also a story of the intensity of young love, and his *Same Time, Next Year* and *Clara's Heart* were also, in a way, about how time and age affect romance. Although his work is uneven, he has always been a serious and sincere artist—both in the early days of the partnership with Alan J. Pakula that produced *Mockingbird,* and since.

Nothing else he has done, however, approaches the purity and perfection of *The Man in the Moon.* As the film arrived at its conclusion without having stepped wrong once, I wondered whether he could do it—whether he could maintain the poetic, bittersweet tone, and avoid the sentimentalism and cheap emotion that could have destroyed this story. Would he maintain the integrity of this material? He would, and he does.

Man of Iron

NO MPAA RATING, 140 m., 1980

Jerzy Radziwilowicz (Tomczyk), Krystyna Janda (Agnieszka), Marian Opania (Winkiel), Lech Walesa (As Himself). Directed by Andrzej Wajda. Screenplay by Aleksander Scibor-Rylski.

As a youth of thirteen, the Polish filmmaker Andrzej Wajda lived in a small town where he witnessed German troops lead thousands of Polish army officers to their deaths in concentration camps. As a young student after the war, he lived through the repressive Stalinist years. In the 1950s he made his first films, betraying a spirit that the party ideologues found too individualistic for their taste. In a speech in 1981 at American University in Washington, D.C., he quoted from "the best review I've ever had." It was from a confidential 1976 Polish censor's report:

. . . *politically and ideologically he is not on our side. He has taken the position, often found among artists, of a "neutral judge" of history and today's times—believing that he has the right . . . to apply the gauge of humanism and morals to all the problems of the world and that*

*he doesn't need Marxism nor any other philo-
sophical-social system to do it.*

Wajda is at it again, judging history, applying the gauge of humanism, not requiring
Marxism, in *Man of Iron,* his extraordinary
film about the birth of the Polish Solidarity
labor movement. This film is a marriage between a fictional story and actual events, and
Wajda took his cameras and his actors right
into the firestorm of the Gdansk demonstrations to record the victorious Solidarity agreement at the Lenin Shipyard.

Wajda is in a strange position in Poland. He
and Krystof Zanussi are the only two Polish
directors still in Poland who have international reputations. He is honored all over the
world, but at home the authorities are a little
reluctant to give him his head; his films do not
promote domestic tranquility.

Man of Iron, filmed during the tumultuous
days of relative freedom when Solidarity
seemed to hold all the cards, was permitted to
be flown out of Warsaw during the closing
days of the 1981 Cannes Film Festival, where it
won the Grand Prize.

It's a sequel of sorts to Wajda's *Man of Marble* (1976), although you needn't have seen the
earlier film, which was about a labor leader
during the years of repressive policies in
Poland. This film is about the same man's son,
who is a Solidarity leader a few steps down in
influence from Lech Walesa. Wajda follows his
fictional characters into the center of real
events (it's sometimes hard to tell where
fiction ends and documentary begins), and he
uses a broadcast newsman as an interviewer—
a technique that allows his film to go places
and ask questions that would be difficult to
cover in "pure" fiction.

Exactly the same two techniques—the use
of a character who is a journalist, and the juxtaposition of a fictional story with actual
events—were used by Haskell Wexler in
Medium Cool, the film about the 1968 Democratic convention demonstrations in Chicago.
The approach leaves some ragged edges, but
when you are filming at the cutting edge of
history you can't stop for rewrites.

Wajda's film is not a polemic, however. That
humanist streak, complained of by the state
censors, sneaks through even at the expense of
the Solidarity politics he wants to celebrate.

Wajda is an artist first, a reporter second or
third, and not really a very good propagandist.
And the best things in *Man of Iron* are the
purely personal moments, the scenes where
Wajda is concerned with the human dimensions of his characters rather than their ideological struggles.

Those dimensions come through most
clearly in the character of Winkiel (Marian
Opania), the alcoholic journalist who is sent by
the party bosses in Warsaw to spy on Solidarity
in the guise of a radio reporter. Winkiel had his
own values once. Meeting the son of the old
labor leader, he remembers the father. Arriving
in Gdansk, Winkiel discovers to his horror that
the area has been declared dry because of the
troubles—he can't get booze. A party agent slips
him a bottle of vodka, but Winkiel breaks it on
the bathroom floor, and in a scene that will profoundly affect the way we understand his later
actions, he desperately tries to soak up some of
the vodka with a towel. He is a man whose spirit
is broken, a man prepared to be a spy. The most
moving of the several stories in *Man of Iron*
concerns his gradual rediscovery of his old values, until he finally decides to side with the
workers and to abandon his undercover role.

Man of Iron is a fascinating and courageous
document—a film of dissent made because
of, or in spite of, the upheaval in Poland.

In that speech in 1981, Wajda closed with
these words: *Someone once asked me a naive
question. It's a question often asked of very old
writers: Do you feel that you've helped to make
history? My answer is this. I don't know whether
I helped make it. I know I didn't stand with my
hands folded. I didn't look on indifferently as
history was being made.*

Manon of the Spring

PG, 113 m., 1987

Yves Montand (Cesar Soubeyran), Daniel Auteuil
(Ugolin), Emmanuelle Beart (Manon), Hippolyte Girardot
(Schoolteacher), Elisabeth Depardieu (Aimee), Gabriel
Bacquier (Victor). Directed by Claude Berri and
produced by Pierre Grunstein. Screenplay by Berri and
Gerard Brach, based on the book by Marcel Pagnol.

There is something to be said for a long story
that unfolds with an inexorable justice. In recent movies, we've become accustomed to

stories that explode into dozens of tiny, dimwitted pieces of action, all unrelated to each other. Cars hurtle through the air, victims are peppered with gunshot holes, heroes spit out clever one-liners, and at the end of it all, what are we left with? Our hands close on empty air.

Manon of the Spring, which is the conclusion of the story that began with *Jean de Florette*, is the opposite kind of movie. It moves with a majestic pacing over the affairs of four generations, demonstrating that the sins of the fathers are visited upon the children. Although *Manon* is self-contained and can be understood without having seen *Jean de Florette*, the full impact of this work depends on seeing the whole story, right from the beginning; only then does the ending have its full force.

In the first part of the story, as you may recall, a young hunchbacked man from Paris (Gerard Depardieu) came with his wife and daughter to farm some land he had inherited in a rural section of France. The locals did not greet him kindly, and one of the local patriarchs (Yves Montand) sabotaged his efforts by blocking the spring that fed his land. The young man worked morning to night to haul water for his goats and the rabbits he wished to raise, but in the end the effort killed him. Montand and his worthless nephew (Daniel Auteuil) were then able to buy the land cheaply.

Montand's plot against the hunchback was incredibly cruel, but the movie was at pains to explain that Montand was not gratuitously evil. His most important values centered around the continuity of land and family, and in his mind, his plot against Depardieu was justified by the need to defend the land against an "outsider." As *Manon of the Spring* opens, some years later, the unmarried and childless Montand is encouraging his nephew to find a woman and marry, so the family name can be continued.

The nephew already has a bride in mind: the beautiful Manon (Emmanuelle Beart), daughter of the dead man, who tends goats on the mountainside and lives in poverty, although she has received a good education. Unfortunately for the nephew, he has a rival for her affections in the local schoolteacher. As

the story unfolds, Manon discovers by accident that the nephew and his uncle blocked her father's spring—and when she accidentally discovers the source of the water for the whole village, she has her revenge by cutting off the water of those who killed her father.

All of this takes place with the implacable pace of a Greek tragedy. It sounds more melodramatic than it is, because the events themselves are not the issue here—the director, Claude Berri, has a larger point he wants to make, involving poetic justice on a scale that spans the generations. There are surprises at the end of this film that I do not choose to reveal, but they bring the whole story full circle, and Montand finally receives a punishment that is perfectly, even cruelly, suited to his crime.

Apart from its other qualities, *Manon of the Spring* announces the arrival of a strong and beautiful new actress from France in Emmanuelle Beart. Already seen in *Date with an Angel*, a comedy in which she supplied the only redeeming virtue, she is very effective in this central role, this time as a sort of avenging angel who punishes the old man and his nephew by giving them a glimpse of what could have been for them, had they not been so cruel.

The Man on the Train
R, 90 m., 2003

Jean Rochefort (Manesquier), Johnny Hallyday (Milan), Charlie Nelson (Max), Pascal Parmentier (Sadko), Jean-François Stévenin (Luigi), Isabelle Petit-Jacques (Viviane). Directed by Patrice Leconte and produced by Philippe Carcassonne. Screenplay by Claude Klotz.

Two men meet late in life. One is a retired literature teacher. The other is a bank robber. Both are approaching a rendezvous with destiny. By chance, they spend some time together. Each begins to wish he could have lived the other's life.

From this simple premise, Patrice Leconte has made one of his most elegant films. It proceeds as if completely by accident and yet foreordained, and the two men—who come from such different worlds—get along well because both have the instinctive reticence and tact of born gentlemen. When the robber asks the teacher if he can borrow a pair of slippers, we get a glimpse of the gulf that separates them: He wants them, not because he needs them, but because, well, he has never worn a pair of slippers.

The teacher is played by Jean Rochefort, seventy-three, tall, slender, courtly. It tells you all you need to know that he was once cast to play Don Quixote. The robber is played by Johnny Hallyday, fifty-nine, a French rock legend, who wears a fringed black leather jacket and travels with three handguns in his valise. This casting would have a divine incongruity for a French audience. In American terms, think of James Stewart and Johnny Cash.

Leconte is a director who makes very specific films, usually with an undertone of comedy, about characters who are one of a kind. His *The Hairdresser's Husband,* which also starred Rochefort, was about a man who loved to watch women cut hair. His *The Girl on the Bridge* was about a sideshow knife-thrower. His *The Widow of Saint Pierre* was about a nineteenth-century community on a French-Canadian fishing island that comes to love a man condemned to death. His *Ridicule* was about an eighteenth-century provincial who has an ecological scheme, and is told that the king favors those who can make him laugh. His *Monsieur Hire* was about a meek little man who spies on a woman, who sees him spying, and boldly challenges him to make his move.

These films have nothing in common except the humor of paradox, and Leconte's love for his characters. He allows them to talk with wit and irony. "Were you a good teacher?" the robber asks the teacher, who replies: "Not one pupil molested in thirty years on the job." "Not bad," the robber says dryly.

I have seen *The Man on the Train* twice, will see it again, cannot find a flaw. The man gets off the train in a drear November in a French provincial town, and falls into conversation with the teacher, who is quietly receptive. The teacher's elegant old house is unlocked ("I lost the key"). The village hotel is closed for the winter. "I know," the teacher says when the man returns. "I'll show you to your room."

Over a period of a few days, they talk, eat together, drink, smoke, gaze at the stars. There is no reason for them to be together, and so they simply accept that they are. There is a coincidence: At 10:00 A.M. on Saturday, the teacher is scheduled for a triple heart bypass, and the man from the train is scheduled to stick up a bank. The teacher offers the man money if he will abandon the plan, but the man cannot, because he has given his word to his confederates.

Early in the film, the teacher goes into the man's room, tries on his leather jacket, and imitates Wyatt Earp in the mirror. A little later, he gets a new haircut, telling the barber he wants a style "halfway between fresh out of jail, and world-class soccer player." One day when the teacher is away, one of his young tutorial pupils appears, and the robber says, "I'll be your teacher today," and leads him through a lesson on Balzac while successfully concealing that he has never read the novel, or perhaps much of anything else.

It is so rare to find a film that is about male friendship, uncomplicated by sex, romance, or any of the other engines that drive a plot. These men become friends, I think, because each recognizes the character of the other. Yes, the bank robber is a criminal, but not a bad man; the teacher tells him, quite sincerely, that he wishes he could help with the holdup. They talk about sex (the teacher points out the two hundred–year-old oil painting he masturbated before when he was young). They agree "women are not what they once were." The robber observes that, after a point, they're simply not worth the trouble. When the teacher's longtime friend Viviane (Isabelle Petit-Jacques) chatters away during dinner, the robber snaps, "He wants tenderness and sex, not news of your brat."

At the end of the film, the two men do exchange places, in a beautiful and mysterious way. Leconte brings his film to transcendent closure without relying on stale plot devices or the clanking of the plot. He resorts to a kind of poetry. After the film is over, you want to sigh with joy, that in this rude world such civilization is still possible.

Man Push Cart

NO MPAA RATING, 87 m., 2006

Ahmad Razvi (Ahmad), Leticia Dolera (Noemi), Charles Daniel Sandoval (Mohammad), Ali Reza (Manish), Farooq "Duke" Mohammad (Duke). Directed by Ramin Bahrani and produced by Bahrani, Bedford Bentley, and Pradip Ghosh. Screenplay by Bahrani.

Man Push Cart was filmed in Manhattan by an American born in Iran and an American born in Pakistan, and it embodies the very soul of Italian neorealism. Free of contrived melodrama and phony suspense, it ennobles the hard work by which its hero earns his daily bread. He owns a stainless steel bagel wagon, which he pushes through the lonely predawn streets. He sells bagels and sweet rolls and juice and coffee, and many customers call him by his first name although they would never think to ask his last one.

The character, named Ahmad (Ahmad Razvi), has had a life before this, but the pushcart now defines the parameters of his existence. He was a Pakistani rock star, although how that career ended and why he came to New York to push a cart (which would be a subject of a more conventional film) is barely suggested. Ahmad's wife is dead, his in-laws will not allow him to see his son, and maybe he originally came to America to seek the child. Now he sells bagels.

We see the world he inhabits outside the cart. He knows the other nearby vendors, including a Hispanic woman at a magazine stand. Romance would be a possibility, except that romance is not a possibility in Ahmad's life. It is too filled with the making of a living. Like so many Americans who work low-wage jobs, sometimes two or even three of them, his work essentially subsidizes his ability to keep on working.

Ramin Bahrani, the writer-director, shot his film on a shoestring in less than three weeks. He often used a concealed camera, shooting what was really happening. There's a scene of unforced spontaneity when Ahmad offers to sell some bootleg videos. The two guys he pitches say they know where they can get bootlegs, two for eight bucks, in Brooklyn. The two guys did not know they were in a movie.

Ahmad's cart is stolen and, therefore, his livelihood. We get a glimpse backstage of how the vending cart economy operates. What can he do without a cart and a way to replace it? He will, we understand, keep pushing, if not the cart, then something. *Man Push Cart* as a title encapsulates human survival at a most fundamental economic level.

Bahrani's film was accepted by Sundance 2006. The festival offered an opportunity for his low-budget effort to find audiences, and I immediately invited it to my Overlooked Film Festival in April 2006. A central Illinois audience reacted, if anything, more favorably than the Sundance crowd. The film's story is simple, and moving, and inescapable.

In a film like this, it is pointless to describe "screenplay," "acting," or "direction." The film is resolutely utilitarian. No effort is made to create a visual look; the camera simply, impassively, regards. Razui's acting never strains for effect; it embodies the bleakness and exhaustion of his character.

Bahrani, as director, not only stays out of the way of the simplicity of his story but also relies on it; less is more, and with restraint he finds a grimy eloquence.

Bahrani was inspired by *The Myth of Sisyphus*, by Albert Camus, the story of a man who spends his life pushing a rock up a hill, only to see it roll down again, and only to push it back up again. Well, what else can he do? *Man Push Cart* is not an indictment of the American economy or some kind of political allegory. It is about what it is about. I think the message may be that it is better, after all, to push the cart than to face a life without purpose at the bottom of the hill.

Mansfield Park

PG-13, 110 m., 1999

Embeth Davidtz (Mary Crawford), Jonny Lee Miller (Edmund Bertram), Alessandro Nivola (Henry Crawford), Frances O'Connor (Fanny Price), Harold Pinter (Sir Thomas Bertram), Lindsay Duncan (Lady Bertram/Mrs. Price), Sheila Gish (Mrs. Norris), James Purefoy (Tom Bertram), Hugh Bonneville (Mr. Rushworth), Justine Waddell (Julia Bertram), Victoria Hamilton (Maria Bertram), Sophia Myles (Susan), Hilton McRae (Mr. Price), Hannah Taylor Gordon (Young Fanny), Charles Edwards (Yates). Directed by Patricia Rozema and produced by Sarah Curtis. Screenplay by Rozema, based on the book by Jane Austen, her letters, and early journals.

Patricia Rozema's *Mansfield Park* makes no claim to be a faithful telling of Jane Austen's novel, and achieves something more interesting instead. Rozema has chosen passages from Austen's journals and letters and adapted them to reflect on Fanny Price, the heroine of *Mansfield Park,* and the result is a film in which Austen's values (and Fanny's) are more important than the romance and melodrama.

The film begins with a young girl whispering a lurid story into the ear of her wide-eyed little sister. This is Fanny (Hannah Taylor Gordon), whose family lives in poverty in a dockside cottage in Portsmouth. Fanny's mother married unwisely for love. Her sister Lady Bertram married for position, and now lives in the great country estate Mansfield Park. Lady Bertram spends her days nodding in a haze of laudanum, but rouses herself sufficiently to send for one of her nieces, and so with no warning Fanny is bundled into a carriage and taken away from her family. "It seems that mother has given me away," she writes her sister. "I can augur nothing but misery with what I have seen at Mansfield Park."

The narrative springs forward, and we meet a twentyish Fanny, now played by Frances O'Connor. Great English country houses in those days were truly family seats, giving shelter and employment to relatives, dependents, and servants, and we meet Lord Bertram (the playwright Harold Pinter, magisterial and firm), his drug-addled wife (Lindsay Duncan), his drunken older son, Tom (James Purefoy), his likable younger son, Edmund (Jonny Lee Miller), his two inconsequential daughters, and the attractive Crawfords, Henry and his sister, Mary (Alessandro Nivola and Embeth Davidtz). The Crawfords have rented the estate's parsonage with the aim of marrying into the Bertram family.

This may seem like a large cast (I have left out three or four characters), but it is important to understand that in that time and place, it would have seemed a small enough one, because these were literally the only people Fanny Price could expect to see on a regular basis. If she is to marry, her husband will probably come from among them, and nobody has to tell her that the candidates are Tom, Edmund, and Henry. All of Austen's novels, in one way or another, are about capable young women trapped in a strata of country society that assigns them to sit in drawing rooms looking pretty while they speculate on their matrimonial chances and risks.

In crossing this theme with the idea that Fanny is a writer, Rozema cuts right to the heart of the matter. We assume that women have always written, but actually until two hundred years ago women authors were rare; Austen found her own way into the profession. Most women did not have the education, the freedom, or the privacy to write. Virginia Woolf is eloquent about this in *A Room of One's Own,* speculating that someone like Austen might literally have never been alone in a room to write, but should be pictured in the corner of a drawing room containing all the other members of her household—writing her novels while conversation and life carried on regardless, dogs barked and children burped.

In *Mansfield Park,* we see Fanny thrilled to receive a quire of writing paper, and sending letters to her sister Susie that contain a great deal more observation and speculation than family correspondence really requires. This young woman could grow up to write—well, *Pride and Prejudice.* We are so accustomed to the notion of Austen's wit and perception that we lose sight of the fact that for her to write at all was a radical break with the role society assigned her.

Women in the early years of the nineteenth century were essentially commodities until they were married, and puppeteers afterward, exerting power through their husbands and children and in the management of their households. Thus all of Austen's novels (and those of George Eliot, Mrs. Gaskell, and the Brontës) can be seen as stories about business and finance—for a woman's occupation and fortune came through marriage.

The key thing about Fanny Price, and about many of Austen's heroines, is that she is ready to say no. Her uncle, Lord Bertram, informs her that Henry Crawford has asked for her hand, and "I have agreed." Fanny does not love Henry. She loves her cousin Edmund, who is engaged to the worthless Mary Crawford. When she says she does not trust Henry, there is a ruthless exchange with her uncle. "Do you trust me?" he asks. "Yes, sir." "Well, I trust him, and you will marry him."

Later in the film there is a bloodcurdling scene in the drawing room after a scandal has threatened the family's reputation. Without revealing too much, let me ask you to listen for Mary Crawford's chilling analysis of the emergency and her plan for what must be done. To modern ears it sounds crass and heartless. In 1806, just such conversations would have sounded reasonable to people schooled to think of the family fortune above any consideration of love or morality.

Mansfield Park is a witty, entertaining film, and I hope I haven't made it sound too serious. Frances O'Connor makes a dark-haired heroine with flashing eyes and high spirits. Harold Pinter is all the country Tory one could possibly hope for. Alessandro Nivola makes a rakish cad who probably really does love Fanny, after his fashion. And Embeth Davidtz's cold-blooded performance as Mary strips bare the pretense and exposes the family for what it is—a business, its fortune based on slave plantations in the Caribbean. This is an uncommonly intelligent film, smart and amusing, too, and anyone who thinks it is not faithful to Austen doesn't know the author but only her plots.

The Man Who Would Be King

PG, 129 m., 1975

Sean Connery (Daniel Dravot), Michael Caine (Peachy Carnahan), Christopher Plummer (Kipling), Saeed Jaffrey (Billy Fish), Shakira Caine (Roxanne). Directed by John Huston and produced by John Foreman. Screenplay by Huston and Gladys Hill.

John Huston's *The Man Who Would Be King* is swashbuckling adventure, pure and simple, from the hand of a master. It's unabashed and thrilling and fun. The movie invites comparison with the great action films like *Gunga Din* and *Mutiny on the Bounty,* and with Huston's own classic *The Treasure of the Sierre Madre:* We get strong characterizations, we get excitement, we even get to laugh every once in a while.

The action epics of the last twenty years seem to have lost their sense of humor; it's as if once the budget goes over five million dollars, directors think they have to be deadly serious. *Lawrence of Arabia* was a great movie, but introspective and solemn, and efforts such as *Doctor Zhivago* and *War and Peace* never dared to smile. Huston's movie isn't like that. It reflects his personality and his own best

films; it's open, sweeping, and lusty—and we walk out feeling exhilarated.

Huston waited a long time to make this film, and its history is a Hollywood legend. He originally cast Bogart and Gable, but then Bogart died, and the project was shelved until 1975. Maybe it's just as well. We need movies like this more now than we did years ago, when Hollywood wasn't shy about straightforward action films. And Huston's eventual casting of Michael Caine and Sean Connery is exactly right.

They work together so well, they interact so easily and with such camaraderie, that watching them is a pleasure. They never allow themselves to be used merely as larger-than-life heroes, photographed against vast landscapes. Kipling's story, and Huston's interpretation of it, requires a lot more than that; it requires acting of a subtle and difficult sort, even if the sheer energy of the movie makes it look easy.

The two of them play former British soldiers who vow to march off into Afghanistan or somewhere and find a kingdom not yet touched by civilization. With their guns and training, they think they'll be able to take over pretty easily, manipulate the local high priests, and set themselves up as rulers. They tell their plan to an obscure colonial editor named Kipling (played very nicely by Christopher Plummer) and then they set off into the mountains. After the obligatory close calls, including an avalanche that somehow saves their lives, they find their lost land and it's just as they expected it would be.

The natives aren't too excited by their new rulers at first, but a lucky Masonic key chain saves the day—never mind how—and Connery finds himself worshiped as a deity. He even gets to like it, and condescends to Caine, who remains a Cockney and unimpressed. The movie proceeds with impossible coincidences, untold riches, romances and betrayals, and heroic last words and—best of all—some genuinely witty scenes between Connery and Caine, and when it's over we haven't learned a single thing worth knowing and there's not even a moral, to speak of, but we've had fun. It's great that someone still has the gift of making movies like this; even Huston, after thirty years, must have wondered whether he still knew how.

Map of the Human Heart

R, 95 m., 1993

Jason Scott Lee (Avik), Robert Joamie (Young Avik), Anne Parillaud (Albertine), Annie Galipeau (Young Albertine), Patrick Bergin (Walter Russell), Clotilde Courau (Rainee Russell), John Cusack (Clark), Jeanne Moreau (Sister Banville). Directed by Vincent Ward and produced by Tim Bevan and Ward. Screenplay by Louis Nowra.

Map of the Human Heart tells a soaring story of human adventure—adventure of the best kind, based not on violence, but on an amazing personal journey. It is incredible sometimes what distances can be traveled in a single human life, and this is a movie about a man who could not have imagined his end in his beginning.

The story begins in the 1930s in the Arctic north, where a young Eskimo boy is fascinated by the mapmaking activities of a visiting British cartographer named Russell (Patrick Bergin). The boy is named Avik (played as a boy by Robert Joamie, and as a man by Jason Scott Lee). Because Avik says "Holy Boy!" when he means "Holy Cow!" he comes to be known as Holy Boy in the movie.

The mapmaker arrives at the Eskimo settlement by airplane, an astonishing sight, and when he leaves he takes the boy with him—because Avik has tuberculosis, and can be treated in Montreal. The city itself is an unbelievable sight for Avik, who did not imagine such places existed. And in the hospital, he makes a lifelong friend—Albertine, played as a girl by Annie Galipeau and later, as a woman, by Anne Parillaud (from *La Femme Nikita*).

She is half-Indian, half-white. Avik is half-Eskimo, half-white. And the movie shows them standing halfway between their two worlds. For Avik, the meeting with Russell will change his life forever, setting in motion a chain of events that eventually leads to Britain during World War II, where Avik becomes an aerial photographer on bombing missions against Germany. And it is in England that he meets Albertine once again—only to find that she is involved with Russell.

This sort of romantic triangle could easily have collapsed into soapy melodrama, but Vincent Ward is too intelligent to go for the obvious treatment of this story. He doesn't allow his characters cheap sentiment, and indeed as Avik and Albertine renew their love from so long ago, we see two of the most astonishing romantic scenes I've ever seen in a movie—one on top of a barrage balloon, the other inside the hollow ceiling of the Royal Albert Hall.

The entire story of Avik is told in flashback. The movie begins in the present, with a new mapmaker (John Cusack) visiting the Eskimo village, where Avik, now an old man, tells him his story. The device at first seems unnecessary, but by the end of the film, as we see how Ward uses it to come full circle, it becomes a strength.

Ward is a young New Zealander whose previous film was also strange and original. *Navigator* (1988) was about medieval adventurers in the time of the plague, who begin to tunnel to what a mystic tells them is salvation, and somehow find their way through a time warp into a modern city—where they begin to climb the spires of a cathedral.

Oddly enough, this theme is very similar to *Map of the Human Heart*, where once again the hero flees disease and finds his destiny in a modern city. Where *Navigator* was sometimes bleak and obtuse, however, *Map of the Human Heart* is a juicier, more involving film.

Much of its power comes from the charisma of the actors. Jason Scott Lee, a newcomer who also stars in *Dragon: The Bruce Lee Story*, brings a joy and freshness to the early scenes, and makes a good contrast to the older Avik, who has lost his way. Anne Parillaud, once again, as in *La Femme Nikita*, is a combination of warmth and steely courage, and she is best in those scenes where she feels empathy for Avik, so far from home. And Patrick Bergin handles a difficult role with delicacy; he is not precisely the villain, and in some ways is a hero in this story, but when the heart is involved all motives can grow murky.

Robert Joamie and Annie Galipeau, the actors who play the young characters, also have special qualities. When Avik and Albertine become friends in the hospital, for example, there is a magical scene, played in a tent made of bed sheets, in which they exchange their deepest secrets. And when Avik leaves the hospital, he takes with him an odd photograph—Albertine's X rays, which will figure throughout the film. It almost makes sense, later, that they communicate through notes on aerial photographs, which Avik takes and Albertine catalogs, and that in turn is the link that leads to an extraordinary scene involving the fire-bombing of Dresden.

One of the best qualities of *Map of the Human Heart* was that I never quite knew where it was going. It is a love story, a war story, a lifetime story, but it manages to traverse all of that familiar terrain without doing the anticipated. The screenplay, by Louis Nowra, based on a story by Ward, deals with familiar emotions but not in a familiar way. The best movies seem to reinvent themselves as they move along, not drawing from worn-out sources, and *Map of the Human Heart* is one of 1993's best films.

Marat/Sade

NO MPAA RATING, 116 m., 1967

Ian Richardson (Jean-Paul Marat), Patrick Magee (Marquis de Sade), Glenda Jackson (Charlotte Corday), Susan Williamson (Marat's mistress), Clifford Rose (Asylum director). Directed by Peter Brook. Screenplay based on a play by Peter Weiss.

The problem of bringing a play to the screen has been approached in many ways, often disastrously, but it is hard to recall a film that solves it so triumphantly as Peter Brook's *Marat/Sade*.

Here was a vexing and difficult play, lacking entirely in the conventional kind of plot and suspense. Because of its peculiar structure, it made us aware at all times of the gap between the stage and reality.

At one level, the inmates of the asylum at Charenton were performing a play about the assassination of the French revolutionary figure Marat. At the next level, we knew that the play was being directed by one of the inmates, the Marquis de Sade, for an audience of powdered and wigged members of Napoleon's court.

At the third level was the tension during the production. Would the inmates, constantly distracted from the play by their various forms of insanity, be able to finish? Would they riot first? Would the director permit the marquis's subversive play to continue even if they did not?

And of course there was the dramatic situation itself. Here was a play ostensibly being performed in 1808 by madmen, before an audience of reactionaries, four years after the Revolution had died. Why should this situation be thought relevant to us in the middle of the twentieth century? Ah ha!

In Brook's original stage production, the levels of the drama were made clear by the theater situation itself. Everyone was present in the flesh. Here were the inmates, putting on their play. Here was the Marquis de Sade, prompting the actors and defending his production to the outraged asylum director. Here were the director, his wife, and daughter. And there, beyond the footlights, was the audience—of both 1808 and 1967.

But how could this dramatic situation be reproduced in a film, where the audience is accustomed to seeing everything and remaining unseen? I can think of two ways Brook might have approached the problem. He might have "expanded" the stage production, providing elaborate sets and dialogue more straightforward than Peter Weiss's terse, enigmatic, incomplete lines. He might, in short, have taken the stage play and written a screenplay "based" on it. He did not. He might also have become a purist, filming the play exactly as it was performed on the stage, as Gielgud and Burton did with their *Hamlet.* This would have preserved the stage production, a worthy aim, but it would have been a recording and not a new work of art. Brook also avoided this course.

Instead, he made a motion picture about a production of the play. He retained the original script, unaltered so far as I could tell. He used most of the members of the Royal Shakespeare Company in their original roles. He more or less reproduced the large communal cell of the stage production. Beyond the bars he placed an audience, which we see only in silhouette. He made one wall of the cell uniformly bright, supplying all the light for the filming.

And then, to what was still essentially a stage play, he added the techniques of cinema. The one power that a film director has, and a stage director does not, is the power to force us to see what he wants us to see. In the theater, we can look anywhere on the stage. But in the movies the camera becomes our eye and the director looks for us.

In *Marat/Sade,* Brook uses two cameras. One is high up under the ceiling, looking down dispassionately on the cell and the audience alike. The other is in the cage with the madmen, probing, investigating, whirling about to look at actors behind it.

When it faces into the light, the characters become surrealistic: There is nothing on the screen but a dazzling whiteness and uncertain green silhouettes that may be human. When it turns away from the light, we see every raw detail: the fever blisters on Marat's skin, the gray stubble on the marquis's cheeks.

The actors are superb. When we first see the marquis (Patrick Magee), he looks steadily into the camera for half a minute and the full terror of his perversion becomes clearer than any dialogue can make it. Glenda Jackson, as Marat's assassin, Charlotte Corday, weaves back and forth between the melancholy of her mental illness and the fire of the role she plays. Ian Richardson, as Marat, still advocates violence and revolution even though thousands have died and nothing has been accomplished.

Brook has achieved the very difficult. He has taken an important play, made it more immediate and powerful than it was on the stage, and at the same time created a distinguished and brilliant film.

Marie Antoinette

PG-13, 123 m., 2006

Kirsten Dunst (Marie Antoinette), Jason Schwartzman (Louis XVI), Judy Davis (Comtesse de Noailles), Rip Torn (Louis XV), Rose Byrne (Duchesse de Polignac), Asia Argento (Madame du Barry), Molly Shannon (Aunt Victoire), Shirley Henderson (Aunt Sophie). Directed by Sofia Coppola and produced by Francis Ford Coppola. Screenplay by Sofia Coppola.

Ten things that occurred to me while watching *Marie Antoinette*:

1. This is Sofia Coppola's third film centering on the loneliness of being female and surrounded by a world that knows how to use you but not how to value and understand you. It shows Coppola once again able to draw notes from actresses who rarely are required to sound them.

2. Kirsten Dunst is pitch-perfect in the title role, as a fourteen-year-old Austrian princess who is essentially purchased and imported to the French court to join with the clueless future Louis XVI (Jason Schwartzman) to produce an heir. She has self-possession, poise, and high spirits, and they are contained within a world that gives her no way to usefully express them. So she frolics and indulges herself, within a cocoon of rigid court protocol.

3. No, the picture is not informative and detailed about the actual politics of the period. That is because we are entirely within Marie Antoinette's world. And it is contained within Versailles, which shuts out all external reality. It is a self-governing architectural island, like Kane's Xanadu, that shuts out politics, reality, poverty, society.

4. Schwartzman, like Bill Murray's character in *Lost in Translation,* plays a sexually passive sad sack who would rather commiserate than take an active role. Danny Huston is priceless as Marie's older brother, brought in from Austria to give the young dauphin a few helpful suggestions about the birds and the bees. The old king, randy Louis XV (Rip Torn), would certainly need no inspiration to perform, as his mistress, Madame du Barry (Asia Argento), immediately observes.

5. All of Coppola's films, and this one most of all, use locations to define the lives of the characters. Allowed complete access to Versailles, she shows a society as single-mindedly devoted to the care and feeding of Marie Antoinette as a beehive centers on its queen.

6. On the border for the "official handover," Marie Antoinette is stopped, stripped, and searched to ascertain, brutally, if she is indeed a virgin and, for that matter, a female. In a deal like this, it pays to kick the tires. I was reminded of the scene in von Sternberg's *The Scarlett Empress* where Catherine arrives at the court of the empress and the royal physician immediately crawls under her skirt to check her royal plumbing. Every detail is covered by the French authorities; they even confiscate her beloved dogs but tell her, "You can have as many French dogs as you like."

7. Coppola has been criticized in some circles for her use of a contemporary pop overlay—hit songs, incongruous dialogue, jarring intrusions of the Now upon the Then. But no one

ever lives as Then; it is always Now. Many characters in historical films seem somehow aware that they are living in the past. Marie seems to think she is a teenager living in the present, which of course she is—and the contemporary pop references invite the audience to share her present with ours. Forman's *Amadeus* had a little of that, with its purple wigs.

8. Everyone in the audience knows Marie Antoinette was beheaded and I fear we anticipate her beheading with an unwholesome curiosity. Coppola brilliantly sidesteps a beheading and avoids bloated mob scenes by employing light, sound, and a balcony to use Marie Antoinette's death as a curtain call. Hired, essentially, to play a princess, she is a good trouper and faithful to her role. It is impossible to avoid thoughts of Diana, Princess of Wales.

9. Every criticism I have read of this film would alter its fragile magic and reduce its romantic and tragic poignancy to the level of an instructional film.

10. It is not necessary to know anything about Marie Antoinette to enjoy this film. Some of what we think we know is mistaken. According to the Coppola version, she never said, "Let them eat cake." "I would never say that," she says indignantly. What she says is, "Let them eat custard." But, paradoxically, the more you know about her, the more you may learn, because Coppola's oblique and anachronistic point of view shifts the balance away from realism and into an act of empathy for a girl swept up by events that leave her without personal choices. Before she was a queen, before she was a pawn, Marie was a fourteen-year-old girl taken from her home, stripped bare, and examined like so much horseflesh. It is astonishing with what indifference for her feelings the court aristocracy uses her for its pleasure, and in killing her disposes of its guilt.

The Marriage of Maria Braun

R, 120 m., 1979

Hanna Schygulla (Maria Braun), Klaus Lowitsch (Hermann Braun), Ivan Desny (Oswald), Gottfried John (Willi), Gisela Uhlen (Mother), R. W. Fassbinder (Peddler). Directed and produced by Rainer Werner Fassbinder. Screenplay by Peter Marthescheimer and Pea Frohlicj.

Rainer Werner Fassbinder had been working his way toward this film for years, ever since he began his astonishingly prodigious output with his first awkward but powerful films in 1969. His films were always about sex, money, and death, and his method was often to explore those three subjects through spectacularly incompatible couples (an elderly cleaning woman and a young black worker, a James Dean look-alike and a thirteen-year-old girl, a rich gay about town and a simpleminded young sweepstakes winner).

Whatever his pairings and his cheerfully ironic conclusions, though, there was always another subject lurking in the background of his approximately thirty-three (!) features. He gave us what he saw as the rise and second fall of West Germany in the three postwar decades-considered in the context of the overwhelming American influence on his country.

With the masterful epic *The Marriage of Maria Braun,* he made his clearest and most cynical statement of the theme, and at the same time gave us a movie dripping with period detail, with the costumes and decor he was famous for, with the elegant decadence his characters will sell their souls for in a late-1940s economy without chic retail goods.

Fassbinder's film begins with a Germany torn by war and ends with a gas explosion and a soccer game. His ending may seem arbitrary to some, but in the context of West German society in the 1970s it may only be good reporting. His central character, Maria Braun, is played with great style and power by Hanna Schygulla, and Maria's odyssey from the war years to the consumer years provides the film's framework.

The film opens as Maria marries a young soldier, who then goes off to battle and presumably is killed. It follows her during a long period of mourning, which is punctuated by a little amateur hooking (of which her mother tacitly approves) and then by a tender and very carefully observed liaison with a large, strong, gentle black American soldier whom she really likes—we guess.

The soldier's accidental death, and her husband's return, are weathered by Maria with rather disturbing aplomb, but then we begin to see that Maria's ability to feel has been atrophied by the war, and her ability to be surprised has withered away. If war makes any plans absolutely meaningless, then why should one waste time analyzing coincidences?

Fassbinder has some rather bitter fun with what happens in the aftermath of the soldier's death (the lovestruck, or perhaps just shell-shocked, husband voluntarily goes to prison, and Maria rises quickly in a multinational corporation). The movie is more realistic in its treatment of characters than Fassbinder sometimes is, but the events are as arbitrary as ever (and why not—events only have the meanings we assign to them, anyway).

The miniapocalypse at the end is a perfect conclusion (an ending with "meaning" would have been obscene for this film) and then I think we are left, if we want it, with the sum of what Fassbinder has to say about the rebuilding of Germany: We got the stores opened again, but we don't know much about the customers yet.

M*A*S*H

R, 116 m., 1970

Donald Sutherland (Hawkeye), Elliott Gould (Trapper John), Tom Skerritt (Duke), Sally Kellerman (Hot Lips Hoolihan), Robert Duvall (Major Burns), Jo Ann Pflug (Lieutenant Dish), Rene Auberjonois (Dago Red). Directed by Robert Altman and produced by Ingo Preminger. Screenplay by Ring Lardner, Jr.

One of the reasons M*A*S*H is so funny is that it's so desperate. It is set in a surgical hospital just behind the front lines in Korea, and it is drenched in blood. The surgeons work rapidly and with a gory detachment, sawing off legs and tying up arteries, and making their work possible by pretending they don't care. And when they are at last out of the operating tent, they devote their lives to remaining sane. The way they do that, in M*A*S*H, is to be almost metaphysically cruel. There is something about war that inspires practical jokes and the heroes (Donald Sutherland, Elliott Gould, and cronies) are inspired and utterly heartless. They sneak a microphone under the bed of Major "Hot Lips" Hoolihan, and broadcast her lovemaking to the entire camp. They drug a general and photograph him in a brothel.

We laugh, not because M*A*S*H is

Sergeant Bilko for adults, but because it is so true to the unadmitted sadist in all of us. There is perhaps nothing so exquisite as achieving (as the country song has it) sweet mental revenge against someone we hate with particular dedication. And it is the flat-out, pokerfaced hatred in M*A*S*H that makes it work. Most comedies want us to laugh at things that aren't really funny; in this one we laugh precisely because they're not funny. We laugh, that we may not cry.

But none of this philosophy comes close to the insane logic of M*A*S*H, which is achieved through a peculiar marriage of cinematography, acting, directing, and writing. The movie depends upon timing and tone to be funny. I had an opportunity to read the original script, and I found it uninteresting. It would have been a failure, if it had been directed like most comedies; but Ring Lardner, Jr., wrote it, I suspect, for exactly the approach Robert Altman used in his direction, and so the angle of a glance or the timing of a pause is funnier than any number of conventional gag lines. This is true, for example, in the football game between the surgeons and the general's team. The movie assumes, first of all, that we are intimate with the rules of football. We are. The game then becomes doubly funny, not just because the M*A*S*H boys have recruited a former pro as a ringer for their side, but because their victory depends upon legal cheating (how about a center-eligible play?). The audience's laughter is triumphant, because our guys have outsmarted the other guys. Another movie might have gone for purely physical humor in the scene (big guy walks over little guy, etc.) and blown it.

The performances have a lot to do with the movie's success. Elliott Gould and Donald Sutherland are two genuinely funny actors; they don't have to make themselves ridiculous to get a laugh. They're funny because their humor comes so directly from their personalities. They underplay everything (and Sutherland and Gould trying to downstage each other could eventually lead to complete paralysis).

Strangely enough, they're convincing as surgeons. During operations, covered with blood and gore, they mutter their way through running commentaries that sound totally professional. Sawing and hacking away at a parade of bodies, they should be driving us away, but they don't. We can take the unusually high gore-level in *M*A*S*H* because it is originally part of the movie's logic. If the surgeons didn't have to face the daily list of maimed and mutilated bodies, none of the rest of their lives would make any sense. When they are matter-of-factly cruel to "Hot Lips" Hoolihan, we cannot quite separate that from the matter-of-fact way they've got to put wounded bodies back together again. "Hot Lips," who is all army professionalism and objectivity, is less human because the suffering doesn't reach her.

I think perhaps that's what the movie is about. Gould and Sutherland and the members of their merry band of pranksters are offended because the army regulars don't feel deeply enough. "Hot Lips" is concerned with protocol, but not with war. And so the surgeons, dancing on the brink of crack-ups, dedicate themselves to making her *feel* something. Her façade offends them; no one could be unaffected by the work of this hospital, but she is. And so if they can crack her defenses and reduce her to their own level of dedicated cynicism, the number of suffering human beings in the camp will go up by one. And even if they fail, they can have a hell of a lot of fun trying. Also, of course, it's a distraction.

Master and Commander: The Far Side of the World

PG-13, 139 m., 2003

Russell Crowe (Captain Jack Aubrey), Paul Bettany (Dr. Stephen Maturin), Billy Boyd (Barrett Bonden), James D'Arcy (Lieutenant Thom Pullings), Lee Ingleby (Hollom), George Innes (Joe Plaice), Mark Lewis Jones (Mr. Hogg) Chris Larkin (Marine Captain Howard), Richard McCabe (Mr. Higgins), Robert Pugh (Mr. Allen), David Threlfall (Killick), Max Pirkis (Lord Blakeney), Edward Woodall (2nd Lieutenant William Mowett), Ian Mercer (Mr. Hollar), Max Benitz (Peter Calamy). Directed by Peter Weir and produced by Samuel Goldwyn, Jr., Duncan Henderson, John Bard Manulis, and Weir. Screenplay by Weir and John Collee, based on the books by Patrick O'Brian.

Peter Weir's *Master and Commander* is an exuberant sea adventure told with uncommon intelligence; we're reminded of well-crafted classics before the soulless age of computerized action. Based on the beloved novels of Patrick O'Brian, it re-creates the world of the British navy circa 1805 with such detail and intensity that the sea battles become stages for personality and character. They're not simply swashbuckling—although they're that, too, with brutal and intimate violence.

The film centers on the spirits of two men, Captain Jack Aubrey and ship's surgeon Stephen Maturin. Readers of O'Brian's twenty novels know them as friends and opposites—Aubrey, the realist, the man of action; Maturin, more intellectual and pensive. Each shares some of the other's qualities, and their lifelong debate represents two sides of human nature. There's a moment in *Master and Commander* when Maturin's hopes of collecting rare biological specimens are dashed by Aubrey's determination to chase a French warship, and the tension between them at that moment defines their differences.

Aubrey, captain of HMS *Surprise*, is played by Russell Crowe as a strong but fair leader of men, a brilliant strategist who is also a student, but not a coddler, of his men. He doesn't go by the book; his ability to think outside the envelope saves the *Surprise* at one crucial moment and wins a battle at another. Maturin is played by Paul Bettany, whom you may recall as Crowe's imaginary roommate in *A Beautiful Mind*. He's so cool under pressure that he performs open-skull surgery on the deck of the *Surprise* (plugging the hole with a coin), and directs the removal of a bullet from his own chest by looking in a mirror. But his passion is biology, and he is onboard primarily because the navy will take him to places where there are beetles and birds unknown to science.

The story takes place almost entirely onboard the *Surprise*, a smaller vessel outgunned by its quarry, the French warship *Acheron*. Using an actual ship at sea and sets in the vast tank in Baja California where scenes from *Titanic* were shot, Weir creates a place so palpable we think we could find our own way around. It is a very small ship for such a large ocean, living conditions are grim, some of the men have been shanghaied on board, and one of the junior officers is thirteen years old. For risking their lives, the men are rewarded with an extra tot of grog, and feel well paid. There are scenes at sea, including the rounding of Cape Horn, which are as good or better than any sea journey ever filmed, and the battle scenes are harrowing in their closeness and ferocity; the object is to get close enough in the face of withering cannon fire to board the enemy vessel and hack its crew to death.

There are only two major battle scenes in the movie (unless you count the storms of the Cape as a battle with nature). This is not a movie that depends on body counts for its impact, but on the nature of life on board such a ship. Maturin and Aubrey sometimes relax by playing classical duets, the captain on violin, the doctor on cello, and this is not an affectation but a reflection of their well-rounded backgrounds; their arguments are as likely to involve philosophy as strategy. The reason O'Brian's readers are so faithful (I am one) is because this friendship provides him with a way to voice and consider the unnatural life of a man at sea: By talking with each other, the two men talk to us about the contest between man's need to dominate and his desire to reflect.

There is time to get to know several members of the crew. Chief among them is young Lord Blakeney (Max Pirkis), the teenager who is actually put in command of the deck during one battle. Boys this young were often at sea, learning in action (Aubrey was not much older when he served under Nelson), and both older men try to shape him in their images. With Maturin he shares a passion for biology, and begins a journal filled with sketches of birds and beetles they encounter. Under Aubrey he learns to lead men, to think clearly in battle. Both men reveal their characters in teaching the boy, and that is how we best grow to know them.

There is a sense here of the long months at sea between the dangers, of loneliness and privation on "this little wooden world." One subplot involves an officer who comes to be considered bad luck—a Jonah—by the men. Another involves the accidental shooting of the surgeon. There is a visit to the far Galapagos, where Darwin would glimpse the underlying engines of life on earth. These passages are punctuation between the battles, which depend more on strategy than firepower—as they must, if the *Surprise* is to stand against the dangerous French ship. Aubrey's charge is to prevent the French from controlling the waters off Brazil, and although the two-ship contest in *Master and Commander* is much scaled down from the fleets at battle in O'Brian's original novel, *The Far Side of the World*, that simply brings the skills of individual men more into focus.

Master and Commander is grand and glorious, and touching in its attention to its characters. Like the work of David Lean, it achieves the epic without losing sight of the human, and to see it is to be reminded of the way great action movies can rouse and exhilarate us, can affirm life instead of simply dramatizing its destruction.

Match Point

R, 124 m., 2006

Jonathan Rhys-Meyers (Chris Wilton), Scarlett Johansson (Nola Rice), Emily Mortimer (Chloe Hewett Wilton), Matthew Goode (Tom Hewett), Brian Cox (Alec Hewett), Penelope Wilton (Eleanor Hewett). Directed by Woody Allen and produced by Letty Aronson, Lucy Darwin, Stephen Tenenbaum, and Gareth Wiley. Screenplay by Allen.

One reason for the fascination of Woody Allen's *Match Point* is that each and every character is rotten. This is a thriller not about good vs. evil but about various species of evil engaged in a struggle for survival of the fittest—or, as the movie makes clear, the luckiest. "I'd rather be lucky than good," Chris, the tennis pro from Ireland, tells us as the movie opens, and we see a tennis ball striking the net; it is pure luck which side it falls on. Chris's own good fortune depends on just such a lucky toss of a coin.

The movie, Allen's best since *Crimes and Misdemeanors* (1989), involves a rich British family and two outsiders who hope to enter it by using their sex appeal. They are the two sexiest people in the movie—their bad luck, since they are more attracted to each other than to their targets in the family. Still, as someone once said (Robert Heinlein, if you must know), money is a powerful aphrodisiac. He added, however, "Flowers work almost as well." Not in this movie, they don't.

The movie stars Jonathan Rhys-Meyers as Chris, a poor boy from Ireland who was on the tennis tour and now works in London as a club pro. He meets rich young Tom (Matthew Goode), who takes a lesson, likes him, and invites him to attend the opera with his family. During the opera, Tom's sister Chloe (Emily Mortimer) looks at Chris once with interest and the second time with desire. Chris does not need to have anything explained to him.

Tom's own girlfriend is Nola (Scarlett Johansson), an American who hopes to become an actress or Tom's wife, not in that order. Tom and Chloe are the children of Alec and Eleanor Hewett (Brian Cox and Penelope Wilton), who have serious money, as symbolized by the country house where the crowd assembles for the weekend. It's big enough to welcome two Merchant-Ivory productions at the same time.

Chloe likes Chris. She wants Chris. Her parents want Chloe to have what she wants. Alec offers Chris a job in "one of my companies"—always a nice touch, that. Tom likes Nola, but to what degree, and do his parents approve? All is decided in the fullness of time, and now I am going to become maddeningly vague in order not to spoil the movie's twists and turns, which are ingenious and difficult to anticipate.

Let us talk instead in terms of the underlying philosophical issues. To what degree are we prepared to set aside our moral qualms in order to indulge in greed and selfishness? I have just finished rereading *The Wings of the Dove* by Henry James, in which a young man struggles heroically with just such a question. He is in love with a young woman he cannot afford to marry, and a rich young heiress is under the impression he is in love with her. The heiress is dying. Everyone advises him he would do her a great favor by marrying her; then after her death, inheriting her wealth, he could afford to marry the woman he loves. But isn't this unethical? No one has such moral qualms in Allen's film, not even sweet Chloe, who essentially has her daddy buy Chris for her. The key question facing the major players is: Greed or lust? How tiresome to have to choose.

Without saying why, let me say that fear also enters into the equation. In a moral universe, it would be joined by guilt, but not here. The fear is that in trying to satisfy both greed and lust, a character may have to lose both, which

would be a great inconvenience. At one point this character sees a ghost, but this is not Hamlet's father, crying for revenge; this ghost drops by to discuss loopholes in a "perfect crime."

When *Match Point* premiered at Cannes 2005, the critics agreed it was "not a typical Woody Allen film." This assumes there is such a thing. Allen has worked in a broad range of genres and struck a lot of different notes, although often he uses a Woody Figure (preferably played by himself) as the hero. *Match Point* contains no one anything like Woody Allen, is his first film set in London, is constructed with a devious clockwork plot that would distinguish a *film noir*, and causes us to identify with some bad people. In an early scene, a character is reading *Crime and Punishment*, and during the movie, as during the novel, we are inside the character's thoughts.

The movie is more about plot and moral vacancy than about characters, and so Allen uses typecasting to quickly establish the characters and set them to their tasks of seduction, deception, lying, and worse. Rhys-Meyers has a face that can express crafty desire, which is not pure lust but more like lust transformed by quick strategic calculations. Goode, as his rich friend, is clueless almost as an occupation. Mortimer plays a character incapable of questioning her own happiness, no matter how miserable it should make her. Johansson's visiting American has been around the block a few times, but like all those poor American girls in Henry James, she is helpless when the Brits go to work on her. She has some good dialogue in the process.

"Men think I may be something special," she tells Chris.

"Are you?"

"No one's ever asked for their money back."

Match Point, which deserves to be ranked with Allen's *Annie Hall, Hannah and Her Sisters, Manhattan, Everyone Says I Love You,* and *Crimes and Misdemeanors,* has a terrible fascination that lasts all the way through. We can see a little way ahead, we can anticipate some of the mistakes and hazards, but the movie is too clever for us, too cynical. We expect the kinds of compromises and patented endings that most thrillers provide, and this one goes right to the wall. There are cops hanging around trying to figure out what, if anything, anyone in the movie might have been up to, but they're too smart and logical to figure this one out. Bad luck.

Matchstick Men

PG-13, 120 m., 2003

Nicolas Cage (Roy), Sam Rockwell (Frank Mercer), Alison Lohman (Angela), Bruce McGill (Frechette), Bruce Altman (Dr. Klein). Directed by Ridley Scott and produced by Sean Bailey, Ted Griffin, Jack Rapke, Scott, and Steve Starkey. Screenplay by Nicholas Griffin and Ted Griffin, based on the book by Eric Garcia.

Ridley Scott's *Matchstick Men* tells three stories, each one intriguing enough to supply a movie. It is: (1) the story of a crisis in the life of a man crippled by neurotic obsessions; (2) the story of two con men who happen onto a big score; and (3) the story of a man who meets the teenage daughter he never knew he had, and finds himself trying to care for her. The hero of all three stories is Roy (Nicolas Cage), who suffers from obsessive-compulsive disorder, agoraphobia, panic attacks, you name it. His con-man partner is Frank (Sam Rockwell). His daughter is Angela (Alison Lohman), and Roy is so fearful that when he decides to contact her, he persuades his shrink to make the phone call.

I wish that you had seen the movie so we could discuss what a sublime job it does of doing full justice to all three of these stories, which add up to more, or perhaps less, than the sum of their parts. The screenplay for *Matchstick Men* is an achievement of Oscar caliber— so absorbing that whenever it cuts away from "the plot," there is another, better plot to cut to. Brothers Ted and Nicholas Griffin adapted it from the novel by Eric Garcia. Cage bought the movie rights before it was published, and no wonder, because the character of Roy is one of the great roles of recent years; he's a nut case, a clever crook, and a father who learns to love, all in one. Cage effortlessly plays these three sides to his character, which by their nature would seem to be in conflict.

As the movie opens, Roy and Frank are playing a sophisticated form of the Pigeon Drop, in which victims are convinced they have a tax refund coming, and are then visited by Frank and Roy themselves, posing as federal agents who want cooperation in catching the tax frauds. Elegant. Frank keeps wondering when Roy will be ready to pull a really big job, but it's all Roy can do to get out of bed in the morning.

An open door can cause a panic attack. He goes into spasms of compulsive behavior, and only the pills prescribed by Dr. Klein (Bruce Altman) seem to hold him together at all. When he spills his pills down the drain and Klein's office is closed, Cage has a scene in a pharmacy that is the equal of his opening moments in *Leaving Las Vegas* as an illustration of a man desperately trying to get what he needs before he implodes.

Enter the mark: Frechette (Bruce McGill), a man who might want to turn a profit laundering large sums of British money that Roy and Frank happen to have on hand. The way they bait this trap, spring it, and then move Frechette up to a really large sum has the fascination of any good con. The secret, Roy explains, is that he doesn't take people's money: "They give it to me." The victims always think it's their own idea. And since they're breaking the law, who can they complain to?

Meanwhile, Dr. Klein learns more about Roy's early, unhappy marriage, which produced a daughter after Roy left. Would it help to meet this girl, who would now be about fifteen? It might. After Klein makes the first advance, Roy approaches Angela after school, his tics and jerks and twitches all in demo mode. Angela comes for a "trial weekend," stays for a while, and eventually becomes a steadying influence for her father. At first Roy is reluctant to tell her about himself, but when he finally does admit he's not very proud of what he does, that's the first moment in the movie when he seems calm and even relaxed.

Nicolas Cage is accused of showboating, but I prefer to think he swings for the fences. Sometimes he strikes out *(Gone in 60 Seconds)*, but more often he connects (he took enormous risks in *Leaving Las Vegas, Bringing Out the Dead,* and *Adaptation*). He has a kind of raging zeal that possesses his characters; what in another actor would be overacting is, with Cage, a kind of fearsome intensity.

Rockwell, Lohman, McGill, and Altman are all perfectly cast, which is essential, since they must convince us without the movie making any effort to insist. Lohman in particular is effective; I learn to my astonishment that she's twenty-four, but here she plays a fifteen-year-old with all the tentative love and sudden vulnerability that the role requires when your dad is a whacko confidence man.

Because this is a movie about con men and a con game, there are elements I must not reveal. But let's talk about the very last scene—the one that begins "One Year Later." This is a scene that could have gone terribly wrong, spoiled by being too obvious, sentimental, angry, or tricky. Ridley Scott and his players know just how to handle it; they depend on who these characters really are. If you consider what the characters have gone through and mean to one another, then this scene has a kind of transcendence to it. It doesn't trash the story or add one more twist just for fun, but looks with dispassionate honesty at what, after all, people must believe who do this sort of thing for a living.

May

R, 95 m., 2003

Angela Bettis (May Canady), Jeremy Sisto (Adam Stubbs), Anna Faris (Polly), James Duval (Blank), Nichole Hiltz (Ambrosia), Kevin Gage (Papa), Merle Kennedy (Mama), Chandler Hect (Young May). Directed by Lucky McKee and produced by Marius Balchunas and Scott Sturgeon. Screenplay by McKee.

May is a horror film and something more and deeper, something disturbing and oddly moving. It begins as the story of a strange young woman, it goes for laughs and gets them, it functions as a black comedy, but then it glides past the comedy and slides slowly down into a portrait of madness and sadness. The title performance by Angela Bettis is crucial to the film's success. She plays a twisted character who might easily go over the top into parody, and makes her believable, sympathetic, and terrifying.

The movie will inevitably be compared with *Carrie*, not least because Bettis starred in the 2002 TV version of that story. Like *Carrie*, it is about a woman who has been wounded by society and finds a deadly revenge. But *May* is not a supernatural film. It follows the traditional outlines of a horror or slasher film, up to a point—and then it fearlessly follows its character into full madness. We expect some kind of a U-turn or cop-out, but no; the writer and director, Lucky McKee, never turns back from his story's implacable logic. This is his solo directing debut, and it's kind of amazing. You get the feeling he's the real thing.

Bettis plays May Canady, who as a girl had a "lazy eye" that made her an outcast at school. After a brief prologue, we meet her in her twenties, as an assistant in a veterinary clinic. She is shy, quirky, askew, but in a curiously sexy way, so that when she meets the good-looking Adam Stubbs (Jeremy Sisto), he is intrigued. "I'm weird," she tells him. "I like weird," he says. "I like weird a lot."

Uh-huh. His idea of weird is attending the revival of a Dario Argento horror film. He shows May his own student film, which begins with a young couple kissing and caressing and then moves on inexorably into mutual cannibalism. May likes it. She snuggles closer to him on the sofa. Afterward, she gives him her review: "I don't think that she could have gotten his whole finger in one bite, though. That part was kind of far-fetched."

Bettis makes May peculiar but fully human. There are scenes here of such close observation, of such control of body language, voice, and behavior, evoking such ferocity and obsession, that we are reminded of Lady Macbeth. It is as hard to be excellent in a horror film as in Shakespeare. Harder, maybe, because the audience isn't expecting it. Sisto's performance as Adam is carefully calibrated to show an intelligent guy who is intrigued, up to a point, and then smart enough to prudently back away. He's not one of those horror movie dumbos who makes stupid mistakes. Notice the look in his eye after he asks her to describe some of the weird stuff that goes on at the animal hospital, and she does, more graphically than he requires.

May's colleague at the clinic is Polly (Anna Faris), a lesbian, always open to new experiences. One day when May cuts herself with a scalpel, Polly is fascinated. Then May unexpectedly cuts her. Polly recoils, screams, considers, and says, "I kind of liked it. Do me again." Like Adam, she is erotically stirred by May's oddness—up to a point. There is an erotic sequence involving May and Polly, not explicit but very evocative, and it's not just a "sex scene," but a way to show that for Polly sex is entertainment and for May it is of fundamental importance.

McKee uses various fetishes in an understated way. May is not a smoker, but she treasures a pack of cigarettes that Adam gave her, and the precious cigarettes are measured out one by one as accomplices to her actions. She has a doll from childhood that gazes from its glass cabinet; in a lesser movie, it would come alive, but in this one it does all the necessary living within May's mind. When May volunteers to work with blind kids, we fear some kind of exploitation, but the scenes are handled to engender suspense, not disrespect.

The movie subtly darkens its tone until, when the horrifying ending arrives, we can see how we got there. There is a final shot that would get laughs in another kind of film, but *May* earns the right to it, and it works, and we understand it.

There are so many bad horror movies. A good one is incredibly hard to make. It has to feel a fundamental sympathy for its monster, as movies as different as *Frankenstein, Carrie,* and *The Silence of the Lambs* did. It has to see that they suffer, too. The crimes of too many horror monsters seem to be for their own entertainment, or ours. In the best horror movies, the crimes are inescapable, and the monsters are driven toward them by the merciless urgency of their natures.

McCabe and Mrs. Miller

R, 120 m., 1971

Warren Beatty (McCabe), Julie Christie (Mrs. Miller), Rene Auberjonois (Shehan), Hugh Millais (Butler), Michael Murphy (Sears), William Devane (Lawyer). Directed by Robert Altman and produced by David Foster and Mitchell Brower. Screenplay by Altman and Brian McKay.

McCabe rides into the town of Presbyterian Church under a lowering sky, dismounts, takes off his buffalo-hide coat, puts on his bowler hat, and mumbles something under his breath that we can't quite make out, but the tone of voice is clear enough. This time, he's not going to let the bastards grind him down. He steps off through the mud puddles to the only local saloon, throws a cloth on the table, and takes out a pack of cards, to start

again. His plan is to build a whorehouse with a bathhouse out in back, and get rich. By the end of the movie, he will have been offered $6,250 for his holdings, and he will be sitting thoughtfully in a snowbank, dead, as if thinking it all over.

And yet Robert Altman's *McCabe and Mrs. Miller* doesn't depend on that final death for its meaning. It doesn't kill a character just to get a trendy existential feel about the meaninglessness of it all. No, McCabe doesn't find it meaningless at all, and once Mrs. Miller explains the mistake he made in his reasoning, he rides all the way into the next town to try to sell his holdings for half what he was asking, because he'd rather not die.

Death is very final in this Western, because the movie is about life. Most Westerns are about killing and getting killed, which means they're not about life and death at all. We spend a time in the life of a small frontier town, which grows up before our eyes out of raw, unpainted lumber and tubercular canvas tents. We get to know the town pretty well, because Altman has a gift for making movies that seem to eavesdrop on activity that would have been taking place anyway.

That was what happened in *M*A*S*H,* where a lot of time didn't have to be wasted in introducing the characters and explaining the relationships between them, because the characters already knew who they were and how they felt about each other. In a lot of movies, an actor appears on the screen and has no identity at all until somebody calls him "Smith" or "Slim," and then he's Smith or Slim. In *McCabe and Mrs. Miller,* Altman uses a tactfully unobtrusive camera, a distinctive conversational style of dialogue, and the fluid movements of his actors to give us people who are characters from the moment we see them; we have the sense that when they leave camera range they're still thinking, humming, scratching, chewing, and nodding to each other in the street.

McCabe and Mrs. Miller are an organic part of this community. We are aware, of course, that they're played by Warren Beatty and Julie Christie, but rarely have stars been used so completely for their talents rather than their fame. We don't ever think much about McCabe being Warren Beatty, and Mrs.

Miller being Julie Christie; they're there along with everybody else in town, and the movie just happens to be about their lives.

Because the movie is about a period in the lives of several people (and not about a series of events that occur to one-dimensional characters), McCabe and Mrs. Miller change during the course of the story. Mrs. Miller is a tough Cockney madam who convinces McCabe that he needs a competent manager for his whorehouse: How would *he* ever know enough about managing women? He agrees, and she lives up to her promise, and they're well on their way to making enough money for her to get out of this dump of a mining town and back to San Francisco, where, she believes, a woman of her caliber belongs.

All of this happens in an indoor sort of a way, and by that I don't mean that the movie looks like it was shot on a sound stage. The outdoors is always there, and people are always coming in out of it and shaking the rain from their hats, and we see the trees whipping in the wind through the windows. But it's a wet autumn and then a cold winter, so people naturally congregate in saloons and grocery stores and whorehouses, and the climate forces a sense of community. Then the enforcers come to town: The suave, Scottish-accented Butler, who kills people who won't sell out to the Company, and his two sidekicks. One of them is slack-jawed and mean, and the other is a nervous blond kid with the bare makings of a mustache. On the suspension bridge that gets you across the river to the general store, he kills another kid—a rawboned, easygoing country kid with a friendly smile—and it is one of the most affecting and powerful deaths there ever has been in a Western.

The final hunt for McCabe takes place in almost deserted streets, because the church is burning down and everybody is out at the edge of town trying to save it. The church burns during a ghostly, heavy daylight snowstorm: fire and ice. And McCabe almost gets away. Mrs. Miller, who allowed him into her bed but always, except once, demanded five dollars for the privilege, caught on long before he did that the Company would rather kill him than go up $2,000. She is down at the foot of town, in Chinatown, lost in an opium dream while the snow drifts against his body.

McCabe and Mrs. Miller is like no other Western ever made.

Me and You and Everyone We Know

R, 95 m., 2005

John Hawkes (Richard), Miranda July (Christine), Miles Thompson (Peter), Brandon Ratcliff (Robby), Carlie Westerman (Sylvie), Hector Elias (Michael), Brad Henke (Andrew), Natasha Slayton (Heather), Najarra Townsend (Rebecca), Tracy Wright (Nancy). Directed by July and produced by Gina Kwon. Screenplay by July.

Miranda July's *Me and You and Everyone We Know* is a film that with quiet confidence creates a fragile magic. It's a comedy about falling in love when, for you, love requires someone who speaks your rare emotional language. Yours is a language of whimsy and daring, of playful mind games and bold challenges. Hardly anybody speaks that language, the movie suggests—only me and you and everyone we know, because otherwise we wouldn't bother knowing them.

As a description of a movie, I suppose that sounds maddening. An example. A young woman walks into a department store, and in the shoe department she sees a young man who fascinates her. His hand is bandaged. She approaches him and essentially offers the gift of herself. He is not interested; he's going through a divorce and is afraid of losing his children. She asks him how he hurt his hand. "I was trying to save my life," he says. We've already seen how it happened: He covered his hand with lighter fluid and set it on fire to delight his two sons. He didn't think lighter fluid really burns you when you do that. He was wrong. He was thinking of rubbing alcohol.

Now imagine these two characters, named Christine (Miranda July) and Richard (John Hawkes), as they walk down the street. She suggests that the block they are walking down is their lives. And so now they are halfway down the street and halfway through their lives, and before long they will be at the end. It is impossible to suggest how poetic this scene is; when it's over, you think, that was a perfect scene, and no other scene can ever be like it.

Richard and Christine are at the center of

the film, but through Richard's sons we meet other characters. His seven-year-old is named Robby, and is played by Brandon Ratcliff, who read my review from Sundance and wrote me a polite and helpful letter in which he assured me he's as smart as an eleven-year-old. In the movie, he visits an online sex chat room even though he knows nothing about sex. He knows enough about computers to sound like he does, however, by cutting and pasting words, and using open-ended questions. Asked what turns him on, he writes "poop," not because it does, but possibly because it is the only word he can spell that he thinks has something to do with the subject.

His fourteen-year-old brother, Peter (Miles Thompson), is being persecuted by two girls in his class named Heather (Natasha Slayton) and Rebecca (Najarra Townsend). They are intensely interested in oral sex, but unsure about its theory and technique. They decide to practice on Peter. I know this sounds perverse and explicit, and yet the fact is, these scenes play with an innocence and tact that is beyond all explaining. They are about what an embarrassment and curiosity sex is when you're old enough to know it exists but too young to know how it's done and what it's for. They are much intrigued by a neighbor who is a dirty old man in theory but not in practice.

Other characters have other plans for perfect lifetimes. Young Peter, once he shakes off the relentless Heather and Rebecca, is fascinated by Sylvie (Carlie Westerman), a ten-year-old neighbor who does comparison shopping to get the best price on kitchen appliances. Peter catches her ironing some towels. They are going straight into her hope chest, she explains. She is preparing her own dowry. Her future husband, when she grows up and finds him, had better be ready to be good and married.

There is also an art curator (Tracy Wright) who has a strange way of evaluating art, as if she's afraid it may violate rules she's afraid she doesn't know. She has a sexual hunger that proves particularly hard to deal with. She is, however, able to project her longings into the uncomprehending world; the strategy she uses, and the result it brings, is a scene of such inevitability and perfection that we laugh at least partly out of admiration.

Miranda July is a performance artist; this is her first feature film (it won the Special Jury Prize at Sundance, and at Cannes won the Camera d'Or as best first film, and the Critics' Week grand prize). Performance art sometimes deals with the peculiarities of how we express ourselves, with how odd and wonderful it is to be alive. So does this film. As Richard slowly emerges from sadness and understands that Christine values him, and he must value her, for reasons only the two of them will ever understand, the movie holds its breath, waiting to see if their delicate connection will hold.

Me and You and Everyone We Know is a balancing act, as July ventures into areas that are risky and transgressive, but uses a freshness that disarms them, a directness that accepts human nature and likes to watch it at work. The MPAA gave it an R rating "for disturbing sexual content involving children," but the one thing it isn't is disturbing. When the movie was over at Sundance, I let out my breath and looked across the aisle at another critic. I wanted to see if she felt how I did. "What did you think?" she said. "I think it's the best film at the festival," I said. "Me too," she said.

Mean Streets
R, 110 m., 1974

Robert De Niro (Johnny Boy), Harvey Keitel (Charlie). Directed by Martin Scorsese and produced by Jonathan T. Taplin. Screenplay by Scorsese and Mardik Martin.

Martin Scorsese's *Mean Streets* isn't so much a gangster movie as a perceptive, sympathetic, finally tragic story about how it is to grow up in a gangster environment. Its characters (like Scorsese himself) have grown up in New York's Little Italy, and they understand everything about that small slice of human society except how to survive in it. The two most important characters, Charlie and Johnny Boy, move through the Mafia environment almost because it's expected of them. Charlie is a Catholic with pathological guilt complexes, but because the mob is the family business, he never quite forces himself to make the connection between right and wrong and what he does. Not that he's very good at being a

Mafioso: He's twenty-seven, but he still lives at home; he's a collector for his uncle's protection racket, but the collections don't bring in much. If he has any luck at all, he will be able to take over a bankrupt restaurant.

He is, at least fitfully, a realist. Johnny Boy, on the other hand, is a violent, uncontrolled product of romanticized notions of criminal street life. Little Italy is all around him, and yet he seems to have formed his style and borrowed half his vocabulary from the movies. He contains great and ugly passions, and can find no way to release them except in sudden violent bursts. Charlie is in love with Johnny Boy's sister, and he also feels a dogged sense of responsibility for Johnny Boy: He goes up on a roof one night when Johnny is shooting out streetlights and talks him down. At least Johnny releases his angers in overt ways. Charlie suppresses everything, and sometimes in desperation passes his hand through a flame and wonders about the fires of hell. He takes his Catholicism literally.

Scorsese places these characters in a perfectly realized world of boredom and small joys, sudden assaults, the possibility of death, and the certainty of mediocrity. He shot on location in Little Italy, where he was born and where he seems to know every nuance of architecture and personality, and his story isn't built like a conventional drama: It emerges from the daily lives of the characters. They hang out. They go to the movies. They eat, they drink, they get in sudden fights that end as quickly as a summer storm. Scorsese photographs them with fiercely driven visual style. We never have the sense of a scene being set up and then played out; his characters hurry to their dooms while the camera tries to keep pace. There's an improvisational feel even in scenes that we know, because of their structure, couldn't have been improvised.

Scorsese got the same feel in his first feature, *Who's That Knocking at My Door?* (1967). *Mean Streets* is a sequel, and Scorsese gives us the same leading actor (Harvey Keitel) to assure the continuity. In the earlier film, he was still on the edge of life, of sex, of violence. Now he has been plunged in, and he isn't equal to the experience. He's not tough enough to be a Mafia collector (and not strong enough to resist). Johnny Boy is played by Robert De Niro

and it's a marvelous performance, filled with urgency and restless desperation.

The movie's scenes of violence are especially effective because of the way Scorsese stages them. We don't get spectacular effects and skillfully choreographed struggles. Instead, there's something realistically clumsy about the fights in this movie. A scene in a pool hall, in particular, is just right in the way it shows its characters fighting and yet mindful of their suits (possibly the only suits they have). The whole movie feels like life in New York; there are scenes in a sleazy nightclub, on fire escapes, and in bars, and they all feel as if Scorsese has been there.

Medium Cool
R, 110 m., 1969

Robert Forster (John), Verna Bloom (Eileen), Peter Bonerz (Gus), Marianna Hill (Ruth), Harold Blankenship (Harold), Christine Bergstrom (Dede). Directed by Haskell Wexler and produced by Tully Friedman and Wexler. Screenplay by Wexler.

I don't think I exactly want to review Haskell Wexler's *Medium Cool*. A formal review (or even my chaotic version of one) would be inappropriate to this most informal and direct of films. What is needed is a response and some speculation.

Besides, you already know pretty much what *Medium Cool* is about. We had a long interview with Wexler six weeks ago in the *Sun-Times*. The national magazines are full of photos of his characters: the TV cameraman, his sidekick, his girl, and her remarkable twelve-year-old son. And by this stage of the game, you don't want to read another rehash. So instead, I'd like to discuss the form of *Medium Cool*—that is, the way the movie was conceived, shot, and edited.

Five years ago, this film would have been considered incomprehensible to the general movie audience. Now it's going into a big first-run house, and you don't hear the Loop exhibitors talking so scornfully about "art films" anymore. So what's going on when an experimental, radical film such as *Medium Cool* can get this sort of exposure?

What's happened, I think, is that moviemakers have at last figured out how bright the average moviegoer is. By that I don't mean they're making more "intelligent" pictures. I mean they understand how quickly we can catch on to things.

Even five years ago, most Hollywood movies insisted on stopping at B on their way from A to C. Directors were driven by a fierce compulsion to explain how the characters got out of that train and up to the top of the mountain. And so their movies crept along slowly, and we spent so much time climbing the mountain that we didn't give a damn what happened when we finally got there.

But a movie named *The Graduate* didn't bother with that. For years, underground and experimental films had stopped using the in-between steps. But now, here was one of the biggest commercial movies of all time, and when Benjamin plunged onto the prone form of Mrs. Robinson, there was a cut in mid-action to Benjamin landing belly-down on a rubber raft in a swimming pool. And no one had to explain why Mrs. Robinson turned into a raft, or how Benjamin got into the pool.

Most of us are so conditioned by the quick-cutting and free association of ideas in TV commercials that we think faster than feature-length movies can move. We understand cinematic shorthand. And we like movies that give us credit for our wit. We didn't like *Shoes of the Fisherman,* no matter how noble its intentions, because it insisted on explaining everything. We liked *Bullitt* because it moved at our speed.

And *Bullitt,* to grab a recent example, did something else. In all movies, from Bogart to James Bond, symbols meant what they were. Bogart got into a souped-up Buick Special and Bond got into an Aston-Martin, and it was the car's prestige that was important. But in fact, the cars mostly sat there being Buicks and Aston-Martins.

Bullitt distilled the power of the car symbol. The *Bullitt* chase was not about what a Mustang and a Charger were—but about what they did. And it was the doing, the action, the speed, that exploited the cars as symbols of power.

A third example and I'm through.

All of us are capable of switching on the TV late show at any point during the movie and figuring out for ourselves what's going on. The other night, I turned on a John Wayne sea epic. In the first thirty seconds, Wayne had given orders to burn the lifeboats for fuel and had sternly ordered a girl to stay off the bridge in time of crisis.

From these two events, it was possible to theorize that the movie was (a) about an endangered mission, most likely undertaken for a crucial purpose—else why the fuel shortage?—and (b) had a romantic subplot that probably involved Wayne's delayed realization that he loved the girl.

I made these brilliant deductions on the basis of having seen countless other Grade B movies, and on a familiarity with the basic Wayne character. Another thirty seconds probably would have revealed where the ship was headed, and why. If I'd held out fifteen minutes, I probably would have gotten to see Wayne kiss the girl.

Conventional movie plots telegraph themselves because we know all the basic genres and typical characters. Wexler's *Medium Cool* is one of several new movies that knows these things about the movie audience (others include *The Rain People, Easy Rider, Alice's Restaurant,* etc.). Of the group, *Medium Cool* is probably the best. That may be because Wexler, for most of his career, has been a very good cinematographer, and so he's trained to see a movie in terms of its images, not its dialogue and story.

In *Medium Cool,* Wexler forges back and forth through several levels. There is a fictional story about the TV cameraman, his romance, his job, his girl, and her son. There is also documentary footage about the riots during the Democratic Convention. There is a series of set-up situations that pretend to be real (women taking marksmanship practice, the TV crew confronting black militants). There are fictional characters in real situations (the girl searching for her son in Grant Park). There are real characters in fictional situations (the real boy, playing a boy, expressing his real interest in pigeons).

The mistake would be to separate the real things from the fictional. They are all significant in exactly the same way. The National Guard troops are no more real than the love scene, or the melodramatic accident that ends the film. All the images have meaning because of the way they are associated with each other.

And *Medium Cool* also does the second thing—sees not the symbols but their function.

Wexler doesn't see the hippie kids in Grant Park as hippie kids. He doesn't see the clothes or the lifestyle, and he doesn't hear the words. He sees their function; they are there entirely because the National Guard is there and vice versa.

Both sides have a function only when they confront each other. Without the confrontation, all you'd have would be the kids, scattered all over the country, and the guardsmen, dressed in civilian clothes and spending the week at their regular jobs. So it's not what they are that's important—it's what they're doing there.

Wexler does the third thing, too. He evokes our memories of the hundreds of other movies we've seen to imply things about his story that he never explains on the screen.

The basic story of the romance (young professional falls in love with war widow, gradually wins friendship of her hostile son) is certainly not original. If Wexler had spelled it out, it would have been conventional and boring.

Instead, he limits himself to the characteristic and significant aspects of this relationship (the boy likes pigeons, the woman is a teacher, the location is Uptown, the time is the Democratic Convention, the woman seems more genuine to the cameraman than the model he's living with). And these are the scenes Wexler shoots. The rest of the romance is implied but never shown; we skip B on our way from A to C.

Finally, *Medium Cool* is so important and absorbing because of the way Wexler weaves all these elements together. He has made an almost perfect example of the new movie. Because we are so aware this is a movie, it seems more relevant and real than the smooth fictional surface of, say, *Midnight Cowboy*.

This is true even of the last scene—that accident that happens for no reason at all. Accidents are always accidents, and they always happen for no reason at all. When we get it, it occurs to us that it's the first movie accident we've ever seen that we weren't expecting for at least five minutes.

Menace II Society

R, 97 m., 1993

Tyrin Turner (Caine), Larenz Tate (O-Dog), Jada Pinkett (Ronnie), MC Eiht (A-Wax), Marilyn Coleman (Grandmama), Arnold Johnson (Grandpapa), Samuel L. Jackson (Tat Lawson). Directed by Allen and Albert Hughes and produced by Darin Scott. Screenplay by Tyger Williams.

Caine, the young man at the center of *Menace II Society*, is not an evil person in the usual sense of the word. He has a good nature and a quick intelligence, and in another world he might have turned out happy and productive. But he was not raised in a world that allowed that side of his character to develop, and that is the whole point of this powerful film.

Caine, like so many young black men from the inner city, has grown up in a world where the strong values of an older generation are being undermined by the temptations of guns, drugs, and violence. As a small boy he sees his father murder a man over a trivial matter. He sees his mother die of an overdose. He takes an older neighborhood man as his mentor, only to see him go to prison. By the time he is in high school, Caine wears a beeper on his belt and is a small-time drug dealer. The film's narration tells us he is society's nightmare: "He's young, he's black, and he doesn't give a shit."

We see that it is more complicated than that. The tragedy of Caine's life is that he cannot stand back a little and get a wider view, and see what alternatives are available to him. He adopts the street values that are based on a corruption of the word "respect." He wants respect, but has done nothing to deserve it. For him, "respect" is the product of intimidation: If you back down because you fear him, you "respect" him.

The movie opens as Caine and O-Dog, his heedless, violent friend, enter a Korean grocery store to buy a couple of beers. The grocer and his wife, who don't want trouble, ask them to make their purchase and leave. Caine and O-Dog engage in a little meaningless verbal intimidation, aware that because they are young and black they can score some points from the couple's fear. "I feel bad for your mother," the grocer says as they are about to leave. That is all O-Dog needs to hear, and he murders the grocer and then forces his wife to hand over the store's security videotape before killing her, too.

Caine is shocked by this sudden violent development. He sees it in terms of his own misfortune: He went out to get a beer, and now he's an accessory to murder. During the course of the movie, O-Dog will use the videotape for entertainment at parties, freeze-framing the moment of the grocer's death. Eventually dozens of people will know who killed the grocer, but nobody will be charged with the crime, because such violence is so common and the laws are such that many murders simply slip through the fingers of the police.

There are people in Caine's life who care for him. A friend who has an athletic scholarship. A teacher at school. His God-fearing grandparents, who eventually throw him out of the house. His mentor's girlfriend, who wants him to move to Atlanta with her and start over.

But Caine's world is narrow and limited. He has the values of his immediate circle, and the lack of imagination: He cannot quite envision a world for himself outside of the limited existence of guns, cars, drugs, and swagger. This movie, like many others, reminds us that murder is the leading cause of death among young black men. But it doesn't blame the easy target of white racism for that: It looks unblinkingly at a street culture that offers its members few choices that are not self-destructive.

If *Boyz N the Hood* was the story of a young man lucky enough to grow up with parents who cared, and who escapes the dangers of the street culture, *Menace II Society* is, tragically, about many more young men who are not so lucky. The movie was directed by Allen and Albert Hughes, twin brothers, and is based on the screenplay they wrote with their friend, Tyger Williams. The brothers were twenty-one when they finished the film, but already they had a track record of many music videos. Their mother gave them a video camera when they were twelve, they told me at the Cannes Film Festival, and that pointed them away from the possibilities they show in their film, and toward their current success.

The message here is obvious: Many of the victims of street and gang violence are a great loss to society, their potential destroyed by a bankrupt value system. The Hughes twins, given a chance, reveal here that they are natural filmmakers. *Menace II Society* is as well-

directed a film as you'll see from America in 1993, an unsentimental and yet completely involving story of a young man who cannot quite manage to see a way around his fate.

It's impressive, the way the filmmakers tell Caine's story without making him seem either the hero or victim; he is presented more as a typical example. He is not bad, but he does bad things and clearly would do more. We are not asked to sympathize with him, but to a degree we do, in the sense of the empathetic prayer, "There, but for the grace of God, go I." It is clear that, given the realities of the society in which he is raised, Caine's fate is likely.

The film is filled with terrific energy. The performances, especially those by Tyrin Turner as Caine, Larenz Tate as O-Dog, and Jada Pinkett as Ronnie, the caring girlfriend, are filled with life and conviction. Because *Menace II Society* paints such an uncompromised picture, and offers no easy hope or optimistic conclusion, it may be seen as a very negative film in some quarters. "If you hate blacks, this movie will make you hate them more," Allen Hughes said during his Cannes visit. "But true liberals will get something sparked in their heads."

That is true. If *Menace II Society* shows things the way they often are—and I believe it does—then the film is not negative for depicting them truthfully. Anyone who views this film thoughtfully must ask why our society makes guns easier to obtain and use than any other country in the civilized world. And that is only the most obvious of the many questions the film inspires.

Men with Guns
R, 128 m., 1998

Federico Luppi (Dr. Fuentes), Damian Delgado (Domingo, the Soldier), Dan Rivera Gonzalez (Conejo, the Boy), Tania Cruz (Graciela, the Mute Girl), Damian Alcazar (Padre Portillo, the Priest), Mandy Patinkin (Andrew), Kathryn Grody (Harriet). Directed by John Sayles and produced by R. Paul Miller and Maggie Renzi. Screenplay by Sayles.

Men with Guns tells the story of a doctor in an unnamed Central American country who makes a trip into the rain forest to visit the young medical students he trained some years earlier. They were supposed to fan out among the Indian villages, fighting tapeworm and other scourges. The doctor has reason to believe many of them have been killed.

The doctor's journey is enlarged by John Sayles into an allegory about all countries where men with guns control the daily lives of the people. Some of the men are with the government, some are guerrillas, some are thieves, some are armed to protect themselves, and to the ordinary people it hardly matters: The man with the gun does what he wants, and his reasons are irrelevant—unknown perhaps even to himself.

The film takes the form of a journey, sometimes harrowing, sometimes poetic. It has a backbone of symbolism, as many great stories do. As the doctor moves from the city to the country, from the shore to the mountains, he also moves through history. We see the ruins of older civilizations that lived in this land, and we see powerless villagers moved here and there according to arbitrary whims. They are killed by the military for helping the guerrillas, and killed by the guerrillas for helping the military, and their men are killed simply because they are men without guns. There is no suggestion that either military or guerrillas have any larger program than to live well off the spoils of power.

The doctor (Federico Luppi), tall and white-haired, has a grave dignity. He is not an action hero, but a man who has been given a pass in life; while he has lived comfortably in the capital with a nice practice, his country's reality has passed him by. As he ventures into the countryside, he gathers four traveling companions. There is an army deserter, now a thief, who first steals from him, then joins him. A former priest ("his church calls it liberation theology, but he preferred to liberate himself"). A young boy who knows the area better than any of them and has an uncanny ability to judge the essence of a situation. And a woman who has not spoken since she was raped.

The critic Tom Keogh suggests that there is an element of *The Wizard of Oz* in the doctor and his companions, who need a heart, a voice, and courage. There are also suggestions of *Treasure of the Sierra Madre* and other stories in which a legendary goal—Oz, gold, El Dorado—is said to be hidden further on. In this case the travelers begin to hear about a village named "The Circle of Heaven," which is so high on a mountain and so deep in the trees that the helicopters cannot find it, and people live free. Sayles tells his story in a series of vignettes—encounters on the road, stories told, flashbacks of earlier experiences, a touch of magic realism.

From time to time, the travelers and their journey are interrupted by two other characters, chatty American tourists (Mandy Patinkin and Kathryn Grody) who are looking for "antiques" and haven't a clue about the reality of the land and people behind them.

The tourists serve a satirical purpose, but I found myself seeing them in a different light. From time to time, reviewing a movie, I'll say the leading characters were shallow but the people in the background seemed interesting. In that sense, *Men with Guns* is about the background. Sayles finances his own films. If he had taken this script to a studio executive, he no doubt would have been told to beef up the American tourist roles and cast the roles with stars. The film would have become an action sitcom with Indians, doctors, priests, and orphans in the background as local color.

If you doubt me, look again at *Medicine Man* (1992), with Sean Connery in the rain forest, or *Anaconda* (1997), with snake-hunters up the Amazon. In my bemusement, every time the American tourists turned up, I thought of them as visitors from the phantom Hollywood revision of this material: magic realism of a different sort. It's as if Sayles is saying, "Here's what the studios would have made this movie into."

When the history of the century's films is written, John Sayles will stand tall as a director who went his own way, made his own films, directed and edited them himself, and operated completely outside the traditional channels of distribution and finance. When we hear Francis Coppola's lament that he has to make a John Grisham film in order to make one of his "own" films, we can only reflect that Sayles has demonstrated that a director can be completely independent if he chooses.

Men with Guns is immensely moving and sad, and yet because it dares so much, it is an exhilarating film. It frees itself from specific stories about *this* villain or *that* strategy to stand back and look at the big picture: at societies in collapse because power has been concentrated in the hands of small men made big with guns. I understand guns in war, in hunting, in sport. But when a man feels he needs a gun to leave his house in the morning, I fear that man. I fear his fear. He believes that the only man more powerless than himself is a dead man.

Mephisto

NO MPAA RATING, 135 m., 1981

Klaus Maria Brandauer (Henrik Hofgon), Krystyna Janda (Barbara Bruckner), Ildiko Bansagi (Nicolette Von Hiebuhr), Karin Boyd (Juliette Martens). Directed and produced by Istvan Szabo. Screenplay by Szabo and Peter Dobel.

There are times in *Mephisto* when the hero tries to explain himself by saying that he's only an actor, and he has that almost right. *All* he is, is an actor. It's not his fault that the Nazis have come to power, and that as a German-speaking actor he must choose between becoming a Nazi and being exiled into a foreign land without jobs for German actors. As long as he is acting, as long as he is not called upon to risk his real feelings, this man can act his way into the hearts of women, audiences, and the Nazi power structure. This is the story of a man who plays his life wearing masks, fearing that if the last mask is removed, he will have no face.

The actor is played by Klaus Maria Brandauer in one of the greatest movie performances I've ever seen. The character, Henrik, is not sympathetic, and yet we identify with him because he shares so many of our own weaknesses and fears. Henrik is not a very good actor or a very good human being, but he is good enough to get by in ordinary times. As the movie opens, he's a socialist, interested in all the most progressive new causes, and is even the proud lover of a black woman. By the end of the film, he has learned that his liberalism was a taste, not a conviction, and that he will do anything, flatter anybody, make any compromise, just to hear applause, even though he knows the applause comes from fools.

Mephisto does an uncanny job of creating its period, of showing us Hamburg and Berlin from the 1920s to the 1940s. And I've never seen a movie that does a better job of showing the seductive Nazi practice of providing party members with theatrical costumes, titles, and pageantry. In this movie, not being a Nazi is like being at a black-tie ball in a brown corduroy suit. Hofgon, the actor, is drawn to this world like a magnet. From his ambitious beginnings in the provincial German theater, he works his way up into more important roles and laterally into more important society. All of his progress is based on lies. He marries a woman he does not love, because her father can do him some good. When the rise of the Nazis destroys his father-in-law's power, he leaves his wife. He continues all this time to maintain his affair with his black mistress. He has a modest, but undeniable, talent as an actor, but prostitutes it by playing his favorite role, Mephistopheles in *Faust,* not as he could but as he calculates he should.

The obvious parallel here is between the hero of this film and the figure of tragedy who sold his soul to the devil. But *Mephisto* doesn't depend upon easy parallels to make its point. This is a human story, and as the actor in this movie makes his way to the top of the Nazi propaganda structure and the bottom of his own soul, the movie is both merciless and understanding. This is a weak and shameful man, the film seems to say, but then it cautions us against throwing the first stone.

Mephisto is not a German but a Hungarian movie, directed by the talented Istvan Szabo, who has led his country's cinema from relative obscurity to its present position as one of the best and most innovative film industries in Europe. Szabo, in his way, has made a companion film to Fassbinder's *The Marriage of Maria Braun.* The Szabo film shows a man compromising his way to the top by lying to himself and everybody else, and throwing aside all moral standards. It ends as World War II is under way. The Fassbinder film begins after the destruction of the war, showing a woman clawing her way out of the rubble and repeating the same process of compromise, lies, and unquestioning materialism.

Both the man in the Szabo film and the woman in the Fassbinder film maintain one love affair all through everything, using their love (he for a black woman, she for a convict) as a sort of token contempt for a society whose corrupt values they otherwise completely accept. The fact that they *can* still love, of course, makes it impossible for them to quite deceive themselves. That is the price they pay for their deals with the devil.

Metropolis

PG-13, 107 m., 2002

With the voices of: Jamieson Price (Duke Red), Yuka Imoto (Tima), Kei Kobayashi (Kenichi), Kouki Okada (Rock), Toshio Furukawa (General), Dave Mallow (Pero), Scott Weinger (Atlas). Directed by Taro Rin and produced by Yutaka Maseba and Haruyo Kanesaku. Screenplay by Osamu Tezuka and Katsuhiro Otomo, based on Tezuka's comic book. Dubbed into English.

There's something about vast futuristic cities that stirs me. Perhaps they awaken memories of my twelfth year, when I sat in the basement on hot summer days and read through the lower reaches of science-fiction magazines: *Imagination, Other Worlds, Amazing.* On the covers, towering cities were linked by sky-bridges, and buses were cigar-shaped rockets. In the foreground a bug-eyed monster was attacking a screaming heroine in an aluminum brassiere. Even now, the image of a dirigible tethered to the top of the Empire State Building is more thrilling to me than the space shuttle, which is merely real.

Those visions are goofy and yet at the same time exhilarating. What I like about Tokyo is that it looks like a 1940s notion of a future city. I placed *Dark City* first on my list of the best films of 1998, loved *Blade Runner*'s visuals more than its story, liked the taxicabs in the sky in *The Fifth Element.* Now here is *Metropolis,* one of the best animated films I have ever seen, and the city in this movie is not simply a backdrop or a location, but one of those movie places that colonize our memory.

The Japanese anime is named after the 1926 Fritz Lang silent classic, and is based on a 1949 *manga* (comic book) by the late Osamu Tezuka, which incorporated Lang's images. The movie was directed by Taro Rin and written by the anime legend Katsuhiro Otomo, who directed *Akira* and wrote *Roujin Z.* It uses the Lang film as a springboard into a surprisingly thoughtful, ceaselessly exciting sci-fi story about a plot to use humanoids to take over the city. In the romance between Tima, the half-human heroine, and Kenichi, the detective's nephew who falls in love with her, the movie asks whether a machine can love. The answer is an interesting spin on *A.I.* and *Blade Runner,* because the debate goes on within Tima herself, between her human and robotic natures.

The film opens with astonishing visuals of the great city, which, like Lang's Metropolis, exists on several levels above- and below-ground. We see the skyscraping Ziggurat, a complex of towers linked by bridges and braces. The building seems to be a symbol of progress, but actually masks a scheme by the evil Duke Red to wrest control of the city from elected officials. Deep inside Ziggurat is a throne suspended in a hall filled with giant computer chips; it is intended for Tima, a humanoid in the image of Duke Red's dead daughter, built for him by the insane Dr. Lawton. Tima's role will be to merge the power of computers and the imagination of the human brain into a force that will possess the city.

Rock, the adopted son of Duke Red, hates this plan and wants to destroy Tima. He is jealous that his father prefers this artificial girl to his son, and believes Duke Red himself should sit on the throne. Other characters include an elderly detective who arrives in the city to explore the mystery of Ziggurat; his nephew Kenichi becomes the hero.

The story is told with enormous energy; animation is more versatile than live action in making cataclysmic events comprehensible. Mob scenes at the beginning and explosions and destruction throughout have a clarity and force that live action would necessarily dissipate. The animation owes less to mainstream American animation than to the comic book or *manga* tradition of Japan, where both comics and animation are considered art forms worthy of adult attention.

In the figures of Tima and Kenichi, the movie follows the anime tradition of heroes who are childlike, have enormous eyes, seem innocent and threatened. The other characters have more realistic faces and proportions, and indeed resemble Marvel superheroes (the contrast between these characters' looks is unusual: Imagine Nancy visiting Spider-Man). The backgrounds and action sequences look like the anime version of big-budget Hollywood f/x thrillers.

The music, too, is Western. The introduction to the city is scored with Dixieland, Joe Primrose sings "St. James Infirmary" at one point, and the climactic scene is accompanied by Ray Charles singing "I Can't Stop Loving You" (the effect is a little like "We'll Meet Again" at the end of *Dr. Strangelove*).

The movie is so visually rich I want to see it again to look in the corners and appreciate the details. Like all the best Japanese anime, it pays attention to little things. There is a scene where an old man consults a book of occult lore. He opens it and starts to read. A page flips over. He flips it back in place. Considering that every action in an animated film requires thousands of drawings, a moment like the page flip might seem unnecessary, but all through the movie we get little touches like that. The filmmakers are not content with ordinary locations. Consider the Hotel Coconut, which seems to be a lobby with a desk clerk who checks guests into ancient luxury railway carriages.

Metropolis is not a simpleminded animated cartoon, but a surprisingly thoughtful and challenging adventure that looks into the nature of life and love, the role of workers, the rights (if any) of machines, the pain of a father's rejection, and the fascist zeal that lies behind Ziggurat. This is not a remake of the 1926 classic, but a wild elaboration. If you have never seen a Japanese anime, start here. If you love them, *Metropolis* proves you are right.

Micki & Maude

PG-13, 115 m., 1984

Dudley Moore (Rob Salinger), Amy Irving (Maude Salinger), Ann Reinking (Micki Salinger), Richard Mulligan (Leo Brody), Lu Leonard (Nurse Verbeck). Directed by Blake Edwards and produced by Tony Adams. Screenplay by Jonathan Reynolds.

The key to the whole thing is Dudley Moore's absolutely and unquestioned sincerity. He loves both women. He would do anything to avoid hurting either woman. He wants to do the right thing but, more than that, he wants to do the kind thing. And that is how he ends up in a maternity ward with two wives who are both presenting him with baby children. If it were not for those good qualities in Moore's character, qualities this movie goes to great lengths to establish, *Micki & Maude* would run the risk of turning into tasteless and even cruel slapstick. After all, these are serious matters we're talking about. But the triumph of the movie is that it identifies so closely with Moore's desperation and his essentially sincere motivation that we understand the lengths to which he is driven. That makes the movie's inevitable climax even funnier.

As the movie opens, Moore is happily married to an assistant district attorney (Ann Reinking) who has no desire to have children. Children are, however, the only thing in life that Moore himself desires; apart from that one void, his life is full and happy. He works as a reporter for one of those TV magazine shows where weird people talk earnestly about their constitutional rights to be weird: For example, nudists defend their right to bear arms. Then he meets a special person, a cello player (Amy Irving) who has stepped in at the last moment to play a big concert. She thinks he has beautiful eyes, he smiles, it's love, and within a few weeks Moore and Irving are talking about how they'd like to have kids. Then Irving gets pregnant. Moore decides to do the only right thing, and divorce the wife he loves to marry the pregnant girlfriend that he also loves. But then his wife announces that she's pregnant, and Moore turns, in this crisis of conscience, to his best friend, a TV producer wonderfully played by Richard Mulligan. There is obviously only one thing he can do: become a bigamist.

Micki & Maude was directed by Blake Edwards, who also directed Moore in *10*, and who knows how to build a slapstick climax by one subtle development after another. There is, for example, the fact that Irving's father happens to be a professional wrestler, with a lot of friends who are even taller and meaner than he is. There is the problem that Moore's original in-laws happen to pass the church where he is having his second wedding. Edwards has a way of applying absolute logic to insane situations, so we learn, for example, that after Moore tells one wife he works days and the other one he works nights, his schedule works out in such a way that he begins to get too much sleep.

Dudley Moore is developing into one of the great movie comedians of his generation. *Micki & Maude* goes on the list with *10* and *Arthur* as screwball classics. Moore has another side as an actor, a sweeter, more serious side, that shows up in good movies like *Romantic Comedy* and bad ones like *Six Weeks,* but it's when he's in a screwball comedy, doing his specialty of absolutely sincere desperation, that he reaches genius. For example: The last twenty minutes of *Micki & Maude,* as the two pregnant women move inexorably forward on their collision course, represents a kind of filmmaking that is as hard to do as anything you'll ever see on a screen. The timing has to be flawless. So does the logic: One loose end, and the inevitability of a slapstick situation is undermined. Edwards and Moore are working at the top of their forms here, and the result is a pure, classic slapstick that makes *Micki & Maude* a real treasure.

Microcosmos

G, 77 m., 1997

A documentary directed by Claude Nuridsany and Marie Perennou and produced by Galatee Films, Jacques Perrin, Christophe Barratier, and Yvette Mallet. Screenplay by Nuridsany and Perrenou.

There are so many different insect species that there's a famous biologists' quip: Essentially *all* species are insects. Their biomass—the combined weight of the creepy-crawly things—is many times greater than the combined weight of everything else that swims, flies, walks, and makes movies. Insects are the great success story on planet Earth; they were here before we arrived and will remain long after we've gone, inhabiting their worlds of mindless and intricate beauty.

Children, being built nearer to the ground and having more time on their hands, are close observers of ants and spiders, caterpillars and butterflies. Adults tune them out; bugs are things you slap, swat, step on, or spray. *Microcosmos* is an amazing film that allows us to peer deeply into the insect world, and marvel at creatures we casually condemn

to squishing. The makers of this film took three years to design their close-up cameras and magnifying lenses, and to photograph insects in such brilliant detail that if they were cars we could read their city stickers.

The movie is a work of art and whimsy as much as one of science. It uses only a handful of words, but is generous with music and amplified sound effects, dramatizing the unremitting struggle of survival that goes on in a meadow in France. If a camera could somehow be transported to another planet, there to photograph alien life forms, would the result be any more astonishing than these invasions into the private lives of snails and bees, mantises and beetles, spiders and flies?

Where did these forms come from? These legs—two, four, six, a thousand? Eyes like bombardiers' turrets? Giant pincers? Honeyed secretions? Metamorphoses from a wormy crawling thing into a glorious flying thing? Grasshoppers that look like plants, and beetles that look like ants? Every one of these amazing creatures represents a successful Darwinian solution to the problem of how to reproduce and make a living. And so do we.

One beautiful creature after another takes the screen. There is a parade of caterpillars. A dung beetle, tirelessly moving his treasure. Two snails engaging in a long and very loving wet kiss. Spiders methodically capturing and immobilizing their prey (what a horrible fate; does the victim understand what has happened to it?). Ants construct lives of meticulous order and then a hungry bird comes along and gobbles up thousands of them. More ants construct more anthills, flawless in design and function, and then the hills are bombed by raindrops that look to them as big as beach balls.

There is a fight to the death between two beetles, and their struggle looks as gargantuan as the battling dinosaurs in *Jurassic Park.* There are tiny insects who live in, on, and for the nectar supplied by plants that are perfectly designed for them. Ladybugs seem so ill-designed to fly that every takeoff looks like a clumsy miracle; do they get sweaty palms? Overhead there is a towering canopy of jungle foliage, consisting of the grasses and flowers of the meadow.

Microcosmos is in a category of its own.

There is no other film like it. If the movies allow us to see places we have not been and people we do not know, then *Microcosmos* dramatically extends the range of our vision, allowing us to see the world of the creatures who most completely and enduringly inhabit Earth.

Sometimes the close-up cameras are almost embarrassingly intimate; should we blush to see these beings engaged in their crucial daily acts of dining, loving, fighting, being born, and dying? You may leave this movie feeling a little like a god. Or like a big, inelegant and energy-inefficient hunk of clunky design. Of course, we're smart and they're not. We know the insects exist, and they don't know we exist. Or need to.

The Mighty Quinn

R, 98 m., 1989

Denzel Washington (Xavier), James Fox (Elgin), Robert Townsend (Maubee), Mimi Rogers (Hadley), M. Emmet Walsh (Miller), Sheryl Lee Ralph (Lola), Art Evans (Jump), Esther Rolle (Ubu Pearl), Norman Beaton (Governor Chalk). Directed by Carl Schenkel and produced by Sandy Lieberson, Marion Hunt, and Ed Elbert. Screenplay by Hampton Fancher, based on the book *Finding Maubee* by A. H. Z. Carr.

The Mighty Quinn is a spy thriller, a buddy movie, a musical, a comedy, and a picture that is wise about human nature. And yet with all of those qualities, it never seems to strain: This is a graceful, almost charmed, entertainment. It tells the story of a police chief on an island not unlike Jamaica, who gets caught in the middle when a wealthy developer is found murdered. Everyone seems to believe the chief's best friend, a no-account drifter named Maubee, committed the crime. Everyone but the chief and the chief's wife, who observes laconically, "Maubee is a lover, not a killer."

The film stars Denzel Washington, in one of those roles that creates a movie star overnight. You might have imagined that would have happened to Washington after he starred in *Cry Freedom*, as the South African hero Steven Biko. He got an Oscar nomination for that performance, but it didn't even begin to hint at his reserves of charm, sexiness, and offbeat humor. In an effortless way that reminds me of Robert Mitchum, Michael Caine, or Sean Connery in the best of the Bond pictures, he is able to be tough and gentle at the same time, able to play a hero and yet not take himself too seriously. He plays Xavier Quinn, a local boy who once played barefoot with Maubee and got into the usual amount of trouble, but who grew up smart, went to America to be trained by the FBI, and has now returned as the police chief. The people of his district call him The Mighty Quinn, after the Bob Dylan song, and there is something both affectionate and ironic in the nickname. He knows everybody in town, knows their habits, and is on good terms even with the island governor (Norman Beaton), a cheerfully corrupt hack who only wants to keep the lid on things.

The murder is a great embarrassment. It is likely to discourage tourism, and perhaps there are more sinister reasons for sweeping the crime under the carpet and blaming Maubee. Quinn is the only one who wants to press an investigation, and it takes him into the decadent lives of the local establishment. He encounters Elgin, the suave local fixer (played by the elegant James Fox, that British specialist in the devious and the evasive). He is powerfully attracted to Elgin's restless wife (Mimi Rogers), and has a private encounter with her that is charged with eroticism precisely because he wants to resist her seductiveness.

Most troublesome of all, he encounters a shambling, overweight, genial American who wanders around with a camera and always seems to be in the wrong place at the right time. This character, Miller, is played by M. Emmet Walsh, one of Hollywood's greatest character actors, who in this movie seems to combine the Sydney Greenstreet and Peter Lorre roles: He is comic relief at first, sinister malevolence later.

As his investigation makes its way through this moral quicksand, Quinn also weathers trouble at home. His wife, Lola (Sheryl Lee Ralph), is rehearsing with a reggae trio and is just a shade too emasculating to make a man truly comfortable around her. A local beauty (Tyra Ferrell) wants to steal Quinn away from her. An old crone (Esther Rolle), who is the island's resident witch, makes prophecies of dire outcomes. And the carefree Maubee himself (played by Robert Townsend) turns up to taunt Quinn with his innocence.

This story, rich enough to fuel one of the great and complicated old Warner Bros. plots, is enriched still further by wall-to-wall music, including a lot of reggae and even a couple of appearances by Rita Marley. And the photography by Jacques Steyn is natural and amused, allowing us to ease into the company of these people instead of confronting us with them.

Denzel Washington is at the heart of the movie, and what he accomplishes is a lesson in movie acting. He has obligatory action scenes, yes, and confrontations that are more or less routine. He handles them easily. But watch the way he and Mimi Rogers play their subtle romantic encounter. The scene develops in three beats instead of two, so that the erotic tension builds. But coexisting with his macho side is a playfulness that allows him to come up behind a woman and dance his fingers along her bare arms, and sashay off again before she knows what has happened.

If Washington is the discovery in this movie, he is only one of its many wonderful qualities. I'd never heard of the director, Carl Schenkel, before, and I learned from the press releases only that he is Swiss and has directed a lot of commercials, but on the basis of this film, he's a natural. He is able in the moderate running time of 98 minutes to create a film that seems as rich and detailed as one much longer. He uses his Jamaican locations and interiors so easily that the movie seems to really inhabit its world, instead of merely being photographed in front of it. And the music helps; reggae somehow seems passionate, lilting, and comforting, all at once. *The Mighty Quinn* was one of 1989's best films.

Million Dollar Baby

PG-13, 132 m., 2004

Clint Eastwood (Frankie Dunn), Hilary Swank (Maggie Fitzgerald), Morgan Freeman (Scrap), Jay Baruchel (Danger), Mike Colter (Big Willie Little), Lucia Rijker (Billie [The Blue Bear]), Brian F. O'Byrne (Father Horvak), Margo Martindale (Earline Fitzgerald). Directed by Eastwood and produced by Tom Rosenberg, Paul Haggis, Albert S. Ruddy, and Eastwood. Screenplay by Haggis, based on stories from *Rope Burns*, by F. X. Toole.

Clint Eastwood's *Million Dollar Baby* is a masterpiece, pure and simple, deep and true. It tells the story of an aging fight trainer and a hillbilly girl who thinks she can be a boxer. It is narrated by a former boxer who is the trainer's best friend. But it's not a boxing movie. It is a movie about a boxer. What else it is, all it is, how deep it goes, what emotional power it contains, I cannot suggest in this review, because I will not spoil the experience of following this story into the deepest secrets of life and death. This is the best film of the year.

Eastwood plays the trainer, Frankie, who runs a seedy gym in Los Angeles and reads poetry on the side. Hilary Swank plays Maggie, from southwest Missouri, who has been waitressing since she was thirteen and sees boxing as the one way she can escape waitressing for the rest of her life. Otherwise, she says, "I might as well go back home and buy a used trailer, and get a deep fryer and some Oreos." Morgan Freeman is Scrap, whom Frankie managed into a title bout. Now he lives in a room at the gym and is Frankie's partner in conversations that have coiled down through the decades. When Frankie refuses to train a "girly," it's Scrap who convinces him to give Maggie a chance: "She grew up knowing one thing. She was trash."

These three characters are seen with a clarity and truth that is rare in the movies. Eastwood, who doesn't carry a spare ounce on his lean body, doesn't have any padding in his movie, either: Even as the film approaches the deep emotion of its final scenes, he doesn't go for easy sentiment, but regards these people, level-eyed, as they do what they have to do.

Some directors lose focus as they grow older. Others gain it, learning how to tell a story that contains everything it needs and absolutely nothing else. *Million Dollar Baby* is Eastwood's twenty-fifth film as a director, and his best. Yes, *Mystic River* is a great film, but this one finds the simplicity and directness of classical storytelling; it is the kind of movie where you sit very quietly in the theater and are drawn deeply into lives that you care very much about.

Morgan Freeman is the narrator, just as he

was in *The Shawshank Redemption,* which this film resembles in the way the Freeman character describes a man who became his lifelong study. The voice is flat and factual: You never hear Scrap going for an effect or putting a spin on his words. He just wants to tell us what happened. He talks about how the girl walked into the gym, how she wouldn't leave, how Frankie finally agreed to train her, and what happened then. But Scrap is not merely an observer; the film gives him a life of his own when the others are offscreen. It is about all three of these people.

Hilary Swank is astonishing as Maggie. Every note is true. She reduces Maggie to a fierce intensity. Consider the scene where she and Scrap sit at a lunch counter, and Scrap tells the story of how he lost the sight in one eye, how Frankie blames himself for not throwing in the towel. It is an important scene for Freeman, but what I want you to observe is how Hilary Swank has Maggie do absolutely nothing but listen. No "reactions," no little nods, no body language except perfect stillness, deep attention, and an unwavering gaze.

There's another scene, at night driving in a car, after Frankie and Maggie have visited Maggie's family. The visit didn't go well. Maggie's mother is played by Margo Martindale as an ignorant and selfish monster. "I got nobody but you, Frankie," Maggie says. This is true, but do not make the mistake of thinking there is a romance between them. It's different and deeper than that. She tells Frankie a story involving her father, whom she loved, and an old dog she loved too.

Look at the way the cinematographer, Tom Stern, uses the light in this scene. Instead of using the usual "dashboard lights" that mysteriously seem to illuminate the whole front seat, watch how he has their faces slide in and out of shadow, how sometimes we can't see them at all, only hear them. Watch how the rhythm of this lighting matches the tone and pacing of the words, as if the visuals are caressing the conversation.

It is a dark picture overall. A lot of shadows, many scenes at night, characters who seem to be receding into their private fates. It is also a "boxing movie" in the sense that it follows Maggie's career, and there are several fight scenes. She wins right from the beginning, but

that's not the point; *Million Dollar Baby* is about a woman who is determined to make something of herself, and a man who doesn't want to do anything for this woman, and will finally do everything.

The screenplay is by Paul Haggis, who has worked mostly on TV but with this work will earn an Oscar nomination. Other nominations, and possibly Oscars, will go to Swank, Eastwood, Freeman, the picture, and many of the technicians—and possibly the original score composed by Eastwood, which always does what is required and never distracts. *[Indeed, the film won four Oscars.]*

Haggis adapted the story from *Rope Burns: Stories from the Corner,* a 2000 book by Jerry Boyd, a seventy-year-old fight manager who wrote it as "F. X. Toole." The dialogue is poetic but never fancy. "How much she weigh?" Maggie asks Frankie about the daughter he hasn't seen in years. "Trouble in my family comes by the pound." And when Frankie sees Scrap's feet on the desk: "Where are your shoes?" Scrap: "I'm airing out my feet." The foot conversation continues for almost a minute, showing the film's freedom from plot-driven dialogue, its patience in evoking character.

Eastwood is attentive to supporting characters, who make the surrounding world seem more real. The most unexpected is a Catholic priest who is seen, simply, as a good man; the movies all seem to put a negative spin on the clergy these days. Frankie goes to Mass every morning and says his prayers every night, and Father Horvak (Brian F. O'Byrne) observes that anyone who attends daily Mass for twenty-three years tends to be carrying a lot of guilt. Frankie turns to him for advice at a crucial point, and the priest doesn't respond with church orthodoxy but with a wise insight: "If you do this thing, you'll be lost, somewhere so deep you will never find yourself." Listen, too, when Haggis has Maggie use the word "frozen," which is what an uneducated backroads girl might say, but is also the single perfect word that expresses what a thousand could not.

Movies are so often made of effects and sensation these days. This one is made out of three people and how their actions grow out of who they are and why. Nothing else. But isn't that everything?

Millions

PG, 97 m., 2005

James Nesbitt (Ronnie Cunningham), Daisy Donovan (Dorothy), Lewis McGibbon (Anthony Cunningham), Alex Etel (Damian Cunningham), Christopher Fulford (The Man). Directed by Danny Boyle and produced by Graham Broadbent, Andrew Hauptman, and Damian Jones. Screenplay by Frank Cottrell Boyce, based on his book.

"It isn't the money's fault it got stolen."

That is the reasoning of Anthony Cunningham, who at nine is more of a realist than his seven-year-old brother, Damian. Therefore, it isn't their fault that a bag containing 265,000 British pounds bounced off a train and into Damian's playhouse and is currently stuffed under their bed.

Danny Boyle's *Millions*, a family film of limitless imagination and surprising joy, follows the two brothers as they deal with their windfall. They begin by giving some of it away, taking homeless men to Pizza Hut. Damian wants to continue their charity work, but Anthony leans toward investing in property. They have a deadline: In one week the U.K. will say goodbye to the pound and switch over to the euro; maybe, thinks Anthony, currency speculation would be the way to go.

Here is a film that exists in that enchanted realm where everything goes right—not for the characters, for the filmmakers. They take an enormous risk with a film of sophistication and whimsy, about children, money, criminals, and saints. Damian collects the saints— "like baseball cards," says Richard Roeper. He knows all their statistics. He can see them clear as day, and have conversations with them. His favorite is St. Francis of Assisi, but he knows them all: When a group of Africans materializes wearing halos, Damian is ecstatic: "The Ugandan martyrs of 1881!"

The boys' mother has died, and Damian asks his saints if they have encountered a Saint Maureen. No luck, but then heaven is limitless. Their dad, Ronnie (James Nesbitt), has recently moved them into a newly built suburb outside Liverpool, where the kids at school are hostile at first. Anthony finds it cost-efficient to bribe them with money and neat stuff. Damian, under advice from St. Francis, wants to continue giving money to the poor. Anthony warns him urgently that throwing around too much money will draw attention to them, but Damian drops 10,000 pounds into a charity collection basket. When the boys find out the money was stolen, Damian thinks maybe they should give it back, which is when Anthony comes up with the excellent reasoning I began with.

Perhaps by focusing on the money and the saints I have missed the real story of *Millions*, which involves the lives of the boys, their father, and the woman (Daisy Donovan) who works at the charity that finds the fortune in its basket. The boys are dealing with the death of their mother, and the money is a distraction. Their father is even lonelier; maybe too lonely to ever marry again, maybe too distracted to protect his boys against the bad guy (Christopher Fulford), who dreamed up the perfect train robbery and is now skulking about the neighborhood looking for his missing bag of loot.

By now you may have glanced back to the top of the review to see if I really said *Millions* was directed by Danny Boyle, who made *Shallow Grave, Trainspotting,* and the zombie movie *28 Days Later.* Yes, *the* Danny Boyle. And the original screenplay and novel are by Frank Cottrell Boyce, who wrote *Hilary and Jackie* and *24 Hour Party People.* What are these two doing making a sunny film about kids?

I don't require an answer for that, because their delight in the film is so manifest. But they are serious filmmakers who do not know how to talk down to an audience, and although *Millions* uses special effects and materializing saints, it's a film about real ideas, real issues, and real kids. It's not sanitized, brainless eye candy. Like all great family films, it plays equally well for adults—maybe better, since we know how unusual it is.

One of its secrets is casting. In Alex Etel and Lewis McGibbon the film has found two of the most appealing child actors I've ever seen. Alex is like the young Macaulay Culkin (*Home Alone*) except that he has no idea he is cute, and like the young Haley Joel Osment (*The Sixth Sense*) in that he finds it perfectly reasonable to speak with dead people. There is no overt cuteness, no affected lovability, not a false note in their performances, and the movie allows them to be very smart, as in Anthony's theory about turning the pounds into dollars and buying back into euros after the new currency falls from its opening-day bounce.

Of course, that involves the difficulty of two boys ages seven and nine trying to convert 265,000 pounds into anything. They can't just walk into a bank with a note from their dad. The movie handles this and other problems with droll ingenuity, while also portraying a new suburban community in the making. An opening shot by Boyle, maybe a sly dig at Lars von Trier's *Dogville,* shows the boys visiting the site of their new neighborhood when it consists only of chalk outlines on the ground. After the new homeowners move in, a helpful policeman cheerfully advises a community meeting that they should expect to be burgled, and he tells them which forms to ask for at the police station.

Boyce, a screenwriter who often works with Michael Winterbottom, is so unpredictable and original in his work that he could be called the British Charlie Kaufman, if they were not both completely distinctive. He got the inspiration for *Millions,* he says, from an interview in which Martin Scorsese said he was reading the lives of the saints.

The idea of characters getting a sudden cash windfall is not new, indeed has been a movie staple for a century. What's original about the movie is the way it uses the money as a device for the young brothers to find out more about how the world really works, and what is really important to them. The closing sequence is a bit of a stretcher, I will be the first to admit, but why not go for broke? One of the tests of sainthood is the performance of a miracle, and since Damian is clearly on the road to sainthood, that is permitted him. For that matter, Boyce and Boyle have performed a miracle with their movie. This is one of the best films of the year.

Minnie and Moskowitz

PG, 114 m., 1971

Gena Rowlands (Minnie), Seymour Cassel (Moskowitz), Val Avery (Zelmo Swift), Tim Carey (Morgan Morgan), Katherine Cassavetes (Sheba Moskowitz), Lady Rowlands (Georgia Moore), Elsie Ames (Florence), David Rowlands (Minister). Directed by John Cassavetes and produced by Paul Donelly and Al Ruben. Screenplay by John Cassavetes.

Minnie works in a museum and has never forgiven the movies for selling her a bill of goods. "The movies lead you on," she tells her friend Florence. "They make you believe in romance and love . . . and, Florence, there just aren't any Clark Gables, not in the real world." Still, Minnie dreams and keeps a romantic secret locked in her heart: She's glad the movies sold her that bill of goods.

Seymour is a car-hiker. He has a magnificent mustache, shoulder-length hair, and very little else to show for his life so far. "An Albert Einstein he's not," his mother exclaims. "Pretty he's not. Look at that face. A future he doesn't have; he parks cars for a living."

And yet, and yet . . . love blossoms somehow between Minnie Moore and Seymour Moskowitz, during four crazy days and nights. Seymour thinks he might be able to improve his position, get a job in a larger garage, maybe. Minnie shakes her head and sighs when she looks at him: "Seymour, look at that face. It's not the face I dreamed of, Seymour."

Consumed by love, Seymour bangs his fist against the roof of his pickup truck: "Minnie, oh, Minnie! Oh, Minnie!" Seymour is not very articulate. He talks about only three things, Minnie says: money, eating, and cars. "Cars are very important to Seymour," Minnie explains to her mother. Her mother nods, a little stunned. "Seymour *cares* about cars."

And all of this is why love scores an altogether unreasonable triumph over common sense in *Minnie and Moskowitz,* a comedy by John Cassavetes. The movie is sort of a fairy tale, Cassavetes says; it's dedicated to all the people who didn't marry the person they should have. It is a movie on the side of love, and it is one of the finest movies of the year.

Cassavetes has always been an interesting director, with an inspired unpredictability to his work. He likes to get the texture of real life in his films, and when his experiments succeed they produce brilliant work, such as *Faces,* which I thought was the best film of 1968. When they don't work, we get embarrassingly disconnected and obscurely personal work, such as *Husbands,* which was maybe the most overrated film of 1971.

Minnie and Moskowitz isn't much like anything Cassavetes has done before, except in its determination to go all the way with actors' performances—even at the cost of the movie's overall form. Cassavetes, an actor himself, is one of the few American directors who really is sympathetic with actors. He lets them go, lets them try new things and take risks. This can lead to terribly indulgent performances, as it did in *Husbands*. But in *Minnie and Moskowitz* it gives us performances by Gena Rowlands and Seymour Cassel that are so beautiful you can hardly believe it.

Rowlands is a lovely, warm actress with a speaking voice that's round and interesting, and not as detached as most performers' voices. Cassel is one of the few actors who can let everything inside hang out, because he's got the stuff inside. A lot of actors throw aside caution and reveal their innermost being, only to raise the curtain on a void. Cassel makes Moskowitz into a convincing, dedicated, pure crazy romantic, and that's why, even in dreary 1971, we can believe he could sweep Minnie off her feet.

Rowlands (who is Mrs. Cassavetes) played the prostitute in *Faces,* and Cassel got an Academy Award nomination for his performance as the hippie in that movie. There are a lot of other members of the Cassavetes circle in *Minnie and Moskowitz:* Cassavetes's mother plays Moskowitz's mother, Rowland's mother plays Minnie's mother, Rowland's father has a cameo as a minister, various children and family friends have walk-ons, and Cassavetes himself turns up, unbilled, as Minnie's loveless lover.

This kind of casting can't help but give the movie an intimate, familiar feeling, and maybe that's why the comedy works as human comedy and not just manufactured laughs. The casting also turns up the funniest mother performance of the year, by Katherine Cassavetes, who is sort of a cross between Ruth Gordon and Mrs. Portnoy and should get several acting offers after this. "Look at my son," she says. "He's a bum. Where will they sleep? What food will they eat? Money will they make?" Yes, but who cares? Not Minnie, not Moskowitz, not love.

Minority Report

PG-13, 145 m., 2002

Tom Cruise (John Anderton), Samantha Morton (Agatha [Precog]), Max von Sydow (Lamarr Burgess), Colin Farrell (Danny Witwer), Tim Blake Nelson (Gideon), Steve Harris (Jad), Neal McDonough (Officer Fletcher). Directed by Steven Spielberg and produced by Jan de Bont, Bonnie Curtis, Gerald R. Molen, and Walter F. Parkes. Screenplay by Scott Frank and Jon Cohen, based on a short story by Philip K. Dick.

At a time when movies think they have to choose between action and ideas, Steven Spielberg's *Minority Report* is a triumph—a film that works on our minds and our emotions. It is a thriller and a human story, a movie of ideas that's also a whodunit. Here is a master filmmaker at the top of his form, working with a star, Tom Cruise, who generates complex human feelings even while playing an action hero.

I complained earlier this summer of awkward joins between live action and computer-generated imagery; I felt the action sequences in *Spider-Man* looked too cartoonish, and that *Star Wars: Episode II,* by using computer effects to separate the human actors from the sets and CGI characters, felt disconnected and sterile. Now here is Spielberg using every trick in the book and matching them without seams, so that no matter how he's achieving his effects, the focus is always on the story and the characters.

The movie turns out to be eerily prescient, using the term "precrime" to describe stopping crimes before they happen; how could Spielberg have known the government would be using the same term in the summer of 2002? In his film, inspired by, but much expanded from, a short story by Philip K. Dick, Tom Cruise is John Anderton, chief of the Department of Precrime in the District of Columbia, where there has not been a murder in six years. Soon, it appears, there will be a murder—committed by Anderton himself.

The year is 2054. Futuristic skyscrapers coexist with the famous Washington monuments and houses from the nineteenth century. Anderton presides over an operation controlling three "precogs," precognitive humans who drift in a flotation tank, their brain waves tapped by computers. They're able to pick up thoughts of premeditated murders and warn the cops, who swoop down and arrest the would-be perpetrators before the killings can take place.

Because this is Washington, any government operation that is high-profile and successful inspires jealousy. Anderton's superior, bureau director Burgess (Max von Sydow), takes pride in him, and shields him from bureaucrats like Danny Witwer (Colin Farrell) from the Justice Department. As the precrime strategy prepares to go national, Witwer seems to have doubts about its wisdom—or is he only jealous of its success?

Spielberg establishes these characters in a dazzling future world, created by art director Alex McDowell, that is so filled with details large and small that we stop trying to figure out everything and surrender with a sigh. Some of the details: a computer interface that floats in midair, manipulated by Cruise with the gestures of a symphony conductor; advertisements that crawl up the sides of walls and address you personally; cars that whisk around town on magnetic cushions; robotic "spiders" that can search a building in minutes by performing a retinal scan on everyone in it. *Blade Runner,* also inspired by a Dick story, shows a future world in decay; *Minority Report* offers a more optimistic preview.

The plot centers on a rare glitch in the visions of the precogs. Although "the precogs are never wrong," we're told, "sometimes . . . they disagree." The dissenting precog is said to have filed a minority report, and in the case of Anderton the report is crucial, because otherwise he seems a certain candidate for arrest as a precriminal. Of course, if you could outsmart the precog system, you would have committed the perfect crime.

Finding himself the hunted instead of the hunter, Anderton teams up with Agatha (Samantha Morton), one of the precogs, who seemed to be trying to warn him of his danger. Because she floats in a fluid tank, Agatha's muscles are weakened (have precogs any rights of their own?), and Anderton has to half-drag her as they flee from the precrime police. One virtuoso sequence shows her foreseeing the immediate future and advising Anderton about what to do to elude what the cops are going to do next. The choreography, timing, and wit of this sequence make it, all by itself, worth the price of admission.

But there are other stunning sequences. Consider a scene where the "spiders" search a rooming house, and Anderton tries to elude capture by immersing himself in a tub of ice water. This sequence begins with an overhead cross section of the apartment building and several of its inhabitants, and you would swear it has to be done with a computer, but no: This is an actual, physical set, and the elegant camera moves were elaborately choreographed. It's typical of Spielberg that, having devised this astonishing sequence, he propels it for dramatic purposes and doesn't simply exploit it to show off his cleverness. And watch the exquisite timing as one of the spiders, on its way out, senses something and pauses in midstep.

Tom Cruise's Anderton is an example of how a star's power can be used to add more dimension to a character than the screenplay might supply. He compels us to worry about him, and even in implausible action sequences (like falls from dizzying heights) he distracts us by making us care about the logic of the chase, not the possibility of the stunt.

Samantha Morton's character ("Agatha" is a nod to Miss Christie) has few words and seems exhausted and frightened most of the time, providing an eerie counterpoint for Anderton's man of action. There is poignance in her helplessness, and Spielberg shows it in a virtuoso two-shot, as she hangs over Anderton's shoulder while their eyes search desperately in opposite directions. This shot has genuine mystery. It has to do with the composition and lighting and timing and breathing, and like the entire movie, it furthers the cold, frightening hostility of the world Anderton finds himself in. The cinematographer, Janusz Kaminski, who has worked with Spielberg before (not least on *Schindler's List*), is able to get an effect that's powerful and yet bafflingly simple.

The plot I will avoid discussing in detail. It is as ingenious as any *film noir* screenplay, and plays far better than some. It's told with such clarity that we're always sure what Spielberg wants us to think, suspect, and know. And although there is a surprise at the end, there is no cheating: The crime story holds water.

American movies are in the midst of a transition period. Some directors place their trust in technology. Spielberg, who is a master of technology, trusts only story and character, and then uses everything else as a workman uses his tools. He makes *Minority Report with* the new technology; other directors seem to be trying to make their movies *from* it. This film is such a virtuoso high-wire act, daring so much, achieving it with such grace and skill. *Minority Report* reminds us why we go to the movies in the first place.

Mirage

NO MPAA RATING, 82 m., 1972

Starring Helena Rojo, Hernán Romero, and Orlando Sacha. Directed by Armando Robles-Godoy and produced by Bernardo Batievsky. Screenplay by Robles-Godoy.

Mirage is a work of stunning subtlety and limitless visual beauty by the Peruvian director Armando Robles-Godoy. We have seen these qualities in his work before, in *The Green Wall* (winner of the Chicago Film Festival's 1970 Golden Hugo award). But *Mirage* is a more complex, difficult, and, finally, more rewarding film.

On one level, it tells a story of the greatest simplicity. In the little desert town of Ica, not too far from Lima, two young boys of about twelve are great friends. The family of one boy is planning to move to Lima, which is all right with him because he thinks the city might offer him a better chance of becoming a soccer star. The other boy is apparently without parents and lives alone in a vast, strange, haunted structure at the edge of the desert.

What is this structure, and why is it there? The priest hints that a great tragedy took place in it one day, a story so sad no one wants to remember it—and that is just as well forgotten, in any case. But the second boy seems to know the story, which has to do with a cruel landowner, his beautiful wife, and the workman she loves. The ways by which the boy understands this story that he could not possibly know are hard to describe. Robles-Godoy does not use dreams, fantasies, or flashbacks. The people he tells us about are all dead by now. But by inhabiting their home, the boy somehow inhabits their space, their lives. He knows about them because they pass through him and in some mystical way are always there.

The story of the love is told by Robles-Godoy with pure and unashamed romanticism; it is so rare to find a film that exists at a wholly adult level and still affirms romantic love and presents it with visual and musical

lushness. And yet there is always something extra in the love, and it is not so much a simple love story as a legend, an often-heard tale in which the characters are doomed because their fates have all long ago been written down.

Mirage was filmed on location in and around the Peruvian desert and is the most visually beautiful film I have seen since a previous Chicago festival winner, *The Fruits of Paradise*. The use of the fluidity of the sand, the simplicity of the life, the disturbingly erotic process of winemaking, is masterful.

And there is a particular sequence in *Mirage* that comes close to a perfect marriage between an idea and the way it is presented. The avaricious landowner insists that his grape pickers whistle while they work—because it is impossible to eat a grape while whistling, and he reckons he is losing 1 percent of his crop to his workers' appetites.

So they whistle. At first their song is a chaotic and tuneless one, but eventually, ever so slowly, the strains of a familiar tune emerge . . . the "Internationale."

Mishima

R, 121 m., 1985

Ken Ogata (Yukio Mishima), Mashayuki Shionoya (Morita), Hiroshi Mikami (First Cadet), Naoko Otani (Mother). Directed by Paul Schrader and produced by Mata Yamamoto and Tom Luddy. Screenplay by Paul and Leonard Schrader.

The Japanese author Yukio Mishima seems to have thought of his life as a work of art, and more than anyone since Hemingway he got other people to think of it that way, too. He was a brilliant self-promoter who not only wrote important novels and plays, but also cultivated the press, posed for beefcake photographs, and founded his own private army. He was an advocate of a return to medieval Japanese values, considered himself a samurai, and died on schedule and according to his own plan: After occupying an army garrison with some of his soldiers, he disemboweled himself while being beheaded by a follower.

Mishima's life obviously supplies the materials for a sensationalistic film. Paul Schrader has not made one. Instead, his *Mishima* takes this most flamboyant of writers and translates his life into a carefully structured examination of three different Mishimas: public, private, and literary.

The film begins with the public Mishima, a literary superstar who begins the last day of his life by ritualistically donning the uniform of his private army. From time to time during the film, we return to moments from that final day, as Mishima is jammed somewhat inelegantly into a tiny car and driven by his followers to an appointment with a Japanese general. The film ends with Mishima holding the general hostage, and winning the right to address the troops of the garrison (who must have been just as astonished as if Norman Mailer turned up at West Point). Although the film ends with Mishima's ritual suicide, it is not shown in the graphic detail that's popular in recent films; Schrader wisely realizes that too much blood would destroy the mood of his film and distract attention from the idea behind Mishima's death.

Mishima's last day is counterpointed with black-and-white sequences showing his childhood and adolescence, and with gloriously stylized color dramatizations of scenes from his novels, *Temple of the Golden Pavilion*, *Kyoko's House*, and *Runaway Horses*. The scenes from the novels were visualized by designer Eiko Ishioka, who seems to have been inspired by fantasy scenes from early Technicolor musicals. They don't summarize Mishima's novels so much as give us an idea about them; as we see the ritualistic aspects of his fantasies, we are seeing Japan through his eyes, as he wished it to be.

The black-and-white biographical sequences show a little boy growing up into a complicated man. Young Yukio, raised by his mother and his grandmother, was a lonely outcast with a painful stammer, and we can see in the insecurities of his youth impulses that led him to build his muscles, to leap for literary glory, and to wrap himself in the samurai ethic.

Mishima is a rather glorious project, in these days of pragmatic commercialism and rank cynicism in the movie industry. Although a sensationalized version of his life might have had potential at the box office (and although Schrader, author of *Taxi Driver*, director of *American Gigolo*, would have been

quite capable of directing it), this is a much more ambitious and intellectual film.

It challenges us to think about Mishima, instead of simply observing the strange channels of his life. What did he prove, on the day when his life ended according to plan? That he was willing to pay the ultimate price to transform his life into an artistic statement—and also, perhaps, that some of his genius was madness. Was it worth it? Who can say who is not Mishima?

Mississippi Burning
R, 127 m., 1988

Gene Hackman (Anderson), Willem Dafoe (Ward), Frances McDormand (Mrs. Pell), Brad Dourif (Deputy Pell), R. Lee Ermey (Mayor Tilman), Gailard Sartain (Sheriff Stuckey), Stephen Tobolowsky (Townley), Michael Rooker (Frank Bailey), Pruitt Taylor Vince (Lester Cowens), Badja Djola (Agent Monk), Kevin Dunn (Agent Bird). Directed by Alan Parker and produced by Frederick Zollo and Robert F. Colesberry. Screenplay by Chris Gerolmo.

Movies often take place in towns, but they rarely seem to live in them. Alan Parker's *Mississippi Burning* feels like a movie made from the inside out, a movie that knows the ways and people of its small southern city so intimately that, having seen it, I know the place I'd go for a cup of coffee and the place I'd steer clear from. This acute sense of time and place—rural Mississippi, 1964—is the lifeblood of the film, which gets inside the passion of race relations in America, and was the best film of 1988.

The film is based on a true story, the disappearance of Chaney, Goodman, and Schwerner, three young civil rights workers who were part of a voter registration drive in Mississippi. When their murdered bodies were finally discovered, their corpses were irrefutable testimony against the officials who had complained that the whole case was a publicity stunt, dreamed up by northern liberals and outside agitators. The case became one of the milestones, like the day Rosa Parks took her seat on the bus or the day Martin Luther King marched into Montgomery, on the long march toward racial justice in this country.

But *Mississippi Burning* is not a documentary,

nor does it strain to present a story based on the facts. This movie is a gritty police drama, bloody, passionate, and sometimes surprisingly funny, about the efforts of two FBI men to lead an investigation into the disappearances. Few men could be more opposite than these two agents: Anderson (Gene Hackman), the good old boy who used to be a sheriff in a town a lot like this one, and Ward (Willem Dafoe), one of Bobby Kennedy's bright young men from the Justice Department. Anderson believes in keeping a low profile, hanging around the barber shop, sort of smelling out the likely perpetrators. Ward believes in a show of force, and calls in hundreds of federal agents and even the National Guard to search for the missing workers.

Anderson and Ward do not like each other very much. Both men feel they should be in charge of the operation. As they go their separate paths, we meet some of the people in the town: The mayor, a slick country-club type, who lectures against rabble-rousing outsiders. The sheriff, who thinks he can intimidate the FBI men. And Pell (Brad Dourif), a shifty-eyed deputy who has an alibi for the time the three men disappeared, and it's a good alibi—except why would he have an alibi so good, for precisely that time, unless he needed one?

The alibi depends on the word of Pell's wife (Frances McDormand), a woman who has taken a lot over the years from this self-hating racist, a man who needs a gun on his belt by day and a hood over his head by night just to gather the courage to stand and walk. Anderson, the Hackman character, singles her out immediately as the key to the case. He believes the sheriff's department delivered the three men over to the local Klan, which murdered them. If he can get the wife to talk, the whole house of cards crashes down.

So he starts hanging around. Makes small talk. Shifts on his feet in her living room like a bashful boy. Lets his voice trail off, so that in the silence she can imagine that he was about to say what a pretty woman she still was. Anderson plays this woman like a piano. And she wants to be played. Because Gene Hackman is such a subtle actor, it takes us a while to realize that he has really fallen for her. He would like to rescue her from the scum she's married to, and wrap her up in his arms.

McDormand is wonderful in the role. She could have turned her role into a flashy showboat performance, but chose instead to show us a woman who had been raised and trained and beaten into accepting her man as her master, and who finally rejects that role simply because with her own eyes she can see that it's wrong to treat black people the way her husband does. The woman McDormand plays is quiet and shy and fearful, but in the moral decision she makes, she represents a generation that finally said, hey, what's going on here is simply not fair.

The relationship between the McDormand and Hackman characters is counterpoint to the main current of the film, which involves good police work, interrogations, searches and—mostly—hoping for tips. There is reason to believe that the local black community has a good idea of who committed the murders, but the Klan trashes and burns the home of one family with a son who might talk, and there is terror in the air in the black neighborhood.

Parker, the director, doesn't use melodrama to show how terrified the local blacks are of reprisals; he uses realism. We see what can happen to people who are not "good nigras." The Dafoe character approaches a black man in a segregated luncheonette and asks him questions. The black refuses to talk to him— and *still* gets beaten by the Klan. Sometimes keeping your mouth shut can be sound common sense. Parker has dealt with intimidating bullies before in his work, most notably in *Midnight Express,* but what makes this film so particular is the way he understates the evil in it. There are no great villains and sadistic torturers in this film, only banal little racists with a vicious streak.

By the end of the film, the bodies have been found, the murderers have been identified, and the wheels of justice have started to grind. We knew the outcome of this case when we started watching. What we may have forgotten, or never known, is exactly what kinds of currents were in the air in 1964. The civil rights movement of the early 1960s was the finest hour of modern American history, because it was the painful hour in which we determined to improve ourselves, instead of others. We grew. The South grew, the whole nation grew more comfortable with the radical idea that all men were created equal and endowed with certain inalienable rights, among them life, liberty, and the pursuit of happiness.

What *Mississippi Burning* evokes more clearly than anything else is how recently in our past those rights were routinely and *legally* denied to blacks, particularly in the South. In a time so recent that its cars are still on the road and its newspapers have not started to yellow, large parts of America were a police state in which the crime was to be black. Things are not great for blacks today, but at least official racism is no longer on the law books anywhere. And no other movie I've seen captures so forcefully the look, the feel, the very smell of racism. We can feel how sexy their hatred feels to the racists in this movie, how it replaces other entertainments, how it compensates for their sense of worthlessness. And we can feel something breaking free, the fresh air rushing in, when the back of that racism is broken.

Mona Lisa

R, 104 m., 1986

Bob Hoskins (George), Cathy Tyson (Simone), Michael Caine (Mortwell), Clarke Peters (Anderson), Kate Hardie (Cathy), Robbie Coltrane (Thomas). Directed by Neil Jordan and produced by Stephen Wooley and Patrick Cassavetti. Screenplay by Jordan and David Leland.

You can tell how much they will eventually like each other by how much they hate each other at first. His name is George. He's a short, fierce, bullet-headed foot-soldier in the London underworld, and he's just gotten out of prison. Her name is Simone. She's a tall, beautiful black woman who works as a high-priced call girl. George goes to Mortwell, who runs the mob, looking for a job. He is assigned to drive Simone around to expensive hotels and private homes and to wait for her while she conducts her business. He is also supposed to protect her if anything goes wrong.

At first he seems hopelessly unsuited to his job. He wears the wrong clothes, and stands out like a sore thumb in the lobbies of hotels like the Ritz. She can't believe she's been sad-dled with this misfit. He thinks she is stuck-up and cold, and puts on too many airs for a whore. They are at each other's throats day and night, fighting about everything, until eventually they realize they enjoy their arguments; they are entertained by one another.

That's the setup for *Mona Lisa,* a British film set in the tattered precincts of Soho, where vice lords run sordid clubs where bewildered provincial girls sell themselves to earn money for drugs. Simone now operates at a higher level in the sex business, but she never forgets where she started, and sometimes she orders George to cruise slowly in the big Jaguar, as she searches for a young girl who used to be her friend when they were on the streets together, and who is still the slave, she fears, of a sadistic pimp. These nighttime journeys are a contrast to her usual routine, which involves visiting wealthy bankers, decadent diplomats, and rich Middle Eastern investors who live on the most expensive streets of Hampstead. George drives her, argues with her, speculates about her, and falls in love with her. And when she asks him to help find the missing girl, he risks his life for her.

Mona Lisa stars Bob Hoskins as George. You may remember him as the ferocious little mob boss in *The Long Good Friday,* where he had it all fixed up to go respectable and then someone started blowing up his pubs. Hoskins is one of the very best new British actors, and this is a great performance—it won him the best actor award at the 1986 Cannes Film Festival. Simone is played by Cathy Tyson, and she is elegant and cool and yet able to project the pain that is always inside. The relationship of their characters in the film is interesting, because both people, for personal reasons, have developed a style that doesn't reveal very much. They have walls, and friendship means being able to see over someone else's wall while still keeping your own intact.

The third major character in the movie, and the third major performance, is by Michael Caine, as Mortwell, the vice boss. In the more than twenty years since I first saw Caine in a movie, I don't believe I've seen him in a bad performance more than once or twice. And I've rarely seen him doing the same thing, which is strange, since in one way or another he usually seems to look and talk like Michael Caine—and yet with subtle differences that are just right for the role. In *Mona Lisa*, he plays one of his most evil villains, a slimebag who trades in the lives and happiness of naive young girls, and he plays the character without apology and without exaggeration, as a businessman. That's why Mortwell is so creepy.

The movie plot reveals itself only gradually. At first *Mona Lisa* seems to be a character study, the story of George and Simone and how they operate within the call-girl industry. After we find out how important the missing girl is to Simone, however, the movie becomes a thriller, as George descends into gutters to try to find her and bring her back to Simone. The movie's ending is a little too neat for my taste. But in a movie like this, everything depends on atmosphere and character, and *Mona Lisa* knows exactly what it is doing.

Monsieur Hire

PG-13, 88 m., 1990

Michel Blanc (Monsieur Hire), Sandrine Bonnaire (Alice), Luc Thuillier (Emile), Andre Wilms (Police Inspector). Directed by Patrice Leconte and produced by Philippe Carcassonne and Rene Cleitman. Screenplay by Leconte and Patrick DeWolf, based on the book by Georges Simenon.

Monsieur Hire's life is organized with the extreme precision of a man who fears that any deviation from routine could destroy him. He lives alone in a neatly ordered room where everything has its place. He dresses carefully and conservatively and goes out every day to work by himself in a small office in the town, where he operates a mail-order business. He comes home to his dinner of a hard-boiled egg. He listens to the same piece of music over and over again. He speaks to people only to observe the formalities: "Good morning." "Nice day."

His sexual life is equally precise. Hour after hour, he stands in his darkened room, looking across the small courtyard of his building into the window of a young woman who lives directly opposite and one floor below. She never pulls her shades. He watches her dress, undress, read, eat, listen to the radio, make love. Hour after hour.

Another young woman is found dead in the neighborhood—her body cast aside in an overgrown vacant lot. Who committed the crime? There are no suspects, but in this neighborhood a man like Monsieur Hire is always a suspect. He has no friends, no associations, no "life." The neighbors have marked him out as peculiar. To look at him you would think it was absurd that he could kill anyone. But suspicion begins to grow.

The story of Monsieur Hire was first told in a novel by Georges Simenon, that endlessly observant Belgian who wrote more than three hundred books, many of them works of genius. This is one of his best stories, a study of character and loneliness. Reading the book some years ago, I formed a picture of Hire in my mind, and seeing this movie I was startled to see how closely my notions matched the appearance of Michel Blanc, who plays the title role.

He is a solemn man with a fringe of black hair around a face that is more than merely pale; he seems to have been sprouted in a basement. He is reclusive, solemn, absorbed with his own thoughts. As he watches the woman across the courtyard, we can only imagine what he is thinking. Somehow the conventional sexual fantasies do not seem to fit him; perhaps he is thinking what a slattern she is, or what an angel.

The woman (Sandrine Bonnaire) has a boyfriend. He is cold, distant, and cruel, and he treats her badly. She does what he says. He does not make her happy, but certain women are attracted to cruel men. Did the boyfriend commit the murder? The movie is not really concerned with the solution to the crime—much less concerned than the Simenon novel. Indeed, when the police inspector turns up in the movie, we're not sure at first who he is. Maybe he's a family friend?

Monsieur Hire is so delicate that you almost hold your breath during the last half-hour. Events of grave subtlety are taking place. The heart of the movie involves two difficult questions: What exactly does the young woman think about Monsieur Hire, and what does he think that she thinks? Of course, the woman knows that Hire is always at his window, watching. She sees him one day, illuminated by lightning. Still she does nothing to conceal herself, and so from that moment on there is a kind of communication between them. Each knows the other is aware.

Monsieur Hire, so middle-aged and nondescript, is certainly not her "type." But is his adoration appealing to her? Is he the one man in the world who regards her simply as she is and finds her wonderful? Does he want nothing more from her than to worship? Does this make her grateful to him, in a sense, considering the mistreatment she gets from the boyfriend? Will she lie to save Hire? Will she lie to save the boyfriend?

The concluding passages of the movie have the weight of sad, inevitable tragedy to them. But nothing prepares us for the movie's extraordinary final shot, in which a swift action contains a momentary pause, a look that seems torn out of the very fabric of life itself. What does the look say? What is this woman trying to communicate? The director, Patrice Leconte, knows that to explain the look is to destroy the movie. *Monsieur Hire* is a film about conversations that are never held, desires that are never expressed, fantasies that are never realized, and murder.

Monster

R, 109 m., 2004

Charlize Theron (Aileen Wuornos), Christina Ricci (Selby Wall), Bruce Dern (Thomas), Scott Wilson (Horton Rohrback), Lee Tergesen (Vincent Corey), Pruitt Taylor Vince (Gene), Annie Corley (Donna Tentler), Marco St. John (Evan). Directed by Patty Jenkins and produced by Mark Damon, Donald Kushner, Clark Peterson, Theron, and Brad Wyman. Screenplay by Jenkins.

What Charlize Theron achieves in Patty Jenkins's *Monster* isn't a performance but an embodiment. With courage, art, and charity, she empathizes with Aileen Wuornos, a damaged woman who committed seven murders. She does not excuse the murders. She simply asks that we witness the woman's final desperate attempt to be a better person than her fate intended.

Wuornos received a lot of publicity during her arrest, trial, conviction, and 2002 execution for the Florida murders of seven men who picked her up as a prostitute (although one wanted to help her, not use her). The headlines, true as always to our compulsion to treat everything as a sporting event or an entry for the *Guinness Book,* called her "America's first female serial killer." Her image on the news and in documentaries presented a large, beaten-down woman who did seem to be monstrous. Evidence against her was given by Selby Wall (Christina Ricci), an eighteen-year-old who became the older woman's naive lesbian lover and inspired Aileen's dream of earning enough money to set them up in a "normal" lifestyle. Robbing her clients led to murder, and each new murder seemed necessary to cover the tracks leading from the previous one.

I confess that I walked into the screening not knowing who the star was, and that I did not recognize Charlize Theron until I read her name in the closing credits. Not many others will have that surprise; she won the Academy Award for Best Actress. I didn't recognize her—but more to the point, I hardly tried, because the performance is so focused and intense that it becomes a fact of life. Observe the way Theron controls her eyes in the film; there is not a flicker of inattention, as she urgently communicates what she is feeling and thinking. There's the uncanny sensation that Theron has forgotten the camera and the script and is directly channeling her ideas about Aileen Wuornos. She has made herself the instrument of this character.

I have already learned more than I wanted to about the techniques of disguise used by makeup artist Toni G. to transform an attractive twenty-eight-year-old into an ungainly street prostitute, snapping her cigarette butt into the shadows before stepping forward to talk with a faceless man who has found her in the shadows of a barren Florida highway. Watching the film, I had no sense of makeup technique; I was simply watching one of the most real people I had ever seen on the screen. Jenkins, the writer-director, has made the best film of the year. Movies like this are perfect when they get made, before they're ground down by analysis. There is a certain tone in the voices of some critics that I detest—that superior way of explaining technique in order to destroy it. They imply that because they can explain how Theron did it, she didn't do it. But she does it.

The movie opens with Wuornos informing

God that she is down to her last $5, and that if God doesn't guide her to spend it wisely she will end her life. She walks into what happens to be a lesbian bar and meets the eighteen-year-old Selby, who has been sent to live with Florida relatives and be "cured" of lesbianism. Aileen is adamant that she's had no lesbian experience, and indeed her sordid life as a bottom-rung sex worker has left her with no taste for sex at all. Selby's own sexuality functions essentially as a way to shock her parents and gratify her need to be desired. There is a stunning scene when the two women connect with raw sexual energy, but soon enough sex is unimportant compared to daydreaming, watching television, and enacting their private soap opera in cheap roadside motels.

Aileen is the protector and provider, proudly bringing home the bacon—and the keys to cars that Selby doesn't ask too many questions about. Does she know that Aileen has started to murder her clients? She does and doesn't. Aileen's murder spree becomes big news long before Selby focuses on it. The crimes themselves are triggered by Aileen's loathing for prostitution—by a lifetime's hatred for the way men have treated her since she was a child. She has only one male friend, a shattered Vietnam veteran and fellow drunk (Bruce Dern). Although she kills for the first time in self-defense, she is also lashing out against her past. Her experience of love with Selby brings revulsion uncoiling from her memories; men treat her in a cruel way and pay for their sins and those of all who went before them. The most heartbreaking scene is the death of a good man (Scott Wilson) who actually wants to help her, but has arrived so late in her life that the only way he can help is to be eliminated as a witness.

Aileen's body language is frightening and fascinating. She doesn't know how to occupy her body. Watch Theron as she goes through a repertory of little arm straightenings and body adjustments and head tosses and hair touchings, as she nervously tries to shake out her nervousness and look at ease. Observe her smoking technique; she handles her cigarettes with the self-conscious bravado of a thirteen-year-old trying to impress a kid. And note that there is only one moment in the movie where she seems relaxed and at peace with herself; you will know the scene, and it will explain itself.

This is one of the greatest performances in the history of the cinema.

Christina Ricci finds the correct note for Selby Wall—so correct some critics have mistaken it for bad acting, when in fact it is sublime acting in its portrayal of a bad actor. She plays Selby as clueless, dim, in over her head, picking up cues from moment to moment, cobbling her behavior out of notions borrowed from bad movies, old songs, and barroom romances. Selby must have walked into a gay bar for the first time only a few weeks ago, and studied desperately to figure out how to present herself. Selby and Aileen are often trying to improvise the next line they think the other wants to hear.

We are told to hate the sin but not the sinner, and as I watched *Monster* I began to see it as an exercise in the theological virtue of charity. It refuses to objectify Wuornos and her crimes and refuses to exploit her story in the cynical manner of true crime sensationalism—insisting instead on seeing her as one of God's creatures worthy of our attention. She has been so cruelly twisted by life that she seems incapable of goodness, and yet when she feels love for the first time she is inspired to try to be a better person.

She is unequipped for this struggle, and lacks the gifts of intelligence and common sense. She is devoid of conventional moral standards. She is impulsive, reckless, angry, and violent, and she devastates her victims, their families, and herself. There are no excuses for what she does, but there are reasons, and the purpose of the movie is to make them visible. If life had given her anything at all to work with, we would feel no sympathy. But life has beaten her beyond redemption.

Monster's Ball
R, 111 m., 2002

Billy Bob Thornton (Hank Grotowski), Halle Berry (Leticia Musgrove), Heath Ledger (Sonny Grotowski), Peter Boyle (Buck Grotowski), Sean "Puffy" Combs (Lawrence Musgrove), Coronji Calhoun (Tyrell Musgrove). Directed by Marc Forster and produced by Lee Daniels. Screenplay by Milo Addica and Will Rokos.

Monster's Ball is about a black woman and a white man who find, for a time anyway, solace in each other for their pain. But their pain remains separate and so do they; this is not a message movie about interracial relationships, but the specific story of two desperate people whose lives are shaken by violent deaths, and how in the days right after that they turn to each other because there is no place else to turn. The movie has the complexity of great fiction, and requires our empathy as we interpret the decisions that are made—especially at the end, when the movie avoids an obligatory scene that would have been conventional and forces us to cut straight to the point.

Billy Bob Thornton and Halle Berry star as Hank and Leticia, in two performances that are so powerful because they observe the specific natures of these two characters and avoid the pitfalls of racial clichés. What a shock to find these two characters freed from the conventions of political correctness and allowed to be who they are: weak, flawed, needful, with good hearts tested by lifetimes of compromise. They live in a small Georgia town, circa 1990. She works the night shift in a diner, has a fat little son, and an ex-husband on death row. He works as a guard on death row, has a mean, racist father and a browbeaten son, and will be involved in her husband's execution. ("Monster's Ball" is an old English term for a condemned man's last night on Earth.)

At first Hank and Leticia do not realize the connection they have through the condemned man. For another movie that would be enough plot. We can imagine the scenes of discovery and revelation. How this movie handles that disclosure is one of its great strengths: how both characters deal with it (or don't deal with it) internally, so that the movie blessedly proceeds according to exactly who they are, what they need, what they must do, and the choices open to them.

The screenplay by Milo Addica and Will Rokos is subtle and observant; one is reminded of short fiction by Andre Dubus, William Trevor, Eudora Welty, Raymond Carver. It specifically does not tell "their" story, but focuses on two separate lives. The characters are given equal weight and have individual story arcs, which do not intersect but simply, inevitably, meet. There is an overlay of racism in the story; Hank's father, Buck (Peter Boyle), is a hateful racist, and Hank mirrors his attitudes. But the movie is not about redemption, not about how Hank overcomes his attitudes, but about how they fall away from him like a dead skin because his other feelings are so much more urgent. The movie, then, is not about overcoming prejudice, but sidestepping it because it comes to seem monstrously irrelevant.

Hank is an abused son and an abusive father. His old man, Buck, confined to a wheelchair and a stroller, still exercises an iron will over the family. All three generations live under his roof, and when Hank's son, Sonny (Heath Ledger), opts out of the family sickness, Buck's judgment is cruel: "He was weak." We do not learn much about Leticia's parents, but she is a bad mother, alternately smothering her son, Tyrell (Coronji Calhoun), with love, and screaming at him that he's a "fat little piggy." She drinks too much, has been served with an eviction notice, sees herself as a loser. She has no affection at all for Tyrell's father, Lawrence (Puffy Combs), on death row, and makes it clear during a visitation that she is there strictly for her son. There is no side story to paint Lawrence as a victim; "I'm a bad man," he tells Tyrell. "You're the best of me."

Leticia is all messed up. She sustains a loss that derails her, and it happens by coincidence that Hank is there when he can perform a service. This makes them visible to each other. It is safe to say that no one else in the community is visible, in terms of human need, to either one. Hank's shy, slow courtship is so tentative it's like he's sleepwalking toward her. Her response is dictated by the fact that she has nowhere else to turn. They have a key conversation in which the bodies of both characters are tilted away from each other, as if fearful of being any closer. And notice another conversation, when she's been drinking, and she waves her hands and one hand keeps falling on Hank's lap; she doesn't seem to notice and, here is the point, he doesn't seem willing to.

Their intimate scenes are ordinary and simple, a contrast to Hank's cold, mercenary arrangement with a local hooker. The film's only flaw is the way Marc Forster allows his camera to linger on Halle Berry's half-clothed beauty; this story is not about sex appeal, and if the camera sees her that way we are pretty sure that Hank doesn't. What he sees, what she sees, is defined not by desire but by need.

Students of screenwriting should study the way the film handles the crucial passages at the end, when she discovers some drawings and understands their meaning. Here is where a lesser movie would have supplied an obligatory confrontation. Leticia never mentions the drawings to Hank. Why not? Because it is time to move on? Because she understands why he withheld information? Because she has no alternative? Because she senses that the drawings would not exist if the artist hated his subject? Because she is too tired and this is just one more nail on the cross? Because she forgives? What?

The movie cannot say. The characters have disappeared into the mysteries of the heart. *Monster's Ball* demonstrates that to explain all its mysteries, a movie would have to limit itself to mysteries that can be explained. As for myself, as Leticia rejoined Hank in the last shot of the movie, I was thinking about her as deeply and urgently as about any movie character I can remember.

Montenegro

R, 96 m., 1981

Susan Anspach (Marilyn), Erland Josephson (Martin), Jamie Marsh (Jimmy), Per Oscarsson (Dr. Pazardjian), Bare Todorovic (Alex), Marianne Jacobi (Cookie), John Zacharias (Grandpa Bill), Svetezar Cvetkovic (Montenegro). Directed by Dusan Makavejev and produced by Christer Abrahamsen, Bo Jönsson, and George Zecevic. Screenplay by Makavejev.

There can be something absolutely liberating about a movie that makes up its rules as it goes along. *Montenegro* is a movie like that. It is about an uptight American wife who escapes from her husband's utterly sedate existence in Stockholm and spends two wild and wooly nights in a sleazy nightclub run by some expatriate Yugoslavians.

She leaves behind a staid, comfortable, affluent Swedish household, in which the only spark of life is the old grandfather's conviction that he is Buffalo Bill and that he can find a bride by advertising in the newspaper. She finds herself in a ghetto inhabited by immigrant workers from southern and eastern Europe. She is surrounded by sex and violence, and, truth to tell, she likes it.

Montenegro is the first movie in seven years from Dusan Makavejev, one of the great free spirits of moviemaking in our time. He does not see it as a protest against the exploitation of his poor countrymen who immigrate to northern Europe in search of jobs. Quite the contrary. He believes that his life-embracing countrymen are doing the uptight Swedes a favor by condescending to live in their dull country. At one point, Makavejev says, he intended to dedicate *Montenegro* to the 11 million "guest workers" of Europe, "who moved north to exploit rich and prosperous people, bringing with them filthy habits, bad manners, and the smell of garlic."

You can guess from that statement something of the spirit in which *Montenegro* was made. The movie stars Susan Anspach, the displaced housewife of *Blume in Love,* as the American wife of a rich Swedish executive. The Swede is Erland Josephson, who played a similar character (from a radically different point of view) in Ingmar Bergman's *Scenes from a Marriage.*

They live with a precocious son a dotty grandfather, and occasionally consult a psychiatrist (Per Oscarsson) who is so sick he may be trying to research insanity from the inside. Their household is a mixture of sterile, efficient creature comforts and buried frustration. Their sex life is not terrific.

Anspach's husband has to make a business trip. She thinks to join him, but at the airport she's waylaid by a band of Yugoslavians, and before she quite understands what has happened, she has posed for a Polaroid with a man with a knife stuck in his forehead and is sharing the backseat of a car with a sheep. The Yugoslavians take her to the Zanzi Bar, a disreputable nightclub, where she witnesses the transformation of a shy Yugoslavian farm girl into an exotic dancer and finds herself powerfully attracted to the garlicky sexuality of a strong young peasant.

The nightclub occupies no known plane of real existence. Like many of the places in Makavejev's movies, it ventures into a fevered fantasy world of eroticism, Marxism, and unbridled excess. We know we're in a strange place when we see the battery-powered, remote-controlled toy U.S. Army tank with a large vibrator mounted on it. For Makavejev, this is no doubt a splendid symbol, enjoining us to make love, not war.

Seeing a Makavejev film is like experiencing a showdown with the director's libido. He has a few major themes: Large bureaucracies are stupid, ideologies are usually misunderstood by their most fervent supporters, most people are too uptight, possessions get in the way of sexuality, and an orgasm a day keeps the doctor away. In this case, the doctor (Oscarsson) and the husband hold frantic conferences about the whereabouts of the missing Anspach, while the Zanzi Bar engages in an unrestrained countdown toward New Year's Day.

Makavejev's movies are very frank about sexuality, but they are not dirty. They have a kind of table-slapping, robust good health to them. Anspach, who is not robust, and who is in fact rather shy and frail, may not seem like a likely candidate to enter this world, but she undergoes a transformation in the movie, from the suppressed, unbalanced housewife into a woman who was born to embrace Rabelaisian excess.

Maybe it's the movie's cheerful collision between the Cuisinart set and raw peasant passion that is pleasing *Montenegro's* audiences (the movie was a big hit among the Lincoln Park crowds at the Biograph). Without knowing it, Makavejev may have stumbled on the cinematic equivalent of a visit to Greek Town. It's liberating to descend into the ethnic dives and dance to the wild zither and dodge flaming cheese and be home in front of the Sony by midnight. That's why I especially love the last scene in *Montenegro,* in which Anspach returns to her affluent cocoon and takes appropriate action.

Monte Walsh

PG, 106 m., 1970

Lee Marvin (Monte Walsh), Jeanne Moreau (Martine), Jack Palance (Chet), Mitch Ryan (Shorty), Jim Davis (Cal Brennan), Bear Hudkins (Sonny Jacobs). Directed by William A. Fraker and produced by Hal Landers and Bobby Roberts. Screenplay by Lukas Heller and David Z. Goodman, based on the book by Jack Schaefer.

Monte Walsh is as lovely a Western as I've seen in a long time. Like a lot of recent Westerns, it's about the end of the old West. Monte, a

friend says to Lee Marvin, "do you realize how many cowpunchers there were out here ten years ago? Well, there's a hell of a lot less now. And no jobs for them." And so Monte Walsh, fiftyish, thinks in a rather disorganized way of getting into some other line of work and maybe even getting married.

The thing that helps make up his mind for him is when his best friend, Chet (Jack Palance), gives up cowpunching, moves into town, and marries the "hardware widow." Chet's wedding starts Monte thinking about marrying the town whore (Jeanne Moreau), who has never taken a penny from him and who clearly loves him.

Times have been hard for her, too. Prostitution, she observes, is a profession of diminishing returns, and she has had to move to a railroad town nearby. With the consolidation of all the ranches into one big spread managed by some financial wizards from back East, jobs for cowboys have become scarce. And thus, inevitably, there has been less call for her services. Monte rides over to the railroad town and asks her what she thinks about the idea of getting married.

Moreau, in a moment of luminous acting, thinks it over and then smiles and says, "I like it," in a way that can't be described. Then she reflects: "Of course, marriage is a common ambition in my profession."

But not in Monte's. "Cowboys don't get married," he observes to Chet. So he toys with the idea of stunt-riding for a Wild West show, but the thought of all those concrete cities without any open spaces is too much for him. And so he is faced, toward the end of the movie, with a very lonely desperation. This may be the first three-handkerchief Western.

There have been, I mentioned, several movies recently about the passing of the old West. They seem to be inspired by different kinds of motives. Some hands in Hollywood seem to believe that the Western itself is dead, that since you can't seriously peddle the old good guy–bad guy plots, you have to dismantle them and bury them.

The Wild Bunch and *The Professionals,* each in its own way, were about the shortage of work for gunslingers. They suggested that violence had gone out of style in the West, that a gun on the hip no longer was required in polite society.

The Wild Bunch seemed to seek death almost suicidally in the last half of that great movie; they'd lived by the gun and they had to die by it, ironically, because they knew no other way to make a living.

Monte Walsh is set at the same psychological moment in the West, but it takes a quieter and, on the whole, more thoughtful approach. There's a fair amount of gunplay, yes, and Marvin has a well-staged action scene where he tries to tame a bronco and succeeds in destroying half a town. But mostly the movie sticks close to ordinary life: to the camaraderie of the bunkhouse and the range, to the everyday life of the working cowboy, and to the shy and beautiful love between the cowboy and the prostitute. The movie is rough but it is almost always tender.

The performances are extraordinary. Marvin has seldom been better; he leaves in the toughness of his usual screen character, but he also reveals a lot of depth. He's often directed wastefully; directors want him for his presence and authority but don't really seem to want a performance from him. And he obliges, usually for lots of bread (*Paint Your Wagon* was a sad example). This time he acts.

Moreau and Palance both seem to relate to him especially well. Given their roles of lover and best buddy, there was a danger of clichés. But you never get that feeling; the scenes seem real. You're reminded once again what a good actor Palance is and how seldom he gets the opportunity to prove it.

A lot of the credit for the movie's taste and emotional depth probably belongs to William Fraker, a talented cinematographer who was directing for the first time. Most first-time directors choose projects they wanted to make long before they got the opportunity. Fraker, whose credits include *Rosemary's Baby,* photographed *Paint Your Wagon* and must have been thinking all during that unfortunate movie about how he'd direct Marvin, if he got the chance. He did get the chance, and *Monte Walsh* was worth waiting for.

Moolaade

NO MPAA RATING, 124 m., 2004

Fatoumata Coulibaly (Colle Ardo Gallo Sy), Maimouna Helene Diarra (Hadjatou), Salimata Traore (Amasatou), Dominique T. Zeida (Mercenaire), Mah Compaore (Doyenne des Exciseuses), Aminata Dao (Alima Ba). Directed and produced by Ousmane Sembene. Screenplay by Sembene.

Sometimes I seek the right words and I despair. What can I write that will inspire you to see *Moolaade*? This was, for me, the best film at Cannes 2004, a story vibrating with urgency and life. It makes a powerful statement and at the same time contains humor, charm, and astonishing visual beauty.

But even my words of praise may be the wrong ones, sending the message that this is an important film, and therefore hard work. Moviegoers who will cheerfully line up for trash are cautious, even wary, about attending a film they fear might be great. And if I told you the subject of the film is female circumcision—would I lose you? And if I placed the story in an African village, have you already decided to see *National Treasure* instead?

All I can tell you is, *Moolaade* is a film that will stay in my memory and inform my ideas long after other films have vaporized. It takes place in a village in Senegal, where ancient customs exist side-by-side with battery-powered radios, cars, and trucks, and a young man returning from Paris. Traditional family compounds surround a mosque; they are made in ancient patterns from sun-baked mud and have the architectural beauty of everything that is made on the spot by the people who will use it, using the materials at hand. The colors of this world are the colors of sand, earth, sky, and trees, setting off the joyous colors of the costumes.

It is the time for several of the young women in the village to be "purified." This involves removing parts of their genitals so they will have no feeling during sex. The practice is common throughout Africa to this day, especially in Muslim areas, although Islam in fact condemns it. Many girls die after the operation, and during the course of this movie two will throw themselves down a well. But men, who in their wisdom assume control over women's bodies, insist on purification. And because men will marry no woman who has not been cut, the older women insist on it too; they have daughters who must find husbands.

Colle (Fatoumata Coulibaly), the second of four wives of a powerful man, has refused to let her daughter be cut. Now six girls flee from a purification ritual, and four of them seek refuge with her. Colle agrees to help them, and invokes "moolaade," a word meaning "protection." She ties a strand of bright yarn across the entrance to her compound, and it is understood by everyone that as long as the girls stay inside the compound, they are safe, and no one can step inside to capture them.

These details are established not in the mood of a dreary ethnographic docudrama, but with great energy and life. The writer, producer, and director is Ousmane Sembene, sometimes called the father of African cinema, who at eighty-one can look back on a life during which he has made nine other films, founded a newspaper, written a novel, and become, in the opinion of his distributor, the art film pioneer Dan Talbot, the greatest living director. Sembene's stories are not the tales of isolated characters; they always exist within a society that observes and comments, and sometimes gets involved. Indeed, his first film, *Black Girl* (1966), is the tragedy of a young African woman who is taken away from this familiarity and made to feel a stranger in Paris.

The village in *Moolaade* has an interesting division of powers. All authority allegedly resides with the council of men, but all decisions seem to be made by the women, who in their own way make up their minds and achieve what they desire. Men insist on purification, but it is really women who enforce it—not just the fearsome women who actually conduct the ceremony, but ordinary women who have undergone it and see no reason why their daughters should be spared.

Colle has seen many girls sicken and die, and does not want to risk her daughter. She knows, as indeed most of those in the village know, that purification is dangerous and unnecessary and has been condemned even by their own government. But if a man will not marry an unpurified daughter, what is a mother to do? This is particularly relevant for Colle, whose own daughter, Amasatou (Salimata Traore), is engaged to be married to a young man who will someday rule their tribe, and who is a successful businessman in Paris. Yes, he is modern, is educated, is cos-

mopolitan, but in returning to his village for a bride, of course he desires one who has been cut.

Local characters stand out in high relief. There is Mercenaire (Dominique T. Zeida), a peddler whose van arrives at the village from time to time with pots, pans, potions, and dry goods, and who brings news from the wider world. There's spontaneous fun in the way the women bargain and flirt with him. And there is the *doyenne des exciseuses* (Mah Compaore), whose livelihood depends on her purification rituals, and who rules a fierce band of assistants who could play the witches in *Macbeth*.

Much of the humor in the film comes from the ineffectual debates of the council of men, who deplore Colle's action but have been checkmated by the invocation of moolaade. One ancient tradition is thwarted by another. Colle's husband, who has been away, returns to the village and insists that she hand over the girls, but she flatly refuses, and in a scene of drama and rich humor, the husband's first wife backs up the second wife's position and supports her.

All of this nonsense is caused by too much outside influence, the men decide. All of the radios in the village are collected and thrown onto a big pile near the mosque—where, in an image that lingers through the last scenes of the film, some of them continue to play, so that the heap seems filled with disembodied voices. Colle stands strong. Then the young man from Paris arrives, and the whole village holds its breath, poised between the past and the future.

Moonlighting

PG, 97 m., 1982

Jeremy Irons (Nowak), Eugene Lipinski (Banaszak), Jiri Stanislav (Wolski), Eugeniusz Haczkiewicz (Kudaj). Directed by Jerzy Skolimowski and produced by Mark Shivas and Skolimowski. Screenplay by Skolimowski.

Moonlighting is a wickedly pointed movie that takes a simple little story, tells it with humor and truth, and turns it into a knife in the side of the Polish government. In its own way, this response to the crushing of Solidarity is as powerful as Andrzej Wajda's *Man of Iron*. It also is more fun. The movie takes place in London, during the weeks just before and after the banning of the Solidarity movement in Poland. It begins, actually, in Warsaw, with a mystifying scene in which a group of plotters are scheming to smuggle some hardware past British customs. They're plotters, all right; their plot is to move into a small house in London and remodel it, knocking out walls, painting ceilings, making it into a showplace for the Polish government official who has purchased it. The official's plan is simplicity itself: By bringing Polish workers to London on tourist visas, he can get the remodeling done for a fraction of what British workmen would cost him. At the same time, the workers can earn good wages that they can take back to Poland and buy bicycles with. The only thing nobody counts on is the upheaval after Solidarity is crushed and travel to and from Poland is strictly regulated.

Jeremy Irons, of *The French Lieutenant's Woman,* plays the lead in the film. He's the only Polish workman who can speak English. Acting as foreman, he guides his team of men through the pitfalls of London and safely into the house they're going to remodel. He advises them to keep a low profile, while he ventures out to buy the groceries and (not incidentally) to read the newspapers. When he finds out about the crisis in Poland, he keeps it a secret from his comrades. The daily life of the renovation project falls into a pattern, which the film's director, Jerzy Skolimowski, intercuts with the adventures of his hero. Jeremy Irons begins to steal things: newspapers, bicycles, frozen turkeys. He concocts an elaborate scheme to defraud the local supermarket, and some of the movie's best scenes involve the subtle timing of his shoplifting scam, which involves the misrepresentation of cash-register receipts. He needs to steal food because he's running out of money, and he knows his group can't easily go home again. There's also a quietly hilarious, and slightly sad, episode involving a salesgirl in a bluejeans store. Irons, pretending to be more naive than he is, tries to pick the girl up. She's having none of it.

Moonlighting invites all kinds of interpretations. You can take this simple story and set it against the events of the last two years, and see it as a kind of parable. Your interpretation is as good as mine. Is the house itself Poland, and the workmen Solidarity—rebuilding it from within, before an authoritarian outside force

intervenes? Or is this movie about the heresy of substituting Western values (and jeans and turkeys) for a homegrown orientation? Or is it about the manipulation of the working classes by the intelligentsia? Or is it simply a frontal attack on the Communist Party bosses who live high off the hog while the workers are supposed to follow the rules?

Like all good parables, *Moonlighting* contains not one but many possibilities. What needs to be insisted upon, however, is how much *fun* this movie is. Skolimowski, a Pole who has lived and worked in England for several years, began writing this film on the day that Solidarity was crushed, and he filmed it, on a small budget and with a small crew, in less than two months: He had it ready for the 1982 Cannes Film Festival where it was a major success. It's successful, I think, because it tells an interesting narrative in a straightforward way. Skolimowski is a natural storyteller. You can interpret and discuss *Moonlighting* all night. During the movie, you'll be more interested in whether Irons gets away with that frozen turkey.

Moonlight Mile
PG-13, 112 m., 2002

Jake Gyllenhaal (Joe Nast), Dustin Hoffman (Ben Floss), Susan Sarandon (JoJo Floss), Holly Hunter (Mona Camp), Ellen Pompeo (Bertie Knox), Dabney Coleman (Mike Mulcahey). Directed by Brad Silberling and produced by Mark Johnson and Silberling. Screenplay by Silberling.

After the funeral is over, and the mourners have come back to the house for coffee and cake and have all gone home, the parents and the boyfriend of Diana, the dead girl, sit by themselves. Her mother criticizes how one friend expressed her sympathy. And the father asks, what *could* she say? "Put yourself in their shoes."

That little scene provides a key to Brad Silberling's *Moonlight Mile.* What do you say when someone dies—someone you cared for? What are the right words? And what's the right thing to do? Death is the ultimate rebuke to good manners. The movie, which makes an unusually intense effort to deal with the process of grief and renewal, is inspired by a loss in Silberling's own life. The TV actress Rebecca Schaeffer, his girlfriend at the time, was killed in

1989 by a fan. Silberling has grown very close to her parents in the years since then, he told me, and more than a decade later he has tried to use the experience as the starting point for a film.

Moonlight Mile, which takes place in 1973, opens in an elliptical way. At first only quiet clues in the dialogue allow us to understand that someone has died. We meet Joe Nast (Jake Gyllenhaal), the fiancé of the dead girl, and her parents, Ben and JoJo Floss (Dustin Hoffman and Susan Sarandon). They talk not in a sentimental way, but in that strange, detached tone we use when grief is too painful to express and yet something must be said.

After the funeral and the home visitation, the film follows what in a lesser film would be called the "healing process." *Moonlight Mile* is too quirky and observant to be described in psychobabble. Joe stays stuck in the Floss house, living in an upstairs bedroom, his plans on hold. Ben, who has lost a daughter, now in a confused way hopes to gain a son, and encourages Joe to join him in his business as a real estate developer. JoJo, protected by intelligence and wit, looks closely and suspects a secret Joe is keeping, which leaves him stranded between the past and future.

Gyllenhaal, who in person is a jokester, in the movies almost always plays characters who are withdrawn and morose. Remember him in *Donnie Darko*, *The Good Girl*, and *Lovely and Amazing*. Here, too, he is a young man with troubled thoughts. At the post office, and again at a bar where she has a night job, he meets Bertie Knox (Ellen Pompeo), who sees inside when others only look at the surface. They begin to talk. She has a loss too: Her boyfriend has been missing in action in Vietnam for three years. While it is possible that they will mend each other's hearts by falling in love, the movie doesn't simple-mindedly pursue that plot path, but meanders among the thoughts of the living.

Silberling's screenplay pays full attention to all of the characters. Ben and JoJo are not simply a backdrop to a romance involving Joe and Bertie. The movie provides key scenes for all of the characters, in conversation and in monologue, so that it is not only about Joe's grieving process but about all four, who have lost different things in different ways.

Anyone regarding the Hoffman character will note that his name is Benjamin and re-

member Hoffman's most famous character, in *The Graduate*. But Joe is the Benjamin of this film, and Hoffman's older man has more in common with another of his famous roles: Willy Loman, the hero of *Death of a Salesman*. Ben occupies a low-rent storefront office on Main Street in Cape Anne, Massachusetts, but dreams of putting together a group of properties and bringing in a superstore like K-Mart. This will be his big killing, the deal that caps his career, even though we can see in the eyes of the local rich man (Dabney Coleman) that Ben is too small to land this fish. Ben's desire to share his dream with his surrogate son Joe also has echoes from the Arthur Miller tragedy.

Sarandon's JoJo is tart, with a verbal wit to protect her and a jaundiced view of her husband's prospects. The deepest conversation JoJo has with Joe ("Isn't it funny, that we have the same name?") is about as well done as such a scene can be. She intuits that Joe is dealing not only with the loss of Diana's life, but with the loss of something else.

Ellen Pompeo, a newcomer, plays Bertie with a kind of scary charisma that cannot be written, only felt. She knows she is attractive to Joe. She knows she likes him. She knows she is faithful to her old boyfriend. She is frightened by her own power to attract, especially since she wants to attract even while she tells herself she doesn't. She is so vulnerable in this movie, so sweet, as she senses Joe's pain and wants to help him.

Holly Hunter is the fifth major player, as the lawyer who is handling the case against Diana's killer. She embodies the wisdom of the law, which knows, as laymen do not, that it moves with its own logic regardless of the feelings of those in the courtroom. She offers practical advice, and then you can see in her eyes that she wishes she could offer emotional advice instead.

Moonlight Mile gives itself the freedom to feel contradictory things. It is sentimental but feels free to offend, is analytical and then surrenders to the illogic of its characters, is about grief and yet permits laughter. Everyone who has grieved for a loved one will recognize the moment, some days after the death, when an irreverent remark will release the surprise of laughter. Sometimes we laugh that we may not cry. Not many movies know that truth. *Moonlight Mile* is based on it.

Moonstruck

PG, 100 m., 1987

Cher (Loretta Castorini), Nicolas Cage (Ronny Cammareri), Vincent Gardenia (Cosmo Castorini), Olympia Dukakis (Rose Castorini), Danny Aiello (Johnny Cammareri), Julie Bovasso (Rita Cappomaggi), John Mahoney (Perry), Louis Guss (Raymond Cappomaggi), Feodor Chaliapin (Old Man). Directed by Norman Jewison and produced by Patrick Palmer and Jewison. Screenplay by John Patrick Shanley.

When the moon hits your eye, like a big-a pizza pie—that's amore!
—Dean Martin

The most enchanting quality about *Moonstruck* is the hardest to describe, and that is the movie's tone. Reviews of the movie tend to make it sound like a madcap ethnic comedy, and that it is. But there is something more here, a certain bittersweet yearning that comes across as ineffably romantic, and a certain magical quality that is reflected in the film's title.

The movie stars Cher, as an Italian-American widow in her late thirties, but she is not the only moonstruck one in the film. There is the moonlit night, for example, that her wise, cynical mother (Olympia Dukakis) goes out for dinner by herself, and meets a middle-aged university professor (John Mahoney) who specializes in seducing his young students, but who finds in this mature woman a certain undeniable sexuality. There is the furtive and yet somehow sweet affair that Cher's father (Vincent Gardenia) has been carrying on for years with the ripe, disillusioned Anita Gillette.

And at the heart of the story, there is Cher's astonishing discovery that she is still capable of love. As the movie opens, she becomes engaged to Mr. Johnny Cammareri (Danny Aiello), not so much out of love as out of weariness. But after he flies to Sicily to be at the bedside of his dying mother, she goes to talk to Mr. Johnny's estranged younger brother (Nicolas Cage), and is thunderstruck when they are drawn almost instantly into a passionate embrace.

Moonstruck was directed by Norman Jewison and written by John Patrick Shanley, and one of their accomplishments is to allow the film to be about all of these people (and several more, besides). This is an ensemble comedy, and a lot of the laughs grow out of the sense of family that Jewison and Shanley create; there are, for example, small hilarious moments involving the exasperation that Dukakis feels for her ancient father-in-law (Feodor Chaliapin), who lives upstairs with his dogs. (In the course of a family dinner, she volunteers: "Feed one more bite of my food to your dogs, old man, and I'll kick you 'til you're dead!")

As Cher's absent fiancé lingers at his mother's bedside, Cher and Cage grow even more desperately passionate, and Cher learns the secret of the hatred between the two brothers: One day Aiello made Cage look the wrong way at the wrong time, and he lost his hand in a bread-slicer. Now he wears an artificial hand, and carries an implacable grudge in his heart.

But grudges and vendettas and old wounds and hatreds are everywhere in this film. The mother knows, for example, that her husband is having an affair with another woman. She asks from the bottom of her heart why this should be so, and a friend replies, "Because he is afraid of dying." She sees at once that this is so. But does that cause her to sympathize with her husband? Hardly. One night he comes home. She asks where he has been. He replies, "Nowhere." She tells him she wants him to know one thing: "No matter where you go, or what you do—you're gonna die."

Some of these moments are so charged with tension they remind us of the great opening scenes of *Saturday Night Fever* (and the mother from that movie, Julie Bovasso, is on hand here as an aunt). But all of the passion is drained of its potential for hurt, somehow, by the influence of the moon, which has enchanted these people and protects them from the consequences of their frailties. Jewison captures some of the same qualities of Ingmar Bergman's *Smiles of a Summer Night,* in which nature itself conspires with lovers to bring about their happiness.

The movie is filled with fine performances—by Cher, 1987's Best Actress Oscar winner, never funnier or more assured; by Olympia Dukakis (who was named Best Supporting Actress) and Vincent Gardenia, as her parents, whose love runs as deep as their exasperation; and by Nicolas Cage as the hapless, angry brother, who is so filled with hurts he has lost track of what caused them. In its warmth and in its enchantment, as well as in its laughs, this is a fine comedy.

Moscow on the Hudson

R, 115 m., 1984

Robin Williams (Vladimir Ivanoff), Maria Conchita Alonso (Lucia Lombardo), Cleavant Derricks (Witherspoon), Alejandro Rey (Orlando Ramirez). Directed and produced by Paul Mazursky. Screenplay by Mazursky and Leon Capetanos.

Mike Royko likes to make fun of foreign born taxi drivers. He uses a lot of phonetic spellings to show how funny dey speeka da Engleesh. Maybe he's missing out on some good conversations. Have you ever *talked* to a taxi driver from Iran or Pakistan or Africa? I have, and usually I hear a fascinating story about a man who has fled from poverty or persecution, who in some cases has left behind a thriving business, and who is starting out all over again in this country. I also usually get the name of a good restaurant.

I thought of some of those experiences while I was watching Paul Mazursky's *Moscow on the Hudson,* a wonderful movie about a man who defects to the United States. His name is Vladimir Ivanoff, he plays the saxophone in a Russian circus, and when the circus visits New York, he falls in love with the United States and defects by turning himself in to a security guard at Bloomingdale's. The Russian is played by Robin Williams, who disappears so completely into his quirky, lovable, complicated character that he's quite plausible as a Russian. The movie opens with his life in Moscow, a city of overcrowded apartments, bureaucratic red tape, long lines for consumer goods, secret pleasures like jazz records, and shortages so acute that toilet paper has turned into a currency of its own. The early scenes are eerily convincing, partly because Williams plays them in Russian. This isn't one of those movies where everybody somehow speaks English. The turning point of the movie occurs in Bloomingdale's, as so many turning points do, and Ivanoff makes two friends right

there on the spot: Witherspoon, the black security guard (Cleavant Derricks), and Lucia, the Italian salesclerk (Maria Conchita Alonso).

They're a tip-off to an interesting casting decision by Mazursky, who populates his movie almost entirely with ethnic and racial minorities. In addition to the black and the Italian, there's a Korean taxi driver, a Cuban lawyer, a Chinese anchorwoman, all of them reminders that all of us came from somewhere else. Ivanoff moves in with the security guard's family, which greatly resembles the one he left behind in Moscow, right down to the pious grandfather. He gets a job selling hot dogs from a pushcart, he works his way up to driving a limousine, and he falls in love with the salesclerk from Italy. That doesn't go so well. She dreams of marrying a "real American," and Ivanoff, even after he trims his beard, will not quite do.

Moscow on the Hudson is the kind of movie that Paul Mazursky does especially well. It's a comedy that finds most of its laughs in the close observations of human behavior, and that finds its story in a contemporary subject Mazursky has some thoughts about. In that, it's like his earlier films *An Unmarried Woman* (women's liberation), *Harry and Tonto* (growing old), *Blume in Love* (marriage in the age of doing your own thing), and *Bob & Carol & Ted & Alice* (encounter groups). It is also a rarity, a patriotic film that has a liberal, rather than a conservative, heart. It made me feel good to be an American, and good that Vladimir Ivanoff was going to be one, too.

The Mother and the Whore

NO MPAA RATING, 215 m., 1973 (rereleased 1999)

Jean-Pierre Leaud (Alexandre), Bernadette Lafont (Marie), Francoise Lebrun (Veronika), Isabelle Weingarten (Gilberte), Jean Douchet (Man at Café Flore), Jean-Noel Picq (Offenbach Lover). Directed by Jean Eustache and produced by Pierre Cottrell. Screenplay by Eustache.

When Jean Eustache's *The Mother and the Whore* was released in 1973, young audiences all over the world embraced its layabout hero and his endless conversations with the woman he lived with, the woman he was dating, the woman who rejected him, and various other women encountered in the cafés of Paris. The character was played by Jean-Pierre Leaud, star of *The 400 Blows* and two other autobiographical films by François Truffaut. In 1977, Truffaut made *The Man Who Loved Women.* This one could have been titled *The Man Who Loved to Hear Himself Talk.*

At three and a half hours, the film is long, but its essence is to be long: Make it any shorter, and it would have a plot and an outcome, when in fact Eustache simply wants to record an existence. Alexandre (Leaud), his hero, lives with Marie (Bernadette Lafont), a boutique owner who apparently supports him; one would say he was between jobs if there were any sense that he'd ever had one. He meets a blind date named Veronika (Francoise Lebrun) in a café, and subjects her to a great many of his thoughts and would-be thoughts. (Much of Lebrun's screen time consists of close-ups of her listening.) In the middle of his monologues, Alexandre has a way of letting his eyes follow the progress of other women through his field of view.

Alexandre is smart enough, but not a great intellect. His favorite area of study is himself, but there he hasn't made much headway. He chatters about the cinema and about life, sometimes confusing them ("films tell you how to live, how to make a kid"). He wears a dark coat and a very long scarf, knotted around his neck and sweeping to his knees; his best friend dresses the same way. He spends his days in cafés, holding (but not reading) Proust. "Look there's Sartre—the drunk," he says one day in Café Flore, and Eustache supplies a quick shot of several people at a table, one of whom may or may not be Sartre. Alexandre talks about Sartre staggering out after his long intellectual chats in the café, and speculates that the great man's philosophy may be alcoholic musings.

The first time I saw *The Mother and the Whore*, I thought it was about Alexandre. After a viewing of the newly restored 35mm print being released for the movie's twenty-fifth anniversary, I think it is just as much about the women, and about the way that women can let a man talk endlessly about himself while they regard him like a specimen of aberrant behavior. Women keep a man like Alexandre around, I suspect, out of curiosity about what new idiocy he will next exhibit.

Of course, Alexandre is cheating—on Marie, whom he lives with, and on Veronika, whom he says he loves. Part of his style is to play with relationships, just to see what happens. The two women find out about each other, and eventually meet. There are some fireworks, but not as many as you might expect, maybe because neither one would be that devastated at losing Alexandre. Veronika, a nurse from Poland, is at least frank about herself: She sleeps around because she likes sex. She has a passionate monologue about her sexual needs and her resentment that women aren't supposed to admit their feelings. Whether Alexandre has sex with Marie is a good question; I suppose the answer is yes, but you can't be sure. She represents, of course, the mother, and Veronika thinks of herself as a whore; Alexandre has positioned himself in the crosshairs of the classic Freudian dilemma.

Jean-Pierre Leaud's best performance was his first, as the fierce young thirteen-year-old who roamed Paris in *The 400 Blows*, idolizing Balzac and escaping into books and trouble as a way of dealing with his parents' unhappy marriage. In a way, most of his adult performances are simply that boy, grown up. Here he smokes and talks incessantly, and wanders Paris like a puppet controlled by his libido. It's amusing the way he performs for the women; there's one shot in particular, where he takes a drink so theatrically it could be posing for a photo titled, "I Take a Drink."

The genuine drama in the movie centers on Veronika, who more or less knows they are only playing at love while out of the sight of Marie. We learn a lot about her life—her room in the hospital, her schedule, her low self-esteem. When she does talk, it is from brave, unadulterated self-knowledge.

The Mother and the Whore made an enormous impact when it was released. It still works a quarter-century later, because it was so focused on its subjects and lacking in pretension. It is rigorously observant, the portrait of an immature man and two women who humor him for a while, paying the price that entails. Eustache committed suicide at forty-three, in 1981, after making about a dozen films, of which this is by far the best-known. He said his film was intended as "the description of a normal course of events without the shortcuts of dramatization," and described Alexandre as a collector of "rare moments" that occupy his otherwise idle time. As a record of a kind of everyday Parisian life, the film is superb. We think of the cafés of Paris as hotbeds of fiery philosophical debate, but more often, I imagine, they are just like this: people talking, flirting, posing, drinking, smoking, telling the truth, and lying, while waiting to see if real life will ever begin.

Mouchette

NO MPAA RATING, 78 m., 1970

Nadine Nortier (Mouchette), Jean-Claude Guilbert (Arsene), Marie Cardinal (La Mere), Paul Hebert (Father). Directed by Robert Bresson and produced by Anatole Dauman. Screenplay by Bresson, based on a book by Georges Bernanos.

Although Robert Bresson is considered to be one of the greatest French filmmakers, his name isn't heard as often as those of Truffaut, Chabrol, Resnais, Malle, and the others—and his films aren't as often seen. His work is austere, meticulously considered, and often very sad; his concerns are often with characters who have little understanding of the world the rest of us haphazardly occupy.

And yet in France his name is spoken with reverence. He makes few films, usually not more than one every three or four years, and he makes them only about the subjects he chooses and in the styles he feels right. He isn't "commercial," but he is totally accessible. He speaks directly about simple people, and for a long time after we see his films their eyes regard us in our memories.

Mouchette, made in 1966 but not released in America until 1970, is a film like that. It's about a young adolescent girl who lives in a French provincial town and is commonly regarded by everyone as the town slut, a judgment she accepts passively. She lives in a shack outside town with her family—a drunken bootlegger father who beats her, a bedridden mother on the edge of death, and the family's new baby, which constantly cries. Outside the shack, trucks roar past all night, shaking it.

Mouchette's an outcast at school: Her clothes are dirty, she can't sing without hitting the wrong notes, the other girls make fun of

her in the streets and she retaliates with mudballs. She keeps house for her family and has a Sunday job washing dishes in a café. Her father keeps her wages. And yet Bresson has the magical ability to show us humanity, humor, and grace still surviving in Mouchette's soul.

There's a wonderful scene, for example, that takes place when a traveling carnival comes to town. Mouchette is given money for one ride on the bumper cars, and strikes up a friendship (of a sort) with a young boy who chooses her car to crash into. They exchange shy smiles, and afterward she begins to walk up to him, but is grabbed away and slapped by her father. The timing and editing of the scene on the carnival ride is an example of Bresson's mastery: He gives us a tawdry setting and an aggressive means of expression and extracts tenderness from them.

The next evening, Mouchette leaves school to walk in the woods and becomes involved in a feud between a poacher and a game warden. The poacher, thinking he has killed the warden, enlists Mouchette to help provide an alibi. And then, drunk, he rapes her. The next morning her mother dies (people are not often happy in Bresson's world). There is great poignancy in the way Mouchette accepts the sympathy (half scornful) of the townspeople, and there is pathos in the way she so simply describes the poacher as "my lover." The film's last sequene is heartbreaking and so inevitable it could have been the first.

Mr. and Mrs. Bridge

PG-13, 127 m., 1991

Paul Newman (Walter Bridge), Joanne Woodward (India Bridge), Margaret Welsh (Carolyn Bridge), Kyra Sedgwick (Ruth Bridge), Blythe Danner (Grace Barron), Robert Sean Leonard (Douglas Bridge), Simon Callow (Dr. Alex Sauer). Directed by James Ivory and produced by Ismail Merchant. Screenplay by Ruth Prawer Jhabvala, based on the books by Evan S. Connell.

Mr. and Mrs. Bridge observes with great care and an almost frightening detachment the precise ways in which an emotionally paralyzed couple gets through life together. The movie is set in an affluent Kansas City neighborhood in the 1930s and 1940s. Manicured lawns surround generous white houses with green shutters, and inside the house of the Bridges lives a man who is absolutely sure he knows how life is best to be lived, but his knowledge is not bringing very much happiness to his family.

Mr. Bridge is a lawyer, played by Paul Newman in one of his most daring and self-effacing performances. Mrs. Bridge is a house-wife, played by Joanne Woodward in a masterful observation of suppression and resignation. It is hard to say exactly what is the matter with Mr. Bridge—whether he is frightened of intimacy, or shy, or simply locked into his view of proper male behavior. Whatever his problem, it involves a subtle sort of psychological wife-beating, in which his wife is essentially his emotional captive. She can communicate with him only by following careful formulas involving what can be said, and how, and when.

Passion has perhaps never existed in this couple—not, at least, joyous passion. Even the first sexual experiences must have been largely physical, involving bodily functions more than personalities. Now life has settled into a routine. The children have nearly grown up, and are hardly known to their father. Their mother knows them better, but is afraid to reveal all she knows, or tell them all she wants to say. Mr. Bridge goes off to his office and does his job and associates in time-honored patterns of ritual with his fellow professional men, and Mrs. Bridge, "keeping house," reminds me of that woman that Stevie Smith wrote about—the woman out in the sea who seemed to be waving, but was not waving, but drowning.

The film is based on two novels by Evan S. Connell, adapted by another novelist, Ruth Prawer Jhabvala, for her longtime collaborators the director James Ivory and the producer Ismail Merchant. Their other work includes *A Room with a View* and *The Bostonians*, and it is not surprising that they were drawn to this carefully seen portrait of social behavior. The film does not have a plot in the ordinary sense of the word, perhaps because a plot would have appeared unseemly to Mr. Bridge; one does not, in his world, do this in order to have that happen. One exists as nearly as possible in the same admirable way, day after day.

Incidents happen. The Bridges have children who want to lead lives that do not correspond to the family values and timetable. They are absolutely forced to rebel in one way or another, because within the family there is no room for compromise. Mrs. Bridge has a friend (Blythe Danner) who is slowly cracking up; the alcoholism that is killing her is her only strategy for surviving. For Mrs. Bridge, this friend is an external sign of her own inner turmoil. Her own life is apparently ordered and serene, and seems placid and happy to the world, but in a way she is as desperate as her friend.

The movie is not heavy-handed. It does not present Mr. Bridge as a monster. He is as trapped in his world as everyone else. Very occasionally he permits himself the smallest of tight-lipped smiles, and once in a very long time, he will unbend a little. But essentially he is the captive of duty, and his duty as a professional white man in Kansas City in the late 1930s is to conform, to do what is expected, to present the proper appearances, and to beware of emotional extremes that could lead him to lose control.

Much is made of the excesses and silliness of the sixties, but it is because of that liberating decade that Mr. Bridge and his world will never quite exist again, and it is worth remembering that the young people of the 1960s were the children of parents who were often very much like the Bridges: parents who were playing out some ideal role of probity and respectability, and who were so wary of their own feelings that they disciplined their children for having feelings at all.

I hope I haven't made *Mr. and Mrs. Bridge* seem like a dreary or depressing film. Bad films are depressing. Good films, no matter what they're about, are exhilarating, and *Mr. and Mrs. Bridge* observes its characters with such attention and care that it is always absorbing. Most movies want us to care about what happens to the characters. This one simply wants us to care about them. The work of Woodward and Newman here is a classic example of a certain kind of acting, of studies of voice and behavior, of fleeting glances and subtle nuances of body language, of people who would almost rather drown than wave.

Mr. Death: The Rise and Fall of Fred A. Leuchter, Jr.

PG-13, 96 m., 2000

A documentary directed by Errol Morris and produced by Michael Williams, David Collins, and Dorothy Aufiero.

The hangman has no friends. That truth, I think, is the key to understanding Fred A. Leuchter, Jr., a man who built up a nice little business designing death-row machines, and then lost it when he became a star on the Holocaust denial circuit. Leuchter, the subject of Errol Morris's documentary *Mr. Death: The Rise and Fall of Fred A. Leuchter, Jr.*, is a lonely man of limited insight who is grateful to be liked—even by Nazi apologists.

This is the seventh documentary by Morris, who combines dreamlike visual montages with music by Caleb Sampson to create a movie that is more reverie and meditation than reportage. Morris is drawn to subjects who try to control that which cannot be controlled—life and death. His heroes have included lion tamers, topiary gardeners, robot designers, wild turkey callers, autistics, death row inmates, pet cemetery owners, and Stephen Hawking, whose mind leaps through space and time while his body slumps in a chair.

Fred Leuchter, the son of a prison warden, stumbled into the death row business more or less by accident. An engineer by training, he found himself inspired by the need for more efficient and "humane" execution devices. He'd seen electric chairs that cooked their occupants without killing them, poison gas chambers that were a threat to the witnesses, gallows not correctly adjusted to break a neck. He went to work designing better chairs, trapdoors, and lethal injection machines, and soon (his trade not being commonplace) was being consulted by prisons all over America.

Despite his success in business, he was not, we gather, terrifically popular. How many women want to date a guy who can chat about the dangers of being accidentally electrocuted while standing in the pool of urine around a recently used electric chair? He does eventually marry a waitress he meets in a doughnut shop; indeed, given his habit of forty to sixty cups of coffee a day, he must have met a lot of waitresses. We hear her offscreen voice as she describes their brief marriage, and demurs at Fred's notion that their visit to Auschwitz was a honeymoon (she had to wait in a cold car, serving as a lookout for guards).

Leuchter's trip to Auschwitz was the turning point in his career. He was asked by Ernst Zundel, a neo-Nazi and Holocaust denier, to be an expert witness at his trial in Canada. Zundel financed Leuchter's 1988 trip to Auschwitz, during which he chopped off bits of brick and mortar in areas said to be gas chambers, and had them analyzed for cyanide residue. His conclusion: The chambers never contained gas. The "Leuchter Report" has since been widely quoted by those who deny the Holocaust took place.

There is a flaw in his science, however. The laboratory technician who tested the samples for Leuchter was later startled to discover the use being made of his findings. Cyanide would penetrate bricks only to the depth of a tenth of a human hair, he says. By breaking off large chunks and pulverizing them, Leuchter had diluted his sample by a hundred thousand times, not even taking into account the fifty years of weathering that had passed. To find cyanide would have been a miracle.

No matter; Leuchter became a favorite after-dinner speaker on the neo-Nazi circuit, and the camera observes how his face lights up and his whole body seems to lean into applause, how happy he is to shake hands with his new friends. Other people might shy away from the pariah status of a Holocaust denier. The hangman is already a pariah, and finds his friends where he can.

Just before *Mr. Death* was shown in a slightly different form at the 1999 Sundance Film Festival, a *New Yorker* article by Mark Singer wondered whether the film would create sympathy for Leuchter and his fellow deniers. After all, here was a man who lost his wife and his livelihood in the name of a scientific quest. My feeling is that no filmmaker can be responsible for those unwilling or unable to view his film intelligently; anyone who leaves *Mr. Death* in agreement with Leuchter deserves to join him on the loony fringe.

What's scary about the film is the way Leuchter is perfectly respectable up until the time the neo-Nazis get their hooks into him.

Those who are appalled by the mass execution of human beings sometimes have no problem when the state executes them one at a time. You can even run for president after presiding over the busiest death row in U.S. history.

Early sequences in *Mr. Death* portray Leuchter as a humanitarian who protests that some electric chairs "cook the meat too much." He dreams of a "lethal injection machine" designed like a dentist's chair. The condemned could watch TV or listen to music while the poison works. What a lark. There is irony in the notion that many American states could lavish tax dollars on this man's inventions, only to put him out of work because of his unsavory connections. The ability of so many people to live comfortably with the idea of capital punishment is perhaps a clue to how so many Europeans were able to live with the idea of the Holocaust: Once you accept the notion that the state has the right to kill someone, and the right to define what is a capital crime, aren't you halfway there?

Like all of Errol Morris's films, *Mr. Death* provides us with no comfortable place to stand. We often leave his documentaries not sure if he liked his subjects or was ridiculing them. He doesn't make it easy for us with simple moral labels. Human beings, he argues, are fearsomely complex, and can get their minds around very strange ideas indeed. Sometimes it is possible to hate the sin and love the sinner. Poor Fred. What a dope, what a dupe, what a lonely, silly man.

Mulholland Dr.

R, 146 m., 2001

Justin Theroux (Adam Kesher), Naomi Watts (Betty Elms), Laura Elena Harring (Rita), Ann Miller (Coco Lenoix), Dan Hedaya (Vincenzo Castigliani), Mark Pellegrino (Joe), Brian Beacock (Studio Singer), Robert Forster (Detective Harry McKnight), Michael J. Anderson (Mr. Roque). Directed by David Lynch and produced by Neal Edelstein, Joyce Eliason, Tony Krantz, Michael Polaire, Alain Sarde, and Mary Sweeney. Screenplay by Lynch.

David Lynch has been working toward *Mulholland Dr.* all of his career, and now that he's arrived there I forgive him *Wild at Heart* and even *Lost Highway*. At last his experiment

doesn't shatter the test tubes. The movie is a surrealist dreamscape in the form of a Hollywood *film noir*, and the less sense it makes, the more we can't stop watching it.

It tells the story of . . . well, there's no way to finish that sentence. There are two characters named Betty and Rita whom the movie follows through mysterious plot loops, but by the end of the film we aren't even sure they're different characters, and Rita (an amnesiac who lifted the name from a *Gilda* poster) wonders if she's really Diane Selwyn, a name from a waitress's name tag.

Betty (Naomi Watts) is a perky blonde, Sandra Dee crossed with a Hitchcock heroine, who has arrived in town to stay in her absent aunt Ruth's apartment and audition for the movies. Rita (Laura Elena Harring) is a voluptuous brunette who is about to be murdered when her limousine is front-ended by drag racers. She crawls out of the wreckage on Mulholland Drive, stumbles down the hill, and is taking a shower in the aunt's apartment when Betty arrives.

She doesn't remember anything, even her name. Betty decides to help her. As they try to piece her life back together, the movie introduces other characters. A movie director (Justin Theroux) is told to cast an actress in his movie or be murdered; a dwarf in a wheelchair (Michael J. Anderson) gives instructions by cell phone; two detectives turn up, speak standard TV cop show dialogue, and disappear; a landlady (Ann Miller—yes, Ann Miller) wonders who the other girl is in Aunt Ruth's apartment; Betty auditions; the two girls climb in through a bedroom window, Nancy Drew style; a rotting corpse materializes; and Betty and Rita have two lesbian love scenes so sexy you'd swear this was a 1970s movie, made when movie audiences liked sex. One of the scenes also contains the funniest example of pure logic in the history of sex scenes.

Having told you all of that, I've basically explained nothing. The movie is hypnotic; we're drawn along as if one thing leads to another—but nothing leads anywhere, and that's even before the characters start to fracture and recombine like flesh caught in a kaleidoscope. *Mulholland Dr.* isn't like *Memento*, where if you watch it closely enough you can hope to explain the mystery. There is no explanation. There may not even be a mystery.

There have been countless dream sequences in the movies, almost all of them conceived with Freudian literalism to show the characters having nightmares about the plot. *Mulholland Dr.* is all dream. There is nothing that is intended to be a waking moment. Like real dreams, it does not explain, does not complete its sequences, lingers over what it finds fascinating, dismisses unpromising plotlines. If you want an explanation for the last half-hour of the film, think of it as the dreamer rising slowly to consciousness as threads from the dream fight for space with recent memories from real life, and with fragments of other dreams—old ones and those still in development.

This works because Lynch is absolutely uncompromising. He takes what was frustrating in some of his earlier films, and instead of backing away from it, he charges right through. *Mulholland Dr.* is said to have been assembled from scenes he shot for a 1999 ABC television pilot, but no network would air (or understand) this material, and Lynch knew it. He takes his financing where he can find it, and directs as fancy dictates. This movie doesn't feel incomplete because it could never be complete—closure is not a goal.

Laura Elena Harring and Naomi Watts take the risk of embodying Hollywood archetypes, and get away with it because they *are* archetypes. Not many actresses would be bold enough to name themselves after Rita Hayworth, but Harring does, because she can. Slinky and voluptuous in clinging gowns, all she has to do is stand there and she's the first good argument in fifty-five years for a *Gilda* remake. Naomi Watts is bright-eyed and bushy-tailed, a plucky girl detective. Like a dream, the movie shifts easily between tones; there's an audition where a girl singer performs "Sixteen Reasons" and "I Told Every Little Star," and the movie isn't satirizing *American Bandstand,* it's channeling it.

This is a movie to surrender yourself to. If you require logic, see something else. *Mulholland Dr.* works directly on the emotions, like music. Individual scenes play well by themselves, as they do in dreams, but they don't connect in a way that makes sense—again, like dreams. The way you know the movie is over is that it ends. And then you tell a friend, "I saw the weirdest movie last night." Just like you tell him you had the weirdest dream.

Munich

R, 164 m., 2005

Eric Bana (Avner), Daniel Craig (Steve), Geoffrey Rush (Ephraim), Mathieu Kassovitz (Robert), Ciaran Hinds (Carl), Hanns Zischler (Hans), Michael Lonsdale (Papa), Mathieu Amalric (Louis), Lynn Cohen (Golda Meir). Directed by Steven Spielberg and produced by Barry Mendel, Kathleen Kennedy, Spielberg, and Colin Wilson. Screenplay by Tony Kushner, based on the book *Vengeance* by George Jonas.

Steven Spielberg's *Munich* is an act of courage and conscience. The director of *Schindler's List,* the founder of the Shoah Foundation, the most successful and visible Jew in the world of film, has placed himself between Israel and the Palestinians, looked at decades of terrorism and reprisal, and had one of his characters conclude, "There is no peace at the end of this." Spielberg's film has been called an attack on the Palestinians and he has been rebuked as "no friend of Israel." By not taking sides, he has taken both sides.

The film has deep love for Israel and contains a heartfelt moment when a mother reminds her son why the state had to be founded: "We had to take it because no one would ever give it to us. Whatever it took, whatever it takes, we have a place on Earth at last." With this statement, I believe, Spielberg agrees to the bottom of his soul. Yet his film questions Israel's policy of swift and full retribution for every attack.

Munich opens with a heart-stopping reenactment of the kidnapping and deaths of Israeli athletes at the 1972 Munich Olympics. It then shows Prime Minister Golda Meir (Lynn Cohen) with her cabinet, stating firmly, "Forget peace for now." It shows the formation of a secret Israeli revenge squad to kill those responsible. It concludes that although nine of the eleven eventually were eliminated, they were replaced and replaced again by men even more dangerous, while the terrorists responded with even more deaths. What was accomplished?

The movie is based upon a book by George Jonas, a 1956 Hungarian freedom fighter, now a conservative Toronto political writer, who has been an acquaintance for twenty-five years. I thought to ask him what he thought of Spielberg's view of his material, but I didn't. I wanted to review the movie as an interested but not expert outsider, sharing (with most of the film's audience) not a great deal more knowledge than the film supplies. Those who know more, who know everything, are often the wrong ones to consult about a film based on fact. The task of the director is to transmute fact into emotions and beliefs—and beliefs, we need to be reminded, are beliefs precisely because they are not facts.

Munich takes the form of a thriller matched with a procedural. Eric Bana stars as Avner, a former bodyguard to Meir, who is made leader of the secret revenge squadron. He and his men are paid off the books, have no official existence, and are handled by a go-between named Ephraim (Geoffrey Rush). Why it is necessary to deny their existence is not quite explained by the film, since they are clearly carrying out Israeli policy and Israel wants that known; they even use bombs instead of bullets to generate more dramatic publicity.

Avner is assigned only four teammates: Robert (Mathieu Kassovitz), a toymaker, expert at disarming bombs, now asked to build them; Carl (Ciaran Hinds), who removes the evidence after every action; Steve (Daniel Craig), the trigger man; and Hans (Hanns Zischler), who can forge letters and documents. They travel with assumed names and false passports, and discover the whereabouts of many of their targets by paying bounties to a shadowy Frenchman named Louis (Mathieu Amalric).

Eventually Avner meets Louis' "Papa" (Michael Lonsdale), who has been selling information for years. Papa fought in the French Resistance and is now disillusioned: "We paid this price so Nazi scum could be replaced by Gaullist scum. We don't deal with governments." The family, he believes, is the only unit worth fighting for. His speech is moving, but does he really believe Avner and his money do not come from a government?

The film's most exciting moments are in the details of assassination. Plastic bombs are planted, booby traps are baited, there is a moment of Hitchcockian suspense when the team waits for a little girl to leave for school before calling her father's telephone; they have failed to see her reenter the house and are astonished when she answers the phone. As the team tries to prevent the explosion, we reflect how it is always more thrilling in a movie, when someone needs to run desperately, for it to be an awkward older man.

The teammates move among world capitals. One night, in a comic screwup with deadly possibilities, Avner's men and a PLO team are booked into the same "safe house." As the operation proceeds, it takes a psychic toll on Avner, who moves his family to Brooklyn, who grows paranoid, who questions the ethical basis of the operation he heads: "Jews don't do wrong because our enemies do wrong," he argues, and "if these people committed crimes we should have arrested them." To which he is told, "Every civilization finds it necessary to negotiate compromises with its own values."

The same debate is going on right now in America. If it is true that civilizations must sometimes compromise their values, the questions remain: What is the cost, and what is the benefit? Spielberg clearly asks if Israel has risked more than it has gained. The stalemate in the Middle East will continue indefinitely, his film argues, unless brave men on both sides decide to break with the pattern of the past. Certainly in Israel itself it is significant that old enemies Ariel Sharon, from the right, and Shimon Peres, from the left, are now astonishingly both in the same new party and seeking a new path to peace. For the Palestinians, it may be crucial that the PLO's corrupt Arafat no longer has a personal stake in the status quo and a new generation of leaders has moved into place.

Spielberg's film is well-timed in view of these unexpected political developments, which he could not have foreseen (Sharon left his Likud Party on November 21, 2005, and Peres left his Labour Party a week later). Far from being "no friend of Israel," he may be an invaluable friend, and for that very reason a friend of the Palestinians as well. Spielberg is using the effective form of a thriller to argue that loops of mutual reprisal have led to endless violence in the Middle East, Ireland, India and Pakistan, the former Yugoslavia, the former Soviet Union, Africa, and on and on. Miraculous that the pariah nation of South Africa was the one place where irreconcilable enemies found a way to peacefully share the same land together.

At crucial times in a nation's history, its best friends may be its critics. Spielberg did not have to make *Munich*, but he needed to. With this film he has dramatically opened a wider dialogue, helping to make the inarguable into the debatable. As a thriller, *Munich* is efficient, absorbing, effective. As an ethical argument, it is haunting. And its questions are not only for Israel but for any nation that believes it must compromise its values to defend them.

Murderball

R, 85 m., 2005

Featuring Mark Zupan, Joe Soares, Keith Cavill, Andy Cohn, Scott Hogsett, and Bob Lujano. A documentary directed by Henry Alex Rubin and Dana Adam Shapiro and produced by Jeffrey Mandel and Shapiro.

"How do you eat your pizza with your elbows?"

It's a natural question for a little boy to ask a quadruple amputee, and Bob Lujano is happy to answer it. He and the other stars of the documentary *Murderball* wish more people would ask more questions, instead of becoming inhibited around people in wheelchairs. After this movie, maybe they will. You don't have to feel shy around quadriplegics who play wheelchair rugby.

This is one of those rare docs, like *Hoop Dreams,* where life provides a better ending than the filmmakers could have hoped for. Also like *Hoop Dreams,* it's not really a sports film; it's a film that uses sport as a way to see into lives, hopes, and fears. These tough all-Americans compete in international championships. Once they were shattered young men waking up in hospital beds and being told they would never walk again.

Consider Mark Zupan, probably the best player in the sport today. He was paralyzed when he was eighteen. He fell asleep in the bed of a pickup driven by his friend Christopher Igoe, who drove away not realizing Mark was aboard. The truck crashed, and Mark was thrown into a canal and wasn't found for thirteen hours. It took them a long time, but he and Igoe are friendly again.

During a discussion after a festival screening of the movie, he was asked, "If you could,

would you turn back the clock on that day?" You could have heard a pin drop as he answered: "No, I don't think so. My injury has led me to opportunities and experiences and friendships I would never have had before. And it has taught me about myself." He paused. "In some ways, it's the best thing that ever happened to me."

This is hard to believe, but from him, I believe it. The movie follows Zupan and his teammates on Team USA during a couple of seasons where the off-court drama is fraught with tension. We meet Joe Soares, an all-American for many years, who with advancing age is dropped from the American team, is angry, and gets revenge by joining the Canadians. Under Soares, Canada beats the United States for the first time in twelve years. There is no love between Soares and Zupan ("If he were on fire, I wouldn't piss on him to put it out").

Wheelchair rugby is a full-contact sport. Chairs are reinforced to take the hammering. One strategy is to knock over your opponent's chair and land him on the floor; that's not a foul, although the referees helpfully put the players back on their wheels. Has anybody been injured *again* while playing the game? So far, no.

Many people think quadriplegics have no control over their four limbs, like Christopher Reeve, but most of them retain some degree of movement. Their level of disability is rated on a scale from 0.5 to 3.5, and a team can have a total of 8 points on the court at once. This leads to an ironic paradox: The athletes spend their lives overcoming and diminishing their disabilities, then hope for higher handicaps.

Although the sports scenes are filled with passion and harrowing wheelchair duels, the heart of the movie is off the court. We follow a young man named Keith Cavill, who has been wounded in a motocross accident and is painfully undergoing the slow process of rehabilitation. Encouragement from wheelchair athletes is crucial to his state of mind. Later, Team USA visits Walter Reed Army Medical Center, where newly arrived casualties from Iraq are facing the new reality of their lives. War injuries such as his are becoming more common; explosions cause more casualties than gunfire in Iraq, and *Harper's* magazine reports that improved body armor has created a large number of wounded soldiers whose body trunks are unblemished but whose arms and legs are devastated.

If Zupan is the hero of the movie, Soares is its enigma. He had a tough childhood. After losing the use of his legs from polio, he dragged himself around for years before his poor Portuguese-American family provided him with a chair. He fought for respect in school, fought for an education, was a fierce competitor on the court, and seems ferocious as he leads Team Canada against his former teammates.

At home, he wants his son Robert to be a jock like Dad. But Robert prefers to play the viola and observes wistfully that one of the household tasks he doesn't like involves "dusting Dad's trophy wall." Then an unexpected development (miraculously caught on camera) causes Soares to take a deep breath and re-evaluate his life and his relationship with his son. Rehabilitation is not limited to the body.

As the players talk frankly about their lives, we learn everything we always wanted to know about quadriplegic sex but were afraid to ask. One player says the chair works like a babe magnet: Women are dying to ask him if he can perform sexually. The answer, according to a documentary quoted in the film, is often "yes," and little animated figures show us some of the moves. We also learn that people in chairs have long since gotten over any self-consciousness in talking about their situation, and they hate it when people avoid looking at them or interacting with them. "I'm a guy in a chair," Zupan says. "I'm just like you, except I'm sitting down."

Murderball, directed by Henry Alex Rubin and Dana Adam Shapiro, produced by Jeffrey Mandel and Shapiro, and photographed by Rubin, works like many great documentaries to transcend its subject and consider the human condition. We may not be in chairs and may not be athletes, but we all have disabilities, sometimes of the spirit. To consider the bleak months and sleepless nights when these men first confronted the reality of their injuries, and now to see them in the full force of athletic exuberance, is to learn something valuable about the human will. Remember Bob Lujano, whom the kid asked about eating pizza? He has a motto: "No arms, no legs, no problem."

Murmur of the Heart

R, 118 m., 1971

Lea Massari (Clara Chevalier), Benoît Ferreux (Laurent Chevalier), Daniel Gélin (Charles Chevalier), Michael Lonsdale (Father Henri). Directed by Louis Malle and produced by Vincent Malle and Claude Nedjar. Screenplay by Louis Malle.

We have it on no less an authority than Leo Tolstoy that all happy families are the same, but each unhappy family is unhappy in its own way. I am not quite sure, however, that Count Tolstoy had in mind a family like the one we meet in *Murmur of the Heart,* Louis Malle's warm, human, very funny movie about incest. You will agree that this family, at least is happy in its own way.

It's an uncommon family, especially by the standards of Dijon, France, circa 1954. The father is a wealthy and successful physician. He is married to a girl fifteen years younger than himself and, worse, the girl is Italian, which profoundly shocked his French bourgeois family at the time of the marriage. No matter. The union has been blessed with three sons, and at the time the movie opens the mother is closer to them (in age and temperament) than to the father.

The movie opens with a good-natured family tussle, and only after it's over do we discover that Lea Massari is the mother. She looks more like an older sister, and she is certainly more of a pal than a mother to her children. The family discipline is administered by a very round, very muscular maid.

The two older sons are pranksters and brats, but the youngest is bookish and thoughtful. To be sure, his taste in reading runs to Henry Miller, de Sade, and *The Story of O,* and his thoughts are of a nature to be dialogue for the confessional. But he's a bright, quiet, likable kid. He is also at that sharp, poignant moment of midadolescence when it begins to seem that carnal knowledge is forever out of reach but just barely.

Malle gives us the family in a series of short, fairly self-contained scenes. There are fights and truces, and the boy learns to smoke cigars, drink brandy, and forge paintings. The youngest son is taken by his brothers to a brothel (in order to be the victim of a cruel practical joke, as it turns out). The mother has an affair, not very discreetly. And then it turns out the young boy has a heart murmur. Summer at a resort is prescribed, and the mother goes along to keep her son company (and to continue her affair).

They take adjoining rooms at the resort hotel, and then Malle sets up for the final scenes so skillfully that the moment of incest, when it occurs, seems almost natural, more fond than carnal, and not terribly significant. How he achieves this effect is beyond me; he takes the most highly charged subject matter you can imagine, and mutes it into simple affection.

The boy is played by a nonactor, Benoît Ferreux. whose puzzlement about growing up, and whose admiration at the possibilities of life, remind us of young Jean-Pierre Leaud in Truffaut's *The 400 Blows* of a decade ago. The two movies deserve comparison in more ways than one. And yet *Murmur of the Heart* isn't really about the boy, but the mother. Lea Massari (you may remember her as the girl in *L'Avventura*) is so irrepressible, so irresponsible, so much a girl and not quite an adult, that her performance takes scenes that might have been embarrassing and makes them simply magical.

My Dinner with André

NO MPAA RATING, 110 m., 1981

Wallace Shawn (Wally), André Gregory (André), Jean Lenauer (Waiter), Roy Butler (Bartender). Directed by Louis Malle and produced by George W. George and Beverly Karp. Screenplay by Shawn and Gregory.

The idea is astonishing in its audacity: a film of two friends talking, just simply talking— but with passion, wit, scandal, whimsy, vision, hope, and despair—for 110 minutes. It sounds at first like one of those underground films of the 1960s, in which great length and minimal content somehow interacted in the dope-addled brains of the audience to provide the impression of deep if somehow elusive profundity. *My Dinner with André* is not like that. It doesn't use all of those words as a stunt. They are alive on the screen, breathing, pulsing, reminding us of endless, impassioned conversations we've had with those few friends worth talking with for hours and hours. Underneath all the other fascinating things in this film beats the tide of friendship, of two people with a genuine interest in one another.

The two people are André Gregory and Wallace Shawn. Those are their real names, and also their names in the movie. I suppose they are playing themselves. As the film opens, Shawn travels across New York City to meet Gregory for dinner, and his thoughts provide us with background: His friend Gregory is a New York theater director, well-known into the 1970s, who dropped out for five years and traveled around the world. Now Gregory has returned, with wondrous tales of strange experiences. Shawn has spent the same years in New York, finding uncertain success as an author and playwright. They sit down for dinner in an elegant restaurant. We do not see the other customers. The bartender is a wraith in the background, the waiter is the sort of presence they were waiting for in *Waiting for Godot*. The friends order dinner, and then, as it is served and they eat and drink, they talk.

What conversation! André Gregory does most of the talking, and he is a spellbinding conversationalist, able to weave mental images not only out of his experiences, but also out of his ideas. He explains that he had become dissatisfied with life, restless, filled with anomie and discontent. He accepted an invitation to join an experimental theater group in Poland. It was *very* experimental, tending toward rituals in the woods under the full moon.

From Poland, he traveled around the world, meeting a series of people who were seriously and creatively exploring the ways in which they could experience the material world. They (and Gregory) literally believed in mind over matter, and as Gregory describes a monk who was able to stand his entire body weight on his fingertips, we visualize that man and in some strange way (so hypnotic is the tale) we share the experience.

One of the gifts of *My Dinner with André* is that we share so many of the experiences. Although most of the movie literally consists of two men talking, here's a strange thing: *We* do not spend the movie just passively listening to them talk. At first, director Louis Malle's sedate series of images (close-ups, two-shots, reaction shots) calls attention to itself, but as Gregory continues to talk, the very simplicity of the visual style renders it invisible. And like the listeners at the feet of a master storyteller, we find ourselves visualizing what Gregory describes, until this film is as filled with visual images as a radio play—*more* filled, perhaps, than a conventional feature film.

What Gregory and Shawn talk about is, quite simply, many of the things on our minds these days. We've passed through Tom Wolfe's Me Decade and find ourselves in a decade during which there will apparently be less for everybody. The two friends talk about inner journeys—not in the mystical, vague terms of magazines you don't want to be seen reading on the bus, but in terms of trying to live better lives, of learning to listen to what others are really saying, of breaking the shackles of conventional ideas about our bodies and allowing them to more fully sense the outer world.

The movie is not ponderous, annoyingly profound, or abstract. It is about living, and Gregory seems to have lived fully in his five years of dropping out. Shawn is the character who seems more like us. He listens, he nods eagerly, he is willing to learn, but—something holds him back. Pragmatic questions keep asking themselves. He can't buy Gregory's vision, not all the way. He'd like to, but this is a real world we have to live in, after all, and if we all danced with the Druids in the forests of Poland, what would happen to the market for fortune cookies?

The film's end is beautiful and inexplicably moving. Shawn returns home by taxi through the midnight streets of New York. Having spent hours with Gregory on a wild conversational flight, he is now reminded of scenes from his childhood. In *that* store, his father bought him shoes. In that one, he bought ice cream with a girlfriend. The utter simplicity of his memories acts to dramatize the fragility and great preciousness of life. He has learned his friend's lesson.

My Family

R, 122 m., 1995

Jimmy Smits (Jimmy), Esai Morales (Chucho), Eduardo Lopez Rojas (Jose), Jenny Gago (Maria), Constance Marie (Toni), Edward James Olmos (Paco), Lupe Ontiveros (Irene Sanchez), Jacob Vargas (Young Jose), Jennifer Lopez (Young Maria), Elpidia Carrillo (Isabel), Enrique Castillo (Memo), Maria Canals (Young Irene). Directed by Gregory Nava and produced by Anna Thomas. Screenplay by Nava and Thomas.

Gregory Nava's *My Family* is like a family dinner with everybody crowded around the table, remembering good times and bad, honoring those who went before, worrying about those still to come. It is an epic told through the eyes of one family, the Sanchez family, whose father walked north to Los Angeles from Mexico in the 1920s, and whose children include a writer, a nun, an ex-convict, a lawyer, a restaurant owner, and a boy shot dead in his prime.

Their story is told in images of startling beauty and great, overflowing energy; it is rare to hear so much laughter from an audience that is also sometimes moved to tears. Few movies like this get made because few filmmakers have the ambition to open their arms wide and embrace so much life. This is the great American story, told again and again, of how our families came to this land and tried to make it better for their children.

The story begins with a man named Jose Sanchez, who thinks it might take him a week or two to walk north from Mexico to "a village called Los Angeles," where he has a relative. It takes him a year. The relative, an old man known as El Californio, was born in Los Angeles when it was still Mexico, and on his tombstone he wants it written, "and where I lie it is *still* Mexico."

El Californio lives in a small house in East Los Angeles, and this house, tucked under a bridge on a dirt street that still actually exists, becomes a symbol of the family, gaining paint and windows and extra rooms and a picket fence, as the family grows. Jose (Jacob Vargas) crosses the bridge to the Anglo neighborhoods to work as a gardener, and there he meets Maria (Jennifer Lopez), who works as a nanny. They are married and have two children, and she is pregnant with a third, in the Depression year of 1932, when government troops round her up with tens of thousands of other Mexican-Americans (most of them, like Maria, U.S. citizens) and ship them in cattle cars to central Mexico, hoping they will never return.

"This really happened," says the narrator,

Paco (Edward James Olmos), a writer who is telling the story of his family. But Maria fights her way back to her family, her baby in her arms. As the action moves from the 1930s to the late 1950s, we meet all the children: Paco; Irene, on her wedding day; Toni, who becomes a nun; Memo, who wants to go to law school; Chucho, who is attracted to the street life; and little Jimmy ("whose late arrival came as a great surprise").

Nava and his cowriter and producer, Anna Thomas, tell their stories in vivid sequences. Irene's wedding is interrupted by the arrival of a gang hostile to the hotheaded Chucho, and as they threaten each other Paco tells us "it was the usual macho bullshit." But eventually Chucho will lose his life because of it, and little Jimmy, seeing him die, will be scarred for many years.

Toni, meanwhile, becomes a nun, goes to South America, gets "political," and comes home to present her family with a big surprise, in one of the many scenes that mix social commentary with humor. Memo does become a lawyer (and tells his Anglo in-laws his name is "basically Spanish for 'Bill'").

In one of the movie's best sequences, Toni (Constance Marie), now an activist in L.A., becomes concerned by the plight of a young woman from El Salvador, who is about to be deported and faces death because of the politics of her family. She convinces Jimmy to marry her and save her from deportation, and in a sequence that is first hilarious and later quite moving, Jimmy does. (Instead of kissing the bride, he mutters "you owe me" ominously at his activist sister.) This relationship, between Jimmy (Jimmy Smits) and Isabel (Elpidia Carrillo) leads to a love scene of great beauty, as they share their stories of pain and loss.

In the scenes set in the 1950s and 1980s, Jose and Maria are played by Eduardo Lopez Rojas and Jenny Gago. They wake up at night worrying about their children ("thank God for Memo going to law school," Paco says, "or they would have never gotten a night's sleep"). Jimmy, so tortured by the loss of his brother, is a special concern. But the family pulls together, and Paco observes, "In my home the difference between a family emergency and a party wasn't that big."

Nava, a Chicano whose earlier films include the great *El Norte* (1983), an Oscar nominee for its screenplay, has an inspired sense of color and light, and his movie has a visual freedom you rarely see on the screen. Working with cinematographer Ed Lachman, he uses color filters, smoke, shafts of sunlight, and other effects to make some scenes painterly with beauty and color—and he has used a painter, Patssi Valdez, to design the interior of the Sanchez home. The movie is not just in color, but in *colors*.

Through all the beauty, laughter, and tears, the strong heart of the family beats, and everything leads up to a closing scene, between old Jose and Maria, that is quiet, simple, joyous, and heartbreaking. Rarely have I felt at the movies such a sense of time and history, of stories and lessons passing down the generations, of a family living in its memories. The story of the Sanchezes is the story of one Mexican-American family, but it is also in some ways the story of all families. Watching it, I was reminded of my own family's legends and heroes and stray sheep, and the strong sense of home. "Another country?" young Jose says, when he is told where Los Angeles is. "What does that mean—'another country'?"

My Father's Glory
G, 110 m., 1991

Philippe Caubere (Joseph), Nathalie Roussel (Augustine), Didier Pain (Uncle Jules), Therese Liotard (Aunt Rose), Julien Ciamaca (Marcel), Joris Molinmas (Lili). Directed by Yves Robert and produced by Alain Poire. Screenplay by Lucette Andrei, based on the story by Marcel Pagnol.

My Father's Glory is the first in a series of two films that creep up on you with small moments of warmth and charm. At first this film and its companion, *My Mother's Castle*, don't seem to be about much of anything. They meander. To a viewer accustomed to the machinery of plots, they play like a simple series of episodes. Then the episodes add up to a childhood. And by the end of the second film, the entire foundation for a life has been recreated, in memories of the perfect days of childhood. Of course the films are sentimental. Who would want it any other way?

My Father's Glory is based on the childhood of Marcel Pagnol, the French novelist and filmmaker whose twinned novels, *Jean de Florette* and *Manon of the Spring*, were turned into wonderful films a few years earlier. Those were stories based on melodrama and coincidence, telling of a poor city man who tries to make a living from the land, the bitter local farmers who hide the existence of a spring from him, and the shocking poetic justice that punishes a cruel old man. The films provided showcases for the considerable talents of Yves Montand and Gérard Depardieu, the two ranking stars of French cinema.

There are no recognizable stars in *My Father's Glory*—and no melodrama, either. The movie is narrated by the hero, Marcel, as an adult. We see him as a young man of ten or twelve. His father, Joseph, is a schoolteacher in the city, and his mother, Augustine, is a paragon of domestic virtue. One summer they journey out to the hills of Provence to take a cottage and spend their vacation. These hills are to become the focus of Marcel's most enduring love affair. He loves the trees and the grasses, the small birds, and the eagle that nests high in a crag, the pathways up rock faces, and the way that voices carry from one side of a valley to another.

His guide and teacher for the lore of Provence is a local boy named Lili, who becomes his fast friend. Together they explore the countryside, which in this film seems bathed in a benevolent light and filled with adventures but not with dangers. The evenings are spent sitting around a battered old table in the yard, under a tree, eating the food that Augustine has prepared from the local markets and orchards.

There are others in his life: Uncle Jules, so full of secrets and wit, who becomes married to the charming Aunt Rose. And all of the local people, who seem through good luck to have found the place, the occupation, and the partner who will make them contented. The nights are filled with stars, and dreams of adventure. The days with Lili are spent learning the names and ways of all the living things that share the valley. Then autumn comes, and school begins again, and Marcel must leave his beloved hills.

The movie has a deliberate nostalgic tone.

It is most definitely intended as a memory. The narrator's voice reminds us of that, but the nature of the events makes it clear, too. What do we remember from our childhoods? If we are lucky, we recall the security of family rituals, our admiration for our parents, and the bittersweet partings with things we love. Childhood ends, in a sense, the day we discover that summer does not last forever.

Because not much "happens" in these films, there is more time for things to happen. There is time to dash out of the rain and into a cave, and discover that a great eagle has gotten there first. Time to run through the dusty orchards and climb up hills to the top of the world. Time to admire the perfect handwriting of Joseph, as he writes out the lessons on the board. Time to bask in the snug bourgeois security of the family, which is blessed, for a time, with perfect happiness.

My Father's Glory was released first, before *My Mother's Castle*, the continuation. That is the best way to see them—the first film about memory becoming a memory itself, to be reawakened by the second. What is surprising about the two films is the way they creep up on you emotionally, until at the end of the second one, when we discover the meaning of the movie's title, there is a deeply moving moment of truth and insight. The films were directed by Yves Robert, whose previous titles, including *The Tall Blond Man with One Black Shoe*, did not prepare me for the joy and serenity of these films. Like all the best movies, these memories of Marcel Pagnol work by becoming our memories, as well.

My Left Foot
R, 103 m., 1989

Daniel Day-Lewis (Christy Brown), Brenda Fricker (Mrs. Brown), Alison Whelan (Sheila), Kirsten Sheridan (Sharon), Declan Croghan (Tom), Eanna MacLiam (Benny), Marie Conmee (Sadie), Cyril Cusack (Lord Castlewelland). Directed by Jim Sheridan and produced by Noel Pearson. Screenplay by Jim Sheridan and Shane Connaughton, based on the book by Christy Brown.

I am trying to imagine what it would be like to write this review with my left foot. Quite seriously. I imagine it would be a great nuisance—unless, of course, my left foot was the only part of my body over which I had control. If that were the case, I would thank God that there was still some avenue down which I could communicate with the world.

That is the story of Christy Brown, born in a large, poor, loving family in a Dublin slum and considered for the first ten years of his life to be hopelessly retarded. He was born with cerebral palsy, and his entire body was in revolt against him—all except for the left foot, with which one day he picked up a piece of chalk and wrote a word on the floor. Everyone was amazed except for Christy's mother, who had always believed he knew what was going on. She could see it in his eyes.

The story of Christy Brown is one of the great stories of human courage and determination. He belongs on the same list with Helen Keller—and yet it is hard to imagine Christy being good company for the saintly Miss Keller, since he was not a saint himself but a ribald, boozing, wickedly gifted Irishman who simply happened to be handicapped.

Jim Sheridan's *My Left Foot* is the story of Brown's life, based on his autobiography and on the memories of those who knew him. He was not an easy man to forget. Tiny and twisted, bearded and unkempt, he managed, despite his late start, to grow into a poet, a novelist, a painter, and a lyrical chronicler of his own life. Like many geniuses, he was not an easy man to live with, and the movie makes that clear in its brilliant opening scene.

Perhaps concerned that we will mistake *My Left Foot* for one of those pious TV docudramas, the movie begins in the middle of one of Brown's typical manipulations. He is backstage in the library of a great British country home, where he is soon to be brought out to be given an award. He has a pint of whiskey hidden in his jacket pocket with a straw to allow him to sip it. But a hired nurse is watching him with a gimlet eye. Trying to get her out of the way for a second, he asks her for a light for his cigarette.

"But Mr. Brown," she says, "you know that smoking is not good for you."

"I didn't ask for a fucking psychological lecture," he replies. "I only asked for a fucking light."

It is the perfect opening scene because it breaks the ice. We know that it is all right to laugh with Christy and not to be intimidated by the great burden of his life. And as the movie develops, it is startling how much of it plays as comedy—startling unless we remember the universal Irish trait of black humor, in which the best laughter, the wicked laughter, is born out of hard times and bad luck.

My Left Foot charts Christy Brown's life from his earliest days until his greatest triumph, but the key scene in the movie may be one that takes place shortly after he is born. His father goes into the local pub to have a pint and consider the fact that his son has been born handicapped, and then he stubbornly makes the statement that no son of his will be sent to a "home." The decision to raise Christy as part of a large and loving family is probably what saved his life—for a man of such intelligence would have been destroyed by an institution. His brilliant mind, trapped inside his imperfect body, would have gone mad from calling for help.

Christy is played in the early scenes by Hugh O'Conor and from his teenage years onward by Daniel Day-Lewis. The two actors fit Brown's life together into one seamless performance of astonishing beauty and strength. There is an early scene in which Christy's brothers and other neighbor kids are playing soccer in the street, and crippled Christy, playing goalie, defends the goal by deflecting the ball with his head. There is great laughter and cheering all around, but the heart of the scene is secure: This child is not being protected in some sort of cocoon of sympathy, but is being raised in the middle of life, hard knocks and all. This is reinforced in other scenes where Christy's siblings dump him in a barrow and wheel him around to their games.

As he watched and listened, the boy was making the observations that would inform his life work. His novel *Down All the Days* and his other writings see Dublin street life with a clarity that is only possible because he was raised right in the middle of it and yet was always an outsider. As a painter, he saw Dublin in the same way: as a stage upon which people did things he was intimately familiar with and yet would never do himself.

Christy's life as a man was not easy. He was willful and arrogant, and right from the first time he tasted whiskey he knew there was at least one way to escape from the cage of his body. Like all men, he desired love, and there is a heartbreaking sequence in which he develops a crush on a teacher who works with him on speech therapy and loves Christy, but not in the romantic way that he imagines. Learning of her engagement, he creates a scene in a restaurant that in the power of its hurt and anger is almost unbearable.

He drank more. He was demanding. Like all bright people forced to depend on the kindness of others, he was filled with frustration. A woman did finally come into his life, a nurse who became his wife and loved him until the end, but by then happiness was conditional for Christy because he was an alcoholic. Since he could not obtain booze on his own—since it had to be brought to him and provided to him—there is the temptation to ask why his loved ones didn't simply shut him off. But of course that would have been a cruel exploitation of his weakness, and then too, Christy was a genius at instilling guilt.

My Left Foot is a great film for many reasons, but the most important is that it gives us such a complete picture of this man's life. It is not an inspirational movie, although it inspires. It is not a sympathetic movie, although it inspires sympathy. It is the story of a stubborn, difficult, blessed, and gifted man who was dealt a bad hand, who played it brilliantly, and who left us some good books, some good paintings, and the example of his courage. It must not have been easy.

My Mother's Castle

PG, 98 m., 1991

Philippe Caubere (Joseph), Nathalie Roussel (Augustine), Didier Pain (Uncle Jules), Therese Liotard (Aunt Rose), Julien Ciamaca (Marcel). Directed by Yves Robert and produced by Alain Poire. Screenplay by Jerome Tonnere, Louis Nucera, and Robert, based on the story by Marcel Pagnol.

And now here we are back again in the hills of Provence, in the second of two remarkable memory-films based on the childhood of the great French writer Marcel Pagnol. If you have seen *My Father's Glory*, the first of the films, these places will be familiar to you, along with some of the people and all of the feelings of Marcel, the young narrator, who has grown a year older and is now aware that there are girls in the world, in addition to hills and valleys and caves and eagles.

My Mother's Castle begins where *My Father's Glory* ended, after a brief look back. (It is best to see the films in order, even though this one is complete in itself.) The effect of the two films is a long, slow, subtle buildup to the enormous emotional payoff at the end of the second film, a moment when gratitude and regret come flowing into the heart of the narrator.

The time is the earlier decades of this century. The hero, Marcel, is now thirteen or fourteen. His father is a schoolteacher, much admired, and his mother is a sweet and loving woman who is still quite young and girlish, although she does not seem that way, of course, to her son. The family had been going every summer and during holidays to the countryside of Provence, and now old friends greet Marcel, including Lili, the local boy who taught him the ways of the countryside. But Lili is no longer the center of the universe; that position is soon taken by an imperious young lady who has read, perhaps, too many historical romances, and treats Marcel as her vassal.

The central set piece of the movie involves the journey the family must make to get to their summer cottage. The legal way is long and tiring, involving a walk that circles several great estates. There is a shortcut that reduces the walk by four-fifths, but it involves walking along the canal path that cuts through the estates, not only trespassing but also somehow getting through the locked gates as the path crosses each property line.

Help comes in the form of a canal guard who was once a student of Marcel's father, Joseph. He has the keys, and sees no need for the family to take the long way around. He gives a key to Joseph, and on each visit the little family takes the shortcut, as the vast private houses look down frowningly upon them from the hills.

One house has a mean, bitter caretaker, and a dog that looks ferocious but would really rather sun itself than bite. Marcel's mother, Augustine, is terrified of dogs, and there comes a day when the dog and the caretaker frighten the family, and it was up to Joseph to somehow salvage his family's self-respect.

All of this sounds as simple as a children's film, I suppose, and yet there are deep currents of pain and memory flowing here, and these scenes set up an emotional payoff at the end of the film that brings the whole experience to a triumphant conclusion.

My Father's Glory and *My Mother's Castle* are linked autobiographical stories by Pagnol, who also wrote the two novels *Jean de Florette* and *Manon of the Spring*. Those stories were more epic in sweep; these are intimate and nostalgic. It is likely that no one, not even Pagnol, had a childhood quite this perfect, and yet all happy childhoods grow happier in memory, and it is the nature of film that we can share some of Pagnol's happiness.

Mystic River

R, 137 m., 2003

Sean Penn (Jimmy Markum), Tim Robbins (Dave Boyle), Kevin Bacon (Sean Devine), Laurence Fishburne (Whitey Powers), Marcia Gay Harden (Celeste Boyle), Laura Linney (Annabeth Markum), Thomas Guiry (Brendan), Emmy Rossum (Katie). Directed by Clint Eastwood and produced by Eastwood, Judie Hoyt, and Robert Lorenz. Screenplay by Brian Helgeland, based on the book by Dennis Lehane.

Clint Eastwood's *Mystic River* is a dark, ominous brooding about a crime in the present that is emotionally linked to a crime in the past. It involves three boyhood friends in an Irish neighborhood of Boston, who were forever marked when one of them was captured by a child molester; as adults, their lives have settled into uneasy routines that are interrupted by the latest tragedy. Written by Brian Helgeland, based on the novel by Dennis Lehane, the movie uses a group of gifted actors who are able to find true human emotion in a story that could have been a whodunit, but looks too deeply and evokes too much honest pain.

The film centers on the three friends: Jimmy (Sean Penn), an ex-con who now runs the corner store; Dave (Tim Robbins), a handyman; and Sean (Kevin Bacon), a homicide detective. All are married; Jimmy to a second wife, Annabeth (Laura Linney), who helps him raise his oldest daughter and two of their own; Dave to Celeste (Marcia Gay Harden), who has given him a son; Sean to an absent, pregnant wife

who calls him from time to time but never says anything. The other major character is Whitey (Laurence Fishburne), Sean's police partner.

Jimmy keeps a jealous eye on his nineteen-year-old daughter, Katie (Emmy Rossum), who works with him at the store. She's in love with Brendan (Thomas Guiry), a boy Jimmy angrily disapproves of. Theirs is a sweet puppy love; they plan to run away together, but before that can happen Katie is found brutally beaten and dead. Sean and Whitey are assigned to the case. Brendan is obviously one of the suspects, but so is Dave, who came home late the night of the murder, covered with blood and talking to his wife in anguish about a mugger he fought and may have killed.

Although elements in *Mystic River* play according to the form of a police procedural, the movie is about more than the simple question of guilt. It is about pain spiraling down through the decades, about unspoken secrets and unvoiced suspicions. And it is very much about the private loyalties of husbands and wives. Jimmy says that he will kill the person who killed his daughter, and we have no reason to doubt him, especially after he hires neighborhood thugs to make their own investigation. Laura Linney, as his wife, has a scene where she responds to his need for vengeance, and it is not unreasonable to compare her character to Lady Macbeth. Marcia Gay Harden, as Celeste, Dave's wife, slowly begins to doubt her husband's story about the mugger, and shares her doubts. We see one wife fiercely loyal, and another who suspects she has been shut out from some deep recess of her husband's soul.

Although the story eventually arrives at a solution, it is not about the solution. It is about the journey, and it provides each of the actors with scenes that test their limits. Both Penn and Robbins create urgent and breathtaking suspense as they are cross-examined by the police. There is tension between Whitey, who thinks Dave is obviously guilty, and Sean, who is reluctant to suspect a childhood friend. There are such deep pools of hatred and blood lust circling the funeral that we expect an explosion at any moment, and yet the characters are all inward, smoldering.

And always that day in the past lingers in their memories. The three boys were writing their names in wet concrete when two men in a car drove up, flashed a badge, and took one of the boys away with them. Flashbacks show that he was abused for days. Compounding his suffering was the uneasiness the other two boys always felt about him; maybe they didn't entirely understand what happened to him, but in some sense they no longer felt the same about their violated friend—whose name, half-finished, remains in the old concrete like a life interrupted in midstream.

This is Clint Eastwood's twenty-fourth film as a director, and one of the few titles where he doesn't also act. He shows here a deep rapport with the characters and the actors, who are allowed lancing moments of truth. Always an understated actor himself, he finds in his three actors pools of privacy and reserve. Robbins broods inside his own miseries and watches vampire movies on TV to find metaphors for the way he feels. Bacon hurts all the time, we feel, because of the absence of his wife. Penn is a violent man who prepares to act violently but has not, we see, found much release that way in the past.

To see strong acting like this is exhilarating. In a time of flashy directors who slice and dice their films in a dizzy editing rhythm, it is important to remember that films can look and listen and attentively sympathize with their characters. Directors grow great by subtracting, not adding, and Eastwood does nothing for show, everything for effect.

N

Naked

NO MPAA RATING, 130 m., 1993

David Thewlis (Johnny), Lesley Sharp (Louise), Katrin
Cartlidge (Sophie), Greg Cruttwell (Jeremy), Claire
Skinner (Sandra), Peter Wight (Brian), Ewen Bremner
(Archie), Susan Vidler (Maggie). Directed by Mike Leigh
and produced by Simon Channing-Williams. Screenplay
by Leigh.

The characters in Mike Leigh's *Naked* look as
if they have lived indoors all of their lives, perhaps down in a cellar. Their pale, pasty skin
looks cold to the touch in the film's blue-gray
lighting. The film is shot in a high-contrast
style that makes everything seem a little more
bleak and narrow than it must. And if you listen carefully to the sound track, you become
aware that it lacks much of the background
ambiance of most movies; we are hearing
voices, flat and toneless, in what sounds like
an empty room.

All of these stylistic choices are right for
Naked, and so is the title, which describes characters who exist in the world without the usual
layers of protection. They are clothed, but not
warmly or cheerfully. They are naked of families, relationships, homes, values, and, in most
cases, jobs. They exist in modern Britain with
few possessions except their words.

The central character in *Naked* is Johnny
(David Thewlis), who as the movie opens has
rough sex with a weeping girl in an alley in
some barren northern city, and then steals a
car and drives down to London. From the way
he talks and certain things he refers to, we
gradually conclude that he has had an education—is an "intellectual," in that his opinions
are mostly formed from words, not feelings.

Something has gone terribly wrong in his
life, leaving him stranded without connections, employment, or hope. He goes to the
flat of an old girlfriend, who is away on holiday, and moves in, establishing a rapport of
the damned with her flatmate Sophie (Katrin
Cartlidge), who is so spaced out on drugs that
she seems barely able to make the connection
between what she says and what she thinks, if
anything.

The "relationship" that develops between
these two people is so pathetic that it can
barely be watched. The "sex" they have is such
a desperate attempt to feel something in the
midst of their separate wastelands that it is
much like watching them wound themselves.
When others appear in the flat—especially the
supercilious, hurtful Jeremy (Greg Cruttwell),
the landlord—they are like visitors from adjacent circles in hell.

Nor do matters improve with the arrival of
Sandra (Claire Skinner), whose name is on the
lease. She has a job, and apparently thinks of
herself as being normal and productive, and
offers free advice and criticism, but the film
invites us to see how precariously close she is
to falling into the same abyss as her friends.

Mike Leigh's method of working is well
known. He gathers his actors, suggests a
theme, and asks them to improvise situations.
A screenplay develops out of their work. This
method has created in *Naked* a group of characters who could not possibly have emerged
from a conventional screenplay; this is the
kind of film that is beyond imagining, and
only observation could have created it. Are
there people like this? Yes, a great many, who
have the ability and intelligence to lead functioning lives but lack the will and—in particular—the opening. Somehow they have
slipped out of the picture. It is not easy to slip
back in.

The movie won the best director award for
Leigh at the 1993 Cannes Film Festival, and a
best actor award for Thewlis, who was also
honored by several critics' groups. His performance never steps wrong. He creates a kind of
heroism in Johnny: It's not that we like him or
approve of him, but that we must admire the
dogged way he sticks to his guns and forges
ahead through misery, anger, and despair.
There is a scene here that is among the best
Leigh has ever done. Johnny strikes up a conversation with a night watchman, who takes
him on a midnight tour of a modern office
building. The subtext is that the watchman
will never do what the employees in the building do in the daytime, but owes his survival to
his job of guarding it for them at night, from
the likes of Johnny, who lacks even that much
of a toehold.

This is a painful movie to watch. But it is also exhilarating, as all good movies are, because we are watching the director and actors venturing beyond any conventional idea of what a modern movie can be about. Here there is no plot, no characters to identify with, no hope. But there is care: The filmmakers care enough about these people to observe them very closely, to note how they look and sound and what they feel.

Leigh has said in an interview that while his earlier films (including *High Hopes* and *Life Is Sweet*) might have embodied a socialist view of the world, this one edges over into anarchy. I agree. It suggests a world in which the operating systems have become distant from such inhabitants as Johnny and the women in the flat. The world is indifferent to them, and they to it. To some degree, they don't even know what's hit them. Johnny has a glimmer. His response is not hope or a plan. It is harsh, sardonic laughter. Destruction is his only response.

Nashville

R, 159 m., 1975

Henry Gibson (Haven Hamilton), Ronee Blakley (Barbara Jean), Timothy Brown (Tommy Brown), Gwen Welles (Sueleen Gay), Michael Murphy (John Triplette), Shelley Duvall (L. A. Joan), Lily Tomlin (Linnea Reese), Ned Beatty (Delbert Reese), Scott Glenn (Private First Class Glenn Kelly), Keith Carradine (Tom Frank), Geraldine Chaplin (Opal), Karen Black (Connie White), Barbara Harris (Albuquerque). Directed and produced by Robert Altman. Screenplay by Joan Tewkesbury.

Robert Altman's *Nashville*, which was the best American movie since *Bonnie and Clyde*, creates in the relationships of nearly two dozen characters a microcosm of who we were and what we were up to in the 1970s. It's a film about the losers and the winners, the drifters and the stars in Nashville, and the most complete expression yet of not only the genius but also the humanity of Altman, who sees people with his camera in such a way as to enlarge our own experience. Sure, it's only a movie. But after I saw it I felt more alive, I felt I understood more about people, I felt somehow wiser. It's that good a movie.

The movie doesn't have a star. It does not, indeed, even have a lead role. Instead, Altman creates a world, a community in which some people know each other and others don't, in which people are likely to meet before they understand the ways in which their lives are related. And he does it all so easily, or seems to, that watching *Nashville* is as easy as breathing and as hard to stop. Altman is the best natural filmmaker since Fellini.

One of the funny things about *Nashville* is that most of the characters never have entrances. They're just sort of there. At times, we're watching an important character and don't even know, yet, why he's important, but Altman's storytelling is so clear in his own mind, his mastery of this complex wealth of material is so complete, that we're never for a moment confused or even curious. We feel secure in his hands, and apart from anything else, *Nashville* is a virtuoso display of narrative mastery.

It concerns several days and nights in the lives of a very mixed bag of Nashville locals and visitors, all of whom, like the city itself, are obsessed with country music. Tennessee is in the midst of a presidential primary, and all over Nashville, there are the posters and sound trucks of a quasi-populist candidate, Hal Philip Walker, who seems like a cross between George Wallace and George McGovern. We never meet Walker, but we meet both his local organizer and a John Lindsay–type PR man. They're trying to round up country-western talent for a big benefit, and their efforts provide a thread around which some of the story is loosely wound.

But there are many stories here, and in the way he sees their connections, Altman makes a subtle but shrewd comment about the ways in which we are all stuck in this thing together. There are the veteran country stars like Haven Hamilton (Henry Gibson), who wears gaudy white costumes, is self-conscious about his short stature, is painfully earnest about recording a painfully banal Bicentennial song, and who, down deep, is basically just a good old boy. There is the reigning queen of country music, Barbara Jean (Ronee Blakley), who returns in triumph to Nashville after treatment at a burn center in Atlanta for unspecified injuries incurred from a fire baton (she's met at the airport by a phalanx of girls from TIT—the Tennessee Institute of Twirling—only to collapse again). There is the corrupted, decadent rock star, played by Keith Carradine, who is so ruthless in his sexual aggression, so evil in his need to hurt women, that he telephones one woman while another is still just leaving his bed, in order to wound both of them.

But these characters are just examples of the people we meet in *Nashville,* not the leads. Everyone is more or less equal in this film, because Altman sees them all with a judicious and ultimately sympathetic eye. The film is filled with perfectly observed little moments: The star-struck young soldier keeping a silent vigil by the bedside of Barbara Jean; the campaign manager doing a double take when he discovers he's just shaken the hand of Elliott Gould ("a fairly well-known actor," Haven Hamilton explains, "and he used to be married to Barbra Streisand"); the awestruck BBC reporter describing America in breathless, hilarious hyperbole; the way a middle-aged mother of two deaf children (Lily Tomlin) shyly waits for an assignation with a rock singer; the birdbrained cheerfulness with which a young groupie (Shelley Duvall) comes to town to visit her dying aunt and never does see her, being distracted by every male over the age of sixteen that she meets.

The film circles around three motifs without, thankfully, ever feeling it has to make a definitive statement about any of them. Since they're all still very open subjects, that's just as well. What Altman does is suggest the ways in which we deal with them—really, in unrehearsed everyday life, not thematically, as in the movies. The motifs are success, women, and politics.

Success: It can be studied most fruitfully in the carefully observed pecking order of the country-and-western performers. There are ones at the top, so successful they can afford to be generous, expansive, well-liked. There are the younger ones in the middle, jockeying for position. There are what can only be described as the professional musicians at the bottom, playing thanklessly but well in the bars and clubs where the stars come to unwind after the show. And at the very bottom, there are those who aspire to be musicians but

have no talent at all, like a waitress (Gwen Welles) who comes to sing at a smoker, is forced to strip, and, in one of the film's moments of heartbreaking truthfulness, disdainfully flings at the roomful of men the sweat socks she had stuffed into her brassiere.

Women: God, but Altman cares for them while seeing their predicament so clearly. The women in *Nashville* inhabit a world largely unaffected by the feminist revolution, as most women do. They are prized for their talent, for their beauty, for their services in bed, but not once in this movie for themselves. And yet Altman suggests their complexities in ways that movies rarely have done before. The Lily Tomlin character, in particular, forces us to consider her real human needs and impulses as she goes to meet the worthless rock singer (and we remember a luminous scene during which she and her deaf son discussed his swimming class). Part of the movie's method is to establish characters in one context and then place them in another, so that we can see how personality—indeed, basic identity itself—is constant but must sometimes be concealed for the sake of survival or even simple happiness.

Politics: I won't be giving very much away by revealing that there is an attempted assassination in *Nashville.* The assassin, a loner who takes a room in a boarding house, is clearly telegraphed by Altman. It's not Altman's style to surprise us with plot. He'd rather surprise us by revelations of character. At this late date after November 22, 1963, and all the other days of infamy, I wouldn't have thought it possible that a film could have anything new or very interesting to say on assassination, but *Nashville* does, and the film's closing minutes, with Barbara Harris finding herself, to her astonishment, onstage and singing, "It Don't Worry Me," are unforgettable and heartbreaking. *Nashville,* which seems so unstructured as it begins, reveals itself in this final sequence to have had a deep and very profound structure—but one of emotions, not ideas.

This is a film about America. It deals with our myths, our hungers, our ambitions, and our sense of self. It knows how we talk and how we behave, and it doesn't flatter us but it does love us.

National Lampoon's Animal House

R, 109 m., 1978

John Belushi (Bluto), Tim Matheson (Otter), John Vernon (Dean Wormer), Verna Bloom (Mrs. Wormer), Thomas Hulce (Pinto), Cesare Danova (Mayor), Donald Sutherland (Jennings), Mary Louise Weller (Mandy), Stephen Furst (Flounder), Mark Metcalf (Neidermeier). Directed by John Landis and produced by Matty Simmons and Ivan Reitman. Screenplay by Harold Ramis, Douglas Kenney, and Chris Miller.

"What we need right now," Otter tells his fraternity brothers, "is a stupid, futile gesture on someone's part." And no fraternity on campus—on any campus—is better qualified to provide such a gesture than the Deltas. They have the title role in *National Lampoon's Animal House*, which remembers all the way back to 1962, when college was simpler, beer was cheaper, and girls were harder to seduce.

The movie is vulgar, raunchy, ribald, and occasionally scatological. It is also the funniest comedy since Mel Brooks made *The Producers*. *Animal House* is funny for some of the same reasons the *National Lampoon* is funny (and Second City and *Saturday Night Live* are funny): Because it finds some kind of precarious balance between insanity and accuracy, between cheerfully wretched excess and an ability to reproduce the most revealing nuances of human behavior.

In one sense there has never been a campus like this movie's Faber University, which was apparently founded by the lead pencil tycoon and has as its motto "Knowledge is Good." In another sense, Faber University is a microcosm of . . . I was going to say *our society*, but why get serious? Let someone else discuss the symbolism of Bluto's ability to crush a beer can against his forehead.

Bluto is, of course, the most animalistic of the Deltas. He's played by John Belushi, and the performance is all the more remarkable because Bluto has hardly any dialogue. He isn't a talker, he's an event. His best scenes are played in silence (as when he lasciviously scales a ladder to peek at a sorority pillow fight).

Bluto and his brothers are engaged in a holding action against civilization. They are in favor of beer, women, song, motorcycles, *Play-boy* centerfolds, and making rude noises. They are opposed to studying, serious thought, the dean, the regulations governing fraternities, and, most especially, the disgusting behavior of the Omegas—a house so respectable it has even given an ROTC commander to the world.

The movie was written by *National Lampoon* contributors (including Harold Ramis, who was in Second City at the same time Belushi was), and was directed by John Landis. It's like an end run around Hollywood's traditional notions of comedy. It's anarchic, messy, and filled with energy. It assaults us. Part of the movie's impact comes from its sheer level of manic energy: When beer kegs and Hell's Angels come bursting through the windows of the Delta House, the anarchy is infectious. But the movie's better made (and better acted) than we might at first realize. It takes skill to create this sort of comic pitch, and the movie's filled with characters that are sketched a little more absorbingly than they had to be, and acted with perception.

For example: Tim Matheson, as Otter, the ladies' man, achieves a kind of grace in his obsession. John Vernon, as the dean of students, has a blue-eyed, rulebook hatefulness that's inspired. Verna Bloom, as his dipsomaniacal wife, has just the right balance of cynicism and desperation. Donald Sutherland, a paranoic early sixties pothead, nods solemnly at sophomoric truisms and admits he's as bored by Milton as everyone else. And stalking through everything is Bluto, almost a natural force: He lusts, he thirsts, he consumes cafeterias full of food, and he pours an entire fifth of Jack Daniel's into his mouth, belches, and observes, "Thanks. I needed that."

He has, as I suggested, little dialogue. But it is telling. When the Delta House is kicked off campus and the Deltas are thrown out of school, he makes, in a moment of silence, a philosophical observation: "Seven years down the drain." What the situation requires, of course, is a stupid, futile gesture on someone's part.

Natural Born Killers

R, 123 m., 1994

Woody Harrelson (Mickey Knox), Juliette Lewis (Mallory Knox), Robert Downey, Jr. (Wayne Gale),

Tommy Lee Jones (McClusky), Tom Sizemore (Jack Scagnetti), Rodney Dangerfield (Mallory's Dad), Russell Means (Indian), Edie McClurg (Mallory's Mom). Directed by Oliver Stone and produced by Jane Hamsher, Don Murphy, and Clayton Townsend. Screenplay by David Veloz, Richard Rutowski, and Stone.

Oliver Stone's *Natural Born Killers* might have played even more like a demented nightmare if it hadn't been for the O. J. Simpson case. Maybe Stone meant his movie as a warning about where we were headed, but because of Simpson it plays as an indictment. We are becoming a society more interested in crime and scandal than in anything else—more than in politics and the arts, certainly, and maybe even more than sports, unless crime *is* our new national sport.

If that's true, then Stone's movie is about the latest all-Americans, Mickey and Mallory (Woody Harrelson and Juliette Lewis), two mass murderers who go on a killing spree across America, making sure everybody knows their names, so they get credit for their crimes. (Terrorists always claim "credit" rather than "blame.") The movie is not simply about their killings, however, but also about the way they electrify the media and exhilarate the public. (One teenager tells the TV cameras, "Mass murder is wrong. But if I *were* a mass murderer, I'd be Mickey and Mallory!")

The boom in courtroom TV has given us long hours to study the faces of famous accused murderers; we have a better view than the jury. Looking into their faces, I sense a curious slackness, an inattention, as if the trial is a mirage, and their thoughts far away. If they're guilty, it's like they're rehearsing their excuses for the crime. If they're innocent, maybe those empty expressions mean the courtroom experience is so alien they can't process it. Not once during his trial did I see a shot of Simpson looking normal in any way I can understand. His expression always seems to be signifying, "Yes, but . . ."

Oliver Stone captures this odd emptiness, this moral inattention, in the faces and behavior of Mickey and Mallory. They're on their own frequency. The casting is crucial: Woody Harrelson and Juliette Lewis are both capable of being frightening, both able to project

amorality and disdain as easily as Jack Lemmon projects ingratiation. There is a scene where a lawman is trying to intimidate Lewis, and he throws his cigarette onto the floor of her cell. She steps on it and rubs it out with her bare foot. Set and match.

Natural Born Killers is not so much about the killers, however, as about the feeding frenzy they inspire. During the period of their rampage, they are the most famous people in America, and the media goes nuts. There are Mickey and Mallory fan clubs and T-shirts; tabloid TV is represented by a bloodthirsty journalist played by Robert Downey, Jr., who is so thrilled by their fame he almost wants to embrace them. The people Mickey and Mallory touch in the law industry are elated to be handling the case; it gives them a brush with celebrity, and a tantalizing whiff of the brimstone that fascinates some cops.

Stone has never been a director known for understatement or subtlety. He'll do anything to get his effect, and that's one of the things I value about him. He understands that celebrity killers have achieved such a bizarre status in America that it's almost impossible to satirize the situation—to get beyond real life. But he goes for broke, in scenes of carnage like a prison riot which is telecast live while the "host" gets caught up in the bloodlust.

Yet you do not see as much actual violence as you think you do in this movie; it's more the tone, the attitude, and the breakneck pacing that gives you that impression. Stone is not making a geek show, with close-ups of blood and guts. Like all good satirists, he knows that too much realism will weaken his effect. He lets you know he's making a comedy. There's an over-the-top exuberance to the intricate crosscut editing, by Hank Corwin and Brian Berdan, and to the hyperactive camera of Robert Richardson. Stylistically, the film is a cinematic bazaar, combining color and black and white, film and video, 35mm and Super 8, sitcom style and animated cartoons, fiction and newsreels. They're throwing stuff at the screen by the gleeful handfuls.

And look how this film blindsided the good citizens of the MPAA classification board. The review panel threatened the film with the dreaded NC-17 rating, and after five appeals and some cutting, finally granted the R rating.

But read their parental warning: "For extreme violence and graphic carnage, for shocking images, and for strong language and sexuality." They've got the fever! I could point to a dozen more violent recent films that have left the MPAA unstirred, but Stone has touched a nerve here, because his film isn't about violence, it's about how we respond to violence, and that truly is shocking.

Stone's basic strategy is to find the current buzzwords and buzz ideas of crime and violence, and project them through the looking glass into a wonderland of murderous satire. It is a commonplace, for example, that many violent criminals were abused as children. All right, then, Stone will give us abuse: We see Mallory's childhood, shot in the style of a lurid TV sitcom, with Rodney Dangerfield as her drunken, piggish father. As he shouts and threatens violence, as he ridicules Mallory's thoroughly cowed mother, as he grabs his daughter and makes lewd suggestions, we hear a sitcom laugh track that grinds out mechanical hilarity. Everything is funny to the "live studio audience," because Dangerfield's timing is right for the punch lines. Never mind how frightening the words are. Who really listens to sitcoms, anyway?

Everything is grist for Stone's mill. Look at Tommy Lee Jones, as Warden McClusky of Batongaville State Prison. He's seen too many prison movies, and he's intoxicated by the experience of being on TV. He rants, he raves, he curses, he runs his prison like a deranged slave plantation. And then here comes Downey, as Wayne Gale, who hosts a clone of *Hard Copy* or *America's Most Wanted*. Using a Robin Leach accent that makes the whole thing into showbiz, he's so thrilled to be in the same frame with these famous killers that he hardly cares what happens to him. Watch his reaction in the final bloody showdown, when he believes he is immune because, after all, he has the camera.

Seeing this movie once is not enough. The first time is for the visceral experience, the second time is for the meaning. *Natural Born Killers* is like a slap in the face, waking us up to what's happening.

Watching the movie, it occurred to me that I didn't meet or talk with anyone who seemed genuinely, personally, angry that Simpson (or anyone else) might have committed those sad murders. Instead, people seem more intrigued and fascinated. The word *grateful* comes to mind. The case has given us all something to talk about. The barking dog. The blood tests. The ice cream that didn't melt. The matching glove. When the subject came up at a party, you could almost feel the relief in the room, as everyone joined in: At last, a topic we could all get worked up about! Once we were shocked that the Romans threw Christians to the lions. Now we figure out a way to recycle the format into a TV show. That's what *Natural Born Killers* is all about.

Network
R, 121 m, 1976

Faye Dunaway (Diana Christenson), William Holden (Alex Schumacher), Peter Finch (Howard Beale), Robert Duvall (Frank Hackett), Wesley Addy (Nelson Chaney), Ned Beatty (Arthur Jensen). Directed by Sidney Lumet and produced by Howard Gottfried. Screenplay by Paddy Chayefsky.

There's a moment near the beginning of *Network* that has us thinking this will be the definitive indictment of national television we've been promised. A veteran anchorman has been fired because he's over the hill and drinking too much and, even worse, because his ratings have gone down. He announces his firing on his program, observes that broadcasting has been his whole life, and adds that he plans to kill himself on the air in two weeks. We cut to the control room, where the directors and technicians are obsessed with getting into the network feed on time. There are commercials that have to be fit in, the anchorman has to finish at the right moment, the buttons have to be pushed, and the station break has to be timed correctly. Everything goes fine. "Uh," says somebody, "did you hear what Howard just said?" Apparently nobody else had.

They were all consumed with form, with being sure the commercials were played in the right order and that the segment was the correct length. What was happening—that a man has lost his career and was losing his mind— passed right by. It wasn't their job to listen to Howard, just as it wasn't his job to run the control board. And what *Network* seems to be telling us is that television itself is like that: an economic process in the blind pursuit of ratings and technical precision, in which excellence is as accidental as banality.

If the whole movie had stayed with this theme, we might have had a very bitter little classic here. As it is, we have a supremely well-acted, intelligent film that tries for too much, that attacks not only television but also most of the other ills of the 1970s. We are asked to laugh at, be moved by, or get angry about such a long list of subjects: sexism and ageism and revolutionary rip-offs and upper-middle-class anomie and capitalist exploitation and Neilsen ratings and psychics and that perennial standby, the failure to communicate. Paddy Chayefsky's script isn't a bad one, but he finally loses control of it. There's just too much he wanted to say. By the movie's end, the anchorman is obviously totally insane and is being exploited by blindly ambitious programmers on the one hand and corrupt businessmen on the other, and the scale of evil is so vast we've lost track of the human values.

And yet, still, what a rich and interesting movie this is. Lumet's direction is so taut, that maybe we don't realize that it leaves some unfinished business. It attempts to deal with a brief, cheerless love affair between Holden and Dunaway, but doesn't really allow us to understand it. It attempts to suggest that multinational corporations are the only true contemporary government, but does so in a scene that slips too broadly into satire, so that we're not sure Chayefsky means it. It deals with Holden's relationship with his wife of twenty-five years, but inconclusively.

But then there are scenes in the movie that are absolutely chilling. We watch Peter Finch cracking up on the air, and we remind ourselves that *this* isn't satire, it was a style as long ago as Jack Paar. We can believe that audiences would tune in to a news program that's half happy talk and half freak show, because audiences *are* tuning in to programs like that. We can believe in the movie's "Ecumenical Liberation Army" because nothing along those lines will amaze us after Patty Hearst. And we can believe that the Faye Dunaway character could be totally cut off from her emotional and sexual roots, could be fanatically obsessed

with her job, because jobs as competitive as hers almost require that. Twenty-five years ago, this movie would have seemed like a fantasy; now it's barely ahead of the facts.

So the movie's flawed. So it leaves us with loose ends and questions. That finally doesn't bother me, because what it does accomplish is done so well, is seen so sharply, is presented so unforgivingly, that *Network* will outlive a lot of tidier movies. And it won several Academy Awards, including those for Peter Finch, awarded posthumously as Best Actor; Chayevsky for his screenplay; Beatrice Straight, as Best Supporting Actress; and Faye Dunaway, as Best Actress. Watch her closely as they're deciding what will finally have to be done about their controversial anchorman. The scene would be hard to believe—if she weren't in it.

A New Leaf

G, 102 m., 1971

Walter Matthau (Henry), Elaine May (Henrietta), Jack Weston (Andrew McPherson), George Rose (Harold), William Redfield (Beckett), James Coco (Uncle Harry). Directed by May and produced by Joe Manduke. Screenplay by May, based on the story "The Green Heart" by Jack Ritchie.

"Perfect!" says Walter Matthau, after Elaine May has dropped her teacup (twice), her glasses, her purse, her gloves, and her composure while trying to master the complexities of a simple tea party. The hostess is dismayed at the damage to her rug, so Matthau deliberately pours his own drink onto it. Then he observes that of all the sexual perversions he has ever witnessed, the neurotic relationship of the hostess and her rug is without doubt the most disgusting. Exit.

Is it any wonder, then, that the enormously wealthy May immediately falls in love with Matthau, whose sole skill, if any, is putting down Turkish-rug fetishists? She is, herself, a botanist who dreams of the day when a frond, herb, or previously unclassified fern will be named for her. That would be, you see, immortality of a sort, to have a frond of one's own.

Elaine May's *A New Leaf* is a love story about these two people, who are in desperate need of each other even if he doesn't know it. Matthau plays an aging bon vivant who has squandered his fortune and is told by his butler that he has few choices: suicide, perhaps, or marrying money. He has no ability or ambition, and work of course would be out of the question. He has dedicated his life to living it comfortably and with style. His butler tells him, as he dons his velvet smoking jacket: "You have preserved in your own lifetime, sir, a way of life that was dead before you were born."

To carry it still further, he borrows $50,000 for six weeks from his rich uncle, a sort of gay Rabelaisian played by James Coco, who spends most of his day eating, drinking, and employing a transistorized pepper mill. Matthau sets out on a search for the right potential wife, with no results until May drops her teacup and he suspects that she may be so incompetent, even dumb, as to marry him.

Their courtship involves finding out about each other's tastes. He savors rare French vintages, for example, and she likes Mogen David and soda, with a drop of lime juice. And so on. For their wedding night, she dons a Grecian gown, inadvertently sticking her head through the armhole. He attempts to readjust her, and as she struggles within the gown for about two minutes you hear more laughter than I've heard in any theater since *The Producers,* which is my yardstick for these matters.

A New Leaf is, in fact, one of the funniest movies of our unfunny age. May reportedly is dissatisfied with the present version; newspaper reports indicate that her original cut was an hour longer and included two murders. Matthau, who likes this version better than the original, has suggested that writer-director-stars should be willing to let someone else have a hand in the editing. Maybe so. I'm generally prejudiced in favor of the director in these disputes.

Whatever the merits of May's case, however, the movie in its present form is hilarious, and cockeyed, and warm.

The New World

PG-13, 130 m., 2006

Colin Farrell (Captain John Smith), Q'Orianka Kilcher (Pocahontas), Christopher Plummer (Captain Newport), Christian Bale (John Rolfe), August Schellenberg (Powhatan), Wes Studi (Opechancanough), David Thewlis (Captain Wingfield). Directed by Terrence Malick and produced by Sarah Green. Screenplay by Malick.

Terrence Malick's *The New World* strips away all the fancy and lore from the story of Pocahontas and her tribe and the English settlers at Jamestown, and imagines how new and strange these people must have seemed to one another. If the Indians stared in disbelief at the English ships, the English were no less awed by the somber beauty of the new land and its people. They called the Indians "the naturals," little understanding how well the term applied.

Malick strives throughout his film to imagine how the two civilizations met and began to speak when they were utterly unknown to each other. We know with four centuries of hindsight all the sad aftermath, but it is crucial to *The New World* that it does not know what history holds. These people regard one another in complete novelty, and at times with a certain humility imposed by nature. The Indians live because they submit to the realities of their land, and the English nearly die because they are ignorant and arrogant.

Like his films *Days of Heaven* and *The Thin Red Line,* Malick's *The New World* places nature in the foreground, instead of using it as a picturesque backdrop as other stories might. He uses voice-over narration by the principal characters to tell the story from their individual points of view. We hear Capt. John Smith describe Pocahontas: "She exceeded the others not only in beauty and proportion, but in wit and spirit, too." And later the settler John Rolfe recalls his first meeting: "When first I saw her, she was regarded as someone broken, lost."

The New World is Pocahontas's story, although the movie deliberately never calls her by any name. She is the bridge between the two peoples. Played by a fourteen-year-old actress named Q'Orianka Kilcher as a tall, grave, inquisitive young woman, she does not "fall in love" with John Smith, as the children's books tell it, but saves his life—throwing herself on his body when he is about to be killed on the order of the chief, her father—for far more complex reasons. The movie implies, rather than says, that she is driven by curiosity about these strange visitors, and empathy with their plight as strangers, and with admiration for

Smith's reckless and intrepid courage. If love later plays a role, it is not modern romantic love so much as a pure, instinctive version.

And what of Smith (Colin Farrell)? To see him is to know he knows the fleshpots of London and has been raised without regard for women. He is a troublemaker, under sentence of death by the expedition leader, Captain Newport (Christopher Plummer), for mutinous grumblings. Yet when he first sees Pocahontas, she teaches him new feelings by her dignity and strangeness. There is a scene where Pocahontas and Smith teach each other simple words in their own languages, words for sky, eyes, and lips, and the scene could seem contrived, but it doesn't because they play it with such a tender feeling of discovery.

Smith is not fair with Pocahontas. Perhaps you know the story, but if you don't, I'll let the movie fill in the details. She later encounters the settler John Rolfe (Christian Bale) and from him finds loyalty and honesty. Her father, the old chief Powhatan (August Schellenberg), would have her killed for her transgressions, but "I cannot give you up to die. I am too old for it." Abandoned by her tribe, she is forced to live with the English. Rolfe returns with her to England, where she meets the king and is a London sensation, although that story, too, is well-known.

There is a meeting that she has in England, however, that Malick handles with almost trembling tact, in which she deals with a truth hidden from her, and addresses it with unwavering honesty. What Malick focuses on is her feelings as a person who might as well have been transported to another planet. Wearing strange clothes, speaking a strange language, she can depend only on those few she trusts, and on her idea of herself.

There are two new worlds in this film, the one the English discover, and the one Pocahontas discovers. Both discoveries center on the word "new," and what distinguishes Malick's film is how firmly he refuses to know more than he should in Virginia in 1607 or London a few years later. The events in his film, including the tragic battles between the Indians and the settlers, seem to be happening for the first time. No one here has read a history book from the future.

There are the familiar stories of the Indians helping the English survive the first winter, of how they teach the lore of planting corn and laying up stores for the winter. We are surprised to see how makeshift and vulnerable the English forts are, how evolved the Indian culture is, how these two civilizations could have built something new together—but could not, because what both societies knew at that time did not permit it. Pocahontas could have brought them together. In a small way, she did. She was given the gift of sensing the whole picture, and that is what Malick founds his film on, not tawdry stories of love and adventure. He is a visionary, and this story requires one.

Note: This review is based on a viewing of the re-edited version of The New World, *which runs about 130 minutes; I also saw the original 150-minute version and noticed no startling changes.*

Night Moves

R, 100 m., 1975

Gene Hackman (Harry Moseby), Harris Yulin (Marty Heller), Jennifer Warren (Paula), Janet Ward (Arlene), Susan Clark (Ellen), Melanie Griffith (Delly), Edward Binns (Ziegler). Directed by Arthur Penn and produced by Robert M. Sherman. Screenplay by Alan Sharp.

There's some kind of irony in the release, so close together, of a movie that claims to be inspired by the detective novels of Ross Macdonald—but isn't—and one that makes no claims but is a triumph in the Macdonald tradition. The first movie was the weary *The Drowning Pool,* in which Paul Newman gave one of his lesser performances. The second is Arthur Penn's *Night Moves,* with Gene Hackman subtle and riveting as the private eye.

Night Moves is one of the best psychological thrillers in a long time, probably since *Don't Look Now.* It has an ending that comes not only as a complete surprise—which would be easy enough—but that also pulls everything together in a new way, one we hadn't thought of before, one that's almost unbearably poignant. If you like private eyes, find it.

The eye this time is named Harry Moseby, perhaps with a nod toward Hackman's great performance as Harry Caul in *The Conversation,* perhaps not. He's a former pro football player and a man of considerable intelligence whose wife (Susan Clark) runs an antiques business. He's a private detective for reasons, vaguely hinted at, involving his childhood.

A Hollywood divorcée, clinging to the last shreds of a glamour that once won her a movie director (and half the other men in town, she claims) hires him to trace down her missing daughter. Harry takes the case, pausing only long enough to track down his own missing wife—who is, it turns out, having a not especially important affair with a man who owns a beach house in Malibu. His confrontation with the man, like so many scenes in the movie, is done with dialogue so blunt in its truthfulness that the characters really do escape their genre.

Harry traces the missing girl to her stepfather, a genial pilot in the Florida Keys, and goes there to bring her back. And from the moment he sets eyes on the stepfather's mistress, the movie, which has been absorbing anyway, really takes off. The mistress is played by a relatively unknown actress and sometime singer named Jennifer Warren, who has the cool gaze and air of competence and tawny hair of that girl in the Winston ads who smokes for pleasure and creates waves of longing in men from coast to coast. Warren creates a character so refreshingly eccentric, so sexy in such an unusual way, that it's all the movie can do to get past her without stopping to admire. But it does.

The plot involves former and present lovers of the girl and her mother, sunken treasure (yes, sunken treasure), conflicts across the generations, and murders more complex by far than they seem at first.

These are all the trademarks of the Lew Archer novels by Ross Macdonald, especially the little-girl-lost theme, and Alan Sharp's screenplay uses them infinitely better than *The Drowning Pool* did—even though that was actually based on a Macdonald book. By the movie's end, and especially during its last shock of recognition, we've been through a wringer. Art this isn't. But does it work as a thriller? Yes. It works as about two thrillers.

Nixon

R, 190 m., 1995

Anthony Hopkins (Nixon), Joan Allen (Pat Nixon), Powers Boothe (Alexander Haig), Ed Harris (E. Howard Hunt), Bob Hoskins (J. Edgar Hoover), E. G. Marshall (John Mitchell), David Paymer (Ron Ziegler), Paul Sorvino (Kissinger), J. T. Walsh (Erlichman), James Woods (Haldeman). Directed by Oliver Stone and produced by Stone, Clayton Townsend, and Andrew G. Vajna. Screenplay by Stephen J. Rivele, Stone, and Christopher Wilkinson.

Oliver Stone's *Nixon* gives us a brooding, brilliant, tortured man, sinking into the gloom of a White House under siege, haunted by the ghosts of his past. Thoughts of Hamlet, Macbeth, and King Lear come to mind; here, again, is a ruler destroyed by his fatal flaws. There's something almost majestic about the process: As Nixon goes down in this film, there is no gloating, but a watery sigh, as of a great ship sinking.

The movie does not apologize for Nixon, and holds him accountable for the disgrace he brought to the presidency. But it is not without compassion for this devious and complex man, and I felt a certain empathy: There, but for the grace of God, go we. I rather expected Stone, the maker of *JFK* and *Natural Born Killers*, to adopt a scorched-earth policy toward Nixon, but instead he blames not only Nixon's own character flaws but also the imperial presidency itself, the system that, once set in motion, behaves with a mindlessness of its own.

In the title role, Anthony Hopkins looks and sounds only generally like Nixon. This is not an impersonation; Hopkins gives us a deep, resonant performance that creates a man instead of imitating an image. Stone uses the same approach, reigning in his stylistic exuberance and yet giving himself the freedom to use flashbacks, newsreels, broadcast voices, montage, and the device of clouds swiftly fleeing over the White House sky as events run ahead of the president's ability to control them.

Nixon is flavored by the greatest biography in American film history, *Citizen Kane*. There are several quotes, such as the opening upward pan from outside the White House fence, the Gothic music on a cloudy night, the *March of Time*–style newsreel, and the scene where the president and Mrs. Nixon sit separated by a long dinner table. The key device Stone has borrowed is the notion of Rosebud, the missing piece of information that might explain a man's life.

In Stone's view, the infamous eighteen-and-a-half-minute gap on the White House tapes symbolizes a dark hole inside the president's soul, a secret that Nixon hints at but never reveals. What is implied is that somehow a secret CIA operation against Cuba, started with Nixon's knowledge during the last years of the Eisenhower administration, turned on itself and somehow led to the assassination of John F. Kennedy.

The movie doesn't suggest that Nixon ordered or desired Kennedy's death, but that he half-understood the process by which the "Beast," as he called the secret government apparatus, led to the assassination. Learning that former CIA Cuba conspirator E. Howard Hunt was involved in the Watergate caper, he murmurs, "He's the darkness reaching out for the dark. Open up that scab, you uncover a lot of pus." And in an unguarded moment, he confides to an aide, "Whoever killed Kennedy came from this thing we created—this Beast."

If the eighteen-and-a-half-minute gap conceals Rosebud, it is like the Rosebud in *Kane,* explaining nothing, but pointing to a painful hole in the hero's psyche created in childhood. *Nixon* shows the president's awkward, unhappy early years, as two brothers die and his strict parents fill him with a sense of purpose and inadequacy. "When you quit struggling, they've beaten you," his father says. And his mother (Mary Steenburgen), speaking in the Quaker language of thees and thous, seems always to hold him to a higher standard than he can hope to reach.

Stone, who was burned by accusations that some of the history in *JFK* was fabricated, opens with the disclaimer that some scenes are based on hypothesis and speculation. Many of the scenes, in fact, come out of our memory book of Nixon's greatest hits: the Checkers speech, "You won't have Nixon to kick around any more," the summit with Mao, the bizarre midnight visit to antiwar protesters at the Lincoln Memorial, and the strange scene, reported in Woodward and Bernstein's *The Final Days,* in which a crushed president asks Henry Kissinger to join him on his knees in prayer.

One theme throughout the film is Nixon's envy of John F. Kennedy. He judges his entire life in terms of his nemesis. Nixon on JFK's 1960 campaign: "All my life he's been sticking it to me. Now he steals from me." Nixon, bitter at not being invited by Kennedy's family to JFK's funeral, reflecting half-enviously: "If I'd been president, they never would have killed me." Nixon, alone at the end, speaking to the portrait of JFK: "When they look at you, they see what they want to be. When they look at me, they see what they are."

Stone has surrounded his Nixon with a gallery of figures we remember from the Watergate years, played by actors of a uniformly high caliber. Bob Hoskins creates a feral, poisonous J. Edgar Hoover, eating melon from the mouth of a handsome pool boy and ogling the marine guards at a White House reception. Paul Sorvino plays Henry Kissinger, reserved, watchful, disbelieving as he gets down on his knees to pray. J. T. Walsh and James Woods are Erlichman and Haldeman, the inner guard, carefully monitoring the nuances between what is said and what is implied. Powers Boothe is the impeccable Alexander Haig, who firmly guides the president toward resignation. When Nixon ponders a cover-up of the tapes, it is Haig who raises the (imaginary?) possibility that backup copies might surface. Notice the precision of his wording: "I know for a fact that it's possible that there was another tape."

The key supporting performance in the movie, however, is by Joan Allen, as Pat Nixon. She emerges as strong-willed and clear-eyed, a truth-teller who sees through Nixon's masks and evasions. She is sick of being a politician's wife. Their daughters, she says, know Nixon only from television. More than anyone else in the film, she supplies the conscience.

Nixon would be a great film even if there had been no Richard Nixon. In its control of mood and personality, in the way the president musters moments of brilliance even as the circle closes, in the way it shows advisers huddled terrified in the corridors of power, it takes on the resonance of classic tragedy. Tragedy requires the fall of a hero, and one of the achievements of *Nixon* is to show that greatness was within his reach. Aristotle advises that the listener to a tragic tale will "thrill with horror and melt with pity." Yes, and so we do, because Nixon was right about his life: The cards *were* stacked against him, even though he dealt most of them himself.

No Direction Home: Bob Dylan

NO MPAA RATING, 225 m., 2005

Featuring Bob Dylan, Joan Baez, Liam Clancy, Peter Yarrow, Dave Van Ronk, Allen Ginsberg, Maria Muldaur, and others. Directed by Martin Scorsese and produced by Margaret Bodde, Susan Lacy, Jeff Rosen, Scorsese, Nigel Sinclair, and Anthony Wall.

It has taken me all this time to accept Bob Dylan as the extraordinary artist he clearly is, but because of a new documentary by Martin Scorsese, I can finally see him freed from my disenchantment. I am Dylan's age, and his albums were the sound track of my college years. I never got involved in the war his fans fought over his acoustic and electric styles: I liked them all, every one.

Then in 1968 I saw *Don't Look Back*, D. A. Pennebaker's documentary about Dylan's 1965 tour of Great Britain. In my review I called the movie "a fascinating exercise in self-revelation" and added, "The portrait that emerges is not a pretty one." Dylan is seen not as a "lone, ethical figure standing up against the phonies," I wrote, but is "immature, petty, vindictive, lacking a sense of humor, overly impressed with his own importance, and not very bright."

I felt betrayed. In the film, he mercilessly puts down a student journalist and is rude to journalists, hotel managers, fans. Although Joan Baez was the first to call him on her stage when he was unknown, after she joins the tour, he does not ask her to sing with him. Eventually she bails out and goes home.

The film fixed my ideas about Dylan for years. Now Scorsese's *No Direction Home: Bob Dylan*, a 225-minute documentary that played in two parts on PBS, creates a portrait that is deep, sympathetic, perceptive, and yet finally leaves Dylan shrouded in mystery, which is where he properly lives.

The movie uses revealing interviews made recently by Dylan, but its subject matter is essentially the years between 1960, when he first came into view, and 1966, when after the British tour and a motorcycle accident he didn't tour for

eight years. He was born in 1941, and the career that made him an icon essentially happened between his twentieth and twenty-fifth years. He was a very young man from a little Minnesota town who had the mantle of a generation placed, against his will, upon his shoulders. He wasn't there at Woodstock; Arlo Guthrie was.

Early footage of his childhood is typical of many Midwestern childhoods: the small town of Hibbing, Minnesota, the homecoming parade, bands playing at dances, the kid listening to the radio and records. The early sounds he loved ran all the way from Hank Williams, Sr. and Webb Pierce to Muddy Waters, the Carter Family, and even Bobby Vee, a rock star so minor that young Robert Zimmerman for a time claimed to be Bobby Vee.

He hitched a ride to New York (or maybe he didn't hitch; his early biography is filled with romantic claims, such as that he grew up in Gallup, New Mexico). In Greenwich Village he found the folk scene, and it found him. He sang songs by Woody Guthrie, Pete Seeger, others, then was writing his own. He caught the eye of Baez, and she mentored and promoted him. Within a year he was—Dylan.

The movie has a wealth of interviews with people who knew him at the time: Baez, Pete Seeger, Mike Seeger, Liam Clancy, Dave Von Ronk, Maria Muldaur, Peter Yarrow, and promoters such as Harold Leventhal. There is significantly no mention of Ramblin' Jack Elliott. The 2000 documentary *The Ballad of Ramblin' Jack* says it was Elliott who introduced Dylan to Woody Guthrie, suggested the harmonica holder around his neck, and essentially defined his stage persona; "There wouldn't be no Bob Dylan without Ramblin' Jack," says Arlo Guthrie, who also is not in the Scorsese film.

Dylan's new friends in music all admired the art but were ambivalent about the artist. Van Ronk smiles now about the way Dylan "borrowed" his "House in New Orleans." The Beat generation, especially Jack Kerouac's *On the Road*, influenced Dylan, and there are many observations by the Beat poet Allen Ginsberg, who says he came back from India, heard a Dylan album, and wept, because he knew the torch had been passed to a new generation.

It is Ginsberg who says the single most perceptive thing in the film: For him, Dylan stood atop a column of air. His songs and his ideas rose up from within him and emerged uncluttered and pure, as if his mind, soul, body, and talent all were one.

Dylan was embraced by the left-wing musical community of the day. His "Blowin' in the Wind" became an anthem of the civil rights movement. His "Only a Pawn in Their Game" saw the killer of Medgar Evers as an insignificant cog in the machine of racism. Baez, Pete Seeger, the Staple Singers, Odetta, and Peter, Paul, and Mary—all sang his songs and considered him a fellow warrior.

But he would not be pushed or enlisted, and the crucial passages in this film show him drawing away from any attempt to define him. At the moment when he was being called the voice of his generation, he drew away from "movement" songs. A song like "Mr. Tambourine Man" was a slap in the face to his admirers, because it moved outside ideology.

Baez, interviewed before a fireplace in the kitchen of her home, still with the same beautiful face and voice, is the one who felt most betrayed: Dylan broke her heart. His change is charted through the Newport Folk Festival: early triumph, the summit in 1964 when Johnny Cash gave him his guitar, the beginning of the end with the electric set in 1965. He was backed by Mike Bloomfield and the Butterfield Blues Band in a folk-rock-blues hybrid that his fans hated. When he took the new sound on tour, audiences wanted the "protest songs" and shouted "Judas!" and "What happened to Woody Guthrie?" when he came onstage. Night after night, he opened with an acoustic set that was applauded and then came back with the Butterfield Blues Band and was booed.

"Dylan made it pretty clear he didn't want to do all that other stuff," Baez says, talking of political songs, "but I did." It was the beginning of the Vietnam era, and Dylan had withdrawn. When he didn't ask Baez onstage to sing with him on the British tour, she says quietly, "It hurt."

But what was happening inside Dylan? Was he the jerk portrayed in *Don't Look Back*? Scorsese looks more deeply. He shows countless news conferences where Dylan is assigned leadership of his generation and assaulted with inane questions about his role, message, and philosophy. A photographer asks him, "Suck your glasses" for a picture. He is asked how many protest singers he thinks there are: "There are 136."

At the 1965 Newport festival, Pete Seeger recalls: "The band was so loud, you couldn't understand one word. I kept shouting, 'Get that distortion out!' If I had an ax I'd chop the mike cable right now!" For Seeger, it was always about the words and the message. For Dylan, it was about the words, and then it became about the words and the music, and it was never particularly about the message.

Were drugs involved in these years? The movie makes not the slightest mention of them, except obliquely in a scene where Dylan and Cash do a private duet of "I'm So Lonesome I Could Cry," and it's clear they're both stoned. There is sad footage near the end of the British tour, when Dylan says he is so exhausted, "I shouldn't be singing tonight."

The archival footage comes from many sources, including documentaries by Pennebaker and Murray Lerner *(Festival)*. Many of the interviews were conducted by Michael Borofsky, and Jeff Rosen was a key contributor. But Scorsese provides the master vision, and his factual footage unfolds with the narrative power of fiction.

What it comes down to, I think, is that Robert Zimmerman from Hibbing, Minnesota, who mentions his father only because he bought the house where Bobby found a guitar, and mentions no other member of his family at all, who felt he was from nowhere, became the focus for a time of fundamental change in music and politics. His songs led that change but they transcended it. His audience was uneasy with transcendence. It kept trying to draw him back down into categories. He sang and sang, and finally, still a very young man, found himself a hero who was booed. "Isn't it something, how they still buy up all the tickets?" he asks, about a sold-out audience that hated his new music.

What I feel for Dylan now and did not feel before is empathy. His music stands and it will survive. Because it embodied our feelings, we wanted him to embody them, too. He had his own feelings. He did not want to embody. We found it hard to forgive him for that. He had the choice of caving in or dropping out. The blues band music, however good it really was, functioned also to announce the end of his days as a standard-bearer. Then after his motorcycle crash in 1966, he stopped touring for eight years and went away into a personal space where he remains.

Watching him singing in *No Direction Home*, we see no glimpse of humor, no attempt to entertain. He uses a flat, merciless delivery, more relentless cadence than melody, almost preaching. But sometimes at the press conferences we see moments of a shy, funny, playful kid inside. And just once, in his recent interviews, seen in profile against a background of black, we see the ghost of a smile.

No End in Sight

NO MPAA RATING, 122 m., 2007

With Campbell Scott (narrator), Barbara Bodine, Chris Allbritton, Colonel Lawrence Wilkerson, Colonel Paul Hughes, Walter Slocombe, Seth Moulton, David Yancey, General Jay Garner, George Packer, Gerald Burke, Hugo Gonzalez, Samantha Power, James Fallows, Linda Bilmes, Major General Paul Eaton, Marc Garlasco, Matt Sherman, Nir Rosen, Paul Pillar, Ray Jennings, Richard Armitage, Robert Hutchings, Yaroslav Trofimov. Written and directed by Charles Ferguson and produced by Alex Gibney.

Remember the scene in *A Clockwork Orange* where Alex has his eyes clamped open and is forced to watch a movie? I imagine a similar experience for the architects of our catastrophe in Iraq. I would like them to see *No End in Sight* the story of how we were led into that war, and more than three thousand American lives and hundreds of thousands of other lives were destroyed.

They might find the film of particular interest because they would know so many of the people appearing in it. This is not a documentary filled with antiwar activists or sitting ducks for Michael Moore. Most of the people in the film were important to the Bush administration. They had top government or military jobs, they had responsibility in Iraq or Washington, they implemented policy, they filed reports, they labored faithfully in service of U.S. foreign policy, and then they left the government. Some jumped, some were

pushed. They all feel disillusioned about the war and the way the White House refused to listen to them about it.

The subjects in this film now feel that American policy in Iraq was flawed from the start, that obvious measures were not taken, that sane advice was disregarded, that lies were told and believed, and that advice from people on the ground was overruled by a cabal of neocon goofballs who seemed to form a wall around the president.

The president and his inner circle *knew*, just *knew*, for example, that Saddam had or would have weapons of mass destruction, that he was in league with al-Qaida and bin Laden, and that in some way it was all hooked up with 9/11. Not all of the advice in the world could penetrate their obsession, and they fired the bearers of bad news.

It is significant, for example, that a Defense Intelligence Agency team received *orders* to find links between al-Qaida and Hussein. That there were none was ignored. Key advisor Paul Wolfowitz's immediate reaction to 9/11 was war on Iraq. Anarchy in that land was all but assured when the Iraqi army was disbanded against the urgent advice of Gen. Jay Garner, the American administrator, who was replaced by the neocon favorite Paul Bremer. That meant that a huge number of competent military men, most of them no lovers of Saddam, were rendered unemployed—and still armed. How was this disastrous decision arrived at? People directly involved said it came as an order from administration officials who had never been to Iraq.

Did Bush know and agree? They had no indication. Perhaps not. A National Intelligence report commissioned in 2004 advised against the war. Bush, who apparently did not read it, dismissed it as guesswork—a word that seems like an ideal description of his own policies.

Who is Charles Ferguson, director of this film? Onetime senior fellow of the Brookings Institute, software millionaire, originally a supporter of the war, visiting professor at MIT and Berkeley, he was trustworthy enough to inspire confidences from former top officials. They mostly felt that orders came from the precincts of Vice President Cheney, that Cheney's group disregarded advice from veteran American officials, and in at least one case channeled a decision to avoid Bush's scrutiny. The president signed, but didn't read, and you can see the quizzical, betrayed looks in the eyes of the men and women in the film, who found that the more they knew about Iraq, the less they were heeded.

Although Bush and the war continue to sink in the polls, I know from some readers that they still support both. That is their right. And if they are so sure they are right, let more young men and women die or be maimed. I doubt if they will be willing to see this film, which further documents an administration playing its private war games. No, I am distinctly *not* comparing anyone to Hitler, but I cannot help be reminded of the stories of him in his Berlin bunker, moving nonexistent troops on a map, and issuing orders to dead generals.

North Country

R, 123 m., 2005

Charlize Theron (Josey Aimes), Frances McDormand (Glory), Sean Bean (Kyle), Richard Jenkins (Hank Aimes), Jeremy Renner (Bobby Sharp), Michelle Monaghan (Sherry), Woody Harrelson (Bill White), Sissy Spacek (Alice Aimes). Directed by Niki Caro and produced by Nick Wechsler. Screenplay by Michael Seitzman, based on the book *Class Action* by Clara Bingham and Laura Leedy Gansler.

After Josey Aimes takes her kids and walks out on the boyfriend who beats her, she doesn't find a lot of sympathy back at home. "He caught you with another man? That's why he laid hands on you?" asks her father. "You can actually ask me that question?" she says. He can. In that place, at that time, whatever happened was the woman's fault. Josey has returned to her hometown in northern Minnesota, where her father works in the strip mines of the Mesabi Iron Range.

She gets a job as a hairdresser. It doesn't pay much. She can make six times more as a miner. She applies for a job and gets one, even though her new boss is not happy: "It involves lifting, driving, and all sorts of other things a woman shouldn't be doing, if you ask me. But the Supreme Court doesn't agree." Out of every thirty miners, twenty-nine are men.

Josey, who is good-looking and has an attitude, becomes a target for lust and hate, which here amount to the same thing.

North Country, which tells her story, is inspired by the life of a real person, Lois Jenson, who filed the first class-action lawsuit for sexual harassment in American history. That the suit was settled as recently as 1991 came as a surprise to me; I would have guessed the 1970s, but no, that's when the original Court decision came down. Like the Court's decisions on civil rights, it didn't change everything overnight.

The filmmakers say Josey Aimes is a character inspired by Jenson's lawsuit but otherwise is fictional; the real Jenson is not an Erin Brockovich–style firebrand and keeps a low profile. What Charlize Theron does with the character is bring compelling human detail. We believe she looks this way, sounds this way, thinks this way. After *Monster*, here is another extraordinary role from an actress who has the beauty of a fashion model but has found resources within herself for these powerful roles about unglamorous women in the world of men.

The difference is that her Aileen Wuornos, in *Monster*, was a murderer, no matter what society first did to her. All Josey Aimes wants is a house of her own, good meals and clothes for her kids, and enough money to buy her son hockey skates once in a while. Reasonable enough, it would seem, but even her father, Hank (Richard Jenkins), is opposed to women working in the mines, because it's not "women's work," and because she is taking the job away from a man "who needs it to support his family." Josey replies, "So do I." But even the women in the community believe there's something wrong if she can't find a man to take care of her.

North Country is the first movie by Niki Caro since the wonderful *Whale Rider*. That was the film about a twelve-year-old Maori girl in New Zealand who is next in an ancestral line to be chief of her people but is kept from the position because she is female. Now here is another woman told what she can't do because she is a woman. *Whale Rider* won an Oscar nomination for young Keisha Castle-Hughes, who lost to Charlize Theron. Now Theron and Caro have gone to the Academy Awards again.

Caro sees the story in terms of two worlds. The first is the world of the women in the community, exemplified by a miner named Glory (Frances McDormand), who is the only female on the union negotiating committee, and has a no-nonsense, folksy approach that disarms the men. She finds a way to get what she wants without confrontation. The other women miners are hardworking survivors who put up with obscenity and worse, and keep their heads down because they need their jobs more than they need to make a point. Josey has two problems: She is picked on more than the others, and one of her persecutors is a supervisor named Bobby Sharp (Jeremy Renner), who shares a secret with her that goes back to high school and has left him filled with guilt and hostility.

In the male world, picking on women is all in a day's work. It's what a man does. A woman operates a piece of heavy machinery unaware that a sign painted on the cab advertises sex for sale. The women find obscenities written in excrement on the walls of their locker room. When McDormand convinces the union to ask for portable toilets for the women, "who can't hold it as long as you fellas," one of the first women to use one has it toppled over while she's inside.

There is also all sorts of touching and fondling, but if a woman is going to insist on having breasts, how can a guy be blamed for copping a feel? After Bobby Sharp assaults Josey, his wife screams at her in public: "Stay away from Bobby Sharp!" It is assumed and widely reported that Josey is a tramp, and she is advised to "spend less time stirring up your female coworkers and less time in the beds of your male coworkers."

She appeals to a local lawyer (Woody Harrelson), who takes the case partly because it will establish new law. It does. The courtroom protocol in the closing scenes is not exactly conventional, but this isn't a documentary about legal procedure; it's a drama about a woman's struggle in a community where even the good people are afraid to support her. The court scenes work magnificently on that level.

North Country is one of those movies that stir you up and make you mad because it dramatizes practices you've heard about but never really visualized. We remember that McDormand played a female police officer in this same area in *Fargo,* and we value that memory because it provides a foundation for Josey Aimes. McDormand's role in this movie is different and much sadder but brings the same pluck and common sense to the screen. Put these two women together (as actors and characters) and they can accomplish just about anything. Watching them do it is a great movie experience.

Northfork

PG-13, 103 m., 2003

Peter Coyote (Eddie), Anthony Edwards (Happy), Duel Farnes (Irwin), Daryl Hannah (Flower Hercules), Nick Nolte (Father Harlan), Mark Polish (Willis O'Brien), James Woods (Walter O'Brien), Claire Forlani (Mrs. Hadfield), Robin Sachs (Cup of Tea), Ben Foster (Cod), Clark Gregg (Mr. Hadfield). Directed by Michael Polish and produced and written by Mark Polish and Michael Polish.

There has never been a movie quite like *Northfork,* but if you wanted to put it on a list, you would also include *Days of Heaven* and *Wings of Desire.* It has the desolate open spaces of the first, the angels of the second, and the feeling in both of deep sadness and pity. The movie is visionary and elegiac, more a fable than a story, and frame by frame it looks like a portfolio of spaces so wide, so open, that men must wonder if they have a role beneath such indifferent skies.

The film is set in Montana in 1955, as the town of Northfork prepares to be submerged forever beneath the waters of a dam. Three two-man evacuation teams travel the countryside in their fat black sedans, persuading the lingering residents to leave. The team members have a motivation: They've all been promised waterfront property on the lake to come. Most of the residents have already pulled out, but one stubborn citizen opens fire on the evacuators, and another plans to ride out the flood waters in his ark, which does not have two of everything but does have two wives, a detail Noah overlooked.

Other lingerers include Irwin (Duel Farnes), a pale young orphan who has been turned back in by his adoptive parents (Claire Forlani and Clark Gregg) on the grounds that he is defective. "You gave us a sick child, Father," they tell Father Harlan, the parish priest (Nick Nolte). "He can't stand the journey." The priest cares for the child himself, although the lonely little kid is able to conjure up company by imagining four angels who come to console him. Or are they imaginary? They are real for little Irwin, and that should be real enough for us.

The town evokes the empty, lonely feeling you get when you make a last tour of a home you have just moved out of. There is a scene where the six evacuators line up at the counter in a diner to order soup. "Bowl or cup?" asks the waitress, and as they consider this choice with grave poker faces, we get the feeling that only by thinking very hard about soup can they avoid exploding in a frenzy of madness. One of Father Harlan's final church services is conducted after the back wall has already been removed from his church, and the landscape behind him looks desolate.

This is the third film by the Polish twins. Michael directs, Mark acts, and Mark and Michael coproduce and cowrite. Their first was the eerie, disquieting *Twin Falls Idaho*, about Siamese twins who deal with the fact that one of them is dying. The next was *Jackpot*, about a man who tours karaoke contests, looking for his big break. Now *Northfork*, which in its visual strategy presents Montana not as a scenic tourist wonderland, but as a burial ground of foolish human dreams. Indeed, one of the subplots involves the need to dig up the bodies in the local cemetery, lest the coffins bob to the surface of the new lake; Walter O'Brien (James Woods), one of the evacuators, tells his son Willis O'Brien (Mark Polish) that if they don't move the coffin of the late Mrs. O'Brien, "When this small town becomes the biggest lake this side of the Mississippi, your mother will be the catch of the day."

Funny? Yes, and so is the soup scene in the diner, but you don't laugh out loud a lot in this film because you fear the noise might echo under its limitless leaden sky. This is like a black-and-white film made in color. In some shots, only the pale skin tones contain any color at all. In talking with the Polish brothers after the film premiered at Sundance 2003, I learned that they limited all the costumes, props, and sets to shades of gray, and the cinematographer, M. David Mullen, has drained

color from his film so that there is a bleakness here that gets into your bones.

Against this cold is the pale warmth of the angels, who are evoked by Irwin. To console himself for being abandoned by his adoptive parents, he believes that he is a lost angel, fallen to Earth and abducted by humans who amputated his wings. Indeed, he has scars on his shoulder blades. The angels include Flower Hercules (Daryl Hannah), who seems neither man nor woman; Cod (Ben Foster), a cowboy who never speaks; Happy (Anthony Edwards), who is almost blind, but perhaps can see something through the bizarre glasses he wears, with their multiple lenses; and Cup of Tea (Robin Sachs), who talks enough to make up for Happy.

Of these the most moving is Flower Hercules, who seems to feel Irwin's loneliness and pain as her/his own. Daryl Hannah evokes a quality of care for the helpless that makes her a tender guardian angel. Since the evacuators have a stock of angel's wings, which they sometimes offer as inducements to reluctant homeowners, the thought persists that angels are meant to be real in the film, just as they are in *Wings of Desire*, and only those who cannot believe think Irwin has dreamed them up.

Northfork is not an entertaining film so much as an entrancing one. There were people at Sundance, racing from one indie hipness to another, who found it too slow. But the pace is well chosen for the tone, and the tone evokes the fable, and the fable is about the death of a town and of mankind's brief purchase on this barren plat of land, and it is unseemly to hurry a requiem. The film suggests that of the thousands who obeyed the call, "Go West, young man!" some simply disappeared into the wilderness and were buried, as Northfork is about to be buried, beneath the emptiness of it all.

Nosferatu
R, 63 m., 1979

Klaus Kinski (Count Dracula), Isabelle Adjani (Lucy Harker), Bruno Ganz (Jonathan Harker). Directed, produced, and written by Werner Herzog.

Set aside for the moment the details of the Dracula story. They've lost their meaning.

They've been run through a thousand vampire movies too many. It's as easy these days to play Dracula as Santa Claus. The suit comes with the job. The kids sit on your knee and you ask them what they want and this year they want blood.

Consider instead Count Dracula. He bears a terrible cross but he lives in a wonderful sphere. He comes backed by music of the masters and dresses in red and black, the colors De Sade found finally the most restful. Dracula's shame as he exchanges intimacies and elegant courtesies with you is that tonight or sometime soon he will need to drink your blood. What an embarrassing thing to know about someone else.

Werner Herzog's *Nosferatu* concerns itself with such knowledge. *Nosferatu.* A word for *the vampire.* English permits "vampire movies"—but a "nosferatu movie?" Say "vampire" and your lips must grin. The other word looks like sucking lemons. Perfect. There is nothing pleasant about Herzog's vampire, and this isn't a movie for Creature Feature fans. There are movies for people who like to yuk it up and make barfing sounds, God love 'em, while Christopher Lee lets the blood dribble down his chin, but they're not the audience for *Nosferatu.* This movie isn't even scary. It's so slow it's meditative at times, but it is the most evocative series of images centered around the idea of the vampire that I have ever seen—since F. W. Murnau's *Nosferatu*, which was made in 1922.

That is why we're wise to forget the details of the basic Dracula story. *Nosferatu* doesn't pay them heed. It is about the mood and *style* of vampirism, about the terrible seductive pity of it all. There is a beautiful passage early in the film showing the hero, Jonathan Harker, traveling from his home village to the castle of Dracula. The count has summoned him because he is considering the purchase of another home. Harker makes the journey by horse path. He enters into a high mountain pass filled with tenuous cloud layers that drift by a little too fast, as if God were sucking in his breath. The music is *not* your standard creepy Loony Tunes, but a fierce melody of exhilaration and dread. Deeper and deeper rides Harker into the cold gray flint of the peaks. Some will say this passage goes on too long

and that nothing happens during it. I wish the whole movie were this empty.

Before long, we are regarding the count himself. He is played totally without ego by Klaus Kinski. The *count* has a monstrous ego, of course—it is Kinski who has none. There is never a moment when we sense this actor enjoying what a fine juicy cornpone role he has, with fangs and long sharp fingernails and a cape to swirl. No, Kinski has grown far too old inside to play Dracula like that: He makes his body and gaunt skull transparent, so the role can flicker through.

Sit through *Nosferatu* twice, or three times. Cleanse yourself of the expectation that things will happen. Get with the flow. This movie works like an LP record: You can't love the music until you've heard the words so often they're sounds. It's in German with English subtitles. It would be just fine with no subtitles, dubbed into an unknown tongue. The need to know what Dracula is saying at any given moment is a bourgeois affectation. Dracula is *always* saying, "I am speaking with you now as a meaningless courtesy in preface to the unspeakable event that we both know is going to take place between us sooner rather than later."

No Way Out

R, 114 m., 1987

Kevin Costner (Tom Farrell), Gene Hackman (David Brice), Sean Young (Susan Atwell), Will Patton (Scott Pritchard), Howard Duff (Senator Duvall), George Dzundza (Sam Hesselman), Jason Bernard (Major Donovan), Iman (Nina Beka). Directed by Roger Donaldson and produced by Laura Ziskin and Robert Garland. Screenplay by Garland.

No Way Out is one of those thrillers like *Jagged Edge,* where the plot gives us a great deal of information, but the more we know, the less we understand. It's like a terrifying jigsaw puzzle. And because the story is so tightly wound and the performances are so good, I found myself really caring about the characters. That's the test of a good thriller: When you stop thinking about the mechanics of the plot and start caring about the people. The movie begins with the same basic situation that was always one of Alfred Hitchcock's favorites: An innocent man stands wrongly accused of a crime, and all the evidence seems to point right back to him. In *No Way Out,* there are a couple of neat twists. One is when the innocent man is placed in charge of the investigation of the crime.

The man is played by Kevin Costner in a performance I found a lot more complex and interesting than his work in *The Untouchables.* He plays a career navy man who is assigned to the personal staff of the secretary of defense (Gene Hackman). Hackman and his devoted assistant (Will Patton) want Costner to handle some sensitive assignments for them involving the secretary's pet defense projects.

All of those details are handled in the first few minutes, and after the movie springs a genuine erotic surprise. Costner goes to a diplomatic reception to meet Hackman. There is a beautiful young woman at the party. Their eyes meet. The chemistry is right. They leave almost immediately, and the woman throws herself at Costner in hungry passion.

They have an affair. The woman (Sean Young) is friendly, but mysterious, and eventually Costner finds out why: She is also Hackman's mistress. And that leads to the night when Hackman attacks her in a jealous rage, and she dies. Because Costner saw Hackman going into her apartment as he was leaving, he knows who committed the crime. But there are reasons why he cannot say what he knows. And then Patton determines to mastermind a cover-up and enlists Costner.

At about this point you may be thinking I have revealed too much of the plot. I haven't. *No Way Out* is truly labyrinthine and ingenious. The director, Roger Donaldson, sometimes uses two or three suspense-building devices at the same time, such as when a search of the Pentagon coincides with Costner's attempt to obtain evidence against Hackman, and the slow progress of a computer that may, or may not, enhance a photograph that could hang Costner.

A lot of what goes on in the film is psychological and not merely plot-driven. For example, there's the interesting performance of Patton, who says early on that he would willingly sacrifice his life for Hackman and who is later revealed to have more than one reason for his devotion. There's another good performance by George Dzundza (*The Deer Hunter*)

as the wheelchair-bound Pentagon computer expert, trying to be a nice guy without ever really understanding what he's in the middle of.

The movie contains some of the ingredients I have declared myself tired of in recent thrillers, including a couple of chases. But here the chases do not exist simply on their own accord; they grow out of the logic of the plot. And as the plot moves on it grows more and more complex, until a final twist that some people will think is simply gratuitous but that does fit in with the overall logic.

Movies such as this are very hard to make. For proof, look at the wreckage of dozens of unsuccessful thrillers every year. *No Way Out* is a superior example of the genre, a film in which a simple situation grows more and more complex until it turns into a nightmare not only for the hero but also for everyone associated with him. At the same time, it respects the audience's intelligence, gives us a great deal of information, trusts us to put it together, and makes the intellectual analysis of the situation one of the movie's great pleasures.

Nowhere in Africa
NO MPAA RATING, 140 m., 2003

Juliane Köhler (Jettel Redlich), Merab Ninidze (Walter Redlich), Lea Kurka (Younger Regina), Karoline Eckertz (Teenage Regina), Sidede Onyulo (Owuor [Cook]), Matthias Habich (Süsskind). Directed by Caroline Link and produced by Peter Herrmann. Screenplay by Link, based on the book by Stefanie Zweig.

It is so rare to find a film where you become quickly, simply absorbed in the story. You want to know what happens next. Caroline Link's *Nowhere in Africa* is a film like that, telling the story of a German Jewish family that escapes from the Nazis by going to live and work on a farm in rural Kenya. It's a hardscrabble farm in a dry region, and the father, who used to be a lawyer, is paid a pittance to be the manager. At first his wife hates it. Their daughter, who is five when she arrives, takes to Africa with an immediate and instinctive love.

We see the mother and daughter, Jettel and Regina Redlich (Juliane Köhler and Lea Kurka), in their comfortable world in Frankfurt. The mother likes clothes, luxury, elegance. Her husband, Walter (Merab Ninidze), reading the ominous signs of the rise of Nazism, has gone ahead to East Africa, and now writes asking them to join him—"and please bring a refrigerator, which we will really need, and not our china or anything like that." What Jettel brings is a ballroom gown, which will be spectacularly unnecessary.

The marriage is a troubled one. Jettel thinks herself in a godforsaken place, and Walter, who works hard but is not a natural farmer, has little sympathy with her. Their sex life fades: "You only let me under your shirt when I'm a lawyer," he tells her once when his advance is turned away. But little Regina loves every moment of every day. She makes friends with the African children her age, with that uncomplicated acceptance that children have, and seems to learn their language overnight. She picks up their lore and stories, and is at home in the bush.

Jettel, meanwhile, has a rocky start with Owuor (Sidede Onyulo), the farm cook. He is a tall, proud, competent man from the regional tribe, the Masai, who soon loves Regina like his own daughter. Jettel makes the mistake of treating him like a servant when he sees himself as a professional. He never compromises local custom regarding cooks. Asked to help dig a well, he explains, "I'm a cook. Cooks don't dig in the ground." And for that matter, "Men don't carry water."

They are outsiders here in three ways: as white people, as Germans, and as Jews. The first presents the least difficulty, because the tribal people on the land are friendly and helpful. Their status as Germans creates an ironic situation when war is declared and they are rounded up by the British colonial authorities as enemy aliens; this is absurd, since they are refugees from the enemy, but before the mistake can be corrected they are transported to Nairobi and interred—ironically, in a luxury hotel that has been pressed into service. As high tea is served to them, a British officer asks the hotel manager if the prisoners need to be treated so well. "These are our standards, and we are not willing to compromise," the manager replies proudly.

To the Africans, they are not Jews, Germans, or aliens, but simply white farmers; the rise of anticolonialism is still in the future in this district. Regina, so young when she left Europe, therefore hasn't tasted anti-Semitism until her parents send her into town to a boarding school. Now a pretty teenager (played by Karoline Eckertz), she is surprised to hear the headmaster say, "The Jews will stand outside the classroom as we recite the Lord's Prayer."

As time passes and the beauty and complexity of the land become clear to Jettel, she begins slowly to feel more at home. Her husband is vindicated in moving his family to Africa; letters arrive with sad news of family members deported to death camps. But he always considers Africa a temporary haven, and his attention is focused on a return to Europe. Each member of the Redlich family has a separate arc: The mother grows to like Africa as the father likes it less, and their daughter loves it always.

The story is told through the eyes of the daughter (Eckertz is the narrator); Caroline Link's screenplay is based on a best-selling German novel by Stefanie Zweig, who treats such matters as Jettel's brief affair with a British officer as they might have been perceived, and interpreted, by the daughter. Link's style permits the narrative to flow as it might in memory, and although there are dramatic high points (such as a fire and a plague of locusts), they are not interruptions but part of the rhythm of African life, and are joined by the sacrifice of a lamb (for rain) and an all-night ritual ceremony that the young girl will never forget.

Link's film, which won five German Oscars, including best film, won the 2003 Academy Award as Best Foreign Film, and comes after another extraordinary film, her 1997 *Beyond Silence*, which was an Oscar nominee. That one was also about the daughter of a troubled marriage; the heroine was the hearing child of a deaf couple. I respond strongly to her interest in good stories and vivid, well-defined characters; this film is less message than memory, depending on the strength of the material to make all of the points. We feel as if we have lived it.

O

An Officer and a Gentleman

R, 126 m., 1982

Richard Gere (Zack Mayo), Debra Winger (Paula Pokrifki), Lou Gossett, Jr. (Sergeant Foley), David Keith (Sid Worley), Robert Loggia (Byron Mayo), Lisa Blount (Lynette), Lisa Eilbacher (Casey Seeger). Directed by Taylor Hackford and produced by Martin Elfand. Screenplay by Douglas Day Stewart.

An Officer and a Gentleman is the best movie about love that I've seen in a long time. Maybe that's because it's not about "love" as a Hollywood concept, but about love as growth, as learning to accept other people for who and what they are. There's romance in this movie, all right, and some unusually erotic sex, but what makes the film so special is that the sex and everything else is presented within the context of its characters finding out who they are, what they stand for—and what they will *not* stand for.

The movie takes place in and around a Naval Aviation Officer Candidate School in Washington state. Every thirteen weeks, a new group of young men and women come here to see if they can survive a grueling session of physical and academic training. If they pass, they graduate to flight school. About half fail. Across Puget Sound, the local young women hope for a chance to meet an eligible future officer. They dream of becoming officers' wives, and in some of their families, we learn, this dream has persisted for two generations.

After the first month of training, there is a Regimental Ball. The women turn out with hope in their hearts and are sized up by the candidates. A man and a woman (Richard Gere and Debra Winger) pair off. We know more about them than they know about one another. He is a loner and a loser, whose mother died when he was young and whose father is a drunk. She is the daughter of an officer candidate who loved and left her mother twenty years before. They dance, they talk, they begin to date, they fall in love. She would like to marry him, but she refuses to do what the other local girls are willing to do—get pregnant or fake pregnancy to trap a future officer. For his part, the man is afraid of commitment, afraid of love, incapable of admitting that he cares for someone. All he wants is a nice, simple affair, and a clean break at the end of OCS.

This love story is told in counterpoint with others. There's the parallel affair between another candidate and another local girl. She *is* willing to trap her man. His problem is, he really loves her. He's under the thumb of his family, but he's willing to do the right thing, if she'll give him the chance.

All of the off-base romances are backdrops for the main event, which is the training program. The candidates are under the supervision of a tough drill sergeant (Lou Gossett, Jr.) who has seen them come and seen them go and is absolutely uncompromising in his standards. There's a love-hate relationship between the sergeant and his trainees, especially the rebellious, resentful Gere. And Gossett does such a fine job of fine-tuning the line between his professional standards and his personal emotions that the performance deserves its Academy Award.

The movie's method is essentially to follow its characters through the thirteen weeks, watching them as they change and grow. That does wonders for the love stories, because by the end of the film we know these people well enough to care about their decisions and to have an opinion about what they should do. In the case of Gere and Winger, the romance is absolutely absorbing because it's so true to life, right down to the pride that causes these two to pretend they don't care for each other as much as they really do. When it looks as if Gere is going to throw it all away—is going to turn his back on a good woman who loves him, just because he's too insecure to deal with her love—the movie isn't just playing with emotions, it's being very perceptive about human behavior.

But maybe I'm being too analytical about why *An Officer and a Gentleman* is so good. This is a wonderful movie precisely because it's so willing to deal with matters of the heart. Love stories are among the rarest of movies these days (and when we finally get one, it's likely to involve an extraterrestrial). Maybe they're rare because writers and filmmakers no longer believe they understand what goes

549

on between modern men and women. *An Officer and a Gentleman* takes chances, takes the time to know and develop its characters, and by the time this movie's wonderful last scene comes along, we know exactly what's happening, and why, and it makes us very happy.

The Official Story

NO MPAA RATING, 110 m., 1985

Hector Alterio (Roberto), Norma Aleandro (Alicia), Chela Ruiz (Sara), Chunchuna Villafane (Ana), Hugo Arana (Enrique). Directed by Luis Puenzo and produced by Marcelo Pineyro. Screenplay by Puenzo and Aida Bortnik.

Five years after the arrival of her adopted daughter, Alicia finds herself asking some questions. Where, exactly, did the little girl come from? Was she indeed obtained through the normal adoption channels in Argentina, as her husband insists, or was she stolen from a mother who was a political prisoner? Is the real mother still alive? Is it moral for her to ignore those questions, just because she loves her adopted daughter so much?

These are the heartbreaking dilemmas of *The Official Story,* a film that deals with the turmoil in Argentina through the story of a single family. Alicia is married to Roberto, a wealthy, powerful man with connections in industry and government. Her life centers on their adopted daughter. She is vaguely aware of some of the unhappy realities of recent Argentinean politics—the roundups of leftists and opponents of the government, who became "missing persons" and presumably were killed in a secret holocaust. But until Ana, an old high school friend, reenters her life, Alicia does not understand how those events might affect her.

At first Ana does not want to talk about the experiences she has been through. But then she begins to reopen her wounds. She tells Alicia that her lover was a leftist opponent of the government. After her lover disappeared, Ana was taken captive by the government and tortured for information about his whereabouts. She could tell them nothing. Eventually she was released.

Ana's story makes Alicia uncomfortable. She tells her husband about it, but he dismisses it as rumor and invention. Alicia begins to realize that her husband may be part of the repressive establishment. One day, walking downtown, she comes across a demonstration by family members of the missing. She hears stories that some of the prisoners were pregnant and that their children were taken away at birth. Could that be the story of her own daughter? In one of the most powerful scenes in the movie, she takes down the clothing her daughter came dressed in and touches it gently, and we can read her mind: She is thinking that her daughter's natural mother was the person who put these clothes on the baby girl.

The Official Story is part polemic, part thriller, part tragedy. It belongs on the list with such films as *Z, Missing,* and *El Norte,* which examine the human aspects of political unrest. It is a movie that asks some very hard questions. Should Alicia search for the real mother of her daughter? Is her own love no less real? What would be "best" for the little girl?

Alicia meets an old woman who may, or may not, be the grandmother of the adopted daughter. The two women become close, in a strange way. Political arrogance and heartlessness may have taken a child from one family and assigned it to another, but at some deep and fundamental level, these two women understand each other. Both of them are made to face the reality of losing a daughter, and although they should be enemies, they find strength from each other. The way this particular relationship is developed is one of the wonders of this film, and provides its emotional center, as love and honor try to find a way to exist in the face of official cruelty.

Alicia is played in the movie by Norma Aleandro, whose performance won the best actress award at the 1985 Cannes Film Festival. It is a performance that will be hard to forget, particularly since so much of it is internal. Some of the key moments in the film come as we watch Aleandro and realize what must be taking place inside her mind, and inside her conscience. Most political films play outside the countries that they are about; *The Official Story* is now actually playing in Argentina, where it must be almost unbearably painful for some of the members of its audiences. It was almost as painful for me.

Oh! What a Lovely War

G, 144 m., 1969

Laurence Olivier (Sir John French), Michael Redgrave (Sir Henry Wilson), John Mills (Sir Douglas Haig), Vanessa Redgrave (Sylvia Pankhurst), John Gielgud (Count von Berchtold), Dirk Bogarde (Stephen), Ralph Richardson (Sir Edward Grey), Maggie Smith (Music Hall Star). Directed by Richard Attenborough and produced by Brian Duffy and Attenborough. Screenplay by Len Deighton, based on the plays by Charles Chilton and Joan Littlewood.

It's a mistake to review *Oh! What a Lovely War* as a movie. It isn't one, but it is an elaborately staged tableau, a dazzling use of the camera to achieve essentially theatrical effects. And judged on that basis, Richard Attenborough has given us a breathtaking evening.

I wasn't lucky enough to see Joan Littlewood's original London stage production of *Lovely War*, back in the early 1960s. I was in London at the time, but I was a rash youth and went to see the Windmill girls instead. No matter. It's a fallacy, I think, to judge a film on the basis of how faithful it is to the book, or to the play, or to anything other than itself.

Like most people, I know World War I at second- or third-hand, through such sources as Robert Graves's *Goodbye to All That*. The most dramatic point Graves makes is that the war almost literally exterminated the generation that would have ruled Britain in the 1930s and 1940s. Something like 90 percent of the field officers were killed on some fronts. Joseph Losey's film *King and Country* shows us Tom Courtenay as the lone survivor of his original unit; every other man had been killed, and many of their replacements had died as well. This apparently was fairly common.

And so this tragic event sank into the bones of the British memory. America, which came into the war rather late and sustained much lighter casualties, could afford the luxury of a "lost generation" in the 1920s. England literally lost her generation; it was dead and buried, and we seem to see it beneath the countless crosses stretching out behind John Mills in the last, stunning graveyard shot in *Oh! What a Lovely War*.

And yet war films and books usually have not recorded this loss, or the enormity of the stupidity that caused it. Those that have (such as *King and Country*) have done it in microcosm; we care for the Courtenay character, but we do not reflect on the total war. *Oh! What a Lovely War* does re-create this time, in a bitter mixture of history, satire, detail, panorama, and music.

Especially music. There is something paradoxical in the thought of singing about a war, and yet cheap popular songs often capture the spirit of a time better than any collection of speeches and histories. Littlewood, and Attenborough after her, present the war as a British music hall review; there's a lot of smiling up front, but backstage you can see the greasepaint and smell the sweat, and the smiles become desperate, and there begins to be blood.

This sense is captured most tellingly in Maggie Smith's scene. She plays a robust, patriotic broad who lures the young men from the audience to the stage with promises of love and implications of heroic death. But death is reserved for the young, not for the old, and John Mills (as Sir Douglas Haig) stays far behind the lines, studying the front from an observation tower. Meanwhile, politicians, kings, and rulers play stupid games of diplomacy and etiquette, and "acceptable losses" are counted in the hundreds of thousands. But always everyone whistles a happy tune. . . .

The film is populated with a gallery of British stars. All the knights and ladies seem to be there, and everyone else, too: Olivier, Gielgud, Richardson, at least three Redgraves (and Vanessa looking especially spirited), and the rest. But the important thing is that Attenborough doesn't use them as a freak show, as Michael Todd did with his cameos in *Around the World in 80 Days*, or as happens in the upcoming *Battle of Britain*. The abilities of these great actors are employed, as well as their names and faces, and together they re-create a horrible war. And the deepest impact of the film comes from the realization that there have been wars even more horrible since this one.

Oldboy

R, 120 m., 2005

Min-sik Choi (Dae-su Oh), Ji-tae Yoo (Woo-jin Lee), Hye-jung Gang (Mido). Directed by Chan-wook Park and produced by Dong-joo Kim. Screenplay by Jo-yun Hwang, Joon-hyung Lim, and Park.

A man gets violently drunk and is chained to the wall in a police station. His friend comes and bails him out. While the friend is making a telephone call, the man disappears from an empty city street in the middle of the night. The man regains consciousness in what looks like a shabby hotel room. A bed, a desk, a TV, a bathroom cubicle. There is a steel door with a slot near the floor for his food tray. Occasionally a little tune plays, the room fills with gas, and when he regains consciousness the room has been cleaned, his clothes have been changed, and he has received a haircut.

This routine continues for fifteen years. He is never told who has imprisoned him, or why. He watches TV until it becomes his world. He fills one journal after another with his writings. He pounds the wall until his fists grow bloody, and then hardened. He screams. He learns from TV that his blood and fingerprints were found at the scene of his wife's murder. That his daughter has been adopted in Sweden. That if he were to escape, he would be a wanted man.

Oldboy, by the Korean director Chan-wook Park, watches him objectively, asking no sympathy, standing outside his plight. When, later, he does talk with the man who has imprisoned him, the man says: "I'm sort of a scholar, and what I study is you."

In its sexuality and violence, this is the kind of movie that can no longer easily be made in the United States; the standards of a puritanical minority, imposed on broadcasting and threatened even for cable, make studios unwilling to produce films that might face uncertain distribution. But content does not make a movie good or bad—it is merely what it is about. *Oldboy* is a powerful film not because of what it depicts, but because of the depths of the human heart it strips bare.

The man, named Dae-su Oh (Min-sik Choi), is a wretch when we first meet him, a drunk who has missed his little daughter's birthday and now sits forlornly in the police station, ridiculously wearing the angel's wings he bought her as a present. He is not a bad man, but alcohol has rendered him useless.

When he suddenly finds himself freed from his bizarre captivity fifteen years later, he is a different person, focused on revenge, ridiculously responsive to kindness. Wandering into a restaurant, he meets a young woman who, he knows from the TV, is Korea's "Chef of the Year." This is Mido (Hye-jung Gang). Sensing that he has suffered, feeling an instinctive sympathy, she takes him home with her, hears his story, cares for him, comes to love him. Meanwhile he sets out on a methodical search to find the secret of his captivity. He was fed pot stickers day after day, until their taste was burned into his memory, and he travels the city's restaurants until he finds the one that supplied his meals. That is the key to tracking down his captors.

It is also, really, the beginning of the movie, the point at which it stops being a mystery and becomes a tragedy in the classical sense. I will not reveal the several secrets that lie ahead for Dae-su, except to say that they come not as shabby plot devices, but as one turn after another of the screws of mental and physical anguish and poetic justice. I can mention a virtuoso sequence in which Dae-su fights with several of his former jailers, his rage so great that he is scarcely slowed by the knife sticking in his back. This is a man consumed by the need for revenge, who eventually discovers he was imprisoned by another man whose need was no less consuming, and infinitely more diabolical.

I am not an expert on the Korean cinema, which is considered in critical circles as one of the most creative in the world (*Oldboy* won the grand jury prize at Cannes 2004). I can say that of the Korean films I've seen, only one (*The YMCA Baseball Team*) did not contain extraordinary sadomasochism. *Oldboy* contains a tooth-pulling scene that makes Laurence Olivier's Nazi dentist in *Marathon Man* look like a healer. And there is a scene during which an octopus is definitely harmed during the making of the movie.

These scenes do not play for shock value, but are part of the whole. Dae-su has been locked up for fifteen years without once seeing another living person. For him the close presence of anyone is like a blow to all of his senses. When he says in a restaurant, "I want to eat something that is alive," we understand (a) that living seafood is indeed consumed as a delicacy in Asia, and (b) he wants to eat the life, not the food, because he has been buried in death for fifteen years.

Why would Mido, young, pretty, and talented, take this wretched man into her life? Perhaps because he is so manifestly helpless. Perhaps because she believes his story, and even the reason why he cannot reclaim his real name or identity. Perhaps because in fifteen years he has been transformed into a man she senses is strong and good, when he was once weak and despicable. From his point of view, love is joined with salvation, acceptance, forgiveness, and the possibility of redemption.

All of this is in place during the several scenes of revelation that follow, providing a context and giving them a deeper meaning. Yes, the ending is improbable in its complexity, but it is not impossible, and it is not unmotivated. *Oldboy* ventures to emotional extremes, but not without reason. We are so accustomed to "thrillers" that exist only as machines for creating diversion that it's a shock to find a movie in which the action, however violent, makes a statement and has a purpose.

Oliver!

G, 146 m., 1968

Mark Lester (Oliver), Ron Moody (Fagin), Oliver Reed (Bill Sikes), Shani Wallis (Nancy), Jack Wild (Artful Dodger), Hug Griffith (Magistrate), Harry Secombe (Mr. Bumble). Directed by Carol Reed and produced by John Woolf. Screenplay by Vernon Harris, based on the musical by Lionel Bart.

Sir Carol Reed's *Oliver!* is a treasure of a movie. It is very nearly universal entertainment, one of those rare films such as *The Wizard of Oz* that appeal in many ways to all sorts of people. It will be immediately exciting to the children, I think, because of the story and the unforgettable Dickens characters. Adults will like it for the sweep and zest of its production. And as a work of popular art, it will stand the test of time, I guess. It is as well made as a film can be.

Not for a moment, I suspect, did Reed imagine he had to talk down to the children in his audience. Not for a moment are the children in the cast treated as children. They're equal participants in the great adventure, and

they have to fend for themselves or bloody well get out of the way. This isn't a watered-down lollipop. It's got bite and malice along with the romance and humor.

The basis of its success, perhaps, is that Reed took a long look at the character of Oliver Twist. The problem with Oliver is that he isn't really very interesting, is he? He's a young, noble, naive lad whose main duty in Dickens's novel is to stand about while a marvelous collection of heroes and villains struggle over his destiny.

The weakness in the stage musical *Oliver!*, and even in David Lean's film *Oliver Twist* (1948), was that they made too much of Oliver and didn't quite know what to do with him. Reed does; he establishes Oliver as a bright, attractive young boy; gives him some scenes so we get to care about him and admire his pluck; and then focuses his movie on the characters who are *really* interesting: Fagin, Bill Sikes, the Artful Dodger, and Nancy. The movie belongs so much to Fagin and the Dodger, in fact, that when we see them marching down the road in their last scene we think the movie should stop right there, instead of giving us a final look at Oliver. Still, Oliver is well acted by Mark Lester (who played the youngest boy in Jack Clayton's *Our Mother's House*).

Reed gives us the seedy underworld of London (with shadows as long and cobblestones as rough as the Vienna of his *The Third Man*). We get Bill Sikes and his mangy dog. We get the rowdy life of the alehouse under an embankment, and we get a Nancy who is, at last, as tough and harshly beautiful as Dickens must have imagined.

And we get Fagin! Ron Moody, who is hardly over thirty, has somehow stepped into this character twice his age and made it his own. When he advises Oliver, *You've Got to Pick a Pocket or Two*, and when he sings "I'm Reviewing the Situation," he creates a marvelous screen portrait.

The other really memorable characterization is by Jack Wild, the quintessence of Artful Dodgerdom. But the film is strong in casting, and we get a villainous Bill Sikes from Oliver Reed and an unctuous Bumble from Harry Secombe; and Shari Wallis, as Nancy, makes us believe in her difficult, complicated character.

The problem with the road show format, as I've observed before, is that the movie has to be longer and more expensive than usual; those are the ground rules. Many a delightful movie has been ruined by being bloated up to road show "standards," and the challenge to a director in this genre is to spend his money wisely and pace his movie well.

Oliver succeeds at both. John Box, the designer, has created magnificent sets that reproduce Victorian England in perfect detail—and never to excess. John Green, musical director at MGM during its "golden age of musicals" in the late 1940s and early 1950s, was brought in to do the music and has hit the right balance.

Oliver! succeeds finally because of its taste. It never stoops for cheap effects and never insults our intelligence. And because we can trust it, we can let ourselves go with it, and we do. It is a splendid experience.

Once Upon a Time in America

R, 227 m., 1984

Robert De Niro (Noodles), James Woods (Max), Elizabeth McGovern (Deborah), Treat Williams (Jimmy), Tuesday Weld (Carol), Burt Young (Joe). Directed by Sergio Leone and produced by Arnon Milchan. Screenplay by L. Benvenuti, P. De Bernardo, E. Medioli, F. Arcalli, F. Ferrini, Leone, and S. Kaminski.

This was a murdered movie, now brought back to life on cassette. Sergio Leone's *Once Upon a Time in America*, which in its intended 227-minute version is an epic poem of violence and greed, was chopped by ninety minutes for U.S. theatrical release into an incomprehensible mess without texture, timing, mood, or sense. The rest of the world saw the original film, which I saw at the Cannes Film Festival. In America, a tragic decision was made. When the full-length version (now available in cassette form) played at the 1984 Cannes Film Festival, I wrote:

"Is the film too long? Yes and no. Yes, in the sense that it takes real concentration to understand Leone's story construction, in which everything may or may not be an opium dream, a nightmare, a memory, or a flashback, and that we have to keep track of characters and relationships over fifty years. No, in the

sense that the movie is compulsively and continuously watchable and that the audience did not stir or grow restless as the epic unfolded."

The movie tells the story of five decades in the lives of four gangsters from New York City—childhood friends who are merciless criminals almost from the first, but who have a special bond of loyalty to each other. When one of them breaks that bond, or thinks he does, he is haunted by guilt until late in his life, when he discovers that he was not the betrayer but the betrayed. Leone's original version tells this story in a complex series of flashbacks, memories, and dreams. The film opens with two scenes of terrifying violence, moves to an opium den where the Robert De Niro character is seeking to escape the consequences of his action, and then establishes its tone with a scene of great power: A ceaselessly ringing telephone, ringing forever in the conscience of a man who called the cops and betrayed his friends. The film moves back and forth in a tapestry of episodes, which all fit together into an emotional whole. There are times when we don't understand exactly what is happening, but never a time when we don't feel confidence in the film's narrative.

That version was not seen in American theaters, although it is now available on cassette. Instead, the whole structure of flashbacks was junked. The telephone rings once. The poetic transitions are gone. The movie has been wrenched into apparent chronological order, scenes have been thrown out by the handful, relationships are now inexplicable, and the audience is likely to spend much of its time in complete bewilderment. It is a great irony that this botched editing job was intended to "clarify" the film.

Here are some of the specific problems with the shortened version. A speakeasy scene comes before a newspaper headline announces that Prohibition has been ratified. Prohibition is then repealed, on what feels like the next day but must be fourteen years later. Two gangsters talk about robbing a bank in front of a woman who has never been seen before in the film; they've removed the scene explaining who she is. A labor leader turns up, unexplained, and involves the gangsters in an inexplicable situation. He later sells out, but to whom? Men come to kill De Niro's girlfriend, a character we've hardly met, and we don't know if they come from the mob or the police. And here's a real howler: At the end of the shortened version, De Niro leaves a room he has never seen before by walking through a secret panel in the wall. How did he know it was there? In the long version, he was told it was there. In the short version, his startling exit shows simple contempt for the audience.

Many of the film's most beautiful shots are missing from the short version, among them a bravura moment when a flash-forward is signaled by the unexpected appearance of a Frisbee, and another where the past becomes the present as the Beatles' "Yesterday" sneaks into the sound track. Relationships are truncated, scenes are squeezed of life, and I defy anyone to understand the plot of the short version. The original *Once Upon a Time in America* gets a four-star rating. The shorter version is a travesty.

Once Upon a Time . . . When We Were Colored

PG, 111 m., 1996

Al Freeman, Jr. (Poppa), Phylicia Rashad (Ma Ponk), Charles Earl (Spud) Taylor, Jr. (Cliff at Five), Willie Norwood, Jr. (Cliff at Twelve), Damon Hines (Cliff at Sixteen), Leon (Melvin), Iona Morris (Showgirl), Richard Roundtree (Cleve), Polly Bergen (Miss Maybry), Paula Kelly (Ma Pearl), Bernie Casey (Mr. Walter), Isaac Hayes (Preacher Hurn). Directed by Tim Reid and produced by Reid and Michael Bennett. Screenplay by Paul W. Cooper, based on the book by Clifton Taulbert.

Tim Reid's *Once Upon a Time . . .When We Were Colored* re-creates the world of a black community in the rural South in the years from 1946 to 1962, as hard-line segregation gradually fell to the assault of the civil rights movement. It is a memory of the close bonds of family, friends, and church that grew up to sustain such communities, in a society where an American version of apartheid was the law.

The key word there is "community," and rarely has a film more movingly shown how people who work, live, and pray together can find a common strength and self-respect. There are eighty-three speaking parts in this ambitious film, which spans four generations and remembers not only the joy of Saturday night dances and Sunday church socials, but also the cruel pain of a little boy learning to spell his first words: "white" and "colored." By the end of the film, we feel we know the people in the "colored town" of Glen Allan, Mississippi, and we understand why such communities produced so many good and capable citizens.

The movie is based on a 1989 book by Clifton Taulbert, who published it with a small Kansas City firm and then saw it reach the best-seller lists after a strong review in the *New York Times;* it was the first book requested by Nelson Mandela after he was released from prison. One of its early readers was the television actor Tim Reid *(WKRP in Cincinnati, Frank's Place),* who determined to film it even though it seemed "commercial" in no conventional sense. He assembled the enormous cast, shot on location in North Carolina, and has made a film that is both an impressive physical production (the period looks and feels absolutely authentic) and a deeply moving emotional experience. In many ways this film compares with *The Color Purple,* although it has a simpler, more direct, less melodramatic quality; it is not about a few lives, but about life itself as it was experienced in the segregated South.

There are so many characters that to attempt a plot summary would be pointless. Better to remember some of the extraordinary scenes. Much of the story is told through the eyes of a young boy named Cliff (played at different ages by three actors), who is raised by his great-grandparents (Al Freeman, Jr. and Paula Kelly). As he watches and learns, so do we, especially in a scene where Poppa, his great-grandfather, takes him to town for a treat. It is on this trip that he makes the mistake of going into the "white" washroom in a gas station, and Poppa carefully traces out the letters "C" and "W" and tells him what words they stand for, and why.

Few scenes in my memory have had a greater impact than the one where the boy, happily supplied with an ice-cream cone, joins his grandfather in watching silently as a Klan parade marches ominously down Main Street. Al Freeman's character never says a word, but his jaw tightens and his eyes compress with pain, and we feel as we seldom have before in the movies how personally hurtful racism is.

But there are happier moments. Many of them involve Cliff's adventures in the neighborhood, especially on a day when a carnival comes to town, and one of the dancing girls is boarded with a local woman named Ma Ponk (Phylicia Rashad). The dancer, played by Iona Morris, is basically no more than a sideshow stripper, but to young eyes she seems impossibly glamorous.

There is a scene that begins conventionally, as the dancer promises to "make over" Ma Ponk by doing her hair and makeup, and putting her in a fancy dress. But the payoff is extraordinary, as the local woman combs out the dancer's hair in front of a mirror and the touch of her hands reminds the dancer of her own mother, whom she has not seen in fifteen years. A wordless communication of understanding and sympathy passes between the women. It is one of those magical scenes you cannot account for; something happens that transcends story and acting, and reaches straight into the heart.

Segregation was wrong and hurtful, but the system did provide a benefit: The black community was self-sufficient, supporting its own tradespeople, schoolteachers, ministers, and craftsmen, who provided role models for young people growing up. The movie remembers one-room schoolhouses, and churches where gospel music and fiery sermons uplifted a congregation after its week of work in the fields. It remembers juke joints and church picnics (with the cards hidden under a hat when the preacher approaches) and the way that old people were respected and consulted.

There are also scenes to show that many of the local white people were good-hearted and well-meaning; a woman named Miss Maybry (Polly Bergen) gives young Cliff books to read, and encourages him to stretch his mind and develop his ambition. (There is a very funny scene where Cliff says things that Miss Maybry perhaps should not be told, and Miss Maybry's maid tries to signal him from behind her employer's back.)

When the civil rights movement first penetrates into this corner of Mississippi, not everyone in the black community is happy to see it come. Many people have a working arrangement with the old system, and are afraid of stirring up trouble, especially since they know that "agitators" can be beaten or killed. There is a meeting in the church that dramatizes that tension.

The changing times come to a head through the person of Cleve (Richard Roundtree), the local iceman, who has hired Cliff to help him on his rounds. A white ice company decides to take over the "colored route," and so the local ice wholesaler refuses to sell to Cliff. He goes to another dealer, miles away. Then the white field foreman announces that anyone not buying ice from the white company will lose their job. And that is when something cracks, and feeling that has been repressed for long years finally breaks through.

It is almost impossible to express the cumulative power of *Once Upon a Time . . . When We Were Colored.* It isn't a slick, tightly packaged docudrama, but a film from the heart, a film that is not a protest against the years of segregation so much as a celebration of the human qualities that endured and overcame. Although the movie is about African-Americans, its message is about the universal human spirit. I am aware of three screenings it has had at film festivals: before a largely black audience in Chicago, a largely white audience in Virginia, and a largely Asian audience in Honolulu. All three audiences gave it a standing ovation. There you have it.

One False Move

R, 105 m., 1992

Bill Paxton (Dale "Hurricane" Dixon), Cynda Williams (Fantasia/Lila), Billy Bob Thornton (Ray Malcolm), Michael Beach (Pluto), Jim Metzler (Dud Cole), Earl Billings (McFeely). Directed by Carl Franklin and produced by Jesse Beaton and Ben Myron. Screenplay by Thornton and Tom Epperson.

Here is a crime movie that lifts you up and carries you along in an ominously rising tide of tension, building to an emotional payoff of amazing power. On the very short list of great movies about violent criminals, *One False Move* deserves a place of honor, beside such different kinds of films as *In Cold Blood, Henry: Portrait of a Serial Killer, Badlands, The Executioner's Song,* and *At Close Range.* It is a great film—one of the best of the year—and announces the arrival of a gifted director, Carl Franklin.

Yet no words of praise can quite reflect the seductive strength of *One False Move*, which begins as a crime story and ends as a human story in which everything that happens depends on the personalities of the characters. It's so rare to find a film in which the events are driven by people, not by chases or special effects. And rarer still to find a story that subtly, insidiously gets us involved much more deeply than at first we realize, until at the end we're torn by what happens—by what has to happen.

The movie was written by Billy Bob Thornton and Tom Epperson, who begin by telling one story—about three criminals on the run from Los Angeles to Arkansas—and end by telling two. The second story involves the interaction between a small-town Arkansas sheriff and two tough Los Angeles cops who fly out to join him in a trap for the fugitives. The movie pays full attention to the dynamics of both groups, the cops and the killers, and then quietly reveals a hidden connection between them—a secret that I will not reveal, because it generates such a moral and emotional force at the end of the film.

The film begins in Los Angeles, with a series of brutal murders of people in the drug underworld. Three people are involved: two men who have teamed up to steal drugs and money, and the girlfriend of one of them. They're played by Billy Bob Thornton, as a violent, insecure redneck type; Cynda Williams, as his lover, a black woman obviously deeply wounded in the past; and Michael Beach as the partner, a black man whose wire-rim glasses and impassive reserve conceal a capacity for sudden, cold violence.

Their original plan is to sell the drugs in Houston, but after they're identified as the fleeing murderers they change course, heading for the small Arkansas town where Williams was born and raised. The movie cuts ahead to the town, where we meet a cheerfully ambitious young sheriff, nicknamed "Hurricane" and played by Bill Paxton as the kind of guy who knows everybody in town and has never had to draw a gun in six years. He is mightily impressed when two Los Angeles detectives (Jim Metzler and Earl Billings) fly out to join him. He thinks he might be able to make the big time in L.A. himself some day.

The screenplay intercuts between these two story lines in a way that makes it increasingly important to us what will happen when the fugitives arrive in town. This isn't the usual formula of the cops and criminals drawing nearer, but a more subtle approach, in which secrets about the past that raise the stakes are gradually revealed.

One of the strengths of the film is the way it draws its interpersonal relationships. As the Thornton and Williams characters veer unhappily between protestations of love and outbursts of accusations, Beach sits quietly to one side—on a motel bed, in the backseat of the car—talking in a low, controlled voice. Most of what he says makes sense, and is disregarded. Meanwhile, in Arkansas, the two visiting cops, one black, one white, joke about the aspirations of the local lawman, who they see as a naive greenhorn. But his knowledge about the town goes very deep, and what he knows about the approaching fugitives will provide the key to the movie's last thirty minutes.

Carl Franklin's career has been mostly in acting until now, on stage and in several TV series. He directed some low-budget exploitation films, attended the American Film Institute, and then got *One False Move* as his first substantial film project. It is a powerful directing job. He starts with an extraordinary screenplay and then finds the right tones and moods for every scene, realizing it's not the plot we care about, it's the people.

One of the unique qualities of the screenplay, and his direction, is that this is a film where the principals are three black people and three white people, and yet the movie is not about black-white "relationships" in the dreary way of so many other recent movies, which are motivated either by idealistic bonhomie or the clichés of ethnic stereotypes. Every character in this film, black and white, operates according to his or her own agenda. That's why we care so very much about what happens to them.

One Sings, the Other Doesn't

NO MPAA RATING, 120 m., 1978

Valerie Mairesse (Pomme), Therese Liotard (Suzanne), Robert Dadies (Jerome). Directed, written, and produced by Agnes Varda.

Suzanne lives with a photographer who isn't much of a man. They aren't married, but he's fathered two of her children. Now she's pregnant again, and there isn't enough money for food as it is. Suzanne is twenty-two. She makes a friend of Pauline, the seventeen-year-old around the corner who everyone calls "Pomme," for "apple," maybe because of her round cheeks.

Pomme helps Suzanne find the money for an abortion and stands by her as a friend during the ordeal. The two women draw closer as the photographer wraps his insecurity around himself. One day, returning to the studio, they find he has hanged himself. So now Suzanne is left with two children, no lover, and an uncertain future.

So begins Agnes Varda's *One Sings, the Other Doesn't*, which, despite its grim beginnings, goes on to become one of the most appealing films by a French director whose best work has always found a balance between the heart and the mind. Varda works close to the human grain; she insists whenever possible on making documentaries between each of her feature films, so she can stay in touch with reality and not fall for the stylistic excesses of the big fiction films.

That restraint isn't always evident in *One Sings, the Other Doesn't*, which contains about three or four songs too many for its subject matter to support. But I'm getting ahead of the story, which is simplicity itself: After her lover's death, Suzanne goes with her children to live on her parents' farm in the country, and Pomme . . . well, Pomme has adventures.

She becomes a pop singer. She becomes a feminist and forms a singing group dedicated to woman's liberation. She falls in love with an Iranian student, who seems one sort of person in France and quite another after she marries him and moves back to Iran to have his child. At home, he's an unreconstructed chauvinist, insisting that his wife fill traditional roles. She can't see it, and they finally part, more or less friends, and she returns to France.

In the meantime, the two women have somehow kept in touch through the years. Sometimes they meet; more often it'll be by letter or postcard, Pomme checking in from some exotic spot and Suzanne (who eventually marries a doctor) replying with news of the reassuring rhythms of life on the farm. Varda's title is a perfect one (and even more melodic in French: *L'une Chante, L'Autre Pas*). Here we have them, she says: Two women, friends, and one sings and the other doesn't, but they'll remain friends and sisters for all of their lives.

The movie's final passages are among the best. Pomme comes with her child and friends to spend some time on the farm, and so several generations are brought together as the two friends approach the middles of their lives. There's a picnic, and kids playing, and wine, and singing (but of too many songs), and what Varda's doing, in a sneaky way, is making her case for feminism in a lyric voice instead of a preachy one.

On Golden Pond

PG, 109 m., 1981

Katharine Hepburn (Ethel Thayer), Henry Fonda (Norman Thayer, Jr.), Jane Fonda (Chelsea), Doug McKeon (Billy Ray), Dabney Coleman (Bill Ray). Directed by Mark Rydell and produced by Bruce Gilbert. Screenplay by Ernest Thompson.

Simple affection is so rare in the movies. Shyness and resentment are also seldom seen. Love is much talked-about, but how often do we really believe that the characters are in love and not simply in a pleasant state of lust and like? Fragile emotions are hard to portray in a movie, and the movies that reach for them are more daring, really, than movies that bludgeon us with things like anger and revenge, which are easy to portray.

On Golden Pond is a treasure for many reasons, but the best one, I think, is that I could believe it. I could believe in its major characters and their relationships, and in the things they felt for one another, and there were moments when the movie was witness to human growth and change. I left the theater feeling good and warm, and with a certain resolve to try to mend my own relationships and learn to start listening better. All of those achievements are small miracles for any movie, but especially for this one, which began as a formula stage play and still contains situations and characters that are constructed completely out of cardboard.

THE ONION FIELD ★ ★ ★ ★ 559

The story of *On Golden Pond* begins with the arrival of an old, long-married couple (Henry Fonda and Katharine Hepburn) at the lakeside cottage where they have summered for many years. They know each other very well. Hepburn, of course, knows Fonda better than he knows her—or himself, for that matter. Fonda is a crotchety, grouchy old professor whose façade conceals a great deal of shyness, we suspect. Hepburn knows that. Before long, three more people turn up at the pond: Their daughter (Jane Fonda), her fiancé (Dabney Coleman), and his son (Doug McKeon).

That's the first act. In the second act, the conflicts are established. Jane Fonda feels that her father has never really given her her due—he wanted a son, or perhaps he never really understood how to be a father, anyway. Jane tells her parents that she's spending a month in Europe with Coleman, and, ah, would it be all right if they left the kid at the lake? Hepburn talks the old man into it. In the central passages of the movie, the old man and the kid grudgingly move toward some kind of communication and trust. There is a crisis involving a boating accident, and a resolution that brings everybody a lot closer to the realization that life is a precious and fragile thing. Through learning to relate to the young boy, old Fonda learns, belatedly, how to also trust his own daughter and communicate with her: The kid provides Henry with practice at how to be a father. There is eventually the sort of happy ending that some people cry through.

Viewed simply as a stage plot, *On Golden Pond* is so predictable we can almost hear the gears squeaking. Forty-five minutes into the movie, almost everyone in the audience can probably predict more or less what is going to happen to the characters, emotionally. And yet *On Golden Pond* transcends its predictability and the transparent role of the young boy, and becomes a film with passages of greatness.

This is because of the acting, first of all, but also because Ernest Thompson, who wrote such a formula play, has furnished it with several wonderful scenes. A conversation between old Henry Fonda and young Coleman is an early indication that this is going to be an unusual movie: A man who is forty-five asks a man who is eighty for permission to sleep in the same room with the man's daughter, and after the old man takes the question as an excuse for some cruel put-downs, the conversation takes an altogether unexpected twist into words of simple truth. That is a good scene. So are some of the conversations between Hepburn and Fonda. And so are some remarkable scenes involving the boating accident, in which there is no doubt that Hepburn, at her age, is doing some of her own stunts. It's at moments like this that stardom, acting ability, character, situation—and what the audience already knows about the actors—all come together into an irreplaceable combination.

As everybody knows, this is the first film in which Hepburn and the two Fondas have acted in any combination with one another. Some reviews actually seem to dismiss the casting as a stunt. I believe it adds immeasurably to the film's effect. If Hepburn and Henry Fonda are legends, seen in the twilight of their lives, and if we've heard that Jane and Henry have had some of the same problems offscreen that they have in this story—does that make the movie simple gossip? No, not if the movie deals honestly with the problems, as this one does. As people, they have apparently learned something about loving and caring that, as actors, they are able to communicate, even through the medium of this imperfect script. Watching the movie, I felt I was witnessing something rare and valuable.

The Onion Field
R, 126 m., 1979

John Savage (Karl Hettinger), James Woods (Greg Powell), Franklyn Seales (Jimmy Smith), Ted Danson (Ian Campbell), Ronny Cox (Pierce Brooks), David Huffman (Phil Halpin), Christopher Lloyd (Jailhouse Lawyer), Diane Hull (Helen Hettinger), Priscilla Pointer (Chrissie Campbell). Directed by Harold Becker and produced by Walter Coblenz. Screenplay by Joseph Wambaugh, based on his book.

Since *The Onion Field* will inevitably inspire comparisons with *In Cold Blood*, we might as well begin with a basic one: Both the book and the film of *In Cold Blood* began with murder instead of ending with it.

The Onion Field does the same thing. It is

also based on real events—the 1963 kidnappings of Los Angeles police officers Karl Hettinger and Ian Campbell, and the eventual cold-blooded murder of Campbell. And Joseph Wambaugh, who wrote the book and personally controlled the film production, didn't reorder the facts to give us a dramatic burst of gunfire at the end. Instead, he places the deadly event of the murder in an onion field at about where it should occur, midway between the criminal preparations that led up to it and the longest single criminal court case in California history, which lasted more than seven years.

For Wambaugh (himself a former policeman), the trial, too, was a crime—and the fact of Campbell's murder had to be considered in the context of the legal travesties that followed it. That attention to the larger context of the kidnap-killing is one thing that makes *The Onion Field* so much more than another cop drama. This movie is about people, about how they behave and why, and about how small accidents and miscalculations can place people in situations they never dreamed of. Life is a very fragile thing; *The Onion Field* knows that in its bones.

The film moves between two basic, completely dissimilar, sets of characters: the two police officers, and the two third-rate hoods who would eventually be convicted of the crime. The cops aren't seen in quite the same sharp focus as the criminals—perhaps because, until the night of the onion field, little they had done in their lives had prepared them for what would follow.

Campbell (Ted Danson), the one who is killed, is seen almost as a memory: a tall, good-looking, black-haired Scottish-American with an obsession for bagpipes. Hettinger (John Savage from *The Deer Hunter*) is seen at the beginning as a cheerful, openfaced young man who will only later, after the onion field, develop very deep hurts and complications.

The hoods are seen more clearly. There's Greg Powell (James Woods), a streetwise smartass with a quick line of talk and an ability to paint situations so other people see them his way. And then there's Jimmy Smith (Franklyn Seales), a disturbed, insecure young black who is a perfect recruit for Powell. They make a suitable team. Powell creates criminal scenarios out of his fantasies; Smith finds them real enough to follow; and in some convoluted way Powell then follows Smith into them.

The Onion Field makes these two characters startlingly convincing: It paints their manners, their speech, their environment, their indecisions in such a way that we can almost understand them as they blunder stupidly into their crimes.

It never quite captures the personality of Campbell, the man who will be killed, but in the aftermath of the killing it begins to develop disturbing insights into Hettinger, the survivor. In a dozen subtle ways he becomes an outcast in the department (he senses, perhaps correctly, that the other cops wonder how he could allow his partner to be killed). Eventually, punishing himself, seeking guilt, he becomes a shoplifter, and is caught and fired from the force. Savage's handling of a scene of near-suicide, late in the film, is so frightening we can hardly stand to watch it.

Those events take place as *The Onion Field* explores the bureaucratic nightmare of the criminal courts system. The case dragged on and on and on—Hettinger was called upon to testify in more than six different trials—and plea bargaining, delays, and continuances, and legal loopholes made the case into an impossible (and almost insoluble) tangle.

So there is a lot of ground for *The Onion Field* to cover. It covers it remarkably well, working both as a narrative and as Wambaugh's cry of protest against the complicated and maddening workings of the courts. The movie is actually a vindication for Wambaugh: He was so displeased with the Hollywood and TV treatments of his novels (especially *The Choirboys*) that he said he would never let this factual story be made into a movie unless he controlled the production.

He did, and he has made it into a strong and honorable film. His instinct in going with Harold Becker, a commercial director with little previous feature experience, was obviously a good one; the movie's craftsmanship is unobtrusive but fine. And the performances (especially James Woods's as Greg Powell) bring the characters into heartbreaking reality. This is a movie that, once seen, cannot be set aside.

On the Ropes

NO MPAA RATING, 90 m., 1999

A documentary featuring boxers Tyrene Manson, George Walton, Noel Santiago, trainer Harry Keitt, manager Mickey Marcello, and Randy Little. Directed and produced by Nanette Burstein and Brett Morgen.

On the Ropes tells the true stories of three young boxers. One of them is sent to prison although she is apparently innocent. We watch as she is represented by an incompetent lawyer, crucified by uncaring prosecutors, and sentenced by a judge who exhibits the worst kind of barbarism: indifference to those whose lives he has power over.

The most amazing thing about the trial and conviction of Tyrene Manson is not that it happened. Justice miscarries all the time in America, frequently when poor black defendants are involved. The new movie *Hurricane* tells the true story of a boxer much more famous than Manson, who was railroaded for life on three fabricated murder convictions.

No, what is amazing is that the lawyer, the prosecutors, and the judge allowed themselves to be filmed as they toyed recklessly with Tyrene Manson's life. You'd think that even the most indifferent of jurists would be on good behavior before the camera. Perhaps the camera itself explains their lack of prudence. *On the Ropes* was filmed by Nanette Burstein and Brett Morgen with a low-tech Sony Handycam; its subjects might not have expected a real movie to result. But it did, and it won the special jury award at Sundance. Now they know.

On the Ropes is a sports documentary as gripping, in a different way, as *Hoop Dreams*. Both films are about ambitious young people from the ghetto who see sports as a road out of poverty. *On the Ropes* centers on the New Bed-Stuy Gym in New York, where a wise trainer, himself a survivor of hard times, guides the careers of three boxers.

The trainer's name is Harry Keitt, and his story will also figure here. The boxers are Tyrene Manson, a young Golden Gloves contender who has already knocked out the defending champion; George Walton, who seems to have genuine professional potential; and Noel Santiago, who is quick and promising, but easily discouraged. As they prepare for upcoming fights, we learn something of their stories.

Tyrene Manson's is the most inspiring—and therefore most heartbreaking. She is determined to be "the first member of my family to make something of myself." Trapped in poverty, she lives in a house with assorted other family members, and is raising two nieces who belong to her Uncle Randy, described in the movie as a crackhead. During her training for the Golden Gloves, disaster strikes when Randy is arrested for selling drugs to undercover police. They search the house, find cocaine in a bedroom, and charge Tyrene with possession with intent to sell.

Now pause a moment for Tyrene's story, which is more than the court did. She is a woman with no previous history of drug crimes. She does not use drugs. Five people shared that bedroom as their sleeping quarters. There was no lock on the door. She had been trying desperately to find other houses for herself and her nieces, to get them away from the crackhead and his life. Why was she the one charged? Because she was there.

Now follow the progress of the court case. Because her court-appointed attorney forgets a key appointment, her trial is postponed until four days before the Golden Gloves. She asks for a postponement so she can fight. Request denied. On the very day of her cancelled fight, she is sentenced to four and a half to nine years, after a "trial" that is an incompetent assembly-line procedure. One wonders if the judge even really saw her. Certainly he took no notice of her story. Her lawyer is so inept we want to shout obvious suggestions from the audience. Her own tearful speech in her own defense does her no good.

The message is clear: The drug epidemic is so widespread and the courts so overburdened and cynical that a defendant without a competent lawyer is more or less routinely doomed to be locked up. In this case, the evidence suggests that Tyrene Manson was innocent. But to be cynical, even if she were guilty, if she had been white, rich, or well represented, she would never have done a day because of the tainted evidence trail.

There is more heartbreak in the film. We watch as George Walton shows such promise that he gets a shot at the big time, and promptly allows himself to be fast-talked by Vegas types, while hardworking Harry Keitt gets left behind. We see how hard Harry works to help Noel Santiago find direction in his life. We learn something about Harry himself, his own past history of drug problems, his homelessness, and how the gym represents his own comeback. And we see the almost unimaginable disappointments he has to bear.

Note: In one of those notes of irony that life produces so freely, Tyrene Manson was given a brief pass out of prison to attend the Oscars when On the Ropes *was nominated for an Academy Award.*

Ordinary People

R, 125 m., 1980

Donald Sutherland (Calvin), Mary Tyler Moore (Beth), Judd Hirsch (Berger), Timothy Hutton (Conrad), M. Emmet Walsh (Swim Coach), Elizabeth McGovern (Jeannine), Dinah Manoff (Karen). Directed by Robert Redford and produced by Ronald L. Schwary. Screenplay by Alvin Sargent.

Families can go along for years without ever facing the underlying problems in their relationships. But sometimes a tragedy can bring everything out in the open, all of a sudden and painfully, just when everyone's most vulnerable. Robert Redford's *Ordinary People* begins at a time like that for a family that loses its older son in a boating accident. That leaves three still living at home in a perfectly manicured suburban existence, and the movie is about how they finally have to deal with the ways they really feel about one another.

There's the surviving son, who always lived in his big brother's shadow, who tried to commit suicide after the accident, who has now just returned from a psychiatric hospital. There's the father, a successful Chicago attorney who has always taken the love of his family for granted. There's the wife, an expensively maintained, perfectly groomed, cheerful homemaker whom "everyone loves." The movie begins just as all of this is falling apart.

The movie's central problems circle almost fearfully around the complexities of love. The parents and their remaining child all "love" one another, of course. But the father's love for the son is sincere yet also inarticulate, almost shy. The son's love for his mother is blocked by his belief that she doesn't really love him—she only loved the dead brother. And the love between the two parents is one of those permanent facts that both take for granted and neither has ever really tested.

Ordinary People begins with this three-way emotional standoff and develops it through the autumn and winter of one year. And what I admire most about the film is that it really *does* develop its characters and the changes they go through. So many family dramas begin with a "problem" and then examine its social implications in that frustrating semi-factual, docudrama format that's big on TV. *Ordinary People* isn't a docudrama; it's the story of these people and their situation, and it shows them doing what's most difficult to show in fiction—it shows them changing, learning, and growing.

At the center of the change is the surviving son, Conrad, played by a wonderfully natural young actor named Timothy Hutton. He is absolutely tortured as the film begins; his life is ruled by fear, low self-esteem, and the correct perception that he is not loved by his mother. He starts going to a psychiatrist (Judd Hirsch) after school. Things are hard for this kid. He blames himself for his brother's death. He's a semi-outcast at school because of his suicide attempt and hospitalization. He does have a few friends—a girl he met at the hospital, and another girl who stands behind him at choir practice and who would, in a normal year, naturally become his girlfriend. But there's so much turmoil at home.

The turmoil centers around the mother (Mary Tyler Moore, inspired casting for this particular role, in which the character masks her inner sterility behind a facade of cheerful suburban perfection). She does a wonderful job of running her house, which looks like it's out of the pages of *Better Homes and Gardens*. She's active in community affairs, she's an organizer, she's an ideal wife and mother—except that at some fundamental level she's selfish, she can't really give of herself, and she *has*, in fact, always loved the dead older son more. The father (Donald Sutherland) is one of those men who wants to do and feel the right things, in his own awkward way. The change he goes through during the movie is one of the saddest ones: Realizing his wife cannot truly care for others, he questions his own love for her for the first time in their marriage.

The sessions of psychiatric therapy are supposed to contain the moments of the film's most visible insights, I suppose. But even more effective, for me, were the scenes involving the kid and his two teenage girlfriends. The girl from the hospital (Dinah Manoff) is cheerful, bright, but somehow running from something. The girl from choir practice (Elizabeth McGovern) is straightforward, sympathetic, able to be honest. In trying to figure them out, Conrad gets help in figuring himself out.

Director Redford places all these events in a suburban world that is seen with an understated matter-of-factness. There are no cheap shots against suburban lifestyles or affluence or mannerisms: The problems of the people in this movie aren't caused by their milieu, but grow out of themselves. And, like it or not, the participants have to deal with them. That's what sets the film apart from the sophisticated suburban soap opera it could easily have become. Each character in this movie is given the dramatic opportunity to look inside himself, to question his *own* motives as well as the motives of others, and to try to improve his own ways of dealing with a troubled situation. Two of the characters do learn how to adjust; the third doesn't. It's not often we get characters who face those kinds of challenges on the screen, nor directors who seek them out. *Ordinary People* is an intelligent, perceptive, and deeply moving film.

Oscar and Lucinda

R, 133 m., 1998

Ralph Fiennes (Oscar Hopkins), Cate Blanchett (Lucinda Leplastrier), Ciaran Hinds (Reverend Dennis Hasset), Tom Wilkinson (Hugh Stratton), Richard Roxburgh (Mr. Jeffris), Clive Russell (Theophilus), Bille Brown (Percy Smith), Josephine Byrnes (Miriam Chadwick), Geoffrey Rush (Narrator). Directed by Gillian Armstrong and produced by Robin Dalton and Timothy White. Screenplay by Laura Jones from the original book by Peter Carey.

"In order that I exist," the narrator of *Oscar and Lucinda* tells us, "two gamblers, one obsessive, one compulsive, must declare themselves." The gamblers are his grandparents,

two oddball nineteenth-century eccentrics, driven by faith and temptation, who find they are freed to practice the first by indulging in the second. Their lives form a love story of enchantment and wicked wit.

When we say two people were born for each other, that sometimes means their lives would have been impossible with anyone else. That appears to be the case with Oscar and Lucinda. Their story, told as a long flashback, begins with Oscar as the shy son of a stern English minister, and Lucinda as the strong-willed girl raised on a ranch in the Australian outback. We see them formed by their early lives; he studies for the ministry, she inherits a glassworks and becomes obsessed with glass, and they meet during an ocean voyage from England to Australia.

They meet, indeed, because they gamble. Oscar (Ralph Fiennes) has been introduced to horse racing while studying to be a clergyman, and is transformed by the notion that someone will actually pay him money for predicting which horse will cross the line first. Lucinda (Cate Blanchett) loves cards. Soon they're playing clandestine card games on board ship, and Oscar is as thrilled by her descriptions of gambling as another man might be by tales of sexual adventures.

Oscar and Lucinda is based on a novel by Peter Carey, a chronicler of Australian eccentricity; it won the 1988 Booker Prize, Britain's highest literary award. Reading it, I was swept up by the humor of the situation and by the passion of the two gamblers. For Oscar, gambling is not a sin but an embrace of the rules of chance that govern the entire universe: "We bet that there is a God—we bet our life on it!"

There is also the thrill of the forbidden. Once ashore in Sydney, where Oscar finds rooms with a pious church couple, they continue to meet to play cards, and when they are discovered, they're defiant. Oscar decides he doesn't fit into ordinary society. Lucinda says it is no matter. Even now they are not in love; it is gambling that holds them together, and Oscar believes Lucinda fancies another minister who has gone off to convert the outback. That gives him his great idea: Lucinda's glassworks will fabricate a glass cathedral, and Oscar will superintend the process of floating it upriver to the remote settlement.

For madness, this matches the obsession in Herzog's *Fitzcarraldo* to move a steamship across a strip of dry land. For inspiration, it seems divine—especially since they make a bet on it. Reading the novel, I pictured the glass cathedral as tall and vast, but of course it is a smaller church, one suitable for a growing congregation, and the photography showing its stately river progress is somehow funny and touching at the same time.

Oscar and Lucinda has been directed by Gillian Armstrong, whose films often deal with people who are right for each other and wrong for everyone else (see her neglected 1993 film *The Last Days of Chez Nous*, about a troubled marriage between an Australian and a Frenchman, or recall her 1979 film *My Brilliant Career*, in which Judy Davis played a character not unlike Lucinda in spirit). Here there is a dry wit, generated between the well-balanced performances of Fiennes and Blanchett, who seem quietly delighted to be playing two such rich characters.

The film's photography, by Geoffrey Simpson, begins with standard, lush nineteenth-century period evocations of landscape and sky, but then subtly grows more insistent on the quirky character of early Sydney, and then cuts loose altogether from the everyday in the final sequences involving the glass church. In many period films, we are always aware that we're watching the past: Here Oscar and Lucinda seem ahead of us, filled with freshness and invention, and only the narration (by Geoffrey Rush of *Shine*) reminds us that they were, incredibly, someone's grandparents.

Oscar and Lucinda begins with the look of a period literary adaptation, but this is not Dickens, Austen, Forster, or James; Carey's novel is playful and manipulative, and so is the film. Oscar is shy and painfully sincere, Lucinda has evaded her century's strictures on women by finding a private passion, and they would both agree, I believe, that people who worship in glass churches should not throw stones.

Out of Africa

PG, 153 m., 1985

Meryl Streep (Karen), Robert Redford (Denys), Klaus Maria Brandauer (Bror), Michael Kitchen (Berkeley), Malick Bowens (Farah), Joseph Thiaka (Kamante), Stephen Kinyanjui (Kinyanjui), Michael Gough (Delamere), Suzanna Hamilton (Felicity). Directed and produced by Sydney Pollack. Screenplay by Kurt Luedtke, based on the book by Isak Dinesen (Karen Blixen).

Earlier, there was a moment when a lioness seemed about to attack, but did not. The baroness had been riding her horse on the veld, had dismounted, had lost her rifle when the horse bolted. Now the lioness seemed about to charge, when behind her a calm voice advised the baroness not to move one inch. "She'll go away," the voice said, and indeed the lioness did skulk away after satisfying its curiosity.

That scene sets up the central moment in Sydney Pollack's *Out of Africa*, which comes somewhat later in the film. The baroness is on safari with the man who owned the cool voice, a big-game hunter named Denys. They happen upon a pride of lions. Once again, the man assumes charge. He will protect them. But then a lion unexpectedly charges from another direction, and it is up to the baroness to fell it, with one shot that must not miss, and does not. After the man and woman are safe, the man sees that the woman has bitten her lip in anxiety. He reaches out and touches the blood. Then they hold each other tightly.

If you can sense the passion in that scene, then you may share my enjoyment of *Out of Africa*, which is one of the great recent epic romances. The baroness is played by Meryl Streep. The hunter is Robert Redford. These are high-voltage stars, and when their chemistry is wrong for romances (as Streep's was for *Falling in Love*, and Redford's for *The Natural*), it is very wrong. This time, it is right.

The movie is based on the life and writings of Baroness Karen Blixen, a Danish woman who, despairing that she would be single forever, married her lover's brother, moved to Kenya in East Africa, ran a coffee plantation on the slopes of Kilimanjaro, and later, when the plantation was bankrupt and the dream was finished, wrote books about her experiences under the name Isak Dinesen.

Her books are glories—especially *Out of Africa* and *Seven Gothic Tales*—but they are not the entire inspiration for this movie. What we have here is an old-fashioned, intelligent, thoughtful love story, told with enough care and attention that we really get involved in the passions between the characters.

In addition to the people Streep and Redford play, there is a third major character, Bror, the man she marries, played by Klaus Maria Brandauer. He is a smiling, smooth-faced, enigmatic man, who likes her well enough, after his fashion, but never seems quite equal to her spirit. After he gives her syphilis and she returns to Denmark for treatment, she is just barely able to tolerate his behavior—after all, he did not ask to marry her—until a New Year's Eve when he flaunts his infidelity, and she asks him to move out.

He turns up once more, asking for money, after Redford has moved his things into the baroness's farmhouse. The two men have a classic exchange. Brandauer: "You should have asked permission." Redford: "I did. She said yes."

The movie takes place during that strange blip in history when the countries of East Africa—Kenya, Uganda, the Rhodesias—were attracting waves of European settlers discontented with life at home in the years around World War I. The best land available to them was in the so-called white highlands of Kenya, so high up the air was cooler and there were fewer insects, and some luck could be had with cattle and certain crops.

The settlers who lived there soon settled into a hard-drinking, high-living regime that has been documented in many books and novels; they were sort of *Dallas* crossed with *Mandingo*. The movie steers relatively clear of the social life, except for a scene where Streep is snubbed at the local club, a few other scenes in town, and an extraordinary moment when she goes down on her knees before the British governor to plead for land for the Africans who live on her bankrupt farm.

Before that moment, she has not seemed particularly interested in Africans, except for an old overseer who becomes a close friend (and this is not true to the spirit of her book, where Africans are of great importance to her). Instead, she is much more involved in the waves of passion that sweep over the veld, as Redford passes through her life like a comet on a trajectory of its own.

He wants to move "his things" in, but does not want to move himself in. He wants commitment, but personal freedom. His ambiguity toward her is something like his ambiguity toward the land, which he penetrates with truck and airplane, leading tours while all the time bemoaning the loss of the virgin veld. Because *Out of Africa* is intelligently written, directed, and acted, however, we do not see his behavior as simply willful and spoiled, but as part of the contradictions he needs to stay an individual in a land where white society is strictly regimented.

The Baroness Blixen needs no such shields; she embodies sufficient contradictions on her own. In a land where whites are foreigners, she is a foreign white. She writes and thinks instead of gossiping and drinking. She runs her own farm. She scorns local gossip. In this hunter, she finds a spirit equal to her own, which is eventually the undoing of their relationship.

Out of Africa is a great movie to look at, breathtakingly filmed on location. It is a movie with the courage to be about complex, sweeping emotions, and to use the star power of its actors without apology. Sydney Pollack has worked with Redford before—notably in another big-sky epic, *Jeremiah Johnson*. He understands the special, somewhat fragile mystique of his star, who has a tendency to seem overprotective of his own image. In the wrong hands, Redford can look narcissistic. This time, he seems to have much to be narcissistic about.

Overlord

NO MPAA RATING, 88 m., 1975 (rereleased 2006)

Brian Stirner (Tom), Davyd Harries (Jack), Nicholas Ball (Arthur), Julie Neesam (The Girl), Sam Sewell (Trained Soldier), John Franklyn-Robbins (Dad), Stella Tanner (Mum). Directed by Stuart Cooper and produced by James Quinn. Screenplay by Christopher Hudson and Cooper.

I wrote from the 2004 Telluride Film Festival:

"The most remarkable discovery at this year's Telluride is *Overlord,* an elegiac 1975 film that follows the journey of one young British soldier to the beaches of Normandy. The film, directed by Stuart Cooper, won the Silver Bear at Berlin—but sank quickly from view after a limited release and was all but forgotten until this Telluride revival.

"Unlike *Saving Private Ryan* and other dramatizations based on D-day, *Overlord* is an intimate film, one that focuses closely on Tom Beddoes (Brian Stirner), who enters the British army, goes through basic training, and is one of the first ashore on D-day. Beddoes is not a macho hero but a quiet, nice boy, who worries about his cocker spaniel and takes along *David Copperfield* when he goes off to war.

"The movie tells his story through a remarkable combination of new and archival footage. It was produced by the Imperial War Museum in London, where Cooper spent three years looking at documentary and newsreel footage from World War II. About 27 percent of the film is archival, and awesomely real—for example, a scene where soldiers and their landing boat are thrown against rocks by furious waves.

"There are sights I had never seen before, including monstrous mechanical wheels that propel themselves across the beach to explode land mines and flatten barbed wire. One of these machines is driven by a ring of rockets around its rim, and as it rolls forward, belching fire and smoke, it looks like a creature of hell.

"*Overlord,* whose title comes from the code word for one of the invasion plans, uses archival footage to show the devastation of bombing raids, from above and below. Cooper's cinematographer, the Kubrick favorite John Alcott, used lenses and film stock that matched the texture of this footage, so the black-and-white film seems all of a piece. Tom's story is not extraordinary; he says good-bye to his parents, survives some hazing during basic training, makes a few close friends, and becomes convinced he will die in the landing. This prospect does not terrify him, and he writes a letter to his parents, consoling them in advance.

"He meets a local girl (Julie Neesam) at a dance, in a club filled with soldiers on leave. All of the clichés of such scenes are abandoned. She is a nice girl, he is a nice boy, they are kind to each other, tender and polite, and agree to meet again on Monday. But on Monday he is part of the early stages of the invasion, which seems, he writes his parents, like an entity that is growing to unimaginable proportions while he becomes a smaller and smaller speck of it. He has a fantasy in which he meets the girl

again; to describe it would reveal too much about this film, which is a rare rediscovery."

I reprint this earlier report because I'm writing this from Cannes and was not able to see the film again before deadline. *Overlord* remains firmly and clearly in my memory as a different kind of war film, one that sees through the eyes of one soldier and follows his story not through exciting adventures but through the routine steps designed to deliver an efficient and useful warrior to a place where he is needed.

The poignancy in the film comes because he knows, and his parents know, and the girl he meets knows, that his future is on hold. He may return home, he may have a future with the girl, and then again, maybe not, and this is the reality they all acknowledge in one sense or another.

The movie has been restored in a new 35mm print and combines its newsreel and fictional footage so effectively that it has a greater impact than all fiction, or all documentary, could have achieved. I still remember the rocket-driven mechanical wheel I wrote about from Telluride. I do not recall ever having seen such a machine depicted in a movie; that it is real is awesome.

Owning Mahowny

R, 107 m, 2003

Philip Seymour Hoffman (Dan Mahowny), Minnie Driver (Belinda), John Hurt (Victor Foss), Maury Chaykin (Frank Perlin), Sonja Smits (Dana Selkirk), Ian Tracey (Ben Lock), Roger Dunn (Bill Gooden). Directed by Richard Kwietniowski and produced by Andras Hamori and Seaton McLean. Screenplay by Maurice Chauvet, based on a book by Gary Ross.

Owning Mahowny is about a man seized helplessly with tunnel vision, in the kind of tunnel that has no light at either end. He is a gambler. Cut off temporarily by his bookie, he asks incredulously, "What am I supposed to do? Go out to the track and *watch?*" Given the means to gamble, he gambles—thoughtless of the consequences, heedless of the risks, caught in the vise of a power greater than himself. Like all addictive gamblers he seeks the sensation of losing more money than he can afford. To win a great deal before losing it all back again creates a kind of fascination: Such gamblers need to confirm over and over that they cannot win.

The film is based on the true story of a Toronto bank vice president who began by stealing exactly as much as he needed to clear his debts at the track ($10,300) and ended by taking his bank for $10.2 million. So intent is he on this process that he rarely raises his voice, or his eyes, from the task at hand. Philip Seymour Hoffman, that fearless poet of implosion, plays the role with a fierce integrity, never sending out signals for our sympathy because he knows that Mahowny is oblivious to our presence. Like an artist, an athlete, or a mystic, Mahowny is alone within the practice of his discipline.

There have been many good movies about gambling, but never one that so single-mindedly shows the gambler at his task. Mahowny has just been rewarded at work with a promotion and a raise. He drives a clunker even the parking lot attendants kid him about. His suits amuse his clients. He is engaged to Belinda (Minnie Driver), a teller who is the very embodiment of a woman who might be really pretty if she took off those glasses and did something about her hair.

He is so absorbed in gambling that even his bookie (Maury Chaykin) tries to cut him off, to save himself the trouble of making threats to collect on the money Mahowny owes him. "I can't do business like this," the bookie complains, and at another point, when Mahowny is so rushed he only has time to bet $1,000 on all the home teams in the National League and all the away teams in the American, the bookie finds this a breach of ethics: He is in business to separate the gambler from his money, yes, but his self-respect requires the gambler to make reasonable bets.

When Mahowny moves up a step by stealing larger sums and flying to Atlantic City to lose them, he encounters a more ruthless and amusing professional. John Hurt plays the manager of the casino like a snake fascinated by the way a mouse hurries forward to be eaten. Hurt has seen obsessive gamblers come and go and is familiar with all the manifestations of their sickness, but this Mahowny brings a kind of grandeur to his losing.

The newcomer is quickly singled out as a high roller, comped with a luxury suite, offered French cuisine and tickets to the Pointer Sisters, but all he wants to do is gamble ("and maybe . . . some ribs, no sauce, and

a Coke?"). Hurt sends a hooker to Mahowny's room, and a flunky reports back: "The only woman he's interested in is Lady Luck." Certainly Mahowny forgets his fiancée on a regular basis, standing her up, disappearing for weekends, even taking her to Vegas and then forgetting that she is upstairs waiting in their suite. (The fiancée is a classic enabler, excusing his lapses, but Vegas is too much for her; she tries to explain to him that when she saw the size of the suite she assumed they had come to Vegas to get married: "That's what normal people do in Vegas.")

It is impossible to like Mahowny, but easy to identify with him, if we have ever had obsessions of our own. Like all addicts of anything, he does what he does because he does it. "He needs to win in order to get more money to lose," one of the casino professionals observes.

Of course he will eventually be caught. He knows it, we know it, but being caught is beside the point. The point is to gamble as long as he can before he is caught. Mahowny refers at one point to having had a lot of luck, and he is referring not to winning, but to being able to finance a great deal of gambling at a level so high that, asked by a psychiatrist to rate the excitement on a scale of zero to one hundred, he unhesitatingly answers, "One hundred." And his greatest excitement in life outside of gambling? "Twenty."

Philip Seymour Hoffman's performance is a masterpiece of discipline and precision. He spends a lot of time adjusting his glasses or resting his fingers on his temples, as if to enhance his tunnel vision. He never meets the eye of the camera, or anyone else. Even when a casino security guard is firmly leading his fiancée away from his table, he hardly looks up to notice that she is there, or to say a word in her defense. He is . . . gambling. The movie has none of the false manipulation of most gambling movies, in which the actors signal their highs and lows. Hoffman understands that for this gambler, it is not winning or losing, but all process.

The movie, written by Maurice Chauvet, has been directed by Richard Kwietniowski, whose only other feature was *Love and Death on Long Island* (1998). That one also starred John Hurt, playing a reclusive British literary intellectual who becomes as obsessed as Mahowny, but with an erotic fixation. So unworldly he does not own a television and never goes to the movies, the Hurt character takes refuge from the rain in a cinema, finds himself watching a teenage comedy starring Jason Priestley, and becomes so fascinated by this young man that he keeps a scrapbook like a starstruck teenager and eventually travels to Long Island just in the hopes of meeting him. We get the impression that the Hurt character has been unaware of his homosexuality and indeed even his sexuality before being thunderstruck by this sudden fixation. In both films, Kwietniowski understands that conscious choice has little to do with his characters, that risk and humiliation are immaterial, that once they are locked in on the subjects of their obsessions, they have no choice but to hurry ahead to their dooms.

P

Pale Rider

R, 113 m., 1985

Clint Eastwood (Preacher), Michael Moriarty (Hull Barrett), Carrie Snodgress (Sarah Wheeler), Chris Penn (Josh LaHood), Richard A. Dysart (Loy LaHood). Directed and produced by Eastwood. Screenplay by Michael Butler and Dennis Shryack.

Clint Eastwood has by now become an actor whose moods and silences are so well known that the slightest suggestion will do to convey an emotion. No actor is more aware of his own instruments, and Eastwood demonstrates that in *Pale Rider,* a film he dominates so completely that only later do we realize how little we really saw of him.

Instead of filling each scene with his own image and dialogue, Eastwood uses sleight of hand: We are shown his eyes, or a corner of his mouth, or his face in shadow, or his figure with strong light behind it. He has few words. The other characters in the movie project their emotions upon him. He may indeed be the pale rider suggested in the title, whose name was death, but he may also be an avenging spirit, come back from the grave to confront the man who murdered him. One of the subtlest things in the movie is the way it plays with the possibility that Eastwood's character may be a ghost, or at least something other than an ordinary mortal.

Other things in the movie are not so subtle. In its broad outlines, *Pale Rider* is a traditional Western, with a story that has been told, in one form or another, a thousand times before. In a small California mining town, some independent miners have staked a claim to a promising lode. The town is ruled by a cabal of evil men, revolving around the local banker and the marshal, who is his hired gun. The banker would like to buy out the little miners, but, lacking that, he will use force to drive them off their land and claim it for his company.

Into this hotbed rides the lone figure of Eastwood, wearing a clerical collar and preferring to be called *Preacher.* There are people here he seems to know from before. The marshal, for example, seems to be trying to remember where he has previously encountered this man. Eastwood moves in with the small miners and becomes close with one group; a miner (Michael Moriarty) who lives with a woman (Carrie Snodgress) and her daughter (Sydney Penny). He urges the miners to take a stand and defend their land, and agrees to help them. That sets the stage for a series of violent confrontations.

As the film's director, Eastwood has done some interesting things with his vision of the West. Instead of making the miners' shacks into early American antique exhibits, he shows them as small and sparse. The sources of light are almost all from the outside. Interiors are dark and gloomy, and the sun is blinding in its intensity. The Eastwood character himself is almost always backlit, so we have to strain to see him and this strategy makes him more mysterious and fascinating than any dialogue could have.

There are some moments when the movie's mythmaking becomes self-conscious. In one scene, for example, the marshal's gunmen enter a restaurant and empty their guns into the chair where Eastwood had been sitting moments before. He is no longer there; can't they see that? In the final shootout, the Preacher has a magical ability to dematerialize, confounding the bad guys, and one shot (of a hand with a gun emerging from a water trough) should have been eliminated—it spoils the logic of the scene.

But *Pale Rider* is, overall, a considerable achievement, a classic Western of style and excitement. Many of the greatest Westerns grew out of a director's profound understanding of his actors' screen presence; consider, for example, John Ford's films with John Wayne and Henry Fonda. In *Pale Rider,* Eastwood is the director, and having directed himself in nine previous films, he understands so well how he works on the screen that the movie has a resonance that probably was not there even in the screenplay.

Panic

R, 88 m., 2001

William H. Macy (Alex), John Ritter (Josh Parks), Neve Campbell (Sarah), Donald Sutherland (Michael), Tracey

Ullman (Martha), Barbara Bain (Deidre), David Dorfman (Sammy). Directed by Henry Bromell and produced by Andrew Lazar, Lori Miller, and Matt Cooper. Screenplay by Bromell.

"I've got two jobs. I run a small mail-order business out of the house. Lawn ornaments, kitchen geegaws, sexual aids—things like that."
  "And the rest of the time?"
  "I work for my father. I kill people."

The sad-eyed patient speaks calmly. His psychiatrist says, "You're kidding, right?" No, he is not kidding. He was raised in the family business. His father was a hit man, and he's a hit man too. Not even his wife knows; she believes the mail-order story. But now he's in his forties, has a young son he loves, and wants to stop murdering for a living.

It tells you something—it may even tell you enough—that the man, named Alex, is played by William H. Macy. This wonderful actor has a gift for edgy unhappiness, repressed resentment, and in *Panic* he speaks too calmly and moves too smoothly, as if afraid of trip wires and booby traps. He spent his childhood afraid to stand up to his father, and in a sense his childhood has never ended.

Henry Bromell's *Panic* seeps with melancholy, old wounds, repressed anger, lust. That it is also caustically funny and heartwarming is miraculous: How does it hit so many different notes and never strain? It has a relationship between Alex and his son, Sammy, that reminds us of *The Sixth Sense*, and one between Alex and the sexy young Sarah (Neve Campbell) that evokes *American Beauty*. And Alex himself, trying to keep everyone happy, trying to keep secrets, trying to separate the compartments of his life, has the desperation of the character Macy played in *Fargo*.

But this is not a movie assembled from spare parts. Bromell began as a writer *(Northern Exposure, Chicago Hope)*, and this is a first film made with joy and with a writer's gift for character and dialogue. It involves a situation rich with irony and comic possibilities but isn't cynical about it; it's the kind of story that is funny when you hear about it from someone else, but not funny if it happens to you.

Alex was raised by his father, Michael (Donald Sutherland), to be a hit man. They started with squirrels and worked up from there. Alex didn't like killing squirrels, and in all of his killings since, it has been his father's finger pulling the trigger of Alex's tortured psyche. Alex is good at his job. But it makes him sick.

In the waiting room of his psychiatrist (John Ritter), he meets the patient of another doctor. This is Sarah, played by Neve Campbell as bright, cheeky, and with a gift for sharp observation. She has a complicated love life, is aware of her appeal, asks Alex if he's a guy in midlife crisis who thinks a sexy young girl might be just the ticket. In *American Beauty*, Kevin Spacey did indeed think that about the pom-pom girl, but Alex is looking not for sex but for approval, forgiveness, redemption; sex with Sarah would be less lust than rehab.

There are other important women in the picture. Tracey Ullman is Martha, Alex's wife, and Barbara Bain is Deidre, his mother. Martha has no idea how Alex really earns his living. Deidre knows all about everything, and when Alex confides that he wants out, she delivers a merciless lecture about how his father spent his whole life building up the family business, and Alex is an ungrateful child to destroy that dream. Yes, this is ironic, discussing murder in business terms, but it is so easy to separate success from morality. This could be any business in which the father insists that the son surrender his own dreams for the old man's.

Alex doesn't confide much in his wife; his secrets have built a wall. He loves her, but hopelessly, and he loves his son (David Dorfman, the little boy in *Bounce*). Their talks at bedtime are long and rich, and Sammy sees that something is deeply troubling his father: "Dad, are you all right?"

The movie takes these strands and weaves them into an emotional and logistical trap for Alex. His relationship with Sarah, a complicated girl, creates more issues than it solves. His father assigns him to perform an execution that demonstrates the old man's inexorable power over his son. Flashbacks show Alex's anguish as a child, and there is also a flashback showing how he met his wife, and how he was attracted to her goofiness.

The elements of the movie stand on their own. The Neve Campbell character is not simply the younger woman in Alex's life, but creates plot space of her own, where Alex is a visitor. The parents, Michael and Deidre, have a relationship that depends on their son but excludes him. Alex and Sammy have a private bond. We come to see Alex as a desperate man running from one secret compartment to another, seeking a place where he can hide.

Macy is as easy to identify with as any actor working. He doesn't push it. As Alex, he approaches his problems doggedly, sometimes bravely, hoping for a reprieve. Sutherland makes the old hit man into a particularly unlikable person: There's something about the way he gobbles an outdoor meal, his hat askew, that sets our teeth on edge. Bain's mother in her cold confidence is even more hateful. Ullmann, that gifted character actress, creates a woman who knows her life is coming apart but doesn't know what her life is. Neve Campbell takes a tricky role and enriches it, brings it a human dimension instead of being content with the "sexpot" assignment. And the little boy is heartbreaking, particularly in a conversation late in the movie. This is one of the year's best films.

Note: Panic *was a success at Sundance 2000, but didn't get a major release after a test audience disliked it. I don't blame the test audience; this is not a look-alike movie. But the executives who believed the audience instead of their own eyes should be ashamed of themselves. Now the film has won a national release and, like* Croupier, *could be discovered by filmgoers who make up their own minds.*

Pan's Labyrinth

R, 112 m., 2006

Ivana Baquero (Ofelia), Sergei López (Capitán Vidal), Maribel Verdu (Mercedes), Doug Jones (Pan/Pale Man), Ariadna Gil (Carmen Vidal), Alex Angulo (Dr. Ferreiro). Directed, produced, and written by Guillermo del Toro.

Pan's Labyrinth is one of the greatest of all fantasy films, even though it is anchored so firmly in the reality of war. On first viewing, it is challenging to comprehend a movie that on the one hand provides fauns and fairies, and on the other hand creates an inhuman sadist in the uniform of Franco's fascists. The fauns and fantasies are seen only by the eleven-year-old heroine, but that does *not* mean she's "only dreaming"; they are as real as the fascist captain who murders on the flimsiest excuses. The coexistence of these two worlds is one of the scariest elements of the film; they both impose sets of rules that can get an eleven-year-old killed. *Pan's Labyrinth* took shape in the imagination of Guillermo del Toro as long ago as 1993, when he began to sketch ideas and images in the notebooks he always carries. The Mexican director responded strongly to the horror lurking under the surface of classic fairy tales, and had no interest in making a children's film, but instead a film that looked horror straight in the eye. He also rejected all the hackneyed ideas for the creatures of movie fantasy and created (with his Oscar-winning cinematographer, art director, and makeup people) a faun, a frog, and a horrible Pale Man whose skin hangs in folds from his unwholesome body and from his face without eyes, nose, or mouth.

The time is 1944 in Spain. Bands of anti-Franco fighters hide in the forest, encouraged by news of the Normandy landings and other setbacks for Franco's friends Hitler and Mussolini. A troop of Franco's soldiers is sent to the remote district to hunt down the rebels, and is led by Capitán Vidal (Sergei López), a sadist undercover as a rigid military man. Commandeering a gloomy old mill as his headquarters, he moves in his new wife, Carmen (Ariadna Gil), who is very pregnant, and her daughter from her first marriage, Ofelia (Ivana Baquero). The girl hates her stepfather, who indeed values Carmen only for breeding purposes. Soon after arriving, Vidal shoots dead two farmers whose rifles, they claim, are only for hunting rabbits. After they die, Vidal finds rabbits in their pouches. "Next time, search these assholes before wasting my time with them," he tells an underling. He orders Mercedes (Maribel Verdu), his chief servant, to cook the rabbits for dinner: "Maybe a stew." What a vile man.

Ofelia encounters a strange insect that looks like a praying mantis. It shudders in and out of frame, and we're reminded of del Toro's affection for odd little creatures (as in *Cronos,* with its deep-biting immortality bug). The insect, friendly and insistent, seems to her like a fairy, and when she says so, the bug becomes a vibrating little man who leads her into a labyrinth and thus to her first fearsome meeting with the faun (Doug Jones, who specializes in acting inside bizarre costumes). Some viewers have confused the faun with Pan, but there is no Pan in the picture and the international title translates as *Labyrinth of the Faun.*

The faun seems to be both good and evil; what are we to make of a mural showing him eating babies, or a huge pile of used shoes, especially worrisome in the time of the Holocaust? But what he actually offers is not good or evil, but the choice between them, and del Toro says in a commentary that Ofelia is "a girl who needs to disobey anything except her own soul." The whole movie he says, is about choices.

The faun fits neatly into Ofelia's worries about her pregnant mother; he gives her a mandrake root to hide under the mother's bed and feed with two drops of blood daily. The mandrake root is said to resemble a penis, but this one, in special effects beyond creepy, looks like a half-baby made from wood, leaves, and earth. Ofelia discovers that Carmen is aiding the rebels, but keeps her secret because she doesn't want to be responsible for hurting anyone, a trait that will benefit her. And then the warfare between the fascists and the rebels ratchets up, and Capitán Vidal behaves with cruel and ruthless precision.

The film is visually stunning. The creatures do not look like movie creations but like nightmares (especially the Pale Man, with eyes in the palms of his hands). The baroque organic look of the faun's lair is unlike any place I have seen in the movies. When the giant frog delivers up a crucial key in its stomach, it does so by regurgitating its entire body, leaving an empty frog skin behind. Meanwhile, Vidal plays records on his phonograph, smokes, drinks, shaves as if tempting himself to slash his throat, speaks harshly to his wife, threatens the doctor, and shoots people.

Del Toro moves between many of these scenes with a moving foreground wipe—an area of darkness, or a wall or a tree that wipes out the military and wipes in the labyrinth, or vice-versa. This technique insists that his two worlds are not intercut, but are part of the same frame. He portrays most of the mill interiors in a cold blue-gray slate, but introduces life tones into the faces of characters we favor

and into the fantasy world. It is no coincidence that the bombs of the rebels introduce red and yellow explosions into the monotone world they attack.

Guillermo del Toro (born 1964) is the most challenging of directors in the fantasy field, because he invents from scratch or adapts into his own vision. He has made six features since his debut at twenty-nine with *Cronos* (1993), and I have admired, even loved, all of them, even those like *Hellboy, Mimic,* and *Blade II* that did not receive the universal acclaim of *Cronos* and *The Devil's Backbone* (a ghost story also set in Franco's Spain). He is above all a visually oriented director, and when he says "films are made of looks," I think he is referring not only to the gazes of his actors but to his own.

Born in Mexico, he has worked there and overseas, like his gifted friends and contemporaries Alfonso Cuarón (born 1961) and Alejandro González Iñárritu (born 1963). Isn't it time to start talking about a new Mexican Cinema, not always filmed in Mexico but always informed by the imagination and spirit of the nation? Think of del Toro's remarkable films, and then consider too Cuarón's *Children of Men, Harry Potter and the Prisoner of Azkaban* (the best-looking Potter film), *Great Expectations* (an overlooked masterpiece), and *Y tu Mama Tambien.* Or Iñárritu's *Amores Perros, 21 Grams,* and *Babel.*

Some of these are in one way or another genre films, but there is so much impact and intensity, and such a richness of visual imagination, that they flatter their genres instead of depending on them. The three directors trade actors and technicians, support each other, make new rules, are successful without compromise. Cuarón's 1998 *Great Expectations,* set in a Spanish-moss-dripping modern Florida and starring Ethan Hawke, Gwyneth Paltrow, and Anne Bancroft (in guess which roles), is a stunning reworking of Dickens and illustrates how all three directors put hands on a project and make it their own.

What makes del Toro's *Pan's Labyrinth* so powerful, I think, is that it brings together two kinds of material, obviously not compatible, and insists on playing true to both, right to the end. Because there is no compromise there is no escape route, and the dangers in both worlds are always present in the other. Del Toro talks of the "rule of three" in fables (three doors, three rules, three fairies, three thrones). I am not sure three viewings of this film would be enough, however.

The Paper Chase

PG, 111 m., 1973

Timothy Bottoms (Hart), Lindsay Wagner (Susan), John Houseman (Kingsfield), Graham Beckel (Ford), Edward Herrmann (Anderson), Bob Lydiard (O'Connor). Directed by James Bridges and produced by Robert C. Thompson and Rodrick Paul. Screenplay by Bridges.

The Paper Chase is about an aggressive, very bright, terribly engaging first-year student at Harvard Law School. The movie respects its hero, respects the school, and most of all respects the venerable Professor Kingsfield, tyrant of contract law.

Kingsfield is really the movie's central character, even though John Houseman gets supporting billing for the role. Everything centers around his absolute dictatorship in the classroom and his icy reserve at all other times. He's the kind of teacher who inspires total dread in his students, and at the same time a measure of hero worship; he doesn't just know contract law, he wrote the book.

Into his classroom every autumn come several dozen would-be Harvard law graduates, who fall into the categories we all remember from school: (a) the drones, who get everything right but will go forth to lead lives of impeccable mediocrity; (b) the truly intelligent, who will pass or fail entirely on the basis of whether they're able to put up with the crap; (c) those with photographic memories, who can remember everything but connect nothing; (d) the students whose dogged earnestness will somehow pull them through; and (e) the doomed.

One of each of these types is in the study group of Hart, the movie's hero, and the one who is truly intelligent. He's a graduate of the University of Minnesota and somewhat out of place among the Ivy League types, but he does well in class because he really cares about the law. He also cares about Kingsfield, to the degree that he breaks into the library archives to examine the master's very own undergraduate notes.

Hart is played by Timothy Bottoms, the star of *The Last Picture Show*. Bottoms is an awfully good actor, and so natural and unaffected that he shows up the mannerisms of actors like Dustin Hoffman or Jon Voight. Bottoms never seems to try; he's just there, complete and convincing. He falls in love, fatefully, with Susan (Lindsay Wagner), who turns out to be, even more fatefully, Kingsfield's daughter. Their relationship is a little hard to follow in the film; we aren't sure why she treats him the way she does—after all, she loves the guy—and the movie jerks abruptly in bringing them back together after a splitup.

But that isn't fatal because the fundamental relationship in the movie is between Hart and Kingsfield. The crusty old professor obviously appreciates the intelligence and independence of his prize student, but he hardly ever lets his affection show; there's a great scene in the classroom where he calls Hart forward, offers him a dime, and says: "Call your mother and tell her you will never be a lawyer." Houseman is able to project subtleties of character even while appearing stiff and unrelenting; it's a performance of Academy Award quality, and resulted in an Oscar for Best Supporting Actor.

Lindsay Wagner, as the daughter, is also a surprise; she made her movie debut in the unfortunate *Two People*, which had Peter Fonda as a conscience-stricken army deserter. She wasn't able to make much of an impression in that one, but *The Paper Chase* establishes her as an actress with class and the saving grace of humor.

What's best about the movie is that it considers interesting adults—young and old—in an intelligent manner. After it's over we almost feel relief; there are so many movies about clods reacting moronically to romantic and/or violent situations. But we hardly ever get movies about people who seem engaging enough to spend half an hour talking with (what would you say to Charles Bronson?). Here's one that works.

Paperhouse

PG-13, 94 m., 1989

Charlotte Burke (Anna), Elliott Spiers (Marc), Glenne Headly (Kate), Ben Cross (Dad), Gemma Jones (Dr. Nichols). Directed by Bernard Rose and produced by

Tim Bevan and Sarah Radclyffe. Screenplay by
Matthew Jacobs, based on the book *Marianne Dreams*,
by Catherine Storr.

Paperhouse is a film in which every image has
been distilled to the point of almost frightening simplicity. It's like a Bergman film, in
which the clarity is almost overwhelming, and
we realize how muddled and cluttered most
movies are. This one has the stark landscapes
and the obsessively circling story lines of a
dream—which is what it is.

The movie takes place during the illness of
Anna (Charlotte Burke), a thirteen-year-old
with a mysterious fever. One day in class,
Anna draws a lonely house on a windswept
cliff and puts a sad-faced little boy in the window. She is reprimanded by the teacher, runs
away from the school, falls in a culvert, and is
knocked unconscious.

And then she dreams of a "real" landscape
just like the one in her drawing, with the very
same house, and with a sad boy's face in an
upper window. She asks him to come outside.
He cannot, because his legs will not move, and
because she has not drawn any stairs in the
house.

Found by a search party, Anna is returned
home, where her behavior is explained by the
fever she has developed. The film alternates
between Anna's sickroom and her dream
landscape, and very few other characters are
allowed into her confined world. Among
them, however, are her mother (Glenne
Headly) and her doctor (Gemma Jones), and
there are flashbacks to her absent father (Ben
Cross), who is the distant and ambiguous father figure of so many frightening children's
stories.

The film develops a simple rhythm. Anna
draws, dreams, and then revises her drawings.
She sketches in a staircase for the young boy,
whose name is Marc, and fills his room with
toys. She adds a fruit tree and flowers to the
garden. And then one day she discovers, to her
astonishment, that her doctor has another patient—a boy named Marc, who faces paralysis, and about whom she is very concerned.

Paperhouse wisely never attempts to provide any kind of a rational explanation for its
story, although we might care to guess that the
doctor is sort of a psychic conduit allowing
Anna and Marc to enter each other's dreams.
Anna rebels briefly against the notion that she
is someone playing God for Marc, but then accepts the responsibility of her drawings and
her dreams.

Paperhouse is not in any sense simply a children's movie, even though its subject may
seem to point it in that direction. It is a
thoughtfully written, meticulously directed
fantasy in which the actors play their roles
with great seriousness. Watching it, I was engrossed in the development of the story, and
found myself accepting the film's logic on its
own terms.

The movie's director is Bernard Rose, a
young Briton who had some success with
music videos before this first feature. He carries some of the same visual inventiveness of
the best music videos over into his images
here, paring them down until only the essential elements are present, making them so
spare that, like the figure of Death in
Bergman's *Seventh Seal*, they seem too concrete to be fantasies.

I will not discuss the end of the movie,
except to say that it surprised and pleased me.
I don't know what I expected—some kind of
conventional plot resolution, I suppose—but
Paperhouse ends instead with a bittersweet
surprise that is unexpected and almost spiritual. This is not a movie to be measured and
weighed and plumbed, but to be surrendered to.

Paper Moon
PG, 102 m., 1973

Ryan O'Neal (Moses Pray), Tatum O'Neal (Addie
Loggins), Madeline Kahn (Trixie Delight), John
Hillerman (Deputy Hardin), P. J. Johnson (Imogene).
Directed and produced by Peter Bogdanovich.
Screenplay by Alvin Sargent, based on the book
Addie Pray by Joe David Brown.

The two kinds of Depression-era movies we
remember best are the ones that ignored the
Depression altogether and the ones such as
The Grapes of Wrath that took it as a subject.
Peter Bogdanovich's *Paper Moon* somehow
manages to make these two approaches into
one, so that a genre movie about a con man
and a little girl is teamed up with the real

poverty and desperation of Kansas and Missouri, circa 1936. You wouldn't think the two approaches would fit together, but, somehow they do, and the movie comes off as more honest and affecting than if Bogdanovich had simply paid tribute to older styles. Maybe that's why Addie Loggins, the little girl, hardly ever smiles: She can see perfectly well there's nothing to smile about. The movie opens at her mother's funeral on a windswept plain. Her mother (we learn from an old photograph) was a flapper of the worst sort, but Addie is a tomboy in overalls and a flannel shirt. At the last moment, an old car comes rattling up and discharges one Moses Pray, con man, alleged Bible salesman and just possibly Addie's father. He promises to deliver the child to relatives in St. Joe, mostly so he can collect $200 in blackmail money.

But then the nine-year-old girl, who somehow resembles Huckleberry Finn more than any little boy I can imagine, turns out to be the more clever con man, and before long they're selling Bibles to widows who are told their husbands ordered them—deluxe editions with the names embossed in gold, of course—before "passing on." The movie is about two con artists, but not really about their con, and that's a relief. We've seen enough movies that depend on the cleverness of confidence tricks—not only 1930s movies, but right down to the recent *The Flim-Flam Man.* No, Bogdanovich takes the con games only as the experience that his two lead characters share and that draws them together in a way that's funny sometimes, but also very poignant and finally deeply touching.

By now everybody knows that Ryan O'Neal and his real-life daughter, Tatum, play the man and the girl. But I wonder how many moviegoers will be prepared for the astonishing confidence and depth that Tatum brings to what's really the starring role. I'd heard about how good she was supposed to be, but I nevertheless expected a kind of clever cuteness, like we got from Shirley Temple or young Elizabeth Taylor. Not at all. Tatum O'Neal creates a character out of thin air, makes us watch her every moment, and literally makes the movie work (in the sense that this key role had to be well played). She has a scene in a Kansas hotel, for example, that isn't at all easy. Moses has picked up a tart from a sideshow, one

Trixie Delight by name, and has designs on her. Addie is jealous and makes a liaison with Trixie's young black maid, Imogene (wonderfully played by P. J. Johnson). Together they concoct a scheme to lure the hotel clerk into Trixie's room and then inform Moses.

Now, this could have been a hotel-corridor farce scene, as Bogdanovich demonstrated he could direct quite well in *What's Up, Doc?* But this time the scene is played for pathos and for the understanding of the child's earnestness, and the two young girls are perfectly matched to it.

Paper Moon doesn't come off, then, as an homage to earlier beloved directors and styles (as Bogdanovich's *What's Up, Doc?* did—and his *The Last Picture Show,* to a smaller extent). No, it achieves something quite different: a period piece that uses generic conventions only when they apply, so that we see the Depression through the eyes of characters who are allowed to be individuals. Whatever Addie and Moses do in this movie, we have the feeling it's because they want to (or have to) and not that the ghost of some 1930s screenwriter is prompting them.

Paradise Lost: The Child Murders at Robin Hood Hills

NO MPAA RATING, 150 m., 1996

A documentary directed and produced by Joe Berlinger and Bruce Sinofsky.

On May 5, 1993, the mutilated bodies of three second-graders were found in a wooded area near West Memphis, Arkansas. A month later, murder charges were filed against three local teenagers, who were accused of killing the children in a satanic ritual. A police officer, asked how good the state's case was, said, "On a scale of 1 to 10, it's an 11." But a hypnotic new documentary suggests that the community and the courtroom, inflamed by emotion and sensationalism, rushed to judgment.

Paradise Lost: The Child Murders at Robin Hood Hills is unique among courtroom documentaries in that the filmmakers, Joe Berlinger and Bruce Sinofsky, seem to have had complete access to both sides of the trial process, including private family meetings, conferences with lawyers, even sessions in the judge's chambers. The film opens with sad police video footage from the crime scene, showing the bodies as they were first discovered, and then reports how wild rumors swept the area about satanic rituals, animal sacrifice, and blood drinking.

A month after the murders, an undersized seventeen-year-old named Jesse Misskelly, with an IQ of 72, testified that he had been present when Damien Wayne Echols, eighteen, and Jason Baldwin, sixteen, killed and mutilated the boys. Local prosecutors brought murder charges against the boys. In the courtroom, they make a poignant trio: Jesse, small and blinking; Jason, who does not testify and indeed hardly speaks except in soft, shy generalities; and Damien, intelligent and articulate, known locally for dressing in black, listening to heavy metal music and reading books on Wicca, or "white magic." There is no significant physical evidence linking them to the crime, and the crime scene itself is without clues. Although one of the victims lost five pints of blood and the others bled freely, there is no blood at the murder site. The state's case is based on Jesse's testimony and hearsay; the defense argues that the statements made by Jesse contained only facts first supplied to him by the police, and there is a fascinating cross-examination in which a police transcript shows Jesse shifting the time of the crimes from morning to noon to after school to evening (when they actually occurred) under leading suggestions by police.

Jesse, whose trial was split off from the others, was found guilty and sentenced to life plus forty years. He was offered a reduced sentence if he would testify at the trial of the other two teenagers, but refused. His mother says she told him she would be sitting right there in the courtroom and didn't want to hear him lie.

At the trial of Damien and Jason, evidence of the satanic orientation of the murders is supplied by a state "expert occultist" who turns out to have his degrees from a mail-order university that did not require any classes or schoolwork. For the defense, a pathologist testifies that it would be so difficult to carry out the precise mutilations on one of the boys that he couldn't do it himself—not without the right scalpel, and certainly not in the dark or in muddy water.

Meanwhile, we meet members of the families on both sides. Time and again, the documentary describes someone as a boyfriend, girlfriend, stepfather, stepmother, ex-wife, or ex-husband; there seem to be few intact original marriages in this milieu. The parents of the murdered children are quick to believe the theories about the crime and are unforgiving. One mother says of Damien, "He deserves to be tortured for the rest of his life." She curses not only the defendants "but the mothers that bore them." In one especially uncomfortable scene, relatives of two of the victims take target practice by shooting at pumpkins they have named after the defendants, aiming at parts of the "bodies" they have not yet hit.

One of these men is John Mark Byers, stepfather of one of the victims, who earlier has been seen in a video at the crime scene, re-creating the crimes in grisly detail while vowing vengeance. In the movie's single most astonishing development, Byers gives the filmmakers a knife. They turn it over to the state. Crime lab reports show traces of blood that apparently came from Byers and his stepson. On the witness stand, he testifies that he beat his stepson with a belt at 5:30 P.M. on the day of his death. The welts from the belt buckle previously had been linked to the ritual killing.

We would like to hear testimony from Byers about whether the other victims were then present, or if his stepson later joined them, and where they were later, and where he was. Either those questions were not asked, or the filmmakers decided not to use them. One of the frustrating things about *Paradise Lost* is that, for all the information it contains, key elements are missing. The three defendants, for example, all claim to have alibis for the night of the murder, but we learn little about them.

The film ends with guilty verdicts against Damien (death by injection) and Jason (life in prison). The sentences are under appeal. At the end of the film I was unconvinced of their guilt.

The film creates a vivid portrait of a subculture in which Satan is a central figure. Where did Damien, Jason, and Jesse hear about satanic rituals? Mostly in church, it would appear. Some members of this community seem to require satanism as part of their world view; they seize upon the devil to explain what dismays them. Their frequent theme is vengeance, and it is blood-curdling to hear relatives of the victims promise that if the defendants are released, they will track them down and kill them.

The only person in the film who defends a traditional Christian belief system is the grandfather of one victim, who says he believes in forgiveness and knows he will be reunited in heaven with his loved ones. The others in the room listen without comprehension. We leave the film unsure about who committed the murders but convinced that an obsession with Satanism extends here far beyond the circle of defendants.

Parenthood

PG-13, 124 m., 1989

Steve Martin (Gil), Mary Steenburgen (Karen), Dianne Wiest (Helen), Jason Robards (Frank), Rick Moranis (Nathan), Tom Hulce (Larry), Martha Plimpton (Julie), Keanu Reeves (Tod). Directed by Ron Howard and produced by Brian Glazer. Screenplay by Lowell Ganz and Babaloo Mandel.

Ron Howard's *Parenthood* is a delicate balancing act between comedy and truth, a movie that contains a lot of laughter and yet is more concerned with character than punch lines. It's the best kind of comedy, where we recognize the truth of what's happening even while we're smiling, and where we eventually acknowledge that there is a truth in comedy that serious drama can never quite reach.

The movie is about a lot of parents and children—four generations, from an ancient matriarch to a three-year-old. Because almost everyone in this movie has both parents and children, almost everyone in the movie is both a child and a parent, and a lot of the film's strength comes from the way it sees each generation in reaction to its parents' notions of parenthood. The complexity of the movie—there are a dozen or more important characters—must have seemed daunting on the writing level, and yet the film's first strength is in the smart, nimble screenplay, which is also very wise.

Parenthood stars Steve Martin and Mary Steenburgen as the parents of three children, with another on the way. Life is not easy for them, although they are surrounded by all of the artifacts of middle-class suburbia, such as a nice home and new uniforms for the Little League team. Martin is engaged in warfare at the office, where he wants to be made a partner, and yet he resists spending too much time at work because he wants to be a good father—a better father than his father (Jason Robards), who was cold and distant.

We can see this for ourselves when we meet the Robards character. Or can we? Robards himself feels little love for his surviving parent, a mother of whom he snarls, "Yeah, she's still alive" at a family gathering. Robards has had four children, and we meet them all in the movie: characters played by Martin, Dianne Wiest, Harley Kozak, and Tom Hulce.

The Hulce character, Robards's youngest child, is in his mid-twenties and is the family's black sheep (he is introduced with the line, "Whatever you do, don't lend him any money"). He is a compulsive gambler and liar, and yet Robards somehow keeps alive a flame of hope for him, and loves him and cares, and so you can see that parenthood has not been simple for him, either.

We learn these and other things in an indirect way; the screenplay, by Lowell Ganz and Babaloo Mandel, with input from director Ron Howard, never reveals an obvious plot line, but instead cuts between several different family situations.

With Martin and Steenburgen, we see an attempt being made to create a typical, wholesome American nuclear family—with Martin driven almost to exhaustion by his determination to be a "good pop." Dianne Wiest plays a divorced mother of two, who is bitter about her former husband, and weary but courageous in her determination to do her best by a strong-willed sixteen-year-old daughter (Martha Plimpton) and a secretive, distracted thirteen-year-old son (Leaf Phoenix).

Kozak plays a sensible mother whose husband (Rick Moranis) is insanely obsessed with his theories about tapping the genius within young children; he reads Kafka at bedtime to their daughter, not yet four, and proudly demonstrates that she can look at a group of paper dots and calculate their square root (Martin and Steenburgen's child is only human and later eats the dots). The Hulce character is the only one not yet married, and indeed, in his gambling and lying and dangerous brinksmanship he seems to have flown entirely out of the orbit of parenthood. Perhaps the best scene in the movie is the one between Robards and Hulce after the old man has decided to make one more sacrifice for his no-good son, and then the son betrays the trust because what he really wants is not help, but simply the freedom to keep on losing.

Howard, Ganz, and Mandel have fifteen children among them, I understand, and that is easy to believe. Even such standard scenes as the annual school play, with the parents beaming proudly from the audience and the kids dropping their lines onstage, is handled here with a new spin. There are many moments of accurate observation, as when kids of a certain age fall in love with terms for excrement, or when kids at a party refuse to have the good time that has been so expensively prepared for them.

What I enjoyed most about the movie was the way so many scenes were thought through to an additional level. Howard and his collaborators don't simply make a point, they make the point and then take another look at it from a new angle, finding a different kind of truth. There is a wonderful moment, for example, in which the old matriarch (Helen Shaw) makes a wise and pithy observation, and then goes out to get into the car. Her dialogue provides a strong exit line, and a lot of movies would have left it at that, but not *Parenthood*, which adds a twist: "If she's so smart," Martin observes, looking out the window, "why is she sitting in the neighbor's car?"

In a movie filled with good performances, I especially admired the work by Martin, Steenburgen, Wiest, and Robards. What we are seeing in their performances, I think, is acting enriched by having lived, having actually gone through some of the doubts and long nights and second thoughts that belong to their characters. For Ron Howard, the movie is a triumph of a different sort: Having emerged from a TV sitcom determined to become a director, he paid his dues with apprentice work like *Grand Theft Auto*, went on to box-office and critical success with *Splash* and *Cocoon*, and now has made a wonderful film that shows him as a filmmaker mature and secure

enough to find truth in comedy, and comedy in truth, even though each hides in the other so successfully.

Paris, Texas
R, 145 m., 1984

Harry Dean Stanton (Travis), Nastassja Kinski (Jane), Hunter Carson (Their Son), Dean Stockwell (Walt), Aurore Clement (Anne), Bernhard Wicki (Dr. Ulmer). Directed by Wim Wenders and produced by Don Guest. Screenplay by Sam Shepard.

A man walks alone in the desert. He has no memory, no past, no future. He finds an isolated settlement where the doctor, another exile, a German, makes some calls. Eventually the man's brother comes to take him back home again. Before we think about this as the beginning of a story, let's think about it very specifically as the first twenty minutes of a movie. When I was watching *Paris, Texas* for the first time, my immediate reaction to the film's opening scenes was one of intrigue: I had no good guesses about where this movie was headed, and that, in itself, was exciting, because in this most pragmatic of times, even the best movies seem to be intended as predictable consumer products. If you see a lot of movies, you can sit there watching the screen and guessing what will happen next, and be right most of the time.

That's not the case with *Paris, Texas*. This is a defiantly individual film, about loss and loneliness and eccentricity. We haven't met the characters before in a dozen other films. To some people, that can be disconcerting; I've actually read reviews of *Paris, Texas* complaining because the doctor is German, and that another character is French. Is it written that the people in movies have to be Middle Americans, like refugees from a sitcom?

The characters in this movie come out of the imagination of Sam Shepard, the playwright of rage and alienation, and Wim Wenders, a West German director who often makes "road movies," in which lost men look for answers in the vastness of great American cities. The lost man is played this time by Harry Dean Stanton, the most forlorn and angry of all great American character actors. We never do find out what personal cataclysm led to his walk in the desert, but as his memory begins to return, we learn how much he has lost. He was married, once, and had a little boy. The boy has been raised in the last several years by Stanton's brother (Dean Stockwell) and sister-in-law (Aurore Clement). Stanton's young wife (Nastassja Kinski) seems to have disappeared entirely in the years of his exile. The little boy is played by Hunter Carson, in one of the least affected, most convincing juvenile performances in a long time. He is more or less a typical American kid, despite the strange adults in his life. He meets Stanton and accepts him as a second father, but of course he thinks of Stockwell and Clement as his family. Stanton has a mad dream of finding his wife and putting the pieces of his past back together again. He goes looking, and finds Kinski behind the one-way mirror of one of those sad sex emporiums where men pay to talk to women on the telephone.

Paris, Texas is more concerned with exploring emotions than with telling a story. This isn't a movie about missing persons, but about missing feelings. The images in the film show people framed by the vast, impersonal forms of modern architecture; the cities seem as empty as the desert did in the opening sequence. And yet this film is not the standard attack on American alienation. It seems fascinated by America, by our music, by the size of our cities, and a land so big that a man like the Stanton character might easily get misplaced. Stanton's name in the movie is Travis, and that reminds us not only of Travis McGee, the private eye who specialized in helping lost souls, but also of lots of American Westerns in which things were simpler, and you knew who your enemy was. It is a name out of American pop culture, and the movie is a reminder that all three of the great German New Wave directors—Herzog, Fassbinder, and Wenders—have been fascinated by American rock music, American fashions, American mythology.

This is Wenders's fourth film shot at least partly in America (the others were *Alice in the Cities, The American Friend,* and *Hammett*). It also bears traces of *Kings of the Road,* his German road movie in which two men meet by chance and travel for a time together, united by their mutual inability to love and understand women. But it is better than those movies—it's his best work so far—because it links the unforgettable images to a spare, perfectly heard American idiom. The Sam Shepard dialogue has a way of allowing characters to tell us almost nothing about themselves, except for their most banal beliefs and their deepest fears.

Paris, Texas is a movie with the kind of passion and willingness to experiment that was more common fifteen years ago than it is now. It has more links with films like *Five Easy Pieces* and *Easy Rider* and *Midnight Cowboy,* than with the slick arcade games that are the box-office winners of the 1980s. It is true, deep, and brilliant.

A Passage to India
PG, 160 m., 1984

Judy Davis (Adela Quested), Victor Banerjee (Dr. Aziz), Peggy Ashcroft (Mrs. Moore), Alec Guinness (Godbole) James Fox (Fielding), Nigel Havers (Ronny Heaslop). Directed by David Lean and produced by John Brabourne and Richard Goodwin. Screenplay by Lean, based on the book by E. M. Forster.

Only connect!

—E. M. Forster

That is the advice he gives us in *Howards End,* and then, in *A Passage to India,* he creates a world in which there are no connections, where Indians and Englishmen speak the same language but do not understand each other, where it doesn't matter what you say in the famous Marabar Caves, since all that comes back is a hollow, mocking, echo. Forster's novel is one of the literary landmarks of this century, and now David Lean has made it into one of the greatest screen adaptations I have ever seen.

Great novels do not usually translate well to the screen. They are too filled with ambiguities, and movies have a way of making all their images seem like literal fact. *A Passage to India* is especially tricky, because the central event in the novel is something that happens offstage, or never happens at all—take your choice. On a hot, muggy day, the eager Dr. Aziz leads an expedition to the Marabar Caves. One by one, members of the party drop out, until finally only Miss Quested, from England, is left. And so the Indian man and the British woman climb the last path alone, at a time when England's rule of India was based on an ingrained, semiofficial racism, and some British, at least, nodded approvingly at Kipling's "East is East, and West is West, and never the twain shall meet."

In Forster's novel, it is never clear exactly what it was that happened to Miss Quested after she wandered alone into one of the caves. David Lean's film leaves that question equally open. But because he is dealing with a visual medium, he cannot make it a mystery where Dr. Aziz is at the time; if you are offstage in a novel, you can be anywhere, but if you are offstage in a movie, you are definitely not where the camera is looking. So in the film version we know, or think we know, that Dr. Aziz is innocent of the charges later brought against him—of the attempted rape of Miss Quested.

The charges and the trial fill the second half of Lean's *A Passage to India.* Lean brings us to that point by a series of perfectly modulated, quietly tension-filled scenes in which Miss Quested (Judy Davis) and the kindly Mrs. Moore (Peggy Ashcroft) sail to India, where Miss Quested is engaged to marry the priggish local British magistrate in a provincial backwater. Both women want to see the "real India"—a wish that is either completely lacking among the locals, or is manfully repressed. Mrs. Moore goes walking by a temple pool by moonlight, and meets the earnest young Dr. Aziz, who is captivated by her gentle kindness. Miss Quested wanders by accident into the ruins of another temple, populated by sensuous and erotic statuary, tumbled together, overgrown by vegetation.

Miss Quested's temple visit is not in Forster, but has been added by Lean (who wrote his own screenplay). It accomplishes just what it needed, suggesting that in Miss Quested the forces of sensuality and repression run a great deal more deeply than her sexually constipated fiancé is ever likely to suspect. Meanwhile, we meet some of the other local characters, including Dr. Godbole (Alec Guinness), who meets every crisis with perfect equanimity, and who believes that what will be, will be. This philosophy sounds like recycled fortune cookies but turns out, in the end, to have been the simple truth. We also meet Fielding (James Fox), one of those tall,

lonely, middle-aged Englishmen who hang about the edges of stories set in the empire, waiting until their destiny commands them to take a firm stand.

Lean places these characters in one of the most beautiful canvases he has ever drawn (and this is the man who directed *Doctor Zhivago* and *Lawrence of Arabia*). He doesn't see the India of travel posters and lurid postcards, but the India of a Victorian watercolorist like Edward Lear, who placed enigmatic little human figures here and there in spectacular landscapes that never seemed to be quite finished. Lean makes India look like an amazing, beautiful place that an Englishman can never quite put his finger on—which is, of course, the lesson Miss Quested learns in the caves.

David Lean is a meticulous craftsman, famous for going to any lengths to make every shot look just the way he thinks it should. His actors here are encouraged to give sound, thoughtful, unflashy performances (Guinness strains at the bit), and his screenplay is a model of clarity: By the end of this movie we know these people so well, and understand them so thoroughly, that only the most reckless among us would want to go back and have a closer look at those caves.

Passion Fish

R, 135 m., 1993

Mary McDonnell (May-Alice), Alfre Woodard (Chantelle), David Strathairn (Rennie), Vondie Curtis-Hall (Sugar), Leo Burmeister (Max), Angela Bassett (Dawn/Rhonda), Lenore Banks (Nurse Quick), Nelle Stokes (Therapist No. 1), Brett Ardoin (Therapist No. 2). Directed by John Sayles and produced by Sarah Green and Maggie Renzi. Screenplay by Sayles.

Her life is essentially going nowhere before her accident. She's in a dead-end career, her marriage has ended, and she's filled with a deep discontent. Then she is paralyzed in an accident, and goes back home to Louisiana to recover, filled with resentment.

In a typical TV docudrama, this would be the setup for a heartwarming tale of uplift and courage. But John Sayles's *Passion Fish* cuts closer to the bone. This is a tough, muscular story about a headstrong woman who wants things to go her way.

The film stars Mary McDonnell as May-Alice, the soap opera star whose life is suddenly changed by fate. She has some money and a home down in the bayou country where her family is from, and after she is finished with rehabilitation therapy (where she is a very poor candidate), she goes back down there to sit in her chair and drink wine and harbor her bitterness.

She has enough money to hire a full-time companion, and she interviews several, all with a lot of problems of their own. A couple of them are hired for varying lengths of time, before they are fired or walk off the job. She is not easy to work for, and she has just about reached the bottom of the local employment pool when Chantelle, a black woman played by Alfre Woodard, arrives.

Woodard is a strong woman, too. She is also determined to keep the job. She needs it, for more reasons than we know. She sizes up the situation, sees that May-Alice needs less coddling and a lot less wine, and tries to take charge. May-Alice fights back. And *Passion Fish* is essentially about the struggle of their wills.

John Sayles says he has been interested in such relationships between client and companion ever since he watched them develop in his own family. It is an interesting division of power: The companion is healthy and able-bodied, and has the freedom of movement. The client, like McDonnell, has power over the sources of money, and can try to control the other person through threats to her economic security. So there is a delicate balance, a struggle, sometimes unacknowledged, that goes on all day long.

Sayles writes his own movies, which range from *Eight Men Out* to *Matewan* to the powerful *City of Hope*, and he has rarely written more three-dimensional characters than this time. Although his subject is a mine field of clichés and the material cries out to be processed into a disease-of-the-week docudrama, he creates vivid, original characters for his story-characters like Uncle Max (Leo Burmeister), who comes to visit and reveals his entire lifetime in a few sentences, or May-Alice's childhood friends, or the actresses who worked with her on television.

Each of these meetings between May-Alice and her past requires her to play a different role, and that's also the case when Rennie (David Strathairn) turns up one day to make some repairs on the house. This was the guy she had a crush on in high school, before she left him and all the rest of her early life behind and moved to New York. Now he is married, and she is in a wheelchair, and it seems as if all possibilities of romance have disappeared. But things are not always as they seem.

At the heart of the movie is the uneasy relationship between May-Alice and Chantelle. May-Alice is used to being willful and spoiled. Chantelle does not find her behavior acceptable. But May-Alice has the money and Chantelle needs the job, for more urgent reasons than we first realize, and so it seems that Chantelle may have to put up with May-Alice's behavior. Yet in a deeper sense, one that only gradually reveals itself to May-Alice, what she needs most of all from Chantelle is the other woman's ability to stand up to her.

There are elements here of a vaguely similar relationship in *Driving Miss Daisy*, but Sayles has made his own film, direct and original, and in the struggle of wills between these two characters he creates two of the most interesting human portraits of 1993. The struggle at the heart of the movie is lightened by the comic portraits of May-Alice's many visitors (I would have liked to see a whole movie about Uncle Max, and an old friend named Precious deserves a short subject of her own). The romance is handled with a delicate, tentative touch that reflects the characters' feelings for one another. *Passion Fish* begins with a scene from May-Alice's soap opera, and by the end we see how far such canned melodrama is from the real lessons of life.

The Passion of the Christ
R, 126 m., 2004

James Caviezel (Jesus, the Christ), Maia Morgenstern (Mary), Monica Bellucci (Mary Magdalene), Mattia Sbragia (Caiphas), Hristo Shopov (Pontius Pilate), Claudia Gerini (Pilate's Wife), Luca Lionello (Judas). Directed by Mel Gibson and produced by Bruce Davey, Gibson, and Stephen McEveety. Screenplay by Gibson and Benedict Fitzgerald.

If ever there was a film with the correct title, that film is Mel Gibson's *The Passion of the*

Christ. Although the word *passion* has become mixed up with romance, its Latin origins refer to suffering and pain; later Christian theology broadened that to include Christ's love for mankind, which made him willing to suffer and die for us. The movie is 126 minutes long, and I would guess that at least 100 of those minutes, maybe more, are concerned specifically and graphically with the details of the torture and death of Jesus. This is the most violent film I have ever seen.

I prefer to evaluate a film on the basis of what it intends to do, not on what I think it should have done. It is clear that Mel Gibson wanted to make graphic and inescapable the price that Jesus paid (as Christians believe) when he died for our sins. Anyone raised as a Catholic will be familiar with the stops along the way; the screenplay is inspired not so much by the Gospels as by the fourteen Stations of the Cross. As an altar boy, serving during the Stations on Friday nights in Lent, I was encouraged to meditate on Christ's suffering, and I remember the chants as the priest led the way from one station to another:

At the Cross, her station keeping . . .
Stood the mournful Mother weeping . . .
Close to Jesus to the last.

For us altar boys, this was not necessarily a deep spiritual experience. Christ suffered, Christ died, Christ rose again, we were redeemed, and let's hope we can get home in time to watch the Illinois basketball game on TV. What Gibson has provided for me, for the first time in my life, is a visceral idea of what the Passion consisted of. That his film is superficial in terms of the surrounding message—that we get only a few passing references to the teachings of Jesus—is, I suppose, not the point. This is not a sermon or a homily, but a visualization of the central event in the Christian religion. Take it or leave it.

David Anson, a critic I respect, finds in *Newsweek* that Gibson has gone too far. ". . . (T)he relentless gore is self-defeating," he writes. "Instead of being moved by Christ's suffering, or awed by his sacrifice, I felt abused by a filmmaker intent on punishing an audience, for who knows what sins." This is a completely valid response to the film, and I quote Anson because I suspect he speaks for many audience

members, who will enter the theater in a devout or spiritual mood and emerge deeply disturbed. You must be prepared for whippings, flayings, beatings, the crunch of bones, the agony of screams, the cruelty of the sadistic centurions, the rivulets of blood that crisscross every inch of Jesus' body. Some will leave before the end.

This is not a Passion like any other ever filmed. Perhaps that is the best reason for it. I grew up on those pious Hollywood biblical epics of the 1950s, which looked like holy cards brought to life. I remember my grin when *Time* magazine noted that Jeffrey Hunter, starring as Christ in *King of Kings* (1961), had shaved his armpits. (Not Hunter's fault; the film's crucifixion scene had to be reshot because preview audiences objected to Jesus' hairy chest.) If it does nothing else, Gibson's film will break the tradition of turning Jesus and his disciples into neat, clean, well-barbered middle-class businessmen. They were poor men in a poor land. I debated Scorsese's *The Last Temptation of Christ* with Michael Medved before an audience from a Christian college, and was told by an audience member that the characters were filthy and needed haircuts.

The Middle East in biblical times was a Jewish community occupied against its will by the Roman Empire, and the message of Jesus was equally threatening to both sides—to the Romans, because he was a revolutionary, and to the establishment of Jewish priests because he preached a new covenant and threatened the status quo. In the movie's scenes showing Jesus being condemned to death, the two main players are Pontius Pilate, the Roman governor, and Caiphas, the Jewish high priest. Both men want to keep the lid on, and while neither is especially eager to see Jesus crucified, they live in a harsh time when such a man is dangerous.

Pilate is seen going through his well-known doubts before finally washing his hands of the matter and turning Jesus over to the priests, but Caiphas, who also had doubts, is not seen as sympathetically. The critic Steven D. Greydanus, in a useful analysis of the film, writes: "The film omits the canonical line from John's gospel in which Caiphas argues that it is better for one man to die for the people that the nation be saved. Had Gibson retained this line, perhaps giving Caiphas a measure of the inner conflict he gave to Pilate, it could have underscored the similarities between Caiphas and Pilate and helped defuse the issue of anti-Semitism."

This scene and others might justifiably be cited by anyone concerned that the movie contains anti-Semitism. My own feeling is that Gibson's film is not anti-Semitic, but reflects a range of behavior on the part of its Jewish characters, on balance favorably. The Jews who seem to desire Jesus' death are in the priesthood, and have political as well as theological reasons for acting; like today's Catholic bishops who were slow to condemn abusive priests, Protestant TV preachers who confuse religion with politics, or Muslim clerics who are silent on terrorism, they have an investment in their positions and authority. The other Jews seen in the film are viewed positively; Simon helps Jesus to carry the cross, Veronica brings a cloth to wipe his face, Jews in the crowd cry out against his torture.

A reasonable person, I believe, will reflect that in this story set in a Jewish land, there are many characters with many motives, some good, some not, each one representing himself, none representing his religion. The story involves a Jew who tried no less than to replace the established religion and set himself up as the Messiah. He was understandably greeted with a jaundiced eye by the Jewish establishment while at the same time finding his support, his disciples, and the founders of his church entirely among his fellow Jews. The libel that the Jews "killed Christ" involves a willful misreading of testament and teaching: Jesus was made man and came to Earth *in order* to suffer and die in reparation for our sins. No race, no religion, no man, no priest, no governor, no executioner killed Jesus; he died by God's will to fulfill his purpose, and with our sins we *all* killed him. That some Christian churches have historically been guilty of the sin of anti-Semitism is undeniable, but in committing it they violated their own beliefs.

This discussion will seem beside the point for readers who want to know about the movie, not the theology. But *The Passion of the Christ*, more than any other film I can recall, depends upon theological considerations. Gibson has not made a movie that anyone would call "commercial," and if it grosses millions, that will not be because anyone was entertained. It is a personal message movie of the most radical

kind, attempting to re-create events of personal urgency to Gibson. The filmmaker has put his artistry and fortune at the service of his conviction and belief, and that doesn't happen often.

Is the film "good" or "great"? I imagine each person's reaction (visceral, theological, artistic) will differ. I was moved by the depth of feeling, by the skill of the actors and technicians, by their desire to see this project through, no matter what. To discuss individual performances, such as James Caviezel's heroic depiction of the ordeal, is almost beside the point. This isn't a movie about performances, although it has powerful ones; or about technique, although it is awesome; or about cinematography (although Caleb Deschanel paints with an artist's eye); or music (although John Debney supports the content without distracting from it). It is a film about an idea. An idea that it is necessary to fully comprehend the Passion if Christianity is to make any sense. Gibson has communicated his idea with a single-minded urgency. Many will disagree. Some will agree, but be horrified by the graphic treatment. I myself am no longer religious in the sense that a long-ago altar boy thought he should be; but I can respond to the power of belief whether I agree or not, and when I find it in a film I must respect it.

Note: I said the film is the most violent I have ever seen. It will probably be the most violent you have ever seen. This is not a criticism but an observation; the film is unsuitable for younger viewers, but works powerfully for those who can endure it. The MPAA's "R" rating is definitive proof that the organization either will never give the NC-17 rating for violence alone, or was intimidated by the subject matter. If it had been anyone other than Jesus up on that cross, I have a feeling that NC-17 would have been automatic.

Patton

PG, 171 m., 1970

George C. Scott (Patton), Karl Malden (Bradley), Stephen Young (Captain Hansen), Michael Strong (General Carver), Karl Michel Vogler (Rommel), Michael Bates (Montgomery). Directed by Franklin J. Schaffner and produced by Frank McCarthy. Screenplay by Francis Ford Coppola and Edward H. North.

We have all of these things buried inside of us, waiting for a movie like *Patton* to release them. The reflex patriotism of World War II is still there, we discover; Vietnam has soured us on war, but not on that war. There is a small corner of our being that will always be thrilled by Patton's dash across Europe after the Germans, and we are still a little bit in admiration of heroes on his arrogant scale. And that is why, make no mistake, *Patton* is not an anti-war film. If I read one, I read half a dozen tortuous liberal rationalizations for this movie, written by people who liked it but felt guilty afterward. *Patton* is really against war, they said; by taking us almost inside the soul of the most fanatically military of all America's generals, *Patton* was supposed to fill us with distaste for militarism. It does not, of course. But neither is it a very hawklike movie. It is such an extraordinarily intelligent film, so sure of its purpose, that it makes war its medium but not its subject. It is not about war but about Patton at war, and it is one of the best screen biographies ever made.

Patton once said something to the effect that war was the supreme human activity because it forced men to operate at the ultimate limit of their abilities. This is not a very good justification for war, but it is a supreme test for men, and the action in *Patton* all takes place at the delicate balance point where the war meets the man. That was a basically brilliant idea in Francis Ford Coppola's original screenplay, but what makes it work so well in *Patton* is the performance of George C. Scott. He is absorbed into the role, and commands it. He is such a good actor that the movie doesn't have to explain a lot of things; we feel we know Patton and so we're sure of our footing. That's good, because it frees director Franklin J. Schaffner from a lot of cluttering props and plot lines. *Patton* is almost three hours long but it is a surprisingly uncomplicated movie, telling its story with clean, simple scenes and shots. Schaffner is at home here; one of the best things about his *Planet of the Apes* was the simplicity of style he found for it. If *Planet* had gotten complicated, we would have laughed at it.

The simplicity of *Patton* does not lead to any loss of subtlety; just the reverse. Because we are freed from those semiobligatory junk scenes that clutter up most war movies (the wife at home, the "human interest" drained from ethnic character actors, the battle scenes that are allowed to run too long because they cost so much) we can concentrate on the man, and we can even begin to believe we understand a warrior like this one. Because it's no good being hypocritical, I guess. Generals should be generals, and not lovable quasi-political figures like Ike or MacArthur. Patton's life was war (and how sad that really was) but he was honest enough to admit it, and the movie takes its stand on that point. And so although we deplore war we find ourselves respecting the movie; *Patton* is written and directed with integrity.

Beyond that, it's an awfully good movie, and one of its best features is the way it gets its laughs. There aren't any cheap laughs in *Patton,* but there are a lot of earned ones, all serving to flesh in our idea of this brilliant, obsessed man. And a lot of the humor is simply there, embodied in the Scott performance. It turns out *Patton* is exactly the war movie we didn't realize how much we wanted to see.

Payday

R, 103 m., 1973

Rip Torn (Maury Dann), Michael C. Gwynne (Clarence McGinty), Ahna Capri (Mayleen Travis), Jeff Morris (Bob Tally), Elayne Heilveil (Rosamond McClintock), Cliff Emmich (Chicago). Directed by Daryl Duke and produced by Martin Fink and Donald Carpenter. Screenplay by Carpenter.

The musician's name is Maury Dann and he's perhaps on the edge of stardom and certainly on the edge of an abyss. He started in life as next to nothing and by the age of thirty-five has worked his way up to his own band, a couple of hit records, a string of groupies, and a chauffeured Cadillac limousine. "You only pass through life once," he is fond of saying, "and it might as well be in a Cadillac." He does not realize he is pronouncing his epitaph.

He more or less lives in the backseat of his Cadillac. He's on the way to Birmingham, and then to Nashville, where he has a booking on the Opry and a sure guest shot on Buck Owens and—maybe—a chance of getting on the *Johnny Cash Show.* Those are his destinations, but they seem somehow insubstantial as he relentlessly moves at ninety-five miles an hour through an endless Alabama. He isn't basically a cruel man, but you would have a hard time proving that by anyone who knows him. He lives on Cokes and Dr Peppers and handfuls of pills, and there are times when he's so strung out that it must be physically painful for him to appear to be present.

He's played by Rip Torn in Daryl Duke's *Payday,* which was released in 1973 to some very favorable reviews and then, inexplicably, never got a proper national release.

It's interesting that *Payday* comes along on the heels of Robert Altman's *Nashville,* because Maury Dann could have wandered through *Nashville* and fit right in: He's cut from the same cloth as the singers in that movie, but he's a little more desperate. The pills are keeping him alive and killing him, all at the same time, and his life is filled with great terrors. He tries to distract himself by expeditions back into his past, where he apparently felt some pleasure, but when he arrives for the birthday of one of his children he finds that he is either four months late or eight months early, and when he joins old friends for some quail-shooting, the day ends in a fight over a dog.

The movie's structure qualifies it as a fairly traditional road picture; we get the series of little towns and sunsets and traffic signs and motels and fast food joints that look about the same in Alabama as anywhere. But the stops along the way are a lot more perceptive than they usually are in road movies, and in particular there's an encounter with a disk jockey that develops genuine corruption.

Maury, acting as straight as he can despite the speed, visits the DJ in his studio and brings along a quart of Wild Turkey as a gift ("Why, Maury, I see you've brought me some wild game!" the DJ snickers). Then follows low-key blackmail in which the DJ tries to talk Maury into returning on Monday for a local fund-raiser, and Maury tries to talk his way out of it, and they both implicitly acknowledge the payola aspect of the whole deal. It's a perfectly observed scene.

There's another sequence in which Maury dumps one of his groupies at roadside, drives off, returns, drives off again, and then returns again; to describe exactly what he's up to would destroy the scene, but it's funny and very hurtful both at once. Duke uses these road scenes to build up a portrait of a man who is deeply cynical, especially about himself, and who uses his little power to protect himself from a world that has so much more. In the end, it turns out he isn't powerful enough.

There's a murder—quick, accidental, almost a surprise—and Maury gets his driver to take the rap for him. It'll be self-defense anyway, but Maury has to make the Birmingham concert. And then his life starts closing in on him. His problems refuse to stay buried; his desperation turns into rage; he has come to the end of the line and he can't fix things anymore—"Not this time," his manager says when he tries to get rid of a cop. The movie's ending provides not so much a tragedy as a deliverance for Maury, and *Payday* is very good at making us see why.

Peggy Sue Got Married

PG-13, 103 m., 1986

Kathleen Turner (Peggy Sue), Nicolas Cage (Charlie), Barry Miller (Richard), Catherine Hicks (Carol), Joan Allen (Maddie). Directed by Francis Ford Coppola and produced by Paul R. Gurian. Screenplay by Jerry Leightling and Arlene Sarner.

We walk like ghosts through the spaces of our adolescence. We've all done it. We stroll unseen across the high school football field. We go back to the drive-in restaurants where we all hung out, all those years ago. We walk into a drugstore for some aspirin, and the magazine rack brings back a memory of sneaking a peek at a Playmate in 1959.

Certain times and places can re-create, with a headstrong rush, what it felt like to be seventeen years old—and we are sometimes more in touch with ourselves at that age than we are with the way we felt a year ago. Have you ever received a telephone message from somebody you were in love with when you were seventeen? And didn't it feel, for a second, as if it came from that long-ago teenager, and not from the adult who left it?

Peggy Sue Got Married is a lot of things—a human comedy, a nostalgic memory, a love story—but there are times when it is just plain creepy, because it awakens such vivid memories in us. It's about a woman who attends her twenty-fifth high school reunion, and passes out, and when she comes to it is 1958 and she inhabits her own teenage body.

Those few details make the movie sound like *Back to the Future,* but give it some thought and you will see that *Peggy Sue* is not a clone, but a mirror image. In *Back to the Future,* the hero traveled backwards through time to meet his own parents when they were teenagers. In *Peggy Sue* the heroine travels backwards to enter her own body as a teenager—and she enters it with her forty-two-year-old mind still intact.

What would you say, knowing what you know now, to the people you loved when you were seventeen? How would you feel if you picked up the telephone, and it was your grandmother's voice? Would you tell her she was going to die in another two years and three months? No, but you would know that, and wouldn't your heart leap into your throat, and wouldn't she wonder what was wrong with you, that you couldn't respond to her simple hello?

Peggy Sue Got Married provides moment after moment like that. It's like visiting a cemetery where all of the people are still alive. And yet it is a comedy. Frank Capra made comedies like this, in which the humor welled up out of a deep, even sentimental, drama of human emotions. There is a scene in the movie where the seventeen-year-old girl (with the mind of the forty-two-year-old woman) sits in the front seat of a car and necks with the teenage boy that (she knows) she will marry and someday decide to divorce. Imagine kissing someone for the first time after you have already kissed them for the last time.

The movie stars Kathleen Turner, in a performance that must be seen to be believed. How does she play a seventeen-year-old? Not by trying to actually look seventeen, because the movie doesn't try to pull off that stunt (the convention is that the heroine looks adult to us, but like a teenager to the other characters). Turner, who is actually thirty-two, plays a teenager by making certain changes in her speech and movement: She talks more impetuously, not waiting for other people to reply, and she walks in that heedless teenage way of those who have not yet stumbled often

enough to step carefully. There is a moment when she throws herself down on her bed, and never mind what she looks like, it feels like a seventeen-year-old sprawled there. Her performance is a textbook study in body language; she knows that one of the symptoms of growing older is that you arrange your limbs more thoughtfully in repose.

The other important character in the movie is Charlie, her boyfriend and later her husband, played by Nicolas Cage. We meet him first as a local businessman in his early forties, and from the way he walks into a room you can tell he's the kind of man who inspires a lot of local gossip. He and his wife are separated and planning to divorce. When we see him again, he's the teenage kid she's dating, and there are two delicate, wonderful scenes where she walks a tightrope, trying to relate to him as if she were a teenager, and as if she hadn't already shared his whole future.

That scene in the front seat of the car is a masterpiece of cross-purposes; she actually wants to go all the way, and he's shocked—shocked not so much by her desire, as by a girl having the temerity to talk and act that way in the 1950s. "Jeez," he says, after she makes her move, "that's a guy's line."

The movie was directed by Francis Coppola, who seems to have been in the right place at the right time. The *Peggy Sue* project got traded around from one actor and director to another (Turner's role was originally cast with Debra Winger, and Coppola was the third director on the project). After several years in which he has tried to make technical and production breakthroughs on his movies, experimenting with new film processes and new stylistic approaches with honorable but uneven results, this time Coppola apparently simply wanted to make a movie, and put some characters on the screen, and tell a story. He has, all right. This was one of the best movies of 1986.

The People vs. Larry Flynt
R, 130 m., 1996

Woody Harrelson (Larry Flynt), Courtney Love (Althea Leasure), Edward Norton (Alan Isaacman), Brett Harrelson (Jimmy Flynt), Donna Hanover (Ruth Carter Stapleton), James Cromwell (Charles Keating), Crispin Glover (Arlo),

Vincent Schiavelli (Chester). Directed by Milos Forman and produced by Oliver Stone, Janet Yang, and Michael Hausman. Screenplay by Scott Alexander and Larry Karaszewski.

"This is it?" the Cincinnati printer asks dubiously, looking at the page proofs for the newsletter Larry Flynt wants him to print. "You've got to have text—like *Playboy*." Flynt is unyielding. He is interested in gynecological detail, not redeeming social merit. Soon his newsletter has blossomed into *Hustler* magazine, although not without difficulties (one editorial conference is devoted to a discussion of why the number of a magazine's pages must be divisible by two).

If you believe that *Hustler* is pornographic and in bad taste, you will not get an argument from Flynt. Flaunting the magazine's raunchiness, he became a millionaire while printing cartoons like the one where "Dorothy has a foursome with the Tin Man, the Cowardly Lion, and the Scarecrow—oh, and Toto." Emboldened by his success, Flynt grew more outrageous, until finally one of his parody ads inspired a $40 million lawsuit from the Rev. Jerry Falwell.

Was Falwell right to be offended? He certainly was; the parody of a Smirnoff ad was in outrageously bad taste. Did Flynt have a right to print the parody? The Supreme Court eventually decided that he did. No one in his right mind could believe that what the ad said was true (as Falwell himself admitted from the witness stand), and the right of free speech includes the right to offend.

The Supreme Court's ruling in the *Hustler* case came under attack at the time, but consider this: If Falwell had won his suit against Flynt, all newspapers would be fundamentally different. The editorial cartoons could not make fun of public officials. The op-ed columns could not risk offending. The lawyers might have questioned a recent review in which I said a film should be cut up into ukulele picks; after all, that might have hurt the director's feelings. And Falwell himself might not have been able to broadcast his sermons, because they might have offended atheists (or you, or me).

"If they'll protect a scumbag like me, then they'll protect all of you," Flynt said after his 1987 court victory. Inelegant, but true. Milos Forman's *The People vs. Larry Flynt* argues that the freedom of speech must apply to unpopular speech or it is meaningless. Beginning with this belief, Forman constructs a fascinating biopic about a man who went from rags to riches by never overestimating the taste of his readers.

If you question the dimensions of *Hustler*'s success, reflect that a modern skyscraper towers in Los Angeles, proclaiming FLYNT PUBLICATIONS from its rooftop. Even if he's only leasing, that's a lot of rent. When Flynt started *Hustler* in 1972, *Playboy* was already twenty years old and *Penthouse* was a success. He aimed below them—at the vulgar underbelly of the market—and offered pictorial details that *Playboy*, at least, has never been interested in printing.

For Flynt, *Hustler* was like winning the lottery. Played by Woody Harrelson, he was a Kentucky moonshiner's son who ran away from home and eventually ran strip clubs in Cincinnati. There he found the love of his life: Althea Leasure (Courtney Love), a bisexual stripper who bluntly told him, "You are not the only person who has slept with every woman in this club."

Hustler's first publicity breakthrough came when Flynt printed nude photos of Jacqueline Onassis, a coup so sensational it forced the media (and the public) to notice the magazine. *The People vs. Larry Flynt* shows Flynt running a loose editorial ship in which his brother Jimmy (Brett Harrelson), hangers-on, and assorted strippers and hookers seem to publish the magazine by committee.

Very early, he meets a man destined to be a lifelong companion: his lawyer, Alan Isaacman (Edward Norton), who wins his spurs defending him in one action after another. An early antagonist is Charles Keating, then head of Citizens for Decent Literature, more recently a figure in the S&L scandals. "I'm your dream client," Flynt tells Isaacman. "I'm fun, I'm rich, and I'm always in trouble."

The movie shows Larry and Althea as a couple deeply into promiscuity; proposing marriage to him in a hot tub, Althea is shocked when Larry thinks she means monogamy. Their marriage survives many tests, not least the one when Flynt is temporarily converted to religion by Ruth Carter Stapleton, sister of the president. (The movie never really makes it clear how sincere Flynt was in his born-again period.)

As the magazine grows, Flynt keeps it on the low road, eventually developing enemies. In 1978, during a trial in Georgia, both he and Isaacman are shot by an unknown gunman, and Flynt is paralyzed from the waist down. That leads to a long dark period, until 1983, when he and Althea hole up in a Los Angeles mansion, using painkillers and whatever other drugs come to hand. The magazine seems to run itself while they cower behind the steel door of their bedroom.

Flynt eventually has an operation that stops his pain, and he kicks drugs. Leasure, not as lucky, sickens and dies of AIDS. Then comes the suit by Falwell, and a journey that ends with Flynt pumping his wheelchair into the Supreme Court.

Larry Flynt is never likely to find his face on a postage stamp, but he has played a role in our era. A negative one, in contributing to the general decay of taste and decorum, and a positive one, in being the point man for a crucial defense of American liberties. As an individual, he seems to have been clueless some of the time and morose much of the time (he plays a cameo role in the film as a judge, and looks unhappy).

But like many another man he was fortunate to find the love of a loyal woman, and Althea, as played by Love, is a quirky free spirit. The product of a tragic childhood (she identified the bodies after her father murdered her family, then went to an orphanage where she was abused), she is made by Love into a kind of life force, misdirected but uncompromised. It is quite a performance; Love proves she is not a rock star pretending to act, but a true actress, and Harrelson matches her with his portrait of a man who has one thing on his mind and never changes it.

Milos Forman's other films have included *Amadeus* and *One Flew Over the Cuckoo's Nest,* both about inspired misfits with the courage of their eccentricity. Now Larry Flynt is another. Who else could have so instinctively combined idealism and cash, declaring at a press conference, "Americans for a Free Press is me. Who do you think is paying for this show?"

A Perfect World

PG-13, 136 m., 1993

Clint Eastwood (Red Garnett), Kevin Costner (Butch Haynes), Laura Dern (Sally Gerber), T. J. Lowther (Phillip Perry), Keith Szarabajka (Terry Pugh), Leo Burmester (Tom Adler), Bradley Whiteford (Bobby Lee). Directed by Eastwood and produced by Mark Johnson and David Valdes. Screenplay by John Lee Hancock.

A Perfect World contains a prison break, the taking of a hostage, a chase across Texas, two murders, various robberies, and a final confrontation between a fugitive and a lawman. It is not really *about* any of those things, however. It's deeper and more interesting than that. It's about the true nature of violence, and about how the child is father of the man.

The film brings together the leading icons of two generations of strong, silent American leading men: Kevin Costner, as a fugitive who takes a boy as hostage, and Clint Eastwood, as the Texas Ranger who leads the pursuit. But the Costner character doesn't seem really focused on his escape, and the Eastwood character seems somewhat removed from the chase. These two men first met long ago, and they both know this isn't about a chase; it's about old, deep wounds.

This is a movie that surprises you. The setup is such familiar material that you think the story is going to be flat and fast. But the screenplay by John Lee Hancock goes deep. And the direction by Clint Eastwood finds strange, quiet moments of perfect truth in the story. Both Costner and Eastwood are fresh from triumphs at the Academy Awards, but in neither *Dances with Wolves* nor *Unforgiven* will you find the subtlety and the sadness that they discover here. Eastwood has directed seventeen films, but his direction is sometimes taken less seriously because he's a movie star. *A Perfect World* is a film that any director alive might be proud to sign.

Costner's character, Butch Haynes, is a young man who drifted into trouble and was sentenced unfairly, to get him out of the way. The Eastwood character, Red Garnett, had something to do with that, and has never felt quite right about it. Escaping from prison, Haynes and another convict break in on a mother and her children at dawn. Soon they're on the road with a hostage, Phillip (T. J. Lowther), nine or ten years old.

Before long the other con is gone from the scene, and the man and the boy are cutting across the back roads of Texas. In pursuit is Red Garnett, riding in a newfangled Airglide trailer that's a "mobile command headquarters." Garnett is saddled with a talky criminologist (Laura Dern) and various other types, including a sinister federal agent who is an expert marksman. The general view is that Haynes is a desperate kidnapper. Both Eastwood and Dern think, for different reasons, it isn't that simple.

And it's not. The heart of the movie is the relationship that develops between the outlaw and the kid. You can look very hard, but you won't be able to guess where this relationship is going. It doesn't fall into any of the conventional movie patterns. Butch isn't a terrifically nice guy, and Phillip isn't a cute movie kid who makes and then loses a friend.

It's not that simple. Butch, we learn, was treated badly as a boy. His father was absent, his mother was a prostitute, the men in her life didn't like him much. Butch talks vaguely about going to Alaska. But as the man and boy drive through the dusty 1963 Texas landscape, it's more like they're going in circles, while the man looks hard at the boy and tries to see what it means to be a boy, what is the right way and the wrong way to talk to one. He's trying to see himself in the kid.

There are, I said, some murders in the film. All of them are off-camera. One body is found in an auto trunk, the other in a cornfield. We don't see either killing; Eastwood makes a decision to stay away from the cliché of a gun firing, a body falling, and it's not until late in the film that someone is shot on-screen, and then in very particular circumstances.

But there is violence in the movie. In the film's key sequence, Butch and Phillip are given shelter for the night by a friendly black farmer (George Haynes). The next morning, Butch watches as the farmer treats his son roughly, slapping him when he doesn't behave. It's the wrong way to treat a kid, but Butch's reaction is so angry, we realize a nerve has been touched. And as a complex series of events unfolds, we discover the real subject of the movie: Treat kids right, and you won't

have to put them in jail later on. The crucial violence, from which later violence springs, is when a child is treated with cruelty.

Eastwood tells the story in unexpected ways. The way Butch starts right out, for example, letting Phillip hold a gun. (But not to shoot someone with it; his reasons for doing this, in fact, are so deep you have to think long about them.) The way Phillip behaves—not as a kidnap victim, not as a friend, but more as a kid keeping his eyes wide open and seeing all he can. And scenes of quirky humor, involving runaway trailers, Halloween masks, barbecued steaks, and other details that break the tension with a certain craziness. (There is, for example, a scene in a roadside diner named "Dottie's Squat and Gobble," which is the best restaurant name I have ever seen in a movie.)

A Perfect World has the elements of a crime genre picture, but it has the depth of thought and the freedom of movement of an art film. Watching it, you may be reminded of *Bonnie and Clyde, Badlands,* or an unsung masterpiece from earlier in 1993, *Kalifornia.* Not because they all tell the same story, but because they all try to get beneath the things we see in a lot of crime movies, and find out what they really mean.

Perfume: The Story of a Murderer
R, 145 m., 2007

Ben Whishaw (Grenouille), Dustin Hoffman (Baldini), Alan Rickman (Richis), John Hurt (Narrator), Rachel Hurd-Wood (Laura), Karoline Herfurth (The Plum Girl), David Calder (Bishop of Grasse). Directed by Tom Tykwer and produced by Julio Fernandez, Andreas Grosch, Samuel Hadida, Manuel Malle, Martin Moskowicz, and Andreas Schmid. Screenplay by Andrew Birkin, Bernd Eichinger, and Tykwer, based on the book by Patrick Suskind.

Not only does *Perfume* seem impossible to film, it must have been almost impossible for Patrick Suskind to write. How do you describe the ineffable enigma of a scent in words? The audiobook, read by Sean Barrett, is the best audio performance I have ever heard; he snuffles and sniffles his way to greatness and you almost believe he is inhaling bliss, or the essence of a stone. I once almost destroyed a dinner party by putting it on for "five minutes," after which nobody wanted to stop listening.

Suskind's famous novel involves a twisted little foundling whose fishwife mother casually births him while chopping off cod heads. He falls neglected into the stinking charnel house that was Paris three-hundred years ago, and is nearly thrown out with the refuse. But Grenouille grows into a grim, taciturn survivor (Ben Whishaw) who possesses two extraordinary qualities: He has the most acute sense of smell in the world and has absolutely no scent of his own.

This last attribute is ascribed by legend to the spawn of the devil, but the movie *Perfume: The Story of a Murderer* makes no mention of this possibility, wisely limiting itself to vile if unnamed evil. Grenouille grows up as a tanner, voluptuously inhaling the world's smells, and eventually talks himself into an apprenticeship with Baldini (Dustin Hoffman), a master perfumer, now past his prime, whose shop is on an overcrowded medieval bridge on the Seine.

Mention of the bridge evokes the genius with which director Tom Tykwer (*Run, Lola, Run*) evokes a medieval world of gross vices, all-pervading stinks, and crude appetites. In this world, perfume is like the passage of an angel—some people think, literally. Grenouille effortlessly invents perfect perfumes, but his ambition runs deeper; he wants to distill the essence of copper, stone, and beauty itself. In pursuit of this last ideal he becomes a gruesome murderer.

Baldini tells him the world center of the perfume art is in Grasse, in southern France, and so he walks there. I was there once myself, during the Cannes festival, and at Sandra Schulberg's villa met les nez de Grasse, "the noses of Grasse," the men whose tastes enforce the standards of a global industry. They sat dressed in neat business suits around a table bearing a cheese, which they regarded with an interest I could only imagine. On the lawn, young folk frolicked on bedsheets strewn with rose petals. You really must try it sometime.

It is in the nature of creatures like Grenouille (I suppose) that they have no friends. Indeed he has few conversations, and they are rudimentary. His life, as it must be, is almost entirely interior, so Tykwer provides a narrator (John Hurt) to establish certain events and facts. Even then, the film is essentially visual, not spoken, and does a remarkable job of es-

tablishing Grenouille and his world. We can never really understand him, but we cannot tear our eyes away.

Perfume begins in the stink of the gutter and remains dark and brooding. To rob a person of his scent is cruel enough, but the way it is done in this story is truly macabre. Still it can be said that Grenouille is driven by the conditions of his life and the nature of his spirit—also, of course, that he may indeed be the devil's spawn.

This is a dark, dark, dark film, focused on an obsession so complete and lonely it shuts out all other human experience. You may not savor it, but you will not stop watching it, in horror and fascination. Whishaw succeeds in giving us no hint of his character save a deep savage need. And Dustin Hoffman produces a quirky old master whose life is also governed by perfume, if more positively. Hoffman reminds us here again, as in *Stranger than Fiction*, what a detailed and fascinating character actor he is, able to bring to the story of Grenouille precisely what humor and humanity it needs, and then tactfully leaving it at that. Even his exit is nicely timed.

Why I love this story, I do not know. Why I have read the book twice and given away a dozen copies of the audiobook, I cannot explain. There is nothing fun about the story, except the way it ventures so fearlessly down one limited, terrifying, seductive dead end and finds there a solution both sublime and horrifying. It took imagination to tell it, courage to film it, and thought to act it, and from the audience it requires a brave curiosity about the peculiarity of obsession.

Permanent Record

PG-13, 92 m., 1988

Alan Boyce (David Sinclair), Keanu Reeves (Chris Townsend), Michelle Meyrink (J. G.), Jennifer Rubin (Lauren), Pamela Gidley (Kim), Michael Elgart (Jake), Richard Bradford (Leo Verdell). Directed by Marisa Silver and produced by Frank Mancuso, Jr. Screenplay by Jarre Fees, Alice Liddle, and Larry Ketron.

The opening shot of *Permanent Record* is ominous and disturbing, and we don't know why. In an unbroken movement, the camera tracks past a group of teenagers who have parked their cars on a bluff overlooking the sea, and are hanging out casually, their friendship too evident to need explaining. There seems to be no "acting" in this shot, and yet it is superbly acted, because it feels so natural that we accept at once the idea that these kids have been close friends for a long time. Their afternoon on the bluff seems superficially happy, and yet there is a brooding quality to the shot, perhaps inspired by the lighting, or by the way the camera circles vertiginously above the sea below.

The following scenes unfold, it seems, almost without plan. We meet a couple of kids who play in a rock band together, and try to sneak into a recording studio, and are thrown out, and arrive at school late. We meet the high school principal, a man who is enormously intriguing because he reveals so little, and yet still succeeds in revealing goodness. We meet the crowd that these two kids hang out with, and we attend some auditions for a school production of *The Pirates of Penzance.* We are impressed by the fact that these teenagers are intelligent, thoughtful, and articulate; they come from a different planet than most movie teenagers.

To describe the opening scenes makes them seem routine, and yet they captured my attention with an intensity I still do not understand. The underlying mystery of many good movies is the way they absorb us in apparently unremarkable details, while bad movies can lose us even with car crashes and explosions. Marisa Silver, who directed this film, and Frederick Elmes, who photographed it, have done something very subtle and strong here, have seen these students and their school in a way that inescapably prepares us for something, without revealing what it is.

The kids all hang out together, but one begins to attract our attention more than the others. He is David (Alan Boyce), an intense, dark-eyed musician who everyone knows is gifted. He leads the rock band, gives lessons to his fellow musicians, and is arranging the music for the production of *Pirates*. In a scene of inexplicable tension, he is told by the principal (Richard Bradford) that he's won a scholarship to a great music school. He tries to seem pleased, but complains that he is so busy—too busy. Bradford quietly reminds him the scholarship isn't until next year.

And then . . . but here I want to suggest that if you plan to see the film, you should read no further and permit yourself its surprises. I began watching this film knowing absolutely nothing about it, and this is the kind of film where that is an advantage. Let the movie unfold like life. Save the review until later.

I found myself impressed, most of all, by the subtlety with which Silver and her writers (Jarre Fees, Alice Liddle, and Larry Ketron) develop David's worsening crisis. This is not a young man made unhappy by the usual problems of TV docudramas. He doesn't use drugs, his girlfriend isn't pregnant, he isn't flunking out of school, and he doesn't have an unhappy home life. But it becomes clear, especially in retrospect, that there is no joy in his life, and we see that most clearly in the understated scene in the bedroom of the girl he sometimes sleeps with. Any other couple who do what they do together, she suggests, would be said to be going together. He nods.

There is something missing here. Some kind of connection with other people. Some exultation in his own gifts and talents. Giving guitar lessons to his friend Chris (Keanu Reeves), he is a little impatient; Chris does not strive hard enough for excellence. David, who is admired by everyone in his school, who is the one singled out by his friends for great success, has a deep sadness inside himself because he is not good enough. And that leads to the scene in which one moment he is on the side of that high bluff, and the next moment he is not.

The rest of the movie is about his friends—about the gulf he has left behind, and about their sorrow, and their rage at him. Again and again, Silver and her writers find authentic ways to portray emotions. We never feel manipulated, because the movie works too close to the heart. Perhaps the best scene in the whole film is the one where Chris, drunk, drives his car into David's yard and almost hits David's younger brother, and then, when David's father comes out on the lawn to shout angrily at him, Chris falls into his arms, weeping and shouting, "I should have stopped him." And the father holds him.

Life goes on. The school production is held. There is a dramatic moment in which David is eulogized, and there is also the sense that years from now his friends will sometimes remember him, be angry with him, and wonder what would have become of him. This is one of the year's best films, and one reason for its power is that it clearly knows what it wants to do, and how to do it. It is not a film about the causes of David's death, and it does not analyze or explain. It is a film about the event, and about the memory of the event. The performances, seemingly artless, are appropriate to the material, and I was especially impressed by the way Bradford suggested so many things about the principal while seeming to reveal so little.

Permanent Record is Marisa Silver's second feature, after the wonderful *Old Enough* (1984), which told the story of a friendship between two thirteen-year-old girls who were from opposite sides of the tracks but were on the same side of adolescence. In that film and this one, she shows that she has a rare gift for empathy, and that she can see right to the bottom of things without adding a single gratuitous note.

Persona

NO MPAA RATING, 83 m., 1966

Bibi Andersson (Nurse Alma), Liv Ullmann (Elisabeth Vogler). Directed and produced by Ingmar Bergman. Screenplay by Bergman.

At first the screen is black. Then, very slowly, an area of dark gray transforms itself into blinding white. This is light projected through film onto the screen, the first basic principle of the movies. The light flickers and jumps around, finally resolving itself into a crude cartoon of a fat lady.

Then the pace picks up. There are shots of cops in old cars, maybe the Keystone Kops. There is a flicker of a tramp; maybe it was Chaplin. There is some footage from an old horror movie, and now there is a sound track too. We hear creepy music. Then some other shots, harder to place.

All this takes several minutes, before the titles for Ingmar Bergman's *Persona* finally appear on the screen. Apparently Bergman intends his film to begin with the invention of the "moving picture" and then to work its way forward in time to the present moment. He is establishing *Persona* as a definite episode in the history of the movies.

Most movies try to seduce us into forgetting we're "only" watching a movie. But Bergman keeps reminding us his story isn't "real." At a crucial moment in his plot the film seemingly breaks, and after it rips for a dozen frames it seems to catch fire within the projector. We see it melting on the screen. Then blackness, then light, and then the old silent comedies again, as *Persona* starts again at the beginning.

Near the end of the film, there is even a transition made by cutting from one of the actresses to a shot of the camera crew. Light men, camera operators, script girls, and Bergman himself look at us dispassionately. Then the on-screen camera turns, and in its view finder we see what will be the next scene. We have been brutally reminded that the story is being filtered through technical equipment.

Bergman's preoccupation with illusion and reality seems to be tied into the plot of *Persona*, which involves a neurotic actress (Liv Ullmann) and her nurse (Bibi Andersson). The actress stopped speaking one night in the middle of a performance and hasn't said a word since. The nurse's duty is to try to win her confidence during a summer of seclusion in the country.

As the two women grow intimate, a strange exchange of personalities seems to occur. "No, no, I'm not you," the nurse cries. "I'm myself." The actress doesn't reply to this or anything else, and the nurse is driven to desperate means in an attempt to get through to her. Who is she? Who is anybody? What is real?

This is a difficult, frustrating film, seeming at times to have more in common with the "personal cinema" of Jean-Luc Godard than with Bergman's usual cool control. The director keeps reminding us that he's right there, creating his film before our eyes. And the distance between his presence and the story he tells is like the distance between what the actress is and what she reveals. The nurse is maddened by the unspeaking actress in the same sense that the audience is frustrated by the movie: Both stubbornly refuse to be conventional and to respond as we expect.

Personal Best

R, 124 m., 1982

Mariel Hemingway (Chris Cahill), Patrice Donnelly (Tory Skinner), Scott Glenn (Coach), Kenny Moore (Denny

Stites). Directed and produced by Robert Towne.
Screenplay by Towne.

Robert Towne's *Personal Best* tells the story of
two women who are competitors for pentath-
lete berths on the 1980 U.S. Olympic team—
the team that did not go to Moscow. The
women are attracted to one another almost at
first sight, and what begins as a tentative exploration develops into a love relationship.
Then the romance gets mixed up with the ferocity of top-level sports competition.

What distinguishes *Personal Best* is that it
creates *specific* characters—flesh-and-blood
people with interesting personalities, people I
cared about. *Personal Best* also seems knowledgeable about its two subjects, which are the
weather of these women's hearts, and the
world of Olympic sports competition.

It is a movie containing the spontaneity of
life. It's about living, breathing, changeable
people and because their relationship seems
to be so deeply felt, so important to them,
we're fascinated by what may happen next.
The movie stars Mariel Hemingway and
Patrice Donnelly as the two women track
stars, Scott Glenn as their coach, and Kenny
Moore as the Olympic swimmer who falls in
love with Hemingway late in the film. These
four people are so right for the roles it's almost
scary; it makes us sense the difference between
performances that are technically excellent
and other performances, like these, that may
sometimes be technically rough but always
find the correct emotional note.

Mariel Hemingway plays a young, naive
natural athlete. We sense that she always has
been under the coaching thumb of her father,
a perfectionist, and that her physical excellence has been won at the cost of emotional
maturity. She knows everything about working out, and next to nothing about her heart,
her sexuality, her own identity. She loses an
important race at a preliminary meet, is
sharply handled by the father, gets sick to her
stomach, is obviously emotionally distraught.

Patrice Donnelly, as a more experienced
athlete, tries to comfort the younger girl. In a
dormitory room that night, they talk. Donnelly shares whatever wisdom she has about
training and running and winning. They

smoke a joint. They kid around. They arm
wrestle. At this point, watching the film, I had
an interesting experience. I did not already
know that the characters in the film were homosexual, but I found myself thinking that
the scene was so erotically charged that, "if
Hollywood could be honest," it would develop
into a love scene. Just then, it did! "This is
scary," Donnelly says, and then she kisses
Hemingway, who returns the kiss.

Personal Best is not simply about their romance, however, it is about any relationship in
which the trust necessary for love is made to
compete with the total egotism necessary for
championship sports. *Can* two people love
each other, and at the same time compete for
the same berth on an Olympic team? Scott
Glenn, the coach, doesn't think so. He accepts
the fact of his two stars' homosexuality, but
what bothers him is a suspicion that Donnelly
may be using emotional blackmail to undercut Hemingway's performance.

This is a very physical movie, one of the
healthiest and sweatiest celebrations of physical exertion I can remember. There is a lot of
nudity in the film—not only erotic nudity, although there is some of that, but also locker
room and steam room nudity, and messing
around nudity that has an unashamed, kidding freshness to it. One scene that shocks
some viewers occurs between Mariel Hemingway and Kenny Moore, when he gets up to go
to the bathroom and she decides to follow
along; the scene is typical of the kind of unforced, natural spontaneity in the whole film.
The characters in *Personal Best* seem to be free
to have real feelings. It is filled with the uncertainties, risks, cares, and rewards of real life,
and it considers its characters' hearts and
minds, and sees their sexuality as an expression of their true feelings for each other.

Peter Rabbit and Tales of Beatrix Potter
G, 90 m., 1971

Frederick Ashton (Mrs. Tiggy-Winkle), Alexander
Wood (Peter Rabbit), Ann Howard (Jemima
Puddle-Duck), Robert Mead (Fox), Michael
Coleman (Jeremy Fisher), Sally Ashby (Mrs.
Pettitoes). Directed by Reginald Mills and
produced by Richard Goodwin. Screenplay by

Goodwin and Christine Edzard, based on the stories of Beatrix Potter.

I have never attended a live ballet performance. I blush to admit it. But it's true. I have in my time attended functions where women danced about on a stage, but I did not confuse them with ballet. Nor wanted to. My ignorance of ballet is based on deep-seated cultural and class prejudices absorbed during my central Illinois childhood; The same forces that sent me panting to the Princess Theater on Saturday afternoons with a dime in my hand made me disinterested in ballet.

Ballet had something to do with the activities of the Fauntleroys who sported about in Thelma Leah Ritter's Dance Studios, which were located upstairs over the Princess Theater. From time to time during quiet scenes in the movies, we could hear them thumping about overhead, and we felt nothing but pity. Pity, and contempt, and hatred, and . . . well, if you've read any of Booth Tarkington's Penrod stories you know how we felt.

I make this confession at this time because I fully expected not to like *Peter Rabbit and Tales of Beatrix Potter*. It is a series of animal tales from the works of Beatrix Potter, a strange Englishwoman who was a little crackers, according to the latest biography, but wrote charming children's stories. The stories are told in dance and pantomime by the Royal Ballet, and the sound track is all music. I thought perhaps four minutes of this ought to be enough for me.

Curiously enough, I stayed and even enjoyed the film. I still would have testified it was too highbrow for kids, though, because as a kid it would have been too highbrow for me. I was programmed against ballet and that was that. Fortunately, I took along three kids who hadn't been told they didn't like ballet and, therefore, didn't know that they were supposed to have a bad time. They had a good time. They were seven, six, and four years old, and among the three of them there were only two expeditions to the john (both by the four-year-old, and one of them a spurious excuse to look for the candy counter).

The stories are told simply and directly and with a certain almost clumsy charm. Instead of going for perfection in the dancing, the Royal Ballet dancers have gone for characterizations instead. The various animals have their quirks and eccentricities, and they are fairly authentic: The frog dances like a frog, for example, and not like Nureyev.

There are a couple of bad moments for the literal-minded, I suppose. Take the scene where Jemima Puddle-Duck is trying to lay an egg. Mr. Fox has in mind the possibilities of preparing Jemima with a sage and onion stuffing, and after Jemima delivers herself of the egg, there is a touchy moment when it just misses becoming an omelet. This kind of confusion between animal-as-character and animal-as-food is a little disquieting; if Jemima Puddle-Duck had eaten the omelet, would she be guilty of incestuous cannibalism? (Movies are getting so perverted these days!)

In any event, I think I can fairly report that your children will enjoy Peter Rabbit and that you will too, especially if you live in the affluent middle-class white communities near the Hillside, Lincoln Village, and Highland Park theaters. Hardly any family movies ever play the South or West Sides; action and violence are shown in those neighborhoods. The entire inner city, including the Near North Side, Rogers Park, Hyde Park, South Shore, and so on, are considered off-limits for high-quality family fare, I guess. It could be that the kids of the urban core (black and white) could use a little whimsical fantasy once in a while, wouldn't you think? I mean, a kid's a kid, right?

Pete Seeger: The Power of Song

NO MPAA RATING, 93 m., 2007

Featuring Pete Seeger, Toshi Seeger, Bob Dylan, Bruce Springsteen, Natalie Maines, Tom Paxton, David Dunaway, Bess Lomax Hawes, Joan Baez, Ronnie Gilbert, Jerry Silverman, Henry Foner, Eric Weissberg, Arlo Guthrie, Peter Yarrow, Mary Travers, Julian Bond, Tommy Smothers, and Bonnie Raitt. Directed by Jim Brown and produced by Michael Cohl and William Eigen.

I don't know if Pete Seeger believes in saints, but I believe he is one. He's the one in the front as they go marching in. *Pete Seeger: The Power of Song* is a tribute to the legendary singer and composer who thought music could be a force for good, and proved it by writing songs that have actually helped shape our times ("If I Had a Hammer" and "Turn, Turn, Turn") and popularizing "We Shall Overcome" and Woody Guthrie's unofficial national anthem, "This Land Is Your Land." Over his long career (he is eighty-eight), he has toured tirelessly with song and stories, never happier than when he gets everyone in the audience to sing along.

This documentary, directed by Jim Brown, is a sequel of sorts to Brown's wonderful *The Weavers: Wasn't That a Time!* (1982), which centered on the farewell Carnegie Hall concert of the singing group Seeger was long associated with. The Weavers had many big hits circa 1950 ("Goodnight Irene," "Kisses Sweeter Than Wine") before being blacklisted during the McCarthy years; called before the House Un-American Activities Committee and asked to name members of the Communist Party, Seeger evoked, not the fifth, but the First Amendment. The Weavers immediately disappeared from the playlists of most radio stations, and Seeger did not appear on television for seventeen years, until the Smothers Brothers broke the boycott.

But he kept singing, invented a new kind of banjo, did more for the rebirth of that instrument than anyone else, cofounded two folksong magazines, and with Toshi, his wife of sixty-two years, did more and sooner than most to live a "green" lifestyle, just because it was his nature. On rural land in upstate New York, they lived for years in a log cabin he built himself, and we see him still chopping firewood and working on the land. "I like to say I'm more conservative than Goldwater," Wikipedia quotes him. "He just wanted to turn the clock back to when there was no income tax. I want to turn the clock back to when people lived in small villages and took care of each other."

With access to remarkable archival footage, old TV shows, home movies, and the family photo album, Brown weaves together the story of the Seegers with testimony by admirers who represent his influence and legacy: Bruce Springsteen, Bob Dylan, Natalie Maines of the Dixie Chicks, Tom Paxton, Joan Baez, Arlo Guthrie, Peter Yarrow, Mary Travers, Julian Bond, and Bonnie Raitt. There is also coverage of the whole Seeger family musical tradition, including brother Mike and sister Peggy.

This isn't simply an assembly of historical materials and talking heads (however eloquent), but a vibrant musical film as well, and Brown has remastered the music so that we feel the real excitement of Seeger walking into a room and starting a sing-along. Unique among musicians, he doesn't covet the spotlight but actually insists on the audience joining in; he seems more choir director than soloist.

You could see that in 2004 at the Toronto Film Festival, in the "final" farewell performance of the Weavers, as he was joined onstage by original group members Ronnie Gilbert and Fred Hellerman, who go back fifty-seven years together, and more recent members Erik Darling and Eric Weissberg. Missing from the original group was the late Lee Hays, who cowrote "If I Had a Hammer."

The occasion was the showing of an interim Brown doc, *Isn't This a Time*, a documentary about a Carnegie Hall "farewell concert" concert in honor of Harold Leventhal's fiftieth anniversary as an impresario. It was Leventhal who booked the Weavers into Carnegie Hall for the first time in the late 1940s, and Leventhal who brought them back to the hall when the group's left-wing politics had made them victims of the show-business blacklist. Although Seeger has sung infrequently in recent years, claiming his voice is "gone," he was in fine form that night in Toronto, his head as always held high and thrown back, as if focused on the future.

Sadly, for many people, Seeger is still associated in memory with the Communist Party USA. Although never a "card-carrying member," he was and is adamantly left-wing; he broke with the party in 1950, disillusioned with Stalinism, and as recently as this year, according to Wikipedia, apologized to a historian: "I think you're right. I should have asked to see the gulags when I was in the USSR."

What I feel from Seeger and his music is a deep-seated, instinctive decency, a sense of fair play, a democratic impulse reflected by singing along as a metaphor. I get the same feeling from Toshi, who coproduced this film and has coproduced her husband's life. How many women would sign on with a folk singer who planned to build them a cabin to live in? The portrait of their long marriage, their children and grandchildren, is one of the most inspiring elements in the film. They actually live as if this land was made for you and me.

Petulia

R, 106 m., 1968

George C. Scott (Archie), Julie Christie (Petulia), Shirley Knight (Polo), Richard Chamberlain (David), Joseph Cotten (Mr. Danner), Pippa Scott (May). Directed by Richard Lester and produced by Raymond Wagner, and Don Devlin. Screenplay by Lawrence B. Marcus.

Richard Lester's *Petulia* made me desperately unhappy, and yet I am unable to find a single thing wrong with it. I suppose that is high praise. It is the coldest, cruelest film I can remember, and one of the most intellectual.

By that I don't mean it's filled with philosophy, like Bergman, or with metaphysics, like *2001*. On the contrary, it's filled with nothing at all. It is lifeless, heartless, bloodless, the expression of Lester's abstract thought about the American way of life. And it is terribly effective.

Most films come with emotions wrapped inside. We pick a movie according to the emotion we desire: a musical to be happy, a Western to be thrilled. *Petulia* doesn't work this way. It provides no built-in emotional response at all. Instead, it glides perfectly across the screen, and the idea is for the audience to provide its own emotion by responding to it.

Offhand, I can think of only two other films that worked this way: Antonioni's *Eclipse* and Resnais's *Last Year at Marienbad*. To one degree or another, both of these inspired impatience, confusion, and irritation. Yet when they were analyzed, they turned out to contain nothing more than the components of everyday life. So what were we irritated at? The lives we lead?

I think so. We are living in an increasingly sanitary, air-conditioned, computerized, Saran-wrapped, Muzaked society. Supermarkets aren't food stores anymore, but hypnotic temples of consumer spending. Public buildings are filled these days with half-audible hums (air conditioning) and buzzes (the lights). Elevators play "Whistle a Happy Tune" at you while you stare at the floor numbers over the door. People unconsciously elevate their manners to fit these clean new environments, nodding graciously to each other in the supermarket aisles as if they were actors in a commercial for living better electrically.

This world is brilliantly re-created in *Petulia*. Lester has buried his characters in material possessions. They live in a modern, efficient, totalitarian society of the sort that used to be called the "city of the future" by *Popular Mechanics*. But now the future has arrived, and we ourselves are those future citizens cooking with invisible rays and sleeping in computerized motels. *Petulia* is almost a poem to artifacts. Its hero, played by George C. Scott, is a doctor in a hospital so efficient that the patients seem incidental to the machines.

Lester's city is also a cruel one. The film is literally filled with violence, with shattered limbs, with beatings, with the Vietnam War on television, with lies and jealousy, and with cruel insults. After Scott examines the torn leg of a little Mexican boy who has been run over by a car, he turns away. The nurse yanks at the leg: "Straighten up, you little spic."

Petulia has more plot than a typical Lester film such as *The Knack* or *A Hard Day's Night*. And Lester's use of quick cuts and jumbled time, which ran wild in *How I Won the War*, is in control this time.

The story mostly involves Scott's relationships with his ex-wife (well played by Shirley Knight) and Julie Christie (as Petulia). There are also Petulia's problems with the Mexican boy, her husband (Richard Chamberlain), and her father (a brilliant performance by Joseph Cotten). But the details of the story are incidental.

Lester's method, I think, is to appeal to the human animal that lives inside the citizen of society. We all live in this world, and we all participate in its indifference. But when we are confronted so directly with the soulless quality of American materialism, as in *Petulia*, we are repelled and disgusted. And that is the idea of the film.

The Phantom of Liberty

R, 104 m., 1974

Adrianna Asti (Prefect's Sister), Jean-Claude Brialy (Mr. Faucaulte), Aldolfo Celi (Dr. Legendre), Michel Piccoli (Second Prefect), Monica Vitti (Mrs. Faucaulte). Directed by Luis Buñuel and produced by Serge Silberman. Screenplay by Buñuel and Jean-Claude Carriere.

Things first began to go wrong, Luis Buñuel teases us, in Spain in 1808, when Napoleon's troops arrived to liberate Toledo. In the opening scenes of Buñuel's savage comedy, *The Phantom of Liberty*, the soldiers execute those who would not be liberated. "Down with freedom!" cries one of the doomed. It is the cry of a defeated social order. The French and American Revolutions have unleashed freedom on a defenseless world, and forevermore the population will be unable to rely on the authoritarian reassurance of church and state.

After a scene of typically Buñuelian surrealism—a drunken soldier tried to embrace a marble woman, and is banged on the head by the sculpture's husband—the film's action moves to contemporary France and stays there. But it doesn't stay in any one place very long. The movie's a fluid, dizzying juggling act of many stories and cheerfully bizarre coincidences.

Buñuel sweeps us into each new vignette so quickly there's no time to hang around while the last one is tidied up. We meet characters, they confront a crisis involving insanity, illegality, doom, fetishism, institutional stupidity, or all of the above, and then, just as the cause of the crisis is revealed as a paradox, the characters cross paths with a new set of characters and we're off on their heels. Buñuel's camera often enters a scene with one set of characters and leaves with another, a device that was used again in *Slacker* (1991).

If I attempted to describe them, Buñuel's interlocking yet disconnected stories would sound bewildering. But his film is strangely lucid; it has the heightened reality of a dream. This material couldn't work if the director weren't supremely confident. And at the age of seventy-five, when most directors are dictating their memoirs, Luis Buñuel was still refining his style and finding new ways to humor his pet personal obsessions. *The Phantom of Liberty* uses his usual prejudices and fetishes to play variations on his favorite theme, which might be stated: In a world cast loose of its moorings by freedom, only anarchy is logical.

Buñuel has always, of course, included an aura of guilty sadomasochism in his movies. His characters are frequently adults pretending to be naughty little boys and girls (like the cardinal who wanted to be a gardener in *The Discreet Charm of the Bourgeoisie*). His fetishes are presented with such exquisite timing, with such a horselaugh in the face of propriety, that we've got to laugh. ("That was a wonderful afternoon little Luis spent on the floor of his mother's closet when he was twelve, and he's been sharing it with us ever since," Pauline Kael once said.)

In *The Phantom of Liberty*, for example, one of the most shocking yet funniest scenes takes place in a wayside inn. Four monks pray for a woman's ailing father. They join her in a poker game, only to be invited to another guest's room for port. The other guest and his female companion disappear, then leap back into sight (she dressed in leather and with a whip), primed for flagellation. As the shocked guests rush out of the room, the would-be victim says plaintively, "Can't at least the monks stay?"

In another scene, a mass killer, found guilty, is released and signs autographs. Guests are cheerfully scatological at the dinner table but sneak into the bathroom to eat their dinner. A man in a playground gives a little girl postcards ("Show them to your friends but not to adults!"). When her parents see the cards, which are views of historical landmarks, they fire the girl's nurse. Another little girl is reported missing at school, even though she is quite clearly there and accompanies her parents to the police station. And so on.

The most impressive thing about the movie is the way Buñuel leads us effortlessly from one wacky parable to the next. We ought to be breathless but we aren't because his editing makes everything seem to follow with inevitable logic. It doesn't, of course, but that's freedom's fault: If people want liberty, they shouldn't be expected to count on anything. *The Phantom of Liberty* is a tour de force, a triumph by a director confronting almost impossible complications and contradictions and mastering them. It's very funny, all right, but remember: With Buñuel, you only laugh when it hurts.

The Piano

R, 121 m., 1993

Holly Hunter (Ada), Harvey Keitel (Baines), Sam Neill (Stewart), Anna Paquin (Flora), Kerry Walker (Aunt Morag), Genevieve Lemon (Nessie), Tungia Baker

(Hira). Directed by Jane Campion and produced by Jan Chapman. Screenplay by Campion.

The Piano is as peculiar and haunting as any film I've seen. It tells a story of love and fierce pride, and places it on a bleak New Zealand coast where people live rudely in the rain and mud, struggling to maintain the appearance of the European society they've left behind. It is a story of shyness, repression, and loneliness; of a woman who will not speak and a man who cannot listen, and of a willful little girl who causes mischief and pretends she didn't mean to.

The film opens with the arrival of a thirty-ish woman named Ada (Holly Hunter) and her young daughter Flora (Anna Paquin) on a stormy gray beach. They have been rowed ashore along with Ada's piano, to meet a local bachelor named Stewart (Sam Neill) who has arranged to marry her. "I have not spoken since I was six years old," Ada's voice tells us on the sound track. "Nobody knows why, least of all myself. This is not the sound of my voice; it is the sound of my mind."

Ada communicates with the world through her piano, and through sign language that is interpreted by her daughter. Stewart and his laborers, local Maori tribesmen, take one look at the piano crate and decide it is too much trouble to carry inland to the house, and so it stays there, on the beach, in the wind and rain. It says something that Stewart cares so little for his new bride that he does not want her to have the piano she has brought all the way from Scotland—even though it is her means of communication. He does not mind quiet women, is one way he puts it.

Ada and Flora settle in. No intimacy grows between Ada and her new husband. One day she goes down to the beach to play the piano, and the music is heard by Baines (Harvey Keitel), a rough-hewn neighbor who has affected Maori tattoos on his face. He is a former whaler who lives alone, and he likes the music of the piano—so much that he trades Stewart land for the piano.

"That is *my* piano—*mine!!*" Ada scribbles on a note she hands to Stewart. He explains that they all make sacrifices and she must learn to, as well. Baines invites her over to play, and thus begins his single-minded seduction, as he offers to trade her the piano for intimacy. There are eighty-eight keys. He'll give her one for taking off her jacket. Five for raising her skirt.

Jane Campion, who wrote and directed *The Piano*, does not handle this situation as a man might. She understands better the eroticism of slowness and restraint, and the power that Ada gains by pretending to care nothing for Baines. The outcome of her story is much more subtle and surprising than Baines's crude original offer might predict.

Campion has never made an uninteresting or unchallenging film (her credits include *Sweetie*, about a family ruled by a self-destructive sister, and *An Angel at My Table*, the autobiography of writer Janet Frame, wrongly confined for schizophrenia). Her original screenplay for *The Piano* has elements of the Gothic in it, of that sensibility that masks eroticism with fear, mystery, and exotic places. It also gives us a heroine who is a genuine piece of work; Ada is not a victim here, but a woman who reads a situation and responds to it.

The performances are as original as the characters. Holly Hunter's Ada is pale, grim, and hatchet-faced at first, although she is capable of warming. Harvey Keitel's Baines is not what he first seems, but has unexpected reserves of tenderness and imagination. Sam Neill's taciturn husband conceals a universe of fear and sadness behind his clouded eyes. And the performance by Anna Paquin, as the daughter, is one of the most extraordinary examples of a child's acting in movie history. She probably has more lines than anyone else in the film, and is as complex, too-able to invent lies without stopping for a breath, and filled with enough anger of her own that she tattles just to see what will happen. She won an Oscar as Best Supporting Actress.

Stuart Dryburgh's cinematography is not simply suited to the story, but enhances it. Look at his cold grays and browns as he paints the desolate coast, and then the warm interiors that glow when they are finally needed. And if you are oddly affected by a key shot just before the end (I will not reveal it), reflect on his strategy of shooting and printing it, not in real time, but by filming at quarter-time and then printing each frame four times, so that the movement takes on a fated, dreamlike quality.

The Piano is one of those rare movies that is not just about a story, or some characters, but about a whole universe of feeling—of how people can be shut off from each other, lonely and afraid, about how help can come from unexpected sources, and about how you'll never know if you never ask.

Pixote

R, 127 m., 1981

Fernando Ramos da Silva (Pixote), Marilla Pera (Sueli), Jorge Juliao (Lilica), Gilberto Moura (Dito). Directed by Hector Babenco and produced by Sylvia B. Naves. Screenplay by Babenco and Jorge Duran.

Kids love to play by the rules. They're great at memorizing them. They repeat them to one another like ancient commandments. They never pause to question them. For the kids in *Pixote,* the rules apply to their lives in the streets as thieves, beggars, and child prostitutes. These kids are only ten or twelve years old, and at the beginning of *Pixote* we learn that there are hundreds of thousands of them living in the streets of Rio and Sao Paolo, Brazil, where more than half the population is younger than eighteen.

Pixote is the story of one of those children, called Pixote because he is small and wide-eyed and solemn-faced and the name seems to fit. He is not a bad kid, but he lives in a fearsome environment, in which all crimes, even the most violent, are part of the daily routine. Some of the children who commit these crimes are too young to even fully understand the gravity of taking a human life. To them, a gun or a knife is a coveted possession, a prize captured from the adult world, and to use it is to gain in stature.

There is no attempt to reform these kids. They're rounded up from time to time, after a particularly well-publicized theft, mugging, or killing. They're thrown into corrupt reformatories that act as schools for crime. For all of them, the overwhelming fact of their society—the only *law* they finally understand—is that they are immune from the full force of the law until they are eighteen. They almost seem to interpret this as a license to steal, a li-cense revoked on their eighteenth birthday, when real life begins.

Hector Babenco's film follows Pixote and several other street children through a crucial passage in their lives. They survive, they steal, they engage in innocent entertainments, they impassively observe the squalor around them, they pass through reformatory jails, they sit on the beach and dream of the future, and their lives lead up to a moment of unplanned, almost accidental violence.

Babenco shot his film on location, on the streets and inside the slum rooms of Brazil's big cities. He also cast it from among the street children themselves. Twenty-one homeless, parentless children play themselves, more or less, in this movie, and the leading character (Fernando Ramos da Silva) is an untrained, uneducated young orphan who succeeds, in this film, in creating a performance of utterly convincing realism. The film's other great performance is by Marilla Pera, as the prostitute who adopts him. (Pera won the National Society of Film Critics award for best actress for this performance; da Silva returned to the streets and was killed by police bullets in 1988.)

Babenco's filmmaking method, of casting actual people to play themselves, and then shooting on the locations where they live and work, has been used before, most successfully by the Italian neorealists. Such films as Vittorio De Sica's *Bicycle Thief* and *Shoeshine* were cast with nonactors and shot on location, and they captured a freshness and actuality that influenced the look and feel of subsequent mainstream films: After the neorealists, there was a movement in the studio films of the 1950s and 1960s toward performances, dialogue, and sets that reflected more of real life and less of the stylized Hollywood fantasies of the 1930s.

De Sica's story lines, however, were heavily, if simply, plotted, and his films drew clear conclusions about the social injustices suffered by his characters. *Pixote* is just as angry and committed as *Bicycle Thief,* but it has more of a documentary freedom. Even though it is loosely based on a novel, Babenco's film sometimes seems to be following characters no matter what they're inclined to do or say.

The one scene in the film that does seem planned is the last one, of a prostitute nursing a mournful child at her breast—and that scene, of course, is directly from John Steinbeck's *The Grapes of Wrath*, where even at the time it seemed contrived and too obviously symbolic.

The film otherwise moves with the very rhythms of life itself. It shows evil deeds (thefts, muggings, killings) that have no evil perpetrators; both criminal and target are victims. And it shows a society that perpetrates a class of child criminals because it is incapable of even really *seeing* them clearly, let alone helping to improve their lives. *Pixote* is one of the very best realistic dramas of modern cinema.

Platoon

R, 119 m., 1986

Tom Berenger (Barnes), Willem Dafoe (Sergeant Elias), Charlie Sheen (Chris), Forest Whitaker (Big Harold), Francesco Quinn (Raah), John C. McGinley (Sergeant O'Nill), Richard Edson (Sal), Kevin Dillon (Bunny). Directed by Oliver Stone and produced by Arnold Kopelson. Screenplay by Stone.

It was François Truffaut who said that it's not possible to make an antiwar movie, because all war movies, with their energy and sense of adventure, end up making combat look like fun. If Truffaut had lived to see *Platoon*, he might have wanted to modify his opinion. Here is a movie that regards combat from ground level, from the infantryman's point of view, and it does not make war look like fun.

The movie was written and directed by Oliver Stone, who fought in Vietnam and who has tried to make a movie about the war that is not fantasy, not legend, not metaphor, not message, but simply a memory of what it seemed like at the time to him.

The movie is narrated by a young soldier (Charlie Sheen) based on Stone himself; a middle-class college kid who volunteers for the war because he considers it his patriotic duty, and who is told, soon after he arrives in the combat zone, "You don't belong here." He believes it.

There are no false heroics in this movie, and no standard heroes; the narrator is quickly at the point of physical collapse, bedeviled by long marches, no sleep, ants, snakes, cuts, bruises, and constant, gnawing fear. In a scene near the beginning of the film, he is on guard duty when he clearly sees enemy troops approaching his position, and he freezes. He will only gradually, unknowingly, become an adequate soldier.

The movie is told in a style that rushes headlong into incidents. There is no carefully mapped plot to lead us from point to point, and instead, like the characters, we are usually disoriented. Anything is likely to happen, usually without warning. From the crowded canvas, large figures emerge: Barnes (Tom Berenger), the veteran sergeant with the scarred face, the survivor of so many hits that his men believe he cannot be killed; Elias (Willem Dafoe), another good fighter, but a man who tries to escape from the reality through drugs; Bunny (Kevin Dillon), the scared kid, who has become dangerous because that seems like a way to protect himself.

There is rarely a clear, unequivocal shot of an enemy soldier. They are wraiths, half-seen in the foliage, their presence scented on jungle paths, evidence of their passage unearthed in ammo dumps buried beneath villages. Instead, there is the clear sense of danger all around, and the presence of civilians who sometimes enrage the troops just by standing there and looking confused and helpless.

There is a scene in the movie that seems inspired by My Lai, although it does not develop into a massacre. As we share the suspicion that these villagers may, in fact, be harboring enemy forces, we share the fear that turns to anger, and we understand the anger that turns to violence.

Some of the men in *Platoon* have lost their bearings, are willing to kill almost anyone on the least pretext. Others still retain some measure of the morality of the situation. Since their own lives may also be at stake in their arguments, there is a great sense of danger when they disagree; we see Americans shooting other Americans, and we can understand why.

After seeing *Platoon*, I fell to wondering why Stone was able to make such an effective movie without falling into the trap Truffaut spoke about—how he made the movie riveting without making it exhilarating. Here's how I think he did it. He abandoned the choreography that is standard in almost all war movies. He abandoned any attempt to make it clear where the various forces were in relation to each other, so that we never know where "our" side stands and where "they" are. Instead of battle scenes in which lines are clearly drawn, his combat scenes involve 360 degrees. Any shot might be aimed at friend or enemy, and in the desperate rush of combat, many of his soldiers never have a clear idea of exactly who they are shooting at, or why.

Traditional movies impose a sense of order upon combat. Identifying with the soldiers, we feel that if we duck behind this tree or jump into this ditch, we will be safe from the fire that is coming from over there. In *Platoon*, there is the constant fear that any movement offers a fifty-fifty chance between a safe place or an exposed one. Stone sets up his shots to deny us the feeling that combat makes sense.

The Vietnam War is the central moral and political issue of the last quarter century for Americans. It has inspired some of the greatest recent American films: *Apocalypse Now, The Deer Hunter, Coming Home, The Killing Fields*. Now here is the film that, in a curious way, should have been made before any of the others. A film that says—as the Vietnam Memorial in Washington says—that before you can make any vast sweeping statements about Vietnam, you have to begin by understanding the bottom line, which is that a lot of people went over there and got killed, dead, and that is what the war meant for them.

The Player

R, 123 m., 1992

Tim Robbins (Griffin Mill), Greta Scacchi (June Gudmundsdottir), Fred Ward (Walter Stuckel), Whoopi Goldberg (Detective Avery), Peter Gallagher (Larry Levy), Dean Stockwell (Andy Civella), Sydney Pollack (Dick Mellen), Dina Merrill (Celia). Directed by Robert Altman and produced by David Brown, Michael Tolkin, and Nick Wechsler. Screenplay by Tolkin, based on his book.

It would be hard to describe Griffin Mill's job in terms that would make sense to anyone who has had to work for a living. He's a vice president at a movie studio, which pays him enormous sums of money to listen to people describe movies to him. When he hears a pitch he likes,

he passes it along. He doesn't have the authority to give a "go" signal himself, and yet for those who beseech him to approve their screenplays, he has a terrifying negative authority. He can turn them down. Griffin starts getting anonymous postcards from a writer who says he is going to kill him. Griffin's crime: He said he would call the writer back, and he never did.

Robert Altman's *The Player*, which tells Griffin's story with a cold, sardonic glee, is a movie about today's Hollywood—hilarious and heartless in about equal measure, and often at the same time. It is about an industry that is run like an exclusive rich boys' school, where all the kids are spoiled and most of them have ended up here because nobody else could stand them. Griffin is capable of humiliating a waiter who brings him the wrong mineral water. He is capable of murder. He is not capable of making a movie, but if a movie is going to be made, it has to get past him first.

This is material Altman knows from the inside and the outside. He owned Hollywood in the 1970s, when his films like *M*A*S*H, McCabe and Mrs. Miller,* and *Nashville* were the most audacious work in town. Hollywood cast him into the outer darkness in the 1980s, when his eclectic vision didn't fit with movies made by marketing studies. Now he is back in glorious vengeance, with a movie that is not simply about Hollywood, but about the way we live now, in which the top executives of many industries are cut off from the real work of their employees and exist in a rarefied atmosphere of greedy competition with one another.

The Player opens with a very long, continuous shot that is quite a technical achievement, yes, but also works in another way, to summarize Hollywood's state of mind in the early 1990s. Many names and periods are evoked: silent pictures, foreign films, the great directors of the past. But these names are like the names of saints who no longer seem to have the power to perform miracles. The new gods are like Griffin Mill—sleek, expensively dressed, noncommittal, protecting their backsides. Their careers are a study in crisis control. If they do nothing wrong, they can hardly be fired just because they never do anything right.

The Player follows Griffin (Tim Robbins) during a period when his big paycheck, his luxury car, and his expensive lifestyle seem to be in danger. There is another shark in the pond, a younger executive (Peter Gallagher) who may be even sleeker and greedier, and who may get Griffin's job. This challenge comes at a bad time: Griffin is shedding a girlfriend (a woman whose superior intelligence he feeds on, while treating the rest of her like a shabby possession). And there are those postcards.

Who is sending the postcards? Griffin racks his memory and his secretary's appointment book. He has lied to so many writers that there is no way to narrow the field. Finally he picks one name and calls the guy for a meeting. The guy's girlfriend says he's out in Pasadena, seeing *The Bicycle Thief* at a revival house. Griffin drives out there, meets the guy, has a conversation with him, follows him back to a parking lot, and kills him. As if Griffin didn't have enough problems already.

The movie then follows Griffin's attempts to protect his position at the studio, evade arrest for murder, and conduct a romance with the dead man's fiancée (Greta Scacchi), who, if anything, is more cynical than Griffin. This story was first told in a novel by Michael Tolkin, who made it so compelling I read it in a single sitting. Now Altman has made it funny as well, without losing any of the lacerating anger and satire. Altman fills his film with dozens of cameos by recognizable stars, most of them saying exactly what's on their minds. And he surrounds Griffin with the kind of oddball characters who seem to roll into Los Angeles, as if the continent was on a tilt: Whoopi Goldberg as a Pasadena police detective who finds Griffin hilarious, Fred Ward as a studio security chief who has seen too many old *Dragnet* episodes, Sydney Pollack as a lawyer who does for the law what Griffin does for the cinema, Lyle Lovett as a sinister figure lurking on the fringes of many gatherings.

Watching *The Player*, we want to despise Griffin Mill, but we can't quite manage that. He is not dumb. He has a certain verbal charm. As played by Tim Robbins, he is tall, with a massive forehead but a Dana Carvey smile, and he wears a suit well. Watching him in some shots, especially when the camera is below eye level and Altman uses a mockheroic composition, we realize with a shock that Griffin looks uncannily like the young Citizen Kane. He has a similar morality, too, but not the breadth of vision.

Altman, who has always had a particular strength with unusual supporting characters, surrounds him with people who all seem to be sketches for movies of their own. The girlfriend played by Scacchi, whose name is June Gudmundsdottir, and who may or may not be Icelandic, is an example: a Southern California combination of artistic self-realization (she paints) and self-interest (for her, romances are like career stages). Peter Gallagher, as the rival young executive, is like the kid at school who could always push your buttons, who was so hateful you could never understand why God didn't strike him dead for smirking at you all the time. And Whoopi Goldberg, as the cop who is almost certain Griffin is a murderer, brings a certain moral detachment to her job: Would she rather apprehend a perpetrator, or enjoy the human comedy?

The Player is a smart movie, and a funny one. It is also absolutely of its time. After the savings and loan scandals, after Michael Milken, after junk bonds and stolen pension funds, here is a movie that uses Hollywood as a metaphor for the avarice of the 1980s. It is the movie *The Bonfire of the Vanities* wanted to be. There was a full-page photo of Robert Altman in one of the newsweeklies, looking sideways at the camera, grinning like someone who has waited a long time, and finally gotten in the last word. As someone who grew up on his great films, it gives me pleasure to see him make another one.

Play It as It Lays
R, 99 m., 1973

Tuesday Weld (Maria), Tammy Grimes (Helene), Anthony Perkins (B. Z.), Adam Roarke (Carter). Directed by Frank Perry and produced by Dominick Dunne and Perry. Screenplay by Joan Didion and John Gregory Dunne, based on the book by Didion.

In the sometimes very cruel world of the movie business, there is a truth so old that hardly anybody even bothers to repeat it anymore: Actors have much longer professional careers than actresses. It has something to do with our sexist tastes in human styles, I suppose. Almost all of the top male movie stars are in their forties or fifties, and most of the top females are under thirty-five.

Whatever else this is (tragic? unnecessary?), it is a fact. And the people who make their living in Hollywood understand it as a fact, the women as well as the men. Joan Didion's *Play It as It Lays,* which has now been made into a movie by Frank Perry, is in many ways a consideration of such a fact. The movie concerns Maria, a woman who began life in a ferociously genuine Montana town but has somehow found her way into the totally illusory world of the movies. She's an actress, and maybe you could say she's a minor star. She had a success in *Angel Beach,* a movie directed by her husband. But now she waits (exists, drifts) through a series of empty weeks while her husband plays big shot with his new movie project.

The thing is, you see, that the real power in Hollywood always belongs to the money brokers, and they are almost always men: the executives, producers, directors. The public knows all about the stars and considers them important, but in the business itself, the important people are the ones with clout, connections, money enough to float a project for real. All of this is implied around the edges of *Play It as It Lays,* which is about the crack-ups of Maria and her best friend, B. Z. Now B. Z. is a producer and, therefore, should be strong, successful, happy. But B. Z. has a problem. He has been cursed with insight, and he suspects in his despairing soul that life—and the novice and everything—adds up to one big fat zero.

Maria is beginning to understand this, too, and she fears it more as she prowls up and down the Los Angeles freeways and through the casinos in Vegas, looking for nothing. Her husband, of course, is involved in his ego trip and does not understand that a million times zero is still. . . . It's not so much that Maria is sick and could get well with professional help. It's more that she really does understand how futile her life has become, and she's cracking up under the realization. She's a person born bleak and raised on skepticism, and at the end of the movie she comes up with a pretty cheerless reason for continuing to live: "Why not?" Why not. I have an Irish friend who says those two words are the handiest in the language and will help you to avoid bar fights for the rest of your life. Anybody says anything, just answer "Why not?" Doesn't even matter what was said: The

words are all-purpose, circular, appropriate for every situation, and meaningless. And they do something else that my friend didn't mention: When you address them to another person, you cause him suddenly to turn his observation, whatever it was, back upon himself.

Apply these words to life itself, and you get an approximation of Maria's state of mind. *Play It as It Lays* is an astringent, cynical movie that ultimately manages to spin one single timid thread of hope. Its happiest moment—the moment of deepest human understanding and mutual love—comes during a suicide.

Didion's book has been recruited by the feminists to illustrate various, no doubt cogent, points. But it isn't a feminist novel; it's a novel about going to pieces. It's about a woman who is confronted with her own lack of worthwhile identity in much the same way Scott Fitzgerald faced his, in *The Crack-Up.*

What makes the movie work so well on this difficult ground is, happily, easy to say: It has been well-written and directed, and Tuesday Weld and Anthony Perkins are perfectly cast as Maria and her friend B. Z. The material is so thin (and has to be) that the actors have to bring the human texture along with them. They do, and they make us care about characters who have given up caring for themselves.

Play Misty for Me

R, 102 m., 1971

Clint Eastwood (Disc Jockey), Jessica Walter (Strange Woman), Donna Mills (Girlfriend), Don Siegel (Bartender). Directed by Eastwood and produced by Robert Daley. Screenplay by Jo Heims and Dean Reisner.

The girl calls up every night at about the same time and asks the disc jockey to play "Misty" for her. Some nights he does. He's the all-night man on a small station in Carmel who plays records, reads poems, and hopes to make it someday in the big city. After work (and before work, for that matter) he drinks free at bars around town, places he sometimes mentions on the air. He had a steady girl for a while, but he's been freelancing recently, and one night he picks up a girl in a bar. Or maybe she picks him up. She's the girl who likes "Misty." She is also mad. She insinuates herself into his life with a passionate jealousy, and we gradually come to understand that she is capable of violence. At the same time, the disc jockey's old love turns up in town, and he wants nothing more than to allow himself, finally, to quit playing the field and marry her. But the new girl doesn't see it that way. And she has this thing for knives.

Play Misty for Me is not the artistic equal of *Psycho*, but in the business of collecting an audience into the palm of its hand and then squeezing hard, it is supreme. It doesn't depend on a lot of surprises to maintain the suspense. There ARE some surprises, sure, but mostly the film's terror comes from the fact that the strange woman is capable of anything.

The movie was Clint Eastwood's debut as a director, and it was a good beginning. He must have learned a lot during seventeen years of working for other directors. In particular, he must have learned a lot from Don Siegel, who directed his previous four movies and has a bit part (the bartender) in this one. There is no wasted energy in *Play Misty for Me*. Everything contributes to the accumulation of terror, until even the ordinary, daytime scenes seem to have unspeakable things lurking beneath them.

In this connection, Eastwood succeeds in filming the first Semi-Obligatory Lyrical Interlude that works. The Semi-OLI, you'll recall, is the scene where the boy and girl walk in the meadow and there's a hit song on the sound track. In Eastwood's movie, he walks in the meadow with the girl, but the scene has been prepared so carefully that the meadow looks ominous. The grass looks muddy, the shadows are deep, the sky is gray, and there is a chill in the air. The whole visual style of the movie is strangely threatening.

The movie revolves around a character played with an unnerving effectiveness by Jessica Walter. She is something like flypaper; the more you struggle against her personality, the more tightly you're held. Clint Eastwood, in directing himself, shows that he understands his unique movie personality. He is strong but somehow passive, he possesses strength but keeps it coiled inside. And so the movie, by refusing to release any emotion at all until the very end, absolutely wrings us dry. There is no purpose to a suspense thriller, I suppose, except to involve us, scare us, to give us moments of vicarious terror. *Play Misty for Me* does that with an almost cruel efficiency.

Pleasantville

PG-13, 116 m., 1998

Tobey Maguire (David/Bud), Reese Witherspoon (Jennifer/Mary Sue), Jeff Daniels (Mr. Johnson), Joan Allen (Betty Parker), William H. Macy (George Parker), J. T. Walsh (Big Bob), Don Knotts (TV Repairman), Paul Walker (Skip), Marley Shelton (Margaret), Jane Kaczmarek (David and Jennifer's Mom). Directed by Gary Ross and produced by Steven Soderbergh, Jon Kilik, and Bob Degus. Screenplay by Ross.

In the twilight of the twentieth century, here is a comedy to reassure us that there is hope— that the world we see around us represents progress, not decay. *Pleasantville*, which is one of the year's best and most original films, sneaks up on us. It begins by kidding those old black-and-white sitcoms like *Father Knows Best*, it continues by pretending to be a sitcom itself, and it ends as a social commentary of surprising power.

The movie opens in today's America, which we have been taught to think of as rude, decadent, and dangerous. A teenager named David languishes in front of the tube, watching a rerun of a 1950s sitcom named *Pleasantville*, in which everybody is always wholesome and happy. Meanwhile, his mother squabbles with her ex-husband and his sister Jennifer prepares for a hot date.

Having heard a whisper or two about the plot, we know that the brother and sister will be magically transported into that 1950s sitcom world. And we're expecting maybe something like *The Brady Bunch Movie*, in reverse. We are correct: While David and Jennifer are fighting over the remote control, there's a knock at the door, and a friendly TV repairman (Don Knotts) offers them a device "with more oomphs." They click it, and they're both in Pleasantville.

The movie has been written and directed by Gary Ross, who wrote *Big*, the 1988 movie where Tom Hanks was a kid trapped in an adult body. Here the characters are trapped in a whole world. He evokes the black-and-white 1950s sitcom world of picket fences and bobby sox, where everybody is white and middle class, has a job, sleeps in twin beds, never uses the toilet, and follows the same cheerful script.

Luckily, this is a world that David (Tobey Maguire) knows well; he's a TV trivia expert. It's a mystery to his sister Jennifer (Reese Witherspoon), so he briefs her: Their names are now Bud and Mary Sue, and their parents are Betty and George Parker (Joan Allen and William H. Macy). "We're, like, stuck in Nerdville!" Jennifer complains.

They are. Geography lessons at the local high school are limited to subjects like "Main Street" and "Elm Street" because the world literally ends at the city limits. Space twists back upon itself in Pleasantville, and "the end of Main Street is just the beginning again." Life always goes according to plan, and during basketball practice every shot goes in. (But things change. After one player experiences sex, he is capable of actually missing a shot; a dead silence falls as it rolls away. "Stand back, boys!" warns the coach. "Don't touch it!")

Pleasantville has fun during these middle sequences, as "Bud and Mary Sue" hang out at the malt shop run by Mr. Johnson (Jeff Daniels) and park on Lover's Lane (just to hold hands). Then sparks from the emerging future begin to land here and there in the blandness. Mary Sue shares information about masturbation with her mother, who of course has never dreamed of such a pastime (as a perfect housewife, she has never done anything just for herself). As her mother relaxes in her bath, a tree outside their house breaks into flames—in full color!

Ross and his cinematographer, John Lindley, work with special effects to show a black-and-white world in which some things and a few people begin switching to color. Is there a system? "Why aren't I in color?" Mary Sue asks Bud. "I dunno," he says. "Maybe it's not just the sex." It isn't. It's the change.

The kids at school are the first to start appearing in colors. They're curious and ready to change. They pepper Bud with questions. "What's outside of Pleasantville?" they ask. "There are places," he says, "where the roads don't go in a circle. They just keep going." Dave Brubeck's "Take Five" subtly appears on the sound track.

Bud shows Mr. Johnson a book of color art reproductions, and the soda jerk is thunderstruck by the beauty of Turner and van Gogh. He starts painting. Soon he and Betty Parker have discovered they're kindred spirits. (After Betty turns up in color, she's afraid to show herself, and in a scene of surprising tenderness her son helps her put on gray makeup.) George Parker, meanwhile, waits disconsolately at home for his routine to continue, and the chairman of the chamber of commerce (J. T. Walsh, in his last performance) notes ominously, "Something is happening in our town."

Yes, something, in a town where nothing ever did. The film observes that sometimes pleasant people are pleasant simply because they have never, ever been challenged. That it's scary and dangerous to learn new ways. The movie is like the defeat of the body snatchers: The people in color are like former pod people now freed to move on into the future. We observe that nothing creates fascists like the threat of freedom.

Pleasantville is the kind of parable that encourages us to reevaluate the good old days, and take a fresh look at the new world we so easily dismiss as decadent. Yes, we have more problems. But also more solutions, more opportunities, and more freedom. I grew up in the 1950s. It was a lot more like the world of *Pleasantville* than you might imagine. Yes, my house had a picket fence, and dinner was always on the table at a quarter to six, but things were wrong that I didn't even know the words for. There is a scene in this movie where it rains for the first time. Of course it never rained in 1950s sitcoms. Pleasantville's people in color go outside and just stand in it.

Note: Pleasantville *contains the last major role by the much-admired character actor J. T. Walsh. He plays the head of the 1950s sitcom chamber of commerce, a man much threatened by change, who warns, "There is something happening in our town"—a town, we know, where nothing has ever happened.*

Walsh, who played roles in nearly sixty movies in a busy acting career that began only in 1983, was also seen recently as an internal affairs investigator in The Negotiator *and a murdering truck driver in* Breakdown. *He died unexpectedly on February 27, 1998, of a heart attack, at age fifty-three.*

"He was so hard on himself," remembers Gary Ross, who directed him in Pleasantville.

"I met J. T. at seven in the morning and he was having a big whipped cream cheese, smoking a cigarette while he was eating. He smoked all the time. Tough on himself. And he was so hard on himself as an actor.

"As a director, you try to sort of find what it is they need, a little bit of reassurance, and with J. T. it was—boy, how do I get him to forgive himself and relax a little bit here? He was so brilliant, and I would go, 'This is great, this is great.' But he never believed it."

Walsh came late to acting, Ross said. "He was an encyclopedia salesman. He was so good right from the start. Remember him in Good Morning, Vietnam?"

He was also in Sling Blade, Nixon *(as John Erlichman),* Contact, Red Rock West, Backdraft, Hoffa *(as union leader Frank Fitzsimmons), and many TV programs (he had a continuing role on* L.A. Law *in 1986).*

In Pleasantville, *he leads the forces of the status quo against the threat of change. "J. T. had the best way of describing the movie," Ross remembered. "He said the kids from the future (who stir up the 1950s sitcom universe) are like the sand that gets in the oyster. It was such a perfect metaphor—the irritation that produces something beautiful."*

As for Walsh's death so soon after filming was completed: "It's just an insane loss."

The Polar Express

G, 100 m., 2004

Body movement performers: Tom Hanks (Hero Boy/Father/Conductor/Hobo/Scrooge/Santa), Michael Jeter (Smokey/Steamer), Nona Gaye (Hero Girl), Peter Scolari (Lonely Boy), Eddie Deezen (Know-It-All), Charles Fleischer (Elf General), Steven Tyler (Elf Lieutenant/Elf Singer), Leslie Zemeckis (Sister Sarah/Mother). Voice performers if different than above: Daryl Sabara (Hero Boy), Andre Sogliuzzo (Smokey/Steamer), Jimmy Bennett (Lonely Boy), Isabella Peregrina (Sister Sarah). Directed by Robert Zemeckis and produced by Gary Goetzman, Steve Starkey, William Teitler, and Robert Zemeckis. Screenplay by Zemeckis and William Broyles, Jr., based on the book by Chris Van Allsburg.

The Polar Express has the quality of a lot of lasting children's entertainment: It's a little creepy. Not creepy in an unpleasant way, but in that sneaky, teasing way that lets you know eerie things could happen. There's a deeper, shivery tone, instead of the mindless jolliness of the usual Christmas movie. This one creates a world of its own, like *The Wizard of Oz* or *Willy Wonka,* in which the wise child does not feel too complacent.

Those who know the Chris Van Allsburg book will feel right at home from the opening moments, which quote from the story: *On Christmas Eve, many years ago, I lay quietly in my bed . . .* The young hero, who is never given a name, is listening for the sound of sleigh bells ringing. He is at just the age when the existence of Santa Claus is up for discussion.

The look of the film is extraordinary, a cross between live action and Van Allsburg's artwork. Robert Zemeckis, the same director whose *Who Framed Roger Rabbit* juxtaposed live action with animation, this time merges them, using a process called "performance capture," in which human actors perform the movements that are translated into lifelike animation. The characters in *The Polar Express* don't look real, but they don't look unreal, either; they have a kind of simplified and underlined reality that makes them visually magnetic. Many of the body and voice performances are by Tom Hanks, who is the executive producer and worked with Zemeckis on *Forrest Gump* (1994)—another film that combined levels of reality and special effects.

The story: As Hero Boy lies awake in bed, there is a rumble in the street and a passenger train lumbers into view. The boy runs outside in his bathrobe and slippers, and the conductor advises him to get onboard. Having refused to visit a department store Santa, having let his little sister put out Santa's milk and cookies, Hero Boy is growing alarmingly agnostic on the Santa question, and *The Polar Express* apparently shuttles such kids to the North Pole, where seeing is believing.

Already on board is Hero Girl, a solemn and gentle African-American, who becomes the boy's friend, and also befriends Lonely Boy, who lives on the wrong side of the tracks and always seems sad. Another character, Know-It-All, is one of those kids who can't supply an answer without sounding obnoxious about it. These four are the main characters, in addition to the conductor, a hobo who lives on top of the train, Santa, and countless elves.

There's an interesting disconnect between the movie's action and its story. The action is typical thrill-ride stuff, with *The Polar Express* careening down a "179-degree grade" and racing through tunnels with a half-inch of clearance, while Hero Boy and the hobo ski the top of the train to find safety before the tunnel. At the North Pole, there's another dizzying ride when the kids spin down a corkscrewing toy chute.

Those scenes are skillful, but expected. Not expected is a dazzling level of creativity in certain other scenes. Hero Girl's lost ticket, for example, flutters through the air with as much freedom as the famous floating feather at the start of *Forrest Gump*. When hot chocolate is served on the train, dancing waiters materialize with an acrobatic song-and-dance. And the North Pole looks like a turn-of-the-century German factory town, filled with elves who not only look mass-produced but may have been, since they mostly have exactly the same features (this is not a cost-cutting device, but an artistic decision).

Santa, in this version, is a good and decent man, matter-of-fact and serious: a professional man, doing his job. The elves are like the crowd at a political rally. A sequence involving a bag full of toys is seen from a high angle that dramatizes Santa's operation, but doesn't romanticize it; this is not Jolly St. Nick, but Claus Inc. There is indeed something a little scary about all those elves with their intense, angular faces and their mob mentality.

That's the magic of *The Polar Express*: It doesn't let us off the hook with the usual reassuring Santa and Christmas clichés. When a helicopter lifts the bag of toys over the town square, of course it knocks a star off the top of the Christmas tree, and of course an elf is almost skewered far below. When Santa's helpers hitch up the reindeer, they look not like tame cartoon characters, but like skittish purebreds. And as for Lonely Boy, although he does make the trip and get his present, and is fiercely protective of it, at the end of the movie we suspect his troubles are not over, and that loneliness may be his condition.

There are so many jobs and so many credits on this movie that I don't know who to praise, but there are sequences here that are really very special. Some are quiet little moments, like a reflection in a hubcap. Some are visual masterstrokes, like a point-of-view that looks straight up through a printed page, with the letters floating between us and the reader. Some are story concepts, like the train car filled with old and dead toys being taken back to the Pole for recycling. Some are elements of mystery, like the character of the hobo, who is helpful and even saves Hero Boy's life but is in a world of his own up there on top of the train and doesn't become anybody's buddy (when he disappears, his hand always lingers a little longer than his body).

The Polar Express is a movie for more than one season; it will become a perennial, shared by the generations. It has a haunting magical quality because it has imagined its world freshly and played true to it, sidestepping all the tiresome Christmas clichés that children have inflicted on them this time of year. The conductor tells Hero Boy he thinks he really should get on the train, and I have the same advice for you.

Note: I've seen the movie twice, once in the IMAX 3-D process that will be available in larger markets. New oversized 3-D glasses, big enough to fit over your own glasses, light enough so you can forget them, made this the best 3-D viewing experience I've ever had. If there's a choice, try the IMAX version. Or go twice. This is a movie that doesn't wear out.

Pollock

R, 122 m., 2001

Ed Harris (Jackson Pollock), Marcia Gay Harden (Lee Krasner), Amy Madigan (Peggy Guggenheim), Jennifer Connelly (Ruth Klingman), Jeffrey Tambor (Clement Greenberg), Bud Cort (Howard Putzel), John Heard (Tony Smith), Val Kilmer (Willem de Kooning). Directed by Harris and produced by Fred Berner, Harris, and John Kilik. Screenplay by Barbara Turner and Susan Emshwiller, based on the book *Jackson Pollock: An American Saga* by Steven Naifeh and Gregory White Smith.

Reporter from *Life* magazine: "How do you know when you're finished with a painting?"

Jackson Pollock: "How do you know when you're finished making love?"

Jackson Pollock was a great painter. He was also a miserable man who made everyone around him miserable a lot of the time. He was an alcoholic and manic-depressive, and he died in a drunken car crash that killed an innocent woman. What Ed Harris is able to show in *Pollock* is that when he was painting, he got a reprieve. He was also reasonably happy during those periods when he stopped drinking. Then the black cloud would descend again.

Pollock avoids the pitfall of making simplistic one-to-one connections between the artist's life and his paintings. This is not a movie about art but about work. It is about the physical labor of making paintings, and about the additional labor of everyday life, which is a burden for Pollock because of his tortured mind and hungover body. It is said that it takes more will for an alcoholic to get out of bed in the morning than for other people to go through the day, and there are times when Pollock simply stops, stuck, and stares into space. He didn't have de Kooning's luck and find sobriety.

Pollock is often depressed, but *Pollock* is not depressing. It contains all the hum and buzz of the postwar New York art world, the vibrant courage of Pollock's wife, Lee Krasner, the measured presence of the art critic Clement Greenberg (who more or less validated abstract expressionism), and the fun-loving energy of the millionaire art patron Peggy Guggenheim, who collected paintings and painters. It was a time when Pollack traded a painting to pay a $56 bill at a store, and found himself in *Life* magazine not long after. Things were on the move.

This is Ed Harris's movie. He started thinking about it fifteen years ago, after reading a book about Pollock. He commissioned the screenplay. He raised the money. He stars in it, and he directed it. He knew he looked a lot like Pollock (his father saw the book and thought the cover photo resembled his son). But his similarity to Pollock is not just superficial; he looks a little like Picasso, too, but is unlikely to find the same affinity. He seems to have made a deeper connection, to have felt an instinctive sympathy for this great, unhappy man.

The movie wears its period lightly. It gets rolling in postwar Greenwich Village. Everybody smokes all the time. Rents are cheap, but the first time Peggy Guggenheim visits Pollock's studio is almost the last: "I do not climb up five flights of stairs to nobody home!" Why did Pollock almost miss his first meeting with

the famous patron? Some damn fool reason. He had a knack for screwing up, and it's arguable that his career would never have happened if Lee Krasner hadn't poked her head around his door one day.

Krasner (played by Marcia Gay Harden, evoking enormous sympathy and patience) comes calling because she wants to see his paintings. She passes her hand over them as if testing their temperature. She knows they are good. She senses that Pollock takes little initiative in personal matters, and takes charge of their relationship, undressing while Pollock is still looking for his cigarettes. She goes in with her eyes open. She knows she's marrying a troubled man, but stands by him, and is repaid with a couple of happy years when they get a place in the country, and he doesn't drink. Then the troubles all start again—a bottle of beer, a fight, an upset table at Thanksgiving, and affairs with hero-worshipping girls like Ruth Klingman (Jennifer Connelly).

I don't know if Ed Harris knows how to paint, but I know he knows how to look like he's painting. There's a virtuoso scene where he paints a mural for Peggy's townhouse, utterly confident, fast and sure, in the flow. And others where we see the famous drip technique (and see that "anyone" could not do it). His judge and jury is the critic Clement Greenberg, played with judicious, plummy certainty by Jeffrey Tambor. He says what he thinks, praising early work and bringing Guggenheim around, then attacking later work even as the world embraces it ("pretentious muddiness").

Pollock is confident, insightful work—one of the best films of the year. Ed Harris is always a good actor but here seems possessed, as if he had a leap of empathy for Pollock. His direction is assured, economical, knows where it's going, and what it wants to do. No fancy visual gimmicks, just the look and feel of this world.

I first saw the movie at the Toronto Film Festival and a day later ran into the painter Julian Schnabel. I mentioned Pollock's suffering. "What happened to Jackson Pollock when he was painting," Schnabel said, "is, he was free." That's what Ed Harris communicates in the film. A man is miserable but he is given a gift. The gift lifts his misery while he employs it. It brings joy to himself and others. It creates space he can hide in, space he can breathe in, space he can escape to. He needs that space, and given his demons, painting is the only way he can find it.

A Prairie Home Companion

PG-13, 105 m., 2006

Woody Harrelson (Dusty), Tommy Lee Jones (Axeman), Garrison Keillor (G. K.), Kevin Kline (Guy Noir), Lindsay Lohan (Lola Johnson), Virginia Madsen (Dangerous Woman), John C. Reilly (Lefty), Maya Rudolph (Molly), Meryl Streep (Yolanda Johnson), Lily Tomlin (Rhonda Johnson), L. Q. Jones (Chuck Akers), Tim Russell (Back Stage Manager), Sue Scott (Makeup Lady), Tom Keith (Effects Man). Directed by Robert Altman and produced by Altman, Wren Arthur, Joshua Astrachan, Tony Judge, and David Levy. Screenplay by Garrison Keillor.

What a lovely film this is, so gentle and whimsical, so simple and profound. Robert Altman's *A Prairie Home Companion* is faithful to the spirit of the radio program, a spirit both robust and fragile, and yet achieves something more than simply reproducing a performance of the show. It is nothing less than an elegy, a memorial to memories of times gone by, to dreams that died but left the dreamers dreaming, to appreciating what you've had instead of insisting on more.

This elegiac strain is explained by the premise that we are watching the last performance of the weekly show. After a final singing of "Red River Valley" (the saddest of all songs), the paradise of the Fitzgerald Theater will be torn down so they can put up a parking lot. After thirty years, the show will be no more.

The show is hosted by a man referred to as G. K., and played by Garrison Keillor as a version of himself, which is about right, because he always seems to be a version of himself. Keillor, whose verbal and storytelling genius has spun a whole world out of thin air, always seems a step removed from what he does, as if bemused to find himself doing it. Here his character refuses to get all sentimental about the last program and has a dialogue with Lola (Lindsay Lohan), a young poet who likes suicide as a subject. It seems to her G. K. should offer up a eulogy; there is sufficient cause, not only because of the death of the program but also because a veteran of the show actually dies during the broadcast.

"I'm of an age when if I started to do eulogies, I'd be doing nothing else," he says.

"You don't want to be remembered?"

"I don't want them to be *told* to remember me."

So the last show is treated like any other. In the dressing room, incredibly cluttered with bric-a-brac and old photos, we meet Lola's mother and her aunt, Yolanda and Rhonda Johnson (Meryl Streep and Lily Tomlin). They are the two survivors from a four-sister singing act: "The Carter Family was like us, only famous." Their onstage duets are hilarious, depending on a timing that rises above the brilliant to the transcendent; they were doing this double act on the Academy Award telecast in March 2006.

We also meet Chuck Akers (L. Q. Jones), an old-time C&W singer, and Dusty and Lefty (Woody Harrelson and John C. Reilly), two cowboy singers who threaten to make the last program endless as they improvise one corny joke after another. We also meet the people who make the show work: one of the stage managers, Molly (Maya Rudolph), and, borrowed from the show itself, the makeup lady (Sue Scott), Al the backstage guy (Tim Russell), the sound effects man (Tom Keith), the bandleader (Rich Dworsky), and the P. H. C. house band. Molly is surely so pregnant she should stay calm, but she is driven to distraction by G. K.'s habit of never planning anything and moseying up to the microphone at the last conceivable moment.

Adding another level is the materialization in the real world of Guy Noir, Private Eye (Kevin Kline). Listeners of the program will know that Keillor and his stock company perform adventures from the life of Noir as a salute to old-time radio drama. In Altman's movie, Noir is a real person, a broken-down gumshoe who handles security for the show (he lights his cigarettes with wooden kitchen matches, just like Philip Marlowe in Altman's *The Long Goodbye*). Guy is visited by a character described as the Dangerous Woman (Virginia Madsen), who may perhaps be an angelic one.

The final visitor to the Fitzgerald Theater is Axeman (Tommy Lee Jones), who represents the investors who have bought the lovely theater and will tear it down. He doesn't recognize the bust of a man in the theater's private box, but we do: It is F. Scott Fitzgerald, that native son of St. Paul in whose honor the theater is named. A little later, Ed Lachman's camera helps Altman observe that Fitzgerald and Guy Noir have profiles so similar as to make no difference.

Like the show that inspired it, *A Prairie Home Companion* is not about anything in particular. Perhaps it is about everything in general: about remembering, and treasuring the past, and loving performers not because they are new but because they have lasted. About smiling and being amused, but not laughing out loud, because in Minnesota loud laughter is seen as a vice practiced on the coasts. About how all things pass away, but if you live your life well, everything was fun while it lasted. There is so much of the ghost of Scott Fitzgerald hovering in the shadows of this movie that at the end I quoted to myself the closing words of *The Great Gatsby*. I'm sure you remember them, so let's say them together: "And so we beat on, boats against the current, borne back ceaselessly into the past."

The President's Analyst

NO MPAA RATING, 102 m., 1967

James Coburn (Dr. Sidney Schaefer), Severn Darden (Kropotkin), Godfrey Cambridge (Masters), Joan Delaney (Nan Butler), Pat Harrington (Arlington Hewes), William Daniels (Wynn Quantrill), Walter Burke (Henry Lux). Directed by Theodore J. Flicker and produced by Stanley Rubin. Screenplay by Flicker.

The phone company is the enemy. Not the commies. The phone company. We hate the phone company every time we get a wrong number. The phone company doesn't like that. It wants to be loved. It spends millions of dollars (our dollars) to make us love it. Doesn't that strike you as sinister?

Every month the little *TeleBriefs* magazine comes with your phone bill. It is the most relentlessly bright, cute, and friendly publication in the world. It is the Doris Day of the printed word. It is filled with stories of heroic telephone operators hauling dogs out of the river. It is overdone. One of the world's largest corporations trying to be folksy is like Godzilla giving Lassie a Milk-Bone.

The President's Analyst fights back against the phone company and its accomplice, J. Edgar Hoover and his Electric G-Men. It is one of the funniest movies of the year, ranking with *The Graduate* and *Bedazzled* in the sharp edge of its satire.

James Coburn stars as an analyst who is called in to give the president someone to talk to. This makes problems. The president is the loneliest man in the world. But the president's analyst is lonelier, especially since the FBI bugs his room and the CIA hires his girlfriend.

The girlfriend also presents problems. The CIA says it's okay for Coburn to have a girlfriend. But the FBI doesn't think that's normal. Its leader believes people entrusted with national secrets should be clean and noble, above suspicion and not fool around with (ugh) girls and disgusting things like that. Coburn begins to go nuts. He escapes into Greenwich Village, joins a hippie rock band, and has a beautiful love scene with one of the hippie girls. But the FBI and the secret services of various foreign powers are after him.

He's saved by two friendly counter-spies: Godfrey Cambridge of the CIA and Severn Darden of the Russian secret police. Cambridge releases his droll, sly humor, and the brilliant Darden is turned loose to portray maniacal normalcy as only he can.

Writer and director Theodore Flicker's satire is modern and biting, and there are many fine, subtle touches in the film. All of the FBI agents are clean-cut, sharp-jawed, impeccably groomed men of exactly four feet, eleven inches tall. And when Coburn is kidnapped by the phone company, there is a nauseatingly pleasant young man who lectures him on why the phone company is his friend. To accompany the lecture, there are animated cartoons like a TV commercial—but done in a peculiar way so all the little dancing men look uncoordinated.

As the girlfriend, Joan Delaney is refreshingly natural and warmly animal. William Daniels, who plays a middle-class creep, has brought this role to perfection in *Two for the Road* and *The Graduate*. Coburn, who has been in lousy movies lately (*In Like Flint, Waterhole No. 3*) regains his form as a comedian. *TeleBriefs* readers of the world, throw off your area codes and love one another.

Prick Up Your Ears

R, 111 m., 1987

Gary Oldman (Joe Orton), Alfred Molina (Kenneth Halliwell), Vanessa Redgrave (Peggy Ramsay), Wallace Shawn (John Lahr), Lindsay Duncan (Anthea Lahr), Julie Walters (Elsie Orton), James Grant (William Orton). Directed by Stephen Frears and produced by Andrew Brown. Screenplay by Alan Bennett, based on the book by Lahr.

For all of their years together, Joe Orton and Kenneth Halliwell lived in a cramped room in the north of London, up near the Angel tube stop where everything seems closer to hell. Even after Orton became famous, even after his plays were hits and he was winning awards and his picture was in the papers, he came home to the tiny hovel where Halliwell was waiting. One night he came home and Halliwell hammered him to death and killed himself.

Prick Up Your Ears is the story of Orton and Halliwell and the murder. They say that most murderers are known to their victims. They don't say that if you knew the victims as well as the murderer did, you might understand more about the murder, but doubtless that is sometimes the case. This movie opens with a brutal, senseless crime. By the time the movie is over, the crime is still brutal, but it is possible to comprehend.

When they met, Orton was seventeen, Halliwell was twenty-five, and they both wanted to be novelists. They were homosexuals, but sex never seemed to be at the heart of their relationship. They lived together, but Orton prowled the night streets for rough trade and Halliwell scolded him for taking too many chances. Orton was, by all accounts, a charming young man-liked by everybody, impish, rebellious, with a taste for danger. Halliwell, eight years older, was a stolid, lonely man who saw himself as Orton's teacher.

He taught him everything he could. Then Orton used what he'd learned to write plays that drew heavily on their life together. His big hits were *Loot* and *What the Butler Saw,* and both are still frequently performed. But when Orton won the *Evening Standard*'s award for the play of the year—an honor like the Pulitzer Prize—he didn't take Kenneth to the banquet, he took his agent.

Halliwell began to feel that he was receiving no recognition for what he saw as the sacrifice of his life. He dabbled in art and constructed collages out of thousands of pictures clipped from books and magazines. But his shows were in the lobbies of the theaters presenting Joe's plays, and people were patronizing to him. That began to drive him mad.

Prick Up Your Ears is based on the biography that John Lahr wrote about Orton, a biography that has become famous for discovering a private life so different from the image seen by the public.

Homosexuality was a crime in the 1960s in England, but Orton was heedless of the dangers. In fact, he seemed to enjoy danger. Perhaps that was why he kept Halliwell around, because he sensed the older man might explode. More likely, though, he kept him out of loyalty and indifference and didn't fully realize how much he was hurting him. One of the early scenes in the film shows Halliwell skulking at home, angry because Orton is late for dinner.

The movie is good at scenes like that. It has a touch for the wound beneath the skin, the hurt that we can feel better than the person who is inflicting it. The movie is told as sort of a flashback, with the Lahr character interviewing Orton's literary agent and then the movie spinning off into memories of its own.

The movie is not about homosexuality, which it treats in a matter-of-fact manner. It is really about a marriage between unequal partners. Halliwell was, in a way, like the loyal wife who slaves at ill-paid jobs to put her husband through medical school, only to have the man divorce her after he's successful because they have so little in common—he with his degree, she with dishwater hands.

The movie was written by Alan Bennett, a successful British playwright who understands Orton's craft. He bases one of his characters on Lahr (played by Wallace Shawn), apparently as an excuse to give Orton's literary agent (Vanessa Redgrave) someone to talk to. The device is awkward, but it allows Redgrave into the movie, and her performance is superb: aloof, cynical, wise, unforgiving.

The great performances in the movie are, of course, at its center. Gary Oldman plays Orton and Alfred Molina plays Halliwell, and these are two of the best performances of 1987. Oldman you may remember as Sid Vicious, the punk rock star in *Sid & Nancy*. There is no point of similarity between the two performances; like a few gifted actors, he is able to reinvent himself for every role. On the basis of these two movies, he is the best young British actor around. Molina has a more thankless role as he stands in the background, overlooked and misunderstood. But even as he whines we can understand his feelings, and by the end we are not very surprised by what he does.

The movie was directed by Stephen Frears, whose previous movie, *My Beautiful Laundrette*, also was about a homosexual relationship between two very different men: a Pakistani laundry operator and his working-class, neofascist boyfriend. Frears makes homosexuality an everyday thing in his movies, which are not about his characters' sexual orientation but about how their underlying personalities are projected onto their sexuality and all the other areas of their lives.

In the case of Orton and Halliwell, there is the sense that their deaths had been waiting for them right from the beginning. Their relationship was never healthy and never equal, and Halliwell, who was willing to sacrifice so much, would not sacrifice one thing: recognition for his sacrifice. If only Orton had taken him to that dinner, there might have been so many more opening nights.

Pride & Prejudice

PG, 127 m., 2005

Keira Knightley (Elizabeth Bennet), Matthew Macfadyen (Darcy), Brenda Blethyn (Mrs. Bennet), Donald Sutherland (Mr. Bennet), Simon Woods (Charles Bingley), Rupert Friend (Lieutenant Wickham), Tom Hollander (William Collins), Rosamund Pike (Jane Bennet), Jena Malone (Lydia Bennet), Judi Dench (Lady Catherine), Carey Mulligan (Kitty Bennet), Talulah Riley (Mary Bennet). Directed by Joe Wright and produced by Tim Bevan, Eric Fellner, and Paul Webster. Screenplay by Deborah Moggach, based on the book by Jane Austen.

It is a truth universally acknowledged, that a single man in possession of a good fortune, must be in want of a wife.

Everybody knows the first sentence of Jane Austen's *Pride & Prejudice*. But the chapter ends with a truth equally acknowledged about Mrs. Bennet, who has five daughters in want of husbands: "The business of her life was to get her daughters married." Romance seems so urgent and delightful in Austen because marriage is a business, and her characters cannot help treating it as a pleasure. *Pride & Prejudice* is the best of her novels because its romance involves two people who were born to be in love, and who care not about business, pleasure, or each other. It is frustrating enough when one person refuses to fall in love, but when both refuse, we cannot rest until they kiss.

Of course all depends on who the people are. When Dorothea marries the Reverend Casaubon in Eliot's *Middlemarch,* it is a tragedy. She marries out of consideration and respect, which is all wrong; she should have married for money, always remembering that where money is, love often follows, since there is so much time for it. The crucial information about Mr. Bingley, the new neighbor of the Bennet family, is that he "has" an income of four or five thousand pounds a year. One never earns an income in these stories, one has it, and Mrs. Bennet (Brenda Blethyn) has her sights on it.

Her candidate for Mr. Bingley's hand is her eldest daughter, Jane; it is orderly to marry the girls off in sequence, avoiding the impression that an older one has been passed over. There is a dance, to which Bingley brings his friend Darcy. Jane and Bingley immediately fall in love, to get them out of the way of Darcy and Elizabeth, who is the second Bennet daughter. These two immediately dislike each other. Darcy is overheard telling his friend Bingley that Elizabeth is "tolerable, but not handsome enough to tempt *me*." The person who overhears him is Elizabeth, who decides she will "loathe him for all eternity." She is advised within the family circle to count her blessings: "If he liked you, you'd have to talk to him."

These are the opening moves in Joe Wright's new film *Pride & Prejudice*, one of the most delightful and heartwarming adaptations made from Austen or anybody else. Much of the delight and most of the heart comes from Keira Knightley, who plays Elizabeth as a girl glowing in the first light of perfection. She is beautiful, she has opinions, she is kind but can be unforgiving. "They are all silly and ignorant like other girls," says her father in the novel, "but Lizzie has something more of quickness than her sisters."

Knightley's performance is so light and yet fierce that she makes the story almost realistic; this is not a well-mannered *Masterpiece Theatre* but a film where strong-willed young people enter life with their minds at war with their hearts. The movie is more robust than most period romances. It is set earlier than most versions of the story, in the late 1700s, when Austen wrote the first draft; that was a period more down to earth than 1813, when she revised and published it. The young ladies don't look quite so much like illustrations for *Vanity Fair*, and there is mud around their hems when they come back from a walk. It is a time of rural realities: When Mrs. Bennet sends a daughter to visit Netherfield Park, the country residence of Mr. Bingley, she sends her on horseback, knowing it will rain and she will have to spend the night.

The plot by this point has grown complicated. It is a truth universally acknowledged by novelists that before two people can fall in love with each other, they must first seem determined to make the wrong marriage with someone else. It goes without saying that Lizzie fell in love with young Darcy (Matthew Macfadyen) the moment she saw him, but her pride has been wounded. She tells Jane: "I might more easily forgive his vanity had he not wounded mine."

The stakes grow higher. She is told by the dashing officer Wickham (Rupert Friend) that Darcy, his childhood friend, cheated him of a living that he deserved. And she believes that Darcy is responsible for having spirited Bingley off to London to keep him out of the hands of her sister Jane. Lizzie even begins to think she may be in love with Wickham. Certainly she is not in love with the Reverend Collins (Tom Hollander), who has a handsome living and would be Mrs. Bennet's choice for a match. When Collins proposes, the mother is in ecstasy, but Lizzie declines and is supported by her father (Donald Sutherland), a man whose love for his girls outweighs his wife's financial planning.

All of these characters meet and circle one another at a ball in the village Assembly Hall, and the camera circles them. The sequence involves one unbroken shot and has the same elegance as Visconti's long single take as he follows the count through the ballrooms in *The Leopard*. We see the characters interacting, we see Lizzie avoiding Collins and enticing Darcy, we understand the politics of these romances, and we are swept up in the intoxication of the dance. In a later scene, as Lizzie and Darcy dance together, everyone else somehow vanishes (in their eyes, certainly) and they are left alone within the love they feel.

But a lot must happen before the happy ending, and I particularly admired a scene in the rain where Darcy and Lizzie have an angry argument. This argument serves two purposes: It clears up misunderstandings, and it allows both characters to see each other as the true and brave people they really are. It is not enough for them to love each other; they must also love the goodness in each other, and that is where the story's true emotion lies.

The movie is well cast from top to bottom; like many British films, it benefits from the genius of its supporting players. Judi Dench brings merciless truth-telling to her role as a society arbiter; Sutherland is deeply amusing as a man who lives surrounded by women and considers it a blessing and a fate; and as his wife, Blethyn finds a balance between her character's mercenary and loving sides. She may seem unforgivably obsessed with money, but better be obsessed with money now than with poverty hereafter.

When Lizzie and Darcy finally accept each other in *Pride & Prejudice*, I felt an almost unreasonable happiness. Why was that? I am impervious to romance in most films, seeing it as a manifestation of box office requirements. Here it is different, because Darcy and Elizabeth are good and decent people who would rather do the right thing than convenience themselves. Anyone who will sacrifice their own happiness for higher considerations deserves to be happy. When they realize that about each other their hearts leap and, reader, so did mine.

Primary Colors
R, 135 m., 1998

John Travolta (Governor Jack Stanton), Emma Thompson (Susan Stanton), Billy Bob Thornton (Richard Jemmons), Kathy Bates (Libby Holden), Adrian Lester

(Henry Burton), Maura Tierney (Daisy), Larry Hagman (Governor Fred Picker), Diane Ladd (Mamma Stanton). Directed and produced by Mike Nichols. Screenplay by Elaine May, based on the book by "Anonymous" (Joe Klein).

Here's the surprising thing: *Primary Colors* would seem just about as good, as tough, and as smart if there had never been a president named Bill Clinton. Of course the movie resonates with its parallels to the lives of Bill and Hillary Clinton, but it's a lot more than a disguised exposé. It's a superb film—funny, insightful, and very wise about the realities of political life.

The director, Mike Nichols, and the writer, his longtime collaborator Elaine May, have put an astonishing amount of information on the screen, yes, but that wasn't the hard part. Their real accomplishment is to blend so many stories and details into an observant picture that holds together. We see that Jack Stanton, the presidential candidate in the film, is a flawed charmer with a weakness for bimbos, but we also see what makes him attractive even to those who know the worst: He listens and cares, and knows how to be an effective politician.

John Travolta and Emma Thompson play Stanton and his wife, Susan, as a couple who, we feel, have spent many long hours and nights in mind-to-mind combat. Her true feelings about his infidelity remain unexpressed, but she is loyal to a larger idea of the man, and not as hurt that he fools around as that she's lied to about it. Much will be written about how much Travolta and Thompson do or do not resemble the Clintons, but their wisest choice as actors is to preserve their mystery.

By *not* going behind their bedroom door, by not eavesdropping on their private moments, the movie avoids having to explain what perhaps can never be understood: why a man is driven to self-destructive behavior, and how his wife might somehow remain at his side anyway. The movie wisely stays a certain distance from the Stantons. There are no important scenes in which they are alone together in a room.

Instead, *Primary Colors* centers its point of view in a character named Henry Burton (Adrian Lester), grandson of a civil rights leader, who doesn't join the campaign so much as get sucked into its wake. Before he has even agreed to join Stanton's team, he finds himself on a chartered plane to New Hampshire with the candidate asleep on his shoulder. Earlier, he saw Stanton at work. At an illiteracy class, a black man (Mykelti Williamson in a powerful cameo) tells of the pain of not being able to read. Stanton empathizes with him, telling the story of his Uncle Charlie, who was a Medal of Honor winner but passed up college scholarships because he was ashamed to admit his illiteracy, and instead "just laid down on his couch and smoked his Luckies."

Of course, the Uncle Charlie story may not be entirely true, and later that day Henry sees Stanton emerging from a hotel bedroom with the flustered woman who runs the illiteracy program, but for Henry and the other campaign workers it eventually comes down to this: All the candidates are flawed in one way or another, but some have good ideas, and of those only a few might be able to win.

John Travolta dominates the movie, in part, by his absence. Nichols and May must have decided it would be a mistake to put him into every scene: A man like Jack Stanton is important because of the way people talk, speculate, and obsess about him in his absence.

Through Henry, we meet the campaign's inner circle. Richard Jemmons (Billy Bob Thornton), obviously based on Clinton's strategist James Carville, is a cynical realist who provides running commentary on the stages of the campaign. Libby Holden (Kathy Bates), the "dust-buster," is a longtime Stanton confidant and recent mental patient who comes out of retirement, foul-mouthed and lusty, to dig up the dirt before the other side can. And Daisy (Maura Tierney), quiet and observant, is a scheduler who eventually finds herself in Henry's bed, not so much out of choice as default. Of the crowd, Bates is the dynamo, playing a hard-living lesbian with a secret center of idealism; it's an Oscar-caliber performance.

The movie ticks off episodes based on real life. There's a woman from the candidate's home state who claims to have had an affair with him and to have tapes to prove it. And a dramatic appearance on national TV, where Susan Stanton holds her husband's hand and defends him (her hand snaps away from his as the show goes off the air). It intercuts these with fiction, created in the novel by "Anonymous," now revealed as ex-*Newsweek* writer Joe Klein. There's the pregnancy of the teenage daughter of Stanton's favorite barbecue chef. And the populist Florida governor (Larry Hagman), who looks good against Stanton until his past returns to haunt him.

Much of the movie's ethical content revolves not around sex, but around how a primary campaign should handle damaging information it turns up about its opponent. Libby argues that they shouldn't use it. Jack says that if they don't, the other side will. Better to get it out before it does more harm.

In the way *Primary Colors* handles this issue, it shows more insight and maturity than all but a handful of recent mainstream movies: This is a grown-up film about real issues in the real world. Among its pleasures is the way it lets us examine the full frame, and observe how characters at the side or in the background react; whole characters are developed in asides.

It is also very funny at times, as when Stanton, Jemmons, and others get in a "mommathon," praising their mothers into the night. Or when Susan snatches Jack's ever-present chicken drumstick out of his hand. Or when the candidate, his wife, and his aides search a roadside for a cell phone thrown from a car in anger. The movie is endlessly inventive and involving: You get swept up in the political and personal suspense, and begin to understand why people are engulfed in political campaigns.

Will *Primary Colors* hurt or help the Clinton presidency? To some degree, neither; it's a treatment of matters the electorate has already made up its mind about. The film has certainly not in any sense "softened" its portrayal of its Clintonesque hero—those rumors are exposed by its almost brutal candor. But in a strange way *Primary Colors* may actually work to help Clinton. While a lesser film would have felt compelled to supply an "answer," this one knows that the fascination is in the complexity, in the strong and weak qualities at war with one another. The secret of what makes Jack Stanton tick is as unanswerable as the meaning of Citizen Kane's "Rosebud." And the resemblance doesn't stop there.

Prince of the City

R, 167 m., 1981

Treat Williams (Daniel Ciello), Jerry Orbach (Gus Levy), Richard Foronjy (Joe Marinaro), Don Billett (Bill Mayo), Jenny Marino (Dom Bando), Bob Balaban (Sentimassino), Lindsay Crouse (Carla Ciello). Directed by Sidney Lumet and produced by Burtt Harris. Screenplay by Jay Presson Allen and Lumet, based on the book by Robert Daley.

He will not rat on his partners. This is his bottom line. He will talk to investigators about all the other guys he knows things about. He will talk about how narcotics cops get involved in the narcotics traffic, how they buy information with drugs, how they string out addicts and use them as informers, how they keep some of the money and some of the drugs after big busts. He will tell what he knows about how the other cops do these things. But he will not talk about his partners in his own unit. This is his code, and, of course, he is going to have to break it.

That is the central situation of Sidney Lumet's *Prince of the City*. While you are watching it, it's a movie about cops, drugs, and New York City, in that order. After the film starts to turn itself over in your mind, it becomes a much deeper piece, a film about how difficult it is to go straight in a crooked world without hurting people you love.

Drugs are a rotten business. They corrupt everyone they come into contact with, because they set up needs so urgent that all other considerations are forgotten. For addicts, the need is for the drug itself. For others, the needs are more complex. The members of the special police drug unit in *Prince of the City*, for example, take on an envied departmental status because of their assignment. They have no hours, no beats, no uniforms. They are elite freelancers, modern knights riding out into the drug underworld and establishing their own rules. They do not look at it this way, but their status depends on drugs. If there were no drugs and no addicts, there would be no narcs, no princes of the city. Of course, their jobs are also cold, dirty, lonely, dangerous, thankless, and never finished. That is the other side of the deal, and that helps explain why they will sometimes keep the money they confiscate in a drug bust. It's as if they're levying their own fines. It also explains why they sometimes supply informers with drugs: They know better than anyone how horrible the addict's life can be. "A junkie can break your heart," the hero of this movie says at one point, and by the movie's end we understand what he means.

The film is based on a book by Robert Daley about Bob Leuci, a New York cop who cooperated with a 1971 investigation of police corruption. In the movie, Leuci is called Ciello, and he is played by Treat Williams in a demanding and grueling performance. Williams is almost always onscreen, and almost always in situations of extreme stress, fatigue, and emotional turmoil. We see him coming apart before our eyes. He falls to pieces not simply because of his job, or because of his decision to testify, but because he is in an inexorable trap and he *will* sooner or later have to hurt his partners.

This is a movie that literally hinges on the issue of perjury. And Sidney Lumet and his cowriter, Jay Presson Allen, have a great deal of respect for the legal questions involved. There is a sustained scene in this movie that is one of the most spellbinding I can imagine, and it consists entirely of government lawyers debating whether a given situation justifies a charge of perjury. Rarely are ethical issues discussed in such detail in a movie, and hardly ever so effectively.

Prince of the City is a very good movie and, like some of its characters, it wants to break your heart. Maybe it will. It is about the ways in which a corrupt modern city makes it almost impossible for a man to be true to the law, his ideals, and his friends, all at the same time. The movie has no answers. Only horrible alternatives.

Princess Mononoke

PG-13, 133 m., 1999

With the voices of: Claire Danes (San [Princess Mononoke]), Minnie Driver (Eboshi), Gillian Anderson (Moro the Wolf), Billy Crudup (Ashitaka), Jada Pinkett-Smith (Toki), Billy Bob Thornton (Jigo), John De Mita (Kohroku), John Di Maggio (Gonza). Directed by Hayao Miyazaki and produced by Toshio Suzuki. Screenplay by Miyazaki, English adaptation by Neil Gaiman.

I go to the movies for many reasons. Here is one of them: I want to see wondrous sights not available in the real world, in stories where myth and dreams are set free to play. Animation opens that possibility because it is freed from gravity and the chains of the possible. Realistic films show the physical world; animation shows its essence. Animated films are not copies of "real movies," are not shadows of reality, but create a new existence in their own right. True, a lot of animation is insipid and insulting, even to the children it is made for. But great animation can make the mind sing.

Hayao Miyazaki is a great animator, and his *Princess Mononoke* is a great film. Do not allow conventional thoughts about animation to prevent you from seeing it. It tells an epic story set in medieval Japan at the dawn of the Industrial Age, when some men still lived in harmony with nature and others were trying to tame and defeat it. It is not a simplistic tale of good and evil, but the story of how humans, forest animals, and nature gods all fight for their share of the new emerging order. It is one of the most visually inventive films I have ever seen.

The movie opens with a watchtower guard spotting "something wrong in the forest." There is a disturbance of nature, and out of it leaps a remarkable creature, a kind of boar-monster with flesh made of writhing snakes. It attacks villagers, and to the defense comes Ashitaka, the young prince of his isolated people. He is finally able to slay the beast, but his own arm has been wrapped by the snakes and is horribly scarred.

A wise woman is able to explain what has happened. The monster was a boar god, until a bullet buried itself in its flesh and drove it mad. And where did the bullet come from? "It is time," says the woman, "for our last prince to cut his hair and leave us." And so Ashitaka sets off on a long journey to the lands of the west, to find out why nature is out of joint, and whether the curse on his arm can be lifted. He rides Yakkuru, a beast that seems part horse, part antelope, part mountain goat.

There are strange sights and adventures along the way, and we are able to appreciate the quality of Miyazaki's artistry. The drawing in this film is not simplistic, but has some of the same "clear line" complexity used by the Japanese graphic artists of two centuries ago, who inspired such modern work as Hergé's Tintin books. Nature is rendered majestically

(Miyazaki's art directors journeyed to ancient forests to make their master drawings) and fancifully (as with the round little forest sprites). There are also brief, mysterious appearances of the spirit of the forest, who by day seems to be a noble beast and at night a glowing light.

Ashitaka eventually arrives in an area prowled by Moro, a wolf god, and sees for the first time the young woman named San. She is also known as Princess Mononoke, but that's more a description than a name; a "mononoke" is the spirit of a beast. San was a human child, raised as a wolf by Moro; she rides bareback on the swift white spirit-wolves, and helps the pack in their battle against the encroachments of Lady Eboshi, a strong ruler whose village is developing ironworking skills and manufactures weapons using gunpowder.

As Lady Eboshi's people gain one kind of knowledge, they lose another, and the day is fading when men, animals, and the forest gods all speak the same language. The lush green forests through which Ashitaka traveled west have been replaced here by a wasteland; trees have been stripped to feed the smelting furnaces, and on their skeletons, yellow-eyed beasts squat ominously. Slaves work the bellows of the forges, and lepers make the weapons.

But all is not black-and-white. The lepers are grateful that Eboshi accepts them. Her people enjoy her protection. Even Jigo, a scheming agent of the emperor, has motives that sometimes make a certain amount of sense. When a nearby samurai enclave wants to take over the village and its technology, there is a battle with more than one side and more than one motive. This is more like mythical history than action melodrama.

The artistry in Princess Mononoke is masterful. The writhing skin of the boar-monster is an extraordinary sight, one that would be impossible to create in any live-action film. The great white wolves are drawn with grace, and not sentimentalized; when they bare their fangs, you can see that they are not friendly comic pals, but animals who can and will kill. The movie does not dwell on violence, which makes some of its moments even more shocking, as when Ashitaka finds that his scarred arm has developed such strength that his arrow decapitates an enemy.

Miyazaki and his collaborators work at Stu-

dio Ghibli, and a few years ago Disney bought the studio's entire output for worldwide distribution. (Disney artists consider Miyazaki a source of inspiration.) The contract said Disney could not change a frame—but there was no objection to dubbing into English, because of course all animation is dubbed, into even its source language, and as Miyazaki cheerfully observes, "English has been dubbed into Japanese for years."

This version of Princess Mononoke has been well and carefully dubbed with gifted vocal talents, including Billy Crudup as Ashitaka, Claire Danes as San, Minnie Driver as Eboshi, Gillian Anderson as Moro, Billy Bob Thornton as Jigo, and Jada Pinkett-Smith as Toki, a commonsensical working woman in the village.

The drama is underlaid with Miyazaki's deep humanism, which avoids easy moral simplifications. There is a remarkable scene where San and Ashitaka, who have fallen in love, agree that neither can really lead the life of the other, and so they must grant each other freedom and only meet occasionally. You won't find many Hollywood love stories (animated or otherwise) so philosophical. Princess Mononoke is a great achievement and a wonderful experience, and one of the best films of 1999.

Note: Some of my information comes from an invaluable book, Hayao Miyazaki: Master of Japanese Animation, by Helen McCarthy, Stone Bridge Press.

Prizzi's Honor

R, 129 m., 1985

Jack Nicholson (Charley Partanna), Kathleen Turner (Irene Walker), Anjelica Huston (Maerose), Robert Loggia (Eduardo Prizzi), John Randolph (Pop Partanna), William Hickey (Don Corrado Prizzi), Lee Richardson (Dominic). Directed by John Huston and produced by John Foreman. Screenplay by Richard Condon and Janet Roach.

John Huston's Prizzi's Honor marches like weird and gloomy clockwork to its relentless conclusion, and half of the time, we're laughing. This is the most bizarre comedy in many a month; a movie so dark, so cynical, and so funny that perhaps only Jack Nicholson and Kathleen Turner could have kept straight faces during the love scenes. They do. They play two professional Mafia killers who meet, fall in love, marry, and find out that the mob may not be big enough for both of them.

Nicholson plays Charley Partanna, a soldier in the proud Prizzi family, rulers of the East Coast, enforcers of criminal order. The godfather of the Prizzis, Don Corrado, is a mean little old man who looks like he has been freeze-dried by the lifelong ordeal of draining every ounce of humanity out of his wizened body. To Don Corrado (William Hickey), nothing is more important than the Prizzis' honor—not even another Prizzi. Charley Partanna is the Don's grandson. He has been raised in this ethic, and accepts it. He kills without remorse. He follows orders. Only occasionally does he disobey the family's instructions, as when he broke his engagement with Maerose Prizzi (Anjelica Huston), his cousin. She then brought disgrace upon herself and, as the movie opens, is in the fourth year of self-imposed exile. But she is a Prizzi, and does not forget, or forgive.

The movie opens like *The Godfather,* at a wedding. Charley's eyes roam around the church. In the choir loft, he sees a beautiful blonde (Kathleen Turner). She looks like an angel. At the reception, he dances with her once, and then she disappears. Later that day, there is a mob killing. Determined to find out the name of the blond angel, Charley discovers even more—that she was the California hitman, brought in to do the job. He turns to Maerose for advice. She counsels him to go ahead: After all, it's good to have interests in common with your wife.

Charley flies to the coast, setting up a running gag as they establish a transcontinental commute. There is instant, electrifying chemistry between the two of them, and the odd thing is, it seems halfway plausible. They're opposites, but they attract. Nicholson plays his hood as a tough Brooklynite; he uses a stiff upper lip, like Bogart, and sounds simple and implacable. Turner, who is flowering as a wonderful comic actress, plays her Mafia killer like a bright, cheery hostess. She could be selling cosmetics.

What happens between them is best not explained here, since the unfolding of the plot is one of the movie's delights. The story is by Richard Condon, a novelist who delights in devious plot construction, and here he takes two absolutes—romantic love and the Prizzis' honor—and arranges a collision between them. Because all of the motivations are so direct and logical, the movie is able to make the most shocking decisions seem inevitable.

John Huston directed this film right after *Under the Volcano,* and what other director could have put those two back-to-back? It is one of his very best films, perhaps because he made it with friends; Condon is an old pal from Ireland, Anjelica Huston is, of course, his daughter, and Nicholson has long been Anjelica's lover. Together they have taken a strange plot, peopled it with carefully overwrought characters, and made *Prizzi's Honor* into a treasure.

Proof

PG-13, 99 m., 2005

Gwyneth Paltrow (Catherine), Anthony Hopkins (Robert), Hope Davis (Claire), Jake Gyllenhaal (Hal). Directed by John Madden and produced by John Hart, Robert Kessel, Alison Owen, and Jeff Sharp. Screenplay by David Auburn and Rebecca Miller, based on the play by David Auburn.

John Madden's *Proof* is an extraordinary thriller about matters of scholarship and the heart, about the true authorship of a mathematical proof and the passions that coil around it. It is a rare movie that gets the tone of a university campus exactly right and at the same time communicates so easily that you don't need to know the slightest thing about math to understand it. Take it from me.

The film centers on two remarkable performances, by Gwyneth Paltrow and Hope Davis, as Catherine and Claire, the daughters of a mathematician so brilliant that his work transformed the field and has not yet been surpassed. But his work was done years ago, and at the age of twenty-six or twenty-seven he began to "get sick," as the family puts it. This man, named Robert and played by Anthony Hopkins, still has occasional moments of lucidity, but he lives mostly in delusion, filling up one notebook after another with meaningless scribbles. Yet he remains on the University of Chicago faculty, where he has already made a lifetime's contribution; his presence and rare remissions are inspiring. Recently he had a year when he was "better."

Catherine was a brilliant math student, too—at Northwestern, because she wanted to be free of her father. But she returned home to care for him when he got worse, and her life has been defined by her father and the family home. Hal (Jake Gyllenhaal), her father's student and assistant, is hopelessly in love with her; she shies away from intimacy and suspects his motives. Most of the movie takes place after the father's death (flashbacks show him in life and imagination), and Hal is going through the notebooks. "Hoping to find something of my dad's you could publish?" Catherine asks him in a moment of anger.

Claire, the older sister, flies in from New York and makes immediate plans to sell the family home to the university: "They've been after it for years." Catherine is outraged, but the movie subtly shows how Claire, not the brilliant sister, is the dominant one. There is the sinister possibility that she thinks (in all sincerity) that Catherine may have inherited the family illness and should not be allowed to stay alone in Chicago. Claire expresses love and support for her sister in terms that are frightening.

There is a locked drawer in Robert's desk. Catherine gives Hal the key. It contains what may be a revolutionary advance on Robert's earlier work; a new mathematical proof of incalculable importance. Did Robert somehow write this in a fleeting moment of clarity? The authorship of the proof brings into play all of the human dynamics that have been established among Catherine and Claire and Hal, and indeed among all of them and the ghostly presence of the father.

Proof, based on the award-winning Broadway and London play by David Auburn, contains one scene after another that is pitch-perfect in its command of how academics talk and live. Having once spent a year as a University of Chicago doctoral candidate, I felt as if I were back on campus. There is a memorial service at which the speaker (Gary Houston) sounds precisely as such speakers sound; his subject is simultaneously the dead mathematician and his sense of his own importance. There is a faculty party at which all of the right notes are sounded. And when Catherine and Hal speak, they talk as friends, lovers, and fellow mathematicians; they communicate in several languages while speaking only one.

What makes the movie deep and urgent is that Catherine is motivated by conflicting desires. She wants to be a great mathematician but does not want to hurt or shame her father. She wants to be a loyal daughter and yet stand alone as herself. She half-believes her older sister's persuasive smothering. She half-believes Hal loves her only for herself. At the bottom, she only half-believes in herself. That's why the Paltrow performance is so fascinating: It's essentially about a woman whose destiny is in her own hands, but she can't make them close on it.

It would be natural to compare *Proof* with *A Beautiful Mind* (2001), another movie about a brilliant and mad mathematician. But they are miles apart. *A Beautiful Mind* tries to enter the world of the madman. *Proof* locates itself in the mind of the madman's daughter, who loves him and sorrows for him, who has lived in his shadow so long she fears the light and the things that go with it.

Note: It doesn't make the movie any better or worse, but it's unique in that all of the locations match. There are no impossible journeys or nonexistent freeway exits. The trip from Hyde Park to Evanston reflects the way you really do get there. So real do the locations feel that it's a shock to find that most of the interiors were filmed in England; they match the Chicago locations seamlessly.

The Proposition

R, 104 m., 2006

Guy Pearce (Charlie Burns), Ray Winstone (Captain Stanley), Danny Huston (Arthur Burns), John Hurt (Jellon Lamb), David Wenham (Eden Fletcher), Emily Watson (Martha Stanley), David Gulpilil (Jacko), Richard Wilson (Mike Burns), Tommy Lewis (Two Bob). Directed by John Hillcoat and produced by Chris Brown, Chiara Menage, Cat Villiers, and Jackie O'Sullivan. Screenplay by Nick Cave.

The Proposition plays like a Western moved from Colorado to hell. The characters are familiar: the desperado brothers, the zealous lawman, his civilized wife, the corrupt mayor, the old coots, the resentful natives. But the setting is the outback of Australia as I have never seen it before. These spaces don't seem wide open because an oppressive sky glares down at the sullen earth; this world is sun-baked, hostile, and unforgiving, and it breeds heartless men.

Have you read *Blood Meridian,* the novel by Cormac McCarthy? This movie comes close to realizing the vision of that dread and despairing story. The critic Harold Bloom believes no other living American novelist has written a book as strong. He compares it with Faulkner and Melville but confesses his first two attempts to read it failed, "because I flinched from the overwhelming carnage."

That book features a character known as the Judge, a tall, bald, remorseless bounty hunter who essentially wants to kill anyone he can, until he dies. His dialogue is peculiar, the speech of an educated man. *The Proposition* has such a character in an outlaw named Arthur Burns, who is much given to poetic quotations. He is played by Danny Huston in a performance of remarkable focus and savagery. Against him is Captain Stanley (Ray Winstone), who is not precisely a sheriff since this land is not precisely a place where the law exists. He is more of an Ahab, obsessed with tracking down Arthur Burns and his brothers Charlie (Guy Pearce) and Mike (Richard Wilson). They are not merely outlaws, desperadoes, and villains but are dedicated to evil for its own sake, and the film opens with a photograph labeled "Scene of the Hopkins Outrage." The Burns boys murdered the Hopkins family, pregnant wife and all, perhaps more for entertainment than gain.

Ray Winstone, who often plays villains, is one of the best actors now at work in movies (see him in *Sexy Beast, Ripley's Game, Last Orders*). Here he plays a man who would be fearsome enough in an ordinary land but pales before the malevolence of the Burns brothers. He lives with Martha (Emily Watson), his fragrant wife from England, who fences off a portion of wilderness, calls it their lawn, plants rosebushes there, serves him his breakfast egg, and behaves, as colonial women did in Victorian times, as if still at "home."

"I will civilize this land," Captain Stanley says. In the 1880s, it is an achievement as likely as Ahab capturing the whale. He is able to capture Charlie and Mike Burns: Mike, a youth like the Kid in *Blood Meridian,* still half-formed but schooled only in desperation, and Charlie, an inward, brooding, damaged man whose feelings are as instinctive as a kicked dog. The captain is not happy with his prisoners because he lacks the real prize. He makes a proposition to Charlie. If Charlie tracks and kills his brother Arthur, the captain will spare both Charlie and Mike.

Charlie sets off on this mission. He feels no particular filial love for Arthur; they are bonded mostly by mutual hatred of others. The captain himself ventures out on the trail, finding such settlers as have chosen to live in exile and punishment. The most colorful—no, "colorful" is not a word for this movie—the most gnarled and cured by the sun is Jellon Lamb, played by John Hurt as if he is made of jerky.

Why do you want to see this movie? Perhaps you don't. Perhaps, like Bloom, it will take you more than one try to face the carnage. But the director, John Hillcoat, working from a screenplay by Nick Cave (the sometime punk rocker and actor in *Johnny Suede*), has made a movie you cannot turn away from; it is so pitiless and uncompromising, so filled with pathos and disregarded innocence, that it is a record of those things we pray to be delivered from. The actors invest their characters with human details all the scarier because they scarcely seem human themselves. In what place within Arthur Burns does poetry reside? What does he feel as he quotes it? What does Martha, the Emily Watson character, really think as she uncrates a Christmas tree she has had shipped in from another lifetime? If Captain Stanley is as tender toward her as he seems, why has he brought her to live in these badlands?

What of the land itself? There is a sense of palpable fear of the outback in many Australian films, from *Walkabout* to *Japanese Story,* not neglecting the tamer landscapes in *Picnic at Hanging Rock.* There is the sense that spaces there are too empty to admit human content. There are times in *The Proposition* when you think the characters might abandon their human concerns and simply flee from the land itself.

And what of the Aborigines, who inhabit this landscape more or less invisibly and have their own treaty with it? The Stanleys have a house servant named Two Bob, played by Tommy Lewis, who sizes up the situation and walks away one day, carefully removing his shoes, which remain in the garden.

The Public Eye

R, 99 m., 1992

Joe Pesci (Leon Bernstein), Barbara Hershey (Kay Levitz), Stanley Tucci (Sal), Jerry Adler (Arthur Nabler), Jared Harris (Doorman). Directed by Howard Franklin and produced by Sue Baden-Powell. Screenplay by Franklin.

The Public Eye contains a couple of great, juicy movie performances. They're from Joe Pesci and Barbara Hershey, playing New York City fringe dwellers who try to make a living from the kinds of people who come out after dark. They also fall in love, I think. You may think differently. They're the kind of people who should ask themselves, am I really in love, or does it just feel so good when I stop hitting myself over the head with this pistol butt?

It's the 1940s. Pesci plays a guy named Bernzy, who is a freelance photographer for the tabloids. He cruises the night in a souped-up coupe with a police radio under the dash and a darkroom in the trunk. He takes pictures of mobsters, politicians, crooks, gamblers, cops, and ladies who ain't no ladies. A lot of these people are dead when they sit for their portraits. When Bernzy sells a picture to the *Daily News,* it runs a credit line that says: "Photo by the Great Bernzini."

He takes his work seriously. Someday he wants to publish a book of his photos. He thinks ordinary pictures of ordinary people can be art. Bernzy reminds me of Weegee, the great New York City street photographer, who also took pictures of the disreputable and the unlovely, and thought his work was art. They laughed at him, but check out his prices in the galleries.

Bernzy is the perpetual outsider. His relationships are all through the viewfinder. One night, Kay Levitz (Hershey) asks him for a favor. She runs a nightclub she inherited from her husband, who was old when she married him and dead shortly after. There are people who think she married him to get the club. Now they want the club, but they don't want to marry her. They want to muscle her out. Kay thinks maybe Bernzy can give her some advice, help her out.

He is willing to try. He is willing, even though his lifetime policy is—don't get in-volved. The writer-director, Howard Franklin, is subtle and touching in the way he modulates the key passages between Pesci and Hershey. There is a lot that goes unsaid between them. We can maybe guess from Bernzy's eyes and actions how he feels about her, but he never tells her. He keeps his distance. He can maybe hope she feels the same way. She plays it close.

The movie surrounds them with a gallery of colorful nighttime characters—vice detectives, rival photographers, mob bosses, broken-down critics who mourn the bad novels they never wrote. The photography occupies the beloved territory of *film noir:* night, wet streets, cars with running boards, dames with low necklines, guys with diamond pinky rings, empty marble newspaper lobbies, guns, highballs, furnished apartments. This was an era when the good guys smoked cigars, and the bad guys smoked cigarettes.

One of the best things about the movie is the way it shows us how seriously Bernzy takes his work. He doesn't talk about it. He does it, with that cigar stuck in his mug, leading the way with the big, ungainly Speed-Graphix with the glass flashbulbs. In the movie's big scene of a mob assassination, he stares death in the face to get a great picture. He doesn't even seem especially noble. It's what he bred himself to do. At one point he is asked to turn off the police radio in his car, and he says, "It doesn't *turn* off." This is his philosophy of life.

The plot of the movie advances the story on the surface, while the romance develops in an unacknowledged subterranean fashion. Everything leads up to a moment when Bernzy turns his head away from Kay and says, "You have no idea what I would have done for you." This is the best kind of love—unrequited. There are moments in *The Public Eye* that made me think a little about *Casablanca,* especially the earlier scenes when Bogart is still mad at Bergman. Higher praise is not necessary.

Public Housing

NO MPAA RATING, 210 m., 1997

A documentary by Frederick Wiseman.

If I told you I've seen a documentary about public housing in Chicago, you might im-mediately assume it shows poverty, illiteracy, welfare, drugs, and crime. If I told you that the documentary had moved me almost to tears with the kindness, courage, tenacity, and hope that it displayed, you might wonder what miracle the filmmaker had witnessed—or evoked. But all Frederick Wiseman has done is point his camera, and look and listen.

His new film *Public Housing,* is the record of a lot of time spent among the residents of the Ida B. Wells homes on the South Side. These are poor people, mostly unemployed, one step from homelessness, preparing for the coming changes in the welfare system.

Watching the film, I came to the uneasy conclusion that the Chicago Housing Authority bureaucracy is a pyramid of jobholders balanced precariously on the backs of the poor. Residents speak helplessly of the steps necessary to get anything done. There's a woman who needs an ink cartridge for a copying machine: Her request has to go through four levels of authorization to be approved. Then it has to be put out for three bids. Then the lowest bid has to go through an approval process. "I finally went out and just bought the thing myself," she says.

Yet many of the people involved at ground level in the system, including maintenance men, residents, volunteers, social workers, and police officers, are so generous and patient in their efforts that their everyday lives take on a sort of quiet heroism.

Yes, heroism. The news is filled with stories about bad cops. But look at the cops in *Public Housing.* Two stand for fifteen minutes on a street corner with a young woman who is apparently involved in the drug business. They find no drugs, but they, and eventually we, can see what's up. Finally one cop tells her: "Six months from now you're gonna have all your teeth broken out, and your eyeball hanging down on your cheek. You still got a life ahead of you. You can beat these drugs. I'm gonna remember you. You're gonna be my special project. Every time I see you I'm gonna pull over."

Then there are two other cops, evicting an old man who is being sent to a nursing home. Look at their tenderness. The old man is surrounded by the scant remains of a lifetime. One cop sighs and shakes open a brown paper bag, and begins to fill it with canned goods.

There's an exterminator, patiently giving a woman tips on how to catch bugs off guard. A plumber, fixing a leaking drain and obviously concerned about a young man who seems to wander through an old woman's apartment at will. A police captain, talking quietly with a man who owes $80 to drug dealers; they both know the man will be beaten later that night. "Have you got any relatives you could go to?" the cop asks. And, "Well, your wife hung in there for a while, huh?"

There is a woman named Helen Finner, who has been president of the Ida B. Wells Resident's Association for twenty years, and who works the phone in her office while a sad young girl sits huddled in a blanket. "You have 200 vacancies waiting for somebody to move into them, and you have mothers with children, homeless, sitting around in the lobby of the hospital, who can't find a place to spend the night," she says into the phone. "If I haven't heard from (you) by one o'clock Monday, then I'm gonna call down there and act crazy."

There are meetings. The Men of Wells sit behind folding tables and discuss commitments for volunteer work. A teacher from a junior college explains ways residents can qualify for funds to start small businesses. There's a meeting about the Child Family Preservation Center, and the speaker tells a story I will not forget. She has just seen a young mother's children taken away from her in court. When her own mother tries to comfort her, the younger woman tells her frankly, "If they had taken me away from you, I wouldn't be here today."

And on and on. Frederick Wiseman has spent his lifetime filming the institutions of society: hospitals, high schools, mental homes, even a monastery. He doesn't bring an attitude to his work. He visits, looks, and listens. To watch his films is to spend some time in the lives of other people.

Those who do not live in public housing have a lot of ideas about those who do. Most of them are formed by crime reports in the news. What you see in *Public Housing* is a neighborhood with many people, some bad, some devastated by drugs, yes—but most just sincerely trying to get by, live right, improve themselves, and stick together. If you were in big trouble, these might be neighbors you would be happy to have.

Pulp Fiction

R, 154 m., 1994

John Travolta (Vincent Vega), Bruce Willis (Butch Coolidge), Samuel L. Jackson (Jules), Uma Thurman (Mia), Harvey Keitel (Mr. Wolf), Tim Roth (Pumpkin), Amanda Plummer (Honey Bunny), Maria de Medeiros (Fabienne), Ving Rhames (Marsellus Wallace), Eric Stoltz (Lance). Directed by Quentin Tarantino and produced by Lawrence Bender. Screenplay by Tarantino and Roger Avary.

Quentin Tarantino is the Jerry Lee Lewis of cinema, a pounding performer who doesn't care if he tears up the piano, as long as everybody is rocking. His movie *Pulp Fiction* is a comedy about blood, guts, violence, strange sex, drugs, fixed fights, dead-body disposal, leather freaks, and a wristwatch that makes a dark journey down through the generations.

Seeing this movie at the Cannes Film Festival, I knew it was either one of the year's best films, or one of the worst. Tarantino is too gifted a filmmaker to make a boring movie, but he could possibly make a bad one: Like Edward D. Wood, Jr., proclaimed the Worst Director of All Time, he's in love with every shot—intoxicated with the very act of making a movie. It's that very lack of caution and introspection that makes *Pulp Fiction* crackle like an ozone generator: Here's a director who's been let loose inside the toy store, and wants to play all night.

The screenplay, by Tarantino and Roger Avary, is so well written in a scruffy, fanzine way that you want to rub noses in it—the noses of those zombie writers who take "screenwriting" classes that teach them the formulas for "hit films." Like *Citizen Kane*, *Pulp Fiction* is constructed in such a nonlinear way that you could see it a dozen times and not be able to remember what comes next. It doubles back on itself, telling several interlocking stories about characters who inhabit a world of crime and intrigue, triplecrosses, and loud desperation.

The title is perfect. Like those old pulp mags named *Thrilling Wonder Stories* and *Official Detective*, the movie creates a world where there are no normal people and no ordinary days—where breathless prose clatters down fire escapes and leaps into the Dumpster of doom.

The movie resurrects not only an aging genre but also a few careers. John Travolta stars as Vincent Vega, a midlevel hit man who carries out assignments for a mob boss. We see him first with his partner Jules (Samuel L. Jackson); they're on their way to a violent showdown with some wayward yuppie drug dealers, and are discussing such mysteries as why in Paris they have a French word for Quarter Pounders. They're as innocent in their way as Huck and Jim, floating down the Mississippi and speculating on how foreigners can possibly understand each other, since they don't speak English.

Travolta's career is a series of assignments he can't quite handle. Not only does he kill people inadvertently ("The car hit a bump!"), but he doesn't know how to clean up after himself. Good thing he knows people like Mr. Wolf (Harvey Keitel), who specializes in messes, and has friends like the character played by Eric Stoltz, who owns a big medical encyclopedia, and can look up emergency situations.

Travolta and Uma Thurman have a sequence that's funny and bizarre. She's the wife of the mob boss (Ving Rhames), who orders Travolta to take her out for the night. He turns up stoned, and addresses an intercom with such grave, stately courtesy Buster Keaton would have been envious. They go to Jack Rabbit Slim's, a 1950s theme restaurant where Ed Sullivan is the emcee, Buddy Holly is the waiter, and they end up in a twist contest. That's before she overdoses and Stoltz, waving a syringe filled with adrenaline, screams at Travolta, "*You* brought her here, *you* stick in the needle! When I bring an O.D. to *your* house, *I'll* stick in the needle!"

Bruce Willis and Maria de Medeiros play another couple: He's a boxer named Butch Coolidge who is supposed to throw a fight, but doesn't. She's his sweet, naive girlfriend, who doesn't understand why they have to get out of town *right away*. But first he needs to make a dangerous trip back to his apartment to pick up a priceless family heirloom—a wristwatch. The history of this watch is described in a flashback, as Vietnam veteran Christopher Walken tells young Butch about how the watch was purchased by his great-grandfather, Private doughboy Orion Coolidge, and has come down through the generations—and through a lot more than generations, for that matter. Walken's monologue builds to the movie's biggest laugh.

The method of the movie is to involve its characters in sticky situations, and then let them escape into stickier ones, which is how the boxer and the mob boss end up together as the captives of weird leather freaks in the basement of a gun shop. Or how the characters who open the movie, a couple of stickup artists played by Tim Roth and Amanda Plummer, get in way over their heads. Most of the action in the movie comes under the heading of crisis control.

If the situations are inventive and original, so is the dialogue. A lot of movies these days use flat, functional speech: The characters say only enough to advance the plot. But the people in *Pulp Fiction* are in love with words for their own sake. The dialogue by Tarantino and Avary is off the wall sometimes, but that's the fun. It also means that the characters don't all sound the same: Travolta is laconic, Jackson is exact, Plummer and Roth are dopey lovey-doveys, Keitel uses the shorthand of the busy professional, Thurman learned how to be a moll by studying soap operas.

It is part of the folklore that Tarantino used to work as a clerk in a video store, and the inspiration for *Pulp Fiction* is old movies, not real life. The movie is like an excursion through the lurid images that lie wound up and trapped inside all those boxes on the Blockbuster shelves. Tarantino once described the old pulp mags as cheap, disposable entertainment that you could take to work with you, and roll up and stick in your back pocket. Yeah, and not be able to wait until lunch, so you could start reading them again.

The Purple Rose of Cairo
PG, 87 m., 1985

Mia Farrow (Cecilia), Jeff Daniels (Tom Baxter/Gil Shepherd), Danny Aiello (Monk), Van Johnson (Larry), Alexander H. Cohen (Raoul Hirsh). Directed by Woody Allen and produced by Robert Greenhut. Screenplay by Allen.

About twenty minutes into Woody Allen's *The Purple Rose of Cairo,* an extraordinary event takes place. A young woman has been going to see the same movie over and over again, because of her infatuation with the movie's hero. From his vantage point up on the screen, the hero notices her out in the audience. He strikes up a conversation, she smiles and shyly responds, and he abruptly steps off the screen and into her life. No explanation is offered for this miraculous event, but then perhaps none is needed: Don't we spend our lives waiting for the same thing to happen to us in the movies?

Life, of course, is never as simple and dreamy as the movies, and so the hero's bold act has alarming consequences. The movie's other characters are still stranded up there on the screen, feeling angry and left out. The Hollywood studio is aghast that its characters would suddenly develop minds of their own. The actor who *played* the hero is particularly upset, because now there are two of him walking around, one wearing a pith helmet. Things are simple only in the lives of the hero and the woman, who convince themselves that they *can* simply walk off into the sunset, and get away with this thing.

The Purple Rose of Cairo is audacious and witty and has a lot of good laughs in it, but the best thing about the movie is the way Woody Allen uses it to toy with the very essence of reality and fantasy. The movie is so cheerful and open that it took me a day or two, after I'd seen it, to realize how deeply Allen has reached this time. If it is true, and I think it is, that most of the time we go to the movies in order to experience brief lives that are not our own, then Allen is demonstrating what a tricky self-deception we practice. Those movie lives consist of *only* what is on the screen, and if we start thinking that real life can be the same way, we are in for a cruel awakening.

The woman in the movie is played by Mia Farrow as a sweet, rather baffled small-town waitress whose big, shiftless lug of a husband bats her around. She is a good candidate for the magic of the movies. Up on the screen, sophisticated people have cocktails and plan trips down the Nile and are recognized by the doormen in nightclubs. The hero in the movie is played by Jeff Daniels (who was Debra Winger's husband in *Terms of Endearment*). He is a genial, open-faced smoothie with all the right moves, but he has a problem: He *only* knows what his character knows in the movie, and his experience is literally limited to what happens to his character in the plot. This can cause problems. He's great at talking sweetly to a woman, and holding hands, and kissing—but just when the crucial moment arrives, the movie fades out, and therefore, alas, so does he.

Many of Allen's best moments come from exploring the paradox that the movie character knows nothing of real life. For example, he can drive a car, because he drives one in the movie, but he can't start a car, because he doesn't turn on the ignition in the movie. Mia Farrow thinks maybe they can work this out. They can learn from each other. He can learn real life, and she can learn the romance of the movies. The problem is, both of them are now living in real life, where studio moguls and angry actors and snoopy reporters are making their life miserable.

Allen's buried subject in *The Purple Rose of Cairo* is, I think, related to the subjects of his less successful movies, *Stardust Memories* (1980) and *Zelig* (1983). He is interested in the conflicts involving who you want to be, and who other people want you to be. *Stardust* was about a celebrity whose fame prevented people from relating to anything but his image. *Zelig,* the other side of the coin, was about a man whose anonymity was so profound that he could gain an identity only by absorbing one from the people around him. In *Purple Rose,* the movie hero has the first problem, and the woman in the audience has the second, and when they get together, they still don't make one whole person, just two sad halves.

Purple Rose is delightful from beginning to end, not only because of the clarity and charm with which Daniels and Farrow explore the problems of their characters, but also because the movie is so intelligent. It's not brainy or intellectual—no one in the whole movie speaks with more complexity than your average 1930s movie hero—but the movie is filled with wit and invention, and Allen trusts us to find the ironies, relish the contradictions, and figure things out for ourselves. While we do that, he makes us laugh and he makes us think, and when you get right down to it, forget about the fantasies; those are two of the most exciting things that could happen to anybody in a movie. The more you think about *The Purple Rose of Cairo,* and about the movies, and about why you go to the movies, the deeper the damned thing gets.

Q

The Queen
PG-13, 97 m., 2006

Helen Mirren (Elizabeth II), Michael Sheen (Tony Blair), James Cromwell (Prince Philip), Sylvia Syms (Queen Mother), Paul Barrett (Trevor Rees-Jones), Helen McCrory (Cherie Blair). Directed by Stephen Frears and produced by François Ivernel, Cameron McCracken, and Scott Rudin. Screenplay by Peter Morgan.

The opening shots of Stephen Frears's *The Queen* simply show Helen Mirren's face as her character prepares for it to be seen. She is Queen Elizabeth II, and we know that at once. The resemblance is not merely physical but also embodies the very nature of the Elizabeth we have grown up with—a private woman who takes her public role with great gravity.

Elizabeth is preparing to meet Tony Blair (Michael Sheen), the new Labor prime minister who has just been elected in a landslide. We see Blair preparing for the same meeting. His election was a fundamental upheaval of British political life after Thatcherism, and at that time, Britain stood on a threshold of uncertain but possibly tumultuous change.

Within months, the queen and Blair find themselves in a crisis that involves not politics but a personal tragedy that was completely unforeseen—the death of Diana, Princess of Wales, in a Paris car crash. *The Queen* tells the story of how her death with her boyfriend, the playboy department-store heir Dodi Fayed, would threaten to shake the very monarchy itself.

Told in quiet scenes of proper behavior and guarded speech, *The Queen* is a spellbinding story of opposed passions—of Elizabeth's icy resolve to keep the royal family separate and aloof from the death of the divorced Diana, who was legally no longer a royal, and of Blair's correct reading of the public mood, which demanded some sort of public expression of sympathy from the Crown for "the People's Princess."

It was extraordinary, the grief that people felt after her death. I was reminded of the weeks after the assassination of John F. Kennedy. Was it out of proportion to Diana's objective importance? She was a young woman almost cynically picked for her marriage, who provided the Crown with its required heirs, who was a photogenic escort for Prince Charles, who found no love from her husband; it was no secret they both had affairs during their marriage. Once divorced, she made peculiar dating choices.

She died in a late-night crash while being pursued by paparazzi. Yet it was as if a saint had been taken from our midst. Yes, Diana devoted much time to doing good. Yes, I believe she was sincere. But doing good was part of her job description; she signed on for it. In death, she had the same impact as if a great national hero had died.

The Queen is told almost entirely in small scenes of personal conflict. It creates an uncanny sense that it knows what goes on backstage in the monarchy; in the movie, Queen Elizabeth, Prince Philip, and the Queen Mother have settled into a sterile domesticity cocooned by servants and civil servants. It shows Tony and Cherie Blair (Helen McCrory) in their own bourgeois domestic environment. Both households, privately, are plain-spoken to the point of bluntness, and Cherie is more left-wing than her husband, less instinctively awed by the monarchy, more inclined to dump the institution.

What Tony clearly sees is that the monarchy could be gravely harmed, if not toppled, by the queen's insistence on sticking to protocol and not issuing a statement about Diana. The press demands that Elizabeth fly the flag at Buckingham Palace at half-mast as a symbolic gesture. Elizabeth stands firm. The palace will not acknowledge the death or sponsor the funeral.

The Queen comes down to the story of two strong women loyal to the doctrines of their beliefs about the monarchy, and a man who is much more pragmatic. The queen is correct, technically, in not lowering the flag to half-mast—it is not a national flag, but her own, flown only when she is in residence. But Blair is correct that the flag has become a lightning rod for public opinion. The queen is correct, indeed, by tradition and history in all she says about the affair—but she is sadly aloof from the national mood. Well, maybe queens should be.

Certainly that's what the Queen Mum thinks. Played by Sylvia Syms, she is shown at ninety-plus years, still tart and sharp-witted. At the last minute, the palace needs a protocol plan for the funeral, and time is so short that the Queen Mum's own funeral plan has to be borrowed and modified. Syms has a priceless reaction where she learns that her honor guard, all servicemen, will be replaced by celebrities—even, gasp, Elton John.

The Queen could have been told as a scandal-sheet story of celebrity gossip. Instead, it becomes the hypnotic tale of two views of the same event—a classic demonstration, in high drama, of how the establishment has been undermined by publicity. I think it possible that Thatcher, if she still had been in office, might have supported the queen. That would be impossible to the populist Blair.

Frears, the director, has made several wonderful films about conflicts and harmonies in the British class system (*My Beautiful Laundrette, Dirty Pretty Things, Prick Up Your Ears*), and *The Queen*, of course, represents the ultimate contrast. No one is more upper class than the queen, and Tony Blair is profoundly middle class.

The screenplay is intense, focused, literate, observant. The dynamic between Elizabeth and Philip (James Cromwell), for example, is almost entirely defined by decades of what has not been said between them—and what need not be said. There are extraordinary, tantalizing glimpses of the "real" Elizabeth driving her own Range Rover, leading her dogs, trekking her lands at Balmoral—the kind of woman, indeed, who seems more like Camilla Parker-Bowles than Diana.

Mirren is the key to it all in a performance sure to be nominated for an Oscar. She finds a way, even in a "behind the scenes" docudrama, to suggest that part of her character will always be behind the scenes. What a masterful performance, built on suggestion, implication, and understatement. Her queen in the end authorizes the inevitable state funeral, but it is a tribute to Mirren that we have lingering doubts about whether, objectively, it was the right thing. Technically, the queen was right to consider the divorced Diana no longer deserving (by her own choice) of a royal funeral. But in terms of modern celebrity worship, Elizabeth was wrong. This may or may not represent progress.

The Quiet American
R, 118 m., 2003

Michael Caine (Thomas Fowler), Brendan Fraser (Alden Pyle), Do Thi Hai Yen (Phuong), Rade Serbedzija (Inspector Vigot), Tzi Ma (Hinh), Robert Stanton (Joe Tunney), Holmes Osborne (Bill Granger), Quang Hai (The General), Ferdinand Hoang (Mr. Muoi). Directed by Phillip Noyce and produced by Staffan Ahrenberg and William Horberg. Screenplay by Christopher Hampton and Robert Schenkkan, based on the book by Graham Greene.

The Englishman is sad and lonely. He suffers from the indignity of growing too old for romance while not yet free of yearning. He is in love for one last time. He doesn't even fully understand it is love until he is about to lose it. He is a newspaper correspondent in Saigon, and she is a dance-hall girl thirty or forty years younger. She loves him because he pays her to. This arrangement suits them both. He tells himself he is "helping" her. Well, he is, and she is helping him.

His name is Fowler, and he is played by Michael Caine in a performance that seems to descend perfectly formed. There is no artifice in it, no unneeded energy, no tricks, no effort. It is there. Her name is Phuong (Do Thi Hai Yen), and like all beautiful women who reveal little of their true feelings, she makes it possible for him to project his own upon her. He loves her for what he can tell himself about her.

Between them steps Alden Pyle (Brendan Fraser), the quiet young American who has come to Vietnam, he believes, to save it. Eventually he also believes he will save Phuong. Young men, like old ones, find it easy to believe hired love is real, and so believe a girl like Phuong would prefer a young man to an old one, when all youth represents is more work.

Graham Greene's novel *The Quiet American* (1955) told the story of this triangle against the background of America's adventure in Vietnam in the early 1950s—when, he shows us, the CIA used pleasant, presentable agents like Pyle to pose as "aid workers" while arranging terrorist acts that would justify our intervention there.

The novel inspired a 1958 Hollywood version in which the director Joseph Mankiewicz turned the story on its head, making Fowler the bad guy and Pyle the hero. Did the CIA have a hand in funding this film? Stranger things have happened: The animated version of *Animal Farm* (1954) was paid for by a CIA front, and twisted Orwell's fable about totalitarianism both East and West into a simplistic anti-Communist cartoon.

Now comes another version of *The Quiet American,* this one directed by the Australian Phillip Noyce and truer to the Greene novel. It is a film with a political point of view, but often its characters lose sight of that in their fascination with each other and with the girl. A question every viewer will have to answer at the end is whether a final death is the result of moral conviction or romantic compulsion.

The film is narrated by Caine's character in that conversational voice weary with wisdom; we are reminded of the tired cynicism of the opening narration in the great film of Greene's *The Third Man.* Pyle has "a face with no history, no problems," Fowler tells us; his own face is a map of both. "I'm just a reporter," he says. "I offer no point of view, I take no action, I don't get involved." Indeed, he has scarcely filed a story in the past year for his paper, the *Times* of London; he is too absorbed in Phuong and opium.

The irony is that Pyle, whom he actually likes at first, jars him into action and involvement. What he finally cannot abide is the younger man's cheerful certainty that he is absolutely right: "Saving the country and saving a woman would be the same thing to a man like that."

As luck would have it, *The Quiet American* was planned for release in the autumn of 2001. It was shelved after 9/11, when Miramax president Harvey Weinstein decided, no doubt correctly, that the national mood was not ripe for a film pointing out that the United States is guilty of terrorist acts of its own. Caine appealed to Weinstein, who a year later allowed the film to be shown at the Toronto Film Festival, where it was well received by the public and critics.

It would be unfortunate if people went to the movie, or stayed away, because of its political beliefs. There is no longer much controversy about the CIA's hand in stirring the Vietnam pot, and the movie is not an exposé but another of Greene's stories about a worndown, morally exhausted man clinging to shreds of hope in a world whose cynicism has long since rendered him obsolete. Both men "love" Phuong, but for Pyle she is less crucial. Fowler, on the other hand, admits: "I know I'm not essential to Phuong, but if I were to lose her, for me that would be the beginning of death." What Phuong herself thinks is not the point with either man, since they are both convinced she wants them.

Fraser, who often stars as a walking cartoon (*Dudley Do-Right, George of the Jungle*), has shown in other pictures, like *Gods and Monsters,* that he is a gifted actor, and here he finds just the right balance between confidence and blindness: What he does is evil, but he is convinced it is good, and has a simple, sunny view that maddens an old hand like Fowler. The two characters work well together because there is an undercurrent of commonalty: They are both floating in the last currents of colonialism, in which life in Saigon can be very good, unless you get killed.

Phillip Noyce made two great pictures close together, this one and *Rabbit-Proof Fence.* He feels anger as he tells this story, but he conceals it, because the story as it stands is enough. Some viewers will not even intercept the political message. It was that way with Greene: The politics were in the very weave of the cloth, not worth talking about. Here, in a rare Western feature shot in Vietnam, with real locations and sets that look well-worn enough to be real, with wonderful performances, he suggests a worldview more mature and knowing than the simplistic pieties that provide the public face of foreign policy.

R

Radio Days
PG, 88 m., 1987

Mia Farrow (Sally White), Seth Green (Joe), Michael Tucker (Father), Josh Mostel (Abe), Tito Puente (Bandleader), Danny Aiello (Rocco), Diane Keaton (New Year's Singer), Wallace Shawn (Masked Avenger), Dianne Wiest (Bea). Directed by Woody Allen and produced by Robert Greenhut. Screenplay by Allen.

I can remember what happened to the Lone Ranger in 1949 better than I can remember what happened to me. His adventures struck deeply into my imagination in a way that my own did not, and as I write these words there is almost a physical intensity to my memories of listening to the radio. Television was never the same. Television shows happened in the TV set, but radio shows happened in my head.

That is one of the truths that Woody Allen evokes in *Radio Days,* his comedy about growing up in the 1940s. Another one is that glamour and celebrity meant something in those days. And for millions of people living in ordinary homes in ordinary neighborhoods, the radio brought images of beings who lived in a shimmering world of penthouses and nightclubs, in dressing rooms and boudoirs.

The hero of *Radio Days* is an ordinary person like that: an adolescent Jewish kid who grows up in Brooklyn in a house full of relatives and listens passionately to the radio. But the movie is not simply his story. It is also the story of 1940s radio itself, and it recreates many of the legends that he remembers hearing.

For example, the story of the burglars who answered the phone in a house they were burgling and won the jackpot on *Name That Tune,* and the prizes were delivered the next day to their bewildered victims. Or the embarrassing plight of the suave radio host who liked to play around and got locked on the roof of a nightclub with the cigarette girl. Or the way the macho heroes of radio adventure serials turned out, in real life, to be short little bald guys. (The one legend Allen leaves out is the scandal of the kiddie-show host who growled "That oughta hold the little bastards" into an open mike.)

Radio Days cuts back and forth between the adolescent hero's working-class neighborhood in Brooklyn and the glamorous radio world of Manhattan. And, like radio, it jumps easily from one level of reality to another. There are autobiographical memories of relatives and school, neighbors and friends, and then there are the glittering radio legends that seeped into these ordinary lives.

Allen is not concerned with creating a story with a beginning and an end, and his movie is more like a revue in which drama is followed by comedy and everything is tied together by music, by dozens of lush arrangements of the hit songs of the 1940s. He has always used popular music in his movies (remember the opening of *Manhattan*?), but never more than this time, where the muscular, romantic confidence of the big-band sound reinforces every memory with the romance of the era.

There are so many characters in *Radio Days,* and they are in so many separate vignettes, that it's hard to give a coherent description of the plot or plots. In form and even in mood, the movie it's closest to is Federico Fellini's *Amarcord,* which also was a memory of growing up—of family, religion, sex, local folk legends, scandalous developments, and intense romantic yearnings, underlined with wall-to-wall band music. In a way, both films have nostalgia itself as one of their subjects. What they evoke isn't the long-ago time itself, but the memory of it. There is something about it being past and gone and irretrievable that makes it more precious than it ever was at the time.

As part of this nostalgic feeling, Allen seems to have made a deliberate attempt to use as many of his former actors as possible. The movie is a roll call of casts from earlier films, from Mia Farrow and Diane Keaton to Tony Roberts, Danny Aiello, Dianne Wiest, Jeff Daniels, and Wallace Shawn. And viewers with good memories will notice there also are many actual radio veterans in the movie, such as Don Pardo and Kitty Carlisle, and the shadows of others, such as Bill Stern, whose inspirational parables about sports heroes are mercilessly satirized.

The one actor who is not visible is Allen. But his teenage alter ego (Seth Green) provides a memory of young Allen in *Take the Money and Run,* and then there is Allen's own voice on the sound track, evoking those golden days of yesteryear. There also is the Allen irreverence in several moments of absolutely inspired comedy, such as a classroom show-and-tell session, or the time the young hero collects dimes for Israel and then spends them on a boxtop secret decoder ring and has to face the rabbi's wrath.

Radio Days is so ambitious and so audacious that it almost defies description. It's a kaleidoscope of dozens of characters, settings, and scenes—the most elaborate production Allen has ever made—and it's inexhaustible, spinning out one delight after another. Although there is no narrative thread from beginning to end, there is a buried emotional thread. Like music, the movie builds toward a climax we can't even guess is coming, and then Allen finds the perfect images for the last few minutes, for a bittersweet evocation of good-bye to all that.

His final moments are staged on a set representing a rooftop on Times Square, with a smoker puffing his cigarette on a Camel billboard, while in another direction a giant neon top hat is lifted and lowered. This set is so overblown and romantic, it's like the moment in *Amarcord* when all of the townspeople get into boats and go out to watch the great ocean liner go past, and we see that the liner is obviously a prop—a vast, artificial Christmas tree of shimmering lights and phony glory. Allen finds the same truth that Fellini did: What actually happens isn't nearly as important as how we remember it.

Raging Bull

R, 119 m., 1980

Robert De Niro (Jake La Motta), Cathy Moriarty (Vickie La Motta), Joe Pesci (Joey), Frank Vincent (Salvy), Nicholas Colasanto (Tommy Como), Theresa Saldana (Lenore), Frank Adonis (Patsy), Mario Gallo (Mario). Directed by Martin Scorsese and produced by Irwin Winkler and Robert Chartoff. Screenplay by Paul Schrader and Mardik Martin.

Martin Scorsese's *Raging Bull* is a movie about brute force, anger, and grief. It is also, like several of Scorsese's other movies, about a man's inability to understand a woman except in terms of the only two roles he knows how to assign her: virgin or whore. There is no room inside the mind of the prizefighter in this movie for the notion that a woman might be a friend, a lover, or a partner. She is only, to begin with, an inaccessible sexual fantasy. And then, after he has possessed her, she becomes tarnished by sex. Insecure in his own manhood, the man becomes obsessed by jealousy—and releases his jealousy in violence.

It is a vicious circle. Freud called it the "madonna-whore complex." Groucho Marx put it somewhat differently: "I wouldn't belong to any club that would have me as a member." It amounts to a man having such low self-esteem that he (a) cannot respect a woman who would sleep with him, and (b) is convinced that, given the choice, she would rather be sleeping with someone else. I'm making a point of the way *Raging Bull* equates sexuality and violence because one of the criticisms of this movie is that we never really get to know the central character. I don't agree with that. I think Scorsese and Robert De Niro do a fearless job of showing us the precise feelings of their central character, the former boxing champion Jake La Motta.

It is true that the character never tells us what he's feeling, that he is not introspective, that his dialogue is mostly limited to expressions of desire, fear, hatred, and jealousy. But these very limitations—these stone walls separating the character from the world of ordinary feelings—tell us all we need to know, especially when they're reflected back at him by the other people in his life. Especially his brother and his wife, Vickie.

Raging Bull is based, we are told, on the life of La Motta, who came out of the slums of the Bronx to become middleweight champion in the 1940s, who made and squandered millions of dollars, who became a pathetic stand-up comedian, and finally spent time in a prison for corrupting the morals of an underage girl. Is this the real La Motta? We cannot know for sure, though La Motta was closely involved with the production. What's perhaps more to the point is that Scorsese and his principal collaborators, actor Robert De Niro and screenwriter Paul Schrader, were attracted to this material. All three seem fascinated by the lives of tortured, violent, guilt-ridden characters; their previous three-way collaboration was the movie *Taxi Driver.*

Scorsese's very first film, *Who's That Knocking at My Door* (1967), starred Harvey Keitel as a kid from Little Italy who fell in love with a girl but could not handle the facts of her previous sexual experience. In its sequel, *Mean Streets* (1974), the same hangup was explored, as it was in *Taxi Driver,* where the De Niro character's madonna-whore complex tortured him in sick relationships with an inaccessible, icy blonde, and with a young prostitute. Now the filmmakers have returned to the same ground, in a film deliberately intended to strip away everything but the raw surges of guilt, jealousy, and rage coursing through La Motta's extremely limited imagination.

Raging Bull remains close to its three basic elements: a man, a woman, and prizefighting. La Motta is portrayed as a punk kid, stubborn, strong, and narrow. He gets involved in boxing, and he is good at it. He gets married, but his wife seems almost an afterthought. Then one day he sees a girl at a municipal swimming pool and is transfixed by her. The girl is named Vickie, and she is played by Cathy Moriarty as an intriguing mixture of unstudied teenager, self-reliant survivor, and somewhat calculated slut.

La Motta wins and marries her. Then he becomes consumed by the conviction she is cheating on him. Scorsese finds a way to visually suggest his jealousy: From La Motta's point of view, Vickie sometimes floats in slow motion toward another man. The technique fixes the moment in our minds; we share La Motta's exaggeration of an innocent event. And we share, too, the La Motta character's limited and tragic hang-ups. This man we see is not, I think, supposed to be any more subtle than he seems. He does not have additional "qualities" to share with us. He is an engine driven by his own rage. The equation between his prizefighting and his sexuality is inescapable, and we see the trap he's in: La Motta is the victim of base needs and instincts that, in his case, are not accompanied by the insights and maturity necessary for him to cope with them. The raging bull. The poor sap.

Raiders of the Lost Ark

PG, 115 m., 1981

Harrison Ford (Indy), Ronald Lacey (Teht), John Rhys-Davies (Sallah), Karen Allen (Marion), Wolf Kahler (Dietrich). Directed by Steven Spielberg and produced by Frank Marshall. Executive producers, George Lucas and Howard Kazanjian. Screenplay by Lucas and Philip Kaufman.

Raiders of the Lost Ark is an out-of-body experience, a movie of glorious imagination and breakneck speed that grabs you in the first shot, hurtles you through a series of incredible adventures, and deposits you back in reality two hours later—breathless, dizzy, wrungout, and with a silly grin on your face. This movie celebrates the stories we spent our adolescence searching for in the pulp adventure magazines, in the novels of Edgar Rice Burroughs, in comics—even in the movies. There used to be a magazine named *Thrilling Wonder Stories,* and every shot in *Raiders of the Lost Ark* looks like one of its covers. It's the kind of movie where the hero gets out of bed wondering what daring exploits and astonishing, cliffhanging, death-defying threats he will have to survive in the next ten seconds.

It's actually more than a movie; it's a catalog of adventure. For locations, it ticks off the jungles of South America, the hinterlands of Tibet, the deserts of Egypt, a hidden submarine base, an isolated island, a forgotten tomb—no, make that *two* forgotten tombs—and an American anthropology classroom. For villains, it has sadistic Nazis, slimy gravediggers, drunken Sherpas, and scheming Frenchmen. For threats, it climaxes with the wrath of God, and leads up to that spectacular development by easy stages, with tarantulas, runaway boulders, hidden spears, falling rock slabs, burning airplanes, runaway trucks, sealed tombs, and snakes. Lots of snakes. For modes of conveyance, it looks like one of those old world's fair panoramas of transportation: It has horse carts, biplanes, motorcycles, submarines, ships, horses, trains, and trucks. No bicycles.

For heroes, it has Indiana Jones (Harrison Ford) and his former and future girlfriend, Marion (Karen Allen). She's the kind of girl . . . well, to make a long story short, when they first met ten years ago, Indiana deflowered her, and that made her so mad at men that she moved to the mountains of Tibet, opened a bar, and started nightly drinking contests with the Sherpas. She'll never forgive him, almost.

The time is 1936. Indy is an American anthropologist who learns that the Nazis think they've discovered the long-lost resting place of the Ark of the Covenant, the golden casket used by the ancient Hebrews to hold the Ten Commandments. Indy's mission: Beat the Nazis to the prize. He flies to Tibet, collects Marion and a priceless medallion that holds the secret of the Ark's location, and then tries to outsmart the Nazis. What is a little amazing about *Raiders of the Lost Ark* is that this plot somehow holds together and makes some sense, even though it functions primarily as a framework for the most incredible series of action and stunt set pieces I've ever seen in a movie. Indiana and Marion spend the entire film hanging by their fingernails—literally, at one point, over a pit of poisonous snakes.

They survive a series of gruesome and dreadful traps, pitfalls, double-crosses, ambushes, and fates worse than death (of which this movie suggests several). And Indiana engages in the best chase scene I've seen in a film. (I include, in second place, the chase from *The French Connection,* with *Bullitt* in third.) The chase involves a truck, three jeeps, a horse, a motorcycle, and an awesomely difficult stunt in which a character is required to make a 360-degree turn of the speeding truck. All of these spectacles are achieved with flawless movie technology brought to a combination of stunts, special visual effects, and sheer sweat. The makers of this film have covered similar ground before, if perhaps never so fluently; George Lucas, the executive producer, gave birth to the *Star Wars* movies, and Steven Spielberg, the director, made *Jaws* and *Close Encounters.* The rest of the all-star crew's work includes photography by veteran British cinematographer Douglas Slocombe, appropriately stirring and haunting music by *Star Wars* composer John Williams, sets by *Star Wars* production designer Norman Reynolds and art director Les Dilley, and countless wonderments by Richard Edlund, who supervised the visual effects.

Two things, however, make *Raiders of the*

Lost Ark more than just a technological triumph: its sense of humor and the droll style of its characters. This is often a funny movie, but it doesn't get many of its laughs with dialogue and only a few with obvious gags (although the biggest laugh comes from the oldest and most obvious gag, involving a swordsman and a marksman). We find ourselves laughing in surprise, in relief, in incredulity at the movie's ability to pile one incident upon another in an inexhaustible series of inventions. And the personalities of the central characters are enormously winning. Harrison Ford, as Indy Jones, does not do a reprise of his *Star Wars* work. Instead he creates a taciturn, understated, stubborn character who might be the Humphrey Bogart of *The Treasure of the Sierra Madre* with his tongue in his cheek. He survives fires, crushings, shootings, burnings. He really hates snakes. Karen Allen plays the female lead with a resilient toughness that develops its own charm. She can handle herself in any situation. She *really* hates snakes.

Raiders of the Lost Ark is a swashbuckling adventure epic in the tradition of *Star Wars, Superman,* the James Bond pictures, and all the other multimillion-dollar special-effects extravaganzas. It wants only to entertain. It succeeds. Watch it with someone you know fairly well. There will be times during the film when it will be necessary to grab somebody.

The Rain People
R, 101 m., 1969

James Caan (Kilgannon), Shirley Knight (Natalie), Robert Duvall (Gordon), Marya Zimmet (Rosalie), Tom Aldredge (Mr. Alfred), Laurie Crewes (Ellen), Andrew Duncan (Artie), Margaret Fairchild (Marlon). Directed by Francis Ford Coppola and produced by Bart Patton and Ronald Colby. Screenplay by Coppola.

In a curious way, Francis Ford Coppola's *The Rain People* is the mirror image of *Easy Rider.* In Coppola's film, a middle-class wife drives the family station wagon west in search of freedom. In *Easy Rider,* two drug freaks make a fortune smuggling cocaine across the border, then head east on motorcycles in search of the middle-class dream of retirement in Florida.

And so you have two opposed American lifestyles crossing paths, somewhere in Oklahoma, like ships in the night. The characters in one movie are seeking what the characters in the other are escaping. Maybe that's what both movies are about; In any case, none of the characters succeed in escaping their pasts or reaching their goals. Or, as Peter Fonda says in *Easy Rider*, "we blew it; we all blew it."

That may not be entirely accurate. Here and there in these states, there are no doubt millions of people who, by and large, are happy. By and large, I'm happy most of the time myself. But the catch is, what are we getting out of it? Should a life contribute something? Should it seem to have a meaning? Is it enough to be happy, or must one be surrounded by a metaphysical glow of significance?

The search for personal fulfillment is such an American theme we hold the patent on it. For a long time, we had the West. If you didn't like it here, you could always head there. But then, about the time of *The Grapes of Wrath* the West fell through as a place to go when things were bad at home. And ever since then, the great American search has to hit the road. Route 66. The Wabash Cannonball. I hear that train a-comin'. . . .

Basically the search is the same no matter how you undertake it. The young wife (Shirley Knight) in *The Rain People* and the Peter Fonda character in *Easy Rider* are lineal descendants of the most typical American searcher of them all, Huckleberry Finn. The rules of the game say these searches are always undertaken by two companions: a sophisticate and an innocent. So Huck Finn takes along the slave, Jim. And Peter Fonda takes along the pothead (played by Dennis Hopper). And Shirley Knight picks up a hitchhiker (James Caan) who was a college football player until he got banged on the head and that made him an innocent.

The function of innocents is to be satisfied and ask obvious questions. They dig things. They like catfish (Jim) and getting stoned (Hopper) and they love a parade (Caan). And they can't understand why their companion on the quest doesn't just settle down and take it easy.

But the big thing about a quest, as Don Quixote explained to Sancho, is that it's only fun as long as you're still on it. That was the trouble with *Midnight Cowboy*—as long as Ratso believed Florida would solve his problems, he was okay. But actually getting on the bus and going to Florida was a fatal mistake. By making his dream real he discovered, alas, it was only a dream.

In *The Rain People* Coppola takes his characters across a carefully observed American landscape. Knight and Caan drive through small country towns and big cities.

But the Knight character filters the landscape through her own disillusionment and despair. (She's trapped in a marriage she doesn't believe in, and she's going to have a child she's not sure she wants.) The *Easy Rider* characters, on the other hand, would like to see groovy things but in their landscape everything seems to be going wrong. The kids in the hippie communes are as screwed up as the rednecks in the roadside café.

Huck Finn had this figured out and he tried to fence off the world by creating his own and taking it with him. There was nothing so nice and smooth and quiet and easy as lying on your back on that raft in the middle of the night, floating down the Mississippi, and watching the stars slide past.

As for Coppola and his world, it's difficult to say whether his film is successful. That's the beautiful thing about a lot of the new, experimental American directors. They'd rather do interesting things and make provocative observations than try to outflank John Ford on his way to the Great American Movie.

So all you can really say, I guess, is here's what Coppola's up to. It is a traditional American pastime and a noble one—exploring the country through the eyes of a dissatisfied searcher. And what the search discovers is no more (and no less) than a crossroads in Oklahoma, a parade in Pennsylvania, long nights on the road, a hero who got banged on the head, and a highway patrolman who is, even so, a human being. And these places and people fit together, they love or hate each other, all because of the accident of being alive at the same time and place.

It takes the innocent (the slave Jim, the simpleton pothead, the football hero) to ask—why aren't you happy? What are you looking for? And it takes the sophisticate (as Huck

Finn understood so well in his long chats with Jim) to say: If you can ask the question you don't need the answer.

Raise the Red Lantern
PG, 126 m., 1992

Gong Li (Songlian), Ma Jingwu (Chen Zuoqian), He Caifei (Third Wife), Cao Cui (Second Wife), Jin Shuyuan (First Wife), Kong Lin (Maid). Directed by Zhang Yimou and produced by Chiu Fu-sheng. Screenplay by Su Tong, based on his book.

The fourth wife of the rich old man comes to live in his house against her will. She has been educated, and thinks herself ready for the wider world, but her mother betrays her, selling her as a concubine, and soon her world is no larger than the millionaire's vast house. Its living quarters are arrayed on either side of a courtyard. There is an apartment for each of the wives. She is quietly informed of the way things work here. A red lantern is raised each night outside the quarters of the wife who will be honored by a visit from the master.

So opens *Raise the Red Lantern,* a Chinese film of voluptuous physical beauty and angry passions. It was one of 1992's Academy Award nominees in the Foreign Language category, directed by Zhang Yimou, whose *Ju Dou* was nominated in 1990. This film, based on the novel *Wives and Concubines* by Su Tong, can no doubt be interpreted in a number of ways—as a cry against the subjection of women in China, as an attack on feudal attitudes, as a formal exercise in storytelling— and yet it works because it is so fascinating simply on the level of melodrama.

We enter into the sealed world of the rich man's house, and see how jealousies fester in its hothouse atmosphere. Each of the four wives is treated with the greatest luxury, pampered with food and care, servants and massages, but they are like horses in a great racing stable, cared for at the whim of the master. The new wife, whose name is Songlian, is at first furious at her fate. Then she begins to learn the routine of the house, and is drawn into its intrigues and alliances. If you are given only one game to play, it is human nature to try to win it.

Songlian is played by Gong Li, an elegant woman who also starred in quite different roles in Zhang Yimou's two previous films. In *Red Sorghum,* she was a defiant young woman, sold into marriage to a wealthy vintner; she takes over his winery after his death and makes it prosperous with the help of a sturdy peasant who has earlier saved her from rape. In *Ju Dou,* she was the young bride of a wealthy old textile merchant, who enslaved both her and his poor young nephew—with the result that she and the nephew fall in love, and the merchant comes to a colorful end in a vat of his own dyes.

Zhang Yimou is obviously attracted to the theme of the rich, impotent old man and the young wife. But in *Raise the Red Lantern,* it is the system of concubinage that he focuses on. The rich man is nowhere to be seen, except in hints and shadows. He is a patriarchal, offstage presence, as his four wives and the household staff scheme among themselves for his favor.

We meet the serene first wife, who reigns over the other wives and has the wisdom of longest experience in this house. Then there are the resigned second wife and the competitive third wife, who is furious that the master has taken a bride younger and prettier than herself. The servants, including the young woman assigned to Songlian, have their own priorities. And there is Dr. Gao (Cui Zhihgang), who treats the wives, and whose medical judgments are instrumental in the politics of the house. The gossip that whirls among the wives and their servants creates the world for these people; little that happens outside ever leaks in.

Zhang Yimou's visual world here is part of the story. His master shot, which is returned to again and again, looks down the central space of the house, which is open to the sky, with the houses of the wives arrayed on either side, and the vast house of the master at the end. As the seasons pass, the courtyard is sprinkled with snow, or dripping with rain, or bathed in hot, still sunlight. The servants come and go. Up on the roof of the house is a little shed that is sometimes whispered about. It has something to do with an earlier wife who did not adjust well.

Zhang uses the bold, bright colors of *Ju Dou* again this time; his film was shot in the classic three-strip Technicolor process, now abandoned by Hollywood, which allows a richness of reds and yellows no longer possible in American films. There is a sense in which *Raise the Red Lantern* exists solely for the eyes. Entirely apart from the plot, there is the sensuous pleasure of the architecture, the fabrics, the color contrasts, the faces of the actresses. But beneath the beauty is the cruel reality of this life, just as beneath the comfort of the rich man's house is the sin of slavery.

Ran

R, 160 m., 1985

Tatsuya Nakadai (Lord Hidetora), Akira Terao (Taro, Eldest Son), Jinpachi Nezu (Jiro, Second Son), Daisuke Ryn (Sahuro, Youngest Son), Mjeko Harada (Lady Kaede, Taro's Wife), Yoshiko Miyazaki (Lady Sue, Jiro's Wife), Masayuki Yui (Tango, Hidetora's Servant), Peter (Kyoami, The Fool). Directed by Akira Kurosawa and produced by Serge Silberman and Masato Hara. Screenplay by Hideo Oquino, Masato Ide, and Kurosawa.

One of the early reviews of Akira Kurosawa's *Ran* said that he could not possibly have directed it at an earlier age. My first impression was to question that act of critical omnipotence. Who is to say Kurosawa couldn't have made this film at fifty or sixty, instead of at seventy-five, as he has? But then I thought longer about *Ran*, which is based on Shakespeare's *King Lear* and on a similar medieval samurai legend. And I thought about Laurence Olivier's Lear and about the *Lear* I recently saw starring Douglas Campbell and I realized that age is probably a prerequisite to fully understanding this character. Dustin Hoffman might be able to play Willy Loman by aging himself with makeup, but he will have to wait another twenty years to play Lear.

The character contains great paradoxes, but they are not the paradoxes of youth; they spring from long habit. Lear has the arrogance of great power, long held. He has wide knowledge of the world. Yet he is curiously innocent when it comes to his own children; he thinks they can do no wrong, can be trusted to carry out his plans. At the end, when his dreams have been broken, the character has the touching quality of a childlike innocence that can see breath on

lips that are forever sealed, and can dream of an existence beyond the cruelties of man. Playing Lear is not a technical exercise. I wonder if a man can do it who has not had great disappointments and long dark nights of the soul.

Kurosawa has lived through those bad times. Here is one of the greatest directors of all time, out of fashion in his own country, suffering from depression, nearly blind. He prepared this film for ten years, drawing hundreds of sketches showing every shot, hardly expecting that the money would ever be found to allow him to make the film. But a deal was finally put together by Serge Silberman, the old French producer who backed the later films of Luis Buñuel (who could also have given us a distinctive Lear). Silberman risked his own money; this is the most expensive Japanese film ever made, and, yes, perhaps Kurosawa could not have made it until he was seventy-five.

The story is familiar. An old lord decides to retire from daily control of his kingdom, yet still keep all the trappings of his power. He will divide his kingdom in three parts among his children. In *Ran*, they are sons, not daughters. First, he requires a ritual statement of love. The youngest son cannot abide the hypocrisy, and stays silent. And so on.

The Japanese legend which Kurosawa draws from contains a famous illustration in which the old lord takes three arrows and demonstrates that when they are bundled, they cannot be broken, but taken one at a time, they are weak. He wishes his sons to remain allies, so they will be strong, but of course they begin to fight, and civil war breaks out as the old lord begins his forlorn journey from one castle to another, gradually being stripped of his soldiers, his pride, his sanity.

Nobody can film an epic battle scene like Kurosawa. He has already abundantly demonstrated that in *The Seven Samurai*, in *Yojimbo*, in *Kagemusha*. In *Ran*, the great bloody battles are counterpointed with scenes of a chamber quality, as deep hatreds and lusts are seen to grow behind the castle's walls.

King Lear is a play that centers obsessively around words expressing negatives. "Nothing? Nothing will come of nothing!" "Never, never, never." "No, no, no, no, no." They express in deep anguish the king's realization that what has been taken apart will never be put together again, that his beloved child is dead and will breathe no more, that his pride and folly have put an end to his happiness. Kurosawa's film expresses that despair perhaps more deeply than a Western film might; the samurai costumes, the makeup inspired by Noh drama, give the story a freshness that removes it from all our earlier associations.

Ran is a great, glorious achievement. Kurosawa must often have associated himself with the old lord as he tried to put this film together, but in the end he has triumphed, and the image I have of him, at seventy-five, is of three arrows bundled together.

The Rapture

R, 92 m., 1991

Mimi Rogers (Sharon), David Duchovny (Randy), Patrick Bauchau (Vic), Kimberly Cullum (Mary), Will Patton (Sheriff Foster). Directed by Michael Tolkin and produced by Nick Wechsler, Nancy Tenenbaum, and Karen Koch. Screenplay by Tolkin.

As flies to wanton boys, are we to the gods; They kill us for their sport.
—Shakespeare, *King Lear*

Her life is a bleak and sinful void. She finds God and is reborn. But then, after a period during which she finds peace through her new beliefs, her life becomes a void again—this time, on God's terms. Sharon, the woman played brilliantly and courageously by Mimi Rogers in *The Rapture*, is a character like Job, tested by God to the breaking point. Unlike Job, she finally refuses to be toyed with any longer.

Her story is told in one of the most challenging and infuriating movies I've seen—a radical, uncompromising treatment of the Christian teachings about the final judgment. Almost all movies with a religious theme are made by people who are themselves religious, or who piously pretend to be. *The Rapture*, written and directed by Michael Tolkin, is seen from a more literal, skeptical point of view: All right, he seems to be saying, if this is what the end of creation is going to be like, then we should stare unblinking at its full and terrifying implications.

As the movie opens, Sharon and her lover, Vic (Patrick Bauchau), are swingers, mate-swappers who cruise the bars together, looking for likely prospects. When they find others who want to swing, they go home for sexual games that Sharon finds increasingly unrewarding. Is this all life is—partying all night and spending her days in a tiny cubicle, working as an operator for the telephone company?

Tolkin uses Sharon's daytime job as a metaphor for modern man, who communicates more easily than ever before, but more impersonally. Sharon's job requires her to talk to hundreds of people all day long, but in a mechanical way. Her nighttime sex life is almost a reaction to the sterile existence of her days.

Then she overhears some of her coworkers talking during a lunch break about "the rapture," about the imminent Second Coming of Christ, about "the boy," who is their prophet. She is curious, and is taken to one of their meetings, and finds that all over the world some people are sharing the same dream of the imminent end of the world. It is a dream she has herself. Torn between her sinful existence and the hope of these believers, she attempts to commit suicide, but instead experiences an overwhelming spiritual experience and is born again.

Ah, but the movie does not lead us where we expect it to go after her experience. She leaves Vic, she finds a partner who is spiritually healthier, she has a daughter, she leads a blameless life, and then, when the girl is about six, Sharon becomes convinced that the Second Coming is imminent. She goes out into the wilderness with her daughter to await the moment when she expects God to gather the two of them into heaven. And she waits. And waits. And a national park policeman takes pity on them, as they stand under the merciless sun.

Sharon is guilty, I believe, of the sin of pride. She thinks she knows when, and how, God will call her. God does not perform according to her timetable. And yet Tolkin does not cheat us with an ending in which Sharon is simply seen as deluded. God does exist in this film, and he does make judgments about individuals such as Sharon, and the world does end, with the fearsome horsemen of the apocalypse in the sky, and the bars falling from the doors of the prison cells.

It is simply that, by the time of the judgment, Sharon has had enough. She commits a shocking action; she tries to stand firm and unflinching in her faith, but she finally comes to believe that God has asked too much of her. Her actions in the last twenty minutes of this film send audiences boiling out of the theater engaged in fierce discussions. After decades of "religious" films that were simply sentimentalized fables, here is a film that demands its audiences make their own peace with the rules of an inflexible diety.

Watching the film, I began to realize that I would feel cheated if Tolkin did not give us some vision of heaven—did not take Sharon to another plane, in one way or another. He does not cheat us, and the closing passages of this film are stunning in their implications. It is true that on a limited budget *The Rapture* is not able to give us sensational special effects— a state-of-the-art heaven, if you will. It doesn't matter. He gives us an idea of heaven that transcends any possible special effect, and brings us face to face with the awful, and aweful, consequences of that day when the saints go marching in.

Ratatouille

G, 114 m., 2007

Patton Oswalt (Remy), Lou Romano (Linguini), Ian Holm (Skinner), Janeane Garofalo (Colette), Brian Dennehy (Django), Peter O'Toole (Anton Ego), Brad Garrett (Gusteau), Peter Sohn (Emile). Directed by Brad Bird and produced by John Lasseter. Written by Bird, based on an original story by Jan Pinkava, Jim Capobianco, and Bird.

A lot of animated movies have inspired sequels, notably *Shrek*, but Brad Bird's *Ratatouille* is the first one that made me positively desire one. Remy, the earnest little rat who is its hero, is such a lovable, determined, gifted rodent that I want to know what happens to him next, now that he has conquered the summit of French cuisine. I think running for office might not be beyond his reach, and there's certainly something De Gaullean about his snout.

Remy is a member of a large family of rats (a horde, I think, is the word) who ply the trash cans and sewers of a Parisian suburb, just like good rats should. "Eat your garbage!" commands Remy's father, Django, obviously a loving parent. The rats are evicted from their cozy home in a cottage kitchen ceiling in a scene that will have rat haters in the audience cringing (and who among us will claim they don't hate rats more than a little?), and they are swept through the sewers in a torrential flood. Students of Victor Hugo will know that the hero Jean Valjean of *Les Miserables* found the Seine because he knew that every sewer must necessarily run downhill toward it, and indeed Remy washes up near the river, in view of the most famous restaurant in "tout le France." This is the establishment of Auguste Gusteau, author of the best seller *Anyone Can Cook*, a title that might not go over very well in France, which is why the book appears to be in English and might well be titled, *Anyone Can Cook Better Than the English*. (Famous British recipe: "Cook until gray.")

Remy (voice by Patton Oswalt) has always been blessed, or cursed, with a refined palate and a sensitive nose, and now he starts skulking around the kitchen of his culinary hero (voice by Brad Garrett). Alas, the monstrous food critic Anton Ego (Peter O'Toole) issues a scathing indictment of Gusteau's recent cooking, the chef dies in a paroxysm of grief, or perhaps it is not a paroxysm, but I like the word, and the kitchen is taken over by the sniveling little snipe Skinner (Ian Holm). Lowest of the low is Gusteau's nephew Linguini (Lou Romano), who must be hired, but is assigned to the wretched job of "plongeur"—literally, one who washes the dishes by plunging them into soapy water.

Linguini and Remy meet, somehow establish trust and communication, and when Linguini gets credit for a soup that the rat has saved with strategic seasonings, they team up. Remy burrows into Linguini's hair, is concealed by his toque, can see through its transparent sides, and controls Linguini by pulling on his hair as if each tuft were a joy stick. Together, they astonish Paris with their genius.

All of this begins as a dubious premise and ends as a triumph of animation, comedy, imagination, and, yes, humanity. What is most lovable about Remy is his modesty and shyness, even for a rat. He has body language so expressive than many humans would trade for it. Many animated characters seem to communicate with semaphores, but Remy has a repertory of tiny French hand gestures, shrugs, and physical expressiveness. Does any other nationality have more ways of moving a finger and an eyebrow less than an inch while signaling something as complex as, "I would do anything for you, monsieur, but as you see, I have only two hands, and these times we live in do not permit me the luxury of fulfilling such requests."

Brad Bird and his coproducer John Lasseter pretty clearly take over leadership in the animation field right now. Yes, Bird made *The Incredibles,* but the one that got away was his wonderful *The Iron Giant,* in which a towering robot was as subtle, gentle, and touching as Remy. His eye for detail is remarkable. Every prop and utensil and spice and ingredient in the kitchen is almost tangible, and I for one would never turn off the Food Channel if Remy hosted a program named *Any Rat Can Cook.*

This is clearly one of the best of the year's films. Every time an animated film is successful, you have to read all over again about how animation isn't "just for children" but "for the whole family" and "even for adults going on their own." No kidding!

Raven's End

NO MPAA RATING, 94 m., 1972

Thommy Berggren (Anders), Keve Hielm (Father), Emy Storm (Mother), Ingvar Hlrdwall (Sixten), Christina Frambeck (Elsie), Agneta Prytz (A Neighbor). Directed by Bo Widerberg. Screenplay by Widerberg.

The young man looks at the empty lives of the people living on his block and writes an angry book about the way they've been treated. A publisher invites him to Stockholm to discuss the manuscript but finally patronizes him: "There is a cry of rage here, but it is still inarticulate." Sobbing with frustration, the young man tells a sympathetic neighbor girl: "Sometimes a cry is so loud it cannot be heard." They make love that night, the girl becomes pregnant, and before long the young man believes that he has been trapped just as his parents were.

This is the simple stuff of *Raven's End,* a film made in 1963 by Bo Widerberg, the Swedish director who went on to great success with *Elvira Madigan* and *Adalen '31.* This is his best film and would have achieved distribution long ago were it not for the strange way we regard foreign directors. In 1963, a long time ago as movie history goes, Ingmar Bergman was just about the whole Swedish film industry as far as American distributors were concerned. *Raven's End* was chosen for the Cannes and New York Film Festivals and then disappeared, apart from infrequent film society screenings. It didn't open commercially in New York until 1970.

It has crept into Chicago for eight days only, as the inaugural premiere of the new Termite Theater in Piper's Alley. The theater is well named, being hidden in the walls beyond the adjacent Aardvark Theater, and containing only eighty-eight seats. It is intended as a showcase for short runs of art films, and Jean-Luc Godard's *Two or Three Things I Know About Her* opens next.

Raven's End is set very convincingly in a working-class district in the north of Sweden during the late years of the 1930s when the Swedish Nazi Party was trying to win power. The young man, who is very introspective and intense and reminds you somewhat of Thomas Wolfe's Eugene Gant, lives with his parents in an apartment block. The father is a failure and blames the social unacceptability of his wife and his own unlucky breaks. In fact, he is an idealistic but disorganized alcoholic with big, empty plans.

The development of the relationship between the three people is done as perceptively, skillfully, and deeply as anything in this line apart from Eric Rohmer's recent work. Widerberg has an incredible eye for details of dialogue, and as the father describes his drunkenness ("the only thing I ever invented—the diving bell; I am inside and it is quiet and I am sinking, sinking....") we're reminded of the alcoholic introspection in Frederick Exley's great novel *A Fan's Notes.*

The father fails at everything, even passing out handbills, but the mother hangs on and takes laundry, and cannot believe that her son would run out on a pregnant girl. He says he isn't running from the girl, but from the doomed life he sees reaching out before him.

She doesn't understand, and maybe he doesn't either. But he has to go. In the beer garden the night before, he asked his father for help and advice: "You're only thirty-nine, Father, you can't give up before you're forty." And the father only said he was sinking, sinking. . . .

Ray

PG-13, 152 m., 2004

Jamie Foxx (Ray Charles), Kerry Washington (Della Bea Robinson), Clifton Powell (Jeff Brown), Harry Lennix (Joe Adams), Terrence Dashon Howard (Gossie McKee), Larenz Tate (Quincy Jones), Richard Schiff (Jerry Wexler), Aunjanue Ellis (Mary Ann Fisher), Bokeem Woodbine (Fathead Newman), Sharon Warren (Aretha Robinson), Curtis Armstrong (Ahmet Ertegun), Regina King (Margie Hendricks), Warwick Davis (Oberon). Directed by Taylor Hackford and produced by Howard Baldwin, Stuart Benjamin, and Hackford. Screenplay by James L. White.

Ray Charles became blind at age seven, two years after witnessing the drowning death of his little brother. In a memory that haunted his life, he stood nailed to the spot while the little boy drowned absurdly in a bath basin. Why didn't Ray act to save him? For the same reason all five-year-olds do dumb and strange things: Because they are newly in possession of the skills of life, and can be paralyzed by emotional overload. No one seeing the scene in *Ray,* Taylor Hackford's considerable new musical biography, would think to blame the boy, but he never forgives himself.

If he had already been blind, he could not have blamed himself for the death, and would not have carried the lifelong guilt that, the movie argues, contributed to his drug addiction. Would he also then have not been driven to become the consummate artist that he was? Who can say? For that matter, what role did blindness play in his genius? Did it make him so alive to sound that he became a better musician? Certainly he was so attuned to the world around him that he never used a cane or a dog; for Charles, blindness was more of an attribute than a handicap.

Jamie Foxx suggests the complexities of Ray Charles in a great, exuberant performance. He doesn't do the singing—that's all Ray Charles on the sound track—but what would be the point? Ray Charles was deeply involved in the project for years, until his death in June 2004, and the film had access to his recordings, so of course it should use them, because nobody else could sing like Ray Charles.

What Foxx gets just right is the physical Ray Charles, and what an extrovert he was. Not for Ray the hesitant blind man of cliché, feeling his way, afraid of the wrong step. In the movie and in life, he was adamantly present in body as well as spirit, filling a room, physically dominant, interlaced with other people. Yes, he was eccentric in his mannerisms, especially at the keyboard; I can imagine a performance in which Ray Charles would come across like a manic clown. But Foxx correctly interprets his body language as a kind of choreography, in which he was conducting his music with himself, instead of with a baton. Foxx so accurately reflects my own images and memories of Charles that I abandoned thoughts of how much "like" Charles he was, and just accepted him as Charles, and got on with the story.

The movie places Charles at the center of key movements in postwar music. After an early career in which he seemed to aspire to sound like Nat "King" Cole, he loosened up, found himself, and discovered a fusion between the gospel music of his childhood and the rhythm and blues of his teen years and his first professional gigs. The result was, essentially, the invention of soul music, in early songs like "I Got a Woman."

The movie shows him finding that sound in Seattle, his improbable destination after he leaves his native Georgia. Before and later, it returns for key scenes involving his mother, Aretha (Sharon Warren), who taught him not to be intimidated by his blindness, to dream big, to demand the best for himself. She had no education and little money, but insisted on the school for the blind, which set him on his way. He heads for Seattle after hearing about the club scene, but why there and not in New York, Kansas City, Chicago, or New Orleans? Certainly his meeting with the Seattle teenager Quincy Jones was one of the crucial events in his life (as was his friendship with the dwarf emcee Oberon, played by Warwick Davis, who turns him on to pot).

The movie follows Charles from his birth in 1930 until 1966, when he finally defeats his heroin addiction and his story grows happier but also perhaps less dramatic. By then he had helped invent soul, had moved into the mainstream with full orchestration, had moved out of the mainstream into the heresy of country music (then anathema to a black musician), and had, in 1961, by refusing to play a segregated concert in Georgia, driven a nail in the corpse of Jim Crow in the entertainment industry.

In an industry that exploits many performers, he took canny charge of his career, coldbloodedly leaving his longtime supporters at Atlantic Records to sign with ABC Paramount and gain control of his catalog. (It's worth noting that the white Atlantic owners Ahmet Ertegun and Jerry Wexler are portrayed positively, in a genre that usually shows music execs as bloodsuckers.) Charles also fathered more children than the movie can tell you about, with more women than the movie has time for, and yet found the lifelong love and support of his wife, Della Bea Robinson (Kerry Washington).

The film is two and a half hours long—not too long for the richness of this story—but to cover the years between 1966 and his death in 2004 would have required more haste and superficial summary than Hackford and his writer, James L. White, are willing to settle for. When we leave him, Ray is safely on course for his glory years, although there is a brief scene set in 1979 where he receives an official apology from his home state of Georgia over the concert incident, and "Georgia on My Mind" is named as the state song.

Charles's addictions were to drugs and women. He beat only drugs, but *Ray* is perceptive and not unsympathetic in dealing with his roving ways. Of the women we meet, the most important is his wife, Della Bea, played by Washington as a paragon of insight, acceptance, and with a certain resignation; when one of his lovers dies, she asks him, "What about her baby?" "You knew?" says Charles. She knew everything.

His two key affairs are with Mary Ann Fisher (Aunjanue Ellis), a blues singer, and Margie Hendricks (Regina King), a member of his backup group, the Raelettes. Who knows what the reality was, but in the film we get the sense that Charles was honest, after his fashion, about his womanizing, and his women understood him, forgave him, accepted him,

and were essential to him. Not that he was easy to get along with during the heroin years, and not that they were saints, but that, all in all, whatever it was, it worked. "On the road," says Margie, in a line that says more than it seems to, "I'm Mrs. Ray Charles."

The movie would be worth seeing simply for the sound of the music and the sight of Jamie Foxx performing it. That it looks deeper and gives us a sense of the man himself is what makes it special. Yes, there are moments when an incident in Ray's life instantly inspires a song (I doubt "What'd I Say?" translated quite so instantly from life to music). But Taylor Hackford brings quick sympathy to Charles as a performer and a man, and we remember that he directed *Hail! Hail! Rock 'n' Roll*, a great documentary about Chuck Berry, a performer whose onstage and offstage moves more than braced Hackford for this film. Ray Charles was quite a man; this movie not only knows it, but understands it.

Red

R, 95 m., 1994

Irene Jacob (Valentine), Jean-Louis Trintignant (the Judge), Frederique Feder (Karin), Jean-Pierre Lorit (Auguste), Samuel Lebihan (Photographer), Marion Stalens (Veterinarian), Teco Celio (Barman), Bernard Escalon (Record Salesman). Directed by Krzysztof Kieslowski and produced by Marin Karmitz and Gerard Ruey. Screenplay by Krzysztof Piesiewicz and Kieslowski.

At this moment, in this café, we're sitting next to strangers. Everyone will get up, leave, and go their own way. And then, they'll never meet again. And if they do, they won't realize that it's not for the first time.

—Krzysztof Kieslowski

One of the opening images in *Red* is of telephone lines, crossing. It is the same in life. We are connected with some people and never meet others, but it could easily have happened otherwise. Looking back over a lifetime, we describe what happened as if it had a plan. To fully understand how accidental and random life is—how vast the odds are against any single event taking place—would be humbling.

That is the truth that Kieslowski keeps returning to in his work. In *The Double Life of Veronique,* there is even a moment when, if the heroine had looked out of a bus window, she might have seen herself on the street; it's as if fate allowed her to continue on one lifeline after choosing another. In *Red,* none of the major characters know each other at the beginning of the movie, and there is no reason they should meet. Exactly.

The film opens in Geneva, in an apartment occupied by a model named Valentine (Irene Jacob). She makes a telephone call, and the phone rings at the same time in an apartment just across the street, occupied by Auguste (Jean-Pierre Lorit), a law student. But she is not calling him. Her call is to her boyfriend, who is in England, and who she rarely sees. As far as we know, Valentine and Auguste have never met. And may never meet. Or perhaps they will.

One day Valentine's car strikes a dog, and she takes it to the home of its owner, a retired judge (Jean-Louis Trintignant). He hardly seems to care for the dog, or for her. He spends his days in an elaborate spying scheme, using wiretaps to monitor an affair being carried on by a neighbor. There is an instant spark that strikes between the old man and the young woman—a contact, a recognition of similarity, or sympathy—but they are forty years apart in age, and strangers to one another, and have met by accident, and . . .

The story becomes completely fascinating. We have no idea where it is going, where it could possibly go. There is no plot to reassure us. No goal that the characters hope to attain. Will the young woman and the judge ever meet again? What will come of that? Does it matter? Would it be good, or bad?

Such questions, in *Red,* become infinitely more interesting than the questions in simpleminded commercial movies, about whether the hero will kill the bad guys, and drive his car fast, and blow things up, or whether his girlfriend will take off her clothes. Seeing a movie like *Red,* we are reminded that watching many commercial films is the cinematic equivalent of reading *Dick and Jane.* The mysteries of everyday life are so much deeper and more exciting than the contrivances of plots.

We learn something about Auguste, the law student who lives across the way. He has a girlfriend named Karin (Frederique Feder). She specializes in "personal weather reports" for her clients, which sounds reasonable, something like having a personal trainer or astrologer, until we reflect that the weather is more or less the same for everybody. But perhaps her clients live in such tight boxes of their own construction that each one has different weather.

Valentine talks to her boyfriend. They are rarely together. He is someone on the phone. Perhaps she "stays" with him to save herself the trouble of a lover whose life she would actually share. She goes back out to the house of the old judge, and talks to him some more. We learn more about the lives he is eavesdropping on. There are melodramatic developments, but no one seems to feel strongly about them.

And Valentine and Auguste. What a good couple they would make! Perhaps. If they ever meet. And if, in the endless reaches of cosmic time, there had been the smallest shift in the lifetimes of Valentine and the judge, they could have been the same age. Or another infinitesimal shift, and they would have lived a century apart. Or never lived at all. Or if the dog had wandered somewhere else, Valentine would not have struck him, and met the judge. Or if the judge had had a cat . . .

Think about these things, reader. Don't sigh and turn the page. Think that I have written them and you have read them, and the odds against either of us ever having existed are greater by far than one to all of the atoms in creation.

Red is the conclusion of Kieslowski's masterful trilogy, after *Blue* and *White,* named for the colors in the French flag. At the end of *Red* the major characters from all three films meet—through a coincidence, naturally. This is the kind of film that makes you feel intensely alive while you're watching it, and sends you out into the streets afterward eager to talk deeply and urgently, to the person you are with. Whoever that happens to be.

Red Beard

NO MPAA RATING, 185 m., 1969

Toshiro Mifune (Dr. Niide [Red Beard]), Yuzo Kayama (Yasumoto), Yoshio Tsuchiya (Mori), Reiko Dan (Osuki), Kyoko Kagawa (The Mantis), Terumi Niki (Otoyo [Young Girl]). Directed by Akira Kurosawa and produced by

Ryuzo Kikushima and Tomoyaki Tanaka. Screenplay by Masato Ide, Hideo Oguni, Ryuzo Kiksuhima, and Kurosawa.

Akira Kurosawa's *Red Beard* is assembled with the complexity and depth of a good nineteenth-century novel, and it is a pleasure, in a time of stylishly fragmented films, to watch a director taking the time to fully develop his characters.

It is also rather startling to find a director who values the positive human impulses; whose film considers not only violence and deception, but also sacrifice and healing. There has been so much despair in recent films—more than we realize, until *Red Beard* provides such a contrast. There is no such thing, perhaps, as the right time or the wrong time to see a film. But somehow, at the end of a decade that has seen so many things go wrong, *Red Beard* seems necessary.

It is a great and moving film, although its length and the number of its characters may put off those not familiar with Kurosawa. Unlike American directors, who are usually forced to work at the commercially feasible length of under two hours, Kurosawa takes the time to develop his story in a leisurely fashion, establishing a rhythm more in time with the way we really live.

His film is about a young doctor (Yuzo Kayama) who comes to a free public clinic, more or less against his will, to work under the famous old doctor Red Beard (Toshiro Mifune). The time is about 1825. Modern advances in medicine are just seeping into Japan, and the young doctor is proud of the advanced training he has received at Nagasaki. He wants to be the personal doctor for a rich family; public clinics repel him. For many days he even refuses to wear a uniform.

But the old doctor, deeply aware of human nature, gradually involves the young man in the daily life of the clinic. He is sent to watch an old man die; it is a profound moment, Red Beard says, but the young doctor is horrified. A few days later, attending his first operation, he passes out. He discovers that medicine is a great deal more than an avenue into a fashionable career.

Kurosawa leaves his central narrative from time to time, to tell us stories about some of the patients in the clinic. He develops a sub-plot about a maltreated young girl, who refuses to talk to anyone and who becomes the young doctor's first real patient. The young doctor becomes sick himself, and old Red Beard subtly encourages the girl to nurse the doctor. By healing him, she is healed; and then she takes upon herself the care of a young thief and pauper in the neighborhood, so that three people are cured instead of one.

This theme of healing, of making some sort of human contribution, is at the heart of my favorite Kurosawa film, *Ikiru* (1952). I suppose it is a terribly square film by our "sophisticated" standards, although it ventures much more deeply into the human condition than almost anything from Hollywood. *Ikiru* is about an old accountant who is told he has about six months to live.

Faced with the fact of death, he goes on a desperate last fling that leads nowhere. Gradually he becomes aware that he has accomplished exactly nothing in life; that the papers he has pushed around have been meaningless. He determines to achieve one good thing before he dies, and settles on reclaiming a small piece of land as a park for children.

This is a small thing but it is something, and that is the sort of gain that Red Beard tries to achieve at his clinic. The social order is corrupt, yes, and conditions at the clinic are discouraging. But each small gain is something.

Reflections in a Golden Eye
NO MPAA RATING, 108 m., 1967

Elizabeth Taylor (Leonora Penderton), Marlon Brando (Major Penderton), Brian Keith (Lieutenant Colonel Langdon), Julie Harris (Alison Langdon), Zorro David (Anacleto), Robert Forster (Private Williams). Directed by John Huston and produced by Ray Stark. Screenplay by Chapman Mortimer and Gladys Hill, from the book by Carson McCullers.

It seemed fishy to begin with that *Reflections in a Golden Eye* crept into town so silently. Here was a movie with Elizabeth Taylor and Marlon Brando, no less, and the director was that great man himself, John Huston. So shouldn't we have read millions of words about it by now? Every time Liz blows her nose, she makes the cover of *Look*. But not this time. Why not? Was the movie so wretchedly bad that Warner Bros. decided to keep it a secret?

Or could it be, perhaps, that it was too good? Perhaps it could. To begin with, somebody slipped up and did an honest screenplay based on the novel by Carson McCullers. And then Huston and his cast journeyed bravely into the dark, twisted world of the McCullers characters, and nobody told them they were supposed to snicker. So they didn't.

The story is set on an army base in the South. Brando plays a major who gives disjointed lectures about leadership and courage as his repressed homosexuality begins to emerge. Taylor, as his wife, plays a domineering, emasculating female who rides a white stallion and carries a whip (in case you missed the symbolism). Next door, a neurotic and self-doubting woman (Julie Harris) lives with her husband, Brian Keith, who is really a pretty decent sort, even though he is Taylor's lover.

The action is fairly simple, beginning with Brando's abortive attempt to ride his wife's horse. It throws him, he whips it, and later, at a party, she whips him in front of the entire officer corps. Brando begins to disintegrate, his carefully built facade of "leadership qualities" destroyed. In a horrifying and effective scene, he goes to pieces in the middle of a lecture.

In this scene and others, Brando regains the peak of his magnificent talent. After his series of six or seven disastrous performances, even his admirers had given him up for lost. But it was too soon. There is a scene in which he slowly breaks down and begins to cry, and his face screws up in misery. The audience laughed, perhaps because it's supposed to be "funny" to see a man cry. The audience should have been taken outside and shot.

Indeed, the audience was perhaps the greatest problem with this very good film. It was filled with matrons, who found it necessary to shriek loudly and giggle hideously through three-quarters of it, and their husbands, who delivered obligatory guffaws in counterpoint. They had never seen anything funnier in their lives, I guess, than Brando nervously brushing down his hair when he thinks a handsome young private is coming to see him.

But if you can set that aside, then *Reflections* is a better film than we had any right to expect. It follows the McCullers story faithfully

and without compromise. The performances are superb. Besides Brando, there is Taylor, proving once again as she did in *Who's Afraid of Virginia Woolf?* that she really can act, believe it or not. There is Keith, all understatement and quiet sympathy. The photography is restrained, shot in a process that drains almost all the color out of color film, leaving only reds and pinks and an occasional hint of blue or green. The result is a bleak landscape, within which lonely and miserable people try to account for themselves.

Return of the Jedi
PG, 136 m., 1983

Mark Hamill (Luke Skywalker), Harrison Ford (Han Solo), Carrie Fisher (Princess Leia), Billy Dee Williams (Lando Calrissian), Anthony Daniels (C-3PO), David Prowse (Darth Vader), James Earl Jones (Vader's Voice), Alec Guinness (Obi-Wan Kenobi). Directed by Richard Marquand and produced by Howard Kazanjian. Screenplay by Lawrence Kasdan and George Lucas.

Here is just one small moment in *Return of the Jedi*, a moment you could miss if you looked away from the screen, but a moment that helps explain the special magic of the Star Wars movies. Luke Skywalker is engaged in a ferocious battle in the dungeons beneath the throne room of the loathsome Jabba the Hutt. His adversary is a slimy, gruesome, reptilian monster made of warts and teeth. Things are looking bad when suddenly the monster is crushed beneath a falling door. And then (here is the small moment) there's a shot of the monster's keeper, a muscle-bound jailer, who rushes forward in tears. He is brokenhearted at the destruction of his pet. Everybody loves somebody.

It is that extra level of detail that makes the Star Wars pictures much more than just space operas. Other movies might approach the special effects. Other action pictures might approximate the sense of swashbuckling adventure. But in *Return of the Jedi*, as in *Star Wars*, and *The Empire Strikes Back*, there's such a wonderful density to the canvas. Things are happening all over. They're pouring forth from imaginations so fertile that, yes, we do halfway believe in this crazy Galactic Empire long ago and far, far away.

Return of the Jedi is both a familiar movie and a new one. It concludes the stories of the major human characters in the saga, particularly Skywalker, Han Solo, Princess Leia, and Darth Vader. It revisits other characters who seem either more or less than human, including Ben (Obi-Wan) Kenobi, Yoda, Chewbacca, and the beloved robots C-3PO and R2-D2. If George Lucas persists in his plan to make nine Star Wars movies, this will nevertheless be the last we'll see of Luke, Han, and Leia, although the robots will be present in all the films.

The story in the Star Wars movies is, however, only part of the film—and a less crucial element as time goes by. What *Jedi* is really giving us is a picaresque journey through the imagination, and an introduction to forms of life less mundane than our own.

In *Jedi,* we encounter several unforgettable characters, including the evil Jabba the Hutt, who is a cross between a toad and the Cheshire Cat; the lovable, cuddly Ewoks, the furry inhabitants of the "forest moon of Endor"; a fearsome desert monster made of sand and teeth; and hateful little ratlike creatures that scurry about the corners of the frame. And there is an admiral for the Alliance who looks like the missing link between Tyrannosaurus rex and Charles de Gaulle.

One thing the Star Wars movies never do is waste a lot of time on introductions. Unlike a lot of special effects and monster movies, where new creatures are introduced with laborious setups, *Jedi* immediately plunges its alien beasts into the thick of the action. Maybe that's why the film has such a sense of visual richness. Jabba's throne room, for example, is populated with several weird creatures, some of them only half-glimpsed in the corner of the frame. The camera in *Jedi* slides casually past forms of life that would provide the centerpiece for lesser movies.

The movie also has, of course, more of the amazing battles in outer space—the intergalactic video games that have been a trademark since *Star Wars.* And *Jedi* finds an interesting variation on that chase sequence in *Star Wars* where the space cruisers hurtled through the narrow canyons on the surface of the Death Star. This time, there's a breakneck chase through a forest, aboard airborne motorcycles. After several of the bad guys have run into trees and gotten creamed, you pause to ask yourself why they couldn't have simply flown above the treetops . . . but never mind. It wouldn't have been as much fun that way.

And *Return of the Jedi* is fun, magnificent fun. The movie is a complete entertainment, a feast for the eyes and a delight for the fancy. It's a little amazing how Lucas and his associates keep topping themselves.

From the point of view of simple moviemaking logistics, there is an awesome amount of work on the screen in *Jedi* (twice as many visual effects as *Star Wars* in the space battles, Lucas claims). The fact that the makers of *Jedi* are able to emerge intact from their task, having created a very special work of the imagination, is the sort of miracle that perhaps Obi-Wan would know something about.

Reversal of Fortune

R, 110 m., 1990

Glenn Close (Sunny von Bulow), Jeremy Irons (Claus von Bulow), Ron Silver (Alan M. Dershowitz), Annabella Sciorra (Carol), Uta Hagen (Maria), Fisher Stevens (David Marriott), Christine Baranski (Andrea Reynolds). Directed by Barbet Schroeder and produced by Edward R. Pressman and Oliver Stone. Screenplay by Nicholas Kazan, based on the book by Dershowitz.

I followed the investigative accounts of the von Bulow case with that special attention I always pay to the troubles of society people. With their advantages and connections, they have a better chance of being involved in a stimulating crime. Some of them, it is true, simply stab or shoot one another, but a few go to the trouble of using classic means—poisons and deceptions, subterfuge and wit. With all the lack of subtlety in modern murder, it is heartening to find that a few people still aspire to the perfect crime.

Having seen *Reversal of Fortune,* the story of Claus von Bulow's two trials on the charge of attempting to murder his wife, I am no closer than before to a clear idea of who did what, or why. That is the charm of the movie. Something terrible happened to Sunny von Bulow on that winter day eleven years ago, and nobody knows exactly what it was. The victim still lingers in a coma. Her husband was convicted of murder, but his conviction was overturned, and there is compelling suspicion that some of the evidence used against him was fishy.

And now we have this film, based on a book by Alan J. Dershowitz, the famous Harvard professor who conducted Claus von Bulow's appeal. It is a surprisingly entertaining film—funny, wicked, sharp-tongued, and devious. It does not solve the case, nor intend to. I am afraid it only intends to entertain. Because Sunny von Bulow does indeed lie in a coma, I felt at first a little guilty that I enjoyed the film so much. But I am in attendance as a critic, not a priest or prosecutor, and, like the other witnesses, I can only testify from my own experience.

The genius of *Reversal of Fortune* is that the story is narrated by Sunny from her sickbed. We hear her voice, wondering aloud at the chain of events caused by that day when she sank into her long sleep. She guides us through the details of the case. She reminisces about the first time she met Claus, about what she felt for him, about how their marriage progressed. She confesses herself as confused as anyone about what happened on her last day of consciousness. "You tell me," she says, and somehow this gives us permission to look at the film in a more genial mood.

The opening shot, taken from a helicopter, shows the great mansions of Newport, Rhode Island. They stand like sentinels at the edge of the sea, flaunting their wealth at the waves. In one of those mansions Sunny von Bulow lived with Claus and the children they had together or previously. How could one not be entertained by living in such a place? And yet, Sunny seems to seek the escape of unconsciousness. She abuses pills and alcohol. After brief forays into the world, she retreats to her bed. She is not really present for her family; her mind is clouded, and her memory shaky. While her body goes through the motions of smoking and drinking and taking pills, her mind yawns and dozes.

One day she nearly dies, probably of an overdose, but is rescued in time. A year later, she is not so lucky, and by the time help is summoned she is in a coma. What happened? The maid says she was worried for hours before Claus would let her call for help. Claus says he thought she was sleeping; she had

often slumbered deeply before. But how did she end up on the bathroom floor? And what about the insulin? Did Claus administer a fatal overdose? Whose insulin was it, anyway? And who found it?

The question of the insulin is what finally brings Alan Dershowitz into the appeal, after Claus is found guilty. The evidence was gathered by private investigators hired by Sunny's children, and then turned over to the authorities, and Dershowitz decides that the rich simply cannot be permitted to hire their own police and decide among themselves which evidence should be made available. It isn't fair. There are also questions about many other aspects of the case—so many that, if Claus is not innocent, there is at least no way to prove that he is guilty.

Reversal of Fortune is above all a triumph of tone. The director, Barbet Schroeder, and the writer, Nicholas Kazan, have not made a docudrama or a sermon, but a film about personalities. The most extraordinary personality in the film is von Bulow's, as he is played by Jeremy Irons. He appears as a man with affections and bizarre mannerisms, a man who speaks as if he lifted his words from an arch drawing-room comedy, who smokes a cigarette as if hailing a taxi. Irons is able to suggest, subtly, that some of this over-the-top behavior is the result of fear. Von Bulow cannot modulate his tone, cannot find the right note, because beneath his façade he is quaking.

And yet he keeps up a brave front. That is one of the best qualities of the film, the way it shows him trying to brazen his way out of an impossible situation. If he wins, he keeps the fortune and the lifestyle. If he loses, he ends his life in jail. The man who can save him is Dershowitz, played by Ron Silver as a hyperkinetic showboat who surrounds himself with students and acolytes, possibly as a protection against the fear of silence. The law students plunge like beavers into their research, triumphantly emerging with new strategies for their leader, who does not like von Bulow much and doubts his innocence, but believes the case raises important legal points.

Glenn Close is important, too, as Sunny. She appears in some flashbacks as well as narrating the film, and we see the things we need to notice: Her beauty and personality when she's got it together, and the vague lost confusion of her alcoholic and tranquilized daydreams. Without nudging us, the film shows us two things. First, why a man might finally be tempted to allow his wife to slip into the oblivion she seems so desperately to desire. Second, how she could have accidentally overdosed in any event.

What happened? Who knows. The movie's strength is its ability to tantalize, to turn the case this way and that, so that the light of evidence falls in one way and then another. You tell me.

Richard Pryor Live on the Sunset Strip

R, 82 m., 1982

Directed by Joe Layton and produced by Richard Pryor.

At the beginning of this film, Richard Pryor is clearly nervous. He is back on a stage for the first time since he set himself on fire. That means he is working with the stand-up comedian's greatest handicap, the audience's awareness of his vulnerability. Whatever else they do, comics must project utter confidence in their material, and when Pryor had his accident, he also had his whole hip image blown out from under him. So it's a shaky start. He begins by almost defiantly using the word "fuck" as an incantation, employing it not so much for shock value (does it still have any?) as for punctuation. His timing is a little off. He is not, at first, the supremely confident, cocky Richard Pryor of his earlier films. But as he gets rolling, as he populates the stage with a whole series of characters, we watch the emergence of a Richard Pryor who is older, wiser, and funnier than before. And the last fifty or sixty minutes of this film are extraordinary.

Richard Pryor Live on the Sunset Strip was filmed at the Hollywood Palladium, down at the unfashionable east end of that legendary street of rock clubs, restaurants, hookers and heroes, hot-pillow motels, and some of the most expensive real estate in the world. The movie opens with a montage of the strip's neon signs (including the Chateau Marmont, where John Belushi died). Then it cuts inside to the Palladium auditorium, and Pryor walks onstage and lays claim to being the most talented one-man stage show in existence right now.

His gift is to be funny and painfully self-analytical at the same time. Like Bill Cosby, he gets a lot of his material out of memories of growing up black in America. But he sees deeper than Cosby, and his vignettes capture small truths and build them into an attitude. In the brilliant middle sections of this film, he uses just his own voice and body to create little one-act plays, such as the one where he recalls working in a Mafia-owned nightclub in Ohio. In that one, his Italian-American-gangster accent is perfectly heard; in another skit, about the animals in Africa, he turns into a gifted physical comedian, getting laughs out of his impressions of the movements of gazelles, water buffaloes, and lions—and ending with a hilarious observation of the body language of two whites passing each other on the street in black Africa.

The whole middle passage of the film is that good. The last twenty minutes is one of the most remarkable marriages of comedy and truth I have ever seen. He talks with great honesty about his drug addiction, his accident, and how his life has changed since he stopped using drugs. He confesses that in the three weeks before his accident, he holed up alone in his room with his cocaine pipe, which talked to him in reassuring, seductive tones uncannily like Richard Nixon's. Then a friend, the actor Jim Brown, came to see him, and asked him flat-out, "Whatcha gonna do?" There was nothing he wanted to do but hide in drugs. What he finally did was set himself on fire.

I saw the film the same day that actor Shay Duffin opened his one-man evening with Brendan Behan at the Apollo Theater Center in Chicago. The papers that day carried the news that Belushi had overdosed. Behan, of course, killed himself with alcohol. Some day, inevitably, an actor will give us an evening with John Belushi. The dramatic structure is all there, for the Behans and Belushis: The genius, the laughter, and the doomed drive to self-destruction. Watching *Richard Pryor Live on the Sunset Strip*, a breathtaking performance by a man who came within a hair of killing himself with drugs, was like a gift, as if Pryor had come back from the dead to perform in his own oneman memory of himself. It is good we still have him. He is better than ever.

Richard Pryor Here and Now

R, 94 m., 1983

A documentary written and directed by Richard Pryor and produced by Bob Parkinson and Andy Friendly.

Is there anyone else in America who could have pulled off this film? *Richard Pryor Here and Now* is a documentary of one man talking. Pryor walks onto the stage of the Saenger Theater in New Orleans, establishes an immediate rapport with the audience, and away he goes. At the end of the movie we have been wrung out with laughter—and with a few other things, too, because Pryor is more than a comedian in this film: He's a social commentator and a man talking honestly about himself.

This is Pryor's third concert film. The first one, *Richard Pryor Live in Concert* (1979), was made before he set himself on fire while freebasing cocaine. The second, *Richard Pryor Live on the Sunset Strip* (1982), recorded his first filmed concert after the accident, and included his description of Jim Brown's attempts to talk him out of drug use, and Pryor's own now-famous dialogue with cocaine. In *Here and Now*, filmed in August 1983 with Brown as executive producer, Pryor firmly says he hasn't used drugs or alcohol for seven months. The arithmetic would seem to suggest that he hadn't stopped using everything when he made the second film, or that he had a relapse after his initial hospitalization. I mention that only because the Richard Pryor we see on screen in *Here and Now* has obviously found some kind of peace with himself that was lacking in the *Sunset Strip* film.

He can smile more easily. He doesn't have to reach for effects. He handles audience interruptions with grace and cool. He is the master of his instrument. And he takes bigger chances. Some of his material covers familiar ground—sex, booze, race, marriages. But all along he's showing his gift for populating the stage with a lot of different characters. He goes in and out of accents, body language, and characters, giving us confused drunks, defensive husbands, shrill wives, uptight WASPs, impenetrable Africans ("Everybody speaks English," one tells him in Zimbabwe, "but what language do you speak at *home?*"). And

then at the end of his act, he goes into an extended characterization of a street black shooting heroin. In this character are humor and pain, self-deception and touching honesty, and the end of the sketch comes closer to tragedy than it does to comedy.

Pryor is a spokesman for our dreams and fears, the things we find funny and the things we're frightened of. He has assumed a role that has previously been filled by such comedians as Will Rogers, Lenny Bruce, Mort Sahl, and Woody Allen—all men who, as Rogers put it, talked about what they'd just seen in the papers. Pryor works off issues and subjects that are absolutely current, and he addresses them with a humor that is aimed so well, we duck. His story could have gone either way. He could have been killed in that wasteful accident. But he was not, and now, given a second chance, he is paying his dues.

The Right Stuff

PG, 193 m., 1983

Sam Shepard (Chuck Yeager), Ed Harris (John Glenn), Fred Ward (Gus Grissom), Dennis Quaid (Gordon Cooper), Scott Glenn (Alan Shepard), Barbara Hershey (Glennis Yeager), Mary Jo Deschanel (Annie Glenn), Pamela Reed (Trudy Cooper). Directed by Philip Kaufman and produced by Irwin Winkler and Robert Chartoff. Screenplay by Kaufman, based on the book by Tom Wolfe.

At the beginning of *The Right Stuff*, a cowboy reins in his horse and regards a strange sight in the middle of the desert: the X-1 rocket plane, built to break the sound barrier. At the end of the film, the seven *Mercury* astronauts are cheered in the Houston Astrodome at a Texas barbecue thrown by Lyndon B. Johnson. The contrast between those two images contains the message of *The Right Stuff*, I think, and the message is that Americans still have the right stuff, but we've changed our idea of what it is.

The original American heroes were loners. The cowboy is the perfect example. He was silhouetted against the horizon and he rode into town by himself and if he had a sidekick, the sidekick's job was to admire him. The new American heroes are team players. No wonder Westerns aren't made much anymore; cowboys don't play on teams. The cowboy at the beginning of *The Right Stuff* is Chuck Yeager, the legendary lone-wolf test pilot who survived the horrifying death rate among early test pilots (more than sixty were killed in a single month) and did fly the X-1 faster than the speed of sound. The movie begins with that victory, and then moves on another ten years to the day when the Russians sent up *Sputnik,* and the Eisenhower administration hustled to get back into the space race.

The astronauts who eventually rode the first *Mercury* capsules into space may not have been that much different from Chuck Yeager. As they're portrayed in the movie, anyway, Gus Grissom, Scott Carpenter, and Gordon Cooper seem to have some of the same stuff as Yeager. But the astronauts were more than pilots; they were a public-relations image, and the movie shows sincere, smooth-talking John Glenn becoming their unofficial spokesman. The X-1 flew in secrecy, but the *Mercury* flights were telecast, and we were entering a whole new era, the selling of space. There was a lot going on, and there's a lot going on in the movie, too. *The Right Stuff* is an adventure film, a special-effects film, a social commentary, and a satire. That the writer-director, Philip Kaufman, is able to get so much into a little more than three hours is impressive. That he also has organized this material into one of the best recent American movies is astonishing. *The Right Stuff* gives itself the freedom to move around in moods and styles, from a broadly based lampoon of government functionaries to Yeager's spare, taciturn manner and Glenn's wonderment at the sights outside his capsule window.

The Right Stuff has been a landmark movie in a lot of careers. It announces Kaufman's arrival in the ranks of major directors. It contains uniformly interesting performances by a whole list of unknown or little-known actors, including Ed Harris (Glenn), Scott Glenn (Alan Shepard), Fred Ward (Grissom), and Dennis Quaid (Cooper). It confirms the strong and sometimes almost mystical screen presence of playwright Sam Shepard, who played Yeager. And it joins a short list of recent American movies that might be called experimental epics: movies that have an ambitious reach through time and subject matter, that spend freely for locations or special effects, but that consider each scene as intently as an art film. *The Right Stuff* goes on that list with *The Godfather, Nashville, Apocalypse Now,* and maybe *Patton* and *Close Encounters.* It's a great film.

Risky Business

R, 96 m., 1983

Tom Cruise (Joel), Rebecca De Mornay (Lana), Curtis Armstrong (Miles), Bronson Pinchot (Barry), Joe Pantoliano (Guido). Directed by Paul Brickman and produced by Joe Avnet and Steve Tisch. Screenplay by Brickman.

Risky Business is a movie about male adolescent guilt. In other words, it's a comedy. It's funny because it deals with subjects that are so touchy, so fraught with emotional pain, that unless we laugh there's hardly any way we can deal with them—especially if we are now, or ever were, a teenage boy. The teenager in the movie is named Joel. His family lives in a suburb on Chicago's North Shore. It's the sort of family that has three cars: the family station wagon, Mom's car, and Dad's Porsche. As the movie opens, Mom and Dad are going off on vacation to a sundrenched consumer paradise and their only son, Joel, is being left alone at home. It's a busy time in Joel's life. He's got college board exams, an interview with a Princeton admissions officer, and finals at high school.

It gets to be an even busier time after his parents leave. Joel gets involved in an ascending pyramid of trouble. He calls a number in one of those sex-contact magazines and meets a young hooker who moves into the house. He runs afoul of the girl's pimp. His mother's expensive Steuben egg is stolen. His dad's Porsche ends up in Lake Michigan. The family home turns into a brothel. He blows two finals. And so on. This description may make *Risky Business* sound like a predictable sitcom. It is not. It is one of the smartest, funniest, most perceptive satires in a long time. It not only invites comparison with *The Graduate,* it earns it. Here is a great comedy about teenage sex.

The very best thing about the movie is its dialogue. Paul Brickman, who wrote and directed, has an ear so good that he knows what to leave out. This is one of those movies where a few words or a single line says everything that needs to be said, implies everything that needs to be implied, *and* gets a laugh. When the hooker tells the kid, "Oh, Joel, go to school. Learn something," the precise inflection of those words defines their relationship for the next three scenes.

The next best thing about the movie is the casting. Rebecca De Mornay somehow manages to take that thankless role, the hooker with a heart of gold, and turn it into a very specific character. She isn't all good and she isn't all clichés: she's a very complicated young woman with quirks and insecurities and a wayward ability to love. I became quietly astounded when I realized that this movie was going to create an original, *interesting* relationship involving a teenager and a hooker. The teenage kid, in what will be called the Dustin Hoffman role, is played by Tom Cruise, who also knows how to imply a whole world by what he won't say, can't feel, and doesn't understand.

This is a movie of new faces and inspired insights and genuine laughs. It's hard to make a good movie and harder to make a good comedy and almost impossible to make a satire of such popular but mysterious obsessions as guilt, greed, lust, and secrecy. This movie knows what goes on behind the closed bathroom doors of the American dream.

Rivers & Tides: Andy Goldsworthy Working with Time

NO MPAA RATING, 90 m., 2002

A documentary directed by Thomas Riedelsheimer.

Have you ever watched—no, better, have you ever been a young child intent on building something out of the materials at hand in the woods, or by a stream, or at the beach? Have you seen the happiness of an adult joining kids and slowly slipping out of adulthood and into the absorbing process of this . . . and now . . . and over here . . . and build this up . . . and it should go like this? The artist Andy Goldsworthy lives in that world of making things. They have no names, they are Things. He brings order to leaves or twigs or icicles and then surrenders them to the process of nature. He will kneel for hours by the ocean-side, creating a cairn of stones that balances precariously, the weight on the top holding the sides in place, and then the tide will come in and wash away the sand beneath, and the cairn will collapse, as it must, as it should.

"The very thing that brought the thing to be is the thing that will cause its death," Goldsworthy explains, as his elegant, spiraled constructions once again become random piles of stones on the beach. As with Andy's stones, so with our lives.

Rivers & Tides: Andy Goldsworthy Working with Time is a documentary that opened in San Francisco in mid-2002 and just kept running, moving from one theater to another, finding its audience not so much through word of mouth as through hand on elbow, as friends steered friends into the theater, telling them that this was a movie they had to see. I started getting e-mails about it months ago. Had I seen it? I hadn't even heard of it.

It is a film about a man wholly absorbed in the moment. He wanders woods and river-banks, finding materials and playing with them, fitting them together, piling them up, weaving them, creating beautiful arrangements that he photographs before they return to chaos. He knows that you can warm the end of an icicle just enough to make it start to melt, and then hold it against another icicle, and it will stick. With that knowledge, he makes an ice sculpture, and then it melts in the sun and is over.

Some of his constructions are of magical beauty, as if left behind by beings who disappeared before the dawn. He finds a way to arrange twigs in a kind of web. He makes a spiral of rocks that fans out from a small base and then closes in again, a weight on top holding it together. This is not easy, and he gives us pointers: "Top control can be the death of a work." Often Andy will be . . . almost there . . . right on the edge . . . holding his breath as one last piece goes into place . . . and then the whole construction will collapse, and he will look deflated, defeated, for a moment ("Damn!"), and then start again: "When I build something, I often take it to the very edge of its collapse, and that's a very beautiful balance." His art needs no explanation. We go into modern art galleries and find work we cannot comprehend as art. We see Damien Hurst's sheep, cut down the middle and embedded in plastic, and we cannot understand how it won the Turner Prize (forgetting that no one thought Turner was making art, either). We suppose that Concepts and Statements are involved.

But with Andy Goldsworthy, not one word of explanation is necessary, because every single one of us has made something like his art. We have piled stones or made architectural constructions out of sand, or played Pick Up Sticks, and we know exactly what he is trying to do—and why. Yes, why, because his art takes him into that Zone where time drops away and we forget our left-brain concerns and are utterly absorbed by whether this . . . could go like this . . . without the whole thing falling apart.

The documentary, directed, photographed, and edited by Thomas Riedelsheimer, a German filmmaker, goes home with Goldsworthy to Penpont, Scotland, where we see him spending time with his wife and kids. It follows him to a museum in the south of France, and to an old stone wall in Canada that he wants to rebuild in his own way. It visits with him old stone markers high in mountains, built by early travelers to mark the path.

And it offers extraordinary beauty. We watch as he smashes stones to release their cyan content and uses that bright-red dye to make spectacular patterns in the currents and whirlpools of streams. We see a long rope of linked leaves, bright green, uncoil as it floats downstream. Before, we saw only the surface of the water, but now the movement of the leaves reveals its current and structure. What a happy man. Watching this movie is like daydreaming.

Rocky

PG, 119 m., 1976

Sylvester Stallone (Rocky), Talia Shire (Adrian), Burt Young (Paulie), Carl Weathers (Apollo Creed), Burgess Meredith (Mickey), Frank Stallone (Timekeeper). Directed by John Avildsen and produced by Robert Chartoff and Irwin Winkler. Screenplay by Sylvester Stallone.

She sits, tearful and crumpled, in a corner of her little bedroom. Her brother has torn apart the living room with a baseball bat. Rocky, the guy she has fallen in love with, comes into the room.

"Do you want a roommate?" she asks shyly, almost whispering.

"Absolutely," says Rocky.

Which is exactly what he should say, and how he should say it, and why *Rocky* is such an immensely involving movie. Its story, about a punk club fighter from the back streets of Philly who gets a crack at the world championship, has been told a hundred times before. A description of it would sound like a cliché from beginning to end. But *Rocky* isn't about a story, it's about a hero. And it's inhabited with supreme confidence by a star.

His name is Sylvester Stallone, and, yes, in 1976 he did remind me of the young Marlon Brando. How many actors have come and gone and been forgotten who were supposed to be the "new Brando," while Brando endured? And yet in *Rocky* he provides shivers of recognition reaching back to *A Streetcar Named Desire*. He's tough, he's tender, he talks in a growl, and hides behind cruelty and is a champion at heart. "I coulda been a contender," Brando says in *On the Waterfront*. This movie takes up from there.

It inhabits a curiously deserted Philadelphia: There aren't any cars parked on the slum street where Rocky lives or the slightest sign that anyone else lives there. His world is a small one. By day, he works as an enforcer for a small-time juice man, offering to break a man's thumbs over a matter of $70 ("I'll bandage it!" cries the guy. "It'll *look* broke"). In his spare time, he works out at Mickey's gym. He coulda been good, but he smokes and drinks beer and screws around. And yet there's a secret life behind his facade. He is awkwardly in love with a painfully shy girl (Talia Shire) who works in the corner pet shop. He has a couple of turtles at home, named Cuff and Link, and a goldfish named Moby Dick. After he wins forty bucks one night for taking a terrible battering in the ring, he comes home and tells the turtles: "If you guys could sing and dance, I wouldn't have to go through this crap." When the girl asks him why he boxes, he explains: "Because I can't sing and dance."

The movie ventures into fantasy when the world heavyweight champion (Carl Weathers, as a character with a certain similarity to Muhammad Ali) decides to schedule a New Year's Eve bout with a total unknown—to prove that America is still a land of opportunity. Rocky gets picked because of his nickname, the Italian Stallion; the champ likes the racial contrast. And even *here* the movie looks like a genre fight picture from the 1940s, right down to the plucky little gymnasium manager (Burgess Meredith) who puts Rocky through training, and right down to the lonely morning ritual of rising at four, drinking six raw eggs, and going out to do roadwork. What makes the movie extraordinary is that it doesn't try to surprise us with an original plot, with twists and complications; it wants to involve us on an elemental, a sometimes savage, level. It's about heroism and realizing your potential, about taking your best shot and sticking by your girl. It sounds not only clichéd but corny—and yet it's not, not a bit, because it really does work on those levels. It involves us emotionally, it makes us commit ourselves: We find, maybe to our surprise after remaining detached during so many movies, that this time we *care*.

The credit for that has to be passed around. A lot of it goes to Stallone when he wrote this story and then peddled it around Hollywood for years before he could sell it. He must have known it would work because he could see himself in the role, could imagine the conviction he's bringing to it, and I can't think of another actor who could quite have pulled off this performance. There's that exhilarating moment when Stallone, in training, runs up the steps of Philadelphia's art museum, leaps into the air, shakes his fist at the city, and you know he's sending a message to the whole movie industry.

The director is John Avildsen, who made *Joe* and then another movie about a loser who tried to find the resources to start again, *Save the Tiger*. Avildsen correctly isolates Rocky in his urban environment, because this movie shouldn't have a documentary feel, with people hanging out of every window: It's a legend, it's about little people, but it's bigger than life, and you have to set them apart visually so you can isolate them morally.

And then there's Talia Shire, as the girl (she was the hapless sister of the Corleone boys in *The Godfather*). When she hesitates before kissing Rocky for the first time, it's a moment so poignant it's like no other. And Burt Young as her brother—defeated and resentful, loyal and bitter, caring about people enough to hurt them just to draw attention to his grief. There's all that, and then there's the fight that ends the film. By now, everyone knows who wins, but the scenes before the fight set us up for it so completely, so emotionally, that when it's over we've had it. We're drained.

Roger & Me
R, 100 m., 1989

A documentary directed, produced, and written by Michael Moore.

The peculiar genius of *Roger & Me* is not that it's a funny film or an angry film, or even a film with a point to make—although it is all three of those things. It connects because it's a revenge comedy, a film in which the stinkers get their comeuppance at last. It generates the same kind of laughter that Jack Nicholson inspired in that immortal scene where he told the waitress what she could do with the chicken salad. It allows the audience to share in the delicious sensation of getting even.

The movie was made by Michael Moore, a native of Flint, Michigan, the birthplace of General Motors. As GM closed eleven plants in Flint and laid off some thirty-three thousand workers, Moore got mad—and this is his response. But it's not a dreary documentary about hard times in the rust belt. It's a stinging comedy that sticks in the knife of satire and twists.

The ostensible subject of the film is the attempt by Moore to get an interview with Roger Smith, chairman of General Motors. We know right away that this is one interview that is unlikely to take place. Moore, a ramshackle manmountain who fancies baseball caps and overflowing Hush Puppies, wanders through the film like a babe in toyland. He's the kind of guy who gets in an elevator in GM headquarters in Detroit and is surprised when the button for the top floor—Smith's office—doesn't light up when it's pressed. The closest he gets to Smith is a slick, oily GM public relations man who explains why the layoffs are regrettable but necessary. (It goes without saying that the spokesman himself is eventually laid off.)

Denied access to Smith, *Roger & Me* pokes around elsewhere in Flint. It follows a deputy sheriff on his rounds as he evicts unemployed auto workers. It covers a Flint Pride parade that marches depressingly past the boarded-up store windows of downtown. It listens to enthusiastic spokesmen for Auto World, an indoor amusement park where Flint citizens can visit a replica of their downtown as it used to look before the boards went up. It listens as a civic booster boasts that Flint's new Hyatt Hotel has escalators and "big plants" in the lobby—just like the Hyatts in Atlanta and Chicago. The hotel and amusement park are supposed to create a tourism industry for Flint, but the biggest convention booked into the hotel is the state Scrabble tournament, and when Auto World goes out of business, the rueful Chamber of Commerce–type speculates that asking people to come to Flint for Auto World "is sort of like asking them to come to Alaska for Exxon World."

Many celebrities wander through the film, brought to Flint by big fees to cheer people up. Anita Bryant sings, Pat Boone suggests that the unemployed workers might become Amway distributors, and Ronald Reagan has pizza with the jobless, but forgets to pick up the check.

Meanwhile, some resourceful victims fight back. A woman advertises "Bunnies as Pets or Rabbits as Meat." Jobless auto workers hire themselves out as living statues who stand around in costume at a *Great Gatsby* charity benefit. Some local industries even improve—there's need for a new jail, for example. And the local socialites hold a charity ball in the jail the night before it opens for business. They have a lot of fun wearing riot helmets and banging each other over the head with police batons.

Roger & Me does have a message to deliver—a message about corporate newspeak and the ways in which profits really are more important to big American corporations than the lives of their workers. The movie is a counterattack against the amoral pragmatism of modern management theory, against the sickness of the *In Search of Excellence* mentality.

Michael Moore has struck a nerve with this movie. There are many Americans, I think,

who have not lost the ability to think and speak in plain English—to say what they mean. These people were driven mad by the 1980s, in which a new kind of bureaucratese was spawned by Ronald Reagan and his soulmates—a new manner of speech by which it became possible to "address the problem" while saying nothing and yet somehow conveying optimism.

Roger Smith and General Motors are good at that kind of talk. *Roger & Me* undercuts it with blunt contradictions. In the movie's single most haunting image, Smith addresses a GM Christmas television hookup, reading from *A Christmas Carol* while Moore shows deputies evicting a jobless GM worker and throwing his Christmas tree in the gutter. A spokesman for GM has attacked this scene as "manipulative." It certainly is. But Smith's treacly Christmas ceremony is manipulative, too, and so is the whole corporate doublespeak that justifies his bottom-line heartlessness. The genius of *Roger & Me* is that it understands the image-manipulating machinery of corporate public relations and fights back with the same cynicism and cleverness. The wonder is that the movie is both so angry and so funny. We knew revenge was sweet. What the movie demonstrates is that it is also hilarious—for the avenged.

Romeo and Juliet

PG, 138 m., 1968

Leonard Whiting (Romeo), Olivia Hussey (Juliet), Michael York (Tybalt), John McEnery (Mercutio), Pat Heywood (Nurse), Milo O'Shea (Friar Lawrence), Paul Hardwick (Lord Capulet), Natasha Parry (Lady Capulet), Antonio Pierfederici (Lord Montague), Esmeralda Ruspoli (Lady Montague). Directed by Franco Zeffirelli and produced by Anthony Havelock-Allan and John Brabourne. Screenplay by Franco Brusati and Masolino D'Amico, based on the tragedy by William Shakespeare.

Like many victims of the American education system, I had a dislike for Shakespeare years before I got my hands on anything he had written. His name was a password to be profaned by twelve-year-olds whose voices had started to change and who, therefore, had to act tough and cynical and, especially at twelve, anti-intellectual.

But part of the problem came later, in the classroom, where we inched through *Julius Caesar* and *Macbeth* at a velocity of ten lines an hour. It was impossible to read Shakespeare as slowly as we did and remember anything from the first three acts by the time we got to the murders. "Who's this Brutus guy?" we whispered. What was needed as an introduction was an approach that caught the spirit and life of Shakespeare and didn't get bogged down prematurely in the language.

With this in mind, I believe Franco Zeffirelli's *Romeo and Juliet* is the most exciting film of Shakespeare ever made. Not because it is greater drama than Olivier's *Henry V,* because it is not. Nor is it greater cinema than Welles's *Falstaff.* But it is greater Shakespeare than either because it has the passion, the sweat, the violence, the poetry, the love, and the tragedy in the most immediate terms I can imagine. It is a deeply moving piece of entertainment, and that is possibly what Shakespeare would have preferred.

To begin with, Zeffirelli's film is the first production of *Romeo and Juliet* I am familiar with in which the romance is taken seriously. Always before, we have had actors in their twenties or thirties or even older, reciting Shakespeare's speeches to each other as if it were the words that mattered. They do not, as anyone who has proposed marriage will agree. Often enough, one cannot even remember what was said at moments of great emotion; the words are outpourings of the soul.

And that is the effect Zeffirelli achieves in two almost impossible scenes: the balcony scene and the double suicide in the tomb. There are some lines in Shakespeare too famous for their own good. When Hamlet winds up for "to be, or not to be," the entire audience is there ahead of him, waiting for those lines, watching them come down the track. The same is true of Juliet's "Romeo, Romeo, oh, wherefore art thou, Romeo?" The very words bring back memories of campfire skits.

It is to the credit of Zeffirelli and his young players (Leonard Whiting and Olivia Hussey) that they have brought the lines and characters of Romeo and Juliet back to life again. In a theater filled to capacity Saturday night, not one single person found it necessary to snicker when Juliet asked so simply where Romeo was; we were looking for him, too.

The success of the film depends upon Whiting and Hussey. Zeffirelli reportedly interviewed hundreds of young actors and actresses before choosing them; if so, then this is the first movie "talent search" worth the trouble. They are magnificent. We can see why Zeffirelli didn't want older actors. The love between Romeo and Juliet, and the physical passion that comes with it, are of that naive and hopeless intensity only those in love for the very first time can comprehend.

Zeffirelli places his lovers within a world of everyday life. With the first shots of the film, we are caught up in the feud between the Capulets and the Montagues. We understand the nature of the quarrel between Tybalt (Michael York) and Mercutio (John McEnery) instinctively because Zeffirelli has picked them for their types: cocky insolence vs. sly mockery. The key supporting roles of Friar Lawrence (Milo O'Shea) and Juliet's nurse (Pat Heywood) are also superbly cast. For once, the nurse and friar are young enough to have empathy with the lovers. In most productions, they are creaking relics.

And all of this is photographed with great intensity (even a handheld camera for the dueling scenes) and beauty. As in his first film, *The Taming of the Shrew,* Zeffirelli has controlled his colors carefully. Everything is red and brown and yellow, dusty and sunlit, except for the fresh green of the garden during the balcony scene and the darkness of the tomb.

A lot of fuss has been made about the brief, beautiful nude love scene. I doubt whether anyone could see it and disapprove of it, but apparently someone has. The Chicago Board of Education, I am informed, objects to the nudity and will not approve the film for educational use after its commercial run. This is stupidity.

If Chicago's educators could show me a city filled with students who rejoice in Shakespeare, I would yield the point. But they cannot, and Zeffirelli is so far ahead of them, so much richer and deeper, so much more inspired in his interpretation of our greatest poet, that the Board of Education, cannot fly with him and must find excuses in half a dozen frames of a joyous film.

A Room with a View

PG-13, 110 m., 1985

Maggie Smith (Charlotte Bartlett), Helena Bonham Carter (Lucy Honeychurch), Denholm Elliott (Mr. Emerson), Julian Sands (George Emerson), Daniel Day-Lewis (Cecil Vyse), Simon Callow (Reverend Beebe), Judi Dench (Miss Lavish), Rosemary Leach (Mrs. Honeychurch). Directed by James Ivory and produced by Ismail Merchant. Screenplay by Ruth Prawer Jhabvala, based on the book by E. M. Forster.

My favorite character in *A Room with a View* is George Emerson, the earnest, passionate young man whose heart beats fiercely with love for Lucy Honeychurch. She is a most respectable young woman from a good family, who has been taken to Italy on the grand tour, with a lady companion, Miss Bartlett. Lucy meets George and his father in their *pensione*. A few days later, while standing in the middle of a waving field of grass, the sun bathing the landscape in a yellow joy, she is kissed by George Emerson, most unexpectedly. He does not ask her permission. He does not begin with small talk. He takes her and kisses her, and for him, something "great and important" has happened between them.

Lucy Honeychurch is not so sure. She catches her breath, and Miss Bartlett appears on top of a hill and summons her back to tea, and a few months later, in England, Lucy announces her engagement to Cecil Vyse, who is a prig. Cecil is the sort of man who would never play tennis, who wears a *pince-nez*, who oils his hair, and who thinks that girls are nice because they like to listen to him read aloud. Cecil does not have many clues as to what else girls might be nice for.

Meanwhile, George Emerson and his father—who is an idealist, a dreamer, and a follower of Thoreau—take a cottage in the neighborhood. And one day George kisses Lucy again. He then delivers himself of an astonishing speech, in which he explains that Love exists between them. (Not love but Love—you can hear the capital letter in his voice.) Lucy must not marry Cecil, he explains,

for Cecil does not understand women and will never understand Lucy, and wants her only for an ornament. George, on the other hand, wants her as his partner in the great adventure of life.

George does not have many big scenes, other than those two. The rest of the time, he keeps a low profile and says little. But his function is clear: He is the source of passion in a society that is otherwise tightly bound up in convention, timidity, and dryness. He is the man to break the chains, to say what he thinks, to free Lucy's spirit. And that he does, with great energy and efficiency. George is my favorite character because he is such a strange bird, so intense, so filled with conviction, so convinced of Lucy's worth.

A Room with a View is the story of George and Lucy, but it is also an attack on the British class system. In the opening scenes of the movie, Lucy and Miss Bartlett have been given a room in the Italian *pensione* that does not have a view. Dear old Mr. Emerson insists that the women take his rooms, which have a view. By the end of the film, George will have offered Lucy a view out of the room of her own life. She has been living a suffocating, proper existence—and he will open the window for her. That's what's exhilarating about the film, that it is not only about perplexing and eccentric characters, it's about how they can change their lives.

The movie has been adapted from the E. M. Forster novel by three filmmakers who have specialized recently in film adaptations of literary works: Director James Ivory, producer Ismail Merchant, and screenwriter Ruth Prawer Jhabvala. Their other recent credits include *The Bostonians, The Europeans,* and *Heat and Dust.* This is the best film they have ever made.

It is an intellectual film, but intellectual about emotions: it encourages us to think about how we feel, instead of simply acting on our feelings. It shows us a young woman, Lucy Honeychurch, who is about to marry the wrong man—not because of her passion, but because of her lack of thought. Only think about your passion, the movie argues, and you will throw over Cecil and marry George. Usually thought and passion are opposed in the movies; this time it's entertaining to find them on the same side.

The story moves at a deliberate pace, with occasionally dramatic interruptions for great passion. The dialogue is stately and abstract, except when all of a sudden it turns direct and honest. The performances are perfectly balanced between the heart and the mind. At the center of everything stands Lucy, who is played by Helena Bonham Carter, that dark-browed, stubborn little girl from *Lady Jane*. Maggie Smith is wonderfully dotty as her companion. Denholm Elliott, the most dependable of all British character actors, steals scene after scene as George's freethinking father ("Leave me my portrait of Thoreau," he insists, as they are moving from their cottage). Julian Sands is the intense young George and Daniel Day-Lewis creates a foppish masterpiece in his performance as Cecil; give him a monocle and a butterfly, and he could be on the cover of the *New Yorker*.

A Room with a View enjoys its storytelling so much that I enjoyed the very process of it; the story moved slowly, it seemed, for the same reason you try to make ice cream last—because it's so good.

Rosemary's Baby

R, 136 m., 1968

Mia Farrow (Rosemary), John Cassavetes (Guy), Ruth Gordon (Minnie Castevet), Sidney Blackmer (Roman Castevet), Maurice Evans (Hutch), Ralph Bellamy (Dr. Sapirstein), Angela Dorian (Terry), Elisha Cook, Jr. (Rental Agent). Directed by Roman Polanski and produced by William Castle. Screenplay by Polanski, based on the book by Ira Levin.

Roman Polanski's *Rosemary's Baby* is a brooding, macabre film, filled with the sense of unthinkable danger. Strangely enough it also has an eerie sense of humor almost until the end. It is a creepy film and a crawly film, and a film filled with things that go bump in the night. It is very good.

As everyone must have heard by now, the movie is based on Ira Levin's novel about modern-day witches and demons. But it is much more than just a suspense story; the brilliance of the film comes more from Polanski's direction, and from a series of genuinely inspired performances, than from the original story.

For this reason, the effectiveness of *Rosemary's Baby* is not at all diminished if you've read the book. How the story turns out, and who (or what) Rosemary's baby really is, hardly matters. The film doesn't depend on a shock ending for its impact.

Although I haven't read Levin's novel, I'm informed that he works in the conventional suspense mode. We meet Rosemary and her husband and the couple next door. We identify with Rosemary during her pregnancy, sharing her doubts and fears, But when the ending comes, I'm told, it is an altogether unexpected surprise.

Polanski doesn't work this way. He gives the audience a great deal of information early in the story, and by the time the movie's halfway over we're pretty sure what's going on in that apartment next door. When the conclusion comes, it works not because it is a surprise but because it is horrifyingly inevitable. Rosemary makes her dreadful discovery, and we are wrenched because we knew what was going to happen—and couldn't help her.

This is why the movie is so good. The characters and the story transcend the plot. In most horror films, and indeed in most suspense films of the Alfred Hitchcock tradition, the characters are at the mercy of the plot. In this one, they emerge as human beings actually doing these things.

A great deal of the credit for this achievement must go to Mia Farrow, as Rosemary, and Ruth Gordon, as Mrs. Castevet, the next-door neighbor. Here are two of the finest performances by actresses this year.

And the interesting thing is how well they work together: Farrow, previously almost untried in the movies, and Gordon, an experienced professional. Because we can believe them as women who live next door to each other, we find it possible to believe the fantastic demands that the Castevets eventually are able to make on Rosemary.

Polanski has also drawn a memorable performance from Sidney Blackmer, as the explicably sinister old smoothy, Roman Castevet. John Cassavetes is competent as Rosemary's husband but not as certain of his screen identity as he was in *The Dirty Dozen*.

The best thing that can be said about the

film, I think, is that it works. Polanski has taken a most difficult situation and made it believable, right up to the end. In this sense, he outdoes even Hitchcock. Both *Rosemary's Baby* and Hitchcock's classic *Suspicion* are about wives, deeply in love, who are gradually forced to suspect the most sinister and improbable things about their husbands.

But Cary Grant in *Suspicion* was only a bounder and perhaps a murderer, and we didn't even really believe that (since he was Cary Grant). Rosemary, on the other hand, is forced into the most bizarre suspicions about her husband, and we share them and believe them. Because Polanski exercises his craft so well, we follow him right up to the end and stand there, rocking that dreadful cradle.

'Round Midnight

R, 130 m., 1986

Dexter Gordon (Dale Turner), Francois Cluzet (Francis Borier), Gabrielle Haker (Berangere), Sandra Reaves-Phillips (Buttercup), Lonette McKee (Darcey Leigh), Christine Pascal (Sylvie), Herbie Hancock (Eddie Wayne), Martin Scorsese (Goodley). Directed by Bertrand Tavernier and produced by Irwin Winkler. Screenplay by David Rayfiel and Tavernier.

In Dexter Gordon's voice in this movie there is a quality that at first sounds like a great weariness. As I listened more carefully, however, I realized that there were other notes also present.

Here is a man (I speak of the character, not the actor) who has gone too far and seen too much, and who knows that in one way or another his death is near. Yet he is not impatient with those who still have long to live; he takes what remains of his precious time to speak carefully with them. And when he speaks of the world around him, it is with a quiet amazement that he is still there to see it.

I mention Gordon's voice because it plays the same notes as the music in this film. As with all great musicians, the notes that come from within are the same as the feelings that come from within. I believe that musicians who use breath to play their instruments—those who play the various horns—arrive sooner or later at a point where they play and speak in the same voice. Dexter Gordon makes it easy to

hear that; the music that comes from his saxophone is sad and tender, and so are his words.

In *'Round Midnight*, he plays a man named Dale Turner, an American jazzman who goes to Paris in 1959 to play at a club called the Blue Note. Turner is about sixty, an alcoholic and drug abuser whose pattern has been to pull things together for a while, and then let them slide. Each slide is closer to death. He is on the wagon in Paris, watched over by a ferocious landlady and a vigilant club owner, who want him sober so he can get his job done. In the smoky little club every night, he plays the new music of Monk and Bird, the standards of Gershwin and Porter, and songs that come up spontaneously while they are being played.

Outside in the rain one night, a young Frenchman stands by a window, listening to the music, not caring if he gets wet. He believes Dale Turner is the greatest sax player in the world, but he doesn't have enough money to go inside to hear him. One night he follows the old man out of the club, and is able to see without very much trouble that Dale needs help. So he offers it.

Dale Turner is the most hopeless kind of alcoholic, the kind who tries to stay dry by depending on his own willpower and the enforcement of others. Sooner or later his willpower will advise him to drink, and sooner or later the others will not be there, so sooner or later he will be drunk. The young Frenchman senses this, and also senses the overwhelming loneliness of Dale's life, and invites him home for food and talk.

That seemingly very slight gesture—a fan trying to help the man he admires—is the heart of *'Round Midnight*. This is not a heavily plotted movie, one of these musical biographies that are weighted down with omens and light on music. It is about a few months in a man's life, and about his music. It has more jazz in it than any other fiction film ever made, and it is probably better jazz; it makes its best points with music, not words.

Dexter Gordon plays the central role with an eerie magnetism. He is a musician, not an actor, and yet no actor could have given this performance, with its dignity, its wisdom, and its pain. He speaks slowly, carefully considering, really making his words mean something, and so even commonplace sentences ("Francois, this is a lovely town you have here") are really meant. He calls everyone "Lady" in the movie, and doesn't explain it, and doesn't need to.

The music was recorded live. The director, Bertrand Tavernier, believes that in earlier jazz films, the audience could sense that the actors were not really playing; that you could see in their eyes that they were not listening to the other musicians onstage with them. In *'Round Midnight*, the music happens as we hear it, played by Gordon, Herbie Hancock on piano, and such others as Freddie Hubbard, Bobby Hutcherson, Ron Carter, and Billy Higgins, with Lonette McKee on vocals. You do not need to know a lot about jazz to appreciate what is going on, because in a certain sense this movie teaches you everything about jazz that you really need to know.

There are side-stories: Dale's old loves, new possibilities, painful memories, battle with drink, and his suicidal decision to return to New York (where he is awaited by a slick agent and a patient, fatalistic heroin dealer). They all add up to the story of the end of a life. The story needs a song, and the movie has the song, *'Round Midnight.*

Ruby in Paradise

NO MPAA RATING, 115 m., 1993

Ashley Judd (Ruby Lee Gissing), Todd Field (Mike McCaslin), Bentley Mitchum (Ricky Chambers), Allison Dean (Rochelle Bridges), Dorothy Lyman (Mildred Chambers), Betsy Douds (Debrah Ann), Felicia Hernandez (Persefina). Directed by Victor Nuñez and produced by Keith Crofford. Screenplay by Nuñez.

The movies are filled with stories about people who escape from unhappy homes and discover personal freedom for themselves. But the freedom they discover is seldom very convincing—it seems made out of the fantasies of lottery winners and *Star Search* finalists. Real freedom, I think, doesn't come from overnight wealth or fame. It comes from finding out what you love to do, and being able to do it.

Ruby in Paradise is a wonderful, life-affirming movie about a young woman who has that kind of luck. It's a celebration of heart, courage, and persistence. It stars Ashley Judd, in one of the very best performances of 1993, as Ruby Lee Gissing, age about twenty, who gets in the car and drives away from her dead-end existence in Tennessee, and finds herself in Florida. We never find out much about what she left behind; she doesn't want to remember it. In Florida, what she basically seeks is a job that pays enough to meet her living expenses, so she can support herself and be independent.

She finds a job, in a beachwear shop run by a woman named Mildred Chambers (Dorothy Lyman). Mildred doesn't really need an employee. It's the slow season. But Ruby stands her ground, looks her in the eye, and gets the job, and after a while she begins to like doing it. She likes dealing with the public and doing inventory and arranging the stock; retail is exciting, and it suits her.

Other aspects of the job are not so thrilling. She has a mild little flirtation, for example, with Mildred's son Ricky (Bentley Mitchum). But he's not her type, and she tries to discourage him. He isn't easily discouraged, is angered with her, tells lies to his mother, and causes her to lose her job.

And then there is a low, bleak period of unemployment and desperation, even involving a brief visit to a topless joint where she considers, and rejects, the idea of becoming a stripper.

In that entire sequence, you can see a different mentality at work than you usually sense behind American movies. Hollywood in general sees strippers and hookers in a curiously positive light, as if the sex business is a good one for a woman to get into. Maybe that's how a lot of men in the movie business feel. Many Hollywood female characters are prostitutes even when there's no earthly reason in the plot for them to be one. See *True Romance*, for example.

Ruby in Paradise has different values. Ruby is filled with stubbornness and pride, and perhaps the best scene in the whole movie comes when Mildred Chambers discovers the truth about Ruby and her son, and goes to visit the young woman, and offers to rehire her. Study that scene—the writing, the acting, the lighting, the direction—and you will be looking at a movie that knows exactly what it is about, and how to achieve it.

Ruby in Paradise was written, directed, and edited by Victor Nuñez, a Floridian whose previous films, *Gal Young Un* and *A Flash of Green*, showed a deep sympathy with his characters. He cares about his people—what they need, how they feel. Here he has found the perfect star in Ashley Judd, who has done some television but is in her first movie role, and brings a simplicity and honesty to the performance that is almost startling in its power.

The key thing, I think, is that Judd and Nuñez allow Ruby to have the halfway feelings of real people, when that's appropriate, instead of casting all her decisions in the black-white exaggeration of most movie plotting. Look at the subtle way the movie handles her relationship with another local man, named Mike McCaslin (Todd Field). He's a pleasant, caring, ethical soul, concerned with ecology and social causes. She likes his sensitivity and his friendship. But eventually she comes to realize that he's too laid-back for her; that she has more drive, and wants to get more places than he cares about.

This is so refreshing, to see her go through these discoveries, since in most movies the women choose their men only according to qualities that would be equally valued among primates in a zoo. What we see is Ruby growing, learning, discovering things about herself. There is an important scene where Mildred takes her to a retail convention in Tampa, and at another table Ruby sees a young woman like herself, carrying a briefcase, engaged in a business meeting. At that instant, I think, Ruby stops thinking of her job as mere employment, and realizes it is a career.

My description of *Ruby in Paradise* may make it sound like events in a boring, everyday world. Nothing could be further from the truth. The greatest adventures in life don't take place in bizarre places with fantasy people. They take place as we size up the world and take our chances with it. And here is a young woman, on her own, smart and capable but still feeling her way, who makes some discoveries about what she can achieve, and what makes her happy.

When successful people tell their stories, you never hear much enthusiasm in their voices as they describe their most recent tri-umph. But their voices glow when they describe their first successes: their first job, or the first time their talent was recognized, or the first time they realized what they were good at doing. That first chapter is the hard one to write. Then the rest of the book takes care of itself. *Ruby in Paradise* is a breathtaking movie about a young woman who opens the book of her life to a fresh page, and begins to write.

Runaway Train

R, 111 m., 1985

Jon Voight (Manny), Eric Roberts (Buck), Rebecca De Mornay (Sara), Kyle T. Heffner (Frank Barstow), John P. Ryan (Ranken), Kenneth McMillan (Eddie). Directed by Andrei Konchalovsky and produced by Menahem Golan and Yoram Globus. Screenplay by Djordje Milicevic, Paul Zindel, and Edward Bunker.

The great adventure movies have all been stories of character, not just tales of action. One of the great losses in the movies of recent years has been that sense of real character: One-dimensional people insert themselves into chases and explosions, and the mindless spectacle on the screen is supposed to replace the presence of plausible human beings.

Runaway Train is a reminder that the great adventures are great because they happen to people we care about. That was true of *The African Queen,* and of *Stagecoach,* and of *The Seven Samurai,* three movies that would otherwise seem to have little in common. And it is also true of this tale of two desperate convicts on board a train that is hurtling through the snows of Alaska.

The movie stars Jon Voight and Eric Roberts, who were both nominated for Oscars. They are two actors with dramatically different styles. Voight is always internalized and moody; Roberts has a collection of verbal and physical tics that are usually irritating, and are sometimes meant to be. Here they are both correctly cast, as two convicts in a maximum-security prison in Alaska, who escape through a drain tunnel and then blunder onto the train that takes them on their hellbound mission.

Voight plays Manny, a convict who is so distrusted by the warden that his cell doors have been welded shut for three years. "He's not a human being—he's an animal," the warden says, and this is not just stock dialogue, but the thesis on which the whole movie will rest. Roberts is Buck, a trusty who works for the prison laundry. The warden is Ranken (John P. Ryan), and he has a personal grudge against Manny. In fact, he releases him from solitary in the wicked hope that Manny will try to escape—he's done it before—and that will give Ranken license to kill him.

The opening passages are intense, but somewhat routine; they're out of the basic kit of prison movie clichés. Then the two convicts escape, and stumble by luck into one of the back cabs of a train that consists of four locomotives linked together. The train starts, the engineer suddenly collapses with a heart attack, and the movie's epic journey has begun.

Runaway Train is based on an original screenplay by the Japanese master Akira Kurosawa, whose best movies use the actors as a means of studying character. After some rewriting, *Runaway Train* was directed by Andrei Konchalovsky, the emigré Russian who figures so memorably (under a pseudonym) as Shirley MacLaine's lover in her bestseller *Dancing in the Light.* He has given the story the kind of wildness and passion it requires; this isn't a high-tech Hollywood adventure movie, but a raw saga that works close to the floor.

Once the train has started to move, the movie follows three threads. One involves the three people on the train (the two men discover after a while that a woman crew member, played by Rebecca De Mornay, is also on board, and also powerless to stop the engines). The second thread involves the railway dispatchers, who quarrel over a computer system that may possibly have the ability to clear the tracks ahead of the runaway. The third involves the ferocious determination of Ranken, the warden, to track the train by helicopter, and kill the men inside. Those elements might be enough to make *Runaway Train* a superior action movie. What makes it more than that is the dynamic inside the cab of the train. Voight is seen as a man who is intelligent enough to realize how desperate the situation is—because he has been caught not just in a physical trap, but also in a psychological one. In an impassioned speech that may be the best single scene he has ever played, he tries to explain to

Roberts how limited their choices are in life. He uses a story of a man with a broom to create a parable about the impossibility of living as a free man.

The Roberts character does not quite understand the story. He is a wild man of limited intelligence, and prison life has made him dangerous—he acts without regard for the consequences. When these two men are joined by a woman, it is not just a plot gimmick; her role as an outsider gives them an audience and a mirror.

The action sequences in the movie are stunning. Frequently, in recent movies, I've seen truly spectacular stunts and not been much excited, because I knew they were stunts. All I could appreciate was their smoothness of execution. In *Runaway Train,* as the characters try to climb along the sides of the ice-covered locomotive, as the train crashes through barriers and other trains, as men dangle from helicopters and try to kill the convicts, there is such a raw, uncluttered desperation in the feats that they put slick Hollywood stunts to shame.

The ending of the movie is astonishing in its emotional impact. I will not describe it. All I will say is that Konchalovsky has found the perfect visual image to express the ideas in his film. Instead of a speech, we get a picture, and the picture says everything that needs to be said. Afterward, just as the screen goes dark, there are a couple of lines from Shakespeare that may resonate more deeply the more you think about the Voight character. This was one of the year's best.

Running on Empty

PG-13, 113 m., 1988

Christine Lahti (Annie Pope), River Phoenix (Danny Pope), Judd Hirsch (Arthur Pope), Jonas Abry (Harry Pope), Martha Plimpton (Lorna Phillips), Ed Crowley (Mr. Phillips), L. M. (Kit) Carson (Gus Winant), Steven Hill (Mr. Patterson), Augusta Dabney (Mrs. Patterson), David Margulies (Dr. Jonah Reiff). Directed by Sidney Lumet. Produced by Amy Robinson and Griffin Dunne. Screenplay by Naomi Foner.

How do you explain it to your children, when you take the family dog and put it out into the street, and say that it will surely find a home—

and then you drive out of town, forever? That's what happens in an early scene of *Running on Empty,* and the most chilling thing about it is that the children take it fairly well. They've abandoned family dogs before. And they've left town a lot of times.

The movie is about the Popes, a married couple who have been underground since the 1960s, and about their children—especially Danny, who is a senior in high school and has never known any other kind of lifestyle. The Popes were involved with radical politics, and they blew up a building, and there was a janitor inside who they didn't know would be there. They've been on the run ever since, changing towns, changing names, learning how to find jobs that don't attract attention, learning to keep the kids home on the day they take the school picture.

But it's a funny thing about the past. The more you run from it, the more it's in your thoughts. And now time is catching up with this family. What, for example, is Danny (River Phoenix) going to do? He is a gifted piano player, and through one of his teachers he gets a scholarship to Juilliard. But he can't claim it unless he produces his high school transcripts— which are scattered back along his trail in many towns under many different names.

Arthur Pope (Judd Hirsch) has taken a hard line for years, and he's not ready to change it now. He believes that the family must stay together, must protect itself against the world. He's built a fortress mentality, and Danny shares it. He knows that if he comes clean and enters the school, he cannot see his family again; he'll have an FBI tail every moment. His mother, Annie (Christine Lahti), feels as if her heart will break. She has been running a long time, and she doesn't regret the sacrifices she made, but she can't bear the thought that Danny will have to sacrifice his future, just as she lost hers.

Life, in the short run, goes on. Danny makes a girlfriend (Martha Plimpton), whose father is the music teacher. They share secrets, but Danny cannot share his deepest one. This is the first time he's had a girlfriend, the first time he's allowed anyone to grow this close, and he has to learn a neat trick, the trick of learning to trust without being trustworthy. Plimpton knows something is wrong, but she doesn't know what.

The family has survived every crisis that came from the outside, every close call with the FBI, every question from a pushy neighbor. But this is a threat that's unanswerable, because it comes from within: It is no longer possible for these people to avoid questioning the very foundations on which they have built their lives. And that questioning leads to the movie's emotional high point, when the Lahti character calls up her father (Steven Hill), and arranges to meet him for lunch. Long ago, she broke his heart. She disappeared from his life for years. Now she wants her parents to take Danny so that he can go to music school. She will lose her son, just as her father lost her. It's ironic, and it's very sad, and by the end of the scene we have been through a wringer.

The movie was directed by Sidney Lumet, who made a movie called *Daniel* in 1983, inspired by the children of the Rosenbergs, who were charged with spying for the Russians. That film never quite came clear on what it thought about the Rosenbergs—not about whether they were guilty or innocent, but whether they were good or bad. They were seen through so many political and historical filters that we never knew who we were looking at. *Running on Empty* doesn't make that mistake. These are people who have made a choice and are living with the consequences, and during the course of the film they will have to reevaluate their decisions.

The family is not really political at all. Politics, ironically, have been left far behind—that kind of involvement would blow the cover of the Pope family. The film is a painful, enormously moving drama in which a choice must be made between sticking together, or breaking up and maybe fulfilling a long-delayed potential. The parents never fulfilled whatever potential they had because of their life underground. Now are they justified in asking their son to abandon his own future? And how will they do that? Push him out of the car and drive away, and trust that he will find a home, just as the dog did?

Lumet is one of the best directors at work today, and his skill here is in the way he takes a melodramatic plot and makes it real by making it specific. All of the supporting characters are convincing, especially Plimpton and her father (Ed Crowley). There is a chilling walk-on by L. M. (Kit) Carson as a radical friend from the old days. And there are great performances in the central roles. River Phoenix essentially carries the story; it's about him. Lahti and Hill have that shattering scene together. And Lahti and Hirsch, huddled together in bed, fearfully realizing that they may have come to a crossroads, are touching; we see how they've depended on each other. This was one of the best films of 1988.

Russia

NO MPAA RATING, 108 m., 1972

A documentary directed by Theodore Holcomb and Kira Muratora.

I suppose we all know in a vague sort of way that the USSR is just what its name suggests, a union of various republics, nationalities, and language groups. But most of the time we think of Russia as . . . just Russia. There's Moscow, Leningrad, Siberia, and the Ukraine, we know, but then our high school geography gets vague.

One of the wonders of Theodore Holcomb's new color documentary, *Russia,* is that he has recorded the look and feel of daily life in places that are totally unlike our notion of Russia. He visited twelve of the fifteen Soviet republics, including exotic central Asian capitals that seem to belong in the *Arabian Nights* rather than in the grip of a superpower. And he has come back with an astonishingly diverse picture of a nation we often regard as monolithic.

Russia is the first uncensored documentary about the Soviet Union made by an outsider. The story of how Holcomb shot it would, I suspect, make a good documentary in itself. Holcomb is an independent filmmaker with an impressive track record of documentaries about out-of-the-way places such as African villages and the foothills of Anapurna. More important for the purposes of *Russia,* he doesn't have any connection, official or otherwise, with the American government.

He had the good luck to find a department of the Russian government that gave him permission to travel freely in the Soviet Union, without a guide or interpreter to oversee him, and he traveled some seventeen thousand miles during six months despite the great puzzlement of the Soviet secret police, the KGB, about how he had entered Russia at all.

Traveling only with his French cameraman, George Elliautou, Holcomb ran into surprisingly little suspicion. He says, "There we were with our big 16-mm Eclair on a tripod, and everybody just seemed to assume we had permission to shoot, or we wouldn't be there." Although tourists' cameras are frequently taken from them and the film exposed, Holcomb ran into no trouble with his thousands of feet of film negative—until the very end.

The secret police, who did not approve of his visit no matter how good his clout was with the government, stopped him at Moscow Airport and exposed all his footage to X-rays designed to ruin it. Through some unexplained miracle, the X-ray machine malfunctioned, and the color print of *Russia* is of excellent quality except for some wayward light fogging caused by X-rays.

What we get, then, is a picture of the Soviet Union that never tends to preach, lecture, or propagandize. The commentary was written by the *New York Times'* old Russia hand, Harrison E. Salisbury, and it is intelligent and doesn't get in the way. Salisbury has a couple of points he wants to make: that academic freedom is terribly scarce in the Soviet Union and that despite its Constitution, the government continues a systematic campaign against organized religion. But *Russia* is not an attack on Russia, or a defense; it is mostly just a portrait.

We see faces, a lot of them. We see young students in Moscow, and incredibly aged peasants outside Tashkent. We go up to a mountaintop in central Asia to hear an ancient stringed instrument played, and we have dinner in a crowded Moscow apartment. We take a ride on the Trans-Siberian Railway, we look at the bleak and ice-bound North, and we float down the ancient canals of Leningrad.

All this is in dramatic contrast to the image of Russia that used to be current in this country. When I was in grade school, during the deep-freeze years of the Cold War, I was given a mental image of Russia as a place where the sun literally did not shine and where slaves worked eighteen-hour days on collective farms. I did not, certainly, have any idea of the quiet, sunny church squares of Lithuania or the soft old mountains of Ukraine. It is good that a film like this one can let us see that there are only people over there, after all, and good that the Russians are now seeing a lot of American films.

Holcomb makes no attempt, however, to suggest that the Russian system of socialism and collectivism is interchangeable with what we have here. Salisbury's commentary is especially pointed in a few places, as when he says that it will be "a very long time" before the Lithuanians and the Latvians accept Moscow's rule.

The film also suggests that an impulse toward free enterprise tends to spring up stubbornly even in the most avid of socialist states. We see Moscow's *Bird Market,* one of the last officially sanctioned havens of free enterprise, where pet fanciers buy, sell, and trade their pigeons, parakeets, goldfish, cats, and dogs. And we see peasants working enthusiastically on the half-acre they're allowed to cultivate for themselves—and selling the produce in town markets.

Russia never presses too hard, never belabors points. A lot of its atmosphere comes from its music, which was recorded mostly on location in the Soviet Union from native musicians playing folk compositions. Holcomb allows the camera to simply watch people during long stretches of film, and from his documentary comes a relaxed and observant record of a nation that most of us don't know nearly enough about.

Russian Ark

NO MPAA RATING, 96 m., 2002

Sergey Dontsov (The Marquis), Mariya Kuznetsova (Catherine the Great), Leonid Mozgovoy (The Spy), Mikhail Piotrovsky (Himself), David Giorgobiani (Orbeli), Aleksandr Chaban (Boris Piotrovsky), Lev Yeliseyev (Himself), Oleg Khmelnitsky (Himself), Maksim Sergeyev (Peter the Great). Directed by Aleksandr Sokurov and produced by Andrey Deryabin, Jens Meuer, and Karsten Stöter. Screenplay by Anatoly Nikiforov, Boris Khaimsky, Svetlana Proskurina, and Sokurov.

Every review of *Russian Ark* begins by discussing its method. The movie consists of one unbroken shot lasting the entire length of the film, as a camera glides through the Hermitage, the repository of Russian art and history in St. Petersburg. The cinematographer, Tilman Buttner, using a Steadicam and high-definition digital technology, joined with some two thousand actors in a high-wire act in which every mark and cue had to be hit without fail; there were two broken takes before the third time was the charm.

The subject of the film, which is written, directed, and (in a sense) hosted by Aleksandr Sokurov, is no less than three centuries of Russian history. The camera doesn't merely take us on a guided tour of the art on the walls and in the corridors, but witnesses many visitors who came to the Hermitage over the years. Apart from anything else, this is one of the best-sustained *ideas* I have ever seen on the screen. Sokurov reportedly rehearsed his all-important camera move again and again with the cinematographer, the actors, and the invisible sound and lighting technicians, knowing that the Hermitage would be given to him for only one precious day.

After a dark screen and the words "I open my eyes and I see nothing," the camera's eye opens upon the Hermitage and we meet the Marquis (Sergey Dontsov), a French nobleman who will wander through the art and the history as we follow him. The voice we heard, which belongs to the never-seen Sokurov, becomes a foil for the Marquis, who keeps up a running commentary. What we see is the grand sweep of Russian history in the years before the Revolution, and a glimpse of the grim times afterward.

It matters little, I think, if we recognize all of the people we meet on this journey; such figures as Catherine II and Peter the Great are identified (Catherine, like many another museum visitor, is searching for the loo), but some of the real people who play themselves, like Mikhail Piotrovsky, the current director of the Hermitage, work primarily as types. We overhear whispered conversations, see state functions, listen as representatives of the shah apologize to Nicholas I for the killing of Russian diplomats, even see little flirtations.

And then, in a breathtaking opening-up, the camera enters a grand hall and witnesses a formal state ball. Hundreds of dancers, elaborately costumed and bejeweled, dance to the music of a symphony orchestra, and then the camera somehow seems to float through the air to the orchestra's stage and moves among the musicians. An invisible ramp must have been put into place below the camera frame for Buttner and his Steadicam to smoothly climb.

The film is a glorious experience to witness, not least because, knowing the technique and understanding how much depends on every moment, we almost hold our breath. How tragic if an actor had blown a cue or Buttner had stumbled five minutes from the end! The long, long single shot reminds me of a scene in *Nostalgia,* the 1982 film by Russia's Andrei Tarkovsky, in which a man obsessively tries to cross and recross a littered and empty pool while holding a candle that he does not want to go out: The point is not the action itself, but its duration and continuity.

It will be enough for most viewers, as it was for me, to simply view *Russian Ark* as an original and beautiful idea. But Stanley Kauffmann raises an inarguable objection in his *New Republic* review, when he asks, "What is there intrinsically in the film that would grip us if it had been made—even excellently made—in the usual edited manner?" If it were not one unbroken take, if we were not continuously mindful of its 96 minutes—what then? "We sample a lot of scenes," he writes, "that in themselves have no cumulation, no self-contained point. . . . Everything we see or hear engages us only as part of a directorial tour de force."

This observation is true, and deserves an answer, and I think my reply would be that *Russian Ark,* as it stands, is enough. I found myself in a reverie of thoughts and images, and sometimes, as my mind drifted to the barbarity of Stalin and the tragic destiny of Russia, the scenes of dancing became poignant and ironic. It is not simply what Sokurov shows about Russian history, but what he does not show— doesn't need to show, because it shadows all our thoughts of that country. Kauffmann is right that if the film had been composed in the ordinary way out of separate shots, we would question its purpose. But it is not, and the effect of the unbroken flow of images (experimented with in the past by directors like Hitchcock and Max Ophuls) is uncanny. If cinema is sometimes dreamlike, then every edit is an awakening. *Russian Ark* spins a daydream made of centuries.

S

The Sacrifice
PG, 145 m., 1986

Erland Josephson (Alexander), Susan Fleetwood (Adelaide), Valerie Mairesse (Julia), Allan Edwall (Otto), Gudrun Gisladottir (Maria), Sven Wollter (Victor), Filippa Franzen (Marta), Tommy Kjellqvist (Little Man). Directed by Andrei Tarkovsky and produced by Anna-Lena Wilborn. Screenplay by Tarkovsky.

The old workman gave the younger workman the use of his shop: Andrei Tarkovsky went to Sweden to shoot a movie on the island of Faro, the same island where Ingmar Bergman lives and makes most of his films.

Tarkovsky's film was produced by the Swedish Film Institute, it was photographed by Sven Nykvist, Bergman's cinematographer, and it starred Erland Josephson, who has acted in many Bergman films.

There are moments when the resulting film, *The Sacrifice*, looks uncannily like a work by Bergman, and I think that is intentional: Tarkovsky, the visitor, an exile from Russia, was working with Bergman's materials and subjects in much the same way that an itinerant Renaissance painter might briefly stop and submerge himself in the school of a master.

Yet Tarkovsky is a master, too. With Bergman, he is one of the five living filmmakers who have concerned themselves primarily with ultimate issues of human morality (the others are Akira Kurosawa, Satyajit Ray, and Robert Bresson). He is the greatest Russian filmmaker since Sergei Eisenstein, and yet he stands outside the Soviet tradition of materialism and dares to say that he is spiritual, that he can "still be summoned by an inner voice." These days, it takes more courage for an artist to admit his spiritual beliefs than to deny them.

When Tarkovsky made *The Sacrifice*, he knew that he was gravely ill. Now he lies dying in a Paris hospital with a brain tumor. He did not choose a small subject for his final statement. His film is about a man who learns, or dreams, that the bombers have gone on their way to unleash World War III. He offers his own life as a sacrifice, if only his family can be spared.

The movie is not easy to watch, and it is long to sit through. Yet a certain joy shines through the difficulty. Tarkovsky has obviously cut loose from any thought of entertaining the audience and has determined, in his last testament, to say exactly what he wants, in exactly the style he wants.

He uses a great many long shots—both long in duration, and with great distances between the camera and the subjects. Long shots inspire thoughtfulness from the audience. We are not so close that we are required to identify with a character. We stand back, and see everything, and have time to think about it. The movie doesn't hurtle headlong toward its conclusion, taking our agreement for granted. There are spaces between events that are large enough for us to ask ourselves if we would do what the man in the movie is doing.

It is his birthday. He plants a tree, carefully, methodically.

There is a belief that it is impossible to plant a tree without thinking of your own lifespan, because in all certainty the tree will be there long after you have gone. As he plants the tree, his small son watches him and then toddles thoughtlessly about on the surface of the planet he does not yet know is a planet.

Some people came to the birthday party: the man's wife, his daughters, some friends, and a mailman who apparently is the island's mystic. In a sense he delivers the cosmic mail, bringing news of inner realities. During the party, the news comes that the war has broken out.

All of this is told slowly, in elegantly composed shots, with silences in between. When the characters speak, it is rarely to engage in small talk; the hero has a long monologue about the quality of our lives and the ways we are heedlessly throwing away the futures of our children. When the man begs to make his sacrifice, he does so not by ranting and raving to heaven, but by choosing one of his own maids—a humble working woman—as a sort of saintly person who might be able to intervene.

The Sacrifice is not the sort of movie most people will choose to see, but those with the imagination to risk it may find it rewarding. Everything depends on the ability to empathize with the man in the movie, and Tarkovsky refuses to reach out with narrative tricks to involve us. Some movies work their magic in the minds of the audience; this one stays resolutely on the screen, going about its urgent business and leaving us free to participate only if we want to.

That is the meaning of a sacrifice, isn't it— that it is offered willingly?

Safe Conduct

NO MPAA RATING, 170 m., 2003

Jacques Gamblin (Jean Devaivre), Denis Podalydès (Jean Aurenche), Charlotte Kady (Suzanne Raymond), Marie Desgranges (Simone Devaivre), Ged Marlon (Jean-Paul Le Chanois), Philippe Morier-Genoud (Maurice Tourneur), Laurent Schilling (Charles Spaak), Maria Pitarresi (Reine Sorignal). Directed by Bertrand Tavernier and produced by Frédéric Bourboulon and Alain Sarde. Screenplay by Jean Cosmos and Tavernier, based on the book by Jean Devaivre.

More than two hundred films were made in France during the Nazi occupation, most of them routine, a few of them good, but none of them, Bertrand Tavernier observes, anti-Semitic. This despite the fact that anti-Semitism was not unknown in the French films of the 1930s. Tavernier's *Safe Conduct* tells the story of that curious period in French film history through two central characters, a director and a writer, who made their own accommodations while working under the enemy.

The leading German-controlled production company, Continental, often censored scenes it objected to, but its mission was to foster the illusion of life as usual during the occupation; it would help French morale, according to this theory, if French audiences could see new French films, and such stars as Michel Simon and Danielle Darrieux continued to work.

Tavernier considers the period through the lives of two participants, the assistant director Jean Devaivre (Jacques Gamblin) and the writer Jean Aurenche (Denis Podalydès). The film opens with a flurry of activity at the hotel where Aurenche is expecting a visit from an actress; the proprietor sends champagne to the room, although it is cold and the actress would rather have tea. Aurenche is a compulsive womanizer who does what he can in a passive-aggressive

way to avoid working for the Germans while not actually landing in jail. Devaivre works enthusiastically for Continental as a cover for his activities in the French Resistance.

Other figures, some well known to lovers of French cinema, wander through: We see Simon so angry at the visit of a Nazi "snoop" that he cannot remember his lines, and Charles Spaak (who wrote *The Grand Illusion* in 1937) thrown into a jail cell, but then, when his screenwriting skills are needed, negotiating for better food, wine, and cigarettes in order to keep working while behind bars.

Like Francois Truffaut's *The Last Metro* (1980), the movie questions the purpose of artistic activity during wartime. But Truffaut's film was more melodramatic, confined to a single theater company and its strategies and deceptions, while Tavernier is more concerned with the entire period of history.

The facts of the time seem constantly available just beneath the veneer of fiction, and sometimes burst through, as in a remarkable aside about Jacques Dubuis, Devaivre's brother-in-law; after he was arrested as a Resistance member, the film tells us, Devaivre's wife never saw her brother again—except once, decades later, as an extra in a French film of the period. We see the moment in a film clip, as the long-dead man collects tickets at a theater. There was debate within the film community about collaborating with the Nazis, and some, like Devaivre, risked contempt for their cooperative attitude because they could not reveal their secret work for the Resistance. Tavernier shows him involved in a remarkable adventure, one of those wartime stories so unlikely they can only be true. Sent home from the set with a bad cold, he stops by the office and happens upon the key to the office of a German intelligence official who works in the same building. He steals some papers, and soon, to his amazement, finds himself flying to England on a clandestine flight to give the papers and his explanation to British officials. They fly him back; a train schedule will not get him to Paris in time, and so he rides his bicycle all the way, still coughing and sneezing, to get back to work. Everyone thinks he has spent the weekend in bed.

You would imagine a film like this would be greeted with rapture in France, but no. The leading French film magazine, *Cahiers du*

Cinema, has long scorned the filmmakers of this older generation as makers of mere "quality," and interprets Tavernier's work as an attack on the New Wave generation that replaced them. This is astonishingly wrongheaded, since Tavernier (who worked as a publicist for such New Wavers as Godard and Chabrol) is interested in his characters not in terms of the cinema they produced but because of the conditions they survived, and the decisions they made.

Writing in the *New Republic,* Stanley Kauffmann observes: "Those who now think that these film people should have stopped work in order to impede the German state must also consider whether doctors and plumbers and teachers should also have stopped work for the same reason." Well, some would say yes. But that could lead to death, a choice it is easier to urge upon others than to make ourselves.

What Tavernier does here is celebrate filmmakers who did the best they could under the circumstances. Tavernier knew many of these characters; Aurenche and Pierre Bost, a famous screenwriting team, wrote his first film, *The Clockmaker of St. Paul,* and Aurenche worked on several others. In the film's closing moments, we hear Tavernier's own voice in narration, saying that at the end of his life, Aurenche told him he would not have done anything differently.

Saint Jack
R, 112 m., 1979

Ben Gazzara (Jack Flowers), Denholm Elliott (William Leigh), James Villiers (Frogget), Joss Ackland (Yardley), Rodney Bewes (Smale), Peter Bogdanovich (Schuman), Monika Subramaniam (Monika), George Lazenby (Senator). Directed by Bogdanovich and produced by Roger Corman. Screenplay by Howard Sackler, Paul Theroux, and Bogdanovich, based on the book by Theroux.

Sometimes a character in a movie inhabits his world so freely, so easily, that he creates it for us as well. Ben Gazzara does that in *Saint Jack,* as an American exile in Singapore who finds himself employed at the trade of pimp. He sticks his cigar in his mouth and walks through the crowded streets in his flowered sport shirts, he knows everyone, he knows all the angles—but this isn't a smart-aleck per-

formance, something borrowed from Damon Runyon. It's a performance that paints the character with a surprising tenderness and sadness, with a wisdom that does not blame people for what they do, and thus is cheerfully willing to charge them for doing it.

The character, Jack Flowers, is out of a book by Paul Theroux, who took a nonfiction look at this same territory in *The Great Railway Bazaar,* one of the best modern books of travel. The film is by Peter Bogdanovich, and what a revelation it is, coming after three expensive flops.

Bogdanovich, who began so surely in *The Last Picture Show,* seemed to lose feeling and tone as his projects became more bloated. But here everything is right again, even his decision to organize the narrative into an hour of atmosphere and then an hour of payoff.

Everything. Not many films are this good at taking an exotic location like Singapore and a life with the peculiarities of Jack Flowers's, and treating them with such casual familiarity that we really feel Jack lives there—knows it inside out. The movie's complex without being complicated. Its story line is a narrative as straight as *Casablanca*'s (with which it has some kinship), but its details teem with life.

We meet the scheming Chinese traders Jack sometimes works for; the forlorn and drunken British exiles who inhabit "clubs" of small hopes and old jokes; the whores who do not have hearts of gold or minds at all; the odd Ceylonese girl who is Jack's match in cynicism, but not his better.

And we meet William Leigh, another remarkable fictional creation. Leigh is a British citizen out from Hong Kong on business, who looks up Jack Flowers because Jack can arrange things. To Jack's well-concealed surprise, William Leigh doesn't want a prostitute. He wants some talk, a drink, some advice about a hotel room. Jack never really gets to know Leigh, but a bond forms between them because Leigh is *decent,* is that rare thing, a good man.

Denholm Elliott, usually seen here in third-rate British horror films, has the role, and triumphs in it. It is a subtle triumph; the movie doesn't give Leigh noble speeches or indeed much of anything revealing to say, but Elliott exudes a kind of cheery British self-pride, mixed with fears of death, that communicates as clearly as a bell.

Jack Flowers, meanwhile, runs into trouble. Singapore hoodlums are jealous of the success of his brothel, so they kidnap him and tattoo insulting names on his arms (altogether a more diabolical and satisfactory form of gangland revenge than the concrete overcoat). Jack has the tattoos redecorated into flowers, as William Leigh gets drunk with him. Then, his Singapore business opportunities at an end, he signs up with an American CIA type (Bogdanovich) to run an army brothel near a rest and recreation center.

One of the joys of this movie is seeing how cleanly and surely Bogdanovich employs the two levels of his plot. One level is Jack's story, and it leads up to an attempted blackmailing scene that's beautifully sustained. The other level is the level of William Leigh, whose life is so different from Jack's, and yet whose soul makes sense to him. The levels come together in a conclusion that is inevitable, quietly noble, wonderfully satisfactory.

All of this works so well because Bogdanovich, assisted by superb script and art direction, shows us Jack Flowers's world so confidently—and because Ben Gazzara makes Jack so special. It's not just a surprise that Gazzara could find the notes and tones to make *Saint Jack* live. He has been a good actor for a long time. What's surprising, given the difficulties of this character, is that anyone could.

Salaam Bombay!

NO MPAA RATING, 113 m., 1988

Shafiq Syed (Krishna/Chaipau), Sarfuddin Qurrassi (Koyla), Raju Barnad (Keera), Raghubir Yadav (Chillum), Aneeta Kanwar (Rekha), Nana Patekar (Baba), Hansa Vithal (Manju), Mohanraj Babu (Salim), Chandrashekhar Naidu (Chungal). Produced and directed by Mira Nair. Screenplay by Sooni Taraporevala.

The history of the making of *Salaam Bombay!* is almost as interesting as the film itself. The filmmakers gathered a group of the street children of Bombay and talked with them about their experiences, visiting the streets and train stations, bazaars and redlight districts where many of them lived. Out of these interviews emerged a screenplay that was a composite of several lives. Then many of the children were enlisted for weeks in a daily workshop, not to teach them "acting" (for that they already knew from hundreds of overacted Indian film melodramas), but to teach them how to behave naturally in front of the camera.

Out of those workshops a cast gradually emerged, and it was clear almost from the start that the star was an eleven-year-old street child named Shafiq Syed, whose history was unknown, but who proved to be such a natural filmmaker that he sometimes reminded the directors of errors in continuity. Using Syed and shooting on actual locations in Bombay, director Mira Nair has been able to make a film that has the everyday, unforced reality of documentary, and yet the emotional power of great drama. *Salaam Bombay!* is one of the best films of 1988.

Shafiq Syed plays its hero, a boy named Chaipau who works for a traveling circus. One day he is sent on an errand—to get some cigarettes from a neighboring village—and when he returns, the circus has packed up and disappeared. He goes to a nearby village and takes a train to Bombay, following some half-formed plan to return to his native village and his mother, who perhaps sold him to the circus. But Chaipau cannot read or write, and he is not quite sure where his village is, or perhaps even what it is named, and he disappears naturally into the ranks of thousands of children who live, and die, on the streets of Bombay.

These streets are without doubt a cruel and dreadful place, but as Nair sees them, they are not entirely without hope. Her Bombay seems to have a kinship with one of the Victorian slums of Dickens, who portrayed a society in which even the lowest classes had identity and a role to play. In that respect, *Salaam Bombay!* is quite different from *Pixote*, the 1981 film about Brazilian street children. Although the two films obviously have much in common, the children of *Pixote* exist in an anarchic and savage world, while those in *Salaam Bombay!* share a community, however humble.

Chaipau is an intelligent boy, stubborn and wily, and he finds a job as a runner for a man who runs a tea stall in the street. Chaipau's job is to race up flights of tenement stairs with trays of tea, and in the tenements he finds a world of poverty, sweatshops, prostitution, and drug dealing. One of the friends he makes is a pathetic sixteen-year-old girl who was sold or kidnapped away from her native village, and is being held captive by a rapacious madam who plans to sell her virginity to the highest bidder. The other characters in the neighborhood include a hopeless drunk and addict who befriends the children as best he can.

One of the subplots of the film involves the relationship between a drug dealer and the prostitute who is his common-law wife. She lives for her child, and exists in daily fear that the child will be taken from her because of the life she leads. Nair treats this woman with such sensitivity that we feel great sympathy for her when the child is threatened, and this illustrates one of the underlying beliefs of *Salaam Bombay!*—that the street life, however hard, is preferable to what happens to people once they are identified by the law and become the victims of official institutions.

It is remarkable how well Nair creates this street world and tells us its rules without seeming to force her story. One of her secrets is location shooting; not a single scene in this movie was shot on a set or in a studio, and some of the scenes—including a funeral procession—were shot with hidden cameras to capture the unrehearsed behavior of the spectators.

It is a well-known truism of filmmaking that color photography tends to make locations look better than they are; we lose the smells and the suffering, and see the bright colors and the sunlight. That happens here, I think; the very act of photographing this society has probably tended to romanticize it somewhat. And yet there are moments that remain raw and painful, as when Chaipau drops his street-smart façade for a second and we see the lonely little boy behind it.

One of the questions asked, but not answered, by the film is what should be done about these children. At one point, Chaipau and some friends are rounded up by the police and herded into a large institution that combines the worst features of an orphanage and a prison, but that doesn't seem to be the answer, and we are left with the troubling impression that in Bombay, at any event, the children seem to fare better on the streets. There they have an identity and a measure of hope. Of course, in the best of possible worlds, something would be "done" about

them, but *Salaam Bombay!* takes place far from such a world, and the movie is about children doing the best they can for themselves.

Santa Sangre

R, 124 m., 1990

Axel Jodorowsky (Fenix), Sabrina Dennison (Alma), Guy Stockwell (Orgo), Blanca Guerra (Concha), Thelma Tixou (Tattooed Woman), Adan Jodorowsky (Fenix, Eight Years), Faviola Elenka Tapia (Alma, Seven Years), Jesus Juarez (Aladin). Directed by Alejandro Jodorowsky and produced by Claudio Argento. Screenplay by Alejandro Jodorowsky, Robert Leoni, and Argento.

Santa Sangre is a throwback to the golden age, to the days when filmmakers had bold individual visions and were not timidly trying to duplicate the latest mass-market formulas. This is a movie like none I have seen before, a wild kaleidoscope of images and outrages, a collision between Freud and Fellini. It contains blood and glory, saints and circuses, and unspeakable secrets of the night. And it is all wrapped up in a flamboyant parade of bold, odd, striking imagery, with Alejandro Jodorowsky as the ringmaster.

Those who were going to the movies in the early 1970s will remember the name. Jodorowsky is the perennial artist in exile who made *El Topo,* that gory cult classic that has since disappeared from view, trapped in a legal battle. Then he made *The Holy Mountain,* another phantasmagoric collection of strange visions, and in recent years he has written a series of fantasy comic books which are bestsellers in France and Mexico. Now he is back with a film that grabs you with its opening frames and shakes you for two hours with the outrageous excesses of his imagination.

The film takes place in Mexico, where the hero, Fenix, travels with his father's circus. His father is a tattooed strongman, and his mother is an aerialist who hangs high above the center ring, suspended from the long locks of her hair. She is also a mystic who leads a cult of women who worship a saint without arms—a woman whose arms were severed from her body during an attack by a man. The blood of this saint is *santa sangre*, holy blood, collected in a pool in a church which the authorities want to bulldoze.

The church is pulled down in the opening moments of the movie, while horrendous events take place under the big top. While the mother is suspended from her hair high in the air, she sees her husband sneak out with the tattooed lady—and she tracks them down to their place of sin, kills her, and maims her husband with acid before he cuts off her arms and then kills himself.

Or is that what actually happened? The young son, who witnesses these deeds, is discovered years later in an insane asylum, sitting up in a tree, refusing all forms of human communication. Then he receives a visitor—his mother, come to deliver him from his madness. When he reenters the outer world, he encounters Alma, the deaf-mute girl who was his childhood friend, and who has now grown into a grave, calm young woman. And he embarks on a journey that leads into the most impenetrable thickets of Freudian and Jungian symbology.

Fenix's mother, still without arms, makes him her psychological slave. He must always walk and sit behind her, his arms thrust through the sleeves of her dresses, so that his hands do her bidding. Together they perform in a nightclub act—she sitting at the piano, he playing. But is this really happening, or is it his delusion?

Jodorowsky hardly pauses to consider such questions, so urgent is his headlong rush to confront us with more spectacle. I will never forget one sequence in the movie, the elephant's burial, where the circus marches in mournful procession behind the grotesquely large coffin of the dead animal. It is tipped over the side into a garbage dump, where the coffin is pounced upon and ripped open by starving scavengers. Another powerful image comes in a graveyard, where the spirits of female victims rise up out of their graves to confront their tormentor. And there is the strange, gentle, almost hallucinatory passage where Fenix joins his fellow inmates in a trip into town; Jodorowsky uses mongoloid children in this sequence, his actors communicating with them with warmth and body contact in a scene that treads delicately between fiction and documentary.

If Jodorowsky has influences—in addition to the psychologists he plunders for complexes—they are Fellini and Buñuel. Federico Fellini, with his love for grotesque and special people and his circuses and parades, and Luis Buñuel, with his delight in depravity and secret perversion, his conviction that respectability was the disguise of furtive self-indulgence. *Santa Sangre* is a movie in which the inner chambers of the soul are laid bare, in which desires become visible and walk into the room and challenge the yearner to possess them.

When I go to the movies, one of my strongest desires is to be shown something new. I want to go to new places, meet new people, have new experiences. When I see Hollywood formulas mindlessly repeated, a little something dies inside of me: I have lost two hours to boors who insist on telling me stories I have heard before. Jodorowsky is not boring. The privilege of making a film is too precious to him, for him to want to make a conventional one. It has been eighteen years since his last work, and all of that time the frustration and inspiration must have been building. Now comes this release, in a rush of energy and creative joy.

Saraband

R, 107 m., 2005

Liv Ullmann (Marianne), Erland Josephson (Johan), Borje Ahlstedt (Henrik), Julia Dufvenius (Karin), Gunnel Fred (Martha). Directed by Ingmar Bergman and produced by Pia Ehrnvall. Screenplay by Bergman.

Ingmar Bergman is balancing his accounts and closing out his books. The great director is eighty-seven years old and announced in 1983 that *Fanny and Alexander* would be his last film. So it was, but he continued to work on the stage and for television, and then he wrote the screenplay for Liv Ullmann's film *Faithless* (2000). Now comes his absolutely last work, *Saraband*, powerfully, painfully honest.

Although you can see the film as it stands, it will have more resonance if you remember Bergman's *Scenes from a Marriage* (1974). That film starred Ullmann and Erland Josephson as Marianne and Johan, a couple married twenty years earlier and divorced ten years earlier, who meet again in the middle of the night in a cabin in the middle of the woods. Their marriage has failed, their relationship has faded, and yet on this night it is more real than anything else. I wrote in 1974: "They are in middle age now but in the night still fond and frightened lovers holding on for reassurance."

Now there is no more reassurance to be had. They must be in their eighties now; in real life, Josephson is eighty-two and Ullmann sixty-six. Because Bergman's films can be seen again and again, and because he believes the human face is the most important subject of the cinema, we are as familiar with these two faces as any we have ever seen. I saw Ullmann for the first time in Bergman's *Persona* (1967), which I reviewed seven months after I became a film critic. Now here she is again. When I interviewed her about *Faithless* at Cannes five years ago, I noted to myself that she had not, like so many actresses, had plastic surgery. She wore her age as proof of having lived, as we all must. Now I see *Saraband* and the movie is possible because she did not allow a surgeon to give her a face yearning for its younger form.

As the film opens, she is looking through some old photographs. Marianne and Johan had two daughters together, who are now middle-aged. She never sees them; one lives in Australia, and the other has gone mad. She tells us she has not seen Johan for all of those years but now thinks she will go to visit him. We follow her and find that Johan is now living in misery left over from an earlier marriage. He is rich, lives in the country, owns a nearby cottage that is occupied by his sixty-one-year-old son, Henrik (Borje Ahlstedt), and Henrik's nineteen-year-old daughter, Karin (Julia Dufvenius). Anna—Henrik's wife, Karin's mother—has been dead for two years. She is missed because she was needed, as cartilage if nothing else, to keep her husband and daughter from wearing each other down.

They are not Marianne's problem. But she visits them and witnesses appalling unhappiness. Johan is scornful of his son, who has value in his eyes only as the parent of Karin. Henrik is bitter that his father has money but doles it out reluctantly, to keep his son in constant need and supplication. Karin, who plays the cello, feels trapped because she wants to develop her career in the city and her father possessively hangs onto her (they sleep, Marianne discovers, in the same bed).

The movie is not about the resolution of this plot. It is about the way people persist in creating misery by placing the demands of their egos above the need for happiness—their own happiness and that of those around them. In some sense, Johan and Henrik live in these adjacent houses, in the middle of nowhere, simply so that they can hate each other. If they parted, each would lose a reason for living. Karin is the victim of their pathology.

Oh, but Bergman is sad, as he lives decade after decade on his island of Faro and writes these stories and assembles his old crew, or their children and successors, to film them. His *Faithless* showed an old filmmaker (working in Bergman's office, living in Bergman's house on Bergman's island). He hires an actress to help him think through a story he wants to write. The actress, who is imaginary, is in fact playing a woman he once loved; their love caused pain to her husband, her child, and even to the director. Now in his old age he is working through it, perhaps trying to make amends. We know from Bergman's autobiography that the story is loosely based on fact. We know, too, that Ullmann, who is directing it, was also Bergman's lover and had his daughter.

If *Faithless* was an attempt to face personal guilt, *Saraband* is a meditation on the pathology of selfish relationships. It is filled with failed parents: All three adults lack love in their bonds with their children. It is filled with unsettled scores: Now that Henrik is sixty-one, what does it matter that he has never become as successful as his father? The game is over. It is time to enjoy the success of his daughter—a success he will not permit because he fears losing her. When Marianne, a witness to this triangle of resentment, returns to her own life, she returns to even less—to nothing, to photographs.

The overwhelming fact about this movie is its awareness of time. Thirty-one years have passed since *Scenes from a Marriage*. The years have passed for Bergman, for Ullmann, for Josephson, and for us. Whatever else he is telling us in *Saraband*, Bergman is telling us that life will end on the terms by which we have lived it. If we are bitter now, we will not be victorious later; we will still be bitter. Here is a movie about people who have lived so long, hell has not been able to wait for them.

Saving Private Ryan

R, 170 m., 1998

Tom Hanks (Captain Miller), Tom Sizemore (Sergeant Horvath), Edward Burns (Private Reiben), Barry Pepper (Private Jackson), Adam Goldberg (Private Mellish), Vin Diesel (Private Caparzo), Giovanni Ribisi (T/4 Medic Wade), Jeremy Davies (Corporal Upham), Harve Presnell (General George Marshall), Matt Damon (Private Ryan). Directed by Steven Spielberg and produced by Spielberg, Ian Bryce, Mark Gordon, and Gary Levinsohn. Screenplay by Robert Rodat.

The soldiers assigned to find Private Ryan and bring him home can do the math for themselves. The army chief of staff has ordered them on the mission for propaganda purposes: Ryan's return will boost morale on the home front and put a human face on the carnage at Omaha Beach. His mother, who has already lost three sons in the war, will not have to add another telegram to the collection. But the eight men on the mission also have parents—and besides, they've been trained to kill Germans, not to risk their lives for publicity stunts. "This Ryan better be worth it," one of the men grumbles.

In Hollywood mythology, great battles wheel and turn on the actions of individual heroes. In Steven Spielberg's *Saving Private Ryan*, thousands of terrified and seasick men, most of them new to combat, are thrown into the face of withering German fire. The landing on Omaha Beach was not about saving Private Ryan. It was about saving your ass.

The movie's opening sequence is as graphic as any war footage I've ever seen. In fierce dread and energy it's on a par with Oliver Stone's *Platoon*, and in scope surpasses it—because in the bloody early stages the landing forces and the enemy never meet eye to eye, but are simply faceless masses of men who have been ordered to shoot at one another until one side is destroyed.

Spielberg's camera makes no sense of the action. That is the purpose of his style. For the individual soldier on the beach, the landing was a chaos of noise, mud, blood, vomit, and death. The scene is filled with countless unrelated pieces of time, as when a soldier has his arm blown off. He staggers, confused, standing exposed to further fire, not sure what to do

next, and then he bends over and picks up his arm, as if he will need it later.

This landing sequence is necessary in order to establish the distance between those who give the order that Private Ryan be saved, and those who are ordered to do the saving. For Captain Miller (Tom Hanks) and his men, the landing at Omaha has been a crucible of fire. For Army Chief George C. Marshall (Harve Presnell), in his Washington office, war seems more remote and statesmanlike; he treasures a letter Abraham Lincoln wrote consoling Mrs. Bixby of Boston about her sons who died in the Civil War. His advisers question the wisdom and indeed the possibility of a mission to save Ryan, but he barks, "If the boy's alive we are gonna send somebody to find him—and we are gonna get him the hell out of there."

That sets up the second act of the film, in which Miller and his men penetrate into French terrain still actively disputed by the Germans, while harboring mutinous thoughts about the wisdom of the mission. All of Miller's men have served with him before—except for Corporal Upham (Jeremy Davies), the translator, who speaks excellent German and French but has never fired a rifle in anger and is terrified almost to the point of incontinence. (I identified with Upham, and I suspect many honest viewers will agree with me: The war was fought by civilians just like him, whose lives had not prepared them for the reality of battle.)

The turning point in the film comes, I think, when the squadron happens upon a German machine-gun nest protecting a radar installation. It would be possible to go around it and avoid a confrontation. Indeed, that would be following orders. But they decide to attack the emplacement, and that is a form of protest: At risk to their lives, they are doing what they came to France to do, instead of what the top brass wants them to do.

Everything points to the third act, when Private Ryan is found and the soldiers decide what to do next. Spielberg and his screenwriter, Robert Rodat, have done a subtle and rather beautiful thing: They have made a philosophical film about war almost entirely in terms of action. *Saving Private Ryan* says things about war that are as complex and difficult as any essayist could possibly express, and does it with broad, strong images, with violence, with profanity, with action, with camaraderie. It is possible to express even the most thoughtful ideas in the simplest words and actions, and that's what Spielberg does. The film is doubly effective because he communicates his ideas in feelings, not words. I was reminded of *All Quiet on the Western Front.*

Steven Spielberg is as technically proficient as any filmmaker alive, and because of his great success he has access to every resource he requires. Both of those facts are important to the impact of *Saving Private Ryan.* He knows how to convey his feelings about men in combat, and he has the tools, the money, and the collaborators to make it possible.

His cinematographer, Janusz Kaminski, who also shot *Schindler's List,* brings a newsreel feel to a lot of the footage, but that's relatively easy compared to his most important achievement, which is to make everything visually intelligible. After the deliberate chaos of the landing scenes, Kaminski handles the attack on the machine-gun nest, and a prolonged sequence involving the defense of a bridge, in a way that keeps us oriented. It's not just men shooting at one another. We understand the plan of the action, the ebb and flow, the improvisation, the relative positions of the soldiers.

Then there is the human element. Hanks is a good choice as Captain Miller, an English teacher who has survived experiences so unspeakable that he wonders if his wife will even recognize him. His hands tremble, he is on the brink of a breakdown, but he does his best because that is his duty. All of the actors playing the men under him are effective, partly because Spielberg resists the temptation to make them zany "characters" in the tradition of World War II movies, and makes them deliberately ordinary. Matt Damon, as Private Ryan, exudes a different energy because he has not been through the landing at Omaha Beach; as a paratrooper, he landed inland, and although he has seen action, he has not gazed into the inferno.

They are all strong presences, but for me the key performance in the movie is by Jeremy Davies, as the frightened little interpreter. He is our entry into the reality because he sees the war clearly as a vast system designed to humiliate and destroy him. And so it is. His survival depends on his doing the very best he can, yes, but even more on chance. Eventually he arrives at his personal turning point, and his action writes the closing words of Spielberg's unspoken philosophical argument.

Saving Private Ryan is a powerful experience. I'm sure a lot of people will weep during it. Spielberg knows how to make audiences weep better than any director since Chaplin in *City Lights.* But weeping is an incomplete response, letting the audience off the hook. This film embodies ideas. After the immediate experience begins to fade, the implications remain, and grow.

Say Amen, Somebody

G, 100 m., 1983

Featuring Willie May Ford Smith, Thomas A. Dorsey, Sallie Martin, the Barrett Sisters, Edward and Edgar O'Neal, and Zella Jackson Price. Directed by George Nierenberg and produced by George and Karen Nierenberg.

Say Amen, Somebody is one of the most joyful movies I've ever seen. It is also one of the best musicals and one of the most interesting documentaries. And it's a terrific good time. The movie is about gospel music, and it's filled with gospel music. It's sung by some of the pioneers of modern gospel, who are now in their seventies and eighties, and it's sung by some of the rising younger stars, and it's sung by choirs of kids. It's sung in churches and around the dining room table; with orchestras and a capella; by an old man named Thomas A. Dorsey in front of thousands of people; and by Dorsey standing all by himself in his own backyard. The music in *Say Amen, Somebody* is as exciting and uplifting as any music I've ever heard on film.

The people in this movie are something, too. The filmmaker, a young New Yorker named George T. Nierenberg, starts by introducing us to two pioneers of modern gospel: Mother Willie May Ford Smith, who is seventy-nine, and Professor Dorsey, who is eighty-three. She was one of the first gospel soloists; he is known as the Father of Gospel Music. The film opens at tributes to the two of them—Mother Smith in a St. Louis church, Dorsey at a Houston convention—and then Nierenberg cuts back and forth between their memories, their families, their music, and the music sung in tribute to them by younger performers.

That keeps the movie from seeming too much like the wrong kind of documentary—the kind that feels like an educational film and is filled with boring lists of dates and places. *Say Amen, Somebody* never stops moving, and even the dates and places are open to controversy (there's a hilarious sequence in which Dorsey and Mother Smith disagree very pointedly over exactly which of them convened the first gospel convention).

What's amazing in all of the musical sequences is the quality of the sound. A lot of documentaries use "available sound," picked up by microphones more appropriate for the television news. This movie's concerts are miked by up to eight microphones, and the Dolby system is used to produce full stereo sound that really rocks. Run it through your stereo speakers, and play it loud.

Willie May Ford Smith comes across in this movie as an extraordinary woman, spiritual, filled with love and power. Dorsey and his longtime business manager, Sallie Martin, come across at first as a little crusty, but then there's a remarkable scene where they sing along, softly, with one of Dorsey's old records. By the end of the film, when the ailing Dorsey insists on walking under his own steam to the front of the gospel convention in Houston, and leading the delegates in a hymn, we have come to see his strength and humanity. Just in case Smith and Dorsey seem too noble, the film uses a lot of mighty soul music as a counterpoint, particularly in the scenes shot during a tribute to Mother Smith at a St. Louis Baptist church. We see Delois Barrett Campbell and the Barrett Sisters, a Chicago-based trio who have enormous musical energy; the O'Neal Twins, Edward and Edgar, whose "Jesus Dropped the Charges" is a showstopper; Zella Jackson Price, a younger singer who turns to Mother Smith for advice; the Interfaith Choir; and lots of other singers.

Say Amen, Somebody is the kind of movie that isn't made very often, because it takes an unusual combination of skills. The filmmaker has to be able to identify and find his subjects, win their confidence, follow them around, and then also find the technical skill to really capture what makes them special. Nierenberg's achievement here is a masterpiece of research, diligence, and direction. But his work would be meaningless if the movie didn't convey the spirit of the people in it, and *Say Amen, Somebody* does that with great and mighty joy. This is a great experience.

Say Anything

PG-13, 103 m., 1989

John Cusack (Lloyd Dobler), Ione Skye (Diane Court), John Mahoney (James Court), Lili Taylor (Corey Flood), Amy Brooks (D. C.), Pamela Segall (Rebecca), Jason Gould (Mike Cameron), Loren Dean (Joe). Directed by Cameron Crowe and produced by Polly Platt. Screenplay by Crowe.

She is the class brain, and so, of course, no one can see that she is truly beautiful—no one except for the sort of weird kid who wants to devote his life to kick-boxing, and who likes her because of her brains. He calls her up and asks her out. She says no. He keeps talking. She says yes. And after their first date, she tells her father she likes him because he is utterly straightforward and dependable. He is a goofy teenager with absolutely no career prospects, but she senses that she can trust him as an anchor.

She discusses him so openly with her father because they have made a pact: They can say anything to one another. When her parents got divorced, she chose to live with her father because of this trust, because of the openness that he encourages. Her father's love for her is equaled by his respect. And she sees him as a good man, who works long hours running a nursing home because he wants to help people.

Honesty is at the core of *Say Anything*, but dishonesty is there, too, and the movie is the story of how the young woman is able to weather a terrible storm and be stronger and better afterward. This was one of the best films of 1989—a film that is really about something, that cares deeply about the issues it contains—and yet it also works wonderfully as a funny, warmhearted romantic comedy.

The young woman, Diane, is played by Ione Skye as a straight-A student with a scholarship to a school in England. She is one of the class beauties, but doesn't date much because she intimidates boys. The boy who finally asks her out is Lloyd (John Cusack), and he dates her not only out of hormonal urging, but because he admires her. Her father (John Mahoney) is a caring, trusting parent who will do anything he can to encourage his daughter—but his secret is that he has done too much. They find that out when IRS agents come knocking on the door with charges of criminal tax evasion.

The movie treats Diane's two relationships with equal seriousness. This is not one of those movies where the father is a dim-witted, middle-aged buffoon with no insights into real life, and it is also not one of those movies where the young man is obviously the hero. Everyone in this film is complicated, and has problems, and is willing to work at life and try to make it better.

The romance between Diane and Lloyd is intelligent and filled with that special curiosity that happens when two young people find each other not only attractive but interesting—when they sense they might actually be able to learn something useful from the other person. Lloyd has no career plans, no educational plans, no plans except to become a champion kick-boxer, and then, after he meets Diane, to support her because she is worthy of his dedication. In the way they trust each other and learn to depend on each other, their relationship reminded me of the equally complex teenage love story between River Phoenix and Martha Plimpton in *Running on Empty.*

What's unique to this movie is how sure-footed it is in presenting the ordinary everyday lives and rituals of kids in their late teens. The parties, the conversations, and the value systems seem real and carefully observed; these teenagers are not simply empty-headed *Animal House* retreads; the movie pays them the compliment of seeing them as actual people with opinions and futures.

Cameron Crowe, who wrote and directed the film, develops its underlying ideas with a precise subtlety. This is not a melodrama about two kids who fall in love and a parent who gets in trouble with the IRS. It considers the story as if it were actually happening, with all the uncertainties of real life. When Diane goes in to confront a government agent, and tells him that he is harassing her father who is a good man, Crowe allows the scene to develop so that we can see more than one possibility; he even cares enough to give the IRS agent—a minor character—three dimensions.

I was also surprised to find that the movie had a third act and a concluding scene that really concluded something. Today's standard movie script contains a setup, some development, and then some kind of violent or comic cataclysm that is intended to pass for a resolution. *Say Anything* follows all the threads of its story through to the end; we're interested in what happens to the characters, and so is the movie.

The performances are perfectly suited to the characters. Ione Skye—who was a model before she was an actress—successfully creates the kind of teenage girl who is over-looked in high school because she doesn't have the surface glitz of the cheerleaders, but who emerges at the tenth class reunion as a world-class beauty. John Cusack, a unique, quirky actor with great individuality, turns in a fast-talking, intensely felt performance that is completely original; he is so good here that if you haven't seen him in *The Sure Thing* or *Eight Men Out,* you might imagine he is simply playing himself. But his performance is a complete and brilliant invention. And John Mahoney (Olympia Dukakis's sad eyed would-be swain in *Moonstruck*) finds the right note for a father who cares, and loves, and deceives both himself and his daughter, and tries to rationalize his behavior *because* he cares and loves.

Say Anything is one of those rare movies that has something to teach us about life. It doesn't have a "lesson" or a "message," but it observes its moral choices so carefully that it helps us see our own. That such intelligence could be contained in a movie that is simultaneously so funny and so entertaining is some kind of a miracle.

Scandal

R, 112 m., 1989

John Hurt (Stephen Ward), Joanne Whalley-Kilmer (Christine Keeler), Bridget Fonda (Mandy Rice-Davies), Ian McKellen (John Profumo), Leslie Phillips (Lord

Astor), Britt Ekland (Mariella Novotny), Daniel Massey (Mervyn Griffith-Jones), Roland Gift (Johnnie Edgecombe), Jean Alexander (Mrs. Keeler). Directed by Michael Caton-Jones and produced by Stephen Woolley. Screenplay by Michael Thomas.

All Stephen Ward ever really wanted to do in life was to move in the right circles, with the right friends, and be left in peace and quiet. His strategy for gaining admission to the world of British society was unorthodox, but not unkind. He found young women with promise but no prospects, and then he groomed them, coached them, took them to the right places, and introduced them to his important friends.

He was, in a sense, the Henry Higgins of his time, and his most successful Eliza Doolittle was a poor but pretty girl he discovered in a strip show. Her name was Christine Keeler, and he lovingly transformed her into a desirable companion for cabinet members, diplomats, and the aristocracy. His only miscalculation was to allow her to sleep with the British defense minister and a Russian military attache during the same period. That was a mistake that brought down a government, and cost Ward his life.

Scandal tells the story of Stephen Ward with a great deal of sympathy for his motives, and a great deal of anger against the British establishment. Although Ward was convicted of living off the earnings of a prostitute—a decision handed down after he committed suicide in the middle of his trial—the film argues that he never accepted any meaningful sums of money from anybody, and his only real motive, a rather touching one, was to do a favor for both the girls and his famous friends. If his method for doing that—arranging illicit sexual relationships—was unconventional or unsavory, let it be noted that none of the participants on either side of the bargain made the slightest complaint until they found their faces on the front pages of the newspapers.

The facts of the Ward affair are part of modern British history. Christine Keeler and her friend, Mandy Rice-Davies, moved in circles that included some of the most famous and powerful men of their time. After one of them, Defense Minister John Profumo, admitted that he had lied to Parliament about his involvement with Keeler, he was forced to resign, and eventually the widening scandal brought down the Conservative government of Harold Macmillan. The movie *Scandal* argues that a scapegoat had to be found to contain the outrage—and Ward, a harmless and gentle osteopath, was the victim. So efficiently and ruthlessly did the establishment circle its wagons to defend itself that even now, twenty-five years later, attempts to make *Scandal* as a TV miniseries were blocked in England, and it has finally appeared as a movie—as a political melodrama that is also an unexpectedly touching love story between almost the only two major players in the episode who never slept with one another, Ward and Keeler.

The movie's strength is that it is surprisingly wise about the complexities of the human heart. Although the newspapers scorned Keeler's claim that she and Ward were simply "close friends," the movie argues that that was quite possible, and true: She felt gratitude for his decision to pluck her from obscurity and groom her for a kind of stardom, and she believed, if she did not fully understand, that his only reward was in seeing his creation pass, respected and unquestioned, in the highest circles. Since England is one of the most class-conscious nations on earth, this sort of transfer in social strata has a powerful hold on the national imagination (cf. the Ascot scene in *My Fair Lady,* with Eliza testing her upperclass accent).

The movie stars John Hurt in one of the best performances of his career as Ward, the chain-smoking, shabbily genteel doctor, who lives in a coach house with Keeler but spends his weekends as the guest of such friends as Lord Astor, who gave him the key to a guest cottage on his estate. In an early scene, Hurt's eyes light up as he sees a pretty girl walking down the street, and somehow Hurt is able to make us understand that he feels, not lust, but simply a deep and genuine appreciation for how wonderful a pretty girl can look on a fine spring day.

Christine Keeler is played by Joanne Whalley-Kilmer, an actress previously unknown to me, and she walks a fine line with great confidence, seeming neither innocent nor sluttish, but more of a smart, ambitious, and essentially honest young woman who finds that it is no more unpleasant to sleep with rich and important men than with her poor and obscure boyfriend. Mandy Rice-Davies (Bridget Fonda) is a different type of woman, more calculating, more cynical, and probably more intelligent, and perhaps it is no accident that Rice-Davies has gone on to a certain success in business and society during the last twenty-five years, while Keeler has returned to a form of the anonymity from which Ward tried to rescue her.

Some of the most evocative scenes in the movie involve backstage moments between the two women, when they casually discuss their lovers, plan their lives, and pay the most painstaking attention to their faces. These women apply themselves more voluptuously to their makeup than to any of the men in their lives.

The movie, written by Michael Thomas and directed by Michael Caton-Jones, has the feeling of having been made from the inside. It moves effortlessly through the mine fields of British government and society, capturing such nuances as the way in which Lord Astor summons Ward to his club to inform him, shamefacedly, that the scandal has forced him to ask for the return of the key to his cottage. Always circling outside the walls of this inner sanctum are the rabble of the British gutter press—and even as a fellow newspaperman, I am willing to describe them in that way, because there is a certain level of decency in news-gathering which they seem never to have glimpsed.

Scandal is a sad story about human nature, which understands why people sometimes sleep in the wrong beds, and takes note that this is understood privately, but not publicly. When the light of day shines on these affairs, lives are destroyed. The saddest moment in the movie comes in the final courtroom scene, when Keeler is called as a witness and is mercilessly battered by the prosecutor until finally Ward stands up in the defendant's box and cries out, "That is not fair!" That is the cry of this movie.

Scarface

R, 170 m., 1983

Al Pacino (Tony Montana), Steven Bauer (Manny Ray), Michelle Pfeiffer (Elvira), Mary Elizabeth Mastrantonio (Gina), Robert Loggia (Frank Lopez). Directed by Brian De Palma and produced by Martin Bregman. Screenplay by Oliver Stone.

The interesting thing is the way Tony Montana stays in the memory, taking on the dimensions of a real, tortured person. Most thrillers use interchangeable characters, and most gangster movies are more interested in action than personality, but *Scarface* is one of those special movies, like *The Godfather,* that is willing to take a flawed, evil man and allow him to be human. Maybe it's no coincidence that Montana is played by Al Pacino, the same actor who played Michael Corleone. Montana is a punk from Cuba. The opening scene of the movie informs us that when Cuban refugees were allowed to come to America in 1981, Fidel Castro had his own little private revenge and cleaned out his prison cells, sending us criminals along with his weary and huddled masses. We see Montana trying to bluff his way through an interrogation by U.S. federal agents, and that's basically what he'll do for the whole movie: bluff. He has no real character and no real courage, although for a short time cocaine gives him the illusion of both.

Scarface takes its title from the 1932 Howard Hawks movie, which was inspired by the career of Al Capone. That Hawks film was the most violent gangster film of its time, and this 1983 film by Brian De Palma also has been surrounded by a controversy over its violence, but in both movies the violence grows out of the lives of the characters; it isn't used for thrills but for a sort of harrowing lesson about self-destruction. Both movies are about the rise and fall of a gangster, and they both make much of the hero's neurotic obsession with his sister, but the 1983 *Scarface* isn't a remake, and it owes more to *The Godfather* than to Hawks.

That's because it sees its criminal so clearly as a person with a popular product to sell, working in a society that wants to buy. In the old days it was booze. For the Corleones, it was gambling and prostitution. Now it's cocaine. The message for the dealer remains the same: Only a fool gets hooked on his own goods. For Tony Montana, the choices seem simple at first. He can work hard, be honest, and make a humble wage as a dishwasher. Or he can work for organized crime, make himself more vicious than his competitors and get the big cars, the beautiful women, and the bootlicking attention from nightclub doormen. He doesn't wash many dishes.

As Montana works his way into the south Florida illegal drug trade, the movie observes him with almost anthropological detachment. This isn't one of those movies where the characters all come with labels attached ("boss," "lieutenant," "hit man") and behave exactly as we expect them to. De Palma and his writer, Oliver Stone, have created a gallery of specific individuals and one of the fascinations of the movie is that we aren't watching crime-movie clichés, we're watching people who are criminals.

Al Pacino does not make Montana into a sympathetic character, but he does make him into somebody we can identify with, in a horrified way, if only because of his perfectly understandable motivations. Wouldn't we all like to be rich and powerful, have desirable sex partners, live in a mansion, be catered to by faithful servants—and hardly have to work? Well, yeah, now that you mention it. Dealing drugs offers the possibility of such a lifestyle, but it also involves selling your soul. Montana gets it all and he loses it all. That's predictable. What is original about this movie is the attention it gives to how little Montana enjoys it while he has it. Two scenes are truly pathetic; in one of them, he sits in a nightclub with his blond mistress and his faithful sidekick, and he's so wiped out on cocaine that the only emotions he can really feel are impatience and boredom. In the other one, trying for a desperate transfusion of energy, he plunges his face into a pile of cocaine and inhales as if he were a drowning man.

Scarface understands this criminal personality, with its links between laziness and ruthlessness, grandiosity and low self-esteem, pipe dreams and a chronic inability to be happy. It's also an exciting crime picture, in the tradition of the 1932 movie. And, like the Godfather movies, it's a gallery of wonderful supporting performances: Steven Bauer as a sidekick, Michelle Pfeiffer as a woman whose need for drugs leads her from one wrong lover to another, Robert Loggia as a mob boss who isn't quite vicious enough, and Mary Elizabeth Mastrantonio, as Pacino's kid sister who

wants the right to self-destruct in the manner of her own choosing. These are the people Tony Montana deserves in his life, and *Scarface* is a wonderful portrait of a real louse.

Scenes from a Marriage
PG, 168 m., 1974

Liv Ullmann (Marianne), Erland Josephson (Johan), Bibi Andersson (Katarina), Jan Malmslo (Peter). Directed by Ingmar Bergman.

They have reached a truce which they call happiness. When we first meet them, they're being interviewed for some sort of newspaper article, and they agree that after ten years of marriage, they're a truly happy couple. The husband, Johan, is most sure: He is successful in his work, in love with his wife, the father of two daughters, liked by his friends, considered on all sides to be a decent chap. His wife, Marianne, listens more tentatively. When it is her turn, she says she is happy, too, although in her work she would like to move in the direction of—but then she's interrupted for a photograph. We are never quite sure what she might have said, had she been allowed to speak as long as her husband. And, truth to tell, he doesn't seem to care much himself. Although theirs is, of course, a perfect marriage.

And so begins one of the truest, most luminous love stories ever made, Ingmar Bergman's *Scenes from a Marriage*. The marriage of Johan and Marianne will disintegrate soon after the film begins, but their love will not. They will fight and curse each other, and it will be a wicked divorce, but in some fundamental way they have touched, really touched, and the memory of that touching will be something to hold to all of their days.

Bergman has been working for years with the theme of communication between two people. At one time, he referred to it as "the agony of the couple." And who can forget the terrible recriminations and psychic bloodshed of the couples in *Winter Light* or *The Passion of Anna*? And here he seems finally to have resolved his crisis.

The years that preceded the making of this film saw a remarkable conciliation going on within the work of this great artist. In *Cries and Whispers,* he was at last able to face the fact of death in a world where God seemed silent. And now, in this almost heartbreaking masterpiece, he has dealt with his fear that all men are, indeed, islands. The film (168 minutes, skillfully and without distraction edited down from six, fifty-minute Swedish television programs) took him four months to make, he has said, but a lifetime to experience.

His married couple are Swedish upper-middle-class. He is a professor, she is a lawyer specializing in family problems (for which, read divorce). They have two daughters, who remain offscreen. They are intelligent, independent. She truly believes their marriage is a happy one (although she doesn't much enjoy sex). One evening, he comes to their summer cottage and confesses that he has gone and fallen in love with someone else. There is nothing to be done about it. He must leave her.

The way in which his wife reacts to this information displays the almost infinite range of Liv Ullmann, who is a beautiful soul and a gifted performer. Her husband (Erland Josephson) has left her literally without an alternative ("You have shut me out. How can I help us?") and still she loves him. She fears that he will bring unhappiness upon himself.

But he does leave, and the film's form is a sometimes harsh, sometimes gentle, ultimately romantic (in an adult and realistic way) view of the stages of this relationship. At first, their sexual attraction for each other remains, even though they bitterly resent each other because of mutual hurts and recriminations. The frustrations they feel about themselves are taken out on each other. At one point, he beats her and weeps for himself, and we've never seen such despair on the screen. But the passage of time dulls the immediate hurt and the feeling of betrayal. And at last, they are able to meet as fond friends and even to make love, as if visiting an old home they'd once been cozy in.

They drift apart, they marry other people (who also remain offscreen), they meet from time to time.

Ten years after the film has opened, they find themselves in Stockholm while both their spouses are out of the country, and, as a nostalgic lark, decide to spend a weekend in their old summer cottage. But it's haunted with memories, and they go to a cottage nearby.

In the last section of the film (subtitled "In the Middle of the Night in a Dark House"), Marianne awakens screaming with a nightmare, and Johan holds her.

And this is twenty years after they were married, and ten years after they were divorced, and they are in middle age now but in the night still fond and frightened lovers holding on for reassurance.

And that is what Bergman has been able to accept, the source of his reconciliation: Beyond love, beyond marriage, beyond the selfishness that destroys love, beyond the centrifugal force that sends egos whirling away from each other and prevents enduring relationships—beyond all these things, there still remains what we know of each other, that we care about each other, that in twenty years these people have touched and known so deeply that they still remember, and still need.

Marianne and Johan are only married for the first part of this film, but the rest of it is also scenes from their marriage.

The Scent of Green Papaya

NO MPAA RATING, 103 m., 1994

Tran Nu Yen-Khe (Mui at Twenty), Lu Man San (Mui at Ten), Truong Thi Loc (The Mother), Nguyen Anh Hoa (Thi, the Old Servant Woman), Vuong Hoa Hoi (Khuyen), Tran Ngoc Trung (The Father), Talisman Vantha (Thu). Directed by Tran Anh Hung and produced by Christophe Rossignon. Screenplay by Hung.

Here is a film so placid and filled with sweetness that watching it is like listening to soothing music. *The Scent of Green Papaya* takes place in Vietnam between the late 1940s and early 1960s, and is seen through the eyes of a poor young woman who is taken as a servant into the household of a merchant family. She observes everything around her in minute detail, and gradually, as she flowers into a beautiful woman, her simple goodness impresses her more hurried and cynical employers.

The woman, named Mui, is an orphan—a child, when she first comes to work for the family. She learns her tasks quickly and well, and performs them so unobtrusively that sometimes she seems almost like a spirit. But she is a very real person, uncomplaining, all-seeing, and the film watches her world through her eyes. For her, there is beauty in the smallest details: a drop of water trembling on a leaf, a line of busy ants, a selfimportant frog in a puddle left by the rain, the sunlight through the green leaves outside the window, the scent of green papaya.

We understand the workings of the household only through her eyes. We see that the father drinks and is unfaithful, and that the mother runs the business and the family. We see unhappiness, and we also see that the mother comes to think of Mui with a special love—she is like a daughter. As Mui grows and the family's fortunes fade, the routine in the household nevertheless continues unchanged, until a day when the father is dead and the business in disarray. Then Mui is sent to work as the servant of a young man who is a friend of the family.

She has known this young man for a long time, ever since they both were children. He was the playmate of her employer's son. Now he has grown into a sleek and sophisticated man about town, a classical pianist, French-speaking, with an expensive mistress. Mui serves him as she served her first family, quietly and perfectly. And we see through small signs that she loves him. These signs are at first not visible to the man.

The Scent of Green Papaya, which was one of 1994's Oscar nominees in the Foreign Language category, is first of all a film of great visual beauty; watching it is like seeing a poem for the eyes. All of the action, indoors and out, is set in Saigon in the period before the Vietnam War, but what is astonishing is that this entire film was made in Paris, on a sound stage. Everything we see is a set. There is a tradition in Asian films of sets that are obviously artificial (see *Kwaidan*, with its artificial snowfalls and forests). But the sets for *Green Papaya* are so convincing that at first we think we are occupying a small, secluded corner of a real city.

The director, Tran Anh Hung, undoubtedly found it impossible to make a film of this type in today's Vietnam, which is hardly nostalgic for the colonial era. That is one reason he recreated his period piece on a sound stage. Another reason may be that he wanted to achieve a kind of visual perfection that real life seldom approaches; every small detail of his frame is idealized in an understated but affecting way, so that Mui's physical world seduces us as much as her beauty.

Some will prefer the first two-thirds of the film to the conclusion: There is a purity to the observation of Mui's daily world that has a power of its own. Toward the end of the film, plot begins to enter, and we begin to wonder when the young pianist will notice the beautiful woman who lives under his roof and loves him so. There is an old, old movie tradition of the scene where a man suddenly sees a woman through fresh eyes, and realizes that the love he has been looking everywhere for is standing right there in front of him. These scenes can be laughable, but they can also sometimes be moving, and when that moment arrives in *The Scent of Green Papaya*, it has been so carefully prepared that there is a true joy to it.

There is another scene of great gladness, when the man begins to teach the young woman to read. So deep is the romanticism of the film that we almost question whether this is an advancement for her: Her simplicity, her unity of self and world, is so deep that perhaps literacy will only be a distraction. It is one of the film's gifts to inspire questions like that.

I have seen *The Scent of Green Papaya* three times now—the first time in May 1994 at Cannes, where it was named the best film by a first-time director. It is a placid, interior, contemplative film—not plot-driven, but centered on the growth of the young woman. As such, you might think it would seem "slower" on later viewings, but I found that the opposite was true: As I understood better what the movie was, I appreciated it more because, like a piece of music, it was made of subtleties that only grew deeper through familiarity. This is a film to cherish.

Schindler's List
R, 184 m., 1993

Liam Neeson (Oskar Schindler), Ben Kingsley (Itzhak Stern), Ralph Fiennes (Amon Goeth), Caroline Goodall (Emilie Schindler), Jonathan Sagalle (Poldek Pfefferberg), Embeth Davidtz (Helen Hirsch). Directed by Steven Spielberg and produced by Spielberg, Gerald R. Molen, and Branko Lustig. Screenplay by Steven Zaillian, based on the book by Thomas Keneally.

Oskar Schindler would have been an easier man to understand if he'd been a conventional hero, fighting for his beliefs. The fact that he was flawed—a drinker, a gambler, a womanizer, driven by greed and a lust for high living—makes his life an enigma. Here is a man who saw his chance at the beginning of World War II, and moved to Nazi-occupied Poland to open a factory and employ Jews at starvation wages. His goal was to become a millionaire. By the end of the war, he had risked his life and spent his fortune to save those Jews, and had defrauded the Nazis for months with a munitions factory that never produced a single usable shell.

Why did he change? What happened to turn him from a victimizer into a humanitarian? It is to the great credit of Steven Spielberg that his film *Schindler's List* does not even attempt to answer that question. Any possible answer would be too simple, an insult to the mystery of Schindler's life. The Holocaust was a vast evil engine set whirling by racism and madness. Schindler outsmarted it, in his own little corner of the war, but he seems to have had no plan, to have improvised out of impulses that remained unclear even to himself. In this movie, the best he has ever made, Spielberg treats the fact of the Holocaust and the miracle of Schindler's feat without the easy formulas of fiction.

The movie is 184 minutes long, and like all great movies, it seems too short. It begins with Schindler (Liam Neeson), a tall, strong man with an intimidating physical presence. He dresses expensively and frequents nightclubs, buying caviar and champagne for Nazi officers and their girls, and he likes to get his picture taken with the top brass. He wears a Nazi Party emblem proudly in his buttonhole. He has impeccable black market contacts, and is always able to find nylons, cigarettes, brandy: He is the right man to know. The authorities are happy to help him open a factory to build enameled cooking utensils which army kitchens can use. He is happy to hire Jews because their wages are lower, and Schindler will get richer that way.

Schindler's genius is in bribing, scheming, conning. He knows nothing about running a factory, and finds Itzhak Stern (Ben Kingsley), a Jewish accountant, to handle that side of things. Stern moves through the streets of Krakow, hiring Jews for Schindler. Because the factory is a protected war industry, a job there may be a guarantee of a longer life.

The relationship between Schindler and Stern is developed by Spielberg with enormous subtlety. At the beginning of the war, Schindler wants only to make money, and at the end he wants only to save "his" Jews. We know that Stern understands this. But there is no moment when Schindler and Stern bluntly state what is happening, perhaps because to say certain things aloud could result in death.

This subtlety is Spielberg's strength all through the film. His screenplay, by Steven Zaillian, based on the novel by Thomas Keneally, isn't based on contrived melodrama. Instead, Spielberg relies on a series of incidents, seen clearly and without artificial manipulation, and by witnessing those incidents we understand what little can be known about Schindler and his scheme.

We also see the Holocaust in a vivid and terrible way. Spielberg gives us a Nazi prison camp commandant named Goeth (Ralph Fiennes), who is a study in the stupidity of evil. From the veranda of his "villa," overlooking the prison yard, he shoots Jews for target practice. (Schindler is able to talk him out of this custom with an appeal to his vanity so obvious it is almost an insult.)

Goeth is one of those weak hypocrites who upholds an ideal but makes himself an exception to it; he preaches the death of the Jews, and then chooses a pretty one named Helen Hirsch (Embeth Davidtz) to be his maid, and falls in love with her. He does not find it monstrous that her people are being exterminated and she is spared on his affectionate whim. He sees his personal needs as more important than right or wrong, life or death. Studying him, we realize that Nazism depended on people able to think like Jeffrey Dahmer.

Shooting in black and white on many of the actual locations of the events in the story (including Schindler's original factory and even the gates of Auschwitz), Spielberg shows Schindler dealing with the madness of the Nazi system. He bribes, he wheedles, he bluffs, he escapes discovery by the skin of his teeth. In the movie's most audacious sequence, when a trainload of his employees is mistakenly routed to Auschwitz, he walks into the death camp himself and brazenly talks the authorities out of their victims, snatching them from death and putting them back on the train to his factory.

What is most amazing about this film is how completely Spielberg serves his story. The movie is brilliantly acted, written, directed, and seen. Individual scenes are masterpieces of art direction, cinematography, special effects, crowd control. Yet Spielberg, the stylist whose films have often gloried in shots we are intended to notice and remember, disappears into his work. Neeson, Kingsley, and the other actors are devoid of acting flourishes. There is a single-mindedness to the enterprise that is awesome.

At the end of the film, there is a sequence of overwhelming emotional impact, involving the actual people who were saved by Schindler. We learn then "Schindler's Jews" and their descendants today number some six thousand, and that the Jewish population of Poland is four thousand. The obvious lesson would seem to be that Schindler did more than a whole nation to spare its Jews. That would be too simple. The film's message is that one man did *something*, while in the face of the Holocaust, others were paralyzed. Perhaps it took a Schindler, enigmatic and reckless, without a plan, heedless of risk, a con man, to do what he did. No rational man with a sensible plan would have gotten as far.

The French author Flaubert once wrote that he disliked *Uncle Tom's Cabin* because the author was constantly preaching against slavery. "Does one have to make observations about slavery?" he asked. "Depict it; that's enough." And then he added, "An author in his book must be like God in the universe, present everywhere and visible nowhere." That would describe Spielberg, the author of this film. He depicts the evil of the Holocaust, and he tells an incredible story of how it was robbed of some of its intended victims. He does so without the tricks of his trade, the directorial and dramatic contrivances that would inspire the usual melodramatic payoffs. Spielberg is not visible in this film. But his restraint and passion are present in every shot.

School of Rock

PG-13, 108 m., 2003

Jack Black (Dewey Finn), Joan Cusack (Rosalie Mullins), Mike White (Ned Schneebly), Sarah Silverman (Patty), Joey Gaydos (Zack), Miranda Cosgrove (Summer), Maryam Hassan (Tomika), Kevin Clark (Kevin), Rebecca Brown (Katie), Robert Tsai (Lawrence),Brian Falduto (Billy). Directed by Richard Linklater and produced by Scott Rudin. Screenplay by White.

Jack Black is a living, breathing, sweating advertisement for the transformative power of rock and roll in *School of Rock*, the first kid movie that parents will like more than their children. He plays Dewey Finn, failed rocker, just kicked out of the band he founded. Rock is his life. When he fakes his way into a job as a substitute fifth-grade teacher, he ignores the lesson plans and turns the class into a rock band; when the kids ask about tests, he promises them that rock "will test your head, and your mind, and your brain, too."

Now that's a cute premise, and you probably think you can guess more or less what the movie will be like. But you would be way wrong, because *School of Rock* is as serious as it can be about its comic subject, and never condescends to its characters or its audience. The kids aren't turned into cloying little clones, but remain stubborn, uncertain, insecure, and kidlike. And Dewey Finn doesn't start as a disreputable character and then turn gooey. Jack Black remains true to his irascible character all the way through; he makes Dewey's personality not a plot gimmick, but a way of life.

If quirky, independent, grown-up outsider filmmakers set out to make a family movie, this is the kind of movie they would make. And they did. The director is Richard Linklater *(Dazed and Confused, Before Sunrise)*, the indie genius of Austin, Texas, who made *Waking Life* in his garage and revolutionized animation by showing that a commercial film could be made at home with a digital camera and a Macintosh. The writer and costar is Mike White, who since 2000 has also written *Chuck and Buck, Orange County* (which costarred Black as a rebel couch potato), and the brilliant *The Good Girl*, with Jennifer Aniston as a married discount clerk who falls in love with the cute checkout kid.

White's movies lovingly celebrate the comic peculiarities of everyday people, and his Dewey Finn is a goofy original—a slugabed who complains, when his roommate (White) asks for the rent, "I've been mooching off of you for years!" He truly believes that rock, especially classic rock, will heal you and make you whole. His gods include Led Zeppelin, The Ramones, and The Who. His own career reaches a nadir when he ends a solo by jumping ecstatically off the stage and the indifferent audience lets him fall to the floor.

He needs money. A school calls for his roommate, he fakes his identity, and later that day is facing a suspicious group of ten-year-olds and confiding, "I've got a terrible hangover." It's an expensive private school, their parents pay $15,000 a year in tuition, and Summer (Miranda Cosgrove), the smarty-pants in the front row, asks, "Are you gonna teach us anything, or are we just gonna sit here?"

The class files out for band practice, Dewey listens to their anemic performance of classical chestnuts, and has a brainstorm: He'll convert them into a rock group and enter them in a local radio station's Battle of the Bands.

The movie takes music seriously. Dewey assigns instruments to the talented students, including keyboardist Lawrence (Robert Tsai), lead guitarist Zack (Joey Gaydos), drummer Kevin (Kevin Clark), and backup singer Tomika (Maryam Hassan), who is shy because of her weight. "You have an issue with *weight?*" Dewey asks. "You know who else has a weight issue? *Me*! But I get up there on the stage and start to sing, and people *worship* me!"

There's a job for everyone. Billy (Brian Falduto) wants to be the band's designer, and produces glitter rock costumes that convince Dewey the school uniforms don't look so bad. Busybody Summer is made the band's manager. Three girls are assigned to be groupies, and when they complain that groupies are sluts, Dewey defines them as more like cheerleaders.

Of course there is a school principal. She is Rosalie Mullins (Joan Cusack) and, miraculously, she isn't the standard old prune that movies like this usually supply, but a good soul who loves her school and has been rumored to be capable, after a few beers, of getting up on the table and doing a Stevie Nicks imitation. The big payoff is the Battle of the Bands, and inevitably all of the angry parents are in the front row, but the movie stays true, if not to its school, at least to rock and roll, and you have a goofy smile most of the time.

I saw a family film named *Good Boy!* that was astonishingly stupid, and treated its audi-

ence as if it had a tragically slow learning curve and was immune to boredom. Here is a movie that proves you can make a family film that's alive and well acted and smart and perceptive and funny—and that rocks.

Note: I have absolutely no clue why the movie is rated PG-13. There's "rude humor and some drug references," the MPAA says. There's not a kid alive who would be anything but delighted by this film. It belongs on the MPAA's List of Shame with Whale Rider *and* Bend It Like Beckham, *two other PG-13 films perfect for the family.*

Searching for Bobby Fischer
PG, 107 m., 1993

Joe Mantegna (Fred Waitzkin), Laurence Fishburne (Vinnie), Joan Allen (Bonnie Waitzkin), Max Pomeranc (Josh Waitzkin), Ben Kingsley (Bruce Pandolfini), David Paymer (Kalev), Michael Nirenberg (Jonathan Poe). Directed by Steven Zaillian and produced by Scott Rudin and William Horberg. Screenplay by Zaillian, based on the book by Fred Waitzkin.

There was a boy, a chess player, once, who revealed that his gift consisted partly in a clear inner vision of potential moves of each piece as objects with flashing or moving tails of coloured light: He saw a live possible pattern of potential moves and selected them according to which ones made the pattern strongest, the tensions greatest. His mistakes were made when he selected not the toughest, but the most beautiful lines of light.

—A. S. Byatt, *The Virgin in the Garden*

Child prodigies are found most often in three fields: chess, mathematics, and music. All three depend upon an intuitive grasp of complex relationships. None depend on social skills, maturity, or insights into human relationships. A child who is a genius at chess can look at a board and see a universe that is invisible to the wisest adult. This is both a blessing and a curse. There is a beauty to the gift, but it does not necessarily lead to greater happiness in life as a whole.

The wonderful film *Searching for Bobby Fischer* contains in its title a reminder of that truth. Bobby Fischer was arguably the greatest chess player of all time. As a boy he faced and defeated the greatest players of his time. In 1972, after a prelude of countless controversies, he won the world chess championship away from the Russians for the first time in years. Then he essentially disappeared into a netherworld of rented rooms, phantom sightings, paranoid outbursts, and allegiance to a religious cult. He reappeared to win a lucrative chess match in Yugoslavia, for which he was willing to lose his citizenship. His games are models of elegance and artistry. His life does not inspire envy.

Searching for Bobby Fischer, a film of remarkable sensitivity and insight, tells a story based on fact, about a "new" Bobby Fischer— a young boy named Josh Waitzkin (Max Pomeranc) who was born with a gift for chess, which he nurtured in the rough-and-tumble world of chess hustlers in New York's Washington Square Park. His parents are at first doubtful of his talent, then proud of it, then concerned about how he can develop it without stunting the other areas of his life.

The film is the first intelligent one I can remember seeing about chess. That is the case even though no knowledge of chess is necessary to understand it, and some of the filmmaking strategies—such as showing most of the moves at lightning speed—simply ignore the long periods of inaction in many games. It is intelligent because it is about the meaning of chess, a game that has been compared to war and plundered for its lurking Freudian undertones, and yet is essentially just an arrangement of logical outcomes.

In the film Josh learns the moves by watching them played in the park. At first his parents, Fred and Bonnie Waitzkin (Joe Mantegna and Joan Allen), are even unaware he can play, and there is a sweet scene in which the boy allows his father to win a game, to spare his feelings. Josh's first teacher is a black chess hustler named Vinnie (Laurence Fishburne), who uses an in-your-face approach and advises unorthodox moves to throw an opponent off. Eventually Fred becomes convinced his son needs more advanced tutelage, and hires the brilliant but prickly Bruce Pandolfini (Ben Kingsley), a difficult case—but then all good chess players are difficult cases.

The difference in strategy between Vinnie and Bruce is much simplified in the film, and comes down to whether or not you should develop your queen at an early stage in the game.

For the film, the queen is just a symbol of their opposed styles; the movie is really about personalities, and how they express themselves through chess.

The screenplay by Steven Zaillian *(Schindler's List)*, based on Fred Waitzkin's autobiographical book, is best when it deals with the issues surrounding competitive chess. Is winning, for example, the only thing? Is chess so important that it should absorb all the attention of a young prodigy, or is his development as a normal little boy also crucial? Why does one play serious chess in the first place? There is a cautionary moment when Fred Waitzkin sees his first professional chess tournament—an ill-fitted room filled with players, mostly men, mostly silent, bending over their boards as if in prayer—and is warned that this is the world his son will inherit.

By the end of *Searching for Bobby Fischer* we have learned something about tournament chess, and a great deal about human nature. The film's implications are many. They center around our responsibility, if any, to our gifts. If we can operate at the genius level in a given field, does that mean we must—even if the cost is the sort of endless purgatory a Bobby Fischer has inhabited? It's an interesting question and this movie doesn't avoid it. At the end, it all comes down to that choice faced by the young player that A. S. Byatt writes about: the choice between truth, and beauty. What makes us men is that we can think logically. What makes us human is that we sometimes choose not to.

The Secret Garden
G, 99 m., 1993

Kate Maberly (Mary Lennox), Heydon Prowse (Colin), Andrew Knott (Dickon), Laura Crossley (Martha), Maggie Smith (Mrs. Medlock), John Lynch (Lord Craven). Directed by Agnieszka Holland and produced by Fred Fuchs, Fred Roos, and Tom Luddy. Screenplay by Caroline Thompson, based on the book by Frances H. Burnett.

Like all great stories for children, *The Secret Garden* contains powerful truths just beneath the surface. There is always a level at which the story is telling children about more than just events; it is telling them about the nature of life.

That was the feeling I had when I read Frances Hodgson Burnett's book many years ago, and it is a feeling that comes back powerfully while watching Agnieszka Holland's new film.

Some "children's films" are only for children. Some can be watched by the whole family. Others are so good they seem hardly intended for children at all, and *The Secret Garden* falls in that category. It is a work of beauty, poetry, and deep mystery, and watching it is like entering for a time into a closed world where one's destiny may be discovered.

The film tells the story, familiar to generations, of a young girl orphaned in India in the early years of this century, and sent home to England, to live on the vast estate of an uncle. Misselthwaite Manor is a gloomy and forbidding pile in Yorkshire—a construction of stone, wood, metal, secrets, and ancient wounds. The heroine, whose name is Mary Lennox (Kate Maberly), arrives from her long sea journey to be met with a sniff and a stern look from Mrs. Medlock (Maggie Smith), who manages the place in the absence of the uncle, Lord Archibald Craven (John Lynch). Mary quickly gathers that this uncle is almost always absent, traveling in far places in an attempt to forget the heartbreaking death of his young bride some years earlier.

There is little for Mary to do in the mansion but explore, and soon she finds secret passageways and even the bedroom of her late aunt—and in the bedroom, a key to a secret garden. She makes friends with a boy named Dickon (Andrew Knott), whose sister is a maid at Misselthwaite, and together they play in the garden, and he whispers the manor's great secret: The aunt died in childbirth, but her son, now nine or ten years old, still lives in the manor, confined to his bed, unable to walk.

Mary goes exploring and finds the little boy, named Colin (Heydon Prowse). He has lived a life of great sadness, confined to his room, able to see only the sky from the windows visible from his bed. Mary determines he must see his mother's secret garden, and she and Dickon are able to wheel him there in an invalid's chair, stealing him out of the house under the very nose of Mrs. Medlock.

All of this could be told in a simple and insipid story, I am sure, with cute kids sneaking around the corridors. But Holland is alert to the buried meanings of her story, and she has encouraged her actors to act their age—to be smart, resourceful, and articulate. They are so good at their jobs that we stop being aware they are children, and enter into full identification with their quest.

More of the story I must not tell, except to mention in passing the gaunt dignity of Uncle Archibald, played by Lynch with the kind of weary, sensual sadness that Jeremy Irons used to have a corner on. By the end of the film I was surprised by how much I was moved; how much I had come to care about the lonely little boy, the orphaned girl, and the garden that a dead woman had prepared for them.

This is Holland's first American film, backed by Francis Ford Coppola and produced by his longtime associates Fred Fuchs, Fred Roos, and Tom Luddy. Holland's earlier work includes *Europa, Europa*, a story of a Jewish boy who is able to save his life by passing for a Nazi youth brigade member, and *Olivier, Olivier*, another case of mysterious identity, about a long-lost son who may or may not have been found again. I found *Europa, Europa* such an incredible story that I rejected it; what lesson can be learned from the freak survival of one potential victim, while millions died? *Olivier, Olivier* I found a more successful film, although I was mystified by the function of an unexplained supernatural element in the story.

In *The Secret Garden* Holland has again made a film about a missing child, but this time her theme and her telling of it are in complete harmony. It is a beautiful, intelligent film—a fable, a lesson, and an entrancing entertainment. And Roger Deakins's photography elevates the secret garden into a place of such harmony and beauty that we almost believe it can restore the lives of those who look on it. The summer of 1993 will be remembered as the time when every child in the world wanted to see *Jurassic Park*. The lucky ones saw this one, too.

Secret Honor

NO MPAA RATING, 90 m., 1984

Philip Baker Hall (Nixon). Directed and produced by Robert Altman. Screenplay by Donald Freed and Arnold M. Stone.

The most tantalizing images in Woodward and Bernstein's *The Final Days* were those stories of a drunken Richard M. Nixon, falling to his knees in the White House, embarrassing Henry Kissinger with a display of self-pity and pathos. Was the book accurate? Even Kissinger said he had no idea who the authors' sources were (heh, heh). But as Watergate fades into history, and as revisionist historians begin to suggest that Nixon might after all have been a great president—apart from the scandals, of course—our curiosity remains. What were the real secrets of this most complex president? Robert Altman's *Secret Honor,* which is one of the most scathing, lacerating and brilliant movies of 1984, attempts to answer our questions. The film is a work of fiction. An actor is employed to impersonate Nixon. But all of the names and many of the facts are real, and the film gives us the uncanny sensation that we are watching a man in the act of exposing his soul.

The action takes place in Nixon's private office, at some point after his resignation. The shelves are lined with books, and with a four-screen video monitor for the security system. The desk top is weighted down with brass and gold. From the walls, portraits peer down. Eisenhower, Lincoln, Washington, Woodrow Wilson, Kissinger. Nixon begins by fiddling with his tape recorder; there is a little joke in the fact that he doesn't know quite how to run it. Then he begins to talk. He talks for ninety minutes. That bare description may make *Secret Honor* sound like *My Dinner with André,* but rarely have I seen ninety more compelling minutes on the screen. Nixon is portrayed by Philip Baker Hall, an actor previously unknown to me, with such savage intensity, such passion, such venom, such scandal, that we cannot turn away. Hall looks a little like the real Nixon; he could be a cousin, and he sounds a little like him. That's close enough. This is not an impersonation, it's a performance.

What Nixon the character has to say may or may not be true. He makes shocking revelations. Watergate was staged to draw attention away from more serious, even treasonous, activities. Kissinger was on the payroll of the shah of Iran, and supplied the shah with young boys during his visits to New York. Marilyn Monroe was indeed murdered by the CIA, and so on. These speculations are interwoven with stories we recognize as part of the official Nixon biography: the letter to his mother, signed "Your faithful dog, Richard"; the feeling about his family and his humble beginnings; his hatred for the Eastern Establishment, which he feels has scorned him.

Truth and fiction mix together into a tapestry of life. We get the sensation of a man pouring out all of his secrets after a lifetime of repression. His sentences rush out, disorganized, disconnected, under tremendous pressure, interrupted by four-letter words that serve almost as punctuation. After a while the specific details don't matter so much; what we are hearing is a scream of a brilliant, gifted man who is tortured by the notion that fate might have made him a loser.

A strange thing happened to me as I watched this film. I knew it was fiction. I didn't approach it in the spirit of learning the "truth about Nixon." But as a movie, it created a deeper truth, an artistic truth, and after *Secret Honor* was over, you know what? I had a deeper sympathy for Richard Nixon than I have ever had before.

Secrets and Lies

R, 142 m., 1996

Timothy Spall (Maurice), Marianne Jean-Baptiste (Hortense), Brenda Blethyn (Cynthia), Phyllis Logan (Monica), Claire Rushbrook (Roxanne), Elizabeth Berrington (Jane), Michele Austin (Dionne), Lee Ross (Paul). Directed by Mike Leigh and produced by Simon Channing-Williams. Screenplay by Leigh.

Moment after moment, scene after scene, *Secrets and Lies* unfolds with the fascination of eavesdropping. We are waiting to see what these people will do next, caught up in the fear and the hope that they will bring the whole fragile network of their lives crashing down in ruin. When they prevail—when common sense and good hearts win over lies and secrets—we feel almost as relieved as if it had happened to ourselves.

Mike Leigh's best films work like that. He finds a rhythm of life—not "real life," but real life as fashioned and shaped by all the art and skill his actors can bring to it—and slips into it, so that we are not particularly aware we're watching a film; he has a scene here, set at a backyard barbecue, that shows exactly how family gatherings are sometimes a process of tiptoeing through minefields. One wrong word and the repressed resentments of decades will blow up in everyone's face.

It would be easy, but wrong, to describe the plot of *Secrets and Lies* as being about an adopted black woman in London who seeks out her natural birth mother, discovers the woman is white, and arranges to meet her. That would be wrong because it sidesteps the real subject of the film, which is how the mother and her family have been all but destroyed by secrets and lies. The young black woman is the catalyst to change that situation, yes, but her life was fine before the action starts and will continue on an even keel afterward.

Given the deep waters it dives into, *Secrets and Lies* is a good deal funnier and more entertaining than we have any right to expect. It begins with the black woman, a thirtyish optometrist with the quintessentially British name Hortense Cumberbatch (Marianne Jean-Baptiste). After the death of her adoptive mother, she goes to an adoption agency to discover the name of her birth mother, and thinks there must have been a mistake, since the papers indicate her mother was white. There was no mistake.

We meet the mother, named Cynthia, who is played as a fearful nervous wreck by Brenda Blethyn (who won the best actress award at Cannes for this performance). She lives in an untidy council house with her daughter, Roxanne (Claire Rushbrook), who works as a street sweeper, is in a foul mood most of the time, and has a boyfriend whom she has thoroughly cowed. Cynthia mourns the fact that her beloved younger brother, Maurice (Timothy Spall), hasn't called her in more than two years, and blames Maurice's wife, Monica (Phyllis Logan), that "toffee-nosed cow," for the long silence.

The phone rings. It is Hortense. "Oh, no, no, no, no, no, dear—there's been some mistake!" says Cynthia. But Hortense persists. Cynthia hangs up. The phone rings again, and she approaches it like an animal sure the trap is set to spring. But she agrees to meet Hortense, and the scene of their meeting—outside a tube station and then in a nearby café—is one of the great sequences in all of Mike Leigh's work, based on incredulity, disbelief, memory, embarrassment, and acceptance. "But you can't be my daughter, dearie!" Cynthia exclaims. "I mean . . . just look at you!" She claims she has never even slept with a black man, and thinks she is telling the truth, but then a moment comes when she arrives at a startling revelation, and we don't know whether to smile or hold our breaths.

Much of the film is devoted to the domestic life of Maurice and Monica. He is a photographer specializing in wedding pictures; she is a loving woman whose life becomes unbearable for herself and her husband every twenty-eight days. Spall, who you may remember as the proprietor of the doomed French restaurant in Leigh's *Life Is Sweet,* is a born conciliator, wanting to make everyone happy and usually failing.

The movie arrives at its magnificent conclusion at the family reunion, the barbecue where Cynthia brings Hortense and introduces her as a "friend from work." Soon the family is trying to puzzle out why an eye doctor would be employed at a cardboard box factory. Leigh and his actors (who develop the characters and dialogue together, in collaboration) play this scene in one unbroken take, in which six characters eat, drink, talk, and stumble across secrets and lies.

I have admired the work of Mike Leigh ever since 1971, when his *Bleak Moments* premiered in the Chicago Film Festival. For many years he was an outcast of British cinema; it's hard to get financing when you don't have a script or even the idea for a film, but Leigh stubbornly persisted in his method of gathering actors and working with them to create the story. In the 1970s and 1980s, he worked mostly in London theater and for the BBC, and then came *High Hopes* (1989), *Life Is Sweet* (1991), and *Naked* (1994).

Now *Secrets and Lies,* which won the Palme d'Or at Cannes, is a flowering of his technique. It moves us on a human level, it keeps us guessing during scenes as unpredictable as life (the visit, for example, of the former owner of the photography studio), and it shows us how ordinary people have a chance of somehow coping with their problems, which are rather ordinary too. One intriguing aspect of the film is the way Leigh handles race: The daughter is black, the mother is white, the family has no idea she had another child, and yet race is not really on anybody's mind in this film. They think they have more important things to worry about, and they're right.

Seven Beauties
R, 115 m., 1976

Giancarlo Giannini (Pasqualino), Fernando Rey (Peoro), Shirley Stoler (Commandant), Elena Flore (Concettina). Directed by Lina Wertmuller and produced by Arrigo Colombo and Wertmuller. Screenplay by Wertmuller.

Lina Wertmuller's *Seven Beauties* is about Pasqualino, a little man who absentmindedly wanders through the Italian fascism of the pre-war years before finally being imprisoned by the Nazis. That doesn't make it unusual; a lot of Italian films have explored the experience of World War II. What does make *Seven Beauties* unique—what makes it one of the strangest and most intriguing of recent European films—is that Pasqualino is a fool. He's not brave, or bright, or even cynical or cowardly. In his best moments he's an opportunist, and at his worst a devout pawn.

He does not, of course, suspect this about himself. He's obsessed with notions of honor, and even goes so far as to assume he possesses a great deal of honor. His honor is a totally macho thing, involving dim-witted ideas about the proper behavior of males in the face of insults to their sisters. And he has his work cut out for him since there are seven sisters in his family, each one more unattractive than the last, each one, in his eyes, a potential candidate for ruin. When the worst finally happens, when one of his sisters takes up with a pimp and goes to work in a brothel, he knows what he has to do.

He kills the pimp. Then he dismembers the body, which is a very large one, and ships it to various Italian cities in bulky suitcases. He is brought to trial, found insane, and sent to an asylum. On his way, he meets a fellow prisoner. He boasts of himself: "The ax-murderer. The Monster of Naples." Any status is welcome. He spends a great deal of time admiring himself in the mirror and striking dashing poses.

He's eventually released from the asylum to serve in the Italian army, and it's in this material that the movie takes its weird and unexpected turn. The pre-war material seems vaguely related to Wertmuller's *The Seduction of Mimi*, in which the hypocrisy of the Italian male sexual code is cheerfully ridiculed. But *Seven Beauties*, despite some very funny scenes, is not a cheerful movie. It's a dark, brooding piece about the ways people are willing to debase themselves, and Pasqualino, for all of his honor, is a worm.

He finds himself in a Nazi concentration camp. The commandant is a very large, plain, forbidding woman. She carries a whip as if it were her handbag.

Pasqualino recalls the advice of his mother, that even the most inaccessible woman can be reached through her heart, and he mounts a romantic campaign against the commandant. She isn't deceived for a moment by his lies, but she does use him, and in the scenes of their coupling Wertmuller provides some of the most disturbing images she's ever filmed. Many of her films see relationships between men and women as elaborations of sadomasochistic themes, but *Seven Beauties* has the darkest and most despairing of her couples.

After Pasqualino successfully makes love to the commandant—in what's easily the least erotic sex scene ever filmed—she sets out to destroy his character, if any. He's forced to select six fellow prisoners for extermination and, later, to put a bullet through the head of his best friend. He does. He suffers as he does so, perhaps, but not as much as he did at the slights to his sister's honor, or over missed meals. *Seven Beauties* isn't the account of a man's fall from dignity, because Pasqualino never had any—and that's what makes it intriguing.

Why did Wertmuller make it? To explore banality and cruelty? To give us a vision of the Nazi experience, in which moral choices are irrelevant and the characters join together in a grim mutual debasement? To make, as an exercise, an ultimate black comedy? I can't say. I'm not sure there is a rational answer; the movie seems to be a working out on a subconscious level of behavior patterns Wertmuller finds both fascinating and inexplicable.

So the movie's absorbing and mysterious. It doesn't explain itself. It presents its funny scenes—Giancarlo Giannini preening himself in the mirror of his own mind, and then unwittingly behaving as a total fool—with the same detachment it uses in scenes of total pessimism. Its virtuoso style, demonstrating once again Wertmuller's mastery of filmmaking, is used to tell us a story that's very opaque, despairing, and bottomless.

Shadowlands

PG, 133 m., 1994

Anthony Hopkins (C. S. Lewis), Debra Winger (Joy Gresham), Edward Hardwicke (Warnie Lewis), John Wood (Professor Riley), Michael Denison (Reverend Harrington), Joseph Mazzello (Douglas Gresham), Peter Firth (Dr. Craig). Directed by Richard Attenborough and produced by Attenborough and Brian Eastman. Screenplay by William Nicholson, based on the play by William Nicholson.

For many years his life has followed the same comfortable patterns. He is a teacher and a writer, a pipe-smoking bachelor who lives in his book-lined Oxford home with his brother. From his children's books, his science fiction, and his pop theology, he has gained a following, and he gives comforting talks about man's place in God's plans. Then the most extraordinary thing takes place. He falls in love.

Shadowlands is the story, based on fact, of an autumnal romance involving the British writer C. S. Lewis and a divorced American woman named Joy Gresham. They met after she wrote him an admiring letter; their correspondence led to her first visit to England, with her young son. Lewis received her as a courtesy, and was so settled in his lifelong professorial routine that he hardly knew what to do when it became clear, even to him, that he was in love.

Shadowlands has found two perfect actors to play this unlikely couple, Anthony Hopkins and Debra Winger. He is shy sometimes to the point of being tongue-tied; he nods and hems and haws and looks away, and retreats behind formulas of courtesy. She is more direct, an outspoken woman who sometimes surprises him by saying out loud what they have both been thinking, but that he would never have said. She sees at a glance

the comfortable rut he is in—the dinners at his college dining hall, the evenings in front of the fire, reading while the wireless provides classical music from the BBC. She isn't out to "catch" him. It's more that he discovers he cannot imagine her going away.

Their courtship is an odd one. He issues invitations lamely, as if sure she will not accept. He is so terrified of marriage that he has to couch his proposal in "practical" terms—if he marries her, she will not be forced to leave Britain. She has to negotiate the clouded waters of university politics, the annual dinners of the college head, the curiosity and pointed questions of his nosy colleagues. When it comes to sex, he hasn't a clue, and she talks him through it: "What do you do when you go to bed?" "I put on my pajamas and say my prayers and get under the covers." "Well, then, that's what I want you to do right now, except that when you get under the covers, I'll be there."

Lewis has been confident in his writings and lectures that he knows the purpose of suffering and pain: It is God's way of perfecting us, of carving away the wrong parts, of leaving a soul ready to enter heaven. But when Joy contracts cancer, when she finds herself in terrible pain, he finds he is not at all sure of his theory. And, facing the possibility that they will be parted, together they create an idea of human life on earth that comforts him more than his theories.

Shadowlands, directed by Richard Attenborough, based on the stage play by William Nicholson, is intelligent, moving, and beautifully acted. It understands that not everyone falls into love through the avenue of physical desire; that for some, the lust may be for another's mind, for inner beauty. Anthony Hopkins, who earlier in 1993 in *Remains of the Day* gave a brilliant performance as a closed-off English butler who was afraid to love, here provides a companion performance, of a buttoned-down English intellectual who surprises himself by finding the courage to love.

Debra Winger, not afraid to look less than her best in early scenes (although her beauty glows later on in the film), is no less extraordinary: She projects a quiet empathy in creating Joy Gresham, a woman who has fallen in love with Lewis through his writings. Her character goes through a series of delicate adjustments as she meets him and realizes he is not as contented as he thinks. She believes that making one another happier is one of their purposes on earth. His ability to share that view is a small triumph, but one few people can claim.

Shakespeare in Love

R, 120 m., 1998

Gwyneth Paltrow (Viola De Lesseps), Joseph Fiennes (Will Shakespeare), Geoffrey Rush (Philip Henslowe), Colin Firth (Lord Wessex), Ben Affleck (Ned Alleyn), Judi Dench (Queen Elizabeth I), Simon Callow (Tilney, Master of the Revels), Rupert Everett (Christopher Marlowe), Martin Clunes (Richard Burbage), Tom Wilkinson (Fennyman), Imelda Staunton (Nurse), Anthony Sher (Dr. Moth). Directed by John Madden and produced by David Parfitt, Donna Gigliotti, Harvey Weinstein, Edward Zwick, and Marc Norman. Screenplay by Norman and Tom Stoppard.

There is a boatman in *Shakespeare in Love* who ferries Shakespeare across the Thames while bragging, "I had Christopher Marlowe in my boat once." As Shakespeare steps ashore, the boatman tries to give him a script to read. The contemporary feel of the humor (like Shakespeare's coffee mug, inscribed "Souvenir of Stratford-upon-Avon") makes the movie play like a contest between *Masterpiece Theatre* and Mel Brooks. Then the movie stirs in a sweet love story, juicy court intrigue, backstage politics, and some lovely moments from *Romeo and Juliet* (Shakespeare's working title: *Romeo and Ethel, the Pirate's Daughter*).

Is this a movie or an anthology? I didn't care. I was carried along by the wit, the energy, and a surprising sweetness. The movie serves as a reminder that Will Shakespeare was once a young playwright on the make, that theater in all times is as much business as show, and that *Romeo and Juliet* must have been written by a man in intimate communication with his libido. The screenplay is by Marc Norman and Tom Stoppard, whose play *Rosencrantz and Guildenstern are Dead* approached *Hamlet* from the points of view of two minor characters.

Shakespeare in Love is set in late Elizabethan England (the queen, played as a young woman by Cate Blanchett in *Elizabeth*, is played as an old one here by Judi Dench). Theater in London is booming—when the theaters aren't closed, that is, by plague warnings or bad debts. Shakespeare (Joseph Fiennes) is not as successful as the popular Marlowe (Rupert Everett), but he's a rising star, in demand by the impecunious impresario Henslowe (Geoffrey Rush), whose Rose Theater is in hock to a money lender, and Richard Burbage (Martin Clunes), whose Curtain Theater has Marlowe and would like to sign Shakespeare.

The film's opening scenes provide a cheerful survey of the business of theater—the buildings, the budgets, the script deadlines, the casting process. Shakespeare meanwhile struggles against deadlines and complains in therapy that his quill has broken (his therapist raises a Freudian eyebrow). What does it take to renew his energy? A sight of the beautiful Viola De Lesseps (Gwyneth Paltrow), a rich man's daughter with the taste to prefer Shakespeare to Marlowe, and the daring to put on men's clothes and audition for a role in Will's new play.

Players in drag were, of course, standard on the Elizabethan stage ("Stage love will never be true love," the dialogue complains, "while the law of the land has our beauties played by pip-squeak boys"). It was conventional not to notice the gender disguises, and *Shakespeare in Love* asks us to grant the same leeway as Viola first plays a woman auditioning to play a man, and later plays a man playing a woman. As the young man auditioning to play Romeo, Viola wears a mustache and trousers, and yet somehow inspires stirrings in Will's breeches; later, at a dance, he sees her as a woman and falls instantly in love.

Alas, Viola is to be married in two weeks to the odious Lord Wessex (Colin Firth), who will trade his title for her father's cash. Shakespeare nevertheless presses his case, in what turns out to be a real-life rehearsal for Romeo and Juliet's balcony scene, and when it is discovered that he violated Viola's bedchamber, he thinks fast and identifies himself as Marlowe. (This suggests an explanation for Marlowe's mysterious stabbing death at Deptford.) The threads of the story come together nicely on Viola's wedding day, which ends with her stepping into a role she could not possibly have foreseen.

The film has been directed by John Madden, who made *Mrs. Brown* (1997), about the affection between Queen Victoria and her horse trainer. Here again he finds a romance that leaps across barriers of wealth, titles, and class. The story is ingeniously Shakespearean in its dimensions, including high and low comedy, coincidences, masquerades, jokes about itself, topical references, and entrances with screwball timing. At the same time we get a good sense of how the audience was deployed in the theaters, where they stood or sat, and what their view was like—and also information about costuming, props, and stagecraft.

But all of that is handled lightly, as background, while intrigues fill the foreground, and the love story between Shakespeare and Viola slyly takes form. By the closing scene, where Viola breaks the law against women on the stage, we're surprised how much of Shakespeare's original power still resides in lines that now have two or even three additional meanings. There's a quiet realism in the development of the romance, which grows in the shadow of Viola's approaching nuptials: "This is not life, Will," she tells him. "It is a stolen season." And Judi Dench has a wicked scene as Elizabeth, informing Wessex of his bride-to-be, "You're a lordly fool; she's been plucked since I saw her last, and not by you. It takes a woman to know it."

Fiennes and Paltrow make a fine romantic couple, high-spirited and fine-featured, and Ben Affleck prances through the center of the film as Ned Alleyn, the cocky actor. I also enjoyed the seasoned Shakespeareans who swelled the progress of a scene or two: Simon Callow as the Master of the Revels; Tom Wilkinson as Fennyman, the usurer; Imelda Staunton as Viola's nurse; Anthony Sher as Dr. Moth, the therapist.

A movie like this is a reminder of the long thread that connects Shakespeare to the kids opening tonight in a storefront on Lincoln Avenue: You get a theater, you learn the lines, you strut your stuff, you hope there's an audience, you fall in love with another member of the cast, and if sooner or later your revels must be ended, well, at least you reveled.

Shine

PG-13, 105 m., 1996

Geoffrey Rush (David [Adult]), Noah Taylor (David [Young Man]), Alex Rafalowicz (David [Boy]), Armin Mueller-Stahl (Peter), Lynn Redgrave (Gillian), John Gielgud (Cecil Parkes), Googie Withers (Katharine Prichard), Nicholas Bell (Ben Rosen). Directed by Scott Hicks and produced by Jane Scott. Screenplay by Jan Sardi.

Wandering in the rain, the man looks like one of the walking wounded. His talk is obsessive chatter, looping back on itself, seizing on words and finding nonsense associations for them. He laughs a lot and seems desperately affable. When he sits down at a piano in a crowded restaurant, he looks like trouble, until he starts to play. His music floods out like a cry of anguish and hope.

This is the central image in Scott Hicks's *Shine,* based on the true story of an Australian pianist who was an international prodigy, suffered a breakdown, and has gradually been able to piece himself back together. The musician's name is David Helfgott. His life story is not exactly as it is shown here, but close enough, I gather, for us to marvel at the way the human spirit can try to heal itself.

The movie circles in time, using three actors to play Helfgott. Alex Rafalowicz is young David, encouraged to excel at music and chess by a domineering father who slams the chessboard and shouts, "You must always win!" He is savage when his son places second in a national competition. Noah Taylor, so good in *Flirting,* plays the adolescent David, who blossoms at the piano but is forbidden by his father from accepting a scholarship offered by Isaac Stern. Geoffrey Rush plays David as an adult who goes mad and then slowly heals with the help of an understanding woman.

But it is all so much more complicated than this makes it sound. We should begin with David's father, Peter (Armin Mueller-Stahl), a Polish Jew who survived the Holocaust but lost most of his family. Now resettled in Australia, he places family above everything; refusing to let David study at the Royal College of Music in London, he screams, "You will destroy your family!" Peter is capable of violence but also tenderness and love; his family is in the grip of his tyranny, and it is little wonder that David comes unglued, torn between his father's demands that he be perfect at the piano, and his refusal to let him follow his musical career where it will lead.

David finds friendship and support from an old woman (Googie Withers) who encourages his music and helps him find the courage to go to London, where his tutor is played wonderfully, with dryness and affection, by Sir John Gielgud. There he is happy for a time, but during a performance of the formidable Rachmaninoff Piano Concerto no. 3, he comes apart.

We see him next as a middle-aged man, a wanderer back in Australia, talking nonsense, his name forgotten by all but a few. I understand that Scott Hicks got the idea for this film when he came across Helfgott playing in a restaurant, and heard his story.

One of the buried motifs of *Shine* is the war that goes on between David's parent figures. His father is a monster and his mother is weak, but the old woman in Perth helps him, and so does the piano teacher (Nicholas Bell). His key helper is a middle-aged astrologer (Lynn Redgrave), who meets him through a friend toward the end of his restaurant days. They fall in love, and love saves him.

Music is one of the areas in which child prodigies often excel; two others are mathematics and chess. All three have the advantage of not requiring much knowledge of life or human nature (for technical proficiency, anyway). David's piano playing is at first a skill that comes naturally to him; only later does it become an art, a way of self-expression.

What is terrifying for him is that the better he gets, the closer he comes to expressing feelings that his father has charged with enormous guilt. The "Rach 3" is a tumult of emotion, and what happens is that David cannot perform it without being destroyed by the feelings it releases.

The father is undergoing a process similar to the one he has inflicted on his son. He, too, cannot deal with the emotions unleashed by his son's playing, which is why he forbids David to study in Europe; if the son becomes good enough, he will fly away on the wings of the music, breaking up the sacred family unit and reopening the father to all the terrors of the Holocaust—terrors against which he has raised up as a bulwark his family in its little suburban house. The last scene of the movie (filmed, I have been told, at Peter Helfgott's actual grave) tries to acknowledge some of

these truths: Peter is a man whose life inflicted great damage, not least upon himself.

There has been much talk about films that said they were based on true stories but were kidding *(Fargo)* and films that said they were based on true stories but might have been lying *(Sleepers)*. Here is a movie that is based on the truth beneath a true story.

The fact that David Helfgott lived the outlines of these events—that he triumphed, that he fell, that he came slowly back—adds an enormous weight of meaning to the film. There was controversy over his subsequent concert tour of North America, but I can understand why many of those who saw the film wanted to hear him—not for the "comeback drama" so much as to hear the music he kept on playing during his years in the wilderness, and which led him back again to his true calling.

Shoah

NO MPAA RATING, 563 m. on five cassettes, 1986

A documentary directed and produced by Claude Lanzmann.

For more than nine hours I sat and watched a film named *Shoah*, and when it was over, I sat for a while longer and simply stared into space, trying to understand my emotions. I had seen a memory of the most debased chapter in human history. But I had also seen a film that affirmed life so passionately that I did not know where to turn with my confused feelings. There is no proper response to this film. It is an enormous fact, a 563-minute howl of pain and anger in the face of genocide. It is one of the noblest films ever made.

The film's title is a Hebrew word for chaos or annihilation—for the Holocaust. The film is a documentary, but it does not contain images from the 1940s. There are no old newsreel shots, no interviews with the survivors of the death camps, no coverage of the war crimes trials. All of the movie was photographed in the last five or six years by a man named Claude Lanzmann, who went looking for eyewitnesses to Hitler's "Final Solution." He is surprisingly successful in finding people who were there, who saw and heard what went on. Some of them, a tiny handful, are Jewish survivors of the camps. The rest are mostly old people, German and Polish, some who worked in the camps, others who were in a position to observe what happened.

They talk and talk. *Shoah* is a torrent of words, and yet the overwhelming impression, when it is over, is one of silence. Lanzmann intercuts two kinds of images. He shows the faces of his witnesses. And then he uses quiet pastoral scenes of the places where the deaths took place. Steam engines move massively through the Polish countryside, down the same tracks where trains took countless Jews, gypsies, Poles, homosexuals, and other socalled undesirables to their deaths. Cameras pan silently across pastures, while we learn that underneath the tranquility are mass graves. Sometimes the image is of a group of people, gathered in a doorway, or in front of a church, or in a restaurant kitchen.

Lanzmann is a patient interrogator. We see him in the corners of some of his shots, a tall, lanky man, informally dressed, chainsmoking. He wants to know the details. He doesn't ask large, profound questions about the meaning of the extermination of millions of people. He asks little questions. In one of the most chilling sequences in the film, he talks to Abraham Bomba, today a barber in Tel Aviv. Bomba was one of the Jewish barbers ordered to cut off the hair of Jewish women before they were killed in Treblinka. His assignment suggests the shattering question: How can a woman's hair be worth more than her life? But Lanzmann does not ask overwhelming and unanswerable questions like this. These are the sorts of questions he asks:

You cut with what? With scissors?
There were no mirrors?
You said there were about sixteen barbers? You cut the hair of how many women in one batch?

The barber tries to answer. As he talks, he has a customer in his chair, and he snips at the customer's hair almost obsessively, making tiny movements with his scissors, as if trying to use the haircut as a way to avoid the questions. Their conversation finally arrives at this exchange, after he says he cannot talk any more:

A. I can't. It's too horrible. Please.
Q. *We have to do it. You know it.*
A. I won't be able to do it.

Q. *You have to do it. I know it's very hard. I know and I apologize.*
A. Don't make me go on, please.
Q. *Please. We must go on.*

Lanzmann is cruel, but he is correct. He must go on. It is necessary to make this record before all of those who were witnesses to the Holocaust have died.

His methods in obtaining the interviews were sometimes underhanded. He uses a concealed television camera to record the faces of some of the old Nazi officials whom he interviews, and we look over the shoulders of the TV technicians in a van parked outside the buildings where they live. We see the old men nonchalantly pulling down charts from the wall to explain the layout of a death camp, and we hear their voices, and at one point when a Nazi asks for reassurance that the conversation is private, Lanzmann provides it. He will go to any length to obtain this testimony.

He does not, however, make any attempt to arrange his material into a chronology, an objective, factual record of how the "Final Solution" began, continued, and was finally terminated by the end of the war. He uses a more poetic, mosaic approach, moving according to rhythms only he understands among the three kinds of faces we see in this film: survivors, murderers, and bystanders. As their testimony is intercut with the scenes of train tracks, steam engines, abandoned buildings, and empty fields, we are left with enough time to think our own thoughts, to meditate, to wonder.

This is a long movie but not a slow one, and in its words it creates something of the same phenomenon I experienced while watching *My Dinner with André*. The words themselves create images in the imagination, as they might in a radio play. Consider the images summoned by these words, spoken by Filip Muller, a Czech Jew assigned to work at the doors of the gas chambers, a man who survived five waves of liquidations at Auschwitz:

A. You see, once the gas was poured in, it worked like this: It rose from the ground upwards. And in the terrible struggle that followed—because it was a struggle—the lights were switched off in the gas chambers. It was dark, no one could see, so the strongest people tried to climb higher. Because they probably realized that the higher they got, the more air there was. They could breathe better. That caused the struggle. Secondly, most people tried to push their way to the door. It was psychological; they knew where the door was; maybe they could force their way out. It was instinctive, a death struggle. Which is why children and weaker people and the aged always wound up at the bottom. The strongest were on top. Because in the death struggle, a father didn't realize his son lay beneath him.

Q. *And when the doors were opened?*

A. They fell out. People fell out like blocks of stone, like rocks falling out of a truck.

The images evoked by his words are inutterably painful. What is remarkable, on reflection, is that Muller is describing a struggle that neither he nor anyone else now alive ever saw. I realized, at the end of his words, that a fundamental change had taken place in the way I personally visualized the gas chambers. Always before, in reading about them or hearing about them, my point of view was outside, looking in. Muller put me inside.

That is what this whole movie does, and it is probably the most important thing it does. It changes our point of view about the Holocaust. After nine hours of *Shoah*, the Holocaust is no longer a subject, a chapter of history, a phenomenon. It is an environment. It is around us. Ordinary people speak in ordinary voices of days that had become ordinary to them. A railroad engineer who drove the trains to Treblinka is asked if he could hear the screams of the people in the cars behind his locomotive:

A. Obviously, since the locomotive was next to the cars. They screamed, asked for water. The screams from the cars closest to the locomotives could be heard very well.

Q. *Can one get used to that?*

A. No, it was extremely distressing. He knew the people behind him were human, like him. The Germans gave

him and the other workers vodka to drink. Without drinking, they couldn't have done it.

Some of the strangest passages in the film are the interviews with the officials who were running the camps and making the "Final Solution" work smoothly and efficiently. None of them, at least by their testimony, seem to have witnessed the whole picture. They only participated in a small part of it, doing their little jobs in their little corners. If they are to be believed, they didn't personally kill anybody, they just did small portions of larger tasks, and somehow all of the tasks, when added up and completed, resulted in people dying. Here is the man who scheduled the trains that took the Jews to die:

Q. *You never saw a train?*

A. No, never. We had so much work, I never left my desk. We worked day and night.

And here is a man who lived 150 feet from a church where Jews were rounded up, held, and then marched into gas vans for the trip to the crematoriums:

Q. *Did you see the gas vans?*

A. No—yes, from the outside. They shuttled back and forth. I never looked inside; I didn't see Jews.

What is so important about *Shoah* is that the voices are heard of people who did see, who did understand, who did comprehend, who were there, who know that the Holocaust happened, who tell us with their voices and with their eyes that genocide occurred in our time, in our civilization.

There is a tendency while watching *Shoah* to try to put a distance between yourself and the events on the screen. These things happened, after all, forty or forty-five years ago. Most of those now alive have been born since the events happened. Then, while I was watching the film, came a chilling moment. A name flashed on the screen in the subtitles, the name of one of the commandants at Treblinka death camp. At first I thought the name was "Ebert"—my name. Then I realized it was "Eberl." I felt a moment of relief, and then a moment of intense introspection as I realized that it made no difference what the subtitle said. The message of this film (if we believe in the brotherhood of man) is that these crimes were committed by people like us, against people like us.

But there is an even deeper message as well, and it is contained in the testimony of Filip Muller, the Jew who stood at the door of a crematorium and watched as the victims walked in to die. One day some of the victims, Czech Jews, began to sing. They sang two songs: "The Hatikvah," and the Czech national anthem. They affirmed that they were Jews and that they were Czechs. They denied Hitler, who would have them be one but not the other. Muller speaks:

A. That was happening to my country-men, and I realized that my life had become meaningless. (His eyes fill with tears.) Why go on living? For what? So I went into the gas chamber with them, resolved to die. With them. Suddenly, some who recognized me came up to me. . . . A small group of women approached. They looked at me and said, right there in the gas chamber . . .

Q. *You were inside the gas chamber?*

A. Yes. One of them said: "So you want to die. But that's senseless. Your death won't give us back our lives. That's no way. You must get out of here alive, you must bear witness to our suffering and to the injustice done to us."

And that is the final message of this extraordinary film. It is not a documentary, not journalism, not propaganda, not political. It is an act of witness. In it, Claude Lanzmann celebrates the priceless gift that sets man apart from animals and makes us human, and gives us hope: the ability for one generation to tell the next what it has learned.

Short Cuts

R, 189 m., 1993

Tim Robbins (Gene Shepard), Madeleine Stowe (Sherri Shepard), Andie MacDowell (Ann Finnigan), Bruce Davison (Howard Finnigan), Julianne Moore (Marian Wyman), Matthew Modine (Dr. Ralph Wyman), Jack Lemmon (Paul Finnigan), Jennifer Jason Leigh (Lois Kaiser), Christopher Penn (Jerry Kaiser), Lily Tomlin (Doreen Piggot), Peter Gallagher (Stormy Weathers). Directed by Robert Altman and produced by Cary Brokaw. Screenplay by Altman and Frank Barhydt, based on stories by Raymond Carver.

Los Angeles always seems to be waiting for something. Permanence seems out of reach; some great apocalyptic event is on the horizon, and people view the future tentatively. Robert Altman's *Short Cuts* captures that uneasiness perfectly, in its interlocking stories about people who seem trapped in the present, always juggling.

The movie is based on short stories by Raymond Carver, but this is Altman's work, not Carver's, and all the film really has in common with its source is a feeling for people who are disconnected—from relatives, church, tradition—and support themselves with jobs that never seem quite real. It is hard work, no doubt, to be a pool cleaner, a chauffeur, a phone-sex provider, a birthday cake decorator, a jazz singer, a helicopter pilot, but these are professions that find you before you find them. How many people end up in jobs they planned for? Altman is fascinated by the accidental nature of life, by the way that whole decades of our lives can be shaped by events we do not understand or even know about.

Short Cuts understands and knows, because it is filmed from an all-seeing point of view. Its characters all live at the same time in the same city, and sometimes their paths even cross, but for the most part they don't know how their lives are changed by people they meet only glancingly.

Imagine the rage of the baker (Lyle Lovett), for example, when he gets stuck with an expensive birthday cake. We could almost comprehend the cruel, anonymous telephone calls he makes to the parents (Andie MacDowell and Bruce Davison) who ordered the cake, if we didn't know their child missed his birthday because he was hit by a car. Imagine what *they* would say to the unknown driver (Lily Tomlin) who struck their child. But we know that she wanted to take him to a doctor; the boy refused because he has been forbidden to get into the cars of strangers, and besides, he seemed okay. If you knew the whole story in this world, there'd be a lot less to be angry about.

The movie's characters all seem to be from

somewhere else, and without parents. Their homes are as temporary as the trailer park two of the characters inhabit, where people come and go, no one knows from where, or to where. The grandparent (Jack Lemmon) of the injured little boy has disappeared for years. Faced with a son and grandson he hardly knows, he spends most of his time talking about himself. The jazz singer would rather drink than know her daughter.

Sad, insoluble mysteries seem right under the surface. Three men go on a fishing trip and discover the drowned body of a woman. They have waited a long time and come a long way for this trip, and if they report the woman, their trip will be ruined. So, since she's already dead, what difference will a few more days make? And what would the police do, anyway? There's a motorcycle cop (Tim Robbins) in the movie, who seems to be a free-lancer, responsible to no one, using his badge simply as a way to get his will, spending a lot of time cheating on his wife (Madeleine Stowe), who finds his lies hilarious.

Almost everybody drinks all through this movie, although only a few characters ever get exactly drunk. It's as if life is a preventable disease, and booze is the medication. Sex places a very slow second. The pool cleaner's wife (Jennifer Jason Leigh) supplements the family income by working as a phone-sex performer, spinning verbal fantasies to strangers on the phone, while sitting bored in her living room, changing her baby's diapers. Her husband (Christopher Penn) is angry: "How come you never talk that way to me?" Think about that. He's married to her. They sleep in the same bed. He can have actual physical sex with her. But he envies the strangers who will never meet her—who value her inaccessibility: She services their fantasies without imposing her own reality.

Some of these characters, if they could find each other, would find the answers to their needs. The baker, for example, has unexplored reserves of tenderness. He could help the sad young woman (Lori Singer) who plays the cello, and waits for those moments when her mother (Annie Ross), the jazz singer, is sober. The cop would probably be happier talking with the phone-sex girl than carrying on his endless affairs, which have no purpose except to anger his wife, who is past caring. He likes the deception more than the sex, and could get off by telling the stranger on the other end of the phone that he'd been cheating with *another* phone-sex girl.

Yet these people have a certain nobility to them. They keep on trying. They hope for better times. The hash-house waitress (Tomlin) loves her husband (Tom Waits), who is so good to her when he's not drinking that she forgives the dark times when he is drinking. The parents of the little boy find an unexpected consolation from the baker. The wife (Anne Archer) of one of the fly-fishermen finds a new resolve and freedom. Life goes on.

Altman has made this kind of film before, notably in *Nashville* (1975) and *The Player* (1992). He doesn't like stories that pretend that the characters control their destinies, and their actions will produce a satisfactory outcome. He likes the messiness and coincidence of real life, where you can do your best, and some days it's just not good enough. He doesn't reproduce Raymond Carver's stories so much as his attitude.

In a Carver story (and you should read one if you never have), there is typically a moment when an ordinary statement becomes crucial, or poetic, or sad. People get blinding glimpses into the real nature of their lives; the routine is peeled aside, and they can see they've been stuck in a rut for years, going through the motions. Sometimes they see with equal clarity that they are free to take charge, that no one has sentenced them to repeat the same mistakes.

Carver died in 1988, at fifty, of a brain tumor. He believed he would have died at forty, of alcoholism, if he hadn't found a way to stop drinking. When he knew the cancer would kill him, he wrote a poem about that bonus of ten years, called "Gravy." Altman, who spent most of the 1980s in a sort of exile after Hollywood declared him noncommercial, continued to make films, but they didn't have the budgets or the distribution a great filmmaker should have had. Then came the comeback of *The Player*, and now here is *Short Cuts*. Gravy.

Shrek
PG, 90 m., 2001

With the voices of: Mike Myers (Shrek), Eddie Murphy (The Donkey), Cameron Diaz (Princess Fiona), John

Lithgow (Lord Farquaad). Directed by Andrew Adamson and Vicky Jenson and produced by Aron Warner and John H. Williams. Screenplay by Ted Elliott, Terry Rossio, Joe Stillman, and Roger S. H. Schulman, based on the book by William Steig.

There is a moment in *Shrek* when the despicable Lord Farquaad has the Gingerbread Man tortured by dipping him into milk. This prepares us for another moment when Princess Fiona's singing voice is so piercing it causes jolly little bluebirds to explode; making the best of a bad situation, she fries their eggs. This is not your average family cartoon. *Shrek* is jolly and wicked, filled with sly in-jokes and yet somehow possessing a heart.

The movie has been so long in the making at DreamWorks that the late Chris Farley was originally intended to voice the jolly green ogre in the title role. All that work has paid off: The movie is an astonishing visual delight, with animation techniques that seem lifelike and fantastical, both at once. No animated being has ever moved, breathed, or had its skin crawl quite as convincingly as Shrek, and yet the movie doesn't look like a reprocessed version of the real world; it's all made up, right down to, or up to, Shrek's trumpet-shaped ears.

Shrek's voice is now performed by Mike Myers, with a voice that's an echo of his Fat Bastard (the Scotsman with a molasses brogue in *Austin Powers: The Spy Who Shagged Me*). Shrek is an ogre who lives in a swamp surrounded by "Keep Out" and "Beware the Ogre!" signs. He wants only to be left alone, perhaps because he is not such an ogre after all but merely a lonely creature with an inferiority complex because of his ugliness. He is horrified when the solitude of his swamp is disturbed by a sudden invasion of cartoon creatures, who have been banished from Lord Farquaad's kingdom.

Many of these creatures bear a curious correspondence to Disney characters who are in the public domain: The Three Little Pigs turn up, along with the Three Bears, the Three Blind Mice, Tinkerbell, the Big Bad Wolf, and Pinocchio. Later, when Farquaad seeks a bride, the Magic Mirror gives him three choices: Cinderella, Snow White ("She lives with seven men, but she's not easy"), and Princess Fiona. He chooses the beauty who has not had the title role in a Disney animated feature. No doubt all

of this, and a little dig at Disney World, were inspired by feelings DreamWorks partner Jeffrey Katzenberg has nourished since his painful departure from Disney—but the elbow in the ribs is more playful than serious. (Farquaad is said to be inspired by Disney chief Michael Eisner, but I don't see a resemblance, and his short stature corresponds not to the tall Eisner but, well, to the diminutive Katzenberg.)

The plot involves Lord Farquaad's desire to wed the Princess Fiona, and his reluctance to slay the dragon that stands between her and would-be suitors. He hires Shrek to attempt the mission, which Shrek is happy to do, providing the loathsome fairy-tale creatures are banished and his swamp returned to its dismal solitude. On his mission, Shrek is joined by a donkey named The Donkey, whose running commentary, voiced by Eddie Murphy, provides some of the movie's best laughs. (The trick isn't that he talks, Shrek observes; "the trick is to get him to shut up.")

The expedition to the castle of the princess involves a suspension bridge above a flaming abyss, and the castle's interior is piled high with the bones of the dragon's previous contenders. When Shrek and The Donkey get inside, there are exuberant action scenes that whirl madly through interior spaces, and revelations about the dragon no one could have guessed. And all along the way, asides and puns, in-jokes and contemporary references, and countless references to other movies.

Voice-overs for animated movies were once, except for the annual Disney classic, quickie jobs that actors took if they were out of work. Now they are starring roles with fat paychecks, and the ads for *Shrek* use big letters to trumpet the names of Myers, Murphy, Cameron Diaz (Fiona), and John Lithgow (Farquaad). Their vocal performances are nicely suited to the characters, although Myers's infatuation with his Scottish brogue reportedly had to be toned down. Murphy in particular has emerged as a star of the voice-over genre.

Much will be written about the movie's technical expertise, and indeed every summer seems to bring another breakthrough on the animation front. After the three-dimensional modeling and shading of *Toy Story*, the even more evolved *Toy Story 2*, *A Bug's Life*, and *Antz*, and the amazing effects in *Dinosaur*, *Shrek* unveils creatures who have been designed from the inside out, so that their skin, muscles, and fat move upon their bones instead of seeming like a single unit. They aren't "realistic," but they're curiously real. The artistry of the locations and setting is equally skilled—not lifelike, but beyond lifelike, in a merry, stylized way.

Still, all the craft in the world would not have made *Shrek* work if the story hadn't been fun and the ogre so lovable. Shrek is not handsome but he isn't as ugly as he thinks; he's a guy we want as our friend, and he doesn't frighten us but stirs our sympathy. He's so immensely likable that I suspect he may emerge as an enduring character, populating sequels and spin-offs. One movie cannot contain him.

Shy People

R, 120 m., 1988

Jill Clayburgh (Diana), Barbara Hershey (Ruth), Martha Plimpton (Grace), Merritt Butrick (Mike), John Philbin (Tommy), Don Swayze (Mark), Pruitt Taylor Vince (Paul), Mare Winningham (Candy). Directed by Andrei Konchalovsky and produced by Menahem Golan and Yoram Globus. Screenplay by Gerard Brach, Konchalovsky, and Marjorie David.

Two great early shots define the two worlds of *Shy People*. The first is circular, the second straight ahead.

The film's opening shot circles at a vertiginous height above Manhattan, showing the canyons of skyscrapers with people scurrying below like ants. The camera moves through a complete circle, finally coming to rest inside a high-rise apartment where a restless teenager and her distracted mother have no idea what to do about each other.

The second shot, a few minutes later in the film, is also taken from a height; we are above a speedboat that drones relentlessly into the heart of the Louisiana bayou country. This shot, inexplicably thrilling, is like scenes from adventure books we read when we were kids. We feel a quickening of excitement as the boat penetrates the unknown.

The two shots define the two women who are at the heart of the film. Jill Clayburgh plays a shallow, sophisticated Manhattan magazine writer, who convinces her bosses at *Cosmopolitan* to let her write about her family

roots. And Barbara Hershey plays Clayburgh's long-lost distant cousin, who lives in isolation in a crumbling, mossy home in the heart of the bayou. The movie is essentially about the differences between these women, about family blood ties, and about the transparent membrane between life and death.

Shy People is one of the great visionary films of recent years, a film that shakes off the petty distractions of safe Hollywood entertainments and develops a large vision. It is about revenge and hatred, about mothers and sons, about loneliness. It suggests that family ties are the most important bonds in the world, and by the end of the film, Clayburgh will discover that Hershey is closer to her "dead" husband than most city-dwellers are to anybody.

Yet the film is not without a wicked streak of humor. Clayburgh invites her precocious daughter (Martha Plimpton) to accompany her into the Louisiana backwaters, where the adolescent girl meets Hershey's ill-assorted sons. One is literally locked in an outbuilding when the New Yorkers arrive, another is light in the head, and still another is disowned and never mentioned, because he dared to move out of the bayou and open a nightclub in town. As the girl flirts with her cousins, and the women warily spar with each other, the darkness of the swamp closes in.

Shy People was directed by Andrei Konchalovsky, the Russian emigre whose other English-language movies include *Runaway Train* and *Duet for One*. Because he is an outsider, he is not so self-conscious about using American images that an American director might be frightened away from. The world of *Shy People* is the world of Erskine Caldwell's *Tobacco Road*, or Faulkner's Snopes family, of Al Capp and Russ Meyer. Hershey and her family are not small, timid people, but caricatures, and it's to Hershey's credit that she is able to play the role to the hilt and yet still make it real.

There are great sequences in the film, including one extraordinary night in which Clayburgh is lost in the swamp, is up to her neck in the fetid waters, and sees, or thinks she sees, the ghost of Hershey's dead husband.

There is a barroom fight in which the wrathful Hershey wades into her son's nightclub with a gun. Most extraordinary of all, there are spooky, quiet moments in which the mosquitoes drone in the sleepy heat of mid-day, while the two women pore over old photograph albums.

Sid & Nancy

R, 111 m., 1986

Gary Oldman (Sid Vicious), Chloe Webb (Nancy Spungen), Drew Schofield (Johnny Rotten), David Hayman (Malcolm McLaren), Debby Bishop (Phoebe), Jude Alderson (Ma Vicious). Directed by Alex Cox and produced by Eric Fellner. Screenplay by Cox and Abbe Wool.

His real name was John Simon Ritchie, and his father was a trombone player who left before he was born. His mother wore her hair long and went to all the hippie festivals with the little boy at her side. They lived in London's East End, within the culture of poverty and drugs. When he was fifteen, Ritchie dropped out of school. When he was seventeen, he was one of the most famous people in England, although by then he was known as Sid Vicious of the notorious Sex Pistols.

What did he respond to when the American girl, Nancy Spungen, came into his life? She was a groupie from New York, but she was also an authority figure who pushed him to try harder, complained when he was not given his due, and plotted to get him better deals and wider exposure. If she had not bled to death that night in New York, she might have made Vicious really amount to something, someday.

The astonishing thing about *Sid & Nancy* is the amount of subtle information it gives us about their relationship, given the fact that the surface of the movie is all tumult and violence, pain and confusion. This movie doesn't take the easy way out and cast these two lovers as Romeo and Juliet, misunderstood waifs. It sees beneath their leather and chains, their torn T-shirts and steel-toed boots, to a basically conventional relationship between an ambitious woman and a man who was still a boy.

They needed each other. Spungen needed someone to mother, and Vicious, according to his friends, needed self-esteem and was immensely proud that he had an American girlfriend. They were meant for each other, but by the end it was all just ashes and bewilderment, because they were so strung out on drugs that

whole days would slip by unnoticed. In their fantasies of doomed romance, they planned to go out together in a suicide pact, but by the end they were too sick to even go out together for a pizza.

By now, everybody knows that Vicious woke up one morning in New York's Chelsea Hotel to find Spungen's dead body. He was booked on suspicion of murder, released on bail, and two months later was dead of a drug overdose. The available evidence strongly suggests that he did not stab Spungen to death, but that she died of one of those untidy accidents that befall drug abusers. A human being is a dangerous thing to let loose in a room with itself, when it cannot think.

There were some good times earlier in their story, but on the evidence of this movie there were not many. By the time Spungen met Vicious in London in the mid-1970s, the Sex Pistols were the most infamous punk rock band in the world. But they were in the position of Gandhi in that apocryphal story where he sees the mob run past and races to get in front of his followers. The punk conceit was a total rejection of conventional society; their credo was the line by Johnny Rotten, the Pistols' lead singer: "Got a problem and the problem is you." For the Pistols to stay in front of that mob, they had to be meaner, more violent, more negative than their followers. How did it feel to stand on a bandstand and make angry music while your fans stood face to face, banging heads until unconsciousness came?

Sid & Nancy suggests that Vicious never lived long enough to really get his feet on the ground, to figure out where he stood and where his center was. He was handed great fame and a certain amount of power and money, and indirectly told that his success depended on staying fucked up. This is a big assignment for a kid who would otherwise be unemployable. Vicious did his best, fighting and vomiting and kicking his way through his brief days and long nights, until Spungen brought him a measure of relief. Some nights she was someone to hold, and other nights she was someone to hold onto. What difference did it make?

Sid & Nancy makes these observations with such complexity, such vividness, and such tenderness that at the end of the film a curious thing happens. You do not weep for Vicious, or Spungen, but maybe you weep for all of us, that we have been placed in a world where it is possible for people to make themselves so unhappy. Vicious was not a hero, just a guy who got himself into a situation he couldn't handle. But to thousands of London kids, he represented an affront to a society that offered no jobs, no training, no education, and no entry into the world of opportunity. If life offers you nothing, the least you can offer it is the finger.

Performances like the ones in this film go beyond movie acting and into some kind of evocation of real lives. Vicious is played by Gary Oldman and Spungen is played by Chloe Webb, and there isn't even a brief period at the top of the movie where we have to get used to them. They are these people, driven and relentless.

The movie was directed by Alex Cox, who made *Repo Man* a couple of years ago, and here he announces himself as a great director. He and his actors pull off the neat trick of creating a movie full of noise and fury, and telling a meticulous story right in the middle of it.

But why should anyone care about a movie about two scabrous vulgarians? Because the subject of a really good movie is sometimes not that important. It's the acting, writing, and direction that count. If a movie can illuminate the lives of other people who share this planet with us and show us not only how different they are but, how even so, they share the same dreams and hurts, then it deserves to be called great. If you have an open mind, it is possibly true that the less you care about Sid Vicious, the more you will admire this movie.

Sideways

R, 124 m., 2004

Paul Giamatti (Miles Raymond), Thomas Haden Church (Jack Lopate), Virginia Madsen (Maya), Sandra Oh (Stephanie). Directed by Alexander Payne and produced by Michael London. Screenplay by Payne and Jim Taylor, based on the book by Rex Pickett.

"There was a tasting last night," Miles Raymond explains, on one of those alcoholic mornings that begin in the afternoon and strain eagerly toward the first drink. That's why he's a little shaky. He's not an alcoholic, you understand; he's an oenophile, which means he can continue to pronounce French wines long after most people would be unconscious. We realize he doesn't set the bar too high when he praises one vintage as "quaffable." No wonder his unpublished novel is titled *The Day After Yesterday*; for anyone who drinks a lot, that's what today always feels like.

Miles is the hero of Alexander Payne's *Sideways*, which is as lovable a movie as *Fargo*, although in a completely different way. He's an English teacher in middle school whose marriage has failed, whose novel seems in the process of failing, whose mother apparently understands that when he visits her, it is because he loves her, and also because he needs to steal some of her money. Miles is not perfect, but the way Paul Giamatti plays him, we forgive him his trespasses, because he trespasses most of all against himself.

Miles's friend Jack is getting married in a week. They would seem to have little in common. Jack is a big, blond, jovial man at the peak of fleshy middle-aged handsomeness, and Miles looks like—well, if you know who Harvey Pekar is, that's who Giamatti played in his previous movie. But Jack and Miles have been friends since they were college roommates, and their friendship endures because together they add up to a relatively complete person.

Miles, as the best man, wants to take Jack on a week-long bachelor party in the California wine country, which makes perfect sense, because whatever an alcoholic says he is planning, at the basic level he is planning his drinking. Jack's addiction is to women. "My best man gift to you," he tells Miles, "will be to get you laid." Miles is so manifestly not layable that for him this would be less like a gift than an exercise program.

Jack (Thomas Haden Church) is a not very successful actor; he tells people they may have heard his voice-over work in TV commercials, but it turns out he's the guy who rattles off the warnings about side effects and interest rates in the last five seconds. The two men set off for wine country, and what happens during the next seven days adds up to the best human comedy of the year—comedy, because it is funny, and human, because it is surprisingly moving.

Of course they meet two women. Maya (Virginia Madsen) is a waitress at a restaurant where Miles has often stopped in the past, to yearn but not touch. She's getting her graduate degree in horticulture, and is beautiful, in a kind way; you wonder why she would be attracted to Miles until you find out she was once married to a philosophy professor at Santa Barbara, which can send a woman down-market in search of relief. The next day they meet Stephanie (Sandra Oh), a pour girl at a winery tasting room, and when it appears that the two women know each other, Jack seals the deal with a double date, swearing Miles to silence about the approaching marriage.

Miles has much to be silent about. He has been in various forms of depression for years, and no wonder, since alcohol is a depressant. He is still in love with his former wife, and mourns the bliss that could have been his, if he had not tasted his way out of the marriage. Although his days include learned discourses about vintages, they end with him drunk, and he has a way of telephoning the poor woman late at night. "Did you drink and dial?" Jack asks him.

The movie was written by Payne and Jim Taylor, from the novel by Rex Pickett. One of its lovely qualities is that all four characters are necessary. The women are not plot conveniences, but elements in a complex romantic and even therapeutic process. Miles loves Maya and has for years, but cannot bring himself to make a move because romance requires precision and tact late at night, not Miles's peak time of day. Jack lusts after Stephanie, and casually, even cruelly, fakes love for her even as he cheats on his fiancée.

What happens between them all is the stuff of the movie, and must not be revealed here, except to observe that Giamatti and Madsen have a scene that involves some of the gentlest and most heartbreaking dialogue I've heard in a long time. They're talking about wine. He describes for her the qualities of the Pinot Noir grape that most attract him, and as he mentions its thin skin, its vulnerability, its dislike for being too hot or cold, too wet or dry, she realizes he is describing himself, and that is when she falls in love with him. Women can actually love us for ourselves, bless their hearts, even when we can't love ourselves. She waits until he is finished, and then responds with words so simple and true they will win her an Oscar nomination, if there is justice in the world. *[They did.]*

Terrible misunderstandings (and even worse understandings) take place, tragedy grows confused with slapstick, and why Miles finds himself creeping through the house of a fat waitress and her alarming husband would be completely implausible if we had not seen it coming every step of the way. Happiness is distributed where needed and withheld where deserved, and at the end of the movie we feel like seeing it again.

Alexander Payne has made four wonderful movies: *Citizen Ruth, Election,* the Jack Nicholson tragicomedy *About Schmidt,* and now this. He finds plots that service his characters, instead of limiting them. The characters are played not by the first actors you would think of casting, but by actors who will prevent you from ever being able to imagine anyone else in their roles.

Signs
PG-13, 120 m., 2002

Mel Gibson (Graham Hess), Joaquin Phoenix (Merrill Hess), Rory Culkin (Morgan Hess), Abigail Breslin (Bo Hess), Cherry Jones (Officer Caroline Paski), Patricia Kalember (Colleen Hess). Directed by M. Night Shyamalan and produced by Frank Marshall, Sam Mercer, and Shyamalan. Screenplay by Shyamalan.

M. Night Shyamalan's *Signs* is the work of a born filmmaker, able to summon apprehension out of thin air. When it is over, we think not how little has been decided, but how much has been experienced. Here is a movie in which the plot is the rhythm section, not the melody. A movie that stays free of labored explanations and a forced climax, and is about fear in the wind, in the trees, in a dog's bark, in a little girl's reluctance to drink the water. In signs.

The posters show crop circles, those huge geometric shapes in fields of corn and wheat, which were seen all over the world in the 1970s. Their origin was explained in 1991 when several hoaxers came forward and demonstrated how they made them; it was not difficult, they said. Like many supernatural events, however, crop circles live on after their unmasking, and most people today have forgotten, or never knew, that they were explained. *Signs* uses them to evoke the possibility that . . . well, the possibility of anything.

The genius of the film, you see, is that it isn't

really about crop circles, or the possibility that aliens created them as navigational aids. I will not even say whether aliens appear in the movie, because whether they do or not is beside the point. The purpose of the film is to evoke pure emotion through the use of skilled acting and direction, and particularly through the sound track. It is not just what we hear that is frightening. It is the way Shyamalan has us listening intensely when there is nothing to be heard. I cannot think of a movie where silence is scarier, and inaction is more disturbing.

Mel Gibson stars, as Father Graham Hess, who lives on a farm in Bucks County, Pennsylvania. We discover he is a priest only belatedly, when someone calls him "father." "It's not 'father' anymore," he says. Since he has two children, it takes us a beat to compute that he must be Episcopalian. Not that it matters, because he has lost his faith. The reason for that is revealed midway in the film, a personal tragedy I will not reveal.

Hess lives on the farm with his brother Merrill (Joaquin Phoenix) and his children, Morgan and Bo (Rory Culkin and Abigail Breslin). There is an old-fashioned farmhouse and barn, and wide cornfields, and from the very first shot there seems to be something . . . out there, or up there, or in there. Hess lives with anxiety gnawing at him. The wind sounds strange. Dogs bark at nothing. There is something *wrong*. The crop circles do not explain the feelings so much as add to them. He catches a glimpse of something in a corn field. Something wrong.

The movie uses TV news broadcasts to report on events around the world, but they're not the handy CNN capsules that supply just what the plot requires. The voices of the anchors reveal confusion and fear. A video taken at a birthday party shows a glimpse of the most alarming thing. "The history of the world's future is on TV right now," Morgan says.

In a time when Hollywood mistakes volume for action, Shyamalan makes quiet films. In a time when incessant action is the style, he persuades us to pay close attention to the smallest nuances. In *The Sixth Sense* (1999) he made a ghost story that until the very end seemed only to be a personal drama—although there was something there, some buried hint, that made us feel all was not as it seemed. In *Unbreakable*

(2000) he created a psychological duel between two men, and it was convincing even though we later discovered its surprising underlying nature, and all was redefined.

In *Signs,* he does what Hitchcock said he liked to do, and plays the audience like a piano. There is as little plot as possible, and as much time and depth for the characters as he can create, all surrounded by ominous dread. The possibility of aliens is the catalyst for fear, but this family needs none, because it has already suffered a great blow.

Instead of flashy special effects, Shyamalan creates his world out of everyday objects. A baby monitor that picks up inexplicable sounds. Bo's habit of leaving unfinished glasses of water everywhere. Morgan's bright idea that caps made out of aluminum foil will protect their brains from alien waves. Hess's use of a shiny kitchen knife, not as a weapon, but as a mirror. The worst attack in the film is Morgan's asthma attack, and his father tries to talk him through it, in a scene that sets the entire movie aside and is only about itself.

At the end of the film, I had to smile, recognizing how Shyamalan has essentially ditched a payoff. He knows, as we all sense, that payoffs have grown boring. The mechanical resolution of a movie's problems is something we sit through at the end, but it's the setup and the buildup that keep our attention. *Signs* is all buildup. It's still building when it's over.

Silent Movie

PG, 88 m., 1976

Mel Brooks (Mel Funn), Marty Feldman (Marty Eggs), Dom DeLuise (Dom Bell), Bernadette Peters (Vilma Kaplan), Sid Caesar (Studio Chief), Harold Gould (Engulf), Ron Carey (Devour), Henny Youngman (Fly-in-Soup Man). Directed by Mel Brooks and produced by Michael Hertzorg. Screenplay by Brooks, Ron Clark, Rudy DeLuca, and Barry Levinson.

There's a moment very early in *Silent Movie* (before the opening credits, in fact) when Mel Brooks, Marty Feldman, and Dom DeLuise are tooling through Los Angeles in a tiny sports car. They pass a pregnant lady at a bus stop. "That's a very pregnant lady!" Brooks says (on a title card, of course, since this is a silent movie). "Let's give her a lift!" The lady gets into the back of the car, which tilts back onto its rear wheels. Mel drives off with the front wheels in the air.

This is far from being the funniest scene in a very funny movie, but it helps to illustrate my point, which is that Mel Brooks will do anything for a laugh. Anything. He has no shame. He's an anarchist; his movies inhabit a universe in which everything is possible and the outrageous is probable, and *Silent Movie*, where Brooks has taken a considerable stylistic risk and pulled it off triumphantly, made me laugh a lot. On the Brooks-Laff-O-Meter, I laughed more than in *Young Frankenstein* and about as much as in *Blazing Saddles*, although not, I confess, as much as in *The Producers*.

Silent Movie is not only funny, it's fun. It's clear at almost every moment that the filmmakers had a ball making it. It's set in contemporary Hollywood, where Big Pictures Studio ("If it's a big picture, we've made it") teeters on the edge of bankruptcy and a takeover from the giant Engulf and Devour conglomerate. Enter Mel Funn (Brooks), a once-talented director whose career was cut short by drunkenness, who vows to save the studio by convincing Hollywood's biggest stars to make a silent movie. This is a situation that gives rise to a lot of inside jokes (I wonder whether executives at Gulf and Western, which took over Paramount, will notice any parallels), but the thing about Brooks's inside jokes is that their outsides are funny, too.

The intrepid gang of Mel, Dom, and Marty set out to woo the superstars, materializing in the shower of one (who counts his hands, puzzled, and finds he has eight) and plucking another out of a nightclub audience. (There are several "actual" stars in the movie, but it would be spoiling the fun to name them.) Everything's done amid an encyclopedia of sight gags, old and new, borrowed and with a fly in their soup. There are gags that don't work and stretches of up to a minute, I suppose, when we don't laugh—but even then we're smiling because of Brooks's manic desire to entertain. There's a story about the days, years ago, when Brooks was a writer for Sid Caesar and Caesar would march into the writers' office, pick up their desks, brandish them and shout *"funnier!"* I think the lesson rubbed off.

In a movie filled with great scenes, these moments are classics: The battle with the Coke machine. The behavior with the horse on the merry-go-round. The nightclub scene. The dramatic reaction of Engulf and Devour's board of directors to the photo of sexpot Vilma Kaplan. The fly in the soup. The Pong game in the intensive-care unit. The . . . but space is limited: Perhaps I should mention, though, that the movie isn't really silent. It's filled with wall-to-wall music, sound effects, explosions, whistles, and crashes and, yes, one word.

Silent Running
G, 90 m., 1972

Bruce Dern (Lowell), Cliff Potts (Wolf), Ron Rivkin (Barker), Jesse Vint (Keenan), Mark Persons, Steven Brown, Cheryl Sparks, Larry Wisenhunt (Drones). Directed by Douglas Trumbull and produced by Michael Gruskoff. Screenplay by Deric Washburn, Mike Cimino, and Steve Bochco.

In the not very distant future, man has at last finished with Earth. The mountains are leveled and the valleys filled in, and there are no growing plants left to mess things up. Everything is nice and sterile, and man's global housekeeping has achieved total defoliation. Out around the rings of Saturn, a few lonely spaceships keep their vigil. They're interplanetary greenhouses, pointed always toward the sun. Inside their acres and acres of forests, protected by geodesic domes that gather the sunlight, the surviving plants and small animals of Earth grow. There are squirrels and rabbits and moonlit nights when the wind does actually seem to breathe in the trees: a ghostly reminder of the dead forests of Earth.

The keeper of one of these greenhouses, Freeman Lowell, loves the plants and animals with a not terribly acute intelligence. *Silent Running* is his story. In an earlier day, he might have been a forest ranger and happily spent the winter all alone in a tower, spotting forest fires. Now he is millions of miles from Earth, but his thoughts are filled with weedings and prunings, fertilizer and the artificial rainfall.

One day the word comes from Earth: Destroy the greenhouses and return. Lowell cannot bring himself to do this, and so he destroys his fellow crew members instead. Then he hijacks his spaceship and directs it out into the deep galactic night. All of this is told with simplicity and a quiet ecological concern, and it makes *Silent Running* a movie out of the ordinary—especially if you like science fiction.

The director is Douglas Trumbull, a Canadian who designed many of the special effects for Stanley Kubrick's *2001*. Trumbull also did the computers and the underground laboratory for *The Andromeda Strain*, and is one of the best science-fiction special-effects men. *Silent Running*, which has deep space effects every bit the equal of those in *2001*, also introduces him as an intelligent, if not sensational, director.

The weight of the movie falls on the shoulders of Bruce Dern, who plays the only man in sight during most of the picture. His only companions are Huey, Louie, and Dewey, who are small and uncannily human robots who help with the gardening. They're okay with a trowel but no good at playing poker, as their human boss discovers during a period of boredom.

Dern is a very good, subtle actor, who was about the best thing in Jack Nicholson's directing debut, *Drive, He Said*. Dern played a basketball coach as a man obsessed with the notion of winning—and the deep-space ecologist this time is a quieter variation on the theme.

Silent Running isn't, in the last analysis, a very profound movie, nor does it try to be. (If it had, it could have been a pretentious disaster.) It is about a basically uncomplicated man faced with an awesome, but uncomplicated, situation. Given a choice between the lives of his companions and the lives of Earth's last surviving firs and pines, oaks and elms, and creepers and cantaloupes, he decides for the growing things. After all, there are plenty of men. His problem is that, after a while, he begins to miss them.

Silkwood

R, 128 m., 1983

Meryl Streep (Karen Silkwood), Kurt Russell (Drew Stephens), Cher (Dolly Pelliker), Craig T. Nelson (Winston). Directed by Mike Nichols and produced by Nichols and Michael Hausman. Screenplay by Nora Ephron and Alice Arlen.

When the Karen Silkwood story was first being talked about as a movie project, I pictured it as an angry political exposé, maybe *The China Syndrome, Part 2*. There'd be the noble, young nuclear worker, the evil conglomerate, and, looming overhead, the death's-head of a mushroom cloud. That could have been a good movie, but predictable. Mike Nichols's *Silkwood* is not predictable. That's because he's not telling the story of a conspiracy, he's telling the story of a human life. There are villains in his story, but none with motives we can't understand. After Karen is dead and the movie is over, we realize this is a lot more movie than perhaps we were expecting.

Silkwood is the story of some American workers. They happen to work in a KerrMcGee nuclear plant in Oklahoma, making plutonium fuel rods for nuclear reactors. But they could just as easily be working in a southern textile mill (there are echoes of *Norma Rae*), or on an assembly line, or for a metropolitan public school district. The movie isn't about plutonium, it's about the American working class. Its villains aren't monsters; they're organization men, labor union hotshots, and people afraid of losing their jobs. As the movie opens, Karen Silkwood fits naturally into this world, and the movie is the story of how she begins to stand out, how she becomes an individual, thinks for herself, and is punished for her freedom. Silkwood is played by Meryl Streep, in another of her great performances, and there's a tiny detail in the first moments of the movie that reveals how completely Streep has thought through the role. Silkwood walks into the factory, punches her time card, automatically looks at her own wristwatch, and then shakes her wrist: It's a self-winding watch, I guess. That little shake of the wrist is an actor's choice. There are a lot of them in this movie, all almost as invisible as the first one; little by little, Streep and her coactors build characters so convincing that we become witnesses instead of merely viewers.

The nuclear plant in the film is behind on an important contract. People are working overtime and corners are being cut. A series of small incidents convinces Karen Silkwood that the compromises are dangerous, that the health of the workers is being needlessly risked, and that the company is turning its back on the falsification of safety and work-manship tests. She approaches the union. The union sees some publicity in her complaints. She gets a free trip to Washington—her first airplane ride. She meets with some union officials who are much more concerned with publicity than with working conditions, and she has a little affair with one of them. She's no angel. At home in Oklahoma, domestic life resembles a revolving door, with her boyfriend (Kurt Russell) packing up and leaving, and her friend (Cher), a lesbian, inviting a beautician to move in. It's a little amazing that established movie stars like Streep, Russell, and Cher could disappear so completely into the everyday lives of these characters.

The real Karen Silkwood died in a mysterious automobile accident. She was on her way to deliver some documents to a *New York Times* reporter when her car left the road. Was the accident caused in some way? Was she murdered? The movie doesn't say. Nor does it point suspicion only toward the company. At the end there were a lot of people mad at Karen Silkwood. *Silkwood* is the story of an ordinary woman, hardworking and passionate, funny and screwed-up, who made those people mad simply because she told the truth as she saw it and did what she thought was right.

A Simple Plan

R, 123 m., 1998

Bill Paxton (Hank Mitchell), Billy Bob Thornton (Jacob Mitchell), Bridget Fonda (Sarah Mitchell), Brent Briscoe (Lou), Gary Cole (Baxter), Becky Ann Baker (Nancy), Chelcie Ross (Carl), Jack Walsh (Mr. Pederson). Directed by Sam Raimi and produced by James Jacks and Adam Schroeder. Screenplay by Scott B. Smith, based on his book.

"You work for the American Dream—you don't steal it." So says a Minnesota family man early in *A Simple Plan,* but he is only repeating an untested theory. Confronted with the actual presence of $4 million in cash, he finds his values bending, and eventually he's trapped in a horror story of greed, guilt, and murder.

The materials of Sam Raimi's *A Simple Plan* are not unfamiliar, but rarely is a film this skillful at drawing us, step by step, into the consequences of criminal action. The central character is Hank Mitchell (Bill Paxton), who in a narration at the beginning gives us his father's formula for happiness: "A wife he loves. A decent job. Friends and neighbors that like and respect him."

His older brother, Jacob (Billy Bob Thornton), trapped in a lifetime of dim loneliness, would like to go out with a girl who really likes him, and someday farm the place they grew up on. Jacob's best friend, Lou (Brent Briscoe), basically wants to get by, get drunk, and hang out. Hank's pregnant wife, Sarah (Bridget Fonda), would like enough money so she could plan the week's dinners without checking the coupons in the grocery ads.

All of these dreams seem within reach when the three men stumble across an airplane that has crashed in a nature preserve. On board they find the body of the pilot, and a cache of $4 million in bills. "You want to keep it?" Hank asks incredulously. The others do. Soon he does too. It should be a simple plan to hide the money, wait until spring, and divide it among themselves. It's probably drug money anyway, they tell themselves. Who will know? Who can complain?

Hank is the smartest of the three, a college graduate. Jacob, bucktoothed and nearsighted, has never been very bright. Lou is a loose cannon. Can Hank keep them all under control? Some of the film's most harrowing moments show Hank watching in agonized frustration as the others make big, dumb blunders. Right after they find the money, for example, a law officer happens by, and what does Jacob do but blurt out to Hank: "Did you tell him about the plane? It sure sounded like a plane."

At home, Hank's wife, Sarah, at first agrees it would be wrong to keep the money, but she turns that moral judgment around in a snap, and is soon making smart suggestions: "You have to return some of the money, so it looks like no one has been there." All three men begin to dream of what they could do with the money. Then circumstances inspire one impulsive, reckless act after another—acts I will not reveal, because the strength of this film is in the way it leads its characters into doing things they could never have contemplated.

A Simple Plan is one of the year's best films for a lot of reasons, including its ability to involve the audience almost breathlessly in a story of mounting tragedy. Like the reprehensible *Very Bad Things*, it is about friends stumbling into crime and then stumbling into bigger crimes in an attempt to conceal their guilt. One difference between the two films is that *A Simple Plan* faces its moral implications instead of mocking them. We are not allowed to stand outside the story and feel superior to it; we are drawn along, step by step, as the characters make compromises that lead to unimaginable consequences.

The performances can only be described as flawless: I could not see a single error of tone or feeling. Paxton, Thornton, Fonda, and Briscoe don't reach, don't strain, and don't signal. They simply embody their characters in performances based on a clear emotional logic that carries us along from the beginning to the end. Like Richard Brooks's *In Cold Blood* (1967), this is a film about ordinary people capable of monstrous deeds.

Thornton and Fonda have big scenes that, in other hands, might have led to grandstanding. They perform them so directly and simply that we are moved almost to tears—we identify with their feelings even while shuddering at their deeds.

Thornton's character, Jacob, has never been very bright, and has watched as Hank went to college and achieved what passes for success. At a crucial moment, when his brotherhood is appealed to, he looks at his friend Lou and his brother Hank and says, "We don't have one thing in common, me and him, except maybe our last name." He has another heartbreaking scene as they talk about women. Hank remembers the name of a girl Jacob dated years ago in high school. Jacob reveals that the girl's friends bet her $100 she wouldn't go steady with him for a month. As for Fonda, her best moment is a speech about facing a lifetime of struggling to make ends meet.

The characters are rich, full, and plausible. Raimi's direction and the screenplay by Scott Smith are meticulous in forming and building the characters, and placing them within a film that also functions as a thriller. There is the danger that the theft will be discovered. The deepening hole of crime they dig for themselves. Suspense over the source of the money. Mystery over the true identity of some characters. And two confrontations in the woods—one suspenseful, one heartbreaking.

All of this is seen against a backdrop of Minnesota in the winter (Raimi's friends the Coen brothers, who made *Fargo*, gave advice about shooting and lighting in the snow). The blanket of snow muffles voices, gives a soft edge to things, underlines the way the characters are isolated indoors, each in their own warm refuge. Outdoors, in the woods, foxes kill chickens and men kill each other. Angry black birds scramble to eat dead bodies. "Those things are always waiting for something to die so they can eat it," Jacob says. "What a weird job."

Sin City
R, 126 m., 2005

Bruce Willis (Hartigan), Jessica Alba (Nancy), Rosario Dawson (Gail), Benicio Del Toro (Jackie Boy), Clive Owen (Dwight), Mickey Rourke (Marv), Brittany Murphy (Shellie), Nick Stahl (Yellow Bastard), Alexis Bledel (Becky), Devon Aoki (Miho), Jaime King (Goldie), Frank Miller (Priest), Powers Boothe (Senator Roark), Michael Clarke Duncan (Manute), Carla Gugino (Lucille). Directed by Robert Rodriguez, Frank Miller, and Quentin Tarantino and produced by Elizabeth Avellan, Miller, and Rodriguez. Screenplay by Rodriguez and Miller, based on the stories of Miller.

If *film noir* was not a genre but a hard man on mean streets with a lost love in his heart and a gat in his gut, his nightmares would look like *Sin City*. The new movie by Robert Rodriguez and Frank Miller plays like a convention at the movie museum in Quentin Tarantino's subconscious. A-list action stars rub shoulders with snaky villains and sexy wenches in a city where the streets are always wet, the cars are ragtops, and everybody smokes. It's a black-and-white world, except for blood that is red, eyes that are green, hair that is blond, and the Yellow Bastard.

This isn't an adaptation of a comic book; it's like a comic book brought to life and pumped with steroids. It contains characters who occupy stories, but to describe the characters and summarize the stories would be like replacing the weather with a weather map.

The movie is not about narrative but about style. It internalizes the harsh world of the Frank Miller *Sin City* comic books and processes it through computer effects, grotesque makeup, lurid costumes, and dialogue that chops at the language of *noir*. The actors are mined for the archetypes they contain; Bruce Willis, Mickey Rourke, Jessica Alba, Rosario Dawson, Benicio Del Toro, Clive Owen, and the others are rotated into a hyperdimension. We get not so much their presence as their essence; the movie is not about what the characters say or what they do, but about who they are in our wildest dreams.

On the movie's Web site there's a slide show juxtaposing the original drawings of Frank Miller with the actors playing the characters, and then with the actors transported by effects into the visual world of graphic novels. Some of the stills from the film look so much like frames of the comic book as to make no difference. And there's a narration that plays like the captions at the top of the frame, setting the stage and expressing a stark, existential world view.

Rodriguez has been aiming toward *Sin City* for years. I remember him leaping out of his chair and bouncing around a hotel room, pantomiming himself filming *Spy Kids 2* with a digital camera and editing it on a computer. The future! he told me. This is the future! You don't wait six hours for a scene to be lighted. You want a light over here, you grab a light and put it over here. You want a nuclear submarine, you make one out of thin air and put your characters into it.

I held back, wondering if perhaps the spy kids would have been better served if the films had not been such a manic demonstration of his method. But never mind; the first two *Spy Kids* were exuberant fun (*Spy Kids 3-D* sucked, in great part because of the 3-D). Then came his *Once Upon a Time in Mexico* (2003), and I wrote it was "more interested in the moment, in great shots, in surprises and ironic reversals and close-ups of sweaty faces, than in a coherent story." Yes, but it worked.

And now Rodriguez has found narrative discipline in the last place you might expect, by choosing to follow the Miller comic books almost literally. A graphic artist has no time or room for drifting. Every frame contributes, and the story marches from page to page in vivid action snapshots. *Sin City* could easily have looked as good as it does and still been a mess, if it were not for the energy of Miller's storytelling, which is not the standard

chronological account of events, but more like a tabloid murder illuminated by flashbulbs.

The movie is based on three of the *Sin City* stories, each more or less self-contained. That's wise, because at this velocity a two-hour, one-story narrative would begin to pant before it got to the finish line. One story involves Bruce Willis as a battered old cop at war with a pedophile (Nick Stahl). One has Mickey Rourke waking up next to a dead hooker (Jaime King). One has a good guy (Clive Owen) and a wacko cop (Benicio Del Toro) disturbing the delicate balance of power negotiated between the police and the leader of the city's hookers (Rosario Dawson), who despite her profession moonlights as Owen's lover. Underneath everything is a deeper layer of corruption, involving a senator (Powers Boothe), whose son is not only the pedophile but also the Yellow Bastard.

We know the Bastard is yellow because the movie paints him yellow, just as the comic book did; it was a masterstroke for Miller to find a compromise between the cost of full-color reproduction and the economy of two-color pages; red, green, and blue also make their way into the frames. Actually, I can't even assume Miller went the two-color route for purposes of economy, because it's an effective artistic decision.

There are other vivid characters in the movie, which does not have leads so much as actors who dominate the foreground and then move on. In a movie that uses nudity as if the 1970s had survived, Rosario Dawson's stripper is a fierce dominatrix, Carla Gugino shows more skin than she could in Maxim, and Devon Aoki employs a flying guillotine that was borrowed no doubt from a circa-1970 Hong Kong exploiter.

Rodriguez codirected, photographed, and edited the movie, collaborated on the music and screenplay, and is coproducer. Frank Miller and Quentin Tarantino are credited as codirectors, Miller because his comic books essentially act as storyboards, which Rodriguez follows with ferocity, Tarantino because he directed one brief scene on a day when Rodriguez was determined to wean him away from celluloid and lure him over to the dark side of digital. (It's the scene in the car with Clive Owen and Del Toro, who has a pistol stuck in his head.) Tarantino also contributed something to the culture of the film, which follows his influential *Pulp Fiction* in its recycling of pop archetypes and its circular story structure. The language of the film, both dialogue and narration, owes much to the hard-boiled pulp novelists of the 1950s.

Which brings us, finally, to the question of the movie's period. Skylines suggest the movie is set today. The cars range from the late 1930s to the 1950s. The costumes are from the trench coat and g-string era. I don't think *Sin City* really has a period, because it doesn't really tell a story set in time and space. It's a visualization of the pulp *noir* imagination, uncompromising and extreme. Yes, and brilliant.

Sky Captain and the World of Tomorrow

PG, 107 m., 2004

Jude Law (Joe "Sky Captain" Sullivan), Gwyneth Paltrow (Polly Perkins), Angelina Jolie (Captain Franky Cook), Giovanni Ribisi (Dex Dearborn), Michael Gambon (Editor Morris Paley), Ling Bai (Mysterious Woman). Directed by Kerry Conran and produced by Jon Avnet, Sadie Frost, Law, and Marsha Oglesby. Screenplay by Conran.

Sky Captain and the World of Tomorrow is even more fun than it sounds like. In its heedless energy and joy, it reminded me of how I felt the first time I saw *Raiders of the Lost Ark*. It's like a film that escaped from the imagination directly onto the screen, without having to pass through reality along the way.

Before I got into serious science fiction, I went through a period when my fantasies were fed by a now-forgotten series of books about Tom Corbett, Space Cadet. There was a gee-whiz vigor to those adventures, a naive faith in science and pluck, evoking a world in which evil existed primarily as an opportunity for Tom to have fun vanquishing it. *Sky Captain* has that kind of innocence.

Jude Law and Gwyneth Paltrow star, as Joe "Sky Captain" Sullivan, a freelance buccaneer for truth and justice, and Polly Perkins, a scoop-crazy newspaperwoman who hitches a ride in his airplane. Manhattan has come under attack from giant mechanical men who lumber through the skies like flying wrestlers, and stomp down the city streets sending civilians scurrying. This is obviously a case for Sky Captain, who must be the richest man on Earth,

judging by his secret hideaway and what seems to be his private air force and science lab.

The robots have been sent by the mysterious Dr. Totenkopf, a World War I–vintage German scientist who has nurtured his plans for world domination ever since. He has kidnapped many leading scientists, and now his metal men will enforce his rule, unless Joe and Polly can stop him. Also on the side of the good guys are Franky (Angelina Jolie), a sexy pilot with her own agenda, and Dex Dearborn (Giovanni Ribisi), Sky Captain's head of research and development.

To summarize the plot would spoil the fun, and be pointless anyway, since the plot exists essentially to inspire silly grins. What needs to be described is the look and technique of the film. *Sky Captain* is filmed halfway between full color and sepiatone, so that it has the richness of color and yet the distance and nostalgic quality of an old photograph. Its production design and art direction remind me of covers for ancient pulp magazines like *Thrilling Wonder Stories*.

Much will be written about the technique, about how the first-time director, Kerry Conran, labored for years to bring forth on his Macintosh a six-minute film illustrating his vision for *Sky Captain*. This film caught the attention of the director Jon Avnet, who agreed to produce Conran's film and presented the idea to Paltrow and Law.

The actors did almost all of their scenes in front of a blue screen, which was then replaced with images generated on computers. The monsters, the city, and most of the sets and props never really existed except as digital files. This permitted a film of enormous scope to be made with a reasonable budget, but it also freed Conran and his collaborators to show whatever they wanted to, because one digital fantasy costs about as much as another.

The film is not good because it was filmed in this way, however; it's just plain good. The importance of the technique is that it allows the movie to show idealized versions of sci-fi fantasies that are impossible in the real world and often unconvincing as more conventional special effects. It removes the layers of impossibility between the inspiration and the audience.

Paltrow and Law do a good job of creating the kind of camaraderie that flourished between the genders in the 1930s and 1940s, in films like *The Lady Eve*, with Henry Fonda and Barbara Stanwyck, or *His Girl Friday*, with Cary Grant and Rosalind Russell. The women in this tradition are tomboys (Katharine Hepburn is the prototype), and although romance is not unknown to them, they're often running too fast to kiss anyone. We gather that Polly and Joe had a romance a few years ago that ended badly (Franky may have had a role in that), but now their chemistry renews itself as they fly off to Nepal in search of Dr. Totenkopf's lair.

The evil doctor is played by Laurence Olivier, who died in 1989, and who is seen here through old shots recycled into a new character. A posthumous performance makes a certain sense, given the nature of Dr. Totenkopf. There's something ghoulish about using a dead actor's likeness without his knowledge, and in the past I've deplored such desecrations as the Fred Astaire dust-buster ads, but surely every actor on his deathbed, entering the great unknown, hopes he has not given his last performance.

Sky Captain will probably not inspire the universal affection of a film like *Indiana Jones*, in part because Steven Spielberg is a better director than Kerry Conran, in part because many of *Sky Captain*'s best qualities are more cinematic than dramatic; I responded to the texture and surfaces and very feel of the images, and felt some of the same quickening I remember from the cover of a new Tom Corbett book. If the Space Cadet ever graduated, he probably grew up to be Sky Captain.

Sleuth

PG, 138 m., 1972

Laurence Olivier (Andrew Wyke), Michael Caine (Milo Tindle), Alec Cawthorne (Inspector Doppler), Eve Channing (Marguerite), John Matthews (Sergeant Talvant), Teddy Martin (Constable Higgs). Directed by Joseph L. Mankiewicz and produced by Morton Gottleib. Screenplay by Anthony Shaffer, based on his play.

We come upon Andrew Wyke, the mystery writer, in an appropriate setting. He's in the middle of his vast garden, which is filled with shrubbery planted to form a maze. There is no way into, or out of, the maze—unless you know the secret. The better we come to know Andrew Wyke, the more this seems like the kind of garden he would have.

Wyke is a game-player. His enormous Tudor country manor is filled with games, robots, performing dolls, dart boards, and chess tables. He also plays games with people. One day poor Milo Tindle comes for a meeting with him. Milo is everything Wyke detests: only half-British, with the wrong accent, and "brand-new country gentleman clothes."

But Milo and Andrew's wife have fallen in love, and they plan to marry. So Andrew has a little scheme he wants to float. He is willing—indeed, happy—to give up his wife, but only if he can be sure she'll stay gone. He wants to be sure Milo can support her, and he suggests that Milo steal the Wyke family jewels and pawn them in Amsterdam. Then Milo will have a small fortune, and Andrew can collect the insurance.

Up to this point, everything in *Sleuth* seems so matter-of-fact that there's no hint how complicated things will get later on. But they do get complicated, and deadly, and reality begins to seem like a terribly fragile commodity. Andrew and Milo play games of such labyrinthine ferociousness that they eventually seem to forget all about Andrew's wife (and his mistress) and to be totally absorbed with stalking each other in a macabre game of cat and mouse.

Sleuth, a totally engrossing entertainment, is funny and scary by turns, and always superbly theatrical. It's the kind of mystery we keep saying they don't make anymore, but sometimes they do, and the British seem to write them better than anyone. The movie is based on the long-running play by Anthony Shaffer, who also wrote Alfred Hitchcock's *Frenzy*. Both films have in common a nice flair for dialogue and a delicate counterpoint between the ironic and the gruesome.

What really makes the movie come alive—what makes it work better than the play, really—are the lead performances by Sir Laurence Olivier, Michael Caine, and Alec Cawthorne. Olivier plays the wealthy mystery writer Andrew Wyke as a true-blue British eccentric: His head, like his house, is cluttered with ornate artifacts largely without function. The hero of his detective stories, the wonderfully named St. John Lord Merridewe, is equally dotty. Olivier is clearly having fun in the role, and he throws in all kinds of accents, asides, and nutty pieces of business. Michael Caine, who might seem an unlikely candidate to play Milo Tindle, turns out to be a very good one. He manages somehow to seem smaller and less assured than Olivier (even while he towers over Sir Laurence). And he is strangely touching as he dresses up in an absurd clown's costume to steal the jewels. Inspector Doppler, the kindly old investigator who suspects that Andrew has murdered Milo, is played by Alec Cawthorne, a veteran stage actor making his movie debut.

It's difficult to say more about *Sleuth* without giving away its plot—which in this case would be a capital offense. Let me just mention that the play makes a remarkably easy transition to the screen because of director Joseph L. Mankiewicz's willingness to respect its timing and dialogue, instead of trying to jazz it up cinematically. And, despite the fact that most of the movie takes place indoors, we never get the sense of visual limitations because Ken Adams's set designs give us such an incredible multitude of things to look at (and through) in the mansion.

Small Change

PG, 104 m., 1976

Geory Desmouceaux (Patrick), Philippe Goldman (Julien), Christine Pelle (Madame), Jean-François Stevenin and Chantal Mercier (The Teachers). Directed by François Truffaut. Screenplay by Truffaut and Suzanne Schiffman.

There's a moment in François Truffaut's *Small Change* that remembers childhood so well we don't know whether to laugh or cry. It takes place in a classroom a few minutes before the bell at the end of the school day. The class cutup is called on. He doesn't have the answer (he never does), but as he stands up his eyes stray to a large clock outside the window. The hand stands at twenty-eight minutes past the hour. Click: twenty-nine minutes. He stalls, he grins, the teacher repeats the question. Click: thirty past, and the class bell rings. The kid breaks out in a triumphant grin as he joins the stampede from the room.

This moment, like so many in Truffaut's magical film, has to be seen to be appreciated. He re-creates childhood, and yet he sees it objectively, too: He remembers not only the funny moments but the painful ones. The agony of a first crush. The ordeal of being the only kid in class so poor he has to wear the same sweater every day. The painful earnestness that goes into the recitation of a dirty joke that neither the teller nor the listeners quite understand.

Truffaut has been over some of this ground before. His first feature, *The 400 Blows*, told the painful story of a Paris adolescent caught between his warring parents and his own better nature. In *Small Change* he returns to similar material in a sunnier mood. He tells the stories of several kids in a French provincial town, and of their parents and teachers. His method is episodic; only gradually do we begin to recognize faces, to pick the central characters out from the rest. He correctly remembers that childhood itself is episodic: Each day seems separate from any other, each new experience is sharply etched, and important discoveries and revelations become great events surrounded by a void. It's the accumulation of all those separate moments that create, at last, a person.

"Children exist in a state of grace," he has a character say at one point. "They pass untouched through dangers that would destroy an adult." There are several such hazards in *Small Change*. The most audacious—Truffaut at his best—involves a two-year-old child, a kitten, and an open window on the tenth floor. Truffaut milks this situation almost shamelessly before finally giving us the happiest of denouements. And he exhibits at the same time his mastery of film; the scene is timed and played to exist exactly at the border between comedy and tragedy, and from one moment to the next we don't know how we should feel. He's got the audience in his hand.

That's true, too, in a scene involving a little girl who has been made to stay at home as a punishment. She takes her father's battery-powered megaphone and announces indignantly to the neighbors around the courtyard that she is hungry, that her parents have gone out to a restaurant without her, and that she has been abandoned. The neighbors lower her food in a basket: Chicken and fruit but not, after all, a bottle of red wine one of the neighborhood kids wanted to put in.

In the midst of these comic episodes, a more serious story is developed. It's about the kid who lives in a shack outside of town. He's abused by his parents, he lives by his wits, he steals to eat. His mistreatment is finally found out by his teachers, and leads to a concluding speech by one of them that's probably unnecessary but expresses Truffaut's thinking all the same: "If kids had the vote," the teacher declares, "the world would be a better and safer place."

Smash Palace

R, 100 m., 1982

Bruno Lawrence (Al Shaw), Anna Jemison (Jacqui Shaw), Greer Robson (Georgie Shaw), Keith Aberdeen (Ray Foley), Des Kelly (Tiny). Directed and produced by Roger Donaldson. Screenplay by Donaldson, Peter Hansard, and Lawrence.

Step by step, this powerful movie takes a man from perfect happiness into a personal hell. By the end of the film, the man is behaving irrationally, but here's the frightening thing: Because we've followed him every step of the way, we have to admit he's behaving as we ourselves might, in the same circumstances. The man in *Smash Palace* is Al Shaw, a Grand Prix driver who leaves the racing circuit to take over his father's auto garage in New Zealand. Played by Bruno Lawrence, Al is a straight-talking, direct man who enjoys working with his hands and takes a vast delight in the affections of his wife and the love of his small daughter. It's a long way from the Grand Prix to repairing transmissions, but he's happy with his work and content to raise a family in peace and quiet. His wife (Anna Jemison) is not so content. She wanted him to leave the racing circuit before he was killed, but now, in the quiet backwaters of New Zealand, she is going quietly stir-crazy. She begins an affair with a local cop (Keith Aberdeen) and finally tells her husband she's leaving him. She's moving into town.

Her decision starts him on a series of wrong moves that may seem logical, one by one, but which eventually add up in the minds of others to a simple conclusion: He has lost his rea-

son. He is jealous—of course. He holds a great fury against his wife and the cop. But, much more important, he misses his daughter. He wants custody. But because he acts in ways that are violent and frightening to his wife (and because her lover is on the police force, which must respond to the domestic emergencies he creates), he works himself into a Catch-22: The more he does to take back his daughter, the closer he is to losing her. Finally, he kidnaps her. He takes her out into the woods where they live together for a time in isolation and happiness. It's an idyll that can't last. But *Smash Palace* doesn't lead up to the inevitable violent conclusion we might expect. All along the way, this film prefers the unexpected turns of actual human behavior to the predictable plot developments we might have expected, and, at the end, there's another turn, a fascinating one.

Smash Palace is one of 1982's best films, an examination of much the same ground as *Shoot the Moon*, but a better film, because it has the patience to explore the ways in which people can become consumed by anger (*Shoot the Moon* contented itself with the outward symptoms). One of the reasons the movie works so well is the performances, which are all the stronger because they come from actors we have not seen before. Bruno Lawrence, bald-headed, wiry, tough, and surprisingly tender, is just right as the man who loses his family. Anna Jemison has a difficult assignment as his wife: We're on his side, and yet we see the logic of her moves. Keith Aberdeen is properly tentative as the other man; he feels love and lust, and yet is not unaware of the unhappiness he is causing. And there's a guy named Des Kelly who plays Tiny, an employee at the Smash Palace who looks on, and sees all, and wishes he knew what to do.

The movie was directed by a young filmmaker named Roger Donaldson, who, in a sense, *is* the New Zealand film industry. He has produced six features for New Zealand television, and his first feature film, *Sleeping Dogs*, starred Warren Oates in a horrifying and plausible fantasy about the American occupation of New Zealand. Now comes this film, so emotionally wise and observant that we learn from it why people sometimes make the front pages with guns in their hands and try to explain that it's all because of love. Love, yes, but also the terrible frustration of trying to control events, to make people do what you want them to do, what you "know" would make them happy—no matter what they think. The hero of *Smash Palace* does not act wisely, but if we are honest, it's hard to see where we might have acted differently.

The Son

NO MPAA RATING, 103 m., 2003

Olivier Gourmet (Olivier), Morgan Marinne (Francis), Isabella Soupart (Magali), Remy Renaud (Philippo), Nassim Hassaini (Omar), Kevin Leroy (Raoul), Felicien Pitsaer (Steve). Directed by Jean-Pierre Dardenne and Luc Dardenne and produced by the Dardennes and Denis Freyd. Screenplay by the Dardennes.

The Son is complete, self-contained, and final. All the critic can bring to it is his admiration. It needs no insight or explanation. It sees everything and explains all. It is as assured and flawless a telling of sadness and joy as I have ever seen.

I agree with Stanley Kauffmann, in the *New Republic,* that a second viewing only underlines the film's greatness, but I would not want to have missed my first viewing, so I will write carefully. The directors, Jean-Pierre Dardenne and Luc Dardenne, do not make the slightest effort to mislead or deceive us. Nor do they make any effort to explain. They simply (not so simply) show, and we lean forward, hushed, reading the faces, watching the actions, intent on sharing the feelings of the characters.

Let me describe a very early sequence in enough detail for you to appreciate how the Dardenne brothers work. Olivier (Olivier Gourmet), a Belgian carpenter, supervises a shop where teenage boys work. He corrects a boy using a power saw. We wonder, because we have been beaten down by formula films, if someone is going to lose a finger or a hand. No. The plank is going to be cut correctly.

A woman comes into the shop and asks Olivier if he can take another apprentice. No, he has too many already. He suggests the welding shop. The moment the woman and the young applicant leave, Olivier slips from the shop and, astonishingly, scurries after them like a feral animal and spies on them through a door open-

ing and the angle of a corridor. A little later, strong and agile, he leaps up onto a metal cabinet to steal a look through a high window.

Then he tells the woman he will take the boy after all. She says the boy is in the shower room. The handheld camera, which follows Olivier everywhere, usually in close medium shot, follows him as he looks around a corner (we intuit it is a corner; two walls form an apparent join). Is he watching the boy take a shower? Is Olivier gay? No. We have seen too many movies. He is simply looking at the boy asleep, fully clothed, on the floor of the shower room. After a long, absorbed look he wakes up the boy and tells him he has a job.

Now you must absolutely stop reading and go see the film. Walk out of the house today, tonight, and see it, if you are open to simplicity, depth, maturity, silence, in a film that sounds in the echo chambers of the heart. *The Son* is a great film. If you find you cannot respond to it, that is the degree to which you have room to grow. I am not being arrogant; I grew during this film. It taught me things about the cinema I did not know.

What did I learn? How this movie is only possible because of the way it was made, and would have been impossible with traditional narrative styles. Like rigorous documentarians, the Dardenne brothers follow Olivier, learning everything they know about him by watching him. They do not point, underline, or send signals by music. There are no reaction shots because the entire movie is their reaction shot. The brothers make the consciousness of the Olivier character into the auteur of the film.

... So now you have seen the film. If you were spellbound, moved by its terror and love, struck that the visual style is the only possible one for this story, then let us agree that rarely has a film told us less and told us all, both at once.

Olivier trains wards of the Belgian state—gives them a craft after they are released from a juvenile home. Francis (Morgan Marinne) was in such a home from his eleventh to sixteenth years. Olivier asks him what his crime was. He stole a car radio.

"And got five years?"

"There was a death."

"What kind of a death?"

There was a child in the car, whom Francis did not see. The child began to cry and would not let go of Francis, who was frightened and "grabbed him by the throat."

"Strangled him," Olivier corrects.

"I didn't mean to," Francis says.

"Do you regret what you did?"

"Obviously."

"Why obviously?"

"Five years locked up. That's worth regretting."

You have seen the film and know what Olivier knows about this death. You have seen it and know the man and boy are at a remote lumberyard on a Sunday. You have seen it and know how *hard* the noises are in the movie, the heavy planks banging down one upon another. How it hurts even to hear them. The film does not use these sounds or the towers of lumber to create suspense or anything else. It simply respects the nature of lumber, as Olivier does and is teaching Francis to do. You expect, because you have been trained by formula films, an accident or an act of violence. What you could not expect is the breathtaking spiritual beauty of the ending of the film, which is nevertheless no less banal than everything that has gone before.

Olivier Gourmet won the award for best actor at Cannes 2002. He plays an ordinary man behaving at all times in an ordinary way. Here is the key: *Ordinary for him.* The word for his behavior—not his performance, his behavior—is "exemplary." We use the word to mean "praiseworthy." Its first meaning is "fit for imitation."

Everything that Olivier does is exemplary. Walk like this. Hold yourself just so. Measure exactly. Do not use the steel hammer when the wooden mallet is required. Center the nail. Smooth first with the file, then with the sandpaper. Balance the plank and lean into the ladder. Pay for your own apple turnover. Hold a woman who needs to be calmed. Praise a woman who has found she is pregnant. Find out the truth before you tell the truth. Do not use words to discuss what cannot be explained. Be willing to say, "I don't know." Be willing to have a son and teach him a trade. Be willing to be a father.

A recent movie got a laugh by saying there is a rule in *The Godfather* to cover every situation. There can never be that many rules. *The Son* is about a man who needs no rules because he respects his trade and knows his

tools. His trade is life. His tools are his loss and his hope.

Songs from the Second Floor

NO MPAA RATING, 98 m., 2000

Lars Nordh (Kalle), Stefan Larsson (Stefan), Torbjörn Fahlstrom (Pelle), Sten Andersson (Lasse), Lucio Vucina (Magician), Hanna Eriksson (Mia), Peter Roth (Tomas), Tommy Johansson (Uffe). Directed by Roy Andersson and produced by Lisa Alwert and Andersson. Screenplay by Andersson.

In a sour gray city, filled with pale drunken salarymen and parading flagellants, everything goes wrong, pain is laughed at, businesses fail, traffic seizes up, and a girl is made into a human sacrifice to save a corporation. Roy Andersson's *Songs from the Second Floor* is a collision at the intersection of farce and tragedy—the apocalypse, as a joke on us.

You have never seen a film like this before. You may not enjoy it, but you will not forget it. Andersson is a deadpan Swedish surrealist who has spent the last twenty-five years making "the best TV commercials in the world" (Ingmar Bergman), and now bites off the hand that fed him, chews it thoughtfully, spits it out, and tramples on it. His movie regards modern capitalist society with the detached hilarity of a fanatic saint squatting on his pillar in the desert.

I saw it at the 2000 Cannes Film Festival. Understandably, it did not immediately find a distributor. Predictably, audiences did not flock to it. When I screened it at my 2001 Overlooked Film Festival, there were times when the audience laughed out loud, times when it squinted in dismay, times when it watched in disbelief. When two of the actors came out onstage afterward, it was somehow completely appropriate that one of them never said a word.

I love this film because it is completely new, starting from a place no other film has started from, proceeding implacably to demonstrate the logic of its despair, arriving at a place of no hope. One rummages for the names of artists to evoke: Bosch, Tati, Kafka, Beckett, Dali. It is "slapstick Ingmar Bergman," says J. Hoberman in the *Village Voice.* Yes, and tragic Groucho Marx.

The film opens ironically with a man in a tanning machine—ironic, because all of the other characters will look like they've spent years in sunless caves. It proceeds with a series of set pieces in which the camera, rarely moving, gazes impassively at scenes of absurdity and despair. A man is fired and clings to the leg of his boss, who marches down a corridor dragging him behind. A magician saws a volunteer in two. Yes. A man with the wrong accent is attacked by a gang. A man burns down his own store and then assures insurance inspectors it was arson, but as they talk we lose interest, because outside on the street a parade of flagellants marches past, whipping themselves in time to their march.

There is the most slender of threads connecting the scenes—the arsonist is a continuing character—but Andersson is not telling a conventional story. He is planting his camera here and there in a city that has simply stopped working, has broken down and is cannibalizing itself. It is a twentieth-century city, but Andersson sees it as an appropriate backdrop for the plague or any other medieval visitation. And its citizens have fallen back on ancient fearful superstition to protect themselves.

Consider the scene where clerics and businessmen, all robed for their offices, gather in a desolate landscape as a young woman walks the plank to her death below. Perhaps the sacrifice of her life will placate the gods who are angry with the corporation. We watch this scene and we are forced to admit that corporations are capable of such behavior: that a tobacco company, for example, expects its customers to walk the plank every day.

Is there no hope in this devastation? A man who corners the market in crucifixes now bitterly tosses out his excess inventory. "I staked everything on a loser," he complains. Does that make the movie anti-Christian? No. It is not anti-anything. It is about the loss of hope, about the breakdown of all systems of hope. Its characters are piggish, ignorant, clueless salarymen who, without salaries, have no way to be men. The movie argues that in an economic collapse our modern civilization would fall from us, and we would be left wandering our cities like the plague victims of old, seeking relief in drunkenness, superstition, sacrifice, sex, and self-mockery.

Oh, but yes, the film is often very funny about this bleak view. I have probably not con-

vinced you of that. It's funny because it stands back and films its scenes in long shot, the camera not moving, so that we can distance ourselves from the action—and we remember the old rule from the silent days: Comedy in long shot, tragedy in close-up. Close shots cause us to identify with the characters, to weep and fear along with them. Long shots allow us to view them objectively, within their environment. *Songs from the Second Floor* is a parade of fools marching blindly to their ruin, and for the moment, we are still spectators and have not been required to join the march. The laughter inspired by the movie is sometimes at the absurd, sometimes simply from relief.

Sophie's Choice
R, 157 m., 1982

Meryl Streep (Sophie), Kevin Kline (Nathan), Peter MacNicol (Stingo), Greta Turken (Leslie Lapidus), Gunther Maria Halmer (Rudolf Hoess). Directed by Alan J. Pakula and produced by Pakula and Keith Barish. Screenplay by Pakula.

Sometimes when you've read the novel, it gets in the way of the images on the screen. You keep remembering how you imagined things. That didn't happen with me during *Sophie's Choice*, because the movie is so perfectly cast and well-imagined that it just takes over and happens to you. It's quite an experience.

The movie stars Meryl Streep as Sophie, a Polish-Catholic woman, who was caught by the Nazis with a contraband ham, was sentenced to a concentration camp, lost her two children there, and then was somehow spared to immigrate to Brooklyn, U.S.A., and to the arms of an eccentric charmer named Nathan. Sophie and Nathan move into an old boardinghouse, and the rooms just below them are taken by Stingo, a jug-eared kid from the South who wants to be a great novelist. As the two lovers play out their doomed, romantic destiny, Stingo falls in love with several things: with his image of himself as a writer, with his idealized vision of Sophie and Nathan's romance, and, inevitably, with Sophie herself.

The movie, like the book, is told with two narrators. One is Stingo, who remembers these people from that summer in Brooklyn, and who also remembers himself at that much earlier age. The other narrator, contained within Stingo's story, is Sophie herself, who remembers what happened to her during World War II, and shares her memories with Stingo in a long confessional. Both the book and the movie have long central flashbacks, and neither the book nor the movie is damaged by those diversions, because Sophie's story is so indispensable to Stingo's own growth, from an adolescent dreamer to an artist who can begin to understand human suffering. The book and movie have something else in common. Despite the fact that Sophie's story, her choices, and her fate are all sad, sad stories, there is a lot of exuberance and joy in the telling of them. *Sophie's Choice* begins as a young southerner's odyssey to the unimaginable North—to that strange land celebrated by his hero, Thomas Wolfe, who took the all-night train to New York with its riches, its women, and its romance. Stingo is absolutely entranced by this plump blond Polish woman who moves so winningly into his life, and by her intense, brilliant, mad lover.

We almost don't notice, at first, as Stingo's odyssey into adulthood is replaced, in the film, by Sophie's journey back into the painful memories of her past. The movie becomes an act of discovery, as the naive young American, his mind filled with notions of love, death, and honor, becomes the friend of a woman who has seen so much hate, death, and dishonor that the only way she can continue is by blotting out the past, and drinking and loving her way into temporary oblivion. It's basically a three-character movie, and the casting, as I suggested, is just right. Meryl Streep is a wonder as Sophie. She does not quite look or sound or feel like the Meryl Streep we have seen before in *The Deer Hunter* or *Manhattan* or *The French Lieutenant's Woman*. There is something juicier about her this time; she is merrier and sexier, more playful and cheerful in the scenes before she begins to tell Stingo the truth about her past. Streep plays the Brooklyn scenes with an enchanting Polish-American accent (she has the first accent I've ever wanted to hug), and she plays the flashbacks in subtitled German and Polish. There is hardly an emotion that Streep doesn't touch in this movie, and yet we're never aware of her

straining. This is one of the most astonishing and yet one of the most unaffected and natural performances I can imagine.

Kevin Kline plays Nathan, the crazy romantic who convinces everyone he's on the brink of finding the cure for polio and who wavers uncertainly between anger and manic exhilaration. Peter MacNicol is Stingo, the kid who is left at the end to tell the story. Kline, MacNicol, and Streep make such good friends in this movie—despite all the suffering they go through—that we really do believe the kid when he refuses to act on an unhappy revelation, insisting, "These are my *friends*. I love them!"

Sophie's Choice is a fine, absorbing, wonderfully acted, heartbreaking movie. It is about three people who are faced with a series of choices, some frivolous, some tragic. As they flounder in the bewilderment of being human in an age of madness, they become our friends, and we love them.

The Sorrow and the Pity
PG, 130 m., 1972

A documentary directed by Marcel Ophuls and produced by André Harris and Alain de Sedovy.

The Sorrow and the Pity leaves you with the peculiar feeling of having spent a good deal of time, over the years, in the small French city of Clermont-Ferrand. You know the inhabitants by name and quite a few of their faces. You even knew some of their secrets, and what they privately think of one another.

You know, for example, that this jolly appliance salesman was the famed *Colonel* Gaspar, hero of the Resistance. That a local public relations man was so impressed by the Third Reich that he signed up with a company of French volunteers and went off to wear the German uniform and fight the Russians. And that a weathered old farmer who fought for the underground knows which of his neighbors turned him in to the Nazis, but doesn't much care.

"What can be done about it at this late date?" he says, sighing, sitting at his kitchen table surrounded by his family, his friends, and several bottles of the excellent regional wine.

His remark is one of the most haunting in the whole four-and-a-half-hour length of this remarkable documentary, because he seems to be speaking for so many of the survivors of the Nazi occupation of France, on both sides. Their passions were high and their loyalties were fierce, and many of them were killed, tortured, or imprisoned.

And yet, thirty years later, they seem to share a kind of intellectual exhaustion on the subject.

The occupation was such a complex matter, so much a matter of human nature, they seem to say. It is hard to explain to an outsider (and maybe even to oneself) exactly how a decision was reached, and why some Frenchmen collaborated with the Germans while others resisted and most simply tried to carry on business as usual.

Director Marcel Ophuls spent more than two years compiling the fifty hours of footage that eventually were edited into *The Sorrow and the Pity*. He spoke with the little people— some of them so anonymous they seem ashamed of their opinions, if indeed they have any—and with the larger figures such as Pierre Mendes-France, Georges Bidault, Anthony Eden, and German armaments czar Albert Speer.

He introduces us to "Colonel" Gaspar and to Gaspar's wartime associate, who says a little bitchily that Gaspar was a hero, yes, but he was greedy for glory.

Ophuls has also found the commander of the German occupation forces in Clermont-Ferrand and obtained a painfully revealing interview with him at his daughter's wedding. (He thinks others resent the fact that he wears his World War II decorations because they're jealous that they don't have medals of their own, and he complains that the Resistance fighters didn't play fair—they disguised themselves as peasants instead of wearing a mark of identification, "some kind of hat or armband, you know.")

The striking thing about all of these people is that, so far as I can remember, no one on either side brings up questions of morality in an attempt to explain his own actions. No one says that he acted as he did because he was right and the other side was wrong. This was certainly the basis for actions of many of the participants, but they seem reluctant to admit to such deep motivation.

Instead, they give reasons that seem banal until you realize how moving their evasions actually are.

The old farmer, for example, went underground and risked his life for years because, he says, he grew tired of being told in restaurants that there was no meat: "And here were the Germans eating all the meat they wanted, and it was our meat, too . . . French beef!"

On the other side, the son of an anti-Semitic aristocratic family says he joined with the Germans "because what else was someone of my class to do? There were two movements that could change the world, communism and fascism, and I couldn't be a communist, obviously. Besides, we were all a little thrilled by Hitler's show; it was like Cecil B. DeMille."

Ophuls makes it clear that the majority of Frenchmen were neither supporters of the Germans nor members of the Resistance. Instead, they went along rather quietly with the wartime collaborationist government of Petain and Laval.

The movie makes the point that France was the only nation that actually collaborated during the war and that de Gaulle's "Free French" in London were in the embarrassing position of not being a government-in-exile, because France's government remained in residence.

Those who "went along" did so not because they were lacking in patriotism or moral backbone but because it seemed the thing to do. Ophuls has pointed out in an interview that the establishment tends to remain the establishment, no matter what. To be in the Resistance, he speculates, "you had to be a misfit, one who wouldn't go along," and this is a point the movie makes.

Even de Gaulle was a misfit, his military career stalled until the war, who refused to accept a French government that looked (sadly) legal to the rest of the world.

What *The Sorrow and the Pity* does more brilliantly than anything else is avoid abstractions and give human portraits of people who tried to land on their feet during chaotic times.

There are unforgettable scenes. Pierre Mendes-France recalls his prison break during the war. He was on top of the wall, ready to jump, when he became aware that a young couple was romancing in the bushes below. "He knew what he wanted, but she was unsure," he recalls. "Her indecision was very inconvenient for me."

It is left to Anthony Eden, whose own political career was destroyed by the Suez crisis, to add the wisest words in the movie, words that express directly and simply what Ophuls seems to be telling us: "One who has not suffered the horrors of an occupying power has no right to judge a nation that has."

Still, there are heroes and villains in *The Sorrow and the Pity,* and a great number of people in between who, we finally come to realize, probably acted not much differently than we might have. In its complexity, its humanity, its refusal to find easy solutions, this is one of the greatest documentaries ever made.

Sounder

G, 105 m., 1972

Cicely Tyson (Rebecca Morgan), Paul Winfield (Nathan Lee Morgan), Kevin Hooks (David Lee Morgan), Carmen Mathews (Mrs. Boatwright), Taj Mahal (Ike), James Best (Sheriff Young), Janet MacLachlan (Camille, the Teacher), Sylvia "Kuumba" Williams (Harriet). Directed by Martin Ritt and produced by Robert B. Radnitz. Screenplay by Lonne Elder III.

Sounder is a story simply told and universally moving. It is one of the most compassionate and truthful of movies, and there's not a level where it doesn't succeed completely. It's one of those rare films that can communicate fully to a child of nine or ten, and yet contains depths and subtleties to engross any adult. The story is so simple because it involves, not so much what people do, but how they change and grow. Not a lot happens on the action level, but there's tremendous psychological movement in *Sounder,* and hardly ever do movies create characters who are so full and real, and relationships that are so loving.

The movie is set in rural Louisiana in about 1933, and involves a black sharecropper family. The boy, David Lee, is twelve or thirteen years old, just the right age to delight in the nighttime raccoon hunts he goes on with his father and their hound, Sounder. The hunts are not recreation but necessity. There is no food and no money, and at last, the father steals a ham in desperation. He's sentenced to a year at hard labor, and it's up to the mother and the

children (two of them too small to be much help) to get the crop in. They do. "We'll do it, because we have to do it," the mother says.

The boy sets out to find the labor camp where his father is being held. He never does, but he comes across a black school where the teacher talks to him of some of the accomplishments of blacks in America. He decides that he would like to attend her school; by special dispensation, he had been attending a segregated school near his home as sort of a back-row, second-class student.

He returns home, the father returns home, and there is a heartbreaking moment when, for the boy, no school in the world could take him away from this family that loves him. He runs away, filled with angry tears, but his father comes after him and talks to him simply and bluntly: "You lose some of the time what you go after, but you lose all of the time what you don't go after."

The father has a totally realistic understanding of the trap that southern society set for black sharecroppers, and he is determined to see his son break out of that trap, or else. The scene between the father (Paul Winfield) and the son (Kevin Hooks) is one of the greatest celebrations of the bond between parents and children that I have ever seen in a movie. But it is only one of the scenes like that in *Sounder.*

The mother is played by Cicely Tyson, and it is a wonder to see the subtleties in her performance. We have seen her with her family, and we know her strength and intelligence. Then we see her dealing with the white power structure, and her behavior toward it is in a style born of cynicism and necessity. She will say what they want to hear in order to get what she wants to get.

The story is about love, loss, anger, and hope. That's all, and it's enough; not many movies deal with even one of those subjects with any honesty or power. Hope is probably the emotion evoked most by *Sounder*—the hope of the parents that the school will free their bright and capable son from the dead end of sharecropping; the hope of the teacher, who is representative of the southern growth of black pride and black studies; and, of course, the boy's hope.

The movie was attacked in a few quarters

because of this orientation. It is merely "liberal," some of its critics say. It isn't realistic, it's deceiving. I don't think so. I think it has to be taken as a story about one black family and its struggle. It is, I suppose, a "liberal" film, and that has come to be a bad word in these times when liberalism is supposed to stand for compromise—for good intentions but no action. This movie stands for a lot more than that, and we live in such illiberal times that *Sounder* comes as a reminder of former dreams. It's not surprising that the boy in the movie reminded Mrs. Coretta Scott King of her husband.

This is a film for the family to see. That doesn't mean it's a children's film. The producer, Robert B. Radnitz, has specialized in authentic and serious family films *(A Dog of Flanders, The Other Side of the Mountain)*. The director, Martin Ritt, is one of the best American filmmakers (his credits include *Hud, The Molly Maguires,* and *The Great White Hope*), and he has made *Sounder* as a serious and ambitious undertaking. There is no condescension in it, no simplification. The relationship between the man and wife is so completely realized on a mature level that it comes as a shock; we'd forgotten that authentic grown-ups can be portrayed in films. We'd thought, for a moment, that to be a movie adult you had to drive a fast car, be surrounded by sexy dames, and pack an arsenal. *Sounder* proves it isn't so.

Spartan

R, 106 m., 2004

Val Kilmer (Robert Scott), Derek Luke (Curtis), William H. Macy (Stoddard), Ed O'Neill (Burch), Tia Texada (Jackie Black), Kristen Bell (Laura Newton). Directed by David Mamet and produced by Art Linson, David Bergstein, Elie Samaha, and Moshe Diamant. Screenplay by Mamet.

Spartan opens without any credits except its title, but I quickly knew it was written by David Mamet because nobody else hears and writes dialogue the way he does. That the film tells a labyrinthine story of betrayal and deception, a con within a con, also stakes out Mamet territory. But the scope of the picture is larger than Mamet's usual canvas: This is a thriller on a global scale, involving the Secret Service, the FBI, the CIA, the White House, a secret Special Ops

unit, and Middle Eastern kidnappers. Such a scale could lend itself to one of those big, clunky action machines based on seven-hundred-page best sellers that put salesmen to sleep on airplanes. But no. Not with Mamet, who treats his action plot as a framework for a sly, deceptive exercise in the gradual approximation of the truth.

Before I get to the plot, let me linger on the dialogue. Most thrillers have simpleminded characters who communicate to each other in primary plot points ("Cover me." "It goes off in ten minutes." "Who are you working for?") *Spartan* begins by assuming that all of its characters know who they are and what they're doing, and do not need to explain this to us in thriller-talk. They communicate in elliptical shorthand, in shoptalk, in tradecraft, in oblique references, in shared memories; we can't always believe what they say, and we don't always know that. We get involved in their characters and we even sense their rivalries while the outline of the plot is still murky. How murky we don't even dream.

Val Kilmer, in his best performance since *Tombstone,* plays a Special Ops officer named Scott, who as the movie opens is doing a field exercise with two trainees: Curtis (Derek Luke) and Jackie Black (Tia Texada). He's called off that assignment after the daughter of the president is kidnapped. The Secret Service was supposed to be guarding her, but . . . what went wrong is one of the movie's secrets. Ed O'Neill plays an agent in charge of the search for the daughter, William H. Macy is a political operative from the White House, and it turns out that the daughter, Laura Newton (Kristen Bell), was taken for reasons that are not obvious, by kidnappers you would not guess, who may or may not know she is the president's daughter. Kilmer's assignment: go anywhere and get her back by any means necessary. Curtis and Jackie want to get involved, too, but Kilmer doesn't want them, which may not be the final word on the subject.

And that is quite enough of the plot. It leaves me enjoying the way Mamet, from his earliest plays to his great films like *House of Games, Wag the Dog, Homicide,* and *The Spanish Prisoner,* works like a magician who uses words instead of cards. The patter is always fascinating, and at right angles to the action. He's like a magician who gets you all involved in his story about the king, the queen, and the jack, while the whole point is that there's a rabbit in your pocket. Some screenwriters study Robert McKee. Mamet studies magic and confidence games. In his plots, the left hand makes a distracting movement, but you're too smart for that, and you quickly look over at the right hand to spot the trick, while meantime the left hand does the business while still seeming to flap around like a decoy.

The particular pleasure of *Spartan* is to watch the characters gradually define themselves and the plot gradually emerge like your face in a steamy mirror. You see the outlines, and then your nose, and then you see that somebody is standing behind you, and then you see it's you, so who is the guy in the mirror? Work with me here. I'm trying to describe how the movie operates without revealing what it does.

William H. Macy, who has been with Mamet since his earliest theater days, is an ideal choice for this kind of work. He always seems like the ordinary guy who is hanging on for retirement. He's got that open, willing face, and the flat, helpful voice with sometimes the little complaint in it, and in *Spartan* he starts out with what looks like a walk-on role (we're thinking David found a part for his old pal) and ends up walking away with it. Val Kilmer, a versatile actor who can be good at almost anything (who else has played Batman and John Holmes?), here plays lean and hard, Sam Jackson style. His character is enormously resourceful with his craft, but becomes extremely puzzled about what he can do safely, and who he can trust. Derek Luke, a rising star with a quiet earnestness that is just right here, disappears for a long stretch and then finds out something remarkable, and Tia Texada, in the Rosario Dawson role, succeeds against all odds in actually playing a woman soldier instead of a sexy actress playing a woman soldier.

I like the safe rooms with the charts on the walls, and I like the casual way that spycraft is explained by being used, and the way Mamet keeps pulling the curtain aside to reveal a new stage with a new story. I suppose the last scene in the film will remind some of our friend the *deus ex machina,* but after reflection I have decided that, in that place, at that time, what happens is about as likely to happen as anything else, maybe likelier.

Speed

R, 115 m., 1994

Keanu Reeves (Jack Traven), Dennis Hopper (Howard Payne), Sandra Bullock (Annie), Joe Morton (Captain McMahon), Jeff Daniels (Harry), Alan Ruck (Stephens), Glenn Plummer (Jaguar Owner). Directed by Jan De Bont and produced by Mark Gordon. Screenplay by Graham Yost.

Speed is like an ingenious wind-up machine. It's a smart, inventive thriller that starts with hostages trapped on an elevator and continues with two chases—one on a bus, one on a subway—so that it's wall-to-wall with action, stunts, special effects, and excitement. We've seen this done before, but seldom so well, or at such a high pitch of energy.

The movie stars Keanu Reeves as a member of the Los Angeles bomb squad. He and his veteran partner (Jeff Daniels) are called in after a mad bomber severs the cables holding an elevator in a high-rise building. Now the terrified passengers are trapped between floors, and the bomber wants three million dollars or he'll push a button and blow off the car's emergency brakes. This situation in itself might make the heart of a thriller, but it's only a curtain-raiser for *Speed,* which turns into a battle of the wills between Reeves and the madman.

The bomber is played by Dennis Hopper, the most dependable and certainly the creepiest villain in the movies right now. He's a former cop with a grudge, an intelligent man with a big bag of tricks who seems able to anticipate every one of Reeves's moves. He wants not only the ransom money but also the satisfaction of humiliating the LAPD, and when he's outsmarted on the elevator caper, his next trick is truly diabolical.

He rigs an ordinary Los Angeles rapid transit bus so that if it exceeds fifty miles an hour, a bomb will be armed—and then, if its speed falls below fifty miles an hour, the bomb will explode. This is an inspiration that will raise many questions for anyone who has ever been in L.A. traffic, but never mind: It provides the basis for an extended, suspenseful chase sequence that comes up with one ingenious crisis after another.

Reeves manages to get himself on board the bus, of course. And after the driver is shot by a passenger, another passenger (Sandra Bullock) grabs the wheel while Reeves tries to think of a way out of the dilemma, and the bus cruises at fifty-five miles an hour—in the wrong lanes, in the wrong directions, sideswiping other cars, causing accidents, and eventually ending up on an empty freeway that would provide clear sailing—if it weren't for a fifty-foot gap in an overpass. Can a bus really leap a fifty-foot space? This is the kind of movie where you don't ask questions like that.

The screenplay, by Graham Yost, piles on complications until the movie's very construction is a delight. Bullock keeps her cool at the wheel while Reeves tries stunts like going under the bus to try to disarm the bomb while it continues to bounce along at high speed. Meanwhile, the story intercuts between Hopper, who is issuing ultimatums and dropping sinister hints, and Daniels, back at headquarters, who is using computers to try to figure out the identity of the blackmailer.

When the bus episode finally ends, we sit back, drained, ready for the movie to end, too. But it has another surprise in store, a chase on a subway train, with Bullock held hostage and handcuffed inside one of the cars. All of this is of course gloriously silly, a plundering of situations from the *Indiana Jones* and *Die Hard* movies all the way back to *The Perils of Pauline*, but so what? If it works, it works.

Keanu Reeves has rarely had a role like this before. In fact, in his previous film, he played the mystical Prince Siddhartha, and generally he tends toward dreamy, sensitive characters. That's why it's sort of amazing to see him so cool and focused here, a completely convincing action hero who is as centered and resourceful as a Clint Eastwood or Harrison Ford in similar situations. He and Bullock have good chemistry; they appreciate the humor that is always flickering just beneath the surface of the preposterous plot. And Hopper's dialogue has been twisted into savagely ironic understatements that provide their own form of comic relief.

Films like *Speed* belong to the genre I call Bruised Forearm Movies, because you're always grabbing the arm of the person sitting next to you. Done wrong, they seem like tired replays of old chase clichés. Done well, they're fun. Done as well as *Speed*, they generate a kind of manic exhilaration. The director, Jan

De Bont, has worked as a cinematographer on many action classics, including *Basic Instinct* and *Die Hard*. Here he shows his own mastery, in a great entertainment.

Spider-Man 2
PG-13, 125 m., 2004

Tobey Maguire (Peter Parker/Spider-Man), Kirsten Dunst (Mary Jane Watson), Alfred Molina (Dr. Otto Octavius/Doc Ock), James Franco (Harry Osborn), Rosemary Harris (Aunt May), J. K. Simmons (J. Jonah Jameson). Directed by Sam Raimi and produced by Avi Arad and Laura Ziskin. Screenplay by Alvin Sargent, Michael Chabon, Miles Millar, and Alfred Gough, based on the comic book by Stan Lee and Steve Ditko.

Now this is what a superhero movie should be. *Spider-Man 2* believes in its story in the same way serious comic readers believe, when the adventures on the page express their own dreams and wishes. It's not camp and it's not nostalgia, it's not wall-to-wall special effects and it's not pickled in angst. It's simply and poignantly a realization that being Spider-Man is a burden that Peter Parker is not entirely willing to bear. The movie demonstrates what's wrong with a lot of other superhero epics: They focus on the superpowers and short-change the humans behind them (has anyone ever been more boring than Clark Kent or Bruce Wayne?).

Spider-Man 2 is the best superhero movie since the modern genre was launched with *Superman* (1978). It succeeds by being true to the insight that allowed Marvel Comics to upturn decades of comic book tradition: Readers could identify more completely with heroes like themselves than with remote, godlike paragons. Peter Parker was an insecure high school student, in grade trouble, inarticulate in love, unready to assume the responsibilities that came with his unexpected superpowers. It wasn't that Spider-Man could swing from skyscrapers that won over his readers; it was that he fretted about personal problems in the thought balloons above his Spidey face mask.

Parker (Tobey Maguire) is in college now, studying physics at Columbia, more helplessly in love than ever with Mary Jane Watson (Kirsten Dunst). He's on the edge of a breakdown: He's lost his job as a pizza deliveryman, Aunt May faces foreclosure on her mortgage, he's missing classes, the colors run together when he washes his Spider-Man suit at the Laundromat, and after his web-spinning ability inexplicably seems to fade, he throws away his beloved uniform in despair. When a bum tries to sell the discarded Spidey suit to Jonah Jameson, editor of the *Daily Bugle,* Jameson offers him $50. The bum says he could do better on eBay. Has it come to this?

I was disappointed by the original *Spider-Man* (2002), and surprised to find this film working from the first frame. Sam Raimi, the director of both pictures, this time seems to know exactly what he should do, and never steps wrong in a film that effortlessly combines special effects and a human story, keeping its parallel plots alive and moving. One of the keys to the movie's success must be the contribution of novelist Michael Chabon to the screenplay; Chabon understands in his bones what comic books are, and why. His inspired 2000 novel, *The Amazing Adventures of Kavalier and Clay,* chronicles the birth of a 1940s comic book superhero and the young men who created him; Chabon worked on the screen story that fed into Alvin Sargent's screenplay.

The seasons in a superhero's life are charted by the villains he faces (it is the same with James Bond). *Spider-Man 2* gives Spider-Man an enemy with a good nature that is overcome by evil. Peter Parker admires the famous Dr. Otto Octavius (Alfred Molina), whose laboratory on the banks of the East River houses an experiment that will either prove that fusion can work as a cheap source of energy, or vaporize Manhattan. To handle the dangerous materials of his experiments, Octavius devises four powerful tentacles that are fused to his spine and have cyber-intelligence of their own; a chip at the top of his spine prevents them from overriding his orders, but when the chip is destroyed the gentle scientist is transformed into Doc Ock, a fearsome fusion of man and machine, who can climb skyscraper walls by driving his tentacles through concrete and bricks. We hear him coming, hammering his way toward us like the drums of hell.

Peter Parker meanwhile has vowed that he cannot allow himself to love Mary Jane because her life would be in danger from Spider-Man's enemies. She has finally given up on Peter, who is always standing her up; she announces her engagement to no less than an astronaut. Peter has heart-to-hearts with her and with Aunt May (Rosemary Harris), who is given full screen time and not reduced to an obligatory cameo. And he has to deal with his friend Harry Osborn (James Franco), who likes Peter but hates Spider-Man, blaming him for the death of his father (a.k.a. the Green Goblin, although much is unknown to the son).

There are special effects, and then there are special effects. In the first movie I thought Spider-Man seemed to move with all the realism of a character in a cartoon. This time, as he swings from one skyscraper to another, he has more weight and dimension, and Raimi is able to seamlessly match the CGI and the human actors. The f/x triumph in the film is the work on Doc Ock's four robotic tentacles, which move with an uncanny life, reacting and responding, doing double-takes, becoming characters of their own.

Watching Raimi and his writers cut between the story threads, I savored classical workmanship: The film gives full weight to all of its elements, keeps them alive, is constructed with such skill that we care all the way through; in a lesser movie from this genre, we usually perk up for the action scenes but wade grimly through the dialogue. Here both stay alive, and the dialogue is more about emotion, love, and values, less about long-winded explanations of the inexplicable (it's kind of neat that Spider-Man never does find out why his web-throwing ability sometimes fails him).

Tobey Maguire almost didn't sign for the sequel, complaining of back pain; Jake Gyllenhaal, another gifted actor, was reportedly in the wings. But if Maguire hadn't returned (along with Spidey's throwaway line about his aching back), we would never have known how good he could be in this role. Kirsten Dunst is valuable, too, bringing depth and heart to a girlfriend role that in lesser movies would be conventional. When she kisses her astronaut boyfriend upside-down, it's one of those perfect moments that rewards fans of the whole saga; we don't need to be told she's remembering her only kiss from Spider-Man.

There are moviegoers who make it a point of missing superhero movies, and I can't blame them, although I confess to a weakness for the genre. I liked both of *The Crow* movies, and *Daredevil, The Hulk,* and *X2,* but not enough to recommend them to friends who don't like or understand comic books. *Spider-Man 2* is in another category: It's a real movie, full-blooded and smart, with qualities even for those who have no idea who Stan Lee is. It's a superhero movie for people who don't go to superhero movies, and for those who do, it's the one they've been yearning for.

Spirited Away

PG, 124 m., 2002

With the voices of: Daveigh Chase (Chihiro), Suzanne Pleshette (Yubaba), Jason Marsden (Haku), Susan Egan (Lin), David Ogden Stiers (Kamaji), Michael Chiklis (Chihiro's Father), Lauren Holly (Chihiro's Mother), John Ratzenberger (Assistant Manager). Directed by Hayao Miyazaki (U.S. production directed by Kirk Wise) and produced by Toshio Suzuki and Donald W. Ernst. Screenplay by Miyazaki, Cindy Davis Hewitt, and Donald H. Hewitt.

Spirited Away has been compared to *Alice in Wonderland,* and indeed it tells of a ten-year-old girl who wanders into a world of strange creatures and illogical rules. But it's enchanting and delightful in its own way, and has a good heart. It is the best animated film of recent years, the latest work by Hayao Miyazaki, the Japanese master who is a god to the Disney animators.

Because many adults have an irrational reluctance to see an animated film from Japan (or anywhere else), I begin with reassurances: It has been flawlessly dubbed into English by John Lasseter *(Toy Story),* it was cowinner of this year's Berlin Film Festival against "regular" movies, it passed *Titanic* to become the top-grossing film in Japanese history, and it is the first film ever to make more than $200 million before opening in America.

I feel like I'm giving a pitch on an infomercial, but I make these points because I come bearing news: This is a wonderful film. Don't avoid it because of what you think you know about animation from Japan. And if you only go to Disney animation—well, this is being released by Disney.

Miyazaki's works *(My Neighbor Totoro, Kiki's Delivery Service, Princess Mononoke)* have a depth and complexity often missing in American animation. Not fond of computers, he draws thousands of frames himself, and there is a painterly richness in his work. He's famous for throwaway details at the edges of the screen (animation is so painstaking that few animators draw more than is necessary). And he permits himself silences and contemplation, providing punctuation for the exuberant action and the lovable or sometimes grotesque characters.

Spirited Away is told through the eyes of Chihiro (voice by Daveigh Chase), a ten-year-old girl, and is more personal, less epic, than *Princess Mononoke.* As the story opens, she's on a trip with her parents, and her father unwisely takes the family to explore a mysterious tunnel in the woods. On the other side is what he speculates is an old theme park; but the food stalls still seem to be functioning, and as Chihiro's parents settle down for a free meal, she wanders away and comes upon the film's version of Wonderland, which is a towering bathhouse.

A boy named Haku appears as her guide, and warns her that the sorceress who runs the bathhouse, named Yubaba, will try to steal her name and thus her identity. Yubaba (Suzanne Pleshette) is an old crone with a huge face; she looks a little like a Toby mug, and dotes on a grotesquely huge baby named Bou. Ominously, she renames Chihiro, who wanders through the structure, which is populated, like *Totoro,* with little balls of dust that scurry and scamper underfoot.

In the innards of the structure, Chihiro comes upon the boiler room, operated by a man named Kamaji (David Ogden Stiers), who is dressed in a formal coat and has eight limbs, which he employs in a bewildering variety of ways. At first he seems as fearsome as the world he occupies, but he has a good side, is no friend of Yubaba, and perceives Chihiro's goodness.

If Yubaba is the scariest of the characters and Kamaji the most intriguing, Okutaresama is the one with the most urgent message. He is the spirit of the river, and his body has absorbed the junk, waste, and sludge that has been thrown into it over the years. At one point he actually yields up a discarded bicycle. I was reminded of a throwaway detail in *My Neighbor Totoro,* where a child looks into a bubbling brook, and there is a discarded bottle at the bottom. No point is made; none needs to be made.

Japanese myths often use shape-shifting, in which bodies reveal themselves as facades concealing a deeper reality. It's as if animation was invented for shape-shifting, and Miyazaki does wondrous things with the characters here. Most alarming for Chihiro, she finds that her parents have turned into pigs after gobbling up the free lunch. Okutaresama reveals its true nature after being freed of decades of sludge and discarded household items. Haku is much more than he seems. Indeed, the entire bathhouse seems to be under spells affecting the appearance and nature of its inhabitants.

Miyazaki's drawing style, which descends from the classical Japanese graphic artists, is a pleasure to regard, with its subtle use of colors, clear lines, rich detail, and its realistic depiction of fantastical elements. He suggests not just the appearances of his characters, but their natures. Apart from the stories and dialogue, *Spirited Away* is a pleasure to regard just for itself. This is one of the year's best films.

Spring, Summer, Fall, Winter, and Spring

R, 103 m., 2003

Oh Young Soo (Old Monk), Kim Ki Duk (Adult Monk), Kim Young Min (Young Adult Monk), Seo Jae Kyung (Boy Monk), Ha Yeo Jin (Girl), Kim Jong Ho (Child Monk), Kim Jung Young (Girl's Mother). Directed and written by Kim Ki Duk. Produced by Karl Baumgartner and Seung-jae Lee.

Rarely has a movie this simple moved me this deeply. I feel as if I could review it in a paragraph, and discuss it for hours. The South Korean film *Spring, Summer, Fall, Winter, and Spring* is Buddhist, but it is also universal. It takes place within and around a small house floating on a small raft on a small lake, and within that compass contains life, faith, growth, love, jealousy, hate, cruelty, mystery, redemption, and nature. Also a dog, a rooster, a cat, a bird, a snake, a turtle, a fish, and a frog.

The one-room house serves the function of a hermitage, or a monk's cell. As the film opens, it is occupied by a monk (Oh Young Soo) and a small boy (Seo Jae Kyung), learning to be a monk. The monk rises, wakes the boy, bows and prays to a figure of the Buddha, and knocks on a hollow bowl that sends a

comfortable resonance out into the forest. We gather the daily routine rarely changes.

Before I describe the action any further, let me better set the scene. The lake is surrounded on all sides by steep walls of forest or stone, broken here and there by ravines. It is approached through two large, painted wooden doors, which swing open to introduce each season of the movie, and frame the floating house. These doors do not keep anyone out, because one would only have to walk around them to find the rest of the shore open and free. But they are always respected.

It is the same inside the house. The master and the boy sleep on palettes on either side of the room. At the foot of each sleeping area is a door. The area is otherwise completely open to the room, and always visible. But when the monk awakens the boy, he is careful to open the door and enter, instead of simply calling out to him or stepping around the door. Several people will occupy these sleeping spaces during the movie, and they will always treat the door as if it had a practical function, except sometimes.

What do we learn from these doors that close nothing out or in? They are not symbols, I think, but lessons. They teach the inhabitants that it is important to follow custom and tradition, to go the same way that others have gone, to respect what has been left for them.

The shore is reached by an old but beautifully painted rowboat. The boy often goes ashore to collect herbs, which his master teaches him about. One day the boy rows to shore and plays in some little ponds. Inspired to mischief, he ties a string around a fish, and a small stone to the other end, to make it hard for the fish to swim. He burbles with laughter. Then he plays the same trick on a frog, and a snake. He does not know that the master has followed and is watching him.

And we do not know how the master got to shore without the rowboat, although more than once he seems to be able to do that. The rowboat seems to moor itself next to an ancient tree in the lake, without tether or anchor, and on one occasion seems to float toward the master at his bidding, but there is no hint earlier that the boat returned for the master. And the movie makes no point at all of the master's inexplicable materialization; some viewers may not notice it. It is at that level of mysticism where you wonder if you really did see something out of the corner of your eye.

The next morning when the boy awakes, he finds a stone tied to his back. the master orders him to return to shore and free the fish, the frog and he snake. If one of them has died, you will always carry that stone in your heart.

End of spring. I will not spoil the film's unfolding during the later seasons (and years), other than to note that when a young girl comes to the hermitage to be cured, she and the boy (now a young man) fall in love. The monk thinks sex might be part of her cure, but warns of anger: Lust awakens the desire to possess. And that awakens the intent to murder.

There is always an animal on the raft to keep the monk company (the dog is glimpsed only briefly at the beginning). The monk feeds them, pets the cat because it is the requirement of cats to be petted, and otherwise simply shares the space, as he does with his student. The lake, the raft, the house, the animals, the forest are there for them, and will be there after them, and the monk accepts the use of them.

The film is by Kim Ki Duk, or in the Korean usage Ki-duk Kim, born in 1960. We see him briefly at the end, playing another monk who has come to the island. I first became aware of his work at Sundance 2000, where he showed *The Isle*, probably the most viscerally violent film I have ever seen. No, it doesn't have explosions or shootings, but what it does with fishhooks is unspeakable. Strange, that the same director made both films. I note that Korean directors have an inclination toward extreme violence and frank sexuality, although it is usually represented as behavior, in long shot, instead of being insisted upon in close-up. The nudity and sexuality in *Spring* is context, not subject.

There must be something about floating isolation that fascinates this director. *The Isle* was about fisherman each occupying a small floating fishing shack on a large lake, their only contact with shore an unspeaking women who rows to them with food, drink, supplies, and prostitutes. His movie *The Bow* (2005) involves a starting situation something like *Spring*. An old man lives on his boat with a girl he has raised since infancy. He expects

(as the monk apparently expects of his student) that the arrangement will continue indefinitely. In both films, a visitor the same age as the protégé comes aboard and introduces the possibility of carnality.

Kim Ki Duk avoids one practice: In his films that I have seen (also including *Three-Iron*, 2004—not a golf picture), he doesn't make his message manifest. There is little or no dialogue, no explanations, no speeches with messages. He descends upon lives that have long since taken their form. If conflict comes, his characters will in some way bring it upon themselves or within themselves. That causes us to pay closer attention. How inferior a film like *Spring* would be if it supplied a rival monk, or visiting tourists, or land developers. The protagonist in this film is life, and the antagonists are time and change. Nor is it that simple, because to be alive you must come to terms with both of those opponents.

STAR 80

R, 102 m., 1983

Mariel Hemingway (Dorothy Stratten), Eric Roberts (Paul Snider), Cliff Robertson (Hugh Hefner), Carroll Baker (Dorothy's Mother), Roger Rees (Aram Nicholas). Directed by Bob Fosse and produced by Wolfgang Glattes and Kenneth Utt. Screenplay by Fosse.

Bob Fosse dresses all in black and makes films about the demonic undercurrents in our lives. Look at his credits: *Cabaret, Lenny, All That Jazz*, and now *STAR 80*. Although his Broadway musicals have been upbeat entertainment, he seems to see the movie camera as a device for peering into our shames and secrets. *STAR 80* is his most despairing film. After the Nazi decadence of *Cabaret*, after the drug abuse and self-destruction in *Lenny*, and the death-obsessed hero of *All That Jazz*, here is a movie that begins with violent death and burrows deeper. There were times when I could hardly keep my eyes on the screen, and a moment near the end when I seriously asked myself if I wanted to continue watching.

And yet I think this is an important movie. Devastating, violent, hopeless, and important, because it holds a mirror up to a part of the world we live in, and helps us see it more clearly. In particular, it examines the connection between fame and obscurity, between those who have a moment of praise and notoriety, and those who see themselves as condemned to stand always at the edge of the spotlight. Like Martin Scorsese's *Taxi Driver*, it is a movie about being an outsider and about going crazy with the pain of rejection.

The movie tells the story of two young people from Vancouver. One of them was Dorothy Stratten, a shy, pretty blonde who thought her hands and feet were too big, who couldn't understand why anyone would value her, and who was close enough to some sort of idealized North American fantasy that she became the 1979 Playmate of the Year. The other was Paul Snider, a Vancouver small-timer who worked as a salesman, con man, and part-time pimp. When Paul saw Dorothy behind the counter of a hamburger stand, he knew she was his ticket to the big time. Dorothy resisted his compliments at first, but he was so relentless in his adoration that she surrendered to his fantasies. Paul masterminded Dorothy's rise. He arranged the photo session that attracted the eye of *Playboy*'s talent scouts. He bought her dresses and flowers. He pushed her into the limelight and then edged into it next to her. But then she went to Los Angeles and found the real stardust, the flattery of the Playboy Mansion, the attentions of young men whose sports cars were bought with their own money, while Paul's was bought with hers.

Paul had a vanity license plate made: STAR 80. But Dorothy had moved out of his world, had been given a taste of a larger world that, frankly, Paul didn't have the class to appreciate. She fell in love with a movie director. She went out of town on location. She and Paul drifted apart, and he went mad with jealousy and resentment. On August 14, 1980, Dorothy went back to the shabby little North Hollywood bungalow they had rented together, and Paul murdered her.

STAR 80 begins with the murder. Everything else is in flashback, and, therefore, the film has no really happy scenes. Dorothy's triumphs are all stained with our knowledge of what will happen. Every time she smiles, it's poignant. We know Paul will go berserk and kill her, and so we can see from the beginning that he's unbalanced. Fosse knows his material is relentlessly depressing, and so he doesn't try

for moments of relief. Although we enter the world of *Playboy* and see Dorothy partying in the mansion and posing in nude modeling sessions, although the whole movie is concerned with aspects of sex, there is never an erotic moment. Fosse keeps his distance, regarding Dorothy more as a case study than as a fantasy. That makes Mariel Hemingway's performance as Dorothy all the more powerful. She has been remade into the sleek, glossy Playmate image, but she still has the adolescent directness and naïveté that she used so well in *Manhattan* and *Personal Best*. She's a big kid. Her eyes open wide when she gets to Los Angeles, and she's impressed by the attention she's receiving. The character she plays is simple, uncomplicated, shallow, and so trusting that she never does realize how dangerous Paul is.

The other performances in the movie are equally strong. Eric Roberts as Paul even succeeds in persuading us to accept him as a suffering human being rather than as a hateful killer. Like Robert De Niro as Travis Bickle in *Taxi Driver*, he fills his role with so much reality that we feel horror, but not blame. Carroll Baker, as Dorothy's mother, is heartbreakingly incapable of connecting in any meaningful way with her daughter.

What is the point of *STAR 80*? I'm not sure, just as I wasn't sure of the points of *In Cold Blood* or *Lacombe, Lucien* or "The Executioner's Song." There is no redemption in the movie, no catharsis. It unblinkingly looks at the short life of a simple, pretty girl, and the tortured man who made her into something he couldn't have, and then killed her for it. The movie seems to be saying: These things happen. After it was over, I felt bad for Dorothy Stratten. In fact, for everybody.

Star Wars
PG, 121 m., 1977

Mark Hamill (Luke Skywalker), Carrie Fisher (Princess Leia), Harrison Ford (Han Solo), Alec Guinness (Obi-Wan Kenobi), David Prowse (Darth Vader), James Earl Jones (Vader's Voice), Kenny Baker (R2-D2), Anthony Daniels (C-3PO). Directed by George Lucas and produced by Gary Kurtz. Screenplay by Lucas.

Every once in a while I have what I think of as an out-of-the-body experience at a movie.

When the ESP people use a phrase like that, they're referring to the sensation of the mind actually leaving the body and spiriting itself off to China or Peoria or a galaxy far, far away. When I use the phrase, I simply mean that my imagination has forgotten it is actually present in a movie theater and thinks it's up there on the screen. In a curious sense, the events in the movie seem real, and I seem to be a part of them.

Star Wars works like that. My list of other out-of-the-body films is a short and odd one, ranging from the artistry of *Bonnie and Clyde* or *Cries and Whispers* to the slick commercialism of *Jaws* and the brutal strength of *Taxi Driver*. On whatever level (sometimes I'm not at all sure) they engage me so immediately and powerfully that I lose my detachment, my analytical reserve. The movie's *happening,* and it's happening to me.

What makes the *Star Wars* experience unique, though, is that it happens on such an innocent and often funny level. It's usually violence that draws me so deeply into a movie—violence ranging from the psychological torment of a Bergman character to the mindless crunch of a shark's jaws. Maybe movies that scare us find the most direct route to our imaginations. But there's hardly any violence at all in *Star Wars* (and even then it's presented as essentially bloodless swashbuckling). Instead, there's entertainment so direct and simple that all of the complications of the modern movie seem to vaporize.

Star Wars is a fairy tale, a fantasy, a legend, finding its roots in some of our most popular fictions. The golden robot, lion-faced space pilot, and insecure little computer on wheels must have been suggested by the Tin Man, the Cowardly Lion, and the Scarecrow in *The Wizard of Oz.* The journey from one end of the galaxy to another is out of countless thousands of space operas. The hardware is from *Flash Gordon* out of *2001,* the chivalry is from *Robin Hood,* the heroes are from Westerns, and the villains are a cross between Nazis and sorcerers. *Star Wars* taps the pulp fantasies buried in our memories, and because it's done so brilliantly, it reactivates old thrills, fears, and exhilarations we thought we'd abandoned when we read our last copy of *Amazing Stories.*

The movie works so well for several reasons, and they don't all have to do with the spectacular special effects. The effects *are* good, yes, but great effects have been used in such movies as *Silent Running* and *Logan's Run* without setting all-time box-office records. No, I think the key to *Star Wars* is more basic than that.

The movie relies on the strength of pure narrative, in the most basic storytelling form known to man, the Journey. All of the best tales we remember from our childhoods had to do with heroes setting out to travel down roads filled with danger, and hoping to find treasure or heroism at the journey's end. In *Star Wars,* George Lucas takes this simple and powerful framework into outer space, and that is an inspired thing to do, because we no longer have maps on Earth that warn, "Here there be dragons." We can't fall off the edge of the map, as Columbus could, and we can't hope to find new continents of prehistoric monsters or lost tribes ruled by immortal goddesses. Not on Earth, anyway, but anything is possible in space, and Lucas goes right ahead and shows us very nearly everything. We get involved quickly, because the characters in *Star Wars* are so strongly and simply drawn and have so many small foibles and large, futile hopes for us to identify with. And then Lucas does an interesting thing. As he sends his heroes off to cross the universe and do battle with the forces of Darth Vader, the evil Empire, and the awesome Death Star, he gives us lots of special effects, yes—ships passing into hyperspace, alien planets, an infinity of stars—but we also get a wealth of strange living creatures, and Lucas correctly guesses that they'll be more interesting for us than all the intergalactic hardware.

The most fascinating single scene, for me, was the one set in the bizarre saloon on the planet Tatooine. As that incredible collection of extraterrestrial alcoholics and bugeyed martini drinkers lined up at the bar, and as Lucas so slyly let them exhibit characteristics that were universally human, I found myself feeling a combination of admiration and delight. *Star Wars* had placed me in the presence of really magical movie invention: Here, all mixed together, were whimsy and fantasy, simple wonderment and quietly sophisticated storytelling.

When Stanley Kubrick was making *2001* in the late 1960s, he threw everything he had into the special effects depicting outer space, but he finally decided not to show any aliens at all—because they were impossible to visualize, he thought. But they weren't at all, as *Star Wars* demonstrates, and the movie's delight in the possibilities of alien life forms is at least as much fun as its conflicts between the space cruisers of the Empire and the rebels.

And perhaps that helps to explain the movie's one weakness, which is that the final assault on the Death Star is allowed to go on too long. Maybe, having invested so much money and sweat in his special effects, Lucas couldn't bear to see them trimmed. But the magic of *Star Wars* is only dramatized by the special effects; the movie's heart is in its endearingly human (and nonhuman) people.

Stavisky

PG, 120 m., 1975

Jean-Paul Belmondo (Alexandre Stavisky), Anny Deperey (Arlette Stavisky), Charles Boyer (Baron Raoul), Francois Perier (Borelli), Roberto Bisaco (Montalvo), Michel Lonsdale (Dr. Mezy). Directed by Alain Resnais and produced by Georges Dancigers and Alexandre Mnouchkine. Screenplay by Jorge Semprun.

Alain Resnais's *Stavisky* shares only its brilliance with his other work. His films have never had a consistent visual style, if only because he begins with such dissimilar material and then tries to find a look for it that's appropriate. But even so, we'd hardly anticipate this elegant, sparkling period piece from the director of *Hiroshima Mon Amour* and *La Guerre Est Finie.*

Resnais sets his film in the France of the early 1930s, when a shaky economy is being held together by the lies and bluffs of the ruling class. One of the greatest of the manipulating financiers, and certainly the most fascinating, is Alexandre Stavisky, the emigre son of a Russian Jewish dentist who has parlayed his personal charm and confidence schemes into a vast stock swindle.

He has, in the process, partially deceived even himself. He's a man of great contradictions who wants, on the one hand, to be embraced by French society (he even changes his first name to the more fashionable Serge) and, on the other hand, to hold his new peer in contempt. He knows how his frauds work and yet, at times, he actually seems to believe in them. He fights with perfect sincerity against inflation and unemployment and, in the process, all but succeeds in destroying the French economy.

To play Stavisky, Renais chose Jean-Paul Belmondo, and it's perfect casting. There's something in Belmondo's screen personality that fundamentally suggests the con man. It was there in the jauntiness of his first movie, *Breathless,* and in *Cartouche,* a movie totally unlike this one except for Belmondo's cocky bravado in the face of certain defeat. Belmondo has grown and become more subtle in fifteen years, and in *Stavisky,* he gives us his most complex and probably his best performance.

As counterpoint there is Charles Boyer, at seventy-five projecting a totally serene elegance, as Baron Raoul, Stavisky's friend and sponsor. The baron was born possessing and representing everything Stavisky yearns for. He defines the French upper classes. And yet he is completely taken in by Stavisky, given over to the kind of fascination with the personality of a man who can come from nowhere and convince the rich and the powerful to follow him. The fascination in time becomes an obsession, and in the end, Baron Raoul follows Stavisky into ruin and defeat. Even when Stavisky's entire pyramid is crumbling, the baron prefers to believe in it, because accepting the truth would require destruction of his illusions.

Resnais places these characters, and Anny Deperey as Stavisky's wife, Arlette, in a world that has as many facets and contradictions as the spa in *Last Year at Marienbad.* Not only is nothing ever as it seems, but no one seems to see it in the same way twice. People define themselves by their relationships to Stavisky, and yet he's never the same to two people, so when his associates meet, they have no common point of reference.

There's also no point of connection between Stavisky and the other historical figure Resnais puts into the film, Leon Trotsky. The story never requires them to meet, but from time to time, Resnais provides a glimpse of Trotsky in exile, perhaps to suggest that at this moment in history, two kinds of economic systems were proving themselves corrupt and bankrupt. In France, traditional predatory capitalism was falling in upon itself, and in Russia, Stalin having prevailed over Trotsky, Marxism was being shaped into a rationale for a totalitarian economy.

The movie is finally about two things, truth and death, both of which Stavisky prefers to avoid at any possible cost. When he loses to them, he loses spectacularly, there are riots in the streets, and the nation for a moment approaches anarchy. Let it not be said his passing went unnoticed. But who was he really? What shaped him and why did he behave as he did? Stavisky didn't know, and Resnais doesn't know, either, and that provides the fascinating central mystery of the film. Like Charles Foster Kane, Alexandre Stavisky is a man of intriguing parts that make up any number of wholes.

Stevie

NO MPAA RATING, 102 m., 1981

Glenda Jackson (Stevie Smith), Mona Washbourne (Her Aunt), Alec McCowen (Freddie), Trevor Howard (The Man). Directed and produced by Robert Enders. Screenplay by Hugh Whitemore, based on his play.

Stevie Smith came across a newspaper clipping one day that told of a man who drowned within a few hundred yards of the shore. The people on the beach saw him waving, and they waved back. The truth, as Stevie expressed it in a famous poem, was the man's problem was just like her own:

I was much too far out all my life
And not waving, but drowning.

In those lines, Stevie Smith made an image of her own life, and it is an image that Glenda Jackson's film *Stevie* expresses with clarity, wit, and love.

Stevie Smith was a British poet of considerable reputation, who died in 1971 at the age of sixty-nine. She spent almost all of her life living in a small home in the London suburb of Palmers Green, where she moved as a child. She worked every day in an office in the city, until her growing reputation as a poet allowed her to take an early retirement. She lived with an old maid aunt, and eventually she became an old maid herself. We watch this process as it is punctuated by a marriage proposal, by a visit to Buckingham Palace for tea with the queen, by a halfhearted suicide attempt. Every night, there was definitely a glass or two or more of sherry, or sometimes gin.

To the world, she must have appeared to be an exemplary example of a talented English eccentric. Her poems were irreverent, sharply satirical, and laconic. She was capable of writing one day:

The Englishwoman is so refined
She has no bosom and no behind.

And on another day, writing about death:

I have a friend
At the end
of the world.
His name is a breath
Of fresh air.

She was not waving, but drowning. The film *Stevie* captures this laconic despair, but it also does a great deal more. It gives us a very particular portrait of a woman's life. The movie is based on a play by Hugh Whitemore, and it contains one of Glenda Jackson's greatest performances. She knows this character well. She played Stevie on the London stage and on a BBC radio production before making this film. She does what great actors can do: She takes a character who might seem uninteresting, and makes us care deeply about the uneventful days of her life.

Although *Stevie* is totally dominated by Jackson's performance, it is not a one-character film by any means. The veteran British actress Mona Washbourne provides a magnificent performance as Stevie's maiden aunt, who is a little dotty and a little giggly and very loving, who likes her glass of sherry and wears flowered print dresses that Stevie says look like a seed catalog illustration titled "They All Came Up." Alec McCowen plays Freddie, the not-so-young man who comes calling, and whose proposal Stevie rejects. And the wonderful Trevor Howard has an ambiguous part as "The Man." On one level, "The Man" is just someone she met at a literary party and conned into giving her rides to poetry readings. At another level, especially when he is seen by himself, telling us about Stevie and reading some of her lines, he is the understanding, forgiving father figure Stevie never had.

Movies like *Stevie* run the risk of looking like photographs of stage plays, but *Stevie* somehow never feels that way. Even though it uses the artifices of the stage (including remarks addressed by Glenda Jackson directly to the audience), and even though a lot of its dialogue is poetry, *Stevie* always feels as if it occupies this woman's life. She is the poet, we are her confidantes, and it is a privilege to get to know her. I have perhaps given the impression that *Stevie* is grim and depressing. It is not at all. It is very sad at times, of course, but there are other times of good humor and barbed wit, when she's not drowning, but waving.

The Sting

PG, 129 m., 1973

Paul Newman (Henry Gondorf), Robert Redford (John Hooker), Robert Shaw (Doyle Lonnegan). Directed by George Roy Hill and produced by Richard D. Zanuck and David Brown. Screenplay by David S. Ward.

The Sting is one of the most stylish movies of the year. That's an especially pleasant surprise because it reunites the costars and the director of *Butch Cassidy and the Sundance Kid,* a movie I thought was overrated.

The director is George Roy Hill, and the stars are those two good old buddies Paul Newman and Robert Redford. This time they play con men who methodically and with great ingenuity fleece a rich mark (Robert Shaw). Their methods are incredibly complex (it would take all of this space to attempt to explain them). A lot of the fun in the movie is watching Hill and his screenwriter, David S. Ward, keep the plot straight.

The movie is set in Chicago in the 1930s, and many of the outdoor scenes were shot there (including an effective platform shot at Union Station). We see a big, confused, lusty, brawling city where the big guys with the muscle are somehow always losing to the guys with the confidence angles. Shaw never figures out what hit him. He's a high-stakes gambler who first gets hooked during a poker game

between New York and Chicago on the 20th Century Limited. Newman and Redford spot him, mark him, and begin to manipulate him. He never figures out they even know each other, and that's part of the charm: They have to play a lot of scenes for him as complete strangers, as Redford casually lets drop that he knows the location of the biggest wire room in Chicago.

The idea, Redford explains, is to allow Shaw to win big on a fixed horse race in order to ... but I wasn't kidding when I said the scheme is complicated. Newman operates the wire room. Or should we say it appears to be operated by Newman. Or, more accurately, it appears to be a wire room, because the entire operation is simply a theatrical set, and everybody in the room is an actor, and the "broadcasts" from the track actually are being made up by an announcer in the back room.

The movie has a nice, light-fingered style to it. Hill gently kids the 1930s with his slight exaggerations of fashions and styles. He tells his story episodically, breaking the movie down into the various plateaus of the con game. And he's awfully good at maintaining a kind of off-balance pacing; we can never quite pin Newman and Redford down. They're always sort of angling into scenes, making enigmatic statements under their breath and staying at least a step ahead of us. Hill's visual style is oblique; instead of stationing his actors in the frame and recording the action, he seems to sneak up on it. Newman and Redford almost seem on their way to another movie. If that sounds like a criticism, it's not meant as one: The style here is so seductive and witty it's hard to pin down. It's like nothing else I've seen by Hill, and at times, it almost reminds me of Jacques Tati crossed with Robert Altman. It's good to get a crime movie more concerned with humor and character than with blood and gore; here's one, as we say, for the whole family.

The Story of Adele H.

PG, 96 m., 1975

Isabelle Adjani (Adele Hugo), Bruce Robinson (Lieutenant Pinson), Sylvia Marriott (Mrs. Saunders), Reubin Darcy (Mr. Saunders), Joseph Blatchley (Mr. Whistler), M. White (Colonel). Directed by Francois Truffaut and produced by Marcel Barbert and Claude

Miller. Screenplay by Jean Gruault, Suzanne Schiffman, and Truffaut, based on the diaries of Adele Hugo.

Francois Truffaut's *The Story of Adele H.* insists at the outset that it's based on real events and real people, perhaps because that assurance will help to anchor us during the film's descent into one woman's mad and obsessive passion. The woman is Adele Hugo, the youngest daughter of Victor Hugo, and in the coded journals she kept during her long life (she died in 1915 at the age of eighty-five) she wrote the history of her doomed love.

The facts seem to be these, more or less: While living in exile with her famous father on the island of Guernsey, she was seduced by one Lieutenant Pinson of the British army. She fell in love with him, and he fell in love with her, too—but only after his fashion, because it was his custom to move on to the next conquest every so often. He proposed marriage, not meaning it, and she accepted with a devotion so ferocious that it would rule, and destroy, her life. When he was posted to Halifax, she followed him there. She trailed him through the streets; she spied on him in the countryside, in town, and in the boudoirs of his lovers. Once she sent him a whore, paid for. She took to calling herself Madame Pinson and wrote to her family that she was married. When Pinson became engaged to a Halifax girl, Adele stuffed a pillow under her blouse, went to the girl's father, and announced that she herself was engaged to Pinson and pregnant by him. Her nights were filled with dreams of drowning.

Truffaut has taken this factual material and made it into a strange, moody film that belongs very much with the darker side of his work. He has two kinds of women in his movies. There are the bright, pleasant, vapid little things, such as the various girls in the life of his autobiographical character, Antoine Doinel. And then there are the obsessed, sometimes insane women whose neurotic or incomplete ideas about sexuality drive them into fatal relationships with men.

In this category we find the Jeanne Moreau characters in *Jules and Jim* and *The Bride Wore Black,* the homicidal mail-order bride played by Catherine Deneuve in *Mississippi Mermaid,* the murderess in *Such a Gorgeous Kid Like Me,* and, especially, the two sisters in *Two English Girls.* Tormented by a sexuality that gives them little release, all of these women try to manipulate, possess, and destroy the men in their lives. It apparently is a theme Truffaut finds fascinating, and you have to look very closely through his films to find a normally developed woman (the Jacqueline Bisset character in *Day for Night* comes close).

Adele H., then, must have seemed the ideal Truffaut heroine when he happened across her diaries. And he has made one of his best films about her. He stars Isabelle Adjani, a dark-haired, dark-eyed, severely beautiful young woman, and then photographs her slowly losing all notion of reality (in the final scenes, she has followed Pinson to Barbados and walks through the streets in a ragged gown, blank-eyed, not even recognizing the love of her life when she sees him). Truffaut's colors are blacks and browns and blues, and he fills the screen with shadows; this is the film of a life into which little happiness found its way.

And yet Truffaut finds a certain nobility in Adele. He quotes one of the passages in her diaries twice: She writes that she will walk across the ocean to be with her lover. He sees this not as a declaration of love but as a statement of a single-mindedness so total that a kind of grandeur creeps into it. Adele was mad, yes, probably—but she lived her life on such a vast and romantic scale that it's just as well Pinson never married her. He would have become a disappointment.

The Straight Story

G, 111 m., 1999

Richard Farnsworth (Alvin Straight), Sissy Spacek (Rose), Jane Heitz (Dorothy), James Cada (Danny Riordan), Everett McGill (Tom the Dealer), Jennifer Edwards (Brenda), Barbara E. Robertson (Deer Woman), John Farley (Thorvald), John Lordan (Priest), Harry Dean Stanton (Lyle). Directed by David Lynch and produced by Alain Sarde and Mary Sweeney. Screenplay by Sweeney and John Roach.

The first time I saw *The Straight Story,* I focused on the foreground and liked it. The second time I focused on the background, too, and loved it. The movie isn't just about Alvin Straight's odyssey through the small towns and rural districts of the Midwest, but about the people he finds to listen to and care for him. You'd think it was a fantasy, this kindness of strangers, if the movie weren't based on a true story.

Straight (Richard Farnsworth) is a seventy-three-year-old man from Laurens, Iowa, who learns that his brother is dying, and wants to see him one last time. His eyes are too bad to allow him to drive. He lives with his daughter Rose (Sissy Spacek), who is somewhat retarded and no good behind the wheel. Nor do they have a car. But they have a tractor-style lawn mower, and the moment Alvin's eyes light on it, he knows how he can drive the three hundred miles to Zion, Wisconsin. The first mower konks out, but he gets another one, a John Deere, hitches a little wagon to it, and stubbornly sets off down the road.

Along the way we will learn a lot about Alvin, including a painful secret he has kept ever since the war. He is not a sophisticated man, but when he speaks the words come out like the bricks of a wall built to last. Like Hemingway's dialogue, the screenplay by John Roach and Mary Sweeney finds poetry and truth in the exact choice of the right everyday words. Richard Farnsworth, who was seventy-nine when he made the film, speaks the lines with perfect repose and conviction.

Because the film was directed by David Lynch, who usually deals in the bizarre (*Wild at Heart, Twin Peaks*), we keep waiting for the other shoe to drop—for Alvin's odyssey to intersect with the Twilight Zone. But it never does. Even when he encounters a potential weirdo, like the distraught woman whose car has killed fourteen deer in one week on the same stretch of highway ("... and I *have* to take this road!"), she's not a sideshow exhibit and we think, yeah, you can hit a lot of deer on those country roads.

Alvin's journey to his brother is a journey into his past. He remembers when they were young and filled with wonder. He tells a stranger, "I want to sit with him and look up at the stars, like we used to, so long ago." He remembers his courtship and marriage. His army service as a sniper whose aim, one day, was too good. And about years lost to drinking and nastiness. He has emerged from the forge of his imperfections as a better man,

purified, simple, and people along the way seem to sense that.

My favorite, of all of his stops, comes in a small town where he's almost killed when he loses a drive belt and speeds out of control down a hill. He comes to rest where some people in lawn chairs are watching the local firemen practicing putting out a fire.

In the town are twin brothers who squabble all the time, even while charging him by the hour to repair the mower, and a retired John Deere employee named Danny Riordan (James Cada), who lets Alvin camp for a while in his backyard (Alvin won't enter the house, even to use the phone). Danny is a rare man of instinctive sweetness and tact, who sees what the situation requires, and supplies it without display. He embodies all of our own feelings about this lovable old—yes, fool. He gently offers advice, but Alvin is firm: "You're a kind man talking to a stubborn man."

If Riordan and the deer lady and the dueling twins (and a forlorn young girl) are the background I was talking about, so are the locations themselves. The cinematographer, Freddie Francis, who once made the vastness of Utah a backdrop for *The Executioner's Song,* knows how to evoke a landscape without making it too comforting. There are fields of waving corn and grain here, and rivers and woods and little red barns, but on the sound track the wind whispering in the trees plays a sad and lonely song, and we are reminded not of the fields we drive past on our way to picnics, but on our way to funerals, on autumn days when the roads are empty.

The faces in this movie are among its treasures. Farnsworth himself has a face like an old wrinkled billfold that he paid good money for and expects to see him out. There is another old man who sits next to him on a bar stool near the end of the movie, whose face is like the witness to time. And look and listen to the actor who plays the bartender in that same late scene, the one who serves the Miller Lite. I can't find his name in the credits, but he finds the right note: He knows how all good bartenders can seem like a friend bringing a present to a sickroom.

The last notes are also just right. Who will this dying brother be, and what will he say? Will the screenplay say too much or reach for easy sentimentality? Not at all. Just because you have to see someone doesn't mean you have a lot to gab about. No matter how far you've come.

Note: I later discovered the actor who plays the bartender is Russell Reed.

Strange Days

R, 145 m., 1995

Ralph Fiennes (Lenny Nero), Angela Bassett (Lornette "Mace" Mason), Juliette Lewis (Faith Justin), Tom Sizemore (Max Peltier), Michael Wincott (Philo Gant), Vincent D'Onofrio (Burton Steckler), Richard Edson (Tick), Glenn Plummer (Jeriko One). Directed by Kathryn Bigelow and produced by James Cameron and Steven-Charles Jaffe. Screenplay by Cameron and Jay Cocks.

We know we want it. We want to see through other people's eyes, have their experiences, stand in their shoes. That's the unspoken promise of the movies, and as the unsettling prospect of computer-generated virtual reality creeps closer, it is possible that millions now living will know *exactly* what it feels like to be somebody else.

Strange Days, which takes place on the last two days of 1999, shows us a Los Angeles torn by crime and violence, where the ultimate high is to "jack in" by attaching a "squid" to your skull—a brain-wave transmitter that creates the impression that you are having someone else's experiences. The squid software tapes the lives of other people and plays them back. The movie shows how it works in an opening scene of savage kinetic energy, as a tapehead goes along on an armed robbery, vicariously sharing the same experience until the robber falls off a rooftop to his death.

The tape is for sale, but Lenny Nero (Ralph Fiennes) doesn't want to buy it. He doesn't deal in "blackjack"—the word for snuff films. This is a scruple *Strange Days* does not share, and some of its scenes are deeply disturbing, involving the audience as voyeurs during scenes of death. But isn't that what we do during all the thrillers we attend? Get entertained by the sight of violent action? By making the process explicit, *Strange Days* requires us to think about it, which is more than all but a few movies can or want to do.

The movie paints a Los Angeles that stands midway between the futuristic nightmare of *Blade Runner* and the mean streets of 1940s *film noir.* Roaming gangs rule the city. Armored limousines protect the rich. Santa gets mugged on Hollywood Boulevard. "Jacking in" is the new drug of choice, and Lenny Nero is addicted to it himself; he likes to play back tapes of happier days, when he was still with Faith (Juliette Lewis), the woman he loved. The camera caresses Fiennes's face during these VR sessions; his face reveals surrender to pleasure as he forgives himself everything.

But Faith has split. Now she belongs to Philo Gant (Michael Wincott), who manages rock stars, including Jeriko One, who was "one of the most important black men in America"—until he was shot dead, inspiring riots. Lenny wants Faith back. He also needs money, desperately. Fiennes plays him as a wheedling con man, forever offering "the Rolex off my wrist" to tough guys who would much rather beat him to a pulp. Lenny used to be a cop, but now he's a loser, surviving by selling contraband tapes and not asking too many questions about how the "playback" was obtained.

Lenny leads us into grungy nightclubs and scummy hotels, dealing with the pathetic needs of his customers. In a set-up scene in a club, he sells playbacks to a timid businessman, seductively explaining the technology ("This is like TV, only better. This is like a piece of someone's life—straight from the cerebral cortex"). He lets the businessman have a taste, and we see the mark's face as he turns soft and narcissistic; he thinks he's a teenage girl having a shower. Then Lenny points out a couple dancing on the other side of the room. "How'd you like to be him? How'd you like to have a hot girlfriend like that? How'd you like to be *her?*"

The movie is a technical tour de force. Director Kathryn Bigelow *(Blue Steel)* and her designers and special-effects artists create the vision of a city spinning out of control. Cinematographer Matthew F. Leonetti's point-of-view shots are virtuoso (especially one where a character falls from a roof in an apparently uninterrupted take). The pacing is relentless, and the editing, by Howard Smith, creates an urgency and desperation.

Working from a screenplay by Jay Cocks and James Cameron (director of the *Terminator* films), Bigelow turns scenes like this into a critique of the central paradox of virtual reality: You cannot share someone else's reality without abandoning your own. As the "virgin brain" in the nightclub experiences the sample tape, he watches—and we watch him—defenseless and without inhibition. It's creepy.

Other scenes in the movie go much further, exploring more twisted horrors. In one, which is disturbing and graphic, a man attacks a woman victim after first forcing her to wear the headpiece—so that she experiences her own death through his eyes. It's revealing, how a scene like that seems so much more sad and distressing than the more graphic scenes of violence we see all the time in the movies: Bigelow is able to exploit the *idea* of what is happening; she forces her audience to deal with the screen reality, instead of allowing us to process it as routine "action."

The plot is in the *noir* tradition, with updates out of recent headlines. Although Jeriko One's murder has pushed the city into anarchy, Lenny Nero's priorities are private. He wants to raise some money, maybe because that will increase his stature in Faith's eyes. Nero gains a companion for his quest: Mace (Angela Bassett), who drives an armored limo, and met Lenny when her husband was murdered and he was the cop who comforted her kids. She sees through his scam-artist's façade and saves his skin.

Strange Days does three things that will make it a cult film. It creates a convincing future landscape; it populates it with a hero who comes out of the *noir* tradition and is flawed and complex rather than simply heroic; and it provides a vocabulary. Look for "tapehead," "jacking in," and the movie's spin on "playback" to appear in the vernacular.

At the same time, depending more on mood and character than logic, the movie backs into an ending that is completely implausible. The police commissioner's sudden appearance on the scene is miraculous; and Bigelow begins a riot and then forgets about it, segueing into a New Year's Eve celebration as if you can turn off anarchy like water from a tap.

What stays from the movie are not the transient plot problems, however, but the overall impact. This is the first movie about virtual reality to deal in a challenging way with the implications of the technology. It's fascinating

how Bigelow is able to suggest so much of VR's impact (and dangers) within a movie—a form of VR that's a century old. As the character Faith observes: "One of the ways movies are still better than playback—the music comes up, and you know it's over."

The Stranger

NO MPAA RATING, 104 m., 1967

Marcello Mastroianni (Meursault), Anna Karina (Marie), Georges Geret (Raymond), Georges Wilson (Prosecutor), Bernard Blier (Defense Lawyer). Directed by Luchino Visconti and produced by Dino DeLaurentiis. Screenplay by Suco Cecchi D'Amico, Georges Conchon, and Emmanuel Robles, based on the book by Albert Camus.

The curious fault of Luchino Visconti's *The Stranger* is that the film follows the book too closely.

If Visconti had tampered with Albert Camus's masterpiece, I suppose I would have responded with knee-jerk indignation. But he has handled Camus with an almost excessive reverence, and halfway through we realize the film will have no surprises.

This doesn't mean *The Stranger* is bad as cinema. Visconti, like Camus, realizes that the meaning of *The Stranger* is to be found not in the plot but in the mood. The mood is ennui, the dominant emotion of a man who hardly cares enough to tell his own story. Meursault, Camus's hero, commits a murder almost absentmindedly.

The point is not so much that he murders a man as that he hardly seems to care. The courtroom is enraged that a man could be so lacking in basic human emotion. The hazard for the director is to show Meursault's boredom without making a boring film, and Visconti succeeds for the most part. Even when very little is happening on the screen, it is happening interestingly. Visconti mutes his colors, preferring blues and grays, an occasional yellow or white or orange, and only a rare splash of anything bright. The surface of his photography is still, at most, passive.

The murder scene is filmed in a deliberately unsensational way; it hardly seems to matter. Against this passive mood, the strong emotions of the other characters clash strongly. There is the opening scene at the funeral for Meursault's mother; an elderly friend faints, but Meursault is unmoved.

In the other rooms of Meursault's building, an old man passionately loves and hates his dog, lovers quarrel, and there are shouts on the stairway, but for Meursault the day is only something to be gotten through.

The people who surround him *care* about the events in their lives; Meursault does not. Marcello Mastroianni is perhaps too striking to play Meursault (I would have preferred a nonentity). But he turns in a good, restrained performance. He is at his best in the scenes with Anna Karina, the girlfriend he hardly cares about. Even when he says he loves her, it is his good nature and not his passion speaking.

He wants to be agreeable. That is why the murder is such a puzzle. Why would such an agreeable, indifferent, passive person murder one of his fellows? But that is the question Camus began with.

Stranger than Paradise

R, 90 m., 1984

John Lurie (Willie), Eszter Balint (Eva), Richard Edson (Eddie), Cecillia Stark (Aunt Lottie), Danny Rosen (Billy), Rammellzee (Man with Money), Tom Decillo (Airline Agent). Directed by Jim Jarmusch and produced by Sara Driver. Screenplay by Jarmusch.

Stranger than Paradise is filmed in a series of uninterrupted shots; the picture fades in, we watch the scene, and when the scene is over, there's a fade to black. Then comes the next fade-in. This is not a gimmick, but a visual equivalent of the film's deadpan characters, who take a lot to get excited.

The movie's hero is Willie (John Lurie), who arrived on these shores from Hungary about ten years ago, and has spent the intervening decade perfecting his New York accent and trying to make nothing out of himself. He lives in an apartment where the linoleum is the highlight. On a good day, he'll sleep late, hang out, play a little poker. His cousin Eva arrives from Budapest. This is the last thing he needs, a sixteen-year-old girl who needs a place to stay. She hates him, too. But she has to kill some time before she goes to Cleveland to

live with her aunt Lottie. She has good taste in American music, but not according to him. Willie's friend, Eddie, comes over occasionally and eyeballs Eva. Nothing much happens. She leaves for Cleveland.

The screen is filled with large letters: ONE YEAR LATER. This in itself is funny, that we'd get such a momentous time cue in a movie where who even knows what day it is. Eddie and Willie get in some trouble over a poker game and Eddie suddenly remembers Willie's cousin in Cleveland. They go to see her. It is cold in Cleveland. Eva has bought the American Dream and is working in a fast-food outlet. They all go to look at the lake, which is frozen. Aunt Lottie turns out to make Clara Peller look like Dame Peggy Ashcroft. The guys say to hell with it and head for Florida. Then they come back and get Eva and take her along with them. They have a postcard that makes Florida look like paradise, but they wind up living at one of those hotels where the permanent guests live in the woodwork. Everything goes sour. Eva wants to go back to Hungary. The guys lose all their money at the dog races. Creeps start hanging around. It will take a miracle to give this movie an upbeat ending. There is a miracle.

Stranger than Paradise is a treasure from one end to the other. I saw it for the first time at the 1984 Cannes Film Festival, where it was having its first public showing. Half the people in the theater probably didn't speak English, but that didn't stop them from giving the movie a standing ovation, and it eventually won the Camera d'Or prize for the best first film. It is like no other film you've seen, and yet you feel right at home in it. It seems to be going nowhere, and knows every step it wants to make. It is a constant, almost kaleidoscopic experience of discovery, and we try to figure out what the film is up to and it just keeps moving steadfastly ahead, fade in, fade out, fade in, fade out, making a mountain out of a molehill.

Streamers

R, 118 m., 1984

Matthew Modine (Billy), Michael Wright (Carlyle), Mitchell Lichtenstein (Richie), David Alan Grier (Roger), Guy Boyd (Rooney), George Dzundza (Cokes). Directed by Robert Altman and produced by Altman and Nick H. Mileti. Screenplay by David Rabe.

Robert Altman's *Streamers* is one of the most intense and intimate dramas I've ever seen on film. It's based on the play by David Rabe, about young soldiers waiting around a barracks for their orders to go to Vietnam. Most directors, faced with a play that takes place on one set, find ways to "open it up" and add new locations. Altman has moved in the opposite direction, taking advantage of the one-room set to tighten the play until it squeezes like a vise. Watching this film is such a demanding experience that both times I've seen it, it has been too much for some viewers, and they've left. Those who stay, who survive the difficult passages of violence, will find at the end of the film a conclusion that is so poetic and moving it succeeds in placing the tragedy in perspective.

It is the era of Vietnam. In a barracks somewhere, three young men wait for their orders. They are Billy, who is white and middle-class; Roger, who is black and middle-class; and Richie, a dreamy young man who likes to tease the others with hints that he is a homosexual. The only other occupants of the barracks are two drunken master sergeants, Rooney and Cokes, who are best friends and who are stumbling through idiotic revelry in an attempt to drown the realization that Cokes has leukemia. Into this little world comes Carlyle, an angry young black man who is gay, and whose conversations with Richie will lead the others into anger and denial before the situation finally explodes.

There are some surprises, but the developments in *Streamers* flow so naturally out of the material that its surprises should be left intact. A lot can be said, however, about the acting, Altman's direction, and Rabe's writing. I didn't see this play on stage and don't know how it worked there, but Altman is so completely the visual master of this material that we're drawn into that barracks room and into its rhythms of boredom, drunkenness, and passion.

The actors are all unknown to me, except for George Dzundza, who plays Cokes. They are all so natural that the dialogue has an eerie double quality: We know it's written dialogue because it has a poetry and a drama unlikely

in life, but Rabe's ear is so accurate it sounds real, and the performers make it so convincing there's never a false note. The two key performances are by Mitchell Lichtenstein, as Richie, and Michael Wright, as Carlyle. Richie is indeed homosexual, as we realize long before his barracks mates are willing to acknowledge it. He likes to tease the others with insinuations that they may be gay, too. Billy boasts that he is straight, but he protests too much. Roger tries to be a peacekeeper. Then Carlyle wanders in from another unit. He is drunk and angry, collapses, sleeps it off, blearily looks around, figures out Richie, and tries to make a connection.

But there is a lot more going on here than sexual competition. *Streamers* uses both sex and race as foreground subjects while the movie's real subject, war, hovers in the background and in several extraordinary monologues—one about snakes, one about a battle, and one about the realities of parachuting. As the veteran master sergeants make their drunken way through the movie, they drop these hard realities into the lives of the unseasoned kids. And when anger turns to violence and a tragedy occurs, it is up to one of the fat old guys (Dzundza) to deliver a monologue that is one of the most revealing, intimate, honest, and moving speeches I've ever heard.

Streetwise

R, 92 m., 1985

Directed by Martin Bell and produced by Cheryl McCall. Reported by Mary Ellen Mark.

The mother is being frank about her daughter. She says she knows the girl is working as a prostitute, but she figures "it's just a phase she's going through." Her daughter is about fifteen years old. That is not the most harrowing moment in *Streetwise*, a heartbreaking documentary about the street children of Seattle. There are worse moments, for example the one where a street kid tries to talk to her mother about the fact that her stepfather "was fooling around . . . doing perverted things with me" when she was a baby. "Yes," says the mother philosophically, "but now he's stopped."

The subject of runaway, abducted, and

abandoned children has received a lot of attention in the news, but never anything remotely like *Streetwise*, which enters into the lives of these underage survivors as they fight for life and love on the streets of Seattle. The movie was inspired by a *Life* magazine article on a group of the kids, who, at an age when other kids are in school, are learning to be hookers, thieves, con men, pushers, and junkies. Now comes this movie, which contains extraordinary everyday footage, which the filmmakers obtained by spending months hanging out with the kids, until they gained their trust and their cameras became accepted.

The street kids lead horrifying lives, but sometimes there are moments of acceptance and happiness. They cling to each other. They relate uneasily with a social worker who seems philosophically resigned to the facts of street life. They try to dodge the cops. They live in an abandoned hotel, get money by begging and prostitution, eat by raiding the Dumpsters behind restaurants. They even have a system for marking garbage so they don't eat food that's too old.

What is amazing is that some of these kids are still in touch with their parents. One girl shrugs that her mother is off to the woods for a weekend: "I've always known she don't love me or shit. So OK." She hugs herself. Another girl tries to talk to her mother, who says, "Be quiet. I'm drinking." A kid named DeWayne goes to visit his father in prison and gets a long lecture about smoking, drinking, and taking drugs, and a pie-in-the-sky speech about how they're going to open a thrift shop when the old man gets out of prison. The next time we see DeWayne, it is at his funeral; he hanged himself in a jail cell.

You walk out of *Streetwise* realizing that these aren't bad kids. They are resourceful, tough, and true to their own standards. They break the law, but then how many legal ways are there for fourteen-year-olds to support themselves? They talk about their parents in a matter-of-fact way that, we suspect, covers up great wounds, as when one girl says she's never met her natural father—"unless maybe I dated him once."

Streetwise is surprising for the frankness of the material it contains. How did the filmmakers get these people to say these things, to allow the cameras into their lives? We see moments of intimacy, of violence, of pain. The answer, I suspect, is that a lot of these kids were so starving for attention and affection that by offering both, the filmmakers were able to get whatever they wanted. Some of the scenes are possibly staged, in the sense that the characters are aware they are in a movie, but none of the scenes are false or contrived. These are children living rough in an American city, and you would blame their parents if you didn't see that the parents are just as alienated and hopeless, and that before long these kids will be damaged parents, too.

Stroszek

NO MPAA RATING, 108 m., 1978

Bruno S. (Stroszek), Eva Mattes (Eva), Clement Scheitz (Scheitz), Wilhelm von Homburg (Pimp), Burkhard Dreist (Pimp), Clayton Szlapinski (Scheitz's Nephew), Ely Rodriguez (Indian). Directed, produced, and written by Werner Herzog.

Werner Herzog has subtitled *Stroszek* as "a ballad," and so it is: It's like one of those bluegrass nonsense ballads in which impossible adventures are described in every verse, and the chorus reminds us that life gets teedjus, don't it? But because Herzog has one of the most original imaginations of anyone now making movies, *Stroszek* is a haunting and hilarious ballad at the same time, an almost unbelievable mixture of lunacy, comedy, tragedy, and the simply human.

Consider. He gives us three main characters who are best friends, despite the fact that they're improbable as people and impossible as friends. There's Stroszek himself, just released from prison in Germany. He's a simple soul who plays the piano and the accordion and never quite understands why people behave as they do. There's Eva, a dim but pleasant Berlin prostitute. And there's old Scheitz, a goofy soul in his seventies who has been invited to live with his nephew in upstate Wisconsin.

This mixture is further complicated by the fact that Stroszek is played by Bruno S., the same actor Herzog used in *Kaspar Hauser*. Bruno S. is a mental patient, described by Herzog as schizophrenic, and it's a good question whether he's "acting" in this movie or simply exercising a crafty survival instinct. No matter: He comes across as saintly, sensitive, and very strange.

The three friends meet when Eva's two pimps beat her up and throw her out. She comes to live with Stroszek. The pimps (evil hoods right out of a Fassbinder gangster movie) later visit Stroszek and Eva and beat them both up, leaving Stroszek kneeling on his beloved piano with a school bell balanced on his derriere.

It is clearly time to leave Berlin, and old Scheitz has the answer: Visit his relatives in America. The nephew lives on a Wisconsin farm in an incredibly barren landscape, but to the Germans it's the American Dream. They buy an enormous mobile home, seventy feet long and fully furnished, and install a color TV in it. Eva gets a job as a waitress, and turns some tricks on the side at the truck stop. Stroszek works as a mechanic, sort of. Old Scheitz wanders about testing the "animal magnetism" of fence posts.

The Wisconsin scenes are among the weirdest I've ever seen in a movie: Notice, for example, the visit Stroszek and Eva get from that supercilious little twerp from the bank, who wants to repossess their TV set and who never seems to understand that nothing he says is understood. Or notice the brisk precision with which an auctioneer disposes of the mobile home, which is then carted away, all seventy feet of it, leaving the bewildered Stroszek looking at the empty landscape it has left behind.

Stroszek gets most hypnotically bizarre as it goes along, because we understand more of the assumptions of the movie. One of them is possibly that Kaspar Hauser might have become Stroszek, had he lived for another century and studied diligently. (Hauser, you might remember, was the "wild child" kept imprisoned in the dark for nineteen years, never taught to speak, and then dumped in a village square.)

The film's closing scenes are wonderfully funny and sad, at once. Stroszek and Scheitz rob a barber shop, and then Stroszek buys a frozen turkey, and then there is an amusement park with a chicken that will not stop dancing (and a policeman reporting "The dancing chicken won't stop"), and a wrecker driving in a circle with no one at the wheel, and an In-

dian chief looking on impassively, and somehow Herzog has made a statement about America here that is as loony and utterly original as any ever made.

Such Good Friends

R, 101 m., 1971

Dyan Cannon (Julie Messinger), James Coco (Dr. Timmy Spector), Jennifer O'Neill (Miranda Graham), Ken Howard (Cal Whiting), Nina Poch (Mrs. Wallman), Laurence Luckinbill (Richard Messinger), Louise Lasser (Marcy Berns), Burgess Meredith (Bernard Kalman). Directed and produced by Otto Preminger. Screenplay by Elaine May, based on the book by Lois Gould.

Otto Preminger's *Such Good Friends* is a hard, unsentimental, deeply cynical comedy about life as it is lived, unfortunately, in New York City. It's Preminger's best film in a long time, probably since *Anatomy of a Murder* in 1959.

That isn't to say that Preminger hasn't created some good films and some great scenes in the years since. But his projects so often have been vast exercises in logistics: this time he spends his energy on the story of a few painfully realized days, and what has been wasted on width now is invested in depth.

The world he examines is the New York society of money-oriented creators: terribly bright, talented people who have arrived on a certain plateau because of their willingness (eagerness?) to lay everything on the line for success. Their success, like their lives, is totally present tense. Although they have histories and backgrounds and occasionally bow dutifully in the direction of their ethnic groups, they're essentially cut off from everything except high-powered performance. Death strikes these people as a particularly awkward embarrassment.

Preminger's story, fashioned with a screenplay by Elaine May into a sort of black-comedy version of Lois Gould's serious novel, concerns the unexpected death of one Richard Messinger. He is the art director of a big magazine (apparently *Life*) and has written a best-selling children's book. He goes into the hospital for the removal of a nonmalignant mole, and a few days later he is dead.

The complications involve his blood, liver, kidneys, and eventually his heart. His doctors do a macabre verbal dance, adding symptoms while reporting progress. At one point, over baked apples in the hospital cafeteria, they reassure Messinger's wife that things are looking up: Hospital care is so slipshod, you see, that you really have a *better* chance of recovery if your illness becomes critical, because then you're moved into intensive care and modern medical science can really get a grip on you.

This sort of double reverse logic, laid on like the carefully insane reasoning in *Catch-22*, is handled with such flat objectivity by Preminger that we laugh and cringe at the same time. He refuses to go for easy releases of tension—there are no double takes, no mugging (not even from James Coco), and everything lies there flat on the table, as it were. The facts are funny, but a man is dying. At one point, his wife asks, "If you come in with major complications, do you leave with a mole?"

While her husband lies dying, the wife (played with an easily wounded but durable integrity by Dyan Cannon) finds out that he's been having affairs with just about all the women they know. His impending death seems such an unlikely chance ("The odds are 20,000 to 1," the doctor consoles her) that his unfaithfulness somehow seems more real. She hates him, loves him, blames him, forgives him, while all the time he drifts in the infuriating neutrality of a coma.

This was serious stuff in the novel, but it takes on a really wounding irony in the Preminger and May treatment. There are funny lines in the movie, but they are rarely allowed to be merely funny; they are also intended to hurt. People hurt and insult one another because, we sense, attack is the best form of defense inside this carnivorous society.

Some of the dialogue is in appallingly bad taste, and some of the critics have blamed the bad taste on Preminger, but it would have taken a lesser director to leave it in.

The vulgarity belongs there because the movie is as tough as the people it's about. Despite the unfortunate death of the husband, it is also about survival. We spend the days of the deathwatch with the Dyan Cannon character, as she works through booze, adultery, hardness, weakness, and the kind of hypocrisy that death seems to attract and inspire. *Such Good Friends* exists in a world where even a bad friend is better than what you've been getting lately.

Sugar Cane Alley

NO MPAA RATING, 103 m., 1983

Garry Cadenat (Jose), Darling Légitimus (M'Man Tine), Douta Seck (Medouze). Directed by Euzhan Palcy and produced by Jean-Luc Ormiéres. Screenplay by Palcy, based on the book by Joseph Zobel.

Sugar Cane Alley seems to grow so directly out of old memories that it's a surprise to discover that the director based it on a novel; it feels so real we assume she based it on her own life. The film tells the story of a young orphan who was born on the French-speaking island of Martinique in 1920 and, when the story begins, is a carefree eleven-year-old playing with the other kids in Sugar Cane Alley—a row of shacks by the cane fields.

These early scenes get right inside a child's point of view; they're as natural as Francois Truffaut's *Small Change*. The kids are left alone all day while their parents work in the fields, and they make up games, get into fights, and poke about where they're not supposed to be. When one of them breaks a precious sugar bowl, the depth of the tragedy underlines the poverty of these people.

The little boy is named Jose. He lives with his grandmother, a vast, hardworking, God-fearing woman with a great fund of love. He is a smart kid—gifted, likable. He makes friends with a very old man, a man so old that he remembers the days of slavery, and tells Jose that the work in the fields is just a new form of slavery. He dreams of going back to Africa someday, and Jose says he'll join him.

But, meanwhile, Jose is doing well in school. His grandmother works long hours to support them so he can break out of the fields and get an education. And the movie follows Jose as he sits for an exam and is accepted by an intermediate school in the island's capital. He gets a scholarship, but it's not enough money, and in one of the great scenes of the movie his grandmother moves them to a packing case on the outskirts of the city and does laundry to support them both.

The film's director, Euzhan Palcy, knows she's dealing with many of the conventions of a rags-to-riches story here, but she avoids a lot of possible stereotypes by making everything very particular, by making Jose into an individual instead of just a good example. When a woman hires Jose and then makes him late for school, for example, Jose conceives a brilliant plan to sneak back and get even with her— while maintaining a perfect alibi.

Sugar Cane Alley sees its world so clearly because it's an inside job; Palcy grew up on Martinique. At the same time, she doesn't lean on their heartwarming story. She's making a movie here, and it's a smart, sometimes hard-edged story that earns its moments of sentiment.

Every once in a while a movie will come out of nowhere. The actors will be people we've never seen before, the location will be an unfamiliar one, the director's name will be brand new, and everything will fit together so naturally that we wonder where these people have been all their lives. In a way, the very story of *Sugar Cane Alley* answers that question.

Sugar Hill

R, 123 m., 1994

Wesley Snipes (Roemello Skuggs), Michael Wright (Raynathan Skuggs), Theresa Randle (Melissa), Clarence Williams III (A. R. Skuggs), Abe Vigoda (Gus Molino), Ernie Hudson (Lolly Jonas). Directed by Leon Ichaso and produced by Rudy Langlais and Gregory Brown. Screenplay by Barry Michael Cooper.

Sugar Hill is a dark, bloody family tragedy, told in terms so sad and poetic that it transcends its genre and becomes eloquent drama. To call this film a "drug thriller" is like describing *Macbeth* as a murder mystery, or *Long Day's Journey Into Night* as a soap opera. In its rich visual style, its powerful acting, and the unexpected grace of its dialogue, it tells a deeply affecting story.

The film stars Wesley Snipes and Michael Wright as Roemello and Raynathan Skuggs, two brothers whose childhoods were seared by drugs. They have seen their mother die of an overdose, and their father crippled by mob bullets after withholding money in a drug deal. Now, as young men in Harlem, they're drug dealers themselves—working with the same Mafia boss who ordered their father shot.

On a materialistic level, life is good for them. Roemello lives in an apartment of dark, burnished woods and deep reds and bronzes; its interiors reminded me of Don Vito's home in *The Godfather*, and indeed, Bojan Bazelli's cinematography throughout the movie creates the same kind of shadowed, luxurious world that was inhabited by the Corleones.

But Roemello is not happy with his life, and Snipes portrays him as a man who has gotten to the point where he can hardly bear to see what goes on around him. A small boy on a bicycle brandishes a handgun. Another gang wants a piece of the action in his territory, and he doesn't want to face the violence that is likely to result. And in a drab apartment, his father (Clarence Williams III) sits paralyzed from the waist down, waiting for his next fix.

Roemello wants out. Nobody wants him out. His brother believes they are on the brink of a breakthrough to the *really* big time. And Gus Molino (Abe Vigoda), the ancient Mafia boss who controls the drugs, thinks it would be a very bad idea for them to quit now— even though he's behind the division of the territory.

Some of these plot elements are not unfamiliar from many other movies, including Snipes's own *New Jack City* and 1993's *Carlito's Way*. But *Sugar Hill* exists in another dimension. Leon Ichaso's direction and Barry Michael Cooper's screenplay are deliberately aiming for the deep human tragedy in this story, and away from the formula crime elements. Sometimes we can be snobs about genres, and think that a Harlem drug story can only exist on a certain level, but as I was watching this film I was reminded of classical tragedy, and of Shakespeare and Eugene O'Neill.

The film's central pain comes from the fact that the suffering caused by drugs goes on and on and on, one generation after the next. The memory of the dead mother and the daily rebuke of the father's sad existence do not stop the Skuggs brothers from dealing the same drugs, from the same supplier, that destroyed their parents' lives. There is even a certain brooding logic to it; Roemello has won revenge by killing the man who actually shot his father. But he has not touched Gus Molino, who ordered the shooting—because at that level it was, after all, business. And Gus Molino has never looked too deeply into who killed his triggerman (of course he knows it was Roemello), because he accepts the feelings that were involved.

There is a certain conservatism here, a certain respect for continuing to do things in the old ways, that both Roemello and Gus understand. It is the entry of the new gang into the neighborhood (led by Ernie Hudson) that threatens the balance. And even more threatening is Roemello's disenchantment. "It's not that I'm scared, man," he tells his brother. "It's just that I see something you don't."

Roemello has met a woman, Melissa (Theresa Randle), and loves her, but she wants nothing to do with him because he is a drug dealer. She's serious; it isn't an act. He tells her he's leaving the business. She will believe that when she sees it. Their relationship goes deeper than romance usually does in this genre; there is quick passion, yes, but also thought for future consequences. She believes it is not enough to love someone. You must also be able to trust him, and to believe he will be alive for you.

Few movies have been this thoughtful and serious about a problem that has been cheapened by so many gun-crazy movies and TV shows. *Sugar Hill* looks unblinkingly at what drugs do—not simply to the bodies of those who use them, but to the lives and future of those touched by them, even if they don't use them. My only problem with the film is with the very last scene, which looks suspiciously tacked on, as if the filmmakers, having taken their story to its logical conclusion, could not leave it there.

Sugar Hill is in danger of being overlooked by its intended audience, and unappreciated by the audience that will be drawn by exploitative ads. Here is a Harlem drug drama starring Wesley Snipes, one of the top action stars in the movies, and it's logical to assume it's a thriller. It's not. It is appropriate for the same audiences who saw and understood *Schindler's List, Philadelphia,* and *The Remains of the Day.* Of course they will hear some words and see some drug abuse and violence they may not be accustomed to, but that is because this passionate tragedy is not about a very nice world.

Sunday Bloody Sunday

R, 110 m., 1971

Glenda Jackson (Alex Greville), Peter Finch (Dr. Daniel Hirsh), Murray Head (Bob Elkin), Peggy Ashcroft (Mrs. Greville), Tony Britton (Businessman), Maurice Denham (Mr. Greville). Directed by John Schlesinger and produced by Joseph Janni. Screenplay by Penelope Gilliatt.

The official East Coast line on John Schlesinger's *Sunday Bloody Sunday* was that it is civilized. That judgment was enlisted to carry the critical defense of the movie; and, indeed, how can the decent critic be against a civilized movie about civilized people? My notion, all the same, is that *Sunday Bloody Sunday* is about people who suffer from psychic amputation, not civility, and that this film is not an affirmation but a tragedy.

The story involves three people in a rather novel love triangle: A London doctor in his forties, a divorced woman in her thirties, and the young man they are both in love with. The doctor and the woman know about each other (the young man makes no attempt to keep secrets) but don't seem particularly concerned; they have both made an accommodation in order to have some love instead of none at all.

The screenplay by Penelope Gilliatt takes us through eight or nine days in their lives, while the young man prepares to leave for New York. Both of his lovers will miss him—and he will miss *them,* after his fashion—but he has decided to go, and between them, they don't have enough pull on him to make him want to stay. So the two love affairs approach their ends, while the lovers go about a melancholy daily existence in London.

Both the doctor and the woman are involved in helping people, he by a kind and intelligent approach to his patients, she through working in an employment agency. The boy, on the other hand, seems exclusively preoccupied with the commercial prospects in America for his sculpture (he does things with glass tubes, liquids, and electricity). He isn't concerned with whether his stuff is any good, but whether it will sell to Americans. He doesn't seem to feel very deeply about anything, in fact. He is kind enough and open enough, but there is no dimension to him, as there is to his lovers.

It is with the two older characters that we get to the core of the movie. In a world where everyone loses eventually, they are still survivors. They survive by accommodating themselves to life as it must be lived. The doctor, for example, is not at all personally disturbed by his homosexuality, and yet he doesn't reveal it to his close-knit Jewish family; maintaining relations-as-usual with them is another way for him to survive. The woman tells us late in the film, "Some people believe something is better than nothing, but I'm beginning to believe that nothing can be better than something." Well, maybe so, but we get to know her well enough to suspect that she will settle for something, not nothing, again the next time.

The glory of *Sunday Bloody Sunday* is supposed to be the intelligent, sophisticated—civilized!—way in which these two people gracefully accept the loss of a love they had shared. Well, they *are* graceful as hell about it, and there is a positive glut of being philosophical about the inevitable. But that didn't make me feel better for them, or about them, the way it was supposed to; I felt pity for them. I insist that they would *not* have been so bloody civilized if either one had felt really deeply about the boy. The fact that they were willing to share him is perhaps a clue: They shared him not because they were willing to settle for half, but because they were afraid to try for all. The three-sided arrangement was, in part, a guarantee that no one would get in so deep that being "civilized" wouldn't be protection enough against hurt.

The acting is flawless. Peter Finch is the doctor, Glenda Jackson the woman, and Murray Head the young man. They are good to begin with and then just right for Gilliatt's screenplay and Schlesinger's direction. They are set down in a very real and sad London (seen mostly in cold twilights), and surrounded by supporting actors who resonate in a way that fills in all the dimensions of the characters. I think *Sunday Bloody Sunday* is a masterpiece, but I don't think it's about what everybody else seems to think it's about. This is not a movie about the loss of love, but about its absence.

Superman

PG, 144 m., 1978

Christopher Reeve (Superman/Clark Kent), Marlon Brando (Jor-El), Gene Hackman (Lex Luthor), Margot Kidder (Lois Lane), Ned Beatty (Otis), Jackie Cooper (Perry White), Glenn Ford (Jonathan Kent), Trevor Howard (First Elder), Valerie Perrine (Miss Teschmacher). Directed by Richard Donner and produced by Pierre Spengler. Screenplay by Mario Puzo, David Newman, Leslie Newman, and Robert Benton.

Superman is a pure delight, a wondrous combination of all the old-fashioned things we never really get tired of: adventure and romance, heroes and villains, earthshaking special effects, and—you know what else? Wit. That surprised me more than anything: That this big-budget epic, which was half a decade making its way to the screen, would turn out to have an intelligent sense of humor about itself.

The wit, to be sure, is a little slow in revealing itself. The film's opening scenes combine great intergalactic special effects with ponderous acting and dialogue—most of it from Marlon Brando, who, as Superman's father, sends the kid to Earth in a spaceship that barely survives the destruction of the planet Krypton. Brando was allegedly paid $3 million for his role, or, judging by his dialogue, $500,000 a cliché. After Superbaby survives his space flight and lands in a Midwestern wheat field, however, the movie gets down to earth, too. And it has the surprising ability to have *fun* with its special effects. That's surprising because special effects on this vast scale (falling airliners, derailing passenger trains, subterranean dungeons, cracks in the earth, volcanic eruptions, dams bursting) are so expensive and difficult that it takes a special kind of courage to kid them a little—instead of regarding them with awe, as in the witless *Earthquake.*

The audience finds itself pleasantly surprised, and taken a little off guard; the movie's tremendously exciting in a comic book sort of way (kids will go ape for it), but at the same time it has a sly sophistication, a kidding insight into the material, that makes it, amazingly, a refreshingly offbeat comedy.

Most of the humor centers, of course,

around one of the central icons of American popular culture, Superman (who, and I quote from our common memory of hundreds of comic books and radio and TV shows, in his dual identity as Clark Kent is a mild-mannered reporter for the *Daily Planet*). The producers held a worldwide talent search for an actor to play Superman, and although "talent searches" are usually 100 percent horsefeathers, this time, for once, they actually found the right guy.

He is Christopher Reeve. He *looks* like the Superman in the comic books (a fate I would not wish on anybody), but he's also an engaging actor, open and funny in his big love scene with Lois Lane, and then correctly awesome in his showdown with the archvillain Lex Luthor. Reeve sells the role; wrong casting here would have sunk everything.

And there would have been a lot to sink. *Superman* may have been expensive, all right, but the money's there on the screen. The screenplay was obviously written without the slightest concern for how much it might cost. After Clark Kent goes to work for the *Daily Planet* (and we meet old favorites Perry White, Lois Lane, and Jimmy Olsen), there's a nonstop series of disasters just for openers: Poor Lois finds herself dangling from one seatbelt after her helicopter crashes high atop the Daily Planet Building; Air Force One is struck by lightning and loses an engine; a thief climbs up a building using suction cups, and so on. Superman resolves his emergencies with, well, tact and good manners. He's modest about his abilities. Snaps a salute to the president. Says he's for "truth, justice, and the American Way." And, of course, falls in love with Lois Lane.

She's played by Margot Kidder, and their relationship is subtly, funnily wicked. She lives in a typical girl reporter's apartment (you know, a penthouse high atop a Metropolis skyscraper), and Superman zooms down to offer an exclusive interview and a free flight over Metropolis. Supposing *you're* a girl reporter, and Superman turns up. What would you ask him? So does she.

Meanwhile, the evil Lex Luthor (Gene Hackman) is planning an apocalyptic scheme to destroy the entire West Coast, plus Hackensack, New Jersey. He knows Superman's weak point: the deadly substance Kryptonite. He also knows that Superman cannot see through lead (Lois Lane, alas, forgets). Luthor lives in a subterranean pad that's a comic inspiration: A half-flooded, subterranean train station. Superman drills through the earth for a visit.

But enough of the plot. The movie works so well because of its wit and its special effects. A word more about each. The movie begins with the tremendous advantage that almost everyone in the audience knows the Superman saga from youth. There aren't a lot of explanations needed; that's brilliantly demonstrated in the first scene where Superman tries to change in a phone booth. Christopher Reeve can be allowed to smile, to permit himself a double entendre, to kid himself.

And then the special effects. They're as good in their way as any you've seen, and they come thick and fast. When the screenplay calls for Luthor to create an earthquake and for Superman to try to stop it, the movie doesn't give us a falling bridge or two, it gives us the San Andreas Fault cracking open. No half measures for Superman. The movie is, in fact, a triumph of imagination over both the difficulties of technology and the inhibitions of money. *Superman* wasn't easy to bring to the screen, but the filmmakers kept at it until they had it right.

Superman II
PG, 127 m., 1981

Christopher Reeve (Superman/Clark Kent), Gene Hackman (Lex Luthor), Ned Beatty (Otis), Margot Kidder (Lois Lane), Terence Stamp (General Zod), Jackie Cooper (Perry White), Sarah Douglas (Ursa), Jack O'Halloran (Non), Valerie Perrine (Eve). Directed by Richard Lester and produced by Alexander and Ilya Salkind and Pierre Spengler. Screenplay by Mario Puzo, David Newman, and Leslie Newman.

I thought the original *Superman* was terrific entertainment—and so I was a little startled to discover that I liked *Superman II* even more. Perhaps the secret of the sequel is that it has more faith in Superman. Before the original *Superman* was released in 1978, the producers knew he could carry a speeding locomotive, all right—but could he carry a movie? They weren't sure, and since they were investing millions of dollars in the project, they didn't want to rest a whole movie on the broad shoulders of their unknown star, Christopher Reeve. So they began *Superman* ponderously, on the planet Krypton, with the presence of Marlon Brando as a sort of totem to convince audiences that this movie was big league. They told us of Superman's origins with a solemnity more befitting a god. They were very serious and very symbolic, and it wasn't until Superman came to Earth that the movie really caught fire. *Then*, half an hour or more into its length, it started giving us what we came for: Superman flying around with his red cape, saving mankind.

Superman II begins in midstream, and never looks back (aside from a brief recap of the first movie). In many ways, it's a repeat of the last ninety minutes of the first film. It has the same key characters, including archvillain Lex Luthor. It continues the love story of Lois Lane and Superman, not to mention the strange relationship of Lois and Clark Kent. It features the return of three villains from Krypton, who when last seen were trapped in a one-dimensional plane of light and cast adrift in space. And it continues those remarkable special effects.

From his earliest days in a comic book, Superman always has been an urban hero. He lived in a universe that was defined by screaming banner headlines and vast symbolic acts, and *Superman II* catches that flavor perfectly with its use of famous landmarks like the Eiffel Tower, the Empire State Building, Niagara Falls, and the Coca-Cola sign in Times Square. He was a pop hero in a pop world, and like Mickey Mouse and the original Coke trademark, he became an instantly recognizable trademark.

That's why the special effects in both *Superman* movies are so crucial. It is a great deal simpler to show a rocket ship against the backdrop of outer space than to show Kryptonian villains hurling a city bus through the air in midtown Manhattan. But the feeling of actuality makes Superman's exploits more fun. It brings the fantastic into our everyday lives; it delights in showing us the reaction of the man on the street to Superman's latest stunt. In the movie, as in the comic book, ordinary citizens seem to spend their days glued to the sidewalk, gazing skyward, and shouting things like "Superman is dead!" or "Superman has saved the world!"

In *Superman II* he saves large portions of the world, all right, but what he preserves most of all is the element of humanity within him. The *Superman* movies made a basic decision to give Superman and his alter ego, Clark Kent, more human feelings than the character originally possessed. So *Superman II* has a lot of fun developing his odd dual relationship with Lois Lane. At long, long last, Lois and Superman make love in this movie (after champagne, but discreetly offscreen in Superman's ice palace). But Lois and Clark Kent also spend the night together in highly compromised circumstances, in a Niagara Falls honeymoon haven. And the movie has fun with another one of those ultimate tests that Lois was always throwing at Clark to make him admit he was really Superman. Lois bets her life on it this time, hurling herself into the rapids below Niagara Falls. Either Clark can turn into Superman and save her—or she'll drown. And what then? All I can say is, Clark does *not* turn into Superman.

This scene has a lot of humor in it, and the whole film has more smiles and laughs than the first one. Maybe that's because of a change in directors. Richard Donner, who made the first *Superman* film and did a brilliant job of establishing a basic look for the series, was followed this time by Richard Lester *(A Hard Day's Night, The Three Musketeers)*, and this is some of Lester's best work. He permits satire to make its way into the film more easily. He has a lot of fun with Gene Hackman, as the still-scheming, thin-skinned, egomaniacal Lex Luthor. And he draws out Christopher Reeve, whose performance in the title role is sly, knowing, and yet still appropriately square. This movie's most intriguing insight is that Superman's disguise as Clark Kent isn't a matter of looks as much as of mental attitude: Clark is disguised not by his glasses but by his ordinariness. Beneath his meek exterior, of course, is concealed a superhero. And, the movie subtly hints, isn't that the case with us all?

The Sweet Hereafter

R, 110 m., 1997

Ian Holm (Mitchell Stephens), Sarah Polley (Nicole Burnell), Bruce Greenwood (Billy Ansell), Tom

McCamus (Sam Burnell), Gabrielle Rose (Dolores Driscoll), Arsinee Khanjian (Wanda Otto), Alberta Watson (Risa Walker), Maury Chaykin (Wendell Walker). Directed by Atom Egoyan and produced by Egoyan and Camelia Frieberg. Screenplay by Egoyan, based on the book by Russell Banks.

A cold, dark hillside looms above the Bide-a-Wile Motel, pressing down on it, crushing out the life with the gray weight of winter. It is one of the strongest images in Atom Egoyan's *The Sweet Hereafter,* which takes place in a small Canadian town, locked in by snow and buried in grief after fourteen children are killed in a school bus accident.

To this town comes a quiet man, a lawyer who wants to represent the residents in a class-action suit. Mitchell Stephens (Ian Holm) lacks the energy to be an ambulance chaser; he is only going through the motions of his occupation. In a way he's lost a child, too; the first time we see him, he's on the phone with his drug-addicted daughter. "I don't know who I'm talking to right now," he tells her.

There will be no victory at the end, we sense. This is not one of those Grisham films in which the lawyers battle injustice and the creaky system somehow works. The parents who have lost their children can never get them back; the school bus driver must live forever with what happened; lawsuits will open old wounds and betray old secrets. If the lawyer wins he gets to keep a third of the settlement; one look in his eyes reveals how little he thinks about money.

Egoyan's film, based on the novel by Russell Banks, is not about the tragedy of dying but about the grief of surviving. In the film the Browning poem about the Pied Piper is read, and we remember that the saddest figure in that poem was the lame boy who could not join the others in following the Piper. In *The Sweet Hereafter,* an important character is a teenage girl who loses the use of her legs in the accident; she survives but seems unwilling to accept the life still left for her.

Egoyan is a director whose films coil through time and double back to take a second look at the lives of their characters. It is typical of his approach that *The Sweet Hereafter* neither begins nor ends with the bus falling through the ice of a frozen lake, and is not really about how the accident happened, or who was to blame.

The accident is like the snow clouds, always there, cutting off the characters from the sun, a vast fact nobody can change.

The lawyer makes his rounds, calling on parents. Egoyan draws them vividly with brief, cutting scenes. The motel owners, Wendell and Risa Walker (Maury Chaykin and Alberta Watson), fill him in on the other parents (Wendell has nothing good to say about anyone). Sam and Mary Burnell (Tom McCamus and Brooke Johnson) are the parents of Nicole, the budding young C&W singer who is now in a wheelchair. Wanda and Hartley Otto (Arsinee Khanjian and Earl Pastko) lost their son, an adopted Indian boy. Billy Ansell (Bruce Greenwood) was following the bus in his pickup, and waved to his children just before it swerved from the road. He wants nothing to do with the lawsuit, and is bitter about those who do. He is having an affair with Risa, the motel owner's wife.

This story. It is not about lawyers or the law, not about small-town insularity, not about revenge (although that motivates an unexpected turning point). It is more about the living dead: About people carrying on their lives after hope and meaning have gone. The film is so sad, so tender toward its characters. The lawyer, an outsider who might at first seem like the source of more trouble, comes across more like a witness, who regards the stricken parents and sees his own approaching loss of a daughter in their eyes.

Ian Holm's performance here is bottomless with its subtlety; he proceeds doggedly through the town, following the routine of his profession as if this is his penance. And there is a later scene, set on an airplane, where he finds himself seated next to his daughter's childhood friend, and remembers, in a heartbreaking monologue, a time in childhood when his daughter almost died of a spider bite. Is it good or bad that she survived, in order now to die of drugs?

Egoyan sees the town so vividly. A hearing is held in the village hall, where folding tables and chairs wait for potluck dinners and bingo nights. A foosball table is in a corner. In another corner, Nicole, in her wheelchair, describes the accident. She lies. It is too simple to say she lies as a form of getting even, because we wonder—if she were not in a wheelchair, would she feel the same way? Does she feel abused, or scorned?

"You'd make a great poker player, kid," the lawyer tells her.

This is one of the best films of 1997, an unflinching lament for the human condition. Yes, it is told out of sequence, but not as a gimmick: In a way, Egoyan has constructed this film in the simplest possible way. It isn't about the beginning and end of the plot, but about the beginning and end of the emotions. In his first scene, the lawyer tells his daughter he doesn't know who he's talking to. In one of his closing scenes, he remembers a time when he did know her. But what did it get him?

Swept Away by an Unusual Destiny in the Blue Sea of August
R, 116 m., 1976

Giancarlo Giannini (Gennarino), Mariangela Melato (Raffaella). Directed by Lina Wertmuller and produced by Romano Cardarelli. Screenplay by Wertmuller.

Lina Wertmuller's *Swept Away by an Unusual Destiny in the Blue Sea of August* resists the director's most determined attempts to make it a fable about the bourgeoisie and the proletariat, and persists in being about a man and a woman. On that level, it's a great success, even while it's causing all sorts of mischief otherwise. We could have deep arguments about the meaning of it all, and no doubt we will, but as a sort of kinky update of *Heaven Knows, Mr. Allison*, the movie works just fine.

It involves a bearded sailor who's a fervent subscriber to the macho school of Italian thought, and a beautiful young blonde, who's the plaything of her rich husband. They're thrown together during a luxurious yacht cruise in the Mediterranean, and the woman takes every opportunity to mock the sailor: He's stupid, he can't get anything right, he smells, he's probably—worst of all—a communist!

Late one day, the woman decides to go out in a dinghy and orders the sailor to operate the boat. He protests that it's dangerous to leave so late in the day, but she insists. The engine fails, they're cast adrift for days, and when the sailor succeeds after great effort in catching a fish, she throws it overboard because it smells.

Eventually they land on a deserted island, and the tables in their relationship begin to turn with a vengeance. Consider: Ashore and on board the yacht, the woman held the unquestioned upper hand because of her husband's money. But on the island, it's the man, with his survival skills and (most controversial, this) his very masculinity, who's the dominant figure. He orders her around. If she wants to eat, she'll have to do his laundry. She screams, she sulks, she argues, but she loses. And she finds herself powerfully attracted to the situation; she's been spoiled so long, it's almost a relief to be ordered around.

It's here that the movie begins to venture into philosophical and sexual mischief-making, because although Wertmuller is a leftist, she is not, apparently, a feminist. She seems to be trying to tell us two things through the episodes on the island: (1) that once the corrupt facade of capitalism is stripped away, it's the worker, with the sweat of his back, who deserves to reap the benefit of his own labor, and (2) that woman is an essentially masochistic and submissive creature who likes nothing better than being swept off her feet by a strong and lustful male. This is a notion feminists have spent the past ten years trying to erase from our collective fantasies, and it must be unsettling, to say the least, to find the foremost female director making a whole movie out of it. And Wertmuller doesn't kid around: Her shipwrecked couple gradually work their way into a sadomasochistic relationship that makes *The Night Porter* look positively restrained. The more the woman submits, the more ecstasy she finds—until finally she's offending the hapless Sicilian by suggesting practices he can't even pronounce.

Eventually, however, the man and woman have to decide between their island and a return to civilization. And the sailor can't bring himself to believe the woman really loves him: She must prove it, he insists, by returning to shore and still staying with him. Well, not to reveal too much, Wertmuller uses the film's ending to demonstrate that the class system still subverts our real human inclinations. None of this feels quite right; the ending is unsatisfactory in the way it follows Wertmuller's political convictions rather than the impulses of her characters. But then I think we're wary, these days, of movies that try to go beyond their particular stories in order to make large statements. When a movie does have a lot to say—as, for example, *Nashville* did—it's a relief when the director finds a way to say it through the characters, instead of to them.

Still, *Swept Away* is an absorbing movie, it tells a story we get involved in, and (despite all I've said) it's often very funny. Giancarlo Giannini, he of the expressive eyes and slow, interior rages, is wonderful in the way he slowly reveals himself to this woman he has despised. And Mariangela Melato, as the woman, does her 180-degree personality change almost as if she doesn't realize what's happening. If the opening scenes in the yacht had been abbreviated and if the movie had been left open-ended—if, in short, Wertmuller had put the story ahead of her politics—I would have admired *Swept Away* more. But it's a pleasure all the same.

The Swimmer

PG, 94 m., 1968

Burt Lancaster (Ned Merrill), Janet Landgard (Julie Hooper), Janice Rule (Shirley Abbott), Tony Bickley (Westerhazy), Marge Champion (Peggy Forsburgh), Nancy Cushman (Mrs. Halloran), Kim Hunter (Barry Graham). Directed by Frank Perry and produced by Frank Perry and Roger Lewis. Screenplay by Eleanor Perry, based on the story by John Cheever.

The Swimmer is the story of a man who begins at the dawn of a new day to swim in the backyard pool of some friends. The water is cool and fresh, and the day is beautiful.

As he has a drink with his friends, it occurs to him that a string of other backyard pools reaches all the way across the valley to his own home. Why not swim every one—swim all the way home, as it were? This sounds like a glorious adventure, and indeed it starts out that way. He even meets a lovely girl who agrees to come along on the journey.

Some of the pool owners are happy to see him. Others hate him. One is a bitter young woman who loved him once. We learn something about this man's life at every poolside, until finally we are able to piece together a story of his disgrace and failure.

The Swimmer begins as a perfectly realistic film. But somewhere along the way we realize it is an allegory, and the ending makes that clear. It is also a very stylized film. As the swimmer (Burt Lancaster) pauses beside each pool, his conversations with the owners sound real enough, and yet somehow they are very stiff, very correct, as if everybody were reading lines or this were a dream.

The photography contributes to this feeling. It is beautiful, but not joyful. It has the same nostalgia as *Elvira Madigan* or the snapshots in an old photo album. At every moment, we have the feeling that something tragic has already happened to these people we see smiling. And, of course, something has.

The Swimmer is based on a John Cheever story from the *New Yorker*, and it's the sort of allegory the *New Yorker* favors. Like assorted characters by John Updike and J. D. Salinger, Cheever's swimmer is a tragic hero disguised as an upper-class suburbanite. There are a lot of tragic heroes hidden in suburbia, I guess, perhaps because so many of them subscribe to the *New Yorker*. You are what you read.

One interesting thing about *The Swimmer* is that it manages so successfully to reproduce the feeling of a short story in the medium of film. It is a very literary movie, and by that I don't mean the characters stand around talking to each other a lot. The film episodes are put together in a rather formal way, like a well-made short story, and there is none of the fluid movement between scenes that you usually expect in movies.

The movement of the film is from morning to dusk, from sunshine to rain, from youth to age, and from fantasy to truth. It would also appear that the swimmer's experiences are not meant to represent a single day, but a man's life.

What we really have here, then, is a sophisticated retelling of the oldest literary form of all: the epic. A hero sets off on a journey. He has many strange adventures along the way, during which he learns the tragic nature of life. At last he arrives at his goal, older and wiser and with many a tale to tell. The journey Cheever's swimmer makes has been made before in other times and lands by Ulysses, Don Quixote, Huckleberry Finn, and Augie March.

Lancaster is superb in his finest performance. In addition to being a fine actor, he is a plausible hero of the Charlton Heston and Kirk Douglas type. And a hero is needed here. We must believe in the swimmer's greatness if we are to find his fate tragic.

There are also fine performances by Janice

Rule (previously buried in Matt Helms and Westerns) as the mistress, by Janet Landgard, as the young girl, and by a host of character actors. The screenplay and direction are by Eleanor and Frank Perry, respectively, and they are the same couple who made *David and Lisa*. Like that film, *The Swimmer*, is a strange, stylized work, a brilliant and disturbing one.

Syriana

R, 126 m., 2005

George Clooney (Robert Barnes), Matt Damon (Bryan Woodman), Jeffrey Wright (Bennett Holiday), Chris Cooper (Jimmy Pope), William Hurt (Stan Goff), Mazhar Munir (Wasim), Tim Blake Nelson (Danny Dalton), Amanda Peet (Julie Woodman), Christopher Plummer (Dean Whiting), Alexander Siddig (Prince Nasir), Akbar Kurtha (Prince Meshal). Directed by Stephen Gaghan and produced by Jennifer Fox, Georgia Kacandes, and Michael Nozik. Screenplay by Gaghan, based on the book by Robert Baer.

Syriana is an endlessly fascinating movie about oil and money, America and China, traders and spies, the Persian Gulf states and Texas, reform and revenge, bribery and betrayal. Its interlocking stories come down to one thing: There is less oil than the world requires, and that will make some people rich and others dead. The movie seems to take sides, but take a step back and look again. It finds all of the players in the oil game corrupt and compromised, and even provides a brilliant speech in defense of corruption by a Texas oil man (Tim Blake Nelson). This isn't about Left and Right but about Have and Have Not.

The movie begins with one of the Gulf states signing a deal to supply its oil to China. This comes as a strategic defeat for Connex, a Texas-based oil company. At the same time, an obscure oil company named Killen signs a deal to drill for oil in Kazakhstan. Connex announces a merger with Killen, to get its hands on the oil, but the merger inspires a Justice Department investigation, and . . .

Let's stop right there. The movie's plot is so complex we're not really supposed to follow it; we're supposed to be surrounded by it. Since none of the characters understands the whole picture, why should we? If the movie shook out into good guys and bad guys, we'd be the good

guys, of course. Or if it was a critique of American policy, we might be the bad guys. But what if everybody is a bad guy because good guys don't even suit up to play this game? What if a CIA agent brings about two assassinations and tries to prevent another one, and is never sure precisely whose policies he is really carrying out?

What if . . . well, here's a possibility the movie doesn't make explicit, but let me try it out on you. There is a moment when a veteran Washington oil analyst points out that while Kazakhstan has a lot of oil, none of it is where Killen has drilling rights. Yet Killen is undoubtedly shipping oil. Is it possible the Chinese are buying oil in the Gulf, shipping it to Kazakhstan, and selling it to the United States through Killen?

I bring up that possibility because I want to suggest the movie's amoral complexity without spoiling its surprises. *Syriana* is a movie that suggests Congress can hold endless hearings about oil company profits and never discover the answer to anything, because the real story is so labyrinthine that no one—not oil company executives, not Arab princes, not CIA spies, not traders in Geneva—understands the whole picture.

The movie has a lot of important roles and uses recognizable actors to help us keep everything straight. Even then, the studio e-mailed critics a helpful guide to the characters. I didn't look at it. Didn't want to. I liked the way I experienced the film: I couldn't explain the story, but I never felt lost in it. I understood who, what, when, where, and why, but not how they connected. That was how I wanted to relate to it. It created sympathy for individual characters in their specific situations without dictating what I was supposed to think about the big picture.

Some of the characters I cared about included Robert Barnes (George Clooney), a veteran CIA field agent; Bryan Woodman (Matt Damon), a trader based in Geneva; Jimmy Pope (Chris Cooper), who runs Killen; Dean Whiting (Christopher Plummer), a well-connected Washington lawyer whose firm is hired to handle the political implications of the merger; Bennett Holiday (Jeffrey Wright), assigned by Whiting to do "due diligence" on the deal, by which is meant that diligence that supports the merger; Prince Nasir (Alexander Siddig), who sold the rights to the Chinese; his younger brother Prince Meshal (Akbar Kurtha), who is backed by those who do not want Nasir to inherit the throne; and the mysterious Stan, played by William Hurt as someone who is keeping a secret from the rest of the movie.

Already I regret listing all of these names. You now have little tic-tac-toe designs on your eyeballs. *Syriana* is exciting, fascinating, absorbing, diabolical, and really quite brilliant, but I'm afraid it inspires reviews that are not helpful. The more you describe it, the more you miss the point. It is not a linear progression from problem to solution. It is all problem. The audience enjoys the process, not the progress. We're like athletes who get so wrapped up in the game we forget about the score.

A recent blog item coined a term like "hyperlink movie" to describe plots like this. (I would quote the exact term, but irony of ironies, I've lost the link.) The term describes movies in which the characters inhabit separate stories, but we gradually discover how those in one story are connected to those in another. *Syriana* was written and directed by Stephen Gaghan, who won an Oscar for his screenplay for *Traffic*, another hyperlink movie. A lot of Altman films, such as *Nashville* and *Short Cuts* use the technique. Also, recently, *Crash* and *Nine Lives*.

In a hyperlink movie, the motives of one character may have to be reinterpreted after we meet another one. Consider the Damon character. His family is invited to a party at the luxurious Spanish villa of the Gulf oil sheik whose sons are Nasir and Meshal. At the party, Damon's son dies by accident. The sheik awards Damon's firm a $100 million contract. "How much for my other son?" he asks. This is a brutal line of dialogue and creates a moment trembling with tension. Later, Damon's wife (Amanda Peet) accuses him of trading on the life of his son. Well, he did take the deal. Should he have turned it down because his son died in an accident? What are Damon's real motives, anyway?

I think *Syriana* is a great film. I am unable to make my reasons clear without resorting to meaningless generalizations. Individual scenes have fierce focus and power, but the film's overall drift stands apart from them. It seems to imply that these sorts of scenes occur, and always have and always will. The movie explains the politics of oil by telling us to stop seeking an explanation. Just look at the behavior. In the short run, you can see who wants oil and how they're trying to get it. In the long run, we're out of oil.

T

Taiga, Part 1

NO MPAA RATING, 199 m., 1995

A documentary directed, produced, and written by
Ulrike Ottinger.

Watching a film like *Taiga* is an undertaking
entirely apart from the usual experiences we
have at the movies. It is eight hours long but
comes in three parts; I have so far seen the first
part, at 199 minutes, and it resides in my
memory with something of the same weight
as an actual journey to another land.

I am fully aware that an epic ethnographic
documentary about the nomadic tribes of
Mongolia is not a film most people think they
want to see (indeed, my own feet dragged on
my way into the theater).

But for those who are curious, *Taiga* is an
experience that causes us to think about why
we live as we do, what it is to be human, and
what is important in life.

The Darkhad and Soyon Uriyanghai peoples
live in a vast valley in northern Mongolia,
much as their ancestors have for centuries.
They move between their summer, autumn
and winter camps, setting up their yurts—
large, portable round tents, each with a front
door and frame made of wood. They tend cattle and sheep. They have peripheral contact
with modern life, and we see motorcycles
among more ancient styles of possessions.
Their religion centers on shamanesses, female
priests whose ceremonies begin at midnight,
who go into trances, and who must be awake by
dawn lest their spirits stay in the other world.

Taiga is the record of a long period German
filmmaker Ulrike Ottinger spent among these
people. She directed, photographed, and
wrote the sparse titles that introduce each segment. What we understand at once is that the
subjects of her film are not people in a hurry.
They live according to the seasons, not the
hours, and the film adopts a certain patience.
It's not one of those once-over-lightly documentaries where we get a quick snapshot of
colorful nomads and then there's a fade to the
sunset.

At first, the approach is disconcerting: Is
anything ever going to happen in this film?
Then we become comfortable with the
rhythms of their daily lives. In part 1, we attend a shamanistic ceremony and a wedding.
We listen to a folk story, see boots being made,
and visit a sacred tree, all adorned with feathers, skins, horsehair, and other gifts from
those who have been here before.

We watch food being prepared. In particular, we follow the slaughter of a lamb through
all of its particulars, as every ounce of the
lamb is used according to traditional practices; the intestines are cleaned, the organs are
set aside, the blood is drained and saved, and
choice cuts of meat are reserved as prizes in a
wrestling tournament. Then we observe all of
the stages in which meat dumplings are made.

Why does Ottinger show us the process in
such detail? Because her film doesn't want to
chatter, "Meat dumplings are a favorite food
of the Mongols"; it wants to say, "Here is exactly how these people raise, tend, slaughter,
dress, prepare, cook, and serve an animal, and
how food serves both a ceremonial and a family purpose." After seeing this film, I could
make dumplings according to the Mongol
way—and maybe I will.

These people, living from the land, use
everything. Their herds give them plentiful
supplies of milk, and, casually, the film documents how many ways they use it. At various
times we see them preparing salted milk tea,
cottage cheese, yogurt, and milk liquor. Then
we witness a milk can employed for an ingenious barbecue: Rocks are heated in a fire, and
then the hot rocks and chunks of meat are
dropped into the can, which is twisted shut to
form a sort of pressure cooker.

One sequence involves a local wrestling
match. What is remarkable is how good-natured it is, as the wrestlers strut in their homemade uniforms and then square off, and their
audience kneels in a ring, absorbed. There is
no applause for the winner, but instead hand
gestures, palms toward the sky, as if to indicate
that the champion has lifted himself above the
ordinary.

The season comes to an end, and the tribes
disassemble their yurts and load them, and all
their other possessions, onto oxen for the trek
to the winter quarters.

What occurred to me, watching the film, is that time does not slip away for these people. They do not ask where the day went, because they were at its side. They respect one another and themselves, they are deeply courteous, they live in harmony with the land, and although their lives seem hard to us, they are not unhappy lives, because everything has a purpose, and the purpose is clear to see.

If you commit yourself to this epic experience, leave your watch at home. This is a long, slow film. There is no narrator imparting breathless banalities. No cute reaction shots of grinning children or wrinkled grannies. No lovable puppies. No clichés about the simple nobility of these ancient tribes. No documentary packaging. Ottinger was invited into the lives of these peoples, and she stayed a long time, watching and listening, and then she made a film about what she saw and heard. That is worth doing, and worth seeing.

Taiga, Part 2

NO MPAA RATING, 150 m., 1995

A documentary directed, produced, and written by Ulrike Ottinger.

In the second part of *Taiga*, the epic eight-hour documentary, a guide takes us to meet his parents, "who have seen no other people for six years." Like the people in the film's first part, they are Mongols who lead a nomadic existence in the distant reaches of Mongolia, living mostly off the land and their reindeer herds, according to the old ways.

We see the old couple first standing in front of their yurt, a sort of tepee made of animal skins. Then we go inside, and the husband tells tales of the old days: how life was better before the herds were nationalized, how sacred objects were banned from the yurts—but hidden and kept anyway—and how hard life is.

Then it is his wife's turn to speak. She is not hopeful for herself. She is old and weak, she says, and fears that her vision is going. She hardly has the health to do anything. From her appearance, she could be seventy, eighty, or ninety; there is no way to tell. But gradually, in an indirect way, as she describes her life, we get a new appreciation for what she means by "hardly doing anything." She herds the rein-

deer, milks them, does the cooking, collects firewood, fetches water, sews, mends, and does repairs around the yurt.

What would be backbreaking labor for a modern Western person of thirty is, for this old woman and her husband, semiretirement, as they sit out their old age inside a small home, in isolation. Watching this couple, listening to them, we are struck again by how many different kinds of lives still exist on this shrinking planet.

The film was directed, written, and photographed by Ulrike Ottinger, a German woman who spent many months among these people, and whose film is slow and watchful. She provides the screen time necessary for us to glimpse something of the way time passes for these people. Early in the film, for example, we watch a hunter prepare for the hunt. He collects twigs and branches. He starts a fire. He nurtures it. He removes a wok from his saddlebags. He warms milk. He brews milk tea. He lights incense. He sprinkles some of the tea to the four winds, as an offering. He shows us the weapons he will use. Then he is ready to begin hunting.

The first part of the film centered on people who live in yurts, portable houses that can be moved from place to place. In part two we see some of the people moving to their winter camp, five days' march away. We also see "log cities," clusters of simple log houses the nomads visit for supplies. There is a general store, with meager provisions but much excitement. There is a telegraph office, although from the way the operator ritualistically recites the same phrase into a phone that does not seem to be working, we get the impression he serves a symbolic, not an actual, function.

There are wrestling matches, tugs-of-war, a stag hunt.

Complaints: "The Party was always telling us what to do," as if Marxist bureaucrats in a city could have possibly understood what was best for nomadic reindeer herders. Life is better now that the Soviet Union has collapsed, allowing the nomads to make their own decisions.

Like part 1, this section of the film proceeds at its own pace, inviting us into lives so different from our own—sharing the same hopes for children and family, the same desire for comfort and security, in an almost unimaginable environment.

I will remember the words of the old man as he and his wife bid farewell to the film crew. We see them standing outside their yurt, ready to resume six years of complete isolation and backbreaking labor. He says, "Our life is neither good nor bad, although we did expect a bit more."

Taiga, Part 3
NO MPAA RATING, 150 m., 1995

A documentary directed, produced, and written by Ulrike Ottinger.

Taiga, the austere documentary about the reindeer-herding nomads of remote Mongolia, shows lives that are unimaginably different from our own. In taking her camera to the remote land where they live, German director Ulrike Ottinger deliberately avoided a "talking heads" documentary in which a narrator explains all. Instead, she allows her camera to sit in the corner of a rude home or dusty field, watching people as they live their lives.

This is, in general, an approach I prefer. But midway through the first hour of *Taiga, Part 3*, the concluding section of the eight-hour documentary, my attention began to flag. The segment deals with a shamaness who is conducting a séance. She dons a heavy coat hung with religious objects and then beats on a large deerskin drum until she goes into a trance.

The camera essentially watches this process, without significant cutting, for more than thirty minutes, often from an awkward vantage point that prevents us from clearly seeing it. Still, you might say, we are privileged: We are inside the shamaness's yurt (portable house), seeing a ceremony few if any Westerners have ever seen before. Yes, I reply, but we saw a very similar scene in the first part of the film. If Ottinger wants to repeat herself, she might explain what is different about this second sequence, but her subtitles are not helpful. (The preceding scene is subtitled "poem about a chief who cannot make decisions," but the lines of the poem remain untranslated.) At some point, a documentarian risks crossing a line between an unwillingness to cut and an inability to judge. Ottinger crosses that line in this segment of the film, I think. She essentially shows us everything. Still, once we leave the shamaness, the film becomes as haunting as the first two segments were. We arrive, for example, at the forgotten trading centers of Hadhal and Hanch—port cities that were busy, when the Soviet Union thrived, with the comings and goings of merchant ships. But the USSR has collapsed, and the sea trade with it. These ports service just one arrival a year: a merchant ship that tows two others behind it. The shots of this crippled flotilla are a stark image of the collapse of a nation's economy.

The people live off the land. In addition to their herds of reindeer, sheep, and bison, which provide milk, meat, skins, and fur, they eat roots, bark, berries, herbs, wild onions, and grains. There is a sequence where they thump on the ground with poles, listening for the hollow sign that betrays the burrows of the suslik—a tunneling squirrel that stockpiles groundroot. When they find a burrow, they rob it, and then the camera tilts up to the mountain vastness that surrounds them.

Other sequences show a silversmith, a wedding palace, an amusement park, and an old lady who is visibly impatient with the camera: "Large herds? Why should there be so many? Ten or twenty reindeer. Do they give milk? Why should they give much milk? What is there to be cheerful about? I can hardly move my limbs." Leaving the theater after seeing all three parts of *Taiga*, I felt I was in possession of some portion of the lives of these people. As I wrote this, they are in the winter camps we saw them trekking toward, perhaps preparing groundroot they stole from the tunneling susliks. Maybe the old woman has died. Maybe she is still complaining.

Taiga is too long and it repeats itself, but it casts a spell.

The Talented Mr. Ripley
R, 140 m., 1999

Matt Damon (Tom Ripley), Gwyneth Paltrow (Marge Sherwood), Jude Law (Dickie Greenleaf), Cate Blanchett (Meredith Logue), Philip Seymour Hoffman (Freddie Miles), Jack Davenport (Peter Smith-Kingsley), James Rebhorn (Herbert Greenleaf), Sergio Rubini (Inspector Roverini), Philip Baker Hall (Alvin MacCarron). Directed by Anthony Minghella and produced by William Horberg and Tom Sternberg. Screenplay by Minghella, based on the book by Patricia Highsmith.

Villains usually last through only one crime novel, while heroes are good for a whole series. That's a great inconvenience for their authors, because villains are usually more colorful than heroes. Patricia Highsmith's novels about Tom Ripley are the exception, a series of books about a man who is irredeemably bad, and yet charming, intelligent, and thoughtful about the price he pays for his amoral lifestyle.

The Talented Mr. Ripley, her first Ripley novel, published in 1955, shows Ripley in the process of inventing himself and finding his life's work. He was a poor man who wanted to be a rich man, an unknown man who wanted not to be famous but simply to be *someone else.* Some men are envious of other men's cars, or wives, or fortunes. Ripley coveted their identities.

The novel shows him annexing the life and identity of a man named Greenleaf. It was filmed in 1960 by Rene Clement as *Purple Noon,* with Alain Delon as Ripley, and now it has been filmed again by Anthony Minghella *(The English Patient),* with Matt Damon in the title role. One of the pleasures of the two adaptations is that the plots are sufficiently different that you can watch one without knowing how the other turns out—or even what happens along the way. That despite the fact that they both revolve around Ripley's decision that he can be Greenleaf as well as, or better than, Greenleaf can be himself.

Purple Noon begins with the two men already friends. *The Talented Mr. Ripley,* adapted by Minghella, has a better idea: Ripley is an opportunist who stumbles onto an opening into Greenleaf's life and takes it. He borrows a Princeton blazer to play the piano at a rooftop party in Manhattan, and a rich couple assume he must have known their son Dickie at Princeton. He agrees.

The Greenleafs are concerned about Dickie (Jude Law), who has decamped to the decadence of Europe and shows no sign of coming home. They offer Tom Ripley a deal: They'll finance his own trip to Europe and pay him $1,000 if he returns with their son. Cut to a beach in Italy, where Dickie suns with Marge Sherwood (Gwyneth Paltrow), and the original deception turns evil.

Remember that Ripley is already impersonating someone—Dickie's old Princeton friend. That works with Dickie ("I've completely forgotten him," he tells Marge), but eventually he wonders if anything Tom tells him is the truth. Ripley, at this point still developing the skills that will carry him through several more adventures, instinctively knows that the best way to lie is to admit to lying, and to tell the truth whenever convenient. When Dickie asks him what his talents are, he replies, "Forging signatures, telling lies, and impersonating almost anyone." Quite true. And then he does a chilling impersonation of Mr. Greenleaf asking him to bring Dickie back to America. "I feel like he's here," Dickie says, as Tom does his father's voice.

By confessing his mission, Tom disarms Dickie, and is soon accepted into his circle, which also includes an epicurean friend named Freddie Miles (Philip Seymour Hoffman). Also moving through Europe at about the same time is a rich girl named Meredith Logue (Cate Blanchett), who believes things about Tom that Dickie must not be allowed to know. But I am growing vague, and must grow vaguer, because the whole point of the movie is to show Tom Ripley learning to use subterfuge, improvisation, and lightning-fast thinking under pressure to become Dickie Greenleaf.

Highsmith wrote *The Talented Mr. Ripley* five years after writing *Strangers on a Train,* which Hitchcock made into a film he sometimes called his favorite. The two stories are similar. *Strangers* is about a man who meets another man and offers to trade crimes with him: I'll kill the person you hate, and you kill the person I hate, and since neither of us has any connection with our victim or any motive for killing him, we'll never be caught. *Talented* has Dickie blamed for the drowning death of a local woman, and Ripley "trading" that death as a cover-up for another.

Hitchcock's film subtly suggested a homosexual feeling in the instigator, and Tom Ripley also seems to have feelings for Dickie Greenleaf—although narcissism and sexuality are so mixed up in his mind that Ripley almost seems to want to become Greenleaf so that he can love himself (both Ripley movies have a scene of Ripley dressed in Dickie's clothes and posing in a mirror). This undercurrent is wisely never brought up to the level of conscious action, because so many of Tom Ripley's complicated needs and desires are deeply buried; he finds out what he wants to do by doing it.

Matt Damon is bland and ordinary as Ripley, and then takes on the vivid coloration of others—even a jazz singer. Jude Law makes Dickie almost deserving of his fate, because of the way he adopts new friends and then discards them. Gwyneth Paltrow's role is tricky: Yes, Dickie is her boyfriend, but he's cold and treats her badly, and there are times when she would intuit the dread secret if she weren't so distracted by the way she already resents Dickie.

The movie is as intelligent a thriller as you'll see this year. It is also insidious in the way it leads us to identify with Tom Ripley. He is the protagonist, we see everything through his eyes, and Dickie is not especially lovable; that means we are a coconspirator in situations where it seems inconceivable that his deception will not be discovered. He's a monster, but we want him to get away with it. There is one sequence in the film, involving an apartment, a landlady, the police, and a friend who knows the real Dickie, that depends on such meticulous timing and improvisation that if you made it speedier, you'd have the Marx brothers.

Talk Radio

R, 110 m., 1988

Eric Bogosian (Barry), Ellen Greene (Ellen), Leslie Hope (Laura), John C. McGinley (Stu), Alec Baldwin (Dan), John Pankow (Dietz), Michael Wincott (Kent), Linda Atkinson (Sheila Fleming). Directed by Oliver Stone and produced by Edward R. Pressman and A. Kitman Ho. Screenplay by Bogosian and Stone, based on the play by Bogosian.

Alan Berg was a Denver talk radio host who was murdered on June 18, 1984. He was a goofy-looking bird, with a thin face and a bristly white beard that hid the ravages of teen-age acne. He wore reading glasses perched far down on his nose, and he dressed in unlikely combinations of checks and stripes and garments that looked leftover from the 1950s. When the members of a lunatic rightwing group gunned him down in the driveway of his home, they could not have mistaken him for anybody else.

I met Berg three or four times. The first time I was going to be on his radio show; I listened to it as I drove from Boulder to Denver. He was chewing out some hapless housewife whose brain was a reservoir of prejudice against anyone who was the slightest bit different from her. Berg was telling her that no one in their right mind would want to be anything like her at all.

Why were you so hard on that lady? I asked him when we were on the air.

"She was asking for it. Why would she call up and feed me all those straight lines if she didn't want me to tell her how stupid she was?"

Cruel, perhaps, but quite possibly correct. Berg was the top radio personality in Denver because he told people exactly what he thought of them. It was unusual to hear somebody on the radio who was not tailoring his words to the sensibilities of his audience. Talking with Berg off the air, I found that he was a man who had been through a lot, including the loss of a law practice in Chicago because of alcoholism. Now he was sober and successful, but I had the feeling that he was grateful every morning for somehow having pulled out of his crash dive. I liked him. When I learned that he had been murdered, my first reaction was disbelief that anyone could have taken him that seriously. Jeez, didn't they know he was just another poor bastard trying to earn a living?

Oliver Stone's film *Talk Radio* is inspired by the murder of Alan Berg, but it is not based on his life. Berg was older, calmer, and more amused by life than Barry Champlain, the tortured talk radio host in the movie. Berg was also not self-destructive or suicidal, and Champlain is both. When he is mailed a suspicious box in a plain brown wrapper, he puts it next to the microphone. When he gets a call from the man who mailed the box, and the man hints that it contains a bomb, Champlain opens it on the air. When another caller rants and raves incoherently about Champlain's beliefs and calls him a coward, Champlain asks him to come over to the radio station—and invites the man, a disheveled, wild-eyed street person, to come into the studio.

Champlain works in a studio in a Texas high-rise, surrounded by other high-rises. I was aware all during the movie of the thousands of windows with a view into his studio. When the man who sent the box says, "I can see you have it," I cringed, because I imagined someone with a sniper-scope. But Barry Champlain, played with rasping, aggressive sarcasm by Eric Bogosian, simply doesn't care. He is gambling with his life in the same self-hating way as people who get drunk and point a speedboat into the blackness of a storm.

Talk Radio is directed by Stone with a claustrophobic intensity. The camera rarely leaves the radio studio—and then it's only for brief flashbacks into the hero's troubled personal life, or for a personal appearance he makes at a basketball game where some of the fans seem to have crawled out from under their rocks for the purpose of acting weirdly toward him. Most of the movie takes place during the long nights of the radio program, and the movie's beginnings as a stage play are evident when several key characters—including Champlain's former wife—turn up on the scene to bare their hearts to him.

Even so, the movie doesn't feel as boxed in as many filmed plays do, perhaps because radio itself is such an intimate, claustrophobic medium. It's not over there in the TV set; it's inside your head. In a sense we become listeners of *The Barry Champlain Show,* and as he pushes his listeners more and more insistently, egging them on, we begin to feel how some of the people out there in the night could go over the edge. *Talk Radio* is based on a play that Bogosian wrote and starred in, and it was the right decision to star him in the movie, too, instead of some famous star. He feels this material from the inside out, and makes the character convincing. That's especially true during a virtuoso, unsettling closing monologue in which we think the camera is circling Bogosian—until we realize the camera and the actor are still, and the backgrounds are circling.

Alan Berg is more famous in death than life. His memory haunts many people, even those who never heard him on the radio, because his death could be read as a message: Be cautious, be prudent, be bland, never push anybody, never say what you really think, offer yourself as a hostage to the weirdos even before they make the first move. These days, a lot of people are opposed to the newfound popularity of "trash television," and no doubt they are right and the hosts of these shows are shameless controversy-mongers. But at least they are not intimidated. Of what use is freedom of speech to those who fear to offend?

Talk to Her

R, 112 m., 2002

Javier Cámara (Benigno Martin), Dario Grandinetti (Marco Zuloaga), Leonor Watling (Alicia Roncero), Rosario Flores (Lydia Gonzalez), Geraldine Chaplin (Katerina Bilova), Mariola Fuentes (Rosa). Directed by Pedro Almodóvar and produced by Agustín Almodóvar. Screenplay by Pedro Almodóvar.

A man cries in the opening scene of Pedro Almodóvar's *Talk to Her,* but although unspeakably sad things are to happen later in the movie, these tears are shed during a theater performance. Onstage, a woman wanders as if blind or dazed, and a man scurries to move obstacles out of her way—chairs, tables. Sometimes she blunders into the wall.

In the audience, we see two men who are still, at this point, strangers to each other. Marco (Dario Grandinetti) is a travel writer. Benigno (Javier Cámara) is a male nurse. The tears are of empathy, and it hardly matters which man cries, because in the film both will devote themselves to caring for helpless women. What's important are the tears. If he had been the director of *The Searchers* instead of John Ford, Almodóvar told the writer Lorenza Munoz, John Wayne would have cried.

Talk to Her is a film with many themes; it ranges in tone from a soap opera to a tragedy. One theme is that men can possess attributes usually described as feminine. They can devote their lives to a patient in a coma, they can live their emotional lives through someone else, they can gain deep satisfaction from bathing, tending, cleaning up, taking care. The bond that eventually unites the two men in *Talk to Her* is that they share these abilities. For much of the movie, what they have in common is that they wait by the bedsides of women who have suffered brain damage and are never expected to recover.

Marco meets Lydia (Rosario Flores) when she is at the height of her fame, the most famous female matador in Spain. Driving her home one night, he learns her secret: She is fearless about bulls, but paralyzingly frightened of snakes. After Marco catches the snake in her kitchen (we are reminded of Annie Hall's spider), she announces she will never be able to go back into that house again. Soon after, she is gored by a bull and lingers in the twilight of a coma. Marco, who did not know her very well, paradoxically comes to know her better as he attends at her bedside.

Benigno has long been a nurse, and for years tended his dying mother. He first saw the ballerina Alicia (Leonor Watling) as she rehearsed in a studio across from his apartment. She is comatose after a traffic accident. He volunteers to take extra shifts, seems willing to spend twenty-four hours a day at her bedside. He is in love with her.

As the two men meet at the hospital and share their experiences, I was reminded of Julien and Cecilia, the characters in François Truffaut's film *The Green Room* (1978), based on the Henry James story "The Altar of the Dead." Julien builds a shrine to all of his loved ones who have died, fills it with photographs and possessions, and spends all of his time there with "my dead." When he falls in love with Cecilia, he offers her his most precious gift: He shares his dead with her. She gradually comes to understand that for him they are more alive than she is.

That seems to be the case with Benigno, whose woman becomes most real to him now that she is helpless and his life is devoted to caring for her. Marco's motivation is more complex, but both men seem happy to devote their lives to women who do not, and may never, know of their devotion. There is something selfless in their dedication, but something selfish, too, because what they are doing is for their own benefit; the patients would be equally unaware of treatment whether it was kind or careless.

Almodóvar treads a very delicate path here. He accepts the obsessions of the two men, and respects them, but as a director whose films have always revealed a familiarity with the stranger possibilities of human sexual expression, he hints, too, that there is something a little creepy about their devotion. The startling outcome of one of the cases, which I will not reveal, sets an almost insoluble moral dilemma for us. Conventional morality requires us to disapprove of actions that in fact may have been inspired by love and hope.

By Almodóvar's standards this is an almost conventional film; certainly it doesn't involve itself in the sexual revolving doors of many of his films. But there is a special-effects sequence of outrageous audacity, a short silent film fantasy in which a little man attempts to please a woman with what can only be described as total commitment.

Almodóvar has a way of evoking sincere responses from material which, if it were revolved only slightly, would present a face of sheer irony. *Talk to Her* combines improbable melodrama (gored bullfighters, comatose ballerinas) with subtly kinky bedside vigils and sensational denouements, and yet at the end we are undeniably touched. No director since Fassbinder has been able to evoke such complex emotions with such problematic material.

Tampopo

NO MPAA RATING, 117 m., 1987

Tsutomu Yamazaki (Ooro), Nobuko Miyamoto (Tampopo [Dandelion]), Koji Miyamoto (Man in White Suit), Ken Watanabe (Gun), Rikiya Yasuoka (Pisken), Kinzo Sakura (Shohei). Directed by Juzo Itami and produced by Itami, Yasushi Tamaoki, and Seigo Hosogoe. Screenplay by Itami.

Tampopo is one of those utterly original movies that seems to exist in no known category. Like the French comedies of Jacques Tati, it's a bemused meditation on human nature, in which one humorous situation flows into another off-handedly, as if life were a series of smiles.

As it opens, the film looks like some sort of Japanese satire of Clint Eastwood's spaghetti Westerns. The hero is Ooro (Tsutomu Yamazaki), a lone rider with a quizzical smile on his face, who rides a semi instead of a horse. Along with some friends, he stages a search for the perfect noodle restaurant, and cannot find it. Then he meets Tampopo (Nobuko Miyamoto), a sweet young woman who has her heart in the right place, but not her noodles.

The movie then turns into the fairly freestyle story of the efforts by Tampopo and her protector to research the perfect noodle and open the perfect noodle restaurant. Like most movies about single-minded obsessions, this one quickly becomes very funny. It might seem that American audiences would know little and care less about the search for the perfect Japanese noodle, but because the movie is so consumed and detailed, so completely submerged in "noodleology," it takes on a kind of weird logic of its own.

Consider, for example, the *tour de force* of a scene near the beginning of the movie, where a noodle master explains the correct ritual for eating a bowl of noodle soup. He explains every ingredient. How to cut it, how to cook it, how to address it, how to think of it, how to regard it, how to approach it, how to smell it, how to eat it, how to thank it, how to remember it. It's a kind of gastronomic religion, and director Juzo Itami languishes in creating a scene that makes noodles in this movie more interesting than sex and violence in many another.

The movie is constructed as a series of episodes along the route to the perfect noodle restaurant. Some of the scenes hardly even seem to apply, but are hilarious anyway—the treatment, for example, of a man who dies in the pursuit of the perfect bowl of noodles. *Tampopo* doesn't limit itself to satirizing one genre of Hollywood film, either; although the central image is of an Eastwood-style hero on an ultimate quest, there are all sorts of other sly little satirical asides, including one so perfectly aimed that even to describe it would take away some of the fun.

Humor, it is said, is universal. Most times it is not. The humor that travels best, I sometimes think, is not "universal" humor at all, but humor that grows so specifically out of one culture that it reaches other cultures almost by seeming to ignore them. The best British comedies were the very specifically British films like *The Lavender Hill Mob* and *School for Scoundrels*. The best Italian comedies were local products like *Seduced and Abandoned*. The funniest French films were by Tati, who seemed totally absorbed in himself. And this very, very Japanese movie, which seems to make no effort to communicate to other cultures, is universally funny almost for that reason. Who cannot identify with the search for the perfect noodle? Certainly any American can, in the land of sweet corn festivals, bake-offs, and contests for the world's best chili.

Tarnation

NO MPAA RATING, 88 m., 2004

With Jonathan Caouette, Renee LeBlanc, Adolph and Rosemary Davis, and David Sanin Paz. A documentary directed by Caouette and produced by Caouette and Stephen Miller. Screenplay by Caouette.

The child is father of the man.

—Wordsworth

Renee LeBlanc was a beautiful little girl; she was a professional model before she was twelve. Then Renee was injured in a fall from the family garage, and descended into depression. Her parents agreed to shock therapy; in two years she had more than two hundred treatments, which her son blames for her mental illness, and for the pain that coiled through his family.

Tarnation is the record of that pain, and a journal about the way her son, Jonathan Caouette, dealt with it—first as a kid, now as the director of this film, made in his early thirties. It is a remarkable film, immediate, urgent, angry, poetic, and stubbornly hopeful. It has been constructed from the materials of a lifetime: old home movies, answering-machine tapes, letters and telegrams, photographs, clippings, new video footage, recent interviews, and printed titles that summarize and explain Jonathan's life. "These fragments I shored against my ruins," T. S. Eliot wrote in *The Waste Land*, and Caouette does the same thing.

His film tells the story of a boy growing up gay in Houston and trying to deal with a schizophrenic mother. He had a horrible childhood. By the time he was six, his father had left the scene, he had been abused in foster homes, and he traveled with his mother to Chicago, where he witnessed her being raped. Eventually they both lived in Houston with her parents, Adolph and Rosemary Davis, who had problems of their own.

Caouette dealt with these experiences by

stepping outside himself and playing roles. He got a video camera, and began to dress up and film himself playing characters whose problems were not unlike his own. In a sense, that's when he began making *Tarnation*; we see him at eleven, dressed as a woman, performing an extraordinary monologue of madness and obsession.

He was lucky to survive adolescence. Drugs came into his life, he tried suicide, he fled from home. His homosexuality seems to have been a help, not a hindrance; new gay friends provided a community that accepted this troubled teenager. He was diagnosed with "depersonalization disorder," characterized by a tendency to see himself from the outside, like another person. This may have been more of a strategy than a disorder, giving him a way to objectify his experiences and shape them into a story that made sense. In *Tarnation* he refers to himself in the third person. The many printed titles that summarize the story are also a distancing device; if he had spoken the narration, it would have felt first-person and personal, but the written titles stand back from his life and observe it.

The *Up* series of documentaries began with several children at the age of seven. It revisits them every seven years (most recently, in *42 Up*). The series makes it clear that the child is indeed the father of the man; every one of its subjects is already, at seven, a version of the adult he or she would become. *Tarnation* is like Caouette's version of that process, in which the young boy, play-acting, dressing up, dramatizing the trauma in his life, is able to deal with it. Eventually, in New York, he finds a stable relationship with David Sanin Paz, and they provide a home for Renee, whose troubles are still not over.

The method of the film is crucial to its success. *Tarnation* is famous for having been made for $218 on a Macintosh, and edited with the free iMovie software that came with the computer. Of course, hundreds of thousands were later spent to clear music rights, improve the sound track, and make a theatrical print (which was invited to play at Cannes). Caouette's use of iMovie is virtuoso, with overlapping wipes, dissolves, saturation, split screens, multiple panes, graphics, and complex montages. There is a danger with such programs that filmmakers will use every bell and whistle

just because it is available, but *Tarnation* uses its jagged style without abusing it.

Caouette's technique would be irrelevant if his film did not deliver so directly on an emotional level. We get an immediate, visceral sense of the unhappiness of Renee and young Jonathan. We see the beautiful young girl fade into a tortured adult. We see Jonathan not only raising himself, but essentially inventing himself. I asked him once if he had decided he didn't like the character life had assigned for him to play, and simply created a different character, and became that character. "I think that's about what happened," he said.

Looking at *Tarnation*, I wonder if the movie represents a new kind of documentary that is coming into being. Although home movies have been used in docs for decades, they were almost always, by definition, brief and inane. The advent of the video camera has meant that lives are recorded in greater length and depth than ever before; a film like *Capturing the Friedmans* (2003), with its harrowing portrait of sexual abuse and its behind-the-scenes footage of a family discussing its legal options, would have been impossible before the introduction of consumer video cameras. Jonathan Caouette not only experienced his life, but recorded his experience, and his footage of himself as a child says what he needs to say more eloquently than any actor could portray it or any writer could describe it.

The film leaves some mysteries. Caouette visits his grandfather and asks hard questions, but gets elusive answers; we sense that the truth is lost in the murkiness of memory and denial. The two hundred shock treatments destroyed his mother's personality, Caouette believes, and they could have destroyed him by proxy, but in *Tarnation* we see him survive. His is a life in which style literally prevailed over substance; he defeated the realities that would have destroyed him by becoming someone they could not destroy.

Tarzan
G, 88 m., 1999

With the voices of: Brian Blessed (Clayton), Glenn Close (Kala), Minnie Driver (Jane), Tony Goldwyn (Tarzan), Nigel Hawthorne (Professor Porter), Lance Henriksen (Kerchak), Wayne Knight (Tantor), Alex D. Linz (Young

Tarzan), Rosie O'Donnell (Terk). Directed by Kevin Lima and Chris Buck and produced by Bonnie Arnold. Screenplay by Tab Murphy, Bob Tzudiker, and Noni White, based on the story "Tarzan of the Apes" by Edgar Rice Burroughs.

Something deep within the Tarzan myth speaks to us, and Disney's new animated *Tarzan* captures it. Maybe it's the notion that we can all inhabit this planet together, man and beast, and get along. The surface of the movie is adventure, comedy, and movement—there are sequences here as exciting as the ballroom scene in *Beauty and the Beast*—but underneath is something of substance. The most durable movie character in history emerges this time as a man who asks the question, "Why are you threatened by anyone different than you?"

This is not the confident Tarzan of so many Edgar Rice Burroughs novels and Johnny Weissmuller movies, discovering cities of gold. It is a Tarzan who knows from the day he compares his hand with the hand of Kala, the ape who has adopted him, that he is different. A Tarzan who is still different even after he meets other humans—because his experience is not the same. The movie doesn't insist on this thread of meaning, but it gives the movie weight. Like all the best Disney animated films, this one is about something other than cute characters and cheerful songs. It speaks even to the youngest members of the audience, who, like Tarzan, must have days when they feel surrounded by tall, rumbling, autocratic bipeds.

The movie is also a lot of fun. It has scenes that move through space with a freedom undreamed of in older animated films, and unreachable by any live-action process. Disney uses a process called Deep Canvas, a computer-assisted animation tool that handles the details during swoops through three dimensions. There's a sequence where Tarzan helps Jane escape from a band of monkeys, and as they hurtle through the treetops and loop-the-loop on byways of vines, it's like a roller-coaster ride.

The origin of Tarzan is one of the great masterstrokes of twentieth-century fiction. Burroughs, who never visited Africa, imagined it in much the same way that a child might, peering into a picture book of gorillas and elephants. The opening sequence of *Tarzan* encapsulates the story of how the young British baby and his parents were shipwrecked on the coast of Africa, built a treehouse, and lived in it. In the film, the infant is discovered by the curious gorilla Kala, after Sabor the leopard has killed his parents (offscreen, mercifully, although of course almost all Disney movies are about orphans in one way or another). She names the baby Tarzan, and brings it home to the family, where her mate, Kerchak, growls, "He can stay—but that doesn't make him my son!"

The look of the African forest is one of the great beauties of the film. There is such a depth to some scenes, and a feeling of great space in shots like the one where a waterfall tumbles off a mountain wall, while tiny birds make their way through the sky. Against this primeval wilderness, the Disney animators strike a sort of compromise with the laws of the jungle. Some animals (the leopard, for example) are true to their natures and are predators. Others, like the humanoid apes, are sentimentalized; Kala, voiced by Glenn Close, sounds like a suburban mom, and Terk, the wacky sidekick, sounds like—well, Rosie O'Donnell.

The leader of the pack, Kerchak (Lance Henrikson), is rumbling and distant, but there's an elephant who talks like a twelve-stepper ("I've had it with you and your emotional constipation"). Oddly, the animals have normal English dialogue when they are heard by one another, but are reduced to soft gutturals in the presence of outside humans. (Tarzan, who has been chatting with Kala for years, is reduced to talking in little coos after Jane turns up, and we are denied what would no doubt have been an invaluable scene in which Kala tells him the facts of life.)

Jane is voiced by Minnie Driver, as a peppy British girl with lots of moxie. She's come with her father, the walrus-faced Professor Porter (Nigel Hawthorne), to study the gorillas; their guide is Clayton (Brian Blessed), with the graying sideburns of Stewart Granger and the sneers of a Victorian villain. The human plot, as you can guess, includes Clayton's nefarious plans for the gorillas and Tarzan's defense of them. The more interesting plot involves the tug-of-war after Tarzan and Jane fall in love ("I'm in a tree with a man who talks with gorillas!"). Will he return to London with her, or will she stay in the jungle? Burroughs had one answer; Disney has another.

There are, of course, no Africans in this movie. (The opening song promises us a paradise unspoiled by man.) This may be just as well. The Tarzan myth doesn't take place in Africa so much as in a kind of archetypal wilderness occupied only by its own characters. Burroughs used some Africans in his books, but that was after Tarzan got involved in politics (fighting the Germans in South West Africa, for example). At the stage of the story where this film is set, the presence of any additional characters would be disastrous, because they would bring in the real world, and this story has to close out reality to work at all. (*The Lion King,* of course, didn't even have room for Tarzan.)

Tarzan, like *The Hunchback of Notre Dame,* represents another attempt by Disney to push the envelope of animation. Taking a page from the Japanese, where animation is an accepted art form for serious films, *Tarzan* isn't a kiddie cartoon but a movie that works on one level for children (who will like the "Trashin' the Camp" production number), and another for adults (who may stir at scenes like the one where the gorillas reveal themselves to their visitors). The Disney animators also borrow a technique that has been useful to the Japanese, of exaggerating the size of eyes and mouths to make emotions clearer.

I saw *Tarzan* once, and went to see it again. This kind of bright, colorful, hyperkinetic animation is a visual exhilaration. Animation cuts loose from what we can actually see, and shows us what we might ideally see. Like *Mulan* and *A Bug's Life,* this is a film where grownups do not need to be accompanied by a nonadult guardian.

Taxi Driver

R, 112 m., 1976

Robert De Niro (Travis Bickle), Jodie Foster (Iris), Albert Brooks (Tom), Harvey Keitel (Sport), Leonard Harris (Palatine), Peter Boyle (Wizard), Cybill Shepherd (Betsy). Directed by Martin Scorsese and produced by Michael Phillips and Julia Phillips. Screenplay by Paul Schrader.

Taxi Driver shouldn't be taken as a New York film; it's not about a city but about the weathers of a man's soul, and out of all New York he selects just those elements that feed and reinforce his obsessions. The man is Travis Bickle, ex-marine, veteran of Vietnam, composer of dutiful anniversary notes to his parents, taxi driver, killer. The movie rarely strays very far from the personal, highly subjective way in which he sees the city and lets it wound him.

It's a place, first of all, populated with women he cannot have: Unobtainable blond women who might find him attractive for a moment, who might join him for a cup of coffee, but who eventually will have to shake their heads and sigh, "Oh, Travis!" because they find him . . . well, he's going crazy, but the word they use is "strange." And then, even more cruelly, the city seems filled with men who *can* have these women—men ranging from cloddish political hacks to street-corner pimps who, nevertheless, have in common the mysterious ability to approach a woman without getting everything wrong.

Travis could in theory look for fares anywhere in the city, but he's constantly drawn back to 42nd Street, to Times Square and the whores, street freaks, and porno houses. It's here that an ugly kind of sex comes closest to the surface—the sex of buying, selling, and using people. Travis isn't into that, he hates it, but Times Square feeds his anger. His sexual frustration is channeled into a hatred for the creeps he obsessively observes. He tries to break the cycle—or maybe he just sets himself up to fail again. He sees a beautiful blonde working in the storefront office of a presidential candidate. She goes out with him a couple of times, but the second time he takes her to a hard-core film and she walks out in disgust and won't have any more to do with him. All the same, he calls her for another date, and it's here that we get close to the heart of the movie. The director, Martin Scorsese, gives us a shot of Travis on a pay telephone—and then, as the girl is turning him down, the camera slowly dollies to the right and looks down a long, empty hallway. Pauline Kael's review called this shot—which calls attention to itself—a lapse during which Scorsese was maybe borrowing from Antonioni. Scorsese calls this shot the most important one in the film.

Why? Because, he says, it's as if we can't bear to watch Travis feel the pain of being rejected. This is interesting, because later, when Travis goes on a killing rampage, the camera goes so far as to adopt slow motion so we can see the horror in greater detail. That Scorsese finds the rejection more painful than the murders is fascinating, because it helps to explain Travis Bickle, and perhaps it goes some way toward explaining one kind of urban violence. Travis has been shut out so systematically, so often, from a piece of the action that eventually he has to hit back somehow.

Taxi Driver is a brilliant nightmare and like all nightmares it doesn't tell us half of what we want to know. We're not told where Travis comes from, what his specific problems are, whether his ugly scar came from Vietnam— because this isn't a case study, but a portrait of some days in his life. There's a moment at a political rally when Travis, in dark glasses, smiles in a strange way that reminds us of those photos of Bremer just before he shot Wallace. The moment tells us nothing, and everything: We don't know the specifics of Travis's complaint, but in a chilling way we know what we need to know of him. The film's a masterpiece of suggestive characterization; Scorsese's style selects details that evoke emotions, and that's the effect he wants. The performances are odd and compelling: He goes for moments from his actors, rather than slowly developed characters. It's as if the required emotions were written in the margins of their scripts: Give me anger— fear—dread. Robert De Niro, as Travis Bickle, is as good as Brando at suggesting emotions even while veiling them from us (and in many of his close-ups, Scorsese uses almost subliminal slow motion to draw out the revelations). Cybill Shepherd, as the blond goddess, is correctly cast, for once, as a glacier slowly receding toward humanity. And there's Jodie Foster, chillingly cast as a twelve-year-old prostitute whom Travis wants to "save." Harvey Keitel, a veteran of all of Scorsese's films (he was the violent maniac in *Alice Doesn't Live Here Anymore*) is the pimp who controls her, and he's got the right kind of toughness that's all bluff.

These people are seen almost in flashes, as if darkness threatens to close over them altogether. *Taxi Driver* is a hell, from the opening shot of a cab emerging from stygian clouds of steam to the climactic killing scene in which the camera finally looks straight down. Scorsese wanted to look away from Travis's rejec-

tion; we almost want to look away from his life. But he's there, all right, and he's suffering.

10

R, 123 m., 1979

Dudley Moore (George), Julie Andrews (Sam), Bo Derek (Jenny), Robert Webber (Hugh), Dee Wallace (Mary Lewis), Sam Jones (David), Brian Dennehy (Bartender). Directed by Blake Edwards and produced by Edwards and Tony Adams. Screenplay by Edwards.

Blake Edwards's *10* is perhaps the first comedy about terminal yearning. Like all great comedies, it deals with emotions very close to our hearts: In this case, the unutterable poignance of a man's desire for a woman he cannot have. The woman, of course, must be unbelievably desirable (and the hero of *10*, on a scale of 1 to 10, gives this particular woman an 11). It helps, too, if the man is short, forty-two years old, and filled with inchoate longings.

You remember inchoate longings. They used to stalk the pages of novels by Thomas Wolfe, back in the years before the Me Generation and the cult of instant gratification. There used to be a time, incredibly, when you couldn't have something *just because you wanted it*—*10* remembers that time. Its hero, Dudley Moore, begins *10* as a man who seems to have more or less what any man could desire. He is a successful composer. His girlfriend is Julie Andrews. He has a great house up in the hills, he drives a Rolls-Royce, he has cable TV with remote tuning.

But then one day, driving his Rolls down Santa Monica Boulevard, he is visited by a vision. She is a preternaturally beautiful young woman in the next car. She turns to regard him, and he is instantly, helplessly, in love. She turns away. She must be about her business. She is dressed in a bridal gown and is on her way to the church to be married.

He follows her. He is stung by a bee in the church. He has six cavities painfully filled by her father, who is a dentist. Groggy from pain pills and brandy, he finds himself aboard an airplane flying to Mexico—where, amazingly, he winds up at the same resort as his ideal woman (and, of course, her husband—one of the vacuous beach-boy types with a smile fit for a Jockey T-shirts model).

Blake Edwards's screenplay now plunges into some slightly more serious waters, where we will not follow. What we're struck with, in *10*, is the uncanny way its humor gets laughs by touching on emotions and yearnings that are very real for us. We identify with the characters in this movie: Their predicaments are funny, yes—but then ours would be, too, if they weren't our own.

The central treasure in the film is the performance by Dudley Moore. There must have been times when Moore wondered if he'd *ever* get the girl. In *10*, he does. He also brings his character such life and dimension that *10* is a lot more than a comedy: It's a study in the follies of human nature.

The girl (the one who scores 11) is played by Bo Derek. She is so desirable, such a pure and cheerful embodiment of carnal perfection, that we're in there with Dudley Moore every step of the way, even when he's slogging it out to Ravel's interminable "Bolero." Julie Andrews has a small but delightful role as the sensible mistress, and the movie also has warm performances by Robert Webber, as Moore's vulnerable gay friend, and by Brian Dennehy, as a particularly understanding bartender in Mexico.

10 is not only one of the best films Blake Edwards has ever made, but was something of a turning point in his career: The previous decade he had alternated between successful Pink Panther movies and non-Panther flops like *The Tamarind Seed, The Wild Rovers,* and *The Carey Treatment.* Did he have another good straight movie in him? Yes, as a matter of fact, he did.

Ten from Your Show of Shows

NO MPAA RATING, 92 m., 1973

Featuring Sid Caesar, Imogene Coca, Carl Reiner, Howard Morris, Louis Nye. Directed and produced by Max Liebman. Screenplay by Mel Brooks and Sid Caesar.

The release of *Ten from Your Show of Shows*— a collection of ten sketches from the legendary Sid Caesar TV show—has inspired a flood of nostalgia from those who remember when Caesar was the most incredibly popular star on the infant medium.

I cannot join in the nostalgia, alas, because I never saw the original *Your Show of Shows.* Television came belatedly to my hometown (I think there was some kind of court battle over who would get the license), and by the time we got TV, Caesar was already off the air. I spent the early 1950s still listening to radio and going to the movies, which possibly accounts for the fact that *my* nostalgia—for Jack Benny, Johnny Dollar, Bob and Ray, Your FBI in Peace and War, and, yes, even the Lone Ranger— draws a lot of blank stares from people who were watching television then.

The fact that I never saw Caesar at the time doesn't mean I wasn't a fan of his. On the contrary, there was nothing I wanted more desperately than to see *Your Show of Shows.* There was one kid in school whose uncle had put up an enormous TV antenna in his backyard and was able to bring in Peoria and even Indianapolis on good nights. Every week after the Caesar show, this kid would do imitations of the skits. Without ever having seen Caesar, I knew by hearsay he was the funniest man in America.

That instinctive opinion turns out to have been mostly true; *Ten from Your Show of Shows* re-creates the moments when television was inventing itself. Today it would seem impossible to do a weekly ninety-minute live comedy program in front of an audience; in 1950, they did it because there wasn't any other way to do it. After all, wasn't radio usually live, too?

The immediacy of the sketches—the fact that they took place in real time before real audiences—made the show funnier than the canned stuff we get today. Timing was so much more important, and it's timing, for example, that makes the show's funniest skit work. Caesar plays a man who is dragged literally kicking and screaming out of the audience for "This Is Your Story." Forced to relive his past, he's saddled with a fanatically affectionate uncle (Howard Morris) who fastens himself to Caesar and won't let go. The sketch builds from an ordinary satire to a berserk madhouse—but at exactly the right pace, so we never feel Caesar pushing.

The other sketches exhibit Caesar's range. There's a hilarious parody of *From Here to Eternity,* and another one called "The Sewing Machine Girl", about silent movies. There's a pantomime in which all the regulars (Caesar,

Morris, Carl Reiner, Imogene Coca) play a Bavarian cuckoo clock. There's a domestic scene between Caesar and Coca in which he gradually discovers that the wife she's telling him about—the one who ran her car into a drugstore—is, in fact, herself. And there's a funny skit in which Caesar, sitting at the movies with about eighteen sticks of gum in his mouth, gets in the middle of a lovers' quarrel. *Ten from Your Show of Shows* works as nostalgia, I suppose, but it doesn't need it. It's funny even if you've never heard of Sid Caesar—which would be, I suppose, an impossibility.

Terms of Endearment

PG, 129 m., 1983

Debra Winger (Emma Horton), Shirley MacLaine (Aurora Greenway), Jack Nicholson (Breedlove), Jeff Daniels (Flap Horton), Danny DeVito (Vernon), John Lithgow (Sam Burns). Directed, produced, and written by James L. Brooks.

When families get together to remember their times together, the conversation has a way of moving easily from the tragedies to the funny things. You'll mention someone who has passed away, and there'll be a moment of silence, and then somebody will grin and be reminded of some goofy story. Life always has an unhappy ending, but you can have a lot of fun along the way, and everything doesn't have to be dripping in deep significance.

The most remarkable achievement of *Terms of Endearment,* which is filled with great achievements, is its ability to find the balance between the funny and the sad, between moments of deep truth and other moments of high ridiculousness. A lesser movie would have had trouble moving between the extremes that are visited by this film, but because *Terms of Endearment* understands its characters and loves them, we never have a moment's doubt: What happens next is supposed to happen, because life's like that. *Terms of Endearment* feels as much like life as any movie I can think of. At the same time, it's a triumph of show business, with its high comic style, its flair for bittersweet melodrama, and its star turns for the actors. Maybe the best thing about this movie is the way it combines

those two different kinds of filmmaking. This is a movie with bold emotional scenes and big laughs, and at the same time it's so firmly in control of its tone that we believe we are seeing real people.

The movie's about two remarkable women, and their relationships with each other and with the men in their lives. The mother is played by Shirley MacLaine. She's a widow who lives in Houston and hasn't dated a man since her husband died. Maybe she's redirected her sexual desires into the backyard, where her garden has grown so large and elaborate that she either will have to find a man pretty quickly or move to a house with a bigger yard. Her daughter, played by Debra Winger, is one of those people who seems to have been blessed with a sense of life and joy. She marries a guy named Flap who teaches English in a series of Midwestern colleges; she rears three kids and puts up with Flap, who has an eye for coeds.

Back in Houston, her mother finally goes out on a date with the swinging bachelor (Jack Nicholson) who has lived next door for years. He's a hard-drinking, girl-chasing former astronaut with a grin that hints of unspeakable lusts. MacLaine, a lady who surrounds herself with frills and flowers, is appalled by this animalistic man and then touched by him.

There are a couple of other bittersweet relationships in the film. Both mother and daughter have timid, mild-mannered male admirers: MacLaine is followed everywhere by Vernon (Danny DeVito), who asks only to be allowed to gaze upon her, and Winger has a tender, little affair with a banker.

The years pass. Children grow up into adolescence, Flap gets a job as head of the department in Nebraska, the astronaut turns out to have genuine human possibilities of becoming quasi civilized, and mother and daughter grow into a warmer and deeper relationship. All of this is told in a series of perfectly written, acted, and directed scenes that flow as effortlessly as a perfect day, and then something happens that is totally unexpected, and changes everything. I don't want to suggest what happens. It flows so naturally that it should be allowed to take place.

This is a wonderful film. There isn't a thing that I would change, and I was exhilarated by the freedom it gives itself to move from the high comedy of Nicholson's best moments to the acting of Debra Winger in the closing scenes. She outdoes herself. It's a great performance. And yet it's not a "performance." There are scenes that have such a casual gaiety that acting seems to have nothing to do with it. She doesn't reach for effects, and neither does the film, because it's all right there.

Tess
PG, 180 m., 1980

Nastassja Kinski (Tess), Peter Firth (Angel Clare), Leigh Lawson (Alec d'Urberville), Rosemary Martin (Mrs. Durbeyfield), Sylvia Coleridge (Mrs. d'Urberville), John Collin (John Durbeyfield), Tony Church (Parson), Brigid Erin Bates (Girl in Meadow). Directed by Roman Polanski and produced by Claude Berri. Screenplay by Gerard Brach, Polanski, and John Brownjohn, based on the book by Thomas Hardy.

Roman Polanski's *Tess* is a love song with a tragic ending—the best kind of love song of all, just so long as it's not about ourselves. He tells the story of a beautiful young girl, innocent but not without intelligence, and the way she is gradually destroyed by the exercise of the male ego. The story is all the more touching because it is not an unrelenting descent into gloom, as it might have been in other hands, but a life lived in occasional sight of love and happiness. Tess is forever just on the brink of getting the peace she deserves.

The movie is based on a novel by Thomas Hardy, but Polanski never permits his film to become a Classics Illustrated; this isn't a devout rendering of a literary masterpiece, but a film that lives and breathes and has a quick sympathy for its heroine. Nastassja Kinski is just right for the title role. She has the youth, the freshness, and the naïveté of a Tess, and none of the practiced mannerisms of an actress engaged to "interpret" the role. That's good because Tess is a character who should stick out like a sore thumb in many scenes, and Kinski's occasional shy awkwardness is just right for the story of a girl who attempts to move up in social class on sheer bravado.

The story involves a young girl who will be the victim, the prey, and sometimes the lover of many men, without ever quite understanding what it is that those men want of her. The first man in her life is her father, a drunken farmer named John Durbeyfield, who discovers from the local parson that he is related to the noble local family of d'Urbervilles. The farmer and his wife immediately send their beautiful daughter, Tess, off to confront the d'Urbervilles and perhaps win a position in their household.

Tess is almost immediately seduced by a rakish cousin. She becomes pregnant, and her child dies soon after it is born. She never tells the cousin. But later, after she falls in love with the son of a local minister and marries him, she confesses her past. This is too much for her new husband to bear; he "married down" because he was attracted to Tess's humble origins. But he is not prepared to accept the reality of her past. He leaves on a bizarre mission to South America. Tess, meanwhile, descends to rough manual labor for a few pennies an hour. She is eventually reunited with her cousin (who is not a complete bastard, and complains that he should have been informed of her pregnancy). She becomes his lover. Then the wayward husband returns, and the physical and psychic contest for Tess ends in tragedy.

As a plot, these events would be right at home in any soap opera. But what happens in Polanski's *Tess* is less important than how Tess feels about it, how we feel about it, and how successfully Polanski is able to locate those events in a specific place and time. His movie is set in England, but was actually photographed in France. It is a beautifully visualized period piece that surrounds Tess with the attitudes of her time—attitudes that explain how restricted her behavior must be, and how society views her genuine human emotions as inappropriate. This is a wonderful film; the kind of exploration of doomed young sexuality that, like *Elvira Madigan*, makes us agree that the lovers should never grow old.

Testament
PG, 90 m., 1983

Jane Alexander (Carol Wetherly), William Devane (Tom Wetherly), Ross Harris (Brad), Roxana Zal (Mary Liz), Lukas Haas (Scottie), Philip Anglim (Hollis), Leon Ames (Henry Abhart), Rebecca De Mornay (Mother with

Baby). Directed by Lynne Littman and produced by Jonathan Bernstein and Littman. Screenplay by John Sacret Young.

Testament may be the first movie in a long time that will make you cry. It made me cry. And seeing it again for a second time, knowing everything that would happen, anticipating each scene before it came, I was affected just as deeply. But the second time I was able to see more clearly that the movie is more than just a devastating experience, that it has a message with a certain hope.

The film is about a suburban American family, and what happens to that family after a nuclear war. It is not a science-fiction movie, and it doesn't have any special effects, and there are no big scenes of buildings blowing over or people disintegrating. We never see a mushroom cloud. We never even know who started the war. Instead, *Testament* is a tragedy about manners: It asks how we might act toward one another, how our values might stand up in the face of an overwhelming catastrophe.

The movie begins with one of those typical families right out of TV commercials. The father (William Devane) is a physical fitness nut. The mother (Jane Alexander) is loving, funny, and a little harried. The kids include a daughter who practices the piano, a son who races his dad up hills on their ten-speed bikes, and a little boy who guards the "treasure" in the bottom drawer of his chest. The movie follows these people long enough for us to know them, to appreciate their personalities, their good and weak points, and then one sunny afternoon the war starts.

Most of the film is about what happens then. Anarchy does not break out. There is some looting, but it is limited. For the most part, the people in the small northern California town stick together and try to do the best that they can. There are meetings in the church. There are public-health measures. A beloved community leader (Leon Ames, of TV's *Life with Father* many years ago) is a ham-radio operator, and makes contact with a few other places. A decision is made to go ahead with the grade-school play. Life goes on . . . but death invades it, as radiation poisoning begins to take a toll, first on the babies, then on the children, until finally the ceme-

tery is filled and the bodies have to be burned on a pyre.

The movie finds dozens of small details to suggest existence after the bomb. All the kids, for example, take the batteries out of their toys and computer games, and turn them in for emergency use. Gasoline is rationed, and then runs out. The survivors have no garbage collection, no electricity, and, worst of all, no word from elsewhere. The sky gradually grows darker, suggesting realistically that a nuclear war would finally kill us all by raising great clouds of dust that would choke Earth's vegetation.

In the midst of this devastation, Jane Alexander, as the mother, tries to preserve love and decency. She stands by her children, watches as they grow in response to the challenges, cherishes them as she sees all her dreams for them disappear. It is a great performance, the heart of the film. In fact, Alexander's performance makes the film possible to watch without unbearable heartbreak, because she is brave and decent in the face of horror. And the last scene, in which she expresses such small optimism as is still possible, is one of the most powerful movie scenes I've ever seen.

Tex
PG, 103 m., 1982

Matt Dillon (Tex), Jim Metzler (Mason), Meg Tilly (Jamie), Bill McKinney (Pop), Frances Lee McCain (Mrs. Johnson), Ben Johnson (Cole Collins). Directed by Tim Hunter and produced by Ron Miller. Screenplay by Charlie Haas and Hunter, based on the book by S. E. Hinton.

There is a shock of recognition almost from the beginning of *Tex*, because we're listening to the sound of American voices in an authentically American world, the world of teenage boys trying to figure things out and make the right decisions. The voices sound right but may be a little unfamiliar, because adolescents on television are often made to talk in pseudohip sitcom nonspeak. Here in *Tex* are the clear voices of two young men who are worthy of attention. Their names are Tex and Mason. They're brothers, one about eighteen, the other fourteen and a half. They live by themselves in a rundown house on some land outside a rural suburb of Tulsa. Their father is a rodeo cowboy who hardly ever stops in at home and forgets to send money for weeks at a time. These two kids are raising themselves and doing a pretty good job of it.

The movie tells the story of a couple of weeks in their lives. These are the kinds of weeks when things can go either well or badly—and if they go badly, we sense, Tex could get his whole life off to the wrong start. The brothers are broke. Mason sells their horses to raise money to buy food and get the gas turned back on. That makes Tex angry and sad; he's a kid looking for trouble.

We meet the other people in their world. There's the rich family down the road, dominated by a stern father who makes his teenagers toe a strict line. His kids are just as unpredictable as anyone else's, but he doesn't believe that. He believes their two undisciplined friends, Tex and Mason, are leading them into trouble and practically dragging them to late-night beer parties. There's another complication. His daughter and Tex are beginning to fall in love.

There's another friend, a local kid who got a girl pregnant, married her, and moved to Tulsa to start a family. He's dealing drugs. Mason knows this intuitively and surely, and knows the kid is heading for trouble. Tex knows it, too, but there comes a time in this story when Tex just doesn't give a damn, and when the drug dealer happens to be there, Tex accepts a ride into Tulsa with him. Tex doesn't do drugs himself, but he gets into a very scary situation with another dealer, and there's a harrowing scene in which Tex wavers just at the brink of getting into serious trouble.

There is more to this movie's story, but the important thing about it isn't what happens, but how it happens. The movie is so accurately acted, especially by Jim Metzler as Mason and Matt Dillon as Tex, that we care more about the characters than about the plot. We can see them learning and growing, and when they have a heart-to-heart talk about "going all the way," we hear authentic teenagers speaking, not kids who seem to have been raised at Beverly Hills cocktail parties.

Tex is based on a famous novel by S. E. Hinton, who has had two of her other novels

filmed by Francis Ford Coppola. She knows a great deal about adolescents, and her work is unaffected by sentimentality and easy romance. It's authentic. But the backgrounds of the two filmmakers are also interesting. Tim Hunter and Charles Haas bought the book and wrote the screenplay, and Hunter directed. Their previous collaboration was a little movie named *Over the Edge,* about teenagers who feel cornered and persecuted by the rigid middle-class rules of a cardboard Denver suburb. That movie, a small masterpiece containing Matt Dillon's first movie appearance, never got a fair chance in theaters. Now here are Hunter and Haas again, still remembering what it's like to be young, still getting the dialogue and the attitudes, the hang-ups and the dreams, exactly right.

That Obscure Object of Desire
R, 103 m., 1977

Fernando Rey (Mathieu), Carole Bouquet and Angela Molina (Conchita). Directed by Luis Buñuel. Screenplay by Buñuel and Jean-Claude Carriere.

The man is middle-aged, impeccably dressed, perfectly groomed, obviously respectable. He has just barely caught his train. A young woman comes running down the station platform, also trying to catch the train. The man's face reflects intense annoyance; he whispers something to the conductor, gives him a tip, and is allowed into the train's restroom. He emerges with a pail of water, which, as the young lady tries to climb aboard, he pours on her head.

Ah, satisfaction . . . he settles down in his seat, only to discover intense curiosity among his fellow travelers. One of them, a psychologist who is a dwarf, finally speaks: "I could not help seeing what you did. I can tell from your appearance that you are a gentleman. Therefore, you must have had an excellent reason. . . ."

"Yes," the gentleman replies pleasantly, "I had a *most* excellent reason." Seeming almost flattered by their curiosity, he tells them a story. And so, on a note both calm and sly, begins Luis Buñuel's *That Obscure Object of Desire.*

Buñuel's characters did battle with erotic desire for more than fifty years. They tended to be vain and fastidious people, middle class, concerned with maintaining their selfrespect. Yet, they had a way of coming off second best to lust, jealousy, and an assortment of peculiar sexual obsessions. And as Buñuel grew older, he seemed to learn more about their weaknesses with every year, and to find their passions increasingly funny. He made this film when he was seventy-seven.

Take, for example, his hero this time, the completely respectable Mathieu (Fernando Rey). He is a widower with no interest in most women; unless he feels true passion, he says, he would just as soon leave them alone. One day a new maid comes to serve him his dinner. She is Conchita; cool, elegant, gently mocking. He is lost. He is hopelessly in love, but his advances serve only to drive Conchita further away.

He tries what he thinks is a civilized approach, arranging with her mother to provide for the family's financial needs in return for, ahem . . . but Conchita protests: "I wanted to give myself to you, but you tried to buy me!" He would by now, indeed, give her anything he has, but she disappears. Then he discovers her again, by accident, in Switzerland. Their life becomes a strange, erotic game of cat-and-mouse, in which the virginal Conchita torments him by her inaccessibility. At last Mathieu is ready to settle for anything—even sleeping with her without touching her. He is totally enthralled.

Buñuel relishes themes of erotic frustration. His most memorable heroines are those who deny themselves, and we remember the niece sleeping in her hair shirt in *Viridiana,* and Catherine Deneuve's masochistic pastimes in *Belle de Jour* and *Tristana.* This time, though, Buñuel seems to be reaching deeper, to be saying something more. Conchita is not simply denying herself to the man who loves her; she is teaching him a lesson about his own complex nature, about his need for a woman who would be always unattainable.

And Buñuel, of course, is exercising his own dry and totally original wit. His film is filled with small, droll touches, with tiny peculiarities of behavior, with moral anarchy, with a cynicism about human nature that somehow seems, in his hands, almost cheerful. His most obvious touch is perhaps his best: to dramatize Conchita's tantalizing elusiveness, he has cast two actresses to play her. So just when poor Mathieu has all but seduced this Conchita, the other emerges from the dressing room. Pour a pail of water on her head? Yes, we imagine Buñuel nodding wisely, a man could easily be driven to such an extreme.

Note: The story behind the casting could make a movie of its own. Buñuel originally cast Maria Schneider, and when they had a falling-out after a month, he cast Carole Bouquet and Angela Molina to replace her, alternating between the two obviously quite different actresses quite arbitrarily, and with no explanation. The lesson, perhaps, is that obsessions are blind, and so self-centered that the objects of desire can be interchangeable.

That's Entertainment!

G, 132 m., 1974

Selected scenes from MGM musicals between 1929 and 1958, introduced by Frank Sinatra, Fred Astaire, Gene Kelly, Mickey Rooney, Liza Minnelli, Elizabeth Taylor, James Stewart, Donald O'Connor, and others. Written, produced, and directed by Jack Haley, Jr.

It used to be said that the trickiest thing about a musical was to figure out a way for the characters to break gracefully into song. Maybe that was all wrong. Maybe the hardest thing was for them to stop, once the singing had started. That's my notion after seeing *That's Entertainment!,* a magical tour through the greatest musicals produced by the king of Hollywood studios, Metro-Goldwyn-Mayer.

This isn't just a compilation film, with lots of highlights strung together. Those kinds of movies quickly repeat themselves. *That's Entertainment!* is more of a documentary and a eulogy. A documentary of a time that began in 1929 and seemed to end only yesterday, and a eulogy for an art form that will never be again.

Hollywood will continue to make musicals, of course (although, curiously enough, the form never has been very popular overseas). But there will never be musicals like this again, because there won't be the budgets, there won't be the sense of joyous abandon, there won't be so many stars in the same place all at once, and—most of all—there won't be the notion that a musical has to be "important."

The various segments of the film are introduced and narrated by MGM stars of the past (Fred Astaire, Gene Kelly), superstars like Frank Sinatra and Elizabeth Taylor, offspring like Liza Minnelli, and even a ringer like Bing Crosby (he was a Paramount star, but never mind). They seem to share a real feeling of nostalgia for MGM, which, in its heyday, was not only a studio, but also a benevolent and protective organization ruled by the paternal Louis B. Mayer. Liza Minnelli sounds at times as if she's narrating a visit to her mother's old high school. The movie avoids the trap of being too worshipful in the face of all this greatness. It's not afraid to kid; we see Clark Gable looking ill at ease as he pretends to enjoy singing and dancing, and we see a hilarious montage of Judy Garland and Mickey Rooney ringing endless changes to the theme, "I know—we'll fix up the old barn and put on a show!"

And then there are the glorious, unforgettable moments from the great musicals. My favorite musical has always been *Singin' in the Rain*, the 1952 comedy about Hollywood's traumatic switch to talkies. *That's Entertainment!* opens with a montage of musicals (neatly surveying three decades of film progress), and later returns to the two most unforgettable numbers in the film: Gene Kelly sloshing through puddles while singing the title song, and Donald O'Connor in his amazing "Make 'em Laugh," in which he leaps up walls, takes pratfalls, and dives through a set.

There are other great moments: The closing ballet from *An American in Paris;* Nelson Eddy and Jeanette MacDonald being hilariously serious in *Rose Marie;* Astaire and Ginger Rogers, so light-footed they seem to float; Gene Kelly's incredible acrobatics as he does his own stunts, swinging from rooftop to rooftop; William Warfield singing "Old Man River" in *Showboat;* Judy Garland singing "You Made Me Love You" to a montage of stills of Clark Gable; Garland, again, with "Get Happy" (and a vignette of little Liza's first movie appearance, aged about three); the acrobatic woodchopper's scene from *Seven Brides for Seven Brothers;* and even Esther Williams rising from the deep.

The movie's fun from beginning to end. It's not camp, and it's not nostalgia: It's a celebration of a time and place in American movie history when everything came together to make a new art form.

They Shoot Horses, Don't They?

PG, 123 m., 1970

Jane Fonda (Gloria), Michael Sarrazin (Robert), Susannah York (Alice), Gig Young (Rocky), Red Buttons (Sailor), Bonnie Bedelia (Ruby), Severn Darden (Cecil). Directed by Sydney Pollack and produced by Irwin Winkler and Robert Chartoff. Screenplay by James Poe and Robert E. Thompson.

Erase the forced smiles from the desperate faces, and what the dance marathons of the 1930s came down to was fairly simple. A roomful of human beings went around and around within four walls for weeks at a time without sleep, populating a circus for others who paid to see them. At the end, those who didn't collapse or drop dead won cash prizes that were good money during the Depression. And the Depression, in an oblique sort of way, was the reason for it all. The marathons offered money to the winners and distraction to everyone else. To be sure, some of the marathons got pretty grim. Contestants tried to dance their way through illnesses and pregnancies, through lice and hallucinations, and the sight of them doing it was part of the show. Beyond the hit tunes and the crepe paper and the free pig as a door prize, there was an elementary sadism in the appeal of the marathons.

Among American spectator sports, they rank with stock-car racing. There was always that delicious possibility, you see, that somebody would die. Or freak out. Or stand helplessly while his partner collapsed and he lost the investment of thousands of hours of his life.

They Shoot Horses, Don't They? is a masterful re-creation of the marathon era for audiences that are mostly unfamiliar with it. In addition to everything else it does, *Horses* holds our attention because it tells us something we didn't know about human nature and American society. It tells us a lot more than that, of course, but because it works on this fundamental level as well it is one of the best American movies of the 1970s. It is so good as a movie, indeed, that it doesn't have to bother with explaining the things in my first two paragraphs; they are all there (and that's where I found them), but they are completely incorporated into the structure of the film.

Director Sydney Pollack has built a ballroom and filled it with characters. They come from nowhere, really; Michael Sarrazin is photographed as if he has walked into the ballroom directly from the sea. The characters seem to have no histories, no alternate lives; they exist only within the walls of the ballroom and during the ticking of the official clock. Pollack has simplified the universe. He has got everything in life boiled down to this silly contest; and what he tells us has more to do with lives than contests.

Sarrazin meets Jane Fonda, and they became partners almost absentmindedly; he wasn't even planning on entering a marathon. There are other contestants, particularly Red Buttons and Bonnie Bedelia in splendid supporting performances, and they are whipped around the floor by the false enthusiasm of Gig Young, the master of ceremonies. "Yowzza! Yowzza!" he chants, and all the while he regards the contestants with the peculiarly disinterested curiosity of an exhausted god.

There are not a lot of laughs in *Horses*, because Pollack has directed from the point of view of the contestants. They are bitter beyond any hope of release. The movie's delicately timed pacing and Pollack's visual style work almost stealthily to involve us; we begin to feel the physical weariness and spiritual desperation of the characters.

The movie begins on a note of alienation and spirals down from there. *Horses* provides us no cheap release at the end; and the ending, precisely because it is so obvious, is all the more effective. We knew it was coming. Even the title gave it away. And when it comes, it is effective not because it is a surprise but because it is inevitable. As inevitable as death.

The performances are perfectly matched to Pollack's grim vision. Jane Fonda is hard, unbreakable, filled with hate and fear. Sarrazin can do nothing, really, but stand there and pity her; no one, not even during the Depression, should have to feel so without hope. Red Buttons, as the sailor who's a veteran of other marathons and cheerfully teaches everybody the ropes, reminds us that the great character actor from *Sayonara* still exists, and that comedians are somehow the best in certain tragic roles.

And that's what the movie comes down to, maybe. The characters are comedians trapped in tragic roles. They signed up for the three square meals a day and the crack at the $1,500 prize, and they can stop (after all) whenever they want to. But somehow they can't stop, and as the hundreds and thousands of hours of weariness and futility begin to accumulate, the great dance marathon begins to look more and more like life.

Thirteen Conversations About One Thing
R, 102 m., 2002

Matthew McConaughey (Troy), John Turturro (Walker), Alan Arkin (Gene), Clea DuVall (Beatrice), Amy Irving (Patricia), Barbara Sukowa (Helen), William Wise (Wade). Directed by Jill Sprecher and produced by Beni Atoori and Gina Resnick. Screenplay by Jill and Karen Sprecher.

Happiness is the subject of *Thirteen Conversations About One Thing*. For that matter, happiness is the subject of every conversation we ever have: the search for happiness, the envy of happiness, the loss of happiness, the guilt about undeserved happiness. The engine that drives the human personality is our desire to be happy instead of sad, entertained instead of bored, inspired instead of disillusioned, informed rather than ignorant. It is not an easy business.

Consider Troy (Matthew McConaughey), the prosecutor who has just won a big conviction. In the movie's opening scene, he's loud and obnoxious in a saloon, celebrating his victory. He spots a sad sack at the bar: Gene (Alan Arkin), who seems to be pessimistic about the possibility of happiness. Gene is a midlevel manager at an insurance company, has to fire someone, and decides to fire Wade, the happiest man in the department, since he can see the sunny side of anything.

Troy buys drinks for Gene. He wants everybody to be happy. Then he drives drunk, hits a pedestrian with his car, and believes he has killed her. As an assistant district attorney he knows how much trouble he's in, and instinctively leaves the scene. His problem becomes an all-consuming guilt, which spoils his ability to enjoy anything in life; he was cut in the accident, and keeps the wound open with a razor blade to punish himself.

The movie finds connections between people who think they are strangers, finding the answer to one person's problem in the question raised by another. We meet Walker (John Turturro), a sardonic college professor, who walks out on his wife (Amy Irving) and begins an affair with a woman (Barbara Sukowa). She realizes that the affair is hardly the point: Walker is going through the motions because he has been told, and believes, that this is how you find happiness. We also meet a house cleaner (Clea DuVall), who is good at her job but works for a client who can only criticize. She is injured for no reason at all, suffers great pain, does not deserve to.

The truth hidden below the surface of the story is a hard one: Nothing makes any sense. We do not get what we deserve. If we are lucky, we get more. If we are unlucky, we get less. Bad things happen to good people, and good things happen to bad people. That's the system. All of our philosophies are a futile attempt to explain it. Let me tell you a story. Not long ago I was in the middle of a cheerful conversation when I slipped on wet wax, landed hard and broke bones in my left shoulder. I was in a fool's paradise of happiness, you see, not realizing that I was working without a net—that in a second my happiness would be rudely interrupted.

I could have hit my head and been killed. Or landed better and not been injured. At best what we can hope for is a daily reprieve from all of the things that can go wrong. *Thirteen Conversations About One Thing* is relentless in the way it demonstrates how little we control our lives. We can choose actions, but we cannot plan outcomes. Follow, for example, the consequences of Alan Arkin's decision to fire the happy man, and then see what happens to Arkin, and then see what happens to the happy man. Or watch as the Matthew McConaughey character grants reality to something he only thinks he knows. Or see how the Turturro character, so obsessed with his personal timetable, so devoted to his daily and weekly routines, is able to arrange everything to his satisfaction—and then is not satisfied.

The movie is brilliant, really. It is philosophy illustrated through everyday events. Most movies operate as if their events are necessary— that B must follow A. *Thirteen Conversations*

betrays B, A, and all the other letters as random possibilities.

The film was directed by Jill Sprecher, and written with her sister, Karen. It's their second, after *Clockwatchers* (1997), the lacerating, funny story about temporary workers in an office and their strategies to prove they exist in a world that is utterly indifferent to them. After these two movies, there aren't many filmmakers whose next film I anticipate more eagerly. They're onto something. They're using films to demonstrate something to us. Movies tell narratives, and the purpose of narrative is to arrange events in an order that seems to make sense and end correctly. The Sprechers are telling us if we believe in these narratives we're only fooling ourselves.

And yet, even so, there is a way to find happiness. That is to be curious about all of the interlocking events that add up to our lives. To notice connections. To be amused or perhaps frightened by the ways things work out. If the universe is indifferent, what a consolation that we are not.

Thirty-Two Short Films About Glenn Gould

NO MPAA RATING, 94 m., 1994

Colm Feore (Glenn Gould), Derek Keurvorst (Gould's Father), Katya Lada (Gould's Mother), Devon Anderson (Young Glenn, Age Three), Joshua Greenblatt (Young Glenn, Age Eight), Sean Ryan (Young Glenn, Age Twelve), Kate Hennig (Chambermaid), Sean Doyle (Porter). Directed by François Girard and produced by Niv Fichman and Barbara Willis-Sweete. Screenplay by Girard and Don McKellar.

How to suggest an actual human life on film? Most biopics shape the enigmatic events of life into the requirements of fiction, so that most lives seem the same, and only the professions and the time periods change. François Girard's *Thirty-Two Short Films About Glenn Gould* brilliantly breaks with tradition and gives us a movie that actually inspires us to *think* about what it was like to be this man.

Glenn Gould (1932–1982), born in Toronto, could play and read music before he was four years old. Taught only by his mother until he was ten, he was soon giving concerts in Canada and the United States, where Leonard Bernstein was one of his admirers. He became one of the great concert pianists of his time, and then, on April 10, 1964, without advance notice, he gave his last concert and refused to perform in public ever again.

That was not the end of his career but the beginning of an extraordinary second career, in which he channeled all of his efforts into making recordings. His choice of the recording studio over the concert stage was explained in different ways at different times; he didn't like the idea of a performer upstaging the music, he would say, or he could not abide the idea that some people in the audience had better seats than others.

He stayed at home, in Toronto recording studios and hotel rooms, cultivating a benign eccentricity, talking to his friends endlessly on the telephone but sparingly in person. And he left behind a rich recorded legacy, including his performances of Bach's Goldberg Variations (one of Gould's Bach performances has since left the solar system on board *Voyager I*).

Thirty-Two Short Films About Glenn Gould was inspired by the Goldberg Variations, and is a series of brief vignettes suggesting variations on the artist's life. Colm Feore plays the pianist, as a calm, physically economical man whose most highly developed sense, we feel, is his hearing. There is a scene midway in the film where Gould enters a roadside diner where he is apparently a familiar face. As he waits for his eggs to arrive, he listens to the conversations around him, and the sound track pieces these words of strangers together in such an intense way that we listen, too. In another scene, he asks a hotel chambermaid to listen to a recording, and then he judges its effect upon her. Again, in a recording studio, he listens to a piece of music twice, and then says, "I think we might really have something there."

The movie does not deliver, or suggest, a rounded life story. But it leaves us with a much richer idea of his life than a conventional biopic might have. We see the young Gould at his piano (from childhood, he always fancied a stool just fourteen inches off the ground, placing his eyes not far above finger-level). And we see him listening intensely to a radio broadcast of a concert. Our imagination is challenged to feel the music entering him.

There are other episodes, some as mundane as a telephone call to a friend, others as startling

as that last concert in 1964, where he soaks his hands in warm water, then walks slowly through backstage corridors, hesitates before walking onstage, and signs a stagehand's program, adding the words, "the last concert."

Some of the "short films" show episodes from a life. Some show ideas inspired by the music. Some are the documentary testimony of friends, including Yehudi Menuhin, who talk with the warm recollection they might use at a memorial service. One brief sequence simply shows Gould sitting in a chair, listening. We gather he became a hermit of sorts, but a contented one, doing what he loved. The movie makes no suggestions at all about his sexual life, does not deal in gossip, and seems almost proud of its outsider's viewpoint. The filmmakers do not claim to know the secrets of Glenn Gould, but only to be fascinated by them.

The notes with the movie recall that when one of the producers, Barbara Willis-Sweete, was working in the late 1970s as a bartender at the hotel where Gould was living, she followed him late one night as he left with a large bag. He eventually dropped it in a garbage can, and she retrieved it, to find it contained only old newspapers. The point of this story, I think, is not what the bag contained, but that the bartender followed him. The film is made in something of the same spirit, as if the filmmakers admire Gould's work, are puzzled by his life, and want to follow him, unobserved. They discover no great answers or revelations, but by the end of the film they, and we, have a remarkable impression of a life lived curiously, but well.

This Is Spinal Tap
R, 87 m., 1984

Rob Reiner (Marty DiBergi), Michael McKean (David St. Hubbins), Christopher Guest (Nigel Tufnel), Harry Shearer (Derek Smalls). Directed by Reiner and produced by Karen Murphy. Screenplay by Guest, McKean, Shearer, and Reiner.

The children born at Woodstock are preparing for the junior prom, and rock 'n' roll is still here to stay. Rock musicians never die, they just fade away, and *This Is Spinal Tap* is a movie about a British rock group that is rocketing to the bottom of the charts.

The movie looks like a documentary filmed

during the death throes of a British rock band named Spinal Tap. It is, in fact, a satire. The rock group does not really exist, but the best thing about this film is that it could. The music, the staging, the special effects, the backstage feuding, and the pseudoprofound philosophizing are right out of a hundred other rock groups and a dozen other documentaries about rock.

The group is in the middle of an American tour. The tour is not going well. Spinal Tap was once able to fill giant arenas, but its audiences have grown smaller and smaller, and concert dates are evaporating as the bad news gets around. No wonder. Spinal Tap is a bad rock 'n' roll band. It is derivative, obvious, phony, and pretentious, and it surrounds itself with whatever images seem commercial at the moment (a giant death's-head on stage, for one). The movie is absolutely inspired in the subtle way it establishes Spinal Tap's badness. The satire has a deft, wicked touch. Spinal Tap is not that much worse than, not that much different from, some successful rock bands. A few breaks here or there, a successful album, and they could be back in business. (Proof of that: A sound track album, "Smell the Glove," is getting lots of air play with cuts like "Sex Farm.")

The documentary is narrated by its director, Marty DiBergi, played by Rob Reiner, the director of the real movie. He explains that he was first attracted to the band by its unusual loudness. He follows them on tour, asking profound questions that inspire deep, meaningless answers, and his cameras watch as the group comes unglued. One of the band members brings in a girlfriend from England. She feuds with the group's manager. Bookings are canceled. The record company doesn't like the cover for the group's new album. One disastrous booking takes Spinal Tap to a dance in a hangar on a military base. The movie is brilliant at telling its story through things that happen in the background and at the edges of the picture: By the end of the film, we know as much about the personalities and conflicts of the band members as if the movie had been straightforward narrative.

There are a lot of great visual jokes, which I don't want to spoil—especially the climax of the band's Stonehenge production number, or another number that involves them being re-born from womblike stage props. There also are moments of inspired satire aimed at previous styles in rock films, as when we get glimpses of Spinal Tap in its earlier incarnations (the band started as sort of a folk group, plunged into the flower-people generation, and was a little late getting into heavy metal, satanism, and punk).

This Is Spinal Tap assumes that audiences will get most of the jokes. I think that's right. *Entertainment Tonight* and music TV and Barbara Walters specials have made show business trade talk into national gossip, and one of the greatest pleasures of the movie is that it doesn't explain everything. It simply, slyly, destroys one level of rock pomposity after another.

This Man Must Die

PG, 110 m., 1971

Michael Duchaussoy (Charles Thenier), Jean Yanne (Paul), Caroline Cellier (Helene), Lorraine Ranier (Jeanne), Marc Di Napoli (Phillipe). Directed by Claude Chabrol and produced by Andre Génovèse. Screenplay by Chabrol and Paul Gegauff, based on the book by Nicholas Blake.

Claude Chabrol's *This Man Must Die* is advertised as a thriller, but that is the least of its accomplishments. It is a macabre, bizarre study of the hazards of revenge, and it thrills us not with chases or cliff-hangers (although the villain does indeed dangle momentarily from a cliff) but with the relationship between good and evil people.

That's sensible. Thrillers that conceal the villain's identity imply that his identity is the most important thing about him; Chabrol would rather introduce you to the killer and let you live with him for an hour or so before he checks out. In *This Man Must Die*, a little boy is killed by a hit-and-run driver, and the boy's father sets out to find and kill the murderer. He speaks for Chabrol: "When I find him, I won't kill him right away. I'll get to know him and savor my revenge."

Through some elementary detective work and a convenient coincidence, the father meets the killer's sister-in-law, an actress. He fakes a love affair with her to gain an introduction to her family, then discovers that the villain is a truly reprehensible beast who is hated by everyone.

Then Chabrol gets sly. He refuses to let the movie unfold along the usual lines of revenge. He has his hero really fall in love with the sister-in-law. He has the villain's son, who hates his father, develop a tremendous respect for the hero. And gradually the shape of the revenge emerges: The hero will not merely kill the murderer, but strip him of his manhood, his family, his son.

Or will he? Just as things begin to seem almost clear, the murderer finds the hero's diary. But then again the diary may have been written just so it could be found. Chabrol handles these twists, one after another, with quiet delight. When the end comes, we are not allowed to be quite sure who did the killing (although we have an idea). It is the moral responsibility for revenge that interests Chabrol, not the mere fact.

Jean Yanne, as the murderer, is delightful. He is surly and brutal and so filled with his own vanity that we almost like him more than the tight-lipped, impassive hero (Michael Duchaussoy). Chabrol gives us scene after scene of carefully observed confrontations, as the cat and mouse circle each other. Usually they're scenes at mealtime; no other director has so delightfully combined murder and roast duck.

In the end, that's what makes Chabrol so fascinating. In being as concerned with the nuances of daily life as he is with the vast fact of murder, he makes the murder itself more horrible, and the revenge more ambiguous. His text finally seems to come from the Bible, which finds a beast in every man, and suggests that the man must die if the beast is to be the same personality, and then give a moment's thought to the person who actually does kill the killer. You can get in pretty deep.

Note: This review applies to the French language version with English subtitles. A preview audience had the misfortune to see one of the worst, most distracting, most damaging jobs of dubbing I've ever endured. If Allied Artists has any hopes for this film, it should abandon the dubbed version and go with subtitles. In a film where nuance is so important, to remove the rhythms and inflections of the actor's own voices is essentially castration.

The Three Burials of Melquiades Estrada
R, 121 m., 2006

Tommy Lee Jones (Pete Perkins), Barry Pepper (Mike Norton), Julio Cedillo (Melquiades Estrada), Dwight Yoakam (Sheriff Belmont), January Jones (Lou Ann Norton), Melissa Leo (Rachel). Directed by Jones and produced by Michael Fitzgerald and Jones. Screenplay by Guillermo Arriaga.

The Three Burials of Melquiades Estrada tells the kind of story that John Huston or Sam Peckinpah might have wanted to film. It begins with a bedrock of loyalty and honor between men and mixes it with a little madness. In an era when hundreds of lives are casually destroyed in action movies, here is an entire film in which one life is honored, and one death is avenged.

The director and star is Tommy Lee Jones, and the story proceeds directly from fundamental impulses we sense in many of his screen appearances. Jones is most at home in characters who mean business and do not suffer fools gladly. Here he plays Pete Perkins, the hardworking operator of a small cattle operation who hires an illegal Mexican immigrant named Melquiades Estrada (Julio Cedillo) to work as a cowboy. When Melquiades is killed in a stupid shooting involving a rookie agent for the Border Patrol, Pete sees that the local sheriff (Dwight Yoakam) is going to ignore the case. So Pete takes justice into his own hands. And not simple justice, which might involve killing the agent, but poetic justice, which elevates the movie into the realm of parable.

All the action takes place in a small border town of appalling poverty of spirit. This is a hard land for men, and a heartbreaking one for women. We meet two in particular. Lou Ann Norton (January Jones) is the wife of Mike, the border patrolman. Rachel (Melissa Leo) is the waitress in the local restaurant, married to Bob the owner but available for afternoons in motel rooms, not because she is a prostitute but because she is friendly and bored.

The story is told in links between the present and the recent past; the writer, Guillermo Arriaga *(21 Grams)*, was honored at Cannes 2005 as best writer, and Jones was named best actor. We see that the Border Patrol agent, Mike Norton (Barry Pepper), is violent and cruel, perhaps as a way of masking his insecurity. He beats up a woman trying to enter the country and is told by his commander, "You were way overboard there, boy." He lives in a mobile home with Lou Ann, who watches soap operas during sex and hangs out at the diner with Rachel because there is absolutely nothing else to do.

The lives of these characters, including Melquiades, are connected in ways that I will not reveal and that show how they all have two avenues of communication: the public and the personal. Some of the hidden connections produce ironies that only we understand, since the characters don't know as much about each other as we do.

The main line of the movie forms as Pete Perkins kidnaps Mike Norton, handcuffs him, and explains to him that Melquiades Estrada, the dead Mexican, was his friend. Melquiades often talked about his village in Mexico, Pete says, and about his wife and family. Now Mike is going to dig up Melquiades's body, and the two men are going to ride into Mexico, return the dead man to his village, and give him a proper burial.

This is a process involving a good deal of gruesome labor. I was reminded of the Peckinpah masterpiece *Bring Me the Head of Alfredo Garcia*, which is also about a journey through Mexico with a dead man—or more exactly, with his head, which suggests that the rest of the man is dead, too, and is quite enough to draw flies. Mike gags as he digs up the body, and Pete is practical about the problems they face: He fills the corpse with antifreeze.

The horseback journey of the two men is a learning experience, shall we say, for Mike the border patrolman. He begins with threats and defiance, tearfully tries to explain how the shooting of Melquiades was a stupid accident, is finally mired in sullen despair. Of their adventures along the way, two are remarkable. One involves an old blind man, living alone, who suspects his son in the city may have died. He welcomes them, offers them what he has, then makes a haunting request. The other comes when Mike is bitten by a snake, and his life is saved by a woman who has no reason to do so. This scene also has a poetic resolution.

The journey and its end will involve more discoveries and more surprises; it traverses the same kinds of doomed landscapes we picture when we read *Blood Meridian* by Cormac McCarthy. What gathers in this story of lonely men and deep impulses is a kind of grandeur; Jones plays Pete Perkins not as a hero but as a man who looks at what has happened to his friend and responds according to the opportunities at hand. He is a man who never puts two and two together without getting exactly four.

There is one word at the end of the film that carries a burden that a long speech could not have dealt with. It is a word that is also used near the beginning of the film. It contains whatever message Jones finds at the end of the journey. As for the rest, the journey of his body and the burials of Melquiades Estrada are an opportunity for all of the characters in the movie to discover who they are and what they are made of. By the end of the film no one is watching TV.

Three Kings

R, 115 m., 1999

George Clooney (Sergeant Major Archie Gates), Mark Wahlberg (Sergeant Troy Barlow), Ice Cube (Chief), Spike Jonze (Conrad Vig), Nora Dunn (Adriana Cruz), Mykelti Williamson (Colonel Horn), Jamie Kennedy (Walter), Cliff Curtis (Amir). Directed by David O. Russell and produced by Charles Roven, Paul Junger Witt, and Edward L. McDonnell. Screenplay by Russell, based on a story by John Ridley.

Three Kings is some kind of weird masterpiece, a screw-loose war picture that sends action and humor crashing head-on into one another and spinning off into political anger. It has the freedom and recklessness of Oliver Stone or Robert Altman in their mad-dog days, and a visual style that hungers for impact. A lot of movies show bodies being hit by bullets. This one sends the camera inside to show a bullet cavity filling up with bile.

David O. Russell, who wrote and directed, announces his arrival as a major player. Like the best films of Scorsese, Stone, Altman, and Tarantino, this one sings with the exhilaration of pure filmmaking, and embodies ideas in its action and characters. Most movies doze in a haze of calculation and formula; *Three Kings* is awake and hyper.

The movie takes place at the end of the Gulf War of 1991 ("Operation Desert Storm," according to the Pentagon publicists). The first words set the tone: "Are we shooting?" The truce is so new that soldiers are not sure, and a guy waving a white flag gets his head shot off in a misunderstanding. Shame. Three U.S. soldiers find an Iraqi with a piece of paper stuck where the sun don't shine. An officer issues a rubber glove and tells a private to pull it out. The guy wants two gloves, but he'll do it with one, he's told: "That's how the chain of command works."

The map shows the location of gold bullion looted from Kuwait by Saddam's troops and buried in secret bunkers. ("Bullion? Is that a little cube you put in hot water?") The three soldiers are Sergeant Troy Barlow (Mark Wahlberg), Chief Elgin (Ice Cube), and Private Conrad Vig (Spike Jonze). They attract the attention of Sergeant Major Archie Gates (George Clooney), a Special Forces veteran who decides on the spot to lead them on an unauthorized mission to steal the treasure. This involves dumping the cable news reporter he's been assigned to escort. She's Adriana Cruz, played by Nora Dunn as a Christiane Amanpour clone so driven by journalistic zeal that she is heedless of her own safety or anything else but a story. The gold, of course, would be a story.

The movie unreels with breakneck energy; it's one of those experiences like *Natural Born Killers,* where death and violence are a drumbeat in the background of every plot point. Russell's screenplay illustrates the difference between a great action picture and the others: The action grows out of the story, instead of the story being about the action. The Clooney character commandeers a Humvee and leads his men on a loony ride through the desert, where their target practice with footballs somehow reminded me of the water-skiing sequence in *Apocalypse Now.*

A political undercurrent bubbles all through the film. A truce has been declared, and Saddam's men have stopped shooting at Americans and fallen back to the secondary assignment of taming unhappy Iraqis who were expecting him to be overthrown. ("Bush told the people to rise up against Saddam. They thought they'd have our support. They didn't. Now they're being slaughtered.") Strange, the irony in

Iraqis killing Iraqis while American gold thieves benefit from the confusion.

Most Hollywood movies stereotype their Arab characters. *Three Kings* is startling in the way it shows how the world is shrinking and cultures are mixing and sharing values. Clooney and his men see a woman shot dead by Saddam's men, and later meet her husband and children. Is this man a tearful anonymous desert simpleton, grateful to his brave saviors? Not at all. "I'm a B-school graduate from Bowling Green," he tells them. "Your planes blew up all my cafés."

It's a small world, made smaller by the culture of war. The TV journalist stands calmly in the middle of danger, accepted by both sides because they think it's natural they should be on television. When the Mark Wahlberg character is captured and locked in a room, he finds it filled with the loot of war, including a lot of cell phones. When he tries to call his wife in America to give her the coordinates of his position, he has to deal with obtuse telephone operators.

Three Kings has plot structure as traditional as anything in *Gunga Din* or an *Indiana Jones* picture, and links it to a fierce political viewpoint, intelligent characters, and sudden bursts of comedy. It renews clichés. We've seen the wounded buddy who has to be dragged along through the action. But we haven't seen one with a lung wound, and a valve hammered into his chest to relieve the built-up air pressure. We've seen desert warfare before, but usually it looks scenic. Russell's cameraman, Newton Thomas Sigel, uses a grainy, bleached style that makes the movie look like it was left out in a sandstorm.

Like many natural action stars, Clooney can do what needs to be done with absolute conviction; we believe him as a leader. Wahlberg and Ice Cube seem caught up in the action, Wahlberg as a natural target, the Cube as a National Guardsman who believes he stands inside a ring of Jesus' grace. Spike Jonze, himself a director *(Being John Malkovich),* is the obligatory hillbilly, needed for the ethnic mix we always get in war movies. It's interesting how Nora Dunn's cable journalist isn't turned into a cheap parody of Amanpour, but focuses on the obsessiveness that possesses any good war correspondent.

This is David O. Russell's third picture, after

Spanking the Monkey (liked by many, unseen by me) and the inventive, unhinged comedy *Flirting With Disaster* (1997). Like that one, *Three Kings* bounces lots of distinct characters against one another and isn't afraid to punctuate the laughs with moments of true observation and emotion. This is his first movie with a studio budget, and it shows not only enthusiasm, but the control to aim that enthusiasm where he wants it to go. *Three Kings* is one of the best movies of 1999, even if I kept wondering why it wasn't named *Four Kings*.

3:10 to Yuma

R, 117 m., 2007

Russell Crowe (Ben Wade), Christian Bale (Dan Evans), Peter Fonda (Byron McElroy), Gretchen Mol (Alice Evans), Ben Foster (Charlie Prince), Dallas Roberts (Grayson Butterfield), Alan Tudyk (Doc Potter), Vinessa Shaw (Emmy Roberts), Logan Lerman (Will Evans), Kevin Durand (Tucker), Luce Rains (Marshal Weathers), Johnny Whitworth (Tommy Darden), Benjamin Petry (Mark Evans). Directed by James Mangold and produced by Cathy Konrad. Screenplay by Halsted Welles, Michael Brandt, Derek Haas, based on a short story by Elmore Leonard.

James Mangold's *3:10 to Yuma* restores the wounded heart of the Western, and rescues it from the morass of pointless violence. The Western in its glory days was often a morality play, a story about humanist values penetrating the lawless anarchy of the frontier. It still follows that tradition in films like Eastwood's *Unforgiven,* but the audience's appetite for morality plays and Westerns seems to be fading. Here the quality of the acting, and the thought behind the film, make it seem like a vanguard of something new, even though it's a remake of a good movie fifty years old.

The plot is so easily told that Elmore Leonard originally wrote it as a short story. A man named Dan Evans (Christian Bale), who lost a leg in the Civil War, has come to the Arizona territory to try his luck at ranching. It's going badly, made worse by a neighboring bully who wants to force him off his land. The territory still fears Indian raids, and just as much the lawless gang led by Ben Wade (Russell Crowe), which sticks up stagecoaches, robs banks, casually murders people, and outguns any opposition. Through

a series of developments that seem almost dictated by fate, Dan Evans finds himself as part of a posse sworn in to escort Wade, captured and handcuffed, to the nearby town of Contention, where the 3:10 P.M. train has a cell in its mail car that will transport Wade to the prison in Yuma and a certain death sentence.

Both Dan and Ben have elements in their characters that come under test in this adventure. Dan fears he has lost the confidence of his wife Alice (Gretchen Mol) and teenage son Will (Logan Lerman), who doubt he can make the ranch work. Still less does Alice see why her transplanted Eastern husband should risk his life as a volunteer. The son Will, who has practically memorized dime novels about Ben Wade, idealizes the outlaw, and when Dan realizes the boy has followed the posse, he orders him to return home. "He ain't following you," Wade says. "He's following me."

That's an insight into Wade. He plays his persona like a performance. He draws, reads, philosophizes, and is incomparably smarter than the scum in his gang. Having spent untold time living on the run with them, he may actually find it refreshing to spend time with Dan, even as his captive. Eventually the two men end up in a room in the Contention Hotel, overlooking the street, in earshot of the train whistle, surrounded outside by armed men who want to rescue Ben or kill him.

These general outlines also describe the 1957 version of *3:10 to Yuma,* directed by Delmer Daves, starring Glenn Ford and Van Heflin in the roles of the rancher and the outlaw. The movie, with its railroad timetable, followed the slowly advancing clock in *High Noon* (1952) and was compared to it; when I saw it in 35 mm at Telluride in the 1980s, I thought it was better than *High Noon,* not least because of the personality shifts it involves.

Mangold's version is better still than the 1957 original, because it has better actors with more thought behind their dialogue. Christian Bale plays not simply a noble hero, but a man who has avoided such risks as he now takes, and is almost at a loss to explain why he is bringing a killer to justice, except that having been mistreated and feeling unable to provide for his family, he is fed up and here he takes his stand. Crowe, on the other hand, plays not merely a merciless killer, although he is that, too, but a man also capable of surprising himself. He is too intelligent to have only one standard behavior that must fit all situations and is perhaps bored of having that expected of him.

Westerns used to be the showcases of great character actors, of whom I was lucky enough to meet Dub Taylor, Jack Elam, Chill Wills Ben Johnson, and, when she wasn't doing a million other things, Shelley Winters. *3:10 to Yuma* has two roles that need a special character flavor, and fills them perfectly. Peter Fonda plays McElroy, a professional bounty hunter who would rather claim the price on Ben Wade's head than let the government execute him for free. And Ben Foster plays Charlie Prince, the second-in-command of Wade's gang, who seems half in love with Wade, or maybe Charlie's half-aware that he's all in love. Wade would know which, and wouldn't care, except as material for his study of human nature.

Locked in the hotel room, surrounded by death for one or the other, the two men begin to talk. Without revealing anything of the plot, let me speculate that each has found the first man he has met in years who is his equal in conversation. Crowe and Bale play this dialogue so precisely that it never reveals itself for what it really is, a process of mutual insight. One test of a great actor is the ability to let dialogue do its work invisibly, something you can also see in *In the Valley of Elah* with Tommy Lee Jones and Charlize Theron. Too many actors are like the guy who laughs at his own joke and then tells it to you again.

James Mangold first came into view with an extraordinary movie named *Heavy* (1995). His *Walk the Line* (2005) won an Oscar for Reese Witherspoon. To remake *3:10 to Yuma* seems an odd choice after such other modern films as *Girl, Interrupted,* but the movie itself proves he had a good reason for choosing it. In hard times, Americans have often turned to the Western to re-set their compasses. In very hard times, it takes a very good Western. Attend well to Ben Wade's last words in this movie, and who he says them to, and why.

Three Times

NO MPAA RATING, 130 m., 2006

Shu Qi (May/Ah Mei/Jing), Chang Chen (Chen/Mr. Chang/Zhen). Directed by Hou Hsiao-hsien and produced by Hua-fu Chang, Wen-Ying Huang, and Ching-Song Liao. Screenplay by Chu Tien-wen.

Three stories about a man and a woman, all three using the same actors. Three years: 1966, 1911, 2005. Three varieties of love: unfulfilled, mercenary, meaningless. All photographed with such visual beauty that watching the movie is like holding your breath so the butterfly won't stir.

The director is Hou Hsiao-hsien, from Taiwan, and this probably will be the first of his seventeen films you've seen. "The movie distribution system of North America is devoted to maintaining a wall between you and Hou Hsiao-hsien," I wrote after seeing this film at Cannes 2005. Here is a factoid from IMDb.com: "Of the ten films that Hou Hsiao-hsien directed between 1980 and 1989, seven received best film or best director awards from prestigious international film festivals. In a 1988 worldwide critics' poll, Hou was championed as one of the three directors most crucial to the future of cinema."

His subject in *Three Times* is our yearning to love and be loved, and the way the world casually dismisses it. His first story, "A Time for Love," set in 1966, involves Chen (Chang Chen), a soldier on his way to the army, who falls in love with the hostess of a pool hall (Shu Qi). The camera perfectly composes the room and the light pouring in from an open door, and the woman, named May, moves gracefully and without hurry to rack the balls, arrange the cues, serve the customers. Does she like Chen? I think she does. When he gets leave, he hurries back to the pool hall, but she is gone. On the sound track, Hou uses the 1959 recording by the Platters of "Smoke Gets in Your Eyes." That is the song that tells us, "They said, some day you'll find, all who love are blind."

In the second story, "A Time for Freedom," set in 1911, the woman is named Ah Mei, and she is a prostitute in a brothel. The man, named Chang, often visits her, and between them a friendship and comfort grows. He is very filled with his own importance and has plans to reform the world, although perhaps he might reflect that his reforms might start by freeing Ah Mei from the brothel. She begins to love him. He loves her, too, I think, but all who love are blind. She never lets him see how she feels. Only we see. The movie is shot like a silent film, although with a fluid moving camera the real films of 1911 certainly lacked. In some sort of accommodation with the rules, Ah Mei cannot be heard to speak in this story, but she can be heard to sing.

The third story, "A Time for Youth," takes place in the present, in modern Taipei. The characters are named Jing and Zhen. She is a pop singer. He works as a photographer. She has a female lover but neglects her while falling in love with the man. In each of the three films, the woman is a professional performer (hostess, prostitute, singer), and the man, in one way or another, is a client. Perhaps the message is that if people meet in a way involving money and their jobs, they are not free to see each other with the perfect clarity required by love. "When your heart's on fire, you must realize, smoke gets in your eyes."

There isn't any deep message in this film. Love never has any deep message. Meryl Streep once said that every good actor knows that the statement "I love you" is a question. We send our love out into the world hoping it will not be laughed at or destroyed. We trust the one we love to accept it. In these stories, acceptance doesn't come with the territory. The pool hall hostess meets a lot of pool players every day. Yes, Chen is nice enough, but when she gets a new job, she doesn't wait for him. The prostitute sees a lot of men. When she falls for Chang, he doesn't notice because he sees himself as her client. And the modern couple are so wrapped up in overlapping relationships and a running parallel life on cell phones that they can barely deal with each other at all.

More than three centuries ago, Andrew Marvell wrote a poem named *To His Coy Mistress*, in which he said they would be free to love, "Had we but world enough, and time." I think these three couples have world enough and time, but the woman in the first, the man in the second, and both in the third are not willing to accept happiness. They can't even see it's there for the having.

This observation is as shallow as a popular song. Maybe there isn't any deeper level. Most of the things we really believe about love are stated most simply and unforgettably in song

lyrics. The lives in *Three Times* are not tragedies, unless the tragedy is that they never become the lives they could have been. Hou Hsiao-hsien shows us people who could make each other happy and be happy themselves, and he watches them miss their chance. "And yet today, my love has gone away. I am without my love."

3 Women
PG, 125 m., 1977

Sissy Spacek (Pinky), Shelley Duvall (Millie), Janice Rule (Willie), Robert Fortier (Edgar), Ruth Nelson (Mrs. Rose), John Cromwell (Mr. Rose), Craig Richard Nelson (Dr. Maas), Maysie Hoy (Doris). Directed, produced, and written by Robert Altman.

Robert Altman's *3 Women* is, on the one hand, a straightforward portrait of life in a godforsaken California desert community, and, on the other, a mysterious exploration of human personalities. Its specifics are so real you can almost touch them, and its conclusion so surreal we can supply our own.

The community exists somewhere in Southern California, that uncharted continent of discontent and restlessness. Some of its people have put themselves down in a place that contains, so far as we can see, a spa where old people take an arthritis cure, a Western-style bar with a shooting range out back, and a singles residential motel with a swimming pool that has the most unsettling murals on its bottom.

Into this outpost one day comes Pinky (Sissy Spacek), a child-woman so naive, so open, so willing to have enthusiasm, that in another century she might have been a saint, a strange one. She takes a job at the spa and is instructed in her duties by Millie (Shelley Duvall), who is fascinated by the incorrect belief that the men in town are hot for her. Millie recruits Pinky as a roommate in the motel.

This whole stretch of the film—the first hour—is a funny, satirical, and sometimes sad study of the community and its people, who have almost all failed at something else, somewhere else. The dominant male is Edgar (Robert Fortier), a onetime stuntman, now a boozer with a beer bottle permanently in his hand. He's married to Willie (Janice Rule), who never speaks, and is pregnant, and is painting the murals. It's all terrifically new to Pinky: Drinking a beer (which she does as if just discovering the principle of a glass), or moving into Millie's apartment (which she solemnly declares to be the most beautiful place she's ever seen).

Then the film arrives at its center point, one of masked sexual horror. Millie comes home with Edgar and throws Pinky out of their bedroom, and Pinky tries to commit suicide by jumping into the pool. She survives, but as she recovers the film moves from realism to a strange, haunted psychological landscape in which, somehow, Pinky and Millie exchange personalities. 3 Women isn't Altman out of Freud via Psychology Today, and so the movie mercifully doesn't attempt to explain what's happened in logical terms (any explanation would be disappointing, I think, compared to the continuing mystery). Somehow we feel what's happened, though, even if we can't explain it in so many words.

The movie's been compared to Bergman's Persona, another film in which women seem to share personalities, and maybe Persona, also so mysterious when we first see it, helps point the way. But I believe Altman has provided his own signposts, in two important scenes, one at the beginning, one at the end, that mirror one another. Millie, teaching Pinky how to exercise the old folks' legs in the hot baths, places Pinky's feet on her stomach and moves them back and forth, just as Pinky sees the apparition of two twins on the other side of the pool.

Later, when the older woman, Willie, is in labor, Millie places her legs in the same way and moves them in the same way, trying to assist the delivery. But the baby is stillborn, and so are the male-female connections in this small society. And so the women symbolically give birth to each other, around and around in a circle, just as (Altman himself suggests) the end of the picture could be seen as the moment just before its beginning.

The movie's story came to Altman during a dream, he's said, and he provides it with a dreamlike tone. The plot connections, which sometimes make little literal sense, do seem to connect emotionally, viscerally, as all things do in dreams. To act in a story like this must be a great deal more difficult than performing straightforward narrative, but Spacek and Duvall go through their changes so well that it's eerie, and unforgettable. So is the film.

Titanic

PG-13, 194 m., 1997

Leonardo DiCaprio (Jack Dawson), Kate Winslet (Rose DeWitt Bukater), Billy Zane (Cal Hockley), Kathy Bates (Molly Brown), Bill Paxton (Brock Lovett), Gloria Stuart (Rose Calvert), Frances Fisher (Ruth DeWitt Bukater), Bernard Hill (Captain E. J. Smith), David Warner (Spicer Lovejoy), Victor Garber (Thomas Andrews), Jonathan Hyde (Bruce Ismay). Directed by James Cameron and produced by Cameron and Jon Landau. Screenplay by Cameron.

Like a great iron Sphinx on the ocean floor, the Titanic faces still toward the West, interrupted forever on its only voyage. We see it in the opening shots of Titanic, encrusted with the silt of eighty-five years; a remote-controlled TV camera snakes its way inside, down corridors and through doorways, showing us staterooms built for millionaires and inherited by crustaceans.

These shots strike precisely the right note; the ship calls from its grave for its story to be told, and if the story is made of showbiz and hype, smoke and mirrors—well, so was the Titanic. She was "the largest moving object created by man," a character boasts. There is a shot of her, early in the film, sweeping majestically beneath the camera from bow to stern, nearly nine hundred feet long and "unsinkable," it was claimed, until an iceberg made an irrefutable reply.

James Cameron's 194-minute, $200 million film of the tragic voyage is in the tradition of the great Hollywood epics. It is flawlessly crafted, intelligently constructed, strongly acted, and spellbinding. If its story stays well within the traditional formulas for such pictures, well, you don't choose the most expensive film ever made as your opportunity to reinvent the wheel.

We know before the movie begins that certain things must happen. We must see the Titanic sail and sink, and be convinced we are looking at a real ship. There must be a human story—probably a romance—involving a few of the passengers. There must be vignettes involving some of the rest, and a subplot involving the arrogance and pride of the ship's builders—and perhaps also their courage and dignity. And there must be a reenactment of the ship's terrible death throes; it took two and a half hours to sink, so that everyone aboard had time to know what was happening, and to consider his actions.

All of those elements are present in Cameron's *Titanic*, weighted and balanced like ballast, so that the film always seems in proportion. The ship was made out of models (large and small), visual effects, and computer animation. You know intellectually that you're not looking at a real ocean liner—but the illusion is convincing and seamless. The special effects don't call inappropriate attention to themselves, but get the job done.

The human story involves an eighteen-year-old woman named Rose DeWitt Bukater (Kate Winslet) who is sailing to what she sees as her own personal doom: She has been forced by her penniless mother to become engaged to marry a rich, supercilious snob named Cal Hockley (Billy Zane), and so bitterly does she hate this prospect that she tries to kill herself by jumping from the ship. She is saved by Jack Dawson (Leonardo DiCaprio), a brash kid from steerage class, and of course they will fall in love during the brief time left to them.

The screenplay tells their story in a way that unobtrusively shows off the ship. Jack is invited to join Rose's party at dinner in the first-class dining room, and later, fleeing from Cal's manservant, Lovejoy (David Warner), they find themselves first in the awesome engine room, with pistons as tall as churches, and then at a rousing Irish dance in the crowded steerage. (At one point Rose gives Lovejoy the finger; did young ladies do that in 1912?) Their exploration is intercut with scenes from the command deck, where the captain (Bernard Hill) consults with Andrews (Victor Garber), the ship's designer, and Ismay (Jonathan Hyde), the White Star Line's managing director.

Ismay wants the ship to break the transatlantic speed record. He is warned that icebergs may have floated into the hazardous northern crossing, but is scornful of danger. The *Titanic* can easily break the speed record, but is too massive to turn quickly at high speed; there is an agonizing sequence that almost seems to play in slow motion, as the ship strains and shudders to turn away from an iceberg in its path, and fails.

We understand exactly what is happening at that moment because of an ingenious story technique by Cameron, who frames and explains the entire voyage in a modern story. The opening shots of the real *Titanic*, we are told, are obtained during an expedition led by Brock Lovett (Bill Paxton), a documentary filmmaker. He seeks precious jewels but finds a nude drawing of a young girl. In England, an ancient woman sees the drawing on TV and recognizes herself. This is Rose (Gloria Stuart), still alive at 101. She visits Paxton and shares her memories ("I can still smell the fresh paint"). And he shows her scenes from his documentary, including a computer simulation of the *Titanic*'s last hours—which doubles as a briefing for the audience. By the time the ship sinks, we already know what is happening and why, and the story can focus on the characters while we effortlessly follow the stages of the *Titanic*'s sinking.

Movies like this are not merely difficult to make at all, but almost impossible to make well. The technical difficulties are so daunting that it's a wonder when the filmmakers are also able to bring the drama and history into proportion. I found myself convinced by both the story and the saga. The setup of the love story is fairly routine, but the payoff—how everyone behaves as the ship is sinking—is wonderfully written, as passengers are forced to make impossible choices. Even the villain, played by Zane, reveals a human element at a crucial moment (despite everything, damn it all, he does love the girl).

The image from the *Titanic* that has haunted me, ever since I first read the story of the great ship, involves the moments right after it sank. The night sea was quiet enough so that cries for help carried easily across the water to the lifeboats, which drew prudently away. Still dressed up in the latest fashions, hundreds froze and drowned. What an extraordinary position to find yourself in after spending all that money for a ticket on an unsinkable ship.

To Live and Die in L.A.

R, 110 m., 1985

William L. Petersen (Richard Chance), Willem Dafoe (Eric Masters), John Pankow (John Vukovich), Debra Feuer (Bianca Torres), John Turturro (Carl Cody), Darlanne Fluegel (Ruth Lanier), Dean Stockwell (Bob Grimes), Robert Downey (Thomas Bateman). Directed by William Friedkin and produced by Irving H. Levin. Screenplay by Gerald Petievich and Friedkin.

In the hierarchy of great movie chase sequences, the recent landmarks include the chases under the Brooklyn elevated tracks in *The French Connection,* down the hills of San Francisco in *Bullitt,* and through the Paris Metro in *Diva.* Those chases were not only thrilling in their own right, but they reflected the essence of the cities where they took place. Now comes William Friedkin, director of *The French Connection,* with a movie that contains a second chase that belongs on that short list. The movie is set in Los Angeles, and so of course the chase centers around the freeway system.

To Live and Die in L.A. is a law enforcement movie, sort of. It's about Secret Service agents who are on the trail of a counterfeiter who has eluded the law for years, and who flaunts his success. At one point, when undercover agents are negotiating a deal with the counterfeiter in his expensive health club, he boasts, "I've been coming to this gym three times a week for five years. I'm an easy guy to find. People know they can trust me."

Meanwhile, he's asking for a down payment on a sale of bogus bills, and the down payment is larger than the Secret Service can authorize. So, Richard Chance (William L. Petersen), the hot-dog special agent who's the hero of the movie, sets up a dangerous plan to steal the advance money from another crook, and uses it to buy the bogus paper and bust the counterfeiter.

Neat. The whole plot is neat, revolving around a few central emotions—friendship, loyalty, arrogance, anger. By the time the great chase sequence arrives, it isn't just a novelty, tacked onto a movie where it doesn't fit. It's part of the plot. The Secret Service agents bungle *their* crime, the cops come in pursuit, and the chase unfolds in a long, dazzling ballet of timing, speed, and imagination.

The great chases are rarely just chases. They involve some kind of additional element—an unexpected vehicle, an unusual challenge, a strange setting. The car-train chase in *The French Connection* was a masterstroke. In *Diva,* the courier rode his motor scooter into one subway station and out another, bouncing up and down the stairs. Or think of John Ford's sustained stagecoach chase in *Stagecoach,* or the way Buster Keaton orchestrated *The General* so that trains chased each other through a railway system.

The masterstroke in *To Live and Die in L.A.* is that the chase isn't just on a freeway. It goes *the wrong way* down the freeway. I don't know how Friedkin choreographed this scene and I don't want to know. It probably took a lot of money and a lot of drivers. All I know is that there are high-angle shots during the chase during which you can look a long way ahead and see hundreds of cars across four lanes, all heading for the escape car which is aimed at them, full-speed. It is an amazing sequence.

The rest of the movie is also first-rate. The direction is the key. Friedkin has made some good movies (*The French Connection, The Exorcist, Sorcerer*) and some bad ones (*Cruising, Deal of the Century*). This is his comeback, showing the depth and skill of the early pictures. The central performance is by William L. Petersen, a Chicago stage actor who comes across as tough, wiry, and smart. He has some of the qualities of a Steve McQueen, with more complexity. Another strong performance in the movie is by Willem Dafoe, as the counterfeiter, cool and professional as he discusses the realities of his business.

I like movies which teach me about something, movies which have researched their subject and contain a lot of information, casually contained in between the big dramatic scenes. *To Live and Die in L.A.* seems to know a lot about counterfeiting, and also about the interior policies of the Secret Service. The film isn't just about cops and robbers, but about two systems of doing business, and how one of the systems finds a way to change itself in order to defeat the other. That's interesting. So is the chase.

Tootsie

PG, 116 m., 1982

Dustin Hoffman (Michael), Jessica Lange (Julie), Charles Durning (Les Nichols), Teri Garr (Sandy), Bill Murray (Roommate), Dabney Coleman (Ron), Doris Belack (Rita), Sydney Pollack (Agent). Directed by Pollack and produced by Dick Richards. Screenplay by Larry Gelbart.

One of the most endearing things about *Tootsie*, a movie in which Dustin Hoffman plays a middle-aged actress, is that the actress is able to carry most of her own scenes as herself—even if she weren't being played by Hoffman. *Tootsie* works as a story, not as a gimmick. It also works as a lot of other things. *Tootsie* is the kind of Movie with a capital M that they used to make in the 1940s, when they weren't afraid to mix up absurdity with seriousness, social comment with farce, and a little heartfelt tenderness right in there with the laughs. This movie gets you coming and going.

Hoffman stars as Michael Dorsey, a character maybe not unlike Hoffman himself in his younger days. Michael is a New York actor: bright, aggressive, talented—and unemployable. "You mean *nobody in New York* wants to hire me?" he asks his agent, incredulously. "I'd go farther than that, Michael," his agent says. "Nobody in Hollywood wants to hire you, either." Michael has a bad reputation for taking stands, throwing tantrums, and interpreting roles differently than the director. How to get work? He goes with a friend (Teri Garr) to an audition for a soap opera. The character is a middle-aged woman hospital administrator. When his friend doesn't get the job, Michael goes home, thinks, decides to dare, and dresses himself as a woman. And, improvising brilliantly, he gets the role.

That leads to *Tootsie*'s central question: Can a fortyish New York actor find health, happiness, and romance as a fortyish New York actress? Dustin Hoffman is actually fairly plausible as "Dorothy," the actress. If his voice isn't quite right, a southern accent allows it to squeak by. The wig and the glasses are a little too much, true, but in an uncanny way the woman played by Hoffman looks like certain actual women who look like drag queens. Dorothy might have trouble passing in Evanston, but in Manhattan, nobody gives her a second look.

Tootsie might have been content to limit itself to the complications of New York life in drag; it could have been *Victor/Victoria Visits Elaine's*. But the movie's a little more ambitious than that. Michael Dorsey finds to his interest and amusement that Dorothy begins to take on a life of her own. She's a liberated eccentric, a woman who seems sort of odd and funny at first, but grows on you and wins your admiration by standing up for what's right. One of the things that bothers Dorothy is the way the soap opera's chauvinist director (Dabney Coleman) mistreats and insults the attractive young actress (Jessica Lange) who plays Julie, a nurse on the show. Dorothy and Julie become friends and finally close confidantes. Dorothy's problem, however, is that the man inside her is gradually growing uncontrollably in love with Julie. There are other complications. Julie's father (Charles Durning), a gruff, friendly, no-nonsense sort, lonely but sweet, falls in love with Dorothy. Michael hardly knows how to deal with all of this, and his roommate (Bill Murray) isn't much help. Surveying Dorothy in one of her new outfits, he observes dryly, "Don't play hard to get."

Tootsie has a lot of fun with its plot complications; we get almost every possible variation on the theme of mistaken sexual identities. The movie also manages to make some lighthearted but well-aimed observations about sexism. It *also* pokes satirical fun at soap operas, New York show-business agents, and the Manhattan social pecking order. *And* it turns out to be a touching love story, after all—so touching that you may be surprised how moved you are at the conclusion of this comedy.

Topsy-Turvy

R, 160 m., 2000

Allan Corduner (Arthur Sullivan), Jim Broadbent (William Schwenck Gilbert), Lesley Manville (Lucy Gilbert ["Kitty"]), Ron Cook (Richard D'Oyly Carte), Timothy Spall (Richard Temple), Wendy Nottingham (Helen Lenoir), Kevin McKidd (Durward Lely), Martin Savage (George Grossmith), Shirley Henderson (Leonora Braham), Alison Steadman (Madame Leon). Directed by Mike Leigh and produced by Simon Channing-Williams. Screenplay by Leigh.

Mike Leigh's *Topsy-Turvy* is the work of a man helplessly in love with the theater. In a gloriously entertaining period piece, he tells the story of the genesis, preparation, and presentation of a comic opera—Gilbert and Sullivan's *The Mikado*—celebrating all the dreaming and hard work, personality conflict and team spirit, inspiration and mundane detail of every theatrical presentation, however inspired or inept. Every production is completely different, and they are all exactly like this.

As the movie opens, Arthur Sullivan and William Schwenck Gilbert rule the London stage. Their comic operettas, produced by the famed impresario Richard D'Oyly Carte, have even paid for the construction of the Savoy Theater—where, alas, their latest collaboration, *Princess Ida*, has flopped so badly that even Gilbert's dentist tells him it went on too long.

Sullivan, the composer, has had enough. Newly knighted by the queen, he decides it is time to compose serious operas: "This work with Gilbert is quite simply killing me." He flees to Paris and a bordello, where D'Oyly Carte tracks him down and learns that there may never be another collaboration between Gilbert (Jim Broadbent) and Sullivan (Allan Corduner). When Sullivan returns to London, he has a meeting with Gilbert, tense and studiously polite, and rejects Gilbert's latest scenario, which is as silly as all of the others: "Oh, Gilbert! You and your world of Topsy-Turvy-dom!"

The two men are quite different. Sullivan is a womanizer and dandy, Gilbert a businessman with an eagle eye for theatrical detail. One day in the middle of the impasse, his wife, Kitty (Lesley Manville), drags him to London's newly opened Japan exhibition, where he observes a Kabuki performance, sips green tea, and buys a sword that his butler nails up over the door. Not long after, as he paces his study, the sword falls down, and inspiration strikes: Gilbert races to his desk to begin writing *The Mikado*.

The world of Gilbert and Sullivan is one of whimsical goofiness, presented with rigorous attention to detail. The fun is in the tension between absurd contrivance and meticulous delivery; consider the song "I Am the Very Model of a Modern Major-General" from *The Pirates of Penzance*, which is delivered with the discipline of a metronome, but at breakneck pace.

The form itself is a poke in the eye for Victorian values: The plots and songs uphold the conventional while making it seem clearly mad.

Mike Leigh might seem to be the last of modern British directors to be attracted to the world of the Savoy operas. His films, which do not begin with finished screenplays but are "devised" by the director in collaboration with his actors, have always been about modern Britain—often about inarticulate, alienated, shy, hostile types, who are as psychologically awkward in his comedies as in his hard-edged work. His credits include *Life Is Sweet, Naked,* and *Secrets and Lies,* and nothing remotely in the same cosmos as Gilbert and Sullivan.

But think again. Leigh has worked as much in the theater as for film, and his films depend more than most on the theatrical disciplines of improvisation and rehearsal. In London his productions have often been in vest-pocket theaters where even details like printing the tickets and hiring the stagehands may not have escaped his attention. He is a man of the theater in every atom of his being, and that is why there is a direct connection between his work and Gilbert and Sullivan.

The earlier reaches of *Topsy-Turvy* resemble in broad outline other films about theater: a flop, a crisis, a vow to never work again, a sudden inspiration, a new start. All well done, but the film begins to glow when the decision is made to go ahead with *The Mikado*. This is not merely a film that goes backstage, but also one that goes into accounting ledgers, hiring practices, costume design, personnel problems, casting decisions, sex lives, and the endless detail work of rehearsal: Hours of work are needed to manufacture and perfect even a silly throwaway moment, so that it is thrown away with style and wit, instead of merely being misplaced.

My favorite scene is one in which Gilbert rehearses his actors in line readings. The actor George Grossmith (Martin Savage) expresses insufficient alarm, and Gilbert reminds him that his character is under sentence of death, "by something lingering. By either boiling oil or melted lead. Kindly bear that in mind." There is also much travail over the correct pronunciation of "corroborative."

Many of the cast members are veterans of earlier Leigh films, including the pear-shaped, pouty-lipped Timothy Spall, whose character blinks back tears as his big song seems doomed in dress rehearsal. Jim Broadbent makes a precise Gilbert, bluff and incisive, and Allan Corduner's Sullivan is a study in the partner who cannot admit that his greatness lies always in collaboration. Leigh's construction is canny as he follows big musical numbers like "Three Little Maids" from rehearsal through opening night, and the costumes and sets faithfully recreate the classic D'Oyly Carte Co. productions.

Not everyone is familiar with Gilbert and Sullivan. Do they need to be to enjoy *Topsy-Turvy*? No more, I suspect, than one needs to know all about Shakespeare to enjoy *Shakespeare in Love*—although with both films, the more you do know, the more you enjoy. The two films have been compared because both are British, both are about theatrical geniuses, both deal with theatrical lore. The difference is that *Shakespeare in Love* centers on a love story, and *Topsy-Turvy* is about love of the theater. Romantic love ages and matures. Love of the theater, it reminds us, is somehow always adolescent—heedless, passionate, guilty.

Touching the Void

NO MPAA RATING, 106 m., 2004

Brendan Mackey (Simpson), Nicholas Aaron (Yates), Joe Simpson (Himself), Simon Yates (Himself). Directed by Kevin Macdonald and produced by John Smithson. Screenplay by Simpson, based on his book.

For someone who fervently believes he will never climb a mountain, I spend an unreasonable amount of time thinking about mountain climbing. In my dreams my rope has come loose and I am falling, falling, and all the way down I am screaming: "Stupid! You're so stupid! You climbed all the way up there just so you could fall back down!"

Now there is a movie more frightening than my nightmares. *Touching the Void* is the most harrowing movie about mountain climbing I have seen, or can imagine. I've read reviews from critics who were only moderately stirred by the film (my friend Dave Kehr certainly kept his composure), and I must conclude that their dreams are not haunted as mine are.

I didn't take a single note during this film. I simply sat there before the screen, enthralled, fascinated, and terrified. Not for me the discussions about the utility of the "pseudo-documentary format," or questions about how the camera happened to be waiting at the bottom of the crevice when Simpson fell in. *Touching the Void* was, for me, more of a horror film than any actual horror film could ever be.

The movie is about Joe Simpson and Simon Yates, two Brits in their mid-twenties who determined to scale the forbidding west face of a mountain named Siula Grande, in the Peruvian Andes. They were fit and in good training, and bold enough to try the "one push" method of climbing, in which they carried all their gear with them instead of establishing caches along the route. They limited their supplies to reduce weight, and planned to go up and down quickly.

It didn't work out that way. Snowstorms slowed and blinded them. The ascent was doable, but on the way down the storms disoriented them and the drifts concealed the hazard of hidden crevices and falls. Roped together, they worked with one man always anchored, and so Yates was able to hold the rope when Simpson had a sudden fall. But it was disastrous: He broke his leg, driving the calf bone up through the knee socket. Both of them knew that a broken leg on a two-man climb, with rescue impossible, was a death sentence, and indeed Simpson tells us he was rather surprised that Yates decided to stay with him and try to get him down.

We know that Simpson survived, because the movie shows the real-life Simpson and Yates, filmed against plain backgrounds, looking straight on into the camera, remembering their adventure in their own words. We also see the ordeal reenacted by two actors (Brendan Mackey as Simpson, Nicholas Aaron as Yates), and experienced climbers are used as stunt doubles. The movie was shot on location in Peru and also in the Alps, and the climbing sequences are always completely convincing; the use of actors in those scenes is not a distraction because their faces are so bearded, frostbitten, and snow-caked that we can hardly recognize them.

Yates and Simpson had a three-hundred-foot rope. Yates's plan was to lower Simpson three hundred feet and wait for a tug on the rope. That meant Simpson had dug in and anchored himself and it was safe for Yates to climb down and repeat the process. A good method in theory, but then, after dark, in a snowstorm, Yates lowered Simpson over a precipice and left him hanging in midair over a drop of unknowable distance. Since they were out of earshot in the blizzard all Yates could know was that the rope was tight and not moving, and his feet were slipping out of the holes he had dug to brace them. After an hour or so he realized they were at an impasse. Simpson was apparently hanging helplessly in midair, Yates was slipping, and unless he cut the rope they would both surely die. So he cut the rope.

Simpson says he would have done the same thing under the circumstances, and we believe him. What we can hardly believe is what happens next, and what makes the film into an incredible story of human endurance.

If you plan to see the film—it will not disappoint you—you might want to save the rest of the review until later.

Simpson, incredibly, falls into a crevice but is slowed and saved by several snow bridges he crashes through before he lands on an ice ledge with a drop on either side. So there he is, in total darkness and bitter cold, his fuel gone so that he cannot melt snow, his lamp battery running low, and no food. He is hungry, dehydrated, and in cruel pain from the bones grinding together in his leg (two aspirins didn't help much).

It is clear Simpson cannot climb back up out of the crevice. So he eventually gambles everything on a strategy that seems madness itself, but was his only option other than waiting for death: He uses the rope to lower himself down into the unknown depths below. If the distance is more than three hundred feet, well, then, he will literally be at the end of his rope.

But there is a floor far below, and in the morning he sees light and is able, incredibly, to crawl out to the mountainside. And that is only the beginning of his ordeal. He must somehow get down the mountain and cross a plain strewn with rocks and boulders; he cannot walk but must try to hop or crawl despite the pain in his leg. That he did it is manifest, since he survived to write a book and appear in the movie. How he did it provides an experience that at times had me closing my eyes against his agony.

This film is an unforgettable experience, directed by Kevin Macdonald (who made *One Day in September*, the Oscar-winner about the 1972 Olympiad) with a kind of brutal directness and simplicity that never tries to add suspense or drama (none is needed!), but simply tells the story, as we look on in disbelief. We learn at the end that after two years of surgeries Simpson's leg was repaired, and that (but you anticipated this, didn't you?) he went back to climbing again. Learning this, I was reminded of Boss Gettys's line about Citizen Kane: "He's going to need more than one lesson." I hope to God the rest of his speech does not apply to Simpson: ". . . and he's going to get more than one lesson."

Toy Story

G, 81 m., 1995

With the voices of: Tom Hanks (Woody), Tim Allen (Buzz Lightyear), Don Rickles (Mr. Potato Head), Jim Varney (Slinky Dog), Wallace Shawn (Rex), John Ratzenberger (Hamm), Annie Potts (Bo Peep), John Morris (Andy). Directed by John Lasseter and produced by Ralph Guggenheim and Bonnie Arnold. Screenplay by Joss Whedon, Andrew Stanton, Joel Cohen, and Alec Sokolow, based on a story by Lasseter, Stanton, Pete Docter, and Joe Ranft.

Toy Story creates a universe out of a couple of kids' bedrooms, a gas station, and a stretch of suburban highway. Its heroes are toys, that come to life when nobody is watching. Its conflict is between an old-fashioned cowboy who has always been a little boy's favorite toy, and the new space ranger who may replace him. The villain is the mean kid next door who takes toys apart and puts them back together again in macabre combinations. And the result is a visionary roller-coaster ride of a movie.

For the kids in the audience, a movie like this will work because it tells a fun story, contains a lot of humor, and is exciting to watch. Older viewers may be even more absorbed, because *Toy Story*, the first feature made entirely by computer, achieves a three-dimensional reality and freedom of movement that is liberating and new. The more you know about how the movie was made, the more you respect it.

Imagine the spectacular animation of the ballroom sequence in *Beauty and the Beast* at feature length and you'll get the idea. The movie doesn't simply animate characters in front of painted backdrops; it fully animates the characters and the space they occupy, and allows its point of view to move freely around them. Computer animation has grown so skillful that sometimes you don't even notice it (the launching in *Apollo 13* took place largely within a computer). Here, you do notice it, because you're careening through space with a new sense of freedom.

Consider, for example, a scene where Buzz Lightyear, the new space toy, jumps off a bed, bounces off a ball, careens off of the ceiling, spins around on a hanging toy helicopter, and zooms into a series of loop-the-loops on a model-car racetrack. Watch Buzz, the background, and the perspective—which stretches and contracts to manipulate the sense of speed. It's an amazing ride.

I learn from the current *Wired* magazine that the movie occupied the attention of a bank of three hundred powerful Sun microprocessors, the fastest models around, which took about eight hundred thousand hours of computing time to achieve this and other scenes—at two to fifteen hours per frame. Each frame required as much as three hundred megabytes of information, which means that on my one-gigabyte hard disk, I have room for about three frames, or an eighth of a second. Of course computers are as dumb as a box of bricks if they're not well-programmed, and director John Lasseter, a pioneer in computer animation, has used offbeat imagination and high energy to program his.

But enough of this propeller-head stuff. Let's talk about the movie. Lasseter and his team open the film in a kid's bedroom, where the toys come to life when their owner is absent. Undisputed king of the toys is Woody, a cowboy with a voice by Tom Hanks. His friends include Mr. Potato Head (Don Rickles), Slinky Dog (Jim Varney), Hamm the Pig (John Ratzenberger), and Bo Peep (Annie Potts). The playroom ingeniously features famous toys from real life (which may be product placement, but who cares), including a spelling slate that does a running commentary on key developments (when Mr. Potato Head finally achieves his dream of Mrs. Potato Head, the message is "Hubba! Hubba!").

One day there's a big shakeup in this little world. The toy owner, named Andy, has a birthday. Woody dispatches all of the troops in a Bucket of Soldiers to spy on developments downstairs, and they use a Playskool walkie-talkie to broadcast developments. The most alarming: the arrival on the scene of Buzz Lightyear (Tim Allen), a space ranger.

Buzz is the most endearing toy in the movie, because he's not in on the joke. He thinks he's a real space ranger, temporarily marooned during a crucial mission, and he goes desperately to work trying to repair his spaceship—the cardboard box he came in. There's real poignancy later in the film when he sees a TV commercial for himself and realizes he's only a toy.

The plot heats up when the human family decides to move, and Woody and Buzz find themselves marooned in a gas station with no idea how to get home. (It puts a whole new spin on the situation when a toy itself says, "I'm a lost toy!")

Seeing *Toy Story*, I felt some of the same exhilaration I felt during *Who Framed Roger Rabbit*. Both movies take apart the universe of cinematic visuals and put it back together again, allowing us to see in a new way. *Toy Story* is not as inventive in its plotting or as clever in its wit as *Rabbit* or such Disney animated films as *Beauty and the Beast*; it's pretty much a buddy movie transplanted to new terrain. Its best pleasures are for the eyes. But what pleasures they are! Watching the film, I felt I was in at the dawn of a new era of movie animation, which draws on the best of cartoons and reality, creating a world somewhere in between, where space not only bends but snaps, crackles, and pops.

Traffic
R, 147 m., 2001

Michael Douglas (Robert Wakefield), Don Cheadle (Montel Gordon), Benicio Del Toro (Javier Rodriguez), Luis Guzman (Ray Castro), Erika Christensen (Caroline Wakefield), Dennis Quaid (Arnie Metzger), Catherine Zeta-Jones (Helena Ayala), Steven Bauer (Carlos Ayala), Albert Finney (Chief of Staff), James Brolin (General Ralph Landry), Jacob Vargas (Manolo Sanchez), Tomas Milian (General Arturo Salazar), Miguel Ferrer (Eduardo Ruiz). Directed by Steven

Soderbergh and produced by Edward Zwick,
Marshall Herskovitz, and Laura Bickford.
Screenplay by Stephen Gaghan.

Our laws against illegal drugs function as a price support system for the criminal drug industry. They do not stop drugs. Despite billions of dollars spent and a toll of death, addiction, crime, corruption, and lives wasted in prison, it is possible today for anyone who wants drugs to get them. "For someone my age," says a high school student in the new film *Traffic,* "it's a lot easier to get drugs than it is to get alcohol."

Who supports the drug law enforcement industry? A good many honest and sincere people, to be sure. Also politicians who may know drug laws are futile, but don't have the nerve to appear soft on the issue. And corrupt lawmen, who find drugs a lucrative source of bribes, kickbacks, and payoffs. And the drug cartels themselves, since the laws make their business so profitable. If the decriminalization of drugs were ever seriously considered in this country, the opponents would include not only high-minded public servants, but the kingpins of the illegal drug industry.

These are the conclusions I draw from *Traffic,* Steven Soderbergh's new film, which traces the drug traffic in North America from the bottom to the top of the supply chain. They may not be your conclusions. Draw your own. Soderbergh himself does not favor legalizing drugs, but believes addiction is a public health problem, not a crime. Certainly drugs breed crime—addicts steal because they must—and a more rational policy would result in a lower crime rate and a safer society.

The movie tells several parallel stories, which sometimes link but usually do not. We meet two Mexican drug enforcement cops. Two San Diego DEA agents. A midlevel wholesaler who imports drugs from Mexico. A high-level drug millionaire who seems to be a respectable businessman. A federal judge who is appointed the U.S. drug czar. And his teenage daughter, who becomes addicted to cocaine and nearly destroys her life. We also meet a Mexican general who has made it his goal to destroy a drug cartel—but not for the reasons he claims. And we see how cooperation between Mexican and American authorities is compromised because key people on both sides may be corrupt, and betray secrets.

The movie is inspired by a five-part *Masterpiece Theater* series named *Traffik,* which ran ten years ago and traced the movement of heroin from the poppy fields of Turkey to the streets of Europe. The story in North America is much the same, which is why adapting this material was so depressingly easy. At every level, the illegal drug business is about making money. If there is anything more lucrative than an addictive substance that is legal, like alcohol or tobacco, it is one that is illegal, like drugs—because the suppliers aren't taxed or regulated and have no overhead for advertising, packaging, insurance, employee benefits, or quality control. Drugs are produced by subsistence-level peasants and move through a distribution chain of street sellers; costs to the end user are kept low to encourage addiction.

Soderbergh's film uses a level-headed approach. It watches, it observes, it does not do much editorializing. The hopelessness of anti-drug measures is brought home through practical scenarios, not speeches and messages—except for a few. One of the most heartfelt comes from a black man who observes that at any given moment in America, one hundred thousand white people are driving through black neighborhoods looking for drugs, and a dealer who can make $200 in two hours is hardly motivated to seek other employment.

The key performance in the movie is by Michael Douglas, as Robert Wakefield, an Ohio judge tapped by the White House as the nation's new drug czar. He holds all the usual opinions, mouths all the standard platitudes, shares all the naive assumptions—including his belief that he can destroy one of the Mexican cartels by cooperating with the Mexican authorities. This is true in theory, but in practice his information simply provides an advantage for one cartel over the other.

Wakefield is a good man. His daughter, Caroline (Erika Christensen), is an honor student. One night at a party with other teenagers, she tries cocaine and likes it, very much. We see how easily the drug is available to her, how quickly she gets hooked, how swiftly she falls through the safety nets of family and society. This is the social cost of addiction, and the rationale for passing laws against drugs—

but we see that it happens *despite* the laws, and that without a profit motive drugs might not be so easily available in her circle.

In Mexico, we meet two hardworking cops in the drug wars, played by Benicio Del Toro and Jacob Vargas, who intercept a big drug shipment but then are themselves intercepted by troops commanded by an army general (Tomas Milian), who is sort of the J. Edgar Hoover of Mexican drug enforcement. In California, we meet a middleman (Miguel Ferrer) who imports and distributes drugs, and two federal agents (Don Cheadle and Luis Guzman) who are on his trail. And we meet the top executive for this operation, a respectable millionaire (Steven Bauer) and his socialite wife (Catherine Zeta-Jones), who has no idea where her money comes from.

Soderbergh's story, from a screenplay by Stephen Gaghan, cuts between these characters so smoothly that even a fairly complex scenario remains clear and charged with tension. Like Martin Scorsese's *GoodFellas*, *Traffic* is fascinating at one level simply because it shows how things work—how the drugs are marketed, how the laws are sidestepped. The problem is like a punching bag. You can hammer it all day and still it hangs there, impassive, unchanged.

The movie is powerful precisely because it doesn't preach. It is so restrained that at one moment—the judge's final speech—I wanted one more sentence, making a point, but the movie lets us supply that thought for ourselves. And the facts make their own argument: This war is not winnable on the present terms, and takes a greater toll in human lives than the drugs themselves. The drug war costs $19 billion a year, but scenes near the end of the film suggest that more addicts are helped by two free programs, Alcoholics Anonymous and Narcotics Anonymous, than by all the drug troops put together.

The Tree of Knowledge

NO MPAA RATING, 101 m., 1982

Eva Gram Scholdager (Elin), Line Arlien-Soborg (Anne-Mette), Jan Johansen (Nils-Ole), Marian Wendelbo (Elsebeth). Directed by Nils Malmros. Screenplay by Frederick Cryer and Malmros.

The Tree of Knowledge is the truest and most moving film I have ever seen about the experience of puberty, about the little joys and great heartbreaks of the crucial first years of adolescence. It is also one of this year's best films on any subject—a creative act of memory about exactly what it was like to be thirteen in 1953.

The movie comes from Denmark, and yet it didn't feel "foreign" to me. At first I was aware that I was watching a Danish picture, and then the universal insights of the story began to reach me so directly that I was just watching a movie about kids anywhere—it could have been made about an American suburb.

That reminded me of the observation by Francois Truffaut (whose own *Small Change* is another of the great films about childhood) that American and European kids are about the same until their later teen years. Only then do cultural and political considerations begin to outweigh the universal language and experience of puberty.

This film is really something. It was shot over a period of two years, so we observe these Danish teenagers as they grow up physically. And the movie is acutely sensitive to their psychic growing pains. The writer and director, Nils Malmros, follows a schoolroom full of bright kids through two school years observing them in classrooms, at home, in school activities, and in weekend parties where they fumble their way into adolescence.

The movie remembers school vividly. We watch a geometry theorem being proved on a blackboard, a spitball fight breaking up a slide show, chorus practice, and a P. E. class. But what really comes alive in this movie is the painful process by which children become acutely aware of their sexual roles. One of the girls in the class develops a little more quickly than the others, and her breasts represent a threat that the others react to by making fun of her. Sides are chosen and cliques are formed, and the question of who is invited to whose party becomes a big deal.

Meanwhile, other couples are forming and dissolving, as these kids get crushes on the opposite sex and form intense friendships with their own sex. The movie remembers everything: the whispers, the giggles, and heartbreaking moments when parents simply do not understand. The most painful moment in the film comes when Elin, the outsider, is given a silver dollar by a boy a year older, whose father has taken a job in America. The dollar is a token of friendship and she treasures it, but her parents order her to send it back, and her mother asks the unforgivable question, "What did you do to get it?"

The movie's performances are unaffected, spontaneous, and cheerful; I may have made the movie sound depressing, but it isn't, really—not any more depressing than being fourteen and not being invited to any parties.

The Trial

NO MPAA RATING, 118 m., 1963 (rereleased 2000)

Anthony Perkins (Joseph K), Jeanne Moreau (Miss Burstner), Orson Welles (Advocate), Madeline Robinson (Mrs. Brubach), Elsa Martinelli (Hilda), Suzanne Flon (Miss Pittl), Akim Tamiroff (Bloch), Romy Schneider (Leni). Directed by Welles and produced by Alexander Salkind. Screenplay by Welles, based on the book by Franz Kafka.

I was once involved in a project to convince Orson Welles to record a commentary track for *Citizen Kane*. Seemed like a good idea, but not to the great one, who rumbled that he had made a great many films other than *Kane* and was tired of talking about it.

One he might have talked about was *The Trial* (1963), his version of the Kafka story about a man accused of—something, he knows not what. It starred Anthony Perkins in his squirmy post-*Psycho* mode, it had a baroque visual style, and it was one of the few times, after *Kane*, when Welles was able to get his vision onto the screen intact. For years the negative of the film was thought to be lost, but then it was rediscovered and restored.

The world of the movie is like a nightmare, with its hero popping from one surrealistic situation to another. Water towers open into file rooms, a woman does laundry while through the door a trial is under way, and huge trunks are dragged across empty landscapes and then back again. The black-and-white photography shows Welles's love of shadows, extreme camera angles, and spectacular sets. He shot it mostly inside the Gare d'Orsay in Paris, which, after it closed as a train station and before it was reborn as a museum, offered vast spaces; the office where Perkins's character works consists of rows of desks and typists extending almost to infinity, like a similar scene in the silent film *The Crowd*.

Franz Kafka published his novel in Prague in 1925; it reflected his own paranoia, but it was prophetic, foreseeing Stalin's Gulag and Hitler's Holocaust, in which innocent people wake up one morning to discover they are guilty of being themselves. It is a tribute to his vision that the word "Kafkaesque" has, like "catch-22," moved beyond the work to describe things we all see in the world.

Anthony Perkins is a good choice to play Joseph K, the bureaucrat who awakens to find strange men in his room, men who treat him as a suspect and yet give him no information. Perkins could turn in an instant from ingratiating smarminess to anger, from supplication to indignation, his voice barking out ultimatums and then suddenly going high-pitched and stuttery. And watch his body language as he goes into his confiding mode, hitching closer to other characters, buddy-style, looking forward to neat secrets.

The film follows his attempts to discover what he is charged with, and how he can defend himself. Every Freudian slip is used against him (he refers to a "pornograph player," and a man in a black suit carefully notes that down). He finds himself in a courtroom where the audience is cued by secret signs from the judge. He petitions the court's official portrait painter, who claims he can fix cases and obtain a "provisional acquittal." And in the longest sequence, he visits the cavernous home of the Advocate, played by Welles as an ominous sybarite who spends much of his time in bed, smoking cigars and being tended by his mistress (Romy Schneider).

The Advocate has obscure powers in matters such as Joseph K is charged with, whatever they are. He has had a pathetic little man living in his maid's room for a long time, hoping for news on his case, kissing the Advocate's hand, falling to his knees. He would like Joseph to behave in the same way. The Advocate's home reaches out in all directions, like a loft, factory, and junk shop, illuminated by hundreds of guttering candles, decorated by portraits of judges, littered with so many bales of old legal papers that one shot looks like the closing scene in *Citizen Kane*. But neither here nor elsewhere can Joseph come to grips with his dilemma.

Perkins was one of those actors everyone thought was gay. He kept his sexuality private, and used his nervous style of speech and movement to suggest inner disconnects. From an article by Edward Guthmann in the *San Francisco Chronicle*, I learn that Welles confided to his friend Henry Jaglom that he knew Perkins was a homosexual, "and used that quality in Perkins to suggest another texture in Joseph K, a fear of exposure."

"The whole homosexuality thing—using Perkins that way—was incredible for that time," Jaglom told Guthmann. "It was intentional on Orson's part: He had these three gorgeous women (Jeanne Moreau, Romy Schneider, Elsa Martinelli) trying to seduce this guy, who was completely repressed and incapable of responding." That provides an additional key to the film, which could be interpreted as a nightmare in which women make demands Joseph is uninterested in meeting, while bureaucrats in black coats follow him everywhere with obscure threats of legal disaster.

But there is also another way of looking at *The Trial*, and that is to see it as autobiographical. After *Citizen Kane* (1941) and *The Magnificent Ambersons* (1942, a masterpiece with its ending hacked to pieces by the studio), Welles seldom found the freedom to make films when and how he desired. His life became a wandering from one place to another. Beautiful women rotated through his beds. He was reduced to a supplicant who begged financing from wealthy but maddening men. He was never able to find out exactly what crime he had committed that made him "unbankable" in Hollywood. Because Welles plays the Advocate, there is a tendency to think the character is inspired by him, but I can think of another suspect: Alexander Salkind, producer of *The Trial* and much later of the *Superman* movies, who like the Advocate, liked people to beg for money and power which, in fact, he did not always have.

Seen in this restored version (available on video from Milestone), *The Trial* is above all a visual achievement, an exuberant use of camera placement and movement and inventive lighting. Study the scene where the screaming girls chase Joseph K up the stairs to the painter's studio and peer at him through the slats of the walls, and you will see what Richard Lester saw before he filmed the screaming girls in *A Hard Day's Night* and had them peer at the Beatles through the slats of a railway luggage car.

The ending is problematical. Mushroom clouds are not Kafkaesque because they represent a final conclusion, and in Kafka's world nothing ever concludes. But then comes another ending: the voice of Orson Welles, speaking the end credits, placing his own claim on every frame of the film, and we wonder, is this his way of telling us *The Trial* is more than ordinarily personal? He was a man who made the greatest film ever made, and was never forgiven for it.

Tristana

NO MPAA RATING, 96 m., 1970

Catherine Deneuve (Tristana), Fernando Rey (Don Lope), Franco Nero (Horacio), Lola Gaos (Saturna). Directed by Luis Buñuel and produced by Buñuel and Robert Dorfman. Screenplay by Julio Alejandro and Buñuel.

Luis Buñuel's *Tristana* is a haunting study of a human relationship in which the power changes hands. Power over human lives is a lifelong theme of Buñuel, that most sadomasochistic of directors, and *Tristana* is his most explicit study of the subject. Not his best, but his most explicit.

Consider: Don Lope, a feisty middle-aged intellectual and atheist, sees his chance when the beautiful young Tristana (Catherine Deneuve) is orphaned. As the girl's guardian, he takes her into his household and (in what seems like no time at all) into his bed. While ravishing her, he excuses himself by rationalizing that she'd fare worse on the streets.

The girl is repelled by the old man's sexual advances, and that provides the key to her character later in the film. She falls in love with a handsome young artist who eventually takes her away and marries her. But then she develops a tumor and her leg must be amputated; she decides to leave the artist and come back again to Don Lope's household.

All that has gone before has been preparation for what happens now, as Tristana has revenge on the man who took her virginity. He is older now, weaker, and has been reduced to playing cards with priests. He does it not because he's lost his atheism but because he craves their company (and they humor him with an eye to gaining his inheritance for the church). Tristana becomes the dominant personality in the household.

Handled by an ordinary director, or even by a great director with no sympathy for the material, this story could have been embarrassingly melodramatic. I was about to say it could have been disgusting—but, of course, it is disgusting, and that was Buñuel's purpose. The subject matter came out of his own lifelong obsessions. His favorite subjects were sadomasochism and anticlericalism ever since his first movie with Salvador Dali, *Un Chien Andalou* (1928), and in the late flowering of his work in his seventies he became undoubtedly the dirtiest old man of genius the cinema has ever produced.

Certain of his scenes have an almost hypnotic power, because Buñuel himself finds their images so fascinating. The vision of Don Lope's amputated head, used as a clapper on a church bell, reportedly refers to a recurring dream Buñuel (that lifelong atheist) has about himself. The long scene where Don Lope plays cards while the one-legged Tristana walks back and forth on her crutches in the upstairs hallway also has a dreamlike quality.

Again, Buñuel introduces a mute young servant into the household, and Tristana tantalizes him mercilessly. He desires her; she repels him coldly, only to reveal herself to him when she is on her balcony and he in the garden. He draws back quickly into the shrubbery. Buñuel's Freudianism is so explicit as to be almost embarrassing, but you never laugh, because he takes it so seriously. That's why his films work—because they're himself, they're personal. Buñuel is in control of every shot and every scene, and he is having at our subconscious like a surgeon.

A few great directors have the ability to draw us into their dream world, into their personalities and obsessions and fascinate us with them for a short time. This is the highest level of escapism the movies can provide for us—just as our elementary identification with a hero or a heroine was the lowest. As children, we went to Saturday matinees and for an afternoon we were cowboys and Indians. As adults, there are more intellectual routes to escapism. A powerful director like Buñuel (or Bergman, Fellini, Hitchcock, or Satyajit Ray) can open up his mind to us, the way an actress can open up her eyes. It is an experience worth having.

Tristram Shandy: A Cock and Bull Story
R, 91 m., 2006

Steve Coogan (Tristram Shandy/Walter/Steve), Rob Brydon (Toby Shandy/Rob), Raymond Waring (Corporal Trim), Dylan Moran (Dr. Slop/Dylan), Keeley Hawes (Elizabeth Shandy/Keeley), Gillian Anderson (Widow Wadman/Gillian), Shirley Henderson (Susannah/Shirley), Jeremy Northam (Mark), Naomie Harris (Jennie), Kelly Macdonald (Jenny). Directed by Michael Winterbottom and produced by Andrew Eaton. Screenplay by Frank Cottrell Boyce and Winterbottom, based on the book *The Life and Opinions of Tristram Shandy, Gentleman* by Laurence Sterne.

I started reading Laurence Sterne's *The Life and Opinions of Tristram Shandy, Gentleman* in 1965, and I intend to finish it any day now. That is true, and also a joke (a small one) involving a novel about procrastination. *Tristram Shandy* begins with its hero about to be born and becomes so sidetracked by digressions that the story ends shortly after his birth. Perhaps Sterne considered writing a sequel describing the rest of Tristram's life but never got around to it (smaller joke).

Now comes *Tristram Shandy: A Cock and Bull Story*, the movie, which never gets around to filming the book. Since the book is probably unfilmable, this is just as well; what we get instead is a film about the making of a film based on a novel about the writing of a novel. As an idea for comedy, this is inspired, and Michael Winterbottom and his screenwriter, Frank Cottrell Boyce, show the filmmakers constantly distracted by themselves. "But enough about me," Darryl Zanuck once said. "What did *you* think of my movie?"

The film takes place on the set of a movie named *Tristram Shandy*. It involves actors named Steve Coogan, Rob Brydon, Gillian Anderson, and others, played by Steve Coogan, Rob Brydon, Gillian Anderson, and others. The opening scene takes place in a makeup room, where Coogan and Brydon discuss their billing and whether Brydon's teeth are too yellow. Coogan has the lead, playing both Tristram and his father, Walter. Brydon plays Tristram's uncle Toby, who devotes his life to constructing a large outdoor model of the battlefield where, as a young man, he suffered an obscure wound. The Widow Wadman (Anderson), who is considering marrying Toby, wants to know precisely how and, ahem, where he was wounded. "Just beyond the asparagus," Toby explains, pointing to his model landscape.

But I digress. Back to the dressing room. Coogan mentions that he has the lead in the movie. Yes, says Brydon, but Toby is "a featured co-lead." Coogan: "Well, we'll see after the edit." Both actors are competitive in that understated British way that involves put-downs hardly less obscure than Toby's wound. Coogan wants the wardrobe department to build up his shoes so that the "featured co-lead" will not be taller than the leading man. Brydon learns that Gillian Anderson has been hired to join the cast, and he is panic-stricken: He is afraid that in a love scene he might blush or be betrayed by stirrings beyond the asparagus.

There are elements of *This Is Spinal Tap* in the film, and a touch of Al Pacino's *Looking for Richard*, a semidocumentary about actors preparing to play *Richard III*. From *Spinal Tap* come the egos of the artists and the shabbiness of their art; from Pacino the film borrows the device of explaining the material to the viewers while it is being explained to the actors (only one person in *Tristram Shandy*, and possibly nobody in the audience, has read the book).

The art is endearingly shabby. There is a screening of some battle footage in which lackluster foot soldiers wander dispiritedly past the camera, looking like extras on their lunch break. And a scene in which a miniature unborn Tristram is seen inside a miniature womb; I was reminded of Stonehenge in *Spinal Tap*. The explanations of the material include witty dinnertime conversation by Stephen Fry, playing himself playing an actor playing a literary theorist. Coogan picks up enough to lecture an interviewer: "This is a postmodern novel before there was any mod-

ernism to be post about." Later it's claimed that *Tristram Shandy* was "No. 8 on the *Observer*'s list of the greatest novels," which cheers everyone until they discover the list was chronological.

Now about that interviewer. He has information about a lap dancer that the actor met one recent drunken evening. It would be embarrassing to see the lap dancer on the front page of the tabloids, but the interviewer is willing to do a deal: He'll tidy the story in return for an exclusive about Coogan's relationship with his girlfriend, Jenny (Kelly Macdonald), who has just given birth to their baby. It would not be good for Jenny to read about the lap dancer.

Jenny, as it happens, has just arrived on the set, where Coogan has been having a flirtation with a production assistant named Jennie (Naomie Harris). Jennie is not merely sexy and efficient, but also is a film buff who offers analysis and theory to people who really want only a drink. She compares the ungainly battle scene to Bresson's work in *Lancelot du Lac*, and has a lot to say about Fassbinder, who Coogan vaguely suspects might have been a German director. Not surprisingly, Jennie is the only person on the set who has read the novel, and she tries to explain why the battle scene isn't exactly important.

Because their work is so varied, director Winterbottom and Boyce, his frequent writer, are only now coming into focus as perhaps the most creative team in British film. Their collaborations include films as different as *Butterfly Kiss, Welcome to Sarajevo, The Claim, Code 46* and *24 Hour Party People.* That the same director and writer could make such different films is almost inexplicable, and consider, too, that Winterbottom directed *Wonderland* and Boyce wrote Danny Boyle's *Millions.*

Boyce told me *Tristram Shandy* might sound a little like Charlie Kaufman's screenplay for *Adaptation*, but he thinks it's closer to Truffaut's *Day for Night.* (Am I sounding a little like Jennie here?) It wonderfully evokes life on a movie set, which for a few weeks or months creates its own closed society. Wives and lovers visit the set but are subtly excluded from its "family," and even such a miraculous creature as a newborn baby is treated like a prop that is very nice, yes, but not needed for the scene. As the final credits roll, Coogan and Brydon are still engaged in their running duel of veiled insults. They are briefly diverted, however, by imitating Pacino as Shylock. Every actor knows what David Merrick meant when he said, "It is not enough for me to succeed; my enemies must fail."

Tron

PG, 96 m., 1982

Jeff Bridges (Flynn/Clu), Bruce Boxleitner (Alan/Tron), David Warner (Dillinger/Sark), Cindy Morgan (Lora/Yori), Barnard Hughes (Gibbs/Dumont), Dan Shor (Ram). Directed by Steven Lisberger and produced by Donald Kushner. Screenplay by Lisberger.

The interior of a computer is a fine and private place, but none, I fear, do there embrace, except in *Tron,* a dazzling movie from Walt Disney in which computers have been used to make themselves romantic and glamorous. Here's a technological sound-and-light show that is sensational and brainy, stylish, and fun.

The movie addresses itself without apology to the computer generation, embracing the imagery of those arcade video games that parents fear are rotting the minds of their children. If you've never played Pac-Man or Space Invaders or the Tron game itself, you probably are not quite ready to see this movie, which begins with an evil bureaucrat stealing computer programs to make himself look good, and then enters the very mind of a computer itself to engage the villain, the hero, and several highly programmable bystanders in a war of the wills that is governed by the rules of both video games and computer programs.

The villain is a man named Dillinger (David Warner). The hero is a bright kid named Flynn (Jeff Bridges) who created the original programs for five great new video games, including the wonderfully named "Space Paranoid." Dillinger stole Flynn's plans and covered his tracks in the computer. Flynn believes that if he can track down the original program, he can prove Dillinger is a thief. To prevent that, Dillinger uses the very latest computer technology to break Flynn down into a matrix of logical points and insert him *into* the computer, and at that point *Tron*

leaves any narrative or visual universe we have ever seen before in a movie and charts its own rather wonderful path.

In an age of amazing special effects, *Tron* is a state-of-the-art movie. It generates not just one imaginary computer universe, but a multitude of them. Using computers as their tools, the Disney filmmakers literally have been able to imagine any fictional landscape, and then have it, through an animated computer program. And they integrate their human actors and the wholly imaginary worlds of Tron so cleverly that I never, ever, got the sensation that I was watching some actor standing in front of, or in the middle of, special effects. The characters *inhabit* this world. And what a world it is! Video gamesmen race each other at blinding speed, hurtling up and down computer grids while the movie shakes with the overkill of Dolby stereo (justified, for once). The characters sneak around the computer's logic guardian terminals, clamber up the sides of memory displays, talk their way past the guardians of forbidden programs, hitch a ride on a power beam, and succeed in entering the mind of the very Master Control Program itself, disabling it with an electronic Frisbee. This is all a whole lot of fun. *Tron* has been conceived and written with a knowledge of computers that it mercifully assumes the audience shares. That doesn't mean we *do* share it, but that we're bright enough to pick it up, and don't have to sit through long, boring explanations of it.

There is one additional observation I have to make about *Tron,* and I don't really want it to sound like a criticism: This is an almost wholly technological movie. Although it's populated by actors who are engaging (Bridges, Cindy Morgan) or sinister (Warner), it is not really a movie about human nature. Like *Star Wars* or *The Empire Strikes Back,* but much more so, this movie is a machine to dazzle and delight us. It is not a human interest adventure in any generally accepted way. That's all right, of course. It's brilliant at what it does, and in a technical way maybe it's breaking ground for a generation of movies in which computer-generated universes will be the background for mind-generated stories about emotion-generated personalities. All things are possible.

Trouble in Mind

R, 111 m., 1985

Kris Kristofferson (Hawk), Keith Carradine (Coop), Lori Singer (Georgia), Genevieve Bujold (Wanda), Joe Morton (Solo), Divine (Hilly Blue), George Kirby (Detective). Directed by Alan Rudolph and produced by Carolyn Pfeiffer and David Blocker. Screenplay by Rudolph.

Here is a movie that takes place within our memories of the movies. The characters and the mysteries and especially the doomed romances are all generated by old films, by remembered worlds of lurid neon signs and deserted areas down by the docks, of sad cafés where losers linger over a cup of coffee, and lonely rooms where the light bulb is a man's only friend. This is a world for which the saxophone was invented, a world in which the American Motors Javelin was a popular car.

The movie begins with a man being released from prison, of course, and he is dressed in black and has a beard and wears a hat, of course, and is named Hawk, of course, and the first place he goes when he arrives in town is Wanda's Café, where Wanda keeps a few rooms upstairs for her old lovers to mend their broken dreams.

The café is on a worn-out old brick street down at the wrong end of Rain City. It's the kind of place that doesn't need to advertise, because its customers are drawn there by their fates. One day a young couple turn up in a broken-down camper. The kid is named Coop, and he knows he always gets into trouble when he comes to the city, but he needs to make some money to support his little family. His girlfriend is named Georgia, and she looks way young to have a baby, but there it is, bawling in her arms. She's a blonde with a look in her eyes that makes the Hawk's heart soar.

Coop falls into partnership with the wrong man, a black man named Solo who sits in a back booth at Wanda's Café and recites poems about anger and hopelessness. Before long, Coop and Solo are involved in a life of crime, and Hawk is telling Georgia she's living with a loser. Wanda stands behind the counter and watches all this happen with eyes that have seen a thousand plans go wrong. She hires Georgia as a waitress. That turns Hawk into a regular customer. Wanda knows Hawk is in

love with Georgia, because Wanda and Hawk used to be in love with each other, and once you learn to hear that note in a man's voice, you hear it even when he's not singing to you.

Coop and Solo are trying to sell some hot wristwatches. Hilly Blue doesn't like that. Hilly is the boss of the local rackets, and lives in a house that is furnished like the Museum of Modern Art. The best way to describe Hilly Blue is to say that if Sydney Greenstreet could have reproduced by parthenogenesis after radioactive damage to his chromosomes, Hilly would have been the issue.

Trouble in Mind is not a comedy, but it knows that it is funny. It is not a fantasy, and yet strange troops patrol the streets of Rain City, and as many people speak Korean as English. It does not take place in the 1940s, but its characters dress and talk and live as if it did. Could this movie have been made if there had never been any movies starring Richard Widmark, Jack Palance, or Robert Mitchum? Yes, but it wouldn't have had any style.

To really get inside the spirit of *Trouble in Mind*, it would probably help to see *Choose Me* first. Both films are the work of Alan Rudolph, who is creating a visual world as distinctive as Fellini's and as cheerful as Edward Hopper's. He does an interesting thing. He combines his stylistic excesses with a lot of emotional sincerity, so that we believe these characters are really serious about their hopes, and dreams, even if they do seem to inhabit a world of imagination. Look at it this way. In Woody Allen's *The Purple Rose of Cairo*, a character stepped out of a movie and off the screen and into the life of a woman in the audience. If that had happened in *Trouble in Mind*, the woman would have asked the character why he even bothered.

Sometimes the names of movie actors evoke so many associations that further description is not necessary. Let's see. Hawk is played by Kris Kristofferson. Coop is Keith Carradine. Wanda is Genevieve Bujold. Hilly Blue is the transvestite Divine, but he is not in drag this time, allegedly. Mix them together, light them with neon reds and greens, and add a blond child-woman (Lori Singer) and a black gangster (Joe Morton) whose shades are his warmest feature, and perhaps you can begin to understand why they call it Rain City.

True Grit

G, 127 m., 1969

John Wayne (Rooster Cogburn), Jeremy Slate (Emmett Quincy), Kim Darby (Mattie Ross), Robert Duvall (Ned Pepper), Glen Campbell ("La Boeuf"), Dennis Hopper ("Moon"). Directed by Henry Hathaway and produced by Hal Wallis. Screenplay by Marguerite Roberts, based on the book by Charles Portis.

There is a moment in *True Grit* when John Wayne and four or five bad guys confront each other across a mountain meadow. The situation is quite clear: Someone will have to back up or die.

Director Henry Hathaway pulls his telephoto lens high up in the sky, and we see the meadow isolated there, dreamlike and fantastic. And then we're back down on the ground, and with a growl Wayne puts his horse's reins in his teeth, takes his rifle in one of his hands and a six-shooter in the other, and charges those bad guys with all barrels blazing. As a scene, it is not meant to be taken seriously.

The night I saw a sneak preview, the audience laughed and even applauded. This was the essence of Wayne, the distillation. This was the moment when you finally realized how much Wayne had come to mean to you. I have on occasion disliked his movies, most particularly *The Green Berets*. But Wayne has a way of surmounting even bad movies, and in forty years he has also made a great many good ones. In the early ones, such as *The Quiet Man* or *The Long Voyage Home*, he was simply an actor or simply a star. But long before many of us were born, John Ford began to sculpt the actor and the star into the presence. Today there is no actor in movies who is more an archetype.

One of the glories of *True Grit* is that it recognizes Wayne's special presence. It was not directed by Ford (who in any event probably couldn't have been objective enough about Wayne), but it was directed by another old Western hand, Hathaway, who has made the movie of his lifetime and given us a masterpiece. This is the sort of film you call a movie, instead of the kind of movie you call a film.

It is one of the most delightful, joyous scary movies of all time. It goes on the list with *National Velvet* and *Robin Hood* and *The African Queen* and *Treasure of the Sierra Madre* and *Gunga Din*. It is not a work of art, but it would be nearly as good if it were. Instead, it is the Western you should see if you see only one Western every three years (an act of denial I cannot quite comprehend in any case).

It is based faithfully on Charles Portis's novel, and it tells the story of Mattie Ross from near Dardanelle, in Yell County. One day her father rides off to the city and is murdered by a cowardly snake. Mattie (played with the freshness of sweet cream by Kim Darby) rides to town to hire somebody to go into the Indian Territory and capture the scoundrel.

She strikes a bargain with U.S. Marshal Rooster Cogburn (Wayne), who is a one-eyed, unwashed, sandpapered, roughshod, fat old rascal with a heart of gold well-covered by a hide of leather. Then a Texas Ranger (Glen Campbell) gets into the act when he turns up and claims he has a reward for the killer (who also, it appears, plugged a state senator in Texas). "It is a small reward," the ranger explains, "but he was not a large senator."

After two horse-trading scenes in which Mattie outtalks the horse trader and drives him to distraction, the three set out into Indian Territory. Rooster and the ranger can't get rid of Mattie, so she comes along. And we embark on a glorious adventure not far removed from Huck Finn's trip down the Mississippi, for this is also an American odyssey. Portis wrote his dialogue in a formal, enchantingly archaic style that has been retained in Marguerite Roberts's screenplay.

Campbell, who needs some acting practice, finds it difficult to make the dialogue convincing, but Hathaway pulls him through. And Darby, especially in the horse-trading scenes, is a wonder. You may even laugh aloud when she observes that geldings, in her experience, are not a good buy if you mean to breed them. And as for Wayne, I believe he can say almost anything and make it sound convincing. (In Otto Preminger's *In Harm's Way* he had to say, "I mean to get into harm's way," and he made even that convincing.)

Wayne, in fact, towers over this special movie. He is not playing the same Western role he always plays. Instead, he can play

Rooster because of all the Western roles he has played. He brings an ease and authority to the character. He never reaches. He never falters. It's all there, a quiet confidence that grows out of forty years of acting. God loves the old pros.

The Truman Show
PG, 104 m., 1998

Jim Carrey (Truman Burbank), Laura Linney (Meryl), Noah Emmerich (Marlon), Natascha McElhone (Lauren/Sylvia), Holland Taylor (Mother), Ed Harris (Christof), Brian Delate (Kirk), Paul Giamatti (Simeon). Directed by Peter Weir and produced by Scott Rudin, Andrew Niccol, Edward S. Feldman, and Adam Schroeder. Screenplay by Niccol.

The Truman Show is founded on an enormous secret, which all of the studio's advertising has been determined to reveal. I didn't know the secret when I saw the film, and was able to enjoy the little doubts and wonderings that the filmmakers so carefully planted. If by some good chance you do not know the secret, read no further.

Those fortunate audience members (I trust they have all left the room?) will be able to appreciate the meticulous way director Peter Weir and writer Andrew Niccol have constructed a jigsaw plot around their central character, who doesn't suspect that he's living his entire life on live television. Yes, he lives in an improbably ideal world, but I fell for that: I assumed the movie was taking a sitcom view of life, in which neighbors greet each other over white picket fences, and Ozzie and Harriet are real people.

Actually, it's Seaside, a planned community on the Gulf Coast near Panama City. Called Seahaven in the movie, it looks like a nice place to live. Certainly Truman Burbank (Jim Carrey) doesn't know anything else. You accept the world you're given, the filmmakers suggest; more thoughtful viewers will get the buried message, which is that we accept almost everything in our lives without examining it very closely. When was the last time you reflected on how really odd a tree looks?

Truman works as a sales executive at an insurance company, is happily married to Meryl (Laura Linney), and doesn't find it suspicious that she describes household products in the language of TV commercials. He is happy, in a way, but an uneasiness gnaws away at him. Something is missing, and he thinks perhaps he might find it in Fiji, where Lauren (Natascha McElhone), the only woman he really loved, has allegedly moved with her family.

Why did she leave so quickly? Perhaps because she was not a safe bet for Truman's world: The actress who played her (named Sylvia) developed real feeling and pity for Truman, and felt he should know the truth about his existence. Meryl, on the other hand, is a reliable pro (which raises the question, unanswered, of their sex life).

Truman's world is controlled by a TV producer named Christof (Ed Harris), whose control room is high in the artificial dome that provides the sky and horizon of Seahaven. He discusses his programming on talk shows, and dismisses the protests of those (including Sylvia) who believe Truman is the victim of a cruel deception. Meanwhile, the whole world watches Truman's every move, and some viewers even leave the TV on all night as he sleeps.

The trajectory of the screenplay is more or less inevitable: Truman must gradually realize the truth of his environment and try to escape from it. It's clever the way he's kept on his island by implanted traumas about travel and water. As the story unfolds, however, we're not simply expected to follow it; we're invited to think about the implications. About a world in which modern communications make celebrity possible, and inhuman.

Until fairly recently, the only way you could become really famous was to be royalty, or a writer, actor, preacher, or politician—and even then, most people had knowledge of you only through words or printed pictures. Television, with its insatiable hunger for material, has made celebrities into "content," devouring their lives and secrets. If you think *The Truman Show* is an exaggeration, reflect that Princess Diana lived under similar conditions from the day she became engaged to Charles.

Carrey is a surprisingly good choice to play Truman. We catch glimpses of his manic comic persona, just to make us comfortable with his presence in the character, but this is a well-planned performance; Carrey is on the right note as a guy raised to be liked and likable, who decides his life requires more risk and hardship. Like the angels in *City of Angels*, he'd like to take his chances.

Ed Harris finds the right notes as Christof, the TV Svengali. He uses the technospeak by which we distance ourselves from the real meanings of our words. (If TV producers ever spoke frankly about what they were really doing, they'd come across like Bulworth.) For Harris, the demands of the show take precedence over any other values, and if you think that's an exaggeration, tell it to the TV news people who broadcast that Los Angeles suicide.

I enjoyed *The Truman Show* on its levels of comedy and drama; I *liked* Truman in the same way I liked Forrest Gump—because he was a good man, honest and easy to sympathize with. But the underlying ideas made the movie more than just an entertainment. Like *Gattaca*, the previous film written by Niccol, it brings into focus the new values that technology is forcing on humanity. Because we can engineer genetics, because we can telecast real lives—of course we must, right? But are these good things to do? The irony is, the people who will finally answer that question will be the very ones produced by the process.

Tsotsi

R, 94 m., 2006

Presley Chweneyagae (Tsotsi), Terry Pheto (Miriam), Mothusi Magano (Boston), Israel Makoe (Tsotsi's Father), Percy Matsemela (Sergeant Zuma), Jerry Mofokeng (Morris), Benny Moshe (Young Tsotsi), Nambitha Mpumlwana (Pumla Dube). Directed by Gavin Hood and produced by Peter Fudakowski. Screenplay by Hood, based on the book by Athol Fugard.

How strange, a movie where a bad man becomes better, instead of the other way around. *Tsotsi*, a film of deep emotional power, considers a young killer whose cold eyes show no emotion, who kills unthinkingly, and who is transformed by the helplessness of a baby. He didn't mean to kidnap the baby, but now that he has it, it looks at him with trust and need, and he is powerless before eyes more demanding than his own.

The movie won the Oscar as Best Foreign Film. It is set in Soweto, the township outside Johannesburg where neat little houses built by the new government are overwhelmed by square miles of shacks. There is poverty and despair here, but also hope and opportunity; from Soweto have come generations of politicians, entrepreneurs, artists, musicians, as if it were the Lower East Side of South Africa. Tsotsi (Presley Chweneyagae) is not destined to be one of those. We don't even learn his real name until later in the film; "tsotsi" means "thug," and that's what he is.

He leads a loose-knit gang that smashes and grabs, loots and shoots, sets out each morning to steal something. On a crowded train they stab a man, and he dies without anyone noticing; they hold his body up with their own, take his wallet, flee when the doors open. Another day's work. But when his friend Boston (Mothusi Magano) asks Tsotsi how he really feels, whether decency comes into it, he fights with him and walks off into the night, and we sense how alone he is. Later, in a flashback, we will understand the cruelty of the home and father he fled from.

He goes from here to there. He has a strange meeting with a man in a wheelchair and asks him why he bothers to go on living. The man tells him. Tsotsi finds himself in an upscale suburb. Such areas in Joburg are usually gated communities, each house surrounded by a security wall, every gate promising "armed response." An African professional woman gets out of her Mercedes to ring the buzzer on the gate so her husband can let her in. Tsotsi shoots her and steals her car. Some time passes before he realizes he has a passenger: a baby boy.

Tsotsi is a killer, but he cannot kill a baby. He takes it home with him, to a room built on top of somebody else's shack. It might be wise for him to leave the baby at a church or an orphanage, but that doesn't occur to him. He has the baby, so the baby is his. We can guess that he will not abandon the boy because he has been abandoned himself and projects upon the infant all of his own self-pity.

We realize the violence in the film has slowed. Tsotsi himself is slow to realize he has a new agenda. He uses newspapers as diapers, feeds the baby condensed milk, carries it around with him in a shopping bag. Finally, in desperation, at gunpoint, he forces a nursing mother (Terry Pheto) to feed the child. She lives in a nearby shack, a clean and cheerful one. As he watches her do what he demands, something shifts inside of him, and all of his hurt and grief are awakened.

Tsotsi doesn't become a nice man. He simply stops being active as an evil one and finds his time occupied with the child. Babies are single-minded. They want to be fed, they want to be changed, they want to be held, they want to be made much of, and they think it is their birthright. Who is Tsotsi to argue?

What a simple and yet profound story this is. It does not sentimentalize poverty or make Tsotsi more colorful or sympathetic than he should be; if he deserves praise, it is not for becoming a good man but for allowing himself to be distracted from the job of being a bad man. The nursing mother, named Miriam, is played by Terry Pheto as a quiet counterpoint to his rage. She lives in Soweto and has seen his kind before. She senses something in him, some pool of feeling he must ignore if he is to remain Tsotsi. She makes reasonable decisions. She acts not as a heroine but as a realist who wants to nudge Tsotsi in a direction that will protect her own family and this helpless baby, and then perhaps even Tsotsi himself. These two performances, by Chweneyagae and Pheto, are surrounded by temptations to overact or cave in to sentimentality; they step safely past them and play the characters as they might actually live their lives.

How the story develops is for you to discover. I was surprised to find that it leads toward hope instead of despair; why does fiction so often assume defeat is our destiny? The film avoids obligatory violence and actually deals with the characters as people. The story is based on a novel by the great South African writer Athol Fugard, directed and written by Gavin Hood. It won the Oscar one year after the South African film *Yesterday* was the first from that nation to be nominated. There are stories in the beloved country that have cried for a century to be told.

Turtles Can Fly

NO MPAA RATING, 95 m., 2005

Soran Ebrahim (Satellite), Avaz Latif (Agrin), Hirsh Feyssal (Henkov). Directed by Bahman Ghobadi and produced by Ghobadi. Screenplay by Ghobadi.

I wish everyone who has an opinion on the war in Iraq could see *Turtles Can Fly*. That would mean everyone in the White House and in Congress, and the newspaper writers, and the TV pundits, and the radio talkers, and you—especially you, because you are reading this and they are not.

You assume the movie is a liberal attack on George W. Bush's policies. Not at all. The action takes place just before the American invasion begins, and the characters in it look forward to the invasion and the fall of Saddam Hussein. Nor does the movie later betray an opinion one way or the other about the war. It is about the actual lives of refugees, who lack the luxury of opinions because they are preoccupied with staying alive in a world that has no place for them.

The movie takes place in a Kurdish refugee camp somewhere on the border between Turkey and Iraq. That means, in theory, it takes place in "Kurdistan," a homeland that exists in the minds of the Kurds even though every other government in the area insists the Kurds are stateless. The characters in the movie are children and teenagers, all of them orphans; there are adults in the camp, but the kids run their own lives—especially a bright wheeler-dealer named Satellite (Soran Ebrahim), who organizes work gangs of other children.

What is their work? They disarm land mines, so they can be resold to arms dealers in the nearby town. The land mines are called "American," but this is a reflection of their value and not a criticism of the United States; they were planted in the area by Saddam Hussein, in one of his skirmishes with Kurds and Turks. (Well, technically, they were supplied to Saddam by the United States.) Early in the film, we see a character named Henkov (Hirsh Feyssal), known to everyone as The Boy With No Arms, who gently disarms a mine by removing the firing pin with his lips.

Satellite pays special attention to a girl named Agrin (Avaz Latif), who is Henkov's sister. They have a little brother named Risa, who is carried about with his arms wrapped around the neck of his armless brother. We *think* he is their brother, that is, until we discover he is Agrin's child, born after she was raped by Iraqi soldiers while still almost a child herself. The armless boy loves Risa; his sister hates him, because of her memories.

Is this world beginning to take shape in your mind? The refugees live in tents and huts. They raise money by scavenging. Satellite is the most resourceful person in the camp, making announcements, calling meetings, assigning work, and traveling ceremonially on a bicycle festooned with ribbons and glittering medallions. He is always talking, shouting, hectoring, at the top of his voice: He is too busy to reflect on the misery of his life.

The village is desperate for information about the coming American invasion. There is a scene of human comedy in which every household has a member up on a hill with a makeshift TV antenna; those below shout instructions: "To the left! A little to the right!" But no signal is received. Satellite announces that he will go to town and barter for a satellite dish. There is a sensation when he returns with one. The elders gather as he tries to bring in a signal. The sexy music video channels are prohibited, but the elders wait patiently as Satellite cycles through the sin until he finds CNN, and they can listen for English words they understand. They hate Saddam and eagerly await the Americans.

But what will the Americans do for them? The plight of the Kurdish people is that no one seems to want to do much for them. Even though a Kurd has recently been elected to high office in Iraq, we get the sense he was a compromise candidate—chosen precisely because his people are powerless. For years the Kurds have struggled against Turkey, Iraq, and other nations in the region, to define the borders of a homeland the other states refuse to acknowledge.

From time to time the aims of the Kurds come into step with the aims of others. When they were fighting Saddam, the first Bush administration supported them. When they were fighting our ally Turkey, we opposed them. The *New York Times Magazine* ran a cover story about Ibrahim Parlak, who for ten years peacefully ran a Kurdish restaurant in Harbert, Michigan, only to be arrested in 2004 by the federal government, which hoped to deport him for Kurdish nationalist activities that at one point we approved. Because I supported Ibrahim's case, I could read headlines on right-wing sites such as, "Roger Ebert Gives Thumbs Up to Terrorism."

I hope Debbie Schlussel, who wrote that column, sees *Turtles Can Fly*. The movie does not agree with her politics, or mine. It simply provides faces for people we think of as abstractions. It was written and directed by Bahman Ghobadi, whose *A Time for Drunken Horses* (2000) was also about Kurds struggling to survive between the lines. Satellite has no politics. Neither does The Boy With No Arms, or his sister, or her child born of rape; they have been trapped outside of history.

I was on a panel at the University of Colorado where an audience member criticized movies for reducing the enormity of the Holocaust to smaller stories. But there is no way to tell a story big enough to contain all of the victims of the Holocaust, or all of the lives affected for good and ill in the Middle East. Our minds cannot process that many stories. What we can understand is The Boy With No Arms, making a living by disarming land mines like the one that blew away his arms. And Satellite, who tells the man in the city he will trade him fifteen radios and some cash for a satellite dish. Where did Satellite get fifteen radios? Why? You need some radios?

24 Hour Party People

R, 117 m., 2002

Steve Coogan (Tony Wilson), Keith Allen (Roger Ames), Rob Brydon (Ryan Letts), Enzo Cilenti (Pete Saville), Ron Cook (Derek Ryder), Chris Coghill (Bez), Paddy Considine (Rob Gretton), Danny Cunningham (Shaun Ryder), Dave Gorman (John the Postman). Directed by Michael Winterbottom and produced by Andrew Eaton. Screenplay by Frank Cottrell Boyce.

---

24 Hour Party People, which tells the story of the Manchester music scene from the first Sex Pistols concert until the last bankruptcy, shines with a kind of inspired madness. It is based on fact, but Americans who don't know the facts will have no trouble identifying with the sublime posturing of its hero, a television personality named Tony Wilson, who takes himself seriously in a way that is utterly impossible to take seriously.

Wilson, a real man, is played by Steve

Coogan, who plays a Wilsonoid TV personality on British TV. That sort of through-the-looking-glass mixing of reality and fancy makes the movie somehow *more* true than a factual documentary would have been. Wilson is a lanky man with the face of a sincere beagle, a flop of hair over his right eyebrow, and an ability to read banal TV copy as if it has earth-shaking profundity. He's usually the only man in the room wearing a suit and tie, but he looks like he put them on without reading the instructions. He is so heartfelt about his lunacies that we understand, somehow, that his mind deals with contradictions by embracing them.

As the film opens, Wilson is attending the first, legendary, Sex Pistols concert in Manchester, England. Here and elsewhere, director Michael Winterbottom subtly blends real newsreel footage with fictional characters so they all fit convincingly into the same shot. Wilson is transfixed by the Pistols as they sing "Anarchy in the UK" and sneer at British tradition. He tells the camera that everyone in the audience will leave the room transformed and inspired, and then the camera pans to show a total of forty-two people, two or three of them halfheartedly dancing in the aisles.

Wilson features the Pistols and other bands on his Manchester TV show. Because of a ban by London TV, his show becomes the only venue for punk rock. Turns out he was right about the Pistols. They let loose something that changed rock music. And they did it in the only way that Wilson could respect, by thoroughly screwing up everything they did, and ending in bankruptcy and failure, followed by Sid Vicious's spectacular murder-suicide flameout. The Sex Pistols became successful because they failed; if they had succeeded, they would have sold out, or become diluted or commercial. I saw Johnny Rotten a few years ago at Sundance, still failing, and it made me feel proud of him.

Tony Wilson, who preaches "anarchism" not as a political position but as an emotional state, knows he has seen the future. He joins with two partners to form Factory Records, which would become one of the most important and least financially successful recording companies in history, and joyously signs the contract in his blood (while declaring "we will have no contracts"). His bands include Joy Division (renamed New Order after the suicide of its lead

singer) and Happy Mondays. His company opens a rave club, the Hacienda, which goes broke because the customers ignore the cash bars and spend all their money on Ecstasy.

Wilson hardly cares. When the club closes, he addresses the final night's crowd: "Before you leave, I ask you to invade the offices and loot them." When he meets with investors who want to buy Factory Records, they are startled to learn he has nothing to sell—no contracts, no back catalog, nothing. "We are not really a company," he explains helpfully. "We are an experiment in human nature. I protected myself from the dilemma of selling out by having nothing to sell."

This is a lovable character, all the more so because his conversation uses the offhand goofy non sequiturs of real speech instead of being channeled into a narrow lane of movie dialogue. The writer, Frank Cottrell Boyce, gives Wilson a distinctive voice we come to love. "I went to Cambridge University!" he tells one of his broadcast bosses. "I'm a serious journalist, living in one of the most important times in human history." Yes, but the next day he's interviewing a midget elephant-trainer. He explains how the invention of broccoli funded the James Bond movies (there is a shred of truth there, actually). He quotes Plutarch and William Blake, he says one of his singers is a poet equal to Yeats, he looks at empty concert halls and observes hopefully that there were only twelve people at the Last Supper (thirteen, actually, counting the talent). And he is courageous in the face of daunting setbacks, pushing on optimistically into higher realms of failure.

The movie works so well because it evokes genuine, not manufactured, nostalgia. It records a time when the inmates ran the asylum, when music lovers got away with murder. It loves its characters. It understands what the Sex Pistols started, and what the 1990s destroyed. And it gets a certain tone right. It kids itself. At one point, Wilson looks straight at the camera and tells us that a scene is missing, "but it will probably be on the DVD."

As the screenwriter of an ill-fated Sex Pistols movie, I met Rotten, Vicious, Cook, Jones, and their infamous manager, Malcolm McLaren, and brushed the fringe of their world. I could see there was no plan, no strategy, no philosophy, just an attitude. If a book on the Sex Pistols had an upraised middle finger on the cover, it wouldn't need any words inside. And yet Tony Wilson goes to see the Pistols and sees before him a delirious opportunity to—to what? Well, obviously, to live in one of the most important times in human history, and to make your mark on it by going down in glorious flames.

The Twilight Samurai

NO MPAA RATING, 129 m., 2004

Hiroyuki Sanada (Seibei Iguchi), Rie Miyazawa (Tomoe Iinuma), Nenji Kobayashi (Choubei Hisasaka), Min Tanaka (Zenemon Yogo), Ren Osugi (Toyotarou Kouda), Mitsuru Fukikoshi (Michinojo Iinuma), Miki Ito (Kayana Iguchi), Erina Hashiguchi (Ito Iguchi). Directed by Yoji Yamada and produced by Hiroshi Fukazawa, Shigehiro Nakagawa, and Ichiro Yamamoto. Screenplay by Yamada Asama and Yoshitaka Asama, based on books by Shuuhei Fujisawa.

One who is a samurai must before all things keep in mind, by day, and by night, the fact that he has to die. That is his chief business.
—Code of Bushido

The Twilight Samurai is set in Japan during the period of the Meiji Restoration, circa 1868—the same period as Kurosawa's great *Seven Samurai* and Edward Zwick's elegant *The Last Samurai*. The three films deal in different ways with a time when samurai still tried to live by the Code of Bushido, even as they faced poverty or unemployment in a changing society. *The Last Samurai* is about samurai opposing the emperor's moves to modernize Japan; ironically, we learn that the hero of *The Twilight Samurai* fought and died in that rebellion—after the story of this movie is over.

His name is Seibei (Hiroyuki Sanada), and he lives under the rule of his clan in northeast Japan, where he spends his days not in battle but as an accountant, keeping track of dried fish and other foods in storage. Seeing him bending wearily over a pile of papers, declining an invitation by his fellow workers to go out drinking, we're reminded of the hero of Kurosawa's film *Ikiru*. Seibei hurries home because he has a senile mother and two young daughters to support, and is in debt after the death of his wife.

His story is told by director Yoji Yamada in muted tones and colors, beautifully re-creating a feudal village that still retains its architecture, its customs, its ancient values, even as the economy is making its way of life obsolete. What kind of a samurai has to pawn his sword and make do with a bamboo replacement? The film is narrated by Seibei's oldest daughter (Erina Hashiguchi), who is young in the film but an old lady on the sound track, remembering her father with love.

After working all day in the office, Seibei hurries home to grow crops to feed his family and earn extra cash. His coworkers gossip that his kimono is torn, and that he smells. One day the lord of the clan comes to inspect the food stores, notices Seibei's aroma, and reprimands him. This brings such disgrace on the family that Seibei's stern uncle reminds him, "Only a generation ago, hara-kiri would have been called for." His uncle advises him to remarry to get another worker into the home to prepare meals and do laundry. It happens that his childhood sweetheart, Tomoe (Rie Miyazawa), has just divorced her wife-beating husband, and begins to help around the house. The girls love her, but Seibei is shy and tired and cannot imagine remarrying.

The clan comes to him with an assignment: He is to kill the unruly Yogo (Min Tanaka), a samurai who has been employed by the clan for only four years, after a long, destitute time of wandering the countryside. Yogo, considered crazy, has declined the clan's suggestion that he kill himself. That seems sane enough to me, but the clan must uphold its standards even as its time is passing, and so the reluctant Seibei is bribed and blackmailed into taking on the assignment.

The closing third of the film is magnificent in the way it gathers all we have learned about Seibei and uses it to bring depth to what could have been a routine action sequence, but is much more. We see Tomoe shyly preparing him for battle ("Allow me to comb your hair"), and after a crucial conversation, he leaves her and goes to Yogo's home, where the body of an earlier emissary lies in the courtyard, covered by a swarm of flies.

I will not, of course, tell you what happens inside the house, or what happens between Seibei and Tomoe. What I can refer to is the extraordinary conversation between Seibei and Yogo, while their swords remain undrawn. "I know, you're all keyed up," Yogo says. "But I'm going to run." He has no desire to fight. He recounts his weary history as a samurai in poverty, or in bondage to a clan: "I was an errand boy, too." At one extraordinary moment he takes the ashes of his dead daughter and crunches a piece of bone between his teeth. Yogo's motive for having this conversation may not be as clear as it seems; it is up to you to decide.

Director Yoji Yamada, now seventy-three, has made at least sixty-six films, according to IMDB.com. *The Twilight Samurai*, the first to be widely released in this country, was Japan's Oscar nominee this year. He has been nominated six times since he was sixty as Japan's best director, and won once. Yet no less than forty-eight of his films were B-pictures, involving the beloved character Tora-san, popular in Japan from 1970 until the death in 1996 of Kiyoshi Atsumi, who played him. Tora-san is little known outside Japan, but for a class on Japanese cinema, I obtained one of his movies from Shochiku Studios and we watched it. Apparently they are all much the same: Tora-san, a meek, self-effacing comic figure (a little Chaplin, a little Jerry Lewis, a little Red Skelton), is a salesman who stumbles into a domestic crisis, makes it worse, and then makes it better.

One can only imagine what it would be like to direct that formula forty-eight times. Perhaps Yamada felt a little like Seibei, as he remained loyal to the studio and this character year after year. Perhaps when Seibei finds, at the end of *The Twilight Samurai*, that he may be poor and stuck in a rut but he still has greatness in him—well, perhaps that's how Yamada felt when he entered the home stretch. There is a kind of perfection in laboring humbly all your life only to show, as the end approaches, that you had greatness all along. I am half-convinced that as Seibei's daughter remembers her father's life, she is also describing Yamada's. I could probably find out if that is true, but I don't want to know. I like it better as a possibility.

Note: The Twilight Samurai swept the 2003 Japanese Academy Awards, winning twelve categories, including best picture, director, screenplay, actor, actress, supporting actor, and cinematography.

Twilight's Last Gleaming

R, 146 m., 1977

Burt Lancaster (Lawrence Dell), Richard Widmark (General MacKenzie), Charles Durning (President Stevens), Melvyn Douglas (Defense Secretary), Paul Winfield (Powell), Burt Young (Garvas), Joseph Cotton (Secretary of State), Roscoe Lee Browne (James Forrest). Directed by Robert Aldrich and produced by Merv Adelson. Screenplay by Ronald M. Cohen and Edward Huebsch, based on the book *Viper Three*, by Walter Wager.

Robert Aldrich's *Twilight's Last Gleaming* is one of the most intelligent and gripping thrillers in a long time, an American version of those savage European political dramas beginning with "Z." Its best sequences are put together with the precision of a master, and we forget how preposterous the plot is, because somehow it doesn't seem all that preposterous after awhile.

It stars Burt Lancaster as a former Air Force general who lost his "objectivity" during five years in the prison camps of North Vietnam. The ordeal didn't make him a hawk, but a dove capable of violence (how long it's been since hawks and doves were at the front of our consciousness). He gains control of a silo containing nine Titan missiles and threatens to launch them against Russia, because he wants the world to share with him a secret decision of the American government.

He was cleared to see top secret National Security Council proceedings, and the minutes of one meeting haunt him: A former president is cold-bloodedly informed by his advisers that Vietnam is a "no-win" war in which the United States has no chance of prevailing—but that we must continue to sacrifice lives there in order to maintain our credibility with the Russians. Although the film's first shot is the usual disclaimer in which the characters are said not to resemble any persons living or dead, etc., the characters in the transcript express opinions not a million miles removed from some of the tragic tactical reasons behind Vietnam.

Aldrich cuts between three parallel stories.

One concerns Lancaster, who was finally busted by the service and framed on a first-degree murder charge. He's broken out of a Montana prison with other inmates (Paul Winfield and Burt Young) he recruited to help occupy the silo. Lancaster helped design the missile bases, knows exactly how they operate, and succeeds in controlling a silo. The second story concerns the current president (Charles Durning) and his advisers, called into emergency session to deal with the extortion threat. The third centers on Richard Widmark, an Air Force general who's an old enemy of Lancaster's and would like to blast him out of the silo with a pocket atomic bomb.

Lancaster's demands are enormous. He wants $10,000,000, safe passage to a foreign country aboard Air Force One, and the president himself as a hostage. He also wants those National Security Council minutes read to the world. The president finds himself agreeing with the last request: As played by Durning, he's a decent (if intellectually mushy) type who can hardly believe the secret minutes when he reads them himself for the first time. But Durning is not so eager to play the role of hostage. He's scared. And he has reason to be, because Aldrich implies that the military-industrial establishment wouldn't let anyone, not even the president, reveal the real nature of its thinking.

There are scenes of brilliant tension. One occurs as Lancaster and the others neutralize the booby traps built into the missile launching system. Another comes when Lancaster, realizing that Widmark has double-crossed him, pushes the button to begin the launch countdown. And there's the excruciating confrontation at the end, when the president, scared stiff but doing his duty, walks into the silo alone.

From a logical basis, we can't buy this ending: It's hard to believe a president would ever allow himself to be held hostage, and hard to believe he would walk into a potentially lethal situation with absolutely no backup, either in personal security or in terms of emergency medical care. But Aldrich has clearly decided to trade logic for emotion in the last scenes; having given us a finely crafted thriller, he moves at the end to a totally cynical conclusion, one that makes the movie's title bitterly appropriate.

Twin Falls Idaho
R, 105 m., 1999

Mark Polish (Blake Falls), Michael Polish (Francis Falls), Michele Hicks (Penny), Lesley Ann Warren (Francine), Patrick Bauchau (Miles), Jon Gries (Jay), Garrett Morris (Jesus), William Katt (Surgeon). Directed by Michael Polish and produced by Marshall Persinger, Rena Ronson, and Steven J. Wolfe. Screenplay by Mark Polish and Michael Polish.

In a hotel like this, we feel, anything could happen. There is a certain kind of fleabag, with a barren lobby and a strange elevator operator, which has developed in the movies as a mythic backdrop for private eyes, addicts, crooks on the lam, would-be novelists—anyone who needs to hide out on a budget.

Twin Falls Idaho opens with a hooker being dropped off in front of the Hotel Idaho and knocking on a room door, which is opened a crack to reveal a sad and solemn face. The room is occupied, we learn, by the Falls brothers, Blake and Francis, who are joined at the hip and share one leg. It is their birthday, and Francis has ordered her as a gift for his brother—and therefore possibly for himself, we speculate, our minds working out how many genitals might accompany three legs.

The hooker, whose name is Penny (Michele Hicks), flees when she understands the situation. She has to return because she has forgotten her purse, and this time she gets drawn into the world of Blake and Francis (played by identical twins Mark and Michael Polish). They aren't angry at her for leaving, just as they didn't seem much aroused by her arrival. Sex, we guess, may be something they have little experience of; this birthday present may have been more of a gesture, an act of defiance. Where did the twins come from? What is their story?

Penny has walked in on a scene making it clear that Francis is sick. She knows a doctor who will make a house call, she tells them, unless he wants his wife to find out about her. Miles (the urbane and yet somehow ominous actor Patrick Bauchau) arrives, and we learn that Francis has a weak heart. Blake's heart is keeping them both alive, but that may not last for long, and then they will both die—or Francis will, leaving Blake with a loneliness so profound, after the life they have led, that he can scarcely imagine it. (He tells Penny he has never been alone, except for the moment before he goes to sleep and the first moment after he wakes up.)

Twin Falls Idaho was written by the Polish brothers and directed by Michael. It is one of those films not much interested in plot but fascinated by what it is like to be somebody, or two somebodies. The movie doesn't depend on special effects to create a shared body (except for one shot that's not especially convincing), and instead uses the performances. Mark and Michael Polish seem constantly to be confiding in one another, and indeed when you spend your life within inches of another person's ear, you learn to murmur. We can imagine their lifetime of isolation from the normal things people do, and there is a heartbreaking dream shot toward the end of the film, just showing two boys riding bicycles.

Soon it is Halloween, and Penny (who is a prostitute by desperation, not through career choice) takes the brothers to a costume party. This could, of course, be the occasion for bad jokes, but it inspires her empathy: "Show some compassion. This is the one night of the entire year when they're both normal." Gradually we get glimpses of where they came from. We meet their enigmatic mother (Lesley Ann Warren). We hear a little of their story. We learn that they may have checked into the hotel to die. Hicks is gentle, tender, and sad with them, setting the film's tone (although there is also room for irony and even some laughter).

I have a special feeling for movies that want to forget about plot and conflict, and spend their time instead in regarding particular lives. Like π or *Happiness,* this film is a meditation on the situation of its characters. There's no payoff, no answer, no solution, no resolution, because how can there be? You are who you are, and life either goes on or it doesn't. The key bond in the film seems to be between the brothers, but then we realize their bond is given, not chosen, and so doesn't mean as much as the bond between the two of them and Penny. Her business is to minister to the lonely and the needy, and these two boys make her feel so helpless that her own solitude is exposed. In its quiet, dark, claustrophobic way, this is one of the best films of 1999.

Two English Girls

R, 108 m., 1972

Jean-Pierre Leaud (Claude), Kika Markham (Anne Brown), Stacey Tendeter (Muriel Brown), Sylvia Marriott (Mrs. Brown), Marie Mansart (Madame Roc), Phillipe Leotard (Diurka), Mark Peterson (Mr. Flint), Irene Tunc (Ruta). Directed by François Truffaut and produced by Claude Miler. Screenplay by Truffaut and Jean Gruault, based on the book by Henri-Pierre Roche.

It's wonderful how offhand François Truffaut's best films feel. There doesn't seem to be any great effort being made; he doesn't push for his effects, but lets them flower naturally from the simplicities of his stories. His film, *Two English Girls,* is very much like that. Because he doesn't strain for an emotional tone, he can cover a larger range than the one-note movies. Here he is discreet, even while filming the most explicit scenes he's ever done; he handles sadness gently; he is charming and funny even while he tells us a story that is finally tragic.

The story is from the second novel by Henri-Pierre Roche, who began writing at the age of seventy-four and whose first novel, *Jules and Jim,* provided the inspiration for nearly everyone's favorite Truffaut film. The two novels (and the two films) are variations on the same theme: What a terrible complex emotional experience it is to have to share love.

We would say that both stories involve romantic triangles, but Roche seems to see them more simply (and poignantly) as the shared dilemmas of people caught helplessly in their situations. Nobody sets out deliberately to involve himself in a triangular relationship—not when the love involved is real. It hurts too much.

Truffaut introduces us to Claude, a young French art critic, and then introduces him to Anne Brown, an English girl visiting in Paris. They form a friendship, and the girl invites him to come and visit her mother and sister in Wales. During the visit, he falls in love (or thinks he does) with the sister, Muriel. They want to marry, but they both have poor health, and it is decided to put off the marriage for a year. Claude returns to Paris, where Anne follows after a while, and then they fall into a sexual relationship that passes for a time as love. The virgin Muriel, meanwhile, remains passionately in love with Claude and nearly has an emotional breakdown when she learns that he no longer plans to marry her.

The story, as it unfolds, is involved but never untrue. Love itself is an elusive prize that passes among them; it is their doom that whenever two of them are together, it is the third who possesses love. The film relates love and loss so closely that we almost forgive Claude for his infidelities and stubbornness. Perversely, he wants to be apart from Muriel (and later Anne) so that he can desire them all the more.

If *Two English Girls* resembles *Jules and Jim* in theme, it has an unmistakable stylistic relationship to Truffaut's little-seen masterpiece of 1970, *The Wild Child*. Both films used diaries, journals, and a spoken narration in order to separate us from the immediate experience of the stories. Truffaut wants us to feel that we're being told a fable, a sad winter's tale, that is all the more touching because these events happened long ago and love is trapped irretrievably in the past.

His visual strategy for creating this feeling is another favorite device from *The Wild Child:* the iris shot. (Put simply, this is the use of a slowly contracting circle to bring a shot to an end, instead of a fade or a cut). The iris isolates one element in the picture, somehow making it feel alone and vulnerable—and past. The film is photographed in a low-keyed color, and the sound recording is also a little muted; this isn't a film for emotional highs, we sense, because it's far and away too late for these lost love opportunities to be regained.

The one scene that violates this tone is as necessary as it is effective; when Muriel finally makes love with Claude we feel the terrible force of her passion, pent up for so many years, and then the camera pans to the blood-stained sheet and goes out of focus. Put in so many words, this probably sounds crude and obvious; in fact, this is almost the only red in the film, and is Truffaut's perfect visual metaphor for the fact that these three people have created a lot of their own unhappiness by avoiding or deflecting the consequences of their emotional feelings.

Jules and Jim was a young man's film (Truffaut was twenty-eight when he made it). *Two English Girls* is the film of a man some ten or twelve years down the road; it is still playful and winsome, but it realizes more fully the consequences of an opportunity lost. The final scene shows Claude, fifteen years later, wandering in the garden where he used to walk with Anne and Muriel. There are English children playing there, and he thinks to ask one of them, "Are you Muriel Brown's daughter?" But he doesn't, because . . . well, because.

The Two of Us

NO MPAA RATING, 86 m., 1968

Michel Simon (Gramp), Alain Cohen (Claude [the boy]), Luce Fabiole (Granny), Roger Caret (Victor), Paul Preboist (Maxime), Charles Denner (Claude's father). Directed by Claude Berri and produced by André Hunebelle and Paul Cadéac. Screenplay by Berri.

Note: This review contains spoilers.

The happy ending, like all clichés, is hard to define. I used to believe all happy endings resembled one another, while every unhappy ending is unhappy in its own fashion. But that will not do.

On the basis of two current films, the splendid *The Two of Us* and the so-so *With Six You Get Eggroll*, I've decided there are at least two kinds of happy endings: the mechanistic and the organic.

The mechanistic happy ending is simply the regular Hollywood ending we know and love. It bears little relationship to what has gone before. Doris Day may just have dumped Brian Keith in the middle of the street in his underpants, but he will somewhere borrow a Good Humor uniform and they'll be together again, in love again, all misunderstandings cleared up.

This sort of ending is simply a mechanical arrangement of characters, designed to reassure us.

The organic happy ending, on the other hand, grows out of the film. It is not only a happy ending but also a logical one. The movie ends well because the characters recognize their problems and solve them. We feel good.

And that is the test, I think. The conventional Hollywood ending satisfies some sort of cheap, shallow desire to have the movie turn out all right. But the other kind fills us with a glow of happiness.

The Two of Us is such a movie and has such an ending.

The story is about two people: an old man and a boy. The old man (Michel Simon) lives in the French countryside on a farm with his wife, dog, son, daughter-in-law, and anti-Semitic prejudices.

The boy (Alain Cohen) is Jewish, and in 1944 his parents send him to the country at the time of the Nazi occupation. His identity must be kept a secret. His parents give him a resounding Christian name, teach him the Lord's Prayer, and send him away with their fingers crossed.

What follows is a series of adventures, some small, some large, involving the old man, the boy, and human prejudice. The old man blames the war on a secret agreement among the Jews, the English, the Freemasons, Winston Churchill, and any other group that happens to occur to him. He listens to the nightly propaganda broadcasts with fervor and solemnly assures the boy that Jews have big noses and eat by candlelight.

The trouble is, the old man's nose is bigger than the boy's. Some other things don't fit either. The boy is worried at first that his identity will be discovered, but he relaxes and begins to humor the old man. For it has become quite clear that the old man, like all of us, has more prejudices than available targets.

A great affection grows up between them, in a series of beautifully acted scenes. There is pure comedy, a great deal of gentle satire, and a scene of tragedy: The boy's head is shaved at school. The old man comforts him, and their friendship is cemented.

The ending is happy, but it isn't phony. If Hollywood had done this film, the old man would have discovered at the end that the boy was Jewish. Then there would have been a fine liberal curtain speech about the brotherhood of man.

But Claude Berri, who wrote and directed *The Two of Us*, doesn't fall into that trap. The old man never finds out and, what's more, doesn't need to.

2001: A Space Odyssey
G, 141 m., 1968

Keir Dullea (Bowman), Gary Lockwood (Poole), William Sylvester (Dr. Heywood Floyd), Daniel Richter (Moonwatcher), Douglas Rain (HAL 9000 [Voice]), Leonard Rossiter (Smyslov), Margaret Tyzack (Elena), Robert Beatty (Halvorsen), Sean Sullivan (Michaels), Frank Miller (Mission Controller). Directed and produced by Stanley Kubrick. Screenplay by Kubrick and Arthur C. Clarke.

It was e. e. cummings, the poet, who said he'd rather learn from one bird how to sing than teach ten thousand stars how not to dance. I imagine cummings would not have enjoyed Stanley Kubrick's *2001: A Space Odyssey*, in which stars dance but birds do not sing. The fascinating thing about this film is that it fails on the human level but succeeds magnificently on a cosmic scale.

Kubrick's universe, and the spaceships he constructed to explore it, are simply out of scale with human concerns. The ships are perfect, impersonal machines which venture from one planet to another, and if men are tucked away somewhere inside them, then they get there, too. But the achievement belongs to the machine. And Kubrick's actors seem to sense this; they are lifelike but without emotion, like figures in a wax museum. Yet the machines are necessary because man himself is so helpless in the face of the universe.

Kubrick begins his film with a sequence in which one tribe of apes discovers how splendid it is to be able to hit the members of another tribe over the head. Thus do man's ancestors become tool-using animals. At the same time, a strange monolith appears on Earth. Until this moment in the film, we have seen only natural shapes: earth and sky and arms and legs. The shock of the monolith's straight edges and square corners among the weathered rocks is one of the most effective moments in the film. Here, you see, is perfection. The apes circle it warily, reaching out to touch, then jerking away. In a million years, man will reach for the stars with the same tentative motion.

Who put the monolith there? Kubrick never answers, for which I suppose we must be thankful. The action advances to the year

2001, when explorers on the moon find another of the monoliths. This one beams signals toward Jupiter. And man, confident of his machines, brashly follows the trail.

Only at this point does a plot develop. The ship is manned by two pilots, Keir Dullea and Gary Lockwood. Three scientists are put on board in suspended animation to conserve supplies. The pilots grow suspicious of the computer, "HAL," which runs the ship. But they behave so strangely—talking in monotones like characters from *Dragnet*—that we're hardly interested.

There is hardly any character development in the plot, then, and as a result little suspense. What remains fascinating is the fanatic care with which Kubrick has built his machines and achieved his special effects. There is not a single moment, in this long film, when the audience can see through the props. The stars look like stars and outer space is bold and bleak.

Some of Kubrick's effects have been criticized as tedious. Perhaps they are, but I can understand his motives. If his space vehicles move with agonizing precision, wouldn't we have laughed if they'd zipped around like props on *Captain Video?* This is how it would really be, you find yourself believing.

In any event, all the machines and computers are forgotten in the astonishing last half-hour of this film, and man somehow comes back into his own. Another monolith is found beyond Jupiter, pointing to the stars. It apparently draws the spaceship into a universe where time and space are twisted.

What Kubrick is saying, in the final sequence, apparently, is that man will eventually outgrow his machines, or be drawn beyond them by some cosmic awareness. He will then become a child again, but a child of an infinitely more advanced, more ancient race, just as apes once became, to their own dismay, the infant stage of man.

And the monoliths? Just road markers, I suppose, each one pointing to a destination so awesome that the traveler cannot imagine it without being transfigured. Or as cummings wrote on another occasion, "Listen—there's a hell of a good universe next door; let's go."

Note: This movie is best viewed in the letterboxed version, which preserves the wide-screen compositions.

U

Uforia

PG, 100 m., 1985

Cindy Williams (Arlene), Harry Dean Stanton (Brother Bud), Fred Ward (Sheldon), Alan Beckwith (Brother Roy), Beverly Hope Atkinson (Naomi), Harry Carey, Jr. (George Martin), Diane Diefendorf (Delores), Robert Gray (Emile). Directed by John Binder and produced by Gordon Wolf. Screenplay by Binder.

I've always wanted to know one of those women you read about in the *National Enquirer,* those intense Midwestern housewives who are sucked up into flying saucers and flown to Mars, where they have their measurements taken, and are told they will be contacted again real soon. It's not that I want to hear about the trip to Mars. I'd just enjoy having her around the house, all filled with a sense of mystery and purpose.

Uforia is a great and goofy comedy about a woman just like that. Her name is Arlene, and she works as a supermarket checker in a backwater town in the Southwest. She reads all the UFO publications and believes every word, and knows in her heart that They are coming. But the movie is not really about whether They come or not. It's about how waiting for Them can give you something wonderful to think about, to pass the time of those dreary, dusty days.

The movie has two other characters who get involved in Arlene's dream. One of them is named Sheldon, and he is the kind of good ol' boy who drives through the desert in a big ol' convertible, with the car on cruise control and his feet propped up on the dashboard and a can of beer in his hand.

The other one is named Brother Bud, a phony faith healer who conducts revival services in a tent outside of town. When Sheldon sees Arlene at the supermarket, he falls in love, and before long he has settled down, sort of, in her mobile home. Sheldon and Brother Bud are brothers, and Sheldon hires on with Bud to portray a guy whose sick leg gets healed every night. Meanwhile, Arlene's faith grows that the UFO will arrive at any moment.

This is one of those movies where you walk in not expecting much, and then something great happens, and you laugh, and you start paying more attention, and then you realize that a lot of great things are happening, that this is one of those rare movies that really has it. *Uforia* is not just another witless Hollywood laugh machine, but a movie with intelligence and a sly, sardonic style of humor. You don't have to shut down half of your brain in order to endure it.

The casting is just perfect. Cindy Williams is the cornerstone, as Arlene, a woman whose hopes and dreams are too big for the small corner of the earth she has been given to occupy. She doesn't know what to do when she meets Sheldon (played by Fred Ward, from *Remo Williams* and *The Right Stuff*). She likes this guy and she hasn't had a man in a long time. But, then again, she always gets her heart "broke" when she falls for a guy, and so she prays for guidance and starts on the tequila.

Ward gives a wicked performance as the good ol' boy Sheldon. He's Smokey and the Bandit with brains. He has a couple of double takes in this movie that are worth the price of a ticket. And he's not a male chauvinist pig, although everything in his background probably points him in that direction. He doesn't see Arlene as a conquest, but as just the lady he's been looking for. He gets a little tired of the flying-saucer stuff, however.

Harry Dean Stanton plays Brother Bud. This is exactly the kind of role Stanton has been complaining that he's tired of: the weary, alcoholic con man with the jolly cynicism. Yet they keep casting him in these roles, and in *Uforia* you can see why: Nobody does a better job. He has an assistant in the movie, a junior evangelist named Brother Roy (Alan Beckwith), whose face shines with conviction and who is always bathed in wonderment and glory. The quiet, offhand way Stanton deals with him is one of the movie's many treasures.

Uforia didn't have a lot of money and a big ad campaign behind it. It doesn't have big stars, unless you are the kind of movie lover for whom the names Cindy Williams, Harry Dean Stanton, and Fred Ward guarantee a movie will at least be interesting.

Like *Repo Man* and *Turtle Diary* and *Hannah and Her Sisters,* it is willing to go for originality in a world that prizes the entertainment assembly line. I was hugging myself during this movie, because it had so many moments that were just right.

The Unbearable Lightness of Being

R, 172 m., 1988

Daniel Day-Lewis (Tomas), Juliette Binoche (Tereza), Lena Olin (Sabina), Derek de Lint (Franz), Erland Josephson (The Ambassador), Pavel Landovsky (Pavel), Donald Moffat (Chief Surgeon), Daniel Olbrychski (Interior Ministry Official), Stellan Skarsgard (The Engineer), Tomek Bork (Jiri). Directed by Philip Kaufman and produced by Saul Zaentz. Screenplay by Jean-Claude Carriere, based on the book by Milan Kundera.

In the title of Philip Kaufman's *The Unbearable Lightness of Being,* the crucial word is "unbearable." The film tells the story of a young surgeon who attempts to float above the mundane world of personal responsibility and commitment, to practice a sex life that has no traffic with the heart, to escape untouched from the world of sensual pleasure while retaining his privacy and his loneliness. By the end of the story, this freedom has become too great a load for him to bear.

The surgeon's name is Tomas, and he lives in Prague; we meet him in the blessed days before the Russian invasion of 1968. He has an understanding with a woman named Sabina, a painter whose goal is the same as his own—to have a physical relationship without an emotional one. The two lovers believe they have much in common, since they share the same attitude toward their couplings, but actually their genitals have more in common than they do. That is not to say they don't enjoy great sex; they do, and in great detail, in this most erotic serious film since *Last Tango in Paris.*

One day the doctor goes to the country, and while waiting in a provincial train station, his eyes fall upon the young waitress Tereza. He orders a brandy. Their eyes meet. They go for a little walk after she gets off of work, and it is clear there is something special between them. He returns to Prague. One day she appears in the city and knocks at his door. She has come to be with him. Against all of his principles, he

allows her to spend the night, and then to move in. He has betrayed his own code of lightness, or freedom.

The film tells the love story of Tomas and Tereza in the context of the events of 1968, and there are shots that place the characters in the middle of the riots against the Russian invaders. Tereza becomes a photographer, and tries to smuggle pictures of the uprising out of the country. Finally, the two lovers leave Prague for Geneva, where Sabina has already gone—and then Tomas resumes his sexual relationship with Sabina because his philosophy, of course, is that sex has nothing to do with love.

Crushed by his decision, Tereza attempts her own experiment with free love, but it does not work because her heart is not built that way. Sabina, meanwhile, meets a professor named Franz who falls in love with her so urgently that he decides to leave his wife. Can she accept this love? Or is she even more committed to "lightness of being" than Tomas, who tutored her in the philosophy? In the middle of Sabina's indecision, Tereza appears at her door with a camera. She has been asked to take some shots for a fashion magazine and needs someone to pose nude. Sabina agrees, and the two women photograph each other in a scene so carefully choreographed that it becomes a ballet of eroticism.

By this point in the movie, a curious thing had happened to me as a viewer. I had begun to appreciate some of the life rhythms of the characters. Most films move so quickly and are so dependent on plot that they are about events, not lives. *The Unbearable Lightness of Being* carries the feeling of deep nostalgia, of a time no longer present, when these people did these things and hoped for happiness, and were caught up in events beyond their control.

Kaufman achieves this effect almost without seeming to try. At first his film seems to be almost exclusively about sex, but then we notice in countless individual shots and camera decisions that he does not allow his camera to become a voyeur. There is a lot of nudity in the film, but no pornographic documentary quality; the camera does not linger, or move for the best view, or relish the spectacle of nudity. The result is some of the most poignant, almost sad, sex scenes I have ever seen—sensuous, yes, but bittersweet.

The casting has a lot to do with this haunting quality. Daniel Day-Lewis plays Tomas with a sort of detachment that is supposed to come from the character's distaste for commitment. He has a lean, intellectual look, and is not a voluptuary. For him, sex seems like a form of physical meditation, rather than an activity with another person. Lena Olin, as Sabina, has a lush, voluptuous body, big-breasted and tactile, but she inhabits it so comfortably that the movie never seems to dwell on it or exploit it. It is a fact of nature. Juliette Binoche, as Tereza, is almost ethereal in her beauty and innocence, and her attempt to reconcile her love with her lover's detachment is probably the heart of the movie.

The film is based on the novel by the Czech novelist Milan Kundera, whose works all seem to consider eroticism with a certain wistfulness, as if to say that while his characters were making love, they were sometimes distracted from the essentially tragic nature of their existence. That is the case here. Kaufman, whose previous films have included *The Right Stuff* and a remake of *Invasion of the Body Snatchers,* has never done anything remotely like this before, but his experiment is a success in tone; he has made a movie in which reality is asked to coexist with a world of pure sensuality, and almost, for a moment, seems to agree.

The film will be noticed primarily for its eroticism. Although major films and filmmakers considered sex with great frankness and freedom in the early and mid-seventies, films in the last decade have been more adolescent, more plot- and action-oriented. Catering to audiences of adolescents, who are comfortable with sex only when it is seen in cartoon form, Hollywood has also not been comfortable with the complications of adult sexuality—the good and the bad. What is remarkable about *The Unbearable Lightness of Being,* however, is not the sexual content itself, but the way Kaufman has been able to use it as an avenue for a complex story, one of nostalgia, loss, idealism, and romance.

Under the Volcano

R, 109 m., 1984

Albert Finney (Geoffrey Firmin), Jacqueline Bisset (Yvonne Firmin), Anthony Andrews (Hugh Firmin), Ignacio Lopez Tarso (Dr. Vigil), Katy Jurado (Senora Gregoria). Directed by John Huston and produced by Michael Fitzgerald. Screenplay by Guy Gallo, based on the book by Malcolm Lowry.

The consul drinks. He has been drinking for so many years that he has arrived at that peculiar stage in alcoholism where he no longer drinks to get high or to get drunk. He drinks simply to hold himself together and continue to function. He has a muddled theory that he can even "drink himself sober," by which he means that he can sometimes find a lucid window through the fog of his life. *Under the Volcano* is the story of the last day in his drinking.

He lives in Cuernavaca, Mexico, in the years just before World War II. He is not really the British consul anymore: he was only a vice consul, anyway, and now that has been stripped from him, and he simply drinks. He has a few friends and a few acquaintances, and his long days are spent in a drunk's never ending occupation, monitoring his own condition. On this morning, for example, he had a bit too much and passed out in the road. One of those things. Earlier, or later, sometime in there, he had stumbled into a church and prayed for the return of his wife, who had left him. Now he sits on his veranda talking with his half-brother. He turns his head. His wife is standing in the doorway. He turns back. It cannot be her. He looks again. She is still there. Turns away. It cannot be. Looks again. A hallucination. But it persists, and eventually he is forced to admit that his wife has indeed returned, in answer to his prayers.

He drinks. He passes out. He wakes. The three of them set off on a bus journey. A peasant is found dead on a roadside. Later, in a bar, there is an unpleasantness with a whore. Still later, the day ends in a ditch. The consul's day is seen largely through his point of view, and the remarkable thing about *Under the Volcano* is that it doesn't resort to any of the usual tricks that movies use when they portray drunks. There are no trick shots to show hallucinations. No spinning cameras. No games with focus. Instead, the drunkenness in this film is supplied by the remarkably controlled performance of Albert Finney as the consul. He gives the best drunk performance I've ever seen in a film. He doesn't overact, or go for pathos, or pretend to be a character. His focus is on communication. He wants, he desperately desires, to penetrate the alcoholic fog and speak clearly from his heart to those around him. His words come out with a peculiar intensity of focus, as if every one had to be pulled out of the small hidden core of sobriety deep inside his confusion.

The movie is based on the great novel by Malcolm Lowry, who used this day in the life of a drunk as a clothesline on which to hang several themes, including the political disintegration of Mexico in the face of the rising tide of Nazism. John Huston, the sure-footed old veteran who directed the film, wisely leaves out the symbols and implications and subtexts and just gives us the man. Lowry's novel was really about alcoholism, anyway; the other materials were not so much subjects as they were attempts by the hero to focus on something between his ears.

The movie belongs to Finney, but mention must be made of Jacqueline Bisset as his wife and Anthony Andrews as his half-brother. Their treatment of the consul is interesting. They understand him well. They love him (and, we gather, each other). They realize nothing can be done for him. Why do they stay with him? For love, maybe, or loyalty, but also perhaps because they respect the great effort he makes to continue to function, to "carry on," in the face of his disabling illness. Huston, I think, is interested in the same aspect of the story, that within every drunk is a man with self-respect trying to get free.

Undertow
R, 107 m., 2004

Jamie Bell (Chris Munn), Devon Alan (Tim Munn), Josh Lucas (Deel Munn), Dermot Mulroney (John Munn), Kristen Stewart (Lila), Shiri Appleby (Violet). Directed by David Gordon Green and produced by Terrence Malick, Lisa Muskat, and Edward R. Pressman. Screenplay by Joe Conway and Green.

The two boys live in a rural area of Georgia with their father. The older, Chris, is quietly building a reputation as a troublemaker; the younger, Tim, is an odd kid who eats mud and paint and explains he is "organizing my books by the way they smell." Their father, John, mourns his dead wife and keeps his boys so isolated that on his birthday Chris complains, "We can't even have friends. What kind of a birthday party is it with just the three of us?"

A fourth arrives. This is Deel, John's brother, fresh out of prison and harboring resentment. "I knew your mom first—she was my girl," he tells Chris. Deel and John's father had a hoard of Mexican gold coins with a legend attached to them: They belonged to the ferryman on the river Styx. Deel believes he should have inherited half of the coins, and believes John has them hidden somewhere around the place.

If this sounds as much like a Brothers Grimm tale as a plot, that is the intention of David Gordon Green, the gifted director of *Undertow*. Still only twenty-nine, he has made three films of considerable power, and has achieved what few directors ever do: After watching one of his films for a scene or two, you know who directed it. His style has been categorized as "southern Gothic," but that's too narrow. I sense a poetic merging of realism and surrealism; every detail is founded on fact and accurate observation, but the effect appeals to our instinct for the mythological. This fusion is apparent when his characters say something that (a) sounds exactly as if it's the sort of thing they would say, but (b) is like nothing anyone has ever said before. I'm thinking of lines like, "He thinks about infinity. The doctor says his brain's not ready for it." Or, "Can I carve my name in your face?"

Undertow, like Green's *George Washington* (2001) and *All the Real Girls* (2003), takes place in a South where the countryside coexists with a decaying industrial landscape. We see not the thriving parts of cities, but the desolate places they have forgotten. His central characters are usually adolescents, vibrating with sexual feelings but unsure how to express them, and with a core of decency they are not much aware of.

In writing *Undertow*, Green said at the Toronto Film Festival, he had in mind stories by the Grimms, Mark Twain, and Robert Louis Stevenson, and also Capote's *In Cold Blood*. He wears these sources lightly. While much is made about the family legends surrounding the gold coins, they inspire not superstition but greed and function in the story just as any treasure would. Although we see two generations in which there is a troubled brother and a strange brother, the parallels are not underlined.

Instead, we see largely through the eyes of Chris (Jamie Bell, from *Billy Elliot* and *Nicholas Nickleby*). He figures in the startling opening sequence, where he tries to get the attention of a girl he likes, is chased away, and lands on a board with a nail in it. The audience recoils in shock. But now watch how he *continues* to hobble along with the board still attached to his foot. This is technically funny, but in a very painful way, and who but Green would think of the moment when an arresting cop gives Chris his board back?

Chris is in rebellion against the isolated life created for them by their father (Dermot Mulroney). So is Tim (Devon Alan), but in an internal way, expressed by the peculiar things he eats and the chronic stomach pain that results. When their Uncle Deel (Josh Lucas) appears one day, he is at first a welcome change, with his laid-back permissiveness. John asks Deel to watch the kids during the day while he's at work, but Deel is not very good at this, and points his nephews toward more trouble than he saves them from.

The bad feeling over the gold coins comes to a head in an instant of violence, and the boys run away from home, entering a world that evokes *The Night of the Hunter* (1955). In both films, two siblings flee from a violent man through a haunted and dreamy southern landscape. The people they meet during their flight all look and sound real enough, but also have the qualities of strangers encountered in fantasies: the kindly black couple who lets them work for food, and the secret community of other kids, living in a junkyard. If these passages add up to a chase scene, Green directs not for thrills but for deeper, more ominous feelings, and the music by Philip Glass doesn't heighten, as it would during a conventional chase scene, but deepens, as if the chase is descending into ominous dread.

Green has a visual style that is beautiful without being pretty. We never catch him photographing anything for its scenic or decorative effect. Instead, his landscapes have the kind of underlined ambiguity you'd find in the work of a serious painter; these are not trees and swamps and rivers, but Trees and Swamps and Rivers—it's here that the

parallel with *The Night of the Hunter* is most visible.

Undertow is the closest Green has come to a conventional narrative, although at times you can sense him pulling away from narrative requirements to stay a little longer in a moment that fascinates him. He is not a director of plots so much as a director of tones, emotions, and moments of truth, and there's a sense of gathering fate even in the lighter scenes. His films remind me of *Days of Heaven,* by Terrence Malick (one of this film's producers), in the way they are told as memories, as if all of this happened and is over with and cannot be changed; you watch a Green film not to see what will happen, but to see what did happen.

Films like *Undertow* leave some audiences unsettled because they do not proceed predictably according to the rules. But they are immediately available to our emotions, and we fall into a kind of waking trance, as if being told a story at an age when we half-believed everything we heard. It takes us a while to get back to our baseline; Green takes us to that place where we keep feelings that we treasure, but are a little afraid of.

Unforgiven
R, 130 m., 1992

Clint Eastwood (William Munny), Gene Hackman (Little Bill Daggett), Morgan Freeman (Ned Logan), Richard Harris (English Bob), Jaimz Woolvett (Schofield Kid), Saul Rubinek (W. W. Beauchamp), Frances Fisher (Strawberry Alice), Anna Thompson (Delilah Fitzgerald). Directed and produced by Eastwood. Screenplay by David Webb Peoples.

Clint Eastwood's *Unforgiven* opens with a shot of the hero, William Munny, standing at the graveside of his wife. The shot is similar to one with John Wayne in John Ford's *She Wore a Yellow Ribbon.* Given Eastwood's familiarity with classic Westerns, it may be a deliberate echo. Women in Westerns have always been a civilizing influence on the violence of the frontier, bringing schools, churches, white picket fences, and apple pies. Men in the West, left to their own devices, imagine and create such a violent world that they can hardly leave the house unarmed.

William Munny was once, we learn, a gunfighter, and not a very nice one. He killed not simply bad guys, but also women and children, and he doesn't feel very good about that. Now he is trying to support his motherless family by working as a hog farmer, and when the word comes of a $1,000 bounty on the heads of two cowboys who have carved up a prostitute, he accepts the challenge. He needs the money, and perhaps he is attracted to his old ways.

The prostitute was attacked in Big Whiskey, Wyoming, a town ruled by Little Bill Daggett (Gene Hackman), a sheriff who mirrors Munny's own ambiguity about violence and domesticity. Daggett does not permit firearms in his town, and tries to settle disputes peaceably. In adjudicating the brawl at the brothel, for example, he orders the two cowboys to give the saloon owner a couple of horses, in lieu of damages. This is justice of a sort, although not, of course, for the scarred young prostitute, who is treated like so much property. An older hooker (Frances Fisher) is enraged, and raises the money for the bounty on the cowboys.

Like the traditional Western it is, *Unforgiven* sets up this situation in detail and at leisure. We sense in the first few minutes that the plot will lead up to a final violent test of William Munny and his partners. And in a Western like this, that means their personalities and characters will be tested; unlike the new violent urban adventures, Westerns place greater weight on the meaning of gunfights and deaths. They aren't simply stunts, providing a moment of activity before being quickly forgotten.

Munny is told about the bounty in the first place by a kid (all Westerns seem to have a kid) named, inevitably, the Schofield Kid and played by Jaimz Woolvett. He's too nearsighted to shoot straight, and knows he needs help. Munny in turn recruits an old partner, Ned Logan (Morgan Freeman), and they ride into Big Whiskey, only to discover that another famous gunfighter, English Bob (Richard Harris), has also arrived on the scene.

English Bob is trailed by a writer for pulp Western magazines (Saul Rubinek), who interviews the sheriff on his theories about killing, and does research for his report on the impending showdown. His presence essentially signals the death of the Old West, which is in its last days as a reality and its first days as

the stuff of legend and entertainment. The movie is filled, in a low-key way, with other inventions and developments signaling the intrusion of the modern.

Unforgiven is not simply about its plot—about whether William Munny collects the bounty, and about who gets killed in the process—but also about what it means to kill somebody, and how a society is affected when people get killed. Hackman's sheriff is a key element in developing this theme. He is capable of being likable, sensible, friendly, and even funny, but he also harbors a streak of violent sadism, and uses his badge as an excuse to beat his victims. He looks so peaceable up there on the roof of his house, nailing shingles, but like the "peaceful" town he takes such pride in, he harbors a vicious streak.

Eastwood's direction of the film, with cinematography by Jack Green, doesn't make the West seem particularly scenic. A lot of the shots are from the inside looking out, so that the figures seem dark and obscure and the brightness that pours through the window is almost blinding. The effect is to diminish the stature of the characters; these aren't heroes, but simply the occupants of a simple, rude society in which death is an everyday fact.

Eastwood bought the story for this movie years ago, and sat on it, he says, until he was old enough to play it. Indeed, all four of the major actors in the film (Eastwood, Hackman, Freeman, and Harris) are on the shady side of sixty, and the enormous success of *Unforgiven*—both at the box office and in the Academy Awards—indicates that somehow this theme, of older men still trapped in a dance of death, rang a bell. The only way to criticize a movie, Jean-Luc Godard once wrote, is to make another movie. For Clint Eastwood, one of the most intelligent and self-aware of filmmakers, *Unforgiven* may have been a reaction to the rising tide of meaningless violence in films and on television. In a way, this is a movie about how, when you kill someone, they're really dead.

United 93

R, 90 m., 2006

J. J. Johnson (Captain Jason Dahl), Ben Sliney (Himself), Gregg Henry (Colonel Robert Marr), Christian

Clemenson (Thomas Burnett), Becky London (Jean Headley Peterson), David Alan Basche (Todd Beamer), Trish Gates (Sandy Bradshaw), Cheyenne Jackson (Mark Bingham), Lewis Alsamari (Saeed Al Ghamdi), Chip Zien (Mark Rothenberg). Directed by Paul Greengrass and produced by Tim Bevan, Eric Fellner, and Lloyd Levin. Screenplay by Greengrass.

It is not too soon for *United 93*, because it is not a film that knows any time has passed since 9/11. The entire story, every detail, is told in the present tense. We know what they know when they know it, and nothing else. Nothing about al-Qaida, nothing about Osama bin Laden, nothing about Afghanistan or Iraq, only events as they unfold. This is a masterful and heartbreaking film, and it does honor to the memory of the victims.

The director, Paul Greengrass, makes a deliberate effort to stay away from recognizable actors, and there is no attempt to portray the passengers or terrorists as people with histories. In most movies about doomed voyages, we meet a few key characters we'll be following: the newlyweds, the granny, the businessman, the man with a secret. Here there's none of that. What we know about the passengers on United 93 is exactly what we would know if we had been on the plane and sitting across from them: nothing, except for a few details of personal appearance.

Scenes on board the plane alternate with scenes inside the National Air Traffic Control Center, airport towers, regional air traffic stations, and a military command room. Here, too, there are no backstories, just technicians living in the moment. Many of them are played by the actual people involved; we sense that in their command of procedure and jargon. When the controllers in the LaGuardia tower see the second airplane crash into the World Trade Center, they recoil with shock and horror, and that moment in the film seems as real as it seemed to me on September 11, 2001.

The film begins on a black screen, and we hear one of the hijackers reading aloud from the Quran. There are scenes of the hijackers at prayer, and many occasions when they evoke God and dedicate themselves to him. These details may offend some viewers but are almost certainly accurate; the hijacking and destruction of the four planes was carried out as

a divine mission. That the majority of Muslims disapprove of terrorism goes without saying; on 9/12, there was a candlelight vigil in Iran for the United States. That the terrorists found justification in religion also goes without saying. Most nations at most times go into battle evoking the protection of their gods.

But the film doesn't depict the terrorists as villains. It has no need to. Like everyone else in the movie, they are people of ordinary appearance, going about their business. *United 93* is incomparably more powerful because it depicts all of its characters as people trapped in an inexorable progress toward tragedy. The movie contains no politics. No theory. No personal chitchat. No patriotic speeches. We never see the big picture.

We watch United 93 as the passengers and crew board the plane and it prepares to depart. Four minutes later, the first plane went into the WTC. Living in the moment, we share the confusion of the air traffic controllers. At first it's reported that a "small plane" crashed into the tower. Then by a process of deduction, it's determined it must have been a missing American flight. The full scope of the plot only gradually becomes clear. One plane after another abandons its flight plan and goes silent. There are false alarms: For more than an hour, a Delta flight is thought to have been hijacked, although it was not. At the FAA national center, the man in charge, Ben Sliney (playing himself), begins to piece things together and orders a complete shutdown of all American air traffic. Given what a momentous decision this was, costing the airlines a fortune and disrupting a nation's travel plans, we are grateful he had the nerve to make it.

As the outline of events comes into focus, there is an attempt to coordinate civilian and military authorities. It is doomed to fail. A liaison post is not staffed. Two jet fighters are sent up to intercept a hijacked plane, but they are not armed; there is discussion of having the fighters ram the jets as their pilots eject. A few other fighters are scrambled but inexplicably fly east, over the ocean. Military commanders try again and again, with increasing urgency, to get presidential authorization to use force against civilian aircraft. An unbearable period of time passes, with no response.

The movie simply includes this in the flow

of events, without comment. Many people seeing the film will remember the scene in *Fahrenheit 9/11* in which George W. Bush sat immobile in a children's classroom for seven minutes after being informed of the attack on the WTC. What was he waiting for? Was he ever informed of the military request? The movie does not know, because the people on the screen do not have the opportunity of hindsight.

All of these larger matters are far off-screen. The third act of the film focuses on the desperation on board United 93, after the hijackers take control, slash flight attendants, kill the pilots, and seem to have a bomb. We are familiar with details of this flight, pieced together from many telephone calls from the plane and from the cockpit voice recorder. Greengrass is determined to be as accurate as possible. There is no false grandstanding, no phony arguments among the passengers, no individual heroes. The passengers are a terrified planeload of strangers. After they learn by phone about the WTC attacks, after an attendant says she saw the dead bodies of the two pilots, they decide they must take action. They storm the cockpit.

Even as these brave passengers charge up the aisle, we know nothing in particular about them—none of the details we later learned. We could be on the plane, terrified, watching them. The famous words "Let's roll" are heard but not underlined; these people are not speaking for history.

There has been much discussion of the movie's trailer, and no wonder. It pieces together moments from *United 93* to make it seem more conventional, more like a thriller. Dialogue that seems absolutely realistic in context sounds, in the trailer, like sound bites and punch lines. To watch the trailer is to sense the movie that Greengrass did not make. To watch *United 93* is to be confronted with the grim, chaotic reality of that summer day in 2001.

The movie is deeply disturbing, and some people may have to leave the theater. But it would have been much more disturbing if Greengrass had made it in a conventional way. He does not exploit, he draws no conclusions, he points no fingers, he avoids "human interest" and "personal dramas" and just simply watches. The movie's point of view reminds me of the angels in *Wings of Desire*. They see what people do and they are saddened, but they cannot intervene.

An Unmarried Woman

R, 124 m., 1978

Jill Clayburgh (Erica), Alan Bates (Saul), Michael Murphy (Martin), Lisa Lucas (Patti), Cliff Gorman (Charlie), Pat Quinn (Sue), Kelly Bishop (Elaine), Linda Miller (Jeannette), Andrew Duncan (Bob), Penelope Russianoff (Tanya). Directed by Paul Mazursky and produced by Mazursky and Tony Ray. Screenplay by Mazursky.

It is, Erica thinks, a happy marriage, although perhaps she doesn't think about it much. It's *there*. Her husband is a stockbroker, she works in an art gallery, their daughter is in a private high school, they live in a high-rise and jog along the East River. In the morning there is "Swan Lake" on the FM radio, and the last sight at night is of the closing stock prices on the TV screen. Had she bargained for more?

One day, though, swiftly and cruelly, it all comes to an end: Her husband breaks down in phony tears on the street and confesses he's in love with another woman. A younger woman. And so her happy marriage is over. At home, consumed by anger, grief, and uncertainty, she studies her face in the mirror. It is a good face in its middle thirties, and right now it looks plain scared.

So end the first, crucial passages of Paul Mazursky's *An Unmarried Woman*. They are crucial because we have to understand how *completely* Erica was a married woman if we're to join her on the journey back to being single again. It's a journey that Mazursky makes into one of the funniest, truest, sometimes most heartbreaking movies I've ever seen. And so much of what's best is because of Jill Clayburgh, whose performance is, quite simply, luminous.

We know that almost from the beginning. There's a moment of silence in the morning, right after Erica's husband and daughter have left the house. "Swan Lake" is playing. She's still in bed. She's just made love. She speaks from her imagination: "The ballet world was thrilled last night. . . ." And then she slips out of bed and dances around the living room in her T-shirt and panties, because she's so happy, so alive . . . and at that moment the movie's got us. We're in this thing with Erica to the end.

The going is sometimes pretty rough, especially when she's trying to make sense out of things after her husband (Michael Murphy) leaves her. She gets a lot of support and encouragement from her three best girlfriends, and some of the movie's very best scenes take place when they meet for long lunches with lots of white wine, or lie around on long Sunday mornings paging through the *Times* and idly wondering why *their* lives don't seem to contain the style of a Bette Davis or a Katharine Hepburn. And then there are the scenes when she talks things over with her daughter (Lisa Lucas), who's one of those bright, precocious teenagers who uses understatement and cynicism to conceal how easily she can still be hurt.

After Erica gets over the period where she drinks too much and cries too much and screams at her daughter when she doesn't mean to, she goes to a woman psychiatrist, who explains that men are the problem, yes, but they are not quite yet the enemy. And so Erica, who hasn't slept with any man but her husband for seventeen years, finds herself having lunch in Chinese restaurants with boors who shout orders at waiters and try to kiss her in the back seat of a cab. There's also the self-styled stud (Cliff Gorman) who's been hanging around the art gallery, and she finally does go up to his place—warily, gingerly, but she has to find a way sometime of beginning her life again.

And then one day a British artist is hanging a show at the gallery, and he asks her if she doesn't think one side of the painting is a little low, and she says she thinks the *whole* painting is too low, and he doesn't even seem to have noticed her as he says, "Let's discuss it over lunch." They fall in love. Oh, yes, gloriously, in that kind of love that involves not only great sex but walking down empty streets at dawn, and talking about each other's childhood. The painter is played by Alan Bates, who is cast, well and true, as a man who is perfectly right for her and perfectly wrong for her, both at the same time.

An Unmarried Woman plays true with all three of its major movements: The marriage, the being single, the falling in love. Mazursky's films have considered the grave and funny business of sex before (most memorably in *Bob & Carol & Ted & Alice* and *Blume in Love*). But he's never before been this successful at really dealing with the complexities and following them through. I wouldn't want to tell you too much about the movie's conclusion, but believe this much: It's honest and it's *right*, because Mazursky and Jill Clayburgh care too much about Erica to dismiss her with a conventional happy ending.

Clayburgh takes chances in this movie. She's out on an emotional limb. She's letting us see and experience things that many actresses simply couldn't reveal. Mazursky takes chances, too. He wants *An Unmarried Woman* to be true, for starters: We have to believe at every moment that life itself is being considered here. But the movie has to be funny, too. He won't settle for less than the truth *and* the humor, and the wonder of *An Unmarried Woman* is that he gets it. I've been reviewing movies for a long time now without ever feeling the need to use dumb lines like "You'll laugh—you'll cry." But I did cry, and I did laugh.

28 Up

NO MPAA RATING, 136 m., 1985

Featuring Tony Walker, Bruce Balden, Suzanne Dewey, Nicholas Hitchon, Peter Davies, Paul Kligerman, John Brisby, Andrew Brackfield, Charles Furneaux, Neil Hughes, Jackie Bassett, Lynn Johnson, Susan Sullivan, and Symon Basterfield. Directed by Michael Apted and produced by Margaret Bottomley and Apted.

The child is father of the man.
—William Wordsworth

Somewhere at home are photographs taken when I was a child. A solemn, round-faced little boy gazes out at the camera, and as I look at him I know in my mind that he is me and I am him, but the idea has no reality. I cannot understand the connection, and as I think more deeply about the mystery of the passage of time, I feel a sense of awe.

Watching Michael Apted's documentary *28 Up*, I had that feeling again and again, the awe that time does pass, and that the same individual does pass through it, grows from a child to an adult, becoming someone new over the passage of years, but still containing some of the same atoms and molecules and fears and gifts that were stored in the child.

This film began in 1964 as a documentary for British television. The assignment for Michael Apted was to interview several seven-year-olds from different British social classes, races, backgrounds, and parts of the country, simply talking with them about what they found important or interesting about their lives. Seven years later, when the subjects were fourteen, Apted tracked them down and interviewed them again. He repeated the process when they were twenty-one, and again when they were twenty-eight, and this film moves back and forth within that material, looking at the same people when they were children, teenagers, young adults, and now warily approaching their thirties.

We have always known that the motion picture is a time machine. John Wayne is dead, but the angle of his smile and the squint in his eye will be as familiar to our children as it is to us. Orson Welles is dead, but a hundred years from now the moment will still live when the cat rubs against his shoe in *The Third Man,* and then the light from the window catches his sardonic grin. What is remarkable about *28 Up* is not, however, that the same individuals have been captured at four different moments in their lives. We quickly grow accustomed to that. What is awesome is that we can see so clearly how the seven-year-old became the adolescent, how the teenager became the young man or woman, how the adult still contains the seeds of the child.

One sequence follows the lives of three upper-class boys who come from the right families and go to all the right schools. One of the boys is a snot, right from the beginning, and by the time he is twenty-one he is a bit of a reactionary prig. We are not surprised when he declines to be interviewed at twenty-eight; we could see it coming. We are curious, though, about whether he will check back in at thirty-five, perhaps having outlived some of his self-importance.

Another little boy is a winsome loner at seven. At fourteen, he is a dreamy idealist, at twenty-one he is defiant but discontented, and at twenty-eight—in the most unforget-table passage in the film—he is an outcast, a drifter who moves around Great Britain from place to place, sometimes living in a shabby house trailer, still a little puzzled by how he seems to have missed the boat, to never have connected with his society.

There is another little boy who dreams of growing up to be a jockey, and who is a stable boy at fourteen, and does get to be a jockey, briefly, and now drives a cab and finds in his job some of the same personal independence and freedom of movement that he once thought jockeys had. There is a determined young Cockney who is found, years later, happily married and living in Australia and doing well in the building trades. There is a young woman who at twenty-one was clearly an emotional mess, a vague, defiant, bitter, and unhappy person. At twenty-eight, married and with a family, she is a happy and self-assured young woman; the transformation is almost unbelievable.

As the film follows its subjects through the first halves of their lives, our thoughts are divided. We are fascinated by the personal progressions we see on the screen. We are distracted by wonderment about the mystery of the human personality. If we can see so clearly how these children become these adults—was it just as obvious in our own cases? Do we, even now, contain within us our own personal destinies for the next seven years? Is change possible? Is the scenario already written?

I was intending to write that certain groups would be particularly interested in this movie. Teachers, for example, would hardly be able to see *28 Up* without looking at their students in a different, more curious light. Poets and playwrights would learn from this film. So would psychiatrists. But then I realized that *28 Up* is not a film by or for experts. It is superb journalism, showing us these people passing through stages of their lives in such a way that we are challenged to look at our own lives. It is as thought-provoking as any documentary I've ever seen.

I look forward to the next edition of this film, when its subjects are thirty-five. I have hope for some, fear for others. It is almost scary to realize this film has given me a fair chance of predicting what lies ahead for these strangers. I almost understand the motives of those who chose to drop out of the experiment.

35 Up

NO MPAA RATING, 127 m., 1992

A documentary film directed and produced by Michael Apted.

35 Up is the latest installment in the most engrossing long-distance documentary project in the history of film. It began twenty-eight years ago, when a group of ordinary British citizens of various backgrounds were interviewed about their views of the world—at the age of seven. Ever since, at seven-year intervals, director Michael Apted has revisited the subjects for an update on their lives and views, and in this new film the children born in the mid-fifties are marching into middle age, for the most part with few regrets.

Before writing this review, I went back to look again at 28 Up (1985), which had just been released on video. I wanted to freshen my memory of Neil, the loner who has become the most worrisome of Apted's subjects. When we first see him, at the age of seven, he is already clear on how he wants to spend his life: He wants to be a bus driver, choosing the route himself, telling all of his passengers what to look at out of the windows. By fourteen, Neil was a visionary with big hopes for his life, but something happened between then and twenty-one, when we found him angry and discontented. At twenty-eight, in an image that has haunted me, he was an outcast, living in a small house trailer on the shores of a bleak Scottish lake, and there was real doubt in my mind whether he would still be alive at thirty-five.

He is. He still lives alone, still harbors the view that people cannot quite be trusted to choose for themselves, still doubts he will find a wife to put up with him. Now he lives in subsidized housing on a Scottish island, where last year he directed the village pageant. He was not invited to direct it again this year, and he complains morosely that if people would only learn to follow instructions, the pageant might have turned out better.

Most of the other subjects of the film have turned out more happily. There is Tony, who at seven wanted to be a jockey and at fourteen had found employment as a stable boy. In an earlier film we saw him studying "the knowledge," the year-long process by which a London cabbie must learn his city before he is granted a license, and now, at thirty-five, his children growing up nicely, he is happy to own his own taxi. He realized his dreams, he says; he was a jockey, briefly, and once got to race against Lester Piggott.

We revisit the three "working-class girls" of the earlier films, who gather around a pub table to assess their lives, with which they are reasonably content. And we see the progress of an upper-class boy who came across as such a snob at twenty-one that he declined to be interviewed at twenty-eight. He is back at thirty-five, somewhat amazingly involved in a relief project for eastern Europe, and we sense that he has grown out of his class snobbery (to a degree; he cannot resist pointing out a portrait of a royal ancestor).

In my review of 28 Up, I quoted Wordsworth: "The child is father of the man." We can see that even more clearly in 35 Up. The faces gather lines and maturity, the hair sometimes is beginning to turn gray, the slenderness of youth has started to sag. But the eyes are the same. The voices are the same—deeper but still expressing the thoughts of the same person who was already there, somehow formed, at the age of seven. And in almost every case the personality and hopes of the seven-year-old has predicted the reality of the adult life. (There is one exception, a woman who seemed depressed and aimless at twenty-one, but has undergone a remarkable transformation into cheerful adulthood; I would like her to talk frankly, sometime, about what happened to her between twenty-one and later.)

Some of the subjects complain ruefully that the project has violated their privacy. One of the working-class women says that she is well content with her life, except every seven years when Apted comes nosing around. Others have opted out of 35 Up because they no longer welcome the attention. Most have remained, apparently with the thought that since they have gone this far, they might as well stay the distance.

Somewhere in the midst of the Up project

lurks the central mystery of life. How do we become who we are? How is our view of ourselves and our world fashioned? Educators and social scientists might look at these films and despair, because the essential ingredients of future life all seem to be in place at seven, formed in the home and even in the womb before school or the greater world has had much impact. Even more touchingly, in the voices and eyes of these people at thirty-five, we see human beings confronting the fact of their own mortality.

Nearly thirty years have passed since the camera first recorded them peering out at the world around them. In another seven years, most of them will be back again. None has yet died. The project will continue as long as any of them cooperate. Eventually the time will come when only two or three are still alive, and then none. And many years in the future, viewers will be able to look at this unique record and contemplate the beauty and mystery of life. I am glad most of the subjects of this project have sacrificed their privacy to us every seven years, because in a sense they speak for us, and help us take our own measure.

42 Up

NO MPAA RATING, 139 m., 2000

A documentary series directed and produced by Michael Apted.

Give me the child until he is seven, and I will show you the man.

—Jesuit saying

In 1964, a British television network began an intriguing experiment. They would interview a group of seven-year-olds, asking them what they wanted to do in life and what kind of a future they envisioned. Then these same subjects would be revisited every seven years to see how their lives were turning out. It was an intriguing experiment, using film's unique ability to act as a time machine—"the most remarkable nonfiction film project in the history of the medium," wrote Andrew Sarris.

Now here is *42 Up*, the sixth installment in the series. I have seen them all since *14 Up*, and every seven years the series measures out my own life too. It is impossible to see the films without asking yourself the same questions—without remembering yourself as a child and a teenager, and evaluating the progress of your life.

I feel as if I know these subjects, and indeed I do know them better than many of the people I work with every day, because I know what they dreamed of at seven, their hopes at fourteen, the problems they faced in their early twenties, and their marriages, their jobs, their children, even their adulteries.

When I am asked for career advice, I tell students that they should spend more time preparing than planning. Life is so ruled by luck and chance, I say, that you may end up doing a job that doesn't even exist yet. Don't think you can map your life, but do pack for the journey. Good advice, I think, and yet I look at *42 Up* and I wonder if our fates are sealed at an early age. Many of the subjects of the series seemed to know at seven what they wanted to do and what their aptitudes were, and they were mostly right. Others produce surprises, and keep on producing them right into middle age.

Michael Apted could not have predicted that his future would include a lifelong commitment to this series. He was a young man at the beginning of his career when he worked as a researcher on *7 Up*, choosing the fourteen subjects who would be followed. He became the director of *14 Up*, and has guided the series ever since, taking time off from a busy career as the director of feature films (*Coal Miner's Daughter, Gorillas in the Mist*). In his introduction to a new book about the series, he says he does not envy his subjects: "They do get notoriety and it's the worst kind of fame—without power or money. They're out in the street getting on with their lives and people stop them and say, 'Aren't you that girl?' or 'Don't I know you?' or 'You're the one,' and most of them hate that."

The series hasn't itself changed their lives, he believes. "They haven't got jobs or found partners because of the film, except in one case when a friendship developed with dramatic results."

That case involves Neil, who for most long-time followers of the series has emerged as the most compelling character. He was a brilliant but pensive boy, who at seven said he wanted to be a bus driver, so he could tell the passengers what to look for out the windows; he saw himself in the driver's seat, a tour guide for the lives of others. What career would you guess for him? An educator? A politician?

In later films he seemed to drift, unhappy and without direction. He fell into confusion. At twenty-eight, he was homeless in the Highlands of Scotland, and I remember him sitting outside his shabby house trailer on the rocky shore of a loch, looking forlornly across the water. He won't be around for the next film, I thought: Neil has lost his way. He survived, and at thirty-five was living in poverty on the rough Shetland Islands, where he had just been deposed as the (unpaid) director of the village pageant; he felt the pageant would be going better if he were still in charge.

The latest chapter in Neil's story is the most encouraging of all the episodes in *42 Up*, and part of the change is because of his fellow film subject Bruce, who was a boarding school boy, studied math at Oxford, and then gave up a career in the insurance industry to become a teacher in London inner-city schools. Bruce has always seemed one of the happiest of the subjects. At forty, he got married. Neil moved to London at about that time, was invited to the wedding, found a job through Bruce, and today—well, I would not want to spoil your surprise when you find the unlikely turn his life has taken.

Apted says in his introduction to the book *42 Up* that if he had the project to do again, he would have chosen more middle-class subjects (his sample was weighted toward the upper and working classes), and more women. He had a reason, though, for choosing high and low: The original question asked by the series was whether Britain's class system was eroding. The answer seems to be: yes, but slowly. Sarris, writing in the *New York Observer*, delivers this verdict: "At one point, I noted that the upper-class kids, who sounded like twits at 7 compared to the more spontaneous and more lovable lower-class kids, became more interesting and self-confident as they raced past their social inferiors. It was like shooting fish in a barrel. Class, wealth, and social position did matter, alas, and there was no getting around it."

None of the fourteen have died yet, although three have dropped out of the project (some drop out for a film and are back for the next one). By now many have buried their parents. Forced to confront themselves at seven, fourteen, twenty-one, twenty-eight, and thirty-five, they seem mostly content with the way things have turned out. Will they all live to forty-nine? Will the series continue until none are alive? This series should be sealed in a time capsule. It is on my list of the ten greatest films of all time, and is a noble use of the medium.

49 Up

NO MPAA RATING, 135 m., 2005

With Bruce Balden, Jacqueline Bassett, Symon Basterfield, Andrew Brackfield, John Brisby, Suzanne Dewey, Nicholas Hitchon, Neil Hughes, Lynn Johnson, Paul Kligerman, Susan Sullivan, and Tony Walker. The latest installment of a documentary series directed by Michael Apted and produced by Bill Jones.

Tony has a vacation home in Spain now, with a veranda and a swimming pool. He's seen some hard times, but at forty-nine, he is basking in contentment. We see him in the pool, tanned, splashing with his family.

When you live with Michael Apted's *Up* series of documentaries, there tends to be one character who most focuses your attention. For me, in *28 Up* through *42 Up*, it was Neil, the troubled loner. As a boy, he wanted to be a tour bus guide, telling people what to look at. As an adult, he still has an impulse to lead and instruct, but it hasn't worked out, and he became a morose loner. In one film there was a shot of him standing next to a lake in Scotland, in front of his shabby mobile home, no one else in sight; I thought, "Neil will be dead by the next film."

It didn't work out that way, and Neil provides the biggest surprise of *42 Up*. But Tony's development in some ways may be as fundamental as a transition. What happens to him helps illustrate the importance, even the nobility, of this most extraordinary series of documentaries.

In 1964, Granada Television in Britain commissioned a film about a group of children born in 1956. Drawn mostly from the upper and lower ends of the British class system, they were asked about their plans and dreams. The idea was to revisit them every seven years and see how they were doing. As a plan, this was visionary, even foolhardy, but here we are at *49 Up*, and the children of the 1964 film have children and grandchildren of their own. Anyone who has followed the series develops a curious fascination with their lives, because they *are* lives. This is not reality TV, with its contrivances and absurdities, but a meditation on lifetimes.

Consider Tony. At seven years old, he wanted to be a racing jockey. Brash, crew-cut, extroverted, he made it all seem clear. He did briefly become a jockey, even racing against the great Lester Piggott, but as an adult he was a London taxi driver.

Apted, the director who has been with the *Up* series from the beginning, was in 1963 a lad who wanted to be a movie director. He grew up to become one. In a sense, he is another of the film's subjects, growing older off-camera. There was a time when he was convinced that Tony would eventually fall into a life of crime, and so he asked some questions and shot some scenes in anticipation of that development.

Tony did not become a criminal, and Apted learned his lesson, he told me. He decided to never anticipate what might happen to his subjects—to simply revisit them and catch up with their lives. Similarly, he decided to bypass politics; prime ministers and governments come and go during these films, but Apted doesn't see his subjects as political creatures; whatever their politics, he is concerned more with what is happening in their lives and how they feel about that.

I am not British, was born fourteen years before the subjects, and yet by now identify intensely with them, because some kinds of human experience—teenage years, work, marriage, illness—are universal. You could make this series in any society. As its installments accumulate in my memory, they cause me to regard the arc of my own life—to ask if I, too, contained at seven the makings of whom I would become.

Certainly between seven and fourteen my path was settled. I wrote for the grade-school newspaper and used a crude "hektograph" machine to write and publish *The Washington Street News*. I was always going to be a journalist, and very old friends who knew me at twelve say, "You haven't changed."

Neither has Tony. He has expanded in his ideas of what his life can provide him, but he is still the overconfident, driving, ebullient personality he was at seven. Bruce, who wanted to be a missionary at seven, got involved in inner-city schools that were a contrast to his upper-class background. Neil's life has contained enormous surprises, but he is always definitely Neil—worried, discontented, fretting that the world is not following his instructions.

You do not have to have seen any of the earlier films to understand this one. George Turner, Apted's cinematographer since *21* and editor since *28*, provides flashbacks to earlier days in each life. By now that is a daunting editing task, but he is able to do it and keep us up to speed.

The early films were shot in black and white. Then Apted went to color. Now he is using digital. The subtle visual alterations help to suggest the passage of time. So do gray hairs and potbellies. None of the original group has died; most have prospered and found happiness. And with the passing of every seven years, the more they look different than they were at seven, the more they are the same.

Michael Apted's *Up* series remains one of the great imaginative leaps in film. I came aboard early in the series and I, too, have grown older along with it. In Tony's eyes at seven, reflecting in his mind his triumphs as a jockey, I can see the same eyes at forty-nine, gazing upon his swimming pool in Spain. He ran the race, and he won.

The Upside of Anger

R, 118 m., 2005

Joan Allen (Terry Wolfmeyer), Kevin Costner (Denny Davies), Erika Christensen (Andy Wolfmeyer), Evan Rachel Wood ("Popeye" Wolfmeyer), Keri Russell (Emily Wolfmeyer), Alicia Witt (Hadley Wolfmeyer), Mike Binder ("Shep" Goodman). Directed by Mike Binder and produced by Jack Binder, Alex Gartner, and Sammy Lee. Screenplay by Mike Binder.

Joan Allen and Kevin Costner achieve something in *The Upside of Anger* that may have been harder than costarring in *Macbeth*. They create two imperfect, alcoholic, resentful ordinary people, neighbors in the suburbs, with enough money to support themselves in the discontent to which they have become accustomed. I liked these characters precisely because they were not designed to be likable—or, more precisely, because they were likable in spite of being exasperating, unorganized, self-destructive, and impervious to good advice. That would be true of most of my friends. They say the same about me.

Allen plays Terry Wolfmeyer, suburban wife and mother of four daughters ("One of them hates me and the other three are working on it"). Her husband has walked out of the marriage, and all signs point to his having fled the country to begin a new life in Sweden with his secretary. "He's a vile, selfish pig," Terry says, "but I'm not gonna trash him to you girls." The girls, of college and high school age, dress expensively, are well groomed, prepare the family meals, and run the household, while their mother emcees with a vodka and tonic; her material is smart and bitter, although she sees the humor in the situation, and in herself.

Costner plays her neighbor, Denny Davies, once a star pitcher for the Detroit Tigers, now a sports-talk host who is bored by sports and talk. He spends his leisure time at the lonely but lucrative task of autographing hundreds of baseballs to sell online and at fan conventions. When Terry's husband disappears, Denny materializes as a friend in need. In need of a drinking partner, mostly. Neither one is a sensational *Barfly/Lost Weekend* kind of alcoholic, but more like the curators of a constant state of swizzledom. They are always a little drunk. Sometimes a little less little, sometimes a little more little.

Allen and Costner are so good at making these characters recognizable that we may not realize how hard that is to do. For Allen, the role comes in a season of triumph; she is also wonderful in Campbell Scott's *Off the Map*, and wait until you see her in Sally Potter's *Yes*. Costner reminds us that he is best when he dials down; he is drawn to epic roles, but here he's as comforting as your boozy best pal.

In *The Upside of Anger*, written and directed by Mike Binder, they occupy a comedy buried in angst. The camaraderie between Terry and Denny is like the wounded affection of two people with hangovers and plenty of time to drink them away. The four daughters have sized up the situation and are getting on with their lives in their own ways, mostly competently. Hadley

(Alicia Witt) is a cool, centered college student; Andy (Erika Christensen) reacts as second children often do, by deciding she will not be Hadley and indeed will accept an offer to be an intern on Denny's radio show—an offer extended enthusiastically by Shep (Binder), the fortyish producer, who is a shameless letch. Emily (Keri Russell) is at war with her mother; she wants to be a dancer, and her mother says there's no money or future in it. Popeye (Evan Rachel Wood) is the youngest, but maturing way too rapidly, like Wood's character in *13*.

Terry deals imperfectly with events in the lives of her daughters, such as Hadley's impending marriage and Andy becoming Shep's girlfriend. Although Terry is wealthy, stylish, and sexy—a thoroughbred temporarily out of training—she has a rebel streak maybe left over from her teens in the late 1970s. At a lunch party to meet Hadley's prospective in-laws, she tells Denny, "I was like a public service ad against drinking."

It is inevitable that Denny and Terry will become lovers. The girls like him. He is lonely, and Terry's house feels more like home than his own, where the living room is furnished primarily with boxes of baseballs. It is also true, given the current state of the drunk driving laws, that alcoholics are wise to choose lovers within walking distance. So the movie proceeds with wit, intelligence, and a certain horrifying fascination. Sometimes Terry picks up the phone to call the creep in Sweden, but decides not to give him the satisfaction.

And then comes an unexpected development. Because *The Upside of Anger* opened a week earlier in New York than in Chicago, I am aware of the despair about this development from A. O. Scott in the *New York Times* (the ending "is an utter catastrophe") and Joe Morgenstern in the *Wall Street Journal* (the ending is "a cheat").

They are mistaken. Life can contain catastrophe, and life can cheat. The ending is the making of the movie, its transcendence, its way of casting everything in a new and ironic light, causing us to reevaluate what went before, and to regard the future with horror and pity. Without the ending, *The Upside of Anger* is a wonderfully made comedy of domestic manners. With it, the movie becomes larger and deeper. When life plays a joke on you, it can have a really rotten sense of humor.

Up the Down Staircase

NO MPAA RATING, 124 m., 1967

Sandy Dennis (Sylvia Barrett), Patrick Bedford (Paul Barringer), Roy Poole (McHabe), Jeff Howard (Joe Ferone), Ellen O'Mara (Alice Blake). Directed by Robert Mulligan and produced by Alan J. Pakula. Screenplay by Tad Mosell, based on the book by Bel Kaufman.

We need more American films like *Up the Down Staircase*. We need more films that might be concerned, even remotely, with real experiences that might once have happened to real people. And we need more actresses like Sandy Dennis, who looks as if she may be alive and not a plastic robot turned out by the little elves who constructed Doris Day and Sandra Dee. Here, at last, is a film made in America by Americans in which no one is murdered by a cigarette lighter.

The film's setting is Calvin Coolidge High School, one of those vast blocks of stone and brick in which our cities educate three thousand students at a shot. Coolidge High is apparently located somewhere in a low-income, racially mixed New York neighborhood, and it is a "problem" school. That makes it bait for an idealistic naive new teacher who wants to "expand vistas."

As the teacher, Sandy Dennis is perfectly cast. She doesn't know how to teach, what to teach, or, in the end, even why she wants to teach. Her first lesson comes in the first two minutes of her first class, when she quotes Emily Dickinson ("There is no frigate like a book") and the students hoot with laughter. A veteran teacher suggests maybe she should have substituted "steamship." These are the things you have to think about if you propose to reach real kids.

As Dennis slowly comes to know the students in her classes, they slowly turn out to be individuals with problems. Like Alice Blake (superbly played by Ellen O'Mara), a chubby, painfully shy girl who falls in love with a handsome English teacher. Or Joe Ferone (Jeff Howard), who can earn good grades when he wants to but gets more attention if he doesn't. Or Harry A. Kagan (Salvatore Rosa), the glib, loud, fat class president who always wears a tie and always tucks it into his belt.

The new teacher starts with fanciful notions, quoting Edna St. Vincent Millay and planning little speeches on *First Impression*. But she gradually feels her way into the minds of her students, and when they make the incredible discovery in *Tale of Two Cities* that today might also be the best of times and the worst of times, she breaks through. It is the best of times, the students say, because we are "surrounded by prosperity"—the words are ironic. It is also the worst of times, they decide, because there are still rats in their bathrooms.

I don't know if Coolidge High is representative of most "problem" schools, but I have a feeling it might be. The process of education goes round and round, but the students are hardly ever involved. Frustrated or defeated, teachers use inane tactics to hold attention. One invents a game called "Hospital Grammar," in which "sick sentences" are treated by students who are "doctors and nurses." When a girl attempts suicide, the only insight found in her "Pupil Personality Profile" is: "Reliable blackboard monitor."

Here is an honest film about one aspect of life as it is lived in our large cities. The school and the students come through with unmistakable authenticity. The camera is alert but not obtrusive, allowing the classroom to emerge spontaneously and not through stagy tricks, and everything is brought together by Dennis's quiet, natural, splendid performance.

V

Vagabond

NO MPAA RATING, 105 m., 1986

Sandrine Bonnaire (Mona), Macha Meril (Madame Lanier), Stephane Friess (JeanPierre), Laurence Cortadellas (Elaine), Marthe Jarnias (Tante Lydie), Yolande Moreau (Yolande), Joel Fosse (Paulo). Directed by Agnes Varda. Screenplay by Varda.

The opening shot moves in ever so slowly across the bleak fields of a French winter landscape. Two trees stand starkly outlined at the top of a hill. There is no joy here. As the camera moves closer, we see in the bottom of a ditch the blue and frozen body of a young woman. A field hand discovers her and sets up a cry. Soon the authorities are there with their clipboards, recording those things which can be known, such as the height and weight and eye color of the corpse, and wondering about all the things which cannot be known, such as her name and why she came to be dead in the bottom of a ditch.

Then we hear Agnes Varda's voice on the sound track, telling us that she became absorbed by the mystery of this young stranger's last months on earth and sought the testimony of those people who had known her. *Vagabond*, however, is the story of a woman who could not be known. And although there are many people who can step forward and say they spoke with the young woman, sheltered her, gave her food and drink, shared cigarettes and even sex with her, there is no one to say that they knew her.

Vagabond tries to feel like a documentary, a series of flashbacks to certain days in the last months of the girl's life. Actually, it is all fiction. And, like all good fiction, it is able to imply much more than it knows. From bits and pieces of information that the girl spreads out among the people that she meets, we learn that she was born of middle-class parents, that she took secretarial training, that she worked in an office but hated it, that eventually she went on the road, carrying her possessions and a tent in a knapsack on her back, begging food and shelter, sometimes doing a little work for a little money.

She looks ordinary enough, with her wide, pleasant face and her quiet smile. People talk about how bad she smells, but we cannot know about that. She rolls her own cigarettes and sometimes prefers them to food. Sometimes in a café, when she is given a few francs, she spends them on the jukebox instead of on bread.

Only gradually do we realize that she contains a great passivity. When a goat herder and his wife take her in, feed her and give her a small trailer to spend the winter in, she does not embrace the opportunity to help them in their work. She sits inside the trailer, staring blankly ahead. She is utterly devoid of ambition. She has gone on the road, not to make her fortune, but to drop out completely from all striving.

It is hard to read her signals. Sometimes she seems to be content, opening the flap of her tent and staring out, half-blinded, at the brightness of the morning sun. She stops for a few days in a chateau and laughs with the old countess who lives there as they get drunk on the countess's brandy and the old lady complains that her son is only waiting for her to die. She seems to respond briefly to a woman professor, an agronomist who takes her along in the car as she inspects a plague among the plane trees. But is she really warming up to these people, or only providing them with a mirror that reflects their own need to touch somebody?

One of the most painful subtleties of this film is the way we see the girl's defenses finally fall. One day after another, almost without seeming to, she sinks lower and lower. The life of the vagabond becomes the life of the outcast, and then the outcast becomes the abandoned. Finally, the abandoned becomes an animal, muddy and unkempt, disoriented, at the bottom, no longer bewildered, frightened, amazed at how low she has fallen. Finally she cries, and we remember how young and defenseless she is, under that tough skin.

What a film this is. Like so many of the greatest films, it tells us a very specific story, strong and unadorned, about a very particular person. Because it is so much her own story and does not seem to symbolize anything—because the director has no parables, only information—it is only many days after the end of the film that we reflect that the story of the vagabond could also be the story of our lives. For how many have truly known us, although many have shared our time?

Vanaja

NO MPAA RATING, 111 m., 2006

Mamatha Bhukya (Vanaja), Urmila Dammannagari (Rama Devi, Landlady), Karan Singh (Shekhar, Her Son), Marianti Ranachandriah (Somayya), Khishna Garlapati (Ran Babu), Krishnamma Gundimalla (Radhamma, Cook), Bhavani Renukunta (Lacchu, Vanaja's Friend), Prabhu Garlapati (Yadigiri, Little Boy). Directed and written by Rajnesh Domalpalli and produced by Andrew Lund.

Vanaja, a beautiful and heart-touching film from India, represents a miracle of casting. Every role, including the challenging central role of a low-caste fourteen-year-old girl, is cast perfectly and played flawlessly, so that it is a renewing pleasure to see these faces on the screen. Then we learn their stories; the actors, naturally and effortlessly true, are all non-professionals who were cast for their looks and presence, and then trained in an acting workshop set up by the director, Rajnesh Domalpalli. He recalls that his luminous star, Mamatha Bhukya, an eighth grader, was untrained and had to learn to act and perform classical Indian dances—during a year of lessons set up in his family's basement!

But this movie is not wonderful because of where the actors started. It is wonderful because of where they arrive, and who they become. Bhukya is a natural star, her eyes and smile illuminating a face of freshness and delight. And the other characters are equally persuasive, especially Urmila Dammannagari, as the district landlady, who has to negotiate a way between her affection for the girl and her love for her son.

But why are you reading this far? An Indian film? Starring Mamatha Bhukya and Urmila Dammannagari? Lesser readers would already have tuned out, but you are curious. And so I can promise you that here is a very special film. It was made by the director as part of his master's thesis in the film department at Columbia University, shot over a period of years on a $20,000 budget, and all I can say is,

$20,000 buys a lot in India, including a great-looking, extraordinary film.

Let me tell you a little of the story. In a rural district of South India, a fourteen-year-old girl named Vanaja (Bhukya) lives with her shambling, alcoholic father. Life is bearable because she makes her own way, and when we first see her she's in the front row of a dance performance with her best friend, Lacchu, where they're giggling like bobby-soxers (a word that will mystify some of my Indian readers, but fair's fair). What beautiful girls these are, and I mean that not in a carnal but a spiritual sense. The sun shines from their skin.

Vanaja's father takes her to the local landlady, Rama Devi (Urmila Dammannagari) and asks for a job for her. Rama Devi, in her late forties, is not a stereotyped cruel landowner, but a strong yet warm woman with a sense of humor who likes the girl's pluck during their interview and hires her—at first to work with the livestock. But Vanaja dreams of becoming a dancer and persuades Rama Devi to give her lessons.

As we know from Satyajit Ray's *The Music Room*, many rural landowners pride themselves on their patronage of the arts; to possess an accomplished dancer in her household would be an adornment for Rama Devi. The lessons go well, and there are dance scenes that show how well the actress learned during her year of basement lessons, but there are no Bollywood-type musical scenes here; indeed, the film industry of this district not far from Hyderabad is known as Tollywood, after the Teluga language. It is also a status symbol to speak English, which Vanaja has never been very good at.

The landlady's twenty-three-year-old son Shekhar (Karan Singh) returns from study in America, prepares to run for office, and notices the new beauty on his mother's staff. And although you may guess what happens next, I won't tell you, except to observe something that struck me. Although there is usually no nudity or even kissing in Indian films (and there is none here) the screenplay is unusually frank in dealing with the realities of sexual life.

Vanaja becomes fifteen, then sixteen. She grows taller. She will be a great beauty. But her lower-caste origins disqualify her for marriage into Rama Devi's family, her drunken father is a worry and burden, the local post-boy is fresh with her, and although the landlady is very fond of her and covets her dancing, her son will always come first. Vanaja's only real allies are her childhood friend, and Radhamma (Krishnamma Gundimalla) the landlady's cook and faithful servant.

In any Indian film many of the pleasures are tactile. There are the glorious colors of saris and room decorations, the dazzle of dance costumes, and the dusty landscape that somehow becomes a watercolor by Edward Lear, with its hills and vistas, its oxen and elephants, its houses that seem part of the land. In this setting, Domalpalli tells his story with tender precision, and never an awkward moment.

The plot reminds me of neorealism crossed with the eccentric characters of Dickens. The poor girl taken into a rich family is also a staple of Victorian fiction. But *Vanaja* lives always in the moment, growing from a simple story into a complex one, providing us with a heroine, yes, but not villains so much as vain, weak people obsessed with their status in society. When the final shot comes, we miss the comfort of a conventional Hollywood ending. But *Vanaja* ends in a very Indian way, trusting to fate and fortune, believing that there is a tide in the affairs of men, which—but you know where it leads. Let's hope it does.

Vanity Fair

PG-13, 137 m., 2004

Reese Witherspoon (Becky Sharp), Eileen Atkins (Matilde Crawley), Jim Broadbent (Mr. Osborne), Gabriel Byrne (Marquess of Steyne), Romola Garai (Amelia Sedley), Bob Hoskins (Sir Pitt Crawley), Rhys Ifans (William Dobbin), Geraldine McEwan (Lady Southdown), James Purefoy (Rawdon Crawley), Jonathan Rhys-Meyers (George Osborne), Tony Maudsley (Joseph Sedley). Directed by Mira Nair and produced by Janette Day, Lydia Dean Pilcher, and Donna Gigliotti. Screenplay by Matthew Faulk, Julian Fellowes, and Mark Skeet, based on the novel by William Makepeace Thackeray.

"I had thought her a mere social climber. I see now she's a mountaineer."

So says one of her fascinated observers as Becky Sharp transforms herself from the impoverished orphan of an alcoholic painter into an adornment of the middle, if not the upper, reaches of the British aristocracy. *Vanity Fair* makes her a little more likable than she was in the 1848 novel—but then, I always liked Becky anyway, because she so admirably tried to obey her cynical strategies and yet so helplessly allowed herself to be misled by her heart.

Reese Witherspoon reflects both of those qualities effortlessly in this new film by Mira Nair, and no wonder, for isn't there a little of Elle Woods, her character in *Legally Blonde*, at work here? Becky, to be sure, never goes through a phase when anyone thinks her stupid, but she does use her sexuality to advantage, plays men at their own game, and scores about as well as possible given the uneven nineteenth-century playing field.

When William Makepeace Thackeray wrote his funny and quietly savage novel, there were few career prospects for an educated young woman who did not fancy prostitution. She could become a governess, a teacher, a servant, a religious, or a wife. The only male profession open to her was writing, which she could practice without the permission or license of men; that accounts for such as Jane Austen, the Brontës, George Eliot, Mrs. Gaskell, and others who, as Virginia Woolf imagined them, wrote their masterpieces in a corner of the parlor while after-dinner chatter surrounded them.

Becky Sharp could probably have written a great novel, and certainly inspired one; Thackeray sees her dilemma and her behavior without sentiment, in a novel that must have surprised its first readers with its realism. We meet Becky just as she's leaving finishing school, where the French she learned from her Parisian mother won her a berth as a boarder and tutor. She made one good friend there: Amelia Sedley (Romola Garai), and now proposes to visit the Sedley family for a few days on her way to her first job, as a governess for the down-at-heels Sir Pitt Crawley (Bob Hoskins).

But working as a governess is not Becky's life goal. She wants to marry well, and since she has neither fortune nor title it would be best if her husband brought both of those attributes into the marriage. Does this make her an evil woman? Not at all; romantic love is a modern and untrustworthy motive for marriage, and in England and India (where both Thackeray and Mira Nair were born), marriage strategies have always involved family connections and financial possibilities.

Amelia likes Becky (she is the only one at school who did, Thackeray observes), and thinks it would be nice if Becky married her brother Joseph (Tony Maudsley). Amelia's own fiancé, Captain George Osborne (Jonathan Rhys-Meyers), discourages this plan, convincing the weak-willed Joseph that Becky is little better than a beggar with vague family irregularities, and would not adorn the Sedley household.

So Becky goes to Crawley Hall, where she mistakes the unshaven Sir Pitt for a servant. Servants, money, and provisions seem in short supply in the Crawley family, but Becky makes one important conquest; Sir Pitt's rich maiden sister, Matilde (played with magnificent, biting wit by Eileen Atkins), admires her pluck and becomes her friend and protector—up to a point. That point is reached when Becky secretly marries her nephew Rawdon Crawley (James Purefoy). As a second son, Rawdon will not inherit the title or house, and as a gambler can't live within his allowance, so this marriage gives Becky a liaison with a good family but not the benefits.

Some of the film's best moments come when characters administer verbal flayings to one another. Matilde is unforgiving when she is crossed. But the most astonishing dialogue comes from a character named Lord Steyne (Gabriel Byrne), whom Becky meets for the first time when she's a young girl in her father's studio. Steyne fancies a portrait of Becky's mother; her father prices it at three guineas, but Becky insists on ten, putting on a good show of sentimental attachment to her departed parent. Now, many years later, Steyne crosses Becky's path again. She reminds him of their first meeting. It occurs to him that having purchased a portrait of the parent, he might purchase the original of the daughter. This sets up a dinner-table scene in the Steyne household at which the lord verbally destroys every member of his family, not sparing the rich mulatto heiress from the Caribbean who married his son for his title even though "the whole world knows he's an idiot."

The peculiar quality of *Vanity Fair*, which

sets it aside from the Austen adaptations like *Sense and Sensibility* and *Pride and Prejudice*, is that it's not about very nice people. That makes them much more interesting. There are some decent blokes in the story, but on the fringes: William Dobbin (Rhys Ifans), for example, who persists in loving Amelia even though she falls for George, a thoroughgoing bounder. Joseph is a good sort, too.

And for that matter, how evil is Lord Steyne, really? He and Becky meet again after her husband, Rawdon, has lost everything at the gambling tables and the bailiff is literally moving their furniture out of the house. Steyne pays off their debts. This would not have been considered by anybody as an act of selfless charity. Of course, he expects Becky to show her gratitude, although oddly enough she shows it more frankly in the 1848 novel than in the 2004 movie; its PG-13 rating no doubt inspired Nair and her writers to suggest to their tender young audiences that Becky can be friendly and grateful without, as the saying goes, Steyne having sex with that young woman. In the real world, the furniture would have been back on the sidewalk.

Is the India-born Mira Nair a strange choice to adapt what some think is the best English novel of the nineteenth century? Not at all. She has an instinctive feel for the comic possibilities of marital alliances, as she showed in her wonderful *Monsoon Wedding* (2001). And she brings to the movie an awareness of the role India played in the English imagination; in the nineteenth century, hardly a well-born family lacked relatives serving or living in India, and wasn't it Orwell who said the two nations deserved each other, because they shared the same love of eccentricity?

Vera Drake

R, 125 m., 2004

Imelda Staunton (Vera Drake), Phil Davis (Stan Drake), Peter Wight (Inspector Webster), Adrian Scarborough (Frank), Heather Craney (Joyce), Daniel Mays (Sid Drake), Alex Kelly (Ethel Drake), Sally Hawkins (Susan), Eddie Marsan (Reg), Ruth Sheen (Lily). Directed by Mike Leigh and produced by Simon Channing Williams and Alain Sarde. Screenplay by Leigh.

Vera Drake is a melodious plum pudding of a woman who is always humming or singing to herself. She is happy because she is useful, and likes to be useful. She works as a cleaning woman in a rich family's house, where she burnishes the bronze as if it were her own, and then returns home to a crowded flat to cook, clean, and mend for her husband, son, and daughter, and cheer them up when they seem out of sorts. She makes daily calls on invalids to plump up their pillows and make them a nice cup of tea, and once or twice a week she performs an abortion.

London in the 1950s. Wartime rationing is still in effect. A pair of nylons is bartered for eight packs of Players. Vera (Imelda Staunton) buys sugar on the black market from Lily (Ruth Sheen), who also slips her the names and addresses of women in need of "help." Lily is as hard and cynical as Vera is kind and trusting. Vera would never think of accepting money for "helping out" young girls when "they got no one to turn to," but Lily charges two pounds and two shillings, which she doesn't tell Vera about.

In a film of pitch-perfect, seemingly effortless performances, Imelda Staunton is the key player, and her success at creating Vera Drake allows the story to fall into place and belong there. We must believe she's naive to be taken advantage of by Lily, but we do believe it. We must believe she has a simple, pragmatic morality to justify abortions, which were a crime in England until 1967, but we do believe it.

Some of the women who come to her have piteous stories; they were raped, they are still almost children, they will kill themselves if their parents find out, or in one case there are seven mouths to feed and the mother lacks the will to carry on. But Vera is not a social worker who provides counseling; she is simply being helpful by doing something she believes she can do safely. Her age-old method involves lye soap, disinfectant, and, of course, lots of hot water, and another abortionist describes her method as "safe as houses."

The movie has been written and directed by Mike Leigh, the most interesting director now at work in England, whose *Topsy-Turvy, High Hopes, All or Nothing,* and *Naked* join this film in being partly "devised" by the actors themselves. His method is to gather a cast for weeks or months of improvisation in which they create and explore their characters. I don't think the technique has ever worked better

than here; the family life in those cramped little rooms is so palpably real that as the others wait around the dining table while Vera speaks to a policeman behind the kitchen door, I felt as if I were waiting there with them. It's not that we "identify" so much as that the film quietly and firmly includes us.

The movie is not about abortion so much as about families. The Drakes are close and loving. Vera's husband, Stan (Phil Davis), who works with his brother in an auto repair shop, considers his wife a treasure. Their son, Sid (Daniel Mays), works as a tailor, has a line of patter, is popular in pubs, but lives at home because of the postwar housing crisis. Their daughter, Ethel (Alex Kelly), is painfully shy, and there is a sweet, tactful subplot in which Vera invites a lonely, tongue-tied bachelor named Reg (Eddie Marsan) over for tea, and essentially arranges a marriage.

Vera Drake tells a parallel story about a rich girl named Susan (Sally Hawkins), the daughter of the family Vera cleans for. Susan is raped by her boyfriend, becomes pregnant, and goes to a psychiatrist who can refer her to a private clinic for a legal abortion. Like everyone in the movie, Susan is excruciatingly shy about discussing sex, and ignorant. "Did he force himself upon you?" the psychiatrist asks, and Susan is not sure how to answer. Leigh's point is that those with £100 could legally obtain an abortion in England in 1950, and those with £2 had to depend on Vera Drake, or on women not nearly as nice as Vera Drake.

Vera's world falls apart when the police become involved in an abortion that almost leads to death, and the tightly knit little family changes when the police knock on the door. Inspector Webster (Peter Wight) is a considerable man, large, imposing, and not without sympathy. He believes in the law and enforces the law, but he quickly understands that Vera was not working for profit, and is not ungentle with her. In a courtroom scene, on the other hand, it is clear that the law makes no room for nuance or circumstance.

Some of the film's best scenes involve the family sitting around the table, shell-shocked (after Vera whispers into her husband's ear, telling him what he had never suspected). There are moments when Leigh uses his technique of allowing a reticent character to stir into conviction. At Vera's final Christmas dinner, Reg, now engaged to Ethel, makes what for him is a long speech: "This is the best Christmas I've had in a long time. Thank you very much, Vera. Smashing!" He knows telling Vera she has prepared a perfect meal means more to her than any speech about rights and wrongs, although later he blurts out: "It's all right if you're rich, but if you can't feed 'em you can't love 'em."

Vera Drake is not so much pro- or antiabortion as it is opposed to laws that do little to eliminate abortion but much to make it dangerous for poor people. No matter what the law says, then or now, in England or America, if you can afford a plane ticket and the medical bill you will always be able to obtain a competent abortion, so laws essentially make it illegal to be poor and seek an abortion.

Even in saying that, I am bringing more ideology into Vera Drake than it probably requires. The strength of Leigh's film is that it is not a message picture, but a deep and true portrait of these lives. Vera is kind and innocent, but Lily, who procures the abortions, is hard, dishonest, and heartless. The movie shows the law as unyielding, but puts a human face on the police. And the enduring strength of the film is the way it shows the Drake family rising to the occasion with loyalty and love.

The Verdict

R, 122 m., 1982

Paul Newman (Frank Galvin), Charlotte Rampling (Laura Fischer), Jack Warden (Mickey Morrissey), James Mason (Ed Concannon), Milo O'Shea (Judge Hoyle), Edward Binns (Bishop Brophy), Julie Bovasso (Maureen Rooney), Lindsay Crouse (Kaitlin Costello). Directed by Sidney Lumet and produced by Richard Zanuck and David Brown. Screenplay by David Mamet.

There is a moment in The Verdict when Paul Newman walks into a room and shuts the door and trembles with anxiety and with the inner scream that people should get off his back. No one who has ever been seriously hung over or needed a drink will fail to recognize the moment. It is the key to his character in The Verdict, a movie about a drinking alcoholic who tries to pull himself together for one last step at salvaging his self-esteem.

Newman plays Frank Galvin, a Boston lawyer who has had his problems over the years—a lost job, a messy divorce, a disbarment hearing, all of them traceable in one way or another to his alcoholism. He has a "drinking problem," as an attorney for the archdiocese delicately phrases it. That means that he makes an occasional guest appearance at his office and spends the rest of his day playing pinball and drinking beer, and his evening drinking Irish whiskey and looking to see if there isn't at least one last lonely woman in the world who will buy his version of himself in preference to the facts. Galvin's pal, a lawyer named Mickey Morrissey (Jack Warden) has drummed up a little work for him: An open-and-shut malpractice suit against a Catholic hospital in Boston where a young woman was carelessly turned into a vegetable because of a medical oversight. The deal is pretty simple. Galvin can expect to settle out-of-court and pocket a third of the settlement—enough to drink on for what little future he is likely to enjoy.

But Galvin makes the mistake of going to see the young victim in a hospital, where she is alive but in a coma. And something snaps inside of him. He determines to try this case, by God, and to prove that the doctors who took her mind away from her were guilty of incompetence and dishonesty. In Galvin's mind, bringing this case to court is one and the same thing with regaining his self-respect—with emerging from his own alcoholic coma. Galvin's redemption takes place within the framework of a courtroom thriller. The screenplay by David Mamet is a wonder of good dialogue, strongly seen characters, and a structure that pays off in the big courtroom scene—as the genre requires. As a courtroom drama, The Verdict is superior work. But the director and the star of this film, Sidney Lumet and Paul Newman, seem to be going for something more; The Verdict is more a character study than a thriller, and the buried suspense in this movie is more about Galvin's own life than about his latest case.

Frank Galvin provides Newman with the occasion for one of his great performances. This is the first movie in which Newman has looked a little old, a little tired. There are moments when his face sags and his eyes seem terribly weary, and we can look ahead clearly to the old men he will be playing in ten years' time. Newman always has been an interesting actor, but sometimes his resiliency, his youthful vitality, have obscured his performances; he has a tendency to always look great, and that is not always what the role calls for. This time, he gives us old, bonetired, hung over, trembling (and heroic) Frank Galvin, and we buy it lock, stock, and shot glass.

The movie is populated with finely tuned supporting performances (many of them by British or Irish actors, playing Bostonians not at all badly). Jack Warden is the old law partner; Charlotte Rampling is the woman, also an alcoholic, with whom Galvin unwisely falls in love; James Mason is the ace lawyer for the archdiocese; Milo O'Shea is the politically connected judge; Wesley Addy provides just the right presence as one of the accused doctors. The performances, the dialogue, and the plot all work together like a rare machine.

But it's that Newman performance that stays in the mind. Some reviewers have found *The Verdict* a little slow-moving, maybe because it doesn't always hum along on the thriller level. But if you bring empathy to the movie, if you allow yourself to think about what Frank Galvin is going through, there's not a moment of this movie that's not absorbing. *The Verdict* has a lot of truth in it, right down to a great final scene in which Newman, still drinking, finds that if you wash it down with booze, victory tastes just like defeat.

Footnote: What was in the cup at the end? I thought whisky. I asked Newman some years later. "Coffee," he said.

Veronika Voss

R, 105 m., 1982

Rosel Zech (Veronika Voss), Hilmar Thate (Robert Krohn), Cornelius Froboess (Henriette), Annemarie Düringer (Dr. Marianne Ratz). Directed by Rainer Werner Fassbinder and produced by Thom Schuhly. Screenplay by Fassbinder and Pea Fröhlich.

Veronika Voss was the next-to-last film made by Rainer Werner Fassbinder, who died June 10, 1982, in Munich of a fatal combination of drugs and alcohol. It tells a story of a German actress, famous in the 1940s, who tried to revive her flagging career with alcohol and drugs, and fell into the hands of a sadistic female doctor who provided the drugs as a means of controlling

rich patients. The film is based on the life of Sybille Schmitz, "the German Garbo," who starred in many glossy postwar West German films before becoming addicted to drugs and killing herself in the late 1950s.

What was Fassbinder trying to tell us in this film? It was made, I understand, during a period when cocaine was making his life unmanageable. He called *Veronika Voss* the third film in his trilogy about the West German "economic miracle" of the 1950s and 1960s; the other two films were *The Marriage of Maria Braun* and *Lola*. Never has a stranger trilogy been made about an economic system.

If *Maria Braun* made its heroine into a symbol of Germany pulling itself together after the end of the war, and *Lola* was about the conflict between corruption and duty, *Veronika Voss* seems to be about Germany's lingering fascination with the images of the 1930s, with the carefully cultivated aesthetic of decadence, domination, perversion, and sinister sexuality.

It gives us a heroine who, at one time in her career, stood for the sort of sophisticated, chic sexuality associated with Marlene Dietrich. But by the time we meet *Veronika Voss*, she can't even pull herself together to do a tiny scene in a movie. She seeks comfort from strangers. She is hopelessly addicted to drugs and is the captive of a psychiatrist who enjoys having a fallen star around the office.

Fassbinder's visual style is the perfect match for this subject. He shoots in the unusual combination of wide-screen and black and white, filling his frame with objects: clothes, jewelry, furniture, paintings, statues, potted palms, kitsch. This is a movie of Veronika Voss's life as Veronika might have pictured it in one of her own nightmares. The elaborate camera moves and the great attention to decor are just right for the performances, which come in two styles: stylized and ordinary. Veronika Voss is elegant even in her degradation, but she is surrounded here by plainer folks such as Robert, the sportswriter she picks up in a café. There are times during the movie when we can almost see everyday, ordinary postwar Germany picking its way distastefully through the smelly rubble of prewar decadence.

Is the movie a statement against drug addiction? Not really. Fassbinder never seems to have seen drug addiction in his movies, despite his personal experience with the subject. *Veronika Voss* seems to believe that drug addiction is more the result of Veronika's fall than its cause. We might ask, of course, what alternatives Veronika had. She could have grown gracefully middle-aged, increased her range of interests, outgrown her obsession with herself and her beauty. But that would not have interested Fassbinder, or Veronika.

Fassbinder seems to believe Veronika's tragedy was inevitable, that she was doomed to a quest for eternal youth, for praise and adulation and a never-ending party. Drugs were the way she continued the quest long after it had become a self-deception. It was no problem finding people to supply them and then consume her remaining energy as their payment. Fassbinder's *Veronika Voss* is a bleak, cheerless, and sometimes savage addition to his trilogy about the collapse of the West German postwar dream, but did he realize that he himself was one of the victims of his stories? This movie makes you wonder.

Vincent

NO MPAA RATING, 99 m., 1989

A documentary written and directed by Paul Cox and produced by Tony Llewellyn-Jones. Words by Vincent van Gogh, read by John Hurt.

How rich art is! If only one can remember what one has seen.

—Vincent van Gogh,
in a letter to his brother

"Dear Theo," the letters always began, and there were more than 750 of them, written by Vincent van Gogh to his brother, Theo. The painter spoke of his life, his finances, his health, his prospects, his opinions of the art world—but most of all he spoke about his paintings, and about the discoveries he was making. To read the letters while looking at the paintings (as you can do if you have the book *Vincent by Himself*) is like having van Gogh take you by the hand and lead you through an exhibit of his work. Few other painters have left such a moving and honest personal correspondence.

If you only read the letters and look at the works, however, you will miss something—the look of the everyday world that van Gogh was transforming into his paintings. What Paul Cox has done in *Vincent*—which is the best film about a painter I have ever seen—is to take his camera to some of the places van Gogh painted, and to re-create some of the others in his imagination. This is not, however, one of those idiotic "art appreciation" films in which we see the windmill and then we see the painting of the windmill; Cox knows too much about art to be that simplistic. Instead, he adopts the role of a disciple of the painter, a man who wants to stand in the same places and see the same things as a simple act of love toward van Gogh's work.

All of the words on the sound track are from Vincent's letters to Theo, read by the British actor John Hurt. On the screen, we see landscapes such as van Gogh might have seen, and we visit some of the places where he painted. But there are fictionalized, created sequences as well: scenes of farmers in their fields, or peasants walking down country lanes, or shadows sweeping across fields of sunflowers. And there is a magical sequence in which the people in a room go about their daily business until they arrange themselves, seemingly by accident, into a reproduction of a painting.

Sometimes Cox makes no effort to photograph specific things that van Gogh might have seen or been influenced by. Instead, his camera visits woods and fields, and watches birds and flowers, and meanders down alleyways populated with people who seem to harbor some of the weariness and fear of so many of van Gogh's models. The words continue over these images as well, creating the illusion that the painter is narrating the film himself.

The best parts of the film are the most specific. Cox uses close-ups to show the smallest details of some of the paintings, while the narration describes the painter's technical discoveries and experiments. There are times when we almost seem to be looking at the very brushstroke that van Gogh is describing in a letter. These moments create a sense of the specific. We aren't looking at stars in the sky, or fields of flowers, or a portrait of the artist; we're looking at frozen moments in time when van Gogh's brush moved just such a way in response to his feeling and his craft. The strokes seem enormous, on the big movie screen, and they call our attention to the detail, to the way that van Gogh's paintings were not about their subjects but about the way he saw his subjects.

So much of the popular image of van Gogh is crude and inaccurate, fed by the notion that he was "mad," fueled by the fact that he cut off his ear. There is an entirely different Vincent here, a poetic, thoughtful man who confides everything to his brother, who is not mad so much as completely open to the full range of his experience, including those parts that most of us prudently suppress. *Vincent* is the most romantic and yet the most sensible documentary about a painter I can imagine.

Vincent, Francois, Paul, and the Others

NO MPAA RATING, 113 m., 1976

Yves Montand (Vincent), Michel Piccoli (Francois), Serge Reggiani (Paul), Gerard Depardieu (Jean), Stephane Audran (Catherine). Directed by Claude Sautet and produced by Raymond Danon and Roland Girard. Screenplay by Jean-Loup Dabadie, based on the book by Claude Néron.

We walk out of *Vincent, Francois, Paul, and the Others* and we think, yeah, that's pretty much the way things are. We don't know whether to smile. The movie takes a group of friends in their forties and observes them for a period of weeks. At the end of that time, we find ourselves recognizing them: They're like friends of ours. They may even be like us.

To begin with, they're always in motion. There's little time for reflection, stock-taking. Marriages break up and there's hardly time for a postmortem before an affair begins. Careers that looked rewarding turn into dead ends. There are money problems. Some of the people they've loved are barely memories, but others leave wounds that will never heal. They have secrets, even from themselves; they feel guilt and remorse and a vague anxiety. They smoke all the time and drink too much, and sometimes they're too tired to sleep at night. And yet this movie about them isn't, finally, depressing. The director, Claude Sautet, doesn't take his slice of French middle-class life and turn it into a portrait of despair. These are tough people. They've survived, and they're resilient. They may have abandoned

specific ambitions, but they're incapable of giving up hope. These are poor, dumb, silly, lovely, doomed, beautiful human beings. The central character is Vincent, played by Yves Montand. He runs a small factory that's mortgaged to the hilt. During the period of the movie, a note falls due that means bankruptcy for him. His young mistress breaks off their affair. His wife (Stephane Audran), whom he still loves but has been separated from for three years, files for divorce. He knows what that means. It means she has found someone else. Francois is played by Michel Piccoli. The first time we see him he's with the others at one of their country homes. Someone has a soccer ball and suggests a game in the field. Piccoli, his country coat too new, his shoes too expensive to ruin in a soccer game, nevertheless runs forward, awkwardly, to join the game. As men stop being young they run standing up straight and with their hands in their pockets. Piccoli is a doctor. Once he ran a clinic for the poor. Now he runs a clinic for the rich.

Paul (Serge Reggiani) is a writer who for some time now hasn't been able to write. Like the others, he gets a borrowed reality out of following the career of one of Vincent's employees, who is a prizefighter. We think of Norman Mailer and Jimmy Breslin buying pieces of a kid from Brooklyn who looks good in the ring: The vicarious psychic energy that can be drained from professional athletes is a tonic for some complaints of middle-aged men.

Sautet does not condemn or satirize these friends; he looks at them with acceptance and compassion. Sure, they're chasing coronaries. Sure, they screw around too much. Sure, they have three drinks too many and tell their best friends to go to hell—and mean it, at the time. And, yes, sure they still possess the ability to love without compromise, to make a grand romantic gesture. It's just that they're so much more protective of that ability.

One of the early images of the film occurs during the soccer game. A shed next to the country house catches fire. Everyone pitches in to put it out. This image is not in the film by accident, we realize after we get to know Vincent, Francois, Paul, and the others. At this point in their lives, they're putting out all sorts of little fires. But the house still stands.

Volver

R, 120 m., 2006

Penelope Cruz (Raimunda), Carmen Maura (Irene), Lola Duenas (Sole), Blanca Portillo (Agustina), Yohana Cobo (Paula), Antonio de la Torre (Paco). Directed by Pedro Almodóvar and produced by Esther Garcia. Screenplay by Almodóvar.

How would you like to spend the afterlife? Hanging around in a tunnel of pure light, welcoming new arrivals from among your family and friends? It seems to me a dreary prospect. You'd run out of customers in a generation or two. And how boring to smile and beckon benevolently all the time. My aunt Martha would more likely be cutting the cards for a game of canasta.

In Pedro Almodóvar's enchanting, gentle, transgressive *Volver,* a deceased matriarch named Irene (Carmen Maura) has moved in with her sister Paula (Chus Lampreave), who is growing senile and appreciates some help around the house, especially with the baking. They live, or whatever you'd call it, in a Spanish town where the men die young and the women spend weekends cheerfully polishing and tending the men's graves, just as if they were keeping house for them. In exemplary classic style, Almodóvar uses a right-to-left tracking shot to show this housekeeping carrying us back into the past, and then a subtle, centered zoom to establish the past as part of the present.

We meet Raimunda (Penelope Cruz) and Sole (Lola Duenas), Irene's daughters; Raimunda's daughter, Paula (Yohana Cobo); and Paco (Antonio de la Torre), Raimunda's beer-swilling, layabout husband. Two deaths occur closely spaced to upset this happy balance: Aunt Paula keels over, and young Paula repulses an advance by her stepfather, Paco, using a large, bloody, very Hitchcockian knife. Paco ends up on the kitchen floor, his arms and legs splayed in an uncanny reminder of the body on the poster of Preminger's *Anatomy of a Murder.*

Where will the ghost of Irene go now? Why, obviously, to the one who needs her most—Raimunda. This is the setup for a confounding gathering of murder, reincarnation, and comedy, also involving Raimunda's almost accidental acquisition of the restaurant where she has one of several part-time jobs.

Almodóvar is above all a director who loves women—young, old, professional, amateur, mothers, daughters, granddaughters, dead, alive. Here his cheerful plot combines life after death with the concealment of murder, success in the restaurant business, the launching of daughters, and with completely serendipitous solutions to (almost) everyone's problems. He also achieves a vivid portrait of life in a village not unlike the one where he was born.

Volver is Spanish for "to return," I am informed. The film reminds me of Fellini's *Amarcord,* also a fanciful revisit to childhood that translates as "I remember." What the directors are doing, I think, is paying tribute to the women who raised them—their conversations, conspiracies, ambitions, compromises, and feeling for romance. (What Fellini does more closely resembles revenge.) These characters seem to get along so easily that even the introduction of a "dead" character can be taken in stride.

Women see time more as a continuity, anyway, don't you think? Don't you often hear them speaking of the dead in the present tense? Their lives are a continuity not limited by dates carved in stone.

What a distinctive filmmaker Almodóvar has become. He is greatly influenced, we are assured, by Hollywood melodramas of the 1950s (especially if that decade had been franker about its secret desires). But he is equally turned on, I think, by the 1950s palette of bright basic colors and cheerful optimism that goes without saying. Here the dominant color is red—for blood, passion, and Pedro.

In this connection, some mention might be made of Cruz's cleavage, including one startling shot also incorporating the murder weapon. It seemed impossible not to mention that shot in an interview at the Cannes Film Festival (where the film won honors for best script and ensemble cast). Almodóvar nodded happily. "Yes, I am a gay man," he said, "but I love breasts."

What is most unexpected about *Volver* is that it's not really about murder or the afterlife, but simply incorporates those awkward developments into the problems of daily living. His characters approach their dilemmas not with metaphysics but with common sense. A dead woman turns up as a ghost and is immediately absorbed into her family's ongoing problems: So what took her so long?

It is refreshing to see Cruz acting in the culture and language that is her own. As it did with Sophia Loren in the 1950s, Hollywood has tried to force Cruz into a series of showbiz categories, when she is obviously most at home playing a woman like the ones she knew, grew up with, could have become.

For Almodóvar, too, *Volver* is like a homecoming. Whenever we are most at ease, we fall most easily and gracefully into our native idioms. Certainly as a young gay man in Franco's Spain, he didn't feel at home, but he felt displaced in a familiar way, and now he feels nostalgia for the women who accepted him as easily as if, well, he had been a ghost.

W

Wag the Dog
R, 97 m., 1998

Dustin Hoffman (Stanley Motss), Robert De Niro (Conrad Brean), Anne Heche (Winifred Ames), Woody Harrelson (Sergeant William Schumann), Denis Leary (Fad King), Willie Nelson (Johnny Green), Andrea Martin (Liz Butsky), Kirsten Dunst (Tacy Lime). Directed by Barry Levinson and produced by Jane Rosenthal, De Niro, and Levinson. Screenplay by David Mamet and Hilary Henkin, based on the book *American Hero* by Larry Beinhart.

So, why *did* we invade Grenada? A terrorist bomb killed all those marines in Beirut, the White House was taking flak, and suddenly our marines were landing on a Caribbean island few people had heard of, everybody was tying yellow ribbons 'round old oak trees, and Clint Eastwood was making the movie. The Grenadan invasion, I have read, produced more decorations than combatants. By the time it was over, the Reagan presidency had proven the republic could still flex its muscle—we could take out a Caribbean Marxist regime at will, Cuba notwithstanding.

Barry Levinson's *Wag the Dog* cites Grenada as an example of how easy it is to whip up patriotic frenzy, and how dubious the motives can sometimes be. The movie is a satire that contains just enough realistic ballast to be teasingly plausible; like *Dr. Strangelove*, it makes you laugh, and then it makes you wonder. Just today, I read a Strangelovian story in the paper revealing that some of Russia's nuclear missiles, still aimed at the United States, have gone unattended because their guards were denied their bonus rations of four pounds of sausage a month. It is getting harder and harder for satire to stay ahead of reality.

In the movie, a U.S. president is accused of luring an underage "Firefly Girl" into an anteroom of the Oval Office, and there presenting her with opportunities no Firefly Girl should anticipate from her commander in chief. A presidential election is weeks away, the opposition candidate starts using "Thank Heaven for Little Girls" in his TV ads, and White House aide Winifred Ames (Anne Heche) leads a spin doctor named Conrad Brean (Robert De Niro)

into bunkers far beneath the White House for an emergency session.

Brean, a Mr. Fixit who has masterminded a lot of shady scenarios, has a motto: "To change the story, change the lead." To distract the press from the Firefly Girl scandal, he advises extending a presidential trip to Asia, while issuing official denials that the new B-3 bomber is being activated ahead of schedule. "But there *is* no B-3 bomber," he's told. "Perfect! Deny it even exists!"

Meanwhile, he cooks up a phony international crisis with Albania. Why Albania? Nobody is sure where it is, nobody cares, and you can't get any news out of it. Nobody can even think of any Albanians except—maybe the Belushi brothers? To produce the graphic look and feel of the war, Brean flies to Hollywood and enlists the services of a producer named Stanley Motss (Dustin Hoffman), who is hard to convince at first. He wants proof that Brean has a direct line to the White House. He gets it. As they watch a live briefing by a presidential spokesman, Brean dictates into a cell phone and the spokesman repeats, word for word, what he hears on his earpiece. (I was reminded of the line in *Broadcast News:* "Goes in here, comes out there.")

Motss assembles the pieces for a media blitz. As spokesmen warn of Albanian terrorists skulking south from Canada with "suitcase bombs," Motss supervises the design of a logo for use on the news channels, hires Willie Nelson to write the song that will become the conflict's "spontaneous" anthem, and fakes news footage of a hapless Albanian girl (Kirsten Dunst) fleeing from rapists with her kitten. (Dunst is an American actress, and the kitten, before it is created with special effects, is a bag of Tostitos.)

But what about a martyr? Motss cooks up "good old Shoe," Sergeant William Schumann (Woody Harrelson), who is allegedly rescued from the hands of the Albanians to be flown back for a hero's welcome. Shoe inspires a shtick, too: Kids start lobbing their old gym shoes over power lines, and throwing them onto the court during basketball games, as a spontaneous display of patriotism.

It's creepy how this material is absurd and

convincing at the same time. Levinson, working from a smart, talky script by David Mamet and Hilary Henkin, based on the book *American Hero* by Larry Beinhart, deconstructs the media blitz that invariably accompanies any modern international crisis. Even when a conflict is real and necessary (the Gulf War, for example), the packaging of it is invariably shallow and unquestioning; like sportswriters, war correspondents abandon any pretense of objectivity and detachment, and cheerfully root for our side.

For Hoffman, this is the best performance in some time, inspired, it is said, by producer Robert Evans. (In power and influence, however, Motss seems more like Ray Stark.) Like a lot of Hollywood power brokers, Hoffman's Motss combines intelligence with insecurity and insincerity, and frets because he won't get "credit" for his secret manipulations. De Niro's Brean, on the other hand, is a creature born to live in shadow, and De Niro plays him with the poker-faced plausibility of real spin doctors, who tell lies as a professional specialty. Their conversations are crafted by Mamet as a verbal ballet between two men who love the jargon of their crafts.

"Why does a dog wag its tail?" Brean asks at one point. "Because the dog is smarter than the tail. If the tail was smarter, it would wag the dog." In the Breanian universe, the tail is smarter, and we, dear readers, are invited to be the dogs.

Waking Life

R, 99 m., 2001

Featuring the voices and animated likenesses of Wiley Wiggins, Trevor Jack Brooks, Robert C. Solomon, Ethan Hawke, Julie Delpy, Charles Gunning, David Sosa, Alex Jones, Aklilu Gebrewald, Carol Dawson, Lisa Moore, Steve Fitch, Steven Prince, Adam Goldberg, Nicky Katt, David Martinez, Tiana Hux, Speed Levitch, Steven Soderbergh, and Richard Linklater. Directed by Linklater and produced by Anne Walker-McBay, Tommy Pallotta, Palmer West, and Jonah Smith. Screenplay by Linklater and the cast members. Animation directed by Bob Sabiston.

Waking Life could not come at a better time. Opening in the sad and fearful days soon after September 11, it celebrates a series of articu-

late, intelligent characters who seek out the meaning of their existence and do not have the answers. At a time when madmen think they have the right to kill us because of what they think they know about an afterlife, which is by definition unknowable, those who don't know the answers are the only ones asking sane questions. True believers owe it to the rest of us to seek solutions that are reasonable in the visible world.

The movie is like a cold shower of bracing, clarifying ideas. We feel cleansed of boredom, indifference, futility, and the deadening tyranny of the mundane. The characters walk around passionately discussing ideas, theories, ultimate purposes—just as we've started doing again since the complacent routine of our society was shaken. When we were students we often spoke like this, but in adult life it is hard to find intelligent conversation. "What is my purpose?" is replaced by "What did the market do today?"

The movie is as exhilarating in its style and visuals as in its ideas—indeed, the two are interlocked. Richard Linklater and his collaborators have filmed a series of conversations, debates, rants, monologues, and speculations, and then animated their film using a new process that creates a shimmering, pulsating life on the screen: This movie seems alive, seems vibrating with urgency and excitement.

The animation is curiously realistic. A still from the film would look to you like a drawing. But go to www.wakinglifemovie.com and click on the clips to see how the sound and movement have an effect that is eerily lifelike. The most difficult thing for an animator may be to capture an unplanned, spontaneous movement that expresses personality. By filming real people and then animating them, *Waking Life* captures little moments of real life: a musician putting down her cigarette, a double-take, someone listening while eager to start talking again, a guy smiling as if to say, "I'm not really smiling." And the dialogue has the true ring of everyday life, perhaps because most of the actors helped create their own words: The movie doesn't sound like a script but like eavesdropping.

The film's hero, not given a name, is played by Wiley Wiggins as a young man who has returned to the town where once, years ago, a playmate's folding paper toy (we used to call them "cootie catchers") unfolded to show him the words, "dream is destiny." He seems to be in a dream, and complains that although he knows it's a dream, he can't awaken. He wanders from one person and place to another (something like the camera did in Linklater's first film, *Slackers*). He encounters theories, beliefs, sanity, nuttiness. People try to explain what they believe, but he is overwhelmed until finally he is able to see that the answer is—curiosity itself. To not have the answers is expected. To not ask questions is a crime against your own mind.

If I have made the movie sound somber and contemplative, I have been unfair to it. Few movies are more cheerful and alive. The people encountered by the dreamer in his journey are intoxicated by their ideas—deliriously verbal. We recognize some of them: Ethan Hawke and Julie Delpy, from Linklater's *Before Sunrise*, continue their conversation. Speed Levitch, the manic tour guide from the documentary *The Cruise*, is still on his guided tour of life. Other characters are long known to Linklater, including Robert C. Solomon, a philosopher at the University of Texas, who comes on-screen to say something Linklater remembers him saying in a lecture years ago, that existentialism offers more hope than predestination, because it gives us a reason to try to change things.

I have seen *Waking Life* three times now. I want to see it again—not to master it, or even to remember it better (I would not want to read the screenplay), but simply to experience all of these ideas, all of this passion, the very act of trying to figure things out. It must be depressing to believe that you have been supplied with all the answers, that you must believe them and that to question them is disloyal or a sin. Were we given minds in order to fear the questions?

Walkabout

PG, 95 m., 1971

Jenny Agutter (The Girl), Lucien John (Brother), David Gumpilil (Aborigine), John Mellon (Father). Directed by Nicolas Roeg and produced by Si Litvinoff. Screenplay by Edward Bond.

It is possible to consider *Walkabout* entirely as the story it seems to be: The story of a four-teen-year-old girl and her little brother, who are abandoned in the Australian outback and then saved through the natural skills of a young aborigine boy. It is simpler and easier to consider it on that level, too, because *Walkabout* is a superb work of storytelling and its material is effortlessly fascinating. There's also a tendency (unfortunate, probably) to read *Walkabout* as a catch-all of symbols and metaphors, in which the Noble Savage and his natural life are tested and found superior to civilization and cities. The movie does, indeed, make this comparison several times. Hundreds of miles from help, the girl turns on her portable radio to hear a philosopher observe: "It is now possible to state that 'that is' is." Well, this isn't exactly helpful, and so we laugh. And more adolescent viewers may have to stifle a sigh and a tear when the girl is seen, at the movie's end, married to a cloddish office clerk and nostalgically remembering her idyllic days in the desert.

The contrast between civilization and man's more natural states is well-drawn in the movie, and will interest serious-minded younger people (just as, at the level of pure story, *Walkabout* will probably fascinate kids). But I don't think it's fruitful to draw all the parallels and then piously conclude that we would all be better off far from the city, sipping water from the ground, and spearing kangaroos for lunch. That sort of comparison doesn't really get you anywhere and leaves you with a movie that doesn't tell you more than you already knew. I think there's more than that to *Walkabout*. And I'm going to have a hard time expressing that additional dimension for you, because it doesn't quite exist in the universe of words. Even in these days of film experiments, most movies have their centers in the worlds of plots and characters. But *Walkabout* . . .

Well, to begin with, the film was directed and photographed by Nicolas Roeg, the cinematographer of *Petulia* and many other British films. Roeg's first stab at direction was as codirector of *Performance*. This was his first work as an individual. I persisted in seeing *Performance* on the level of its perfectly silly plot, and on that level it was a wretched movie indeed. People told me I should forget the plot and simply enjoy the movie itself, but I have a built-in resistance to that notion, usually. Perhaps I should have listened. Because Roeg's *Walkabout* is a very rare example of that kind of movie, in which the "civilized" characters and the aborigine exist in a wilderness that isn't really a wilderness but more of an indefinite place for the story to be told. Roeg's desert in *Walkabout* is like Beckett's stage for *Waiting for Godot*. That is, it's nowhere in particular, and everywhere.

Roeg's photography reinforces this notion. He is careful to keep us at a distance from the physical sufferings of his characters. To be sure, they have blisters and parched lips, but he pulls up well short of the usual clichés of suffering in the desert. And his cinematography (and John Barry's otherworldly music) make the desert seem a mystical place, a place for visions. So that the whole film becomes mystical, a dream, and the suicides which frame it set the boundaries of reality. Within them, what happens between the boy and the girl, and the boy and the little brother, is not merely "communication" or "survival" or "cooperation," but the same kind of life-enhancement that you imagine people feel when they go into the woods and eat berries and bring the full focus of their intelligence to bear on the problem of coexisting with nature.

A Walk in the Clouds

PG-13, 102 m., 1995

Keanu Reeves (Paul Sutton), Aitana Sanchez-Gijon (Victoria Aragon), Anthony Quinn (Don Pedro Aragon), Giancarlo Giannini (Alberto Aragon), Angelica Aragon (Marie Jose Aragon), Evangelina Elizondo (Guadelupe Aragon), Freddy Rodriguez (Pedro Aragon, Jr.), Debra Messing (Betty Sutton). Directed by Alfonso Arau and produced by Gil Netter, David Zucker, and Jerry Zucker. Screenplay by Robert Mark Kamen, Mark Miller, and Harvey Weitzman.

A Walk in the Clouds is a glorious romantic fantasy, aflame with passion and bittersweet longing. One needs perhaps to have a little of these qualities in one's soul to respond fully to the film, which to a jaundiced eye might look like overworked melodrama, but which to me sang with innocence and trust.

The movie, set in the vineyards of northern California in the months right after World War II, tells the story of a young man and woman who meet at a time of crisis in both of their lives, who agree to pretend to be married, and who end up desperately in love just when the pretense is about to fail. The plot lovingly constructs one barrier after another to their happiness, so that we can rejoice as each one falls, only to be even more alarmed at the next. And it sets their story in a place of breathtaking beauty.

The director is Alfonso Arau, the Mexican who had an unexpected success with *Like Water for Chocolate*. Once again, he throws caution to the wind and goes for unabashed sentiment, for glorious excess, for love so idealistic it seems never to have heard of the twentieth century. At a time when movies seem obligated to be cynical, when it is easier to snicker than to sigh, what a relief this film is!

The movie opens with Paul (Keanu Reeves) returning home from the war, to a wife he married one day before he shipped out. He doesn't know her, and she hardly understands him. There should never have been a marriage. Now nothing is left. Paul leaves San Francisco on a bus; another passenger is Victoria Aragon (Aitana Sanchez-Gijon). They have a classic Meet Cute: He defends her from some aggressive guys, is thrown off the bus, walks on dejectedly, and finds her standing in the middle of the road with her suitcases. This is her home.

But first a word about the road. It is a picturesque country lane, with leaves arching overhead, and looks not even remotely like the kind of highway Greyhound or Trailways might travel. For Arau, that is just fine; he is concerned here with the landscape of romance, not realism, and look at a scene soon after, where Victoria shows Paul the valley where her family has its vineyard. There has never been a valley this beautiful, this rolling, misty, sun-drenched, and blessed; Arau uses special effects at several points in the film to push his landscapes beyond the real, into the ideal.

Victoria is sad, and begins to cry. She is pregnant and forlorn, abandoned by a worthless man. She is afraid to go home to her father and confess her sin. Paul sees a way he might help: He could pretend to be her husband, they could make up a story, and he could leave in the morning. The grateful Victoria snatches at this straw, and they walk down to the family farm.

The Aragon family is big and colorful and secure, Mexican Americans who have lived on this land for generations. Alberto (Giancarlo Giannini), the father, plays his role to the hilt: He is stern and unyielding, perhaps to conceal the softness of his heart. His wife, Marie Jose Aragon (Angelica Aragon), is good and generous, and perhaps suspects something about the "marriage" but keeps her thoughts to herself. And then there is the patriarch, Don Pedro Aragon (Anthony Quinn), who sees and understands everything, and may even know Paul and Victoria are in love before they realize it themselves.

The movie now alternates between melodramatic crisis and picturesque set pieces. On the one hand, there is the growing suspicion of Alberto, who wonders why, if this boy is married to this girl, he sleeps on the floor. On the other, there is the generosity of Don Pedro, who takes Paul on an early morning walk to show him the root from which the entire vineyard has grown.

Then there is the problem that Paul has not told Victoria that he is married—in name, at least—and thus not free to act on his feelings. For he is certainly falling in love, not only with Victoria but with her family and its land. He tells her he was raised as an orphan: "When I was a kid, I made a wish on every star in the sky to have what you have here." She asks, "And have everyone telling you what to do?" He says, "Better than no one." And this theme leads up to a moment when Anthony Quinn says a line that perhaps only he could utter with complete solemnity and grace: "You are an orphan no longer."

Arau gives us wonderful scenes which would, in a musical, be production numbers. There is the grape-stomping dance, and the scene of ethereal beauty when frost threatens the vines, and all the family and its workers go into the field, using big butterfly wings to fan the warmth from oil heaters down around the grapes. And a scene of near-tragedy, which I will not describe.

Keanu Reeves brings to the role an artless simplicity. He realizes that this material cannot be touched with the slightest hint of self-awareness: Paul must be completely in and of this story. Reeves's performance is almost transparent, and that is the highest compliment I can pay it. Of course the casting of the young woman is crucial, and Aitana Sanchez-Gijon is a luminous discovery. The child of an Italian mother and Spanish father, she has been acting in Spain since she was nine, and here, in excellent English, she creates a heroine both vulnerable and brave.

For me, the most touching scene in the movie is the one where Paul stands beneath Victoria's window, singing a Mexican love song which he has just learned. I know this scene has no business in a movie made in 1995. I know it belongs in an old Italian opera. But so what?

A Walk in the Clouds is the kind of film you have to give yourself to, open yourself to. Logic and cynicism will get you nowhere with this one. Oh, it will show you're tough, and can't be fooled, and no one can slip these ancient romantic notions past you. But if you can resist the scene where he sings beneath her window, then for you I offer this wish, that no one ever sing beneath your window.

War and Peace

NO MPAA RATING, 415 m., 1969 (rereleased 2007)

Lyudmila Savelyeva (Natasha), Sergei Bondarchuk (Pierre), Vyacheslav Tikhonov (Andrei), Victor Stanitsyn (Count Rostov), Kira Golovkolvanova (Countess Rostova), Oleg Tabakov (Nikolai). Directed by Bondarchuk from a screenplay by Bondarchuk and Vasily Solovyov, based on the book by Leo Tolstoy.

The movies have done a lot of borrowing during their long climb to the status of an art form, but they've also invented an approach or two. It is impossible to think of gangsters or cowboys without thinking of the movies, and perhaps epics also belong on the list of genres that are uniquely cinematic. No other medium, except literature, is so well suited to the epic form.

It would take a film historian to evaluate the dozens—hundreds?—of times Hollywood has marshaled casts of thousands and budgets of millions to create yet another epoch-shattering spectacular. There were the pioneering epics, such as *Birth of a Nation* and *Gone with the Wind*. There were the epics that made it, such as *Spartacus,* and the ones that didn't, such as *Cleopatra*. There was blood and thunder in *Ben-Hur,* beauty and romance in *Doctor Zhivago,* Charlton Heston in half of them, Peter Ustinov in the rest, Rome falling daily, slaves rising weekly, wars won at least once a month, and several miracles a year from Cecil B. DeMille.

Like Westerns and gangster movies, epics almost always were made by Hollywood. What other nation had the means to spend $44 million on *Cleopatra*—even if it was a flop? What happened, though, was that *Cleopatra* brought an end to the epic budget race. If you couldn't make it for $11 million (*Spartacus*) or $14 million (*2001*) or even $19 million (*Dr. Zhivago*), then perhaps you shouldn't make it at all.

For this reason, among many others, the Russian version of *War and Peace* is a magnificently unique film. Money isn't everything, but you can't make an epic without it. And *War and Peace* is the definitive epic of all time. It is hard to imagine that circumstances will ever again combine to make a more spectacular, expensive, and—yes—splendid movie. Perhaps that's just as well; epics seem to be going out of favor, replaced instead by smaller, more personal films. Perhaps this greatest of the epics will be one of the last, bringing the epic form to its ultimate statement and at the same time supplying the epitaph.

By now the statistics regarding *War and Peace* are well known, but forgive me if I recite them with a certain relish anyway: The film was five years in the making at a cost of $100 million, with a cast of one hundred twenty thousand, all clothed in authentic uniforms, and the Red Army was mobilized to re-create Napoleon's battles exactly (it is claimed) as they happened.

The prestige of the Soviet film industry rested on *War and Peace* for half a decade, and the result looks like it. You are never, ever going to see anything to equal it.

It is easy enough to praise director Sergei Bondarchuk for his thundering battle scenes, or his delicate ballroom scenes, or the quality of his actors. But these were almost to be expected. What is extraordinary about *War and Peace* is that Bondarchuk was able to take the enormous bulk of Leo Tolstoy's novel and somehow transform it into this great chunk of film without losing control along the way. The trouble with a lot of long epic films is that the makers can't keep everything in hand. Many a film is smothered by its own production. An example: Samuel Bronston's *The Fall of the Roman Empire,* a dreadfully expensive, chaotic production that eventually resulted in the fall of Bronston's own empire.

Bondarchuk, however, is able to balance the spectacular, the human, and the intellectual. Even in the longest, bloodiest battle scenes there are vignettes that stand out: a soldier demanding a battlefield commendation, a crazed horse whirling away from an explosion, an enigmatic exchange between Napoleon and his lieutenants. Bondarchuk is able to bring his epic events down to comprehensible scale without losing his sense of the spectacular. And always he returns to Tolstoy's theme of men in the grip of history.

It is impossible not to compare *War and Peace* with *Gone with the Wind.* They are, I suppose, the two greatest epic films. Both deal with the most crucial wars of their countries' experience. Both center on larger-than-life heroes and heroines. Both are romantic and glorious. But in all fairness, I think, *War and Peace* must be listed as the greater film. Although it is vulgar in the way all epic films must be vulgar (because they place value on sheer numbers and a massive production scheme), *War and Peace* is a great deal more intelligent, tasteful, and complete than *GWTW.*

The performances are interesting throughout. All of the actors look a little larger, nobler, and more heroic than life—which is the idea in these undertakings. Yet none of them looks conventionally handsome. Perhaps Vyacheslav Tikhonov, as Prince Andrei, comes closest, with his chiseled face.

Bondarchuk made a happy choice when he cast the beautiful Lyudmila Savelyeva as Natasha. She is a ballerina, not an actress, although her acting ability is equal to the role. Audiences applaud her two dances; one is in the graceful ballroom scene, the other is a folk dance in a rude hunting lodge.

Bondarchuk cast himself as Pierre, the self-tormented intellectual, and it is his strong performance that provides the central thread of the complicated story. He looks something like Rod Steiger and acts something like him, with bemused comments to himself and a quiet face concealing a furnace of emotion.

Despite its length, the movie is not too long. When I saw it at the New York premiere in 1969, I quite frankly expected to be bored. But I was completely absorbed in the story; both halves together seem shorter than many a ninety-minute potboiler.

Perhaps the dubbing has something to do with this: The voices are so well dubbed into English that after fifteen minutes you don't even look at the lips anymore. I usually object to dubbing on the grounds that it cheats us of the actor's own voice and intonation. But I am willing to concede that six subtitles would be rather too much for most audiences, more like reading the book.

And it is to a mass audience, not an intellectual minority, that *War and Peace* is directed. The cinema lends itself magnificently to spectacle, and *War and Peace* is great cinema. It is as spectacular as a movie can possibly be and yet it has a human fullness. Considering its cost and the vast effort that went into its making, such a film can be made only once in our time. The wonder, indeed, is that it was made at all.

The War Game

NO MPAA RATING, 121 m., 1967

A documentary directed, produced and written by Peter Watkins.

Quite apart from its disturbing and shocking impact, Peter Watkins's *The War Game* is one of the most skillful documentary films ever made. It won the 1966 Academy Award for documentaries, an award all the more striking because the film "documents" an event that hasn't happened. In the style of a television news program, Watkins covers the effect of a small-scale nuclear attack on an airfield near Kent, in England. The film was produced for British television but was never shown. The British Broadcasting Corporation feared it would depress and frighten TV viewers. And so it would.

The movie begins with an impassive British voice reading news over the radio. The Red Chinese have invaded South Vietnam in support of the Vietcong. The United States has threatened to use tactical nuclear devices in retaliation. Forced to support China, the Rus-

sians have sealed the Berlin corridor in a hawk-like gesture.

The Russians and Americans trade threats and bluffs, although neither wants to get involved in a real conflict while the Chinese are acting uncontrollably. Unwilling to move large numbers of troops to Berlin because of the escalation in Vietnam, the United States deploys NATO field nuclear weapons instead.

The Russians call the American bluff, and a limited nuclear exchange takes place. Watkins deliberately ignores the effect of the bombs on America and Russia. Instead, he "documents" the side effects in England, which has seventy-five or so targets of military consequence.

The British mobilize on an emergency basis and evacuate women and children to rural areas. Hardware and building supply stores are mobbed by householders who want to purchase materials for bomb shelters. One woman tells an interviewer she can afford only seventeen shillings and sixpence. "With her money," the voice observes, "she can buy six sandbags and two boards."

When the bomb falls, its effect is not as bad as it could have been. It is a small bomb, and it misses its target and explodes in the air forty miles away. If it had hit, of course, there would have been nothing left to document.

The cameras follow the consequences. There are more than eight-hundred casualties for every doctor. Food supplies run out. The police are armed. In the area where the bomb struck, a "firestorm" begins—just as they actually did begin at Dresden, at Hamburg, and at Hiroshima.

In the firestorm footage, Watkins achieves remarkable authenticity. Using a handheld camera and grainy newsreel film, he shows firemen dying of gas poisoning as the flames explode. The heat generated in the center of a firestorm, we are told, reaches eight hundred degrees. It creates an updraft so powerful that trees, automobiles, and human bodies are sucked into it by 150 mph winds. All oxygen is drained from the atmosphere. As the voice continues, we see firemen plucked from the ground and literally blown into the flames. "This phenomenon actually occurred in 1945," the voice observes dispassionately.

But there is more. A doctor explains that victims with burns on more than 50 percent of their bodies are being put in a "holding section" to die without drugs. The drugs are needed for those who might live. As a means of identification, wedding rings are taken from the dead. They fill a bucket.

These sections are certainly the most horrifying ever put on film (although, to be sure, greater suffering has taken place in real life, and is taking place today). Orphaned children stare into the camera, their arms and chests a mass of scar tissue. Men who have escaped injury go into a state of fear and shock from the things they have seen. One cannot hold his spoon to eat some soup, and it tinkles against the side of his bowl. The police shoot at a crowd of men rioting for food, and then a mob overturns a munitions truck and breaks into a food depot, killing the policemen. The camera examines a woman who stands over a dead policeman, her arms filled with loot. "This is Mrs. Joyce Fisher," the voice says. "She was a housewife."

After the bombings of Japan, we are told, the population fell into a state of dejection and apathy. The streets were lined with men and women staring blankly into space. Life had come to seem a hollow joke. In probably the saddest and most heart-wrenching scene in *The War Game*, the interviewer asks four little boys what they want to be when they grow up. "I don't want to be nothing," says the first tiny, barely audible voice. "Neither do I want to be nothing," says the next.

They should string up bedsheets between the trees and show *The War Game* in every public park. It should be shown on television, perhaps right after one of those half-witted war series in which none of the stars ever gets killed.

And, somehow, it should be shown to the leaders of the world's nuclear powers, the men who have their fingers on the doomsday button. If the button is ever pushed, the world's nuclear arsenal contains the equivalent of 20 million tons of TNT apiece for you, and for me, and for every blessed person on this earth. Will the survivors envy the dead?

WarGames

PG, 110 m., 1983

Matthew Broderick (David), Dabney Coleman (McKittrick), John Wood (Falken), Ally Sheedy (Jennifer), Barry Corbin (General Beringer). Directed by John Badham and produced by Harold Schneider. Screenplay by Lawrence Lasker and Walter F. Parkes.

Sooner or later, a self-satisfied, sublimely confident computer is going to blow us all off the face of the planet. That is the message of *WarGames*, a scary and intelligent thriller that is one of the best films of 1983. The movie stars Matthew Broderick as a bright high school senior who spends a lot of time locked in his bedroom with his home computer. He speaks computerese well enough to dial by telephone into the computer at his school and change grades. But he's ready for bigger game. He reads about a toy company that's introducing a new computer game. He programs his computer for a random search of telephone numbers in the company's area code, looking for a number that answers with a computer tone. Eventually, he connects with a computer. Unfortunately, the computer he connects with does not belong to a toy company. It belongs to the Defense Department, and its mission is to coordinate early warning systems and nuclear deterrents in the case of World War III. The kid challenges the computer to play a game called "Global Thermonuclear Warfare," and it cheerfully agrees.

As a premise for a thriller, this is a masterstroke. The movie, however, could easily go wrong by bogging us down in impenetrable computerese, or by ignoring the technical details altogether and giving us a *Fail Safe* retread. *WarGames* makes neither mistake. It convinces us that it knows computers, and it makes its knowledge into an amazingly entertaining thriller. (Note: I do not claim the movie is *accurate* about computers—only convincing.) I've described only the opening gambits of the plot, and I will reveal no more. It's too much fun watching the story unwind. Another one of the pleasures of the movie is the way it takes cardboard characters and fleshes them out. Two in particular: the civilian chief of the U.S. computer operation, played by Dabney Coleman as a man who has his own little weakness for simple logic, and the air force general in charge of the war room, played by Barry Corbin as a military man who argues that men, not computers, should make the final nuclear decisions.

WarGames was directed by John Badham, best known for *Saturday Night Fever* and *Blue Thunder,* a thriller that I found considerably less convincing on the technical level. There's not a scene here where Badham doesn't seem to know what he's doing, weaving a complex web of computerese, personalities, and puzzles; the movie absorbs us on emotional and intellectual levels at the same time. And the ending, a moment of blinding and yet utterly elementary insight, is wonderful.

Warrendale

NO MPAA RATING, 100 m., 1969

A documentary directed and produced by Allan King.

Allan King's *Warrendale* is a very special sort of film, and it probably requires a special audience. It is not "entertaining," but not everyone goes to the movies to be entertained: Sometimes it is enough to see life as it is.

Warrendale was a center in Canada where emotionally disturbed children were brought to live in groups of twelve, each with a trained staff of eight. A note at the beginning of the film emphasizes that these are not brain-damaged or retarded children. They are of normal intelligence, but gravely disturbed.

The treatment at Warrendale was experimental, involving a maximum amount of physical contact as a direct way to express love and reassurance. The children were encouraged to release all their anger and aggression while being held tightly by two or three adult staff members. During these "holding sessions," they were told they were not responsible for anything they might do. They were being given a safe way to drain off the latent violence that seemed to be associated with their problems.

I am not competent to say whether this treatment was wise or effective, and the film does not make a special argument for it. Instead, King and his crew have acted entirely as observers, using portable, unobtrusive equipment to record some six weeks of the life at Warrendale. Like the best of cinema verité, *Warrendale* would rather show life than judge it.

A structure was given to the film almost accidentally when Warrendale's cook died unexpectedly. The news is broken to the children in a group meeting. Some of them appear indifferent ("She wasn't any relative of mine"). Others react hysterically, and the staff members hold one young girl while she sobs and cries at the top of her voice, "It's a lie! It's a lie!" Another of the young patients blames herself, and a staff worker calmly repeats over and over: "It's not your fault. You didn't cause Dorothy's death. It's not your fault."

In these scenes of sustained and heartbreaking emotion, we begin to understand the Warrendale experience. The children are victims of the same isolation and loneliness that plagues all men, and their early environments apparently did not provide them with socially approved ways of coping with these feelings. So they began to act strangely in order to call attention to themselves, and perhaps to attract help. Some became delinquents, others self-destructive (one young girl combs her hair violently and painfully, and a staff member says, "You don't have to hurt yourself. Your hair is beautiful").

Still other children developed enormous feelings of guilt, blaming themselves for almost anything. These are perhaps the most pathetic, and the Warrendale treatment encouraged them to release their fear and grief. In these scenes we see a human closeness that is often lacking from life, and almost always from the screen. This depth of emotion may embarrass some audiences, but it is the only way to deal honestly with material of this importance.

Note: Warrendale *shared the 1967 Cannes Festival award with* Blow-Up, *and was named the best documentary of the year by the National Society of Film Critics and the British Film Critics Society.*

The War Zone

NO MPAA RATING, 99 m., 2000

Ray Winstone (Dad), Tilda Swinton (Mum), Lara Belmont (Jessie), Freddie Cunliffe (Tom), Colin J. Farrell (Nick), Aisling O'Sullivan (Carol), Kate Ashfield (Lucy). Directed by Tim Roth and produced by Sarah Radclyffe and Dixie Linder. Screenplay by Alexander Stuart, based on his book *The War Zone.*

It must have been something like this in medieval times, families living in isolation, cut off from neighbors, forced indoors by the weather, their animal and sexual functions not always shielded from view. Tim Roth's *The War Zone*, brilliant and heartbreaking, takes place in the present but is timeless; most particularly it is cut off from the fix-it culture of psychobabble, which defines all the politically correct ways to consider incest. The movie is not about incest as an issue, but about incest as a blow to the heart and the soul—a real event, here, now, in a family that seems close and happy. Not a topic on a talk show.

The movie takes place in winter in Devon, which is wet and gray, the sky squeezing joy out of the day. The family has moved from London "to make a fresh start," the mother says. They live in a comfortable cottage, warm and sheltered, life centering around the big kitchen table. Mom (Tilda Swinton) is very pregnant. Dad (Ray Winstone) is bluff and cheery, extroverted, a good guy. Tom (Freddie Cunliffe) is a fifteen-year-old, silent and sad because he misses his friends in London. Jessie (Lara Belmont) is eighteen years old, ripe with beauty. This looks like a cheerful story.

Roth tells it obliquely, sensitive to the ways families keep secrets even from themselves. Early in the film the mother's time comes and the whole family rushes to the hospital; there's a car crash, but a happy ending, as they gather in the maternity ward with the newcomer, all of them cut and bruised, but survivors. Back at home, there is a comfort with the physical side of life. Mom nurses her child in kitchen scenes like renaissance paintings. Tom is comfortable with his sister's casual nudity while they have a heart-to-heart talk. Mum helps wash her men at the kitchen sink, Jessie dries her brother's hair in the laundry room, the family seems comfortable with one another.

Then Tom glimpses a disturbing part of a moment between his father and his sister. He challenges Jessie. She says nothing happened. Something did happen, and more will happen, including a scene of graphic hurtfulness. But this isn't a case of Tom discovering incest in his family and blowing the whistle. It's much more complicated. How does he feel about his sister and about her relationship with her new boyfriend, Nick? What about his father's eerie split personality, able to deny his behavior and see Tom's interference as an assault on their

happy family? What about the mother's willingness not to know? What about his sister's denial? Does it spring from shame, fear, or a desire to shield Tom and her mother from the knowledge?

And what about a curious episode when Jessie and Tom visit London, and Jessie almost seems to have set up Tom to sleep with one of her friends—as what? Consolation? A bribe? Revenge? The movie's refusal to declare exactly what the London episode means is admirable, because this is not a zero-sum accounting of good and evil, but a messy, elusive, painfully complex tragedy in which no one is driven by just one motive.

When Tom is accused of destroying the family and having a filthy mind, there is a sense in which he accepts this analysis. One critic of the film wrote that a "teenaged boy (from the big city, no less) would surely be more savvy—no matter how distraught—about the workings and potential resolutions of such a situation." Only in textbooks. When you're fifteen, what you learn in social studies and from talk shows is a lot different from how you confront your own family.

Incest is not unfamiliar as a subject for movies, but most incest stories are about characters simplified into monsters and victims. We know intellectually that most child abusers were abused children, but few films pause to reflect how that lifelong hurt reflects itself in real situations. The father here is both better and worse because of his own probably traumatic childhood. He must long ago have often promised himself that he would be different than his own father, that he would be a good dad—loving, kind, warm, cheerful—and so he is, all except for when he is not. When he's accused of evil, he explodes in anger—the anger of the father he is now and also the anger of the child he once was. For a moment his son is, in a sense, the abuser, making Dad feel guilty and shameful just as his own father must have, and tearing down all his efforts to be better, to be different.

Unsurprisingly, *The War Zone* affects viewers much more powerfully than a simple morality tale might. It is not simply about the evil of incest, but about its dynamic, about the way it plays upon guilt and shame and addresses old and secret wounds. The critic James Berardinelli says that when he saw the movie at the Toronto Film Festival, a viewer ran from the theater saying he couldn't take it anymore, and went looking to pull a fire alarm. Tim Roth was standing near the exit and intercepted him, becoming confessor for an emotional outpouring that the movie had inspired.

Roth is one of the best actors now working, and with this movie he reveals himself as a director of surprising gifts. I cannot imagine *The War Zone* being better directed by anyone else, even though Ingmar Bergman and Ken Loach come to mind. Roth and his actors, and Stuart's screenplay, understand these people and their situation down to the final nuance, and are willing to let silence, timing, and visuals reveal what dialogue would cheapen. Not many movies bring you to a dead halt of sorrow and empathy. This one does.

The Weavers: Wasn't That a Time!

PG, 78 m., 1982

Featuring Lee Hays, Ronnie Gilbert, Fred Hellerman, and Pete Seeger. Directed by Jim Brown and produced by Brown, George Stoney, and Harold Leventhal.

Here is one of the most joyous musical documentaries in a long time, a celebration of the music and the singers that made up the Weavers. There are, I suppose, a lot of people who don't know who the Weavers were, but for a time in the fifties they were the top pop quartet in America, and for twenty years their recordings were a key influence on modern American folk music.

The owners of old Weavers record albums treasure them. I have four or five, and when things get depressing and the sky turns overcast and grim, I like to play one of them. There's just something magical about the joy with which the Weavers sing "Goodnight, Irene" or "Kisses Sweeter than Wine" or "The Sloop John B." or "This Land is Your Land."

The Weavers reached their popular peak in the fifties, with a string of Top Ten hits, which also included "On Top of Old Smokey," "Tzena, Tzena," and "If I Had a Hammer" (which was written by the Weavers, and not, as many people believe, by Bob Dylan). The height of their popularity unfortunately coincided with the height of McCarthyism, and the Weavers, all of them longtime left-wing activists, were blacklisted. They couldn't get jobs on television or in nightclubs, and their records were banned.

For several years in the late fifties, the group existed primarily on records. And the artists went their separate ways: Ronnie Gilbert into theater, Fred Hellerman into San Franciso-area media projects, Pete Seeger into a successful solo concert career, and Lee Hays into semiretirement on his New England farm.

There were many calls for a Weavers reunion (in some circles, an event more fervently desired than the Beatles reunion). And in May of 1980, Lee Hays himself convened such a reunion, inviting the other Weavers and their families and friends to a picnic on his farm. As they sat around and sang and played, the idea of a public reunion began to take shape, and on November 28 and 29 of 1980, they held one last historic concert at Carnegie Hall.

The Weavers: Wasn't That a Time! is not simply a concert film, however, but a documentary about the Weavers. The director, Jim Brown, was a neighbor of Hays, and grew to admire the old man who kept on singing after his legs were amputated for diabetes and his heart needed a pacemaker.

Brown's film begins with the picnic at Hays's farm, flashes back to newsreel and archive footage of the Weavers in their prime, and then concludes with the concert in Carnegie Hall. It is impossible not to feel a lump in your throat as the Weavers gather once again on stage, and it's hard not to tap your feet when they start to sing.

Seeing this film is a wonderful experience. I'd recommend it wholeheartedly to those who don't know about the Weavers. I imagine that Weavers fans won't need any encouragement.

Wedding in White

R, 103 m., 1973

Donald Pleasence (Jim), Paul Bradley (Jimmie), Carol Kane (Jeannie), Doug McGrath (Billy), Doris Petrie (Mary), Christine Thomas (Sarah), Leo Phillips (Sandy), Bonnie Carol Case (Dollie). Directed by William Fruet and produced by John Vidette. Screenplay by Fruet.

Jeannie is the kind of girl you can never remember from high school: sort of pretty in a faded way, not very bright, and weighted down with a vast lack of confidence. She's sixteen years old and very much in awe of her friend Dollie, who uses lipstick and has lots of nice clothes and an extensive collection of cheap costume jewelry. The admiration she feels for Dollie, in fact, is about the only sharp emotion in her life; for the rest, she's listless and indifferent.

She lives with her family in Canada, in about 1943. Her father is a beer-guzzling good old boy in the Home Guard, and her brother is in the army. One weekend he comes home with a friend, and what with one thing leading to another the friend sort of rapes her, and she confesses to her mom, "I think I'm in trouble." Her father, enraged, beats her and plans to send her away, but one drunken night he conceives a plan to marry her off to his best buddy, Sandy. Now, Sandy is a drunken and worthless character of about sixty, but so what? "No other man would touch her," her father says.

Out of this commonplace story about ordinary people, the Canadian writer and director William Fruet has fashioned *Wedding in White*, a poignant, bitter, sometimes surprisingly funny slice of life. It really does re-create its wartime society. Everything about it is right: the clothes, the dialogue and particularly the prejudices and ignorance. We don't feel we're being told a story; it's more like we're glimpsing the small joys and tragedies of unfortunate relatives. The movie, which won the Canadian Film Festival, works so well, I think, because the performances are good; this material could never stand being fancied up by overacting. Donald Pleasence, that superb actor who is unsurpassed in his ability to project banal evil, provides the force behind the plot as the father. Carol Kane, as Jeannie, seems almost transparently vulnerable. Doris Petrie, who plays the mother, has a wonderful scene toward the end—she pleads with her husband to understand their child—that seems just right in revealing that she has been defeated by life in everything except a stubborn, lingering hope.

The movie examines its small Canadian town with some of the same attention Peter Bogdanovich revealed in *The Last Picture Show*. The girls go to a dance, for example, and

the band is made up of three elderly women on accordion, drums, and piano; their two-step dance rhythms sound memorized to death. The dime stores, the soda fountains, the slang, and all work toward the final effect.

And the effect is simply that of a small domestic tragedy. The girl's life has been ruined, not by her pregnancy but by her father's ignorance. Yet she's too dim to even quite understand that. It's impossible for her to rebel, unthinkable to question her father. The movie ends without a message, without a statement, without any indication that the characters understand their own motivations. In most movies, that would be a weakness, but here it's a strength, because Fruet wants only to show us these people as they are. The result is one of the most merciless, strangely touching portraits of character I've ever seen in a movie: only Mike Leigh's *Bleak Moments*, comes to mind in comparison.

Weekend

NO MPAA RATING, 100 m., 1967

Mireille Darc (Corinne), Jean Yanne (Roland), Jean-Pierre Kalfon (Leader of FLSO), Valerie Lagrange (His Moll), Jean-Pierre Leaud (Man in Phone Booth). Directed by Jean-Luc Godard. Screenplay by Godard.

Year after year, Jean-Luc Godard has been chipping away at the language of cinema. Now, in *Weekend*, he has just about gotten down to the bare bones. This is his best film, and his most inventive. It is almost pure movie. It is sure to be ardently disliked by a great many people, Godard fans among them. But revolutionary films always take some time for audiences to catch up.

Weekend is about violence, hatred, the end of ideology, and the approaching cataclysm that will destroy civilization. It is also about the problem of how to make a movie about this. Movies about The Bomb are almost never effective; the subject is too large. So Godard abandons any attempt to show us "real" war or destruction. Instead, he shows us attitudes: the casual indifference to suffering that saturates our society.

The film begins with motorists, perhaps because driving a car quickly inspires the animal in us. We see people offhandedly machine-gunning each other over dented fenders, or using insect spray. Then we see a married couple leaving for a weekend motoring holiday, and their journey will in fact be a tour through the horrors of the consumer civilization.

The opening scenes are hilarious. But we first begin to understand this is extraordinary Godard when his couple gets onto the highway. There is a traffic jam. It is a very long traffic jam, and the protagonists pull out into the other lane to pass it. This begins perhaps the most famous single shot in Godard's work.

It is a traveling shot, with the camera parallel to the line of cars, that continues without interruption for perhaps three-quarters of a mile. At some point, we realize that the subject of the shot is not the traffic jam but the fact that the shot is so extended. "Politics is a traveling shot," Godard told us a few years ago, and now we know what he meant. The technique itself makes the point.

The traffic jam shows us a civilization that has gotten clogged up in its own artifacts. Finally abandoning their car, the motorists set out cross-country on the most peculiar odyssey since Gulliver's. They meet historical figures, they walk through scenes from other movies, they are casually raped, they see bodies set afire. This is a radical, bitter view of society, and Godard is at pains to dismiss any optimistic liberal solutions.

It used to be thought, in the days of John Dewey, that universal education would be the salvation of mankind. So Godard provides a scene in which culture is brought to the masses: A grand piano is set up in a barnyard, and the pianist begins to play. In a startling shot, Godard places his camera in the center of the barnyard and moves it through two complete 360-degree revolutions. We see the entire barnyard (pianist, listeners, passersby, the camera crew) twice in sequence. Why? Why not?

There are some other strange things. Two long political speeches are delivered, and we cannot understand why (a) they are so stupid if meant to be taken seriously, or (b) why they are so serious if meant as a joke. This is the case, I would say, with about 95 percent of the rhetoric inspired by currently fashionable radicalism.

Godard also gives us an allegorical ending in which various animals and members of the cast are killed and eaten and other things. But by now we are totally lost in this new Godard universe. Everything makes sense, but nothing holds together. Are people talking to each other, or to us? What's going on? It's as bad as life.

Welcome to the Dollhouse

R, 87 m., 1996

Heather Matarazzo (Dawn Wiener), Eric Mabius (Steve), Brendan Sexton, Jr. (Brandon McCarthy), Telly Pontidis (Jed), Herbie Duarte (Lance). Directed and produced by Todd Solondz. Screenplay by Solondz.

Welcome to the Dollhouse remembers with brutal and unforgiving accuracy the hell of junior high school. Many movies reconstruct those years as a sort of adolescent paradise; it's a shock, watching this film, to remember how cruel kids can be to one another, and how deeply the wounds cut.

I can recall today with perfect accuracy the names and faces of eleven-year-olds who made my life miserable. If I met them today, so many years later, would I forgive and forget? Not a chance. I still hate them. Was I also cruel? Did I have my own victims? Strange, but I can't remember . . .

Welcome to the Dollhouse stars Heather Matarazzo in a dead-on performance as Dawn Wiener, an unpopular seventh-grader whose glasses are wrong, whose hair is wrong, whose complexion is wrong, whose clothes are wrong, and who is as gawky and geeky as it is humanly possible to be. The first time we see her, she's performing one of the most painful rituals in life: walking through the school cafeteria with a loaded tray, trying to choose a table. Her objective is to sit with students as far up the school social scale as she dares, without being rejected.

"Can I sit here?" she asks, regarding an empty space. "Someone barfed there third period," she's informed.

Because Dawn's family name is Wiener, she is inevitably known as "Wiener Dog" in school (I was "Eggbert"). She is also known as "Lesbo" and "Stupid," and when she asks a classmate why she hates her, she gets a refreshingly direct answer: "You're ugly." She isn't ugly, simply unformed in that in-between way, but she projects the vibes of a potential victim, and there are always going to be sadists whose antennae lead them straight to their targets. Inevitably, her only friend in school is a boy much smaller than she is, who is regularly beaten up and called a "faggot." Do the "lesbo" and "faggot" words indicate homophobia? Not necessarily. Kids that age are fascinated by sex and terrified by their own ignorance, so they attack others to assert self-confidence. Any difference at all, real or imaginary, makes someone a target. What qualifies as a difference? Anything you are that I am not, or that I fear becoming.

But I'm making *Welcome to the Dollhouse* sound like some sort of grim sociological study, and in fact it's a funny, intensely entertaining film: intense, because it focuses so mercilessly on the behavior of its characters that we are forced to confront both the comedy and the pain.

Dawn lives in a split-level house with an older brother who is a nerd, and a younger sister who is a ballerina. Her parents claim they love all of their children equally. They are lying. Her brother, Mark (Matthew Faber), is focused on getting into a good college, and everything he does is planned to enrich his application. He starts a garage band and recruits a popular student named Steve (Eric Mabius) as his lead singer. Steve is a mature, handsome hunk, and Dawn gets weak-kneed just looking at him. He's the kind of guy who will break a woman's heart just for the pleasure of hearing it snap, but of course Dawn's heart is far beneath his attention. Nor is he much interested in the band. ("That doesn't sound much like 'Satisfaction,'" he notes, after a clarinet passage by Mark.) Dawn is very badly informed about sex but willing to learn. She will essentially do anything for Steve, who can't be bothered; there is a well-written scene in which she has him alone at home and plies him with junk food.

Meanwhile, she's tormented by Brandon (Brendan Sexton, Jr.), who makes her life miserable. Dawn is smart enough to sense or guess that boys Brandon's age often express affection through hostility, and she puts up with him because he's essentially the only game in school. In one of the movie's best scenes (which works only because it is perfectly written, acted, and understood), Brandon actually makes a date with her to "rape" her, and she turns up for it. Of course nothing

resembling rape takes place, although I'm not sure whether Brandon knows that.

Scene after scene, *Welcome to the Dollhouse* piles on its details, re-creating the acute daily misery of being an unpopular adolescent and remembering, too, how resilient a girl like Dawn can be—how self-absorbed, how hopeful, how philosophical, how enduring.

Dawn's revenge, we hope, is that someday she will be rich, famous, and admired, while the snotty little cheerleaders who persecuted her will have been sucked into the primeval slime of the miserable lives they deserve.

Welcome to the Dollhouse, which won the grand prize at the 1996 Sundance Film Festival, is a first film for its writer-director, Todd Solondz. He shows the kind of unrelenting attention to detail that is the key to satire. It isn't the big picture that matters to a girl like Dawn, but the details: how she looks today in the mirror, and how this dress looks, and what small hopeful signs might have been sighted, or imagined, on the far emotional horizon. If you can see this movie without making a mental hit list of the kids who made your eleventh year a torment, then you are kinder, or luckier, than me.

Werckmeister Harmonies

NO MPAA RATING, 145 m., 2000

Lars Rudolph (Janos), Peter Fitz (Gyorgy Eszter), Hanna Schygulla (Auntie Tunde). Directed by Bela Tarr and produced by Franz Goess, Paul Saadoun, Miklos Szita, and Joachim von Vietinghoff. Screenplay by Tarr and Laszlo Krasznahorkai, based on his book, *The Melancholy of Resistance*.

Bela Tarr's *Werckmeister Harmonies* is maddening if you are not in sympathy with it, mesmerizing if you are. If you have not walked out after twenty or thirty minutes, you will thereafter not be able to move from your seat. "Dreamlike," Jim Jarmusch calls it. Nightmarish as well; doom-laded, filled with silence and sadness, with the crawly feeling that evil is penetrating its somber little town. It is filmed elegantly in black and white, the camera movements so stately they almost float through only thirty-nine shots in a film of one hundred forty-five minutes.

To know where we stand as the film begins,

we should start with these words by the director, Tarr: "I despise stories, as they mislead people into believing that something has happened. In fact, nothing really happens as we flee from one condition to another. . . . All that remains is time. This is probably the only thing that's still genuine—time itself; the years, days, hours, minutes, and seconds."

And what is time anyway but our agreement to divide one rotation of the earth around the sun into those units? Could there be hours, minutes, seconds, on a planet without our year? Why would one earth second need to exist except as part of one earth year? Perhaps such questions lead us into the extraordinary, funny, ingenious eleven-minute shot at the start of the picture.

It is the dead of winter, almost closing time in a shabby pub. An eclipse of the sun is due, and Janos, the local paper carrier, takes it upon himself to explain what will happen in the heavens. He pushes the furniture to the walls and enlists a drunk to stand in the center of the floor and flutter his hands, like the sun's rays, he says. Then he gets another pal to be the earth, and walk in circles around the sun. And then a third is the moon, making his own circles around the earth. All of these circles are choreographed, all the drunks rotating, and then the moon comes between the sun and the earth, and there is an eclipse: "The sky darkens, then goes all dark," Janos says. "The dogs howl, rabbits hunch down, the deer run in panic, run, stampede in fright. And in this awful, incomprehensible dusk, even the birds . . . the birds, too, are confused and go to roost. And then . . . complete silence. Everything that lives is still. Are the hills going to march off? Will heaven fall upon us?"

Janos continues, the others listening in bewilderment because in their village at this hour there is nowhere else to go, nothing else to do, and as he has explained, "All I ask is that you step with me into the boundlessness, where constancy, quietude and peace, infinite emptiness reign." And now I've got you through the first eleven minutes of your twenty- or thirty-minute test, and you certainly haven't left yet. The pub owner announces closing time and throws them all out, and Janos goes to the newspaper office to pick up his papers. There, and at a hotel that is his first stop, he begins to hear alarming rumors, almost Shakespearean portents, that all is not right on heaven and earth, that a circus is coming to town with a huge stuffed whale and "the Prince," who has darkling powers. Whole families have started to disappear. . . .

The shot of the arriving circus truck is haunting. It appears first, and for a long time, as a huge, square shadow on the house fronts. I was reminded of the monster shadow in *The Third Man* that turns out to be only a balloon vendor. Then headlights. Then the truck itself, outsize, gargantuan, large enough to hold, well, a whale. Its full length passes Janos and he stands and regards.

Janos is well-liked in the town. "How's our Janos?" he's asked. He receives a visit from his Auntie Tunde (Hanna Schygulla), who insists he visit her estranged husband, Uncle Gyorgy (Peter Fitz), and enlist him in leading the townspeople against unnamed but imminent threats. She gives him a suitcase to take along, a case that is never opened or explained. Uncle Gyorgy is a musicologist who believes the world went wrong when Andreas Werckmeister (1645–1706) popularized a system of harmonics that interfered with the music of the celestial spheres. Janos and Gyorgy walk to the town square, held in frame in an extraordinary, very long, shot, until they arrive at clumps of people hunched in the cold around the truck containing the whale. Later, when Janos buys his ticket and goes inside, he regards the whale's enormous, lifeless, staring eye.

I will not describe the whole movie, even though it seems I'm about to. I will touch on a scene where a mob rips apart the local hospital and attacks the patients, until they are stilled by the most unanswerable sight. And I could pause for details like the way three tin buckets are stacked into a personal lunch carrier, like tiffin boxes in India. Little details of little lives.

Bela Tarr (born 1955), is a Hungarian director more talked about than viewed, in part because few audiences have an appetite for, and few theaters the time to play, his films like *Satantango* (1994), which is four hundred fifteen minutes long. For all of my time on the festival circuit, I had never seen one of his films until this one, which I obtained through

Facets Multimedia of Chicago, the American distributor of Tarr's work on DVD. When you're at a festival and seeing one film means missing four others, you tend to take the path of least resistance, unless you are Jonathan Rosenbaum or Susan Sontag, and I am not. But Tarr's name kept swimming reproachfully into my view, even in that book *1,001 Movies You Must See Before You Die,* where I proudly checked off movie after movie until I came to . . . Bela Tarr.

And now I find that Tarr does, in fact, make films both completely unique and original, and in a style I find beautiful. I prefer the purity of black and white to color, I like very long takes if they serve a purpose and are not simply stunts, I am drawn into an air of mystery, I find it compelling when a film establishes an immediate, tangible, time and place. For all of his phantasmal themes, *Werckmeister Harmonies* is resolutely realistic. Every person, every room, every street, every action, every line of dialogue, feels as much like *cinema verite* as the works of Frederick Wiseman. It is even possible that a stuffed whale could go on tour. And as for "the Prince," well, what do we learn of him that is not in some way possible?

I think there is a state of film reverie that longer films can create (and at 145 minutes, *Werckmeister* is after all shorter than, say, *Zodiac*). You are lured away from the clock ticking in your mind and drift in a nontemporal state. Tarr's camera drifts as well; it is rock-steady (even though hand-held at times), and glides smoothly through unbroken takes that become long shots, tracking shots, close-ups, framing shots, all without haste or indecision, all without a cut. (Average shot length, if you're one of David Bordwell's ASL collectors: 3–7 minutes, as compared to, say, *Bourne Supremacy* at 1.9 seconds.)

So do you just sit there, friends will ask, and look at the shots? Well, yes, that's what everybody does when they watch a film. But they don't always *see* them. Bela Tarr seems to be trying to regard his characters with great intensity and respect, to observe them without jostling them, to follow unobtrusively as they move through their worlds, which look so ordinary and are so awesome, just like ours.

Wetherby

R, 118 m., 1985

Vanessa Redgrave (Jean Travers), Ian Holm (Stanley Pilborough), Judi Dench (Marcia Pilborough), Marjorie Yates (Verity Braithwaite), Tim McInnerny (John Morgan), Suzanna Hamilton (Karen Creasy), Joely Richardson (Young Jean). Directed by David Hare and produced by Simon Relph. Screenplay by Hare.

A man kills himself among strangers. They never knew who he was, and they do not know why he chose to die. A man dying among strangers is like a tree falling unobserved in the forest. Death, especially suicide, requires resonance from those who knew the living person before it can be assigned its proper meaning. That is why *Wetherby* is such a haunting film, because it dares to suggest that the death of the stranger is important to everyone it touches—because it forces them to decide how alive they really are.

The movie begins with a woman who is living a sort of dead life. Her name is Jean Travers (played by Vanessa Redgrave); she was once in love with a young man who went off to fight the war and was killed. He was not killed gloriously, but stupidly, while getting involved in someone else's drunken quarrel, but he was dead all the same. As the movie opens, Jean has been teaching school in the small town of Wetherby, where her life is on hold. She doesn't walk around in a state of depression, she does have friends, she is a good teacher, but she is not engaged in life because she put all of her passion into the boy who died so many years ago.

One night she throws a small dinner party. Everyone drinks wine and sits around late, talking. One of the men at the table, John Morgan, sits mute all evening and finally makes a short speech about pain and love and honesty that sounds as if every word were written with his own bitter tears. The next day, John Morgan comes back to Jean's house, sits down for a cup of tea, and kills himself. A funny thing comes out in the investigation: John Morgan was not known to any of the people at the dinner party. Apparently he invited himself.

The film moves from this beginning into an examination of the people who were touched by the death. In addition to Jean, there are the Pilboroughs (Ian Holm and Judi Dench), the local constable (Tom Wilkinson), and a young woman (Suzanna Hamilton) who knew the dead man. Some small suspense develops for a while when it appears that Jean spent some time upstairs with John Morgan during the evening of her party—but that, and many other things, seem to be dead ends.

The movie flashes back into events in Jean's youth, and she is played as a young girl by Joely Richardson, Redgrave's daughter. There is an innocence and tenderness in those early scenes, as young Jean and her boyfriend kiss and neck and make promises, and as Jean gradually realizes that she is looking forward to marriage but he is much more excited by the prospect of putting on a uniform and going overseas. He goes overseas, and in some ways this movie is about the fact that Jean has become a middle-aged woman still waiting for him to come back.

Wetherby was written and directed by David Hare, who also wrote the film *Plenty.* Both films are about women who were never able to fully live their lives after what happened to them during the war. I admire both films, but I found *Wetherby* more moving, because the heroine of *Plenty* was essentially a disturbed woman using her war memories as a crutch, and Jean Travers is a whole and healthy woman who only needs to give herself the permission to live. I left the movie thinking that was the lesson she learned from John Morgan. Hoping so, anyway.

Whale Rider

PG-13, 105 m., 2003

Keisha Castle-Hughes (Pai), Rawiri Paratene (Koro Flowers), Vicky Haughton (Nanny Flowers), Cliff Curtis (Porourangi), Grant Roa (Rawiri), Mana Taumaunu (Hemi), Rachel House (Shilo), Taungaroa Emile (Dog). Directed by Niki Caro and produced by John Barnett, Frank Hubner, and Tim Sanders. Screenplay by Caro, based on the book by Witi Ihimaera.

Whale Rider arrives in theaters already proven as one of the great audience-grabbers of recent years. It won the audience awards as the most popular film at both the Toronto and Sundance Film Festivals, played to standing ovations, left

audiences in tears. I recite these facts right at the top of this review because I fear you might make a hasty judgment that you don't want to see a movie about a twelve-year-old Maori girl who dreams of becoming the chief of her people. Sounds too ethnic, uplifting, and feminist, right?

The genius of the movie is the way it sidesteps all of the obvious clichés of the underlying story and makes itself fresh, observant, tough, and genuinely moving. There is a vast difference between movies for twelve-year-old girls, and movies about twelve-year-old girls, and *Whale Rider* proves it.

The movie, which takes place in the present day in New Zealand, begins with the birth of twins. The boy and the mother die. The girl, Pai (Keisha Castle-Hughes), survives. Her father, Porourangi (Cliff Curtis), an artist, leaves New Zealand, and the little girl is raised and much loved by her grandparents, Koro and Nanny Flowers.

Koro is the chief of these people. Porourangi would be next in line, but has no interest in returning home. Pai believes that she could serve as the chief, but her grandfather, despite his love, fiercely opposes this idea. He causes Pai much hurt by doubting her, questioning her achievements, insisting in the face of everything she achieves that she is only a girl.

The movie, written and directed by Niki Caro, inspired by a novel by Witi Ihimaera, describes these events within the rhythms of daily life. This is not a simplistic fable, but the story of real people living in modern times. There are moments when Pai is lost in discouragement and despair, and when her father comes for a visit she almost leaves with him. But, no, her people need her—whether or not her grandfather realizes it.

Pai is played by Keisha Castle-Hughes, a newcomer of whom it can only be said: This is a movie star. She glows. She stands up to her grandfather in painful scenes, she finds dignity, and yet the next second she's running around the village like the kid she is. The other roles are also strongly cast, especially Rawiri Paratene and Vicky Haughton as the grandparents.

One day Koro summons all of the young teenage boys of the village to a series of compulsory lessons on how to be a Maori, and the leader of Maoris. There's an amusing sequence where they practice looking ferocious to scare their enemies. Pai, of course, is banned from these classes, but eavesdrops, and enlists a wayward uncle to reveal some of the secrets of the males.

And then—well, the movie doesn't end as we expect. It doesn't march obediently to standard plot requirements, but develops an unexpected crisis, and an unexpected solution. There is a scene set at a school ceremony, where Pai has composed a work in honor of her people, and asked her grandfather to attend. Despite his anger, he will come, won't he? The movie seems headed for the ancient cliché of the auditorium door that opens at the last moment to reveal the person whom the child onstage desperately hopes to see—but no, that's not what happens.

It isn't that Koro comes or that he doesn't come, but that something else altogether happens. Something on a larger and more significant scale, that brings together all of the themes of the film into a magnificent final sequence. It's not just an uplifting ending, but a transcendent one, inspired and inspiring, and we realize how special this movie really is. So many films by and about teenagers are mired in vulgarity and stupidity; this one, like its heroine, dares to dream.

What's Eating Gilbert Grape?

PG-13, 117 m., 1994

Johnny Depp (Gilbert Grape), Juliette Lewis (Becky), Mary Steenburgen (Betty Carver), Leonardo DiCaprio (Arnie Grape), John C. Reilly (Tucker Van Dyke), Darlene Cates (Momma), Laura Harrington (Amy Grape), Mary Kate Schellhardt (Ellen Grape), Crispin Glover (Bobby McBurney), Kevin Tighe (Mr. Carver). Directed by Lasse Hallstrom and produced by Meir Teper, Bertil Ohlsson, and David Matalon. Screenplay by Peter Hedges, based on his book.

In the small but eventful world of Gilbert Grape, emergencies are a natural state. His younger brother, Arnie, has a way of climbing the town water tower and refusing to come back down. His mother, who weighs five hundred pounds, spends days at a time just sitting on the sofa. His best friend, Bobby, is an apprentice at his dad's funeral parlor and loves to talk about the tricks of the trade. His boss, who runs the local grocery store, is under threat from the big new supermarket on the edge of town, which has live lobsters in a tank—something the folks in Endora, Iowa (pop. 1,091), can't stop talking about.

Gilbert Grape is more or less equal to these challenges, but life is not easy for him. What helps is the small town itself. In a big city, we sense, the Grape family would be isolated and dysfunctional, but in Endora, where everybody knows everybody and Gilbert fits right in, life is more possible, and the family is at least quasi functional.

What's Eating Gilbert Grape? makes of these materials an enchanting story of people who aren't misfits only because they don't see themselves that way. Nor does the film take them with tragic seriousness; it is a problem, yes, to have a retarded younger brother. And it is a problem to have a mother so fat she never leaves the house. But when kids from the neighborhood sneak around to peek at the fat lady in the living room, Gilbert sometimes gives them a boost up to the window. What the hell.

The movie, written by Peter Hedges and based on his novel, has been directed by a Scandinavian, Lasse Hallstrom, for whom families seem to exert a special pull. His credits include *My Life as a Dog* (1985), about a young boy's coming of age amid eccentric Swedish rural people and first love; and the underrated 1991 film *Once Around*, in which Richard Dreyfuss married into a family that was appalled by his abrasiveness.

The special quality of *What's Eating Gilbert Grape?* is not its oddness, however, but its warmth. Johnny Depp, as Gilbert, has specialized in playing outsiders *(Edward Scissorhands, Benny and Joon)*, and here he brings a quiet, gentle sweetness that suffuses the whole film. Leonardo DiCaprio, who plays Arnie, the retarded kid brother, was nominated for an Academy Award, and deserved it. His performance succeeds in being both convincing and likable. We can see both why he's almost impossible to live with, and why Gilbert and the rest of the Grapes choose to, with love.

For all of their resiliency, however, the Grapes seem stuck in a rut in Endora. Gilbert, who appears to be around twenty-one years old, hangs out with other guys his age, drinking coffee and making small talk and quizzing

Bobby about the undertaking business. On his delivery rounds for the grocery store, he makes frequent stops at the home of Mrs. Carver (Mary Steenburgen), a lonely housewife who is always much less lonely after Gilbert's visits. At home, Gilbert oversees his two younger sisters; the household runs according to rituals, and for some time the kitchen table, with dinner on it, has been brought to Momma (Darlene Cates) so that she won't have to go to it.

Then a young woman named Becky (Juliette Lewis) arrives in town, in an RV driven by her grandmother (Penelope Branning). They're on vacation, traveling from nowhere to nowhere, and they pause in Endora long enough for Becky and Gilbert to begin a romance. And love, as it often does, acts as a catalyst for the Grapes, breaking the patterns that might have held them for a lifetime. When Gilbert brings Becky to meet Momma, we sense a tension and an excitement that is breaking the pattern of years.

One of the movie's best qualities is its way of looking at the fat mother and the retarded brother with sympathy, but not pity. Darlene Cates, making her movie debut, has an extraordinary presence on the screen. We see that she is fat, but we see many other things, too, including the losses and disappointments in her life, and the ability she finds to take a grip and make a new start. And DiCaprio, as Arnie, somehow finds a way to be difficult and invaluable at the same time.

Movies like *What's Eating Gilbert Grape?* are not easily summarized; they don't have that slick "high concept" one-sentence peg that makes them easy to sell. Maybe all I've said still leaves you wondering what the movie is about. But some of the best movies are like this: They show everyday life, carefully observed, and as we grow to know the people in the film, maybe we find out something about ourselves. The fact that Hallstrom is able to combine these qualities with comedy, romance, and even melodrama makes the movie very rare.

When a Man Loves a Woman
R, 126 m., 1994

Andy Garcia (Michael Green), Meg Ryan (Alice Green), Lauren Tom (Amy), Tina Majorino (Jess Green), Mae Whitman (Casey Green), Ellen Burstyn (Emily). Directed by Luis Mandoki and produced by Jordan Kerner and Jon Avnet. Screenplay by Ronald Bass and Al Franken.

Here is a wise and ambitious film about the way alcoholism affects the fabric of a marriage. So many movies about the disease simplify it into a three-step process: gradual onset, spectacular bottom, eventual recovery. It isn't that simple; most alcoholics never even give themselves a chance to recover. And recovery is a beginning, not an end. *When a Man Loves a Woman* is about an alcoholic who recovers—and about her husband, who in some ways dealt with her better when she was drunk.

The movie stars Meg Ryan as Alice, a San Francisco junior high school counselor who drinks all day, every day. Her husband, Michael, an airline pilot played by Andy Garcia, knows she gets loaded on occasion, but has no idea of the extent of her drinking. "It starts at four in the morning," she finally confesses, telling him some of her secrets ("You know how we'll be in the car and then I have to run back in the house because I forgot something?"). The movie opens as she begins a steep dive toward her bottom. One day after school she goes out drinking with a friend, and forgets to come home until after midnight. Another day, drunk, she slaps her older daughter and then passes out in the shower, landing on the bathroom floor in a crash of glass, water, and blood.

It's a relief for her to admit her addiction. She's been hiding it too long. Her husband is warm and understanding, arranging for her to check into a treatment facility. It's after Alice sobers up that Michael's unhappiness begins. Early in the film we have seen how much in love he is, how attentive, how accepting. To some degree, he is giving himself points for being a nice guy. Sure, she hid a lot of her drinking (a practiced alcoholic can easily drink three or four times more booze than others might be aware of). But the drinking she couldn't hide (the episode with the eggs, the scene in Mexico, the night she locks herself out of the house) would be unacceptable to many spouses. Not good-hearted, accepting Michael, who is, in recovery jargon, a born enabler.

At the treatment facility, Alice begins learning to live with the disease. She makes close friendships with other recovering alcoholics. On visiting day, when a fairly fearsome-looking fellow patient offers to play with their daughter, she reassures her husband: "He's not a child molester. He's an armed robber." Back home, Alice attends a lot of AA meetings, and confides in friends she meets there. Michael is not sure he likes this so much. One evening he comes home to find Alice deep in a tête-à-tête with a man she met in the treatment center. "I can't remember how long it's been since *we* sat and talked that way," Michael says.

They have fights, mostly because Michael still has the habit of handling everything, settling problems with the children, making decisions. Now that Alice is ready to participate more fully in the family, he feels threatened. And she is emotionally fragile, too. One day she's in a foul mood and he wants to know why, so he can help, and she explains that she is simply having a very bad day and there is nothing either one of them can do about it, and he can't accept that. He needs to know the reason, so he can fix it. They fight.

What makes that scene so good is that it ends inconclusively. The movie doesn't pretend to be able to fix things, either. The strength of the screenplay by Ronald Bass and Al Franken is that it pays close attention to the feelings of both characters. It isn't just about Alice's recovery. It's about Michael's recovery *from* Alice's recovery. The writers make an unusual team: Bass won an Oscar for writing *Rain Man;* Franken writes and plays the twelve-step guru Stuart Smalley on *Saturday Night Live*. In the SNL bits, the jargon of twelve-step groups is kidded ("I'm good enough, I'm smart enough, and doggone it, people like me"). In the screenplay, the movie understands how AA helps alcoholics create a language to describe their feelings and deal with them.

Yet *When a Man Loves a Woman* is not simply a docudrama about the disease of the month. It's fresh and original in the way it sees its characters. The director, Luis Mandoki *(White Palace)*, is even-handed in seeing events through the eyes of both Michael and Alice—and of their young daughters, who see and hear more than the grown-ups realize, and ask hard questions ("Are you getting di-vorced?"). I couldn't find a false note in Ryan's performance—and only one in Garcia's, a smarmy Hollywood speech at the end of the movie that must, I think, be blamed on the filmmakers. (The movie's obvious close was one speech earlier.)

Then there is the character of the couple's pregnant nanny and housekeeper, Amy, played by Lauren Tom. Amy is on-screen only briefly, but is written and acted with such a perfect feel for tone and dialogue that she seems immediately real. She knows all about not enabling. One night as the kids are screaming and Michael is going berserk, she roots herself in the kitchen, preparing her own dinner. She knows what is her problem and what is not her problem. She has a line of dialogue ("It worked") that, in context, is both unexpected and perfect.

Alcoholism has been called a disease of denial. What *When a Man Loves a Woman* understands is that those around the alcoholic often deny it, too, and grow accustomed to their relationship with a drunk. When the drunk gets sober, he or she becomes a fuller and more competent person, and that can threaten the old relationship. That's why professionals call alcoholism a "family disease." It's a hard concept to understand, but here is a movie that understands it.

When Will I Be Loved
R, 81 m., 2004

Neve Campbell (Vera), Fred Weller (Ford), Dominic Chianese (Count Tommaso), Karen Allen (Alexandra), Barry Primus (Victor), Mike Tyson (Himself). Directed by James Toback and produced by Ron Rotholz. Screenplay by Toback.

When Will I Be Loved is like a jazz solo that touches familiar themes on its way to a triumphant and unexpected conclusion. Neve Campbell plays the soloist, a rich girl who likes to walk on the wild side, is open to the opportunities of the moment, and improvises a devious and spontaneous revenge when her boyfriend betrays her. Here is a movie that doesn't start out to be about a con, but ends up that way.

Campbell's performance is carnal, verbally facile, physically uninhibited, and charged with intelligence. Not many actresses could have played this character, and fewer still could give us the sense she's making it up as she goes along. She plays Vera, daughter of wealth, girlfriend of a persuasive street hustler named Ford (Fred Weller). Ford is smart, quick, cynical, and believes in making his own opportunities. He's engaged in trying to scam Count Tommaso (Dominic Chianese), an Italian millionaire who turns out to be interested in only one thing Ford might have to offer: his girlfriend.

The count suggests an introduction. Ford mentions money. Money is not a problem. The count is a man of the world, cultivated, with taste but without scruples. He would never make the mistake of implying that cash will be exchanged for sex. He uses the soothing language of money as a gift or tribute or simply a gesture, as if Vera deserves his money because she is so splendid a person.

Ford pitches the idea to Vera, after a scene in which they have enthusiastic sex; Vera has earlier had spontaneous sex with a girlfriend, and is a thoroughly sensual creature. We begin to understand why she is attracted to Ford, why she even likes him, why she's entertained by the audacity of his pitch to the world. But Ford is poor and needs money, and pushes too hard in the wrong way.

Vera agrees to meet with the count, as much for her own amusement as anything. She quickly ups the talking price from $100,000 to $1 million—both sums negligible to the count. She discovers that Ford, as the middle man, was going to cheat her on her share. She is dealing with a man who wants to sell her and another who wants to buy her, and neither one understands two things: (1) She is offended by being bought and sold, and (2) she doesn't need the money.

Toback began as a writer *(The Gambler)* before going on to write and direct such films as *Fingers* and *Black and White,* and to write *Bugsy* for Warren Beatty. In his work and in his life, he likes risk, likes gambling, likes women, and once tried to pick up so many in a short span of time that the late *Spy* magazine ran a four-page foldout chart of whom he hit on, what he told them, and how he scored. There's a little of Ford in his character, but also a little of Vera and the count, especially in his delight in verbal negotiation.

The centerpiece of the film is an extended scene between Vera and the count, as they discuss the amount of money and what it is being paid for. Vera is very specific about the money, and the count is politely vague about exactly what he expects for it, until Vera makes it clear that the count is likely to be pleased with the outcome. It is possible that Vera might have gone through with the deal, not for $1 million but for the danger, excitement, and audacity of negotiating for the $1 million and then delivering; the count is not young, but he is trim, elegant, sophisticated, and probably good company—at dinner, you know, and the opera, and at what he means when he mentions dinner and the opera.

Now I can tell you no more of the plot, except to say that it involves Vera's evolving response to a situation that develops in ways no one could have foreseen. I've seen countless movies in which people were conned or double-crossed or trapped by a con within a con (*Criminal* is an example). They all have to clear one hurdle: How could the characters predict so accurately who would do what, right on schedule, to make the pieces fall into place?

What is fascinating and ingenious about *When Will I Be Loved* is that nothing need be anticipated, not even the possibility of a con. In scenes of flawless timing, logic, and execution, Vera improvises in a fluid situation and perhaps even surprises herself at where she ends up. The third act of this movie is spellbinding in the way Vera distributes justice and revenge, and adapts to the unexpected and creates, spontaneously and in the moment, a checkmate.

Toback's structure backs into his perfect ending. There's an early scene where he plays a professor who is interviewing Vera for a job as his assistant, and then the two of them begin to speak openly about what is "really" going on; that's the curtain-raiser for the later high-stakes negotiation. There is a scene with Mike Tyson (so effective in *Black and White*) that plays like comic relief, until you think about it in the context of the movie. There's the lesbian scene, which seems gratuitous at the time but later seems necessary to establish Vera's carnal curiosity and Ford's ignorance of her complexity.

And the verbal sparring between Vera and the count is an exercise in the precise and stylish use of language to communicate exact meanings while using inexact euphemisms. Dominic Chianese and Neve Campbell are like virtuoso soloists with conversation as their instrument; the way they test and challenge each other is underlined by their obvious joy in performance. Both characters seem pleased to find another person who can engage them on their level of emotional negotiation.

The song "When Will I Be Loved" is about someone who complains, "I've been cheated—been mistreated." In the movie, the cheater and the mistreater have no idea who they're dealing with.

Who Framed Roger Rabbit

PG, 103 m., 1988

Bob Hoskins (Eddie Valiant), Christopher Lloyd (Judge Doom), Joanna Cassidy (Dolores), Charles Fleischer (Roger's voice), Stubby Kaye (Marvin Acme). Directed by Robert Zemeckis and produced by Robert Watts and Frank Marshall. Screenplay by Jeffrey Price and Peter S. Seaman.

I stopped off at a hot dog stand before the screening of *Who Framed Roger Rabbit*, and ran into a couple of the other local movie critics. They said they were going to the same screening. I asked them what they'd heard about the film. They said they were going to see it for the second time in two days. That's the kind of word of mouth that money can't buy.

And *Who Framed Roger Rabbit* is the kind of movie that gets made once in a blue moon, because it represents an immense challenge to the filmmakers: They have to make a good movie while inventing new technology at the same time. Like *2001, Close Encounters,* and *E.T.,* this movie is not only a great entertainment, but a breakthrough in craftsmanship—the first film to convincingly combine real actors and animated cartoon characters in the same space in the same time and make it look real.

I've never seen anything like it before. Roger Rabbit and his cartoon comrades cast real shadows. They shake the hands and grab the coats and rattle the teeth of real actors. They change size and dimension and perspective as they move through a scene, and the camera isn't locked down in one place to make it easy, either—the camera in this movie moves around like it's in a 1940s thriller, and

the cartoon characters look three-dimensional and seem to be occupying real space.

In a way, what you feel when you see a movie like this is more than appreciation. It's gratitude. You know how easy it is to make dumb, no-brainer action movies, and how incredibly hard it is to make a movie like this, where every minute of screen time can take days or weeks of work by the animators. You're glad they went to the trouble. The movie is a collaboration between the Disney studio and Steven Spielberg, the direction is by Robert *(Back to the Future)* Zemeckis, and the animation is by Raymond Williams. They made this a labor of love.

How did they do it? First they plotted every scene, shot by shot, so they knew where the live actors would be, and where the animated characters would be. Then they shot the live action, forcing actors like Bob Hoskins, the star, to imagine himself in a world also inhabited by cartoons (or "Toons," as the movie calls them). Then they laboriously went through the movie frame by frame, drawing in the cartoon characters. This is not a computer job. Real, living animators did this by hand, and the effort shows in moments like the zowie zoom shots where the camera hurtles at Roger Rabbit and then careens away, with the rabbit changing size and perspective in every frame.

But I'm making the movie sound like homework for a movie class. *Who Framed Roger Rabbit* is sheer, enchanted entertainment from the first frame to the last—a joyous, giddy, goofy celebration of the kind of fun you can have with a movie camera. The film takes place in Hollywood in 1947, in a world where humans and Toons exist side by side. The Toons in the movie include not only new characters like Roger Rabbit and his wife, the improbably pneumatic Jessica, but also established cartoon stars like Bugs Bunny, Betty Boop, Dumbo, Mickey Mouse, and both of the great ducks, Donald and Daffy (they do an act together as a piano duo).

The Toons live in Toontown, a completely animated world where the climax of the movie takes place, but most of the time they hang out in a version of Hollywood that looks like it was borrowed from a 1940s private-eye movie. The plot revolves around the murder of a movie tycoon, and when Roger Rabbit is framed for the murder, private eye Hoskins gets caught in the middle of the action. As plots go, this one will be familiar to anyone who has ever seen a hard-boiled '40s crime movie—except, of course, for the Toons.

The movie is funny, but it's more than funny, it's exhilarating. It opens with what looks like a standard studio cartoon (Mother goes shopping and leaves Roger Rabbit to baby-sit her little brat, who immediately starts causing trouble). This cartoon itself, seen apart from the movie, is a masterpiece; I can't remember the last time I laughed so hard at an animated short. But then, when a stunt goes wrong and the cartoon "baby" stalks off the set and lights a cigar and tells the human director to go to hell, we know we're in a new and special universe.

The movie is filled with throwaway gags, inside jokes, one-liners, and little pokes at the screen images of its cartoon characters. It is also oddly convincing, not only because of the craft of the filmmakers, but also because Hoskins and the other live actors have found the right note for their interaction with the Toons. Instead of overreacting or playing up their emotions cartoon-style, Hoskins and the others adopt a flat, realistic, matter-of-fact posture toward the Toons. They act as if they've been talking to animated rabbits for years.

One tricky question is raised by a movie like this: Is it for kids, or adults, or both? I think it's intended as a universal entertainment, like *E.T.* or *The Wizard of Oz*, aimed at all audiences. But I have a sneaky hunch that adults will appreciate it even more than kids, because they'll have a better appreciation of how difficult it was to make, and how effortlessly it succeeds. Kids will love it too—but instead of being amazed at how they got the rabbits in with the humans, they'll be wondering what adults are doing walking around inside a cartoon.

The Widow of St. Pierre

R, 112 m., 2001

Juliette Binoche (Madame La), Daniel Auteuil (Le Capitaine), Emir Kusturica (Neel Auguste), Michel Duchaussoy (Le Gouverneur), Philippe Magnan (President Venot), Christian Charmetant (Commissaire de la Marine), Philippe Du Janerand (Chef Douanier), Reynald Bouchard (Louis Olliver). Directed by Patrice Leconte and produced by Frederic Brillion and Gilles Legrand. Screenplay by Claude Faraldo.

A man gets drunk and commits a senseless murder. He is condemned to death by guillotine. But in the 1850s on a small French fishing island off the coast of Newfoundland, there is no guillotine, and no executioner. The guillotine can be shipped from France. But the island will have to find its own executioner, because superstitious ship's captains refuse to allow one on board.

Time passes, and a strange and touching thing happens. The murderer repents of his crime, and becomes a useful member of the community. He saves a woman's life. He works in a garden started by the wife of the captain of the local military. The judge who condemned him frets, "His popularity is a nuisance." An islander observes, "We committed a murderous brute and we're going to top a benefactor."

The Widow of St. Pierre is a beautiful and haunting film that tells this story, and then tells another subterranean story, about the seasons of a marriage. Le Capitaine (Daniel Auteuil) and his wife, referred to by everyone as Madame La (Juliette Binoche), are not only in love but in deep sympathy with each other. He understands her slightest emotional clues. "Madame La only likes desperate cases," someone says, and indeed she seems stirred by the plight of the prisoner. Stirred and . . . something else. The film is too intelligent and subtle to make obvious what the woman herself hardly suspects, but if we watch and listen closely we realize she is stirred in a sensual way by the prospect of a prisoner who has been condemned to die. Le Capitaine understands this and, because his wife is admirable and he loves her, he sympathizes with it.

The movie becomes not simply a drama about capital punishment, but a story about human psychology. Some audience members may not connect directly with the buried levels of obsession and attraction, but they'll sense them—sense something that makes the movie deeper and sadder than the plot alone can account for. Juliette Binoche, that wonderful actress, is the carrier of this subtlety, and the whole film resides in her face. Sad that most of those who saw her in *Chocolat* will never see, in this film, how much more she is capable of.

The Widow of St. Pierre is a title that carries extra weight. The French called a guillotine a "widow," and by the end of the film it has created two widows. And it has made a sympathetic character of the murderer, named Neel and played by the dark, burly Yugoslavian director Emir Kusturica. It accomplishes this not by soppy liberal piety, but by leading us to the same sort of empathy the islanders feel. Neel and a friend got drunk and murdered a man for no reason, and can hardly remember it. The friend is dead. Neel is prepared to die, but it becomes clear that death would redress nothing and solve nothing—and that Neel has changed so fundamentally that a different man would be going to the guillotine.

The director is Patrice Leconte, whose films unfailingly move me, and often (but not this time) make me smile. He is obsessed with obsession. He first fascinated me with *Monsieur Hire* (1990), based on a Simenon story about a little man who begins to spy on a beautiful woman whose window faces his. She knows he is looking, and plays her own game, until everything goes wrong. Then there was *The Hairdresser's Husband* (1990), about a man obsessed with hair and the women who cut it. Then *Ridicule* (1996), about a provincial landowner in the reign of Louis XVI, who wants to promote a drainage scheme at court and finds the king will favor only those who make him laugh. Then *The Girl on the Bridge* (1999), about a knife-thrower who recruits suicidal girls as targets for his act—because what do they have to lose?

The Widow of St. Pierre is unlike these others in tone. It is darker, angrier. And yet Leconte loves the humor of paradox, and some of it slips through, as in a scene where Madame La supplies Neel with a boat and advises him to escape to Newfoundland. He escapes, but returns, because he doesn't want to get anyone into trouble. When the guillotine finally arrives, he helps bring it ashore, because he doesn't want to cause work for others on his account. He impregnates a local girl and is allowed to marry, and the islanders develop an affection for him and begin to see the judge as an alien troublemaker from a France they believe "doesn't care about our cod island."

Now watch closely during the scene where Neel marries his pregnant bride. Madame La

hides it well during the ceremony, but is distraught. "It's all right; I'm here," Le Capitaine tells her. What's all right? I think she loves Neel. It's not that she wants to be his lover; in the 1850s such a thought would probably not occur. It's that she is happy for him, and is marrying him and having his child vicariously. And Le Capitaine knows that, and loves her the more for it.

The movie is not even primarily about Neel, his crime, his sentence, and the difficulty of bringing about his death. That is the subplot. It is really about the captain and his wife. About two people with good hearts who live in an innocent, less self-aware time, and how the morality of the case and their deeper feelings about Neel all get mixed up together. Eventually Le Capitaine takes a stand, and everyone thinks it is based on politics and ethics, but if we have been paying attention we know better. It is based on his love for his wife, and the ethics are an afterthought.

The Wild Bunch: The Director's Cut
R, 144 m., 1969

William Holden (Pike), Ernest Borgnine (Dutch), Robert Ryan (Thornton), Edmond O'Brien (Sykes), Warren Oates (Lyle Gorch), Jaime Sanchez (Angel), Ben Johnson (Tector Gorch), Emilio Fernandez (Mapache). Directed by Sam Peckinpah and produced by Phil Feldman. Screenplay by Walon Green and Peckinpah.

In an early scene of *The Wild Bunch*, the bunch rides into town past a crowd of children who are gathered with excitement around their game. They have trapped some scorpions and are watching them being tortured by ants. The eyes of Pike (William Holden), leader of the bunch, briefly meet the eyes of one of the children. Later in the film, a member of the bunch named Angel is captured by Mexican rebels, and dragged around the town square behind one of the first automobiles anyone there has seen. Children run after the car, laughing. Near the end of the film, Pike is shot by a little boy who gets his hands on a gun.

The message here is not subtle, but then Sam Peckinpah was not a subtle director, preferring sweeping gestures to small points. It is that the mantle of violence is passing from the old professionals like Pike and his bunch, who operate according to a code, into the hands of a new generation that learns to kill more impersonally, as a game, or with machines.

The movie takes place in 1913, on the eve of World War I. "We gotta start thinking beyond our guns," one of the bunch observes. "Those days are closing fast." And another, looking at the newfangled auto, says, "They're gonna use them in the war, they say." It is not a war that would have meaning within his intensely individual frame of reference; he knows loyalty to his bunch, and senses it is the end of his era.

This new version of *The Wild Bunch*, carefully restored to its original running time of 144 minutes, includes several scenes not widely seen since the movie had its world premiere in 1969. Most of them fill in details from the earlier life of Pike, including his guilt over betraying Thornton (Robert Ryan), who was once a member of the bunch but is now leading the posse of bounty hunters on their trail. Without these scenes, the movie seems more empty and existential, as if Pike and his men seek death after reaching the end of the trail. With them, Pike's actions are more motivated: He feels unsure of himself and the role he plays.

I saw the original version at the world premiere in 1969, as part of a week-long boondoggle during which Warner Bros. screened five of its new films in the Bahamas for 450 critics and reporters. It was party time, not the right venue for what became one of the most controversial films of its time—praised and condemned with equal vehemence, like *Pulp Fiction*. At a press conference the following morning, Holden and Peckinpah hid behind dark glasses and deep scowls. After a reporter from *Reader's Digest* got up to attack them for making the film, I stood up in defense; I felt, then and now, that *The Wild Bunch* is one of the great defining moments of modern movies.

But no one saw the 144-minute version for many years. It was cut, not because of violence (only quiet scenes were removed), but because it was too long to be shown three times in an evening. It was successful, but it was read as a celebration of compulsive, mindless violence; see the uncut version, and you get a better idea of what Peckinpah was driving at.

The movie is, first of all, about old and worn men. Holden and his fellow actors (Ernest Borgnine, Warren Oates, Edmund O'Brien, Ben Johnson, and the wonderful Robert Ryan) look lined and bone-tired. They have been making a living by crime for many years, and although Ryan is now hired by the law, it is only under threat that he will return to jail if he doesn't capture the bunch. The men provided to him by a railroad mogul are shifty and unreliable; they don't understand the code of the bunch.

And what is that code? It's not very pleasant. It says that you stand by your friends and against the world, that you wrest a criminal living from the banks, the railroads, and the other places where the money is, and that while you don't shoot at civilians unnecessarily, it is best if they don't get in the way.

The two great violent set pieces in the movie involve a lot of civilians. One comes through a botched bank robbery at the beginning of the film, and the other comes at the end, where Pike looks at Angel's body being dragged through the square, and says "God, I hate to see that," and then later walks into a bordello and says "Let's go," and everybody knows what he means, and they walk out and begin the suicidal showdown with the heavily armed rebels. Lots of bystanders are killed in both sequences (one of the bunch picks a scrap from a woman's dress off of his boot), but there is also cheap sentimentality, as when Pike gives gold to a prostitute with a child, before walking out to die.

In between the action sequences (which also include the famous scene where a bridge is bombed out from beneath mounted soldiers), there is a lot of time for the male bonding that Peckinpah celebrated in most of his films. His men shoot, screw, drink, and ride horses. The quiet moments, with the firelight and the sad songs on the guitar and the sweet tender prostitutes, are like daydreams, with no standing in the bunch's real world. This is not the kind of film that would likely be made today, but it represents its set of sad, empty values with real poetry.

The undercurrent of the action in *The Wild Bunch* is the sheer meaninglessness of it all. The first bank robbery nets only a bag of iron washers—"a dollar's worth of steel holes." The train robbery is well planned, but the bunch cannot hold onto their takings. And at the end, after the bloodshed, when the Robert Ryan character sits for hours outside the gate of the compound, just thinking, there is the payoff: A new gang is getting together, to see what jobs might be left to do. With a wry smile he gets up to join them. There is nothing else to do, not for a man with his background.

The movie was photographed by Lucien Ballard, in dusty reds and golds and browns and shadows. The editing, by Lou Lombardo, uses slow motion to draw the violent scenes out into meditations on themselves. Every actor was perfectly cast to play exactly what he could play; even the small roles need no explanation. Peckinpah possibly identified with the wild bunch. Like them, he was an obsolete, violent, hard-drinking misfit with his own code, and did not fit easily into the new world of automobiles and Hollywood studios.

Seeing this restored version is like understanding the film at last. It is all there: why Pike limps, what passed between Pike and Thornton in the old days, why Pike seems tortured by his thoughts and memories. Now, when we watch Ryan, as Thornton, sitting outside the gate and thinking, we know what he is remembering. It makes all the difference in the world.

The Wild Child

G, 83 m., 1970

Francois Truffaut (Dr. Itard), Jean-Pierre Cargol (The Wild Child). Directed by Truffaut and produced by Marcel Berbert. Screenplay by Truffaut and Jean Gruault.

Francois Truffaut's *The Wild Child* is the story of a "wolf boy" who lived like an animal in the woods, and about the doctor who adopted him and tried to civilize him. The story is essentially true, drawn from an actual case in eighteenth-century France, and Truffaut tells it simply and movingly. It becomes his most thoughtful statement on his favorite subject: the way young people grow up, explore themselves, and attempt to function creatively in the world.

This process was the subject of Truffaut's first film, *The 400 Blows*, and he returned to the same autobiographical ground with his recent *Stolen Kisses*. Now, again using Jean-Pierre Cargol as the actor, he's at work on the third film in the trilogy. In this one, reportedly, the autobiographical character survives adolescence and enters bravely into manhood.

That is a happy ending forever out of the reach of the Wild Child, who has been so traumatically affected by his forest life that he can hardly comprehend the idea of language. There's even a question, at first, as to whether he can hear. He can but makes little connection between the sounds of words and their meanings. The doctor makes slow progress, or none, for months at a time. Then perhaps there's a small breakthrough. He records it all in his journal, and Truffaut's spoken English narration from the journal carries most of the ideas in the film.

The Wild Child is about education at its most fundamental level—about education as the process by which society takes millions of literally savage infants every year and gradually seduces them into sharing the conventions of everybody else. There's a question, of course, as to whether "civilization" is good for man, or if he'd be happier in a natural state.

That question is at the root of *The Wild Child*. Since the boy can never function "normally" in society, should he have been left in the woods? It's a question for us, in this uncertain age, but not for the doctor, who shares the rational optimism of Jefferson and never seriously questions the worth of his efforts. He believes in the nobility of man and detests the idea of a human being scavenging for survival in the forest.

Truffaut places his personal touch on every frame of the film. He wrote it, directed it, and plays the doctor himself. It is an understated, compassionate performance, a perfect counterpoint to Jean-Pierre Cargol's ferocity and fear. The day-to-day record of the doctor's attempts to teach the boy to walk upright, to dress himself, to eat properly, to recognize sounds and symbols, is endlessly fascinating. So often movies keep our attention by flashy tricks and cheap melodrama; it is an intellectually cleansing experience to watch this intelligent and hopeful film.

Note: Because Truffaut's narration is in English and the boy speaks hardly at all, there are very few subtitles to be read and the movie is completely accessible even to, say, third- or fourth-graders. I imagine most children would find it completely fascinating.

Willy Wonka and the Chocolate Factory

G, 98 m., 1971

Gene Wilder (Willy Wonka), Jack Albertson (Grandpa Joe), Peter Ostrum (Charlie), Michael Bollner (Augustus Gloop), Aubrey Wood (Mr. Bill), Gunter Meissner (Mr. Slugwork). Directed by Mel Stuart and produced by Stan Margulies and David L. Wolper. Screenplay by Roald Dahl, based on his book.

Kids are not stupid. They are among the sharpest, cleverest, most eagle-eyed creatures on God's Earth, and very little escapes their notice. You may not have observed that your neighbor is still using his snow tires in mid-July, but every four-year-old on the block has, and kids pay the same attention to detail when they go to the movies. They don't miss a thing, and they have an instinctive contempt for shoddy and shabby work. I make this observation because nine out of ten children's movies are stupid, witless, and display contempt for their audiences, and that's why kids hate them. Is that all parents want from kids' movies? That they not have anything bad in them? Shouldn't they have something good in them—some life, imagination, fantasy, inventiveness, something to tickle the imagination? If a movie isn't going to do your kids any good, why let them watch it? Just to kill a Saturday afternoon? That shows a subtle kind of contempt for a child's mind, I think.

All of this is preface to a simple statement: *Willy Wonka and the Chocolate Factory* is probably the best film of its sort since *The Wizard of Oz.* It is everything that family movies usually claim to be, but aren't: Delightful, funny, scary, exciting, and, most of all, a genuine work of imagination. *Willy Wonka* is such a surely and wonderfully spun fantasy that it works on all kinds of minds, and it is fascinating because, like all classic fantasy, it is fascinated with itself.

It's based on the well-known Roald Dahl children's book, and it was financed by the Quaker Oats Company as an experiment in providing high-quality family entertainment. It

succeeds. It doesn't cut corners and go for cheap shortcuts like Disney. It provides a first-rate cast (Gene Wilder as the compulsively distrustful chocolate manufacturer, Jack Albertson as the game old grandfather), a first-rate production, and—I keep coming back to this—genuine imagination.

The story, like all good fantasies, is about a picaresque journey. Willy Wonka is the world's greatest chocolate manufacturer, and he distributes five golden passes good for a trip through his factory and a lifetime supply of chocolate. Each pass goes to a kid, who may bring an adult along, and our hero Charlie (a poor but honest newsboy who supports four grandparents and his mother) wins the last one.

The other four kids are hateful in one way or another, and come to dreadful ends. One falls into the chocolate lake and is whisked into the bowels of the factory. He shouldn't have been a pig. Another is vain enough to try Wonka's new teleportation invention, and winds up six inches tall—but the taffy-pulling machine will soon have him back to size, right? If these fates seem a little gruesome to you, reflect that all great children's tales are a little gruesome, from the Brothers Grimm to Alice to Snow White, and certainly not excluding Mother Goose. Kids are not sugar and spice, not very often, and they appreciate the poetic justice when a bad kid gets what's coming to him.

Wings of Desire

NO MPAA RATING, 130 m., 1988

Bruno Ganz (Damiel), Solveig Dommartin (Marion), Otto Sander (Cassiel), Curt Bois (Homer), Peter Falk (Himself). Directed by Wim Wenders. Screenplay by Wenders and Peter Handke.

In notes that he wrote after directing *Wings of Desire,* Wim Wenders reflected that it would be terrible to be an angel: "To live for an eternity and to be present all the time. To live with the essence of things—not to be able to raise a cup of coffee and drink it, or really touch somebody." In his film, this dilemma becomes the everyday reality of two angels, who move through Berlin observing people, listening, reflecting, caring. They can see and hear, but are cut off from the senses of touch, taste, and smell. Human life appears to them as if it were a movie.

The angels look like two ordinary men, with weary and kind faces. They can move through the air free of gravity, but in all other respects they appear to the camera to be just as present as the human characters in a scene. Their role is a little unclear. They watch. They listen. Sometimes, when they are moved by the plight of a human they care about, they are able to stand close to that person and somehow exude a sense of caring or love, which seems to be vaguely perceived by the human, to whom it can provide a moment of hope or release.

The angel we are most concerned with in the film is Damiel, played by Bruno Ganz, that everyman of German actors whose face is expressive because it is so lived-in, so tired. He moves slowly through the city, hearing snatches of conversation, seeing moments of lives, keenly aware of his existence as a perpetual outsider. One day he comes across Marion (Solveig Dommartin), a trapeze artist, and is moved by her sadness. He helps her in the ways that he can, but eventually he realizes that he does not want to end her suffering so much as to share it.

That is the problem with being an angel. He can live forever, but in a sense, he can never live. To an angel, a being who exists in eternity, human lives must seem to be over in a brief flash of time, in a wink of history, and yet during our brief span, at least humans are really alive—to grow, to learn, to love, to suffer, to drink a cup of coffee, while an angel can only imagine the warmth of the cup, the aroma of the coffee, the taste, the feel.

Damiel determines to renounce immortality and accept human life with all its transience and pain. And in that act of renunciation, he makes one of the most poignant and romantic of gestures. He is accepting the limitations not only of his loved one, but of life itself.

Wings of Desire was directed by Wenders (whose credits include *Paris, Texas* and *The American Friend*), and cowritten by Wenders and Peter Handke, the German novelist who also wrote and directed *The Left-Handed Woman*. They are not interested in making some kind of soft-hearted, sentimental Hollywood story in which harps play and everybody feels good afterward.

Their film is set in divided Berlin, most insubstantial of cities because its future always seems deferred. Most of the film is shot in black and white, the correct medium for this story, because color would be too realistic to reflect the tone of their fable. Many of the best moments in the film have no particular dramatic purpose, but are concerned only with showing us what it is like to be forever an observer. Ganz walks quietly across empty bridges. He looks into vacant windows. He sits in a library and watches people as they read. He is there, and he is not there. The sterility of his existence almost makes us understand the choice of Lucifer in renouncing heaven in order to be plunged into hell, where at least he could suffer, and therefore, feel.

This is the kind of film that needs to be seen in a meditative frame of mind. It doesn't much matter what happens in the story, but it does matter how well we are able to empathize with it, how successfully we are able to enter into the state of mind of an angel. Leaving the movie, I reflected that sometimes we are bored by life, and feel as if nothing exciting is happening. But if we had spent eternity as an angel, observing life without feeling it, and then were plunged into a human body with its physical senses, think what a roar and flood of sensations would overwhelm us! It would be almost too much to bear. It would be everyday life.

Withnail & I
R, 104 m., 1987

Richard E. Grant (Withnail), Paul McGann (Marwood), Richard Griffiths (Monty), Ralph Brown (Danny), Michael Elphick (Jake), Daragh O'Malley (Irishman), Michael Wardle (Isaac Parkin), Una Brandon-Jones (Mrs. Parkin). Directed by Bruce Robinson and produced by Paul M. Heller. Screenplay by Robinson.

Withnail & I takes place in England at the end of the Swinging Sixties. Two would-be actors live in squalor and poverty in a mean little flat in a wretched section of London. They are cold, desperate, broke, and hung over. They dream of glory but lurk about in the corners of pubs to keep warm.

One of them is Withnail, who is tall, craggy, and utterly cynical. He affects a kind of weary bitterness. The other is Marwood, younger, more optimistic, more impressionable. Their situation is desperate. "Something has to happen," Withnail says, "or I'm going to crack."

Then he has an inspiration: His rich and eccentric uncle Monty has some sort of a place in the country. They'll talk him into lending it to them, and perhaps the change of scenery will give them the courage to carry on. The scene that begins when they appear at the door of Monty's London mansion is sly and droll, filled with hazardous currents and undertows as Monty takes a fancy to young Marwood. He agrees to lend them his country place.

The country is bitter, cold, angry, and hostile. Neighbors will not talk to them. Farmers will not sell them firewood. Their wives will not part with eggs or milk. Huddled over a wretched blaze made of Uncle Monty's furniture, Withnail and Marwood contemplate a bleak prospect: They have no food, fuel, money, or (worst of all) drink. Outside the door, the idyllic countryside is roamed by randy bulls.

Then uncle Monty arrives unexpectedly and sets himself on a determined romantic pursuit of young Marwood, who wants nothing to do with him. Withnail confesses that he told his uncle that Marwood was gay, "because otherwise how would we have gotten the cottage?" Uncle Monty is, however, not only gay but also rich and fat, and the erotic tension in the cottage is interrupted by large and leisurely meals.

The performances make the movie, and Richard Griffiths is wonderful as Uncle Monty: overfed, burbling with secondhand eloquence, yet with a cold intelligence lurking behind his bloodshot eyes. It's the best supporting performance in a British movie since Denholm Elliott in *A Room with a View*. Withnail and Marwood, played by Richard E. Grant and Paul McGann, are like Rosencrantz and Guildenstern: They know all their lines but are uncertain about which direction the play is taking.

Withnail & I is a comedy, but a grimly serious one. Nothing is played for laughs. The humor arises from poverty, desperation, and bone-numbing cold. It is not the portrait of two colorful, lovable characters, but of two comrades in emotional shipwreck. The movie is rigorously dyspeptic, and that's why I liked it: It doesn't go for the easy laughs or sentimentalized poverty, but finds its humor in the unforgiving study of selfish human nature.

Witness

R, 120 m., 1985

Harrison Ford (John Book), Kelly McGillis (Rachel), Josef Sommer (Schaeffer), Lukas Haas (Samuel), Alexander Godunov (Daniel Hochleitner). Directed by Peter Weir and produced by Edward S. Feldman. Screenplay by Earl Wallace.

Witness comes billed as a thriller, but it's so much more than a thriller that I wish they hadn't even used the word "murder" in the ads. This is, first of all, an electrifying and poignant love story. Then it is a movie about the choices we make in life and the choices that other people make for us. Only then is it a thriller—one that Alfred Hitchcock would have been proud to make.

The movie's first act sets up the plot, leaving it a lot of time to deal with the characters and learn about them. The film begins on an Amish settlement in Pennsylvania, where for two hundred years a self-sufficient religious community has proudly held onto the ways of their ancestors. The Amish are deeply suspicious of outsiders and stubbornly dedicated to their rural lifestyle, with its horses and carriages, its communal barn raisings, its gas lanterns instead of electricity, hooks instead of buttons.

An Amish man dies. His widow and young son leave on a train journey. In the train station in Philadelphia, the little boy witnesses a murder. Harrison Ford plays the tough big-city detective who gets assigned to the case. He stages lineups, hoping the kid can spot the murderer. He shows the kid mug shots. Then it turns out that the police department itself is implicated in the killing. Ford is nearly murdered in an ambush. His life, and the lives of the widow and her son, are in immediate danger. He manages to drive them all back to the Amish lands of Pennsylvania before collapsing from loss of blood.

And it's at this point, really, that the movie begins. Up until the return to Amish country, *Witness* has been a slick, superior thriller. Now it turns into an intelligent and perceptive love story. It's not one of those romances where the man and woman fall into each other's arms because their hormones are programmed that way. It's about two independent, complicated people who begin to love each other because they have shared danger, they work well together, they respect each other—*and* because their physical attraction for each other is so strong it almost becomes another character in the movie.

Witness was directed by Peter Weir, the gifted Australian director of *The Year of Living Dangerously.* He has a strong and sure feeling for places, for the land, for the way that people build their self-regard by the way they do their work.

In the whole middle section of this movie, he shows the man from the city and the simple Amish woman within the context of the Amish community. It is masterful filmmaking. The thriller elements alone would command our attention. The love story by itself would be exciting. The ways of life in the Amish community are so well-observed that they have a documentary feel. But all three elements work together so well that something organic is happening here; we're *inside* this story.

Harrison Ford has never given a better performance in a movie. Kelly McGillis, the young actress who plays the Amish widow, has a kind of luminous simplicity about her; it is refreshing and even subtly erotic to see a woman who doesn't subscribe to all the standard man-woman programmed responses of modern society.

The love that begins to grow between them is not made out of clichés; the cultural gulf that separates them is at least as important to both of them as the feelings they have. When they finally kiss, it is a glorious, sensuous moment, because this kiss is a sharing of trust and passion, not just another plug-in element from your standard kit of movie images.

We have been getting so many pallid, bloodless little movies—mostly recycled teenage exploitation films made by ambitious young stylists without a thought in their heads—that *Witness* is like a fresh new day. It is a movie about adults, whose lives have dignity and whose choices matter to them. And it is also one hell of a thriller.

A Woman's Decision/The Balance

NO MPAA RATING, 98 m., 1977

Maja Komorowska (Marta), Piotr Fronczewski (Jan), Marek Piwowski (Jacek), Zofia Mrozowska (Jan's Mother). Directed and written by Krzysztof Zanussi.

If you care about the changing images of women in the movies, you've probably already seen *Julia* and *The Turning Point,* and perhaps you admired them. I did, to varying degrees. But now here's a film that has so much to say about one particular woman, and says it so eloquently, that nobody since Bergman has seen a woman character more clearly. The film is *A Woman's Decision,* by Krzysztof Zanussi, who was already Poland's best director and now graduates to grandmaster class.

The woman, Marta, the mother of a little boy, and an accountant in a state office. She is also in the habit of poking her nose in where it allegedly doesn't belong. She stands up for underdogs: She's the union representative in the office and defends a friend who's unfairly accused of having stolen some money. She is also a restless woman, vaguely unsatisfied with her marriage, sort of on the lookout for something different. One day she's given a ride by a good-looking guy who drives a van for the university. And she falls into something. Love, maybe, when the light is right.

Descriptions can be frustrating. This is one of the year's best movies, and so far I've made it sound like a socialist soap opera. Zanussi and Maja Komorowska, who plays the lead, take this material and turn it inside out. They take the most ordinary human situations and see them so clearly that the movie gives meanings even to things in our own lives.

Notice the way, for example, Zanussi develops Marta's marriage. He doesn't proceed in a straightforward fashion, and he doesn't tell us things—he lets us figure them out. And he frames the two characters in their apartment so that they often seem kept apart by the glass wall in the kitchen. The husband, quiet, tactful, knows that she's cracking up, or breaking out, or having an affair. What does he think?

One night she comes home late and he's passed out drunk, the bottle smashed at his feet. She awakens him. "Miss Marta," he says, "Miss Marta." The words are torn from him. "What do you want here?" She gasps, drops to her knees, clears away the broken glass, and tenderly places his feet so he will not cut himself. All done in a few moments, all saying more about the deepness of the anguish here—and the surviving affection—than a thousand words of dialogue.

Marta's progress through the film is a series of confrontations with men, alternating with moments of almost sad fellowship with women. She and her friend at the office, for example—the one accused of theft—they meet in the lavatory to plan their strategy, the other woman looking bitterly into nowhere as she wonders who forged her signature.

Marta finally faces down their boss, refusing to leave his office, telling him she knows that he doesn't really think the other woman is guilty. He tries to bully her, he pushes her, but by allowing herself to be abused by him she wins her case. And somehow we know she had it figured out that way: He is bigger and stronger and more crude, but he never had a chance because he didn't understand what was really being argued about.

Marta herself doesn't have a chance with the young van driver, though. He's pleasant enough, pleased on occasion to take her out, but essentially not reliable. Maybe that's okay. Maybe this whole thing is just Marta testing herself—discovering the limits of her discontent. He helps her find them, all right. And then the film moves to the tremulous humanity of its last great scenes. I search for comparisons. Do you remember Harriet Andersson dying in Bergman's *Cries and Whispers?* Nobody dies in *A Woman's Decision,* but the emotional intensity of the closing moments is strong.

The movie is not all that bleak. Komorowska, who is Poland's best-known actress, projects spunk, humor, and resiliency in the central role. There's life in her. She fights back. She looks kind of naive in some scenes, then terribly wise in others. She has the capacity to love and give. And then, when things go wrong, she's open enough to admit vulnerability, especially in the scene at the end of the long night's wait—the scene where she opens her mouth and permits herself a mournful shout of anguish.

This is a movie for adults. Not because it has content that would be disturbing to younger viewers—although it does—but because you have to have been around for a while to understand all that Zanussi is saying.

I wonder if the movie will find its audience; it's in Polish with English subtitles. *A Woman's*

Decision is so emotionally complex, so sympathetic about Marta's hungers and needs, that it combines great subtlety and wisdom with the absolute ground-level heartbreak of a song by Tammy Wynette. Yes, all at the same time.

A Woman's Tale

PG-13, 94 m., 1992

Sheila Florance (Martha), Gosia Dobrowolska (Anna), Norman Kaye (Billy), Chris Haywood (Jonathan), Ernest Gray (Peter), Myrtle Woods (Miss Inchley). Directed by Paul Cox and produced by Cox and Santhana Naidu. Screenplay by Cox.

Paul Cox's *A Woman's Tale* is a portrait of an old lady of great wit and courage, who faces death as she has faced everything else, on her own terms. *A Woman's Tale* does not sentimentalize its heroine, does not make her cute or lovable or pull any of those other tricks we use to deny the realities of old age. It allows her strong opinions and a skeptical irony, and makes her into one of the great characters of recent movies.

The old woman's name is Martha. She is played by Sheila Florance, who won the Australian Academy Award for her performance. She is about eighty years old, and lives in a flat with a cat, a parakeet, and a few prized possessions, and she gets around well enough to look after Billy, the disintegrating old man who lives next door.

Her other important relationships include an unpleasant one, with her son, who wants to shelve her in a nursing home; a loving one, with Anna (Gosia Dobrowolska), the visiting nurse; an amused one, with Miss Inchly, who is nearly ten years older; and a fighting one, with her landlord, who wants her to move.

Martha's secret is that she is dying. She knows it, Anna knows it, and the others will not be given the satisfaction of being told. She wants to die as she has lived, in her own way, in her own apartment, and the zest with which she defends herself is one of the movie's great joys.

The film has been written by Cox as several days in Martha's life, during which she does as much living as some of us would be lucky to manage in a year. She is a coconspirator in

Anna's affair with a married man, and lets the lovers use her bed ("I am going to die in it; you had might as well love in it"). She sees Billy through his usual crises, chats with her pets, goes for walks to check out the neighborhood, and at night, when the pain keeps her awake, she listens to the radio talk shows and calls in with pointed advice.

The movie is not just about her activities, however. It is also about her continued occupation of a body that has served her for eight decades and is now failing her. The movie is quite frank about Martha's physicality. Her face is a mass of wrinkles, her body is too thin, and when we see her in her bath, we are moved with compassion that such a great spirit should inhabit such a frail vessel.

She has her memories, including some erotic ones, and she takes a frank interest in the life of a neighborhood prostitute. At eighty, it is not so much that she approves or disapproves as that she has lived a long time and knows what goes on in this world. Her greatest threat comes through an alliance between her landlord, who battles to get rid of her, and her well-meaning son, who thinks he is helping her by his efforts to rid her of independence.

Paul Cox, born in Holland, long a resident of Australia, is one of the best directors of our time. His films often deal with loneliness; his credits include *Man of Flowers,* starring Norman Kaye (the Billy of this film) as a gentle recluse, *Lonely Hearts,* about a disastrous dating service match, and *Cactus,* about the possibility of blindness. *A Woman's Tale* is one of his best works—one of the best films of the year.

Sheila Florance, who spent most of her life as an actress in Australia, was dying when she made this film about a woman who is dying. She knew it, Cox knew it, and although she was sometimes in pain she focused on the performance and made it her message to the rest of us, about a process we will all face in one way or another. She died some months after finishing the film; here she still lives, in humor, dignity, and a fine proud anger.

A Woman Under the Influence

R, 155 m., 1974

Peter Falk (Nick Longhetti), Gena Rowlands (Mabel Longhetti), Katherine Cassavetes (Mama Longhetti), Lady Rowlands (Martha Mortensen), Fred Draper (George Mortensen). Directed by John Cassavetes and produced by Sam Shaw. Screenplay by John Cassavetes.

John Cassavetes's *A Woman Under the Influence* gives us a woman whose influences only gradually reveal themselves. And as they do, they give us insight not only into one specific, brilliantly created, woman, but into some of the problems of surviving in a society where very few people are free to be themselves. The woman is Mabel Longhetti, wife and mother and (in some very small, shy, and faraway corner) herself. Her husband, Nick, is the head of a construction gang and a gregarious type with an expansive nature; he's likely to bring his whole crew home at 7 A.M. for a spaghetti dinner.

Mabel isn't gregarious, but she tries. She tries too hard, and that's her problem. She desperately wants to please her husband, and when they're alone, she does. They get along, and they do love one another. But when people are around, she gets a little wacky. The mannerisms, the strange personal little ways she has of expressing herself, get out of scale. She's not sure how to act, because she's not sure who she is. "I'll be whatever you want me to be," she tells Nick, and he tells her to be herself. But who is that?

The film takes place before and after six months she spends in a mental institution. Her husband has her committed, reluctantly, after she begins to crack up. There have been some indications that she's in trouble. She behaves strangely when some neighbor children are brought over to stay for a while with her own, and the neighbor is afraid to leave his kids because of the way she's acting. But what, exactly, is "strange"? Well she's insecure, hyper, manic. She laughs too much and pushes too hard. She's not good with other people around. So her husband does what he thinks he has to do and commits her. But what about him? What kind of a guy is he? It's here that *A Woman Under the Influence* gets to be complicated, involved, and fascinating—a revelation. Because if Mabel is disturbed, then so is he. He's as crazy as she is, maybe more so. But because he's a man and has channels for his craziness, he stays at home and she gets sent away.

Their ways with kids, for example, are revealing. She feels insecure around them. She's not confident enough to be a mother, and almost wants to be another kid. But the father, when he takes over the responsibility of raising them, yanks them out of school in the middle of the day and drags them, bewildered, to the seashore for the most depressing, compulsory day at the beach we can imagine. And then on the way home, he lets them share a six-pack with him. If Mabel wants to be one of the kids, Nick wants them to be three of the boys.

I don't suppose (although I'm not sure) that real families like this exist, and I don't think Cassavetes wants us to take the film as a literal record. The characters are larger than life (although not less convincing because of that), and their loves and rages, their fights and moments of tenderness, exist at exhausting levels of emotion.

Nick, as played by Peter Falk, shouts and storms and is always on. Mabel (Gena Rowlands, who won an Oscar nomination), seems so touchingly vulnerable to every kind of influence around her that we don't want to tap her, because she might fall apart. Because their personalities are so open, so visible, we see what might be hidden in a quieter, tidier film: that Nick no less than Mabel is trapped in a society where people are assigned roles, duties, and even personalities that have little to do with what they really think and who they really are. This is where Cassavetes is strongest as a writer and filmmaker: at creating specific characters and then sticking with them through long, painful, uncompromising scenes until we know them well enough to read them, to predict what they'll do next, and even to begin to understand why.

Mabel and Nick and their relatives and friends are fully realized, convincing, fictional creations, even though Cassavetes does sometimes deliberately push them into extreme situations. There's a scene, for example, where Nick goes almost berserk in throwing a party for Mabel, who's due home from the institution, then tells all the nonfamily guests to leave immediately and then berates the family, and Mabel, and himself, in a painful confrontation around the dining room table. The scene's just too extreme to take literally. But as psychodrama, or whatever you want to call it, it abandons any niceties or evasions and deals directly with what the characters are really thinking.

There's also the scenes of great quiet comedy, as when one of Nick's coworkers somehow dumps his entire plate of spaghetti into his lap and the others battle between decorous table manners and their desire to laugh. There's Gena Rowlands's incredible command of her physical acting resources to communicate what Mabel feels at times when she's too unsure or intimidated to say. There's Falk, in a performance totally unlike his Columbo, creating this character who's so tender, so much in love, and so screwed up. I have a friend who said, after seeing *A Woman Under the Influence*, that she was so affected, she didn't know whether to cry or throw up. Well, sometimes that's the choice life presents you with—along with the laughs.

Wonder Boys
R, 112 m., 2000

Michael Douglas (Grady Tripp), Tobey Maguire (James Leer), Frances McDormand (Sara Gaskell), Robert Downey, Jr. (Terry Crabtree), Katie Holmes (Hannah Green), Richard Thomas (Walter Gaskell), Rip Torn (Q). Directed by Curtis Hanson and produced by Scott Rudin and Hanson. Screenplay by Steve Kloves, based upon the book by Michael Chabon.

My father was an electrician at the University of Illinois. He never taught me a thing about electricity. "Every time I walk through the English building," he said, "I see the professors in their offices with their feet up on the desk, reading books and smoking their pipes. Now that's the life for you."

I thought I would be an English professor. Then I got into this game. Sometimes I am overwhelmed with a sense of loss: I remember myself walking across the snowy campus at dusk, a book bag thrown over my shoulder, on the way to the seminar room to drink coffee and talk about Cather or Faulkner. And I remember the endless weekends, driving around town in somebody's oversize American car, following rumors of parties. And the emotional and romantic confusion that played out at those parties, where everyone was too smart and too high and filled with themselves.

Wonder Boys is the most accurate movie

about campus life I can remember. It is accurate, not because it captures intellectual debate or campus politics, but because it knows two things: (1) students come and go but the faculty actually lives there, and (2) many faculty members stay stuck in graduate student mode for decades. Michael Douglas plays a character like that. It is his best performance in years, muted, gentle, and wondering. He is a boy wonder long past his sell-by date, a fiftyish English professor named Grady Tripp who wrote a good novel seven years ago and now, everyone believes, has writer's block.

Wonder Boys follows him around a Pittsburgh campus in winter during a literary festival, as characters drift in and out of focus on his emotional viewfinder. His wife (we never see her) has just left him. His boss is Walter Gaskell (Richard Thomas), the head of the English department. Walter's wife, Sara (Frances McDormand), is the chancellor. Grady is having an affair with Sara. His New York editor, Crabtree (Robert Downey, Jr.), is in town for the festival, and wonders where the new manuscript is. The famous writer "Q" (Rip Torn) is a visiting speaker. Two of Grady's students occupy his attention: James Leer (Tobey Maguire), who has written a novel and is moody and difficult and a pathological liar; and Hannah Green (Katie Holmes), who rents a room in Grady's house and would probably share his bed, although it has not come to that.

Because Grady is tired, depressed, and continuously stoned on pot, these characters all have more or less equal importance. That is, when he's looking at them they represent problems, and when they're absent, he can forget about them.

The movie is an unsprung screwball comedy, slowed down to real-life speed. Mishaps trip over one another in their eagerness to mess with Grady's mind. One thing leads to another. He goes to a party at the Gaskells' house and Sara tells him she is pregnant. He steps outside for a reefer, sees James standing in the dark with a gun, invites him in, and sneaks him upstairs to show him a secret closet where Walter Gaskell keeps his treasure (the suit Marilyn Monroe wore on her wedding day). Then the Gaskells' blind dog bites him and James shoots the dog dead.

At a certain velocity, this would be wacky.

One of the wise decisions of *Wonder Boys* is to avoid that velocity. Grady plods around town in a pink bathrobe, trying to repair damage, tell the truth, give good advice, be a decent man, and keep his life from falling apart. The brilliance of the movie can be seen in its details: (1) Hannah is brought onstage as an obvious love interest, but is a decoy; (2) Crabtree picks up a transvestite on the airplane, but dumps him for James, who is not exactly straight or gay (neither is Crabtree); (3) when the transvestite needs a ride, Grady says, "I'm your man" but their drive results not in sex but in truth-telling; and (4) Sara is not hysterical about being pregnant and is understanding, actually, about Grady's chaotic lifestyle.

So all the obvious payoffs are short-circuited. No mechanical sex scenes. No amazing revelation that the transvestite is not a woman (everyone in the movie clocks him instantly). No emotional show-offs. And the sex in the movie, gay and straight, is handled sanely, as a calming pastime after long and nutty evenings. (Notice how comfortable the Downey character is with his weaknesses of the flesh.)

Let me give one more example of how the movie uses observation instead of wheezy clichés. When Q, the writer, is giving his speech, he pontificates about piloting the boat of inspiration to the shore of achievement. James utters a loud, high-pitched giggle. In a lesser movie James would have continued, making some kind of angry and rebellious statement. Not in *Wonder Boys,* where James thinks Q is ludicrous, laughs rudely once, and then shuts up.

And listen to the dialogue. Grady has been working on his second novel so long it now runs well over two thousand single-spaced pages. Hannah suggests tactfully that by including the "genealogies of everyone's horses, and their dental records," Grady's work "reads as if you didn't make any choices." The right line in a movie that does make choices. She also wonders if the book would have more shape if he hadn't been stoned when he wrote it. Yes, his brilliant first book was written on reefer, but then a lot of first novels are written long before they're actually put down on paper.

Wonder Boys is the first movie by Curtis Hanson since his *L.A. Confidential.* In a very different way, it is as accomplished. The screenplay by Steve Kloves, based on a novel by Michael Chabon, is European in its preference for character over plot. This is a funny and touching story that contains dead dogs, Monroe memorabilia, a stolen car, sex, adultery, pregnancy, guns, dope, and cops, but it is not about any of those things. It is about people, and especially about trying to be a good teacher.

Could one weekend on a real campus possibly contain all of these events? Easily, given the tendency of writers to make themselves deliberately colorful. Grady knows exactly what he's doing. Of Hannah he observes: "She was a junkie for the printed word. Lucky for me, I manufactured her drug of choice."

Woodstock

R, 225 m., 1994

Directed by Michael Wadleigh and produced by Bob Maurice.

The movies are, of course, a time capsule, and I have rarely felt that more sharply than while watching the twenty-fifth anniversary edition of *Woodstock* (1994). What other generation has so completely captured its youth on film, for better and worse, than the Woodstock Nation? Watching the film today, for someone like me who also saw it on the day it was premiered, inspires meditation as well as joy, dark thoughts as well as hopeful ones.

The making of the film was a happy accident. I remember meeting the director, Michael Wadleigh, in an editing room up in a loft in New York City, months before the movie was released. He talked about how he and his partner, producer Bob Maurice, threw together a production team at the last moment, and descended on the Woodstock site because they had a hunch it might be more than just another rock concert.

What they came away with was 120 miles of footage, which an editing team headed by Thelma Schoonmaker and Martin Scorsese assembled into a three-hour film. The balance was perhaps 60 percent about the music and 40 percent about the event itself—about how four hundred thousand people were drawn to a farm in upstate New York, where the facilities could not remotely sustain or feed them,

and where a thunderstorm soaked them, but where somehow they celebrated, as the film's subtitle has it, "three days of peace and music."

This new "director's cut," available on tape and laserdisc, adds an additional forty-five minutes, including sets by Janis Joplin and Jefferson Airplane that were not in the original film. It also expands the film's final performance, by Jimi Hendrix, which includes his pyrotechnic version of "The Star-Spangled Banner."

That performance was attacked by some at the time as a desecration of the national anthem. Hearing it again the other day, I found it the most stirring version of the song I have ever heard. Hendrix tortured his electric guitar to create the sound of bombs bursting in air, as they were at that moment in Vietnam, and like a jazzman he improvised, working in bits of other songs (I've heard this version many times, but only on this hearing did I pick up fifteen notes of "Taps"). As Hendrix plays, the camera shows the last act of Woodstock. Most of the four hundred thousand have gone home. A few forlorn wanderers walk barefoot across the muddy fields, trying to find shoes that will fit. Trash crews pick up the debris. The event is over. And then the editors slowly reverse the time flow, so that the field fills again, horizon to horizon, with a mass of humanity. It was then and probably still is the largest crowd ever gathered.

It is probable that Woodstock would not have been possible without Vietnam. They are two sides of the same coin: the grinning nun flashing a peace sign to the camera at the concert, and the war. One of the heroes of the film is the Port-a-San man, in charge of servicing the portable toilets. After swabbing out a few units, he confides to the camera that he has a son out there in the crowd somewhere—"and another one in the DMZ, flying helicopters."

The concert, with its pot smoking, its skinny-dipping, its warnings about "bad acid," its famous shot of a couple disrobing and making love in a meadow, and Country Joe leading a sing-along of "Feel Like I'm Fixin' to Die Rag," was in its own way a peace rally. Without the war to polarize American society, these four hundred thousand people might not have felt so much in common. I remembered that time when strangers flashed the peace sign to each other, when costume and attitude created a feeling of camaraderie, when it was believed that music made a difference and could affect society. All of that is gone, gone, gone.

So are some of the performers, dead of drugs. Hendrix, of course, and Janis Joplin, who has always seemed weathered in my memory, but here seems touchingly young, because she did not grow older with the rest of us. Others were survivors: Roger Daltry, Joan Baez, Grace Slick, who in the Airplane set looks like a fresh-faced college girl. Even Country Joe McDonald looks young here. It was all so long ago.

The structure of the documentary is roughly chronological. We see the fields being prepared, the stage being built, the massive traffic jams forming. We see crowds trampling over the fences, and there is the moment when the event, conceived as a profit-making enterprise, is officially declared a "free concert." (There is an amusing moment when the late Bill Graham, a concert promoter who always kept his eye on the gate, advises the organizers, facetiously I think, to fill ditches with flaming oil to keep the gate-crashers out.)

Woodstock was made at a time before rock concerts were routinely filmed (although earlier documentaries about the Stones, Bob Dylan, and the Newport Jazz Festival pointed the way). The stars were not performing for the camera. Richie Havens casually stops in the middle of a set to tune his guitar. Sha-Na-Na does a cornball double-time version of "At the Hop" and doesn't care how it looks. Joan Baez puts down her guitar and sings "Swing Low, Sweet Chariot," and nobody worries that it will slow down the show. Night follows day, day follows night, Hugh Romney of the Hog Farm announces, "What we have in mind is breakfast in bed for 400,000 people." Army helicopters drop food, blankets, medical supplies—and flowers. Babies are born and no one is killed, and for a moment it seems that the spirit of Woodstock Nation could prevail.

Looking up my old review of the movie, I find that I began it with a quote from the Chicago Seven trial. Accused conspirator Abbie Hoffman is asked where he resides, and he replies, "Woodstock Nation." His attorney

asks him to explain to the judge and jury where that is. "It is a nation of alienated young people," Hoffman says. "We carry it around with us as a state of mind, in the same way the Sioux Indians carry the Sioux nation with them. . . ."

Yes, I thought, looking at the old clipping. And look what happened to the Sioux.

Working Girl
R, 116 m., 1988

Melanie Griffith (Tess McGill), Harrison Ford (Jack Trainer), Sigourney Weaver (Katharine Parker), Alec Baldwin (Mick Dugan), Joan Cusack (Cyn), Philip Bosco (Oren Trask), Nora Dunn (Ginny), Olympia Dukakis (Personnel Director). Directed by Mike Nichols and produced by Douglas Wick. Screenplay by Kevin Wade.

The problem with working your way up the ladder of life is that sometimes you can't get there from here. People look at you and make a judgment call, and then, try as you might, you're only spinning your wheels. That's how Tess McGill feels in the opening scenes of *Working Girl.* She is intelligent and aggressive, and she has a lot of good ideas about how to make money in the big leagues of high finance. But she is a secretary. A secretary with too much hair. A secretary who rides the Staten Island ferry to work. A secretary who started talking like a little girl because it was cute when she was eleven and is still talking the same way, except now she is thirty. There is no way anybody is ever going to take her seriously.

One day, Tess (Melanie Griffith) gets a new boss at the mergers and acquisitions firm where she works. The boss (Sigourney Weaver) is a woman of almost exactly Tess's age, but with a different set of accessories. For example, she talks in a low, modulated voice, and wears more businesslike clothes, and has serious hair. "If you want to get ahead in business," Tess muses, "you've got to have serious hair." She gets along fine with her boss until the boss goes on a skiing holiday and breaks her leg and ends up in traction for six weeks. Then Tess goes into her boss's computer, and finds that the boss was about to steal one of Tess's brilliant suggestions and claim it as her own.

This makes her fighting mad, and so she begins an elaborate deception in which she masquerades as an executive at the firm, and figures out a way to meet a guy named Jack Trainer (Harrison Ford), who is the right guy at another firm to make the deal happen. She meets Trainer at a party and gets drunk and ends up in bed with him, even though she *explained* to him, "I have a head for business and a bod for sin." Will he ever take her seriously now? Yes, it turns out he will, because he likes her, and because he thinks her idea really is pretty brilliant.

That's the setup for *Working Girl*, which is one of those entertainments where you laugh a lot along the way, and then you end up on the edge of your seat. Structurally, the film has some parallels with *The Graduate*, Nichols's 1967 classic—including a climactic scene where an important ceremony is interrupted by the wrong person bursting in through the door. But this movie is the other side of the coin. *The Graduate* was about a young man who did not want to make money in plastics. *Working Girl* is about a young woman who very definitely wants to make money in mergers.

This is Melanie Griffith's movie in the same way that *The Graduate* belonged to Dustin Hoffman. She was not an obvious casting choice, but she is the right one, and in an odd way her two most famous previous roles, in *Body Double* and *Something Wild*, work for her. Because we may remember her from those sex-drenched roles, there is a way in which both Griffith and her character are both trying to get respectable—to assimilate everything that goes along with "serious hair."

Supporting roles are crucial in movies like this. The Sigourney Weaver role is a thankless one—she plays the pill who gets humiliated at the end—and yet it is an interesting assignment for an actor with Weaver's imagination. From her first frame on the screen, she has to say all the right things while subtly suggesting that she may not mean any of them. If she is subtle, so is Harrison Ford, an actor whose steadiness goes along with a sort of ruminating passion; when he's in love with a woman, he doesn't grab her, he just seems to ponder her a lot. Weaver and Ford provide the indispensable frame within which the Griffith character can be seen to change.

The plot of *Working Girl* is put together like clockwork. It carries you along while you're watching it, but reconstruct it later and you'll see the craftsmanship. The Kevin Wade screenplay is sort of underhanded, the way it diverts us with laughs and with a melodramatic subplot involving Griffith's former boyfriend, while all the time it's winding up for the suspenseful climax. By the time we get to the last scenes, the movie plays like a thriller, and that's all the more effective because we weren't exactly bracing for that. *Working Girl* is Mike Nichols returning to the top of his form, and Melanie Griffith finding hers.

A World Apart

PG, 112 m., 1988

Barbara Hershey (Diana Roth), Jodhi May (Molly Roth), Jeroen Krabbe (Gus Roth), Carolyn Clayton-Cragg (Miriam Roth), Linda Mvusi (Elsie). Directed by Chris Menges and produced by Sarah Radclyffe. Screenplay by Shawn Slovo.

A World Apart was written by a woman who grew up in South Africa in the 1960s, while her parents were involved in the antiapartheid movement, and it is very much a daughter's story; even though her parents were brave and dedicated, their child still nurses a sense of resentment because she did not get all of the attention she felt she deserved. *A World Apart* is both political and personal—a view of a revolutionary as the middle-class mother of a normal thirteen-year-old girl.

The girl's name is Molly (Jodhi May), and the film opens with episodes from her typical childhood in an affluent white South African community. She takes ballet lessons, she is picked up after class in a big American convertible piloted by her friend's mother, she attends the usual birthday parties, and splashes in a neighbor's swimming pool. The only thing unusual about her life is that some of her parents' friends are black—and in white South Africa in 1963, that is very unusual indeed.

Her parents are the Roths, Diana and Gus, and they are involved in a lot of activities she knows nothing about. One night her father comes to say good-bye to her, and the next day he is gone, having fled the country one step ahead of arrest on charges of communist subversion. Her mother stays behind, works for an antigovernment newspaper, and moves in left-wing circles. A law is passed authorizing the government to detain anyone for up to ninety days on suspicion of subversive activities, and Diana Roth (Barbara Hershey) is one of the first to be detained.

We see this detention in two ways. Through the eyes of the mother, it is a terrifying form of torture, in which she is separated from her family and given no certain future to look forward to. She is interrogated daily by a government official who tries to ingratiate himself with her as kind of a good guy—he falls a little in love with her—but she adopts a stoic mask of determined resistance.

Hershey's own mother steps in to take care of the family during the period. For Molly, everything in her life turns out to have changed. Her best friend, for example, is suddenly cold toward her. She isn't invited to any more birthday or pool parties. Her parents are criminals and so she is somehow a criminal and a pariah, too. Meanwhile, on another front, the brother of the family's maid dies in the hands of the police, and political turmoil begins to simmer.

From a certain point of view, there is an irony here. Why should we care that a thirteen-year-old is not invited to swimming parties, when millions of black South Africans are denied elementary civil rights? From another point of view, A World Apart is stronger because it chooses to deal with the smaller details of specific lives. Unlike Cry Freedom, which was painted on such a large canvas that subtlety was lost, A World Apart is about the specific ways in which individual lives are affected by a legal system in which one's rights depend on one's race.

I spent a year in South Africa, in 1965, at the University of Cape Town, and I have often been disturbed by the ways in which so many fictional depictions of the country seem unable to communicate what it is like to live there. For most people of all races in South Africa, most days are fairly routine, devoted to the various activities of family and work, getting and spending and caring, that are the bedrock of lives everywhere. The country is not some sort of permanent political passion play. It is possible to fall into a workable, even comfortable, routine. It is by showing the placid surface of everyday life that A World

Apart is able to dramatize how close beneath that surface the police state resides. For those who do not rock the boat, South Africa can be a very pleasant place to live.

Diana Roth rocks the boat, and through her daughter's eyes we see the result of that action. As played by Barbara Hershey, Roth is not an ideal mother, although she is a dutiful one; there is a certain hardness in her, an edge of anger that focuses on injustice and sometimes overlooks the needs of her family in what seem to be the more urgent needs of society. This is another fine, strong performance by Hershey, who has emerged in recent years as one of our best actresses.

Jodhi May, as young Molly, is equally impressive, and in many ways this is her movie. The screenplay (by Shawn Slovo, based on her own memories) gives May much to work with, but the ways in which her eyes express hurt and rejection are all her own. (Hershey, May, and Linda Mvusi, who plays the family's maid, shared the best actress award at the 1988 Cannes Film Festival.)

A World Apart has moments of almost unbearable hurt. One of them is at the moment when Hershey thinks her imprisonment is over, and is wrong. Another is when young Molly discovers the truth of a friend's rejection. Another, very powerful, is at the funeral of the murdered black man—a scene smaller, but more powerful, than the similar scene in Cry Freedom. The film is the first directorial work by Chris Menges, the cinematographer of The Killing Fields and The Mission. It is strong, angry, and troubling.

W.R.—Mysteries of the Organism

x, 85 m., 1972

Milena Dravic (Milena), Jagoda Kaloper (Jagoda), Ivica Vidovic (Vladimir), Zoran Radmilovic (Radmilovic), Tuli Kupferberg (Guerrilla Poet), Jackie Curtis (Transvestite), Michael Gelovani (Stalin). Directed, produced, and written by Dusan Makavejev.

If only we were not so rigid, not so unbending in our minds and bodies we could release our dammed-up human energy in a glooorrrrrious outflowing of love and self-realization. And if we could do that, why ... we could not only achieve greater sexual satisfaction, but maybe even cure what ails Soviet Marxism, and solve the problems of American Puritanism, too. And have a good time.

That is as close as I can get to the argument of *W.R.—Mysteries of the Organism,* an insanely brilliant comedy by one Dusan Makavejev. He has come this way before; his *Innocence Unprotected* won the 1968 Chicago International Film Festival, and *W.R.* took the best director award at the 1971 Chicago Festival. It has also made the rounds of the other big festivals; around-the-clock screenings had to be scheduled at Cannes, there was an uproar at New York, it was banned in Yugoslavia and at the Venice Film Festival, etc.

Makavejev himself is a large, happy, open-faced Yugoslavian who says he is astonished that his film has caused such controversy. He is not really astonished at all, of course; his films are designed so that there's a little something in all of them to offend somebody. But with *W.R.* he has outdone himself, taking on the state religions of two superpowers: Marxism (Russia) and psychiatry (America). In the East, his film was banned because it might offend the Russians. In the West, followers of Wilhelm Reich charged that Makavejev had cannibalized the work of that late persecuted genius. In England, they thought the film was pornographic. And so on.

"Maybe it is like a mirror," Makavejev said one late night while walking up Lincoln Avenue. "People hold it up to themselves and see reflected only what they are most offended by."

What was he doing on Lincoln Avenue past midnight? His trip was in the nature of a pilgrimage. He wished to see the place where "Jawn Deeelingher" had been shot. He thought perhaps "Deeelingher" would make an interesting movie.

In the world of Makavejev, you can be sure of one thing only: His film of "Deeelingher"

will not be a gangster movie. He will claim it is, but somehow other scenes will sneak in, footage from ancient Soviet epics, a musical number or two. He works in collage, I guess you'd say. He gets his effects by juxtaposing scenes that have little to do with one another. In *W.R.,* he's all over the map.

The main sequences involve (a) an irreverent documentary about Reich, including interviews with family members and former associates; (b) scenes from a wheezy Russian movie idolizing Stalin fervently but not too well; (c) a melodrama in which a Russian ice-skating star experiences his first orgasm through the cooperation of a young Yugoslavian follower of Reich, and then beheads her with his ice skate ("It's a Champion—the best," the morgue attendant says, examining the skate); and (d) assorted documentary footage of New York freaks, transvestites, painters, and—well, you know, New York folks.

All of this is done as sort of an ideological juggling act, with Makavejev at the center, deadpan, yet always with his eyes slightly widened at the bizarre variety of human experience. As a Yugoslavian, he is naturally weary of doctrinaire Soviet Marxism—not because he is anti-Marxist, but because the Soviets have so little sense of humor about politics.

And if the Russians cannot smile about politics, we Americans are positively long-faced about sex. He wants to loosen us up a little, maybe shock us if that's what we need, but get us to smile, smile, smile, and bankrupt the industry in how-to sex manuals. He takes the things we take most seriously and shows us how absurd they look from a certain light. If he can reduce everything to the absurd, who knows? We may be left in a world where people can take off their ideological overcoats, roll up their shy shirtsleeves, and give the old organism a suntan.

Y

The Year of Living Dangerously
PG, 114 m., 1983

Mel Gibson (Guy Hamilton), Linda Hunt (Billy Kwan), Sigourney Weaver (Jill Bryant), Michael Murphy (Pete Curtis), Noel Ferrier (Wally O'Sullivan), Bill Kerr (Colonel Henderson). Directed by Peter Weir and produced by Jim McElroy. Screenplay by David Williamson, Weir, and C. J. Koch.

The Year of Living Dangerously achieves one of the best re-creations of an exotic locale I've ever seen in a movie. It takes us to Indonesia in the middle 1960s, a time when the Sukarno regime was shaky and the war in Vietnam was just heating up. It moves us into the life of a foreign correspondent, a radio reporter from Australia who has just arrived in Jakarta, and who thrives in an atmosphere heady with danger. How is this atmosphere created by Peter Weir, the director? He plunges into it headfirst. He doesn't pause for travelogue shots. He thrusts us immediately into the middle of the action—into a community of expatriates, journalists, and embassy people who hang out in the same bars, restaurants, and clubs, and speculate hungrily on the possibility that Sukarno might be deposed. That would be a really big story, a corrective for their vague feelings of being stuck in a backwater.

Guy Hamilton, the journalist (Mel Gibson), is a lanky, Kennedyesque, chain-smoking young man who has a fix on excitement. He doesn't know the ropes in Indonesia, but he learns them quickly enough, from a dwarfish character named Billy Kwan. Billy is half-Oriental and half-European, and knows everybody and can tell you where all the bodies are buried. He has a warm smile and a way of encouraging you to do your best, and if you sometimes suspect he has unorthodox political connections—well, he hasn't crossed you yet. In all the diplomatic receptions he's a familiar sight in his gaudy tropical shirts. *The Year of Living Dangerously* follows Guy and Billy as they become friends, and something more than friends; they begin to share a common humanity and respect. Billy gets Guy a good interview with the local Communist Party chief. He even introduces Guy to Jill Bryant (Sigourney Weaver), a British attaché

with two weeks left on her tour. As the revolution creeps closer, as the stories get bigger, Guy and Jill become lovers and Billy, who once proposed to Jill, begins to feel pushed aside.

This sounds, no doubt, like a foreign correspondent plot from the 1940s. It is not. *The Year of Living Dangerously* is a wonderfully complex film about personalities more than events, and we really share the feeling of living in that place, at that time. It does for Indonesia what Bogdanovich's *Saint Jack* did for Singapore. The direction is masterful; Weir (whose credits include *Picnic at Hanging Rock*) is as good with quiet little scenes (like Billy's visit to a dying child) as big, violent ones (like a thrilling attempt by Guy and Billy to film a riot).

The performances of the movie are a good fit with Weir's direction, and his casting of the Billy Kwan character is a key to how the film works. Billy, so small and mercurial, likable and complicated and exotic, makes Indonesia seem more foreign and intriguing than any number of standard travelogue shots possibly could. That means that when the travelogue shots *do* come (and they do, breathtakingly, when Gibson makes a trip into the countryside), they're not just scenery; they do their work for the film because Weir has so convincingly placed us in Indonesia. Billy Kwan is played, astonishingly, by a woman—Linda Hunt, a New York stage actress who enters the role so fully that it never occurs to us that she is not a man. This is what great acting is, a magical transformation of one person into another. Mel Gibson (of *The Road Warrior*) is just right as a basically conventional guy with an obsessive streak of risk-taking. Sigourney Weaver has a less interesting role but is always an interesting actress. This is a wonderfully absorbing film.

A Year of the Quiet Sun
NO MPAA RATING, 106 m., 1986

Scott Wilson (Norman), Maja Komorowska (Emilia), Hanna Skarzanka (Mother), Ewa Dalkowska (Stella), Jerzy Stuhr (Adzio). Directed by Krzysztof Zanussi and produced by Hartwig Schmidt. Screenplay by Zanussi.

Imagine a landscape that seems to contain no joy. An American soldier has been assigned

here, far from his home. He is an uncomplicated man, not young anymore, who has
never really felt that be belonged to anyone.
Also living here is a single woman, not young,
who tends to her dying mother in the home
they have scraped together out of the rubble.
It is shortly after the end of World War II.

The woman speaks Polish. She lives in an
area of Europe that is perhaps Poland, perhaps Germany, depending on how the politicians are drawing their lines on the map.
There was a time when she and her mother
lived comfortably and were respectable, and
now there is the terrible shame of having to
wear torn clothes and live in a few rooms of a
house that is falling to pieces. After the long
years of war, there is no lightness in her life, no
joy except for one thing: Sometimes she finds
a little time to paint.

The soldier sees her painting. He is touched
by her determination to find some small
beauty in this landscape. They communicate
awkwardly because neither speaks the other's
language. They talk with their eyes.

The soldier has little to do—at times he
seems half-forgotten in this backwater
town—and he begins to court the woman.
With his GI's pay and privileges, he is rich by
local standards, and he is able to help the
mother and daughter. Soon he asks the
woman to marry him.

There is a problem. The woman will not
leave her mother. She cannot leave her to fend
for herself in brutal poverty. The mother sees
this but also sees that, for her daughter, this
man represents a chance for escape and happiness. So the mother tries to make the escape
possible. But there is the suggestion that escape from this life will never be possible, that
the war went on too long, the suffering was
too great, and the reality of present poverty is
too crushing for the woman to summon the
imagination to see how it could be different.

A Year of the Quiet Sun is a new film by
Krzysztof Zanussi, the Polish director who is
arguably the best filmmaker in Europe right
now. It stars one of his favorite actresses, Maja
Komorowska, as the younger woman, and the
American actor Scott Wilson (still best known
for *In Cold Blood*) as the lonely GI.

This is a small, quiet film of enormous
power. It is not generated by any genre, by any

plot that we can anticipate; it is the particular
story of the people in this time and place. It
doesn't even make a statement, really. Given
the fact of the war and its aftermath, Zanussi
has no suggestions to make. He simply wants
to tell the story of these people whose human
needs persist.

I have no insights into the personal lives of
Komorowska or Wilson, but I imagine they
must have some source from which to draw
the sadness that they project in this film. There
are scenes that depend entirely on their ability
to find the strength to smile, to hope for a moment that their lives can be better, and the way
they do that is enormously convincing.

Although a movie like this doesn't usually
find a large audience, it represents what I find
most valuable about filmmaking: the ability to
record the emotions during precise moments in
the lives of other people. It's not the story that
matters here, and it's not even all that important
whether the man and woman marry. What's
important is that they succeed, across the barriers of language and culture, in insisting on their
right to be happy together no matter what.

Yes

R, 99 m., 2005

Joan Allen (She), Simon Abkarian (He), Sam Neill
(Anthony), Shirley Henderson (Cleaner), Sheila
Hancock (Aunt), Samantha Bond (Kate), Stephanie
Leonidas (Grace), Gary Lewis (Billy). Directed by Sally
Potter and produced by Christopher Sheppard and
Andrew Fierberg. Screenplay by Potter.

Sally Potter's *Yes* is a movie unlike any other I
have seen or heard. Some critics have treated it
as ill-behaved, as if its originality is offensive.
Potter's sin has been to make a movie that is
artistically mannered and overtly political;
how dare she write her dialogue in poetry, provide a dying communist aunt, and end the film
in Cuba? And what to make of the house-
cleaner who sardonically comments on the
human debris shed by her rich employers? The
flakes of skin, the nail clippings, the wisps of
dead hair, the invisible millions of parasites?

I celebrate these transgressions. *Yes* is alive
and daring, not a rehearsal of safe material and
styles. Potter easily could have made a well-
mannered love story with passion and pain at

appropriate intervals; or perhaps, for Potter, that would not have been so easy, since all of her films strain impatiently at the barriers of convention. She sees no point in making movies that have been made before. See, for example, *Orlando*, in which Tilda Swinton plays a character who lives for centuries and trades genders.

Yes is a movie about love, sex, class, and religion, involving an elegant Irish-American woman (Joan Allen) and a Lebanese waiter and kitchen worker (Simon Abkarian). They are known only as She and He. She is a scientist, married lovelessly to a rich British politician (Sam Neill). He was a surgeon in Beirut, until he saved a man's life only to see him immediately shot dead. Refusing to heal only those with the correct politics, he fled Lebanon and now uses his knives to chop parsley instead of repairing human hearts.

They meet at a formal dinner. They do it with their eyes. He smiles, she smiles. Neither turns away. An invitation has been offered and accepted. Their sex is eager and makes them laugh. They are not young; they are grateful because of long experience with what can go wrong.

There is a scene in the movie of delightful eroticism. It involves goings-on under the table in a restaurant. The camera regards not the details of this audacity, but the eyes and faces of the lovers. They take their time getting to where they are almost afraid to go. They look at each other, enjoying their secret, he looking for a reaction, she wary of revealing one. Her release is a barely subdued shudder of muffled ecstasy. This is what sex is about: two people knowing each other and using their knowledge. Compared to it, the sex scenes in most movies are calisthenics.

She was born in Belfast, raised in America, is Christian, probably Catholic. He is Arabic and Muslim. Both come from lands where people kill each other in the name of God. They are above all that. Or perhaps not. They have an economic imbalance: "You buy me with a credit card in a restaurant," he says in a moment of anger. And: "Even to pronounce my name is an impossibility." With his fellow kitchen workers he debates the way Western women display their bodies, the way their husbands allow them to be looked at by other men. He is worldly, understands the West, and yet his inherited beliefs about women are deeply ingrained, and available when he needs a vocabulary to express his resentment.

She, on the other hand, displays her body with a languorous, healthy pride to him, and to us as we watch the movie. There is no explicit nudity. There is a scene where she goes swimming with her goddaughter, and we see that she is athletic, subtly muscled, with the neck and head of a goddess. To recline at the edge of the pool in casual physical perfection is as natural to She as it is disturbing to He. Their passion cools long enough for them to realize that they cannot live together successfully in either of their cultures.

Now about the dialogue. It is written in iambic pentameter, the rhythm scheme of Shakespeare. It is a style poised between poetry and speech; "to be or not to be, that is the question," and another question is, does that sound to you like poetry or prose? To me, it sounds like prose that has been given the elegance and discipline of formal structure. The characters never sound as if they're reciting poetry, and the rhymes, far from sounding forced, sometimes can hardly be heard at all. What the dialogue brings to the film is a certain unstated gravity; it elevates what is being said into a realm of grace and care.

There is her dying aunt, an unrepentant Marxist who provides us her testament in an interior monologue while she is in a coma. This monologue, and others in the film, are heard while the visuals employ subtle, transient freeze-frames. The aunt concedes that communism has failed, but "what came in its place? A world of greed. A life spent longing for things you don't need." The same point is made by She's house-cleaner (Shirley Henderson) and other maids and lavatory attendants seen more briefly. They clean up after us. We move through life shedding a cloud of organic dust, while minute specks of life make their living by nibbling at us. These mites and viruses in their turn cast off their own debris, while elsewhere galaxies are dying; the universe lives by making a mess of itself.

Can She and He live together? Is there a way for their histories and cultures to coexist as comfortably as their genitals? The dying aunt makes She promise to visit Cuba. "I want my death to wake you up and clean you out," she says. You and I know that Cuba has not worked, and I think the aunt knows it, too. But at least in Cuba the dead roots of her hopes might someday rise up and bear fruit. And Cuba has the advantage of being equally alien to both of them. Neither is an outsider when both are.

Potter has said, "I think 'yes' is the most beautiful and necessary word in the English language"—a statement less banal the more you consider it. Doesn't it seem to you sometimes as if we are fighting our way through a thicket of no? When He and She first meet, their eyes say yes to sex. By the end of the film, they are preparing to say yes to the bold overthrow of their lives up until then, and yes to the beginning of something hopeful and unknown.

You Can Count on Me

R, 109 m., 2000

Laura Linney (Sammy Prescott), Mark Ruffalo (Terry Prescott), Rory Culkin (Rudy), Matthew Broderick (Brian), Jon Tenney (Bob), J. Smith-Cameron (Mabel), Ken Lonergan (Priest). Directed by Lonergan and produced by Barbara De Fina, John Hart, Larry Meistrich, and Jeff Sharp. Screenplay by Lonergan.

Sammy is a divorced mom, has an eight-year-old son, works as a loan officer at the bank, is making ends meet, dates a guy named Bob who doesn't excite her, and hates her new boss. Terry is her easy-come, easy-go brother, one of those charmers that drive you nuts because you love them but you can't count on them. *You Can Count on Me*, a film of great, tender truth, begins as they meet again after one of Terry's long, unexplained silences.

As the film opens, Terry (Mark Ruffalo) has left behind a girlfriend and come to visit Sammy (Laura Linney) in the little town of Scottsville, New York. She glows with happiness to see him; they raised each other after their parents died in an accident. Gradually her joy fades as she realizes he hasn't come home to stay, but just wants to borrow money. It's the same old story.

We meet Rudy (Rory Culkin), Sammy's son, a good kid, close to his mother, suspicious of Terry at first, then growing crazy about him—because Rory aches for his absent father, and Terry does dadlike stuff, like taking him to a pool hall. Sammy is bitter about her ex-husband, won't talk to her son about him, has closed that chapter.

At the bank, the new manager is Brian (Matthew Broderick). He's one of those infu-riating midlevel executives who has been promoted beyond his competence. The bank, like many other corporations, mistakes his tactlessness for tough managerial skills. Brian has no empathy and takes cover behind the regulations. "Is there anyone else who can pick your son up after school?" he asks Sammy, who gives up her lunch hour so she can slip out every afternoon and meet Rudy. It goes without saying that Brian's regard for the rules does not extend to himself, which is why he is willing to have an affair with Sammy even though he has a pregnant wife at home.

Sammy's personal life is limited. In a small town, there are few available men. Bob (Jon Tenney) is a nice enough guy, but forgets to call her for weeks at a time, and seems reluctant to commit—not that she thinks she wants to marry him anyway. One of the truest scenes in the movie comes when Sammy calls him one day to arrange a meeting for sex. Kind of like calling the plumber.

The situation in Scottsville is static when Terry comes to town. Because he's unpredictable and irresponsible, but good-hearted in his half-baked way, he acts as a catalyst. Yes, he forgets to meet Rudy after school. Yes, he ignores his commitments. Yes, it is irresponsible for him to take that eight-year-old kid to a pool hall. But when he lifts Rudy up to the table and Rudy takes a shot and sinks the ball, *this is what the kid needs!* He needs a guy in his life to take the place of the absent father he is so curious about.

Of course, Terry knows Rudy, Sr., the ex-husband. They probably went to school together. He takes matters into his own hands and drives the kid to the house of his father, the louse, in a well-written scene where what happens is kind of inevitable.

The characters in *You Can Count on Me* have been freed from the formulas of fiction and set loose to live lives where they screw up, learn from their mistakes, and bumble hopefully into the future. Ken Lonergan, the writer-director, is willing to leave things open. He shows possibilities without immediately sealing them with decisions. Laura Linney and Mark Ruffalo are open actors who give the impression of spontaneous notions; they are not programmed. We like them. We share their frustration. We despair of Terry even while we see he means well.

I admire the way Linney shows Sammy

struggling with issues of right and wrong. Yes, she sleeps with the married bank manager— and with Bob. She doesn't feel right about it. She goes to her priest, played by Lonergan, the filmmaker. "What is the church's official position on fornication and adultery?" she asks, although she should have a good working knowledge of the answer. "Well," says the priest, wanting to be helpful, aware of situational ethics, "it's a sin . . ."

Yes. But after seeing the film I want you to ponder three possibilities. (1) The priest is quietly attracted to Sammy himself, although he would probably never act on his feelings. (2) Sammy's reason for sleeping with Brian, the bank manager, may have originated in passion, but includes a healthy component of office politics. (3) She may be coming around to the notion that Bob is not entirely unacceptable as a mate.

I call these possibilities because the movie does not seal them, or even take a position on them. They're serious matters, but the movie can be funny about them. Not funny like a comedy, but funny like at the office when some jerk makes enemies, and his enemies pounce. Then there are quiet little sarcastic asides around the watercooler, where you share your joy at the downfall of an ass. Such moments can be so enormously rewarding.

Beyond and beneath that is the rich human story of *You Can Count on Me*. I love the way Lonergan shows his characters in flow, pressed this way and that by emotional tides and practical considerations. This is not a movie about people solving things. This is a movie about people living day to day with their plans, fears, and desires. It's rare to get a good movie about the touchy adult relationship of a sister and brother. Rarer still for the director to be more fascinated by the process than the outcome. This is one of the best movies of the year.

Young Frankenstein

PG, 108 m., 1974

Gene Wilder (Dr. Frankenstein), Peter Boyle (His Monster), Madeline Kahn (Elizabeth), Cloris Leachman (Frau Blucher), Gene Hackman (Blind Man), Teri Garr (Inga). Directed by Mel Brooks and produced by Michael Gruskoff. Screenplay by Wilder and Brooks.

The moment, when it comes, has the inevitability of comic genius. Young Victor Frankenstein, grandson of the count who started it all, returns by rail to his ancestral home. As the train pulls into the station, he spots a kid on the platform, lowers the window, and asks: "Pardon me, boy; is this the Transylvania station?" It is, and director Mel Brooks is home with *Young Frankenstein,* his most disciplined and visually inventive film (it also happens to be very funny). Victor is a professor in a New York medical school, trying to live down the family name and giving hilarious demonstrations of the difference between voluntary and involuntary reflexes. He stabs himself in the process, dismisses the class, and is visited by an ancient family retainer with his grandfather's will.

Frankenstein quickly returns to Transylvania and the old ancestral castle, where he is awaited by the faithful houseboy Igor, the voluptuous lab assistant Inga, and the mysterious housekeeper Frau Blucher, whose very name causes horses to rear in fright. The young man had always rejected his grandfather's medical experiments as impossible, but he changes his mind after he discovers a book entitled *How I Did It* by Victor Frankenstein. Now all that's involved is a little grave-robbing and a trip to the handy local Brain Depository, and the Frankenstein family is back in business.

In his two best comedies, before this, *The Producers* and *Blazing Saddles,* Brooks revealed a rare comic anarchy. His movies weren't just funny, they were aggressive and subversive, making us laugh even when we really should have been offended. (Explaining this process, Brooks once loftily declared, "My movies rise below vulgarity.") *Young Frankenstein* is as funny as we expect a Mel Brooks comedy to be, but it's more than that: It shows artistic growth and a more surehanded control of the material by a director who once seemed willing to do literally anything for a laugh. It's more confident and less breathless.

That's partly because the very genre he's satirizing gives him a strong narrative he can play against. Brooks's targets are James Whale's *Frankenstein* (1931) and *Bride of Frankenstein* (1935), the first the most influential and the second probably the best of the 1930s Hollywood horror movies. Brooks uses carefully controlled black-and-white photography that catches the feel of the earlier films. He uses old-fashioned visual devices and obvious special effects (the train ride is a study in manufactured studio scenes) He adjusts the music to the right degree of squeakiness. And he even rented the original *Frankenstein* laboratory, with its zaps of electricity, high-voltage special effects, and elevator platform to intercept lightning bolts.

So the movie is a send-up of a style and not just of the material (as Paul Morrissey's dreadful *Andy Warhol's Frankenstein* was). It looks right, which makes it funnier. And then, paradoxically, it works on a couple of levels: first as comedy, and then as a weirdly touching story in its own right. A lot of the credit for that goes to the performances of Gene Wilder, as young Frankenstein, and Peter Boyle as the monster. They act broadly when it's required, but they also contribute tremendous subtlety and control. Boyle somehow manages to be hilarious and pathetic at the same time.

There are set pieces in the movie that deserve comparison with the most famous scenes in *The Producers*. Demonstrating that he has civilized his monster, for example, Frankenstein and the creature do a soft-shoe number in black tie and tails. Wandering in the woods, the monster comes across a poor, blind monk (Gene Hackman, very good) who offers hospitality and winds up scalding, burning, and frightening the poor creature half to death.

There are also the obligatory town meetings, lynch mobs, police investigations, laboratory experiments, love scenes, and a cheerfully ribald preoccupation with a key area of the monster's stitched-together anatomy. From its opening title (which manages to satirize *Frankenstein* and *Citizen Kane* at the same time) to its closing, uh, refrain, *Young Frankenstein* is not only a Mel Brooks movie but also a loving commentary on our love-hate affairs with monsters. This time, the monster even gets to have a little love-hate affair of his own.

Your Friends and Neighbors

R, 99 m., 1998

Jason Patric (Cary), Nastassja Kinski (Cheri), Ben Stiller (Jerry), Catherine Keener (Terri), Aaron Eckhart (Barry), Amy Brenneman (Mary). Directed by Neil LaBute and produced by Steve Golin and Patric. Screenplay by LaBute.

Neil LaBute's *Your Friends and Neighbors* is a film about monstrous selfishness—about people whose minds are focused exclusively on their own needs. They use the language of sharing and caring when it suits them, but only to their own ends. Here is the most revealing exchange in the film:

"Are you, like, a good person?"

"Hey! I'm eating lunch!"

The movie looks at sexual behavior with a sharp, unforgiving cynicism. And yet it's not really about sex. It's about power, about enforcing your will on another, about having what you want when you want it. Sex is only the medium of exchange. LaBute is merciless. His previous film, *In the Company of Men,* was about two men who play a cruel trick on a woman. In this film, the trick is played on all the characters by the society that raised and surrounded them. They've been emotionally shortchanged and will never hear a lot of the notes on the human piano.

LaBute's *Your Friends and Neighbors* is to *In the Company of Men* as Tarantino's *Pulp Fiction* was to *Reservoir Dogs.* In both cases, the second film reveals the full scope of the talent, and the director, given greater resources, paints what he earlier sketched. In LaBute's world, the characters are deeply wounded and resentful, they are locked onto their own egos, they are like infants for which everything is either "me!" or "mine!" Sometimes this can be very funny—for the audience, not for them.

Of course they have fashionable exteriors. They live in good "spaces," they have good jobs, they eat in trendy restaurants, and are well-dressed. They look good. They know that. And yet there is some kind of a wall closing them off from one another. Early in the film, the character played by Aaron Eckhart frankly confesses that he is his own favorite sexual partner. A character played by Catherine Keener can't stand it when her husband (Ben Stiller) talks during sex, and later, after sex with Nastassja Kinski, when she's asked, "What did you like the best?" she replies, "I liked the silence best."

Ben Stiller and Keener are a couple; Eckhart and Amy Brenneman are a couple. In addition to Kinski, who works as an artist's assistant, there is another single character played by

Jason Patric. During the course of the movie these people will cheat on and with one another in various ways.

A plot summary, describing who does what and with whom, would be pointless. The underlying truth is that no one cares for or about anybody else very much, and all of the fooling around is just an exercise in selfishness. The other day I spent a long time looking at the penguins in the Shedd Aquarium. Every once in a while two of them would square off into a squawking fit over which rock they were entitled to stand on. Big deal. Meanwhile, they're helpless captives inside a system that has cut them off from their full natures, and they don't even know it. Same thing in this movie.

LaBute, who writes and directs, is an intriguing new talent. His emphasis is on writing: As a director, he is functional, straightforward, and uncluttered. As a writer, he composes dialogue that can be funny, heartless, and satirical all at once. He doesn't insist on the funny moments, because they might distort the tone, but they're fine, as when the Keener character tells Kinski she's a writer—"if you read the sides of a tampon box." She writes ad copy, in other words. Later, in a store, Kinski reads the sides of a tampon box and asks, "Did you write this?" It's like she's picking up an author's latest volume in a bookstore, although in this case the medium is carefully chosen.

The Jason Patric character, too, makes his living off the physical expression of sex: He's possibly a gynecologist (that's hinted, but left vague). The Aaron Eckhart character, who pleasures himself as no other person can, is cheating on his wife with . . . himself, and likes the look of his lover. The Brenneman character is enraged to be treated like an object by her new lover, but of course is treated like one by Eckhart, her husband. And treats him like one. Only the Kinski character seems adrift, as if she wants to be nice and is a little puzzled that Keener can't seem to receive on that frequency.

LaBute deliberately isolates these characters from identification with any particular city, so we can't categorize them and distance ourselves with an easy statement like, "Look at how they behave in Los Angeles." They live in a generic, affluent America. There are no exteriors in the movie. The interiors are modern homes, restaurants, exercise clubs, offices, bedrooms, bookstores. These people are not someone else. In the immortal words of Pogo, "We has met the enemy, and it is us."

This is a movie with the impact of the original stage production of Albee's *Who's Afraid of Virginia Woolf.* It has a similar form, but is more cruel and unforgiving than *Carnal Knowledge.* Mamet has written some stuff like this. It contains hardly any nudity and no physical violence, but the MPAA at first slapped it with an NC-17 rating, perhaps in an oblique tribute to its power (on appeal, it got an R). It's the kind of date movie that makes you want to go home alone.

Y Tu Mama Tambіén

NO MPAA RATING, 105 m., 2002

Maribel Verdu (Luisa Cortes), Gael Garcia Bernal (Julio Zapata), Diego Luna (Tenoch Iturbide). Directed by Alfonso Cuaron and produced by Alfonso Cuaron and Jorge Vergara. Screenplay by Alfonso Cuaron and Carlos Cuaron.

Y Tu Mama Tambіén is described on its Web site as a "teen drama," which is like describing *Moulin Rouge* as a musical. The description is technically true but sidesteps all of the reasons to see the movie. Yes, it's about two teenage boys and an impulsive journey with an older woman that involves sexual discoveries. But it is also about the two Mexicos. And it is about the fragility of life and the finality of death. Beneath the carefree road movie that the movie is happy to advertise is a more serious level—and below that, a dead serious level.

The movie, whose title translates as *"And Your Mama, Too,"* is another trumpet blast that there may be a new Mexican Cinema a-bornin'. Like *Amores Perros,* which also stars Gael Garcia Bernal, it is an exuberant exercise in interlocking stories. But these interlock not in space and time, but in what is revealed, what is concealed, and in the parallel world of poverty through which the rich characters move.

The surface is described in a flash: Two Mexican teenagers named Tenoch and Julio, one from a rich family, one middle class, are free for the summer when their girlfriends go to Europe. At a wedding they meet a cousin named Luisa, ten years older, who is sexy and playful. They suggest a weekend trip to the legendary beach named Heaven's Mouth. When her fiancé cheats on her, she unexpectedly agrees, and they set out together on a lark.

This level could have been conventional but is anything but, as directed by Alfonso Cuaron, who cowrote the screenplay with his brother Carlos. Luisa kids them about their sex lives in a lighthearted but tenacious way, until they have few secrets left, and at the same time she teases them with erotic possibilities. The movie is realistic about sex, which is to say, franker and healthier than the smutty evasions forced on American movies by the R rating. We feel a shock of recognition: This is what real people do and how they do it, sexually, and the MPAA has perverted a generation of American movies into puerile, masturbatory snickering.

Whether Luisa will have sex with one or both of her new friends is not for me to reveal. More to the point is what she wants to teach them, which is that men and women learn to share sex as a treasure they must carry together without something spilling—that women are not prizes, conquests, or targets, but the other half of a precarious unity. This is news to the boys, who are obsessed with orgasms (needless to say, their own).

The progress of that story provides the surface arc of the movie. Next to it, in a kind of parallel world, is the Mexico they are driving through. They pass police checkpoints, see drug busts and traffic accidents, drive past shantytowns, and are stopped at a roadblock of flowers by villagers who demand a donation for their queen—a girl in bridal white, representing the Virgin. "You have a beautiful queen," Luisa tells them. Yes, but the roadblock is genteel extortion. The queen has a sizable court that quietly hints a donation is in order.

At times during this journey the sound track goes silent and we hear a narrator who comments from outside the action, pointing out the village where Tenoch's nanny was born, and left at thirteen to seek work. Or a stretch of road where, two years earlier, there was a deadly accident. The narration and the roadside images are a reminder that in Mexico and many other countries a prosperous economy has left an uneducated and penniless peasantry behind.

They arrive at the beach. They are greeted by a fisherman and his family, who have lived here for four generations, sell them fried fish, rent them a place to stay. This is an unspoiled paradise. (The narrator informs us the beach will be purchased for a tourist hotel, and the fisherman will abandon his way of life, go to the city in search of a job, and finally come back here to work as a janitor.) Here the sexual intrigues that have been developing all along will find their conclusion.

Beneath these two levels (the coming-of-age journey, the two Mexicos) is hidden a third. I will say nothing about it, except to observe there are only two shots in the entire movie that reflect the inner reality of one of the characters. At the end, finally knowing everything, you think back through the film—or, as I was able to do, see it again.

Alfonso Cuaron is Mexican but his first two features were big-budget American films. I thought *Great Expectations* (1998), with Ethan Hawke, Gwyneth Paltrow, and Anne Bancroft, brought a freshness and visual excitement to the updated story. I liked *A Little Princess* (1995) even more. It is clear Cuaron is a gifted director, and here he does his best work to date. Why did he return to Mexico to make it? Because he has something to say about Mexico, obviously, and also because Jack Valenti and the MPAA have made it impossible for a movie like this to be produced in America. It is a perfect illustration of the need for a workable adult rating: too mature, thoughtful, and frank for the R, but not in any sense pornographic. Why do serious film people not rise up in rage and tear down the rating system that infantilizes their work?

The key performance is by Maribel Verdu, as Luisa. She is the engine that drives every scene she's in, as she teases, quizzes, analyzes, and lectures the boys, as if impatient with the task of turning them into beings fit to associate with an adult woman. In a sense she fills the standard role of the sexy older woman, so familiar from countless Hollywood comedies, but her character is so much more than that—wiser, sexier, more complex, happier, sadder. It is true, as some critics have observed, that *Y Tu Mama* is one of those movies where "after that summer, nothing would ever be the same again." Yes, but it redefines "nothing."

Z

Z

PG, 127 m., 1969

Yves Montand (The Deputy), Irene Papas (His Widow), Jean-Louis Trintignant (The Investigator), Charles Denner (Manuel), George Geret (Nick, the Witness), Jacques Perrin (Journalist), Bernard Fresson (Matt), Pierre Dux (General), Francois Perier (Public Prosecutor) Marcel Bozzufi (Vago). Directed by Costa-Gavras and produced by Perrin and Hamed Rachedi. Screenplay by Costa-Gavras and Jorge Semprun, based on the book by Vassili Vassilikos.

Some things refuse to be covered over. It would be more convenient, yes, and easier for everyone if the official version were believed. But then the facts begin to trip over one another, and contradictions emerge, and an "accident" is revealed as a crime.

The film *Z* is about one of these things: about the assassination, six years ago, of a leader of the political opposition in Greece. It is also about all the rest of them. For Americans, it is about the My Lai massacre, the killing of Fred Hampton, the Bay of Pigs. It is no more about Greece than *The Battle of Algiers* was about Algeria. It is a film of our time. It is about how even moral victories are corrupted. It will make you weep and will make you angry. It will tear your guts out.

It is told simply, and it is based on fact. On May 22, 1963, Gregorios Lambrakis was fatally injured in a "traffic accident." He was a deputy of the opposition party in Greece. The accident theory smelled, and the government appointed an investigator to look into the affair.

The investigator's tacit duty was to reaffirm the official version of the death, but his investigation convinced him that Lambrakis had, indeed, been assassinated by a clandestine right-wing organization. High-ranking army and police officials were implicated. The plot was unmasked in court and sentences were handed down—stiff sentences to the little guys (dupes, really) who had carried out the murder, and acquittal for the influential officials who had ordered it.

But the story was not over. When the army junta staged its coup in 1967, the right-wing generals and the police chief were cleared of all charges and "rehabilitated." Those responsible for unmasking the assassination became political criminals.

These would seem to be completely political events, but the young director Costa-Gavras has told them in a style that is almost unbearably exciting. *Z* is at the same time a political cry of rage and a brilliant suspense thriller. It even ends in a chase—not through the streets but through a maze of facts, alibis, and official corruption.

Like Gillo Pontecorvo, who directed *Battle of Algiers*, Costa-Gravas maintains a point of view above the level of the events he photographs. His protagonist changes during the film as he leads us from an initial personal involvement to the indictment of an entire political system. At first, we are interested in Yves Montand, the wise and gentle political leader who is slain. Then our attention is directed to the widow (Irene Papas) and to the opposition leaders who will carry on (Charles Denner and Bernard Fresson).

And then, in the masterful last third of the film, we follow the stubborn investigator (Jean-Louis Trintignant) as he resists official pressure to conceal the scandal. He puts together his evidence almost reluctantly; he has no desire to bring down the government, but he must see justice done if he can. His sympathies are neutral, and a truly neutral judge is the most fearsome thing the establishment can imagine. What good is justice if it can be dealt out to the state as well as to the people?

The movie at first seems to end with triumph. The rotten core of the government is exposed. The military men and the police chief are indicted for murder, official misconduct, obstructing justice. One of the assassinated leader's young followers races to bring the widow the good news. He finds her waiting by the seashore. He is triumphant; justice will be done; the government will fall. Papas hears his news silently and then turns and looks out to sea. Her face reflects no triumph, only suffering and despair. What is really left for her to say?

Nothing, as we know now. The right wing won in the long run and controls Greece today. This film's director, writer, and composer, and Papas are all banned in Greece ("banned"—that terrible word we heard from Russia and South Africa, and now from Greece). Even the letter Z (which means "he is alive") is banned in Greece.

When this film was shown at the San Francisco Film Festival, it was attacked in some quarters as being anti-American, but does it not tell the simple truth? We do support the Greek junta. We do recognize the government that murdered Lambrakis. We did permit the junta to prevent free elections in Greece. And in Vietnam, the candidate who placed second in the "free elections" we sponsored sits in a Saigon jail today. His name is also banned.

Zodiac

R, 158 m., 2007

Mark Ruffalo (Inspector David Toschi), Jake Gyllenhaal (Robert Graysmith), Robert Downey, Jr. (Paul Avery), Anthony Edwards (Inspector William Armstrong), Brian Cox (Melvin Belli), Charles Fleischer (Bob Vaughn), Zack Grenier (Mel Nicolai), Philip Baker Hall (Sherwood Morrill), Elias Koteas (Sergeant Jack Mulanax), John Lacy (Zodiac 4), Donal Logue (Captain Ken Narlow), John Carroll Lynch (Arthur Leigh Allen), Dermot Mulroney (Captain Marty Lee), Chloë Sevigny (Melanie), Ed Setrakian (Al Hyman), John Getz (Templeton Peck), John Terry (Charles Thieriot), Candy Clark (Carol Fisher), Adam Goldberg (Duffy Jennings), James Le Gros (Officer George Bawart). Directed by David Fincher and produced by Louis Phillips. Screenplay by James Vanderbilt, based on the book by Robert Graysmith.

Zodiac is the *All the President's Men* of serial killer movies, with Woodward and Bernstein played by a cop and a cartoonist. It's not merely based on California's infamous killings, but seems to exude the very stench and provocation of the case. The killer, who was never caught, generously supplied so many clues that Sherlock Holmes might have cracked the case in his sitting room. But only a newspaper cartoonist was stubborn enough, and tunneled away long enough, to piece together a convincing case against a man who was *perhaps* guilty.

The film is a police procedural crossed with a newspaper movie, but free of most of the clichés of either. Its most impressive accomplishment is to gather a bewildering labyrinth of facts and suspicions over a period of years, and make the journey through this maze frightening and suspenseful. I could imagine becoming hopelessly mired in the details of the investigation, but director David Fincher *(Seven)* and his writer, James Vanderbilt, find their way with clarity through the murk. In a film with so many characters, the casting by Laray Mayfield is also crucial; like the only eyewitness in the case, we remember a face once we've seen it.

The film opens with a sudden, brutal, bloody killing, followed by others not too long after—five killings the police feel sure Zodiac committed, although others have been attributed to him. But this film will not be a bloodbath. The killer does his work in the earlier scenes of the film, and then, when he starts sending encrypted letters to newspapers, the police and reporters try to do theirs.

The two lead inspectors on the case are David Toschi (Mark Ruffalo) and William Armstrong (Anthony Edwards). Toschi, famous at the time, tutored Steve McQueen for *Bullitt* and was the role model for Clint Eastwood's Dirty Harry. Ruffalo plays him not as a hotshot but as a dogged officer who does things by the book because he believes in the book. The Edwards character, his partner, is more personally worn down by the sheer vicious nature of the killer and his taunts.

At the *San Francisco Chronicle*, although we meet several staffers, the key players are ace reporter Paul Avery (Robert Downey, Jr.), bearded, chain-smoking, alcoholic, and editorial cartoonist Robert Graysmith (Jake Gyllenhaal). These characters are real, and indeed the film is based on Graysmith's books about the case.

I found the newspaper office intriguing in its accuracy. For one thing, it is usually fairly empty, and it was true on a morning paper in those days that the office began to heat up closer to deadline. Among the few early arrivals would have been the cartoonist, who was expected to work up a few ideas for presentation at the daily news meeting, and the office alcoholics, perhaps up all night, or already starting their recovery drinking. Yes, reporters drank at their desks forty years ago, and smoked and smoked and smoked.

Graysmith is new on the staff when the first cipher arrives. He's like the curious new kid in school fascinated by the secrets of the big boys. He doodles with a copy of the cipher, and we think he'll solve it, but he doesn't. He strays off his beat by eavesdropping on cops and reporters, making friends with the boozy Avery, and even talking his way into police evidence rooms. Long after the investigation has cooled, his obsession remains, eventually driving his wife (Chloë Sevigny) to move herself and their children back in with her mom. Graysmith seems oblivious to the danger he may be drawing into his home, even after he appears on TV and starts hearing heavy breathing over the phone.

What makes it authentic is the way it avoids chases, shoot-outs, grandstanding, and false climaxes, and just follows the methodical progress of police work. Just as Woodward and Bernstein knocked on many doors and made many phone calls and met many very odd people, so do the cops and Graysmith walk down strange pathways in their investigation. Because Graysmith is unarmed and civilian, we become generally worried about his naiveté and risk taking, especially during a trip to a basement that is, in its way, one of the best scenes I've ever seen along those lines.

Fincher gives us times and days and dates at the bottom of the screen, which serve only to underline how the case seems to stretch out to infinity. There is even time-lapse photography showing the Transamerica building going up. Everything leads up to a heart-stopping moment when two men look, simply look, at one another. It is a more satisfying conclusion than Dirty Harry shooting Zodiac dead, say, in a football stadium.

David Fincher is not the first director you would associate with this material. In 1992, at thirty, he directed *Alien 3*, which was the least of the *Alien* movies, but even then had his eye (*Alien 3* is one of the best-looking bad movies I have ever seen). His credits include *Seven* (1995), a superb film about another serial killer with a pattern to his crimes; *The Game* (1997), with Michael Douglas caught in an ego-smashing web; *Fight Club* (1999) beloved by most, not by me; the ingenious terror of Jodie Foster in *Panic Room* (2002); and now, five years between features, his most thoughtful, involving film.

He seems to be in reaction against the slice-and-dice style of modern crime movies; his composition and editing are more classical, and he doesn't use nine shots when one will do. (If this same material had been put through an Avid to chop the footage into five times as many shots, we would have been sending our own ciphers to the studio.) Fincher is an elegant stylist on top of everything else, and here he finds the right pace and style for a story about persistence in the face of evil. I am often fascinated by true crime books, partly because of the way they amass ominous details (the best I've read is *Blood and Money*, by Thomas Thompson), and Fincher understands that true crime is not the same genre as crime action. That he makes every character a distinct individual is proof of that; consider the attention given to Graysmith's choice of a mixed drink.

Index

A